July 25–28, 2016
Chicago, IL, USA

Association for
Computing Machinery

Advancing Computing as a Science & Profession

PODC'16

Proceedings of the 2016 ACM Symposium on

Principles of Distributed Computing

Sponsored by:

ACM SIGACT and ACM SIGOPS

Supported by:

Microsoft Research - Inria Joint Centre, VMWare, Akamai, Oracle Labs, & IBM Research

Association for
Computing Machinery

Advancing Computing as a Science & Profession

The Association for Computing Machinery
2 Penn Plaza, Suite 701
New York, New York 10121-0701

ISBN: 978-1-4503-3964-3 (Digital)

ISBN: 978-1-4503-4621-4 (Print)

Additional copies may be ordered prepaid from:

ACM Order Department
PO Box 30777
New York, NY 10087-0777, USA

Phone: 1-800-342-6626 (USA and Canada)
+1-212-626-0500 (Global)
Fax: +1-212-944-1318
E-mail: acmhelp@acm.org
Hours of Operation: 8:30 am – 4:30 pm ET

Printed in the USA

PODC 2016 PC Chair's Welcome

It is our great pleasure to welcome you to the 35th ACM SIGACT-SIGOPS Symposium on Principles of Distributed Computing (PODC 2016). This year's symposium continues its tradition of being the premier forum for presentation of research on all aspects of distributed computing, including the theory, design, implementation and applications of distributed algorithms, systems and networks. During the years, PODC has been the stage where many landmark results have been presented that have increased our understanding of this exciting and fundamental research endeavor. In the best tradition of theoretical discovery, the insights that have been provided have not only elucidated fundamental conceptual issues but also found their way into the real world of systems and applications.

The call for papers attracted 137 regular submissions and 12 brief announcement submissions. The Program Committee accepted 40 regular papers and 24 brief announcements (some of which come from the regular submissions that could not be accepted due to lack of space) that cover a wide variety of topics. Every submitted paper was read and evaluated by at least three reviewers. The final decisions regarding acceptance or rejection of each paper were made through electronic Program Committee discussions held during April 2016. Revised and expanded versions of a few selected papers will be considered for publication in a special issue of the journal Distributed Computing and in the Journal of the ACM.

The Program Committee selected the paper *Analysing Snapshot Isolation*, by Andrea Cerone and Alexey Gotsman, for this year's Best Paper Award. Moreover, the Program Committee decided to split the Best Student Paper Award between two papers: *A Distributed* $(2+\epsilon)$*-Approximation for Vertex Cover in* $O(\log\Delta/\epsilon\log\log\Delta)$ *Rounds*, by Reuven Bar-Yehuda, Keren Censor-Hillel and Gregory Schwartzman, and *The Greedy Spanner is Existentially Optimal*, by Arnold Filtser and Shay Solomon. Three keynote talks will be given by Andrew A. Chien, Faith Ellen, and Phillip B. Gibbons.

The 2016 Edsger W. Dijkstra Prize in Distributed Computing was split between two papers: *A Fast and Simple Randomized Parallel Algorithm for the Maximal Independent Set Problem*, by Noga Alon, Lászl6 Babai, and Alon Itai (published in the Journal of Algorithms 1986), and *A Simple Parallel Algorithm for the Maximal Independent Set Problem* by Michael Luby (published at STOC 1985 and in SIAM Journal on Computing 1986). The Prize will be presented at the conference. Finally, this year we will celebrate the 60th birthday of Faith Ellen.

Putting together PODC 2016 was a team effort. We first thank the authors for providing the content of the program. We are grateful to the Program Committee and the sub-reviewers, who worked very hard in reviewing papers and providing feedback for authors. The help of the Steering Committee and of the Conference Committee was timely and invaluable. Finally, we thank our sponsors, ACM SIGOPS, and ACM SIGACT, and our generous corporate supporters: Microsoft Research - INRIA Joint Center, VMware University Research Fund: a fund at Vanguard Charitable, Akamai, Oracle Labs, and IBM Research.

We hope that you will find this program interesting and thought-provoking and that the symposium will provide you with a valuable opportunity to share ideas with other researchers from institutions around the world. I would like to extend my personal thanks to the Program Committee for enduring my uncountable prompts and reminders. It was probably hard to stand but it was for a good cause.

Andrzej Pelc
PODC'16 Program Chair

Table of Contents

Session 3

Session Chair: Wojciech Golab *(University of Waterloo)*

Keynote Lecture 2

Session 4

Session Chair: Andrea Richa *(Arizona State)*

Session 5

Session Chair: Merav Parter *(MIT)*

Session 6

Session Chair: Gadi Taubenfeld *(IDC Herzliya)*

Keynote Lecture 3

Session 7

Session Chair: Yehuda Afek *(Tel-Aviv University)*

PODC 2016 Symposium Organization

General Chair: George Giakkoupis *(INRIA, France)*

Workshop Coordinator: Chen Avin *(Ben-Gurion University, Israel)*

Communication Co-Chairs: Avery Miller *(University of Manitoba, Canada)*
Jukka Suomela *(Aalto University, Finland)*

Program Committee Chair: Andrzej Pelc *(Université du Québec en Outaouais, Canada)*

Treasurer: Elad Schiller *(Chalmers University of Technology, Sweden)*

Publicity Chair: Mark Tuttle *(Intel, USA)*

Organizing Chair: Nitin Vaidya *(University of Illinois, USA)*

Steering Committee Chair: Nitin Vaidya *(University of Illinois, USA)*

Steering Committee: Shlomi Dolev *(Ben-Gurion University, Israel)*
Pierre Fraigniaud *(CNRS, Université Paris-Diderot, France)*
George Giakkoupis *(INRIA, France)*
Andrzej Pelc *(Université du Québec en Outaouais, Canada)*
Elad Schiller *(Chalmers University of Technology, Sweden)*
Paul Spirakis *(University of Liverpool, UK)*

Program Committee: Ittai Abraham *(VMware Research Group, USA)*
Yehuda Afek *(Tel-Aviv University, Israel)*
Marcos K. Aguilera *(VMware Research Group, USA)*
Dan Alistarh *(Microsoft Research, Cambridge, UK)*
James Aspnes *(Yale University, USA)*
Leonid Barenboim *(The Open University of Israel, Israel)*
Shiri Chechik *(Tel-Aviv University, Israel)*
Colin Cooper *(King's College London, UK)*
Oksana Denysyuk *(University of Calgary, Canada)*
Ittay Eyal *(Cornell University, USA)*
Hugues Fauconnier *(LIAFA, Paris Diderot, France)*
Pascal Felber *(Université de Neuchâtel, Switzerland)*
Wojciech Golab *(University of Waterloo, Canada)*
Rachid Guerraoui *(EPFL, Lausanne, Switzerland)*
Bernhard Haeupler *(Carnegie Mellon University, USA)*
Anne-Marie Kermarrec *(INRIA, Rennes, France)*
Valerie King *(University of Victoria, Canada)*
Adrian Kosowski *(LIAFA, Paris Diderot, France)*

Program Committee (continued):

Shay Kutten *(Technion, Israel)*
Christoph Lenzen *(MPI Saarbruecken, Germany)*
Achour Mostéfaoui *(Université de Nantes, France)*
Calvin Newport *(Georgetown University, USA)*
Merav Parter *(MIT, USA)*
Sergio Rajsbaum *(UNAM, Mexico)*
Andrea Richa *(Arizona State, USA)*
Liam Roditty *(Bar-Ilan University, Israel)*
Nicola Santoro *(Carleton University, Canada)*
Thomas Sauerwald (*University of Cambridge, UK)*
Jukka Suomela *(Aalto University, Finland)*
Gadi Taubenfeld *(IDC Herzliya, Israel)*
Philipp Woelfel *(University of Calgary, Canada)*
Haifeng Yu *(National University of Singapore, Singapore)*
Vassilis Zikas *(ETH, Zurich, Switzerland)*

Additional reviewers:

Zahra Aghazadeh
Hagit Attiya
Chen Avin
Yossi Azar
Foteini Baldimtsi
Luca Becchetti
Petra Berenbrink
Vibhor Bhatt
Jeremy Blackthorne
Peva Blanchard
Lucas Boczkowski
Janna Burman
Christian Cachin
Irina Calciu
Keren Censor-Hillel
Ran Cohen
Sandro Coretti
Artur Czumaj
Shantanu Das
Sebastian Daum
Carole Delporte
Giuseppe Antonio Di Luna
Danny Dolev
Shlomi Dolev
Aleksandar Dragojevic
Martin Dyer
Faith Ellen
Robert Elsässer
Babak Farzad
Pierre Fraigniaud
Stephan Friedrichs
Matthias Függer
Eli Gafni
Anat Ganor
Juan Garay
Leszek Gasieniec
Rati Gelashvili
Mohsen Ghaffari
George Giakkoupis
Robert Gmyr
Lee-Ad Gottlieb
Adam Groce
Christoph Haase
Vassos Hadzilacos
Sima Hajiaghaei
Michal Hanckowiak
Juho Hirvonen
Stephan Holzer
Tomasz Jurdzinski
Dominik Kaaser
Erez Kantor
Petteri Kaski
Idit Keidar
Michael Kerber
Janne H. Korhonen
Sebastian Krinninger

Additional reviewers (continued):

Fabian Kuhn
Ranjit Kumaresan
Petr Kuznetsov
Silvio Lattanzi
Tuomo Lempiäinen
Zvi Lotker
Thanasis Loukopoulos
Nancy Lynch
Alexander Matveev
Yannic Maus
Moti Medina
Hammurabi Mendes
Yoram Moses
Mahnush Movahedi
Shay Mozes
Cameron Musco
Danupon Nanongkai
Emanuele Natale
Christopher Nitta
Ariel Nof
Dominik Pajak
Gopal Pandurangan
Anat Paskin-Cherniavsky
David Peleg
Sriram Pemmaraju
Richard Peng
Matthieu Perrin
Seth Pettie
Maria Potop-Butucaru
Christopher Purcell
Pavel Raykov
Nicolás Rivera
Peter Robinson
Scott Roche
Michał Różański
Aviad Rubinstein
Eric Ruppert
Navin Rustagi
Joel Rybicki
Jared Saia
Christian Scheideler
Elad Michael Schiller
Stefan Schmid
Stefan Schneider
Michele Scquizzato
Shantanu Sharma
Yangguang Shi
Shay Solomon
Grzegorz Stachowiak
Julien Stainer
Thim Strothmann
Hsin-Hao Su
Moshe Sulamy
He Sun
Orr Tamir
Kanat Tangwongsan
Vanessa Teague
Tigran Tonoyan
Roei Tov
Corentin Travers
Eran Tromer
Daniel Tschudi
Eli Upfal
Przemysław Uznański
Nitin Vaidya
Giovanni Viglietta
Ellen Vitercik
Adrian Vladu
Jennifer Walter
Jennifer Welch
Christian Wulff-Nilsen
Yukiko Yamauchi
Dongxiao Yu

Sponsors and Supporters of PODC 2016

Sponsors:

SIGACT

acm SIGOPS

Supporters:

Microsoft Research - Inria JOINT CENTRE

vmware

Akamai

Oracle Labs

IBM Research

The 2016 Edsger W. Dijkstra Prize in Distributed Computing

The Dijkstra Prize Committee has decided to grant the 2016 Edsger W. Dijkstra Prize in Distributed Computing jointly to Noga Alon, László Babai, Alon Itai, and Michael Luby, for the following two papers:

- **A Fast and Simple Randomized Parallel Algorithm for the Maximal Independent Set Problem** by Noga Alon, László Babai, and Alon Itai, published in *Journal of Algorithms*, 7(4):567-583, 1986
- **A Simple Parallel Algorithm for the Maximal Independent Set Problem** by Michael Luby, published in the *Proceedings of the 17th Annual ACM Symposium on Theory of Computing (STOC)*, pp.1-10, May 1985, and in *SIAM Journal on Computing*, 15(4):1036-1053, 1986

The Prize is awarded for outstanding papers on the principles of distributed computing, whose significance and impact on the theory and/or practice of distributed computing have been evident for at least a decade.

In these seminal works, the authors present, simultaneously and independently, an O(log n) time randomized distributed/parallel algorithm for the Maximal Independent Set (MIS) problem. MIS is regarded as a crown jewel of distributed symmetry breaking problems, and a central problem in the area of locality in distributed computing. The nominated papers provide a fascinatingly simple, elegant, and efficient randomized solution for this problem. While many variations exist, at their core, the algorithms are as simple as this:

> *Repeat until done: each node picks an O(log n)-bit random number; strict local minima join the MIS, and get removed from the graph along with their neighbors.*

The algorithm has played a significant role in popularizing Distributed Computing to the broader Computer Science community. It is one of the most well-known distributed algorithms, and perhaps the one covered most frequently in general algorithms courses and textbooks, especially those on randomized algorithms.

The algorithm leads to O(log n) time randomized distributed/parallel algorithms for many other basic symmetry breaking problems such as $(\Delta+1)$-coloring, Maximal Matching, and Ruling Sets. The awarded papers were among the pioneers in demonstrating the striking power of randomization in Distributed Computing, and have received more than 1,000 citations. Interestingly, they were also among the first in observing the simple yet powerful fact that one can derandomize parallel/centralized algorithms that use only d-wise independent randomness for constant d. This fact is used in the papers to derive deterministic parallel MIS algorithms, and it is now viewed as one of the basic derandomization techniques.

Thanks to its simplicity, the algorithm and its variations have been in widespread use, in various settings, from wireless networks to biological systems where symmetry breaking is required. This algorithmic result has also given rise to a host of fundamental and rich theoretical questions. Although to this day many of the questions remain open and continue intriguing the researchers, the follow up work on these questions has advanced our understanding of locality considerably.

The E.W. Dijkstra Prize is sponsored jointly by the ACM Symposium on Principles of Distributed Computing (PODC) and the EATCS Symposium on Distributed Computing (DISC). The prize is presented annually, with the presentation taking place alternately at PODC and DISC. This year it will be presented at PODC to be held at Chicago, IL, USA, July 25-29, 2016.

The 2016 Dijkstra Prize Committee:

Shlomi Dolev	*Ben-Gurion University of the Negev*
Pierre Fraigniaud	*CNRS and University Paris Diderot*
Cyril Gavoille	*University of Bordeaux (Chair)*
Dahlia Malkhi	*VMware Research*
Andrzej Pelc	*Université du Québec en Outaouais*
David Peleg	*Weizmann Institute*

New Opportunities for PODC? Massive, Volatile, but Highly Predictable Resources

Andrew A. Chien
The University of Chicago
Argonne National Laboratory

ABSTRACT
Classical models for distributed systems focus on fine-grained resources and failures (e.g. single processes and fail-stop or byzantine). Cheap hardware, the rise of the worldwide web, and now the rise of cloud computing has transformed distributed systems practice. Instead of single resources, application sites have ten-thousands of virtual machines, and in addition to independent failures, there are a raft of correlated failure modes.

Motivated by the reality the computing is the fastest growing consumer of electric power (and associated carbon emissions), we are creating new model for cloud computing systems, Zero-carbon Cloud, that taps a growing phenomenon of "stranded power" -- energy that is generated, but has no economic value. Stranded power is significant today (7.7 terawatt-hours in the Midwest power grid in 2014, perhaps 50 TWH worldwide), and growing rapidly as concerns about climate change drive a conversion of the grid to intermittent renewable energy generation such as wind and solar.

Zero-carbon cloud resources have several novel properties. First, they have correlated availability at massive scale – 10K-1M cores in an entire data center will go on or offline at once. Second, these periods may be highly predictable -- external factors such as weather, predicted load, and power markets shape the availability of stranded power. Third, these properties can be engineered – for example, a small amount of energy storage can be used to "delay" unavailability.

We will propose Zero-carbon cloud, or massive volatile resources based on stranded power as an interesting new model for a variety of classical distributed systems challenges (consistency, etc.) and new challenges for optimization.

More information is available at http://zccloud.cs.uchicago.edu/

Brief Biography
Dr. Andrew A. Chien is the William Eckhardt Distinguished Service Professor in Computer Science, Director of the CERES Center for Unstoppable Computing, and Senior Fellow in the Computation Institute at the University of Chicago. He also serves as a Senior Computer Scientist at the Argonne National Laboratory. Dr. Chien served as Vice President of Research at Intel Corporation, leading long-range and "disruptive technologies" research at Intel Research. At Intel, he also led Intel's external research programs, including government and higher education engagements. In this role, Chien launched imaginative new efforts in robotics, wireless power, sensing and perception, nucleic acid sequencing, networking, cloud, and ethnography. Working with Microsoft and NSF, Chien was instrumental in creation of the Universal Parallel Computing Research Centers (UPCRC) focused on parallel software, the Open Cirrus Consortium focused on Cloud computing, and Intel's Exascale Research program.

For more than 25 years, Chien has been a global research and education leader, and an active researcher in parallel computing, computer architecture, programming languages, networking, clusters, grids, and cloud computing. Previous academic positions include the SAIC Chair Professor in Computer Science and Engineering, and founding Director of the Center for Networked Systems at the University of California at San Diego (1998-2005). While at UCSD, he also founded Entropia, a widely-known Internet Grid computing startup. From 1990 to 1998, Chien was a Professor of Computer Science at the University of Illinois at Urbana-Champaign with joint appointments at the National Center for Supercomputing Applications (NCSA) where he was a research leader for parallel computing software and hardware, and developed the well-known Fast Messages, HPVM, and Windows NT Supercluster systems.

Dr. Chien is a Fellow of the American Association for Advancement of Science (AAAS), Fellow of the Association for Computing Machinery (ACM), Fellow of Institute of Electrical and Electronics Engineers (IEEE), and has published over 150 technical papers. His research has been recognized for excellence, and supported by the National Science Foundation (NSF), Defense Advanced Research Projects Administration (DARPA), Department of Energy (DOE), National Aeronautics and Space Agency (NASA), Office of Naval Research (ONR), and numerous industry sponsors. Chien served on the Board of Directors for the Computing Research Association (CRA), Advisory Board of the National Science Foundation's Computing and Information Science and Engineering (CISE) Directorate, and is currently on the Editorial Board of the Communications of the Association for Computing Machinery (CACM), ACM's Transactions on Parallel Computing (TOPC), and the Journal of Grid Computing (JOGC). Chien received his Bachelor's in electrical engineering, Master's and Ph.D. in computer science from the Massachusetts Institute of Technology.

PODC'16, July 25-28, 2016, Chicago, IL, USA.
ACM 978-1-4503-3964-3/16/07.
http://dx.doi.org/10.1145/2933057.2933122

A Distributed $(2+\epsilon)$-Approximation for Vertex Cover in $O(\log\Delta/\epsilon\log\log\Delta)$ Rounds

Reuven Bar-Yehuda
Technion, Department of Computer Science
reuven@cs.technion.ac.il

Keren Censor-Hillel *
Technion, Department of Computer Science
ckeren@cs.technion.ac.il

Gregory Schwartzman
Technion, Department of Computer Science
gregorys@cs.technion.ac.il

ABSTRACT

We present a simple deterministic distributed $(2+\epsilon)$ approximation algorithm for minimum weight vertex cover, which completes in $O(\log\Delta/\epsilon\log\log\Delta)$ rounds, where Δ is the maximum degree in the graph, for any $\epsilon > 0$ which is at most $O(1)$. For a constant ϵ, this implies a constant approximation in $O(\log\Delta/\log\log\Delta)$ rounds, which contradicts the lower bound of [KMW10].

1. INTRODUCTION

We present a simple deterministic distributed $(2+\epsilon)$-approximation algorithm for minimum weight vertex cover (MWVC), which completes in $O(\log\Delta/\epsilon\log\log\Delta)$ rounds, where Δ is the maximum degree in the graph, for any $\epsilon > 0$ which is at most $O(1)$, and in particular $o(1)$. If $\Delta \leq 16$ then our algorithm simply requires $O(1/\epsilon)$ rounds. Our algorithm adapts the *local ratio* technique [BYE85] to the distributed setting in a novel simple manner. Roughly speaking, in the simplest form of this technique, one repeatedly reduces the same amount of weight from both endpoints of an arbitrary edge, while not going below zero for any vertex. Terminating this process at the time in which for every edge there is at least one endpoint with no remaining weight, gives that the set of vertices with no remaining weight is a 2-approximation for MWVC. This can be extended to produce a $(2+\epsilon)$-approximation if instead the process terminates at the time in which for every edge there is at least one endpoint with a remaining weight of at most an ϵ' fraction of its initial weight, where $\epsilon' = \epsilon/(\epsilon+2)$.

The challenge in translating this framework to the distributed setting is that the weights we can reduce from endpoints of neighboring edges must depend on each other. This is because we need to make sure that no weight goes below zero. However, as common to computing in this setting, we cannot afford long chains of dependencies, as these directly translate to a large number of communication rounds. Our key method is to divide the weight of a vertex into two parts, a *vault* from which it initiates requests for weight reductions with its neighbors, and a *bank* from which it reduces weight in response to requests from its neighbors. Carefully balancing these two reciprocal weight reductions at each vertex gives the claimed $(2+\epsilon)$ approximation factor and $O(\log\Delta/\epsilon\log\log\Delta)$ time complexity.[1]

In fact, in our distributed algorithm, each vertex v with degree $d(v)$ completes in $O(1/\epsilon)$ rounds if $d(v) \leq 16$, and in $O(\log d(v)/\epsilon\log\log d(v))$ rounds otherwise (and requires no knowledge of n or Δ). The algorithm also works in anonymous networks, i.e., no IDs are required. Moreover, the vertices are not required to start at the same round: as long as each vertex starts no later than after the first message has been sent to it, then each vertex completes within $O(\log d(v)/\epsilon\log\log d(v))$ rounds after it starts (or in $O(1/\epsilon)$ rounds if $d(v) \leq 16$). Finally, provided that the weights of all vertices as well as the ratio between the maximal and minimal weights fit in $O(\log n)$ bits, our algorithm can be modified to work in the CONGEST model.

For any constant ϵ, our algorithm provides a constant approximation in $O(\log\Delta/\log\log\Delta)$ rounds. Apart from improving upon the previous best known complexity for distributed $(2+\epsilon)$-approximation algorithm for minimum weight vertex cover and providing a new way of adapting the sequential local ratio technique to the distributed setting, our algorithm has the consequence of contradicting the lower bound of [KMW10]. The latter states that a constant approximation algorithm requires $\Omega(\log\Delta)$ rounds. Its refutation implies that the current lower bound is $\Omega(\log\Delta/\log\log\Delta)$ from [KMW04], which means that our algorithm is tight.

In Section 5 we pinpoint the flaw in the lower bound of [KMW10]. This also includes refuting the second result of [KMW10], which is a lower bound in terms of n, of $\Omega(\sqrt{\log n})$ rounds for a constant approximation al-

*Supported in part by the Israel Science Foundation (grant 1696/14).

PODC'16, July 25-28, 2016, Chicago, IL, USA
© 2016 ACM. ISBN 978-1-4503-3964-3/16/07...$15.00
DOI: http://dx.doi.org/10.1145/2933057.2933086

[1] Under some restrictions on ϵ, the dependence of the number of rounds on ϵ can be improved via a more involved analysis, see Section 6.

gorithm. Roughly speaking, we claim that the statement of the main theorem is only correct for some smaller range of parameters than claimed, and hence, in particular, one cannot apply it for a number of rounds that is $\Theta(\log \Delta)$ or $\Theta(\sqrt{\log n})$. We emphasize that, as far as we are aware, this bug *does not* occur in the previous version of the lower bound [KMW04], implying that the current lower bounds are $\Omega(\sqrt{\log n / \log \log n})$ in terms of n, and $\Omega(\log \Delta / \log \log \Delta)$ in terms of Δ.

Related Work.

Minimum vertex cover is known to be one of Karp's 21 NP-hard problems [Kar72]. For the unweighted case, a simple polynomial-time 2-approximation algorithm is obtained by taking the endpoints of a greedy maximal matching (see, e.g., [CLRS09, GJ79]). For the weighted case, the first polynomial-time 2-approximation algorithm was given in [NJ75] and observed by [Hoc82]. The first linear-time 2-approximation algorithm is due to [BE81] using the primal-dual framework, and [BYE85] gives a linear-time 2-approximation local-ratio algorithm. Conditioned on the unique games conjecture, minimum vertex cover does not have a $(2 - \epsilon)$ polynomial-time approximation algorithm [KR08].

In the distributed setting, an excellent summary of approximation algorithms is given in [ÅS10], which we overview in what follows. For the unweighted case, it is known how to find a 2-approximation in $O(\log^4 n)$ rounds [HKP01] and in $O(\Delta + \log^* n)$ rounds [PR01]. With no dependence on n, [ÅFP+09] give a $O(\Delta^2)$-round 2-approximation algorithm, and [PS09] give an $O(\Delta)$-round 3-approximation algorithm. The maximal matching algorithm of [BEPS12] gives a 2-approximation for vertex cover in $O(\log \Delta + (\log \log n)^4)$ rounds. This can be made into a $(2 + 1/\text{poly}\Delta)$-approximation within $O(\log \Delta)$ rounds [Pet16].

For the weighted case, [GKP08] give a randomized 2-approximation algorithm in $O(\log n + \log W)$ rounds, where W is the maximal vertex weight. Later, [KY11] were the first to give a randomized 2-approximation algorithm in $O(\log n)$ rounds, i.e., in a running time that is logarithmic in n and independent of the weights. In [PR01], a 2-approximation algorithm which requires $O(\Delta + \log^* n)$ rounds, and in [KVY94], a $(2 + \epsilon)$-approximation algorithm is given, requiring $O(\log \epsilon^{-1} \log n)$ rounds. With no dependence on n, [KMW06] give a $(2+\epsilon)$-approximation algorithm in $O(\epsilon^{-4} \log \Delta)$, [ÅFP+09] give a 2-approximation algorithm in $O(1)$ rounds for $\Delta \leq 3$, and [ÅS10] give a 2-approximation algorithm in $O(\Delta + \log^* W)$ rounds, where W is the maximal weight.

Distributed algorithms have also been devised for additional problems, which are related to vertex cover. The first distributed algorithm that uses the local ratio technique is due to [PRS12], who give an approximation for a variant of a maximum coverage problem (which is a minimization problem). In [GKPS08], a bi-criteria $(2 + \epsilon)$-approximation algorithm for the capacitated vertex cover problem is given, in which each vertex has a limited capacity for the number of edges it can cover and the solution violates the capacity constraints by a factor of at most $(4 + \epsilon)$.

2. A LOCAL RATIO TEMPLATE FOR APPROXIMATING MWVC

In this section we provide the template for using the local-ratio technique for obtaining a $(2 + \epsilon)$-approximation for MWVC. This template does not assume any specific computation model and only describes the paradigm and correctness. It can be proven either using the primal-dual framework [BE81], or the local-ratio framework [Bar00], which are known to be equivalent [BR05]. A similar idea, though in the primal-dual framework, was given in [KVY94] which obtained a $(2 + \epsilon)$-approximation as well, but with a larger number of rounds. Our distributed implementation is more efficient and allows us to obtain a faster algorithm. Here we provide the template and proof for completeness. In Section 3 we provide a distributed implementation of the template and analyze its running time.

We assume a given weighted graph $G = (V, w, E)$, where $w : V \to \mathbb{R}^+$ is an assignment of weights for the vertices. Let $\delta : E \to \mathbb{R}^+$ be a function that assigns weights to edges. We say that δ is *G-valid* if for every $v \in V$, $\sum_{e:v \in e} \delta(e) \leq w(v)$, i.e., the sum of weights of edges that touch a vertex is at most the weight of that vertex in G.

Fix any G-valid function δ. Define $\tilde{w}_\delta : V \to \mathbb{R}^+$ by $\tilde{w}_\delta(v) = \sum_{e:v \in e} \delta(e)$, and let $w'_\delta : V \to \mathbb{R}^+$ be such that $w'_\delta(v) = w(v) - \tilde{w}_\delta(v)$. Since δ is G-valid, it holds that $w'_\delta(v) \geq 0$ for every $v \in V$.

Let $S_\delta = \{v \in V \mid w'_\delta(v) \leq \epsilon' w(v)\}$, where $\epsilon' = \epsilon/(2 + \epsilon)$. The following theorem states that if S_δ is a vertex cover, then it is a $(2 + \epsilon)$-approximation for MWVC.

THEOREM 2.1. *Fix $\epsilon > 0$ and let δ be a G-valid function. Let OPT be the sum of weights of vertices in a minimum weight vertex cover S_{OPT} of G. Then $\sum_{v \in S_\delta} w(v) \leq (2 + \epsilon) OPT$. In particular, if S_δ is a vertex cover then it is a $(2 + \epsilon)$-approximation for MWVC for G.*

PROOF. For every $v \in V$ we have that $w'_\delta(v) = w(v) - \tilde{w}_\delta(v)$, which implies that $w(v) = w'_\delta(v) + \tilde{w}_\delta(v)$. For every $v \in S_\delta$ it holds that $w'_\delta(v) \leq \epsilon' w(v)$, and therefore $w(v) \leq \epsilon' w(v) + \tilde{w}_\delta(v)$. Put otherwise, for every $v \in S_\delta$ we have $w(v) \leq (1/(1 - \epsilon')) \tilde{w}_\delta(v)$. This gives:

$$\begin{aligned}
\sum_{v \in S_\delta} w(v) &\leq \frac{1}{(1 - \epsilon')} \sum_{v \in S_\delta} \tilde{w}_\delta(v) \\
&\leq \frac{1}{(1 - \epsilon')} \sum_{v \in S_\delta} \sum_{e:v \in e} \delta(e) \\
&\leq \frac{1}{(1 - \epsilon')} \sum_{v \in V} \sum_{e:v \in e} \delta(e) \\
&\leq \frac{1}{(1 - \epsilon')} \cdot 2 \sum_{e \in E} \delta(e).
\end{aligned}$$

The above is at most $(2/(1 - \epsilon'))OPT$ because $OPT \geq \sum_{e \in E} \delta(e)$. To see why $OPT \geq \sum_{e \in E} \delta(e)$, associate each edge e with its endpoint v_e in S_{OPT} (choose an arbitrary endpoint if both are in S_{OPT}). The weight $w(v)$

of each $v \in S_{OPT}$ is at least $\sum_{e:v_e=v} \delta(e)$, because it is at least $\sum_{e:v\in e} \delta(e)$. Hence, $OPT = \sum_{v\in S_{OPT}} w(v) \geq \sum_{v\in S_{OPT}} \sum_{e:v_e=v} \delta(e) = \sum_{e\in E} \delta(e)$. Hence the sum of weights in S_δ is at most a factor $2/(1-\epsilon')$ larger than OPT. Since $\epsilon' = \epsilon/(2+\epsilon)$, we have that $2/(1-\epsilon') = (2-2\epsilon'+2\epsilon')/(1-\epsilon') = 2(1+\epsilon'/(1-\epsilon')) = 2+\epsilon$, which completes the proof. □

In the next section, we show how to implement efficiently in a distributed setting an algorithm that finds a function δ that is G-valid, for which the set S_δ is a vertex cover. This immediately gives a distributed $(2+\epsilon)$-approximation for MWVC.

3. A FAST DISTRIBUTED IMPLEMENTATION

Our goal in this section is to find a G-valid function δ such that S_δ is a vertex cover. Since every vertex knows whether it is in S_δ, this immediately gives a distributed $(2+\epsilon)$-approximation algorithm for MWVC. Our algorithm is deterministic and requires for every vertex v only $O(\log d(v)/\epsilon' \log\log d(v))$ rounds, where $d(v)$ is the degree of v in G, or $O(1/\epsilon')$ if $d(v) \leq 16$. Here $\epsilon' = \epsilon/(2+\epsilon)$ where $\epsilon = O(1)$, which means that $\epsilon' = \Theta(\epsilon)$. For clarity of presentation, in this section we describe an implementation for the LOCAL model. In Section 4 we show how this can be easily be adapted to the CONGEST model in which the message size is limited to $O(\log n)$ bits, provided that the initial weights of the vertices and the ratio between the maximal and minimal weights can be expressed by $O(\log n)$ bits.

In our algorithm, each vertex converges to agreeing with each of its neighbors on a function δ that is G-valid, by iterating the process of decreasing the weight of neighbors by the same amount, until either its weight is below a small fraction of its original weight or it has no more neighbors in the graph induced by the vertices that remain so far. This would imply that the set of vertices whose weight decreased below the above threshold is a vertex cover, and by Theorem 2.1 its weight is a $(2+\epsilon)$-approximation to the weight of a minimal vertex cover.

Overview of Algorithm 1.

The algorithm consists of iterations, each of which has a constant number of communication rounds. Each vertex v splits its current weight $w_i(v)$ into two amounts. The first amount is $vault(v)$, which is equal to its threshold $\epsilon' w_0(v)$, and the second amount is $bank_i(v)$, which contains the rest of the weight $w_i(v) - vault(v)$. Notice that $\epsilon' < 1$ because $\epsilon' = \epsilon/(2+\epsilon)$ and therefore these amounts are well-defined.

In each iteration, vertex v sends a $request_i(v,u)$ request to its neighbor u, which is the amount in its $vault(v)$ divided by the current number of neighbors of v. This guarantees that any weight decrease that results for v from this part does not exceed its total remaining weight. The second amount is used to respond to $request_i(u,v)$ requests from its neighbors. The vertex v processes these requests one by one in any arbitrary order, and responds with the amount $budget_i(v,u)$ which is the largest amount by which v can currently decrease its weight, and no more than the request $request_i(u,v)$. This amount is decreased from $bank_i(v)$, and hence it is also guaranteed that decreasing this amount does not exceed the total remaining weight.

Once the weight of v reaches its threshold, v completes its algorithm, returning `InCover` after notifying its neighbors of this fact. If the weight is still above the threshold then v only removes its edges to neighbors that notified they are returning `InCover`. This gives that each edge has at least one endpoint returning `InCover`, and hence the set of all such vertices is a vertex cover, and by Theorem 2.1 its weight is a $(2+\epsilon)$-approximation to the weight of a minimal vertex cover. The analysis of the number of rounds is based on the observation that for each of the neighbors u of v, either it decreases its weight by responding to $request_i(v,u)$ with the entire amount and thereby contributes to decreasing the weight of v by this amount, or it does not have the required budget in its $bank_i(u)$, in which case it contributes to decreasing the number of neighbors of v by 1.

We proceed by the full pseudocode, followed by an explicit analysis.

THEOREM 3.1. *For every $\epsilon = O(1)$, Algorithm 1 is a deterministic distributed $(2+\epsilon)$-approximation algorithm for MWVC in which each vertex v with degree $d(v)$ completes in $O(1/\epsilon)$ rounds if $d(v) \leq 16$, and in $O(\log d(v)/\epsilon \log\log d(v))$ rounds otherwise.*

We split the proof into two parts, showing correctness and complexity separately. We begin by showing correctness in the following lemma. Essentially, we show that the algorithm finds a function δ that is G-valid and for which S_δ is a vertex cover.

LEMMA 3.2. *Algorithm 1 is a deterministic distributed $(2+\epsilon)$-approximation algorithm for MWVC.*

PROOF. We first show that Algorithm 1 is a $(2+\epsilon)$-approximation algorithm for MWVC. That is, we claim that the set $C = \{v \in V \mid v \text{ outputs } \texttt{InCover}\}$ is a vertex cover, and that $\sum_{v\in C} w(v) \leq (2+\epsilon)OPT$, where $OPT = \sum_{v\in S_{OPT}} w(v)$ for some optimal vertex cover S_{OPT}. For this, we show that the sum of amounts deducted by neighbors can be used to define a G-valid function over the edges. This will be exactly the function according to which the vertices decide whether to output `InCover` or `NotInCover`.

For every $e = \{v,u\} \in E$ and every $i = 0, 1 \ldots$, let $\delta_i(e) = budget_i(u,v) + budget_i(v,u)$. Let $\delta(e) = \sum_{i=0,1,\ldots} \delta_i(e)$. We claim that δ is G-valid, i.e., for every vertex v it holds that $\sum_{e:v\in e} \delta(e) \leq w(v)$. Let j be the value of i when v returns, that is, v participates in iterations $i = 0, \ldots, j-1$. For each iteration $i = 0, \ldots j-1$ it holds that

$$\sum_{u_k\in N_i(v)} budget_i(u_k, v) \leq \sum_{u_k\in N_i(v)} vault(v)/d_i(v) = vault(v),$$

where $N_i(v) = \{u_1, \ldots, u_{d_i(v)}\}$ is the set of neighbors of v at the beginning of iteration i. Further, since for $u_k \in$

$w_0(v) = w(v)$
$d_0(v) = d(v)$
$N_0(v) = N(v)$
$i = 0$
$vault(v) = \epsilon' w_0(v)$
while *true* **do**
  $bank_i(v) = w_i(v) - vault(v)$
  $w_{i+1}(v) = w_i(v)$
  $N_{i+1}(v) = N_i(v)$
  foreach $u \in N_i(v)$ **do**
    $request_i(v, u) = vault(v)/d_i(v)$
    Send $request_i(v, u)$ to u
    Let $budget_i(u, v)$ be the response from u
    $w_{i+1}(v) = w_{i+1}(v) - budget_i(u, v)$
    if $budget_i(u, v) < request_i(v, u)$ **then**
      $N_{i+1}(v) = N_{i+1}(v) \setminus \{u\}$
  Let $u_1 \dots u_{d_i(v)}$ be an order of $N_i(v)$
  foreach $k = 1, \dots, d_i(v)$ **do**
    Let $request_i(u_k, v)$ be received from $u_k \in N_i(v)$
    $budget_i(v, u_k) = \min\{request_i(u_k, v), bank_i(v) - \sum_{t=1}^{k-1} budget_i(v, u_t)\}$
    Send $budget_i(v, u_k)$ to u_k
  $bank_{i+1}(v) = bank_i(v) - \sum_{k=1}^{d_i(v)} budget_i(v, u_k)$
  $w_{i+1}(v) = w_{i+1}(v) - \sum_{k=1}^{d_i(v)} budget_i(v, u_k)$
  $d_{i+1}(v) = |N_{i+1}(v)|$
  $i = i + 1$
  if $w_i(v) \le \epsilon' w_0(v)$ **then**
    Send $(v, cover)$ to all neighbors
    Return `InCover`
  foreach $(u, cover)$ *received from* $u \in N_i(v)$ **do**
    $N_i(v) = N_i(v) \setminus \{u\}$
    $d_i(v) = d_i(v) - 1$
  if $d_i(v) = 0$ **then**
    Return `NotInCover`

Algorithm 1: A distributed $(2+\epsilon)$-approximation algorithm for MWVC, code for vertex v.

$N_i(v)$, $budget_i(v, u_k) = \min\{request_i(u_k, v), bank_i(v) - \sum_{t=1}^{k-1} budget_i(v, u_t)\}$, we have that

$$\sum_{u_k \in N_i(v)} budget_i(v, u_k) \le bank_i(v).$$

Since $bank_i(v) = w_i(v) - vault(v)$ it holds that $\sum_{e=\{v,u_k\}:u_k \in N_i(v)} \delta_i(e) \le w_i(v)$. Since $w_{i+1}(v) = w_i(v) - \sum_{(u,v)\in E} (budget_i(u, v) + budget_i(v, u))$, we have that $w_{i+1}(v) = w_i(v) - \sum_{e:v\in e} \delta_i(e) \ge 0$. This gives that $w(v) = \sum_{i=0}^{j-1} (w_i(v) - w_{i+1}(v)) + w_j(v) = \sum_{i=0}^{j-1} \sum_{e:v\in e} \delta_i(e) + w_j(v) \ge 0$, and hence $w(v) - \sum_{e:v\in e} \delta(e) = w_j(v) \ge 0$.

This proves that δ is G-valid, which gives that for $C = \{v \in V \mid v \text{ outputs } \texttt{InCover}\}$ it holds that $\sum_{v\in C} w(v) \le (2+\epsilon)OPT$, where $OPT = \sum_{v\in S_{OPT}} w(v)$ for some optimal vertex cover S_{OPT}, by Theorem 2.1. This is because a vertex v outputs `InCover` at the end of iteration $i = j - 1$ if and only if $w_j(v) \le \epsilon' w_0(v)$. It remains to show that C is a vertex cover. To see why, consider an edge $e = \{v, u\} \in E$. We claim that if u, v have both returned by the end of iteration i, then at least one of them is in C. This is because otherwise $d_{i+1}(v), d_{i+1}(u) \ge 1$, which implies that both have not returned yet. This completes the proof that C is indeed a $(2+\epsilon)$-approximation for MWVC. □

It remains to bound the number of rounds. We do so in the following lemma, in which we show that in each iteration either enough weight is reduced or enough neighbors enter the vertex cover.

LEMMA 3.3. *In Algorithm 1, each vertex v with degree $d(v)$ completes in $O(1/\epsilon)$ rounds if $d(v) \le 16$, and in $O(\log d(v)/\epsilon \log\log d(v))$ rounds otherwise.*

PROOF. Let $K_v > 1$ be a parameter to be chosen later. Let i be an iteration at the beginning of which a vertex $v \in V$ has not yet returned. We claim that either $d_{i+1}(v) \le d_i(v)/K_v$ or $w_{i+1}(v) \le w_i(v) - \epsilon' w_0(v)/K_v$. To see why, suppose $d_{i+1}(v) > d_i(v)/K_v$. This means that for at least $\lceil d_i(v)/K_v \rceil$ vertices $u \in N_i(v)$, it holds that $budget_i(u, v) = request_i(v, u)$, and hence

$$\begin{aligned} w_{i+1}(v) &\le w_i(v) - \left\lceil \frac{d_i(v)}{K_v} \right\rceil \cdot \frac{vault(v)}{d_i(v)} \\ &\le w_i(v) - \frac{d_i(v)}{K_v} \cdot \frac{\epsilon' w_0(v)}{d_i(v)} \\ &\le w_i(v) - \epsilon' w_0(v)/K_v. \end{aligned}$$

Next, we claim that v returns after at most $K_v/\epsilon' + \log d(v)/\log K_v$ iterations of the algorithm. This is because at most $\log_{K_v} d(v) = \log d(v)/\log K_v$ of the iterations i can be such that $d_{i+1}(v) \le d_i(v)/K_v$ (since v returns when $d_i(v) = 0$), and at most K_v/ϵ' iterations i can be such that $w_{i+1}(v) \le w_i(v) - \epsilon' w_0(v)/K_v$ (since v returns when $w_i(v) \le \epsilon' w_0(v)$).

Finally, we set K_v as follows. If $d(v) \le 16$ we set $K_v = d(v) + 1$. This guarantees $K_v > 1$ (an isolated vertex simply outputs `NotInCover`) and gives $O(1/\epsilon)$ rounds for v to complete.

Otherwise, we set $K_v = \log d(v)/\log\log d(v)$. Since $d(v) > 16$, it holds that K_v is well defined (as $\log\log d(v) > 1$) and that $K_v > 1$. It also holds that $\log K_v > 1$ which is used in what follows. This gives that vertex v returns after at most j iterations, where

$$\begin{aligned} j &\le K_v/\epsilon' + \log d(v)/\log K_v \\ &= \frac{\log d(v)}{\epsilon' \log\log d(v)} + \log d(v)/\log K_v \\ &= \frac{\log d(v)}{\epsilon' \log\log d(v)} + \frac{\log d(v)}{\log(\log d(v)/\log\log d(v))} \\ &= \frac{\log d(v)}{\epsilon' \log\log d(v)} + \frac{\log d(v)}{\log\log d(v) - \log\log\log d(v)} \\ &\le O\left(\frac{\log d(v)}{\epsilon \log\log d(v)}\right), \end{aligned}$$

where the last inequality follows because $\epsilon' = \epsilon/(2+\epsilon)$ (and since ϵ is at most $O(1)$ and so $\epsilon' = \Theta(\epsilon)$) and $\log\log d(v)$ dominates $\log\log\log d(v)$, completing the proof. □

Theorem 3.1 follows directly from Lemmas 3.2 and 3.3.

4. ADAPTATION TO THE CONGEST MODEL

Our algorithm is described for the LOCAL model, but can be easily adapted to the CONGEST model in which the message size is limited to $O(\log n)$ bits, provided that the initial weights of the vertices and the ratio between the maximal and minimal weights can be expressed by $O(\log n)$ bits. In order to accommodate $O(\log n)$-bit messages, we slightly modify the messages that are sent as follows. First, in an initial round, each vertex v sends $w_0(v)$ to all of its neighbors. Then, instead of sending $request_i(v,u)$ to neighbor u in some iteration i, vertex v only needs to send $d_i(v)$ to its neighbor u and u can locally compute $request_i(v,u) = vault(v)/d_i(v)$ since all vertices know the value of ϵ as part of their algorithm.

Second, we need to handle the messages of type $budget_i(v,u)$. In general, this amount can be an arbitrary fraction which might not fit in $O(\log n)$ bits. However, we notice that we can avoid sending this explicit amount. To do this, we slightly modify $vault(v)$ to be $\epsilon' w_0(v)/2$. Then, upon receiving a $request_i(u,v)$ message, if $budget_i(v,u) = request_i(u,v)$ then vertex v replies with a predefined message *accept*, and otherwise, v responds with the maximal integer t such that $t\epsilon' w_0(v)/2 \le budget_i(v,u)$. The amount $t\epsilon' w_0(v)/2$ can be locally computed by u, and u can infer that v returns `InCover`. This is because the remainder of weight in vertex v will be another value of at most $\epsilon' w_0(v)/2$ on top of the at most $\epsilon' w_0(v)/2$ value which might remain in $vault(v)$, summing to no more than $\epsilon' w_0(v)$, as needed.

5. DISCUSSION OF [KMW10]

The main result of [KMW10] is the following:

Theorem 9 from [KMW10].

For every constant $\epsilon > 0$, there are graphs G, such that in k communication rounds, every distributed algorithm for the minimum vertex cover problem on G has approximation ratios at least

$$\Omega\left(n^{\frac{1/4-\epsilon}{k^2}}\right) \text{ and } \Omega\left(\Delta^{\frac{1-\epsilon}{k+1}}\right),$$

where n and Δ denote the number of nodes and the highest degree in G, respectively.

The argument in [KMW10] is that in order for the above approximation factors to be constant, the number of rounds, k, has to be $\Omega(\sqrt{\log n})$ and $\Omega(\log \Delta)$, respectively.

However, we argue that the above lower bounds only hold under the conditions that $k = O((\log n)^{1/3})$ and $k = O(\sqrt{\log \Delta})$, respectively. This means that they cannot be applied to $k = \Theta(\sqrt{\log n})$ or $k = \Theta(\log \Delta)$, and therefore do not imply the claimed bounds for constant approximation factors.

To justify our claim, we elaborate upon the proof of the theorem. Previous lemmas in the paper[2] show that the approximation factor of any k-round algorithm is $\Omega(\delta)$, where δ satisfies the following two constraints[3]. First, it holds that $n \le 2^{2k^3+4k}\delta^{4k^2}$ and second, it holds that $\Delta = 2^{k(k+1)/2}\delta^{k+1}$.

The first constraint implies that

$$\delta \ge \frac{n^{1/4k^2}}{2^{(2k^3+4k)/4k^2}} = \frac{n^{1/4k^2}}{n^{(2k^3+4k)/4k^2 \log n}} = n^{1/4k^2-(2k^3+4k)/4k^2 \log n}.$$

Hence, in order to deduce that $\delta = \Omega(n^{\frac{1/4-\epsilon}{k^2}})$, it needs to hold that $(2k^3+4k)/4k^2 \log n \le \epsilon/k^2$. However, for this to happen, it must be that $2k^3+4k \le 4\epsilon \log n$, and in particular k has to be within $O((\log n)^{1/3})$.

The second constraint implies that

$$\delta = \frac{\Delta^{1/(k+1)}}{2^{k/2}} = \frac{\Delta^{1/(k+1)}}{\Delta^{k/2\log\Delta}} = \Delta^{1/(k+1)-k/2\log\Delta}.$$

Hence, in order to deduce that $\delta = \Omega(\Delta^{\frac{1-\epsilon}{k+1}})$, it needs to hold that $k/2\log\Delta \le \epsilon/(k+1)$. However, for this to happen, it must be that $k(k+1) \le 2\epsilon \log \Delta$, and in particular k has to be within $O(\sqrt{\log \Delta})$.

We emphasize again that this last step in the proof of the lower bound is different in the previous version [KMW04], and hence we do not suggest that there is a flaw in [KMW04].

6. A TIGHTER BOUND ON THE NUMBER OF COMMUNICATION ROUNDS

In the previous section, we set $K_v = \log d(v)/\log\log d(v)$ to get a bound of $O(\log d(v)/(\epsilon' \log\log d(v)))$ communication rounds. One may notice that plugging $K_v = \epsilon' \log d(v)/\log\log d(v)$ yields the much better bound of $O(\log d(v)/(\log\log d(v) - \log \epsilon'))$. However, for small values of ϵ' this expression becomes undefined or negative.

The reason for this is that for the proof to make sense, we need the condition $K_v > 1$ to hold. If we set $K_v = \epsilon' \log d(v)/\log\log d(v)$, the condition does not hold for small values of ϵ'. We can still get a better dependence on ϵ' with a slightly more careful analysis.

We note that if $\epsilon' \le \log\log d(v)/\log d(v)$, then $K_v > 1$ cannot hold for $K_v = \epsilon' \log d(v)/\log\log d(v)$. Instead, for such values of ϵ', we set $K_v = 2$, which yields a bound of $O(1/\epsilon' + \log d(v))$. If $\epsilon' > \log\log d(v)/\log d(v)$ we still get the previous bound of $O(\log d(v)/(\log\log d(v) - \log \epsilon'))$ rounds, which for these values of ϵ is $O(\log d(v)/(\log\log d(v)))$.

Acknowledgements.

We thank Seri Khoury and Dror Rawitz for many discussions and helpful suggestions. We also thank the anonymous reviewers for their helpful suggestions.

[2]We refer the reader to [KMW10] for exact details.

[3]We use the notation δ as this is the notation in [KMW10]. Notice that it is unrelated to the function δ that we use in our framework in previous sections of this paper.

7. REFERENCES

[ÅFP+09] Matti Åstrand, Patrik Floréen, Valentin Polishchuk, Joel Rybicki, Jukka Suomela, and Jara Uitto. A local 2-approximation algorithm for the vertex cover problem. In *Distributed Computing, 23rd International Symposium, DISC 2009, Elche, Spain, September 23-25, 2009. Proceedings*, pages 191–205, 2009.

[ÅS10] Matti Åstrand and Jukka Suomela. Fast distributed approximation algorithms for vertex cover and set cover in anonymous networks. In *SPAA 2010: Proceedings of the 22nd Annual ACM Symposium on Parallelism in Algorithms and Architectures, Thira, Santorini, Greece, June 13-15, 2010*, pages 294–302, 2010.

[Bar00] Reuven Bar-Yehuda. One for the price of two: a unified approach for approximating covering problems. *Algorithmica*, 27(2):131–144, 2000.

[BE81] Reuven Bar-Yehuda and Shimon Even. A linear-time approximation algorithm for the weighted vertex cover problem. *J. Algorithms*, 2(2):198–203, 1981.

[BEPS12] Leonid Barenboim, Michael Elkin, Seth Pettie, and Johannes Schneider. The locality of distributed symmetry breaking. In *53rd Annual IEEE Symposium on Foundations of Computer Science, FOCS 2012, New Brunswick, NJ, USA, October 20-23, 2012*, pages 321–330, 2012.

[BR05] Reuven Bar-Yehuda and Dror Rawitz. On the equivalence between the primal-dual schema and the local ratio technique. *SIAM J. Discrete Math.*, 19(3):762–797, 2005.

[BYE85] Reuven Bar-Yehuda and Shimon Even. A local-ratio theorem for approximating the weighted vertex cover problem. *North-Holland Mathematics Studies*, 109:27–45, 1985.

[CLRS09] Thomas H. Cormen, Charles E. Leiserson, Ronald L. Rivest, and Clifford Stein. *Introduction to Algorithms, Third Edition*. The MIT Press, 3rd edition, 2009.

[GJ79] M. R. Garey and David S. Johnson. *Computers and Intractability: A Guide to the Theory of NP-Completeness*. W. H. Freeman, 1979.

[GKP08] Fabrizio Grandoni, Jochen Könemann, and Alessandro Panconesi. Distributed weighted vertex cover via maximal matchings. *ACM Transactions on Algorithms*, 5(1), 2008.

[GKPS08] Fabrizio Grandoni, Jochen Könemann, Alessandro Panconesi, and Mauro Sozio. A primal-dual bicriteria distributed algorithm for capacitated vertex cover. *SIAM J. Comput.*, 38(3):825–840, 2008.

[HKP01] Michal Hanckowiak, Michal Karonski, and Alessandro Panconesi. On the distributed complexity of computing maximal matchings. *SIAM J. Discrete Math.*, 15(1):41–57, 2001.

[Hoc82] Dorit S. Hochbaum. Approximation algorithms for the set covering and vertex cover problems. *SIAM J. Comput.*, 11(3):555–556, 1982.

[Kar72] Richard M. Karp. Reducibility among combinatorial problems. In *Proceedings of a symposium on the Complexity of Computer Computations, held March 20-22, 1972, at the IBM Thomas J. Watson Research Center, Yorktown Heights, New York.*, pages 85–103, 1972.

[KMW04] Fabian Kuhn, Thomas Moscibroda, and Roger Wattenhofer. What cannot be computed locally! In *Proceedings of the Twenty-Third Annual ACM Symposium on Principles of Distributed Computing, PODC 2004, St. John's, Newfoundland, Canada, July 25-28, 2004*, pages 300–309, 2004.

[KMW06] Fabian Kuhn, Thomas Moscibroda, and Roger Wattenhofer. The price of being near-sighted. In *Proceedings of the Seventeenth Annual ACM-SIAM Symposium on Discrete Algorithms, SODA 2006, Miami, Florida, USA, January 22-26, 2006*, pages 980–989, 2006.

[KMW10] Fabian Kuhn, Thomas Moscibroda, and Roger Wattenhofer. Local computation: Lower and upper bounds. *CoRR*, abs/1011.5470, 2010.

[KR08] Subhash Khot and Oded Regev. Vertex cover might be hard to approximate to within 2-epsilon. *J. Comput. Syst. Sci.*, 74(3):335–349, 2008.

[KVY94] Samir Khuller, Uzi Vishkin, and Neal E. Young. A primal-dual parallel approximation technique applied to weighted set and vertex covers. *J. Algorithms*, 17(2):280–289, 1994.

[KY11] Christos Koufogiannakis and Neal E. Young. Distributed algorithms for covering, packing and maximum weighted matching. *Distributed Computing*, 24(1):45–63, 2011.

[NJ75] George L. Nemhauser and Leslie E. Trotter Jr. Vertex packings: Structural properties and algorithms. *Math. Program.*, 8(1):232–248, 1975.

[Pet16] Seth Pettie. Personal communication. 2016.

[PR01] Alessandro Panconesi and Romeo Rizzi. Some simple distributed algorithms for sparse networks. *Distributed Computing*, 14(2):97–100, 2001.

[PRS12] Boaz Patt-Shamir, Dror Rawitz, and Gabriel Scalosub. Distributed approximation of cellular coverage. *J. Parallel Distrib. Comput.*, 72(3):402–408, 2012.

[PS09] Valentin Polishchuk and Jukka Suomela. A simple local 3-approximation algorithm for vertex cover. *Inf. Process. Lett.*, 109(12):642–645, 2009.

The Greedy Spanner is Existentially Optimal

[Extended Abstract]

Arnold Filtser*
Department of Computer Science
Ben-Gurion University of the Negev
Be'er Sheva, 8410501, Israel
arnoldf@cs.bgu.ac.il

Shay Solomon
School of Computer Science
Tel Aviv University
Tel Aviv 69978, Israel
solo.shay@gmail.com

ABSTRACT

The greedy spanner is arguably the simplest and most well-studied spanner construction. Experimental results demonstrate that it is at least as good as any other spanner construction, in terms of both the size and weight parameters. However, a rigorous proof for this statement has remained elusive.

In this work we fill in the theoretical gap via a surprisingly simple observation: The greedy spanner is *existentially optimal* (or existentially near-optimal) for several important graph families. Focusing on the weight parameter, the state-of-the-art spanner constructions for both general graphs (due to Chechik and Wulff-Nilsen [SODA'16]) and doubling metrics (due to Gottlieb [FOCS'15]) are complex. Plugging our observation on these results, we conclude that the greedy spanner achieves near-optimal weight guarantees for both general graphs and doubling metrics, thus resolving two longstanding conjectures in the area.

Further, we observe that approximate-greedy algorithms are existentially near-optimal as well. Consequently, we provide an $O(n \log n)$-time construction of $(1+\epsilon)$-spanners for doubling metrics with constant lightness and degree. Our construction improves Gottlieb's construction, whose runtime is $O(n \log^2 n)$ and whose number of edges and degree are unbounded, and remarkably, it matches the state-of-the-art Euclidean result (due to Gudmundsson et al. [SICOMP'02]) in all the involved parameters (up to dependencies on ϵ and the dimension).

CCS Concepts

•Theory of computation → Sparsification and spanners;

Keywords

Doubling metric, graph spanner, greedy algorithm, greedy spanner, light spanner.

*Partially supported by the Lynn and William Frankel Center for Computer Sciences, ISF grant No. (523/12) and by the European Union Seventh Framework Programme (FP7/2007-2013) under grant agreement $n^\circ 303809$.

PODC'16, July 25-28, 2016, Chicago, IL, USA
© 2016 ACM. ISBN 978-1-4503-3964-3/16/07...$15.00
DOI: http://dx.doi.org/10.1145/2933057.2933114

1. INTRODUCTION

1.1 Graph Spanners

Given a (connected and undirected) n-vertex m-edge graph $G = (V, E, w)$ with positive edge weights and a parameter $t \geq 1$, a subgraph $H = (V, E', w)$ of G ($E' \subseteq E$) is called a *t-spanner* for G if for all $u, v \in V$, $\delta_H(u,v) \leq t \cdot \delta_G(u,v)$. (Here $\delta_G(u,v)$ and $\delta_H(u,v)$ denote the distances between u and v in the graphs G and H, respectively.) The parameter t is called the *stretch* of H. Spanners constitute a fundamental graph structure, and have been extensively and intensively studied since they were introduced [48, 49].

In many practical applications one is required to construct a spanner that satisfies a number of useful properties, while preserving a small stretch. First, the spanner H should have a small number of edges. Second, its *weight* $w(H) = \sum_{e \in E} w(E)$ should be close to the weight of a minimum spanning tree (MST) of the graph G. We henceforth refer to the normalized notion of weight $\Psi(H) = \frac{w(H)}{w(MST(G))}$, which is called *lightness*; a *light* spanner is one with small lightness. Third, its *degree* $\Delta(H)$, defined as the maximum number of edges incident on a vertex, should be small.

Light and sparse spanners are particularly useful for efficient broadcast protocols in the message-passing model of distributed computing [3, 4], where efficiency is measured with respect to both the total communication cost (corresponding to the spanner's size and weight) and the speed of message delivery at all destinations (corresponding to the spanner's stretch). Additional applications of such spanners in distributed systems include network synchronization and computing global functions [2, 49, 3, 4, 47]. Light and sparse spanners were also found useful for various data gathering and dissemination tasks in overlay networks [8, 61, 44], in wireless and sensor networks [62, 6, 56], for VLSI circuit design [16, 17, 18, 55], for routing [63, 49, 50, 60], to compute distance oracles and labels [46, 59, 53], and to compute almost shortest paths [15, 54, 22, 25, 29]. Low degree spanners are also very useful in many of these applications. For example, the degree of the spanner is what determines local memory constraints when using spanners to construct network synchronizers and efficient broadcast protocols. In compact routing schemes, the use of low degree spanners enables the routing tables to be of small size. More generally, viewing vertices as processors, in many applications the degree of a processor represents its *load*, hence a low degree spanner guarantees that the load on all the processors in the network will be low.

The *greedy spanner* by Althöfer et al. [1] is arguably the simplest and most well-studied spanner construction. Althöfer et al. showed that for every weighted n-vertex graph $G = (V, E, w)$ and an integer parameter $k \geq 1$, the *greedy algorithm* (see Algorithm 1) constructs a $(2k-1)$-spanner with $O(n^{1+1/k})$ edges;

assuming Erdős' girth conjecture [26], this size bound is asymptotically tight. Althöfer et al. also showed that the lightness of the greedy spanner is $O(n/k)$. Chandra et al. [12] improved the lightness bound, and showed that the greedy spanner for stretch parameter $t = (2k-1) \cdot (1+\epsilon)$ (here $k > 1$, $\epsilon > 0$) has lightness $O(k \cdot n^{1/k} \cdot (1/\epsilon)^{1+1/k})$. Two decades later, Elkin, Neiman and the second author [23] improved the analysis of [12] and showed that the greedy $(2k-1)\cdot(1+\epsilon)$-spanner has lightness $O(n^{1/k} \cdot (1 + k/(\epsilon^{1+1/k} \log k)))$. Very recently Chechik and Wulff-Nilsen [13] improved the lightness bound all the way to $O(n^{1/k}(1/\epsilon)^{3+2/k})$. Assuming Erdős' girth conjecture [26] and ignoring dependencies on ϵ, the bound of [13] on the lightness is asymptotically tight, thus resolving a major open question in this area. However, the result of Chechik and Wulff-Nilsen [13] is not due to a refined analysis of the greedy spanner. Instead, they devised a different construction, which is far more complex, and bounded the lightness of their own construction. The following question was left open.

QUESTION 1. *Is the lightness analysis of [23] for the greedy spanner optimal, or can one refine it to derive a stronger bound? In particular, is the spanner of [13] lighter than the greedy spanner?*

1.2 Spanners for Euclidean and Doubling Metrics.

Consider a set P of n points in $\mathbb{R}^d$, $d \geq 2$, and a stretch parameter $t \geq 1$. A graph $G = (P, E, w)$ in which the weight $w(p,q)$ of each edge $e = (p,q) \in E$ is equal to the Euclidean distance $\|p-q\|$ between p and q is called a *Euclidean graph*. We say that the Euclidean graph G is a *t-spanner* for P (or equivalently, for the corresponding Euclidean metric $(P, \|\cdot\|)$) if for every pair $p, q \in P$ of distinct points, there exists a path $\Pi(p,q)$ in G between p and q whose weight (i.e., the sum of all edge weights in it) is at most $t \cdot \|p-q\|$. The path $\Pi(p,q)$ is said to be a *t-spanner path* between p and q. For Euclidean metrics, one usually focuses on the regime $t = 1+\epsilon$, for $\epsilon > 0$ being an arbitrarily small parameter. Euclidean spanners were introduced by Chew [14], and were subject to intensive ongoing research efforts since then. We refer to the book "Geometric Spanner Networks" [45], which is devoted almost exclusively to Euclidean spanners and their numerous applications. As with general graphs, it is important to devise Euclidean spanners that achieve small size, lightness and degree.

The *doubling dimension* of a metric space (M, δ) is the smallest value ddim such that every ball B in the metric space can be covered by at most 2^{ddim} balls of half the radius of B. This notion generalizes the Euclidean dimension, since the doubling dimension of the Euclidean space $\mathbb{R}^d$ is $\Theta(d)$. A metric space is called *doubling* if its doubling dimension is constant. Spanners for doubling metrics were also subject of intensive research [30, 10, 9, 40, 52, 32, 34, 57, 24, 11, 58]. The basic line of work in this context is to generalize the known Euclidean spanner results for arbitrary doubling metrics.

Das et al. [19] showed that, in low-dimensional Euclidean metrics, the greedy $(1+\epsilon)$-spanner has constant degree (and so $O(n)$ edges) and constant lightness. In n-point doubling metrics, the greedy $(1+\epsilon)$-spanner has $O(n)$ edges and lightness $O(\log n)$ [57]. As for the degree, there exist n-point metric spaces with doubling dimension 1 for which the greedy spanner has a degree of $n-1$ [41, 57]. It has been a major open question to determine whether any doubling metric admits a $(1+\epsilon)$-spanner with sub-logarithmic lightness. Recently Gottlieb [31] answered this question in the affirmative by devising such a spanner construction with constant lightness. Again, this result is not due to a refined analysis of the greedy spanner. Instead, Gottlieb devised a different construction, which is far more complex, and bounded the lightness of his own construction. The following question was left open.

QUESTION 2. *Is the lightness analysis of [57] for the greedy spanner optimal, or can one refine it to derive a stronger bound? In particular, is the spanner of [31] lighter than the greedy spanner?*

The high runtime of the greedy spanner is a major drawback. The state-of-the-art implementation of the greedy spanner in both Euclidean and doubling metrics requires time $O(n^2 \log n)$ [7]. Building on [19], Das and Narasimhan [20] devised a much faster algorithm that follows the greedy approach. The runtime of their "approximate-greedy" algorithm is $O(n \log^2 n)$, yet its degree and lightness are both bounded by constants (as with the greedy spanner). Gudmundsson et al. [38] improved the result of [20], implementing the approximate-greedy algorithm within time $O(n \log n)$. For doubling metrics, however, the only spanner construction with sub-logarithmic lightness is that of [31]; the runtime of Gottlieb's construction is $O(n \log^2 n)$ rather than $O(n \log n)$, and the size and degree of his construction are unbounded. Hence, there is a big gap in this context between Euclidean and doubling metrics, leading to the following question.

QUESTION 3. *Can one compute $(1+\epsilon)$-spanners with constant lightness in doubling metrics within time $O(n \log n)$? Furthermore, can one extend the state-of-the-art Euclidean result of [38] to arbitrary doubling metrics?*

There have been numerous experimental studies on Euclidean spanners. (See [28, 27], and the references therein.) The conclusion emerging from these experiments is that the greedy Euclidean spanner outperforms the other popular Euclidean spanner constructions, with respect to the size and lightness bounds. (Specifically, the greedy spanner was found to be 10 times sparser and 30 times lighter than any other examined spanner.) It is reasonable to assume that a similar situation occurs in arbitrary doubling metrics.

1.3 Our Contribution

In this work we fill in the theoretical gap by making three important observations.

1. Our first observation is surprisingly simple: The greedy spanner is *existentially optimal* with respect to both the size and the lightness, for any graph family that is closed under edge removal. Applying this observation to the family of general weighted graphs, we conclude that the greedy spanner is just as light as the spanner of [13], thus answering Question 1.

2. The first observation does not hold for doubling metrics. Our second observation is that the greedy spanner is existentially *near*-optimal with respect to both the size and the lightness, for the family of doubling metrics. In particular, it is just as light as the spanner of [31], thus answering Question 2.

3. Our third observation concerns the optimality of the approximate-greedy algorithm of [20, 38] in doubling metrics, and is more intricate than the first two observations. Informally, it states that the approximate-greedy spanner with stretch parameter t is existentially near-optimal with respect to the lightness, for the family of doubling metrics, but when compared to spanners with a slightly smaller stretch parameter $t' < t$. This enables us to conclude that the lightness of the approximate-greedy spanner is close to that of [31]. In this way we manage to extend the state-of-the-art Euclidean

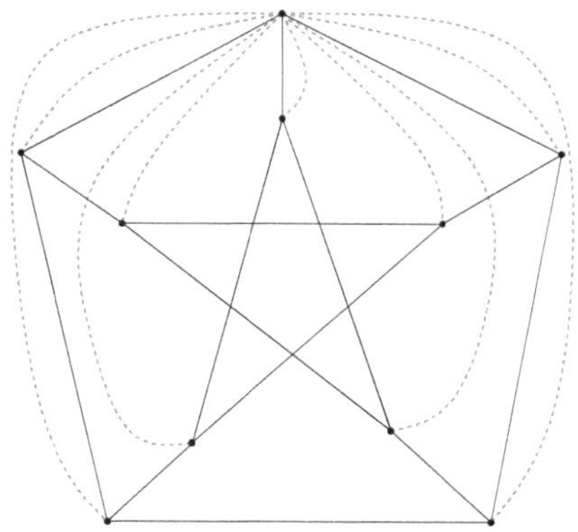

Figure 1: The graph H in the figure is the Petersen graph on 10 vertices, with girth 5 and 15 edges. All edges of H have weight 1, and are colored black. The red dashed edges are the edges of the star S of weight $1 + \epsilon$. The greedy 3-spanner for the graph G obtained as the union of the black and red edges in the figure includes all 15 edges of H, whereas the optimal 3-spanner for G consists of the 9 edges of S.

result of [38] to arbitrary doubling metrics, thus answering Question 3.[1]

To clarify the meaning of *existential optimality*, suppose that the greedy spanner is existentially optimal with respect to the lightness, for some graph family $\mathcal{F}$. This does not imply that for any graph $G \in \mathcal{F}$, the lightness of the greedy spanner for G is bounded by the optimal lightness of any spanner for G. It simply means that for any graph $G \in \mathcal{F}$, there *exists* a graph $G' \in \mathcal{F}$, such that the lightness of the greedy spanner for G is bounded by the optimal lightness of any spanner for G'. Put in other words, for a graph $G \in \mathcal{F}$, let $l(G) = l_t(G)$ denote the optimal lightness of any t-spanner for G, for an arbitrary stretch parameter $t \geq 1$, and let $l(\mathcal{F}) = \max\{l(G) \mid G \in \mathcal{F}\}$ denote the maximum value $l(G)$ over all graphs G in $\mathcal{F}$. Then, for any graph $G \in \mathcal{F}$, although the lightness of the greedy t-spanner for G may well exceed $l(G)$, it must be upper bounded by $l(\mathcal{F})$. For example, let $\mathcal{F}$ be the family of general weighted graphs on n vertices, and let H be an n-vertex dense graph of high girth, namely, with girth $t+2$ and $n^{1+\Theta(1/t)}$ edges, where all edge weights are 1. Also, let S be a star on the same vertex set as H rooted at an arbitrary vertex, so that all edges of S that belong to H have weight 1 and all edges of S that do not belong to H have weight $1 + \epsilon$. Finally, let G be the graph containing all edges of H and all edges of S with weight $1+\epsilon$. Note that the greedy t-spanner for G includes all $n^{1+\Theta(1/t)}$ edges of the high girth graph H, whereas the optimal t-spanner (assuming $t \geq 2+2\epsilon$) consists of the edges of the star S, hence is much sparser and lighter. (See Figure 1 for an illustration.) This example, however, does not contradict the existential optimality of the greedy spanner: Although the lightness of the greedy t-spanner for G exceeds $l(G)$, it can be shown that it is equal to $l(H)$, which, in turn, is bounded by $l(\mathcal{F})$.

The meaning of *existential near-optimality* is similar, except that we are allowed to have some *slack*, which may depend on the stretch parameter t as well as on parameters of the graph family of interest $\mathcal{F}$. As mentioned, in our third observation we compare the lightness of the greedy spanner with a certain stretch parameter t to the optimal lightness of any spanner, but with a slightly smaller stretch parameter t'. This is just one example of how the slack parameter can be used. Another example is to compare the greedy spanner in some graph family $\mathcal{F}$ to the optimal spanner, but with respect to a different (closely related) graph family $\mathcal{F}'$. In particular, in our second and third observations we compare the lightness of the greedy spanner in metric spaces of bounded doubling dimension to the optimal lightness of any spanner, but with respect to metric spaces of slightly larger doubling dimension. (See Section 2 for the definition of doubling dimension.) It would be interesting to study additional ways of using the slack parameter, as they may lead to new results in this area.

We remark that light spanners were extensively studied in various graph families such as planar graphs [1, 43], apex graphs [37], bounded pathwidth graphs [36, 42], bounded catwidth graphs [42], bounded genus graphs [35, 37, 21], bounded treewidth graphs [21, 42], and graphs excluding fixed minors [35, 21]. Since all these graph families are closed under edge removal, our first observation implies that the greedy spanner for them is just as good as any other spanner.

1.4 Organization

In Section 2 we present the notation that is used throughout the paper, and summarize some statements from previous work that are most relevant to us. In Section 3 we show that the greedy spanner is existentially optimal for graph families that are closed under edge removal. The basic optimality argument of Section 3 is extended to doubling metrics in Section 4. Finally, in Section 5 we show that the approximate-greedy spanner in doubling metrics is light.

2. PRELIMINARIES

Let $G = (V, E, w)$ be a (connected and undirected) graph with positive edge weights. The weight $w(P)$ of a path P is the sum of all edge weights in it, i.e., $w(P) = \sum_{e \in P} w(e)$. For a pair of vertices $u, v \in V$, let $\delta_G(u, v)$ denote the distance between u and v in G, i.e., the weight of a shortest path between them. We denote by $M_G = (V, \delta_G)$ the (shortest path) metric space *induced* by G; we will view M_G as a complete weighted graph $(V, \binom{V}{2}, w)$ over the vertex set V, where the weight $w(u, v)$ of an edge (u, v) is given by the graph distance $\delta_G(u, v)$ between its endpoints. A subgraph $H = (V, E', w)$ of G (where $E' \subseteq E$) is called a *t-spanner* for G if for all $u, v \in V$, $\delta_H(u, v) \leq t \cdot \delta_G(u, v)$. The parameter t is called the *stretch* of the spanner H. If $\delta_H(u, v) \leq t \cdot \delta_G(u, v)$ for all edges $(u, v) \in E$, then it also holds that $\delta_H(u, v) \leq t \cdot \delta_G(u, v)$ for all pairs of vertices $u, v \in V$. Therefore, to bound the stretch of the spanner, one may restrict the attention to the edges of the graph. Let $|H| = |E'|$ denote the *size* of H, and let $w(H) = w(E') = \sum_{e \in E'} w(e)$ denote its *weight*. The *lightness* $\Psi(H)$ of H is the ratio between the weight of H and the weight of an MST for G, i.e., $\Psi(H) = \frac{w(H)}{w(MST(G))}$. (Throughout the paper all logarithms are in base 2.)

The result of Chechik and Wulff-Nilsen [13] is summarized in the following theorem.

Theorem 1 **([13])** *For every weighted n-vertex graph $G = (V, E, w)$ and parameters $k \geq 1$ and $0 < \epsilon < 1$, there exists a $(2k-1) \cdot (1+\epsilon)$-spanner with $O(n^{1+1/k})$ edges and lightness $O(n^{1/k}(1/\epsilon)^{3+2/k})$. Such a spanner can be constructed in polynomial time.*

2.1 Doubling metrics

The following lemma gives the standard packing property of doubling metrics (see, e.g., [39]).

[1]The $O(n \log n)$ runtime bound of [38] holds in the traditional algebraic computation-tree model with the added power of indirect addressing. Our result applies with respect to the same computation model.

LEMMA 1. *Let (M, δ) be a metric space with doubling dimension* ddim. *If $S \subseteq M$ is a subset of points with minimum interpoint distance r that is contained in a ball of radius R, then $|S| \leq \left(\frac{2R}{r}\right)^{O(\mathrm{ddim})}$.*

The following theorem states that any doubling metric admits a constant degree $(1+\epsilon)$-spanner.

Theorem 2 ([10, 33]) *For any n-point metric space (M, δ) with doubling dimension* ddim *and parameter $0 < \epsilon < 1/2$, there exists a $(1+\epsilon)$-spanner with degree $\epsilon^{-O(\mathrm{ddim})}$. The runtime of this construction is $\epsilon^{-O(\mathrm{ddim})}(n \log n)$.*

The result of Gottlieb [31] is summarized in the following theorem.

Theorem 3 ([31]) *For any n-point metric space (M, δ) with doubling dimension* ddim *and parameter $0 < \epsilon < 1/2$, there exists a $(1+\epsilon)$-spanner with lightness $(\mathrm{ddim}/\epsilon)^{O(\mathrm{ddim})}$. The runtime of this construction is $(\mathrm{ddim}/\epsilon)^{O(\mathrm{ddim})}(n \log^2 n)$.*

2.2 The Greedy Spanner and its Basic Properties

Algorithm 1 `Greedy`$(G = (V, E, w), t)$

$H = (V, \emptyset, w)$.
for each edge $(u, v) \in E$, in non-decreasing order of weight, **do**
  if $\delta_H(u, v) > t \cdot w(u, v)$ **then**
    Add the edge (u, v) to $E(H)$.
  end if
end for

The greedy spanner algorithm is presented in Algorithm 1. Let $H = (V, E_H, w)$ be the output of an arbitrary execution of the greedy algorithm with stretch parameter t. It is immediate that H has stretch at most t. If the edge weights in the graph are distinct, then H is uniquely defined, but this does not hold in general; nevertheless, by letting H designate an arbitrary such spanner, we may henceforth refer to it as the *greedy t-spanner*. The following observation is immediate (see, .e.g., [23, 13]).

OBSERVATION 2. *H contains all edges of some MST of G, denoted Z. (Hence Z is also an MST of H.)*

3. THE BASIC OPTIMALITY PROOF

In this section we show that the greedy spanner is existentially optimal, with respect to both the size and the lightness, for any graph family that is closed under edge removal.

We start by making the basic observation that the only t-spanner of the greedy t-spanner is itself.

LEMMA 3. *Let $G = (V, E, w)$ be any weighted graph, let $t \geq 1$ be any stretch parameter, and let H be the greedy t-spanner of G. If H' is a t-spanner for H, then $H' = H$.*

PROOF. Assume for contradiction that H' is a t-spanner for H yet there is an edge $e \in H \setminus H'$. Let P be a shortest path in H' between the endpoints of e. As H' is a t-spanner of H, it holds that $w(P) \leq t \cdot w(e)$. Consider the last edge examined by the greedy algorithm among the edges of P and e, denoted e'. By the description of the greedy algorithm, we have $w(e) \leq w(e')$. Consequently, by the time the greedy algorithm examines edge e', all the edges of the path $(P \cup e) \setminus e'$ must have already been added

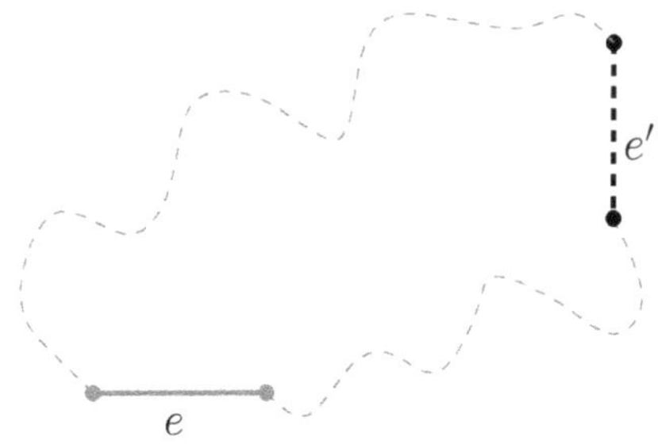

Figure 2: The path P in H' between the endpoints of edge e is depicted by a dashed line. The path $P \cup e \setminus e'$ between the endpoints of edge e', all edges of which have been added to H by the time the greedy algorithm examines edge e', is colored red.

to the greedy spanner. (See Figure 2 for an illustration.) This path connects the endpoints of e', and its weight is given by

$$w(P) - w(e') + w(e) \leq w(P) \leq t \cdot w(e) \leq t \cdot w(e').$$

Hence the greedy algorithm will not add edge e' to H, a contradiction. $\square$

Equipped with Lemma 3, we now turn to the basic optimality proof.

Theorem 4 (Greedy is optimal) *Let $\mathcal{G}$ be any family of n-vertex graphs that is closed under edge removal, and let $t = t(n)$ be any stretch parameter. Assume that for every graph $G \in \mathcal{G}$, there exists a t-spanner for G with at most $m(n,t)$ edges and lightness at most $l(n,t)$. Then for every graph $G \in \mathcal{G}$, the greedy t-spanner H of G has at most $m(n,t)$ edges and lightness at most $l(n,t)$.*

PROOF. Consider an arbitrary graph G in $\mathcal{G}$, and let H be the greedy t-spanner of G. Since $\mathcal{G}$ is closed under edge removal and H is a subgraph of G, H belongs to $\mathcal{G}$. Hence, there exists a t-spanner $\mathcal{H}$ of H with at most $m(n,t)$ edges and lightness at most $l(n,t)$. Lemma 3 implies that $\mathcal{H} = H$, from which the size bound on H immediately follows. The lightness bound is slightly trickier, as the spanner $\mathcal{H}$ is computed on top of the greedy spanner H rather than the original graph G. Nevertheless, Observation 2 implies that G and H have the same MST Z. Since the lightness of $\mathcal{H}$ is at most $l(n,t)$ and Z is an MST for H, it follows that

$$l(n,t) \geq \Psi(\mathcal{H}) = \frac{w(\mathcal{H})}{w(MST(H))} = \frac{w(\mathcal{H})}{w(Z)},$$

hence $w(\mathcal{H}) \leq l(n,t) \cdot w(Z)$. Using the fact that $\mathcal{H} = H$, we conclude that the lightness of H satisfies

$$\begin{aligned} \Psi(H) &= \frac{w(H)}{w(MST(G))} = \frac{w(H)}{w(Z)} \\ &= \frac{w(\mathcal{H})}{w(Z)} \leq \frac{l(n,t) \cdot w(Z)}{w(Z)} = l(n,t). \end{aligned}$$

$\square$

As the family of weighted graphs is closed under edge removal, we can apply Theorem 4 on it. Hence the greedy spanner for general graphs has size and lightness at least as good as in Theorem 1.

COROLLARY 4. *For every weighted graph $G = (V, E, w)$ on n vertices and m edges and parameters $k \geq 1$ and $0 < \epsilon < 1$, the greedy $(2k-1) \cdot (1+\epsilon)$-spanner has $O(n^{1+1/k})$ edges* *and lightness $O(n^{1/k}(1/\epsilon)^{3+2/k})$. (A naive implementation of the greedy algorithm requires $O(mn^{1+1/k})$ time.)*

In [5] it was proved that for any parameter $0 < \delta < 1$ and any stretch parameter $t = t(n)$, if every n-vertex weighted graph admits a t-spanner with at most $m(n,t)$ edges and lightness at most $l(n,t)$, then for every such graph there also exists a t/δ-spanner with at most $m(n,t)$ edges and lightness at most $1 + \delta \cdot l(n,t)$.[2] Applying Theorem 4 again, we derive the following result.

COROLLARY 5. *For every weighted n-vertex graph $G = (V, E, w)$ and parameter $0 < \delta < 1$, the greedy $O(\log n/\delta)$-spanner has $O(n)$ edges and lightness at most $1 + \delta$.*

As mentioned in the introduction, a plethora of graph families that are closed under edge removal were studied extensively in the spanner literature. This includes the families of planar graphs, bounded genus graphs, bounded treewidth graphs, graphs excluding fixed minors, and more. For all these graph families, Theorem 4 shows that the greedy spanner is existentially optimal.

4. THE OPTIMALITY ARGUMENT IN DOUBLING METRICS

The basic optimality argument of Section 3 applies to graph families that are closed under edge removal. Note that metric spaces do not fall into this category. Nevertheless, for metric spaces, the basic optimality argument suffices: On the one hand, the upper bound for general weighted graphs applies to any metric space, and on the other hand, the lower bound due to high girth graphs naturally applies to the induced metric spaces (see, e.g., [1, 51]).

In this section we study the optimality of the greedy spanner for *doubling metrics*. For such metric spaces, one would like to obtain spanners with stretch $1+\epsilon$, where ϵ is arbitrarily close to 0. We will show that the greedy $(1+\epsilon)$-spanner is existentially near-optimal in doubling metrics, with respect to both the size and the lightness.

The next observation and subsequent lemma will be used for proving the lightness optimality.

OBSERVATION 6. *Consider the metric space M_G induced by an arbitrary weighted graph $G = (V, E, w)$. Then any MST of M_G is a spanning tree of G. (Hence there is a common MST for G and M_G, denoted Z.)*

PROOF. Consider an MST Z for M_G, and suppose for contradiction that Z contains an edge e outside G. Since e belongs to $M_G \setminus G$, any path in G between the endpoints of e consists of at least two edges. Consider the (multi) graph obtained from Z by replacing edge e with a shortest path in G between the endpoints of e. It is a spanning subgraph of M_G of weight $w(Z)$, which contains at least $n + 1$ edges (some of which may be multiple edges), and thus at least one cycle. By breaking cycles in this subgraph, we obtain a spanning tree of M_G of weight strictly smaller than $w(Z)$, yielding a contradiction to the weight minimality of Z. □

LEMMA 7. *Let (M, δ) be any metric space, $t \geq 1$ be some stretch parameter, and H be the greedy t-spanner of M. For every t-spanner H' of the metric space M_H induced by H, we have $w(H) \leq w(H')$.*

PROOF. Let H' be a t-spanner of M_H, and define H'' as the subgraph of H obtained from H' by replacing each edge e of H' with a shortest path in H between the endpoints of e. Clearly, the distances in H'' are no greater than the respective distances in H'. Since H'' is a subgraph of H, it follows that H'' is a t-spanner for H. Lemma 3 implies that $H'' = H$. Finally, noting that $w(H'') \leq w(H')$, we have $w(H) = w(H'') \leq w(H')$. □

The following lemma will be used for proving the size optimality.

LEMMA 8. *Let (M, δ) be any metric space, $t < 2$ be some stretch parameter, and H be the greedy t-spanner of M. For every t-spanner H' of the metric space M_H induced by H, we have $|H| \leq |H'|$.*

PROOF. For every edge $e' \in H'$, let $P_{e'}$ be a shortest path between the endpoints of e' in H. We say that edge $e' \in H'$ *covers* all edges of $P_{e'}$, and all these edges are *covered* by e'. An edge $e' \in H \cap H'$ covers itself.

For each edge e in $H \setminus H'$, let $\mathcal{Q}_e$ be a shortest path between the endpoints of e in H'. Since H' is a t-spanner for M_H, we have $w(\mathcal{Q}_e) \leq t \cdot w(e)$. Observe that the edges in $\cup_{e' \in \mathcal{Q}_e} P_{e'}$ form a path Π_e in H between the endpoints of e. (It will be shown next that the path Π_e is not simple.) We have

$$w(\Pi_e) \leq \sum_{e' \in \mathcal{Q}_e} w(P_{e'}) = \sum_{e' \in \mathcal{Q}_e} w(e') = w(\mathcal{Q}_e) \leq t \cdot w(e).$$

Next, we argue that the edge e must belong to Π_e. Indeed, otherwise the edges of Π_e contain a simple path in H between the endpoints of e of weight bounded by $t \cdot w(e)$, implying that the heaviest edge among the edges of this path and e would not be added to the greedy t-spanner H. Consequently, at least one edge e' in $\mathcal{Q}_e$ must cover e.

We define an injection $f : H \to H'$ as follows. For each edge $e \in H \cap H'$, $f(e)$ is defined as e; in this case edge $e = f(e)$ covers itself. For each $e \in H \setminus H'$, $f(e)$ is defined to be an arbitrary edge of $\mathcal{Q}_e$ that covers e. To see that f is injective, suppose for contradiction the existence of two distinct edges e_1 and e_2 in H and an edge $e' \in H'$ such that $f(e_1) = f(e_2) = e' \in H'$. It must hold that e_1 and e_2 are in $H \setminus H'$. Assume without loss of generality that $w(e_1) \leq w(e_2)$. Since both e_1 and e_2 are covered by e', it follows that $w(e') \geq w(e_1) + w(e_2) \geq 2 \cdot w(e_1)$. On the other hand, by the definition of f, the shortest path $\mathcal{Q}_{e_1}$ in H' between the endpoints of e_1 contains the edge $e' = f(e_1)$. Hence the weight of a shortest path in H' between the endpoints of e_1 is given by $w(\mathcal{Q}_{e_1}) \geq w(e') \geq 2 \cdot w(e_1) > t \cdot w(e_1)$, which contradicts the fact that H' is a t-spanner for H. It follows that f is injective, from which we conclude that $|H| \leq |H'|$. □

The following observation shows that a small "stretching" of any metric space does not change the doubling dimension of the metric space by much.

OBSERVATION 9. *Let (M, δ) be a metric space with doubling dimension* ddim. *Let H be a t-spanner of M, for $t \leq 2$. Then the metric space M_H induced by H has doubling dimension at most $2 \cdot \mathrm{ddim}$.*

PROOF. Clearly, any ball of radius r in the "stretched" metric space M_H is contained in the respective ball of the original metric space M. By definition, this ball can be covered by $2^{2 \cdot \mathrm{ddim}}$ balls of radius $\frac{r}{4}$ in M, and so by $2^{2 \cdot \mathrm{ddim}}$ balls of radius $t \cdot \frac{r}{4} \leq \frac{r}{2}$ in the stretched metric space M_H. □

The existential near-optimality result for doubling metrics is summarized in the following theorem.

[2]This reduction appears in the full version of [5], which is currently available via http://www.cs.bgu.ac.il/~arnoldf/BFN16.pdf.

Theorem 5 (Greedy is near-optimal in doubling metrics) *Assume that for every n-point metric space (M, δ) with doubling dimension* ddim *and any stretch parameter $t < 2$, there is a t-spanner with at most $m(n, \mathrm{ddim}, t)$ edges and lightness at most $l(n, \mathrm{ddim}, t)$. Then for every n-point metric space (M, δ) with doubling dimension* ddim*, the greedy t-spanner has at most $m(n, 2\cdot\mathrm{ddim}, t)$ edges and lightness at most $l(n, 2 \cdot \mathrm{ddim}, t)$.*

PROOF. Let M be an arbitrary n-point metric space with doubling dimension ddim, let $H = (V, E)$ be the greedy t-spanner for M, and let M_H be the metric space induced by H. By Observation 9, the doubling dimension of M_H is bounded by $2 \cdot \mathrm{ddim}$. Our assumption implies that there exists a t-spanner $\mathcal{H}$ for M_H with at most $m(n, 2\cdot\mathrm{ddim}, t)$ edges and lightness at most $l(n, 2\cdot\mathrm{ddim}, t)$. Lemma 8 implies that $|H| \leq |\mathcal{H}|$, from which the size bound on H immediately follows. As for the lightness bound on H, note that $\mathcal{H}$ is computed on top of M_H rather than the original metric space M. Nevertheless, Observation 2 and Observation 6 imply that M and M_H have the same MST Z. Since the lightness of $\mathcal{H}$ is at most $l(n, 2 \cdot \mathrm{ddim}, t)$, it follows that

$$l(n, 2 \cdot \mathrm{ddim}, t) \geq \Psi(\mathcal{H}) = \frac{w(\mathcal{H})}{w(MST(M_H))} = \frac{w(\mathcal{H})}{w(Z)},$$

hence $w(\mathcal{H}) \leq l(n, 2 \cdot \mathrm{ddim}, t) \cdot w(Z)$. By Lemma 7, we have $w(H) \leq w(\mathcal{H})$, hence the lightness of H satisfies

$$\begin{aligned}\Psi(H) &= \frac{w(H)}{w(MST(M))} = \frac{w(H)}{w(Z)} \leq \frac{w(\mathcal{H})}{w(Z)} \\ &\leq \frac{l(n, 2 \cdot \mathrm{ddim}, t) \cdot w(Z)}{w(Z)} = l(n, 2 \cdot \mathrm{ddim}, t)\,.\end{aligned}$$

□

It is known that the greedy $(1 + \epsilon)$-spanner for n-point doubling metrics has $O(n)$ edges and lightness $O(\log n)$ [57], where the O-notation hides a multiplicative term of $(1/\epsilon)^{O(\mathrm{ddim})}$. Applying Theorem 5 in conjunction with the result of Theorem 3, we reduce the lightness bound of the greedy spanner to constant.

COROLLARY 10. *For every metric space (M, δ) with doubling dimension* ddim *and any parameter $0 < \epsilon < \frac{1}{2}$, the greedy $(1+\epsilon)$-spanner has $n(1/\epsilon)^{O(\mathrm{ddim})}$ edges and lightness $(\mathrm{ddim}/\epsilon)^{O(\mathrm{ddim})}$.*

Remark. Corollary 10 shows that the greedy $(1 + \epsilon)$-spanner in doubling metrics achieves optimal bounds on the size and the lightness, *disregarding dependencies on ϵ and the doubling dimension*. However, improving these dependencies is a fundamental challenge of practical importance. By Theorem 5, any improvement whatsoever in the dependencies on ϵ and the doubling dimension on either the size or the lightness of *any spanner construction* for doubling metrics – would trigger a similar improvement to the greedy spanner.

5. THE APPROXIMATE-GREEDY SPANNER IN DOUBLING METRICS IS LIGHT

Corollary 10 shows that the greedy $(1 + \epsilon)$-spanner in doubling metrics achieves near-optimal bounds on the size and the lightness. Nevertheless, this spanner has two major disadvantages. First, as mentioned in the introduction, there exist metric spaces with doubling dimension 1 for which its degree may be unbounded. (This is in contrast to d-dimensional Euclidean metrics, where the greedy $(1 + \epsilon)$-spanner has degree $\epsilon^{-O(d)}$.) Second, it cannot be constructed within sub-quadratic time in doubling metrics due to a lower bound of [41]. In fact, even in d-dimensional Euclidean metrics, the state-of-the-art implementation of the greedy $(1 + \epsilon)$-spanner requires time $\epsilon^{-O(d)}(n^2 \log n)$ [7].

Building on [19, 20], Gudmundsson et al. [38] devised a much faster algorithm that follows the greedy approach, hereafter Algorithm `Approximate-Greedy`. The runtime of this algorithm is $\epsilon^{-O(d)}(n \log n)$, yet the degree and lightness of the approximate-greedy spanner produced by the algorithm are both bounded by $\epsilon^{-O(d)}$, just as with the greedy spanner for Euclidean metrics. The runtime analysis of Algorithm `Approximate-Greedy` [38] does not exploit any properties of Euclidean geometry. Specifically, it relies on the triangle inequality, which applies to arbitrary metric spaces, and on standard packing arguments (cf. Lemma 1), which apply to arbitrary doubling metrics. Therefore, the runtime of Algorithm `Approximate-Greedy` remains $\epsilon^{-O(\mathrm{ddim})}(n \log n)$ in arbitrary doubling metrics. Moreover, the degree bound of $\epsilon^{-O(d)}$ applies to arbitrary doubling metrics as well. (We refer to Chapter 15 in [45] for an excellent description of this algorithm and its analysis.)

In this section we show that the approximate-greedy spanner of [38] has constant lightness in arbitrary doubling metrics. Consequently, Algorithm `Approximate-Greedy` provides an $O(n \log n)$-time construction of $(1+\epsilon)$-spanners in doubling metrics with lightness and degree both bounded by constants.

5.1 A Rough Sketch of Algorithm Approximate-Greedy

In this section we provide a very rough sketch of Algorithm `Approximate-Greedy`, aiming to highlight the high-level ideas behind it. This outline is not required for the analysis that is given in Section 5.2; it is provided here for clarity and completeness.

In metric spaces, the greedy algorithm sorts the $\binom{n}{2}$ interpoint distances and examines the edges by non-decreasing order of weight. For each edge that is examined for inclusion in the spanner, the distance between its endpoints in the current spanner is computed. This is expensive for two reasons: (1) The number of examined interpoint distances is quadratic in n. (2) Computing the *exact* spanner distance between two points is costly.

Suppose we aim for a stretch of $t = 1 + \epsilon$, and let t' be an appropriate parameter satisfying $t' = 1 + O(\epsilon) < t$. (Refer to [38, 45] for the exact constant hiding in the O-notation of $O(\epsilon)$.) Instead of examining all $\binom{n}{2}$ interpoint distances, Algorithm `Approximate-Greedy` computes a bounded degree $\sqrt{t/t'}$-spanner $G' = (M, E', \delta)$ for the input metric space (M, δ), and simulates the greedy algorithm with stretch parameter $\sqrt{t \cdot t'}$ only on the edges of G'. The output of the algorithm is a $\sqrt{t \cdot t'}$-spanner $G = (M, E, \delta)$ for G', which is a t-spanner for the original metric space (M, δ) by the "transitivity" of spanners. A spanner G' of degree $\epsilon^{-O(\mathrm{ddim})}$ can be constructed in $\epsilon^{-O(\mathrm{ddim})}(n \log n)$ time via Theorem 2. Since the output t-spanner G for (M, δ) is a subgraph of G', its degree will be at most $\epsilon^{-O(\mathrm{ddim})}$.

The greedy simulation is applied only on the edges of G' that are sufficiently "heavy". Formally, let D denote the maximum weight of any edge of the bounded degree spanner G', and let E_0 be the set of *light edges* in E', namely, of weight at most D/n. As $|E_0| \leq |E'| = O(n)$, we have $w(E_0) = O(D) = O(MST(M))$. All light edges are taken to the output spanner G, and the greedy simulation is applied only on the edges of $E' \setminus E_0$. (So the output spanner G will contain *all* edges of E_0 and *some* edges of $E' \setminus E_0$.)

As mentioned, computing the *exact* distance between two points is costly; using Dijkstra's algorithm, it requires $O(n \log n)$ time (see, e.g., Section 2.5 and Corollary 2.5.10 in [45]). Since G' has $O(n)$ edges, the overall runtime will be $O(n^2 \log n)$. To speed up the computation time, Algorithm `Approximate-Greedy` does not compute the exact distance between two points, but rather an approximation of that distance. This is achieved by maintaining a much simpler and coarser *cluster graph* that approximates the original distances, on which the distance queries are performed. More specifically, the algorithm partitions the edge set $E' \setminus E_0$ into $\log_\mu n$ buckets, for an appropriate parameter $1 < \mu = O(\log n)$, such that edge weights within each bucket differ by at most a factor of μ. Then it examines the edges of $E' \setminus E_0$ by going from one bucket to the next, examining edges by non-decreasing order of weight. Whenever all edges of some bucket have been examined, the cluster graph is updated according to the new edges that were added to the spanner. The idea is to periodically make the cluster graph simpler and coarser, so that the shortest path computations made on it will be fast. The bottom-line is that one does not simulate the greedy algorithm (with stretch parameter $\sqrt{t \cdot t'}$) on the edge set $E' \setminus E_0$, but rather an *approximate version* of it.

5.2 Bounding the Lightness of the Approximate-Greedy Spanner

As mentioned, the runtime of Algorithm `Approximate-Greedy` is $\epsilon^{-O(\mathrm{ddim})}(n \log n)$ in arbitrary doubling metrics. In what follows let $G = (M, E, \delta)$ be the t-spanner for (M, δ) returned by Algorithm `Approximate-Greedy`. Since G is a subgraph of the bounded degree spanner $G' = (M, E', \delta)$, its degree is $\epsilon^{-O(\mathrm{ddim})}$.

It remains to bound the lightness of G. The lightness argument of [38], which relies on previous works [19, 20], is based on rather deep properties from Euclidean geometry, most notably the *leapfrog property*. In particular, this argument does not apply to arbitrary doubling metrics.

Instead, we employ the following lemma, which lies at the heart of the lightness analysis of [38]. While this lemma applies to arbitrary doubling metrics, the way it was used in [38] does not extend to arbitrary doubling metrics. Specifically, it was used in [38] to show that the edge set $E \setminus E_0$ satisfies the leapfrog property. (Recall that E_0 is the set of light edges in $G' = (M, E', \delta)$, all of which are taken to the approximate-greedy spanner $G = (M, E, \delta)$.) In Euclidean metrics, it has been proved [19, 45] that any edge set satisfying the leapfrog property has constant lightness, but this proof does not carry over to arbitrary doubling metrics.

Lemma 11 (Lemma 17 in [38]) *Let $e = (u, v) \in E \setminus E_0$. The weight of the second shortest path between u and v in the approximate-greedy spanner G is greater than $t' \cdot w(e)$. (If there are multiple shortest paths between u and v, then the weight of the second shortest path equals the weight of the shortest path.)*

Remark. The parameter t' in the statement of this lemma depends on the stretch parameters of the spanners G' and G that are constructed by Algorithm `Approximate-Greedy`. Specifically, recall that the output spanner G is a $\sqrt{t \cdot t'}$-spanner for G', which is, in turn, a $\sqrt{t/t'}$-spanner for the input metric space M.

We make the following simple observation.

OBSERVATION 12. *Let H be an arbitrary weighted graph, and let t be any stretch parameter. For any t-spanner H' of H, $w(MST(H')) \le t \cdot w(MST(H))$.*

PROOF. Consider an MST Z for H. Replace each edge of Z by a t-spanner path in H' between the endpoints of that edge, and then break cycles. The resulting structure Z' is a spanning tree of H', hence $w(MST(H')) \le w(Z')$, and we have $w(MST(H')) \le w(Z') \le t \cdot w(Z) = t \cdot w(MST(H))$. □

The following lemma bounds the lightness of G. Its proof is based on the somewhat surprising observation that the lightness of the t-spanner G produced by Algorithm `Approximate-Greedy` is existentially near-optimal with respect to stretch parameter $t' < t$ (rather than t). We remark that G is not a greedy spanner, but rather an approximate-greedy spanner, and it is inherently different than the greedy t-spanner and the greedy t'-spanner. In particular, its weight may be larger than the weights of both these greedy spanners. Nevertheless, our existential near-optimality argument suffices to derive the required lightness bound.

LEMMA 13. *The lightness of G is $(\frac{\mathrm{ddim}}{t'-1})^{O(\mathrm{ddim})}$.*

PROOF. Recall that $G = (M, E, \delta)$ is a t-spanner for M, where $t = 1 + \epsilon, \epsilon < 1$, and let M_G be the metric space induced by G. By Observation 9, the doubling dimension of M_G is bounded by $2 \cdot \mathrm{ddim}$. Let H' be the t'-spanner of M_G with lightness $(\mathrm{ddim}/(t'-1))^{O(\mathrm{ddim})}$ that is guaranteed by Theorem 3, where $t' = 1 + O(\epsilon) < t$ is the parameter appearing in the statement of Lemma 11, which is optimized as part of Algorithm `Approximate-Greedy`. As in the proof of Lemma 7, we transform H' into a t'-spanner H'' of G of weight at most $w(H')$. By Observation 6 and Observation 12, the MST weights for all graphs M, G, M_G, H' and H'' are the same, up to a factor of $t \cdot t' = O(1)$.

We argue that every edge $e \in E \setminus E_0$ belongs to H''. Suppose for contradiction that there is an edge $e \in E \setminus E_0$ that does not belong to H''. Let P be a shortest path between the endpoints of e in H''. Since H'' is a t'-spanner of G, we have $w(P) \le t' \cdot w(e)$. Note that this path is contained in G. Since $e \in G$ and M is a metric space, the weight of the second shortest path between u and v is at most $w(P) \le t' \cdot w(e)$. On the other hand, By Lemma 11, the weight of this path is greater than $t' \cdot w(e)$, a contradiction. It follows that

$$
\begin{aligned}
w(G) &= w(E \setminus E_0) + w(E_0) \\
&\le w(H'') + w(E_0) \\
&\le w(H') + w(E_0) \\
&= \left(\frac{\mathrm{ddim}}{t'-1}\right)^{O(\mathrm{ddim})} \cdot w(MST(M)).
\end{aligned}
$$

□

Setting $t = 1 + \epsilon$ and $t' = 1 + c \cdot \epsilon$ (for an appropriate constant c; see [38, 45]), we conclude:

THEOREM 6. *For any metric space (M, δ) with doubling dimension ddim and parameter $0 < \epsilon < \frac{1}{2}$, Algorithm `Approximate-Greedy` returns a $(1+\epsilon)$-spanner with lightness $(\frac{\mathrm{ddim}}{\epsilon})^{O(\mathrm{ddim})}$ and degree $\epsilon^{-O(\mathrm{ddim})}$. The runtime of Algorithm `Approximate-Greedy` is $\epsilon^{-O(\mathrm{ddim})}(n \log n)$.*

Remark. Theorem 6 should be compared to Theorem 3 due to [31]. Both constructions achieve the same lightness bound, but the degree and number of edges in the spanner construction of [31] are unbounded. Moreover, the runtime of the construction of [31] is $(\mathrm{ddim}/\epsilon)^{O(\mathrm{ddim})}(n \log^2 n)$, whereas that of Theorem 6 is $\epsilon^{-O(\mathrm{ddim})}(n \log n)$. By combining the light spanner H_1 of [31] with a bounded degree spanner H_2, one can obtain a spanner with constant degree and lightness. Specifically, such a spanner $\mathcal{H}$ is obtained by replacing each edge of H_1 with a shortest (or approximately shortest) path in H_2 between the endpoints of that edge. The lightness of the resulting spanner $\mathcal{H}$ will not exceed that of H_1 by much, whereas the degree bound will follow from that of H_2.

There is a major problem with this approach: The runtime needed for computing spanner $\mathcal{H}$ may be very high. Indeed, although there are efficient ways to estimate the weight of an approximately shortest path in H_2 between two points, we must *compute* the corresponding path in H_2. In particular, to achieve the degree bound of H_2, one may not use edges outside H_2. Moreover, even regardless of this computation time, such a path may contain many edges that already belong to the gradually growing spanner $\mathcal{H}$. Deciding which edges of this path should be added to $\mathcal{H}$ may be very costly by itself.

Acknowledgements

We are grateful to Michael Elkin and Ofer Neiman for fruitful discussions.

6. REFERENCES

[1] I. Althöfer, G. Das, D. P. Dobkin, D. Joseph, and J. Soares. On sparse spanners of weighted graphs. *Discrete & Computational Geometry*, 9:81–100, 1993.

[2] B. Awerbuch. Communication-time trade-offs in network synchronization. In *Proc. of 4th PODC*, pages 272–276, 1985.

[3] B. Awerbuch, A. Baratz, and D. Peleg. Cost-sensitive analysis of communication protocols. In *Proc. of 9th PODC*, pages 177–187, 1990.

[4] B. Awerbuch, A. Baratz, and D. Peleg. Efficient broadcast and light-weight spanners. *Manuscript*, 1991.

[5] Y. Bartal, A. Filtser, and O. Neiman. On notions of distortion and an almost minimum spanning tree with constant average distortion. In *Proc. of 27th SODA*, pages 873–882, 2016.

[6] Y. Ben-Shimol, A. Dvir, and M. Segal. SPLAST: a novel approach for multicasting in mobile wireless ad hoc networks. In *Proc. of 15th PIMRC*, pages 1011–1015, 2004.

[7] P. Bose, P. Carmi, M. Farshi, A. Maheshwari, and M. H. M. Smid. Computing the greedy spanner in near-quadratic time. *Algorithmica*, 58(3):711–729, 2010.

[8] R. Braynard, D. Kostic, A. Rodriguez, J. Chase, and A. Vahdat. Opus: an overlay peer utility service. In *Prof. of 5th OPENARCH*, 2002.

[9] H. T.-H. Chan and A. Gupta. Small hop-diameter sparse spanners for doubling metrics. In *Proc. of 17th SODA*, pages 70–78, 2006.

[10] H. T.-H. Chan, A. Gupta, B. M. Maggs, and S. Zhou. On hierarchical routing in doubling metrics. In *Proc. of 16th SODA*, pages 762–771, 2005.

[11] T.-H. H. Chan, M. Li, L. Ning, and S. Solomon. New doubling spanners: Better and simpler. In *Proc. of 40th ICALP*, pages 315–327, 2013.

[12] B. Chandra, G. Das, G. Narasimhan, and J. Soares. New sparseness results on graph spanners. In *Proc. of 8th SOCG*, pages 192–201, 1992.

[13] S. Chechik and C. Wulff-Nilsen. Near-optimal light spanners. In *Proc. of 27th SODA*, pages 883–892, 2016.

[14] L. P. Chew. There is a planar graph almost as good as the complete graph. In *Proc. of 2nd SOCG*, pages 169–177, 1986.

[15] E. Cohen. Fast algorithms for constructing t-spanners and paths with stretch t. In *Proc. of 34th FOCS*, pages 648–658, 1993.

[16] J. Cong, A. B. Kahng, G. Robins, M. Sarrafzadeh, and C. K. Wong. Performance-driven global routing for cell based ics. In *Proc. of 9th ICCD*, pages 170–173, 1991.

[17] J. Cong, A. B. Kahng, G. Robins, M. Sarrafzadeh, and C. K. Wong. Provably good algorithms for performance-driven global routing. In *Proc. of 5th ISCAS*, pages 2240–2243, 1992.

[18] J. Cong, A. B. Kahng, G. Robins, M. Sarrafzadeh, and C. K. Wong. Provably good performance-driven global routing. *IEEE Trans. on CAD of Integrated Circuits and Sys.*, 11(6):739–752, 1992.

[19] G. Das, P. J. Heffernan, and G. Narasimhan. Optimally sparse spanners in 3-dimensional Euclidean space. In *Proc. of 9th SOCG*, pages 53–62, 1993.

[20] G. Das and G. Narasimhan. A fast algorithm for constructing sparse Euclidean spanners. *Int. J. Comput. Geometry Appl.*, 7(4):297–315, 1997.

[21] E. D. Demaine, M. Hajiaghayi, and B. Mohar. Approximation algorithms via contraction decomposition. *Combinatorica*, 30(5):533–552, 2010.

[22] M. Elkin. Computing almost shortest paths. *ACM Transactions on Algorithms*, 1(2):283–323, 2005.

[23] M. Elkin, O. Neiman, and S. Solomon. Light spanners. In *Proc. of 41th ICALP*, pages 442–452, 2014.

[24] M. Elkin and S. Solomon. Fast constructions of light-weight spanners for general graphs. In *Proc. of 24th SODA*, pages 513–525, 2013.

[25] M. Elkin and J. Zhang. Efficient algorithms for constructing (1+epsilon, beta)-spanners in the distributed and streaming models. *Distributed Computing*, 18(5):375–385, 2006.

[26] P. Erdős. Extremal problems in graph theory. In *Proc. of Sympos. Smolenice*, pages 29–36, 1964.

[27] M. Farshi. *A theoretical and experimental study of geometric networks*. PhD thesis, 2008.

[28] M. Farshi and J. Gudmundsson. Experimental study of geometric t-spanners. In *Proc. of 13th ESA*, pages 556–567, 2005.

[29] J. Feigenbaum, S. Kannan, A. McGregor, S. Suri, and J. Zhang. Graph distances in the streaming model: the value of space. In *Proc. of 16th SODA*, pages 745–754, 2005.

[30] J. Gao, L. J. Guibas, and A. Nguyen. Deformable spanners and applications. In *Proc. of 20th SoCG*, pages 190–199, 2004.

[31] L. Gottlieb. A light metric spanner. In *Proc. of 56th FOCS*, pages 759–772, 2015.

[32] L. Gottlieb and L. Roditty. Improved algorithms for fully dynamic geometric spanners and geometric routing. In *Proc. of 19th SODA*, pages 591–600, 2008.

[33] L. Gottlieb and L. Roditty. Improved algorithms for fully dynamic geometric spanners and geometric routing. In *Proc. of 19th SODA*, pages 591–600, 2008.

[34] L. Gottlieb and L. Roditty. An optimal dynamic spanner for doubling metric spaces. In *Proc. of 16th ESA*, pages 478–489, 2008.

[35] M. Grigni. Approximate TSP in graphs with forbidden minors. In *Proc. of 27th ICALP*, pages 869–877, 2000.

[36] M. Grigni and H. Hung. Light spanners in bounded pathwidth graphs. In *Proc. of 37th MFCS*, pages 467–477, 2012.

[37] M. Grigni and P. Sissokho. Light spanners and approximate TSP in weighted graphs with forbidden minors. In *Proc. of 13th SODA*, pages 852–857, 2002.

[38] J. Gudmundsson, C. Levcopoulos, and G. Narasimhan. Fast greedy algorithms for constructing sparse geometric spanners. *SIAM J. Comput.*, 31(5):1479–1500, 2002.

[39] A. Gupta, R. Krauthgamer, and J. R. Lee. Bounded geometries, fractals, and low-distortion embeddings. In *Proc. of 44th FOCS*, pages 534–543, 2003.

[40] S. Har-Peled and M. Mendel. Fast construction of nets in low-dimensional metrics and their applications. *SIAM J. Comput.*, 35(5):1148–1184, 2006.

[41] S. Har-Peled and M. Mendel. Fast construction of nets in low-dimensional metrics and their applications. *SIAM J. Comput.*, 35(5):1148–1184, 2006.

[42] H. Hung. Light spanner and monotone tree. *CoRR*, abs/1207.3807, 2012.

[43] P. N. Klein. A linear-time approximation scheme for planar weighted TSP. In *Proc. of 46th FOCS*, pages 647–657, 2005.

[44] D. Kostic and A. Vahdat. Latency versus cost optimizations in hierarchical overlay networks. *Technical report, Duke University*, (CS-2001-04), 2002.

[45] G. Narasimhan and M. Smid. *Geometric Spanner Networks*. Cambridge University Press, 2007.

[46] D. Peleg. Proximity-preserving labeling schemes and their applications. In *Proc. of 25th WG*, pages 30–41, 1999.

[47] D. Peleg. *Distributed Computing: A Locality-Sensitive Approach*. SIAM, Philadelphia, PA, 2000.

[48] D. Peleg and A. Schäffer. Graph spanners. *J. Graph Theory*, 13(1):99–116, 1989.

[49] D. Peleg and J. D. Ullman. An optimal synchronizer for the hypercube. *SIAM J. Comput.*, 18(4):740–747, 1989.

[50] D. Peleg and E. Upfal. A trade-off between space and efficiency for routing tables. *J. ACM*, 36(3):510–530, 1989.

[51] Y. Rabinovich and R. Raz. Lower bounds on the distortion of embedding finite metric spaces in graphs. *Discrete & Computational Geometry*, 19(1):79–94, 1998.

[52] L. Roditty. Fully dynamic geometric spanners. In *Proc. of 23rd SoCG*, pages 373–380, 2007.

[53] L. Roditty, M. Thorup, and U. Zwick. Deterministic constructions of approximate distance oracles and spanners. In *Proc. of 32nd ICALP*, pages 261–272, 2005.

[54] L. Roditty and U. Zwick. On dynamic shortest paths problems. In *Proc. of 32nd ESA*, pages 580–591, 2004.

[55] F. S. Salman, J. Cheriyan, R. Ravi, and S. Subramanian. Approximating the single-sink link-installation problem in network design. *SIAM Journal on Optimization*, 11(3):595–610, 2001.

[56] H. Shpungin and M. Segal. Near optimal multicriteria spanner constructions in wireless ad-hoc networks. *IEEE/ACM Transactions on Networking*, 18(6):1963–1976, 2010.

[57] M. H. M. Smid. The weak gap property in metric spaces of bounded doubling dimension. In *Proc. of Efficient Algorithms*, pages 275–289, 2009.

[58] S. Solomon. From hierarchical partitions to hierarchical covers: optimal fault-tolerant spanners for doubling metrics. In *Proc. of 46th STOC*, pages 363–372, 2014.

[59] M. Thorup and U. Zwick. Approximate distance oracles. In *Proc. of 33rd STOC*, pages 183–192, 2001.

[60] M. Thorup and U. Zwick. Compact routing schemes. In *Proc. of 13th SPAA*, pages 1–10, 2001.

[61] J. Vogel, J. Widmer, D. Farin, M. Mauve, and W. Effelsberg. Priority-based distribution trees for application-level multicast. In *Proc. of 2nd NETGAMES*, pages 148–157, 2003.

[62] P. von Rickenbach and R. Wattenhofer. Gathering correlated data in sensor networks. In *Proc. of DIALM-POMC*, pages 60–66, 2004.

[63] B. Y. Wu, K. Chao, and C. Y. Tang. Light graphs with small routing cost. *Networks*, 39(3):130–138, 2002.

MST in Log-Star Rounds of Congested Clique

Mohsen Ghaffari
MIT
ghaffari@mit.edu

Merav Parter
MIT
parter@mit.edu

ABSTRACT

We present a randomized algorithm that computes a Minimum Spanning Tree (MST) in $O(\log^* n)$ rounds, with high probability, in the *Congested Clique* model of distributed computing. In this model, the input is a graph on n nodes, initially each node knows only its incident edges, and per round each two nodes can exchange $O(\log n)$ bits.

Our key technical novelty is an $O(\log^* n)$ *Graph Connectivity* algorithm, the heart of which is a (recursive) forest growth method, based on a combination of two ideas: a *sparsity-sensitive sketching* aimed at sparse graphs and a *random edge sampling* aimed at dense graphs.

Our result improves significantly over the $O(\log\log\log n)$ algorithm of Hegeman et al. [PODC 2015] and the $O(\log\log n)$ algorithm of Lotker et al. [SPAA 2003; SICOMP 2005].

1. INTRODUCTION AND RELATED WORK

Congested Clique is a basic model of distributed computing that was introduced by Lotker, Patt-Shamir, Pavlov, and Peleg [LPPSP03]. Since its introduction, this model has received extensive attention and it is receiving increasingly more, recently [PST11, DLP12, BHP12, Len13a, DKO14, Nan14, HPS14, HP14, CHKK+15, HPP+15, BFARR15, Gha16]. In this model, initially each of the n nodes knows only its incident edges in the graph $G = (V, E)$, communications happen in synchronous rounds, and per round, each two nodes exchange $O(\log n)$ bits. Note that unlike the classical CONGEST model [Pel00], here even non-adjacent nodes of G can communicate. While at first glance this seems unorthodox, there are at least two strong motives for studying this *complete communication* model:

The Practical Motivation, *Overlay Networks* and *Large-Scale Graph Processing*: The traditional viewpoint in distributed network algorithms was that processors running the algorithm reside in network nodes and two processors can communicate only if their nodes are adjacent. This implicitly assumes that the whole network, or a connected subgraph of it, runs the algorithm. In many practical cases, this would not be realistic, e.g., most high-level protocols running on the Internet do not control such a subgraph. A more common scenario is that of *overlay networks*, where a number of processors spread over the whole network are running the distributed algorithm. These processors are not necessarily adjacent in the base network but are instead connected via an overlay that provides point-to-point communications between any two of them.

Congested Clique also relates to two models of processing large-scale graphs, the k-machine model [KNPR15] and the MapReduce model [DG08, KSV10, HP15].

The Theoretical Motivation, *Taking Locality Out of the Picture*: Two central challenges in distributed computing are *congestion* and *locality* [Pel00]. Studying these challenges together, as is necessary in the CONGEST model, creates a complex mix. From a theoretician's perspective, a natural step towards understanding these two issues is to decouple them, i.e., to first understand each of them separately. The LOCAL model [Lin92, Pel00], which is by now quite well-studied, is a perfect model in taking the congestion out of the picture and focusing on *locality*. The Congested Clique model can be viewed as the complement, which instead takes locality out and focuses on *congestion*. For instance, the usual locality-based $\Omega(D)$ lower bound of the CONGEST model—where D denotes the network diameter—disappears in the Congested Clique model.

MST in Congested Clique: At the center of the study of the Congested Clique model is the problem of computing a *Minimum Spanning Tree* (MST); in fact the model started with this problem [LPPSP03]. It is easy to see that the 1926 approach of Boruvka [NMN01] can be adapted to solve MST in $O(\log n)$ rounds of this model. While introducing the model, the main result of Lotker et al. [LPPSP03] was to show that MST can be solved faster, particularly in $O(\log\log n)$ rounds. Progress was scarce afterward, for more than a decade, until recently when Hegeman et al. [HPP+15] presented an $O(\log\log\log n)$ algorithm. Considering these gradually shrinking bounds, there has been a growing anticipation in the community that the optimal bound should be much smaller. Though, the question of improving the bound remained *"tantalizing"* [HPP+15] and open.

Our Result: In this paper, we show that MST can indeed be solved significantly faster:

This work was partially funded by the following grants: AFOSR FA9550-13-1-0042, NSF CCF-1461559, CCF-1217506, CCF-0939370.

PODC'16, July 25-28, 2016, Chicago, IL, USA

© 2016 ACM. ISBN 978-1-4503-3964-3/16/07...$15.00

DOI: http://dx.doi.org/10.1145/2933057.2933103

Theorem 1.1. *There is a randomized algorithm in the Congested Clique model that computes a minimum spanning tree in $O(\log^* n)$ rounds, with high probability.*

The time complexity of our algorithm improves gracefully when larger messages are allowed. If the message size is $\Theta(b \log n)$, then the round complexity becomes $O(\log^* n - \log^* b)$. Thus, the round complexity is $O(1)$ rounds for $b = \log\log \ldots \log n$ for c time iterated logarithm, for any constant $c \geq 1$. Contrasting this with a result of Hegeman et al. [HPP+15], it can be phrased as improving the message size of $O(1)$-round algorithms from $O(\log^4 n)$ to almost $O(\log n)$. Our connectivity algorithm also leads to improvements in several other problems, using standard connections:

Corollary 1.2. *In the congested clique model, (1) there are randomized algorithms that solve the following verification problems in $O(\log^* n)$ rounds with high probability*[1]*: Bipartiteness verification, cut verification, s-t connectivity and cycle containment. (2) There is an $O(\log \Delta + \log^* n)$ round randomized MIS algorithm.*

1.1 Our Approach, in a Nutshell

The main technical novelty in our result is an $O(\log^* n)$ *Graph Connectivity* algorithm. The extension from this to MST is based on a mostly known method and will be described in Section 3.

The heart of our connectivity algorithm is growing a maximal forest. To explain this forest growth, suppose that the graph is connected; the method generalizes to disconnected graphs as we describe later. The key in our forest growth is an $O(1)$-round algorithm with the following guarantee:

Forest Growth: *The forest grows from $O(\frac{n}{\log^2 x})$ to $\frac{n}{x}$ components, in $O(1)$ rounds, w.h.p.*

To get a maximal forest, we apply this forest growth for $O(\log^* n)$ iterations, where in the ith iteration we set $x = 2 \uparrow\uparrow \Theta(i)$. Here, $2 \uparrow\uparrow k$ denotes a power tower with base 2 and height k [Knu76].

The Algorithm's Intuition: To explain the intuition behind this $O(1)$-round forest growth algorithm, we next discuss two opposite extremes of the scenario we can face: a *dense* and a *sparse* scenario. In reality, we will not be in either of these extremes *per se*. Nonetheless, the algorithm is an interpolation of the two solutions and we will prove that it always enjoys the fast growth. (I) DENSE SCENARIO: Suppose that each of the current components is incident on at least x^6 outgoing edges. We make each component select a uniformly random outgoing edge, to be added to the forest. One can prove that due to the high density, once these randomly selected edges are added to the forest, w.h.p., the number of connected components is at most n/x. Roughly speaking, the reason is that each new component will (be expected to) have at least x nodes.

(II) SPARSE SCENARIO: Suppose that each of the current components is incident on at most x^6 outgoing edges, and assume that this remains true even as we merge components. For this case, our solution makes use of a simple linear sketching that we designed for this particular case. We note that this is in part inspired by the work of Hegeman et al. [HPP+15] whose approach was, in a nutshell, as follows: grow forest components using Lotker et al's [LPPSP03] algorithm till there are $O(n/\operatorname{poly}(\log n))$ components, and then use $O(\operatorname{poly}(\log n))$-bit ℓ_0-sampler sketches, following Ahn et al. [AGM12], to finish the problem in $O(1)$ extra rounds[2].

In our solution, a key point is to design a *sparsity-sensitive linear sketching* which allows us to reduce the sketch size when the graph is sparse. Particularly, considering that each component is assumed to have at most x^6 outgoing edges, we compute $L = \Theta(\log x)$ many special *linear sketches* in each component, where each sketch has size $O(\log x \log n)$ bits. We discuss these sketches shortly. Then, we gather all these sketches—which is a total of $O(\frac{n}{\log^2 x}) \cdot O(\log x) \cdot O(\log x \log n) = O(n \log n)$ bits—in a leader node, in $O(1)$ rounds. The leader then simulates $\Theta(\log x)$ iterations of Boruvka's component-merging algorithm locally using these sketches. At the end of these locally-computed merges, the forest has at most n/x components.

Our sketches are very simple. Each sketch is composed of $10 \log x$ rows, and each row has $\Theta(\log n)$ bits. To compute the ith row, we do as follows: mark each edge with probability $1/2^i$. Then, the ith row in the sketch of each node v is the bit-wise XOR of the identifiers[3] of the marked edges incident on v. The sketch of a component is defined to be the bit-wise XOR of the sketches of its nodes.

The intuition for this sketch design is as follows: We argue that for each component C, with constant probability, a sketch of C provides an edge going out of C. Notice that the edges internal to C do not affect the sketch of C, because even if such an edge is marked, it gets added twice to the XOR, once from each endpoint, and thus gets canceled out. Let k be the number of edges with exactly one endpoint in C. Note that due to the sparsity assumption, we have $k \in [1, x^6]$. In the ith row of the sketch of C, where $i = \lceil \log k \rceil$, the probability that exactly one outgoing edge of C is marked for this row is at least a constant. If that happens, the ith row is simply the identifier of one outgoing edge, i.e., the sketch of C provides an edge going out of C. Now this happens for each component with constant probability. Thus, if the leader adds all the outgoing edges extracted from the first sketch of all components, w.h.p., the number of components decreases by a constant factor.

The leader can continue this process locally for all L sketches. When two components merge, the sketch of the resulting merged component is simply the XOR of their sketches. Hence, the leader can locally compute the new component sketches and continue. Repeating this for L iterations, once for each sketch, reduces the number of connected components to $n/2^{\Theta(L)} = n/x$.

2. CONNECTIVITY IN $O(\log^* N)$ ROUNDS

In this section, we describe our graph connectivity algorithm, which leads to the following result:

[1] As standard, the term *high probability* indicates a probability exceeding $1 - 1/n^c$, for an arbitrary constant $c \geq 2$.

[2] Sketching based solutions for the connectivity problems were also employed for the centralized dynamic setting [KKM13] and in the k-machine model [PRS15].

[3] We will assign certain $\Theta(\log n)$-bit random identifiers to the edges. These ids will let us determine w.h.p. if a row is exactly only one identifier, or the XOR of two or more identifiers. This will be discussed in Section 2.2.3.

Theorem 2.1. *There exists a randomized algorithm in the congest clique model that identifies the connected components in the graph G in $O(\log^* n)$ communication rounds, with high probability*[4].

This algorithm computes a *maximal forest* F of G, by starting with the trivial forest $F = (V, \emptyset)$ with no edges, and gradually adding edges of G to F—which thus merges some connected components of F with each other—until F is maximal. For the sake of analysis, we call each connected component C of F *growable* if it is not equal to the component of G that contains C, i.e., if C has at least one outgoing edge to vertices in other components and hence it can still grow. In the algorithm, each component C of F is either *active* or *inactive*, and the algorithm ensures that a component becomes inactive only if it is *not* growable anymore.

The key in our method is an algorithm called $\mathsf{ReduceCC}(x)$, which reduces the number of active connected components of F from $O(n/\log^2 x)$ to n/x, in $O(1)$ rounds. The connectivity algorithm is simply made of $O(\log^* n)$ calls to $\mathsf{ReduceCC}(x)$, where in the ith call we set $x = 2 \uparrow\uparrow \Theta(i)$. In the sequel, we describe and analyze the Algorithm $\mathsf{ReduceCC}(x)$.

2.1 The Algorithm's Outline

Our approach for growing the forest is, to some extent, in the spirit of Boruvka's 1926 algorithm. Let us briefly recall Boruvka's algorithm. This algorithm works in $O(\log n)$ iterations, where in each iteration, from each growable component, we pick an outgoing edge. We then add all these outgoing edges to the forest, while ignoring cycle-creating edges. Each such iteration reduces the number of growable components by a 2 factor. Hence, after $O(\log n)$ iterations, we reach to a maximal forest.

As mentioned above, to reduce the number of active components from n to 0 in $O(\log^* n)$ rounds, our task boils down to reducing the number of active components from $O(n/\log^2 x)$ to n/x within $O(1)$ rounds. To achieve this, our approach has two main forest growth steps, as well as a simple clean up step. First, we reduce the number of active components whose number of outgoing edges is at most x^6. We call these components *low-degree* components. Then, the second forest growth step is aimed mainly at *high-degree* components, those (new components) with at least x^6 outgoing edges. After this, we perform a clean up step that deactivates some components that are not growable. At the end, we get that the number of active connected components decreases to at most n/x. We next briefly explain these three steps. A more detailed description follows.

To reduce the number of growable low-degree components to at most n/x, we would like to locally simulate $\Theta(\log x)$ iterations of Boruvka's algorithm at a given leader node u^*. The main challenge in doing so is that *a priori* a node v cannot predict the sequence of the components to which it might belong throughout the process of component merging. Thus v does not know which of its edges will be outgoing for these components. To overcome this, we will design and use a special *linear sketching* procedure that handles all components with at most x^6 outgoing edges.

Our key observation is as follows: an outgoing edge of a *low-degree* component can be computed by letting each node sketch the identifiers of its incident edges into $O(\log x \log n)$ bits. Since there are $O(n/\log^2 x)$ active components, we in fact have sufficient capacity to send $\Theta(\log x)$ such sketches per component to the leader u^*; this will be proven formally. The leader then will use these sketches to locally simulate $\Theta(\log x)$ iterations of Boruvka's algorithm. We will show that the number of growable low-degree components at the end of this step, in the output decomposition $\mathcal{C}'$, is at most $n/(4x)$.

Next, we focus on high-degree components in $\mathcal{C}'$, where we use the following simple yet powerful observation: a single randomly sampled edge of a high-degree component of cardinality at most $(8x)$ is with a "good" probability an outgoing edge. Thus, such an edge is likely to reduce the number of connected components. We will show that by letting each node send one random edge to the leader, and the leader adding them to the forest (while ignoring cycles), the number of high-degree components gets reduced, such that we have at most $n/(2x)$ growable components.

The third step then identifies the non-growable components that have less than $(8x)$ nodes and deactivates them. Note that there are at $n/(8x)$ non-growable components with more than $8x$ nodes. Hence, at the end of this clean up step, what remains will be at most n/x active components. We next provide a compact and high level description of the algorithm, after which we discuss each of the steps in detail, each in one of the subsequent subsections.

Algorithm $\mathsf{ReduceCC}(x)$

Input: a forest F with a set $\mathcal{C}$ of at most $O(n/\log^2 x)$ active components.
Output: a forest F' with a set $\mathcal{C}_{out}$ of at most n/x active components.

- **(S1): Handling low-degree components**
  - Each node v computes $L = \Theta(\log x)$ many linear sketches $\mathsf{Sketch}_1(v)$, $\mathsf{Sketch}_2(v)$, ..., $\mathsf{Sketch}_L(v)$, where each of these sketches has $O(\log x \log n)$ bits.
  - For every active connected component $C \in \mathcal{C}$, let $\mathsf{Sketch}_i(C) = \sum_{v \in C} \mathsf{Sketch}_i(v)$.
  - Route the sketches $\mathsf{Sketch}_i(C)$ of all active components $C \in \mathcal{C}$ to the leader node u^*.
  - Let u^* locally simulates $\Theta(\log x)$ rounds of the basic connectivity algorithm, resulting in the new component decomposition $\mathcal{C}' = \{C'_1, \ldots, C'_k\}$.
- **(S2): Handling high-degree components**
  - Every node sends a random edge to the leader.
  - The leader u^* merges components using these edges, resulting in the output decomposition $\mathcal{C}_{out} = \{C''_1, \ldots, C''_{k'}\}$.
- **(S3): Clean Up**
  - The leader identifies and deactivates components of $\mathcal{C}_{out}$ that are not *growable* and are *small*—having less than $8x$ nodes.

[4]We remark that, by slight adjustments, one can make the message complexity of this algorithm be $O(n\,\mathrm{poly}(\log n))$. Details are deferred to the full version.

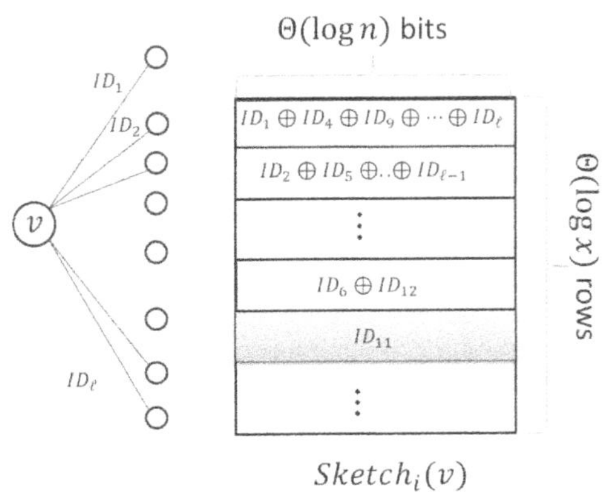

Figure 1: An illustration of a single copy $\mathsf{Sketch}_i(v)$ of the sketch for vertex v. The degree of vertex v is $\ell \le x$. The sketch contains $\Theta(\log x)$ rows, each contains $\Theta(\log n)$ bits. For each row j, the edges are sampled with probability 2^{-j}, and the row contains the bitwise XOR of these sampled edges. The row $\ell' = \lceil \log \ell \rceil$ contains the ID of a single edge with constant probability.

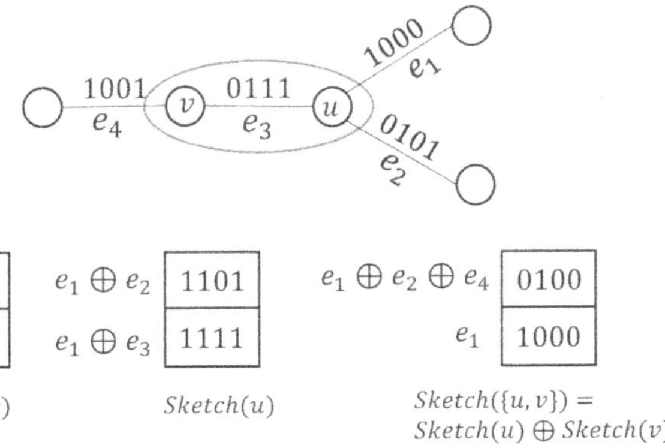

Figure 2: A simple illustration of the sketches and the effect after a merge.

2.2 Step (S1): Handling the Low-Degree Components

2.2.1 *The Algorithm of Step (S1)*

Let $\mathcal{I} = \{\mathrm{ID}(e_1), \ldots, \mathrm{ID}(e_m)\}$ be a set of random edge identifiers, each having $\Theta(\log n)$ bits. The construction of these edge identifiers is described in Section 2.2.3. For a subset of edges $S \subseteq E$, let $\mathsf{XOR}(S)$ be the bitwise XOR of the IDs of edges in S, i.e., $\mathsf{XOR}(S) = \oplus_{e \in S} \mathrm{ID}(e)$.

Sketch Description: Each sketch of node v is composed of $10 \log x$ rows, and each row has $\Theta(\log n)$ bits. Let $E_j \subseteq E$ be a subset of the graph edges, where each $e \in E$ is included in E_j independently with probability 2^{-j}. Let $E_j(v)$ be the subset of E_j edges that are incident on v. The jth row of the sketch of v is the bit-wise XOR of the edge identifiers in $E_j(v)$. The node v computes $\Theta(\log x)$ independent copies of the sketch, where each $\mathsf{Sketch}_i(v)$ is a matrix consists of $10 \log x$ rows as follows

$$\mathsf{Sketch}_i(v) = [\mathsf{XOR}(E_1(v)), \ldots, \mathsf{XOR}(E_{10 \log x}(v))]. \quad (1)$$

See Fig. 1 for an illustration.

We remark that we will ensure that for each edge $e = (u, v)$, nodes u and v know consistently whether $e \in E_i$ or not. Thus, $e = (u, v)$ either appears in both $E_i(v)$ and $E_i(u)$ or in neither. This property is critical, cf. Observation 2.2. In Section 2.2.3, we explain how to achieve this property for all sketches using merely $O(\log n)$ bits of communication between u and v.

Local simulation of Boruvka's algorithm: Let $\mathcal{C} = \{C_1, \ldots, C_k\}$ be the initial collection of $k = O(n/\log^2 x)$ active connected components. For each i, the ith sketch of a component C is defined to be the bit-wise XOR of the ith sketches of its nodes. In Lemma 2.6, we explain the routing that in $O(1)$ rounds, delivers to the leader $\Theta(\log x)$ sketches $\mathsf{Sketch}_i(C)$ per each component C in $\mathcal{C}$.

Each of the $\Theta(\log x)$ sketches of a given component would be used to obtain *one* outgoing edge. The ith sketches $\mathsf{Sketch}_i(C)$ are used in the ith iteration of simulation of Boruvka's algorithm, where $\mathsf{Sketch}_i(C)$ will provide (at most) one edge going out of C. By Lemma 2.4, the random identifiers are constructed in a way that allows the leader to determine w.h.p. whether a row has exactly only one identifier or it is a XOR of two or more identifiers. The leader then looks for a row (among the $10 \log x$ rows) in $\mathsf{Sketch}_i(C)$ that contains one sampled edge. If such an outgoing edge is found, then this edge is added to the forest and the components of the corresponding two endpoint nodes are merged into a single component. For each $j \ge i$, the jth sketch of the new component is simply the bitwise XOR of the two components' j^{th} sketches. At the end of these $\Theta(\log x)$ merge iterations of Boruvka's algorithm, let $\mathcal{C}'$ be the resulting intermediate component decomposition.

2.2.2 *Analysis of Step (S1)*

The following simple observation is useful in this analysis.

Observation 2.2. *Let C be a connected component and let E_{out} be the set of edges with exactly one endpoint in C. Then for each $i \in [1, 10 \log x]$, the ith row of $\mathsf{Sketch}(C)$ is simply the XOR of a subset S of edges E_{out}, where each edge $e \in E_{out}$ appears in S independently with probability $1/2^i$. Particularly, the set of edges with zero or with two endpoints in C do not affect this sketch.*

We say that a component is *large* if it has at least $8x$ nodes, and *small* otherwise. Also recall that a component is called *high-degree* if the number of edges going out of it is at least x^6, and *low-degree* otherwise. Let $\mathcal{C}'$ be the component decomposition at the end of step (S1).

Lemma 2.3. *W.h.p., the number of growable low-degree components in $\mathcal{C}'$ is at most $n/(4x)$.*

Proof. Given any component decomposition, let us call a component (and thus also all of its nodes) *blue* if its outgoing degree is at least $2x^6$, or if it contains a node/component that was colored blue in the past component decompositions. Otherwise, the component is called *red*.

We first argue that the total number of blue low-degree components in $\mathcal{C}'$ is at most $n/(8x)$. Consider a blue component $C' \in \mathcal{C}'$. There are two cases. Case 1: either C' is large, in which case there are at most $n/(8x)$ such components. Case 2: C' is small, in which case since C' contains a blue node, its outgoing degree is at least $2x^6 - (8x)^2 \ge x^6$ and hence C' is not low-degree. Therefore, the total number of blue low-degree components in $\mathcal{C}'$ is at most $n/(8x)$.

Clearly, this also means the number of such components that are also growable is at most $n/(8x)$.

To complete the proof, we next show that, w.h.p., the number of the growable red low-degree components of $\mathcal{C}'$ is at most $n/(8x)$. To prove this, we consider $\Theta(\log x)$ iterations of Boruvka's algorithm as simulated locally by the leader u^*. For each iteration i, let $\mathcal{C}_i$ be the component decomposition at the beginning of this iteration and let y_i be the number of red growable components in $\mathcal{C}_i$. The argument will be provided in two similar parts, first when $\log x \leq O(\log n)$ and second when $\log x \geq \Omega(\log n)$. In the first case, we argue that w.h.p. $y_{i+1} \leq 39y_i/40$. Thus, we would get that $y_k \leq n/(8x)$ for $k = c \log x$ for large enough constants c. In the second case, we argue that $\mathbb{E}[y_{i+1}] \leq 39y_i/40$, and then use the large value of x to show that after $k = c \log x$ merges, w.h.p., $y_k \leq n/(8x)$.

Let us focus on the case where $\log x \leq O(\log n)$ and consider the ith iteration; here we want to prove that w.h.p. $y_{i+1} \leq 39y_i/40$. Let us first examine the expected number of outgoings edges that are decoded successfully using the ith sketch. Consider a red growable component C in $\mathcal{C}_i$ and let t be the number of its outgoing edges $E_{OUT}(C)$. Note that since this is growable component and since it is red, we have $t \in [1, 2x^6]$, which implies $\ell = \lceil \log t \rceil \in [1, 10 \log x]$. Consider the ℓth row of the sketch $\mathsf{Sketch}_i(C)$. Recall that this row is the bitwise XOR of a sampling of edges of $E_{OUT}(C)$, where each edge is sampled independently with probability $2^{-\ell}$. Therefore, the probability that this sampling contains exactly one edge is at least $\frac{t}{2^\ell}(1-1/2^\ell)^{t-1} \geq 1/10$. That is, with probability at least $1/10$, this row provides the identifier of one edge going out of C.

From above, we can conclude that in expectation, the number of outgoing edges that were successfully sampled from the sketches of growable components with only red nodes is at least $y_i/10$. Since $y_i \geq \log n$, by Chernoff bound, we get that w.h.p. the number of outgoing edges is at least $y_i/20$. Therefore, once we add these edges to the forest, the number of red growable components in $\mathcal{C}_{i+1}$ is at most $39y_i/40$. Notice that it is crucial in this argument that no new red component gets introduced, meaning that each component that is red in $\mathcal{C}_{i+1}$ is made solely of red components of $\mathcal{C}_i$, which holds because of the way we defined colors blue and red. Therefore, we have that w.h.p. $y_{i+1} \leq 39/40 \cdot y_i$, which completes the proof for the $\log x \leq O(\log n)$ case.

Let us consider the case where $\log x \geq \Omega(\log n)$. Using arguments as above, we get that $\mathbb{E}[y_{i+1}] \leq 39y_i/40$. Invoking this expectation for $k = c \log x$ iterations, and noting that $\log x \geq \Omega(\log n)$, we get that $\mathbb{E}[y_k] \leq 1/n^5$. Hence, by Markov's inequality, the probability that $y_k \geq 1$ is at most $1/n^5$. That is, w.h.p, $y_k = 0$. This completes the proof. □

2.2.3 Smaller Algorithmic Details of Step (S1)

Assigning random edge identifiers: Our edge identifier construction is based on the notion of ϵ-*bias* sets [NN93]. The construction is randomized and guarantees that, w.h.p., the XOR of each given subset of edges $S \subseteq E$, for $|S| \geq 2$, is not a legal edge identifier (i.e., is not equal to correspond to an ID of an edge that exists). The construction of the edge IDs is randomized and uses a seed of only $O(\log n)$ random bits, which can be chosen by the leader and delivered to all nodes of the network in $O(1)$ rounds. This allows all nodes to know the their corresponding edge IDs. Furthermore, the leader will be able to detect whether a given $O(\log n)$ bits corresponding to an $\mathsf{XOR}(S)$ is a legal ID (in which case, S contains a single edge) or not, w.h.p.

Lemma 2.4. *There is an algorithm that creates a collection $\mathcal{I} = \{\mathrm{ID}(e_1), \ldots, \mathrm{ID}(e_M)\}$ of $M = \binom{n}{2}$ random identifiers for edges, each of $O(\log n)$-bits, and where each node learns the identifiers of its incident edges, within $O(1)$ rounds. These identifiers are such that for each subset $E' \subseteq E$, where $|E'| \neq 1$, we have $\Pr[\mathsf{XOR}(E') \in \mathcal{I}] \leq 1/n^{10}$.*

Proof. Let $\ell = O(\log n)$ be the length of the edge identifier. To compute $\mathcal{I}$, we use an ϵ-*bias* set $S_j \in \{0,1\}^M$ for each of the $j \in [\ell]$ coordinates of the edge identifiers. That is, for each $j \in [\ell]$, the set $S_j = [b_1, \ldots, b_M]$ specifies the jth bit for the identifier of each of the possible $M = \binom{n}{2}$ graph edges. Next, we first define the ϵ-bias property of these sets, and then explain how they can be constructed using $O(\log^2 n)$ bits of communication. Finally, we argue why the ϵ-bias property guarantees that $\Pr[\mathsf{XOR}(S) \in \mathcal{I}] \leq 1/n^{10}$ for each subset $S \subseteq E$ such that $|S| \neq 1$.

The randomly chosen set $S_j = [b_1, \ldots, b_M]$ satisfies the ϵ-*biased property* if for each set of indices $I \subseteq \{1, \ldots, M\}$, it holds that

$$\Pr[\oplus_{i \in I} b_i = 1] \in [1/2 \pm \epsilon] . \qquad (2)$$

For our proposes, it is sufficient to set $\epsilon = 1/10$. Naor and Naor [NN93] provide a deterministic construction of an ϵ-bias space with size $O(M/\operatorname{poly}(\epsilon))$. That is, they particularly provide a collection $\mathcal{F}$ of functions, where $|F| = O(M/\operatorname{poly}(\epsilon))$, where each $f \in \mathcal{F}$ is a function mapping $[M]$ to $\{0,1\}$, and if we pick a random function $f \in \mathcal{F}$, we would have $\Pr[\oplus_{i \in I} f(i) = 1] \in [1/2 \pm \epsilon]$ for all nonempty subsets I. The randomness in this statement is in the choice of $f \in \mathcal{F}$. We define the set S_j in our identifier construction by picking simply one random function f_j from $\mathcal{F}$. Note that choosing one such random function requires $\log |\mathcal{F}| = \Theta(\log M) = \Theta(\log n)$ bits.

Since the construction of $\mathcal{F}$ is deterministic, all vertices can compute locally the family function $\mathcal{F}$ and the only thing that needs to be communicated between the nodes is the random bits used for selecting the ℓ random functions f_j in $\mathcal{F}$. Since electing a random function in $\mathcal{F}$ requires $\Theta(\log |\mathcal{F}|)$ bits, overall the total number of bits required for specifying these $\ell = \Theta(\log n)$ functions is $\Theta(\log^2 n)$ bits. Clearly, this is achievable in $O(1)$ rounds in the Congested Clique, e.g., by letting a leader node select the $\Theta(\log^2 n)$ bits using private randomness, and then communicating them to all nodes via the help of $O(\log n)$ relay nodes. This completes the description of the construction of $\mathcal{I}$.

Now, we argue that this construction satisfies the property we desire from these random edge identifiers. Consider a subset $E' \subset E$ such that $|E'| \neq 1$. We bound the probability that $\mathsf{XOR}(E') = \mathrm{ID}(e)$. To do that, we distinguish between two cases. First, assume that $e \in E'$. Then if $\mathsf{XOR}(E') = \mathrm{ID}(e)$, it holds that $\mathsf{XOR}(T) = [0, 0, ..., 0]$ where $T = E' \setminus \{e\} \neq \emptyset$. Hence, by Equation (2), we get that $\Pr[\mathsf{XOR}(E') = \mathrm{ID}(e)] = \Pr[\mathsf{XOR}(T) = [0, 0, ..., 0]] \leq 0.4^{\log n} = 1/n^c$. Next, consider the complementary case where $e \notin E'$. In this case, $\mathsf{XOR}(E') = \mathrm{ID}(e)$ implies that $\mathsf{XOR}(T) = [0, 0, ..., 0]$ where $T = E' \cup \{e\} \neq \emptyset$ and again, by Equation (2), this happens with probability at most $1/n^c$. By union bounding over all m edges, we get that $\Pr[\mathsf{XOR}(E') \in \mathcal{I}] \leq 1/n^{10}$. □

Consistent edge sampling for the sketches: Our goal is that for each edge $e = (u, v)$, nodes u and v will know consistently whether the edge e is sampled or not in the sketch. To do that, only the endpoint of the larger id, let it be u, makes the random choices regarding whether the edge is sampled. The node u then sends to v on their edge (u, v) a description concerning all the indices in which the edge (u, v) has been sampled in all of its sketches[5]. These indices will be described in the message by putting a special separation mark between two indices of the same sketch and a different mark between indices of different sketches. We now show that this message contains $O(\log n)$ bits:

Lemma 2.5. *The message describing the indices of successful samplings has $O(\log n)$ bits, w.h.p.*

Proof. Consider a edge $e = (u, v)$ and without loss of generality let u be the node with the larger identifier. Note that overall the iterations of our connectivity algorithm, the number of sketches computed by each node u is $O(\log n) + O(\log\log n) + \ldots + O(1) = O(\log n)$. We now show that indices of these samplings in which e is sampled can be written, w.h.p., in $O(\log n)$ bits. That is, the message containing the sampled indices for *all* these $O(\log n)$ sketches has at most $O(\log n)$ bits, w.h.p.

Consider the ith sketch of u and let r_i be the random variable indicating the sum of indices of the rows for which (u, v) has been sampled. Note that the sampled indices can be described using $O(r_i)$ bits, that is, using a number of bits is linear in the summation of the indices of the sampled rows. We first argue that the probability distribution of this random variable r_i is upper bounded by that of a geometric random variable. Particularly, we upper bound the probability that $r_i = y$ for each integer $y \geq 1$ by a function exponentially decaying in y. Then, we invoke a concentration of summation of geometrically distributed random variables to conclude the proof.

Note that if $r_i = y$, then the sum of the indices of the sampled rows is y and the probability that the edge (u, v) has been sampled into these particular rows is at least 2^{-y}. This is regardless of the particular set of indices whose sum is y. To see this, consider an arbitrary possible set of row indices $i_1, \ldots, i_\ell$ satisfying $\sum_j^\ell i_j = y$. Then, the probability that e has been sampled to these rows is at most $\prod_j^\ell 2^{-i_j} = 2^{\sum_j^\ell i_j} = 2^{-y}$. To bound the probability that $r_i = y$, we then union bound over all distinct ways of representing y as a sum of natural numbers. By a *partition number*[6] result of Erdős [Erd42], there are at most $2^{\Theta(\sqrt{y})}$ such options. Since the probability that edge e is sampled for each such options (i.e, that e was sampled to these exact rows) is bounded by 2^{-y}, overall $\Pr[r_i = y] \leq 2^{\Theta(\sqrt{y})} \cdot 2^{-y} \leq 2^{-y/2}$.

Let z_i be a random variable with a geometric distribution with parameter $1/2$, i.e., where $\Pr[z_i = y] = 2^{-y}$ for $y \in \mathbb{N}$. We have $\Pr[r_i = y] \leq \Pr[z_i = y/2]$. Let $Z = \sum_{i=1}^k z_i$ and $R = \sum_{i=1}^k r_i$ where $k = O(\log n)$ is the total number of sketches computed by u throughout the algorithm. Hence, $\Pr[R \geq 20k] \leq \Pr[Z \geq 10k]$. It is known that the summation of geometric random variables is distributed according to a negative binomial distribution and it is concentrated around its expectation. More precisely, $\Pr[Z \geq 20k] \leq exp(-k) = 1/n^5$. Therefore, $\Pr[R \geq 40\log n] \leq 1/n^5$, thus completing the proof. □

[5]Note that the sketch information is independent of the current component decomposition and hence the node can compute in the beginning of the algorithm all the sketches and send to its neighbor this consistency information.

[6]The *partition number* of an integer y is the number of ways to represent y as a summation of positive integers.

Lemma 2.6. *Consider the setting where a leader node u^* knows a forest with $O(n/\log^2 x)$ active connected components $\mathcal{C} = \{C_1, \ldots, C_k\}$. There is an $O(1)$-round routing scheme that delivers the sketches of all these components to the leader u^*.*

Proof. Recall that every node has $\Theta(\log x)$ sketches, each of size $O(\log x \log n)$ bits, and that each component sketch is simply the bit-wise XOR of the corresponding node sketches. We next describe how to deliver these component sketches to the leader in $O(1)$ rounds. The leader u^* partitions the node-set of each active component C_i into $\lceil |C_i|/(n/k) \rceil$ subsets, each of size at most n/k. This is a total of at most $2k \ll n$ subsets. The leader u^* then elects a distinct relay node w_i for each subset, and sends the id of w_i to all the nodes in that subset.

Next, we deliver the component sketches from the nodes to the leader in a two-step manner, using the help of these relay nodes. First, all nodes send their sketches to their corresponding relay nodes. Then, each relay node computes the bitwise XOR of its received sketches and forwards the result to the leader u^*, who can readily compute the component sketches. We next argue that each of these steps can be performed in $O(1)$ rounds, using Lenzen's routing [Len13b].

Lenzen [Len13b] provides a routing scheme such that if each node is the source for $O(n)$ messages and each node is the the designation for $O(n)$ messages, then all these messages can be routed from their sources to their destinations within $O(1)$ rounds. In the first forwarding step above, each node needs to send $O(\log^2 x \log n)$ bits—which is equivalent to $O(\log^2 x)$ messages—to its relay and each relay needs to receive at most $n/k \ll n$ messages from the nodes in its subset. Further, in the second forwarding step, each relay node needs to send $O(\log^2 x)$ messages to the leader u^* and the leader needs to receive at most $2k \cdot O(\log^2 x) = O(n/\log^2 x) \cdot O(\log^2 x) = O(n)$ messages from the relays. Hence, both of these steps can be easily performed using Lenzen's routing. □

2.3 Step (S2): Handling the High-Degree Components

In the second step (S2), each node v randomly and uniformly picks one of the edges incident on v and sends this edge to the leader u^*. The leader adds these edges to the forest, one by one, ignoring the cycles. This results in a new component decomposition $\mathcal{C}_{out}$. We next show the following.

Lemma 2.7. *W.h.p, the decomposition $\mathcal{C}_{out}$ contains at most $n/(2x)$ growable components.*

Proof. First note that by Lemma 2.3, the number of growable low-degree components in $\mathcal{C}'$ is at most $n/(4x)$. Hence, the total number of components of $\mathcal{C}_{out}$ that contain at least one growable low-degree component of $\mathcal{C}'$ is at most $n/(4x)$. Note that if a component in $\mathcal{C}_{out}$ contains a component of $\mathcal{C}'$ that was not growable, this actually means that the two components are the same and both are not growable. To complete the proof, we show that the number of components of $\mathcal{C}_{out}$ that *do not* contain any low-degree component of $\mathcal{C}'$ is also at most $n/(4x)$.

Recall that for each component of $\mathcal{C}_{out}$, we call it *small* if it has less than $8x$ nodes, and *large* otherwise. Clearly, the number of large components of $\mathcal{C}_{out}$ is at most $n/(8x)$. Hence, to complete the proof, what remains is to show that in $\mathcal{C}_{out}$, the number of small components that *do not* contain a low-degree component from $\mathcal{C}'$ is at most $n/(8x)$.

To prove this, we consider the random process of adding edges to the forest gradually, as follows: This process is performed only for the sake of analysis. Throughout, we maintain a counter κ, which at the end will provide an upper bound on the number of small connected components in $\mathcal{C}_{out}$ that do not contain a low-degree component of C'.

First, mark all low-degree components of C' as *processed*, whereas all the high-degree components of C' are considered *unprocessed*. We gradually process unprocessed components and add the related sampled edges to the forest. For clarity, we perform this in phases. In phase $i \geq 1$, pick an arbitrary unprocessed small component C and let it be the head-component of the ith chain. We then sample an edge – as will be described next – from the component C' that was joined last to this chain, where at the start, C' is simply C. To sample an edge from C', we pick an arbitrary vertex $v' \in C'$ of degree at least $x^5/8$ – and sample one of its edges uniformly at random. Since C' is both small and high-degree, such vertex v' exists.

If this randomly sampled edge connects to an unprocessed component C'', then we mark C'' as processed and add C'' to the chain. On the other hand, if the sampled edge connects C' to a component that is already processed, then the extension of the chain is halted and we update the counter κ in the following manner: If the sampled edge connects C' to a processed component within the *same* chain, and the total number of nodes in the connected component created by this chain is less than $8x$, then increment the counter κ by 1. If the sampled edge connects C' to a component in some previous chain, or to one of the low-degree components, then the counter κ remains as is. At this point, phase i ends. We continue this process until all components are marked as processed. See Figure 3 for an illustration.

If this randomly sampled edge connects to an unprocessed component C'', then we mark C'' as processed and add C'' to the chain. If the sampled edge connects C' to a component that is already processed, then the extension of the chain is halted and we update the counter κ in the following manner: If the sampled edge connects C' to a processed component within the *same* chain, and the total number of nodes in the connected component created by this chain is less than $8x$, then increment the counter κ by 1. On the other hand, if the sampled edge connects C' to a component in some previous chain, or to one of the low-degree components, then the counter κ remains as is. At this point, phase i ends. We continue this process until all components are marked as processed. See Figure 3 for an illustration.

Since the counter is incremented only when the chain consists of at most $8x$ nodes and when the random edge does not connect it to a previously counted component, we get that at the end, the number of low-cardinality components that do not contain a low-degree component from C' is upper bounded by κ. To complete the proof, we next show that with high probability, $\kappa \leq n/(8x)$.

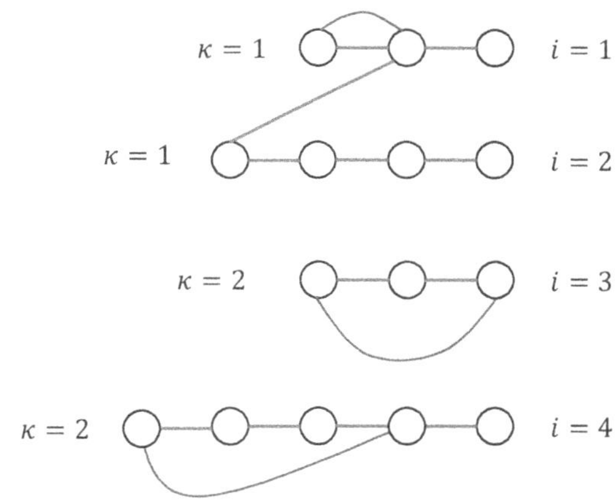

Figure 3: Illustration for Lemma 2.7. The figure shows the chain created at steps $i = 1, 2, 3, 4$. The counter κ is increased only when the sampled edge of the last added component is internal to the chain and the number of vertices in the chain's components is small. For example, the counter is not incremented in step $i = 2$, since the sampled edge hits the chain of step $i = 1$. In addition, the counter is not incremented in step $i = 4$, because the total number of vertices in the chain's components is above $8x$.

To prove this claim, let κ_i be the value of the counter at the end of phase i and let ℓ be the total number of phases. We first claim that for every $i \in \{1, \ldots, \ell\}$, $\mathbb{E}[\kappa_i | \kappa_{i-1}] \leq \kappa_{i-1} + 1/x^2$. Consider the ith chain $[C_{i_1}, \ldots, C_{i_k}]$ generated at phase i and let $v_{i_j} \in C_{i_j}$ be the vertex whose edge has been taken (i.e., the vertex with degree at least $x^5/8$) for every $j \in \{1, \ldots k\}$. The probability that the counter is increased by 1 at the end of the phase is bounded by the probability that somewhere throughout the steps during which the chain had at most $4x$ nodes, the following happens: for at least one of the nodes $v_{i_j} \in C_{i_j}$ which was sampled for an edge, the randomly selected edge had both of its endpoints in the same chain. Throughout these steps, for every $j \in \{1, \ldots, k\}$, since the out-degree of the vertex v_{i_j} is greater than $x^5/8 - (8x)^2 \geq x^5/16$, the probability that a random edge of the node $v_{i_j} \in C_{i_j}$ connects to some node in $\bigcup_{\ell=1}^{j} C_{i_\ell}$ is at most $\frac{(8x)^2}{x^5/16} \leq c \cdot x^3$. Hence, by applying the union bound on all $8x$ "bad" events, we get that the probability that at least one of these edges is internal is $c' \cdot x^2$. Thus, $\mathbb{E}[\kappa_i | \kappa_{i-1}] \leq \kappa_{i-1} + c'/x^2$. This implies $\mathbb{E}[\kappa_\ell] \leq c' \cdot n/x^2$. Next, note that probabilistic events of the counter being increased by 1 are independent among different chains, as in the case of each chain i, the event only depends on the random edges sampled from the component under consideration during phase i, and this component will not be processed again in later phases. In addition, since there are high-degree components, $x^6 \leq n$ which means $2n/x^2 = \Omega(\log n)$. Hence, by Chernoff bound, w.h.p., $\kappa_\ell \leq 2c' \cdot n/x^2 \leq n/(8x)$. □

2.4 Step (S3): Clean Up

We now explain how in $O(1)$ rounds, we can identify and deactivate small connected components of $\mathcal{C}_{out}$ that are not growable. By Lemma 2.7 the number of growable components is at most $n/(2x)$. Moreover, the number of (non-growable) large components is at most $n/(8x)$. Therefore, once we deactivate small non-growable components, the total number of active components would be at most

$n/(8x)+n/(2x) \leq n/x$, as desired. We remark that we perform this clean up step only when $x \leq O(\log^2 n)$, that is, for all iterations of our connectivity algorithm except the very last one where we set $x = (n+1)$. Notice that in that last iteration, w.h.p., after step (S1), all components are non-growable—i.e., the forest is maximal—and thus we do not need to continue steps (S2) and (S3).

Lemma 2.8. *In $O(1)$ rounds, we can identify and deactivate component of F that are small and non-growable.*

Proof. Note that the leader u^* knows the whole forest F at the end of step (S2). For each small component C_i of F—that is, each component that has less than $8x$ nodes—the leader picks one relay node w_i. Then, the leader sends the identifiers of all nodes of component C_i to the relay node w_i, simultaneously for all small components, in O(1) rounds, using Lenzen's routing [Len13a]. Then, each relay node w_i that has received identifiers $v_1, \ldots, v_\ell$ of its corresponding component, delivers all of these identifiers to all of them ℓ nodes. That is, relay w_i creates ℓ messages destined for each of these nodes v_i where each of the messages describes the identifiers of $v_1, \ldots, v_\ell$, for a total of at most $(8x)^2 \leq O(\log^4 n)$ messages. We then use Lenzen's routing [Len13a] to deliver all these messages from relay nodes to nodes of small components. Note that this can be done because each node needs to send $(8x)^2 \leq O(\log^4 n)$ messages and each node needs to receive at most $(8x) \leq O(\log^2 n)$ messages. Finally, each node in these small components that now has received the identifiers of all its component-mates checks whether it has an edge going out of its component and informs the leader about this, using a single message, all of which get delivered to the leader in one round. Hence, at the end, the leader knows which of these small components are not growable, and then it marks them as deactivated. □

3. MST IN $O(\log^* N)$ ROUNDS

Here, we explain how using the graph connectivity algorithm presented in the previous section, we can compute a Minimum Spanning Tree (MST) of a weighted graph $G = (V, E, w)$ in $O(\log^* n)$ rounds.

Technically, the solution relies on three components: (1) a result of Karger, Klein, and Tarjan (KKT) [KKT95] that reduces the general MST problem to MST on sparse graphs, (2) a method of Hegeman et al. [HPP+15] which turns MST of graphs with low sparsity into many independent instances of the graph connectivity problem, and (3) an extension of our connectivity algorithm from the previous section that solves many instances of the connectivity problem simultaneously in $O(\log^* n)$ rounds. In the following, we discuss these three components.

MST Sparsification via KKT: We explain how a randomized trick of Karger, Klein, and Tarjan (KKT) [KKT95] transforms the MST problem on graph G into two MST problems on graphs G_1 and G_2, each with $O(n^{3/2})$ edges.

We first need some notations. For a graph G, let F be a forest, and for two nodes u and v, let $w_F(u, v)$ be the heaviest edge on the path connecting u and v in F; if there is no such path, let $w_F(u, v) = \infty$. We call an edge $e = (u, v)$ is *F-heavy* if $w(u, v) > w_F(u, v)$, and F-light otherwise. Notice that F-heavy edges cannot be in the MST of G.

To transform MST on G to MST on two graphs G_1 and G_2 with with $O(n^{3/2})$ edges each, let $p = \frac{1}{\sqrt{n}}$ and let $G_1 = G(p)$ be a randomly selected subgraph of G where each G-edge is included in $G(p)$ independently with probability p. W.h.p., G_1 has $O(n^{3/2})$ edges. Now suppose we have already computed an *minimum spanning forest* F of G_1, let E_2 be the set of F-light edges of G, and let $G_2 = (V, E_2)$. Clearly, an MST of G_2 is an MST G. The result of Karger, Klein, and Tarjan (KKT) [KKT95] shows that G_2 has at most $O(n/p) = O(n^{3/2})$ edges, w.h.p. Hence, the task of computing an MST of G is reduced to computing an MST F of G_1, identifying the set E_2 of F-light edges, and then computing an MST of G_2. Since in the Congested Clique the forest F can be made known to all nodes in $O(1)$ round, the task is reduced to solving MST in two graphs each with $O(n^{3/2})$ edges, one after the other. Next we explain how to solve each of these problems in $O(\log^* n)$ rounds.

From Sparse MST to Many Connectivity Problems: Consider a weighted graph $G' = (V, E', w)$ with $O(n^{3/2})$ edges. Consider the ordering π of the edges E' by increasing weight. Notice that an edge $e = (u, v)$ is in the MST of G' if and only if in the graph edge-induced by the set of edges lighter than e—i.e., those appearing before e in this ordering π—nodes u and v are in two different components. We next show, following [HPP+15], that one can check this condition for all edges of E' simultaneously—thus computing the MST—by solving $\Theta(\sqrt{n})$ graph connectivity problems.

For i from 1 to $K = \Theta(\sqrt{n})$, define subset E_i to be the edges with rank in $[(i-1)n+1, in]$ in the aforementioned ordering π of edges in E'. Use the Congested Clique sorting result of Lenzen [Len13a] so that in $O(1)$ rounds, each node knows the ranking of its incident edges in the ordering. Thus, each node knows for each of its incident edges e, to which edge-set E_i edge e belongs. Pick K leader nodes $u_1, \ldots, u_K$, and then using Lenzen's routing [Len13a], in $O(1)$ rounds, make each leader node u_i know all the edges in set E_i. Leader u_i will be responsible for detecting which of the edges in E_i belong to the MST. Let $H_i = (v, \cup_{j=1}^{i-1} E_j)$. If u_i knows the connected components—or equivalently, a maximal forest F_i—of H_i, then it can locally identify which of E_i edges belong to the MST, as follows: u_i processes the E_i edges one by one in the increasing weight order; each time it adds the new edge to the forest F_i, and also to the MST of G', and then discards all the unprocessed E_i edges e such that $F_i + e$ has a loop, that is, edges e that are internal to a component of F_i.

Thus, to solve MST of G', what remains is that each leader node u_i should learn the connected components (equivalently, a maximal forest) of graph H_i and this should happen for all $K = \Theta(\sqrt{n})$ graphs H_i. This is where our $O(\log^* n)$ connectivity algorithm comes in, as we discuss next.

Solving Many Connectivity Problems: Here, we explain how to extend the algorithm of the previous section to solve connectivity in many graphs simultaneously. Particularly, this extension will allow the leaders $u_1, u_2, \ldots, u_K$ to know, respectively, the connected component decompositions of graphs $H_1 = (V, E_1)$, $H_2 = (V, E_2) \ldots$, $H_K = (V, E_K)$, in $O(\log^* n)$ rounds.

Recall from Section 2 that to solve one instance of the graph connectivity problem, our main subroutine had three steps: (S1) a step where we deliver the sketches of components to the leader, (S2) a step where we deliver to the leader one randomly selected edge incident on each node, and (S3) a clean-up step where we identify and deactivate small connected components that cannot grow.

Clearly, the step (S2) can be performed in parallel for all the K graphs $H_1, H_2, \ldots, H_k$, in just one round. This is because, each node v can directly send one message to each leader u_i, describing the (at most) one edge in H_i incident on v that it sampled. We next explain how steps (S1) and (S3) can also be performed in $O(1)$ rounds, simultaneously for all graphs H_i.

In the next lemma, we show that step (S1) can be performed in $O(1)$ rounds, simultaneously for all the K graphs H_i. This is by a simple extension of Lemma 2.6, as follows:

Lemma 3.1. *Consider the setting where each leader node u_i knows a forest F_i with at most $k = O(n/\log^2 x)$ active connected components in graph H_i. There is an $O(1)$-round routing scheme that, for all $i \in [1, K]$, simultaneously delivers the sketches of all components of F_i to the leader u_i.*

Proof. The approach is mostly the same as in Lemma 2.6. Here we just point out the simple changes that need to be made. As in Lemma 2.6, each leader u_i partitions the node-set of each of the active connected components of F_i into subsets of size n/k where $k = \Theta(n/\log^2 x)$. This breaks the forest F_i into at most $2k$ subsets. Leader u_i picks (at most) $2k$ relay nodes $w_1, w_2, \ldots, w_{2k}$, one for each of these subsets. In fact, we can allow all the leaders to pick the same $2k$ relay nodes, particularly the $2k$ nodes with smallest IDs (although the assignments will be different). Then each leader u_i delivers the ID of relay node w_j to the nodes in the jth subset in the partition of F_i. We can do this at the same time for all the K leaders because to deliver these relay node IDs, each node v needs to receive one ID from each leader u_i, and it can directly receive it from the leader.

Now, each node v sends its sketch for each graph H_i to its corresponding relay node. This requires v to send out a total of $K \cdot \Theta(\log^2 x) \leq \Theta(\sqrt{n}\log^2 n) \ll n$ messages and it requires each relay node to receive at most $K \cdot n/k = \Theta(\sqrt{n}\log^2 n) \ll n$ messages. Hence, the step of delivering sketches from nodes to relays can be done in $O(1)$ rounds, using Lenzen's routing [Len13b].

Finally, we need to deliver the sketches from the relay nodes to the leaders. This requires each relay to send at most $\Theta(K\log^2 x) \leq \Theta(\sqrt{n}\log^2 n) \ll n$ messages and each leader to receive at most $2k \cdot \Theta(\log^2 x) = O(n/\log^2 x) \cdot \Theta(\log^2 x) = O(n)$ messages. Thus, this again be done in $O(1)$ rounds using Lenzen's routing [Len13b]. □

We remark how Lemma 2.5 extends to solving K connectivity problems simultaneously. Recall that Lemma 2.5 discusses how two nodes u and v connected by an edge $e = (u, v) \in G$ can know consistently whether e is sampled in each of the sketch subsets or not, simply by $O(\log n)$ bits of communication. Instead of repeating this for the K graph connectivity problems we want to solve, we make the $O(\log n)$ bits describe the sampling outcomes in the union graph $\cup_{i\in[K]} H_i$, and then u and v can use the edge e for the computation of each graph H_i, considering whether $e \in H_i$ or not. That is, we use the same $O(\log n)$ bits of randomness for all the connectivity problems. This makes the execution of these graph connectivity problems probabilistically dependent. However, since we know that each of them succeeds with high probability, and since they run independent of each other, we do not need any independence; we can do a simple union bound and say that, with high probability, all the graph connectivity instances succeed.

Finally, it remains to explain how Lemma 2.8 can be extended to perform step (S3) for all the graphs:

Lemma 3.2. *In $O(1)$ rounds, simultaneously we can identify and deactivate components of the forests $F_1, F_2, \ldots, F_k$ of graphs $H_1, H_2, \ldots, H_k$ that are small and non-growable.*

Proof. The procedure for each graph is the same as in Lemma 2.8. The only point to note is that, all these messages can be routed simultaneously using Lenzen's routing. Particularly, each relay node will need to receive at most $K(8x) \leq K \cdot O(\log^2 n) \leq O(\sqrt{n}\log^2 n)$ messages from the corresponding leaders and each relay node will need to send at most $K(8x)^2 \leq O(\sqrt{n}\log^4 n)$ messages to the nodes. Both of these bounds are much smaller than n and thus, Lenzen's routing [Len13a] can route all these messages simultaneously in $O(1)$ rounds. □

4. REFERENCES

[AGM12] Kook Jin Ahn, Sudipto Guha, and Andrew McGregor. Analyzing graph structure via linear measurements. In *Proc. of ACM-SIAM Symp. on Disc. Alg. (SODA)*, pages 459–467, 2012.

[BFARR15] Florent Becker, Antonio Fernandez Anta, Ivan Rapaport, and Eric Reémila. Brief announcement: A hierarchy of congested clique models, from broadcast to unicast. In *the Proc. of the Int'l Symp. on Princ. of Dist. Comp. (PODC)*, PODC '15, pages 167–169. ACM, 2015.

[BHP12] Andrew Berns, James Hegeman, and Sriram V Pemmaraju. Super-fast distributed algorithms for metric facility location. In *Automata, Languages, and Programming*, pages 428–439. Springer, 2012.

[CHKK⁺15] Keren Censor-Hillel, Petteri Kaski, Janne H. Korhonen, Christoph Lenzen, Ami Paz, and Jukka Suomela. Algebraic methods in the congested clique. In *the Proc. of the Int'l Symp. on Princ. of Dist. Comp. (PODC)*, pages 143–152. ACM, 2015.

[DG08] Jeffrey Dean and Sanjay Ghemawat. Mapreduce: simplified data processing on large clusters. *Communications of the ACM*, 51(1):107–113, 2008.

[DKO14] Andrew Drucker, Fabian Kuhn, and Rotem Oshman. On the power of the congested clique model. In *the Proc. of the Int'l Symp. on Princ. of Dist. Comp. (PODC)*, pages 367–376. ACM, 2014.

[DLP12] Danny Dolev, Christoph Lenzen, and Shir Peled. âĂIJtri, tri againâĂİ: Finding triangles and small subgraphs in a distributed setting. In *Distributed Computing*, pages 195–209. Springer, 2012.

[Erd42] Pául Erdos. On an elementary proof of some asymptotic formulas in the theory of partitions. *Annals of Mathematics*, pages 437–450, 1942.

[Gha16] Mohsen Ghaffari. An improved distributed algorithm for maximal independent set. In *Proc. of ACM-SIAM Symp. on Disc. Alg. (SODA)*, 2016.

[HP14] James W Hegeman and Sriram V Pemmaraju. Lessons from the congested clique applied to MapReduce. In *the Proceedings of the International Colloquium on Structural Information and Communication Complexity*, pages 149–164. Springer, 2014.

[HP15] James W Hegeman and Sriram V Pemmaraju. Lessons from the congested clique applied to mapreduce. *Theoretical Computer Science*, 608:268–281, 2015.

[HPP+15] James W. Hegeman, Gopal Pandurangan, Sriram V. Pemmaraju, Vivek B. Sardeshmukh, and Michele Scquizzato. Toward optimal bounds in the congested clique: Graph connectivity and MST. In *the Proc. of the Int'l Symp. on Princ. of Dist. Comp. (PODC)*, pages 91–100. ACM, 2015.

[HPS14] James W Hegeman, Sriram V Pemmaraju, and Vivek B Sardeshmukh. Near-constant-time distributed algorithms on a congested clique. In *Distributed Computing*, pages 514–530. Springer, 2014.

[KKM13] Bruce M Kapron, Valerie King, and Ben Mountjoy. Dynamic graph connectivity in polylogarithmic worst case time. In *Proceedings of the Twenty-Fourth Annual ACM-SIAM Symposium on Discrete Algorithms*, pages 1131–1142. SIAM, 2013.

[KKT95] David R Karger, Philip N Klein, and Robert E Tarjan. A randomized linear-time algorithm to find minimum spanning trees. *Journal of the ACM (JACM)*, 42(2):321–328, 1995.

[KNPR15] Hartmut Klauck, Danupon Nanongkai, Gopal Pandurangan, and Peter Robinson. Distributed computation of large-scale graph problems. In *Proceedings of the Twenty-Sixth Annual ACM-SIAM Symposium on Discrete Algorithms*, pages 391–410. SIAM, 2015.

[Knu76] Donald Ervin Knuth. Mathematics and computer science: coping with finiteness. *Science (New York, NY)*, 194(4271):1235–1242, 1976.

[KSV10] Howard Karloff, Siddharth Suri, and Sergei Vassilvitskii. A model of computation for mapreduce. In *Proceedings of the twenty-first annual ACM-SIAM symposium on Discrete Algorithms*, pages 938–948. Society for Industrial and Applied Mathematics, 2010.

[Len13a] Christoph Lenzen. Optimal deterministic routing and sorting on the congested clique. In *the Proc. of the Int'l Symp. on Princ. of Dist. Comp. (PODC)*, pages 42–50, 2013.

[Len13b] Christoph Lenzen. Optimal deterministic routing and sorting on the congested clique. In *the Proc. of the Int'l Symp. on Princ. of Dist. Comp. (PODC)*, pages 42–50, 2013.

[Lin92] Nathan Linial. Locality in distributed graph algorithms. *SIAM Journal on Computing*, 21(1):193–201, 1992.

[LPPSP03] Zvi Lotker, Elan Pavlov, Boaz Patt-Shamir, and David Peleg. MST construction in $O(\log logn)$ communication rounds. In *the Proceedings of the Symposium on Parallel Algorithms and Architectures*, pages 94–100. ACM, 2003.

[Nan14] Danupon Nanongkai. Distributed approximation algorithms for weighted shortest paths. In *Proc. of the Symp. on Theory of Comp. (STOC)*, 2014.

[NMN01] Jaroslav Nešetřil, Eva Milková, and Helena Nešetřilová. Otakar boruvka on minimum spanning tree problem translation of both the 1926 papers, comments, history. *Discrete Mathematics*, 233(1):3–36, 2001.

[NN93] Joseph Naor and Moni Naor. Small-bias probability spaces: Efficient constructions and applications. *SIAM journal on computing*, 22(4):838–856, 1993.

[Pel00] David Peleg. *Distributed Computing: A Locality-sensitive Approach*. Society for Industrial and Applied Mathematics, Philadelphia, PA, USA, 2000.

[PRS15] Gopal Pandurangan, Peter Robinson, and Michele Scquizzato. Almost optimal distributed algorithms for large-scale graph problems. *arXiv preprint arXiv:1503.02353*, 2015.

[PST11] Boaz Patt-Shamir and Marat Teplitsky. The round complexity of distributed sorting. In *the Proc. of the Int'l Symp. on Princ. of Dist. Comp. (PODC)*, pages 249–256, 2011.

Distributed Algorithms for Planar Networks I: Planar Embedding

Mohsen Ghaffari
MIT
ghaffari@mit.edu

Bernhard Haeupler
CMU
haeupler@cs.cmu.edu

ABSTRACT

This paper presents the first (non-trivial) distributed planar embedding algorithm. We consider this a crucial first step in a broader program to design efficient distributed algorithms for planar networks.

We work in the standard distributed model in which nodes can send an $O(\log n)$-bit message to each of their neighbors per round. In a planar network, with n nodes and diameter D, our deterministic planar embedding algorithm uses $O(D \cdot \min\{\log n, D\})$ rounds to compute a combinatorial planar embedding, which consists of each node knowing the clockwise order of its incident edges in a fixed planar drawing. The complexity of our algorithm is near-optimal and matches the trivial lower bound of $\Omega(D)$ up to a $\log n$ factor. No algorithm outperforming the trivial round complexity of $O(n)$ was known prior to this work.

1. INTRODUCTION

In this paper, which is a part of a broader effort to extend the algorithmic theory of planar graphs to the distributed realm, we present the first (non-trivial) distributed planar embedding algorithm:

Theorem 1.1. *There is a deterministic planar embedding algorithm which on any planar network $G = (V, E)$, with n nodes and diameter D, computes a combinatorial planar embedding in $O(D \cdot \min\{\log n, D\})$ rounds.*

In this theorem and throughout the paper, we use the standard distributed message passing model called CONGEST [Pel00], where communications occur in synchronous round and per round, an $O(\log n)$-bit message can be sent along each edge. We note that the complexity of the algorithm is near-optimal and matches the trivial (folklore) lower bound[1] of $\Omega(D)$ up to a $\log n$ factor. No algorithm outperforming the trivial[2] round complexity of $O(n)$ was known prior to this work.

As we discuss later, this algorithm is a crucial first step in designing efficient distributed algorithms for global network optimization problems in planar networks. Generally, it can be viewed as the first distributed counterpart to the classic centralized planar embedding algorithm of Hopcroft and Tarjan [HT74], which plays a key role in essentially all planar graph algorithms. Our distributed planar embedding particularly is used, in a black-box manner, in the result reported in the other part of this project [GH16]: those results particularly compute minimum spanning tree and minimum cut in $\tilde{O}(D)$ rounds, in planar networks.

1.1 Motivations

General Interest in (Near-)Planar Networks: Planar graphs have always been a primary graph family of interest, since the very beginning of graph theory in Euler's 1735 *Seven Bridges of Königsberg* paper. This interest has even led to courses [KM, Kle, DMST] and textbooks [KMft, NC88] dedicated solely to planar and near-planar graphs. This vast interest is because of the natural and frequent occurrence of (near-)planar structures in reality, and perhaps more so due to the rich theoretical aspects found in them. For most network optimizations, much better centralized algorithms are known for (near-) planar graphs, often requiring quite deep ideas; see [DMST, Lecture 1].

Unfortunately, almost nothing is known about how *distributed* algorithms can utilize planarity for (global) network optimization problems such as minimum spanning tree, shortest paths, min-cut, or max-flow. This gets us to another motive, peculiar to distributed computation:

Further Motivation for *Distributed* Study of Planar Networks: For many basic network optimization problems, including those listed above, $\tilde{\Omega}(D + \sqrt{n})$ is a round complexity lower bound for any distributed algorithm in general graphs [PR99, Elk04b, DSHK+11], and this even holds for

This research was supported in part by the NSF award *Distributed Algorithms for Near Planar Networks* (CCF-1527110) and the NSF grant CCF-BSF:*Coding for Distributed Computing*.

PODC'16, July 25-28, 2016, Chicago, IL, USA

DOI: http://dx.doi.org/10.1145/2933057.2933109

[1]Consider the 4-node complete graph K_4 and replace each edge with a $\Theta(D)$ long path. In any planar embedding, degree-3 nodes must output consistent clockwise ordering of their edges. This requires coordination between nodes that are $\Theta(D)$ hops apart, thus proving that, even with unbounded message sizes, $\Omega(D)$ rounds are needed.

[2]Note that any graph problem can be solved in $O(m)$ rounds in the CONGEST model, simply by gathering the whole network topology and solving the problem locally, and in planar graphs, this is $O(m) = O(n)$ rounds.

any non-trivial approximation. Although more and more algorithms are known to achieve or get close to this bound, for various problems (see e.g., [KP95,Elk04a,LPS13,GK13, Nan14,LPS14,CHGK14,NS14,GL14,Gha14,GKK+15]), this now well-known barrier is becoming somewhat of *plateau*. We believe that it is thus important to examine what can be achieved when these lower bound graphs are ruled out, i.e., in special graph families. However, the lower bound graphs are extremely simple and fit within many basic graph families: particularly, they are *everywhere sparse*, with arboricity 2, and can be even made to have maximum degree 3. Planar (or near-planar) graphs seem to be the main natural graph family that rules out these $\tilde{\Omega}(D+\sqrt{n})$ lower bound graphs.

Motivation for Planar Embedding: Computing a planar embedding is almost always the first algorithmic step, as it makes the planar structure accessible/manageable for algorithms. See e.g. step 1 in the planar separator of Lipton and Tarjan [LT79, Section 3], which itself is a base for many of the planar graph algorithms. In the centralized setting, it is easy to assume that the embedding is already available, thanks to the celebrated $O(n)$ algorithm of Hopcroft and Tarjan [HT74].

We think that our distributed planar embedding will probably play an analogous role, especially because it has an $\tilde{O}(D)$ complexity, which is close to the trivial $\Omega(D)$ lower bound and should typically get dominated by the complexity of the other algorithmic parts. Particularly, in the other part of this project [GH16], we make (black-box) usage of this planar embedding to give near-optimal distributed algorithms for a number of fundamental network optimization problems including minimum spanning tree and minimum cut. These algorithms achieve a complexity of $\tilde{O}(D)$ in planar networks, thus bypassing the $\tilde{\Omega}(D+\sqrt{n})$ lower bound of general graphs [DSHK+11].

1.2 Our Technical Contributions, in Contrast with Centralized Algorithms

Theorem 1.1 borrows two ideas from (some of) its centralized/parallel counterparts [LEC66,KR88,BM04,HT08]: (A) Gradually adding more nodes, while maintaining the embedding, and (B) using (essentially) biconnected component decompositions to keep track of all the partial embeddings of the already added nodes. The former is inspired by the *vertex addition* method [LEC66], but we will need a quite different framework, as discussed in Sections 3 and 4, because for instance we cannot afford to add nodes one by one. The latter is where the *PQ-trees* data structures [BL76] are used in centralized/parallel algorithms. We do not use these data structures *per se*, but we have to deal with many other communication related issues, a few of which have a flavor similar to those faced in implementations of PQ-trees. Generally, there are major differences in the challenging aspects of the centralized algorithms and Theorem 1.1. A partial reasoning is as follows:

Computation vs. Communication: The core matter in centralized planarity tests is *computational* efficiency; this particularly takes special data structures, which is where much of their technicalities lie in. On the other hand, Theorem 1.1 is a statement mainly about *communication*. Note that in the CONGEST model, communication is restricted but nodes have unbounded computational power[3]. In this regard, Theorem 1.1 implies something information theoretic: While it is easy to show cases in which a node must exchange information with up to $\Theta(n)$ many other nodes that are $\Theta(D)$ hops far way, Theorem 1.1 implies, quite surprisingly, that it is possible to summarize/compress and route/communicate this information such that (I) no pair of adjacent nodes needs to exchange $\tilde{\omega}(D)$ bits, and (II) no information needs to be routed along paths (much) longer than the necessary distance of D.

We hope that, besides the distributed algorithms made possible by Theorem 1.1, the study of planar networks from the *communication centered* perspective of distributed computing will also lead to new structural insights[4], similar to the success of the computationally centered studies.

The Novelties in Our Approach: On a more concrete level, to obtain our distributed embedding algorithm, we use a number of seemingly novel ideas. A sampling includes:

- In Section 3 we extend the *vertex addition* framework significantly, such that there is enough flexibility to not just treat the parallel addition of constraints but also to keep the diameter of any partial embedding small. The latter is vital in order to operate distributedly on these partial embeddings in an efficient manner. Our generalized framework is quite clean and we expect it to be useful on its own, beyond this work.
- In Section 4, we present a recursive embedding order, which forms the backbone of our algorithm. This order is very different from prior approaches such as *DFS-orderings* or *s-t orderings* used in [LEC66,KR88, BM04,HT08]. This, too, is necessary mainly to guarantee low-diameter sub-problems, a requirement fairly unique to the distributed setting.
- Our embedding algorithm also contains two new distributed symmetry breaking routines. In particular, in Theorem 5.3 we give an algorithm that can be extended to give a deterministic $\Theta(\log^* n)$ algorithm which, for any (outer-)planar graph G, computes an independent vertex set in the line graph $L(G)$ that is also dominating in $L(G)^2$. In Section 7.1.3 of the full version, we furthermore give a distributed deterministic algorithm which allows every vertex in an everywhere sparse graph to learn the graph induced by its neighborhood in only $O(1)$-rounds. This is used to compute a low arboricity orientation. This symmetry breaking algorithm uses ideas from coding theory and Slepian-Wolf style distributed source coding to achieve this communication efficiency. To our knowledge this is the first time that these tools from coding and information theory have been used in distributed symmetry breaking.
- Achieving a (near) optimal communication efficiency throughout the algorithm also leads to many other challenges and new solutions that are not as easy to recap. The need for a *compressed* variant of PQ-trees

[3] Although, we note that in our algorithm, they will be required to perform at most poly(n) computations.

[4] Perhaps, the existence of *low-congestion shortcuts* for planar graphs, which we prove in the subsequent work, could already be considered as a step in this direction.

that summarizes only essential degrees of freedom is one such example (see Section 7.1.4 of the full version).

In our presentation, we have tried to give one *modular top-down* description, with clean interfaces and levels of abstraction, and with many pictorial illustrations. We hope that this will help in understanding the many details involved in making the algorithm work in the end.

2. SOME PRELIMINARIES

Planar Embeddings: A *geometric embedding* of a graph $G = (V, E)$ is a *drawing* of it on a plane in which any node maps to a point and any edge maps to a curve that connects the points associated with the two vertices it is adjacent to. The geometric embedding is planar if no two curves are intersecting. Given a planar network, our objective is to find a *combinatorial planar embedding* of the network in the format of a *rotation system*, which for each vertex v determines the the clockwise cyclic ordering of edges incident on v around v, where these cyclic orders are equal to those in one fixed geometric planar embedding. By a result of Edmonds [Edm60], it is known that the geometric/topological and the combinatorial definitions are equivalent. Throughout the paper, we are concerned with only simple graphs $G = (V, E)$, that is, G does not have parallel edges or self-loops.

Distributed Input and Output Format in Planar Embedding: The input is that each vertex has a unique identifier and at the start of the execution, each vertex learns the ids of its neighbors. This is the only knowledge initially given to the vertices. When we say a combinatorial planar embedding is computed in a distributed manner, the output format is that each vertex must learn the clockwise ordering of its own edges around itself, in this particular embedding.

Note that in $O(D)$ rounds, nodes can easily compute both the number of nodes n and a 2-approximation of D, using a BFS. Thus, these will be assumed known throughout the paper.

3. GENERAL ALGORITHMIC PLANARITY FRAMEWORK

At any stage, our planarity algorithm maintains a partitioning $\mathcal{P} = \{P_1, P_2, \ldots, P_k\}$ of the set of vertices V, i.e., $\forall i \neq j: \ P_i \cap P_j = \emptyset$ and $\bigcup_i P_i = V$. We call an edge $e = \{u, v\}$ *embedded* if both endpoints are in the same part P_i, and *half-embedded* otherwise. Initially each vertex forms its own part and all edges are half-embedded.

We always maintain that each part induces a connected subgraph of G. Furthermore, we call a part P_i *trivial* if it induces a tree. Throughout the embedding algorithm, our partitioning will preserve the following safety-property:

Definition 3.1. ***(Safety Property)*** *A partition of the vertices V into connected parts $P_1, P_2, \ldots, P_k$ is* safe *if and only if for every non-trivial part P_i the subgraph induced by $V \setminus P_i$ is connected.*

The important insight that motivates this safety property is that it guarantees that in any planar embedding, the half-embedded edges of any part P_i have to lie in a single face (with respect to the internal embedding of P_i). It is often helpful to picture this face as the outside face. See Figure 1. Furthermore, whether or not a partial embedding for a part P_i can be extended to a global planar embedding depends only on the cyclic order of the half-embedded edges around this face. Therefore, to find a planar embedding (or also for a planarity test), all that is needed is to keep track of all possible cyclic orders of half-embedded edges of P_i that have a corresponding planar embedding of P_i. We call this set of cyclic orders the *interface* of P_i.

While there can be a large number of possible cyclic orders, they have a nice structure that is intimately connected to the bi-connected component decomposition of the subgraph induced by P_i. In particular, while each bi-connected component can have many (internal) combinatorial embeddings, its interface—that is, the cyclic order of the vertices connecting to half-embedded edges—is fixed and is always the same up to a flip (reversal). See Figure 2. For each cut-vertex, on the other hand, there is no restrictions on how the bi-connected components it connects to are arranged, as long as no two components that lead to a half-embedded edge are enclosed in each other. See Figure 3.

These observations can be used to fully characterize all degrees of freedom in the interface of a part: Given a combinatorial embedding of P_i with half-embedded edges on the outer face, one can obtain all cyclic orders of these edges in the interface by, successive steps of, flipping a bi-connected component or permuting the order of bi-connected components around a cut-vertex. See Figure 4.

Observation 3.2. *The interface for a part P_i is uniquely identified by the bi-connected component decomposition of P_i and the fixed cyclic order interface of the bi-connected components.*

Hence, throughout the planarity algorithm, for each part, we simply need to keep track of the biconnected component decomposition of it along with one embedding for each of the bi-connected components. We use the straightforward distributed representation of this information:

Distributed Representation of Biconnected Decomposition: Each biconnected component has an ID, which will simply be equal to the smallest edge ID among the edges in the component[5]. Each vertex v knows the IDs of all the biconnected components v it belongs to. Note that v is a cut-vertex if and only if it belongs to two or more biconnected components, and hence this way, v also knows if it is a cut-vertex. Moreover, for each pair of neighboring vertices u and v there is always exactly one biconnected component that includes both v and u. Every vertex knows for each of its neighbors which component this is. Finally, for each biconnected component that includes v, vertex v knows a linear order of all its neighbors u that are in the same component. This order is consistent with a fixed planar embedding of the biconnected component. This fully describes the input and output format of partial embeddings used in our algorithm and its subroutines.

4. ALGORITHM OUTLINE

In this section, we present the outline of our distributed embedding algorithm. In later sections, we then fill in the concrete details of this outline.

Our general strategy for distributed embedding is to use *divide and conquer*. There are a number of important is-

[5]The edge-ID of an edge $e = \{u, v\}$ is equal to $ID(e) = (ID(u), ID(v))$ where u is such that $ID(u) < ID(v)$.

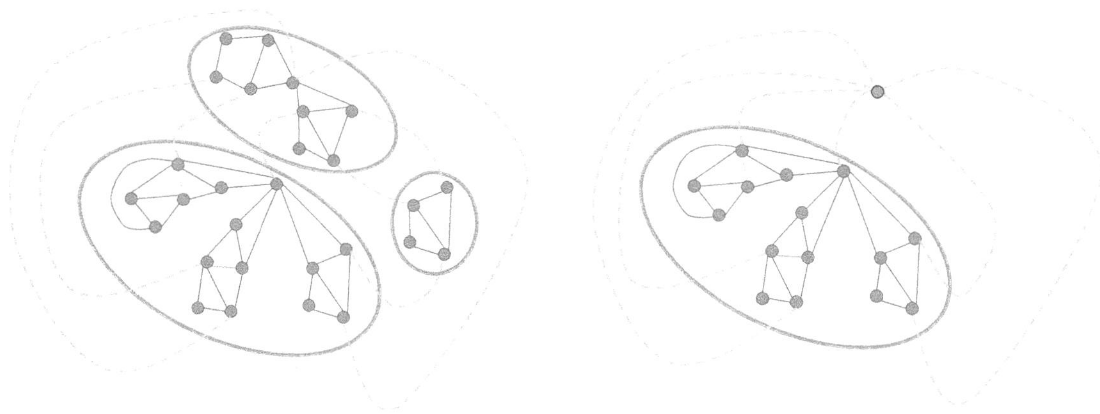

(a) (b)

Figure 1: (a) A planar embedding of three parts with the half-embedded edges between them. In the planar embedding of each part, all half-embedded edges (more formally all nodes incident on half-embedded edges) lie in one face, i.e., the outside face, in regards to the embedding of the part itself. (b) For one of the parts P_1, the rest of the graph, that is $G \setminus P_1$, is contracted into a single node. Note that these contractions do not change the order of the vertices adjacent to half-embedded edges of P_1 around P_1.

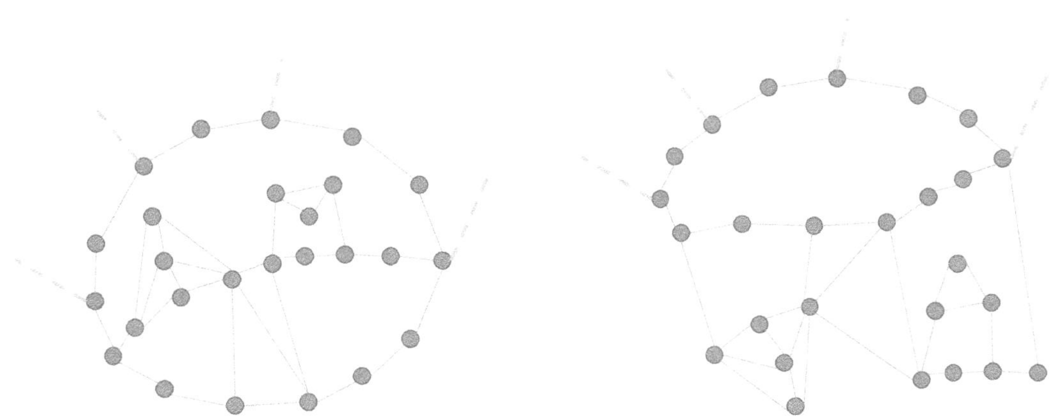

(a) (b)

Figure 2: Two different planar drawings of one bi-connected component. Both drawings lead to the same external cyclic order of the vertices adjacent to half-embedded edges but cyclic orders of the edges around some vertices are different, and even the set of vertices appearing on the outside face are different.

sues that need to be taken into account while instantiating this divide and conquer. We next describe these issues and provide some intuition for each of them.

Considerations when using Divide and Conquer: In the divide and conquer method, we will partition the vertex set into a number of disjoint parts P_1 to P_k, find (a succinct representation of) all possible embeddings of each of the parts, and then merge these into (a succinct representation of) all possible embeddings for the union of the parts.

For this approach to be correct, we need the partition to satisfy the safety property presented in Theorem 3.1. That is, removing each non-trivial part should leave a connected subgraph. Moreover, there are a number of properties that we need due to efficiency considerations: Since the parts are disjoint, we will be able to run distributed algorithms in different parts in parallel. Hence, the overall complexity is determined by the depth of the recursion and the time complexity of each "divide" and "merge". Regarding the first parameter, we would like to have a small recursion depth—e.g., $O(\log n)$. Furthermore, since we want to run distributed algorithms in each of the parts, it is vital that each of the parts has a low diameter, ideally a diameter of $O(D)$. Finally, the division should be such that, we should be able to compute the division fast—i.e., in $O(D)$ time—and more crucially, we should be able to perform the merge step, which puts the partial embeddings of the parts together, distributedly and efficiently—i.e., also in $O(D)$ time.

To recap, we require the partition to: (1) satisfy the safety property of Theorem 3.1; (2) have low recursion depth, ideally $O(\log n)$; (3) lead to parts each with induced diameter $O(D)$; (4) admit efficient $O(D)$ time merging of the partial embeddings of the parts.

We next describe our partitioning method and explain why it satisfies these properties.

Our Approach: Our algorithm first picks a vertex s^* arbitrarily as the starting point of the embedding and marks it for being on the outside face of the embedding of G. This can be for instance the vertex with the largest ID, which can

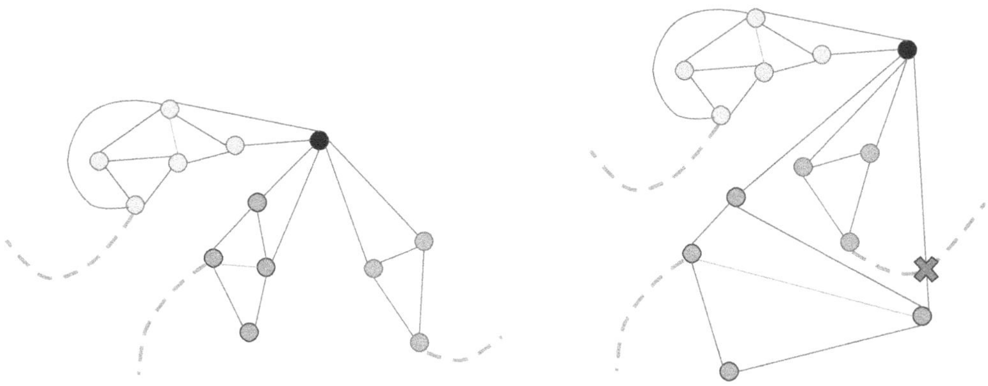

(a) (b)

Figure 3: A cut-vertex (black) and the bi-connected components adjacent to it (colored blue, green, and orange). The biconnected components can have any order around the cut-vertex, but if we ignore the biconnected components that do not have a half-embedded edge, the edges of each other bi-connected component must appear consecutively in the cyclic order around the cut-vertex. That is, a component that leads to a half-embedded edge cannot be enclosed in another.

be computed in $O(D)$ rounds. We then compute a BFS T rooted at this vertex and we work with this BFS throughout the algorithm. For each vertex v, let T_v be the subtree of T induced by v and its descendants.

In each recursion step, we have a subgraph H of G, which is induced by the T-subtree T_s rooted at a vertex s. Furthermore, we have a number of half-embedded edges each with only one endpoint in H, that is, these half-embedded edges go out from H to $G \setminus H$. We want to compute all the possible cyclic orderings of the half-embedded edges around H, along with an embedding of H for each of these orders. We next explain how we partition this problem:

The Partitioning: We find a vertex $v \in T_s$ such that when we remove v from T_s, each of the remaining T_s-components has size at most $2|T_s|/3$. Note that such a vertex v always exists and furthermore, it can be computed distributedly in $O(d)$ time where $d = depth(T_s)$. Define part P_0 to be the unique path in T_s connecting s and v. Let $v_1, \ldots, v_k$ be the vertices in T_s that are T_s-adjacent to P_0. Respectively, define $P_1, \ldots, P_k$ to be the vertex subsets where each P_i includes the set of all T_s-vertices for which the T_s-path to P_0 goes through v_i. See Figure 5, which shows a pictorial example.

Analysis: We next explain why this partition satisfies properties (1) to (3) stated above. Explaining property (4)—i.e., how we can perform the merges in $O(D)$ rounds—will be the challenging part and the topic of the next sections.

Lemma 4.1. *The partition with parts $P_0, P_1, P_2, \ldots, P_k, G \setminus H$ is a safe partition.*

Proof. First notice that P_0 is a trivial part because the subgraph of G induced by the P_0-vertices only includes the edges of the BFS-tree path connecting s to v and no other edge. That is, any extra edge would be in contradiction with the definition of a BFS. For each of the parts $P_1, \ldots, P_k, G \setminus H$, removing this part leaves a connected graph because the other parts are connected via P_0. Thus, the safety property is satisfied. □

We note that similarly, this safety property also holds throughout the recursions. More concretely, consider the partition that happens on P_1 when we have the recursive call of embedding P_1 and let the related parts be $P_{10}, P_{11}, P_{12}, \ldots, P_{1k'}$. Then it is true that for each nontrivial part P_{1i} where $i \geq 1$, subgraph $G \setminus P_{1i}$ is connected. This is because, $G \setminus P_1$ is connected and it includes P_0, and moreover for any $j \geq 1$, subgraph P_{1j} is connected to P_{10} which itself is connected to P_0.

Properties (2) and (3) are easy to establish:

Lemma 4.2. *Each part P_i induces a subgraph with diameter at most $depth(T_s) - 1$ and contains at most $2|T_s|/3$ vertices.*

Lemma 4.3. *The recursion depth is at most $\min\{O(\log n), D\}$. Thus, assuming each level can be performed in $O(D)$ rounds, the overall round complexity is $O(\min\{D \log n, D^2\})$.*

In the next sections, we talk about how we perform the merging of the partial embeddings of parts P_0 and P_1 to P_k.

5. MERGING PARTS: OUTLINE AND SUBROUTINE DESCRIPTIONS

In this section, we give more details on how the algorithm outlined in the previous section merges the parts $P_0, P_1, \ldots, P_k$ in a recursive call. In particular, in Section 5.1 we first explain why essentially any sequence of merges that does not involve P_0 is safe. In Section 5.2 we then describe a number of merging patterns which we call *pairwise merge*, *star merge*, *vertex coordinated merge*, and *path coordinated merge*. These merging patterns build on top of each other and are increasingly more powerful. In particular, in Section 5.3 we explain how a full-fledged path coordinated merge—which is the main thing we need for merging parts $P_0, P_1, \ldots, P_k$—can be performed through a sequence of pairwise, star, and vertex coordinated merging steps and a final simpler case of path-coordinated merge somewhat similar to vertex coordinated merge.

5.1 Safety Considerations for Merges

In this section we give simple sufficient conditions which ensure that the merges that we perform are safe. Let us

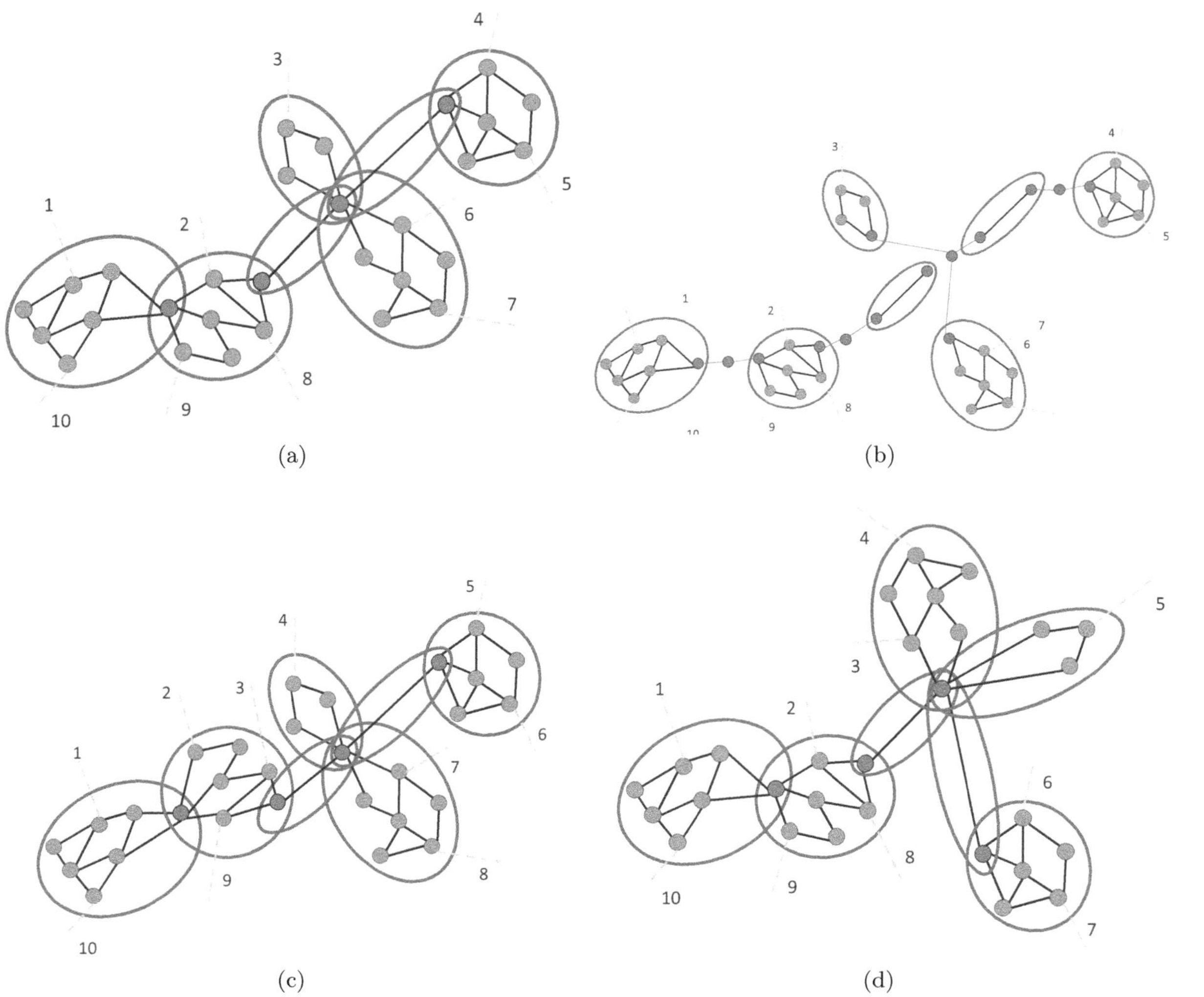

Figure 4: (a) biconnected component decomposition of a planar graph, (b) the related (virtual) tree of the biconnected component decomposition, (c) a flip of one of the biconnected components, (d) a permutations of the biconnected components around a cut-vertex. Red vertices are cut vertices, and oval shapes indicate the biconnected components. Orange dashed edges are half-embedded edges, which connect to the rest of the graph. Their cyclic order around the part changes during (c) and (d), as a result of the flip and permutation.

begin by considering a simple merge of two parts. In this situation, there is a simple (sufficient) safety condition:

Definition 5.1 (Safety of a merge)**.** *Given a safe partition $\mathcal{P} = \{P_1, P_2, \dots, \}$, merging two adjacent parts $P_i, P_j \in \mathcal{P}$ into a new part $P' = P_i \cup P_j$ is safe iff $\mathcal{P}' = \mathcal{P} \setminus \{P_i, P_j\} \cup \{P'\}$ is a safe partition.*

Figure 6 shows parts of a safe-merge and two pairwise merges, one that is safe and one that is not safe. In addition to using the above criterion for the safety of a pairwise merge, there is another situation that easily implies safety for merges:

Proposition 5.2. *Suppose that in a safe partition $\mathcal{P}$, a subset of parts $\mathcal{P}' \subset \mathcal{P}$ are all connected (via half-embedded edges) to a part $P \in \mathcal{P}'$ and suppose that the vertices in $(\mathcal{P} \setminus \mathcal{P}') \cup \{P\}$ are connected. Then, any sequence of merges within $\mathcal{P}'$ not involving P is safe.*

We remark that the condition of not involving the part P in the merge is necessary as any merge that includes P might transform P from a trivial part into a non-trivial part, thus violating safety. All in all, Theorem 5.2 tells us that any merges within a recursive call of our partitionings are safe, so long as the trivial center part P_0 is not involved. Our algorithm(s) thus first perform merges that combine any connected parts except P_0, before the final merge with P_0 is performed.

5.2 Merging Patterns

The general merging setting that we have, as described in the previous section, is an induced-path part P_0 along with a number of parts P_1 to P_k such that each of these parts has diameter $O(D)$ and as expressed in Theorem 4.1, partition $\mathcal{P} = \{P_0, P_1, P_2, \dots, P_k, G \setminus H\}$ is safe. Our ultimate goal is to be able to merge all parts P_0 to P_k. We call this merge setting an *unrestricted path coordinated merge*. This term *unrestricted* is used as opposed to a restricted path coordinated merge, which has at most $O(D)$ parts. Note that in the unrestricted case, k can be as large as $\Theta(n)$. To perform the *unrestricted path coordinated merge*, we use a number of merge subroutines:

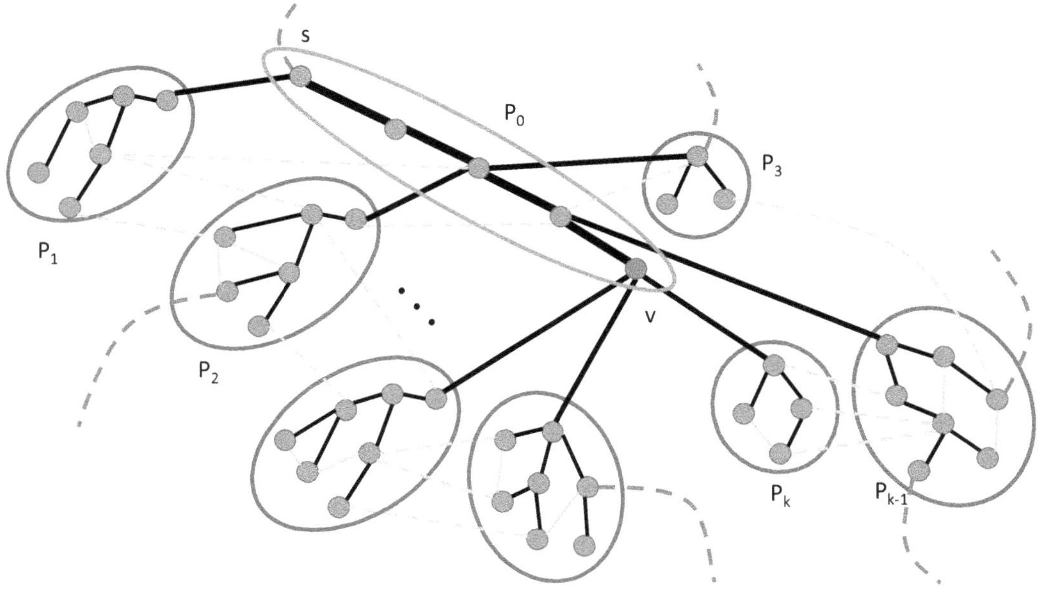

Figure 5: The partition to path P_0 and hanging parts P_1 to P_k. Black links indicate edges of the BFS tree, the brown links are half-embedded edges connecting to $G \setminus H$, and the dashed orange edges are those which fall between parts and will be regarded as half-embedded in the lower levels of recursion. The vertex s which is the root of the BFS subtree of H is indicated with green and the vertex v which breaks the subtree into semi-balanced parts is indicated with red. The path connecting s to v is the P_0 part.

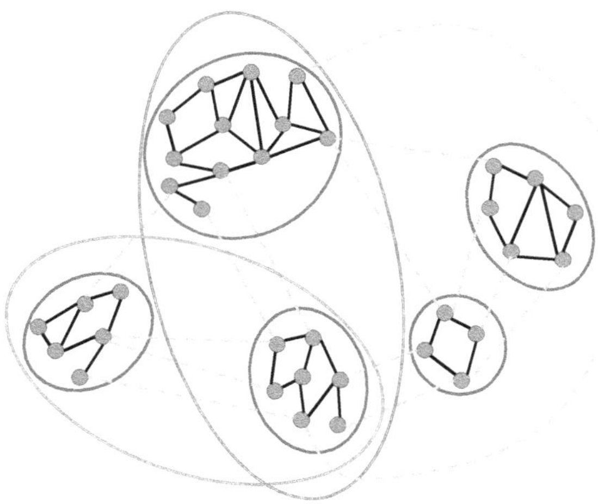

Figure 6: The green and the red curves respectively show a safe and an unsafe pairwise merge.

Merge Patterns: We use the following merging patterns:

- *Pairwise merge*, which merges two parts P_1 and P_2.
- *Star merge*, which merges a part P_1 with several of its neighbors $P_2, P_3, \dots$ as long as they do not share any edges, i.e., as long as $P_1, P_2, P_3, \dots$ induce a star in $G_{\mathcal{P}}$.
- *Vertex coordinated merge*, which merges a trivial part P_1 consisting of a single vertex v with several of its neighbors $P_2, P_3, \dots$ irrespective of what graph $P_2, P_3, \dots$ induce in $G_{\mathcal{P}}$.
- *Path coordinated merge*, which is the same as a vertex coordinated merge except that the trivial part P_1 is allowed to be a path. If there are at most $O(D)$ parts, we call this a *restricted path coordinated merge*. Otherwise, it is called *unrestricted*.

Implementations of pairwise and star coordinated merges are given in Section 6 of the full version, while those of vertex coordinated and restricted path coordinated merges appear in its Section 7.

Remarks, Intuition, and Motivation for the Merge Patterns:

- Pairwise Merge: This is the simplest merging pattern, and we will be using it as the basis of all the other merges.
- Star Merge: The star merge generalizes the pairwise merge and is essentially identical to ℓ pairwise merges, each being between a star center part and one side part, all performed in parallel. It is critically necessary that these ℓ pairwise merges parallelize efficiently as we will need to perform star merges with very large degrees and thus, performing the related pairwise merges one by one would not be sufficient.
- Vertex Coordinated Merge: While Theorem 5.2 shows that any merges in $G_{\mathcal{P}} \setminus P_0$ are safe, just performing local merges on this part cannot lead to an efficient algorithm. To see this, note that $G_{\mathcal{P}} \setminus P_0$ can be any outerplanar graph and thus have a diameter of up to $\Theta(n) \gg D$. Operating on this graph in a distributed fashion would require $\Theta(n)$ rounds. When merging $P_1, P_2, \dots, P_k$, it is thus important to have some communication go over shorter paths, which are in P_0. A simple case of this is when all this shortcut communication can be through a single vertex of P_0. This is exactly vertex-coordinated merge. Given that parts can be up to $\Theta(n)$ large and have rich interactions re-

sulting from up to $\Theta(n)$ edges, it is perhaps surprising that all long-range interactions can be efficiently communicated via the coordinator v even though v might only have a single (capacity-restricted) edge to each part.

- Restricted and Unrestricted Path Coordinated Merge: While the path coordinated merges ideally should function similar to a vertex coordinated merge, the path structure imposes further limitations on the communications that can be performed through the coordinator. In particular, we will be able to only directly handle path coordinated merges when the number of parts k is at most $O(D)$. This is because, when $k = O(D)$, the information that needs to be routed via the coordinator is small enough to not cause congestion on the path edges, beyond what can be handled in $O(D)$ rounds. On the other hand, once $k = \omega(D)$, the amount of information to be shared over the path P_0 can exceed what the path edges can deliver within $O(D)$ rounds. For this reason, we will turn the general *unrestricted path coordinated merge* into a case of *restricted path coordinated merge* (with only $O(D)$ parts) by utilizing a sequence of pairwise, star and vertex coordinated merges. Then, we will use our restricted path coordinate merge to solve the problem for this reduced case with $O(D)$ parts.

5.3 Unresticted Path Coordinated Merge using Other Merge Patterns

As stated in Section 5.2, starting from the general setting of unrestricted path coordinated merge, we will use a sequence of star and vertex coordinated merging steps on parts other than P_0 to reduce the number of parts to $O(D)$, thus leaving us with a restricted path coordinated merge setting. In this section, we explain this step which turns an unrestricted path coordinated merge setting to a restricted one.

To determine which star and vertex coordinated merges are performed here and how these are computed in a distributed fashion, we design a symmetry breaking algorithm. The ideal goal of this algorithm is to partition parts other than P_0 into star merging groups $V_1, V_2, \ldots$ such that (1) every part merges with at least one other part and (2) every group induces a star. However, this is not always possible, e.g., simply when some parts form a triangle. To fix this issue, roughly speaking, we will have two such groupings such that each part P_i participates in at least one of them. Formally, our symmetry breaking algorithm's interface is captured by the following lemma:

Lemma 5.3 (Symmetry Breaking Algorithm). *Suppose $G = (V, E)$ is an undirected outer-planar network with a proper node coloring. There exists a deterministic algorithm that for any such G computes in $O(1)$ rounds:*

- *disjoint node sets $V_1, V_2, \ldots \subseteq V$ of size at least two, each inducing a star in G*
- *a partition of $G' = (V', E')$ into disjoint node sets $V_1', V_2', \ldots$, such that, each V_i' either induces a star in G' or is a path in G' and contains no two G'-nodes with the same color. Here G' is obtained from G by contracting each V_i into V_i's center and keeping the color of the center for the resulting node.*

Remark 1: We note that in reality, we will be running this algorithm on parts, each acting as one node of this algorithm, and where each part has $O(D)$ diameter. That is, the vertices of the same part should work together to run the operations of the single part. However, it is easy to see that for each single round of the above algorithm, the related operations of a single part—which are of the type compute max, min, sum, etc of some variables—can actually be simulated in $O(D)$ rounds on a BFS of the part, using standard upcast and downcast techniques. Hence, the $O(1)$ rounds of Theorem 5.3 translate to $O(D)$ rounds. We skip stating the exact details of how these communications happen on the BFS, as they are standard.

The algorithm of Theorem 5.3 and its analysis appear in Section 5.4 of the full version. Here, we show how we use it to reduce the unrestricted path-coordinated merge to a restricted one. We start with an intuitive (but imprecise and incomplete) explanation, and then we present the algorithm.

Intuition and Outline: Consider the path P_0 and the parts P_1 to P_k connected to it. If we had the property that each part P_i has half-embedded edges connecting to at least three different vertices of P_0, then we could use planarity to prove that in this case, the number of parts could not be more than $O(D)$. Having this in mind, given parts that do not necessarily satisfy this property, the high-level line of attack is to perform small iterations of vertex coordinated or induced-star merges such that at the end of these merges, the merged parts satisfy this property of each having edges to at least three P_0-vertices.

Notice that at the start, each part P_i has edges connecting to at least one of the P_0 vertices. To reach the state where each part has at least three such connection vertices in P_0, we work in two functionally identical iterations, each of which performs merges that (try to) increase this number of connections by at least one, if it is possible. There will be some parts for which such an increase is not possible. We will be able to handle these parts with simpler schemes and discard them afterward.

Each of the iterations works roughly as follows: to make sure that when we combine two neighboring parts we actually increase the number of their connection points, we would like to have the property that these neighboring parts have connections to different P_0 vertices. This is not satisfied at the start. To remedy this, we number the P_0-vertices 1, 2, $\ldots$, $|P_0|$ from one end to the other, and color each part by assigning to it (the number of) its lowest P_0 connection vertex . We then merge the (connected subsets of) nodes of the same color using a vertex coordinated merge where the shared connection vertex i is the coordinator. This might increase the part diameters significantly so we add a copy of this coordinator v to each of the parts colored with i, which reduces the diameter of parts back to $O(D)$. We will argue that this operation does not destroy the planarity, and furthermore, since only different edges of a vertex can communicate different messages, this separate copy of v can operate independently.

Once these merges are done, we remove some *simply-connected parts* of it (made precise in the algorithm) and then compute induced-stars or color-monotone paths of these parts using Theorem 5.3, put the paths aside and perform star merges on the induced stars. Now merging these stars ensures that the number of the connection points in their parts essentially increases by one (as the center and a leaf of the star have different low connection points). Thus, we have managed to increase the number of connections by at least one. Again there will be some *simply-connected parts* for which such an increase is not possible, but these will be handled separately using a simpler scheme.

Algorithm: Having this intuitive idea of what should roughly happen in the algorithm, we are now ready to describe the algorithm.

`Unrestricted Path-Coordinated Merge`:

1. Number the vertices of the P_0 path $1, 2, \ldots, |P_0|$
2. For two iterations, do:
   (a) Each part P_j computes what is the lowest-numbered P_0-vertex it connects to.
   (b) For each vertex $i \in P_0$, perform a vertex coordinated merge on all parts that their low-connection is i, where i operates as the coordinator. The subsets of these parts that are connected get merged, each forming a new merged part.
   (c) Any merged part P_j that is only connected to a single P_0-vertex i (i.e., and not to $G \setminus H$ or $H \setminus (P_j \cup P_0 \setminus \{i\})$) computes one fixed embedding (using a pairwise merge with $\{i\}$), and then it delivers the order of the edges connecting to i to vertex i. After that, this part does not participate in the remaining algorithm.
   (d) Any merged part P_j that is only connected to a single P_0-vertex i and to $G \setminus H$ computes the order of the edges connecting to i (using a pairwise merge with $\{i\}$) and delivers this order to vertex i. It also informs i that it has at least one $G \setminus H$ connection. After that, this part does not participate in the algorithm until the very last step.
   (e) For any other merged part, *split off* a copy of i and add it to this part. That is, vertex i is broken into a primary copy and a number of secondary copies, where these copies form a star with the center being the primary copy. The primary copy is kept in the P_0-path and each secondary copy is added to one of the merged parts. During the second iteration, the primary copy will be kept and some more secondary copies will be created.
   (f) Run the symmetry breaking algorithm from Theorem 5.3 on the inter-part graph $G_{\mathcal{P}}$, where the low-connection numbers are the coloring of G_P, thus computing part-sets V and V'.
   (g) Perform induced-star merges on all V-star sets.
   (h) Perform induced-star merges on all V'-star sets (including paths of length one).
   (i) Parts belonging to V'-paths of lengths 3 or more do not perform any merge and moreover, they do not participate in the next (i.e., second) iteration.
3. Any part P_ℓ that is only connected to P_0 (and not to any other part or to $G \setminus H$) determines whether it is connected to exactly two vertices in P_0. If this is the case, then it informs both of these P_0-vertices simply by reporting its own part-ID and the numbers of the two connection points. Then, it solves for an embedding of P_ℓ by running a pairwise merge with each of these two vertices, one by one (in an arbitrary order). Then, P_ℓ informs each of the two vertices $i \in P_0$ about the order of the edges connecting to i.
4. Any path P_0-vertex i, for any other P_0-vertex j such that that there is a part P_ℓ with only connections to i and j, does as follows: in its cyclic ordering, i orders all its half-embedded edges that connect to each of the parts connecting exactly only to i and j consecutively and according to the ordering received from that part. Moreover, i orders different (i, j)-connecting parts in an increasing order of IDs if $i > j$ and in a decreasing order if $i < j$.
5. For each pair of i, j of P_0 vertices, only the highest ID (i, j)-connecting part is kept and all other (i, j)-connecting parts do not participate in the algorithm until the very last step.
6. Perform a restricted coordinated merge using P_0 as the coordinator.

6. CONCLUDING REMARKS

This paper presents a distributed planar embedding with a near-optimal round complexity of $O(D \cdot \min\{\log n, D\})$. We consider this an important step in obtaining efficient distributed algorithms for planar networks. Particularly, in a subsequent work, we show how to obtain distributed algorithms for minimum spanning tree and minimum cut problems, in planar networks, with near-optimal round complexity of $\tilde{O}(D)$. Those results make (blackbox) use of the embedding given here.

There are many important questions left open. Perhaps obtaining an efficient distributed algorithm to compute an embedding for *bounded genus* graphs is the immediate next step.

7. REFERENCES

[BL76] Kellogg S Booth and George S Lueker. Testing for the consecutive ones property, interval graphs, and graph planarity using pq-tree algorithms. *Journal of Computer and System Sciences*, 13(3):335–379, 1976.

[BM04] John M Boyer and Wendy J Myrvold. On the cutting edge: Simplified O (n) planarity by edge addition. *J. Graph Algorithms Appl.*, 8(2):241–273, 2004.

[CHGK14] Keren Censor-Hillel, Mohsen Ghaffari, and Fabian Kuhn. Distributed connectivity decomposition. In *the Proc. of the Int'l Symp. on Princ. of Dist. Comp. (PODC)*, pages 156–165, 2014.

[DMST] Erik Demaine, Shay Mozes, Christian Sommer, and Siamak Tazari. Algorithms for planar graphs and beyond. http://courses.csail.mit.edu/6.889/fall11/. Accessed: July 2015.

[DSHK+11] Atish Das Sarma, Stephan Holzer, Liah Kor, Amos Korman, Danupon Nanongkai, Gopal Pandurangan, David Peleg, and Roger

Wattenhofer. Distributed verification and hardness of distributed approximation. In *Proc. of the Symp. on Theory of Comp. (STOC)*, pages 363–372, 2011.

[Edm60] Jack Edmonds. A combinatorial representation of polyhedral surfaces. *Notices of the American Mathematical Society*, 7, 1960.

[Elk04a] Michael Elkin. A faster distributed protocol for constructing a minimum spanning tree. In *Proceedings of the fifteenth annual ACM-SIAM symposium on Discrete algorithms*, pages 359–368. Society for Industrial and Applied Mathematics, 2004.

[Elk04b] Michael Elkin. Unconditional lower bounds on the time-approximation tradeoffs for the distributed minimum spanning tree problem. In *Proc. of the Symp. on Theory of Comp. (STOC)*, pages 331–340, 2004.

[GH16] Mohsen Ghaffari and Bernhard Haeupler. Distributed algorithms for planar networks II: Low-congestion shortcuts, mst, and min-cut. In *Pro. of ACM-SIAM Symp. on Disc. Alg. (SODA)*, page to appear, 2016.

[Gha14] Mohsen Ghaffari. Near-optimal distributed approximation of minimum-weight connected dominating set. In *the Proc. of the Int'l Colloquium on Automata, Languages and Programming (ICALP)*, 2014.

[GK13] Mohsen Ghaffari and Fabian Kuhn. Distributed minimum cut approximation. In *Proc. of the Int'l Symp. on Dist. Comp. (DISC)*, pages 1–15, 2013.

[GKK+15] Mohsen Ghaffari, Andreas Karrenbauer, Fabian Kuhn, Christoph Lenzen, and Boaz Patt-Shamir. Near-optimal distributed maximum flow. In *the Proc. of the Int'l Symp. on Princ. of Dist. Comp. (PODC)*, 2015.

[GL14] Mohsen Ghaffari and Christoph Lenzen. Near-optimal distributed tree embedding. In *Proc. of the Int'l Symp. on Dist. Comp. (DISC)*, pages 197–211, 2014.

[HT74] John Hopcroft and Robert Tarjan. Efficient planarity testing. *Journal of the ACM (JACM)*, 21(4):549–568, 1974.

[HT08] Bernhard Haeupler and Robert E Tarjan. Planarity algorithms via PQ-trees. *Electronic Notes in Discrete Mathematics*, 31:143–149, 2008.

[Kle] Philip Klein. Topics in algorithms: Planar graph algorithms. http://cs.brown.edu/courses/csci2950-r/. Accessed: July 2015.

[KM] Philip Klein and Claire Mathieu. Optimization algorithms for planar graphs. http://cs.brown.edu/courses/cs250/. Accessed: July 2015.

[KMft] Philip Klein and Shay Mozes. *Optimization Algorithms for Planar Graphs.* http://www.planarity.org/, draft.

[KP95] Shay Kutten and David Peleg. Fast distributed construction of k-dominating sets and applications. In *the Proc. of the Int'l Symp. on Princ. of Dist. Comp. (PODC)*, pages 238–251, 1995.

[KR88] Philip N Klein and John H Reif. An efficient parallel algorithm for planarity. *Journal of Computer and System Sciences*, 37(2):190–246, 1988.

[LEC66] Abraham Lempel, Shimon Even, and Israel Cederbaum. An algorithm for planarity testing of graphs. *Theory of graphs*, 8(2):215–232, 1966.

[LPS13] Christoph Lenzen and Boaz Patt-Shamir. Fast routing table construction using small messages: Extended abstract. In *Proc. of the Symp. on Theory of Comp. (STOC)*, pages 381–390, 2013.

[LPS14] Christoph Lenzen and Boaz Patt-Shamir. Improved distributed steiner forest construction. In *the Proc. of the Int'l Symp. on Princ. of Dist. Comp. (PODC)*, pages 262–271, 2014.

[LT79] Richard J Lipton and Robert Endre Tarjan. A separator theorem for planar graphs. *SIAM Journal on Applied Mathematics*, 36(2):177–189, 1979.

[Nan14] Danupon Nanongkai. Distributed approximation algorithms for weighted shortest paths. In *Proc. of the Symp. on Theory of Comp. (STOC)*, pages 565–573, 2014.

[NC88] Takao Nishizeki and Norishige Chiba. *Planar graphs: Theory and algorithms.* Elsevier, 1988.

[NS14] Danupon Nanongkai and Hsin-Hao Su. Almost-tight distributed minimum cut algorithms. In *Proc. of the Int'l Symp. on Dist. Comp. (DISC)*, pages 439–453, 2014.

[Pel00] David Peleg. *Distributed Computing: A Locality-sensitive Approach.* Society for Industrial and Applied Mathematics, Philadelphia, PA, USA, 2000.

[PR99] David Peleg and Vitaly Rubinovich. A near-tight lower bound on the time complexity of distributed MST construction. In *Proc. of the Symp. on Found. of Comp. Sci. (FOCS)*, pages 253–, 1999.

Brief Announcement: Labeling Schemes for Power-Law Graphs

Casper Petersen
University of Copenhagen
Universitetsparken 5
2100 Copenhagen, Denmark
cazz@di.ku.dk

Noy Rotbart
University of Copenhagen
Universitetsparken 5
2100 Copenhagen, Denmark
noyro@di.ku.dk

Jakob Grue Simonsen
University of Copenhagen
Universitetsparken 5
2100 Copenhagen, Denmark
jakob@di.ku.dk

Christian Wulff-Nilsen
University of Copenhagen
Universitetsparken 5
2100 Copenhagen, Denmark
koolooz@di.ku.dk

Keywords

Labeling schemes, Power-law graphs

1. INTRODUCTION

A labeling scheme is a method of distributing the information about the structure of a graph among its vertices by assigning short *labels*, such that a selected function on pairs of vertices can be computed using *only* their labels. A labeling scheme consists of an *encoder* that has access to the entire graph and assigns labels to vertices, and a *decoder* that has access to only the labels of a smaller set of vertices (typically a pair) and returns information about this subset (e.g., whether two vertices are adjacent, or the distance between them in the graph). The main objective is to minimize the *maximum label size*: the maximum number of bits used in a label of any vertex. Among the applications of labeling schemes are XML search engines, mapping services, and internet routing.

Adjacency labeling schemes for general graphs, bounded degree graphs, trees and various important graph families were studied (See [2] for a comprehensive table), yielding remarkably close upper and lower bounds[1]. It is thus surprising that the important family of *power-law graphs* has not yet been studied for this question[2].

An n-vertex graph is power-law if the number of its vertices of degree k is proportional to n/k^{α} for some positive α. To solidify this somewhat vague definition, numerous probabilistic and deterministic definitions of power-law graphs are given in the literature. A recent deterministic model, called shifted power-law distribution, has recently proven to capture a vast number of such definitions, both in theory and experimentally in [4].

Power-law graphs (also called scale-free graphs in the literature) have been used to model numerous types of network (see, e.g., [7] for an overview). In our work, we perform the first theoretical and practical study of adjacency labeling schemes for classes of graphs whose statistical properties– in particular their *degree distribution*–more closely resemble that of real-world networks.

We assert that our research can also assist the study of storage of real-world networks, and efficient distribution thereof. Rather than graph compression or dissemination of the underlying graphs of these networks over several machines [8], we propose to disseminate the structural information of the graph to its vertices. This *peer-to-peer* strategy allows inferring the graph's local topology using only local information stored in each vertex without using costly access to large, global data structures. In particular, it can be useful to address privacy concerns and ensure a high survivability rate.

2. OUR CONTRIBUTION

In our full version [11] we contribute the following results for power-law graphs:

A discrete and simple characterisation of power-law graphs. We define and prove useful properties for two simple families of graphs, $\mathcal{P}_h$ and $\mathcal{P}_l$, where $\mathcal{P}_h$ contains and $\mathcal{P}_l$ is contained by the standard definitions of power-law graphs in the literature, including recent ones [4]. We use $\mathcal{P}_h$ and $\mathcal{P}_l$ to study upper and lower bounds respectively.

An $O(\sqrt[\alpha]{n}(\log n)^{1-1/\alpha})$ adjacency labeling scheme. The scheme is based on two ideas: (i) a labeling *strategy* that partitions the vertices of G into high ("fat") and low degree ("thin") vertices based on a threshold degree, and (ii) a threshold *prediction* that depends only on the coefficient α of a power-law curve fitted to the degree distribution of G. These ideas are illustrated in Figure 1. We also show that applying our labeling scheme for random graphs with a power-law distribution results in a small expected worst-case label size.

[1]e.g. the current label size gap for general graphs stands on 4 bits.
[2]Routing labeling schemes however were studied in [5].

PODC'16 July 25-28, 2016, Chicago, IL, USA

ACM ISBN 978-1-4503-3964-3/16/07.
DOI: http://dx.doi.org/10.1145/2933057.2933060

Real-Life Graphs							
Data set	Vertices	Edges	Predicted	Empirical	Upper-Bound	c-sparse	Bounded degree
INTERNET	$22,963$	$48,436$	$1,426$	$1,156$	$8,181$	$4,700$	$17,925$
ENRON	$36,692$	$183,830$	$2,609$	$2,577$	$15,835$	$9,735$	$11,056$
WWW	$325,729$	$1,117,563$	$5,245$	$3,060$	$29,225$	$28,445$	$101,840$
Synthetic Graphs							
Data set	Vertices	Edges	Predicted	Empirical	Upper-Bound	c-sparse	Bounded degree
$\mathrm{s1M}^{\alpha=2.8}$	$1,000,000$	$751,784$	$2,101$	$2,061$	$10,081$	$24,566$	$16,920$
$\mathrm{s300}^{\alpha=2.8}$	$300,000$	$227,247$	$1,350$	$1,312$	$6,244$	$12,849$	$17,499$

Table 1: Label size in bits for various labeling schemes. The *predicted* and *empirical* label sizes are explained below. The upper bound is the guarantee of performance by our algorithm, and we report the label size for the graphs using the sparse and bounded degree [1] labeling schemes.

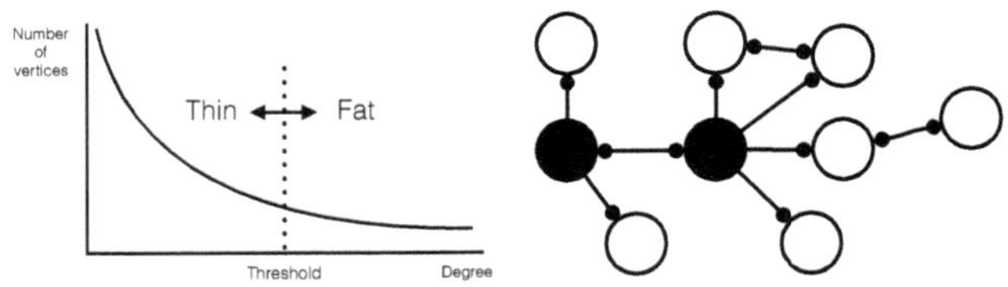

(a) (b)

Figure 1: Two illustrations of the main idea: Figure (a) demonstrates the threshold assignment, figure (b) demonstrates the label assignment, in which fat (black) vertices do not store adjacency to thin (white) vertices.

Real-world power-law graphs rarely exceed 10^{10} vertices. Given that those typically have $2 \leq \alpha \leq 3$, our labeling scheme theoretically achieves label size of $10^4 - 10^5$ bits, well within the processing capabilities of current hardware. This along with their simplicity implies that our labeling scheme may be appealing in practice. Using the same ideas, and as a stepping stone, we also get an asymptotically near-tight $O(\sqrt{n \log n})$ labeling scheme for sparse graphs.

A lower bound of $\Omega(\sqrt[\alpha]{n})$ *for any adjacency labeling scheme.* We use our restrictive subclass of power-law graphs and show that it requires label size $\Omega(\sqrt[\alpha]{n})$ for n-vertex graphs. This lower bound shows that our upper bound above is asymptotically optimal, bar a $(\log n)^{1-1/\alpha}$ factor. By the connections between adjacency labeling schemes and universal graphs, we also obtain upper and lower bounds for induced universal graphs for power-law graphs.

An $O(\log n)$ *adjacency labeling scheme in two restricted settings.* We bypass the aforementioned lower bound in two restricted settings: (i) all power law graphs that are created using the popular Barabasi-Albert [3] model, and (ii) using a variant of labeling schemes called "labeling scheme with a query" [9], which allows for the decoder to consult the labels and fetch a third label to determine the query.

An experimental investigation of our labeling scheme. To test our $O(\sqrt[\alpha]{n}(\log n)^{1-1/\alpha})$ labeling scheme, we label both synthetic graphs (300K-1M vertices) and ones that are considered by practitioners as power-law (23K-3M vertices). We first note that our selected *strategy* is optimal when the threshold chosen balances the largest fat and thin vertex. Using this observation, we can estimate the quality of the *predicted* threshold given in our theoretical approach to the *empirical* optimum. We observe the following:

- As seen in Figure 2, our threshold *prediction* performs close to the *empirical* optimum using this *strategy*, in particular to graphs with a degree distribution close to power-law.
- As seen in Table 1, our labeling scheme achieves maximum label size that is several orders of magnitude smaller than the state-of-the-art labeling schemes for more general graph families [1].

A $o(n)$ *distance labeling scheme.* We demonstrate the usefulness of our strategy to arrive at a $o(n)$ distance labeling scheme. Our labeling scheme outperforms competing labeling schemes for small distances, in accordance to Chung and Lu's findings [6] on the small expected diameter of power-law graphs.

3. THE LABELING SCHEME

To demonstrate our technique we present our adjacency labeling scheme for the case of c-sparse[3] graphs. This family contain all power-law graphs, and can be explained succinctly without the additional definitions required for the case of power-law graphs as described in the full version [11]. As mentioned, we partition the vertices into *thin* vertices which are of low degree and *fat* vertices of high degree. The *degree threshold* for the scheme is the lowest possible degree of a fat vertex.

THEOREM 3.1. *There is a* $\sqrt{2cn \log n} + 2\log n + 1$ *labeling scheme for c-sparse graphs.*

PROOF. Let $G = (V, E)$ be an n-vertex c-sparse graph. Let $\tau(n)$ be the degree threshold for n-vertex graphs; we choose $\tau(n)$ below. Let k denote the number of fat vertices of G, and assign each fat vertex a unique identifier between 1 and k. Each thin vertex is given a unique identifier between $k+1$ and n.

For a $v \in V$, the first part of the label $\mathcal{L}(v)$ is a single bit indicating whether v is thin or fat followed by a string of $\log n$ bits representing its identifier. If v is thin, the last part of $\mathcal{L}(v)$ is the concatenation of the identifiers of the neighbors of v. If v is fat, the last part of $\mathcal{L}(v)$ is a *fat bit*

[3]Graphs of n vertices and at most cn edges.

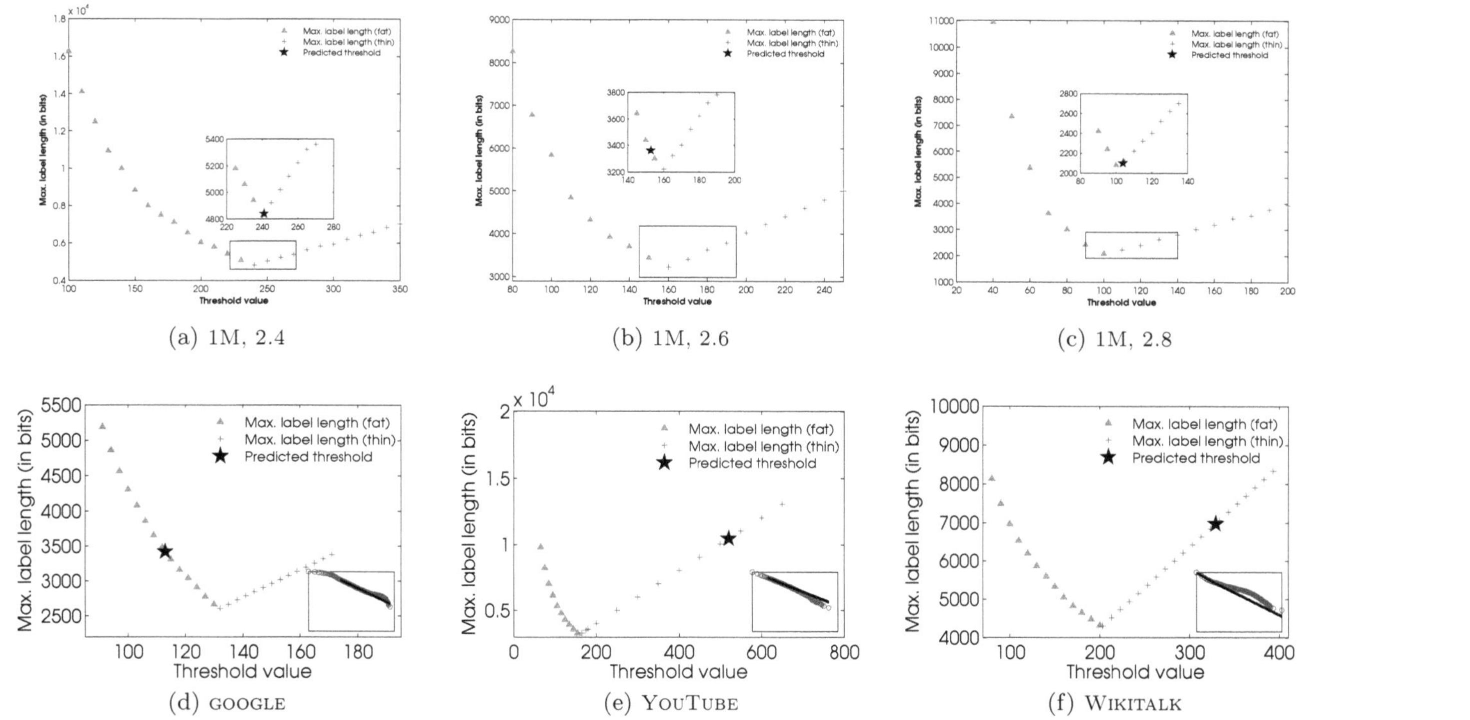

Figure 2: A demonstration of the maximum label size given a choice of threshold, for both synthetic graphs of million vertices and $\alpha = 2.4, 2.6, 2.8$ (top row) and for the real-life claimed power-law graphs GOOGLE, YOUTUBE and WIKITALK (taken from [10]). Our predicted threshold, marked in a black star, provides a close estimation for the location of this minimum.

string of length k where the ith bit is 1 iff v is incident to the (fat) vertex with identifier i.

Decoding a pair $(\mathcal{L}(u), \mathcal{L}(v))$ is straightforward: if one of the vertices, say u, is thin, u and v are adjacent iff the identifier of v is part of the label of u. If both u and v are fat then they are adjacent iff the ith bit of the fat bit string of $\mathcal{L}(u)$ is 1 where i is the identifier of v. Both decoding processes can be computed in $O(\log n)$ time using standard assumptions.

Since $|E| \leq cn$, we have $k \leq 2cn/\tau(n)$. A fat vertex thus has label size $1 + \log n + k \leq 1 + \log n + 2cn/\tau(n)$ and a thin vertex has label size at most $1 + \log n + \tau(n) \log n$. To minimize the maximum possible label size, we solve $2cn/x = x \log n$. Solving this gives $x = \sqrt{2cn/\log n}$ and setting $\tau(n) = \lceil x \rceil$ gives a label size of at most $1 + \log n + (\sqrt{2cn/\log n} + 1) \log n \leq 1 + 2\log n + \sqrt{2cn \log n}$. □

4. ACKNOWLEDGMENTS

The work is supported in part by the Sapere Aude project Complexity via Logic and Algebra (COLA).

5. REFERENCES

[1] S. Alstrup, S. Dahlgaard, and M. B. T. Knudsen. Optimal induced universal graphs and adjacency labeling for trees. FOCS '15, 2015.

[2] S. Alstrup, H. Kaplan, M. Thorup, and U. Zwick. Adjacency labeling schemes and induced-universal graphs. *The 47th symposium on Theory of computing (STOC)*, 2015.

[3] A.-L. Barabási and R. Albert. Emergence of scaling in random networks. *Science*, 286(5439):509–512, 1999.

[4] P. Brach, M. Cygan, J. Lacki, and P. Sankowski. Algorithmic complexity of power law networks. SODA 2016.

[5] W. Chen, C. Sommer, S.-H. Teng, and Y. Wang. A compact routing scheme and approximate distance oracle for power-law graphs. *TALG*, 9, 2012.

[6] F. Chung and L. Lu. The average distance in a random graph with given expected degrees. *Internet Mathematics*, 1(1):91–113, 2004.

[7] A. Clauset, C. R. Shalizi, and M. E. Newman. Power-law distributions in empirical data. *SIAM review*, 51(4):661–703, 2009.

[8] J. E. Gonzalez, Y. Low, H. Gu, D. Bickson, and C. Guestrin. Powergraph: Distributed graph-parallel computation on natural graphs. In *OSDI*, 2012.

[9] A. Korman and S. Kutten. Labeling schemes with queries. In *Structural Information and Communication Complexity*, pages 109–123. Springer, 2007.

[10] J. Leskovec and A. Krevl. SNAP Datasets: Stanford large network dataset collection. http://snap.stanford.edu/data, June 2014.

[11] C. Petersen, N. Rotbart, J. G. Simonsen, and C. Wulff-Nilsen. Near-optimal adjacency labeling scheme for power-law graphs. *To appear in ICALP 16'.*

Brief Announcement: Sublinear-Space Distance Labeling Using Hubs*

Paweł Gawrychowski
Institute of Informatics
University of Warsaw, Poland
P.Gawrychowski@mimuw.edu.pl

Adrian Kosowski
Inria and IRIF
Paris Diderot University, France
adrian.kosowski@inria.fr

Przemysław Uznański†
Dept. of Computer Science
ETH Zürich, Switzerland
przemyslaw.uznanski@inf.ethz.ch

ABSTRACT

A distance labeling scheme is an assignment of bit-labels to the vertices of an undirected, unweighted graph such that the distance between any pair of vertices can be decoded solely from their labels. We propose a series of new labeling schemes within the framework of so-called hub labeling (HL, also known as landmark labeling or 2-hop-cover labeling), in which each node u stores its distance to all nodes from an appropriately chosen set of hubs $S(u) \subseteq V$. For a queried pair of nodes (u, v), the length of a shortest u–v-path passing through a hub node from $S(u) \cap S(v)$ is then used as an upper bound on the distance between u and v.

We present a hub labeling which allows us to decode exact distances in sparse graphs using labels of size sublinear in the number of nodes. For graphs with at most n nodes and average degree Δ, the tradeoff between label bit size L and query decoding time T for our approach is given by $L = \mathcal{O}(n \log \log_\Delta T / \log_\Delta T)$, for any $T \leq n$. Our simple approach is thus the first sublinear-space distance labeling for sparse graphs that simultaneously admits small decoding time (for constant Δ, we can achieve any $T = \omega(1)$ while maintaining $L = o(n)$), and it also provides an improvement in terms of label size with respect to previous slower approaches.

By using similar techniques, we then present a 2-additive labeling scheme for general graphs, i.e., one in which the decoder provides a 2-additive-approximation of the distance between any pair of nodes. We achieve the same label size-time tradeoff $L = \mathcal{O}(n \log^2 \log T / \log T)$, for any $T \leq n$. To our knowledge, this is the first additive scheme with constant absolute error to use labels of sublinear size. The corresponding decoding time is then small (any $T = \omega(1)$ is sufficient).

*An extended version of this paper is available at `http://arxiv.org/abs/1507.06240`

†Most of the work was done while PU was affiliated to Aalto University, Finland.

PODC'16 July 25-28, 2016, Chicago, IL, USA

ACM ISBN 978-1-4503-3964-3/16/07.

DOI: http://dx.doi.org/10.1145/2933057.2933077

CCS Concepts

•Theory of computation → Distributed algorithms; *Data structures design and analysis;*

Keywords

Distributed Data Structures; Graphs; Distance Labeling; Distance Oracles; Algorithms

1. INTRODUCTION

Distance labeling schemes, popularized by Gavoille et al. [8], are among the most fundamental distributed data structures for graph data. The design problem combines two major challenges. First of all, distance labelings serve the role of a *distance oracle*, i.e., a data structure which for a given undirected graph $G = (V, E)$ can answer queries of the form: "what is the distance between the nodes $s, t \in V$?". Throughout most of this paper, we will assume that G is an unweighted graph with n nodes and m edges. The efficiency of a distance oracle is measured by the interplay between the *space* requirement of the data structure representation, the *encoding time* required to set up the oracle for a given graph, and perhaps more importantly, its *decoding time*, that is, the time of processing a $s - t$ distance query. Moreover, a distance labeling scheme is defined more restrictively than a distance oracle, as an assignment of a binary string (label) $\mathsf{label}(u)$ to each node $u \in V$, so that the graph distance between u and v is uniquely determined by the pair of labels: $\mathsf{label}(u)$ and $\mathsf{label}(v)$. The *size* of a distance labeling scheme is now the maximum length of a node label in the graph. In this way, distance labelings add an extra layer of complexity to the graph distance decoding problem, by imposing a distributed representation of information in the labels $(\mathsf{label}(u) : u \in V)$. Whereas the concatenation of all n labels in a distance labeling forms a centralized distance oracle, distance labelings can also be applied in a distributed setting, in which the label of each node is stored at a distinct location in the network. This is the case, for instance, in applications in compact routing protocols, where the goal is to find a shortest path from a source node to a target node with a known label [6].

An interesting characteristic of the problem of distance oracle design for sparse graph is its inherent link to an underlying set intersection task. On the side of lower bounds, this is most clearly observed, following Pătraşcu and Roddity [9], when we consider a pair of vertices belonging to the same partition of a bipartite graph. The distance between them is 2 if and only if the sets of their neighbors intersect, and at least 4 otherwise. Consequently, assuming a plausible conjecture on the space required to decide intersection of a set of small sets, it follows that any oracle for graphs with $\widetilde{\mathcal{O}}(1)$ maximum degree, which admits constant decoding time, requires $\widetilde{\Omega}(n^2)$ space. (Here, the $\widetilde{O}$ and $\widetilde{\Omega}$ notation disregards polylogarithmic factors in n.) By contrast, many efficient algorithms for answering distance queries in real-world scenarios rely on the premise that the distance between a pair of nodes can be computed using an intersection-type query on a pair of small sets. In the basic framework of hub labelings, see [1], (introduced in [7] under the name of 2-hop covers, and also referred to as landmark labelings [3]), each node $u \in U$ stores the set of its distances to some subset $S(u) \subseteq V$ of other nodes of the graph. Then, the computed distance value $\delta'(u, v)$ for a queried pair of nodes $u, v \in V$ is returned as:

$$\delta'(u, v) := \min_{w \in S(u) \cap S(v)} \delta(u, w) + \delta(w, v), \tag{1}$$

where δ denotes the shortest path distance function between a pair of nodes. The computed distance between all pairs of nodes u and v is exact if set $S(u) \cap S(v)$ contains at least one node on some shortest u–v path. This property of the family of sets $(S(u) : u \in V)$ is known as *shortest path cover*. The hub-based method of distance computation is in practice effective for two reasons. First of all, for transportation-type networks it is possible to show bounds on the sizes of sets S, which follow from the network structure. Notably, Abraham et al. [2] introduce the notion of highway dimension h of a network, which is presumed to be a small constant e.g. for road networks, and show that an appropriate cover of all shortest paths in the graph can be achieved using sets S of size $\widetilde{\mathcal{O}}(h)$. Moreover, the order in which elements of sets $S(u)$ and $S(v)$ is browsed when performing the minimum operation is relevant, and in some schemes, the operation can be interrupted once it is certain that the minimum has been found, before probing all elements of the set.

In this work, we make use of the hub set techniques to obtain better (distributed) distance labelings. Whereas $\Omega(n)$ is a lower bound of the size of a hub set for general graphs, we provide hub-based schemes using smaller sets for specific case, leading to labels which can be encoded on $o(n)$. Our scheme provides a shortest-path cover in the class of sparse graphs (with average degree $\Delta = 2m/n$ subpolynomial in n).

The implications of our result can be seen as twofold. First of all, our approach directly leads to labeling of smaller size (and smaller decoding time) for exact distance queries in sparse graphs than all previous distance labeling approaches. Additionally, an important corollary of our result concerns the case of k-*additive* approximate distance labeling, in which the distance decoder is required to return an upper bound on the shortest path length which is within an additive factor of at most k from the optimum. So far, no way to construct k-additive distance labels using labels of sublinear size in n was known for any constant $k > 0$. (This question was considered previously in, e.g., [5]). We provide a way to construct a 2-additive distance labeling in general graphs using distance labels of size $o(n)$. (This result is essentially the best possible, since a 1-additive distance labeling requires distance labels of size at least $n/4$ already on the class of bipartite graphs.)

All distance encodings presented herein rely on the following preprocessing step (cf. e.g. [5]). We fix an arbitrary spanning tree of the graph and assign preorder numbers in the tree to the nodes, i.e., node numbered 1 corresponds to the root and so on. The preorder number of a node u is denoted by $\mathsf{name}(u)$. Such a numbering has the following useful property: if $v_1, v_2, \ldots, v_n$ is the preorder sequence of all nodes, then, for any node u, $\sum_{i=2}^{n} |\delta(u, v_{i-1}) - \delta(u, v_i)| \leq 2n$.

2. EXACT DISTANCE LABELING IN SPARSE GRAPHS

We first consider the case of graphs of bounded maximum degree, assuming that $\deg(u) \leq \Delta$ for every node u. We consider distance labeling schemes characterized by a time parameter T. Intuitively, in the construction, $R = \frac{\log T}{\log \Delta}$ will be a threshold parameter, distinguishing small distances from large distances in the graph — a node will be able to afford to explicitly store the distances and identifiers of all nodes up to some distance $\mathcal{O}(R)$ from itself in its distance label.

THEOREM 2.1. *Fix any value $\Delta \leq T \leq n$ and let $R = \frac{\log T}{\log \Delta}$. In bounded-degree graphs, there is a labeling scheme of size $\mathcal{O}(\frac{n}{R} \log R)$ and decoding time $\mathcal{O}(T)$.*

The definition of the corresponding labeling is the following. Let us denote $R' = \lfloor R \rfloor$. Since $R' \geq 1$, we can bound $R \geq R' \geq \frac{1}{2}R$. Without loss of generality, we can assume that $T \leq \sqrt{n}$, since claimed label size is the same for any $T = \mathrm{poly}(n)$. Consider a node u. The ball of radius r centered at u, denoted $B_u(r)$, is the set of nodes which can be reached from u by following at most r edges. Because the degrees of all nodes are bounded by Δ, $|B_u(r)| = \mathcal{O}(\Delta^r)$. The k-th layer centered at u, denoted $L_u(k)$, consists of all nodes v such that $\ell(u, v) = k \pmod{R}'$. Because the layers are disjoint, there exists an $\mathsf{offset}(v) \in \{0, 1, \ldots, R' - 1\}$ such that $|L_u(\mathsf{offset}(u))| \leq \frac{n}{R'}$.

We define the hub set of node u, to which it stores all its distances, as $S(u) := B_u(R') \cup L_u(\mathsf{offset}(u))$, see Fig. 1. Formally, the label of u in a graph of bounded maximum degree consists of the following elements:

1. n and $\mathsf{name}(u)$,
2. $\mathsf{name}(v)$ and $\delta(u, v)$ for every $v \in B_u(R')$,
3. $\mathsf{name}(v)$ and $\delta(u, v)$ for every $v \in L_u(\mathsf{offset}(u))$.

Our technique can be adapted to the case of bounded average degree by extending the approach for graphs of bounded maximum degree.

THEOREM 2.2. *Fix any $T \leq n$ and Δ, and let $R = \frac{\log T}{\log \Delta}$. There exists an exact distance labeling for graphs with average degree Δ using labels of size $\mathcal{O}(\frac{n}{R} \log R)$ and a corresponding decoding scheme requiring time $\mathcal{O}(T)$.*

3. 2-ADDITIVE DISTANCE LABELING IN GENERAL GRAPHS

We will apply a similar distance labeling scheme as for sparse graphs, obtaining a 2-additive approximation of the distance between any pair of with label sizes of $o(n)$ per node. In this approximate scheme, the hub sets will have the

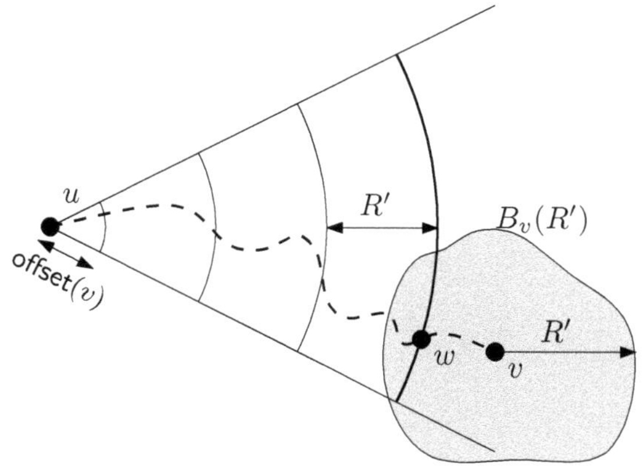

Figure 1: Shortest path from u to v goes through w which belongs to both $B_v(R')$ and $L_u(\mathsf{offset}(u))$.

following property. The label of each node $u \in V$ will provide an encoding of the node identifiers of a subset $S(u) \subseteq V$ and of the distances from u to all elements of $S(u)$. The sets $S(u)$ will be defined so that for any pair u, v, there exists a node $w \in S(u) \cap S(v)$, such that either w or a neighbor of w lies on the shortest path from u to v in G. We will decode the approximate distance as before, using Eq. (1); clearly, $\delta'(u,v) \in \delta(u,v) + \{0,1,2\}$.

The construction of sets $S(u)$ is performed as follows. Let $\tau < \frac{1}{2}\log n$ be an appropriately chosen threshold value of vertex degree. Let $V' = \{v \in V : \deg(v) > \tau\}$, and let $S' \subseteq V$ be a minimum dominating set for V', i.e., a minimum subset of V with the property: $\forall_{w \in V'} B_w(1) \cap S' \neq \emptyset$. By a straightforward application of the probabilistic method (cf. [4, proof of Theorem 1.2.2]), we have $|S'| \leq \frac{1+\ln(\tau+1)}{\tau+1} n < \frac{2\ln\tau}{\tau} n$. For every $u \in V$, we define $B'_u(r)$ as the set of nodes of the ball of radius r around u in the subgraph $G[V \setminus V']$. Finally, we define $R = \frac{\tau}{\log\tau}$ and let L_u, R', and $\mathsf{offset}(u)$ be defined as in Section 2, and let S'_u be a minimal subset of S' such that for every $w \in V'$ on the boundary of $B'_u(R')$, i.e. $B_w(1) \cap B'_u(R') \neq \emptyset$, we have $B_w(1) \cap S'_u \neq \emptyset$.

The approximate distance label of u now consists of the following elements:

1. n and $\mathsf{name}(u)$,
2. $\mathsf{name}(v)$ and $\delta(u,v)$ for every $v \in B'_u(R')$,
3. $\mathsf{name}(v)$ and $\delta(u,v)$ for every $v \in L_u(\mathsf{offset}(u))$.
4. $\mathsf{name}(v)$ and $\delta(u,v)$ for every $v \in S'_u$,
5. $\mathsf{name}(v)$ and $\delta(u,v)$ for every $v \in S' \setminus S'_u$.

In the above, the separation of S' into S'_u and $S' \setminus S'_u$ in the label is done to allow efficient decoding.

THEOREM 3.1. *There is a 2-additive distance labeling scheme for general graphs, which achieves decoding time T using labels of size $\mathcal{O}(n\frac{\log^2\log T}{\log T})$, for any $T \leq n$.* □

Finally, we remark on some implications of our result. By a standard argument, converting a 2-additive approximate distance labeling into an exact one requires an additional label of size $\frac{\log_2 3}{2} n$ bits per node (and an additional $\mathcal{O}(\frac{n}{\log n})$ overhead in the space, which is negligible), with each node u encoding the difference between the approximate and real distance value, $\delta'(u,v) - \delta(u,v)$, for all $v \in \{(u+1) \bmod n, \ldots, (u + \lfloor\frac{n}{2}\rfloor) \bmod n\}$. The time overhead of the corresponding decoding is $\mathcal{O}(1)$.

COROLLARY 3.2. *The proposed exact distance labeling scheme achieves T decoding time using labels of size $\frac{\log_2 3}{2} n + \mathcal{O}(n\frac{\log^2\log T}{\log T})$, for any $T \leq n$.*

In an analogous manner, converting a 2-additive approximate distance labeling into an 1-additive approximate one requires an additional label of size $\frac{1}{2}n$ bits per node.

COROLLARY 3.3. *The proposed exact distance labeling scheme achieves T decoding time using labels of size $\frac{1}{2}n + \mathcal{O}(n\frac{\log^2\log T}{\log T})$, for any $T \leq n$.*

Thus, setting τ as an arbitrarily small increasing function of n, for any desired decoding time $T = \omega(1)$ we can make use of labels of size $o(n)$, $\frac{1}{2}n + o(n)$ and $\frac{\log_2 3}{2} n + o(n)$ respectively for 2-additive, 1-additive and exact distances. Moreover, using this scheme, $\mathcal{O}(1)$ decoding time can be achieved for labels of size εn, $(\frac{1}{2} + \varepsilon) \cdot n$ and $(\frac{\log_2 3}{2} + \varepsilon) \cdot n$, for any absolute constant $\varepsilon > 0$.

4. REFERENCES

[1] I. Abraham, D. Delling, A. V. Goldberg, and R. F. Werneck. Hierarchical hub labelings for shortest paths. In *Proceedings of the 20th Annual European Conference on Algorithms*, ESA'12, pages 24–35, Berlin, Heidelberg, 2012. Springer-Verlag.

[2] I. Abraham, A. Fiat, A. V. Goldberg, and R. F. Werneck. *Highway Dimension, Shortest Paths, and Provably Efficient Algorithms*, chapter 64, pages 782–793.

[3] I. Abraham and C. Gavoille. On approximate distance labels and routing schemes with affine stretch. In *In International Symposium on Distributed Computing (DISC)*, pages 404–415, 2011.

[4] N. Alon and J. H. Spencer. *The Probabilistic Method*. J. Wiley & Sons, New York, 2nd edition, 2000.

[5] S. Alstrup, C. Gavoille, E. B. Halvorsen, and H. Petersen. Simpler, faster and shorter labels for distances in graphs. In R. Krauthgamer, editor, *Proceedings of the Twenty-Seventh Annual ACM-SIAM Symposium on Discrete Algorithms, SODA 2016, Arlington, VA, USA, January 10-12, 2016*, pages 338–350. SIAM, 2016.

[6] V. Chepoi, F. F. Dragan, B. Estellon, M. Habib, Y. Vaxès, and Y. Xiang. Additive spanners and distance and routing labeling schemes for hyperbolic graphs. *Algorithmica*, 62(3-4):713–732, 2012.

[7] E. Cohen, E. Halperin, H. Kaplan, and U. Zwick. Reachability and distance queries via 2-hop labels. *SIAM J. Comput.*, 32(5):1338–1355, May 2003.

[8] C. Gavoille, D. Peleg, S. Pérennes, and R. Raz. Distance labeling in graphs. *J. Algorithms*, 53(1):85–112, Oct. 2004.

[9] M. Pătraşcu and L. Roditty. Distance oracles beyond the Thorup-Zwick bound. *SIAM J. Comput.*, 43(1):300–311, 2014.

Brief Announcement: Optimal Leader Election In Multi-Hop Radio Networks *

Artur Czumaj
Department of Computer Science
Centre for Discrete Mathematics and its Applications
University of Warwick
A.Czumaj@warwick.ac.uk

Peter Davies
Department of Computer Science
Centre for Discrete Mathematics and its Applications
University of Warwick
P.W.Davies@warwick.ac.uk

ABSTRACT

We present optimal randomized leader election algorithms for multi-hop radio networks, which run in expected time asymptotically equal to that required to broadcast one message to the network. We first observe that, under certain assumptions, a simulation approach of Bar-Yehuda, Goldreich and Itai (1991) can be used to obtain an algorithm that for *directed and undirected networks* elects a leader in $O(D \log \frac{n}{D} + \log^2 n)$ expected time, where n is the number of the nodes and D is the eccentricity of the network. We then extend this approach to present an algorithm which operates on *undirected radio networks with collision detection* (and in fact the weaker *beep model*) and elects a leader in $O(D + \log n)$ expected time.

We also give an algorithm for the model without collision detection which runs in time $O((D \log \frac{n}{D} + \log^2 n) \cdot \sqrt{\log n})$, and succeeds with high probability. While slightly slower than the algorithm of Ghaffari and Haeupler (2013), it has the advantage of working in *directed networks*, and is the fastest leader election algorithm to achieve a high-probability bound therein.

CCS Concepts

•Networks → Network control algorithms; •Theory of computation → *Self-organization;*

Keywords

Leader Election, Radio Networks, Randomized Algorithms

1. MULTI-HOP RADIO NETWORKS

We consider the classical model of *radio networks* with *unknown structure*. A *radio network* is modeled by a network (directed or undirected graph) $\mathcal{N} = (V, E)$, where nodes represent transmitter-receiver stations. A directed edge $(v, u) \in E$ means that the node v can send a message to the node u. To make the global communication feasible, we assume that $\mathcal{N}$ is strongly connected. We assume that a node does not have any prior knowledge about the topology of the network, its degree, or the set of its neighbors, but does know linear upper bounds for the size of the network n, and the *eccentricity* of the network D.

We assume that all nodes have access to a global clock and work *synchronously* in discrete time steps. When we refer to the "running time" of an algorithm, we mean the number of time steps which elapse before completion (i.e., we are not concerned with the number of calculations nodes perform within time steps). In each time step a node can either *transmit* a message to all of its out-neighbors at once or can remain silent and *listen* to the messages from its in-neighbors. The distinguishing feature of radio networks is the interfering behavior of transmissions. We are concerned with two variants of the model:

In the *model without collision detection*, if a node v listens in a given round and precisely one of its in-neighbors transmits, then v receives the message. In all other cases v receives nothing; in particular, v is unable to distinguish between multiple in-neighbors transmitting and zero.

The *model with collision detection* is less restrictive: listening nodes can distinguish between the cases of zero and multiple transmitting in-neighbors. However, rather than directly studying this model directly, we instead work in the strictly weaker *beep model*, introduced recently by Cornejo and Kuhn [5]. In this model, in synchronous time steps, each node can either beep or not beep. If a node beeps, then it does not receive any information in this time step. If a node does not beep, then it can tell whether zero neighbors beeped, or whether at least one did. Any algorithm designed for the beep model can be directly used for the standard multi-hop radio network model with collision detection.

2. LEADER ELECTION

Leader election is the problem of ensuring that all nodes agree on a single node to be designated leader. Specifically, at the conclusion of a leader election algorithm, all nodes should output the same node ID, and precisely one node should identify this ID as its own. Leader election is a fundamental primitive in distributed computations and, as the most fundamental means of breaking symmetry within radio networks, it is used as a preliminary step in many more com-

*A full version of this paper is available at https://arxiv.org/abs/1505.06149

PODC'16 July 25-28, 2016, Chicago, IL, USA

ACM ISBN 978-1-4503-3964-3/16/07.

DOI: http://dx.doi.org/10.1145/2933057.2933076

plex communication tasks. For example, many fast multi-message communication protocols require construction of a breadth-first search tree (or some similar variant), which in turn requires a single node to act as source (for more examples, cf. [4, 8], and the references therein).

3. PREVIOUS WORK.

The study of leader election in radio networks started with the *single-hop network model*, in which all nodes are directly reachable by all others. Willard [11] gave an algorithm with the expected running time of $O(\log\log n)$ and showed that this bound is asymptotically optimal, assuming that nodes do not know the value of n.

In the seminal work initiating the study of communication protocols in *multi-hop radio networks*, Bar-Yehuda et al. [2] developed a general randomized framework of simulating single-hop networks with collision detection by multi-hop networks without collision detection. As an application, the authors noted that simulating Willard's algorithm yields a leader election algorithm in multi-hop networks running in $O(T_{BC} \cdot \log\log n)$ expected time, where T_{BC} is the time required to broadcast a message from a single source to the entire network. Plugging in a $O(D\log n + \log^2 n)$-time broadcasting algorithm also due to Bar-Yehuda et al. gave leader election in $O((D\log n + \log^2 n)\log\log n)$ expected time.

Faster broadcasting algorithms [7, 9] subsequently improved this expected leader election time to $O((D\log\frac{n}{D} + \log^2 n)\log\log n)$. Recent work by Ghaffari and Haeupler [8] took a new approach to yield leader election algorithms with improved high-probability running times, but their expected running times were no quicker.

Let us finally emphasize that leader election takes at least as long as broadcasting an $\Omega(\log n)$ bit message (cf. [8]), and, as such, is subject to the lower bounds $\Omega(D\log\frac{n}{D} + \log^2 n)$ for broadcasting without collision detection (cf. [1, 10]), and $\Omega(D+\log n)$ for broadcasting with collision detection or in the beep model [6].

4. OUR RESULTS

We present a simple framework combining the simulation approach of Bar-Yehuda et al. [2] with basic communication primitives that enables us to obtain *new, asymptotically optimal or almost optimal leader election algorithms*.

We begin with noting that, under certain assumptions, the simulation approach of Bar-Yehuda et al. [2] can be used to obtain an algorithm with the *asymptotically optimal expected time complexity* for the task of randomized leader election in multi-hop radio networks without collision detection (Algorithm 1). The algorithm runs in $O(D\log\frac{n}{D} + \log^2 n)$ expected time, where n is the number of the nodes and D is the eccentricity or the diameter of the network; the expected running time complexity of this algorithm is asymptotically equal to the time required to broadcast a single message.

This improves by a $O(\log\log n)$ factor over the expected running time claimed by Bar-Yehuda et al. [2], and, in the case of undirected networks, by a similar $O(\log\log n)$ factor over the high probability bound of Ghaffari and Haeupler [8].

While our algorithm could be seen as a variation of the approach by Bar-Yehuda et al. [2], the obtained result has not previously been noted despite substantial research into the model (see, e.g., [8] and the references therein).

We then present another algorithm which follows a similar outline but exploits the properties of the collision detection mechanism (Algorithm 3). The algorithm operates on *undirected multi-hop radio networks with collision detection* (as well as the strictly weaker *beep model*) and has $O(D+\log n)$ expected running time, which matches the amount of time required to broadcast a single $\Theta(\log n)$ bit message to the network. It is the first known leader election algorithm in this model with the asymptotically optimal expected running time performance.

The algorithms above achieve the asymptotically optimal expected running time performance. For situations when good worst-case running time is required, we present a Monte Carlo algorithm for *directed networks without collision detection* which takes a fixed $O((D\log\frac{n}{D} + \log^2 n)\sqrt{\log n})$ time and succeeds with high probability (Algorithm 4). While this algorithm is not necessarily optimal, and for undirected networks is slightly slower than the algorithm of [8], it is the *fastest known algorithm* for *high probability* leader election in *directed networks*.

5. EXPECTED TIME ALGORITHMS

The approach in our optimal expected-time leader election, Algorithm 1, can be described as follows: we repeatedly attempt to randomly select a single leadership candidate, and then run a process to check whether we have indeed done so. If we have, we terminate the algorithm, and if not, we continue. Since we can achieve a constant probability of selecting one candidate, the expected number of iterations required to do so is also constant.

We can employ the optimal broadcasting algorithm of [7] to have candidates broadcast their IDs to the network; this ensures that all nodes hear a candidate ID. We can then use the classic Decay procedure, first introduced by Bar-Yehuda et al. [3], to locally broadcast. This has the result that any node with at least one in-neighbor who heard a different candidate ID will hear such a differing ID from such a neighbor. Details are given in the full version of this paper. We can then employ the global broadcasting algorithm again to have nodes hearing candidate ID 'clashes' report back to the whole network.

These three stages constitute one iteration of the algorithm, and one can easily show that in expectation only a constant number of iterations are required before the leader election is successful.

Algorithm 1 Leader Election, expected time

```
loop
    each node becomes a candidate with probability 1/n
    candidates choose O(log n)-bit IDs uniformly at random
    candidates broadcast their IDs
    nodes locally broadcast to check for differing IDs
    any node aware of differing IDs broadcasts this to network
    if nodes heard an ID but no 'differing IDs' message, halt
end loop
```

THEOREM 1. *Algorithm 1 terminates in $O(D\log\frac{n}{D}+\log^2 n)$ expected time and correctly performs leader election with high probability, in both directed and undirected networks.*

The algorithm can be seen as being equivalent to simulating Algorithm 2 using the framework of [2] and the broadcasting algorithm of [7]:

Algorithm 2 Leader Election, single-hop networks with collision detection

loop
 each node becomes a **candidate** with probability $\frac{1}{n}$
 candidates choose $O(\log n)$-bit IDs uniformly at random
 candidates transmit their IDs
 if a candidate succeeded in transmitting, halt
end loop

We extend this approach to exploit the mechanism of collision detection, and yield a faster algorithm for networks where this mechanism is available. Specifically, we give an algorithm (Algorithm 3) for the *beep model* which runs in optimal expected time.

The idea of the algorithm is similar: we again repeatedly attempt to randomly select a single leadership candidate, and then check whether we were successful. Here the global broadcasting mechanism we employ is that of *beep waves*, introduced in [8] and formalized in [6]. This technique involves using waves of transmission collisions to carry the bits of a message. By utilizing properties of the beep wave method and restricting the range of possible IDs, we can ensure that nodes become aware of candidate ID clashes without need of a local broadcast phase. Then, we use beep waves once more to broadcast this information back to the network, thus completing an iteration of the algorithm.

Algorithm 3 Leader Election, beep model, expected time

loop
 each node becomes a **candidate** with probability $O(\frac{1}{n})$
 candidates choose $O(\log n)$-bit ID with exactly $k = O(\log n)$ **1**s at random
 candidates broadcast their IDs using beep-waves
 nodes hearing more than k **1**s broadcast this information
 if nodes heard an ID but no 'too many **1**s' message, halt
end loop

THEOREM 2. *Algorithm 3 terminates in $O(D+\log n)$ expected time, performing leader election with high probability.*

6. MONTE CARLO ALGORITHM

We next give a Monte Carlo algorithm designed to yield better worst-case running times, at the expense of expected time. This algorithm works as follows: first nodes choose to be candidates with probability $O(\frac{\log n}{n})$ to ensure that there are $\Theta(\log n)$ candidates. The candidates choose IDs, and we then narrow down the field of candidates by using a binary search procedure to find the first $O(\sqrt{\log n})$ bits of the lowest ID. Details of this procedure can be found in the full version of the paper, but the idea is that we can use the broadcasting algorithm of [7] to have the network agree on a single bit, and so agreeing on $O(\sqrt{\log n})$ bits takes $O(\sqrt{\log n})$ times broadcasting time.

One can show that at most $O(\sqrt{\log n})$ candidates share this lowest ID prefix. We can then remove one candidate at a time by using a slightly strengthened version of the method of Algorithm 1, until only one remains. Each removal stage takes the running time of global broadcast, so reducing $O(\sqrt{\log n})$ candidates down to one again takes $O(\sqrt{\log n})$ times broadcasting time.

Algorithm 4 Leader Election, high probability

each node becomes a **candidate** with probability $O(\frac{\log n}{n})$
candidates choose $O(\log n)$-bit IDs uniformly at random
binary search for the first $O(\sqrt{\log n})$ bits of the lowest ID
candidates with different ID prefixes drop out
loop $O(\sqrt{\log n})$ times
 candidates broadcast their IDs
 nodes locally broadcast to check for differing IDs
 any node aware of differing IDs broadcasts the highest ID it knows to the network
 any node which hears a higher ID than its own drops out
 if nodes heard an ID but no 'differing IDs' message, halt
end loop

THEOREM 3. *Algorithm 4 always runs in time $O((D\log\frac{n}{D}+\log^2 n)\cdot\sqrt{\log n})$, and performs leader election with high probability. It works in both undirected and directed networks.*

7. REFERENCES

[1] N. Alon, A. Bar-Noy, N. Linial, and D. Peleg. A lower bound for radio broadcast. *Journal of Computer and System Sciences*, 43(2):290–298, 1991.

[2] R. Bar-Yehuda, O. Goldreich, and A. Itai. Efficient emulation of single-hop radio network with collision on multi-hop radio network with no collision detection. *Distributed Computing*, 5:67–71, 1991.

[3] R. Bar-Yehuda, O. Goldreich, and A. Itai. On the time-complexity of broadcast in multi-hop radio networks: An exponential gap between determinism and randomization. *Journal of Computer and System Sciences*, 45(1):104–126, 1992.

[4] B. S. Chlebus, D. R. Kowalski, and A. Pelc. Electing a leader in multi-hop radio networks. In *Proceedings of the 16th International Conference on Principles of Distributed Systems (OPODIS)*, pages 106–120, 2012.

[5] A. Cornejo and F. Kuhn. Deploying wireless networks with beeps. In *Proceedings of the 24th International Symposium on Distributed Computing (DISC)*, pages 148–262, 2010.

[6] A. Czumaj and P. Davies. Communicating with beeps. In *Proceedings of the 19th International Conference on Principles of Distributed Systems (OPODIS)*, 2015.

[7] A. Czumaj and W. Rytter. Broadcasting algorithms in radio networks with unknown topology. In *Proceedings of the 44th IEEE Symposium on Foundations of Computer Science (FOCS)*, pages 492–501, 2003.

[8] M. Ghaffari and B. Haeupler. Near optimal leader election in multi-hop radio networks. In *Proceedings of the 24th Annual ACM-SIAM Symposium on Discrete Algorithms (SODA)*, pages 748–766, 2013.

[9] D. Kowalski and A. Pelc. Broadcasting in undirected ad hoc radio networks. *Distributed Computing*, 18(1):43–57, 2005.

[10] E. Kushilevitz and Y. Mansour. An $\Omega(D\log(N/D))$ lower bound for broadcast in radio networks. *SIAM Journal on Computing*, 27(3):702–712, 1998.

[11] D. E. Willard. Log-logarithmic selection resolution protocols in a multiple access channel. *SIAM Journal on Computing*, 15(2):468–477, 1986.

Brief Announcement: The Small World of Curious Beings

Soroush Alamdari *

ABSTRACT

We present a strategic model of network creation that satisfies all known theoretically verifiable properties of the small-world phenomenon. We consider a population that is uniformly distributed in a low-dimensional space, and show that in such a society if each individual follows the status of a subset of others by investing attention in order to satisfy curiosity, then small-world properties appear naturally as a side effect.

1. THE SMALL-WORLD PHENOMENON

Foretold by observant minds, the small-world phenomenon was confirmed in an experiment carried by Milgram [3] in which randomly selected individuals in Nebraska and Kansas where sent an information packet with instruction asking them to help the packet reach an individual in Boston Massachuset, specified by basic information. In case they did not know the target individual personally, the recipient was instructed to pass the packet on to someone they knew personally who was most likely to personally know the target. So each initial recipient started a chain of correspondence, some of which ended before reaching the target due to lack of participation. Among the chains that reached the target, the average length of a chain was just bellow six. An observation we have been trying to explain since.

Consider the network whose nodes are residents of united states at the time of the experiment, and let there be a link from a node v to a node u, if v has the address of u and personally knows them. Minus oddities, the experiment essentially shows that in this network any two nodes are connected via a short chain. This is particularly fascinating as each individual only knows a very small group of others compared to the total population. Satisfying these two constraints simultaneously is a challenge even in an abstract mathematical setting:

*Cornell University, Ithaca, USA alamdari@cs.cornell.edu

PODC'16 July 25-28, 2016, Chicago, IL, USA

ACM ISBN 978-1-4503-3964-3/16/07.

DOI: http://dx.doi.org/10.1145/2933057.2933067

1. **Degree:** The number of others that any node has links to, that is the *degree* of that node, is small relative to the total population.
2. **Diameter:** For any recipient and any target, the length of the shortest chain of links that starts from the recipient and ends in the target is very small. The length of the longest such chain in a network is referred to as the *diameter* of that network.

To address this, Watts and Strogatz [5] showed that in a society with a population of n that are sitting around a ring, if each individual has links to the n^{ε} others that are sitting on each side of it plus n^{ε} random other nodes, then each pair of nodes are connected via a chain of expected length smaller than $1/\varepsilon$. While this satisfies both Constraints 1 and 2, it does not explain how such a chain is found by the participants in the experiment. In fact, this is a much more restricting constraint, as each node is unaware of who others know personally and thus cannot decide who among the people it has a link to are closest to the target in the underlying network. This observation allows us to strengthen Constraint 2:

3. **Limited information:** Each node is unaware of the links maintained by other nodes. We refer to this condition as the limited information constraint.
4. **Observable diameter:** For any recipient and any target, a very short chain connecting the recipient to the target can be found if each recipient chooses the next recipient based on similarity with target. We refer to the length of the longest such chain in a network as the *observable diameter* of that network.

Closer analysis of the experiment has shown that participants favor geographical information when deciding the next recipient [4]. Kleinberg [2] argues that such information is sufficient for satisfying Constraint 4, by showing that in a population that is distributed homogeneously over the plane, if each node has a link to a node of geographical distance l with probability $1/l^{\alpha}$, then iteratively choosing the next recipient based on geographical proximity to the target almost always produces a short chain. Particularly, when $\alpha = 2$, both the expected length of the chain that is found and the expected number of links that each node creates can be bounded by $O(\log n)$.

Although Kleinberg's model satisfies all of the constraints with a natural explanation, it has not been able to end the search for the cause of the small-world phenomenon. It remains curious whether the small-world phenomenon exists

	$\alpha < d+1$	$\alpha = d+1$	$d+1 < \alpha$
Maximum degree	$o(n^{1-\delta\frac{\alpha}{d+1}} \log\log n)$	$O(\log n)$	$O(\log_{\frac{\alpha}{d+1}} \log n)^*$
Observable diameter	$O(\log_{\frac{d+1}{\alpha}} \log n)$	$O(\log n)$	$o(n^{1-\frac{\delta}{\alpha-d}} \log\log n)$

Table 1: The bounds on maximum degree and observable diameter at stability, for different values of α relative to the dimension d. Here δ can be any constant smaller than 1.

by coincidence, or if it is designed by our collective minds. While it is possible that our social experience is dominated by random encounters, it seems more plausible that a selfish drive connects us in this particular way. And so we add one more constraint, although it is not immediately verifiable:

5. **Strategic choice:** Each node create links by making choices in order to satisfy some objective.

To address this, researchers have been trying to find the right game-theoretic model that would be able to explain the astonishing properties of our social networks. However, by considering a game-theoretic model where individuals make choices strategically based on the choices of others, the limited information constraint is immediately violated. So we argue that if a game-theoretic model that is able to produce the small-world properties is established based on the correct objective, then the small-world properties should persist even when the full information assumption is relaxed.

Among various game-theoretic models of network formation, we bring to attention the work of Even-Dar and Kearns [1], where the population is distributed uniformly on the plane and each agent v chooses its links in order to minimize the total cost of maintaining the links plus the average distance to other nodes through the network. In their model, a link to a node of geographical distance l induces a cost of l^α. Particularly, they show that in this model when $\alpha < 2$, the diameter can be bounded by a constant.

When attempting to derandomize the work of Kleinberg [2] at the critical point where logarithmic bounds appear, we come upon a strategic model of network creation that achieves similar bounds and satisfies all of our constraints. When analysing the objective function that archives this we see a natural interpretation that hints towards the role of curiosity in the appearance of the small-world phenomenon.

2. THE MODEL

Consider a d-dimensional grid of n nodes representing the geographical space upon which the population is distributed. Here we consider d to be a constant. For nodes u and v we use $d(u, v)$ to refer to the grid-distance of u and v, which corresponds to the geographical distance of them. Also, for a node u and a set of nodes V we use $d(u, V)$ to refer to the grid-distance of u to its closest member in V, that is, $d(u, V) = \min_{v \in V} d(u, v)$.

A network N, assigns to each node v a set $N(v)$ of nodes that is the set of nodes that v has links to. To model the creation of such a network we introduce a cost that each agent incurs at a given setting. Let $c_N(v)$ be such a function that calculates the cost induced to a node v in N. There are two components to this cost function; the cost of maintaining the links that v has to other nodes and the cost induced by the information that v is missing regarding the nodes that it does not have a link to. For a node u, let $l_N(v, u)$ be the former and $s_N(v, u)$ be the latter. We have

$$c_N(v) = \sum_{u \in N(v)} l_N(v, u) + \sum_{u \notin N(v)} s_N(v, u). \qquad (1)$$

Let us say that the cost that a node v pays for maintaining a link to a node u is proportional to the geographical distance of them to some power α, that is, $l_N(v, u) \propto d^\alpha(v, u)$.

It remains for us to define $s_N(v, u)$, that is, the cost that v pays for not having a link to u. Let this cost to be proportional to the grid-distance between u and the node closest to u that v has a link to, that is, $s_N(v, u) \propto d(u, N(v))$.

We can now express the cost function $c_N(v)$ such that it only depends on $N(v)$ and the position of the nodes on the underlying grid:

$$c_N(v) = \beta \sum_{u \in N(v)} d^\alpha(v, u) + \sum_{u \notin N(v)} d(u, N(v)) \qquad (2)$$

where β is the normalizing factor, assumed to be a small constant here.

As an indicator of equilibrium, we say that a node v is *stable* in N if v cannot reduce its cost $c_N(v)$ by adding or removing a link, and we say a network N is stable if all nodes are stable in N.

Consider the tradeoff between the length of the chains that connect the nodes and the number of links maintained by each node. When $\alpha < \frac{1}{\log_{\beta-1} n}$ every link has a cost smaller than 1 and therefore in stability each agent benefits from having a link to any other node, and when $\alpha > \log(\beta^{-1}n^2)$ no agent can justify a link to a node of distance > 1. We analyse the intermediary values of α around the threshold $\alpha = d + 1$, achieving the bounds depicted in Table 1.

It is imaginable that α has been reduced significantly through the course of history. It seems reasonable to assume that with writing and a postal service, the cost of maintaining the status of another increases relative to geographical distance with a power no more than 2. If that is the case, when considering the United States at the time of the experiment we would expect the bounds for $\alpha < d + 1$ to apply, explaining the short length of chains found in the experiment.

Perhaps the most significant application of our results concern the swarm. Imagine a cloud of drones flying over a terrain in a grid formation that stretches and expands to perform maneuvers and let obstacles through. Suppose that these machines communicate by broadcasting their status on unique frequencies, and each agent wishes to approximate the current position of the others by following a small number of broadcasts. Let us estimate the error in calculation of the position of another drone to be its grid-distance from the closest drone with a known location. If each drone v chooses whose status to listen for by minimizing:

$$c_N(v) = \beta \sum_{u \in N(v)} d^\alpha(v, u) + \sum_{u \notin N(v)} w_v(u) d(u, N(v)) \qquad (3)$$

where $w_v(u)$ represents the relative importance of u for v, then some degree of small-world properties are established as a side effect depending on parameters α and β, and the correlation between relative importance and proximity.

At this point, many directions remain unexplored. Particularly, it is curious as to what happens to the threshold for larger values of β. When we set $\beta = n$, our cost function closely resembles the objective function upon which the model of Even-Dar and Kearns [1] is based. Although their model is inherently different, the tradeoff is there and a similar threshold with features of its own appears. So there is probably a much bigger picture here, one whose pieces are yet to be revealed and put together.

3. REFERENCES

[1] E. Even-Dar and M. J. Kearns. A small world threshold for economic network formation. In *Advances in Neural Information Processing Systems 19*, pages 385–392. MIT Press, 2007.

[2] J. Kleinberg. The small-world phenomenon: An algorithmic perspective. In *ACM Symposium on Theory of Computing 33*, pages 163–170, New York, NY, USA, 2000.

[3] S. Milgram. The Small World Problem. *Psychology Today*, 2:60–67, 1967.

[4] J. Travers and S. Milgram. An experimental study of the small world problem. *Sociometry*, 32:425–443, 1969.

[5] D. J. Watts and S. H. Strogatz. Collective dynamics of'small-world'networks. *Nature*, 393(6684):409–10, 1998.

Analysing Snapshot Isolation

Andrea Cerone
IMDEA Software Institute

Alexey Gotsman
IMDEA Software Institute

ABSTRACT

Snapshot isolation (SI) is a widely used consistency model for transaction processing, implemented by most major databases and some of transactional memory systems. Unfortunately, its classical definition is given in a low-level operational way, by an idealised concurrency-control algorithm, and this complicates reasoning about the behaviour of applications running under SI. We give an alternative specification to SI that characterises it in terms of transactional dependency graphs of Adya et al., generalising serialization graphs. Unlike previous work, our characterisation does not require adding additional information to dependency graphs about start and commit points of transactions. We then exploit our specification to obtain two kinds of static analyses. The first one checks when a set of transactions running under SI can be chopped into smaller pieces without introducing new behaviours, to improve performance. The other analysis checks whether a set of transactions running under a weakening of SI behaves the same as when it running under SI.

Keywords

Snapshot isolation; transaction chopping; robustness

1. INTRODUCTION

Transactions simplify concurrent programming by enabling computations on shared data that are isolated from other concurrent computations and resilient to failures. They are commonly provided by databases [7] and, more recently, by transactional memory systems [22]. Ideally, programmers would like to get strong guarantees about the isolation of transactional computations, formalised by the notion of *serializability* [7]: the results of concurrently executing a set transactions could be obtained if these transactions executed atomically in some order. Unfortunately, ensuring serializability carries a significant performance penalty. For this reason, transactional systems often provide weaker guarantees about transaction processing, formalised by *weak consistency models*. Snapshot isolation (SI) [6] is one of the most popular such models, implemented by major centralised databases (e.g., MS SQL Sever, Oracle), distributed databases [14, 27, 29] and transactional memory systems [1, 8, 15, 25].

PODC'16, July 25 - 28, 2016, Chicago, IL, USA

ISBN 978-1-4503-3964-3/16/07... $15.00

DOI: http://dx.doi.org/10.1145/2933057.2933096

Informally, SI is defined by a multi-version concurrency control algorithm as follows. A transaction T reads values of shared objects from a snapshot taken at its start. The transaction commits only if it passes a *write-conflict* detection check: since T started, no other committed transaction has written to any object that T also wrote to. If the check fails, T aborts. Once T commits, its changes become visible to all transactions that take a snapshot afterwards. This concurrency-control algorithm allows unserializable behaviours, called *anomalies*. One of them, *write skew*, is graphically illustrated in Figure 2(d). Each of the transactions T_1 and T_2 checks that the combined balance of two accounts exceeds 100 and, if so, withdraws 100 from one of them. Under SI, both transactions may pass the checks and make the withdrawals from different accounts, resulting in the combined balance going negative. This outcome cannot occur under serializability. Given such anomalies, reasoning about the behaviour of applications executing under SI is far from trivial. This task is further complicated by the fact that the specification of SI is given in a low-level operational way, by a concurrency control algorithm. To facilitate reasoning about applications using SI and establishing useful results about this consistency model, we need a more declarative specification that abstracts from implementation-level details as much as possible.

An approach that yields such consistency model specifications was proposed by Adya et al. [2, 3]. In this approach, an execution of a set of transactions is described by three kinds of *dependencies* between pairs of transactions T_1 and T_2: *read dependencies* record when T_1 reads the value of an object written by T_2; *write dependencies* record when T_1 overwrites the value of an object written by T_2; finally, *anti-dependencies* are derived from read and write dependencies in a certain way (§3). A set of transactions and dependencies between them form a *dependency graph*, generalising classical serialization graphs [7]. Then the set of executions allowed by a given consistency model is defined by those dependency graphs that lack certain cycles; in particular, serializable executions are characterised by acyclic dependency graphs. This way of specifying consistency models has been shown to be particularly appropriate for designing static analyses [12, 19, 23, 30, 38], run-time monitoring [9, 37] and proving concurrency-control algorithms correct [16, 24, 36]. In particular, specifications in terms of dependency graphs facilitate exploring possible program executions in a static analysis, because the analysis can determine which dependencies can possibly exist at run time by looking for pairs of read or write accesses to the same object in the code of different transactions. In contrast, it is hard to predict statically more low-level information about transaction execution, such as the order in which transactions commit.

Specifications in terms of dependency graphs have been proposed for ANSI isolation levels such as serializability, Read Committed and Repeatable Read [2], as well as more recent proposals of consistency models [5, 36]. But surprisingly, there is no such specification of SI. This is not for the want of trying: Adya did propose a definition of SI that refers to dependency graphs [2]. However, to capture the subtle semantics of SI, this definition extends the graphs by a relation describing low-level information about transaction execution, which negates their benefits.

In this paper we propose the first characterisation of SI solely in terms of dependency graphs (§4) and apply it to develop new static analyses (§5 and §6). Namely, we show that SI allows exactly the executions represented by dependency graphs that contain only cycles with at least two adjacent anti-dependency edges. The proof of this fact is highly non-trivial and represents a key technical contribution of this paper. It requires showing that, given a dependency graph satisfying the above acyclicity condition, we can construct certain relations describing how the transactions can be processed by the SI concurrency control, e.g., the order in which transactions commit. Constructing these relations from transactional dependencies is challenging, and the main insight of our proof is given by a procedure for this construction, based on solving certain kinds of inequalities over relations.

To illustrate the benefits of our dependency graph characterisation of SI, we exploit it to develop two kinds of static analyses. First, we propose a new static analysis for the classical problem of *transaction chopping* [4, 30, 35]—checking when transactions in an application can be chopped into smaller pieces without introducing new behaviours (§5). When applied to long-running transactions executing under SI, chopping can improve performance, because the longer an SI transaction runs, the higher the chances are that it will abort due to a write conflict. There are analyses for transaction chopping under serializability [30] and parallel SI [12], a recently-proposed weaker version of SI for large-scale databases [32]. However, there has been no such analysis under SI, despite the widespread use of this consistency model.

Our dependency graph characterisation of SI is instrumental in deriving the static analysis for transaction chopping, and not only due to the feasibility of determining possible dependencies statically. In more detail, chopping transforms transactions in a program into *sessions* [14, 33] (aka *chains* [38]) of smaller transactions, which ensure that the transactions will be executed in the order given, but provide no isolation guarantees. A chopping is correct if each SI execution of the resulting program can be *spliced* into an SI execution that has the same operations as the original one, but where all operations from each session are executed inside a single transaction. Showing the existence of the spliced execution is challenging on SI because it is non-trivial to pick the order in which its transactions should commit. Our characterisation of SI in terms of transactional dependencies avoids this complication, because unlike low-level aspects of an execution, these dependencies do not change significantly during splicing, and this makes it easy to construct the spliced execution.

The other kind of static analyses that we consider checks whether an application is *robust* [19, 31] against weakening consistency: it behaves the same regardless of whether it uses a database providing a weak consistency model or a database proving a stronger model (§6). When this is the case, the application programmer can reap the performance benefits of using the weaker model, yet can reason about the correctness of the application assuming the stronger one. We first show that our SI characterisation allows easily deriving a variant of an existing analysis that checks whether an application executing under SI behaves the same as when executing under serializability [19] (robustness *against SI*, §6.1). We then propose a new static analysis that checks whether an application executing under the recently-proposed parallel SI [32] behaves the same as when executing under the stronger classical SI (robustness *against parallel SI towards SI*, §6.2). To derive this static analysis, we formulate a dependency graph characterisation of parallel SI, which can be given more easily than for classical SI. Again, our characterisations of consistency models in terms of dependency graphs greatly facilitate deriving the above robustness analyses, since the characterisations allow us to easily map between executions on different models.

Due to space constraints, we defer some of the proofs to [11, §A].

2. SNAPSHOT ISOLATION

We start by formally defining snapshot isolation (SI), as well as serializability. Rather than using the classical definition of SI by a concurrency-control algorithm (§1), it is technically convenient for us to build on a more declarative specification that we previously proposed and proved equivalent to the standard one [10]. Even though this specification is stated in terms of lower-level relations than transactional dependencies, it avoids referring explicitly to times at which a transaction takes a snapshot in the SI concurrency-control algorithm. We first introduce mathematical structures that represent transaction execution in the specification.

We consider a transactional system managing a set of integer-valued ***objects*** $\mathsf{Obj} = \{x, y, \ldots\}$. Transactions read and write the objects, and in our representation of executions, we denote each invocation of such an operation by an ***event*** from a set $\mathsf{Event} = \{e, f, \ldots\}$. A function $\mathsf{op} : \mathsf{Event} \rightarrow \mathsf{Op}$ for $\mathsf{Op} = \{\mathtt{read}(x, n), \mathtt{write}(x, n) \mid x \in \mathsf{Obj}, n \in \mathbb{Z}\}$ determines the operation a given event denotes: reading a value n from an object x or writing n to x. We call a binary relation a ***strict partial order*** if it is transitive and irreflexive. We call it a ***total order*** if it additionally relates any pair of distinct elements one way or another. We represent an execution of a single transaction by the following structure, recording a set of operations and the order in which they were invoked.

DEFINITION 1. *A* ***transaction*** $T, S, \ldots$ *is a pair* (E, po), *where* $E \subseteq \mathsf{Event}$ *is a finite, non-empty set of events and the* ***program order*** $\mathsf{po} \subseteq E \times E$ *is a total order.*

For simplicity, all transactions in this paper are assumed to be committed: our specifications do not constrain values read inside aborted or ongoing transactions; this limitation could be lifted following [2, 17, 21]. We denote components of transactions and similar structures as in E_T and po_T.

To allow transaction chopping (§5), we assume that the transactional system allows its clients to group several transactions into a session [33], which establishes an ordering on the transactions. Thus, instead of classical SI and serializability, we actually define their ***strong session*** variants [13, 14]. We represent the client-visible results of an execution of a set of sessions by a *history*.

DEFINITION 2. *A* ***history*** *is a pair* $\mathcal{H} = (\mathcal{T}, \mathsf{SO})$, *where* $\mathcal{T}$ *is a finite set of transactions with disjoint sets of events and the* ***session order*** $\mathsf{SO} \subseteq \mathcal{T} \times \mathcal{T}$ *is a union of total orders defined on disjoint subsets of* $\mathcal{T}$, *which correspond to transactions in different sessions.*

For simplicity, we elide the treatment of infinite computations, and thus histories are always finite. A consistency model, such as SI or serializability, is specified by a set of histories. To define this set, we extend histories with two relations, declaratively describing how the transactional system processes transactions.

DEFINITION 3. *An* ***abstract execution*** *(or just an execution) is a tuple* $\mathcal{X} = (\mathcal{T}, \mathsf{SO}, \mathsf{VIS}, \mathsf{CO})$, *where* $(\mathcal{T}, \mathsf{SO})$ *is a history and the* ***visibility*** *and* ***commit orders*** $\mathsf{VIS}, \mathsf{CO} \subseteq \mathcal{T} \times \mathcal{T}$ *are such that* $\mathsf{VIS} \subseteq \mathsf{CO}$ *and* CO *is total.*

$\forall (E, \mathsf{po}) \in \mathcal{T}. \forall e \in E. \forall x, n. \mathsf{op}(e) = \mathtt{read}(x, n) \wedge \{f \mid \mathsf{op}(f) = \_(x, \_) \wedge f \xrightarrow{\mathsf{po}} e\} \neq \emptyset \implies$ $\mathsf{op}(\max_{\mathsf{po}}\{f \mid \mathsf{op}(f) = \_(x, \_) \wedge f \xrightarrow{\mathsf{po}} e\}) = \_(x, n)$ (INT)	$\mathsf{SO} \subseteq \mathsf{VIS}$ (SESSION) $\mathsf{CO} \,;\, \mathsf{VIS} \subseteq \mathsf{VIS}$ (PREFIX)
$\forall T \in \mathcal{T}. \forall x, n. T \vdash \mathtt{read}(x, n) \implies \max_{\mathsf{CO}}(\mathsf{VIS}^{-1}(T) \cap \mathsf{WriteTx}_x) \vdash \mathtt{write}(x, n)$ (EXT)	$\mathsf{CO} = \mathsf{VIS}$ (TOTALVIS)
$\forall T, S \in \mathcal{T}. \forall x. (T, S \in \mathsf{WriteTx}_x \wedge T \neq S) \implies (T \xrightarrow{\mathsf{VIS}} S \vee S \xrightarrow{\mathsf{VIS}} T)$ (NOCONFLICT)	

Figure 1: Axioms constraining an abstract execution $(\mathcal{T}, \mathsf{SO}, \mathsf{VIS}, \mathsf{CO})$.

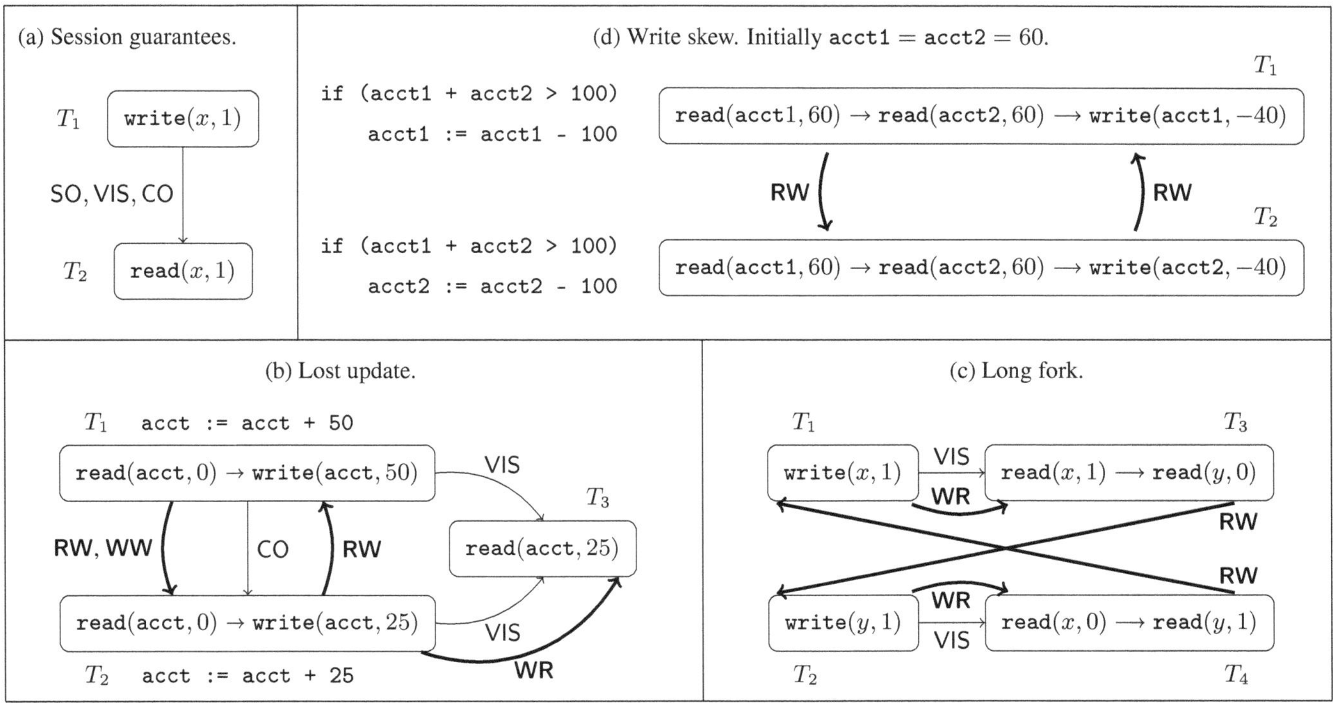

Figure 2: Abstract executions illustrating SI and serializability. Boxes represent transactions, and arrows inside boxes represent the program order. We omit irrelevant CO edges. We also omit a special transaction that writes initial versions of all objects and precedes all the other transactions in VIS and CO. The bold edges are explained in §3.

We write $T \xrightarrow{\mathsf{VIS}} S$ and $(T, S) \in \mathsf{VIS}$ interchangeably, and similarly for other relations. For $\mathcal{H} = (\mathcal{T}, \mathsf{SO})$ we shorten $(\mathcal{T}, \mathsf{SO}, \mathsf{VIS}, \mathsf{CO})$ to $(\mathcal{H}, \mathsf{VIS}, \mathsf{CO})$. In terms of the SI concurrency-control algorithm sketched in §1, $T \xrightarrow{\mathsf{VIS}} S$ means that the writes done by the transaction T are included into the snapshot taken by the transaction S; $T \xrightarrow{\mathsf{CO}} S$ means that T commits earlier than S. The constraint $\mathsf{VIS} \subseteq \mathsf{CO}$ ensures that the snapshot taken by a transaction may only include previously committed transactions. SI or serializability allow those histories that can be extended to an abstract execution satisfying certain ***consistency axioms*** from Figure 1, which specify the corresponding guarantees about transaction processing.

DEFINITION 4. *The sets of executions and histories* ***allowed by (strong session) SI and serializability*** *are:*

$$\mathsf{ExecSI} = \{\mathcal{X} \mid \mathcal{X} \models \text{INT} \wedge \text{EXT} \wedge \text{SESSION} \wedge \text{PREFIX} \wedge \text{NOCONFLICT}\};$$
$$\mathsf{ExecSER} = \{\mathcal{X} \mid \mathcal{X} \models \text{INT} \wedge \text{EXT} \wedge \text{SESSION} \wedge \text{TOTALVIS}\};$$
$$\mathsf{HistSI} = \{\mathcal{H} \mid \exists \mathsf{VIS}, \mathsf{CO}. (\mathcal{H}, \mathsf{VIS}, \mathsf{CO}) \in \mathsf{ExecSI}\};$$
$$\mathsf{HistSER} = \{\mathcal{H} \mid \exists \mathsf{VIS}, \mathsf{CO}. (\mathcal{H}, \mathsf{VIS}, \mathsf{CO}) \in \mathsf{ExecSER}\}.$$

We now explain the axioms in Figure 1, as well as anomalies that SI allows or disallows; the latter are summarised in Figure 2. We use the following notation. For a set A and a total order $R \subseteq A \times A$, we let $\max_R(A)$ be the element $a \in A$ such that $\forall b \in A. a = b \vee (b, a) \in R$; if $A = \emptyset$, then $\max_R(A)$ is undefined. In the following, the use of $\max_R(A)$ in an expression implicitly assumes that it is defined. We define $\min_R(A)$ similarly. For a relation $R \subseteq A \times A$ and an element $a \in A$, we let $R^{-1}(a) = \{b \mid (b, a) \in R\}$. We define the sequential composition of relations R_1 and R_2 as

$$R_1 \,;\, R_2 = \{(a, b) \mid \exists c. (a, c) \in R_1 \wedge (c, b) \in R_2\}.$$

We write _ for a value that is irrelevant and implicitly existentially quantified.

The INT and EXT axioms in Figure 1 ensure that a transaction reads from a snapshot of object states and its own writes. The ***internal consistency axiom*** INT ensures that a read event e on an object x returns the same value as the last write to or a read from x preceding e in the same transaction. If a read is not preceded in the same transaction by an operation on the same object, then its value is determined in terms of writes by other transactions using the ***external consistency axiom*** EXT. For $T = (E, \mathsf{po})$, we let $T \vdash \mathtt{write}(x, n)$ if T writes to x and the last value written is n:

$$\mathsf{op}(\max_{\mathsf{po}}\{e \mid \mathsf{op}(e) = \mathtt{write}(x, \_)\}) = \mathtt{write}(x, n).$$

We let $T \vdash \mathtt{read}(x, n)$ if T reads from x before writing to it and n is the value returned by the first such read:

$$\mathsf{op}(\min_{\mathsf{po}}\{e \mid \mathsf{op}(e) = \_(x, \_)\}) = \mathtt{read}(x, n).$$

We also let $\mathsf{WriteTx}_x = \{T \mid T \vdash \mathtt{write}(x, \_)\}$. Then EXT ensures that, if a transaction T reads an object x before writing to it, then the value read is determined by the transactions that are included into T's snapshot according to VIS and that wrote to x; T reads the value written by the transaction from this set that committed last according to CO. For simplicity, we consider only executions where the above set is always non-empty; this can be ensured by introducing a special transaction that writes initial values of all objects. The executions in Figures 2(a) and 2(b) satisfy EXT.

Our specification determines the snapshot that a transaction reads from based on an arbitrary visibility relation and does not require the snapshot to be "latest"; this is similar to so-called ***generalised SI*** [18]. However, following strong session SI [13, 14], the SESSION axiom requires the snapshot to include the effects of all preceding transactions in the same session. For example, in the execution in Figure 2(a), the session order between T_1 and T_2 induces a visibility edge according to SESSION.

The PREFIX axiom ensures that, if the snapshot taken by a transaction T includes a (committed) transaction S, then this snapshot also includes all transactions that committed before S. Note that PREFIX and the property $\mathsf{VIS} \subseteq \mathsf{CO}$ in Definition 4 imply that VIS is transitive. PREFIX disallows the ***long fork*** anomaly shown in Figure 2(c), which is allowed by some weakening of SI (such as parallel SI [32]). There transactions T_1 and T_2 concurrently write to objects x and y. Transaction T_3 sees the write by T_1, but not the write by T_2; conversely, transaction T_4 sees the write by T_2, but not the write by T_1. Thus, from the perspectives of T_3 and T_4, the writes of T_1 and T_2 happen in different orders. PREFIX disallows any execution with the history in Figure 2(c), because in such an execution T_1 and T_2 have to be related by CO one way or another; but then by PREFIX, either T_4 has to observe the write to x or T_3 has to observe the write to y.

The axioms explained so far do not prevent the ***lost update*** anomaly, illustrated by the execution in Figure 2(b). This execution could arise from the code in the figure that uses transactions T_1 and T_2 to make deposits into an account. The two transactions read the initial balance of the account and concurrently modify it, resulting in one deposit getting lost. This anomaly is disallowed by the NOCONFLICT axiom: if two distinct transactions write to the same object, then one of them has to be aware of the other. This axiom rules out any execution with the history in Figure 2(b): it forces T_1 and T_2 to be ordered by VIS, so that they cannot both read 0 from `acct`. In the SI concurrency control this is ensured by the write-conflict detection check (§1).

The set HistSI (Definition 4) defined using the consistency axioms explained so far is exactly the one produced by the SI concurrency-control algorithm [10]. The axioms allow the execution in Figure 2(d) with the characteristic SI anomaly of ***write skew*** (§1), disallowed by serializability. We formalise the latter by the axiom TOTALVIS, which requires visibility to totally order all transactions. Then the axioms INT and EXT ensure that the transactions are processed according to the usual sequential semantics. We thus have $\mathsf{HistSER} \subset \mathsf{HistSI}$.

3. DEPENDENCY GRAPHS

From an abstract execution we can extract several kinds of dependencies between its transactions, which are used in consistency model specifications in the style of Adya et al. [2, 3].

DEFINITION 5. *Let $\mathcal{X} = (\mathcal{H}, \mathsf{VIS}, \mathsf{CO})$ be an execution. For $x \in \mathsf{Obj}$, we define the following relations on $\mathcal{T}_\mathcal{H}$:*

- ***read dependency**: $T \xrightarrow{\mathsf{WR}_\mathcal{X}(x)} S \iff$ $S \vdash \mathtt{read}(x, \_) \wedge T = \max_{\mathsf{CO}}(\mathsf{VIS}^{-1}(S) \cap \mathsf{WriteTx}_x)$;*
- ***write dependency**: $T \xrightarrow{\mathsf{WW}_\mathcal{X}(x)} S \iff$ $T \xrightarrow{\mathsf{CO}} S \wedge T, S \in \mathsf{WriteTx}_x$;*
- ***anti-dependency**: $T \xrightarrow{\mathsf{RW}_\mathcal{X}(x)} S \iff$ $T \neq S \wedge \exists T'.\, T' \xrightarrow{\mathsf{WR}_\mathcal{X}(x)} T \wedge T' \xrightarrow{\mathsf{WW}_\mathcal{X}(x)} S$.*

Informally, $T \xrightarrow{\mathsf{WR}_\mathcal{X}(x)} S$ means that S reads T's write to x (cf. the EXT axiom in Figure 1); $T \xrightarrow{\mathsf{WW}_\mathcal{X}(x)} S$ means that S overwrites T's write to x; $T \xrightarrow{\mathsf{RW}_\mathcal{X}(x)} S$ means that S overwrites the write to x read by T. For example, the dependencies of the executions in Figures 2(b), 2(d) and 2(c) are shown there with bold arrows (keep in mind that the pictures omit a special initialisation transaction). We often abuse notation and use the symbol $\mathsf{WR}_\mathcal{X}$ to also denote the relation $\bigcup_{x \in \mathsf{Obj}} \mathsf{WR}_\mathcal{X}(x) \subseteq \mathcal{T}_\mathcal{H} \times \mathcal{T}_\mathcal{H}$, and similarly for $\mathsf{WW}_\mathcal{X}$ and $\mathsf{RW}_\mathcal{X}$.

A key goal of this paper is to characterise SI solely in terms of dependencies: we want to determine whether SI allows a given history by looking for appropriate dependencies between its transactions rather than visibility and commit orders, as in Definition 4. To this end, we extend histories to *dependency graphs* (aka direct serialization graphs) [2], which include relations representing the dependencies.

DEFINITION 6. *A **dependency graph** is a tuple $\mathcal{G} = (\mathcal{T}, \mathsf{SO}, \mathsf{WR}, \mathsf{WW}, \mathsf{RW})$, where $(\mathcal{T}, \mathsf{SO})$ is a history and*

- *$\mathsf{WR} : \mathsf{Obj} \to 2^{\mathcal{T} \times \mathcal{T}}$ is such that:*
  - $\forall T, S \in \mathcal{T}.\, \forall x.\, T \xrightarrow{\mathsf{WR}(x)} S \implies$ $\exists n.\, T \neq S \wedge T \vdash \mathtt{write}(x, n) \wedge S \vdash \mathtt{read}(x, n)$;
  - $\forall S \in \mathcal{T}.\, \forall x.\, S \vdash \mathtt{read}(x, \_) \implies \exists T.\, T \xrightarrow{\mathsf{WR}(x)} S$;
  - $\forall T, T', S \in \mathcal{T}.\, \forall x.\, (T \xrightarrow{\mathsf{WR}(x)} S \wedge T' \xrightarrow{\mathsf{WR}(x)} S) \implies$ $T = T'$.
- *$\mathsf{WW} : \mathsf{Obj} \to 2^{\mathcal{T} \times \mathcal{T}}$ is such that for every $x \in \mathsf{Obj}$, $\mathsf{WW}(x)$ is a total order on the set $\mathsf{WriteTx}_x$;*
- *$\mathsf{RW} : \mathsf{Obj} \to 2^{\mathcal{T} \times \mathcal{T}}$ is derived from WR and WW as in Definition 5.*

PROPOSITION 7. *For any $\mathcal{X} \in \mathsf{ExecSI}$, $\mathsf{graph}(\mathcal{X}) = (\mathcal{T}_\mathcal{X}, \mathsf{SO}_\mathcal{X}, \mathsf{WR}_\mathcal{X}, \mathsf{WW}_\mathcal{X}, \mathsf{RW}_\mathcal{X})$ is a dependency graph.*

Note that the constraints on WR in Definition 6 ensure that it uniquely determines the values read by transactions. For $\mathcal{H} = (\mathcal{T}, \mathsf{SO})$ we write $(\mathcal{H}, \mathsf{WR}, \mathsf{WW}, \mathsf{RW})$ for $(\mathcal{T}, \mathsf{SO}, \mathsf{WR}, \mathsf{WW}, \mathsf{RW})$.

We write $\mathcal{T} \models$ INT if a set of transactions $\mathcal{T}$ satisfies the internal consistency axiom INT in Figure 1. (Strong session) serializability can be characterised by the set of acyclic dependency graphs with internally consistent transactions [2].

THEOREM 8. *Let*

$$\mathsf{GraphSER} = \{\mathcal{G} \mid (\mathcal{T}_\mathcal{G} \models \text{INT}) \wedge ((\mathsf{SO}_\mathcal{G} \cup \mathsf{WR}_\mathcal{G} \cup \mathsf{WW}_\mathcal{G} \cup \mathsf{RW}_\mathcal{G}) \text{ is acyclic})\}.$$

Then

$$\mathsf{HistSER} = \{\mathcal{H} \mid \exists \mathsf{WR}, \mathsf{WW}, \mathsf{RW}.\ (\mathcal{H}, \mathsf{WR}, \mathsf{WW}, \mathsf{RW}) \in \mathsf{GraphSER}\}.$$

For example, the histories in Figures 2(b), 2(d) and 2(c) are not serializable, and they cannot be extended to acyclic dependency graphs; in particular, the graphs shown in the figures with bold edges satisfy the conditions of Definition 6, but contain cycles. We now set out to find a characterisation of the above form for SI.

4. SI CHARACTERISATION

For a set $\mathcal{T}$ and a relation $R \subseteq \mathcal{T} \times \mathcal{T}$ let $R? = R \cup \{(T, T) \mid T \in \mathcal{T}\}$. We show that (strong session) SI is characterised by dependency graphs that contain only cycles with at least two adjacent anti-dependency edges.

THEOREM 9. *Let*

$$\mathsf{GraphSI} = \{\mathcal{G} \mid (\mathcal{T}_{\mathcal{G}} \models \textsc{Int}) \wedge (((\mathsf{SO}_{\mathcal{G}} \cup \mathsf{WR}_{\mathcal{G}} \cup \mathsf{WW}_{\mathcal{G}}) \,;\, \mathsf{RW}_{\mathcal{G}}?) \textit{ is acyclic})\}.$$

Then

$$\mathsf{HistSI} = \{\mathcal{H} \mid \exists \mathsf{WR}, \mathsf{WW}, \mathsf{RW}.\ (\mathcal{H}, \mathsf{WR}, \mathsf{WW}, \mathsf{RW}) \in \mathsf{GraphSI}\}.$$

According to the theorem, to determine whether a particular history is allowed by SI, we can look for dependencies that extend it to a graph in GraphSI. As we demonstrate in §5 and §6, this way of defining SI is particularly suitable for developing static analyses for this consistency model. The history in Figure 2(d) is allowed by SI, and indeed the dependency graph shown in the figure contains only cycles with two adjacent anti-dependencies (e.g., $T_1 \xrightarrow{\mathsf{RW}} T_2 \xrightarrow{\mathsf{RW}} T_1$). In contrast, the histories in Figures 2(b) and 2(c) are not allowed by SI, and they cannot be extended to graphs where every cycle has at least two adjacent anti-dependencies. In particular, the graphs shown in the figures contains cycles without these: e.g., $T_1 \xrightarrow{\mathsf{WW}} T_2 \xrightarrow{\mathsf{RW}} T_1$ in Figure 2(b) and $T_1 \xrightarrow{\mathsf{WR}} T_3 \xrightarrow{\mathsf{RW}} T_2 \xrightarrow{\mathsf{WR}} T_4 \xrightarrow{\mathsf{RW}} T_1$ in Figure 2(c).

To prove Theorem 9, we prove a slightly stronger result, showing that we can establish a correspondence between executions in ExecSI and graphs in GraphSI that preserves histories and dependencies.

THEOREM 10.
(i) ***Soundness:*** $\forall \mathcal{G} \in \mathsf{GraphSI}.\ \exists \mathcal{X} \in \mathsf{ExecSI}.\ \mathsf{graph}(\mathcal{X}) = \mathcal{G}$.
(ii) ***Completeness:*** $\forall \mathcal{X} \in \mathsf{ExecSI}.\ \mathsf{graph}(\mathcal{X}) \in \mathsf{GraphSI}$.

As we explain in §7, the easier completeness direction of this theorem actually follows from existing results [19]. Our main technical contribution is the more challenging proof of the soundness direction, which is required for the static analyses that we propose (§5 and §6). We present this proof first.

The main challenge is to construct a total commit order in the desired execution $\mathcal{X}$ from the dependencies given by $\mathcal{G}$ while satisfying the SI axioms (Definition 4). We do this incrementally; at intermediate stages of the construction we get structures similar to abstract executions, but where the commit order can be partial.

DEFINITION 11. *A tuple* $\mathcal{P} = (\mathcal{T}, \mathsf{SO}, \mathsf{VIS}, \mathsf{CO})$ *is a* ***pre-execution*** *if it satisfies all the conditions of Definition 3, except* CO *is a strict partial order that may not be total. We let* PreExecSI *be the set of pre-executions satisfying the SI axioms (Figure 1):*

$$\mathsf{PreExecSI} = \{\mathcal{P} \mid \mathcal{P} \models \textsc{Int} \wedge \textsc{Ext} \wedge \textsc{Session} \wedge \textsc{Prefix} \wedge \textsc{NoConflict}\}.$$

$$\begin{cases} \mathsf{SO} \cup \mathsf{WR} \cup \mathsf{WW} \subseteq \mathsf{VIS} & \text{(S1)} \\ \mathsf{CO} \,;\, \mathsf{VIS} \subseteq \mathsf{VIS} & \text{(S2)} \\ \mathsf{VIS} \subseteq \mathsf{CO} & \text{(S3)} \\ \mathsf{CO} \,;\, \mathsf{CO} \subseteq \mathsf{CO} & \text{(S4)} \\ \mathsf{VIS} \,;\, \mathsf{RW} \subseteq \mathsf{CO} & \text{(S5)} \end{cases}$$

Figure 3: Requirements on a pre-execution $\mathcal{P} = (\mathcal{H}, \mathsf{VIS}, \mathsf{CO})$ constructed from a dependency graph $\mathcal{G} = (\mathcal{H}, \mathsf{WR}, \mathsf{WW}, \mathsf{RW})$.

Thus, an execution is a pre-execution whose commit order is total. In the following, we apply the `graph` function of §3 also to pre-executions; for $\mathcal{P} \in \mathsf{PreExecSI}$, $\mathsf{graph}(\mathcal{P})$ is indeed a dependency graph.

We first obtain auxiliary results that, given a dependency graph $\mathcal{G} = (\mathcal{T}, \mathsf{SO}, \mathsf{WR}, \mathsf{WW}, \mathsf{RW}) \in \mathsf{GraphSI}$, allow us to construct a pre-execution $\mathcal{P} = (\mathcal{T}, \mathsf{SO}, \mathsf{VIS}, \mathsf{CO}) \in \mathsf{PreExecSI}$ such that $\mathsf{graph}(\mathcal{P}) = \mathcal{G}$. Later we show how to extend $\mathcal{P}$ to a desired execution $\mathcal{X} \in \mathsf{ExecSI}$. We start by restating the requirements on the pre-execution $\mathcal{P}$ in a way more suitable for guiding its construction; these are given by the system of inequalities in Figure 3. First, to ensure $\mathsf{graph}(\mathcal{P}) = \mathcal{G}$, by Definition 5 at the very least we must have $\mathsf{WR} \cup \mathsf{WW} \subseteq \mathsf{VIS}$. For $\mathcal{P}$ to satisfy the SESSION axiom we must also have $\mathsf{SO} \subseteq \mathsf{VIS}$. These two observations motivate (S1). This inequality also implies that $\mathcal{P}$ satisfies NOCONFLICT, since according to Definition 5, WW is total over transactions that write to a given object. Inequality (S2) is equivalent to PREFIX, and inequality (S3) states a relationship between VIS and CO inherited by Definition 11 from Definition 3. Inequality (S4) requires CO to be transitive; (S2) and (S3) ensure that so is VIS.

As we now explain, (S5) ensures the axiom EXT. Consider the dependency graph $\mathcal{G} \in \mathsf{GraphSI}$ in Figure 4, which we use as our running example in this section and in §5. Its transactions could arise from the programs, also shown in the figure, that make a transfer between two accounts and query their balances or the sum thereof. The transactions arising from `lookup1` and `lookup2` see the initial state of the database, while the transactions arising from `lookupAll` see its state in the middle of a transfer. The VIS and CO relations shown by the solid arrows give a pre-execution satisfying inequalities (S1)-(S4) and, in fact, all the SI axioms. Suppose we want to construct a pre-execution with a bigger CO by adding an edge $T \xrightarrow{\mathsf{CO}} S'$ (shown dotted). Since $S' \xrightarrow{\mathsf{VIS}} S$, for the resulting pre-execution to satisfy PREFIX we also need to add an edge $T \xrightarrow{\mathsf{VIS}} S$. But then the pre-execution violates EXT: S sees the write to `acct2` by T, but reads the value from the initialisation transaction (elided from Figure 4) that writes 0 to `acct2` and precedes T in CO and WW; the latter fact is witnessed by the edge $S \xrightarrow{\mathsf{RW}} T$. On the other hand, adding an edge $S' \xrightarrow{\mathsf{CO}} T$ (shown dashed), which belongs to VIS ; RW, does not violate EXT. This example illustrates a general pattern. First, as the following lemma shows, (S5) must hold in any SI execution.

LEMMA 12. $\forall \mathcal{X} \in \mathsf{ExecSI}.\ \mathsf{VIS}_{\mathcal{X}} \,;\, \mathsf{RW}_{\mathcal{X}} \subseteq \mathsf{CO}_{\mathcal{X}}$.

Conversely, the system of inequalities in Figure 3 can be used to ensure that a pre-execution $\mathcal{P} = (\mathcal{T}, \mathsf{SO}, \mathsf{VIS}, \mathsf{CO})$ satisfies EXT and has other desired properties.

LEMMA 13. *Let* $\mathcal{G} = (\mathcal{T}, \mathsf{SO}, \mathsf{WR}, \mathsf{WW}, \mathsf{RW})$ *be a dependency graph such that* $\mathcal{T} \models \textsc{Int}$ *and* $\mathsf{VIS}, \mathsf{CO} \subseteq \mathcal{T} \times \mathcal{T}$ *be acyclic relations satisfying the system of inequalities in Figure*

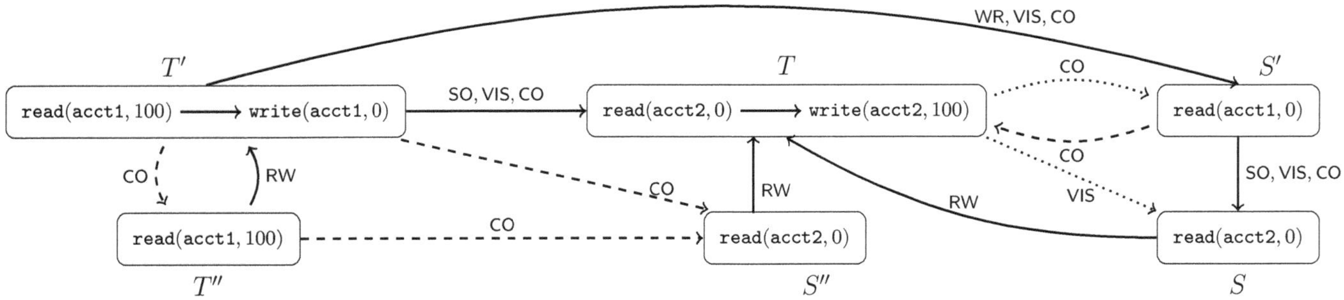


```
T',T: session transfer   { tx { acct1 = acct1 - 100 }; tx { acct2 = acct2 + 100 } }
  T'': session lookup1    { tx { return acct1 } }
  S'': session lookup2    { tx { return acct2 } }
S',S: session lookupAll  { tx { var1 = acct1 }; tx { var2 = acct2 }; return var1 + var2 }
```

Figure 4: An illustration of constructing an execution from a dependency graph (§4) and splicing an execution (§5). We omit an initialisation transaction that sets $\texttt{acct1} = 100$ **and** $\texttt{acct2} = 0$**.**

3. *Then* $\mathcal{P} = (\mathcal{T}, \mathsf{SO}, \mathsf{VIS}, \mathsf{CO})$ *is a pre-execution such that* $\mathcal{P} \in \mathsf{PreExecSI}$ *and* $\mathsf{graph}(\mathcal{P}) = \mathcal{G}$.

The proof of Lemma 12 depends on the following characterisation of anti-dependencies in terms of visibility edges.

PROPOSITION 14.

$$\forall \mathcal{X} \in \mathsf{ExecSI}.\, \forall T, S \in \mathcal{T}_{\mathcal{X}}.\, S \xrightarrow{\mathsf{RW}_{\mathcal{X}}} T \iff S \neq T \wedge$$
$$\exists x.\, S \vdash \texttt{read}(x, \_) \wedge T \vdash \texttt{write}(x, \_) \wedge \neg(T \xrightarrow{\mathsf{VIS}_{\mathcal{X}}} S).$$

Informally, if we had $S \xrightarrow{\mathsf{RW}_{\mathcal{X}}} T$ and $T \xrightarrow{\mathsf{VIS}_{\mathcal{X}}} S$, then S would have to read a value of x at least as up-to-date as that written by T, contradicting the definition of $\mathsf{RW}_{\mathcal{X}}$.

PROOF OF LEMMA 12. Consider $\mathcal{X} \in \mathsf{ExecSI}$ and $T, S', S \in \mathcal{T}_{\mathcal{X}}$ such that $S' \xrightarrow{\mathsf{VIS}_{\mathcal{X}}} S \xrightarrow{\mathsf{RW}_{\mathcal{X}}} T$. If $T = S'$, then $S' \xrightarrow{\mathsf{VIS}_{\mathcal{X}}} S \xrightarrow{\mathsf{RW}_{\mathcal{X}}} S'$, contradicting Proposition 14. If $T \xrightarrow{\mathsf{CO}_{\mathcal{X}}} S'$ (see Figure 4), then by PREFIX we get $T \xrightarrow{\mathsf{VIS}_{\mathcal{X}}} S$, contradicting Proposition 14. Then, since $\mathsf{CO}_{\mathcal{X}}$ is total, we must have $S' \xrightarrow{\mathsf{CO}_{\mathcal{X}}} T$. □

PROOF OF LEMMA 13. We only prove that $\mathcal{P} \models \text{EXT}$ and $\mathsf{WR}_{\mathcal{P}} = \mathsf{WR}$; discharging the other obligations is straightforward. Consider $S \in \mathcal{T}$ such that $S \vdash \texttt{read}(x, n)$. Then there exists a unique T' such that $T' \xrightarrow{\mathsf{WR}(x)} S$. Let $T = \max_{\mathsf{CO}}(\mathsf{VIS}^{-1}(S) \cap \mathsf{WriteTx}_x)$. This is defined because: CO is acyclic; by (S1) and (S3) we have $\mathsf{WW} \subseteq \mathsf{CO}$, so that CO is total over $\mathsf{WriteTx}_x$; and by (S1) we have $\mathsf{WR} \subseteq \mathsf{VIS}$, so that $T' \in \mathsf{VIS}^{-1}(S) \cap \mathsf{WriteTx}_x$. We now show that $T = T'$, which entails the required.

Assume the contrary: $T \neq T'$. We have $T, T' \in \mathsf{VIS}^{-1}(S) \cap \mathsf{WriteTx}_x$. Hence, T and T' are related by WW. Since $\mathsf{WW} \subseteq \mathsf{CO}$, they are related in the same way by the acyclic $\mathsf{CO}(x)$. Then by the definition of T we must have $T' \xrightarrow{\mathsf{CO}(x)} T$ and $T' \xrightarrow{\mathsf{WW}} T$. From the latter and $T' \xrightarrow{\mathsf{WR}(x)} S$ we get $S \xrightarrow{\mathsf{RW}} T$. But $T \xrightarrow{\mathsf{VIS}} S$, so from (S5) we get $T \xrightarrow{\mathsf{CO}} T$. This contradicts the assumption that CO is acyclic. Hence, we must have $T = T'$. □

According to Lemma 13, to construct a desired pre-execution $\mathcal{P} = (\mathcal{T}, \mathsf{SO}, \mathsf{VIS}, \mathsf{CO}) \in \mathsf{PreExecSI}$ from a dependency graph $\mathcal{G} = (\mathcal{T}, \mathsf{SO}, \mathsf{WR}, \mathsf{WW}, \mathsf{RW})$, it is sufficient to find a solution to the system of inequalities in Figure 3 in terms of *acyclic* relations VIS and CO. This is not completely trivial because of the recursive nature of the inequalities: according to them, adding more edges into VIS forces adding more edges into CO and vice versa, increasing the risk of tying a cycle. Our insight is to look for the solution that is *smallest* and, hence, least likely to contain cycles. The following lemma gives a closed form for this solution. In anticipation of using the lemma when extending a pre-execution to an execution, we state it in a generalised form that gives the smallest solution where CO contains at least a given set of edges R. We use $^+$ and * to denote the transitive closure and the transitive and reflexive closure of a given relation.

LEMMA 15. *Let* $\mathcal{G} = (\mathcal{T}, \mathsf{SO}, \mathsf{WR}, \mathsf{WW}, \mathsf{RW})$ *be a dependency graph. For any* $R \subseteq \mathcal{T} \times \mathcal{T}$, *the relations*

$$\begin{aligned} \mathsf{VIS} &= (((\mathsf{SO} \cup \mathsf{WR} \cup \mathsf{WW})\, ;\, \mathsf{RW}?) \cup R)^*\, ; \\ &\quad (\mathsf{SO} \cup \mathsf{WR} \cup \mathsf{WW}); \\ \mathsf{CO} &= (((\mathsf{SO} \cup \mathsf{WR} \cup \mathsf{WW})\, ;\, \mathsf{RW}?) \cup R)^+ \end{aligned} \tag{1}$$

are a solution to the system of inequalities in Figure 3. They also are the smallest solution to the system for which $\mathsf{CO} \supseteq R$*: for any other solution* $(\mathsf{VIS}', \mathsf{CO}')$ *with* $\mathsf{CO}' \supseteq R$ *we have* $\mathsf{VIS} \subseteq \mathsf{VIS}'$ *and* $\mathsf{CO} \subseteq \mathsf{CO}'$.

In particular, for $R = \emptyset$, Lemma 15 gives the smallest solution $(\mathsf{VIS}_0, \mathsf{CO}_0)$ to the system of inequalities in Figure 3.

If $\mathcal{G} \in \mathsf{GraphSI}$, then CO_0 is acyclic, and by (S3), so is VIS_0 (in fact, Lemma 15 is our motivation for defining $\mathsf{GraphSI}$ the way we did). Hence, by Lemma 13, $\mathcal{P}_0 = (\mathcal{T}, \mathsf{SO}, \mathsf{VIS}_0, \mathsf{CO}_0)$ is a pre-execution such that $\mathcal{P}_0 \in \mathsf{PreExecSI}$ and $\mathsf{graph}(\mathcal{P}_0) = \mathcal{G}$, which is what we originally set out to construct. We now proceed to prove Theorem 10(i) by extending the pre-execution $\mathcal{P}_0$ to an execution $\mathcal{X} \in \mathsf{ExecSI}$.

PROOF OF THEOREM 10(I). Assume $\mathcal{G} = (\mathcal{T}, \mathsf{SO}, \mathsf{WR}, \mathsf{WW}, \mathsf{RW}) \in \mathsf{GraphSI}$. To construct $\mathcal{X}$, we define a sequence of pre-executions $\{\mathcal{P}_i = (\mathcal{T}, \mathsf{SO}, \mathsf{VIS}_i, \mathsf{CO}_i)\}_{i=0}^{n}$ for some $n \geq 0$ and let $\mathcal{X} = \mathcal{P}_n$. The sequence is such that $\mathsf{VIS}_i \subseteq \mathsf{VIS}_{i+1}$ and $\mathsf{CO}_i \subset \mathsf{CO}_{i+1}$ for $i = 0..(n-1)$; furthermore, CO_n is total, so that $\mathcal{P}_n$ is an execution. That is, on every step of our construction we add edges to the commit order until it becomes total. Each pair $(\mathsf{VIS}_i, \mathsf{CO}_i)$ gives an acyclic solution to the system in Figure 3. Then by Lemma 13, $\mathcal{P}_i \in \mathsf{PreExecSI}$ and $\mathsf{graph}(\mathcal{P}_i) = \mathcal{G}$. In particular, $\mathcal{P}_n \in \mathsf{ExecSI}$ and $\mathsf{graph}(\mathcal{P}_n) = \mathcal{G}$, as required.

We start the construction of the sequence by taking as $\mathcal{P}_0$ the pre-execution that we constructed above. For example, for the dependency graph in Figure 4, VIS_0 and CO_0 consist of the solid edges in the figure and the dashed edge $S' \xrightarrow{\mathsf{CO}} T$. If the relation CO_0 is not total, then we pick an arbitrary pair of transactions (T_1, S_1) unrelated by CO_0 and construct VIS_1 and CO_1 as the smallest solution to the system of inequalities in Figure 3 such that $\mathsf{CO}_1 \supseteq \{(T_1, S_1)\}$. By Lemma 15 this solution is given by (1) for $R = \{(T_1, S_1)\}$. For example, in Figure 3 the transactions T' and T'' are unrelated by the commit order. If we pick as (T_1, S_1) the pair (T', T'') in Figure 4, then we get $\mathsf{VIS}_1 = \mathsf{VIS}_0$, and $\mathsf{CO}_1 = \mathsf{CO}_0 \cup \{(T', T'')\}$. In general, the construction continues in the same way: while CO_i is not total, we pick an arbitrary pair of transactions (T_i, S_i) unrelated by CO_i and force CO_{i+1} to include it. In our example, CO_1 does not relate the transactions T'' and S''. By picking as (T_2, S_2) the pair (T'', S''), we construct VIS_2 and CO_2 by letting $R = \{(T', T''), (T'', S'')\}$ in (1); this corresponds to all the solid and dashed edges in Figure 4. Note that CO_2 also includes the edge (T', S''). Since CO_2 is total in this example, the construction terminates: $\mathcal{X} = \mathcal{P}_2$.

Formally, in addition to VIS_i and CO_i we construct sets $R_i = \{(T_k, S_k) \mid k = 1..i\}$, $i = 0..n$ that accumulate the edges enforced in the commit order at every step. The relations VIS_i and CO_i and the sets R_i are defined recursively as follows: we let VIS_i and CO_i be defined by (1) for $R = R_i$; we let $R_0 = \emptyset$ and $R_{i+1} = R_i \cup \{(T_i, S_i)\}$, where (T_i, S_i) is an arbitrary pair of transactions unrelated by CO_i; such a pair must exist if CO_i is not total. By Lemma 15, each $(\mathsf{VIS}_i, \mathsf{CO}_i)$ is a solution to the system of inequalities in Figure 3. It is easy to check that $\mathsf{CO}_{i+1} = (\mathsf{CO}_i \cup \{(T_i, S_i)\})^+$, $i = 0..(n-1)$. Since CO_0 is acyclic, by the choice of the edges (T_i, S_i) it follows that CO_i, $i = 1..n$ are acyclic as well. Hence, the sequence $\{\mathcal{P}_i\}_{i=0}^n$ constructed above satisfies the properties stated at the beginning of the proof, as required. □

PROOF OF THEOREM 10(II). Consider $\mathcal{X} = (\mathcal{T}, \mathsf{SO}, \mathsf{VIS}, \mathsf{CO}) \in \mathsf{ExecSI}$. As follows from Lemma 12, VIS and CO give a solution to the system of inequalities of Figure 3 for $\mathsf{WR} = \mathsf{WR}_{\mathcal{X}}$, $\mathsf{WW} = \mathsf{WW}_{\mathcal{X}}$, $\mathsf{RW} = \mathsf{RW}_{\mathcal{X}}$. We now apply Lemma 15 for $R = \emptyset$; the minimality of the solution given by Lemma 15 implies that $((\mathsf{SO} \cup \mathsf{WR} \cup \mathsf{WW}) \,;\, \mathsf{RW}?)^+ \subseteq \mathsf{CO}$. Then $((\mathsf{SO} \cup \mathsf{WR} \cup \mathsf{WW}) \,;\, \mathsf{RW}?)^+$ is acyclic because so is CO. This establishes $\mathsf{graph}(\mathcal{X}) \in \mathsf{GraphSI}$. □

5. TRANSACTION CHOPPING UNDER SI

In this section, we exploit our characterisation of SI in terms of dependency graphs to derive a static analysis that checks when transactions in an application executing under SI can be ***chopped*** [30] into sessions of smaller transactions without introducing new behaviours (the sessions are also called ***chains*** in this context [38]). To this end, the analysis must check that any SI execution of the application with chopped transactions can be *spliced* into an SI execution that has the same operations as the original one, but where all operations from each session are executed inside a single transaction. We first establish a *dynamic chopping criterion* that checks whether a single SI execution, represented by a dependency graph, is spliceable. From this we then derive a static analysis that checks whether this is the case for all executions produced by a given chopped application.

For a history $\mathcal{H}$, let $\approx_{\mathcal{H}} = \mathsf{SO}_{\mathcal{H}} \cup \mathsf{SO}_{\mathcal{H}}^{-1} \cup \{(T, T) \mid T \in \mathcal{T}_{\mathcal{H}}\}$ be the equivalence relation grouping transactions from the same session. We let $\boxed{T}_{\mathcal{H}}$ be the result of splicing all transactions in the session to which T belongs in $\mathcal{H}$ into a single transaction: $\boxed{T}_{\mathcal{H}} = (E, \mathsf{po})$, where $E = (\bigcup\{E_S \mid S \approx_{\mathcal{H}} T\})$ and

$$\mathsf{po} = \{(e, f) \mid (\exists S.\, e, f \in E_S \wedge e \xrightarrow{\mathsf{po}_S} f \wedge S \approx_{\mathcal{H}} T) \vee (\exists S, S'.\, e \in E_S \wedge f \in E_{S'} \wedge S \xrightarrow{\mathsf{SO}_{\mathcal{H}}} S' \wedge S' \approx_{\mathcal{H}} T)\}.$$

We let $\mathsf{splice}(\mathcal{H})$ be the history resulting from splicing all sessions in a history $\mathcal{H}$: $\mathsf{splice}(\mathcal{H}) = \left(\left\{\boxed{T}_{\mathcal{H}} \mid T \in \mathcal{T}_{\mathcal{H}}\right\}, \emptyset\right)$. A dependency graph $\mathcal{G} \in \mathsf{GraphSI}$ is ***spliceable*** if there exists a dependency graph $\mathcal{G}' \in \mathsf{GraphSI}$ such that $\mathcal{H}_{\mathcal{G}'} = \mathsf{splice}(\mathcal{H}_{\mathcal{G}})$. For a dependency graph $\mathcal{G}$, we let $\approx_{\mathcal{G}} = \approx_{\mathcal{H}_{\mathcal{G}}}$ and $\boxed{T}_{\mathcal{G}} = \boxed{T}_{\mathcal{H}_{\mathcal{G}}}$.

For example, the graph $\mathcal{G}_1$ in Figure 4 is not spliceable, because $\mathsf{splice}(\mathcal{H}_{\mathcal{G}_1}) \notin \mathsf{HistSI}$: informally, $\boxed{S}_{\mathcal{G}_1}$ observes the write by $\boxed{T}_{\mathcal{G}_1}$ to `acct1`, but not its write to `acct2`. On the other hand, let $\mathcal{G}_2$ be the graph obtained by removing the transactions S and S' from $\mathcal{G}_1$. Then $\mathcal{G}_2$ is spliceable, as witnessed by the graph $\mathcal{G}_2 \in \mathsf{GraphSI}$ with $\mathcal{H}_{\mathcal{G}_2} = \mathsf{splice}(\mathcal{H}_{\mathcal{G}_2})$ and only the edges $\boxed{T''}_{\mathcal{G}_2} \xrightarrow{\mathsf{RW}_{\mathcal{G}_2}} \boxed{T}_{\mathcal{G}_2}$ and $\boxed{S''}_{\mathcal{G}_2} \xrightarrow{\mathsf{RW}_{\mathcal{G}_2}} \boxed{T}_{\mathcal{G}_2}$.

Given a dependency graph $\mathcal{G}$, we let the ***dynamic chopping graph*** corresponding to $\mathcal{G}$ be the graph $\mathsf{DCG}(\mathcal{G})$ obtained by removing $\mathsf{WR}_{\mathcal{G}}, \mathsf{WW}_{\mathcal{G}}$ and $\mathsf{RW}_{\mathcal{G}}$ edges between transactions related by $\approx_{\mathcal{G}}$, and by extending $\mathcal{G}$ with edges in the reverse of the session order: $\mathsf{SO}_{\mathcal{G}}^{-1}$. We refer to the latter edges as ***predecessor*** edges, to those in $\mathsf{SO}_{\mathcal{G}}$ as ***successor*** edges, and to those in $(\mathsf{WR}_{\mathcal{G}} \cup \mathsf{WW}_{\mathcal{G}} \cup \mathsf{RW}_{\mathcal{G}}) \setminus \approx_{\mathcal{G}}$ as ***conflict*** edges. A cycle in a chopping graph $\mathsf{DCG}(\mathcal{G})$ is ***critical*** if: *(i)* it does not contain two occurrences of the same vertex; *(ii)* it contains a fragment of three consecutive edges of the form "conflict, predecessor, conflict"; and *(iii)* any two anti-dependency edges ($\mathsf{RW}_{\mathcal{G}} \setminus \approx_{\mathcal{G}}$) on the cycle are separated by at least one read ($\mathsf{WR}_{\mathcal{G}} \setminus \approx_{\mathcal{G}}$) or write ($\mathsf{WW}_{\mathcal{G}} \setminus \approx_{\mathcal{G}}$) dependency edge. Our ***dynamic chopping criterion*** is as follows.

THEOREM 16. *For $\mathcal{G} \in \mathsf{GraphSI}$, if $\mathsf{DCG}(\mathcal{G})$ contains no critical cycles, then $\mathcal{G}$ is spliceable.*

For example, the above graph $\mathcal{G}_2$ (Figure 4) contains no critical cycles, and the graph $\mathcal{G}_1$ contains a critical cycle

$$T' \xrightarrow{\mathsf{WR}_{\mathcal{G}_1}} S' \xrightarrow{\mathsf{SO}_{\mathcal{G}_1}} S \xrightarrow{\mathsf{RW}_{\mathcal{G}_1}} T \xrightarrow{\mathsf{SO}_{\mathcal{G}_1}^{-1}} T'.$$

To prove Theorem 16, we exhibit a particular dependency graph $\mathsf{splice}(\mathcal{G})$ such that $\mathsf{splice}(\mathcal{G}) \in \mathsf{GraphSI}$ and $\mathcal{H}_{\mathsf{splice}(\mathcal{G})} = \mathsf{splice}(\mathcal{H}_{\mathcal{G}})$. We define read dependencies $\mathsf{WR}_{\mathsf{splice}(\mathcal{G})}$ by lifting those in $\mathsf{WR}_{\mathcal{G}}$ to spliced transactions:

$$\forall T, S \in \mathcal{T}_{\mathcal{G}}.\, \forall x \in \mathsf{Obj}.\, \boxed{T}_{\mathcal{G}} \xrightarrow{\mathsf{WR}_{\mathsf{splice}(\mathcal{G})}(x)} \boxed{S}_{\mathcal{G}} \iff \boxed{T}_{\mathcal{G}} \neq \boxed{S}_{\mathcal{G}} \wedge T \xrightarrow{\approx_{\mathcal{G}} ; \mathsf{WR}_{\mathcal{G}}(x) ; \approx_{\mathcal{G}}} S. \quad (2)$$

We define $\mathsf{WW}_{\mathsf{splice}(\mathcal{G})}$ similarly and derive $\mathsf{RW}_{\mathsf{splice}(\mathcal{G})}$ from $\mathsf{WR}_{\mathsf{splice}(\mathcal{G})}$ and $\mathsf{WW}_{\mathsf{splice}(\mathcal{G})}$ as in Definition 5. As the following lemma shows, $\mathsf{RW}_{\mathsf{splice}(\mathcal{G})}$ defined in this way can be decomposed into a form similar to (2).

LEMMA 17. *Let $\mathcal{G} \in \mathsf{GraphSI}$ be such that $\mathsf{DCG}(\mathcal{G})$ contains no critical cycles. Then*

$$\forall T, S \in \mathcal{T}_{\mathcal{G}}.\, \forall x \in \mathsf{Obj}.\, \boxed{T}_{\mathcal{G}} \xrightarrow{\mathsf{RW}_{\mathsf{splice}(\mathcal{G})}(x)} \boxed{S}_{\mathcal{G}} \implies \boxed{T}_{\mathcal{G}} \neq \boxed{S}_{\mathcal{G}} \wedge T \xrightarrow{\approx_{\mathcal{G}} ; \mathsf{RW}_{\mathcal{G}}(x) ; \approx_{\mathcal{G}}} S.$$

To prove Theorem 16, we assume $\mathsf{splice}(\mathcal{G}) \notin \mathsf{GraphSI}$ and use Theorem 9 to obtain a cycle in $(\mathsf{WR}_{\mathsf{splice}(\mathcal{G})} \cup \mathsf{WW}_{\mathsf{splice}(\mathcal{G})})$;

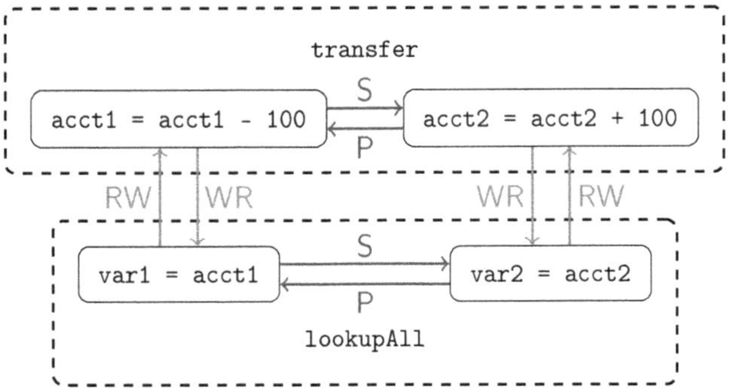

Figure 5: The static chopping graph of the programs $\{\texttt{transfer}, \texttt{lookupAll}\}$ from Figure 4. Dashed boxes group program pieces into sessions.

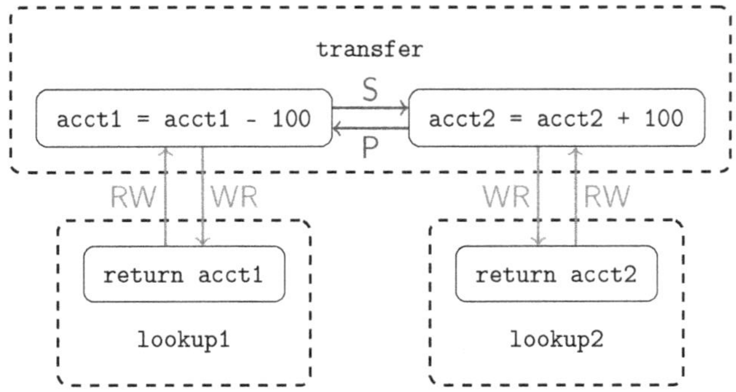

Figure 6: The static chopping graph of the programs $\{\texttt{transfer}, \texttt{lookup1}, \texttt{lookup2}\}$ from Figure 4.

$\mathsf{RW}_{\mathsf{splice}(\mathcal{G})}$?. We then use (2) and Lemma 17 to decompose this cycle into a critical cycle in $\mathsf{DCG}(\mathcal{G})$, yielding a contradiction.

We now derive a static analysis from Theorem 16. Assume a set of ***programs*** $\mathcal{P} = \{P_1, P_2, \ldots\}$, each defining the code of sessions resulting from chopping the code of a single transaction. We leave the precise syntax of the programs unspecified, but assume that each P_i consists of k_i ***program pieces***, defining the code of the transactions in the sessions. We further assume that we are given the sets R^i_j and W^i_j of all objects that can respectively be read and written by the j-th piece of P_i. For example, the program `transfer` in Figure 4 consists of two pieces; the first one has the read and write sets equal to $\{\texttt{acct1}\}$ and the second, to $\{\texttt{acct2}\}$. The program `lookup1` consists of a single piece with the read set $\{\texttt{acct1}\}$ and the write set $\emptyset$.

Following Shasha et al. [30], we make certain assumptions about the way clients execute programs. We assume that, if a transaction initiated by a program piece aborts, it will be resubmitted repeatedly until it commits, and, if a piece is aborted due to system failure, it will be restarted. We also assume that the client does not abort transactions explicitly.

A history $\mathcal{H}$ ***can be produced*** by the programs $\mathcal{P}$, if there is a one-to-one correspondence between every session in $\mathcal{H}$ and a program $P_i \in \mathcal{P}$ whose read and write sets cover the sets of objects read or written by the corresponding transactions in the session. For example, the history in Figure 4 can be produced by the programs in the figure. The chopping defined by the programs $\mathcal{P}$ is ***correct*** if every dependency graph $\mathcal{G} \in \mathsf{GraphSI}$, where $\mathcal{H}_{\mathcal{G}}$ can be produced by $\mathcal{P}$, is spliceable.

We check the correctness of $\mathcal{P}$ using its ***static chopping graph*** $\mathsf{SCG}(\mathcal{P})$. It is a directed graph whose nodes are pairs of indices identifying the pieces in $\mathcal{P}$: $\{(i,j) \mid i = 1..|\mathcal{P}|,\ j = 1..k_i\}$. We have an edge $((i_1, j_1), (i_2, j_2))$ if and only if one of the following holds: $i_1 = i_2$ and $j_1 < j_2$ (a ***successor*** edge); $i_1 = i_2$ and $j_1 > j_2$ (a ***predecessor*** edge); $i_1 \neq i_2$ and $W^{i_1}_{j_1} \cap R^{i_2}_{j_2} \neq \emptyset$ (a ***read dependency*** edge); $i_1 \neq i_2$ and $W^{i_1}_{j_1} \cap W^{i_2}_{j_2} \neq \emptyset$ (a ***write dependency*** edge); or $i_1 \neq i_2$ and $R^{i_1}_{j_1} \cap W^{i_2}_{j_2} \neq \emptyset$ (an ***anti-dependency*** edge). The notion of a critical cycle introduced above for dynamic graphs is also applicable to static ones. The edge set of a static graph $\mathsf{SCG}(\mathcal{P})$ over-approximates the edge sets of dynamic graphs $\mathsf{DCG}(\mathcal{G})$ corresponding to dependency graphs $\mathcal{G}$ produced by the programs $\mathcal{P}$. From this observation and Theorem 16 we easily get our static analysis.

COROLLARY 18. *The chopping defined by $\mathcal{P}$ is correct if $\mathsf{SCG}(\mathcal{P})$ contains no critical cycles.*

In Figure 5 we show the static chopping graph of the programs $\{\texttt{transfer}, \texttt{lookupAll}\}$, which contains a critical cycle:

$$(\texttt{var1} = \texttt{acct1}) \xrightarrow{\mathsf{RW}} (\texttt{acct1} = \texttt{acct1} - 100) \xrightarrow{\mathsf{S}} (\texttt{acct2} = \texttt{acct2} + 100) \xrightarrow{\mathsf{WR}} (\texttt{var2} = \texttt{acct2}) \xrightarrow{\mathsf{P}} (\texttt{var1} = \texttt{acct1}).$$

In fact, since the dependency graph in Figure 4 is not spliceable, the chopping defined by the above programs is incorrect. In Figure 6 we show the static chopping graph of the programs $\{\texttt{transfer}, \texttt{lookup1}, \texttt{lookup2}\}$. This graph contains no critical cycles, and hence, the chopping defined by these programs is correct: they behave the same as when `transfer` is implemented by a single transaction.

Our SI characterisation is instrumental in deriving the above static analysis due to the ease of splicing a dependency graph (cf. (2)). As we explain in [11, §B], splicing abstract executions directly would be problematic.

In [11, §B], we also show that the conditions on chopping required by Corollary 18 are laxer than those of the analysis for serializability [30], but stricter than those for parallel SI [12]. In particular, this implies that the classical transaction chopping analysis for serializability is also sound for SI. This result is non-trivial: the correctness of a chopping requires that the set of histories produced by the chopped program be included into the set of histories produced by the original program. Enlarging both sets when switching from serializability to SI may not preserve the inclusion.

6. ROBUSTNESS CRITERIA FOR SI

We now consider another type of a static analysis that checks whether an application is ***robust*** against weakening consistency: executing it under a weak consistency model produces the same client-observable behaviour as executing it under a stronger one.

6.1 Robustness against SI

We first show that our SI characterisation allows deriving a variant of an existing analysis that checks whether an application executing under SI behaves the same as when executing under serializability [19][1] (robustness ***against SI***). For this the analysis checks that the application code may produce no histories in $\mathsf{HistSI} \setminus \mathsf{HistSER}$. Like for transaction chopping (§5), we first establish a ***dynamic robustness criterion*** that checks whether a single execution, represented by a dependency graph, is in $\mathsf{GraphSI} \setminus \mathsf{GraphSER}$. This easily follows from Theorems 8 and 10.

[1] Our analysis does not take into account the notion of a *vulnerable* dependency from [19].

THEOREM 19. *For any $\mathcal{G}$, we have $\mathcal{G} \in \mathsf{GraphSI} \setminus \mathsf{GraphSER}$ if and only if $\mathcal{T}_\mathcal{G} \models$ INT, $\mathcal{G}$ contains a cycle, and all its cycles have at least two adjacent anti-dependency edges.*

Fekete et al. previously established a result corresponding to the "only if" direction of the above theorem [19]. The "if" direction strengthens their result by showing that the criterion in the theorem is complete for checking whether a given dependency graph is admitted by SI, but not serializability.

The dependency graph $\mathcal{G}_3$ of the write skew anomaly in Figure 2(d) contains a cycle: $T_1 \xrightarrow{\mathsf{RW}_{\mathcal{G}_3}} T_2 \xrightarrow{\mathsf{RW}_{\mathcal{G}_3}} T_1$. Furthermore, it is easy to see that all its cycles have two adjacent anti-dependencies, so that $\mathcal{G}_3 \in \mathsf{GraphSI} \setminus \mathsf{GraphSER}$. The dependency graph $\mathcal{G}_1$ from Figure 4 does not contain any cycles, so that $\mathcal{G}_1 \notin \mathsf{GraphSI} \setminus \mathsf{GraphSER}$; in fact, $\mathcal{G}_1 \in \mathsf{GraphSER}$. Finally, the dependency graph $\mathcal{G}_4$ of the long fork anomaly in Figure 4 contains a cycle, but without two adjacent anti-dependencies; hence, $\mathcal{G}_4 \notin \mathsf{GraphSI} \setminus \mathsf{GraphSER}$, and in fact, $\mathcal{G}_4 \notin \mathsf{GraphSI}$.

We can derive a static analysis from Theorem 19 similarly to how it was done in §5. Namely, the analysis assumes that the code of transactions in an application is defined by a set of programs $\mathcal{P}$ with given read and write sets. Based on these sets, it constructs a ***static dependency graph***, over-approximating possible dependencies that can exist in executions of the programs $\mathcal{P}$. The analysis then checks that the graph has no cycles with at least two adjacent anti-dependency edges. By Theorem 19 this implies that the programs $\mathcal{P}$ produce no histories in $\mathsf{HistSI} \setminus \mathsf{HistSER}$, and hence, the corresponding application is robust against SI. Note that the dependency graphs characterisation of consistency models greatly facilitates deriving the above static analysis, since the characterisations allow us to easily establish correspondences between executions on different models with the same histories.

6.2 Robustness against parallel SI towards SI

We now use our SI characterisation to derive a static analysis that checks whether an application executing under parallel SI [32] behaves the same as when executing under the classical SI (robustness ***against parallel SI towards SI***). To specify parallel SI in the framework of §2, we drop the axiom PREFIX, while still requiring visibility to be transitive, a property that we refer to as TRANSVIS [10].

DEFINITION 20. *The sets of executions and histories **allowed by parallel SI** are:*

$$\mathsf{ExecPSI} = \{\mathcal{X} \mid \mathcal{X} \models \text{INT} \wedge \text{EXT} \wedge \text{SESSION} \wedge \text{TRANSVIS} \wedge \text{NOCONFLICT}\};$$

$$\mathsf{HistPSI} = \{\mathcal{H} \mid \exists \mathsf{VIS}, \mathsf{CO}.\, (\mathcal{H}, \mathsf{VIS}, \mathsf{CO}) \in \mathsf{ExecSI}\}.$$

Note that this specification essentially does not use the commit order CO: according to NOCONFLICT, its edges used in EXT are uniquely determined by VIS.

The axiom TRANSVIS ensures that transactions ordered by VIS are observed by others in this order. However, it allows two transactions unrelated by VIS to be observed in different orders; in particular, parallel SI allows the long fork anomaly of Figure 2(c), disallowed by the axiom PREFIX in SI.

Following [12, extended version, Lemma 14], we can give a characterisation of parallel SI in terms of dependency graphs.

THEOREM 21. *Let*

$$\mathsf{GraphPSI} = \{\mathcal{G} \mid (\mathcal{T}_\mathcal{G} \models \text{INT}) \wedge (((\mathsf{SO}_\mathcal{G} \cup \mathsf{WR}_\mathcal{G} \cup \mathsf{WW}_\mathcal{G})^+ \,;\, \mathsf{RW}_\mathcal{G}?) \text{ is irreflexive})\}.$$

Then

$$\mathsf{HistPSI} = \{\mathcal{H} \mid \exists \mathsf{WR}, \mathsf{WW}, \mathsf{RW}.\, (\mathcal{H}, \mathsf{WR}, \mathsf{WW}, \mathsf{RW}) \in \mathsf{GraphPSI}\}.$$

Thus, parallel SI is characterised by dependency graphs that contain only cycles with at least two anti-dependency edges. For example, consider the dependency graph $\mathcal{G}_4$ in Figure 2(c). It is easy to see that all its cycles contain at least two anti-dependencies, and therefore $\mathcal{G}_4 \in \mathsf{GraphPSI}$. On the other hand, let $\mathcal{G}_5$ be the dependency graph in Figure 2(b). The graph $\mathcal{G}_5$ contains a cycle with exactly one anti-dependency ($T_1 \xrightarrow{\mathsf{WW}_{\mathcal{G}_5}} T_2 \xrightarrow{\mathsf{RW}_{\mathcal{G}_5}} T_1$), and therefore $\mathcal{G}_5 \notin \mathsf{GraphPSI}$. As a corollary of Theorems 9 and 21, we obtain a dynamic robustness criterion that checks whether a given dependency graph is in $\mathsf{GraphPSI} \setminus \mathsf{GraphSI}$.

THEOREM 22. *For any $\mathcal{G}$, we have $\mathcal{G} \in \mathsf{GraphPSI} \setminus \mathsf{GraphSI}$ if and only if $\mathcal{T}_\mathcal{G} \models$ INT, $\mathcal{G}$ contains at least one cycle with no adjacent anti-dependency edges, and all its cycles have at least two anti-dependency edges.*

For example, we have already noted that in the dependency graph $\mathcal{G}_4$ of the long fork anomaly all cycles have at least two anti-dependencies. Furthermore, $\mathcal{G}_4$ also has a cycle with no adjacent anti-dependencies: $T_1 \xrightarrow{\mathsf{WR}_{\mathcal{G}_4}} T_3 \xrightarrow{\mathsf{RW}_{\mathcal{G}_4}} T_2 \xrightarrow{\mathsf{WR}_{\mathcal{G}_4}} T_4 \xrightarrow{\mathsf{RW}_{\mathcal{G}_4}} T_1$, so that $\mathcal{G}_4 \in \mathsf{GraphPSI} \setminus \mathsf{GraphSI}$. The dependency graph $\mathcal{G}_3$ of the write skew anomaly in Figure 2(d) contains only cycles with at least two adjacent anti-dependencies, so that $\mathcal{G}_3 \notin \mathsf{GraphPSI} \setminus \mathsf{GraphSI}$; in fact, $\mathcal{G}_3 \in \mathsf{GraphSI}$. The dependency graph $\mathcal{G}_5$ of the lost update anomaly contains a cycle with exactly one anti-dependency, so that $\mathcal{G}_5 \notin \mathsf{GraphPSI} \setminus \mathsf{GraphSI}$; in fact, $\mathcal{G}_5 \notin \mathsf{GraphPSI}$.

From Theorem 22 it follows that the desired static analysis can check that the static dependency graph of an application contains no cycles where there are at least two anti-dependency edges and no two anti-dependency edges are adjacent.

7. RELATED WORK

Snapshot isolation was originally defined by an idealised algorithm formulated in terms of implementation-level concepts [6]. Since then there have been proposals of more declarative SI specifications [2, 10, 28], one of which [10] was our starting point (§2). However, these specifications are stated in terms of relations which make it challenging to obtain results such as transaction chopping and robustness analyses.

Fekete et al. [19] proposed the analysis for robustness against SI that we considered in §6.1. To this end, they have proved a fact roughly equivalent to our completeness result (Theorem 10(ii)), but they did not establish an analogue of our soundness result (Theorem 10(i)). The latter more challenging result is the one that is needed to obtain analyses for transaction chopping under SI and for robustness against parallel SI towards SI: both require proving that an execution with a particular dependency graph is in SI, rather than the other way round. We also hope that our specification of SI will be beneficial in other domains where dependency graphs have been useful, such as run-time monitoring [9, 37] and proving the correctness of concurrency-control algorithms [16, 36]. Finally, we expect that the approach to constructing a total commit order from transactional dependencies in the proof of our soundness theorem can be used to give dependency graph characterisations to other consistency models whose formulation includes similar total orders, such as *prefix consistency* [34].

The constraint on dependency graphs that we use to characterise SI also arose in the work of Lin et al. [24], who used it to formulate conditions under which a replicated database guarantees SI provided every one of its replicas does so. In comparison to them, we solve a more general problem of characterising SI regardless of how it is implemented and handle a variant of SI that does not require transactions to see the latest snapshot.

Transaction chopping has recently received a lot of attention. In particular, researchers have demonstrated that transactions arising in web applications can be chopped in a way that drastically improves their performance when executed under serializability [26, 36, 38]. There have also been proposals of consistency models for transactional memory that weaken consistency guarantees in a way similar to chopping [4, 20, 35]. Our chopping analysis enables bringing these benefits to transactional systems providing SI. We have previously proposed a chopping analysis for parallel SI [12], which also relies on a dependency graph characterisation of this consistency model (Theorem 21). But since parallel SI can be formulated without using an analogue of SI's commit order, its dependency graph characterisation did not present the challenges that we had to deal with when establishing our soundness theorem.

Acknowledgements. We thank Hongseok Yang, who participated in early stages of this work. We also thank Hagit Attiya, Ricardo Jiménez-Peris and Pierre Sutra for comments that helped improve the paper. This work was supported by an EU project ADVENT.

References

[1] The Clojure language: Refs and transactions. http://clojure.org/refs.

[2] A. Adya. Weak consistency: A generalized theory and optimistic implementations for distributed transactions. PhD thesis, MIT, 1999.

[3] A. Adya, B. Liskov, and P. E. O'Neil. Generalized isolation level definitions. In *ICDE*, 2000.

[4] Y. Afek, H. Avni, and N. Shavit. Towards consistency oblivious programming. In *OPODIS*, 2011.

[5] P. Bailis, A. Fekete, A. Ghodsi, J. M. Hellerstein, and I. Stoica. Scalable atomic visibility with RAMP transactions. In *SIGMOD*, 2014.

[6] H. Berenson, P. Bernstein, J. Gray, J. Melton, E. O'Neil, and P. O'Neil. A critique of ANSI SQL isolation levels. In *SIGMOD*, 1995.

[7] P. A. Bernstein, V. Hadzilacos, and N. Goodman. *Concurrency Control and Recovery in Database Systems*. Addison-Wesley, 1987.

[8] A. Bieniusa and T. Fuhrmann. Consistency in hindsight: A fully decentralized STM algorithm. In *IPDPS*, 2010.

[9] M. J. Cahill, U. Röhm, and A. D. Fekete. Serializable isolation for snapshot databases. *ACM Trans. Database Syst.*, 34(4), 2009.

[10] A. Cerone, G. Bernardi, and A. Gotsman. A framework for transactional consistency models with atomic visibility. In *CONCUR*. Dagstuhl, 2015.

[11] A. Cerone and A. Gotsman. Analysing snapshot isolation (extended version). Available from www.software.imdea.org/~gotsman, 2016.

[12] A. Cerone, A. Gotsman, and H. Yang. Transaction chopping for parallel snapshot isolation. In *DISC*, 2015. Extended version available from www.software.imdea.org/~gotsman.

[13] K. Daudjee and K. Salem. Lazy database replication with ordering guarantees. In *ICDE*, 2004.

[14] K. Daudjee and K. Salem. Lazy database replication with snapshot isolation. In *VLDB*, 2006.

[15] R. J. Dias, J. M. Lourenço, and N. Preguiça. Efficient and correct transactional memory programs combining snapshot isolation and static analysis. In *HotPar*, 2011.

[16] N. Diegues and P. Romano. Time-warp: Lightweight abort minimization in transactional memory. In *PPoPP*, 2014.

[17] S. Doherty, L. Groves, V. Luchangco, and M. Moir. Towards formally specifying and verifying transactional memory. *Formal Aspects of Computing*, 25(5), 2013.

[18] S. Elnikety, W. Zwaenepoel, and F. Pedone. Database replication using generalized snapshot isolation. In *SRDS*, 2005.

[19] A. Fekete, D. Liarokapis, E. O'Neil, P. O'Neil, and D. Shasha. Making snapshot isolation serializable. *ACM Trans. Database Syst.*, 30(2), 2005.

[20] P. Felber, V. Gramoli, and R. Guerraoui. Elastic transactions. In *DISC*, 2009.

[21] R. Guerraoui and M. Kapalka. On the correctness of transactional memory. In *PPoPP*, 2008.

[22] M. Herlihy and J. E. B. Moss. Transactional memory: Architectural support for lock-free data structures. In *ISCA*, 1993.

[23] S. Jorwekar, A. Fekete, K. Ramamritham, and S. Sudarshan. Automating the detection of snapshot isolation anomalies. In *VLDB*, 2007.

[24] Y. Lin, B. Kemme, R. Jiménez-Peris, M. Patiño-Martínez, and J. E. Armendáriz-Iñigo. Snapshot isolation and integrity constraints in replicated databases. *ACM Trans. Database Syst.*, 34(2), 2009.

[25] H. Litz, D. Cheriton, A. Firoozshahian, O. Azizi, and J. P. Stevenson. SI-TM: Reducing transactional memory abort rates through snapshot isolation. In *ASPLOS*, 2014.

[26] S. Mu, Y. Cui, Y. Zhang, W. Lloyd, and J. Li. Extracting more concurrency from distributed transactions. In *OSDI*, 2014.

[27] D. Peng and F. Dabek. Large-scale incremental processing using distributed transactions and notifications. In *OSDI*, 2010.

[28] M. Saeida Ardekani, P. Sutra, M. Shapiro, and N. Preguiça. On the scalability of snapshot isolation. In *Euro-Par*, 2013.

[29] D. Serrano, M. Patiño-Martínez, R. Jiménez-Peris, and B. Kemme. Boosting database replication scalability through partial replication and 1-copy-snapshot-isolation. In *PRDC*, 2007.

[30] D. Shasha, F. Llirbat, E. Simon, and P. Valduriez. Transaction chopping: Algorithms and performance studies. *ACM Trans. Database Syst.*, 20(3), 1995.

[31] D. Shasha and M. Snir. Efficient and correct execution of parallel programs that share memory. *ACM Trans. Program. Lang. Syst.*, 10(2), 1988.

[32] Y. Sovran, R. Power, M. K. Aguilera, and J. Li. Transactional storage for geo-replicated systems. In *SOSP*, 2011.

[33] D. B. Terry, A. J. Demers, K. Petersen, M. Spreitzer, M. Theimer, and B. W. Welch. Session guarantees for weakly consistent replicated data. In *PDIS*, 1994.

[34] D. B. Terry, V. Prabhakaran, R. Kotla, M. Balakrishnan, M. K. Aguilera, and H. Abu-Libdeh. Consistency-based service level agreements for cloud storage. In *SOSP*, 2013.

[35] L. Xiang and M. L. Scott. Software partitioning of hardware transactions. In *PPoPP*, 2015.

[36] C. Xie, C. Su, C. Littley, L. Alvisi, M. Kapritsos, and Y. Wang. High-performance ACID via modular concurrency control. In *SOSP*, 2015.

[37] K. Zellag and B. Kemme. Consistency anomalies in multi-tier architectures: Automatic detection and prevention. *The VLDB Journal*, 23(1), 2014.

[38] Y. Zhang, R. Power, S. Zhou, Y. Sovran, M. Aguilera, and J. Li. Transaction chains: Achieving serializability with low latency in geo-distributed storage systems. In *SOSP*, 2013.

Recoverable Mutual Exclusion

[Extended Abstract]

Wojciech Golab
Dept. of Electrical and Computer Engineering
University of Waterloo, Canada
wgolab@uwaterloo.ca

Aditya Ramaraju
Dept. of Electrical and Computer Engineering
University of Waterloo, Canada
a2ramaraju@uwaterloo.ca

ABSTRACT

Mutex locks have traditionally been the most common mechanism for protecting shared data structures in parallel programs. However, the robustness of such locks against process failures has not been studied thoroughly. Most (user-level) mutex algorithms are designed around the assumption that processes are reliable, meaning that a process may not fail while executing the lock acquisition and release code, or while inside the critical section. If such a failure does occur, then the liveness properties of a conventional mutex lock may cease to hold until the application or operating system intervenes by cleaning up the internal structure of the lock. For example, a process that is attempting to acquire an otherwise starvation-free mutex may be blocked forever waiting for a failed process to release the critical section. Adding to the difficulty, if the failed process recovers and attempts to acquire the same mutex again without appropriate cleanup, then the mutex may become corrupted to the point where it loses safety, notably the mutual exclusion property. We address this challenge by formalizing the problem of recoverable mutual exclusion, and proposing several solutions that vary both in their assumptions regarding hardware support for synchronization, and in their time complexity. Compared to known solutions, our algorithms are more robust as they do not restrict where or when a process may crash, and provide stricter guarantees in terms of time complexity, which we define in terms of remote memory references.

Keywords

Mutual exclusion; recovery; fault tolerance; concurrency; shared memory; multi-core algorithms; non-volatile main memory; persistent data structures.

1. INTRODUCTION

Parallel programs running on multi-core architectures empower essential applications and services today, ranging from mundane desktop computing to massive back-end infrastructures that drive web search, e-commerce, and online social networks. Mutex locks have traditionally been the most popular mechanism for protecting shared data structures in parallel programs owing to their simplicity: any sequential data structure can be made thread-safe by protecting operations on the data structure using a critical section. Mutual exclusion is therefore one of the oldest problems addressed in the area of shared memory synchronization, starting with Dijkstra's seminal paper [11]. Over decades of research, locks have evolved from simple two-process algorithms to scalable mechanisms that provide elaborate correctness properties, such as fairness and local spinning [4]. One technical aspect of mutual exclusion, however, has remained nearly constant throughout history: a typical mutex lock cannot survive the failure of even one process while it is accessing the lock.

Failures in parallel programs are an increasingly important reality, and may arise in several ways. For example, individual processes or threads of control in a program may terminate abruptly due to software bugs or deadlock resolution mechanisms. Similarly, processes may be affected by a loss of electrical power or faulty interconnect, especially in large-scale multiprocessor architectures that incorporate multiple system boards connected by a complex network of electronic and optical components. The straightforward approach to dealing with such failures in lock-based programs is to shut down the entire program and restart it. Thus, all in-memory data structures are thrown away, and may be reconstructed using data from a recovery log in non-volatile secondary storage. In comparison, recovery by repairing in-memory data structures directly is potentially much less disruptive as it avoids sequential logs and bypasses secondary storage altogether. The same mechanism can even be used to recover from system-wide failures, such as during a prolonged power outage, in forthcoming architectures that incorporate non-volatile main memory (NVRAM) [32].

Restoring a data structure protected by a mutex lock following a failure entails solving two technical problems: (1) completing or rolling back any actions in the critical section that may have been interrupted by the failure; and (2) repairing the internal state of the lock, if needed, to preserve safety and liveness. The first problem is arguably easier because the critical section entails sequential reading and writing, and can be solved using Functional Recovery Routines [17]. The second problem involves more intricate lock acquisition and release code that deals with race conditions. If a process crashes while executing this code, then the liveness properties of a conventional mutex lock may cease to hold until the lock is repaired. For example, a process that

PODC'16, July 25 - 28, 2016, Chicago, IL, USA

ISBN 978-1-4503-3964-3/16/07...$15.00

DOI: http://dx.doi.org/10.1145/2933057.2933087

Sec.	Algorithm	Failure-Free RMR Complexity	Worst-Case RMR Complexity	Synchronization Primitives Used
3.1	two out of N processes	$O(1)$	$O(1)$	reads and writes
3.2	N-process arbitration tree	$O(\log N)$	$O(\log N)$	reads and writes
4.1	base mutex → recoverable mutex	same as base	grows with # of failures	base + reads and writes
4.2	bounds RMR complexity in transformation from Sec. 4.1	same as base in Sec. 4.1	$O(N)$ when base mutex uses $O(N)$ RMRs and $O(N)$ space	same as base in Sec. 4.1 + Compare-And-Swap

Figure 1: Summary of recoverable mutual exclusion algorithms presented.

is attempting to acquire an otherwise starvation-free mutex lock may be blocked forever, waiting for a crashed process to release the critical section. Adding to the difficulty, if the failed process recovers and attempts to acquire the same mutex again without appropriate cleanup, then the mutex may be corrupted to the point where it loses safety, particularly the mutual exclusion property.

Hybrid architectures that integrate both volatile and non-volatile main memories simplify the problem under consideration by allowing the shared data structure to reside in NVRAM, while the internal state of the mutex remains volatile and is reset to zero in the event of recovery following a system crash. Under these assumptions, a system crash reverts some mutex algorithms (e.g., [30]) cleanly back to their initial state, which obviates the need for repairs, and yet a small amount of non-volatile memory can be used to record lock ownership for critical section cleanup. In contrast to this simple technique, our solutions in this paper add recoverability to arbitrary mutual exclusion algorithms, and tolerate process crashes without assuming that such failures reset shared state automatically.

The recoverable locks of Bohannon et al. [8, 9] address some, but not all of the technical challenges associated with recovering from process failures. These techniques add recoverability to modern spin locks by introducing a centralized recovery process that relies on support from the operating system to detect process crashes. In comparison, our model is weaker in the sense that processes are permitted to execute recovery actions concurrently, and to crash inside the recovery protocol. On the other hand, we assume that a crashed process is revived for a period of time sufficient to complete recovery actions, whereas [8, 9] consider permanent crash failures.

Our contributions in this paper begin with a formal definition of recoverable mutual exclusion with respect to the following crash-recovery failure model: a process that crashes while accessing a mutex lock eventually recovers and resumes execution at the start of the lock acquisition code. This model of recovery assumes that either the application or the operating system performs appropriate failure detection, which is beyond the scope of the paper. We then present a collection of recoverable mutex algorithms, summarized in Figure 1. We start with a two-process solution in Section 3.1 that uses atomic read and write operations only, then progress to an N-process solution in Section 3.2 using reads and writes, and finally present a pair of algorithms in Sections 4.1–4.2 that can transform any conventional mutex (i.e., "base mutex") into a recoverable mutex (i.e., "target mutex") while preserving time complexity in the absence of failures. The latter transformation can be used to add recoverability to scalable queue-based locks, which take advantage of read-modify-write primitives (e.g., MCS [30]).

2. MODEL

We consider N asynchronous unreliable processes, labeled $p_1, p_2, \ldots, p_N$, that communicate by accessing variables in shared memory. These processes compete for an exclusive lock (mutex), which protects a shared resource, by following the execution path illustrated in Figure 2. In the *non-critical section* (NCS), processes do not access the lock or the shared resource. In the *recovery protocol*, denoted `Recover`, a process cleans up the internal structure of the lock, if needed, following a crash failure. In the *entry protocol*, denoted `Enter`, a process attempts to acquire the lock and waits, if required, for the lock to become available. Access to the shared resource is confined to the *critical section* (CS). In the *exit protocol*, denoted `Exit`, a process releases the lock and makes the shared resource available to other processes.

Correctness properties for mutex algorithms are expressed in reference to *histories* that record the actions of processes as they execute the pseudo-code in Figure 2. Formally, a history H is a sequence of *steps* that come in two varieties: *ordinary steps* and *crash steps*. An ordinary step is a shared memory operation combined with bounded local computation such as arithmetic operations, accessing one or more private variables, and advancing the program counter (if required). A crash step denotes a process failure that resets the private variables of a process to their initial values, including the program counter, which is reset to the non-critical section. The next step a process takes after a crash step is either another crash step, or the first step of `Recover`. A *passage* is a sequence of steps taken by a process from when it begins `Recover` to when it completes `Exit`, or crashes, whichever occurs first. We say that a process is *in cleanup* if it is executing `Recover` following a passage that ended with a crash step. A passage is called *failure-free* if it does not end with a crash step, and *cleanup-concurrent* if it begins in cleanup or overlaps with a passage of another process that begins in cleanup.

```
loop forever
    Non-Critical Section (NCS)
    Recover
    Enter
    Critical Section (CS)
    Exit
```

Figure 2: Execution path of a process participating in recoverable mutual exclusion.

The set of histories generated by possible executions of a mutex algorithm is prefix-closed. For any finite history H, we denote the length of H (i.e., number of steps in H) by

$|H|$. Given a history H and a process p_i, we say that p_i is *active in* H if it takes at least one step in H. A history H is *fair* if it is finite, or if it is infinite and every active process either executes infinitely many steps or stops taking steps after completing a failure-free passage. We assume that the critical section is bounded.

The correctness properties of our recoverable mutex algorithms are derived from Lamport's formalism [27], which considers only permanent crashes ("unannounced death") and Byzantine failures ("malfunctioning"). Differences between our definitions and Lamport's are highlighted in *italics* for clarity. Note that mutual exclusion and deadlock freedom are the only properties considered essential for correctness; the others are optional.

Mutual Exclusion (ME): For any finite history H, at most one process is in the CS at the end of H.

Deadlock Freedom (DF): For any infinite fair history H, if a process p_i leaves the NCS in some step of H then eventually some process p_j (possibly $j \neq i$) is in the CS, *or else there are infinitely many crash steps in* H.

Starvation Freedom (SF): For any infinite fair history H, if a process p_i leaves the NCS in some step of H then eventually p_i itself enters the CS, *or else there are infinitely many crash steps in* H. (SF implies DF.)

We also introduce a new property to constrain the time complexity of the recovery protocol:

Bounded Recovery (BR): For any infinite history H, any execution of `Recover` by a process p_i completes in a bounded number of p_i's steps unless p_i's passage is cleanup-concurrent.

Finally, we propose a property that simplifies recovery from a crash in the critical section:

Critical Section Re-entry (CSR): For any history H and for any process p_i, if p_i crashes inside the CS then no other process may enter the CS before p_i re-enters the CS.

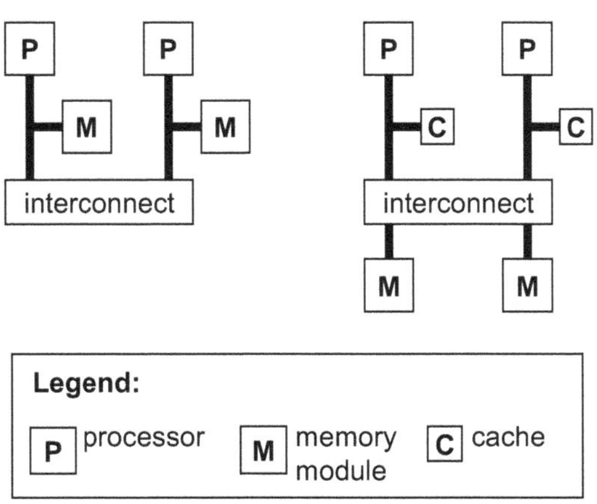

Figure 3: Abstract models of shared memory architectures—DSM (left) and CC (right).

Aside from fundamental safety and liveness properties, we are interested in the time complexity of mutex algorithms, particularly with respect to the number of *remote memory references* (RMRs) executed per passage. The precise definition of RMRs depends on the hardware architecture, and in this paper we consider both the cache-coherent (CC) and distributed shared memory (DSM) models [4], which are illustrated in Figure 3. In the CC model, any memory location can be made locally accessible to a process by creating a copy of it in the corresponding processor's cache. A distributed coherence protocol ensures that when a memory location is overwritten by one processor, cached copies held by other processors are either invalidated or updated. In contrast, the DSM model lacks (coherent) caches but allows each processor to locally access a portion of the address space corresponding to its attached memory module.[1]

Loosely speaking, an RMR in the CC or DSM model is any memory operation that traverses the interconnect shown in Figure 3. In the CC model, we (conservatively) count each shared memory operation as an RMR with the exception of an *in-cache* read, which occurs when a process p_i reads a variable v that it has already read in an earlier step, following which step no process has accessed v except by a read operation. In the DSM model, each shared variable is local to exactly one process (assuming a one-to-one mapping between processes and processors), which is determined statically at initialization. A mutex algorithm is called *local spin* if its worst-case RMR complexity per passage is bounded.

3. SOLUTIONS USING ATOMIC READS AND WRITES

Although modern multiprocessors support a variety of powerful read-modify-write primitives, algorithms that use only atomic reads and writes can be made recoverable more easily. Therefore, we first present two such algorithms, and then use them in Section 4 as building blocks of more advanced solutions that attain better RMR complexity in the absence of failures by leveraging read-modify-write primitives. Specifically, the N-process algorithm described shortly in Section 3.2 is used to protect the recovery protocol of the algorithms presented later on in Section 4.

3.1 A Two-Process Algorithm

Our first algorithm is obtained by transforming Yang and Anderson's two-process local-spin mutex [37]. Processes executing the algorithm have two identifiers: a distinct *short ID* from the set $\{\mathsf{left}, \mathsf{right}\}$, and a distinct *long ID* in the range $1..N$. The long ID is fixed, as described in Section 2, whereas the short ID is adopted temporarily for each passage. The short ID of process p_i is denoted by $\mathsf{side}(i)$, and may change only inside the NCS following a failure-free passage. If two processes access the mutex concurrently then they must have distinct short IDs.

The recoverable two-process mutex algorithm is presented in Figure 4 for the process with long ID p_i. It uses three shared variables: T is used to break symmetry at line 10; C is an array used to track the progress of a process at lines 9, 20, 22, and 26; and P is an array of spin variables used for busy-waiting at lines 17 and 19. The entry and exit protocols generally follow the structure of Yang and Anderson's algorithm, but there are several important differences: (i) the elements of array C, which hold the long IDs of processes competing for the CS in the original algorithm, are augmented with an integer tag that indicates progress through

[1]Despite the prevalence of cache-coherent architectures, the DSM model remains important in practice because of its inherent scalability. Intel's Single-chip Cloud Computer, for example, sacrifices cache-coherence "to simplify the design, reduce power consumption and to encourage the exploration of datacenter distributed memory software models" [21].

Shared variables:

- T: long process ID or $\perp$, initially $\perp$
- $C[...]$: array indexed by left and right, each element a tuple of the form $\langle$long process ID or $\perp$, integer$\rangle$, each element initially $\langle\perp, 0\rangle$
- $P[1..N]$: array of integer spin variables, element $P[i]$ local to process p_i in the DSM model, initially all elements zero

Definitions:

- $\mathsf{other}(z) = \begin{cases} \mathsf{left} & \text{if } z = \mathsf{right} \\ \mathsf{right} & \text{if } z = \mathsf{left} \end{cases}$

```
   // *** Recover ***
1  if C[side(i)] = ⟨i, 1⟩ then
2  |  ⟨rival, ...⟩ := C[other(side(i))]
3  |  if rival ∉ {i, ⊥} then
4  |  |_ P[rival] := 2
5  else if C[side(i)] = ⟨⊥, 3⟩ then
6  |_ execute lines 23–26 of the exit protocol and continue
      to entry protocol

   // *** Enter ***
7  if C[side(i)] = ⟨i, 2⟩ then
8  |_ goto line 21
9  C[side(i)] := ⟨i, 1⟩
10 T := i
11 P[i] := 0
12 ⟨rival, ...⟩ := C[other(side(i))]
13 if rival ≠ ⊥ then
14 |  if T = i then
15 |  |  if P[rival] = 0 then
16 |  |  |_ P[rival] := 1
17 |  |  await P[i] ≥ 1
18 |  |  if T = i then
19 |_ |_ |_ await P[i] = 2
20 C[side(i)] := ⟨i, 2⟩
21 Critical Section (CS)
   // *** Exit ***
22 C[side(i)] := ⟨⊥, 3⟩
23 rival := T
24 if rival ∉ {i, ⊥} then
25 |_ P[rival] := 2
26 C[side(i)] := ⟨⊥, 0⟩
```

Figure 4: Recoverable extension of Yang and Anderson's two-process mutex for process p_i.

a passage; (ii) lines 7–8 of `Enter` are added to bypass the entry protocol after recovery from a crash in the critical section; and (iii) an additional write to C is added at line 26 of `Exit` so that a recovering process can detect whether it crashed in the exit protocol. In the body of `Enter`, starting at line 9, a process proceeds directly to the CS unless it encounters a rival at line 13, in which case the busy-wait loop at line 17 ensures that both processes have progressed past line 10, and the second busy-wait loop at line 19 gives priority to the process that executed line 10 the earliest. `Exit` checks for a rival at line 23, and hands over the critical section at line 25, if required.

The recovery protocol at lines 1–6 is a new addition, and is executed whenever a process transitions out of the NCS. If process p_i is not in cleanup then $C[\mathsf{side}(i)] = \langle\perp, 0\rangle$ holds while it executes `Recover`, and so the conditions tested at lines 1 and 5 are both false. In that case, p_i proceeds directly to `Enter`, as required for bounded recovery. Otherwise, p_i tries to determine where it failed. Lines 1–4 handle a crash inside `Enter`, in which case p_i determines at line 2 whether it has a rival p_j. If so, then p_i assigns $P[j] = 2$ at line 4 to ensure that the rival is not stuck at line 17 or 19, and then repeats the entry protocol. Lines 5–6 handle a crash inside `Exit`, in which case p_i repeats the body of the exit protocol and then proceeds to the entry protocol. A crash failure inside the critical section is handled in `Enter` at lines 7–8, as explained earlier. In this case p_i branches directly to the CS at line 8.

The correctness properties of the algorithm are captured in Theorem 1, whose proof is omitted due to lack of space.

THEOREM 1. *The two-process algorithm satisfies ME, SF, BR, and CSR. Furthermore, its worst-case RMR complexity per passage is $O(1)$ in the CC and DSM models.*

3.2 An N-Process Algorithm

Our N-process solution is modeled after Yang and Anderson's N-process algorithm [37], which is based upon the arbitration tree of Kessels [24]. The algorithm is structured as a binary tree of height $O(\log N)$ where each node is a two-process mutex implemented using the algorithm described in Section 3.1. Each process is mapped statically to a leaf node in the tree as follows: process p_i enters at leaf node number $\lceil i/2 \rceil$ counting from 1. Furthermore, $\mathsf{side}(i) = \mathsf{left}$ at leaf level if i is odd and $\mathsf{side}(i) = \mathsf{right}$ if i is even.

The entry protocol of the N-process algorithm entails executing the recovery and entry protocol (back to back) of each two-process mutex on the path from the designated leaf node of a process to the root, in that order. The exit protocol releases the two-process mutex instances in the opposite order, namely from root to leaf. The recovery protocol is empty since no additional recovery actions are required beyond those performed internally by the two-processes instances. Due to lack of space we omit the pseudo-code for the N-process algorithm, which is identical to the non-recoverable N-process algorithm in [37] except that the two-process instances are implemented using our recoverable two-process mutex.

The correctness properties of the algorithm are captured in Theorem 2, whose proof is omitted due to lack of space.

THEOREM 2. *The N-process algorithm satisfies ME, SF, BR, and CSR. Furthermore, its worst-case RMR complexity per passage is $O(\log N)$ in the CC and DSM models.*

4. GENERAL SOLUTIONS

In this section we develop recoverable mutual exclusion algorithms that improve on the N-process solution from Section 3 in terms of RMRs in the absence of failures. Such algorithms necessarily require synchronization primitives other than atomic reads, writes, and Compare-And-Swap (CAS), otherwise they are subject to the lower bound of $\Omega(\log N)$ for worst-case RMR complexity per passage [6]. In asynchronous failure-free models, the best known solutions in terms of RMRs are queue locks [4] such as Mellor-Crummey and Scott's algorithm (MCS) [30], which has $O(1)$ RMR complexity in the CC and DSM models, and uses both CAS and Fetch-And-Store (FAS) in addition to atomic reads and writes.

The high-level idea underlying our constructions in this section is to augment an ordinary mutex with a recovery procedure that restores the internal structure of the lock, such as the process queue in MCS, in the event of a failure. To our knowledge, Bohannon et al.'s recoverable MCS lock [8] is the first to follow this approach. However, their solution makes two simplifying assumptions: crash failures are permanent, and the recovery protocol is executed in a single dedicated process that is itself reliable. The algorithm achieves $O(1)$ RMR complexity per passage in the CC and DSM models, but only when the recovery process is not active, and does not require any synchronization primitives beyond those used in MCS. Our initial attempt to generalize this approach to crash-recovery failures [33] led to an algorithm that has $O(1)$ RMR complexity in the CC and DSM models in a failure-free passage and $\Theta(N)$ RMRs in the worst case, but requires a powerful Fetch-And-Store-And-Store (FASAS) primitive that is not supported by modern multiprocessors except through transactional memory. Note that [8] and [33] both require $\Omega(N)$ RMRs in the worst case to execute the recovery protocol alone (ignoring the cost of interacting with the operating system to detect failures in [8]) due to some form of interaction with every other process. In [8], this entails checking if the other processes are attempting to acquire the lock, and in [33], it entails traversing the queue structure to test whether the recovering process is already in it. In comparison, our construction in Section 4.2 transforms the MCS lock (among other algorithms) into a recoverable mutex that incurs $O(1)$ RMRs in a passage that is not cleanup-concurrent, $O(N)$ RMRs per passage in the worst case, and uses only widely-supported synchronization primitives.

4.1 Transformation for Recoverability

Our first algorithm, presented in Figure 5, is a general transformation of ordinary mutex algorithms (base algorithms) into recoverable ones (target algorithms), and therefore operates in a fundamentally different way from the recoverable MCS locks discussed earlier. Specifically, our construction is agnostic with regard to the internal structure of the base algorithm in that we deal with failures by resetting the base algorithm to its initial state, rather than by attempting to repair it. This requires careful synchronization between processes executing the recovery protocol (i.e., processes in cleanup) and other processes that may be accessing the base algorithm. We simplify this task by protecting the core of the recovery protocol using an auxiliary recoverable mutex, namely the one described in Section 3.2, which incurs additional RMRs for a process in cleanup but does not affect the RMR complexity in the absence of failures. In the critical section of the auxiliary mutex, the process in cleanup first "breaks" the base mutex in a manner that allows other processes to leave the base entry and exit protocols in a bounded number of their own steps. It then waits for every process to either arrive at a gating mechanism that prevents further access to the base mutex, or to crash and recover, in both cases raising a signal by writing a spin variable. Finally, the process in cleanup resets the base mutex, opens the gate, and releases the auxiliary mutex.

In the absence of failures, a process executing the target mutex bypasses the recovery protocol at line 27, executes the body of the target entry protocol where it acquires the base mutex at line 52, completes the critical section at line 55, and finally releases the base mutex in the target exit protocol at line 57. If a failure occurs, the execution path is steered carefully using the gating mechanism, which is implemented using an array $Gate[1..N]$ of spin variables. The gate is controlled in the core of the recovery protocol at lines 32–42, which are protected by $mutexA$, the recoverable auxiliary mutex. A process in cleanup first closes the gate at lines 33–34, and then re-opens it at lines 40–41. The base mutex is re-initialized at line 39, which is only executed while the gate is closed.

One of the technical challenges in implementing the recovery protocol of the target algorithm is to suspend access to the base mutex, denoted $mutexB$, without sacrificing liveness. Consider for example a scenario where process p_1 waits inside the base entry protocol for process p_2 to release the base mutex, then p_2 crashes, closes the gate while in cleanup with respect to the target algorithm, and waits for p_1 to release the base mutex so that it can be reset safely. To prevent deadlock, executions of the base entry protocol at line 52 and base exit protocol at line 57 are modified as follows: process p_i repeatedly checks $Gate[i]$ while accessing the base mutex, and returns immediately to the target entry or exit protocol if it observes $Gate[i] \neq \bot$, meaning that the gate is closed. In this context, "repeatedly checks" means that p_i reads $Gate[i]$ after executing each step of the base mutex protocol (or at least after each step of a busy-wait loop). Thus, when the gate is closed by a process in cleanup, p_i is able to leave the base mutex in a bounded number of its own steps, allowing the recovery protocol to make progress.

The recovery protocol only deals with crash failures that occurred outside the NCS and CS, which are detected at line 27, including cases where recovery itself was interrupted by a crash. After assigning $C[i] = 5$ at line 28, process p_i reads $Gate[i]$ at line 29 to determine whether the gate is already closed, either by p_i itself prior to failure or by another process in cleanup. If it is closed, then $Gate[i]$ holds the ID of the process in cleanup, and p_i signals this process at line 31. This step is required to prevent deadlock, as explained earlier, if p_i crashed while holding the base mutex. Next, p_i acquires the auxiliary mutex at line 32, closes the gate at lines 33–34, waits for other processes to clear out of the base mutex at lines 35–38, resets the base mutex at line 39, opens the gate at lines 40–41, and finally releases the auxiliary mutex at line 42.

In the entry protocol, process p_i first checks at line 44 whether it is recovering from a crash in the target critical section. If so, then p_i bypasses the body of the entry protocol and proceeds directly to the CS. Otherwise, p_i checks whether the gate is closed at lines 46–47, and waits at line 49 until the gate is opened, if required. Prior to busy-waiting, p_i signals the process in cleanup at line 48 to prevent deadlock. When the gate is released, p_i updates its status to

Shared variables:

- *mutexA*: auxiliary mutex implemented using the algorithm from Section 3.2
- *mutexB*: base mutex, starvation-free
- $C[1..N]$: array of integer or $\perp$, element $C[i]$ local to process p_i in the DSM model, all elements initially zero
- $P[1..N][1..N]$: array of Boolean spin variables, elements $P[i][1..N]$ local to process p_i in the DSM model, all elements initially false
- $Gate[1..N]$: array of process ID or $\perp$, element $Gate[i]$ local to process p_i in DSM model, all elements initially $\perp$

```
   // *** Recover ***
27 if C[i] ∉ {0, 3} then
28     C[i] := 5
       // signal process in cleanup
29     incleanup := Gate[i]
30     if incleanup ≠ ⊥ then
31         P[incleanup][i] := true
       // clean up the base mutex
32     execute the recovery and entry protocols of mutexA
       // close gate
33     for j ∈ 1..N do
34         Gate[j] := i
       // wait for other processes to clear base
          mutex
35     for j ∈ 1..N do
36         P[i][j] := false
37         if j ≠ i ∧ C[j] ∈ {2, 3, 4} then
38             await P[i][j] = true
39     reset mutexB to its initial state
       // re-open gate
40     for j ∈ 1..N do
41         Gate[j] := ⊥
42     execute exit protocol of mutexA
       // recovery complete
43     C[i] := ⊥
```

```
   // *** Enter ***
44 if C[i] ≠ 3 then
45     C[i] := 1
       // wait at gate if needed
46     incleanup = Gate[i]
47     if incleanup ≠ ⊥ then
           // signal process in cleanup
48         P[incleanup][i] := true
           // wait for gate to re-open
49         await Gate[i] = ⊥
50     C[i] := 2
       // check gate again
51     if Gate[i] ≠ ⊥ then goto line 45
52     execute the entry protocol of mutexB, but break to
       line 53 if Gate[i] ≠ ⊥
       // check gate again
53     if Gate[i] ≠ ⊥ then goto line 45
54     C[i] := 3
55 Critical Section (CS)
   // *** Exit ***
56 C[i] := 4
57 execute the exit protocol of mutexB, but break to
   line 58 if Gate[i] ≠ ⊥
58 C[i] := 0
   // signal process in cleanup
59 incleanup = Gate[i]
60 if incleanup ≠ ⊥ then
61     P[incleanup][i] := true
```

Figure 5: Transformation from N-process base mutex to N-process recoverable target mutex. Algorithm shown for process p_i.

$C[i] = 2$ at line 50 and then checks the gate again at line 51. If the gate is once again closed, p_i must restart the entry protocol to ensure that it does not access the base mutex at line 52 concurrently with a process in cleanup. Note that checking the gate earlier at line 46 does not suffice for this purpose because at that point p_i has a different status (i.e., $C[i] = 1$ then vs. $C[i] = 2$ now), which is inspected in the recovery protocol at line 37. On the other hand, if the gate is still open at line 51, then p_i executes the entry protocol of the base mutex at line 52 until it either acquires the base critical section or detects that another process has closed the gate. It then checks the gate yet again at line 53 and restarts the entry protocol if required, which prevents unsafe progress into the target critical section. At line 57, p_i executes the base exit protocol until it either succeeds or detects that another process has closed the gate. It then checks the gate at lines 59–60, and if the gate is closed, p_i signals the process in cleanup at line 61.

The correctness properties of the transformation are captured in Theorem 3, whose proof is omitted due to lack of space.

THEOREM 3. *The target algorithm satisfies ME, SF, BR, and CSR. Furthermore, the worst-case RMR complexity per passage in the CC and DSM models for a process p_i is as follows, assuming the base mutex incurs $O(B)$ RMRs and uses V shared variables:* `Recover` *incurs $O(N+V)$ RMRs if p_i is in cleanup, and $O(1)$ otherwise;* `Enter` *and* `Exit` *incur $O(B+F)$ RMRs where F denotes the number of passages that are cleanup-concurrent with p_i's.*

4.2 Transformation for Bounding RMR Complexity

The construction presented in Section 4.1, when instantiated with a local-spin base mutex, has bounded RMR complexity in failure-free histories, and unbounded RMR complexity in the worst case as there may be arbitrarily many crash failures while a process is attempting to complete the entry protocol. In this section we describe a further transformation that bounds RMR complexity in the worst case and preserves it, up to a constant factor, in the absence of failures. Our technique is inspired by two ideas: Scott and Scherer's *abortable mutual exclusion* [35], in which a process that is waiting in the entry protocol may give up its interest in the critical section by executing a bounded *abort protocol*; and Lamport's *fast path* mechanism [28], which improves the time complexity of a mutex algorithm in the absence of contention.

The new transformation, illustrated in Figure 6, uses the construction from Section 4.1 as its base mutex, and augments it with an abort protocol that is activated when a process in cleanup is detected. A process that breaks out of the base entry protocol in this manner is diverted to a *bounded path* that guarantees bounded RMR complexity but may be slower than the default path in the absence of contention. To ensure mutual exclusion, both the bounded path and the default path are protected by an auxiliary recoverable mutex implemented using the algorithm from Section 3.2. In the absence of failures, the auxiliary mutex is accessed only along the default path where it is already protected by the base mutex, and so contention is minimal. Therefore, augmenting the auxiliary mutex with a suitable fast path ensures that the target mutex has the same RMR complexity asymptotically as the base mutex in the absence of failures.

Augmenting the construction from Section 4.1 with an abort protocol is straightforward because we only need to deal with the case when a process p_i aborts from lines 46–49 in Figure 5, where $C[i] = 1$ holds continuously. It suffices for process p_i to reset $C[i]$ back to 0 and return to the NCS, somewhat similarly to executing the exit protocol from line 58. This action is safe because p_i has not yet accessed the base mutex in its current passage, aside from possibly resetting it earlier at line 39. Liveness is not jeopardized either because a process in cleanup never waits for p_i while $C[i] \in \{0, 1\}$ (see line 37). Finally, there is no penalty for p_i in terms of RMRs because p_i bypasses the recovery protocol at line 27 in its next passage.

Adding a fast path to the recoverable auxiliary mutex is more challenging as the natural approach of generalizing a known fast path implementation to crash-recovery failures leads to some undesirable technicalities. Lamport's use of the fast path [28], for example, leads to unbounded RMR complexity. Yang and Anderson's adaptation of Lamport's mechanism to local-spin algorithms [37] bounds the RMR complexity but only at $\Theta(N)$ in the worst case. Finally, Anderson and Kim's mechanism [2] bounds the RMR complexity at $\Theta(\log N)$ in the worst case, but introduces identifiers that grow without bound. We avoid these issues altogether by using Compare-And-Swap (CAS) to open and close the fast path instead of relying on atomic reads and writes only. This is a reasonable design choice because the two transformations presented in Section 4 are intended to be used with RMR-efficient base algorithms that already rely on atomic read-modify-write primitives. Note that Golab et al.'s RMR-efficient simulation of CAS from reads and writes is not applicable in this context as it assumes reliable processes [15].

The pseudo-code for the target algorithm is presented in Figure 7. The construction uses three mutexes as building blocks: *mutexB* is the base mutex obtained by instantiating the construction from Section 4.1; $mutexA_N$ is the N-process auxiliary mutex that protects the critical section in the default and bounded paths, as explained earlier; and $mutexA_2$ is a two-process auxiliary mutex required to synchronize $mutexA_N$ with the fast path. Both $mutexA_N$ and $mutexA_2$ are implemented using the algorithms presented in Section 3. In the absence of failures, a process p_i executes the base recovery protocol at line 62, the base entry protocol at line 63, and then attempts to capture the fast path by executing a Compare-And-Swap operation (denoted `CAS`) at line 68. (The "$\wedge$" operator at line 68 should be interpreted like && in C++, meaning that the right operand is evaluated only if the left operand is true.) Since the base mutex protects lines 68–83 in the absence of failures, there is no contention on the fast path and so p_i successfully swaps its ID into F. Next, p_i acquires $mutexA_2$ at line 69, completes the target critical section at line 74, releases $mutexA_2$ at line 76, and releases the fast path (by overwriting F with $\perp$) at line 77.

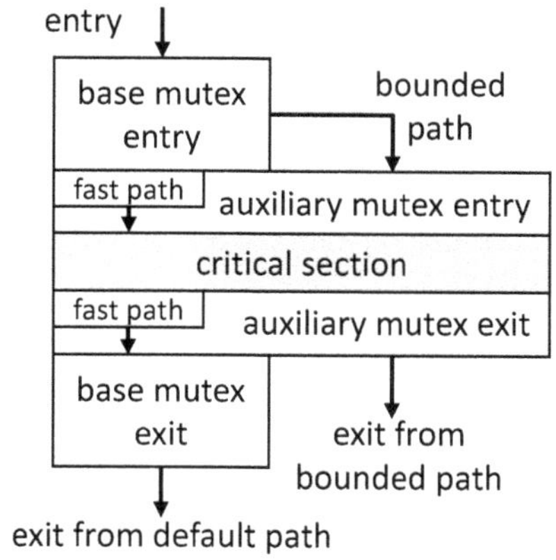

Figure 6: Conceptual structure of the target algorithm with default (left) and bounded (right) paths.

In the presence of failures by other processes, p_i may abort from the base entry protocol at line 63. This event is recorded in *Bypass*[i] at line 65 so that p_i remembers not to execute the base exit protocol later on at line 83, as otherwise it would be departing from the execution path illustrated earlier in Figure 2 with respect to *mutexB*. In this case we treat p_i as transitioning directly from the base entry protocol to the base NCS by aborting, which ends the passage with respect to *mutexB*. The rest of the target entry and exit protocols is executed as in the failure-free case, except that *mutexB* no longer serializes executions of the fast path, leading to the possibility that p_i fails to capture the fast path at line 68 due to contention. In that case, p_i falls back on the bounded path in which it acquires $mutexA_N$ at line 72, acquires $mutexA_2$ at line 73, completes the target critical section at line 74, releases $mutexA_2$ at line 79, and finally releases $mutexA_N$ at line 80. *Bounded*[i] is used at lines 71 and 81 to record p_i's presence in the bounded path for recovery.

If p_i itself crashes, then on recovery it executes the target recovery and entry protocols up to line 68, as described earlier. If p_i failed inside the bounded path (i.e., *Bounded*[i] = `true`), then by the test at line 68 it proceeds to line 71 where it re-enters the bounded path. In this case, p_i cannot enter the fast path at line 68 as otherwise it will acquire $mutexA_2$

Shared variables:

- *mutexA*$_N$ and *mutexA*$_2$: auxiliary N-process and two-process recoverable mutexes implemented using the algorithms from Section 3
- *mutexB*: base mutex implemented using the algorithm from Section 4.1
- F: holds process ID or $\perp$, initially $\perp$
- *Bounded*[1..N]: array of Boolean, initially all elements false
- *Bypass*[1..N]: array of Boolean, element i private to process p_i, initially all elements false

```
   // *** Recover ***
62 execute the recovery protocol of mutexB
   // *** Enter ***
63 execute entry protocol of mutexB, abort if line 48 of
   the base mutex (see Figure 5) is reached
64 if aborted entry protocol of mutexB at line 63 then
65 |  Bypass[i] := true
66 else
67 |_ Bypass[i] := false
   // try to capture the fast path using CAS
68 if Bounded[i] = false ∧ CAS(F, ⊥, i) ∈ {⊥, i} then
69 |  execute the recovery and entry protocols of
   |  mutexA_2 with side(i) = left
70 else
71 |  Bounded[i] := true
72 |  execute the recovery and entry protocols of
   |  mutexA_N
73 |  execute the recovery and entry protocols of
   |_ mutexA_2 with side(i) = right

74 Critical Section (CS)
   // *** Exit ***
75 if F = i then
76 |  execute the exit protocol of mutexA_2 with
   |  side(i) = left
   |  // release the fast path
77 |  F := ⊥
78 else
79 |  execute the exit protocol of mutexA_2 with
   |  side(i) = right
80 |  execute the exit protocol of mutexA_N
81 |_ Bounded[i] := false
82 if Bypass[i] = false then
83 |_ execute the exit protocol of mutexB
```

Figure 7: Transformation for bounding worst-case RMR complexity in the algorithm from Section 4.1. Algorithm shown for process p_i.

with side(i) = left at line 69 before it has a chance to recover its prior passage through *mutexA*$_2$ from line 73 with side(i) = right, which breaks the assumptions stated in Section 3. Otherwise, if p_i failed outside the bounded path (i.e., *Bounded*[i] = false), then it attempts to capture the fast path, and falls back on the bounded path only if necessary. If p_i was already in the fast path when it crashed, then $F = i$ holds and the response of the CAS at line 68 indicates that it is safe for p_i to re-enter the fast path. After completing the target critical section, p_i releases the auxiliary mutexes and the fast path in the target exit protocol at lines 75–81.

The RMR complexity of the target algorithm in the absence of failures is dominated by *mutexB* since the auxiliary two-process mutex used in the fast path (*mutexA*$_2$) requires only $O(1)$ RMRs. Failures affect RMRs in two ways: (i) the complexity of the base recovery protocol increases, which affects line 62; and (ii) aborts at line 63 raise pressure on the fast path and deflect processes into the bounded path, which incurs an additional $\Theta(\log N)$ RMRs per passage. Note that (i) applies only while some process is in cleanup with respect to *mutexB*, hence with respect to the target algorithm as well. In contrast, contention on the fast path in (ii) lingers on until the last process drains out of the bounded path, which could occur long after *mutexB* has been cleaned up. As a result, (ii) affects the RMR complexity of any passage that is, or overlaps with, a cleanup-concurrent passage.

The correctness properties of the transformation are captured in Theorem 4, whose proof is omitted due to lack of space.

THEOREM 4. *The target algorithm satisfies ME, SF, BR, and CSR. Furthermore, the worst-case RMR complexity in the CC and DSM models for a process p_i is as follows, assuming the base mutex used inside mutexB (see Figure 5) incurs $O(B)$ RMRs and uses V shared variables:* `Recover` *incurs $O(N+V)$ RMRs if p_i is in cleanup, and $O(1)$ RMRs otherwise;* `Enter` *and* `Exit` *incur $O(\max(B, \log N))$ RMRs if p_i's passage is, or overlaps with, a cleanup-concurrent passage, and $O(B)$ RMRs otherwise.*

5. RELATED WORK

Literature on mutual exclusion begins with Dijkstra's seminal paper [11], although the first known solution to the problem is credited to Dekker, who proposed a two-process algorithm that uses one-bit read/write registers. Lamport advanced the state of the art by formalizing the correctness properties of mutual exclusion [26, 27], and also introduced the famous Bakery algorithm as an example of first-come-first-served (FCFS) fairness [25]. Whereas the Bakery uses only reads and writes, and orders processes using numerical tickets, more scalable FCFS algorithms implement various queue structures using read-modify-write primitives [5, 29, 16, 30]. For a detailed treatment of progress in mutual exclusion research up to 2003, the reader is referred to [4, 34].

Local spin mutual exclusion algorithms, which guarantee bounded RMR complexity per passage by busy-waiting only on locally accessible shared variables, have been studied intensively due to their performance benefits [5]. For the class of algorithms that use reads, writes and comparison primitives, the tight bound on RMRs per passage in the worst case is $\Theta(\log N)$. Yang and Anderson [37] proved the upper bound in the CC and DSM models using an arbitration tree modeled after Kessels [24]. Attiya, Hendler, and Woelfel [6] later proved the matching lower bound, building on a series of earlier results [3, 10, 13, 15]. In comparison, queue-based locks achieve $O(1)$ RMR complexity but require additional primitives, such as atomic Fetch-And-Store or Fetch-And-Add.

Recovery from failures is featured prominently in the seminal work of Lamport [27], who formalized two types of faulty process behavior: "unannounced death", similar to a crash in our model but permanent, and "malfunctioning", whereby the private state and communication variables of a process assume arbitrary values. Lamport's Bakery algorithm [25] tolerates the first type of failure provided that a faulty process returns to the non-critical section and its communication variables (i.e., the single-writer shared registers written by it) are reset eventually to zero—an assumption that is false in our model.

Taubenfeld's treatment of fault-tolerant mutual exclusion focuses on a crash-recovery model where process failures affect the values of shared variables in well-defined ways [36]. This model is defined around single-writer registers, and assumes that only those variables that a process "owns" (i.e., has write access to) may be affected by its failure. In one variation, the program counter is reset to the non-critical section on failure, and any variables a process owns are reset to default values. In another variation, the program counter and variables owned by a process may adopt arbitrary values, possibly leading to temporary violations of safety and liveness. Solutions in the latter category are based upon Dijkstra's self-stabilization paradigm [12]. In comparison, a failure in our model resets the program counter deterministically and does not affect shared variables at all. Furthermore, we consider multi-writer registers in Section 3, as well as read-modify-write primitives in Section 4.

Bohannon et al. [9] proposed a technique for determining the ownership of a Test-And-Set lock following a permanent crash failure, which is the most difficult aspect of recovery in this case given that the mutex algorithm itself is quite simple. In a follow-up paper, Bohannon et al. [8], added recoverability to Mellor-Crummey and Scott's queue-based mutex algorithm [30] by designing an intricate mechanism to repair the queue structure after a process fails while enqueuing or dequeuing itself. Both papers augment the mutex lock with additional shared variables to detect the intent of a process to enter the CS, and perform corrective actions inside a dedicated recovery process that is able to detect failures by querying the operating system. This process is itself assumed to be reliable. In terms of RMR complexity, Bohannon et al.'s recoverable MCS lock [8] does not bound the number of RMRs per passage in the CC or DSM models, even if there is only one failure in the DSM model. In comparison, our model allows both failures and concurrency in the recovery protocol, and three of our algorithms guarantee bounded RMR complexity per passage irrespective of the number of failures.

Michael and Kim proposed another fault-tolerant mutex lock in which an active process that is waiting to acquire a lock can "usurp" the lock if it determines that the previous lock holder has crashed permanently [31]. This technique is not applicable in our model since we assume that a crashed process eventually recovers and attempts to clean up the lock.

Research on mutual exclusion, and more generally on concurrent objects, has focused mostly on models where the memory is reliable. In this body of work, a limited form or resilience against unreliable processes follows immediately from liveness guarantees in an asynchronous environment, where a slow process cannot be distinguished from one that has crashed permanently. For example, Herlihy introduced *wait-free* objects [19], which guarantee the progress of each correct process individually. In comparison, only a handful of papers consider computation using unreliable memory, focusing on minor corruptions such as bit flips. Afek et al. [1] considered the consensus problem in this general context, Moscibroda and Oshman [1] focused on mutual exclusion, and Jayanti et al. [22] proposed implementations of shared objects from unreliable base objects. In contrast to these techniques, which break if the number of corruptions exceeds a specified bound, Hoepman et al. [20], as well as Johnen and Higham [23], proposed self-stabilizing shared objects that can tolerate any number of memory failures but may lose their safety properties temporarily after a failure.

6. CONCLUSION

In this paper, we formalized the recoverable mutual exclusion problem and presented four solutions, three of which guarantee bounded RMR complexity per passage in the CC and DSM models irrespective of failures (see Figure 1). Our work leaves open several research questions: Can this problem be solved using $o(\log N)$ RMRs per passage in the worst case using commonly supported primitives? Can randomized solutions beat deterministic ones in terms of RMRs, as has been shown for ordinary mutual exclusion [6, 7, 14, 18]? Is it possible to solve the problem for N processes using bounded RMRs in the DSM model and only $O(N)$ shared variables, thus improving on the space complexity of our N-process algorithms? (Simple optimizations reduce the space complexity of our solutions to $O(N)$ in the CC model.) How would one design a recoverable reader-writer lock?

7. ACKNOWLEDGMENTS

The authors are supported in part by the Natural Sciences and Engineering Research Council (NSERC) of Canada, Discovery Grants Program. Peter Buhr and Patrick Lam are gratefully acknowledged for their detailed feedback on Aditya Ramaraju's Master's thesis, on which this paper is based.

8. REFERENCES

[1] Y. Afek, D. S. Greenberg, M. Merritt, and G. Taubenfeld. Computing with faulty shared memory. In *Proc. of the 11th ACM Symposium on Principles of Distributed Computing (PODC)*, pages 47–58, 1992.

[2] J. Anderson and Y.-J. Kim. A new fast-path mechanism for mutual exclusion. *Distributed Computing*, 14(1):17–29, 2001.

[3] J. Anderson and Y.-J. Kim. An improved lower bound for the time complexity of mutual exclusion. *Distributed Computing*, 15(4):221–253, 2002.

[4] J. Anderson, Y.-J. Kim, and T. Herman. Shared-memory mutual exclusion: Major research trends since 1986. *Distributed Computing*, 16(2-3):75–110, 2003.

[5] T. Anderson. The performance of spin lock alternatives for shared-memory multiprocessors. *IEEE Transactions on Parallel and Distributed Systems*, 1(1):6–16, 1990.

[6] H. Attiya, D. Hendler, and P. Woelfel. Tight RMR lower bounds for mutual exclusion and other problems. In *Proc. of the 40th ACM Symposium on Theory of Computing (STOC)*, pages 217–226, 2008.

[7] M. A. Bender and S. Gilbert. Mutual Exclusion with $O(\log^2 \log n)$ Amortized Work. In *Proc. of the 52nd Symposium on Foundations of Computer Science (FOCS)*, pages 728–737, 2011.

[8] P. Bohannon, D. F. Lieuwen, and A. Silberschatz. Recovering scalable spin locks. In *Proc. of the 8th IEEE Symposium on Parallel and Distributed Processing (SPDP)*, pages 314–322, 1996.

[9] P. Bohannon, D. F. Lieuwen, A. Silberschatz, S. Sudarshan, and J. Gava. Recoverable user-level mutual exclusion. In *Proc. of the 7th IEEE Symposium on Parallel and Distributed Processing (SPDP)*, pages 293–301, 1995.

[10] R. Cypher. The communication requirements of mutual exclusion. In *Proc. of the 7th ACM Symposium on Parallel Algorithms and Architectures (SPAA)*, pages 147–156, 1995.

[11] E. W. Dijkstra. Solution of a problem in concurrent programming control. *Communications of the ACM*, 8(9):569, 1965.

[12] E. W. Dijkstra. Self-stabilizing systems in spite of distributed control. *Communications of the ACM*, 17(11):643-644, 1974.

[13] R. Fan and N. Lynch. An $\Omega(n \log n)$ lower bound on the cost of mutual exclusion. In *Proc. of the 25th ACM Symposium on Principles of Distributed Computing (PODC)*, pages 275–284, 2006.

[14] G. Giakkoupis and P. Woelfel. Randomized Mutual Exclusion with Constant Amortized RMR Complexity on the DSM. In *Proc. of the 55th Symposium on Foundations of Computer Science (FOCS)*, pages 504–513, 2014.

[15] W. Golab, V. Hadzilacos, D. Hendler, and P. Woelfel. RMR-efficient implementations of comparison primitives using read and write operations. *Distributed Computing*, 25(2):109–162, 2012.

[16] G. Graunke and S. Thakkar. Synchronization algorithms for shared-memory multiprocessors. *IEEE Computer*, 23(6):60–69, 1990.

[17] J. Gray and A. Reuter. *Transaction Processing: Concepts and Techniques*. Morgan Kaufmann, 1993.

[18] D. Hendler and P. Woelfel. Randomized mutual exclusion with sub-logarithmic RMR-complexity. *Distributed Computing*, 24(1):3–19, 2011.

[19] M. Herlihy. Wait-free synchronization. *ACM Transactions on Programming Languages and Systems*, 13(1):124–149, 1991.

[20] J.-H. Hoepman, M. Papatriantafilou, and P. Tsigas. Self-stabilization of wait-free shared memory objects. In *Proc. of the 9th International Workshop on Distributed Algorithms (WDAG)*, pages 273–287, 1995.

[21] Intel Corporation. Single-chip cloud computer. http://www.intel.com/content/dam/www/public/us/en/documents/technology-briefs/intel-labs-single-chip-cloud-overview-paper.pdf.

[22] P. Jayanti, T. Chandra, and S. Toueg. Fault-tolerant wait-free shared objects. In *Proc. of the 33rd Symposium on Foundations of Computer Science (FOCS)*, pages 157–166, 1992.

[23] C. Johnen and L. Higham. Fault-tolerant implementations of regular registers by safe registers with applications to networks. In *Proc. of 10th International Conference of Distributed Computing and Networking (ICDCN)*, pages 337–348, 2009.

[24] J. Kessels. Arbitration without common modifiable variables. *Acta Informatica*, 17:135–141, 1982.

[25] L. Lamport. A new solution of Dijkstra's concurrent programming problem. *Communications of the ACM*, 17(8):453–455, 1974.

[26] L. Lamport. The mutual exclusion problem: part I – a theory of interprocess communication. *Journal of the ACM*, 33(2):313–326, 1986.

[27] L. Lamport. The mutual exclusion problem: part II – statement and solutions. *Journal of the ACM*, 33(2):327–348, 1986.

[28] L. Lamport. A fast mutual exclusion algorithm. *ACM Transactions on Computer Systems*, 5(1):1–11, 1987.

[29] P. Magnusson, A. Landin, and E. Hagersten. Queue locks on cache coherent multiprocessors. In *Proc. of the 8th International Parallel Processing Symposium (IPPS)*, pages 165–171, 1994.

[30] J. Mellor-Crummey and M. Scott. Algorithms for scalable synchronization on shared-memory multiprocessors. *ACM Transactions on Computer Systems*, 9(1):21–65, 1991.

[31] M. Michael and Y. Kim. Fault tolerant mutual exclusion locks for shared memory systems. US Patent 7,493,618, 2009.

[32] D. Narayanan and O. Hodson. Whole-system persistence. In *Proc. of the 17th International Conference on Architectural Support for Programming Languages and Operating Systems (ASPLOS)*, pages 401–410, 2012.

[33] A. Ramaraju. RGLock: Recoverable mutual exclusion for non-volatile main memory systems. Master's thesis, University of Waterloo, 2015. https://uwspace.uwaterloo.ca/handle/10012/9473.

[34] M. Raynal. *Algorithms for Mutual Exclusion*. MIT Press, 1986.

[35] M. Scott and W. Scherer. Scalable queue-based spin locks with timeout. In *Proc. of the 8th ACM SIGPLAN symposium on Principles and Practices of Parallel Programming (PPoPP)*, pages 44–52, 2001.

[36] G. Taubenfeld. *Synchronization Algorithms and Concurrent Programming*. Prentice Hall, 2006.

[37] J.-H. Yang and J. Anderson. A fast, scalable mutual exclusion algorithm. *Distributed Computing*, 9(1):51–60, 1995.

A Randomized Concurrent Algorithm for Disjoint Set Union

Siddhartha V. Jayanti
Department of Computer Science
Princeton University
Princeton, NJ 08540
sjayanti@princeton.edu

Robert E. Tarjan
Department of Computer Science
Princeton University, Princeton, NJ 08540
& Intertrust Technologies, Sunnyvale, CA 94085
ret@princeton.edu

ABSTRACT

Disjoint set union is a basic problem in data structures with a wide variety of applications. We extend a known efficient sequential algorithm for this problem to obtain a simple and efficient concurrent wait-free algorithm running on an asynchronous parallel random access machine (APRAM). Crucial to our result is the use of randomization. Under a certain independence assumption, for a problem instance in which there are n elements, m operations, and l processes, our algorithm does $\Theta\big(m\left(\alpha\big(n, \frac{m}{nl}\big) + \log\left(\frac{nl}{m}+1\right)\right)\big)$ expected work, where the expectation is over the random choices made by the algorithm and α is a functional inverse of Ackermann's function. In addition, each operation takes $O(\log n)$ steps with high probability.

We point out some gaps in the earlier work on this problem by Anderson and Woll [1]. More importantly, our algorithm is significantly simpler than theirs. Finally, under our independence assumption our algorithm achieves speedup close to linear for applications in which all or most of the processes can be kept busy, thereby partially answering an open problem posed by them.

Keywords

disjoint set union, set union, union-find, data structures, graph algorithms, randomized, algorithms, concurrent, parallel, multiprocessor, linearizable, wait-free

1. INTRODUCTION

The disjoint set union problem, sometimes called the union-find problem, requires maintaining a collection of disjoint sets under on-line union operations. Applications include storage allocation in compilers [14], finding minimum spanning trees [16], finding dominators in flow graphs [7], testing percolation [16], and computing strongly connected components in directed graphs [2,3]. The classical compressed-tree data structure solves the problem sequentially in almost-constant amortized and logarithmic worst-case time per operation. In some applications the problem instances can be enormous. A notable example is model checking [19], which requires computing strongly connected components of implicitly defined, potentially huge directed graphs. A concurrent set union algorithm may well significantly improve performance in such an application, as the work of Bloemen et al. [2,3] suggests.

To our knowledge the only previous work on concurrent algorithms for set union is that of Anderson and Woll [1]. (Another paper [15] addresses the more restricted problem of doing a number of set unions simultaneously, using a distributed memory.) Anderson and Woll's computer model is an asynchronous parallel random-access machine (APRAM) [5, 9], in which a number of processes, each with a local memory, share a common memory that contains the data structure. Concurrent reading is allowed, but not concurrent writing. There is no synchronization among the processes: any process can run arbitrarily slowly as compared to any other. The main correctness criterion is *linearizability*, the requirement that each operation can be viewed as occurring atomically at some point during its execution [12]. An important goal in this model is to avoid having one process wait for another to finish. A concurrent algorithm in which each process can make progress no matter what other processes are doing is *wait-free* [11]. A useful primitive in building wait-free algorithms is CAS(x, y, z), which tests whether $x = y$ and if so assigns $x \leftarrow z$ and returns *true*; if not, it merely returns *false*. This operation is atomic: if the test is *true*, no other process can change x after the test but before x is changed to y. *Total work*, the total number of primitive steps done (summed over all processes) is the natural efficiency metric in this model. Anderson and Woll study concurrent APRAM algorithms for disjoint set union built using CAS, with each set operation done by one process. Our work significantly improves theirs given an independence assumption on the linearization order of some of the operations.

Anderson and Woll propose a concurrent wait-free version of a sequential algorithm, namely *linking by rank* with *path-halving* [18]. They claim a total work bound of $\Theta(m(l + \alpha(m, 0)))$ for m operations executed by l processes. Here α is a functional inverse of Ackermann's function (defined in Section 2), constant for all practical purposes. The bound for the corresponding sequential (one-process) algorithm is $\Theta\left(m \cdot \alpha(n, m/n)\right)$ where n is the number of nodes. Thus, if we consider a situation in which l processes of equal speed are kept active simultaneously through an execution, the total time taken by Anderson and Woll's multiprocessor algorithm to do m operations would be asymptotically the same

PODC'16, July 25 - 28, 2016, Chicago, IL, USA

ISBN 978-1-4503-3964-3/16/07...$15.00

DOI: http://dx.doi.org/10.1145/2933057.2933108

as the total time taken by a sequential algorithm to do the same m operations up to a factor of α. Thus, we say that Anderson and Woll's algorithm has insignificant *speedup*. Also, to obtain their result they add a level of indirection to the data structure and add an extra computation to the union operation, both of which complicate the algorithm. Furthermore, their justification for their claimed work bound is flawed. Even assuming their work bound (and their more-complicated results based on it) are correct, there remains the question of whether there is a simple concurrent algorithm with linear or close-to-linear speedup. Indeed, they leave this question as an open problem. We answer it in the affirmative given a certain independence assumption.

Crucial to our result is randomization, specifically the use of randomized linking [10]. We develop a wait-free concurrent algorithm with an expected total work bound of

$$\Theta\left(m\left(\alpha\left(n,\frac{m}{nl}\right)+\log\left(\frac{nl}{m}+1\right)\right)\right)$$

and a high-probability bound of $O(\log n)$ steps for each set operation. Our computation model is that of Anderson and Woll. Our result significantly simplifies and improves theirs.

The remainder of our paper consists of five sections. Section 2 reviews efficient sequential algorithms for disjoint set union. Section 3 develops our concurrent algorithm, and Section 4 analyzes it. Section 5 discusses some variants to the algorithm, and Section 6 contains some final remarks.

2. SEQUENTIAL SET UNION USING COMPRESSED TREES

The *disjoint set union problem*, sometimes called the *union-find problem*, requires the maintenance of a collection of disjoint sets under the operation of set union. There are various versions of the problem, but we shall study the following one: Given n elements, each initially in a singleton set, perform a sequence of on-line conditional update operations of the following kind:

UNITE(x, y): Given elements x and y, if x and y are in the same set, return *true*; otherwise, unite the sets containing x and y, and return *false*.

Sometimes it is useful to have a second operation that merely tests whether two elements are in the same set:

SAMESET(x, y): If elements x and y are in the same set, return *true*; otherwise, return *false*.

The classical sequential solution [17, 18] to this problem is to represent each set by a *compressed tree*. This is a rooted tree whose nodes are the elements of the set, with each node x storing a pointer $x.p$ to its parent if it has one or to itself if it is a root. Operations UNITE and SAMESET use an auxiliary function FIND(x) that traverses the path of parents from x to the root of the tree containing x and returns the root. Operation SAMESET(x, y) returns *true* if FIND(x) = FIND(y), *false* otherwise. Operation UNITE(x, y) returns *true* if FIND(x) = FIND(y); otherwise, it makes FIND(x) the parent of FIND(y) and returns *false*.

The path of nodes visited by a FIND is the *find path*. Optionally, a FIND can *compact* the find path by replacing one or more parents by nodes farther along the path. Compaction affects only efficiency, not correctness. Three classical compaction methods are *compression*, *splitting*, and *halving*. Compression replaces the parent of every node on the find path by the last node on the path (the root returned by the FIND); splitting replaces the parent of every node on the path by its grandparent; halving replaces the parent of every other node on the find path by its grandparent, starting with the first node on the path. Compression requires two passes over the find path, splitting or halving only one.

The step in UNITE that makes FIND(x) the parent of FIND(y) is called *linking* FIND(x) to FIND(y). Optionally, UNITE can choose to link FIND(y) to FIND(x) instead of linking FIND(x) to FIND(y). This choice affects only efficiency, not correctness. One classical choice is *linking by size* [17], which maintains the size of each root, defined to be the number of nodes in its tree, and links the root of smaller size to the root of larger size, breaking a tie arbitrarily. A related choice is *linking by rank* [18], which maintains a rank for each root, initially zero, and links the root of smaller rank to the root of larger rank; in case of a tie, it breaks the tie by increasing the rank of one of the roots by one. Both linking by size and linking by rank are deterministic; each requires maintaining a value (size or rank respectively) with each root. A more recently studied method is *randomized linking* [10], which chooses a fixed total order of the elements uniformly at random, and links the smaller root with respect to the total order to the larger.

Any of the three compaction methods can be combined with any of the three linking methods, giving a total of nine different algorithms. Each of these has a time bound of $O(m\cdot\alpha(n, m/n))$ for m operations [10, 18], worst-case for linking by size or rank, expected for randomized linking. Here α is a functional inverse of Ackermann's function, defined as follows: Let $A(i, j)$ (Ackermann's function) be the function on non-negative integers defined recursively by $A(0, j) = j+1, A(i, 0) = A(i-1, 1)$ for $i > 0$, and $A(i, j) = A(i-1, A(i, j-1))$ for $i > 0$ and $j > 0$. For k a non-negative integer and d a non-negative real number, $\alpha(k, d) = \min\{i > 0 | A(i, \lfloor d\rfloor) > k\}$.

3. WAIT-FREE CONCURRENCY VIA RANDOMIZED LINKING

Our goal is to extend one or more of the sequential algorithms for disjoint set union to allow several set operations to be done at the same time, by separate processes. To obtain the wait-free property using conditional assignment, every update of the data structure must produce a legal state. This makes it hard or impossible to use linking by size or rank, since both methods need to simultaneously update both a parent and a size or rank. (Anderson and Woll implement a method related to linking by rank, using indirection in an attempt to handle the simultaneous updating problem, but they still have to handle rank ties in the data structure, which results in either an unsatisfactory work bound or a very complicated method.) Randomized linking only changes one value at a time, however, making it the method of choice for us.

Each node in our data structure has two fields, its parent $x.p$ and its *ID* $x.id$. The forest structure is formed by the parent pointers, while the randomized linking order is given by the order of the nodes by ID. In the initial state, we assume that each node x is a singleton tree, i.e. $x.p = x$ and that the order given by the $x.id$'s is chosen uniformly randomly. Anderson and Woll used one level of indirection to ensure that both the parent and the rank could be compared and updated atomically in a single CAS. We are able to do away with the indirection as our ID fields are unchanged over the duration of the algorithm, and thus only parent fields need to be compared and updated atomically.

We base our concurrent implementations of SAMESET and UNITE on those of Anderson and Woll. Our implementation of SAMESET is essentially the same as theirs; our implementation of UNITE is simpler in that it does not need to do simultaneous updates and avoids indirection. In the pseudocode below, linearization points are marked by asterisks. That is, some steps are marked with asterisks, and in each procedure the last step with an asterisk to be executed is the linearization point. When an asterisk is on a FIND, the linearization point of the corresponding FIND is the intended step. Finally, if x and y are nodes, we use the comparison $x < y$ to mean $x.id < y.id$.

Algorithm 1 Returns the root of x's tree.

```
procedure FIND(x)
    u ← x
    while (u ≠ u.p)* do
        u ← u.p
    return u
```

Algorithm 2 Returns whether x and y are in the same set.

```
procedure SAMESET(x, y)
    u ← x    v ← y
    while (true) do
        u ← FIND(u)
        v ← FIND(v)*
        if (u = v) then return true
        if (u = u.p) then return false
```

Algorithm 3 Unites x's and y's sets and returns whether x and y were in the same set.

```
procedure UNITE(x, y)
    u ← x    v ← y
    while (true) do
        u ← FIND(u)
        v ← FIND(v)
        if (u < v) then
            if CAS(u.p, u, v)* then return false
        else if (u = v)* then return true
        else
            if CAS(v.p, v, u)* then return false
```

In SAMESET and UNITE, the linearization points are at the last execution of a step with an asterisk. These implementations rely on two key observations of Anderson and Woll: once $u = v$, nodes x and y are in the same set now and in the future; if $u < v$ and u is a root, then x and y are for the moment in different sets. The implementations are more complicated than the sequential implementations described in Section 2 because they must handle the possibility that, even though u is a root immediately after it is updated, u can become a non-root by the time v is next updated, by having another process change $u.p$. When this happens, both u and v must be updated again.

Algorithm 1 does FIND without compaction. We can improve overall efficiency by doing some form of compaction. The following versions of FIND do concurrent splitting and halving, respectively.

Algorithm 4 Find with splitting.

```
procedure FIND(x)
    u ← x
    while (true) do
        v ← u.p
        w ← v.p
        if (v = w)* then
            return v
        else
            CAS(u.p, v, w)
            u ← v
```

Algorithm 5 Find with halving.

```
procedure FIND(x)
    u ← x
    while (true) do
        v ← u.p
        w ← v.p
        if (v = w)* then
            return v
        else
            CAS(u.p, v, w)
            u ← u.p
```

This gives us three different concurrent set union algorithms, depending on the choice of FIND method. We analyze these methods in the next section. In the remainder of this section, we sketch a proof of correctness of all three methods.

We define the *reference forest* to be the forest constructed by links in UNITEs, ignoring all parent changes done by FINDs.

LEMMA 1. *Each link in* UNITE *makes a root the child of a node in a different tree. Each parent update in* FIND *replaces a parent by one of the parent's proper ancestors in the reference forest. if x is not a root $x < x.p$; if x is a root, $x = x.p$.*

PROOF. The lemma follows by induction on the number of parent changes. Observe that when UNITE links u to v, v may no longer be a root, even though v was a root when it was last updated, since in the meantime another process could have made v a child of another node. Symmetrically, when UNITE links v to u, u may no longer be a root. □

LEMMA 2 (LINEARIZABILITY). *Consider any concurrent execution of set operations. The last executions of the steps marked by asterisks in each operation give a linearization. That is, let $\mathcal{O}$ be the order of operations given by the proposed linearization points. If the operations are executed sequentially in order $\mathcal{O}$, then their returned values will be the same as in the concurrent execution.*

PROOF. The lemma follows by induction on the number of steps. □

LEMMA 3 (WAIT-FREEDOM). *The operations are wait-free.*

PROOF. By Lemma 1, each update of u in FIND replaces u by a proper ancestor of u in the reference forest, and each pair of calls of FIND(u) and FIND(v) in SAMESET and UNITE replaces at least one of u and v by a proper ancestor in the reference forest. It follows that any execution of SAMESET or UNITE finishes in $O(h+1)$ steps, where h is the height of the reference forest. □

THEOREM 1. *The concurrent implementation is correct with any of the three versions of* FIND.

PROOF. The theorem follows from Lemmas 1, 2, and 3. □

4. EFFICIENCY ANALYSIS

Now we study the efficiency of the methods proposed in Section 3. We bound the total work (the total number of steps) taken by l processes executing m operations on n elements. We assume that each operation is done by a single process, so at most l operations overlap. In stating bounds we assume $n > 1$ (otherwise the problem is trivial) and $m \geq n/2$ (otherwise some elements are never found and can be ignored). We rely on bounds obtained by Goel et al. [10] for sequential disjoint set union with randomized linking. Number the elements from 1 to n consistent with the random total order. Identify elements by number. Define the *rank* $x.r$ of an element x to be $\lfloor \lg n \rfloor - \lfloor \lg(n-x+1) \rfloor$ where lg is the base-2 logarithm. Thus, the rank of n is $\lfloor \lg n \rfloor$, that of $n-1$ and $n-2$ is $\lfloor \lg n \rfloor - 1$ and so on. Since ranks are monotonic in node ID (though not strictly), $x.r \leq x.p.r$ for any node x. For purposes of the analysis we assume that the random node order is independent of the linearization of the links done by the UNITE operations.

LEMMA 4. *Each time a root u is linked to a node v, the probability that $u.r < v.r$ is at least $\frac{1}{2}$, independent of all previous links.*

PROOF. The proofs of Lemma 2.3 and Theorem 2.1 in [10] apply to our concurrent linking algorithm. Their proof of Theorem 2.1 contains the statement of the lemma. □

LEMMA 5. *Let $h \geq 1$. For any node x, the expected number of ancestors of x in the reference forest of rank less than h is at most $2h$, and this number is at most $2ch$ with probability at least $1 - e^{\frac{-(c-1)^2 h^2}{2c}}$, for any constant $c > 1$.*

PROOF. Call a link of u to v a *success* if $v.r > u.r$. Let x be any node, and consider the links that give x a new ancestor. When the hth success occurs, the new ancestor of x has rank at least h, as do all ancestors added by later links. The number of links required to obtain h successes is stochastically dominated by a negative binomial distribution with $p = \frac{1}{2}$, and hence has mean at most $2h$ [6]. Furthermore, for any $c > 1$ the probability that $2ch$ links include less than h successes is at most $e^{\frac{-(c-1)^2 h^2}{2c}}$ by a Chernoff bound [4]. □

COROLLARY 1. *With probability at least $1 - \frac{1}{n}$, all nodes have $O(\log n)$ ancestors in the reference forest.*

PROOF. Choose $h = \log n$ and c such that $e^{\frac{-(c-1)^2 h^2}{2c}} \leq \frac{1}{n^2}$. By Lemma 5, any given node has more than $2c \log n + 1$ ancestors in the reference forest with probability at most $\frac{1}{n^2}$. (The $+1$ counts the one possible ancestor of rank $\lfloor \log n \rfloor$.) Hence with probability at least $1 - \frac{1}{n}$, all nodes have at most $2c \log n + 1$ ancestors in the reference forest. □

Given an input x or y to a SAMESET or UNITE, we define the *find sequence* of x or y to be the sequence of values of u or v, respectively, during the operation. By Lemma 1, each find sequence is a sequence of distinct, not necessarily consecutive ancestors in the reference forest. The number of steps done by SAMESET(x, y) or UNITE(x, y) is $O(1)$ plus a constant times the number of nodes on the find sequences of x and y.

THEOREM 2. *With any of the three versions of* FIND, *the probability that every operation does $O(\log n)$ steps, and hence that the total work is $O(m \log n)$, is at least $1 - \frac{1}{n}$.*

PROOF. By Corollary 1, with probability at least $1 - \frac{1}{n}$, every find sequence contains $O(\log n)$ nodes. □

Remark 1. We can increase the success probability in Corollary 1 and Theorem 2 to $1 - \frac{1}{n^{c \log n}}$ for any positive constant c, at the cost of increasing the constant hidden in the big-O notation.

Remark 2. This also confirms the conjecture that the reference forest in the sequential version of randomized linking is of logarithmic height with high probability, an open problem from [10].

By Theorem 2, concurrent randomized linking has linear speedup with high probability over a sequential method that uses any linking rule but no compaction, as long as each set operation is executed by a single process.

To obtain a better work bound for FIND with splitting or halving, we need to delve into the analysis of Goel et al. We use the *potential method* of amortized analysis: we assign to each configuration of the data structure a real-valued *potential* and define the *amortized cost* of an operation to be its actual cost plus the net increase in potential it causes. The total cost of a sequence of operations is then the sum of their amortized costs plus the initial potential minus the final potential. In the analysis of set union, the potential is always non-negative; thus the total cost of a sequence of operations is at most the sum of their amortized costs plus the initial potential.

We need to extend the analysis of Goel et al. to deal with one process changing a parent pointer while other processes are visiting the same node. This would seem to increase the work bound by a factor of l over the sequential time bound, but we are able to reduce this to roughly a logarithmic factor by combining two ideas: we multiply the node potential of Goel et al. by a factor of $2l$, and we give positive potential only to nodes of sufficiently high rank, of which there are very few. The need to count steps that fail to change parent pointers was missed by Anderson and Woll, who claimed (falsely) that an $O(m \cdot \alpha(n, m/n))$ time bound for a sequential set union algorithm implies an $O(m \cdot \alpha(n, m/n))$ work bound for a concurrent version of the same algorithm. We analyze concurrent splitting. The analysis of concurrent halving is similar.

Let $d = \frac{m}{nl}$. We define the *index function* $b(i, k)$ for integers i and k by $b(i, k) = \min\{j \geq 0 | A(i, j) > k\}$. We define the *level function* $a(k, j)$ for non-negative integers k, j by $a(k, j) = \min(\{\alpha(k, d) + 1\} \cup \{i \leq \alpha(k, d) | A(i, b(i, k)) > j\})$. For each node x, we define a *level* $x.a$, *index* $x.b$, and *count* $x.c$ as follows: $x.a = a(x.r, x.p.r)$; $x.b = b(x.a - 1, x.p.r)$ if $x.a > 0$, 0 otherwise; $x.c = x.a(x.r - 2) + x.b$.

Goel et al. proved the following:

i. The level of a node is non-negative and non-decreasing.

ii. The count of a node is non-negative and non-decreasing.

iii. If x is any node such that x, $x.p$, and $x.p.p$ are distinct and $u.a \leq u.p.a$, then changing the parent of u to $u.p.p$ or any higher node increases $x.c$ by at least 1; furthermore, if $u.a < u.p.a$, then changing the parent of u to $u.p.p$ or any higher node increases $x.a$ to at least $u.p.a$.

We use these three properties to bound the total work done by our algorithm if FINDs use splitting or halving.

THEOREM 3. *If* FINDs *are done with splitting or halving, the expected total work done by the concurrent set union algorithm is* $O\left(m\left(\alpha(n, \frac{m}{nl}) + \log\left(\frac{nl}{m} + 1\right)\right)\right)$ *for any fixed linearization of the links in* UNITE.

PROOF. We consider two cases. The simpler one is $d \geq 1$; that is, $\frac{m}{nl} \geq 1$. We define the potential of a node x to be $2l$ times the sum of the number of proper ancestors of x of the same rank and $\max\{0, (\alpha(x.r, d)+1) \times (x.r+2)+d+1-x.c\}$, and the potential of the data structure to be the sum of the node potentials. It follows from results of Goel et al. that the potential of a node is non-negative and non-decreasing, and the expected total node potential is $O(n(d+1)l) = O(m)$.

The total work is $O(m)$ plus at most a constant times the number of occurrences of nodes on find paths. The number of FINDs is at most $2m + 2nl \leq 4m$, since each SAMESET or UNITE does at least two FINDs, and each link, of which there are at most $n-1$, can give rise to $2l$ additional FINDs. We define the cost of a FIND to be the number of nodes on the find path. We give each FIND a potential of $\alpha(n, d) + 3$. We prove that the amortized cost per FIND is non-positive. It follows that the total work is bounded by a constant times the sum of the initial total node potential and the sum of the find potentials, which is $O(m \cdot \alpha(n, d))$.

To keep track of the cost of a FIND, we charge it 1 each time it updates variable u, plus 1 for the last node visited (the root), which is assigned to both v and w (and possibly u) in the last iteration of the loop in FIND. Of the $\alpha(n, d)+3$ units of potential assigned to a FIND, two pay for the initial assignment to u (outside the loop in FIND) and the last node visited. We prove that the loop in FIND maintains the invariant that the FIND has a potential of at least $u.a$, the level of u. Since $u.a$ is non-negative, the invariant implies that the amortized cost of the FIND is non-positive, as desired.

The invariant holds just after u is initialized, since the FIND has $\alpha(n, d) + 1$ units of potential not counting those spent on the first and last nodes of the find path, and the level of any node, including the initial value of u, is at most $\alpha(n, d)+1$. Suppose the invariant holds after some setting of u. Consider the interval of time after this setting and before the next setting of w. If during this interval $u.a$ increases, the potential of node u drops by at least $2l$ times the increase in $u.a$ by (iii). When such an increase occurs, we assign $1/l$ of the potential drop (at least 2 units per level increase) to each of the at most l processes currently visiting u. This is more than enough to maintain the invariant; indeed, if $u.a$ increases at all we get one extra unit of potential to pay for the next setting of u. Thus, the invariant holds when w is set. Call this time t.

We consider three possibilities at time t. If at t, $u.a > v.a$, then the FIND has at least $v.a+1$ units of potential, and this is maintained until u is set to v by the argument above applied to v. Of the $v.a + 1$ units of potential, one pays for the new setting of u, and the rest preserves the invariant. If at t, $u.a = v.a$, then the FIND has at least $v.a$ units of potential, and this is maintained until the CAS operation. Furthermore by (iii), when the CAS operation occurs or earlier, but after t, u will drop in potential, releasing at least two units of potential to the FIND, giving it at least $v.a + 1$ units of potential, and the invariant holds until u is next set, as in the first possibility. The third possibility is $u.a < v.a$, and the difference is some positive $\Delta = v.a - u.a$. In this case the FIND has at least $v.a - \Delta$ units of potential until the CAS operation, with any increase in $v.a$ covered by node potential released from v. By (iii), between t and the time the CAS occurs, at least $2\Delta \geq \Delta + 1$ units of potential will have been released to the FIND from u. Thus when the CAS occurs, the FIND has at least $v.a + 1$ units of potential, and this is maintained until u is next set, as in the first two possibilities.

We conclude that the invariant holds throughout each FIND. Hence the expected total work is $O(m \cdot \alpha(n, d))$.

The second case is $d < 1$; that is, $m < nl$. In this case we apply the argument in the first case only to nodes of high-rank, and use a separate argument to bound the number of occurrences of low-rank nodes on find paths. We call a node *low* if its rank is less than $\lg(1/d)$, and *high* otherwise, where lg is the base-2 logarithm. By Lemma 5, the expected number of low nodes in a find sequence is at most $2\lg(1/d)$. Hence the expected total number of occurrences of low nodes on find sequences is $O(m \cdot \log(1/d))$.

It remains to count the number of occurrences of high nodes in find sequences. We call a FIND *high* if its find path contains at least one high node. The find paths of the high finds contain all the occurrences of high nodes on find sequences. There are $O(\frac{n}{2^{\lg(1/d)}}) = O(nd) = O(m/l)$ high nodes. The number of high finds is at most $2m$ (two per set operation) plus $O(lm/l)$ (at most $2l$ per link of a high node to another (high) node) for a total of $O(m)$. If we define node potentials as in the first case, but only for high nodes, the argument above shows that the expected total number of occurrences of nodes on high find paths is $O(m \cdot \alpha(n, d))$ (the total find potential) plus $O(m)$ (the expected total node potential). Hence the expected total number of occurrences of high nodes on find paths is $O(m \cdot \alpha(n, d))$.

Combining the bounds for low and high nodes, we conclude that the total work is $O(m \cdot (\alpha(n, d) + log(1/d)))$. Combining the results for the first and second cases finishes the proof. □

The following lemma helps us show that the bound in Theorem 3 is tight to within a constant factor.

LEMMA 6. *For any* k, *a suitable sequence of* $k-1$ UNITE*s with* FIND*s done by halving or splitting will build a* k*-node tree whose average node depth is* $\Omega(\log k)$.

PROOF. The proof is constructive and is similar to the construction of binomial trees. The idea is the same as that used to build binomial trees; namely, start with singletons, unite them in pairs, unite the resulting trees in pairs, and repeat until there is one tree. The only complication is that the construction process does not have direct access to the tree roots but can only access them via FINDs, which do compaction. By choosing the parameters to the UNITEs properly, we can guarantee that the compactions have little effect.

Specifically, suppose k is a power of 2. Begin with k singletons, each of whose nodes is the representative of its set. Repeat the following $\lg k$ times: Pair up the existing sets, unite the pairs by calling UNITE on the representatives of the two sets, and designate either of the representatives of the two old sets to be the representative of the new set. This process maintains the following invariants:

1. After i rounds of UNITEs, each tree contains 2^i nodes.
2. Each representative has depth at most 2.
3. After i rounds of UNITEs, the subtree of any node x of depth δ contains at most $2^{i-\delta}$ nodes.

Invariant (1) is immediate. Invariant (2) follows by induction on the number of rounds of UNITEs, since if (2) holds for a representative, a FIND on it reduces its depth to at most 1, and a subsequent link can increase its depth to at most 2. Invariant (3) follows since splitting or halving can only decrease the number of descendants of a non-root.

Now consider the sum of the depths of all k nodes as UNITEs proceed. Consider a UNITE in round $i+1$ that combines two trees with representatives x and y, respectively. The FIND on x can decrease one or more node depths only if x has depth 1 before the FIND and 1 after, in which case it decreases the sum of node depths by at most 2^{i-2} by (3). Similarly, the FIND on y can decrease the sum of node depths by at most 2^{i-2}. The link after the two FINDs increases the sum of node depths by 2^i, for a net increase of 2^{i-1}. The entire round increases the sum of node depths by at least $\frac{k}{4}$. We conclude that after all $\lg k$ rounds, the average node depth is at least $\frac{1}{4}\lg k$.

If k is not a power of 2, we apply the argument above to the largest power of 2 no larger than k (at least $\frac{k}{2}$) to form a tree T, form an arbitrary tree out of enough singletons to bring the total number of nodes to k, and unite the two trees, doing the find in T on its representative. □

THEOREM 4. *The bound in Theorem 3 is tight to within a constant factor. That is, for any m, n, and l, there is a sequence of set operations that take*

$$\Omega\Big(m\cdot\Big(\alpha\Big(n,\frac{m}{nl}\Big)+\log\Big(\frac{nl}{m}+1\Big)\Big)\Big)$$

expected work.

PROOF. Fredman and Saks [8] proved a sequential lower bound of $\Omega(m\cdot\alpha(n,m/n))$ that holds for randomized algorithms. Our version of the problem only exposes UNITE and SAMESET operations; but we can do exactly the same amount of work as a FIND(x) if we simply add an extra node ξ so that there are a total of $n+1$ nodes, and then do a SAMESET(x,ξ) instead of doing a FIND(x). Thus, if operations are done sequentially using our algorithm, there must be a sequence of M operations that do $\Omega(M\cdot\alpha(n,M/n))$ work. Now, we simply allow $M=\frac{m}{l}$ and let each of the l processes do the same operations. If the operations happen to run in lock-step (where all the processes are moving up the find paths together and are thereby not benefitting from any of the compactions in any given set of l steps), then we get a sequence of operations in our algorithm that do work:

$$\Omega\Big(l\cdot\frac{m}{l}\cdot\alpha\Big(n,\frac{m}{nl}\Big)\Big)=\Omega\Big(m\cdot\alpha\Big(n,\frac{m}{nl}\Big)\Big)$$

Simply ensuring that each set of l operations is finished before the next set is started ensures that the linearization order of the links is fixed.

In the case that the $\log\left(\frac{nl}{m}\right)$ term dominates the α term, we know that $nl>m$. Let $\delta=\frac{1}{3d}=\frac{nl}{3m}$ for simplicity of notation in the lower bound example below, and note that $\delta<n$, since $n<2m$ and $l<m$. Below is an explicit sequence of operations that take $\Omega(m\log(\delta))$ expected time (we assume without loss of generality that δ divides n):

1. Use one of the processes to create $\frac{n}{\delta}$ trees $T_1,\ldots,T_{\frac{n}{\delta}}$ each with expected node depth $\Omega(\log\delta)$. This can be done by Lemma 6 using at most n UNITE operations.
2. Pick nodes $x_1,\ldots,x_{\frac{n}{\delta}}$ randomly from the trees $T_1,\ldots,T_{\frac{n}{\delta}}$ respectively.
3. Perform the operation SAMESET(x_i,x_i) with each of the l processes for each $i\in\{1,\ldots,\frac{n}{\delta}\}$. Now, if the processes run in lock-step, then each operation is expected to take $\Omega(\log\delta)$ work.

Note that since $m=\Omega(n)$, at least a constant fraction of the operations in the above process are SAMESET operations from step 3. It follows from the above that the worst-case total expected work of the above sequence of operations is:

$$\Omega\Big(\frac{n}{\delta}\cdot l\cdot\log(\delta)\Big)=\Omega(m\log(\delta))=\Omega\Big(m\cdot\log\Big(\frac{nl}{m}\Big)\Big)$$

□

THEOREM 5 (EFFICIENCY RESULT). *For a fixed linearization of the links in UNITE operations, our algorithm with FIND using halving or splitting does worst case expected work:*

$$\Theta\Big(m\Big(\alpha\Big(n,\frac{m}{nl}\Big)+\log\Big(\frac{nl}{m}+1\Big)\Big)\Big)$$

PROOF. This result follows from Theorem 3 and Theorem 4. □

5. EXTENSIONS

We now present variants of the UNITE and SAMESET procedures that satisfy the efficiency bound in Theorem 3. These variants terminate some FINDs early, exploiting the total order of nodes by ID. We name these variants *early-linking* UNITE and *early-recognition* SAMESET to emphasize the early termination.

The key property of linking in UNITE(x,y) that is needed for the efficiency bounds is that the root whose parent is changed has lower ID than its new parent. This allows us to extend Goel et. al.'s sequential implementation of early-linking UNITE, which traverses the find sequences of x and y simultaneously and stops as soon as one root's ID is smaller than that of the next node in the other sequence to get our concurrent version.

Algorithm 6 Unite implemented with early-linking.

```
procedure UNITE(x, y)
    u ← x    v ← y
    while (true) do
        if (u = v)* then return true
        if (v < u) then SWAP(u, v)
        if CAS(u.p, u, v)* then return false
        z ← u.p
        w ← z.p
        CAS(u.p, z, w)
        u ← z
```

A similar idea can be applied to SAMESET(x, y). When x and y are indeed in the same set, we notice that we can identify this at the least common ancestor of x and y rather than go all the way up to the root. Also, when x and y are in different sets, we notice that we can identify this as soon as we see a root of one of the trees has lower ID than some node in the other tree. These observations lead to the following early-recognition version of SAMESET.

Algorithm 7 Same-set implemented with early-recognition.

```
procedure SAMESET(x, y)
    u ← x    v ← y
    while (true) do
        if (u = v)* then return true
        if (v < u) then SWAP(u, v)
        if (u = u.p)* then return false
        z ← u.p
        w ← z.p
        CAS(u.p, z, w)
        u ← z
```

Goel et al. also analyze two more types of compaction: *splicing* and *compression*. Splicing performs UNITE(x, y) by intermixing the find sequences of x and y. This method has no wait-free linearizable extension, since mixing nodes in the two trees before the linearization point of the UNITE could cause inconsistencies in the return values that make linearization impossible. Compression on the other hand is the only form of compaction analyzed by Goel et al. that is not local. We conjecture that a concurrent FIND with compression would yield an algorithm with the same efficiency guarantees as those with splitting and halving. However, we believe that splitting and halving should be the methods of choice as they require only a single traversal up the tree, as opposed to compression which requires two traversals.

6. REMARKS

We have designed a wait-free concurrent algorithm for disjoint set union, and have shown a tight efficiency bound under the assumption that the linearized order of UNITE operations is independent of the random order on the nodes (we conjecture that this efficiency bound will reflect the actual work done in practice). There is some flexibility in the algorithm. In particular, FINDs can be done using either halving or splitting, and indeed different FINDs can use different methods. Furthermore, UNITEs and SAMESETs can be done by either the classical or early-linking/recognition procedures, and each SAMESET and UNITE can be done by a different method. The bounds in Theorem 2 and 3 hold for any combination of these methods. See [10] for further details.

Our algorithm assumes that nodes are numbered randomly during an initialization phase, but the numbering can be done incrementally if nodes are created on the fly, as can happen in applications. All that is necessary is that a newly created node be assigned a number uniformly at random from a large enough universe that collisions are unlikely. If the nodes are stored in a hash table, for example, the storage location of the node can be used as its number.

Whereas for the sequential version of the problem randomization does not give an asymptotic improvement in efficiency [10], for the concurrent version it does. We have recently shown that we can obtain the efficiency bound in Theorem 3 deterministically and without any independence assumptions using the two word compare-and-swap primitive DCAS [13]. However, we conjecture that this bound cannot be achieved using regular one word CAS. We leave this question of obtaining an efficient deterministic algorithm matching our bounds, or showing that it is impossible to do so, as an open problem.

7. REFERENCES

[1] R. J. Anderson and H. S. Woll. Wait-free parallel algorithms for the union-find problem. In *Full version of STOC '91: Proceedings of the 23rd ACM Symposium on Theory of Computation.* Unpublished Manuscript, 1994.

[2] V. Bloemen. On-The-Fly Parallel Decomposition of Strongly Connected Components. Master's thesis, University of Twente, 2015.

[3] V. Bloemen, A. Laarman, and J. van de Pol. Multi-core on-the-fly scc decomposition. In *Proceedings of the 21st ACM SIGPLAN symposium on Principles and practice of parallel programming*, PPoPP '16, page to appear, 2016.

[4] F. Chung and L. Lu. *Concentration Inequalities and Martingale Inequalities: A Survey*, pages 79–127. 2005.

[5] R. Cole and O. Zajicek. The apram: Incorporating asynchrony into the pram model. In *Proceedings of the First Annual ACM Symposium on Parallel Algorithms and Architectures*, SPAA '89, pages 169–178, New York, NY, USA, 1989. ACM.

[6] W. Feller. *An Introduction to Probability Theory and Its Applications*, volume 1. Wiley, January 1968.

[7] W. Fraczak, L. Georgiadis, A. Miller, and R. E. Tarjan. Corrections to "finding dominators via disjoint set union" [J. discrete algorithms 23 (2013) 2-20]. *J. Discrete Algorithms*, 26:106–110, 2014.

[8] M. L. Fredman and M. E. Saks. The cell probe complexity of dynamic data structures. In *Proceedings of the 21st Annual ACM Symposium on Theory of Computing, May 14-17, 1989, Seattle, Washigton, USA*, pages 345–354, 1989.

[9] P. B. Gibbons. A more practical pram model. In *Proceedings of the First Annual ACM Symposium on Parallel Algorithms and Architectures*, SPAA '89, pages 158–168, New York, NY, USA, 1989. ACM.

[10] A. Goel, S. Khanna, D. H. Larkin, and R. E. Tarjan. Disjoint set union with randomized linking. In *Proceedings of the Twenty-Fifth Annual ACM-SIAM*

Symposium on Discrete Algorithms, SODA 2014, Portland, Oregon, USA, January 5-7, 2014, pages 1005–1017, 2014.

[11] M. Herlihy. Wait-free synchronization. *ACM Trans. Program. Lang. Syst.*, 13(1):124–149, Jan. 1991.

[12] M. Herlihy and J. M. Wing. Linearizability: A correctness condition for concurrent objects. *ACM Transactions on Programming Languages and Systems*, 12(3):463–492, Jul 1990.

[13] S. V. Jayanti and R. E. Tarjan. An efficient deterministic concurrent algorithm for disjoint set union. In *To Appear.*

[14] C. Lattner and V. Adve. Automatic pool allocation for disjoint data structures. *SIGPLAN Not.*, 38(2 supplement):13–24, June 2002.

[15] F. Manne and M. M. A. Patwary. A scalable parallel union-find algorithm for distributed memory computers. In *Proceedings of the 8th International Conference on Parallel Processing and Applied Mathematics: Part I*, PPAM'09, pages 186–195, Berlin, Heidelberg, 2010. Springer-Verlag.

[16] R. Sedgewick and K. Wayne. *Algorithms, 4th Edition.* Addison-Wesley, 2011.

[17] R. E. Tarjan. Efficiency of a good but not linear set union algorithm. *J. ACM*, 22(2):215–225, Apr. 1975.

[18] R. E. Tarjan and J. van Leeuwen. Worst-case analysis of set union algorithms. *J. ACM*, 31(2):245–281, Mar. 1984.

[19] P. Wolper. Lectures on formal methods and performance analysis. chapter Constructing Automata from Temporal Logic Formulas: A Tutorial, pages 261–277. Springer-Verlag New York, Inc., New York, NY, USA, 2002.

Self-stabilizing Balls & Bins in Batches

The Power of Leaky Bins [Extended Abstract]*

Petra Berenbrink
Simon Fraser University,
Burnaby, BC V5A 1S6, Canada.
University of Hamburg,
20148 Hamburg, Germany.
petra@cs.sfu.ca

Tom Friedetzky
Durham University
Durham DH1 3LE
U.K.
tom.friedetzky@dur.ac.uk

Peter Kling
Simon Fraser University
Burnaby, BC V5A 1S6
Canada
pkling@sfu.ca

Frederik Mallmann-Trenn
École normale supérieure
75005 Paris, France.
Simon Fraser University
Burnaby, BC V5A 1S6, Canada.
mallmann@di.ens.fr

Lars Nagel
Johannes
Gutenberg-Universität Mainz
55128 Mainz
Germany
nagell@uni-mainz.de

Christopher Wastell
Durham University
Durham DH1 3LE
U.K.
christopher.wastell@dur.ac.uk

ABSTRACT

A fundamental problem in distributed computing is the distribution of requests to a set of uniform servers without a centralized controller. Classically, such problems are modelled as static balls into bins processes, where m balls (tasks) are to be distributed to n bins (servers). In a seminal work, Azar et al. [4] proposed the sequential strategy GREEDY[d] for $n = m$. When thrown, a ball queries the load of d random bins and is allocated to a least loaded of these. Azar et al. showed that $d = 2$ yields an exponential improvement compared to $d = 1$. Berenbrink et al. [7] extended this to $m \gg n$, showing that the maximal load difference is independent of m for $d = 2$ (in contrast to $d = 1$).

We propose a new variant of an *infinite* balls into bins process. In each round an expected number of λn new balls arrive and are distributed (in parallel) to the bins and each non-empty bin deletes one of its balls. This setting models a set of servers processing incoming requests, where clients can query a server's current load but receive no information about parallel requests. We study the GREEDY[d] distribution scheme in this setting and show a strong self-stabilizing property: For *any* arrival rate $\lambda = \lambda(n) < 1$, the system load is time-invariant. Moreover, for *any* (even super-exponential) round t, the maximum system load is (w.h.p.) $O(\frac{1}{1-\lambda} \cdot \log \frac{n}{1-\lambda})$ for $d = 1$ and $O(\log \frac{n}{1-\lambda})$ for $d = 2$. In particular, GREEDY[2] has an exponentially smaller system load for high arrival rates.

*See [10] for the full version of this paper.

PODC'16, July 25–28, 2016, Chicago, IL, USA.

ISBN 978-1-4503-3964-3/16/07...$15.00

DOI: http://dx.doi.org/10.1145/2933057.2933092

1. INTRODUCTION

One of the fundamental problems in distributed computing is the distribution of requests, tasks, or data items to a set of uniform servers. In order to simplify this process and to avoid a single point of failure, it is often advisable to use a simple, randomized strategy instead of a complex, centralized controller to allocate the requests to the servers. In the most naïve strategy (*1-choice*), each client chooses the server where to send its request uniformly at random. A more elaborate scheme (*2-choice*) chooses two (or more) servers, queries their current loads, and sends the request to a least loaded of these. Both approaches are typically modelled as balls-into-bins processes [2, 4, 5, 7, 14, 21, 23], where requests are represented as balls and servers as bins. While the latter approach leads to considerably better load distributions [4, 7], it loses some of its power in parallel settings, where requests arrive in parallel and cannot take each other into account [2, 23].

We propose and study a new infinite and batchwise balls-into-bins process to model the client-server scenario. In a round, each server (bin) consumes one of its current tasks (balls). Afterward, (expectedly) λn tasks arrive and are allocated using a given distribution scheme. The *arrival rate* λ is allowed to be a function of n (e.g., $\lambda = 1 - 1/\operatorname{poly}(n)$). Standard balls-into-bins results imply that, for high arrival rates, with high probability[1] (w.h.p.) in each round there is a bin that receives $\Theta(\log n)$ balls.

Most other infinite processes limit the total number of concurrent balls in the system by n [4, 5] and show a fast recovery. Since we do not limit the number of balls, our process can, in principle, result in an arbitrary high system load. In particular, if starting in a high-load situation (e.g., exponentially many balls), we cannot recover in a polynomial number of steps. Instead, we adapt the following notion of *self-stabilization*: The system is positive recurrent (expected return time to a low-load situation is finite) and taking a snapshot of the load situation at an *arbitrary* (even super-exponential large) time yields (w.h.p.)

[1] An event $\mathcal{E}$ occurs *with high probability* (w.h.p.) if $\Pr(\mathcal{E}) = 1 - n^{-\Omega(1)}$.

a low maximum load. Positive recurrence is a standard notion for stability and basically states that the system load is time-invariant. For irreducible, aperiodic Markov chains it implies the existence of a unique stationary distribution (cf. Section 1.2). While this alone does not guarantee a good load in the stationary distribution, together with the snapshot property we can look at an arbitrary time window of polynomial size (even if it is exponentially far away from the start situation) and give strong load guarantees. In particular, we give the following bounds on the load in addition to showing positive recurrence:

1-choice Process: The maximum load at an arbitrary time is (w.h.p.) bounded by $O\left(\frac{1}{1-\lambda} \cdot \log \frac{n}{1-\lambda}\right)$. We also provide a lower bound which is asymptotically tight for $\lambda \leq 1 - 1/\operatorname{poly}(n)$. While this implies that already the simple 1-choice process is self-stabilizing, the load properties in a "typical" state are poor: even an arrival rate of only $\lambda = 1 - 1/n$ yields a superlinear maximum load.

2-choice Process: The maximum load at an arbitrary time is (w.h.p.) bounded by $O\left(\log \frac{n}{1-\lambda}\right)$. This allows to maintain an exponentially better system load compared to the 1-choice process; for any $\lambda = 1 - 1/\operatorname{poly}(n)$ the maximum load remains logarithmic.

1.1 Related Work

Let us continue with an overview of related work. We start with classical results for sequential and finite balls-into-bins processes, go over to parallel settings, and give an overview over infinite and batch-based processes similar to ours. We also briefly mention some results from queuing theory (which is related but studies slightly different quality of service measures and system models).

Sequential Setting.

There are many strong, well-known results for the classical, sequential balls-into-bins process. In the sequential setting, m balls are thrown one after another and allocated to n bins. For $m = n$, the maximum load of any bin is known to be (w.h.p.) $(1 + o(1)) \cdot \ln(n)/\ln\ln n$ for the 1-choice process [14, 21] and $\ln\ln(n)/\ln d + \Theta(1)$ for the d-choice process with $d \geq 2$ [4]. If $m \geq n \cdot \ln n$, the maximum load increases to $m/n + \Theta\left(\sqrt{m \cdot \ln(n)/n}\right)$ [21] and $m/n + \ln\ln(n)/\ln d + \Theta(1)$ [7], respectively. In particular, note that the number of balls above the average grows with m for $d = 1$ but is independent of m for $d \geq 2$. This fundamental difference is known as the *power of two choices*. A similar (if slightly weaker) result was shown by Talwar and Wieder [24] using a quite elegant proof technique (which we also employ and generalize for our analysis in Section 3). Czumaj and Stemann [12] study adaptive allocation processes where the number of a ball's choices depends on the load of queried bins. The authors subsequently analyze a scenario that allows reallocations.

Berenbrink et al. [9] adapt the threshold protocol from [2] (see below) to a sequential setting and $m \geq n$ bins. Here, ball i randomly chooses a bin until it sees a load smaller than $1 + i/n$. While this is a relatively strong assumption on the balls, this protocol needs only $O(m)$ choices in total (allocation time) and achieves an almost optimal maximum load of $\lceil m/n \rceil + 1$.

Parallel Setting.

Several papers (e.g., [2, 23]) investigated parallel settings of multiple-choice games for the case $m = n$. Here, all m balls have to be allocated in parallel, but balls and bins might employ some (limited) communication. Adler et al. [2] consider a trade-off between the maximum load and the number of communication rounds r the balls need to decide for a target bin. Basically, bounds that are close to the classical (sequential) processes can only be achieved if r is close to the maximum load [2]. The authors also give a lower bound on the maximum load if r communication rounds are allowed, and Stemann [23] provides a matching upper bound via a collision-based protocol.

Infinite Processes.

In infinite processes, the number of balls to be thrown is not fixed. Instead, in each of infinitely many rounds, balls are thrown or reallocated and bins (possibly) delete old balls. Azar et al. [4] consider an infinite, sequential process starting with n balls arbitrarily assigned to n bins. In each round one random ball is reallocated using the d-choice process. For any $t > cn^2 \log\log n$, the maximum load at time t is (w.h.p.) $\ln\ln(n)/\ln d + O(1)$.

Adler et al. [1] consider a system where in each round $m \leq n/9$ balls are allocated. Bins have a FIFO queue, and each arriving ball is stored in the queue of two random bins. After each round, every non-empty bin deletes its frontmost ball (which automatically removes its copy from the second random bin). It is shown that the expected waiting time is constant and the maximum waiting time is (w.h.p.) $\ln\ln(n)/\ln d + O(1)$. The restriction $m \leq n/9$ is the major drawback of this process. A differential and experimental study of this process was conducted in [6]. The balls' arrival times are binomially distributed with parameters n and $\lambda = m/n$. Their results indicate a stable behaviour for $\lambda \leq 0.86$. A similar model was considered by Mitzenmacher [19], who considers ball arrivals as a Poisson stream of rate λn for $\lambda < 1$. It is shown that the 2-choice process reduces the waiting time exponentially compared to the 1-choice process.

Czumaj [11] presents a framework to study the recovery time of discrete-time dynamic allocation processes. In each round one of n balls is reallocated using the d-choice process. Two models are considered: In the first, the ball to reallocate is chosen by taking a ball of a random bin. In the second, the ball to reallocate is chosen by selecting a random ball. From an arbitrary initial assignment, the system is shown to recover to the maximum load from [4] within $O(n^2 \ln n)$ rounds in the former and $O(n \ln n)$ rounds in the latter case. Becchetti et al. [5] consider a similar (but parallel) process. In each round one ball is chosen from every non-empty bin and reallocated to a randomly chosen bin (one choice per ball). The authors show that (w.h.p.) starting from an arbitrary configuration, it takes $O(n)$ rounds to reach a configuration with maximum load $O(\log n)$. Moreover, if the process starts in a configuration with maximum load $O(\log n)$, then the maximum load stays in $O(\log n)$ for $\operatorname{poly}(n)$ rounds. An interesting connection to our work is that the analysis of [5] is based on an auxiliary TETRIS-process. This process can be seen a special version of our 1-choice process and is defined as follows: Starting from a state with at least $n/4$ empty bins, in each round every non-empty bin deletes one ball. Subsequently, exactly $(3/4)n$ new balls are allocated to the bins (one choice per ball).

Batch-Processes.
Batch-based processes allocate m balls to n bins in batches of (usually) n balls each, where each batch is allocated in parallel. They lie between (pure) parallel and sequential processes. For $m = \tau \cdot n$, Stemann [23] investigates a scenario with n players each having m/n balls. To allocate a ball, every player independently chooses two bins and allocates copies of the ball to both of them. Every bin has two queues (one for first copies, one for second copies) and processes one ball from each queue per round. When a ball is processed, its copy is removed from the system and the player is allowed to initiate the allocation of the next ball. If $\tau = \ln n$, all balls are processed in $\mathrm{O}(\ln n)$ rounds and the waiting time is (w.h.p.) $\mathrm{O}(\ln \ln n)$. Berenbrink et al. [8] study the d-choice process in a scenario where m balls are allocated to n bins in batches of size n each. The authors show that the load of every bin is (w.h.p.) $m/n \pm \mathrm{O}(\log n)$. As noted in Lemma 3.5, our analysis can be used to derive the same result by easier means.

Queuing Processes.
Batch arrival processes have also been considered in the context of queuing systems. A key motivation for such models stems from the asynchronous transfer mode (ATM) in telecommunication systems. Tasks arrive in batches, are stored in a FIFO queue and served by a fixed number of servers which remove the tasks from the queue and process them. Several papers [3, 16, 17, 22] consider scenarios where the number of arriving tasks is determined by a finite state Markov chain. Results study steady state properties of the system to determine properties of interest (e.g., waiting times or queue lengths). Sohraby and Zhang [22] use spectral techniques to study a multi-server scenario with an infinite queue. Alfa [3] considers a discrete-time process for n identical servers and tasks with constant service time $s \geq 1$. To ensure a stable system, the arrival rate λ is assumed to be at most n/s and tasks are assigned cyclical, allowing to study an arbitrary server (instead of the complete system). Kamal [16] and Kim et al. [17] study a system with a finite capacity. The tasks which arrive when the buffer is full are lost. The authors study the steady state probability and give empirical results to show the decay of waiting times as n increases.

1.2 Model & Preliminaries

We model our load balancing problem as an infinite, parallel balls-into-bins process. Time is divided into discrete, synchronous rounds. There are n bins and n generators, and the initial system is assumed to be empty. At the start of each round, every non-empty bin deletes one ball. Afterward, every generator generates a ball with a probability of $\lambda = \lambda(n) \in [0,1]$ (the *arrival rate*). This generation scheme allows us to consider arrival rates that are arbitrarily close to one (like $1 - 1/\operatorname{poly}(n)$). Generated balls are distributed in the system using a distribution process. In this paper we analyze two specific distribution processes: (a) The 1-choice process GREEDY[1] assigns every ball to a randomly chosen bin. (b) The 2-choice process GREEDY[2] assigns every ball to a least loaded among two randomly chosen bins.

Notation.
The random variable $X_i(t)$ denotes the load (number of balls) of the i-th fullest bin[2] at the end of round t. Thus, the load situation (configuration) after round t can be described by the load vector $\boldsymbol{X}(t) = (X_i(t))_{i \in [n]} \in \mathbb{N}^n$. We define $\varnothing(t) := \frac{1}{n}\sum_{i=1}^{n} X_i(t)$ as the average load at the end of round t. The value $\nu(t)$ denotes the fraction of non-empty bins after round t and $\eta(t) := 1 - \nu(t)$ the fraction of empty bins after round t. It will be useful to define $1_i(t) := \min(1, X_i(t))$ and $\eta_i(t) := 1_i(t) - \nu(t)$ (which equals $\eta(t)$ if i is a non-empty bin and $-\nu(t)$ otherwise).

Markov Chain Preliminaries.
The evolution of the load vector over time can be interpreted as a Markov chain, since $\boldsymbol{X}(t)$ depends only on $\boldsymbol{X}(t-1)$ and the random choices during round t. We refer to this Markov chain as $\boldsymbol{X}$. Note that $\boldsymbol{X}$ is time-homogeneous (transition probabilities are time-independent), irreducible (every state is reachable from every other state), and aperiodic (path lengths have no period; in fact, our chain is lazy). Recall that such a Markov chain is positive recurrent (or ergodic) if the probability to return to the start state is 1 and the expected return time is finite. In particular, this implies the existence of a unique stationary distribution. Positive recurrence is a standard formalization of the intuitive concept of stability. See [18] for an excellent introduction into Markov chains and the involved terminology.

2. THE 1-CHOICE PROCESS

We present two main results for the 1-choice process: Theorem 2.1 states the stability of the system under the 1-choice process for an arbitrary λ, using the standard notion of positive recurrence (cf. Section 1). In particular, this implies the existence of a stationary distribution for the 1-choice process. Theorem 2.2 strengthens this by giving a high probability bound on the maximum load for an *arbitrary* round $t \in \mathbb{N}$. Together, both results imply that the 1-choice process is self-stabilizing.

THEOREM 2.1 (STABILITY). *Let $\lambda = \lambda(n) < 1$. The Markov chain $\boldsymbol{X}$ of the 1-choice process is positive recurrent.*

THEOREM 2.2 (MAXIMUM LOAD). *Let $\lambda = \lambda(n) < 1$. Fix an arbitrary round t of the 1-choice process. The maximum load of all bins is (w.h.p.) bounded by $\mathrm{O}\left(\frac{1}{1-\lambda} \cdot \log \frac{n}{1-\lambda}\right)$.*

Note that for high arrival rates of the form $\lambda(n) = 1 - \varepsilon(n)$, the bound given in Theorem 2.2 is inversely proportional to $\varepsilon(n)$. For example, for $\varepsilon(n) = 1/n$ the maximal load is $\mathrm{O}(n \log n)$. Theorem 2.3 shows that this dependence is unavoidable: the bound given in Theorem 2.2 is tight for large values of λ. In Section 3, we will see that the 2-choice process features an exponentially better behaviour for large λ.

THEOREM 2.3. *Let $\lambda = \lambda(n) \geq 0.5$ and consider step $t := 9\lambda \log(n)/(64(1-\lambda)^2)$. With probability $1 - o(1)$ there is a bin i in step t with load $\Omega\left(\frac{1}{1-\lambda} \cdot \log n\right)$.*

The proofs of these results can be found in the following subsections. We first prove a bound on the maximum load

[2] In the proofs we assume that bins are sorted by their load in descending order.

(Theorem 2.2), afterward we prove stability of the system (Theorem 2.1), and finally we prove the lower bound (Theorem 2.3).

2.1 Maximum Load

PROOF OF THEOREM 2.2 (MAXIMUM LOAD). In the following, we prove Theorem 2.2 using a (slightly simplified) drift theorem from [15] (cf. Theorem A.2 in Appendix A). Remember that, as mentioned in Section 1.2, our process is a Markov chain, such that we need to condition only on the previous state (instead of the full filtration from Theorem A.2). Our goal is to bound the load of a fixed bin i at time t using Theorem A.2 and, subsequently, to use this with a union bound to bound the maximum load over all bins. To apply Theorem A.2, we have to prove that the maximum load difference of bin i between two rounds is is exponentially bounded (Majorization) and that, given a high enough load, the system tends to lose load (Negative Bias). We start with the majorization. The load difference $|X_i(t+1)-X_i(t)|$ is bounded by $\max(1, B_i(t)) \leq 1 + B_i(t)$, where $B_i(t)$ is the number of tokens resource i receives during round $t+1$. In particular, we have $(|X_i(t+1) - X_i(t)| \mid \boldsymbol{X}(t)) \prec 1 + B_i(t)$. Note that $B_i(t)$ is binomially distributed with parameters n and λ/n (each of the n balls has probability of $\lambda \cdot 1/n$ to end up in i). Using standard inequalities we bound $\Pr(B_i(t) = k)$

$$\leq \binom{n}{k} \cdot \left(\frac{\lambda}{n}\right)^k \leq \left(\frac{e \cdot n}{k}\right)^k \cdot \left(\frac{1}{n}\right)^k = \frac{e^k}{k^k} \tag{1}$$

and calculate $\mathbb{E}\left[e^{B_i(t)+1}\right]$

$$\begin{aligned} &= e \cdot \sum_{k=0}^{n} e^k \cdot \frac{e^k}{k^k} \leq e \cdot \sum_{k=0}^{\lceil e^3-1 \rceil} \frac{e^{2k}}{k^k} + e \cdot \sum_{k=e^3}^{\infty} \frac{e^{2k}}{k^k} \\ &\leq \Theta(1) + \sum_{k=1}^{\infty} e^{-k} = \Theta(1). \end{aligned} \tag{2}$$

This shows that the Majorization condition from Theorem A.2 holds (with $\lambda' = 1$ and $D = \Theta(1)$). To see that the Negative Bias condition is also given, note that if bin i has non-zero load, it is guaranteed to delete one ball and receives in expectation $n \cdot \lambda / n = \lambda$ balls. We get $\mathbb{E}[X_i(t+1) - X_i(t) \mid X_i(t) > 0] \leq \lambda - 1 < 0$, establishing the Negative Bias condition (with $\varepsilon_0 = 1 - \lambda$). We finally can apply Theorem A.2 with $\eta := \min(1, (1-\lambda)/2D, 1/(2-2\lambda)) = (1-\lambda)/(2D)$ and get for $b \geq 0$ that $\Pr(X_i(t) \geq b)$

$$\begin{aligned} &\leq e^{-b \cdot \eta} + \frac{2D}{\eta \cdot (1-\lambda)} \cdot e^{\eta \cdot (1-b)} \leq \frac{2 \cdot (2D)^2}{(1-\lambda)^2} \cdot e^{\frac{(1-\lambda)\cdot(1-b)}{2D}} \\ &= \frac{c}{(1-\lambda)^2} \cdot e^{-\frac{b \cdot (1-\lambda)}{c}}, \end{aligned} \tag{3}$$

where c denotes a suitable constant. Applying a union bound to all n bins and choosing $b := \frac{c}{1-\lambda} \cdot \ln\left(\frac{c \cdot n^{a+1}}{(1-\lambda)^2}\right)$ yields that $\Pr\left(\max_{i \in [n]} X_i(t) \geq b\right) \leq n^{-a}$. The theorem's statement now follows from

$$\begin{aligned} b &= \frac{c}{1-\lambda} \cdot \ln\left(\frac{c \cdot n^{a+1}}{(1-\lambda)^2}\right) \leq \frac{c \cdot (a+1) + 1}{1-\lambda} \cdot \ln\left(\frac{n}{1-\lambda}\right) \\ &= \mathrm{O}\left(\frac{1}{1-\lambda} \cdot \ln\left(\frac{n}{1-\lambda}\right)\right). \ \square \end{aligned}$$

2.2 Stability

In the following, we provide an auxiliary lemma that will prove useful to derive the stability of the 1-choice process.

LEMMA 2.4. *Let $\lambda = \lambda(n) < 1$. Fix an arbitrary round t of the 1-choice process and a bin i. There is a constant $c > 0$ such that the expected load of bin i is bounded by $\frac{6c}{1-\lambda} \cdot \ln\left(\frac{e \cdot c}{1-\lambda}\right)$.*

PROOF. To get a bound on the expected load of bin i, note that the probability in Equation (3) (see proof of Theorem 2.2) is 1 for $b \leq \gamma := \frac{c}{1-\lambda} \cdot \ln\left(\frac{e \cdot c}{(1-\lambda)^2}\right)$. Considering time windows of γ rounds each, we calculate $\mathbb{E}[X_i(t)]$

$$\begin{aligned} &\leq \sum_{b=1}^{\gamma} b \cdot \Pr(X_i(t) = b) + \sum_{k=1}^{\infty} \sum_{b=k \cdot \gamma}^{(k+1)\gamma} b \cdot \Pr(X_i(t) = b) \\ &\leq \gamma + \sum_{k=1}^{\infty} (k+1) \cdot \gamma \cdot \Pr(X_i(t) \geq k \cdot \gamma) \\ &\leq \gamma + \sum_{k=1}^{\infty} (k+1) \cdot \gamma \cdot e^{-k} \leq 3\gamma \leq \frac{6c}{1-\lambda} \cdot \ln\left(\frac{e \cdot c}{1-\lambda}\right). \end{aligned}$$

This finishes the proof. $\square$

PROOF OF THEOREM 2.1 (STABILITY). We prove Theorem 2.1 using a result from Fayolle et al. [13] (cf. Theorem A.1 in Appendix A). Note that $\boldsymbol{X}$ is a time-homogenous irreducible Markov chain with a countable state space. For a configuration $\boldsymbol{x}$ we define the auxiliary potential $\Psi(\boldsymbol{x}) := \sum_{i=1}^{n} x_i$ as the total system load of configuration $\boldsymbol{x}$. Consider the (finite) set $C := \{\, \boldsymbol{x} \mid \Psi(\boldsymbol{x}) \leq n^4/(1-\lambda)^2 \,\}$ of all configurations with not too much load. To prove positive recurrence, it remains to show that Condition (a) (expected potential drop if not in a high-load configuration) and Condition (b) (finite potential) of Theorem A.1 hold. In the following, let $\Delta := \frac{n^3}{(1-\lambda)^2}$.

Let us start with Condition (a). So fix a round t and let $\boldsymbol{x} = \boldsymbol{X}(t) \notin C$. By definition of C, we have $\Psi(\boldsymbol{x}) > n^4/(1-\lambda)^3$, such that there is at least one bin i with load $x_i \geq \Psi(\boldsymbol{x})/n > n^3/(1-\lambda)^2$. In particular, note that $x_i \geq \Delta$, such that during each of the next Δ rounds exactly one ball is deleted. On the other hand, bin i receives in expectation $\Delta \cdot \lambda n \cdot \frac{1}{n} = \lambda\Delta$ balls during the next Δ rounds. We get $\mathbb{E}[X_i(t+\Delta) - x_i \mid \boldsymbol{X}(t) = \boldsymbol{x}] = \lambda\Delta - \Delta = -(1-\lambda) \cdot \Delta$. For any bin $j \neq i$, we assume pessimistically that no ball is deleted. Note that the expected load increase of each of these bins can be majorized by the load increase in an empty system running for Δ rounds. Thus, we can use Lemma 2.4 to bound the expected load increase in each of these bins by $\frac{6c}{1-\lambda} \cdot \ln\left(\frac{e \cdot c}{1-\lambda}\right) \leq \frac{6e \cdot c^2}{(1-\lambda)^2} \leq \Delta/n^2$. We get $\mathbb{E}[\Psi(\boldsymbol{X}(t+\Delta)) \mid \boldsymbol{X}(t) = \boldsymbol{x}]$

$$\leq -(1-\lambda) \cdot \Delta + (n-1) \cdot \frac{\Delta}{n^2} \leq -\Delta \cdot \frac{1-\lambda}{2}. \tag{4}$$

This proves Condition (a) of Theorem A.1. For Condition (b), assume $\boldsymbol{x} = \boldsymbol{X}(t) \in C$. We bound the system load after Δ rounds trivially by $\mathbb{E}[\Psi(\boldsymbol{X}(t+\Delta)) \mid \boldsymbol{X}(t) = \boldsymbol{x}]$

$$\leq \Psi(\boldsymbol{x}) + \Delta \cdot n \leq \frac{n^4}{(1-\lambda)^2} + \Delta \cdot n < \infty \tag{5}$$

(note that the finiteness in Theorem A.1 is with respect to time, not n). This finishes the proof. $\square$

2.3 Lower Bound on Maximum Load

PROOF OF THEOREM 2.3 (LOWER BOUND). To show this result we will use a bound by Raab and Steger [21, Theorem 1] which lower bounds the the maximum number of balls a bin receives when m balls are allocated into m bins. The idea of the proof is as follows. We assume that we start at an empty system and apply [21, Theorem 1] on $m = \lambda tn$ many balls. The theorem says that one of the bins is likely to get greater than λt many balls, which allows us to show that the load of this bin is large, even if the bin was able to delete a ball during each of the t observed time steps.

Let $m(t')$ the the number of balls allocated during the first t' steps and let $b_u(t')$ the number of these balls that are allocated to bin u. Set $t = 9\lambda \log(n)/(64(1-\lambda)^2)$, assume $\lambda > 0.5$ and assume $\lambda nt \le n \cdot (\log n)^c$ for a constant c. Since the expected number of balls is $\lambda nt \ge n \log n$ we can use Chernoff bounds to show that (w.h.p.) at least $(1-\epsilon) \cdot m(t)$ balls are generated for very small ϵ. Then $\mathbb{E}[m(t')] = \frac{9\lambda \log n}{64(1-\lambda)^2} \cdot \lambda n$. Using Chernoff's inequality we can show that w.h.p. $m(t) \ge (1-\epsilon) \cdot \frac{9\lambda \log n}{64(1-\lambda)^2} \cdot \lambda n$ for an arbitrary small constant ϵ. By [21, Theorem 1] (Case 3) with $\alpha = \sqrt{8/9}$ we get (w.h.p.) $b_u(t)$

$$\ge (1-\epsilon) \cdot \frac{9\lambda \log n}{64(1-\lambda)^2} \cdot \lambda + \sqrt{(1-\epsilon) \cdot \frac{16 \cdot 9\lambda(\log n)^2}{9 \cdot 64(1-\lambda)^2} \cdot \lambda}.$$

We derive $X_u(t)$

$$\begin{aligned}
&\ge (1-\epsilon) \cdot \frac{9}{64} \frac{\lambda^2 \log n}{(1-\lambda)^2} \\
&\quad + \sqrt{(1-\epsilon) \cdot \frac{16 \cdot 9\lambda^2 \cdot (\log n)^2}{9 \cdot 64(1-\lambda)^2}} - \frac{9\lambda \log n}{64(1-\lambda)^2} \\
&= \lambda \cdot (1-\epsilon) \cdot \frac{9}{64} \frac{\lambda \log n}{(1-\lambda)^2} \\
&\quad + \sqrt{\frac{(1-\epsilon)}{4}} \cdot \frac{\lambda \log n}{(1-\lambda)} - \frac{9\lambda \log n}{64(1-\lambda)^2} \\
&= \sqrt{\frac{(1-\epsilon)}{4}} \cdot \frac{\lambda \log n}{(1-\lambda)} + (\lambda \cdot (1-\epsilon) - 1) \cdot \frac{9\lambda \log n}{64(1-\lambda)^2} \\
&\ge \sqrt{\frac{(1-\epsilon)}{4}} \cdot \frac{\lambda \log n}{(1-\lambda)} + ((1-\epsilon') - 1) \cdot \frac{9\lambda \log n}{64(1-\lambda)^2} \\
&\ge \sqrt{\frac{(1-\epsilon)}{4}} \cdot \frac{\lambda \log n}{(1-\lambda)} - \epsilon' \cdot \frac{9}{64} \frac{\lambda \log n}{(1-\lambda)} = \Omega\left(\frac{\lambda \log n}{1-\lambda}\right). \square
\end{aligned}$$

3. THE 2-CHOICE PROCESS

We continue with the study of the 2-choice process. Here, new balls are distributed according to GREEDY[2] (cf. description in Section 1.2). Our main results are the following theorems, which are equivalents to the corresponding theorems for the 1-choice process.

THEOREM 3.1 (STABILITY). *Let $\lambda = \lambda(n) \in [1/4, 1)$. The Markov chain $\boldsymbol{X}$ of the 2-choice process is positive recurrent.*

THEOREM 3.2 (MAXIMUM LOAD). *Consider $\lambda = \lambda(n) \in [1/4, 1)$. Fix an arbitrary round t of the 2-choice process. The maximum load of all bins is (w.h.p.) $O(\log \frac{n}{1-\lambda})$.*

Note that Theorem 3.2 implies a much better behaved system than we saw in Theorem 2.2 for the 1-choice process. In particular, it allows for an exponentially higher arrival rate: for $\lambda(n) = 1 - 1/\text{poly}(n)$ the 2-choice process maintains a maximal load of $O(\log n)$. In contrast, for the same arrival rate the 1-choice process results in a system with maximal load $\Omega(\text{poly}(n))$.

Our analysis of the 2-choice process relies to a large part on a good bound on the *smoothness* (the maximum load difference between any two bins). This is stated in the following lemma. This result is of independent interest, showing that even if the arrival rate is $1 - e^{-n}$, where we get a polynomial system load, the maximum load difference is still logarithmic.

LEMMA 3.3 (SMOOTHNESS). *Let $\lambda = \lambda(n) \in [1/4, 1]$. Fix an arbitrary round t of the 2-choice process. The load difference of all bins is (w.h.p.) bounded by $O(\ln n)$.*

Analysis Overview.

To prove these results, we combine three different potential functions: For a configuration $\boldsymbol{x}$ with average load $\varnothing$ and for a suitable constant α (to be fixed later), we define

$$\begin{aligned}
\Phi(\boldsymbol{x}) &:= \sum_{i \in [n]} e^{\alpha \cdot (x_i - \varnothing)} + \sum_{i \in [n]} e^{\alpha \cdot (\varnothing - x_i)}, \\
\Psi(\boldsymbol{x}) &:= \sum_{i \in [n]} x_i \quad \text{, and} \quad \Gamma(\boldsymbol{x}) := \Phi(\boldsymbol{x}) + \tfrac{n}{1-\lambda} \cdot \Psi(\boldsymbol{x}).
\end{aligned} \tag{6}$$

The potential Φ measures the *smoothness* (basically the maximum load difference to the average) of a configuration and is used to prove Lemma 3.3 (Section 3.1). The proof is based on the observation that whenever the load of a bin is far from the average load, it decreases in expectation. The potential Ψ measures the *total load* of a configuration and is used, in combination with our results on the smoothness, to prove Theorem 3.2 (Section 3.2). The potential Γ entangles the smoothness and total load, allowing us to prove Theorem 3.1 (Section 3.3). The proof is based on the fact that whenever Γ is large (i.e., the configuration is not smooth or it has a huge total load) it decreases in expectation.

Before we continue with our analysis, let us make a simple but useful observation concerning the smoothness: For any configuration $\boldsymbol{x}$ and value $b \ge 0$, the inequality $\Phi(\boldsymbol{x}) \le e^{\alpha \cdot b}$ implies (by definition of Φ) $\max_i |x_i - \varnothing| \le b$. That is, the load difference of any bin to the average is at most b and, thus, the load difference between any two bins is at most $2b$. We capture this in the following observation.

OBSERVATION 3.4. *Let $b \ge 0$ and consider a configuration $\boldsymbol{x}$ with average load $\varnothing$. If $\Phi(\boldsymbol{x}) \le e^{\alpha \cdot b}$, then $|x_i - \varnothing| \le b$ for all $i \in [n]$. In particular, $\max_i(x_i) - \min_i(x_i) \le 2b$.*

3.1 Bounding the Smoothness

The goal of this section is to prove Lemma 3.3. To do so, we show the following bound on the expected smoothness (potential Φ) at an arbitrary time t:

LEMMA 3.5. *Let $\lambda \in [1/4, 1]$. Fix round t of the 2-choice process. There is a const. $\varepsilon > 0$ with[3] $\mathbb{E}[\Phi(\boldsymbol{X}(t))] \le \frac{n}{\varepsilon}$.*

[3]For Φ, the condition $\lambda \ge 1/4$ can be substituted with $\lambda = \Omega(1)$ and only minor changes in the analysis. Moreover, the analysis can be easily adapted for a process that (deterministically) throws $\lambda \cdot n$ balls in each round, even for $\lambda > 1$ as long as it is a constant. Finally, one can easily

Note that Lemma 3.5 together with Observation 3.4 immediately implies Lemma 3.3 by a simple application of Markov's inequality to bound the probability that $\Phi(\boldsymbol{X}(t)) \geq n^2/\varepsilon$.

Our proof of Lemma 3.5 follows the lines of [20, 24], who used the same potential function to analyze variants of the sequential d-choice process without deletions. While the basic idea of showing a relative drop when the potential is high combined with a bounded absolute increase in the general case is the same, our analysis turns out much more involved. In particular, not only do we have to deal with deletions and throwing balls in batches but the size of each batch is also a random variable. Once Lemma 3.5 is proven, Lemma 3.3 emerges by combining Observation 3.4, Lemma 3.5, and Markov's inequality as follows:

$$\Pr\Big(\max_i X_i(t) - \min_i X_i(t) \geq \frac{4}{\alpha} \cdot \ln\Big(\frac{n}{\varepsilon}\Big)\Big) \leq \Pr\Big(\Phi(\boldsymbol{X}(t)) \geq \frac{n^2}{\varepsilon^2}\Big) \leq \frac{\varepsilon}{n}. \tag{7}$$

It remains to prove Lemma 3.5. Remember the definition of $\Phi(\boldsymbol{x})$ from Equation (6). We split the potential in two parts $\Phi(\boldsymbol{x}) := \Phi_+(\boldsymbol{x}) + \Phi_-(\boldsymbol{x})$. Here, $\Phi_+(\boldsymbol{x}) := \sum_i e^{\alpha\cdot(x_i - \varnothing)}$ denotes the *upper potential* of $\boldsymbol{x}$ and $\Phi_-(\boldsymbol{x}) := \sum_i e^{\alpha\cdot(\varnothing - x_i)}$ denotes the *lower potential* of $\boldsymbol{x}$. For a fixed bin i, we use $\Phi_{i,+}(\boldsymbol{x}) := e^{\alpha\cdot(x_i-\varnothing)}$ and $\Phi_{i,-}(\boldsymbol{x}) := e^{\alpha\cdot(\varnothing - x_i)}$ to denote i's contribution to the upper and lower potential, respectively. When we consider the effect of a fixed round $t+1$, we will sometimes omit the time parameter and use prime notation to denote the value of a parameter at the end of round $t+1$. For example, we write X_i and X_i' for the load of bin i at the beginning and at the end of round $t+1$, respectively.

We start with two simple but useful identities regarding the potential drop $\Delta_{i,+}(t+1)$ (and $\Delta_{i,-}(t+1)$) due to a fixed bin i during round $t+1$.

OBSERVATION 3.6. *Fix a bin i, let K denote the number of balls that are placed during round $t+1$ and let $k \leq K$ be the number of these balls that fall into bin i. Then*

(a) $\Delta_{i,+}(t+1) = \Phi_{i,+}(\boldsymbol{X}(t)) \cdot \left(e^{\alpha\cdot(k-\eta_i(t)-K/n)} - 1\right)$ *and*

(b) $\Delta_{i,-}(t+1) = \Phi_{i,-}(\boldsymbol{X}(t)) \cdot \left(e^{-\alpha\cdot(k-\eta_i(t)-K/n)} - 1\right)$.

We now derive the main technical lemma that states general bounds on the expected upper and lower potential change during a single round. This will be used to derive bounds on the potential change in different situations. For this, let $p_i := (\frac{i}{n})^2 - (\frac{i-1}{n})^2 = \frac{2i-1}{n^2}$ (the probability that a ball thrown with GREEDY[2] falls into the i-th fullest bin). We also define $\hat{\alpha} := e^\alpha - 1$ and $\check{\alpha} := 1 - e^{-\alpha}$. Note that $\hat{\alpha} \in (\alpha, \alpha+\alpha^2)$ and $\check{\alpha} \in (\alpha - \alpha^2, \alpha)$ for $\alpha \in (0, 1.7)$. This follows easily from the Taylor approximation $e^x \leq 1+x+x^2$, which holds for any $x \in (-\infty, 1.7]$ (we will use this approximation several times in the analysis). Finally, let $\hat{\delta}_i := \lambda n \cdot (1/n \cdot \check{1} - p_i \cdot \hat{\alpha}/\alpha)$ and $\check{\delta}_i := \lambda n \cdot (1/n \cdot \hat{1} - p_i \cdot \check{\alpha}/\alpha)$, where $\check{1} := 1 - \alpha/n < 1 < \hat{1} := 1 + \alpha/n$. These $\hat{\delta}_i$ and $\check{\delta}_i$ values can be thought of as upper/lower bounds on the expected difference in the number of balls that fall into bin i under

adapt the analysis to cover the process without deletions by setting $\eta_i(t) = 0$ (see Observation 3.6). Using Markov's inequality, this yields the same result as [8] using a simpler analysis.

the 1-choice and 2-choice process, respectively (note that $\hat{1}$, $\check{1}$, $\hat{\alpha}/\alpha$, and $\check{\alpha}/\alpha$ are all constants close to 1).

LEMMA 3.7. *Consider bin i, round t, and a const. $\alpha \leq 1$.*

(a) For the expected change of i's upper potential during round $t+1$ we have $\mathbb{E}[\Delta_{i,+}(t+1) \mid \boldsymbol{X}(t)]/\Phi_{i,+}(\boldsymbol{X}(t))$
$$\leq -\alpha \cdot \left(\eta_i + \hat{\delta}_i\right) + \alpha^2 \cdot \left(\eta_i + \hat{\delta}_i\right)^2.$$

(b) For the expected change of i's lower potential during round $t+1$ we have $\mathbb{E}[\Delta_{i,-}(t+1) \mid \boldsymbol{X}(t)]/\Phi_{i,-}(\boldsymbol{X}(t))$
$$\leq \alpha \cdot (\eta_i + \check{\delta}_i) + \alpha^2 \cdot (\eta_i + \check{\delta}_i)^2.$$

PROOF. For the first statement, we use Observation 3.6 to calculate $\mathbb{E}[\Delta_{i,+}(t) \mid \boldsymbol{X}]/\Phi_{i,+}$

$$= \sum_{K=0}^{n}\sum_{k=0}^{K} \binom{n}{K}\binom{K}{k} \cdot (p_i\lambda)^k \cdot ((1-p_i)\lambda)^{K-k} \cdot (1-\lambda)^{n-K} \cdot \left(e^{\alpha\cdot(k-\eta_i-K/n)} - 1\right)$$

$$= \sum_{K=0}^{n} \binom{n}{K} (1-\lambda)^{n-K} \cdot \lambda^K \sum_{k=0}^{K} \binom{K}{k} \cdot p_i^k \cdot (1-p_i)^{K-k} \cdot \left(e^{\alpha\cdot(k-\eta_i-K/n)} - 1\right)$$

$$= \sum_{K=0}^{n} \binom{n}{K} (1-\lambda)^{n-K} \cdot \lambda^K \cdot \left(e^{-\alpha(\eta_i + \frac{K}{n})} \sum_{k=0}^{K} \binom{K}{k} \cdot (e^\alpha \cdot p_i)^k \cdot (1-p_i)^{K-k} - 1\right)$$

$$= \sum_{K=0}^{n} \binom{n}{K} (1-\lambda)^{n-K} \cdot \lambda^K \cdot \left(e^{-\alpha(\eta_i + K/n)} \cdot (1 + \hat{\alpha}\cdot p_i)^K - 1\right),$$

where we first apply the law of total expectation together with Observation 3.6 and, afterward, twice the binomial theorem. Continuing the calculation using the aforementioned Taylor approximation $e^x \leq 1 + x + x^2$ (which holds for any $x \in (-\infty, 1.7]$), and the definition of $\hat{\delta}_i$ yields

$$\begin{aligned}
&= e^{-\alpha\eta_i} \cdot \left(1 - \lambda + \lambda e^{-\alpha/n} \cdot (1 + \hat{\alpha}\cdot p_i)\right)^n - 1 \\
&\leq e^{-\alpha\eta_i} \cdot \left(1 - \lambda(1 - e^{-\alpha/n}) + \lambda \cdot \hat{\alpha} \cdot p_i\right)^n - 1 \\
&\leq e^{-\alpha\eta_i} \cdot \left(1 - \frac{\lambda\cdot\alpha}{n} \cdot (1 - \alpha/n) + \lambda \cdot \hat{\alpha} \cdot p_i\right)^n - 1 \\
&\leq e^{-\alpha\eta_i} \cdot \left(1 - \frac{\alpha}{n} \cdot \hat{\delta}_i\right)^n - 1 \leq e^{-\alpha\cdot(\eta_i + \hat{\delta}_i)} - 1.
\end{aligned}$$

Now, the claim follows by another application of the Taylor approximation. The second statement follows similarly. □

Using Lemma 3.7, we derive different bounds on the potential drop that will be used in the various situations. The proofs for the following statements can all be found in the full version [10].

We start with a result that will be used when the potential is relatively high.

Lemma 3.8. *Consider a round t and a constant $\alpha \le \ln(10/9)$ ($< 1/8$). Let $R \in \{+,-\}$ and $\lambda \in [1/4, 1]$. For the expected upper and lower potential drop during round $t+1$ we have*

$$\mathbb{E}[\Delta_R(t+1) \mid \boldsymbol{X}(t)] < 2\alpha\lambda \cdot \Phi_R(\boldsymbol{X}(t)). \tag{8}$$

The next lemma derives a bound used to bound the upper potential change in reasonably balanced configurations.

Lemma 3.9. *Consider a round t. Let $\lambda \in [1/4, 1]$ and assume $X_{\frac{3}{4}n}(t) \le \varnothing(t)$. There are constants ε and $\alpha \le \min(\ln(10/9), \varepsilon/4)$ such that*

$$\mathbb{E}[\Delta_+(t+1) \mid \boldsymbol{X}(t)] \le -\varepsilon\alpha\lambda \cdot \Phi_+(\boldsymbol{X}(t)) + 2\alpha\lambda n. \tag{9}$$

The next lemma derives a bound used to bound the lower potential drop in reasonably balanced configurations.

Lemma 3.10. *Consider a round t. Let $\lambda \in [1/4, 1]$ and assume $X_{\frac{n}{4}}(t) \ge \varnothing(t)$. There are constants ε and $\alpha \le \min(\ln(10/9), \varepsilon/8)$ such that*

$$\mathbb{E}[\Delta_-(t+1) \mid \boldsymbol{X}(t)] \le -\varepsilon\alpha\lambda \cdot \Phi_-(\boldsymbol{X}(t)) + \frac{\alpha\lambda n}{2}. \tag{10}$$

The next lemma derives a bound that will be used to bound the potential drop in configurations with many balls far below the average to the right.

Lemma 3.11. *Consider round t. Let $\lambda \in [1/4, 1]$ and assume $X_{\frac{3}{4}n}(t) \ge \varnothing(t)$ and $\mathbb{E}[\Delta_+(t+1) \mid \boldsymbol{X}(t)] \ge -\frac{\varepsilon\alpha\lambda}{4} \cdot \Phi_+(\boldsymbol{X}(t))$. There are constants $\alpha \le 1/46$ ($< \ln(10/9)$) and $\varepsilon \le 1/3$ such that either $\Phi_+(\boldsymbol{X}(t)) \le \frac{\varepsilon}{4} \cdot \Phi_-(\boldsymbol{X}(t))$ or $\Phi(\boldsymbol{X}(t)) = \varepsilon^{-8} \cdot \mathrm{O}(n)$.*

The next lemma derives a bound that will be used to bound the potential drop in configurations with many balls far above the average to the left.

Lemma 3.12. *Consider round t. Let $\lambda \in [1/4, 1]$ and assume $X_{\frac{n}{4}}(t) \le \varnothing(t)$ and $\mathbb{E}[\Delta_-(t+1) \mid \boldsymbol{X}(t)] \ge -\frac{\varepsilon\alpha\lambda}{4} \cdot \Phi_-(\boldsymbol{X}(t))$. There are constants $\alpha \le 1/32$ ($< \ln(10/9)$) and $\varepsilon \le 1$ such that either $\Phi_-(\boldsymbol{X}(t)) \le \frac{\varepsilon}{4} \cdot \Phi_+(\boldsymbol{X}(t))$ or $\Phi(\boldsymbol{X}(t)) = \varepsilon^{-8} \cdot \mathrm{O}(n)$.*

Putting all these lemmas together, we can derive the following bound on the potential change during a single round.

Lemma 3.13. *Consider an arbitrary round $t+1$ of the 2-choice process. Let $\lambda \in [1/4, 1]$. There are constants ε and $\alpha \le \min(\ln(10/9), \varepsilon/8)$ such that we have*

$$\mathbb{E}[\Phi(\boldsymbol{X}(t+1)) \mid \boldsymbol{X}(t)] \le \left(1 - \frac{\varepsilon\alpha\lambda}{4}\right) \cdot \Phi(\boldsymbol{X}(t)) + \varepsilon^{-8} \cdot \mathrm{O}(n).$$

We use this result in a simple induction to prove Lemma 3.5.

Proof of Lemma 3.5. Lemma 3.13 gives us a $\gamma < 1$ and $c > 0$ such that $\mathbb{E}[\Phi(\boldsymbol{X}(t+1)) \mid \boldsymbol{X}(t)] \le \gamma \cdot \Phi(\boldsymbol{X}(t)) + c$ holds for all rounds $t \ge 0$. Taking the expected value on both sides yields $\mathbb{E}[\Phi(\boldsymbol{X}(t+1))] \le \gamma \cdot \mathbb{E}[\Phi(\boldsymbol{X}(t))] + c$. Using induction and the linearity of the expected value, it is easy to check that $\mathbb{E}[\Phi(\boldsymbol{X}(t))] \le \frac{c}{1-\gamma}$ solves this recursion. Using the values from Lemma 3.13 for γ and c (substituting ε' for ε) we get $\mathbb{E}[\Phi(\boldsymbol{X}(t))] \le \frac{4\varepsilon'^{-8}}{\varepsilon'\alpha\lambda} \cdot \mathrm{O}(n)$. The lemma's statement follows for the constant $\varepsilon = \mathrm{O}(\varepsilon'^{-9}/(\alpha\lambda))$. □

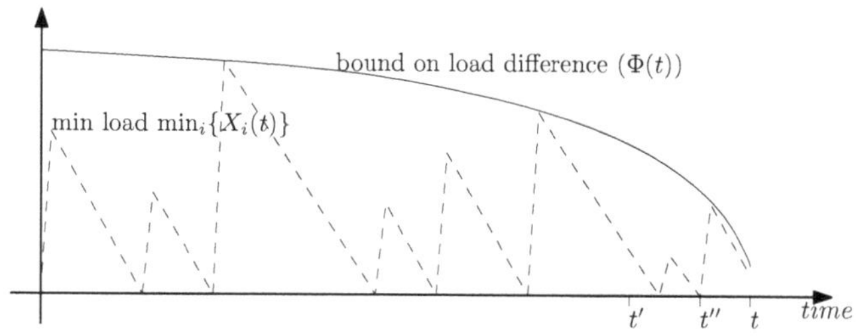

Figure 1: To bound the system load at time t, consider the minimum load and our bound on the load difference over time. There was a last time t'' when there was an empty bin. The system load can only increase if there is an empty bin, and this increase is bounded by our bound on the load difference. Exploiting that the system load decreases linearly in time while every increase is bounded by our logarithmic bound on the load difference, we find a small interval $[t', t]$ containing t''.

3.2 Bounding the Maximum Load

The goal of this section is to prove Theorem 3.2. Remember the definitions of $\Phi(\boldsymbol{x})$ and $\Psi(\boldsymbol{x})$ from Equation (6). For any fixed round t, we will prove that (w.h.p.) $\Psi(\boldsymbol{X}(t)) = \mathrm{O}(n \cdot \ln n)$, so that the average load is $\varnothing = \mathrm{O}(\ln n)$. Using a union bound and Lemma 3.3, we see that (w.h.p.) the the maximum load at the end of round t is bounded by $\varnothing + \mathrm{O}(\ln n) = \mathrm{O}(\ln n)$.

It remains to prove a high probability bound on $\Psi(\boldsymbol{X}(t))$ for arbitrary t. To get an intuition for our analysis, consider the toy case $t = \mathrm{poly}(n)$ and assume that exactly $\lambda \cdot n \le n$ balls are thrown each round. Here, we can combine Observation 3.4 and Lemma 3.5 to bound (w.h.p.) the load difference between any pair of bins and for all $t' < t$ by $\mathrm{O}(\ln n)$ (via a union bound over $\mathrm{poly}(n)$ rounds). Using the combinatorial observation that, while the load distance to the average is bounded by some $b \ge 0$, the bound $\Psi \le 2b \cdot n$ is invariant under the 2-choice process (Lemma 3.14), we get for $b = \mathrm{O}(\ln n)$ that $\Psi(\boldsymbol{X}(t)) \le 2b \cdot n = \mathrm{O}(n \cdot \ln n)$, as required. The case for $t = \omega(\mathrm{poly}(n))$ is considerably more involved. In particular, the fact that the number of balls in the system is only guaranteed to decrease when the total load is high *and* the load distance to the average is low makes it challenging to design a suitable potential function that drops fast enough when it is high. Thus, we deviate from this standard technique and elaborate on the idea of the toy case: Instead of bounding (w.h.p.) the load difference between any pair of bins by $\mathrm{O}(\ln n)$ for all $t' < t$ (which is not possible for $t \gg \mathrm{poly}(n)$), we prove (w.h.p.) an *adaptive bound* of $\mathrm{O}(\ln(t-t') \cdot f(\lambda))$ for all $t' < t$, where f is a suitable function (Lemma 3.15). Then we consider the last round $t'' < t$ with an empty bin. Observation 3.4 yields a bound of $\Psi(\boldsymbol{X}(t'')) = 2 \cdot \mathrm{O}(\ln(t-t'') \cdot f(\lambda)) \cdot n$ on the total load at time t''. Using the same combinatorial observation as in the toy case, we get that (w.h.p.) $\Psi(\boldsymbol{X}(t)) \le \Psi(\boldsymbol{X}(t'')) = 2 \cdot \mathrm{O}(\ln(t-t'') \cdot f(\lambda)) \cdot n$. The final step is to show that the load at time t'' (which is logarithmic in $t - t''$) decreases *linearly* in $t - t''$, showing that the time interval $t - t''$ cannot be too large (or we would get a negative load at time t). See Figure 1 for an illustration.

Lemma 3.14. *Let $b \ge 0$ and consider a configuration $\boldsymbol{x}$ with $\Psi(\boldsymbol{x}) \le 2b \cdot n$ and $\Phi(\boldsymbol{x}) \le e^{\alpha \cdot b}$. Let $\boldsymbol{x}'$ denote the* *configuration after one step of the 2-choice process. Then* $\Psi(\boldsymbol{x}') \leq 2b \cdot n$.

PROOF. We distinguish two cases: If there is no empty bin, then all n bins delete one ball. Since the maximum number of new balls is n, the number of balls cannot increase. That is, we have $\Psi(\boldsymbol{x}') \leq \Psi(\boldsymbol{x}) \leq 2b \cdot n$. Now consider the case that there is at least one empty bin. Let $\eta \in (0, 1]$ denote the fraction of empty bins (i.e., there are exactly $\eta \cdot n > 0$ empty bins). Since the minimal load is zero, Observation 3.4 implies $\max_i x_i \leq 2b$. Thus, the total number of balls in configuration $\boldsymbol{x}$ is at most $(1 - \eta)n \cdot 2b$. Exactly $(1-\eta)n$ balls are deleted (one from each non-empty bin) and at most n new balls enter the system. We get $\Psi(\boldsymbol{x}') \leq (1-\eta)n \cdot 2b - (1-\eta)n + n = (1-\eta)n \cdot (2b-1) + n \leq 2b \cdot n$. □

LEMMA 3.15. *Let* $\lambda \in [1/4, 1)$. *Fix a round* t. *For* $i \in \mathbb{N}$ *with* $t - i \cdot \frac{8 \log n}{1-\lambda} \geq 0$ *define* $\mathcal{I}_i := [t - i \cdot \frac{8 \ln n}{1-\lambda}, t]$. *Let* Y_i *be the number of balls which spawn in* $\mathcal{I}_i$.

(a) *Define the (good) smooth event* $\mathcal{S}_t := \bigcap_{t'<t} \big(\Phi(\boldsymbol{X}(t')) \leq |t - t'|^2 \cdot n^2\big)$. *Then* $\Pr(\mathcal{S}_t) = 1 - \mathrm{O}(n^{-1})$.

(b) *Define the (good) bounded balls event* $\mathcal{B}_t := \bigcap_i \big(Y_i \leq \frac{1+\lambda}{2} \cdot |\mathcal{I}_i| \cdot n\big)$. *Then* $\Pr(\mathcal{B}_t) = 1 - \mathrm{O}(n^{-1})$.

PROOF. Consider an arbitrary time $t' < t$. By Lemma 3.5 we have $\mathbb{E}[\Phi(t')] \leq n/\varepsilon$. Using Markov's inequality, this implies $\Pr(\Phi(t') \geq |t - t'|^2 \cdot n^2) \leq 1/(\varepsilon \cdot |t - t'|^2 \cdot n)$. Using the union bound over all $t' < t$ we calculate

$$\begin{aligned} \Pr(\bar{\mathcal{S}}_t) &\leq \sum_{t'<t} \Pr(\Phi(t') \geq |t - t'|^2 \cdot n^2) \\ &\leq \frac{1}{\varepsilon n} \cdot \sum_{t'<t} \frac{1}{|t - t'|^2} \leq \frac{\pi^2}{6\varepsilon \cdot n} = \mathrm{O}(n^{-1}), \end{aligned} \tag{11}$$

where the last inequality applies the solution to the Basel problem. This proves the first statement.

For the second statement, let $Z_i := |\mathcal{I}_i| \cdot n - Y_i$ be the number of balls that did not spawn during $\mathcal{I}_i$. Note that Z_i is a sum of $|\mathcal{I}_i| \cdot n$ independent indicator variables with $\mathbb{E}[Z_i] = (1 - \lambda) \cdot |\mathcal{I}_i| \cdot n = 8i \cdot \ln n$. Chernoff now yields $\Pr(Z_i \leq (1 - \lambda) \cdot |\mathcal{I}_i| \cdot n/2) \leq e^{-8i \cdot \ln n/8} = n^{-i}$. The desired statement follows by applying the identity $Z_i = |\mathcal{I}_i| \cdot n - Y_i$ and taking the union bound. □

LEMMA 3.16. *Fix a round* t *and assume that both* $\mathcal{S}_t$ *and* $\mathcal{B}_t$ *hold. Then* $\Psi(\boldsymbol{X}(t)) \leq \frac{9n}{\alpha} \cdot \ln\big(\frac{n}{1-\lambda}\big)$.

PROOF. Let $t' < t$ be the last time when there was an empty bin and set $\Delta := t - t'$. Note that t' is well defined, as we have $X_i(0) = 0$ for all $i \in [n]$. Since $\mathcal{S}_t$ holds, we have $\Phi(\boldsymbol{X}(t')) \leq \Delta^2 \cdot n^2 = \exp\big(\ln(\Delta^2 \cdot n^2)\big)$. By choice of t' we have $\min_i X_i(t') = 0$. Together with Observation 3.4 we get $\max_i X_i(t') \leq 2\ln\big(\Delta^2 \cdot n^2\big)/\alpha$. Summing up over all bins (and pulling out the square), this implies $\Psi(\boldsymbol{X}(t')) \leq 4n \cdot \ln\big(\Delta \cdot n\big)/\alpha$. Applying Lemma 3.14 yields $\Psi(\boldsymbol{X}(t'+1)) \leq 4n \cdot \ln\big(\Delta \cdot n\big)/\alpha$. By choice of t', there is no empty bin in $\boldsymbol{X}(t'')$ for all $t'' \in \{t'+1, t'+2, \ldots, t-1\}$. Thus, during each of these rounds exactly n balls are deleted. To bound the number of deleted balls, let i be maximal with $\mathcal{I}_i \subseteq [t', t]$ (as defined in Lemma 3.15). Since $\mathcal{B}_t$ holds and using the maximality of i, the number of balls Y that spawn during $[t', t]$ is at most $(1+\lambda)|\mathcal{I}_i| \cdot n/2 + \frac{8 \ln n}{1-\lambda} \cdot n \leq (1+\lambda)\Delta \cdot n/2 + \frac{8 \ln n}{1-\lambda} \cdot n$. We calculate

$$\begin{aligned} \Psi(\boldsymbol{X}(t)) &\leq \Psi(\boldsymbol{X}(t'+1)) - \Delta \cdot n + Y \\ &\leq \frac{4n}{\alpha} \cdot \ln(\Delta \cdot n) - \frac{1-\lambda}{2}\Delta \cdot n + \frac{8 \ln n}{1-\lambda} \cdot n \\ &= \frac{1-\lambda}{2} \cdot n \cdot \left(\frac{8}{\alpha(1-\lambda)} \cdot \ln(\Delta \cdot n) - \Delta + \frac{16 \ln n}{(1-\lambda)^2}\right) \\ &\leq \frac{1-\lambda}{2} \cdot \Delta \cdot n \cdot \left(\frac{24}{\alpha(1-\lambda)^2} \cdot \frac{\ln(\Delta \cdot n)}{\Delta} - 1\right). \end{aligned}$$

With $f = f(\lambda) := 24/\big(\alpha(1-\lambda)^2\big)$ the last factor becomes $f \cdot \ln(\Delta \cdot n)/\Delta - 1$. It is negative if and only if $\Delta > f \cdot \ln(\Delta \cdot n)$. This inequality holds for any $\Delta > -f \cdot W_{-1}(-\frac{1}{f \cdot n})$, where W_{-1} denotes the lower branch of the Lambert W function[4]. This implies that $\Delta \leq -f \cdot W_{-1}(-1/fn)$, since otherwise we would have $\Psi(\boldsymbol{X}(t)) < 0$, which is clearly a contradiction. Using the Taylor approximation $W_{-1}(x) = \ln(-x) - \ln\big(\ln(-1/x)\big) - \mathrm{o}(1)$ as $x \to -0$, we get

$$\begin{aligned} \Delta &\leq -f \cdot W_{-1}\left(-\frac{1}{f \cdot n}\right) \\ &\leq f \cdot \ln(f \cdot n) + f \cdot \ln\big(\ln(f \cdot n)\big) + f \leq 2f \cdot \ln(f \cdot n). \end{aligned}$$

Finally, we use this bound on Δ to get $\Psi(\boldsymbol{X}(t))$

$$\begin{aligned} &\leq \Psi(\boldsymbol{X}(t'+1)) \leq \frac{4n}{\alpha} \cdot \ln(\Delta \cdot n) \leq \frac{4n}{\alpha} \cdot \ln\big(2fn \cdot \ln(fn)\big) \\ &\leq \frac{4n}{\alpha} \cdot \ln\left(\frac{48n}{\alpha(1-\lambda)^2} \cdot \ln\left(\frac{24n}{\alpha(1-\lambda)^2}\right)\right) \\ &\leq \frac{9n}{\alpha} \cdot \ln\left(\frac{n}{1-\lambda}\right). \end{aligned}$$ □

Now, by combining Lemma 3.16 with the fact that the events $\mathcal{S}_t$ and $\mathcal{B}_t$ hold with high probability (Lemma 3.15), we immediately get that (w.h.p.) $\Psi(\boldsymbol{X}(t)) = \mathrm{O}(n \cdot \ln n)$. As described at the beginning of this section, combining this with Lemma 3.3 proves Theorem 3.2.

3.3 Stability

This section proves Theorem 3.1. The first auxiliary lemma states that for sufficiently high value of Γ, this potential decreases.[5]

LEMMA 3.17 (NEG. BIAS Γ). *Let* $\lambda \in [1/4, 1)$. *If* $\Gamma(\boldsymbol{X}(t)) \geq 2\frac{n^4}{(1-\lambda)^2\lambda}$, *then* $\mathbb{E}[\Gamma(\boldsymbol{X}(t+1)) - \Gamma(\boldsymbol{X}(t)) \mid \boldsymbol{X}(t)] \leq -1$.

PROOF. Assume $\boldsymbol{X}(t) = x$ is fixed. By definition of $\Gamma(\cdot)$, we have $\Phi(x) \geq \Gamma(x)/2$ or $\Psi(x) \geq \Gamma(x)/2$. We now show that in both cases $\mathbb{E}[\Gamma(\boldsymbol{X}(t+1)) - \Gamma(x) \mid \boldsymbol{X}(t) = x] \leq -1$.

(a) If $\Phi(x) \geq \Gamma(x)/2$, then we have, by Lemma 3.13, a potential drop of $\mathbb{E}[\Phi(\boldsymbol{X}(t+1)) - \Phi(x) \mid \boldsymbol{X}(t) = x]$

$$\begin{aligned} &\leq -(\varepsilon\alpha\lambda/4) \cdot \Phi(x) + n \log n \\ &\leq -(\varepsilon\alpha\lambda/8) \cdot \Gamma(x) + n \log n. \end{aligned}$$

Note that, by definition of Ψ, $\Psi(\boldsymbol{X}(t+1)) - \Psi(x) \leq n$. Together with $\Gamma(x) \geq \frac{8(n \log n + n^2/(1-\lambda)+1)}{\varepsilon\alpha\lambda}$,

$$\begin{aligned} &\mathbb{E}[\Gamma(\boldsymbol{X}(t+1)) - \Gamma(x) \mid \boldsymbol{X}(t) = x] \\ &\leq -(\varepsilon\alpha\lambda/8) \cdot \Gamma(x) + n \log n + (n/(1-\lambda)) \cdot n \leq -1. \end{aligned}$$

[4]Note that $-\frac{1}{f \cdot n} \geq -1/e$, so that $W_{-1}(-\frac{1}{f \cdot n})$ is well defined.

[5]It looks tempting to use Γ together with Hajek's theorem to derive a bound on the maximum load of system. However, this requires (exponentially) sharper bounds on Φ.

(b) Otherwise, i.e., if $\Phi(x) < \Gamma(x)/2$, we have that

(i) the load difference is, by Observation 3.4, bounded by $2\ln(\Gamma(x)/2)/\alpha$, and

(ii) $\Psi(x) \geq \Gamma(x)/2$ must hold. This implies that $\varnothing \geq \frac{1}{n}\left(\frac{\Gamma(x)/2}{\frac{n}{1-\lambda}}\right) = \frac{(1-\lambda)\cdot\Gamma(x)}{2n^2}$.

From (i) and (ii) we have that the minimum load is at least $\frac{(1-\lambda)\cdot\Gamma(x)}{2n^2} - \ln(\Gamma(x)/2)/\alpha$. From Lemma 3.18 and $\Gamma(x) \geq 2\frac{n^4}{(1-\lambda)^2\lambda}$, it follows that every bin has load at least load 1. Thus each bin will delete one ball and the number of balls arriving is λn in expectation. Hence, $\mathbb{E}[\Psi(\boldsymbol{X}(t+1)) - \Psi(x) \mid \boldsymbol{X}(t) = x] = -\frac{n}{1-\lambda}(1-\lambda)n$. Now, we calculate $\mathbb{E}[\Gamma(\boldsymbol{X}(t+1)) - \Gamma(x) \mid \boldsymbol{X}(t) = x]$

$$= \mathbb{E}[\Phi(\boldsymbol{X}(t+1)) - \Phi(x) \mid \boldsymbol{X}(t) = x] - \frac{n}{1-\lambda}(1-\lambda)n$$
$$\leq n\log n - \frac{n}{1-\lambda}(1-\lambda)n \leq -1.$$

Thus, $\mathbb{E}[\Gamma(\boldsymbol{X}(t+1)) - \Gamma(x) \mid \boldsymbol{X}(t) = x] \leq -1$, which yields the claim. □

LEMMA 3.18. *For all* $x \geq 2\frac{n^4}{(1-\lambda)^2\lambda}$ *it holds that* $\frac{(1-\lambda)\cdot x}{2n^2} - 2\ln(x/2)/\alpha \geq 1$.

PROOF. Define $f(x) = \frac{(1-\lambda)\cdot x}{2n^2} - 2\ln(x/2)/\alpha$. We have $f\left(2\frac{n^4}{(1-\lambda)^2\lambda}\right) \geq \frac{n^2}{(1-\lambda)\lambda} - \frac{2}{\alpha}\ln\left(\frac{n^4}{(1-\lambda)^2\lambda}\right) \geq 1$, where the last inequality holds for large enough of n since α is a constant. Moreover, for all $x \geq 2\frac{n^4}{(1-\lambda)^2\lambda}$ we have $f'(x) = \frac{1-\lambda}{n^2} - \frac{2}{\alpha x} \geq 0$. Thus, the claim follows. □

We are ready to prove Theorem 3.1.

PROOF OF THEOREM 3.1. The proof proceeds by applying Theorem A.1. We now define the parameters of Theorem A.1. Let $\zeta(t) = \boldsymbol{X}(t)$ and hence Ω is the state space of X. First we observe that Ω is countable since there are a constant number of bins (n is consider a constant in this matter) each having a load which is a natural number. We define $\phi(\boldsymbol{X}(t))$ to be $\Gamma(\boldsymbol{X}(t))$. We define $C = \{ x \mid \Gamma(x) \leq 2\frac{n^4}{(1-\lambda)^2\lambda} \}$. Define $\beta(x) = 1$ and $\eta = 1$. We now show that the preconditions (a) and (b) of Theorem A.1 are fulfilled.

- Let $x \notin C$. By definition of C and $\phi(\boldsymbol{X}(t))$, and from Lemma 3.17 we have $E[\phi(X(t+1)) - \phi(x)|\boldsymbol{X}(t) = x]$
$$\leq E[\Gamma(\boldsymbol{X}(t+1)) - \Gamma(x)|\boldsymbol{X}(t) = x] \leq -1. \quad (12)$$
- Let $x \in C$. Recall that $\Gamma(\boldsymbol{X}(t)) = \Phi(\boldsymbol{X}(t)) + \Psi(\boldsymbol{X}(t))$. By Lemma 3.12 and the fact the the number of balls arriving in one round is bounded by n, we derive,
$$\begin{aligned} & E[\phi(X(t+1))|\boldsymbol{X}(t) = x] \\ = \ & E[\Phi(\boldsymbol{X}(t+1))|\boldsymbol{X}(t) = x] \\ & + E[\Psi(\boldsymbol{X}(t+1))|\boldsymbol{X}(t) = x] \\ \leq \ & \left(\left(1 - \frac{\varepsilon\alpha\lambda}{4}\right)2\frac{n^4}{(1-\lambda)^2\lambda}\right) + \frac{n}{1-\lambda}n < \infty. \end{aligned}$$

The claim follows by applying Theorem A.1 with Equations (12) and (13). □

Acknowledgments

Petra Berenbrink is supported by the Natural Sciences and Engineering Research Council of Canada (NSERC). Peter Kling is partly supported by the Natural Sciences and Engineering Research Council of Canada (NSERC) and the Pacific Institute for the Mathematical Sciences (PIMS). Lars Nagel is supported by the German Ministry of Education and Research under Grant 01IH13004. Christopher Wastell is supported by EPSRC.

References

[1] M. Adler, P. Berenbrink, and K. Schröder. Analyzing an infinite parallel job allocation process. In *Proceedings of the 6th Annual European Symposium on Algorithms*, ESA '98, pages 417–428, London, UK, UK, 1998. Springer-Verlag. ISBN 3-540-64848-8. URL http://dl.acm.org/citation.cfm?id=647908.740138.

[2] M. Adler, S. Chakrabarti, M. Mitzenmacher, and L. Rasmussen. Parallel randomized load balancing. *Random Structures & Algorithms*, 13(2):159–188, 1998. ISSN 1098-2418. . URL http://dx.doi.org/10.1002/(SICI)1098-2418(199809)13:2<159::AID-RSA3>3.0.CO;2-Q.

[3] A. S. Alfa. Algorithmic analysis of the bmap/d/k system in discrete time. *Adv. in Appl. Probab.*, 35(4): 1131–1152, 12 2003. . URL http://dx.doi.org/10.1239/aap/1067436338.

[4] Y. Azar, A. Z. Broder, A. R. Karlin, and E. Upfal. Balanced allocations. *SIAM Journal on Computing*, 29(1):180–200, 1999. .

[5] L. Becchetti, A. E. F. Clementi, E. Natale, F. Pasquale, and G. Posta. Self-stabilizing repeated balls-into-bins. In G. E. Blelloch and K. Agrawal, editors, *Proceedings of the 27th ACM on Symposium on Parallelism in Algorithms and Architectures, SPAA 2015, Portland, OR, USA, June 13-15, 2015*, pages 332–339. ACM, 2015. ISBN 978-1-4503-3588-1. . URL http://doi.acm.org/10.1145/2755573.2755584.

[6] P. Berenbrink, A. Czumaj, T. Friedetzky, and N. D. Vvedenskaya. Infinite parallel job allocation (extended abstract). In *Proceedings of the Twelfth Annual ACM Symposium on Parallel Algorithms and Architectures*, SPAA '00, pages 99–108, New York, NY, USA, 2000. ACM. ISBN 1-58113-185-2. . URL http://doi.acm.org/10.1145/341800.341813.

[7] P. Berenbrink, A. Czumaj, A. Steger, and B. Vöcking. Balanced allocations: The heavily loaded case. *SIAM Journal on Computing*, 35(6):1350–1385, 2006. .

[8] P. Berenbrink, A. Czumaj, M. Englert, T. Friedetzky, and L. Nagel. Multiple-choice balanced allocation in (almost) parallel. In A. Gupta, K. Jansen, J. Rolim, and R. Servedio, editors, *Approximation, Randomization, and Combinatorial Optimization. Algorithms and Techniques*, volume 7408 of *Lecture Notes in Computer Science*, pages 411–422. Springer Berlin Heidelberg, 2012. ISBN 978-3-642-32511-3. . URL http://dx.doi.org/10.1007/978-3-642-32512-0_35.

[9] P. Berenbrink, K. Khodamoradi, T. Sauerwald, and A. Stauffer. Balls-into-bins with nearly optimal load distribution. In *Proceedings of the Twenty-fifth Annual ACM Symposium on Parallelism in Algorithms and Architectures*, SPAA '13, pages 326–335, New York, NY, USA, 2013. ACM. ISBN 978-1-4503-1572-2. . URL http://doi.acm.org/10.1145/2486159.2486191.

[10] P. Berenbrink, T. Friedetzky, P. Kling, F. Mallmann-Trenn, L. Nagel, and C. Wastell. Self-stabilizing balls & bins in batches. *CoRR*, abs/1603.02188, 2016. URL http://arxiv.org/abs/1603.02188.

[11] A. Czumaj. Recovery time of dynamic allocation processes. In *Proceedings of the Tenth Annual ACM Symposium on Parallel Algorithms and Architectures*, SPAA '98, pages 202–211, New York, NY, USA, 1998. ACM. ISBN 0-89791-989-0. . URL http://doi.acm.org/10.1145/277651.277686.

[12] A. Czumaj and V. Stemann. Randomized allocation processes. In *Foundations of Computer Science, 1997. Proceedings., 38th Annual Symposium on*, pages 194–203, Oct 1997. .

[13] G. Fayolle, V. Malyshev, and M. Menshikov. *Topics in the Constructive Theory of Countable Markov Chains.* Cambridge University Press, 1995. ISBN 9780521461979. URL https://books.google.ca/books?id=lTJltFEnnHcC.

[14] G. H. Gonnet. Expected length of the longest probe sequence in hash code searching. *J. ACM*, 28(2): 289–304, Apr. 1981. ISSN 0004-5411. . URL http://doi.acm.org/10.1145/322248.322254.

[15] B. Hajek. Hitting-time and occupation-time bounds implied by drift analysis with applications. *Advances in Applied Probability*, 14(3):502–525.

[16] A. Kamal. Efficient solution of multiple server queues with application to the modeling of atm concentrators. In *INFOCOM '96. Fifteenth Annual Joint Conference of the IEEE Computer Societies. Networking the Next Generation. Proceedings IEEE*, volume 1, pages 248–254 vol.1, Mar 1996. .

[17] N. K. Kim, M. L. Chaudhry, B. K. Yoon, and K. Kim. A complete and simple solution to a discrete-time finite-capacity bmap/d/c queue. 2012.

[18] D. A. Levin and Y. Perres. *Markov Chains and Mixing Times.* American Mathematical Society, December 2008. ISBN 978-0-8218-4739-8.

[19] M. Mitzenmacher. The power of two choices in randomized load balancing. *IEEE Trans. Parallel Distrib. Syst.*, 12(10):1094–1104, 2001. . URL http://doi.ieeecomputersociety.org/10.1109/71.963420.

[20] Y. Peres, K. Talwar, and U. Wieder. The $(1+\beta)$-choice process and weighted balls-into-bins. In *Proceedings of the 21st Annual ACM-SIAM Symposium on Discrete Algorithms (SODA)*, SODA '10, pages 1613–1619, Philadelphia, PA, USA, 2010. Society for Industrial and Applied Mathematics. ISBN 978-0-898716-98-6.

[21] M. Raab and A. Steger. "balls into bins" - A simple and tight analysis. In M. Luby, J. D. P. Rolim, and M. J. Serna, editors, *Randomization and Approximation Techniques in Computer Science, Second International Workshop, RANDOM'98, Barcelona, Spain, October 8-10, 1998, Proceedings*, volume 1518 of *Lecture Notes in Computer Science*, pages 159–170. Springer, 1998. ISBN 3-540-65142-X. . URL http://dx.doi.org/10.1007/3-540-49543-6_13.

[22] K. Sohraby and J. Zhang. Spectral decomposition approach for transient analysis of multi-server discrete-time queues. In *INFOCOM'92. Eleventh Annual Joint Conference of the IEEE Computer and Communications Societies, IEEE*, pages 395–404. IEEE, 1992.

[23] V. Stemann. Parallel balanced allocations. In *Proceedings of the Eighth Annual ACM Symposium on Parallel Algorithms and Architectures*, SPAA '96, pages 261–269, New York, NY, USA, 1996. ACM. ISBN 0-89791-809-6. . URL http://doi.acm.org/10.1145/237502.237565.

[24] K. Talwar and U. Wieder. Balanced allocations: A simple proof for the heavily loaded case. In J. Esparza, P. Fraigniaud, T. Husfeldt, and E. Koutsoupias, editors, *Automata, Languages, and Programming*, volume 8572 of *Lecture Notes in Computer Science*, pages 979–990. Springer Berlin Heidelberg, 2014. ISBN 978-3-662-43947-0. . URL http://dx.doi.org/10.1007/978-3-662-43948-7_81.

APPENDIX

A. AUXILIARY RESULTS

THEOREM A.1 (FAYOLLE ET AL. [13, THEOREM 2.2.4]). *A time-homogeneous irreducible aperiodic Markov chain ζ with a countable state space Ω is positive recurrent if and only if there exists a positive function $\phi(x), x \in \Omega$, a number $\eta > 0$, a positive integer-valued function $\beta(x), x \in \Omega$, and a finite set $C \subseteq \Omega$ such that the following inequalities hold:*

(a) $E[\phi(\zeta(t+\beta(x))) - \phi(x) | \zeta(t) = x] \leq -\eta\beta(x),\ x \notin C$

(b) $E[\phi(\zeta(t+\beta(x))) | \zeta(t) = x] < \infty,\ x \in C$

THEOREM A.2 ([15, THM. 2.3], SIMPL.). *Let $(Y(t))_{t\geq 0}$ be a sequence of random variables on a probability space $(\Omega, \mathcal{F}, P)$ with respect to the filtration $(\mathcal{F}(t))_{t\geq 0}$. Assume the following two conditions hold:*

(i) (Majorization) There exists a random variable Z and a constant $\lambda' > 0$, such that $\mathbb{E}[e^{\lambda' Z}] \leq D$ for some finite D, and $(|Y(t+1) - Y(t)| | \mathcal{F}(t)) \prec Z$ for all $t \geq 0$; and

(ii) (Negative Bias) There exist $a, \varepsilon_0 > 0$, such for all t we have

$$\mathbb{E}[Y(t+1) - Y(t) \mid \mathcal{F}(t), Y(t) > a] \leq -\varepsilon_0.$$

Let $\eta = \min\{\lambda', \varepsilon_0 \cdot \lambda'^2/(2D), 1/(2\varepsilon_0)\}$. Then, for all b and t we have

$$\Pr(Y(t) \geq b \mid \mathcal{F}(0)) \leq e^{\eta(Y(0)-b)} + \frac{2D}{\varepsilon_0 \cdot \eta} \cdot e^{\eta(a-b)}.$$

Brief Announcement: Local Independent Set Approximation

Marijke H. L. Bodlaender
ICE-TCS
School of Computer Science
Reykjavik University
Iceland
marijke12@ru.is

Magnús M. Halldórsson
ICE-TCS
School of Computer Science
Reykjavik University
Iceland
mmh@ru.is

Christian Konrad
ICE-TCS
School of Computer Science
Reykjavik University
Iceland
christiank@ru.is

Fabian Kuhn
Computer Science Dept.
University of Freiburg
Germany
kuhn@cs.uni-freiburg.de

Keywords

Local algorithms, maximum independent set, network decompositions

1. LOCAL INDEPENDENT SET COMPUTATION

Local Algorithms. A central question in distributed computing is what can be computed locally, i.e., in O(1) communication rounds. Local algorithms have many desirable properties, e.g., they can recover quickly from failures, changes in the topology, or changes in the input [11].

Linial [7] showed that computing a maximal independent set on the ring requires $\Omega(\log^* n)$ communication rounds, where n is the number of nodes in the network, thus dashing the hope for local maximal independent set algorithms. In this work, we drop the maximality requirement of independent sets and aim at maximizing their sizes instead. Since the maximum independent set problem is NP-hard and is hard to approximate within a factor $n^{1-\epsilon}$, for any $\epsilon > 0$ [5], we cannot expect to obtain polynomial-time local algorithms.

Our Results. We give a $O(n^{\epsilon})$-approximation, $O(\frac{1}{\epsilon})$ round distributed algorithm for the maximum independent set problem in general graphs. In general graphs, exponential time computations are unavoidable due to the hardness of the problem, but in graph classes that allow the computation of a maximum independent set (or a good approximate thereof) efficiently such as bipartite graph, polynomial time suffices. Furthermore, we show that our algorithm is best possible, even for bipartite graphs.

Our algorithm employs the first phase of the Linial-Saks network decomposition algorithm [8]. A network decomposition is a partition of the vertex set V of a graph $G = (V, E)$ into connected subsets of vertices $(V_i)_i$, denoted clusters, each of bounded diameter, and a coloring of the clusters using a limited number of colors, such that adjacent clusters have different colors. Various network decomposition methods with different characteristics are known [1, 8, 10, 2, 3] and are employed as building blocks in a multitude of distributed algorithms.

Related Work. The work of Barenboim [2] and the follow-up work by Barenboim et al. [3] are closest to our work: They give local distributed algorithms for the minimum vertex coloring problem with approximation factors $\tilde{O}(\sqrt{n})$ (in [2]) and $\tilde{O}(n^{\epsilon})$ (in [3]), where nodes run exponential time algorithms. While our work makes use of the network decomposition of Linial and Saks [8], new network decomposition methods better suited to coloring problems are designed in [2] and [3].

Lower bounds for local algorithms are usually proved by pointing out pairs of graphs that are locally indistinguishable, but their global properties are quite different. In the context of independent sets/colorings, this technique has previously been applied for example for computing maximal independent sets [6] and coloring trees [7].

2. ALGORITHM

In each iteration of the Linial-Saks [8] network decomposition algorithm, a partial assignment of vertices into clusters is computed. The algorithm requires an integer parameter B and a probability p. Parameter B determines the maximum cluster diameter and thus the number of rounds required by the algorithm. Parameter p influences the average cluster diameter, which in turn influences the number of nodes that join a cluster (cf. Lemma 1). Each cluster consists of a cluster leader l and a subset of vertices $C_l \subseteq \Gamma_G^B[l]$, where $\Gamma_G^r[l]$ denotes the set of nodes in G at distance at most r from l including l (i.e., the inclusive r-neighborhood). Importantly, vertices of different clusters are not adjacent. Each iteration requires $2B$ rounds.

The key property that ensures the approximation factor of our algorithm is as follows:

PODC'16 July 25-28, 2016, Chicago, IL, USA

ACM ISBN 978-1-4503-3964-3/16/07.
DOI: http://dx.doi.org/10.1145/2933057.2933068

LEMMA 1 (LINIAL, SAKS [8]). *For every v, the probability that v joins some cluster is at least $p(1-p^B)^n$.*

Our maximum independent set algorithm proceeds as follows: We set $B=\lceil\frac{1}{\epsilon}\rceil$ and $p=n^{-\frac{1}{B}}$, for the given $\epsilon>0$, and run the first iteration of the Linial-Saks decomposition in $2B=2\lceil\frac{1}{\epsilon}\rceil$ rounds, obtaining a set L of cluster leaders. At the same time, nodes collect the topologies of their B-neighborhoods. Each cluster leader $l\in L$ computes a maximum independent set I_l in the subgraph induced by C_l (in exponential time in general graphs). Finally, cluster leaders notify nodes of C_l in at most B rounds whether they are included in the independent set.

THEOREM 1. *For every $\epsilon>0$, there is a randomized distributed algorithm for the maximum independent set problem with expected approximation ratio $(2e\cdot n^{\frac{1}{\epsilon}})$ that runs in $3\lceil\frac{1}{\epsilon}\rceil$ rounds.*

PROOF. First, recall that clusters are disconnected in the input graph, and thus the output $I=\cup_{l\in L}I_l$ is an independent set, establishing correctness of the algorithm.

Let $I^*\subseteq V$ denote a maximum independent set in the input graph, and let $C=\cup_{l\in L}C_l$ denote the set of nodes that are contained in some cluster. Then:

$$\begin{aligned}\mathbb{E}|I^*\cap C| &= \sum_{i\in I^*}\mathbb{P}[i\in C]\geq\sum_{i\in I^*}n^{-B^{-1}}(1-n^{-B^{-1}\cdot B})^n\\ &\geq \sum_{i\in I^*}\frac{1}{n^\epsilon}(1-\frac{1}{n})^n\geq|I^*|\frac{1}{n^\epsilon}\frac{1}{2e},\end{aligned}\tag{1}$$

applying Lemma 1. Then, due to the local optimality of I_l,

$$|I|=\sum_{l\in L}|I_l|\geq\sum_{l\in L}|I^*\cap C_l|=|I^*\cap C|.$$

Taking expectations and applying Inequality 1 yields the approximation factor.

Running the first iteration of Linial-Saks and collecting the topology of local B-neighborhoods requires $2B$ rounds, and notifying nodes whether they are part of the independent set requires additional B rounds. □

Our algorithm can also give a $(1+\epsilon)$-approximation that runs in $O(\log(\frac{n}{\epsilon})/\epsilon)$ rounds by employing parameters $B=c\log(\frac{n}{\epsilon})/\epsilon$, for a small enough constant c, and $p=1-\frac{\epsilon}{2}$,

3. LOWER BOUND

Let $H_1=(V_1,E_1),H_2=(V_2,E_2)$ be d-regular graphs with girths at least g, and suppose that H_1 is bipartite. Let $n_i=|V_i|$, for $i\in\{1,2\}$. Furthermore, for $i\in\{1,2\}$, we label the vertices of H_i such that each vertex $v\in V_i$ receives a unique label (or ID) $\mathcal{L}_i(v)$, where the labeling function $\mathcal{L}_i$ is chosen uniformly at random from the set of injections from V_i to $\{1,\ldots,\max\{n_1,n_2\}\}$.

In the following, we denote the size of a maximum independent set in a graph F by $\alpha(F)$.

LEMMA 2. *Let H_1 and H_2 be as defined above. Every possibly randomized $\lceil g/2\rceil-1$ rounds distributed algorithm for the bipartite maximum independent set problem computes an independent set of expected size at most $\alpha(H_2)\frac{n_1}{n_2}$ on H_1, where the expectation is taken over the labelings of H_1 and the random coin flips.*

PROOF. Let $\mathcal{A}$ be a randomized distributed algorithm for the bipartite maximum independent set problem, and denote by I the independent set computed by $\mathcal{A}$ on graph H_1. For a vertex $v\in V_1$, let $p_v=\mathbb{P}[v\in I]$, where the probability is taken over the random coin flips of the algorithm and the labelings.

Let $g'=\lceil g/2\rceil-1$. Since algorithm $\mathcal{A}$ runs in g' rounds, the outcome of $\mathcal{A}$ when executed on vertex v depends on the structure and labels of the inclusive g'-neighborhood $\Gamma^{g'}_{H_1}[v]$, and on the random bits used by nodes of $\Gamma^{g'}_{H_1}[v]$. Since the girth of H_1 is g, each local neighborhood $\Gamma^{g'}_{H_1}[u]$ is isomorphic to a d-ary tree of depth g' rooted at u. Further, since labels are assigned uniformly at random, and random bits are uniform, the values p_u and p_v are identical, for every $u,v\in V_1$. Denote this value by p (i.e., $p=p_v$ for an arbitrary $v\in V_1$). Then, $\mathbb{E}|I|=\sum_{v\in V_1}p_v=n_1p$.

We consider now the performance of $\mathcal{A}$ on graph H_2. Similar as in H_1, every local neighborhood $\Gamma^{g'}_{H_2}[u]$ is isomorphic to a d-ary tree of depth g' rooted at u. Furthermore, it can easily be seen that the output I' of $\mathcal{A}$ on H_2 constitutes an independent set. Similar considerations as before show that the expected size of I' computed by $\mathcal{A}$ on graph H_2 is $\mathbb{E}|I'|=n_2p$, which is in turn is bounded from above by $\alpha(H_2)$. Thus, $p\leq\alpha(H_2)/n_2$, and hence $\mathbb{E}|I|\leq\alpha(H_2)\frac{n_1}{n_2}$. □

Next, in order to obtain our lower bound result, we employ the Ramanujan graphs of Lubotzky, Phillips, and Sarnak [9]. For p,q distinct primes congruent to 1 mod 4, there are $(p+1)$-regular graphs $X^{p,q}$ on n vertices with girth $\Omega(\log_p(q))$ that satisfy: If the Legendre symbol $\left(\frac{p}{q}\right)=-1$ then $X^{p,q}$ is bipartite and $n=q(q^2-1)$, while if $\left(\frac{p}{q}\right)=1$ then $\alpha(X^{p,q})=\mathrm{O}(\frac{n}{\sqrt{p}})$ and $n=q(q^2-1)/2$. Equipped with these graphs, we are ready to prove our lower bound result.

THEOREM 2. *For every $\epsilon>0$, there is an infinite family of bipartite graphs $\mathcal{G}$ such that every possibly randomized $\frac{1}{\epsilon}$-rounds distributed algorithm for the bipartite maximum independent set problem has approximation factor $n^{\Omega(\epsilon)}$ on every graph $G\in\mathcal{G}$, where n is the number of vertices of G.*

PROOF. Let p,q_1,q_2 be distinct primes congruent to 1 mod 4 such that $\left(\frac{p}{q_1}\right)=-1$, $\left(\frac{p}{q_2}\right)=1$, and $q_1,q_2\in p^{\Theta(\frac{1}{\epsilon})}$. Let $H_1=X^{p,q_1}$, $H_2=X^{p,q_2}$, and for $i\in\{1,2\}$, let n_i be the number of vertices of graph H_i. Then, $n_1,n_2\in p^{\Theta(\frac{1}{\epsilon})}$. H_1 and H_2 have girths $\Omega(\frac{1}{\epsilon})$ and are $(p+1)$-regular. Furthermore, H_1 is bipartite and $\alpha(H_2)=\mathrm{O}(n_2^{1-\Theta(\epsilon)})$.

By Lemma 2, for a small enough C, every possibly randomized $C\frac{1}{\epsilon}$-round distributed bipartite maximum independent set algorithm computes an independent set of size at most $\alpha(H_2)\frac{n_1}{n_2}=n_1/n_2^{\Theta(\epsilon)}=n_1^{1-\Theta(\epsilon)}$ on H_1. Since H_1 is bipartite, it contains an independent set of size at least $n_1/2$, implying approximation ratio of $\Omega(n_1^{\Theta(\epsilon)})$. □

4. CONCLUSION

Since our results provide tight bounds (even for bipartite graphs), an interesting question is to determine graph classes for which local algorithms with sub-polynomial approximations can be obtained. Progress has been made for example for *polynomially bounded-independence graphs* such as unit disc graphs, where poly-logarithmic approximation ratios can be achieved in a single communication round [4]. The same paper [4] implies a constant factor approximation for planar graphs, and, more generally, an O(d)-approximation for graphs with average degree d.

5. ACKNOWLEDGEMENTS

Marijke H. L. Bodlaender, Magnús M. Halldórsson and Christian Konrad are supported by Icelandic Research Fund grants 120032011 and 152679-051. Fabian Kuhn is supported by ERC Grant No. 336495 (ACDC).

6. REFERENCES

[1] Baruch Awerbuch, Andrew V. Goldberg, Michael Luby, and Serge A. Plotkin. Network decomposition and locality in distributed computation. In *30th Annual Symposium on Foundations of Computer Science, Research Triangle Park, North Carolina, USA, 30 October - 1 November 1989*, pages 364–369, 1989.

[2] L. Barenboim. On the locality of some NP-complete problems. In *Automata, Languages, and Programming - 39th International Colloquium, ICALP 2012, Warwick, UK, July 9-13, 2012, Proceedings, Part II*, pages 403–415, 2012.

[3] L. Barenboim, M. Elkin, and C. Gavoille. A fast network-decomposition algorithm and its applications to constant-time distributed computation - (extended abstract). In *Structural Information and Communication Complexity - 22nd International Colloquium, SIROCCO 2015, Montserrat, Spain, July 14-16, 2015, Post-Proceedings*, pages 209–223, 2015.

[4] Magnús M. Halldórsson and Christian Konrad. Distributed large independent sets in one round on bounded-independence graphs. In Yoram Moses, editor, *Distributed Computing*, volume 9363 of *Lecture Notes in Computer Science*, pages 559–572. Springer Berlin Heidelberg, 2015.

[5] Johan Håstad. Clique is hard to approximate within $n^{1-\epsilon}$. *Acta Mathematica*, 182:105–142, 1999.

[6] Fabian Kuhn, Thomas Moscibroda, and Roger Wattenhofer. What Cannot Be Computed Locally! In *23rd ACM Symposium on the Principles of Distributed Computing (PODC), St. Johns, Newfoundland, Canada*, July 2004.

[7] N. Linial. Locality in distributed graph algorithms. *SIAM J. Comput.*, 21(1):193–201, 1992.

[8] N. Linial and M. E. Saks. Low diameter graph decompositions. *Combinatorica*, 13(4):441–454, 1993.

[9] A. Lubotzky, R. Phillips, and P. Sarnak. Ramanujan graphs. *Combinatorica*, 8(3):261–277, September 1988.

[10] Alessandro Panconesi and Aravind Srinivasan. On the complexity of distributed network decomposition. *J. Algorithms*, 20(2), March 1996.

[11] J. Suomela. Survey of local algorithms. *ACM Comput. Surv.*, 45(2):24:1–24:40, March 2013.

Deterministic Objects: Life Beyond Consensus

Yehuda Afek
Tel Aviv University, Israel
afek@post.tau.ac.il

Faith Ellen
University of Toronto, Canada
faith@cs.toronto.edu

Eli Gafni
UCLA, USA
eli@ucla.edu

ABSTRACT

For all integers $m \geq 2$, we construct an infinite sequence of deterministic objects of consensus number m with strictly increasing computational power. In particular, this refutes the Common2 Conjecture, which claimed that every deterministic object of consensus number 2 has a deterministic, wait-free implementation from 2-consensus objects and registers in a system with any finite number of processes.

Keywords

deterministic consensus hierarchy; set-consensus; valency argument; simulation; consistent ordered partition

1. INTRODUCTION

Herlihy's consensus hierarchy has been used to classify the power of an object by its *consensus number*, the number of processes which can solve wait-free consensus using any number of copies of this object and registers [18, 23]. An important consequence of this hierarchy is that it is not always possible to implement an object using multiple copies of another object and registers in asynchronous environments: If object T has consensus number n and object T' has a larger consensus number, then there is no wait-free implementation of object T' shared by more than n processes from copies of object T and registers.

Herlihy also proved that n-consensus objects are *universal* for systems of n processes: n-consensus objects and registers can be used to provide a deterministic implementation of any object in a system of n or fewer processes [18]. In fact, any object with consensus number n is universal for systems of n processes, since there is a deterministic algorithm to solve consensus using only copies of this objects and registers. This also implies that any solvable task for n processes has a deterministic solution using only registers and objects of consensus number n and registers.

However, the computational power of objects with consensus number n in systems of more than n processes is not well-understood. Initially, it was conjectured that any object of consensus number n could be implemented from n-consensus objects and registers, even in systems with more than n processes. This is false: Herlihy [17] constructed a nondeterministic object with consensus number 1 that cannot be deterministically implemented from registers in a system of 2 processes.

Subsequently, it was shown that, within level 1 of the consensus hierarchy, there are an infinite number of incomparable nondeterministic objects. Specifically, the following relationships among set-consensus objects are known [6, 9, 12, 19]. Note that an $(n, 1)$-set consensus object is simply an n-consensus object, which has consensus number n.

THEOREM 1. *Let $n > k$ and $m > j$ be positive integers. Then there is a wait-free (or non-blocking) implementation of an (n, k)-set consensus object from (m, j)-set consensus objects and registers in a system of n or more processes if and only if $k \geq j$, $n/k \leq m/j$, and either $k \geq j\lceil n/m\rceil$ or $k \geq j\lfloor n/m\rfloor + n - m\lfloor n/m\rfloor$.*

In particular, for $m > j \geq 2$, there is no non-blocking implementation of a (2,1)-set consensus object from (m, j)-set consensus objects and registers. Hence (m, j)-set consensus objects have consensus number 1. Moreover, for any integer $k \geq 2$, there is no non-blocking algorithm using only registers that solves k-set consensus in a system of $n > k$ processes [7, 20, 26]. Since k-set consensus can be solved in a system of $n > k$ processes using a single (n, k)-set consensus object, there is no non-blocking implementation of an (n, k)-set consensus object from registers. Recently, Shavit and Taubenfeld [27] defined another family of nondeterministic objects that have consensus number 1, but cannot be implemented from registers in a wait-free manner.

Herlihy [18] asked whether every object of consensus number 2 has a deterministic implementation from fetch&add objects and registers in a system of three or more processes. *Common2* [2, 1] is the family of objects that have deterministic, wait-free implementations from 2-consensus objects and registers in a system of n processes, for all positive integers n. Examples of objects in *Common2* include test&set objects, fetch&add objects, swap objects, and stacks. The Common2 Conjecture claims that every object of consensus number 2 is in Common2. This is equivalent to saying that the answer to Herlihy's question is affirmative. The Common2 Conjecture is a special case of the *Consensus Hierarchy Conjecture*, which claims that, for all $n \geq 2$, any object of consensus number at most n has a deterministic implementation from n-consensus objects and registers in a system with any finite number of processes.

PODC'16, July 25-28, 2016, Chicago, IL, USA
© 2016 ACM. ISBN 978-1-4503-3964-3/16/07...$15.00
DOI: http://dx.doi.org/10.1145/2933057.2933116

Rachman [25] defined a family of nondeterministic objects, one of consensus number m for every positive integer m, and sketched a proof that they cannot be deterministically implemented from registers in a system of 3 processes or from n-consensus objects and registers in a system of $2n+1$ processes, for any integer $n \geq 2$. In particular, there is a nondeterminstic object of consensus number 2 that cannot be deterministically implemented from 2-consensus objects and registers in a system of 5 processes. Since a fetch&add object can be deterministically implemented from 2-consensus obejects and registers in a system of 5 processes, this nondeterministic object cannot be deterministically implemented from fetch&add objects and registers in a system of 5 processes. Thus, the answer to Herlihy's question is no.

Like many other researchers, we thought that the answer might be different for deterministic objects. It has been conjectured that the queue is not in *Common2*, but this remains open [1, 13, 24]. More recently, Gafni and Kuznetsov [16] proved that any algorithm using only deterministic objects of consensus number at most n can be deterministically emulated using only n-consensus objects and registers in a system of $n+1$ processes. This implies that the answer to Herlihy's question is yes for deterministic objects in a system of 3 processes.

We prove that the Consensus Hierarchy Conjecture is false. Specifically, all integers $m, k \geq 2$, we construct a deterministic object $O_{m,k}$ of consensus number m which has no deterministic, non-blocking implementation from m-consensus objects and registers in a system of $km+k-1$ or more processes (Theorem 6). In particular, $O_{2,2}$ cannot be implemented from 2-consensus objects and registers in a system of 5 processes, which refutes the Common2 conjecture.

Furthermore, we show that an $O_{m,k}$ object can be implemented from an $O_{m,k+1}$ object (Lemma 2), but an $O_{m,k+1}$ object cannot be implemented from $O_{m,k}$ objects and registers in a system of $mk+m+k$ or more processes (Theorem 12). Thus $O_{m,2}, O_{m,3}, \ldots$ is an infinite sequence of increasingly more powerful objects, all of consensus number m.

We define the $O_{m,k}$ object in Section 3 and explain how to implement an $O_{m,k}$ object from an $O_{m,k+1}$ object. In Section 4, we prove that $O_{m,k}$ has consensus number m. We use a valency argument to prove that it has consensus number at most m. The fact that it has consensus number at least m is an easy consequence of its definition. It also follows, by construction, that it can be used to implement an $(mk+k-1,k)$-set-consensus object. Since an $(mk+k-1,k)$-set-consensus object cannot be implemented from m-consensus objects and registers for $k \geq 2$, this proves Theorem 6. In Section 5, we define a *consistent ordered partition object* and mention some of its properties. The proof of Theorem 12 is a simulation argument which uses this object. It appears in Section 6.

2. MODEL

We consider an asynchronous shared memory system, in which processes communicate with one another by applying atomic operations, called steps, to shared objects. Each object has a set of possible values or states. Each operation (together with its inputs) is a partial mapping taking each state to a set of states. A shared object is *deterministic* if each operation takes each state to a single state and its associated response is a function of the state to which the operation is applied.

A *configuration* specifies the state of every process and the value of every shared object. An *execution* is an alternating sequence of configurations and steps, starting from an initial configuration. A faulty process can stop taking steps, but, otherwise, must behave in accordance with the algorithm it is executing. If C is a configuration and s is a sequence of steps, we denote by Cs the configuration (or in the case of nondeterministic objects, the set of possible configurations) when the sequence of steps s is performed starting from configuration C.

An *implementation* of a sequentially specified object O consists of a representation of O from a set of shared base objects and algorithms for each process to apply each operation supported by O. The implementation is *deterministic* if all its algorithms are deterministic. The implementation is *linearizable* if, in every execution, there is a sequential ordering of all completed operations on O and a (possibly empty) subset of the uncompleted operations on O such that (a) if op is completed before op' begins, then op occurs before op' in this ordering and (b) the behaviour of each operation in the sequence is consistent with its sequential specification (in terms of its response and its effect on shared objects). Linearizable implementations can be composed: If an object O has a linearizable implementation from a set of objects S and each object in S has a linearizable implementation from copies of objects in set T, then O has a linearizable implementation from copies of objects in set T [21].

An implementation of an object O is *wait-free* if, in every execution, each process that does not crash completes each of its operations on O in a finite number of its own steps. The implementation is *non-blocking* if, starting from every configuration in every infinite execution, some process completes one of its operations within a finite number of steps. In the rest of this paper, we are concerned with deterministic, linearizable, non-blocking implementations.

A *task* specifies what combinations of output values are allowed to be produced, given the input value of each process and the set of processes producing output values. A wait-free or non-blocking solution to a task is an algorithm in which each process that does not crash produces an output value in a finite number of its own steps such that the collection of output values satisfies the specification of the task, given the input values of the processes.

In the *consensus task*, each process, p_i, has an input value x_i and, if it is non-faulty, must output a value y_i that satisfies the following two properties.

- **validity:** Every output is the input of some process.
- **agreement:** All outputs are the same.

We say that an execution of an algorithm solving consensus *decides a value* if that value is the output of some process. *Binary consensus* is the restriction of the consensus task in which each input value $x_i \in \{0, 1\}$.

The *k-set consensus task*, introduced by Chaudhuri [11], is defined in the same way, except that agreement is replaced by the following property.

- **k-agreement:** There are at most k different values output.

Note that the 1-set consensus task is the same as the consensus task.

An object has *consensus number n* if there is a wait-free algorithm that uses only copies of this object and registers to solve consensus for n processes, but there is no such algorithm for $n+1$ processes. An object has infinite consensus number if there is such an algorithm for each positive integer n.

There are objects of consensus number n for every positive integer n. For $n \geq 2$, the n-consensus object is an example. It supports one operation, `propose`, which takes a single non-negative integer as input. The first `propose` operation applied to an n-consensus object returns its input. The next $n-1$ `propose` operations return the same value as the first operation. All subsequent `propose` operations return $\bot$.

For all positive integers $k < n$, an (n,k)-set consensus object [9] supports one operation, `propose`, which takes a single non-negative integer as input. The value of an (n,k)-set consensus object is a set of at most k non-negative integers, which is initially empty, and a count of the number of `propose` operations that have been performed on it (to a maximum of n). The first `propose` operation adds its input to the set. Any other `propose` operation can nondeterministically choose to add its input to the set, provided the set has size less than k. Each of the first n `propose` operations performed on the object nondeterministically returns an element from the set as its output. All subsequent `propose` operations return $\bot$. For $2 \leq k < n$, an (n,k)-set consensus object has consensus number 1. The consensus number of a (read-write) register is also 1.

Likewise, there are many objects with consensus number 2. One example is a (resettable) test&set object. It supports two operations: `test&set`, which sets the value of the object to 1 and returns the value it had, and `reset`, which resets the value of the object to 0. Another example is a fetch&increment object. It supports the single operation `fetch&increment`, which increments the value of the object (by 1) and returns the value it had. A readable fetch&increment object also supports `read`, but still has consensus number 2.

A *conflict detector* is an object that supports a single operation `check`(v). Each `check` operation *op* returns a Boolean response which satisfies the following properties:

- If all `check` operations that begin before *op* returns have the same input, then *op* returns false.
- If a `check` operation *op*$'$ with a different input begins before *op* returns, then either *op* or *op*$'$ returns true.

There are simple wait-free implementations of conflict detectors from registers [3, 4]. They are nonlinearizable, since two concurrent `check` operations with different inputs can both return true. Conflict detectors are closely related to adopt-commit objects [15, 4].

3. THE $O_{m,k}$ OBJECT

For all integers $m, k \geq 2$, consider the following deterministic object, which we call $O_{m,k}$. It supports one operation, `suggest`, which takes a single non-negative integer as input. The value of this object can be represented by $k+1$ numbers: $a_1, \ldots, a_k \in \mathbb{N}$ and $cnt \in \{0, \ldots, mk+k-1\}$. These numbers are all initially 0. The number of `suggest` operations that have been performed on the object are recorded in cnt, to a maximum of $mk+k-1$. If $cnt = (j-1)m$ for $j \in \{1, \ldots, k\}$, then `suggest`(v) sets a_j to v; otherwise, it leaves the values of $a_1, \ldots, a_r$ unchanged. If $(j-1)m \leq cnt \leq jm-1$ for $j \in \{1, \ldots, k\}$, then the operation increments cnt and returns a_j, if $cnt = mk+k-j-1$ for $j \in \{1, \ldots, k-1\}$, it increments cnt and returns a_j, and if $cnt = mk+k-1$, it simply returns $\bot$. Pseudocode for this operation appears in Figure 1.

`suggest`(v):
if $cnt = mk+k-1$ then {return($\bot$)}
if $cnt < km$ then {
    $j \leftarrow \lfloor cnt/m \rfloor + 1$
    if $cnt = (j-1) \times m$ then $\{a_j \leftarrow v\}\}$
else $\{j \leftarrow km+k-1-cnt\}$
$cnt \leftarrow cnt+1$
return(a_j)

Figure 1: The `suggest` operation

Another, more intuitive, way to think about $O_{m,k}$ is to consider the string

$$S_{m,k} = A_1^m A_2^m \cdots A_k^m A_{k-1} \cdots A_1$$

of length $km+k-1$ over the alphabet $\{A_1, \ldots, A_k\}$. If `suggest`(v) is the c'th operation applied to $O_{m,k}$ and A_j is the c'th letter in $S_{m,k}$, then this operation returns the value of a_j. Moreover, if this letter is the first occurrence of A_j in $S_{m,k}$, then this operation sets a_j to v. If $c \geq km+k$, then this operation returns $\bot$.

$O_{m,k+1}$ objects are at least as powerful as $O_{m,k}$ objects.

LEMMA 2. *For $m, k \geq 2$, an $O_{m,k}$ object can be implemented from an initialized $O_{m,k+1}$ object.*

PROOF. The implementation uses an $O_{m,k+1}$ object O with cnt initialized to m and a_1 initialized to 0. To perform `suggest`(v) on the implemented object, it performs `suggest`$(v+1)$ on O. If it receives a positive integer v' in response, it returns $v'-1$. Otherwise, it returns $\bot$. □

4. THE CONSENSUS NUMBER OF $O_{m,k}$

Consider the simple algorithm for m processes in which each process p_i with input x_i performs `suggest`(x_i) on the same $O_{m,k}$ object and returns its response. This algorithm solves consensus in a system of m processes. Therefore $O_{m,k}$ has consensus number at least m.

Using a valency argument [14, 5], we can prove that the consensus number of the $O_{m,k}$ object is exactly m. A configuration is *v-univalent* if all executions starting from this configuration that decide a value decide the value v. Note that, if C is v-univalent, then all configurations reachable from C are also v-univalent. A configuration is *univalent* if it is v-univalent for some $v \in \{0,1\}$. A configuration is *bivalent* if it is not univalent. A configuration is *critical* if it bivalent, but a step by any process results in a univalent configuration. Two configurations C and C' are *indistinguishable* to a set of processes if all processes in the set have the same state in both configurations and, for every sequence of steps by these processes, the responses to each of these steps is the same when they are applied starting from C and starting from C'.

LEMMA 3. *For $m, k \geq 2$, there is no deterministic algorithm that solves binary consensus among $m+1$ processes using only $O_{m,k}$ objects and registers.*

PROOF. To obtain a contradiction, suppose there is such an algorithm. Then, starting from any bivalent initial configuration, it is possible to reach a critical configuration C. Let s_i denote the step that process p_i is poised to perform in configuration C. Without loss of generality, suppose that configuration Cs_0 is 0-univalent and configuration Cs_1 is 1-univalent. We will construct a 0-univalent configuration reachable from C and a 1-univalent configuration reachable from C that are indistinguishable to some process. There is a solo execution by this process starting from this 0-univalent configuration that decides 0. By indistinguishability, this process decides 0 when it performs the same sequence of steps starting from the 1-univalent configuration. This contradicts the definition of 1-univalent.

First, note that s_1 must be an operation on the same object as s_0 and both cannot be `read` operations. Otherwise, the operations commute, i.e. $Cs_0s_1 = Cs_1s_0$. However, Cs_0 and, hence, Cs_0s_1 are 0-univalent and Cs_1 and, hence, Cs_1s_0 are 1-univalent. If s_0 is a `write` to a register, then the configurations Cs_0 and Cs_1s_0 are indistinguishable to process p_0. Likewise, s_1 cannot be a `write` to a register. Therefore, both s_0 and s_1 must be operations on the same $O_{m,k}$ object O. Every other operation s_i must also be an operation on O; otherwise s_0 and s_1 each commute with s_i. Therefore, each s_i is `suggest`(v_i) on O for some non-negative integer v_i.

Suppose that $cnt \neq (j-1)m$ in configuration C, for all $j \in \{1,\ldots,k\}$. Then, when performed in C, neither s_0 nor s_1 changes the value of any of $a_1,\ldots,a_k$, and either both increment cnt or neither increments cnt. Hence, the configurations Cs_0 and Cs_1 are indistinguishable to process p_m. Therefore, in configuration C, $cnt = (j-1)m$ for some $j \in \{1,\ldots,k\}$.

If $j = k$, then, $cnt = km$ in configurations $Cs_0s_1s_2\cdots s_{m-1}$ and $Cs_1s_0s_2\cdots s_{m-1}$. Thus all accesses to O after either of these configurigations will return $a_1,\ldots,a_{k-1}$ or $\perp$. Note that $a_1,\ldots,a_{k-1}$ do not change after C, so these two configurations are indistinguishable to process p_m. Therefore $j < k$.

Note that process p_0 has the same state in configurations Cs_0 and $Cs_1s_2\cdots s_ms_0$, because it receives response v_0 from s_0 in both. All objects other than O have the same values in both these configurations as they had in C. Since Cs_0 is 0-univalent, $Cs_1s_2\cdots s_ms_0$ is 1-univalent, and the next $m-1$ `suggest` operations on O will return v_0 in any execution starting from either of these configurations, process p_0 must access O at least m more times in a solo execution starting from Cs_0. Let σ_0 be the sequence of steps in the longest prefix of this solo execution in which p_0 accesses O only $m-1$ times. Then the next step, s_0', of p_0 in $Cs_0\sigma_0$ is a `suggest` operation on O. Process p_0 gets the same sequence of responses when performing σ_0 starting from Cs_0 or from $Cs_1s_2\cdots s_ms_0$. Since $p_1,\ldots,p_m$ each receive response v_1 from $s_1\cdots s_m$ performed starting from C or $Cs_0\sigma_0$, the state of each process is the same in $C_0 = Cs_0\sigma_0s_1s_2\cdots s_m$ and $C_1 = Cs_1s_2\cdots s_ms_0\sigma_0$. Note that C_0 is 0-univalent and C_1 is 1-univalent. In both these configurations, O has $cnt = (j+1)m$ and $a_i = 0$ for $j+2 \leq i \leq k$. The only difference is that, in C_0, $a_j = v_0$ and $a_{j+1} = v_1$, whereas, in C_1, $a_j = v_1$ and $a_{j+1} = v_0$. The value of every object other than O is the same in both these configurations.

Suppose $j = k-1$. Since p_0 has the same state in C_0, C_1 and $Cs_0\sigma_0$, it follows that s_0' is also the next step of p_0 in configurations C_0 and C_1. In C_0s_0' and C_1s_0', $cnt = km+1$, so all accesses to O after either of these configurations will return $a_1,\ldots,a_{k-2}$ or $\perp$. Note that $a_1,\ldots,a_{k-2}$ do not change after C, so these two configurations are indistinguishable to process p_m. However, C_0s_0' is 0-univalent and C_1s_0' is 1-univalent. Therefore $j \leq k-2$.

Consider any solo execution by p_1 starting from C_0 in which p_1 accesses O at most $(k-j-1)m+k-j-2$ times. Then p_1 gets the same sequence of responses when it performs the same sequence of steps starting from C_1. Therefore, p_1 must access O at least $(k-j-1)m+k-j-1$ more times in a solo execution starting from C_0. Let σ_1 be the sequence of steps in the shortest prefix of this solo execution in which p_1 performs $(k-j-1)m+k-j-1$ `suggest` operations on O. Since p_0 has the same state in $C_0\sigma_1$, $C_1\sigma_1$ and $Cs_0\sigma_0$, it follows that s_0' is also the next step of p_0 in configurations $C_0\sigma_1$ and $C_1\sigma_1$. In $C_0\sigma_1s_0'$ and $C_1\sigma_1s_0'$, $cnt = km+k-j$, so all accesses to O after either of these configurations will return $a_1,\ldots,a_{j-1}$ or $\perp$. Note that $a_1,\ldots,a_{j-1}$ do not change after C, so these two configurations are indistinguishable to process p_m. This is impossible, since $C_0\sigma_1s_0'$ is 0-univalent and $C_1\sigma_1s_0'$ is 1-univalent. □

COROLLARY 4. *The consensus number of $O_{m,k}$ is m.*

Notice that the above proof does not hold when $m = 1$. In fact, an $O_{1,2}$ object (i.e. with associated string $A_1A_2A_1$) has consensus number 2. Consider an $O_{1,2}$ object initialized with $cnt = 1$ and $a_1 = 2$. To solve binary 2-consensus, each process p_i first writes its input x_i to a single-writer register and then performs `suggest`(x_i). If the value returned is equal to x_i, p_i decides x_i; otherwise, it decides the value stored in the single-writer register of the other process.

The object defined in the same way as $O_{2,3}$, but using the string $A_1A_1A_2A_2A_1A_3A_3A_2$ instead of $A_1A_1A_2A_2A_3A_3A_2A_1$ has consensus number 3, not 2. Suppose it is initialized with $cnt = 2$ and $a_1 = 2$. To perform binary 3-consensus, each process p_i performs `suggest`(x_i), where $x_i \in \{0,1\}$ is its input. If it gets response $a_2 \in \{0,1\}$, it decides a_2. Otherwise, p_i is the third process to access the object and it gets response 2. It then performs `suggest`(x_i) three more times and decides the response it gets from the last of these, which is also a_2.

It is easy to prove that an $O_{m,k}$ object is as at least as powerful as an $(mk+k-1,k)$-set-consensus object. Each process simply performs `suggest`(v) on an $O_{m,k}$ object in place of `propose`(v) on the $(mk+k-1,k)$-set-consensus object.

OBSERVATION 5. *For $m,k \geq 2$, an $(mk+k-1,k)$-set-consensus object can be implemented from an $O_{m,k}$ object.*

This enables us to prove that, even though $O_{m,k}$ objects have consensus number m, they are more powerful than m-consensus objects.

THEOREM 6. *For $m,k \geq 2$, an $O_{m,k}$ object cannot be implemented from m-consensus objects and registers in a system of $mk+k-1$ or more processes.*

PROOF. To obtain a contradiction, suppose that an $O_{m,k}$ object can be implemented from m-consensus objects and registers in a system of $mk+k-1$ processes. Then, by Observation 5, an $(mk+k-1,k)$-set-consensus object can be implemented from m-consensus objects and registers. But this contradicts Theorem 1, since $(mk+k-1)/k = m+1-1/k > m/1$. □

Lemma 4 and Theorem 6 refute the Consensus Hierarchy Conjecture and, in particular, the Common2 Conjecture.

5. CONSISTENT ORDERED PARTITION

A one-shot immediate snapshot object [8] supports one access by each process. When a process accesses this object, it returns the subset of processes that accessed it previously or concurrently with itself. More formally, each process p that accesses the object is supposed to return a subset $S[p]$ of the process such that, for all processes $p' \neq p$, **(a)** $p \in S[p]$, **(b)** $S[p] \subseteq S[p']$ or $S[p'] \subseteq S[p]$, and **(c)** if $p \in S[p']$, then $S[p] \subseteq S[p']$. If $\mathcal{S} = \{S_1, \ldots, S_r\}$ is the set of subsets returned by the processes that accessed the object, where $\phi = S_0 \subseteq S_1 \subsetneq S_2 \subsetneq \cdots \subsetneq S_r$, then $S_1 - S_0, S_2 - S_1, \ldots, S_r - S_{r-1}$ is an ordered partition of the set of processes that accessed it such that, for all $1 \leq i \leq r$, the processes in $S_i - S_{i-1}$ accessed it concurrently and, for all $1 \leq j < i \leq r$, the processes in $S_j - S_{j-1}$ accessed it before the processes in $S_i - S_{i-1}$.

The *immediate ordered partition* object X, presented in Figure 2 is closely related to the atomic snapshot object. It supports two operations, ARRIVE(X, g) for $g \in \{1, \ldots, k\}$, and GET-PARTITION(X). Each of these operations may be performed any number of times by every process. The first time some process begins ARRIVE(X, g) (by performing its first step), we say that element g has *arrived.* GET-PARTITION(X) returns an array $\mathcal{H}[1..k]$, each component of which is a subset of $\{1, \ldots, k\}$, such that $\cup\{\mathcal{H}[g] \mid 1 \leq g \leq k\}$ contains all the elements that arrived before this operation began (and possibly some elements that arrived during the operation). Furthermore, for all elements $g, g' \in \{1, \ldots, k\}$, **(a)** if $\mathcal{H}[g] \neq \phi$ then $g \in \mathcal{H}[g]$, **(b)** $\mathcal{H}[g] \subseteq \mathcal{H}[g']$ or $\mathcal{H}[g'] \subseteq \mathcal{H}[g]$, **(c)** if $g \in \mathcal{H}[g']$, then $\mathcal{H}[g] \subseteq \mathcal{H}[g']$, **(d)** if g' arrives before g, $g' < g$, and $g \in \mathcal{H}[g'']$, then $g' \in \mathcal{H}[g'']$, and **(e)** if some call of ARRIVE(X, g') completes before g arrives, then before the call completes, there is some component of $\mathcal{H}$ that contains g' but does not contain g. Suppose $\{\mathcal{H}_1, \ldots, \mathcal{H}_r\}$ is the set of nonempty subsets of $\{1, \ldots, k\}$ that are stored in components of $\mathcal{H}$, where $\phi = \mathcal{H}_0 \subsetneq \mathcal{H}_1 \subsetneq \cdots \subsetneq \mathcal{H}_r$. Then $\mathcal{H}_1 - \mathcal{H}_0, \ldots, \mathcal{H}_r - \mathcal{H}_{r-1}$ is an ordered partition of the set of elements that have arrived. If some elements have not arrived, then we can add $\{1, \ldots, k\} - \mathcal{H}_r$ to get an ordered partition of $\{1, \ldots, k\}$. We call this collection of sets the *ordered partition* (of $\{1, \ldots, k\}$) *induced by* the array $\mathcal{H}$. If $\mathcal{H}'$ is returned by GET-PARTITION(X) after $\mathcal{H}$, then the ordered partition induced by $\mathcal{H}'$ is a (not necessarily proper) refinement of the ordered partition induced by $\mathcal{H}$.

In our implementation, H is a k-component atomic snapshot object and all components of H initially contain ϕ. The partition induced by H at the beginning of the execution is the trivial partition consisting of the single set $\{1, \ldots, k\}$. The algorithm also uses a k^2-component multi-writer Boolean snapshot object $M[1..k, 1..k]$, viewed as a matrix and a matrix $D[2..k, 1..k]$ of conflict detectors [4].

Each component of M is initially 0 and is only updated from 0 to 1. Column g of M corresponds to element g. The rows or levels of M are used to record the progress of elements. We say that element g has *reached level* ℓ if $M[\ell, g] = 1$ and it is *at level* ℓ if it has reached level ℓ, but has not reached level $\ell - 1$.

```
ARRIVE(X, g):
UPDATE(M[k, g], 1)
MOVE-DOWN(X)
return

GET-PARTITION(X):
MOVE-DOWN(X)
return(SCAN(H))

MOVE-DOWN(X):
for g ← 1 to k do {a[g] ← k + 1}
scanM: 𝓜 ← SCAN(M)
S ← {j | 𝓜[1, j] = 1} % elements at level 1
if S ≠ φ then {
     for all g ∈ S do {
          if a[g] > 1 then {
               a[g] ← 1
               UPDATE(H[g], S)
               goto scanM}}}
for ℓ ← 2 to k do {
     S ← {j | 𝓜[ℓ, j] = 1}% elements that reach level ℓ
     if |S| < ℓ then {continue ← 1} else {continue ← 0}
     for all g ∈ S in order from smallest to largest do {
          if a[g] > ℓ then {
               a[g] ← ℓ
               if not check(D[ℓ, g], continue) then {
                    if continue = 1
                    then {% move g down to level ℓ − 1
                         UPDATE(M[ℓ − 1, g], 1)}
                    else {% report that g stops at level ℓ
                         UPDATE(H[g], S)}}
               goto scanM}}}
```

Figure 2: Consistent Ordered Partition Object X

ARRIVE(X, g) updates $M[k, g]$ to have value 1 and then calls MOVE-DOWN(X). The first time ARRIVE(X, g) is performed, $M[k, g]$ is updated from 0 to 1, so element g starts at level k. MOVE-DOWN(X) helps elements move down levels, one level at a time. GET-PARTITION(X) calls MOVE-DOWN(X) and then returns a snapshot of H.

An element g at level ℓ moves down to level $\ell - 1$ (by updating $M[\ell - 1, g]$ from 0 to 1) when there are fewer than ℓ elements that have reached level ℓ.

LEMMA 7. *At most ℓ elements reach level ℓ.*

An element that reaches level 1 stops there. An element stops at level $\ell > 1$ if it does not reach level $\ell - 1$ and there are exactly ℓ elements that have reached level ℓ. If element g stops at level ℓ, a process helping element g can update $H[g]$ to contain the set of ℓ elements that have reached level ℓ.

A problem can arise when multiple processes are trying to help the same element g at level $\ell > 1$. One helper might see fewer than ℓ elements at level ℓ and proceed to move element g down to level $\ell - 1$. Later, another helper might see ℓ elements at level ℓ and might think that g has stopped at level ℓ. To prevent this from happening, the processes helping g at level ℓ use the conflict detector $D[\ell, g]$. In the first case, the helper performs `check` with input 1, indicating that it thinks that element g should continue down to level $\ell - 1$. In the second case, the helper performs `check` with input 0, indicating that it thinks that element g should stop at level ℓ. In any execution in which all `check` operations on $D[\ell, g]$ have the same input value, they all get false, indicating there is no conflict. If an execution contains both `check`($D[\ell, g]$,0) and `check`($D[\ell, g]$,1), then at least one of these two operations returns true, indicating a conflict. Thus, if a helper does not detect a conflict, it can safely move element g to level $\ell - 1$ or safely update $H[g]$, depending on its input value to the conflict detector. A helper that detects a conflict cannot help element g at level ℓ. However, if some other helper moves element g to a lower level, it may be able to help g at that lower level.

LEMMA 8. *Once $H[g]$ has been updated from ϕ, it will never be updated to contain a different set.*

Hence, the collection of subsets contained in $H \cup \{\phi\}$ can only increase as an execution proceeds.

COROLLARY 9. *The partition induced by H at any point in an execution is a refinement of the partition induced by H at any earlier point in the execution.*

Each process has a local array $a[1..k]$. If $a[g] = 1$, then the process has seen that element g is at level 1. If $1 < a[g] \leq k$, then $a[g]$ is the lowest level ℓ at which the process has performed (or is about to perform) `check`($D[\ell, g]$,continue) on line 28 . When the process sets $a[g]$ to ℓ on line 19 or 27, it knows that g has reached level ℓ, since g is in the set $S = \{j \mid \mathcal{M}[\ell, j] = 1\}$ it computed on line 15 or 23. If the process moves element g down to level $\ell - 1$ on line 31, it is only moving g down one level. Each component $a[g]$ is initialized to $k + 1$ on line 13, indicating that the process has not performed `check` on $D[\ell, g]$ at any level.

LEMMA 10. *The implementation in Figure 2 is wait-free.*

PROOF. Each time the execution of MOVE-DOWN jumps to scanM (from line 21 or 34), at least one component of a decreases in value (on line 19 or 27). Since all components of a are positive integers and they never increase in value, MOVE-DOWN eventually terminates. □

6. AN ∞ HIERARCHY AT EACH LEVEL OF THE CONSENSUS HIERARCHY

In Lemma 2, we showed that $O_{m,k+1}$ objects are at least as powerful as $O_{m,k}$ objects. In this section, we show that the $O_{m,k}$ objects, for $k \geq 2$, form an infinite hierarchy within level m of the consensus hierarchy.

We do this by showing how to simulate any $(k + 1)$-set-consensus algorithm for $mk + m + k$ threads that uses only $O_{m,k}$ objects and registers by $mk + m + 1$ processes using only m-consensus objects and registers.

LEMMA 11. *If there is a non-blocking $(k+1)$-set-consensus algorithm for $mk + m + k$ threads that communicate using $O_{m,k}$ objects and registers, then there is a non-blocking $(k+1)$-set-consensus algorithm for $mk+m+1$ processes that communicate using only m-consensus objects and registers.*

Using our simulation, we prove that $O_{m,k+1}$ objects are strictly more powerful than $O_{m,k}$ objects.

THEOREM 12. *For all integers $m, k \geq 2$, an $O_{m,k+1}$ object cannot be implemented from $O_{m,k}$ objects and registers in a system of $mk + m + k$ processes.*

PROOF. Suppose that an $O_{m,k+1}$ object can be implemented from $O_{m,k}$ objects and registers in a system of $mk + m + k$ processes. By Lemma 5, an $(mk + m + k, k + 1)$-set-consensus object can be implemented from an $O_{m,k+1}$ object. Therefore, $mk + m + k$ processes can solve $(k + 1)$-set consensus using only $O_{m,k}$ objects and registers. Hence, by Lemma 11, $mk + m + 1$ processes can solve $(k + 1)$-set-consensus using only m-consensus objects and registers and, thus, an $(mk+m+1, k+1)$-set consensus object can be implemented from m-consensus objects and registers. But this contradicts Theorem 1, since $(mk + m + 1)/(k + 1) = m + 1/(k + 1) > m/1$. □

Consider a non-blocking $(k + 1)$-set-consensus algorithm for $mk+m+k$ threads that communicate using $O_{m,k}$ objects and registers. Without loss of generality, we may assume that the registers are single-writer and each thread q'_j, has exactly one single-writer register R'_j to which it can write.

Our approach is to simulate this $(k + 1)$-set-consensus algorithm using $mk + m + 1$ simulating processes. In addition to m-consensus objects and registers, our simulation uses readable fetch&increment objects, test&set objects, and resettable test&set objects. These objects are all in COMMON2, so they can be implemented from m-consensus objects and registers in a system with any number of processes.

In existing simulations of a collection of threads by a different number of processes [5, 8, 10, 22], simulating processes choose the input for each thread and simulate the successive steps of each thread one step at a time. A lock, based on safe agreement or `test&set` enable the simulating processes to agree on which of them will simulate the next step of that thread. Each simulating process tries to acquire the lock for a thread. If it is unsuccessful, it continues on to the next thread in round-robin order. If it is successful, it simulates the next step of that thread, releases the lock, and then goes to the next thread in round-robin order.

We associate a multi-writer register R_j and a resettable test&set object T_j with each thread q'_j. Simulating processes use T_j as a lock to decide which of them will simulate the next step of q'_j, giving them exclusive write access to R_j. The *contents* of R'_j, the *state* of q'_j, and an *index* in $\{0, \ldots, k-1\}$ are stored in three fields of R_j. At the beginning of the simulation, the initial value of R'_j is stored in $R_j.contents$, $\perp$ is stored in $R_j.state$ (denoting that the input to q'_j has not yet been determined), and 0 is stored in $R_j.index$. The index is used during the simulation of `suggest` operations.

Let p_i be a simulating process that has successfully acquired the lock for a thread q'_j by winning T_j. After acquiring the lock, it reads R_j. If it crashes while it holds the lock, no further steps of thread q'_j are simulated. In other words, thread q'_j crashes in the simulated execution. Depending on the step thread q'_j is poised to perform, there are a number of different cases to consider.

If $R_j.state = \perp$, then p_i writes the initial state of q'_j to $R_j.state$, using its own input as the input to q'_j. Then p_i releases the lock by resetting T_j. If $R_j.state \neq \perp$, then it contains the current state of q'_j in the simulated execution. Local computation that q'_j wants to perform is simulated locally by process p_i, which then updates $R_j.state$.

If thread q'_j is poised to return a decision value v for the

```
h ← R_j.index
if h = 0 then {
    f ← fetch&increment(F)
    if f ≥ (m+1)k then {return(⊥)}
    if f ≤ mk then {
        g ← ⌈f/m⌉ %member of group g
        v ← propose(C[g], u)
        write v to G[g]
        for 1 ≤ g' < g in increasing order do {
            if G[g'] ≠ ⊥ then {ARRIVE(X, g')}}
        f' ← read(F)
        if f' > mg then {ARRIVE(X, g)}
        return(v)}
    %mk < f < (m+1)k
    R_j.index ← (m+1)k − f
    return()}
for 1 ≤ g' ≤ k in increasing order do{
    if G[g'] ≠ ⊥ then {ARRIVE(X, g')}}
𝓗 ← GET-PARTITION(X)
Let φ = S_0 ⊊ S_1 ⊊ S_2 ⊊ ··· ⊊ S_r be the sets in 𝓗 ∪ {φ}
if h > |S_r| then {return()}
%second half of suffix step h
d ← min{y ∈ {1,...,r} : |S_y| ≥ h}
b ← S_d − S_{d−1}
write b to B[h]
b' ← φ
repeat {
    for all g ∈ b − b' in increasing order do {
        if test&set(U[g]) = 0 then {return(G[g])}}
    %suffix thread j has failed on all elements in b
    b' ← b
    𝓑 ← COLLECT B
    b ← smallest box in 𝓑 that properly contains b'}
```

Figure 3: Simulating suggest(u) by thread q'_j

set-consensus algorithm, process p_i resets T_j, returns v as its decision value, and terminates.

If thread q'_j is poised to **write** the value w to R'_j, process p_i writes w to $R_j.contents$, updates the state field of R_j, and resets T_j.

If thread q'_j is poised to **read** R'_h, then process p_i reads $R_h.contents$, updates the state field of R_j based on the value it read and resets T_j.

Finally, suppose thread q'_j is poised to perform **suggest**(u) on an $O_{m,k}$ object. In this case, the simulation is more complicated. It is presented in Figure 3. For each instance of an $O_{m,k}$ object used by the threads, there are three arrays of size k: Each component of $C[1..k]$ is an m-consensus object and each component of $G[1..k]$ and $B[1..k]$ is a multi-writer register. All components of these arrays are initially $\bot$. There is also an array $U[1..k]$ of test&set objects, all of which are initially 0 and a readable fetch&increment object F, which is initially 1. Finally, there is a consistent ordered partition object X, which is initialized to reflect no arrivals.

The first mk simulated steps that begin accessing a particular $O_{m,k}$ object are called its *prefix steps* and the next $k-1$ steps are called its *suffix steps*. The prefix steps are divided into k *groups* of size m, corresponding to m consecutive accesses of the $O_{m,k}$ object. The prefix steps in the same group all return the same value, which is the input value of the first prefix step in the group to be linearized. We call this value the *output* of the group. Each suffix step returns the output of a different group. Therefore, the simulation of a suffix step may be required to wait until enough groups have made their outputs available.

If a process p that begins the simulation of a suffix step is the only process that can complete it, then p can either wait until enough groups have outputs available or start simulating other steps. In the first case, crashes by some of the processes simulating prefix steps could prevent p from finishing the simulation, even though it has not crashed. In the second case, if p crashes, it could block the completion of the simulations of too many threads. The key idea is to divide the simulation of a suffix step into two halves, which may be performed by different processes. The second half is only performed when sufficiently many groups have made their outputs available. Until then, processes simply continue onto the next thread to be simulated.

To begin the simulation of **suggest**(u) by thread q'_j, process p_i reads $R_j.index$. If it contains 0 (indicating that no process has yet started the simulation of this step), process p_i performs **fetch&increment**(F), which returns some value f.

If $f \geq (m+1)k$, then the response from the simulated $O_{m,k}$ object is $\bot$. In this case, p_i simply updates the state field of R_j based on this response and resets T_j.

Simulated steps for which $1 \leq f \leq mk$ are the prefix steps. The m simulated steps that receive values between $m(g-1)+1$ and mg from F constitute *group* $g = \lceil f/m \rceil$. To complete the simulation of a prefix step, p_i proposes its input u to the consensus object $C[g]$ and writes the result v to register $G[g]$. ARRIVE(X, g) should be performed once $G[g] \neq \bot$ and all the prefix steps in group g have started. Because all prefix steps in all previous groups start before any prefix step in group g starts, process p_i calls ARRIVE(X, g') for all $1 \leq g' < g$, in increasing order, such that $G[g'] \neq \bot$. It also reads F. If F has value greater than mg, which indicates that all the prefix steps in group g have started, process p_i calls ARRIVE(X, g). Finally, it updates the state field of R_j based on the simulated response v from the $O_{m,k}$ object and resets T_j.

Simulated steps for which $mk+1 \leq f \leq mk+k-1$ are the *suffix steps*. Recall that a suffix step is simulated in two halves. To complete the first half of the simulation of a suffix step, p_i writes $(m+1)k - f$ to the index field of R_j, and resets T_j. Note that immediately after the first half of the suffix step has been simulated, the index field contains a value between 1 and $k-1$. If the index field of R_j contains the value h, we say that h is the *index* of the simulated suffix step that q'_j is poised to perform.

When process p_i reads $h \in \{1, \ldots, k-1\}$ from $R_j.index$, it decides whether to simulate the second half of the suffix step q'_j is poised to perform. If not, it simply resets T_j.

A straightforward approach is to simulate the second half of suffix step h when $G[h] \neq \bot$. Then the value in $G[h]$ can be returned as the response of this suffix step, the state of q'_j can be updated based on this response, and T_j can be reset. Unfortunately, there is a problem with this approach. To see why, suppose that, in the simulated algorithm, $mk + k - 1$ of the threads access the same $O_{m,k}$ object and they are all simulated by different processes. Let the processes simulating the mk prefix steps all crash before computing outputs for their groups, so the threads they are simulating, as well as the $k-1$ threads performing suffix steps are all blocked. Now, suppose that the $m+1$ remaining threads all access a second $O_{m,k}$ object and they are each simulated by a different one of the $m+1$ remaining processes. Let the processes simulating the first m prefix steps all crash before computing the output for group 1. Then one thread and one simulating process remain. Suppose this remaining thread continues to access the second $O_{m,k}$ object a total of $m(k-1)+(k-1)$ times. In its last access, the thread is blocked, since group 1 has not produced an output. Thus, the remaining process cannot continue the simulation.

Thus, a more complicated approach is needed. Each suffix step is associated with a different group and it returns the output of that group. To ensure that two suffix steps cannot be associated with the same group, an array of test&set objects, $U[1..k]$, is used. Provided enough groups have written their outputs to G, the process p_i simulating the second half of a suffix step by a thread q'_j performs **test&set** on the objects in $U[1..k]$, in some order, until it wins one. If it wins $U[g]$, then this suffix step is associated with group g. It updates the state of q'_j based on the value stored in $G[g]$ as the response from the suffix step and then resets T_j, completing the simulation of this suffix step. The key is to use the consistent ordered partition object X to decide the order in which each process simulating a suffix thread should try these test&set objects.

ARRIVE(X, g) is performed only after the output of group g has been stored in $G[g]$. Thus, if element g is in one of the parts of the partition returned by GET-PARTITION(X) and process p_i wins $U[g]$, there is a value other than $\perp$ in $G[g]$, which can be returned as the response to the suffix step it is simulating.

Before proceeding with the simulation of the second half of suffix step h, p_i calls ARRIVE(X, g') for all $1 \leq g' \leq k$ such that $G[g'] \neq \perp$. This ensures that if a suffix step starts being simulated after the output of a group has been written to G, it will see that element g has arrived.

Next, p_i calls GET-PARTITION(X). Let $H[1..k]$ denote the array returned. If fewer than h different elements appear in the sets in H, i.e. if $\# \cup \{H[g] \mid 1 \leq g \leq k\} < h$, then p_i simply resets T_j. If there are at least h different elements, then p_i finishes the simulation of suffix step h before simulating any other step. In this case, we will say that the second half of suffix step h is *enabled*.

Note that, from the specification of a consistent ordered partition object, $\cup\{H[g] \mid 1 \leq g \leq k\}$ includes all elements g that arrived before p_i invoked GET-PARTITION(X). Thus, when the second half of suffix step h is enabled, at least h elements have arrived. Let $H_1 \subsetneq H_2 \subsetneq \cdots \subsetneq H_r$ be the different sets stored in components of $H[1..k]$ and let $H_0 = \phi$. For any part $H_y - H_{y-1}$ of this partition, define its *range* to be $[|H_{y-1}|+1..|H_y|]$. If H_d is the smallest among $H_1, \ldots, H_r$ that has size at least h, then, by definition, $h \in range(H_d - H_{d-1})$.

Now, process p_i sets its local variable b to $H_d - H_{d-1}$ and writes it into $B[h]$. By construction, $h \in range(B[h])$. We call each nonempty set stored in B a *box*. The following properties are consequences of properties of the consistent ordered partition object and the definition of *range*.

OBSERVATION 13. *Let b and b' be any two boxes.*
Either $b \subseteq b'$, $b' \subseteq b$, or $b \cap b' = \phi$.
If $b \cap b' = \phi$, then $range(b) \cap range(b') = \phi$.
If $b \subseteq b'$, then $range(b) \subseteq range(b')$.

Next, process p_i performs **test&set**$(U[g])$ on the elements $g \in b$, in increasing order, until it wins one. Only a process that is simulating some suffix thread h' whose second half is enabled and has written a box to $B[h']$ accesses test&set objects in $U[1..k]$.

Now, suppose that p_i has lost **test&set**$(U[g])$ for all elements $g \in b$ while simulating suffix step h. Then it sets b' to b, finds the smallest box b in B that properly contains b', and performs **test&set**$(U[g])$ on the elements $g \in b - b'$, in increasing order, until it wins one. If it loses all of them, it repeats these steps.

The next lemma ensures that this can always be done. While p_i is simulating suffix step h, no elements are removed from b, so, by Lemma 13, h is always an element of $range(b)$.

LEMMA 14. *If p_i has lost* **test&set**$(U[g])$ *for all elements $g \in b$ while simulating suffix step h, then there exists a box b' in B that properly contains b.*

PROOF. Suppose that p_i has lost a **test&set** on each object in $\{U[g] \mid g \in b\}$. Since each test&set object is won by a process simulating a different suffix step and $|b| = |range(b)|$, there exist $h' \notin range(b)$ such that the process $p_{i'}$ simulating suffix step h' won **test&set**$(U[g'])$ for some $g' \in b$.

Suppose $p_{i'}$ chose g' from box b'. Then $h' \in range(b')$. Since $g' \in b \cap b'$, Lemma 13 implies that $range(b) \cap range(b') \neq \phi$. But $h' \in range(b') - range(b)$, so, by Lemma 13, $range(b) \subsetneq range(b')$. □

COROLLARY 15. *The simulation of the second half of a suffix step is wait-free.*

PROOF. ARRIVE and GET-PARTITION are both wait-free. Thus, if a process takes an infinite number of steps while simulating the second half of a suffix step, the set of elements stored in its local variable b will grow without bound. But this is impossible, since $b \subseteq \{1, \ldots, k\}$. □

Next, we prove that our simulation is non-blocking.

LEMMA 16. *Suppose that $mk+m+1$ processes simulate a non-blocking $(k+1)$-set-consensus algorithm for $mk+m+k$ threads as described in this section. Then every non-faulty process can determine the value decided by some thread.*

PROOF. The algorithm being simulated is non-blocking and each process can simulate steps of any thread. Thus, the only difficulty that can arise is when processes crash, blocking the simulation of simulated threads. It suffices to show that, even if $mk+m$ simulating processes crash, at least one simulated thread remains unblocked. Then the remaining process can finish the simulation of a thread and determine the value it decided.

Each process that crashes while simulating any step other than a prefix step only blocks the thread that it is simulating. If fewer than m processes crash while simulating prefix steps belong to the same group g of an $O_{m,k}$ object, then group g outputs a value (the value of $G[g]$ gets changed from $\perp$). If c simulating processes crash while simulating prefix steps that access the same $O_{m,k}$ object, then at most $\lfloor c/m \rfloor$ groups will not output a value, so at most $\lfloor c/m \rfloor$ elements will not arrive at the consistent ordered partition object used to simulate the $O_{m,k}$ object. Thus, in addition to blocking the c simulated threads that perform these steps, at most $\lfloor c/m \rfloor - 1$ threads performing suffix steps will be blocked. In particular, if mk processes crash while simulating the prefix steps of the same $O_{m,k}$ object, only $k-1$ additional threads are blocked. Hence, if $mk+m$ simulating processes crash, at most $mk+(k-1)+m$ threads are blocked. Thus, at least one thread remains unblocked. □

To prove that the simulation is correct, it remains to show how the simulated steps of the threads can be linearized. Each read and write step that is performed on behalf of a thread is linearized when it is performed during the execution. All of the prefix steps that access a particular $O_{m,k}$ object are linearized before all of the suffix steps that access it. The suffix steps and the steps that return $\perp$ are linearized in increasing order of the values they receive from F. In particular, this means that suffix steps are linearized in decreasing order of their indices and all simulated steps that return $\perp$ are all linearized after suffix step 1.

The prefix steps in each group g are linearized consecutively, in the order in which they performed `propose` on $C[g]$. They all return the same value, namely the value decided by $C[g]$, which is stored in $G[g]$. By the semantics of a consensus object, this value was proposed by the prefix step in group g that was linearized first.

The groups are linearized in increasing order of the indices of the suffix steps to which they are associated. In particular, the prefix steps in the group associated with suffix step 1 are linearized first. Since there are k groups and only $k-1$ suffix steps, at least one group is not associated with any suffix steps. If there is exactly one such group, it is linearized last. Thus, prefix steps are not necessarily linearized in increasing order of the values the processes that simulate them receive from the fetch&increment object F.

Since the suffix step associated with group g returns the value output by prefix steps in group g, the sequence of values returned by the linearized operations performed on an $O_{m,k}$ object satisfies the semantics of the object. The difficult part is showing that if the prefix steps of group g are linearized before the prefix steps of group $g' < g$, then all these prefix threads must be concurrent.

LEMMA 17. *Suppose that the simulation of some prefix step in group g' completes before the simulation of the last prefix step in group $g > g'$ begins. Then, before g arrives, some call of ARRIVE(X, g') is completed.*

PROOF. Any process simulating a prefix step in a group prior to g does not call ARRIVE(X, g). When a process p begins simulating a prefix step in a group after g or a suffix step, the simulation of the last prefix step in group g has already begun, so the simulation of some prefix step in group g' has completed. In particular, the value output by group g' has already been written to $G[g']$. Thus when p performs line 44 or 51 for g', it sees that $G[g'] \neq \perp$ and calls ARRIVE(X, g'). Since $g' < g$, if p calls ARRIVE(X, g), then it does so after its call of ARRIVE(X, g') is completed.

Now suppose that p is simulating a prefix step in group g. If it sees that it sees that $G[g'] \neq \perp$ when it performs line 44, it calls ARRIVE(X, g') before possibly calling ARRIVE(X, g) on line 46. Suppose that p sees that $G[g'] = \perp$. Let p' be the process that is simulating the prefix step in group g' that completes first. Then, after writing to $G[g']$, p' sees that $F > mg'$ on line 45, since a prefix step in group g has already started. Thus p' performs ARRIVE(X, g') on line 46 before finishing its simulation of this prefix step, which is before the simulation of the last prefix step in group g begins, which is before process p can perform ARRIVE(X, g) on line 46. □

COROLLARY 18. *If groups g and g' are in the same box, then the simulations of all prefix steps in groups g and g' are concurrent.*

PROOF. Since the simulation of a prefix step begins with **fetch&inc**(F), the simulation of all prefix steps in group $g' < g$ start before the simulation of all prefix steps in group g. Thus, when the last prefix step in group g begins, either the simulation of no prefix step in group g' has completed, in which case the simulations of all prefix steps in groups g' and g are concurrent, or the simulation of some prefix step in group g' has completed. In the second case, by Lemma 17, some call of ARRIVE(X, g') is completed before g arrives. Then, by property **(e)**, before this call of ARRIVE(X, g') completes, there is a set in H that contains g' but does not contain g.

Consider the array $\mathcal{H}$ that is the response from GET-PARTITION(X) performed by some process p. Let $\phi = S_0 \subsetneq S_1 \subsetneq S_2 \subsetneq \cdots \subsetneq S_r$ be the sets in $\mathcal{H} \cup \{\phi\}$. If $g \in S_r$, then g arrived before p performed SCAN(H) on line 12. Hence, there exists $1 \leq d < r$ such that $g' \in S_d$, but $g \notin S_d$. Thus g' and g are in different parts of the partition induced by $\mathcal{H}$ and hence are not in the same box. Therefore, no box in B contains both g' and g. □

LEMMA 19. *The simulated steps of an $O_{m,k}$ object can be linearized.*

PROOF. Since suffix steps start in decreasing order of their indices following the start of all prefix steps, the suffix steps can be linearized in decreasing order of their indices following all prefix threads. All simulated steps that return $\perp$ can be linearized after suffix step 1 in the order they begin, which is in increasing order of the values they receive from F.

Consider the array B at the end of any extension of the execution in which the simulations of all mk prefix steps and all $k-1$ suffix steps are completed. Then every prefix step, except one, is associated with some suffix step. Let $\mathcal{B}'$ be the collection of all maximal boxes in B, where a box is maximal if it is not strictly contained in any other box. Then, by Observation 13, $\mathcal{B}'$ induces an ordered partition of $\{1, \ldots, k\}$. Moreover, the ranges of the boxes in $\mathcal{B}'$ are disjoint. Note that suffix step $k-1$ does not complete until there is a box that contains $k-1$ in its range. Thus, there is at most one group that is not in $\cup\{b \mid b \in \mathcal{B}'\}$. All groups in earlier parts of the partition induced by $\mathcal{B}'$ are linearized before groups in later parts of this partition.

From the code, suffix step h only performs **test&set**($U[g]$) for groups $g \in b$ (and, hence, can only be associated with a group in b) if $h \in range(b)$. By Corollary 18, for each $b \in \mathcal{B}'$, the simulations of all prefix steps in the groups in b are concurrent and, therefore, they can be linearized in any order relative to one another. In particular, the groups in b can be linearized in increasing order of the indices of the suffix steps that are associated with them.

Suppose that the simulation of some prefix step in group g' completes before the simulation of some prefix step in group g begins. Then it completes before the the simulation of the last prefix step in group g begins and $g' < g$. By Lemma 17, some call of ARRIVE(X, g') is completed before

g arrives. By property **(d)**, every set $H[g'']$ that contains g also contains g'. Thus g' is in the same part of the partition induced by $\mathcal{B}'$ or an earlier part of this partition. But, by Corollary 18, g and g' are not in the same box. Thus g' is in an earlier part of the partition induced by $\mathcal{B}'$ and, so, is linearized before g. □

This completes the proof of Lemma 11.

Acknowledgments

Yehuda Afek and Eli Gafni were jointly supported by the United States-Israel Binational Science Foundation (grant 2014226). Yehuda Afek was also supported by the Israel Science Foundation (grant 1386/11). Faith Ellen was supported by the Natural Science and Engineering Research Council of Canada.

7. REFERENCES

[1] Y. Afek, E. Gafni, and A. Morrison. Common2 extended to stacks and unbounded concurrency. *Distributed Computing*, 20(4):239–252, 2007.

[2] Y. Afek, E. Weisberger, and H. Weisman. A completeness theorem for a class of synchronization objects (extended abstract). In *Proceedings of the Twelfth Annual ACM Symposium on Principles of Distributed Computing (PODC)*, pages 159–170, 1993.

[3] J. Aspnes. A modular approach to shared-memory consensus, with applications to the probabilistic-write model. *Dist. Comput.*, 25(2):179–188, 2012.

[4] J. Aspnes and F. Ellen. Tight bounds for adopt-commit objects. *Theory Comput. Syst.*, 55(3):451–474, 2014.

[5] H. Attiya and F. Ellen. *Impossibility Results for Distributed Computing*. Synthesis Lectures on Distributed Computing Theory. Morgan & Claypool Publishers, 2014.

[6] E. Borowsky. *Capturing the power of resiliency and set consensus in distributed systems*. PhD thesis, University of California, Los Angeles, 1995.

[7] E. Borowsky and E. Gafni. Generalized FLP impossibility result for t-resilient asynchronous computations. In *Proceedings of the Twenty-Fifth Annual ACM Symposium on Theory of Computing (STOC)*, pages 91–100, 1993.

[8] E. Borowsky and E. Gafni. Immediate atomic snapshots and fast renaming (extended abstract). In *Proceedings of the Twelfth Annual ACM Symposium on Principles of Distributed Computing (PODC)*, pages 41–51, 1993.

[9] E. Borowsky and E. Gafni. The implication of the Borowsky-Gafni simulation on the set-consensus hierarchy. Technical Report 930021, UCLA Computer Science Dept., 1993.

[10] T. D. Chandra, V. Hadzilacos, P. Jayanti, and S. Toueg. Generalized irreducibility of consensus and the equivalence of t-resilient and wait-free implementations of consensus. *SIAM J. Computing*, 34(2):333–357, 2005.

[11] S. Chaudhuri. More choices allow more faults: Set consensus problems in totally asynchronous systems. *Information and Computation*, 105(1):132–158, 1993.

[12] S. Chaudhuri and P. Reiners. Understanding the set consensus partial order using the Borowsky-Gafni simulation (extended abstract). In *Proceedings of the 10th International Workshop on Distributed Algorithms (WDAG)*, pages 362–379, 1996.

[13] M. David. A single-enqueuer wait-free queue implementation. In *Proceedings of the 18th International Conference on Distributed Computing (DISC)*, pages 132–143, 2004.

[14] M. J. Fischer, N. A. Lynch, and M. Paterson. Impossibility of distributed consensus with one faulty process. *J. ACM*, 32(2):374–382, 1985.

[15] E. Gafni. Round-by-round fault detectors: Unifying synchrony and asynchrony. In *Proceedings of the Seventeenth Annual ACM Symposium on Principles of Distributed Computing (PODC)*, pages 143–152, 1998.

[16] E. Gafni and P. Kuznetsov. N-consensus is the second strongest object for N+1 processes. In *Proceedings of the 11th International Conference on the Principles of Distributed Systems (OPODIS)*, pages 260–273, 2007.

[17] M. Herlihy. Impossibility results for asynchronous PRAM (extended abstract). In *Proceedings of the Third Annual ACM Symposium on Parallel Algorithms and Architectures (SPAA)*, pages 327–336, 1991.

[18] M. Herlihy. Wait-free synchronization. *ACM Trans. Program. Lang. Syst.*, 13(1):124–149, 1991.

[19] M. Herlihy and S. Rajsbaum. Set consensus using arbitrary objects (preliminary version). In *Proceedings of the Thirteenth Annual ACM Symposium on Principles of Distributed Computing (PODC)*, pages 324–333, 1994.

[20] M. Herlihy and N. Shavit. The topological structure of asynchronous computability. *J. ACM*, 46(6):858–923, 1999.

[21] M. Herlihy and J. M. Wing. Linearizability: A correctness condition for concurrent objects. *ACM Trans. Program. Lang. Syst.*, 12(3):463–492, 1990.

[22] D. Imbs and M. Raynal. The multiplicative power of consensus numbers. In *Proceedings of the Twenty Ninth Annual ACM Symposium on Principles of Distributed Computing (PODC)*, pages 26–35, 2010.

[23] P. Jayanti. Robust wait-free hierarchies. *J. ACM*, 44(4):592–614, 1997.

[24] Z. Li. Non-blocking implementation of queues in asynchronous distributed shared-memory systems. Master's thesis, University of Toronto, 2001.

[25] O. Rachman. Anomalies in the wait-free hierarchy. In *Proceedings of the 8th International Workshop on Distributed Algorithms (WDAG)*, pages 156–163, 1994.

[26] M. E. Saks and F. Zaharoglou. Wait-free k-set agreement is impossible: The topology of public knowledge. *SIAM J. Comput.*, 29(5):1449–1483, 2000.

[27] N. Shavit and G. Taubenfeld. The computability of relaxed data structures: Queues and stacks as examples. In *Proceedings of the 22nd International Colloquium on Structural Information and Communication Complexity (SIROCCO)*, pages 414–428, 2015.

Unbeatable Set Consensus via Topological and Combinatorial Reasoning*

Armando Castañeda
Universidad Nacional Autónoma de México (UNAM)
armando.castaneda@im.unam.mx

Yannai A. Gonczarowski
The Hebrew University of Jerusalem and Microsoft Research
yannai@gonch.name

Yoram Moses
Technion — Israel Institute of Technology
moses@ee.technion.ac.il

ABSTRACT

The ***set consensus*** problem has played an important role in the study of distributed systems for over two decades. Indeed, the search for lower bounds and impossibility results for this problem spawned the topological approach to distributed computing, which has given rise to new techniques in the design and analysis of protocols. The design of efficient solutions to set consensus has also proven to be challenging. In the synchronous crash failure model, the literature contains a sequence of solutions to set consensus, each improving upon the previous ones.

This paper presents an ***unbeatable*** protocol for nonuniform k-set consensus in the synchronous crash failure model. This is an efficient protocol whose decision times *cannot* be improved upon. Moreover, the description of our protocol is extremely succinct. Proving unbeatability of this protocol is a nontrivial challenge. We provide two proofs for its unbeatability: one is a subtle constructive combinatorial proof, and the other is a topological proof of a new style. These two proofs provide new insight into the connection between topological reasoning and combinatorial reasoning about protocols, which has long been a subject of interest. In particular, our topological proof reasons in a novel way about subcomplexes of the protocol complex, and sheds light on an open question posed by Guerraoui and Pochon (2009). Finally, using the machinery developed in the design of this unbeatable protocol, we propose a protocol for uniform k-set consensus that beats all known solutions by a large margin.

Keywords

k-set consensus; uniform k-set consensus; optimality; unbeatability; topology; knowledge

*A full version of this paper with complete proofs is available on arXiv.org [5].
Part of the results of this paper were announced in [3].

PODC'16, July 25-28, 2016, Chicago, IL, USA

ISBN 978-1-4503-3964-3/16/07...$15.00
DOI: http://dx.doi.org/10.1145/2933057.2933120

1. INTRODUCTION

The ***k-set consensus*** problem [7], which allows processes to decide on up to k distinct values, has played an important role in the study of distributed systems for more than two decades. Its analysis provided deep insights into concurrency and solvability of tasks in fault-tolerant settings, both synchronous and asynchronous (e.g. [1, 2, 8, 14, 15, 22, 28]). Whereas combinatorial techniques sufficed for the study of the traditional (1-set) consensus problem [13], establishing lower bounds and impossibility results for the more general k-set consensus has proven to be more challenging. Tackling these has given rise to the introduction of topological techniques to the theory of distributed systems, and these have become a central tool (see [19] for a detailed treatment of the subject).

In the synchronous message passing model, the literature distinguishes between uniform and nonuniform variants of the classic consensus problem. In nonuniform consensus only the correct processes (the ones that do not crash) are required to decide on the same value, while values decided on by processes who crash are allowed to deviate from the value decided by correct processes. In uniform consensus, however, all decisions must be the same. In asynchronous models the two variants coincide, since there is never a guarantee that a silent process has crashed. Perhaps due to the fact that k-set consensus was first studied in the asynchronous setting, only its uniform variant (in which the total number of distinct values decided by correct *and faulty* processes is no greater than k) has been considered in the literature.

This paper is concerned with k-set consensus in the synchronous message-passing model. In this setting, there are well-known bounds relating the degree of coordination that can be achieved (captured by the parameter k), the number of process crashes that occur in a given execution (typically denoted by f), and the time required for decision, which is $\lfloor f/k \rfloor + 2$ in the uniform case (see [1, 14, 15]). Given an *a priori* bound of $\boldsymbol{t}$ on the total number of crashes in a run, the worst-case lower bound for decision is $\lfloor t/k \rfloor + 1$ [8].

We consider both uniform and nonuniform variants of k-set consensus. For the nonuniform case, we present a protocol that we call $\textsc{Opt}_{\min[k]}$, which is ***unbeatable***, in the sense of [4]. Unbeatability is a very strong form of optimality: A k-set consensus protocol P that always decides at least as soon as $\textsc{Opt}_{\min[k]}$ cannot have even one process ever decide strictly earlier than when that process decides in $\textsc{Opt}_{\min[k]}$. For the uniform case, we present a protocol that we call $\textsc{u-P}_{\min[k]}$, which is built using methods similar to those used for $\textsc{Opt}_{\min[k]}$, and which strictly beats all known protocols, often by a large margin. In many cases, $\text{U-P}_{\min[k]}$ decides in 2 rounds against an adversary for which the best known early-deciding protocols would decide in $\lfloor t/k \rfloor + 1$ rounds. Whether $\text{U-P}_{\min[k]}$ is unbeatable remains an open problem.

The first unbeatable protocols for consensus (in both uniform and nonuniform variants) were presented in [4]. The analysis of those unbeatable consensus protocols shows that the notion of a ***hidden path*** is central to the inability to decide in consensus. Roughly speaking, a hidden path w.r.t. a process i at the end of round m is a sequence of processes that crash one after the other and could inform some process j at time m of an initial value unknown to i.

Our improved k-set consensus protocols are based on an observation that the time required for decision does not depend simply on the number of processes that crash in each round. Only failures that occur in a very specific pattern, maintaining what we call a ***hidden capacity*** of k, can prevent processes from being able to decide. The hidden capacity is a generalization of the notion of a hidden path, which, as mentioned above, was shown in [4] to play an important role in consensus.

The main contributions of this paper are:

- We provide new solutions to k-set consensus in the synchronous message passing model with crash failures. For the nonuniform case, we present the first unbeatable protocol for k-set consensus, called $\text{OPT}_{\min[k]}$: No protocol can beat the decision times of $\text{OPT}_{\min[k]}$. For uniform k-set consensus, we present a protocol $\text{U-P}_{\min[k]}$ that strictly beats all known early-deciding solutions in the literature [1, 8, 14, 15, 26], in some cases beating (all of) them by a large margin.

- We identify a quantity called the hidden capacity of a given execution w.r.t. a process i at time m, which plays a major role in determining the decision times in runs of k-set consensus. Roughly speaking, once its hidden capacity drops below k, process i can decide. Maintaining a hidden capacity of k requires at least k processes to crash in every round. However, they must crash in a very particular fashion. In previous solutions to k-set consensus in this model (see, e.g., [14]), a process that observes k or more new failures per round will not decide. In our protocols, decision can be delayed only as long as failures maintain a hidden capacity of k or more.

- Proving unbeatability has the flavor of a lower bound or impossibility proof. Unsurprisingly, proving the unbeatability of $\text{OPT}_{\min[k]}$ is extremely subtle. We present two different proofs of its unbeatability. One is a completely constructive, combinatorial proof, while the other is a nonconstructive, topological proof based on Sperner's lemma. The latter is a new style of topological proof, since it addresses the local question of when an individual process can decide, rather than the more global question of when the last decision is made. This sheds light on the open problem and challenge posed by Guerraoui and Pochon in [16] regarding how topological reasoning can be used to obtain bounds on local decisions. Topological lower bounds for k-set consensus (e.g. [8, 15]) have established that $k-1$ connectivity (in addition to a Sperner coloring) precludes the possibility that all processes decide. Our analysis provides further insight into the topological analysis for local decisions, illustrating that hidden capacity of k implies $k-1$ connectivity of a subcomplex of the protocol complex in a given round. The hidden capacity thus explains the source of topological connectivity that underlies the lower-bound proofs for k-set consensus. To the best of our knowledge, this is the first time knowledge and topological techniques directly interact to obtain a topological characterization.

The full paper [5] contains the detailed technical analysis that supports the claims in this extended abstract. This includes full proofs of all technical claims. In particular, both the full combinatorial proof of unbeatability and the corresponding topological proof are presented there.

2. PRELIMINARY DEFINITIONS

2.1 Computation and Communication Model

Our model of computation is a synchronous, message-passing model with benign crash failures. A system has $n \geq 2$ processes denoted by $\mathsf{Procs} = \{1, 2, \ldots, n\}$. Each pair of processes is connected by a two-way communication link, and each message is tagged with the identity of the sender. Processes share a discrete global clock that starts at time 0 and advances by increments of one. Communication in the system proceeds in a sequence of ***rounds***, with round $m+1$ taking place between time m and time $m+1$. Each process starts in some ***initial state*** at time 0, usually with an ***input value*** of some kind. In every round, each process first performs a local computation, and performs local actions, then it sends a set of messages to other processes, and finally receives messages sent to it by other processes during the same round. We consider the local computations and sending actions of round $m+1$ as being performed at time m, and the messages are received at time $m+1$.

A faulty process fails by ***crashing*** in some round $m \geq 1$. It behaves correctly in the first $m-1$ rounds and sends no messages from round $m+1$ on. During its crashing round m, the process may succeed in sending messages on an arbitrary subset of its links. At most $\boldsymbol{t} \leq n-1$ processes fail in any given execution.

It is convenient to consider the state and behavior of processes at different (process-time) nodes, where a ***node*** is a pair $\langle i, m\rangle$ referring to process i at time m. A ***failure pattern*** describes how processes fail in an execution. It is a layered graph F whose vertices are all nodes $\langle i, m\rangle$ for $i \in \mathsf{Procs}$ and $m \geq 0$. An edge has the form $(\langle i, m-1\rangle, \langle j, m\rangle)$ and it denotes the fact that a message sent by i to j in round m would be delivered successfully. Let $\mathsf{Crash}(\boldsymbol{t})$ denote the set of failure patterns in which all failures are crash failures, and at most $\boldsymbol{t}$ crash failures can occur. An ***input vector*** describes what input the processes receive in an execution. The only inputs we consider are initial values that processes obtain at time 0. An input vector is thus a tuple $\vec{v} = (v_1, \ldots, v_n)$ where v_j is the input to process j. We think of the input vector and the failure pattern as being determined by an external scheduler, and thus a pair $\alpha = (\vec{v}, \mathsf{F})$ is called an ***adversary***.

A ***protocol*** describes what messages a process sends and what decisions it takes, as a deterministic function of its local state at the start of the round. Messages received during a round affect the local state at the start of the next round. We assume that a protocol P has access to the number of processes n and to the bound t, typically passed to P as parameters.

A ***run*** is a description of an infinite behavior of the system. Given a run r and a time m, the ***local state*** of process i at time m in r is denoted by $r_i(m)$, and the ***global state*** at time m is defined to be $r(m) = \langle r_1(m), r_2(m), \ldots, r_n(m)\rangle$. A protocol P and an adversary α uniquely determine a run, and we write $r = P[\alpha]$.

Since we restrict attention to benign failure models and focus on decision times and solvability in this paper, Coan showed that it is sufficient to consider *full-information* protocols (*fip*'s for short), defined below [9]. There is a convenient way to consider such protocols in our setting. With an adversary $\alpha = (\vec{v}, \mathsf{F})$ we associate a ***communication graph*** $\mathcal{G}_\alpha$, consisting of the graph F extended by labeling the initial nodes $\langle j, 0\rangle$ with the initial states v_j according to α. With every node $\langle i, m\rangle$ we associate a subgraph $\mathcal{G}_\alpha(i, m)$ of $\mathcal{G}_\alpha$, which we think of as i's ***view*** at $\langle i, m\rangle$. Intuitively, this graph represents all nodes $\langle j, \ell\rangle$ from which $\langle i, m\rangle$ has heard, and the initial values it has seen. Formally, $\mathcal{G}_\alpha(i, m)$ is defined by induction on m. $\mathcal{G}_\alpha(i, 0)$ consists of the node $\langle i, 0\rangle$, labeled by the initial value v_i. Assume that $\mathcal{G}_\alpha(1, m), \ldots, \mathcal{G}_\alpha(n, m)$ have been defined, and let $J \subseteq \mathsf{Procs}$ be the set of processes j such that $j = i$ or $e_j = (\langle j, m\rangle, \langle i, m+1\rangle)$ is an edge of F. Then $\mathcal{G}_\alpha(i, m+1)$ consists of the node $\langle i, m+1\rangle$, the union of all graphs $\mathcal{G}_\alpha(j, m)$ with $j \in J$, and the edges $e_j = (\langle j, m\rangle, \langle i, m+1\rangle)$ for all $j \in J$. We say that (j, ℓ) is ***seen*** by $\langle i, m\rangle$ if (j, ℓ) is a node of $\mathcal{G}_\alpha(i, m)$. Note that this occurs exactly if F allows a (Lamport) message chain from $\langle j, \ell\rangle$ to $\langle i, m\rangle$.

A full-information protocol P is one in which at every node $\langle i, m\rangle$ of a run $r = P[\alpha]$ the process i constructs $\mathcal{G}_\alpha(i, m)$ after receiving its round m nodes, and sends $\mathcal{G}_\alpha(i, m)$ to all other processes in round $m + 1$. In addition, P specifies what decisions i should take at $\langle i, m\rangle$ based on $\mathcal{G}_\alpha(i, m)$. Full-information protocols thus differ only in the decisions taken at the nodes. Finally, in a run $r = P[\alpha]$, we define the local state $r_i(m)$ of a process i at time m to be the pair $\langle \beta, \mathcal{G}_\alpha(i, m)\rangle$, where $\beta =$ '$\bot$' if i is undecided at time m, and if $\beta = \mathtt{v}$ in case i has decided $\mathtt{v}$ at or before time m.

For ease of exposition and analysis, all of our protocols are *fip*'s. However, in fact, they can all be implemented in such a way that any process sends any other process a total of $O(n \log n)$ bits throughout any execution (see the full paper [5] for more details).

2.2 Domination and Unbeatability

A protocol P is a ***worst-case optimal*** solution to a decision problem S in a given model if it solves S, and decisions in P are always taken no later than the *worst-case* lower bound for decisions in this problem, in a given model of computation. However, this protocol can be strictly improved upon by ***early stopping*** protocols, which are also worst-case optimal, but can often decide much faster than the original ones. In this paper, we are interested in protocols that are efficient in a much stronger sense.

Consider a context $\gamma = (\vec{\mathtt{V}}, \mathcal{F})$, where $\vec{\mathtt{V}}$ is a set of initial vectors. A decision protocol Q ***dominates*** a protocol P in γ, denoted by $Q \preceq_\gamma P$ if, for all adversaries α and every process i, if i decides in $P[\alpha]$ at time m_i, then i decides in $Q[\alpha]$ at some time $m'_i \leq m_i$. Moreover, we say that Q ***strictly dominates*** P if $Q \preceq_\gamma P$ and $P \not\preceq_\gamma Q$. I.e., if it dominates P and for some $\alpha \in \gamma$ there exists a process i that decides in $Q[\alpha]$ *strictly before* it does so in $P[\alpha]$.

Following [20], a protocol P is said to be an ***all-case optimal*** solution to a decision task S in a context γ if it solves S and, moreover, P dominates every protocol P' that solves S in γ. For the standard (*eventual*) variant of consensus, in which decisions are not required to occur simultaneously, Moses and Tuttle showed that no all-case optimal solution exists [25]. Consequently, Halpern, Moses and Waarts in [18] initiated the study of a natural notion of optimality that is achievable by eventual consensus protocols:

Definition 1. [18] A protocol P is an ***unbeatable*** solution to a decision task S in a context γ if P solves S in γ and no protocol Q solving S in γ strictly dominates P.[1]

Thus, P is unbeatable if for all protocols Q that solve S, if there exist an adversary α and process i such that i decides in $Q[\alpha]$ strictly earlier than it does in $P[\alpha]$, then there must exist some adversary β and process j such that j decides strictly earlier in $P[\beta]$ than it does in $Q[\beta]$. An unbeatable solution for S is $\preceq$-minimal among the solutions of S.

2.3 Set Consensus

In the k-set consensus problem, each process i starts out with an initial value $v_i \in \{0, 1, \ldots, k\}$.[2] Denote by $\exists\mathtt{v}$ the fact that at least one of the processes started out with initial value $\mathtt{v}$. In a protocol for (nonuniform) k-set consensus, the following properties must hold in every run r:

> **k-Agreement**: The set of values that correct processes decide on has cardinality at most k,
>
> **Decision**: Every correct process must decide on some value, and
>
> **Validity**: For every value $\mathtt{v}$, a decision on $\mathtt{v}$ is allowed only if $\exists\mathtt{v}$ holds.

In uniform k-set consensus [6, 11, 17, 23, 27, 29], the **k-Agreement** property is replaced by

> **Uniform k-Agreement**: The set of values decided on has cardinality at most k.

In uniform k-set consensus, values decided on by failing processes (before they have failed) are counted, whereas in the nonuniform case they are not counted. The two notions coincide in asynchronous settings, since it is never possible to distinguish at a finite point in time between a crashed process and a very slow one. Uniformity may be desirable when elements outside the system can observe decisions, as in distributed databases when decisions correspond to commitments to values.

[1]Unbeatable protocols were called *optimal* in [18]. Following [4], we prefer the term *unbeatable* because "optimal" is used very broadly, and inconsistently, in the literature.

[2]The set of values in k-set consensus is often assumed to contain more than $k + 1$ values. We choose this set for ease of exposition. Our results apply equally well with minor modifications if a larger set of values is assumed. See Footnote 4.

3. UNBEATABLE (1-SET) CONSENSUS

Before introducing our protocols for k-set consensus, we briefly review the analysis and the unbeatable protocol for nonuniform (1-set) consensus given in [4]. In this version of the problem, all processes start with binary initial values $v_i \in \{0,1\}$, decisions must satisfy the validity condition, and all correct processes decide on the same value. Recall that we are assuming that the processes follow a full-information protocol, so a protocol can be specified simply by giving the rules by which a process decides on value $\mathtt{v}$, for $\mathtt{v} = 0, 1$.

By Validity, $\exists\mathtt{v}$ is a necessary condition for deciding on a value $\mathtt{v} \in \{0,1\}$. Consequently, a process cannot decide $\mathtt{v}$ unless it knows that some process had initial value $\mathtt{v}$.[3] Clearly, a process knows $\exists\mathtt{v}$ if it sees a value of $\mathtt{v}$, either as its own initial value or reported in a message that the process receives. [4] consider the design of a protocol that will decide on 0 as soon as possible, namely at the first point at which a process knows $\exists 0$. They proceed to consider when a process can decide 1, given that all processes decide 0 if they ever come to know that $\exists 0$. Clearly, we should consider the possibility of deciding 1 only for processes that do not know that $\exists 0$. By the (1-)**Agreement** property, correct processes must decide on the same value. Thus, a process cannot decide 1 if another process is deciding 0. Let us consider when a process can know that nobody is deciding 0.

Our analyses will make use of the different types of information that a process i at time m can know about the state of a process j at time ℓ, in runs of an *fip*. (We denote such process-time pairs by $\langle i,m\rangle$, $\langle j,\ell\rangle$, etc.) We say that $\langle j,\ell\rangle$ is ***seen by*** $\langle i,m\rangle$ if i has received a message by time m containing the state at $\langle j,\ell\rangle$. We say that $\langle j,\ell\rangle$ is ***guaranteed crashed*** at $\langle i,m\rangle$ if i has proof at time m that j crashed *before* time ℓ (i heard from someone who did not hear from j in some round $\leq \ell$). Finally, we say that $\langle j,\ell\rangle$ is ***hidden from*** $\langle i,m\rangle$ if it is neither seen by $\langle i,m\rangle$ nor guaranteed crashed there. As far as i is concerned, j may have sent messages in round $\ell+1$, and since i does not see $\langle j,\ell\rangle$, it may not know at m what information j's messages contained.

Fig. 1 illustrates a case in which process i does not know $\exists 0$ at time 2, while process i_3 decides 0 at time 2. This is possible only if there is a ***hidden path*** with respect to $\langle i,2\rangle$, in the terminology of [4]: at each time ℓ from 0 up to the current time $m=2$, there is a node $\langle j,\ell\rangle$ that is hidden from $\langle i,2\rangle$.

In general, if there is a hidden path with respect to $\langle i,m\rangle$ in a given execution, and process i does not know $\exists 0$ at time m, then i cannot be guaranteed that no correct process is currently deciding 0. It thus cannot decide 1. If no such path exists, i.e., if there is some time $k \leq m$ that contains no hidden node w.r.t. $\langle i,m\rangle$, then i knows that nobody is deciding 0. Moreover, in that case i knows that no value of 0 is known to any active process, and so nobody will ever decide 0. Based on this analysis, [4] proposes the following protocol:

[3]This is an instance of the so-called *Knowledge of Preconditions* principle of [24], which states that if φ is a necessary condition for process i performing an action a, then i must *know* φ when it performs a. For more details on the use of this principle in our setting, see both the full paper [5] and [4].

Protocol OPT_0 (for an undecided process i at time m) [4]:

if seen 0 **then** $\mathsf{decide}(0)$
elseif some time $k \leq m$ contains no hidden node **then** $\mathsf{decide}(1)$

As shown in [4], OPT_0 is an unbeatable protocol for nonuniform consensus. Moreover, it strictly dominates all previously known early stopping protocols for consensus, in some cases deciding in 3 rounds when the best previously known protocol would decide in $t+1$ rounds.

Hidden paths, first defined in [4], are implicit in many lower-bound proofs for consensus in the crash failure model [10, 12]. They play a crucial role in the correctness and unbeatability proof of OPT_0. In this paper, we extend the notion of a hidden path, and use it to provide an unbeatable protocol for set consensus, as well as a protocol for uniform set consensus that beats all previously known protocols.

4. UNBEATABLE *K*-SET CONSENSUS

The design and especially the analysis of protocols for k-set consensus are typically considerably more subtle than that of protocols for (1-set) consensus. Indeed, since processes may decide on different values, their decisions no longer depend on hearing about concrete values. Nevertheless, as we now show, it is possible to extend the above notions to obtain a simple protocol for nonuniform k-set consensus. While the protocol is natural to derive and simple to state, it is unbeatable. Moreover, its proof of unbeatability is highly nontrivial and extremely subtle.

4.1 Protocol Description and Correctness

Recall that the set of possible initial values is assumed to be $\{0,1,\ldots,k\}$. As in the case of 1-set consensus, our goal is to define the rules by which a process will decide on $\mathtt{v}$, for every value $\mathtt{v}$ in this set. Define by $Min\langle i,m\rangle$ the minimal value that process i has seen by time m (i.e., the minimal value $\mathtt{v}$ s.t. i knows that $\exists\mathtt{v}$) in a given run of the *fip*. Moreover, we say that process i is ***low*** at time m if $Min\langle i,m\rangle < k$. We set out to design a protocol in which a process i that decides at time m decides on $Min\langle i,m\rangle$.

Suppose that we choose to allow a process that becomes low to immediately decide on $Min\langle i,m\rangle$. This is analogous to allowing a process that sees 0 to immediately decide on 0 in 1-set consensus. When should a process be able to decide on the value k? As already specified, every low process decides on a ***low value***, i.e., a value smaller than k as soon as possible; therefore, we are only concerned about when high processes (processes that are not low) should decide on a high value, i.e., on k. Of course, a process i should be able to decide on k if it knows that doing so will not violate the properties of k-set consensus, and in particular, the ***k*-Agreement** property, which disallows the correct processes to decide on more than k values. I.e., if i considers it to be possible that there is a correct process deciding on each of the values $0,\ldots,k-1$, then i should not decide on k. In other words, i can decide on k only when it knows that at most $k-1$ of the low values will be decided on. Notice that this is not the same as there being only $k-1$ possible low initial values in the run, but rather that at most $k-1$ values can serve as $Min\langle j,m\rangle$ for any process j that decides at time m. Consider the following generalization of the notion of a hidden path:

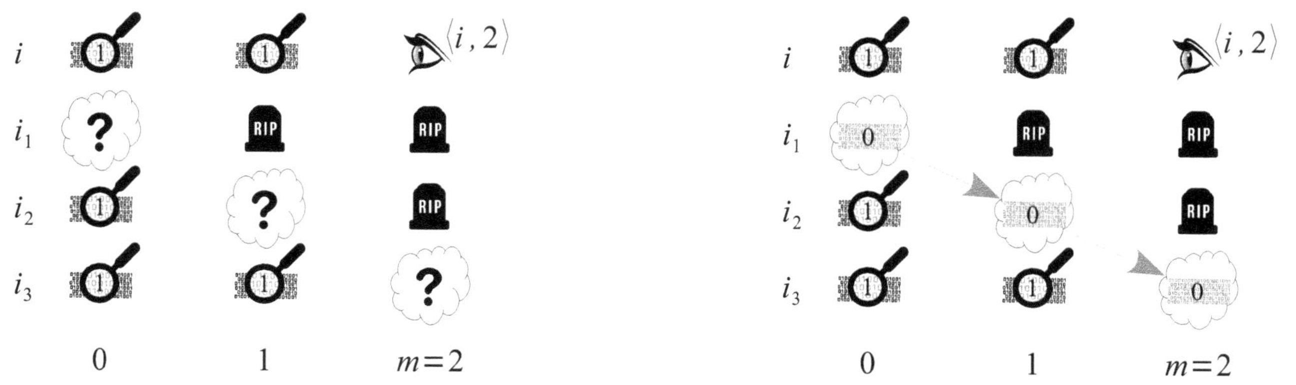

(a) A hidden path w.r.t. $\langle i, 2\rangle$.

(b) A run i considers at 2 to be possible, in which 0 is held by a correct process at 2.

Figure 1: A hidden path at time $m{=}2$ indicates that a value unknown to i may exist in the system.

Definition 2. Fix a run r. We define the ***hidden capacity*** of process i at time m, denoted by $\mathsf{HC}\langle i,m\rangle$, to be the maximum number c such that for every $\ell \le m$, there exist c distinct nodes $\langle i_1^\ell,\ell\rangle,\ldots,\langle i_c^\ell,\ell\rangle$ at time ℓ that are hidden from $\langle i,m\rangle$. The nodes $\langle i_b^\ell,\ell\rangle$ are said to be ***witnesses to the hidden capacity of*** i at m.

Put another way, the hidden capacity of $\langle i,m\rangle$ is at least c iff at each time $\ell \le m$ there are at least c nodes that are hidden from $\langle i,m\rangle$. In particular, a hidden path implies that the hidden capacity is at least 1. Recall that $\langle i,m\rangle$ does not see what happens at nodes $\langle j,\ell\rangle$ that are hidden from it, and does not know who they heard from in round ℓ and whether they communicated to others in round $\ell+1$.

As we now show, the hidden capacity is very closely related to the ability of a process to decide k at a given time. If the hidden capacity of $\langle i,m\rangle$ is c, then there could be up to c *disjoint* hidden paths, where each failing process that belongs to one of the hidden paths sends in its crashing round a message solely to its successor in that path. Fig. 2(a) illustrates the node $\langle i,2\rangle$ with hidden capacity 3, while Fig. 2(b) illustrates three disjoint hidden paths. If such disjoint paths begin in nodes with distinct initial values, they can end at c nodes, each of which sees a distinct minimal value. It follows that a node $\langle i,m\rangle$ with hidden capacity k must consider it possible that there are k nodes $\langle j_0,m\rangle,\ldots,\langle j_{k-1},m\rangle$ with $Min\langle j_b,m\rangle = b$ for every $b = 0,\ldots,k-1$. Therefore, i is not be able to decide on the value k at time m without risking violating ***k*-Agreement**.

Interestingly, when the hidden capacity drops below k, it becomes possible to decide on k. Suppose that the hidden capacity of $\langle i,m\rangle$ is smaller than k. This means that there must be some time $\ell < m$ such that some $c < k$ nodes at time ℓ are hidden from $\langle i,m\rangle$. Each of these nodes has a single minimal value. Assuming that $Min\langle i,m\rangle = k$, we have that for time ℓ nodes seen by $\langle i,m\rangle$, the minimal value is k. Since this is the *fip*, every active process after time ℓ will have one of these $c+1 \le k$ minimal values. It follows that i can safely decide on k at time m if its hidden capacity is lower than k.

The above discussion suggests the following protocol for nonuniform k-set consensus:

Protocol $\textsc{Opt}_{\min[k]}$ (for an undecided process i at time m):

if i is low or i has hidden capacity $< k$
then $\mathsf{decide}(Min\langle i,m\rangle)$

Our protocol $\textsc{Opt}_{\min[k]}$ directly generalizes the unbeatable consensus protocol $\textsc{Opt}_0$. Being low in this case corresponds to seeing 0, while $\mathsf{HC}\langle i,m\rangle < k = 1$ corresponds to there being no hidden path. Recall that the decision rules of $\textsc{Opt}_0$ may be thought of as follows: a process i decides on the value 0 as soon as it knows that some node had initial value 0, and it decides on the value 1 as soon as it knows that no correct process will ever decide on the value 0 (hence **Agreement** is not violated). In $\textsc{Opt}_{\min[k]}$, a process i decides on a low value $\mathtt{v}$ (i.e., a value $\mathtt{v} \in \{0,\ldots,k-1\}$) as soon as it knows that some node had initial value $\mathtt{v}$, and decides on the high value $\mathtt{v} = k$ (indeed, for a high node $\langle i,m\rangle$, we have $Min\langle i,m\rangle = k$) as soon as it knows that at most $k-1$ values smaller than $\mathtt{v}$ will ever be decided on by correct processes (thus satisfying ***k*-Agreement**).

Based on the above analysis, we obtain:[4]

Proposition 1. $\textsc{Opt}_{\min[k]}$ *solves k-set consensus, and all processes decide by time* $\lfloor f/k \rfloor + 1$.

4.2 Unbeatability

Proving that $\textsc{Opt}_{\min[k]}$ is unbeatable is nontrivial.[5] The main technical challenge along the way is, roughly speaking, showing that, e.g., in the scenario depicted in Fig. 2, each of the hidden processes at time $m{=}2$ (i.e., i_b^2 for $b = 1,2,3$) decides on the unique low value (v_b) known to it, not merely in $\textsc{Opt}_{\min[k]}$, but in *any* protocol P that dominates $\textsc{Opt}_{\min[k]}$.

[4]We note that Proposition 1, as well as all other the results that we present, including Theorems 1–3 below, as well as all proofs in the full paper [5], hold verbatim even if the set of possible initial values is $\{0,\ldots,d\}$, for some $d \ge k$. (In this case, all values in $\{k,k+1,\ldots,d\}$ are considered high.) In particular, the definition for this case of all protocols, including $\textsc{Opt}_{\min[k]}$, is unchanged.

[5]In particular, the challenges involved are significantly greater than those in involved in proving that $\textsc{Opt}_0$ is unbeatable for (1-set) consensus (as is often the case with problems regarding k-set consensus vs. their (1-set) consensus counterparts).

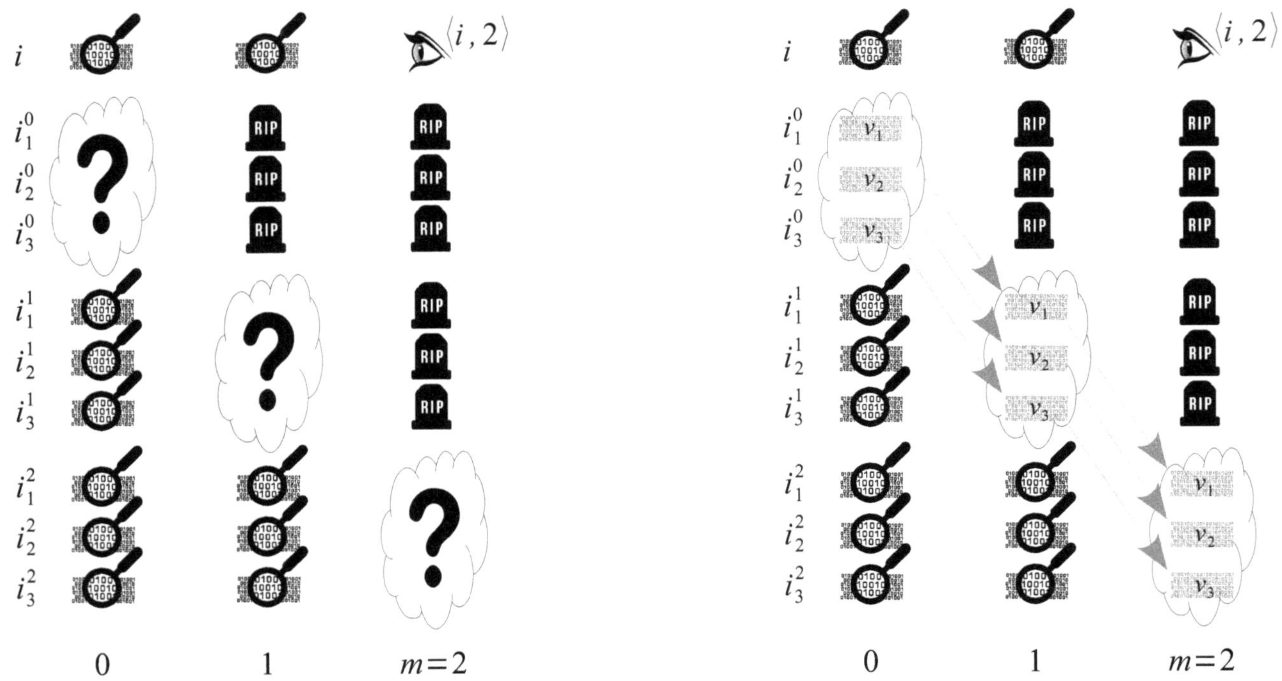

(a) $\langle i, 2\rangle$ has hidden capacity 3.

(b) A run i considers at 2 to be possible, in which v_1, v_2, v_3 are held by distinct processes at 2.

Figure 2: A hidden capacity of $c = 3$ at time $m = 2$ indicates that any arbitrary c values unknown to i may exist in the system, each held by a distinct process (cf. Fig. 1).

Indeed, in the scenario depicted in Fig. 2, one could imagine a hypothetical protocol in which all active nodes decide at time 2 on some high value, say the initial value of process i, thus guaranteeing that i will not violate ***k*-Agreement** by deciding on this value immediately as well. The claim that such a hypothetical protocol does not exist is made precise in Lemma 1 (see also a discussion in Section 4.3 below).

LEMMA 1. *Let P be a protocol solving nonuniform k-set consensus. Assume that in P, every process i that is low at any time m must decide by time m at the latest. Let r be a run of P, let i be a process and let m be a time. If the following conditions hold in r:*

1. *i is low at m for the first time,*
2. *i has seen a single low value v by time m,*
3. *$\mathsf{HC}\langle i, m\rangle \geq k-1$, and*
4. *there exist k distinct processes $j_1, \ldots, j_k$ s.t. $\langle j_b, m-1\rangle$ is high and $\langle j_b, m\rangle$ is hidden from $\langle i, m\rangle$, for all $b = 1, \ldots, k$.*

then i decides in r on its unique low value v at time m.

We note that for $k = 3$, the nodes i_b^2 in Fig. 2 indeed meet the requirements of Lemma 1 at time $m = 2$. (E.g., for i_1^2, we may take the processes called i, i_2^2, i_3^2 in Fig. 2 to serve as the processes $j_1, \ldots, j_k$ in the statement of the lemma.) Given Lemma 1, using reasoning similar to our discussion above regarding the decision rules in $\textsc{Opt}_{\min[k]}$, we conclude that a high process with hidden capacity at least k (such as process i at time $m = 2$ in Fig. 2, for $k = 3$) cannot decide in any protocol P that dominates $\textsc{Opt}_{\min[k]}$ without risking violating ***k*-Agreement**, from which the unbeatability of $\textsc{Opt}_{\min[k]}$ follows (indeed, all undecided nodes in $\textsc{Opt}_{\min[k]}$ are high and have hidden capacity at least k, and are therefore undecided under P as well).

THEOREM 1. *$\textsc{Opt}_{\min[k]}$ is an unbeatable protocol for nonuniform k-set consensus in the crash failure model.*

We stress that $\textsc{Opt}_{\min[k]}$ is implementable in such a way that each process sends each other process $O(n \log n)$ bits throughout the run, and each process requires $O(n)$ local steps in every round. Thus, unbeatability for k-set consensus is attainable at a modest price.

4.2.1 Last-decider unbeatability

In [4] the authors also consider a variation on the notion of unbeatability, called ***last-decider unbeatability***, which compares runs in terms of the time at which the last correct process decides. This notion neither implies, nor is implied by, unbeatability as defined above. Interestingly, $\textsc{Opt}_{\min[k]}$ is unbeatable in this sense as well:

THEOREM 2. *$\textsc{Opt}_{\min[k]}$ is last-decider unbeatable for nonuniform k-set consensus in the crash failure model.*

4.3 A Constructive Combinatorial Approach vs. A Nonconstructive Topological Approach

In the full paper [5], we provide two proofs for Lemma 1. One is combinatorial and completely constructive, devoid of any topological arguments, while the other is nonconstructive and topological, based on Sperner's lemma. Our topological proof reasons in a novel way about subcomplexes of the protocol complex. Both proofs of Lemma 1 are by induction. In both proofs, the induction hypothesis and the (proof of the) base case are the same. The proofs differ only in the induction step.

In the terminology of Lemma 1, both proofs start by showing that there exists a run that $\langle i,m\rangle$ finds possible in which each of the $k-1$ nodes at time $m-1$ that are hidden from $\langle i,m\rangle$ holds a distinct low value other than v; therefore, by the induction hypothesis, had these $k-1$ nodes not failed, they would have each decided on its unique low value. Hence, each of the nodes $j_1,\ldots,j_k$ must consider it possible that all of the hidden nodes that it sees from time $m-1$ have actually decided and are correct. The challenge is to show, without any information about P except for the initial assumption that it dominates $\textsc{Opt}_{\min[k]}$, that there must exist a run r' of P that $\langle i,m\rangle$ finds possible (i.e., a way to adjust the messages received by $j_1,\ldots,j_k$ at time m) in which $j_1,\ldots,j_k$ collectively decide on all low values (including v) at time m; see Fig. 3. Therefore, i cannot decide on a high value without violating ***k*-Agreement** (and since it must decide, it must do so on a low value, and therefore on the only low value that is has seen, namely v).

Our combinatorial proof for the induction step constructively builds such a possible run r' as required (providing a "recipe" for how to adjust the messages received by $j_1,\ldots,j_k$ at time m so that they collectively decide on all low values). In contrast, our topological proof uses Sperner's lemma to show that if process $\langle i,m\rangle$ does not decide on a low value, then there must exist a run of the protocol that violates ***k*-Agreement** (i.e., a run r' as described above). It is interesting that the topological proof essentially shows that $\langle i,m\rangle$ is forced to decide on a low value in the run r because the star complex, denoted $\mathsf{St}(\langle i,m\rangle,\mathcal{P}_m)$, of the node $\langle i,m\rangle$ in the protocol complex $\mathcal{P}_m$ of the protocol P at time m, is $(k-1)$-connected. Intuitively, $\mathsf{St}(v,\mathcal{P}_m)$ is the "part" of $\mathcal{P}_m$ containing all executions that are indistinguishable to $\langle i,m\rangle$. That $\mathsf{St}(\langle i,m\rangle,\mathcal{P}_m)$ is $(k-1)$-connected is the reason why the proof can map a subdivision of k-simplexes to process states; indeed, the subdivision is mapped to a subcomplex of $\mathsf{St}(\langle i,m\rangle,\mathcal{P}_m)$. Therefore, $\langle i,m\rangle$ has no other choice than to decide on a low value, because if it does not do so, then its decision induces a Sperner coloring, which ultimately (together with the connectivity of $\mathsf{St}(\langle i,m\rangle,\mathcal{P}_m)$) implies that the ***k*-Agreement** property is violated.

It is worth noticing that in this topological analysis we only care about the connectivity of a proper subcomplex of the protocol complex, contrary to all known time-complexity lower-bound proofs [15, 21] for k-set consensus, which care about the connectivity of the whole protocol complex in a given round. While connectivity of the whole protocol complex is the "right" thing to consider for lower-bound proofs about when *all* processes can decide, we show that for proving unbeatability, i.e., when concerned with the time at which a *single* process can decide, the "right" thing to consider is the connectivity of just a subcomplex (the star complex of a given process state).

This analysis sheds light on the open question posed by Guerraoui and Pochon in [16] asking for extensions to previous topology techniques that deal with optimality of protocols. In summary, while all-decide lower bounds have to do with the whole protocol complex (e.g. [21]), optimal-single-decision lower bounds have to do with just subcomplexes of the protocol complex. Our topological proof of unbeatability here is the first proof that we are aware of that makes this distinction.

Finally, we emphasize that the connectivity properties of the star complex $\mathsf{St}(\langle i,m\rangle,\mathcal{P}_m)$ are due to the hidden capacity of $\langle i,m\rangle$ in the hypothesis of Lemma 1. Indeed, one can formally relate the connectivity of $\mathsf{St}(\langle i,m\rangle,\mathcal{P}_m)$ to the hidden capacity of $\langle i,m\rangle$, as we now show.

PROPOSITION 2. *Let $\mathcal{P}_m$ be the m-round protocol complex containing all m-round executions of a fip P. If $\langle i,m\rangle$ is a vertex of $\mathcal{P}_m$ whose view corresponds to a local state with hidden capacity at least k in each of the m rounds, then the star complex $\mathsf{St}(\langle i,m\rangle,\mathcal{P}_m)$ of $\langle i,m\rangle$ in $\mathcal{P}_m$ is $(k-1)$-connected.*

Proposition 2 speaks about a local property in protocol complexes, which turns out to be important for optimality analysis. It is unknown whether the converse of this lemma is true, namely, whether $(k-1)$-connectivity of the star complex implies hidden capacity at least k in every round.

5. UNIFORM SET CONSENSUS

We now turn to consider *uniform* k-set consensus. In [4], the concepts of hidden paths and hidden nodes are used to present an unbeatable protocol $\textsc{u-Opt}_0$ for (1-set) uniform consensus. In this section, we present a protocol called $\textsc{u-P}_{\min[k]}$ that generalizes the unbeatable $\textsc{u-Opt}_0$ to k values (i.e. for $k=1$, it behaves exactly like $\textsc{u-Opt}_0$). As in the nonuniform case, the analysis of the case $k>1$ is significantly more subtle and challenging; in fact, generalizing the protocol statement in the uniform case is considerably more involved than in the nonuniform case.

While in the protocol $\textsc{Opt}_{\min[k]}$ (which is defined in Section 4 for nonuniform consensus) an undecided process i decides on its minimal value if and only if i is low or has hidden capacity $< k$, in $\textsc{u-P}_{\min[k]}$ we have to be more careful. Indeed, we must ensure that a value (even a low one) that process i decides upon will not "fade away". This could happen if i is the only one knowing the value, and if i crashes without successfully communicating it to active processes. The case analysis here is also significantly more subtle than in the case of (1-set) uniform consensus. To phrase the exact conditions for decision, we begin with a definition; recall that t is an upper bound on the number of faulty nodes in any given run, and is available to all processes; while curiously the knowledge of t cannot be used to speed up $\textsc{Opt}_{\min[k]}$, it is indeed useful for speeding up decisions in the uniform case.

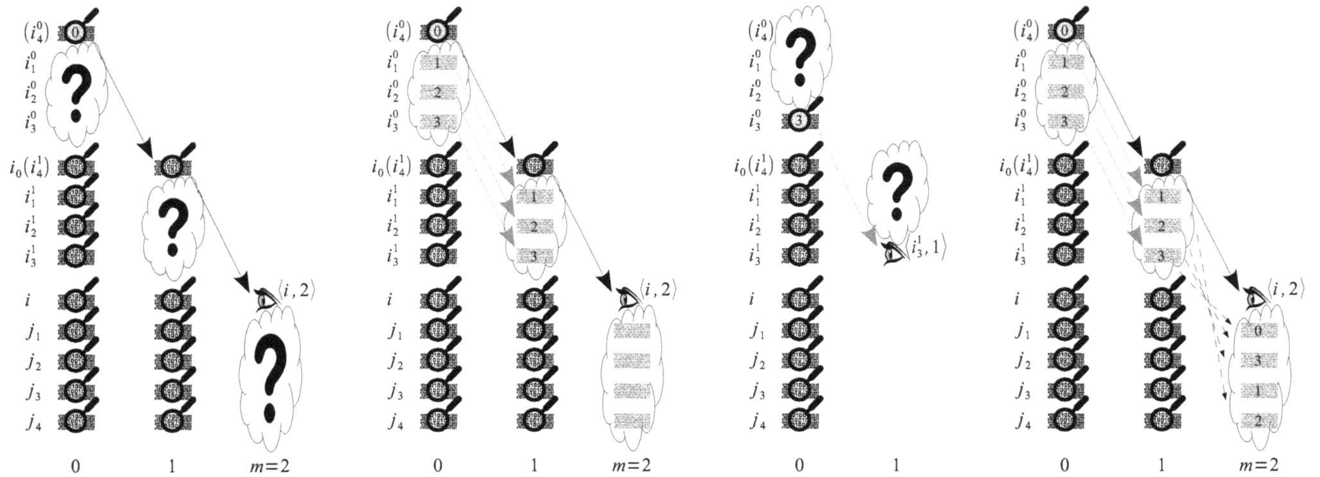

(c) r', as seen by $\langle i_3^1, 1\rangle$. The induction hypothesis dictates i_3^1 decides on 3 at 1.

(d) We aim to adjust the messages received by $j_1, \ldots, j_4$ at 2 in r', so that they collectively decide on all low values.

Figure 3: The proof strategy for the induction step of Lemma 1 (for $m = 2$, $k = 4$).

Definition 3. [4] Let r be a run and assume that i knows of $\boldsymbol{d}$ failures at time m in run r. We say that i ***knows that the value*** v ***will persist*** at time m if (at least) one of the following holds.

- $m > 0$, and i both is active at time m and has seen the value v by time $m - 1$, or
- $\langle i, m\rangle$ sees at least $(\boldsymbol{t} - \boldsymbol{d})$ distinct nodes $\langle j, m-1\rangle$ of time $m - 1$ that have seen the value v.

As shown in [4], if i knows at time m that v will persist, then all active nodes at time $m+1$ will know $\exists$v. Everyone's minimal value will be no larger than v from that point on.

In U-$\mathrm{P}_{\min[k]}$, an undecided process i decides on a value v if and only if v is the minimal value s.t. i knows that both

- v was at some stage the min value known to a process that was low or had hidden capacity $< k$, and
- v will be known to all processes deciding strictly after i.

As mentioned above, designing U-$\mathrm{P}_{\min[k]}$ to check that these conditions hold requires a careful statement of the protocol, which we now present.

Protocol U-$\mathrm{P}_{\min[k]}$ (for an undecided process i at time m):

if $\big(i$ is low or $\mathsf{HC}\langle i, m\rangle < k\big)$ and
i knows that $Min\langle i, m\rangle$ will persist
then $\mathsf{decide}(Min\langle i, m\rangle)$
elseif $m > 0$ and
$\big(\langle i, m-1\rangle$ was low or $\mathsf{HC}\langle i, m-1\rangle < k\big)$
then $\mathsf{decide}(Min\langle i, m-1\rangle)$
elseif $m = \lfloor t/k \rfloor + 1$ **then** $\mathsf{decide}(Min\langle i, m\rangle)$

The correctness and worst-case complexity of U-$\mathrm{P}_{\min[k]}$ are stated in Theorem 3. The reader is referred to its proof in the full paper [5] for a precise analysis of the decision conditions. We remark that, roughly speaking, the second condition decides on $Min\langle i, m-1\rangle$ and not on $Min\langle i, m\rangle$ because the latter value is not guaranteed to persist, while the former value is.

THEOREM 3. *U-$\mathrm{P}_{\min[k]}$ solves **uniform** k-set consensus in the crash failure model, and all processes decide by time* $\min\{\lfloor t/k \rfloor + 1, \lfloor f/k \rfloor + 2\}$.

As shown by Theorem 3, the protocol U-$\mathrm{P}_{\min[k]}$ meets the worst-case lower bound for uniform k-set consensus from [15, 1]. We emphasize that U-$\mathrm{P}_{\min[k]}$ strictly dominates all existing uniform k-set consensus protocols in the literature [8, 14, 16, 26]. Essentially, in each of these protocols, a process remains undecided as long as it discovers at least k new failures in every round. The fact that U-$\mathrm{P}_{\min[k]}$ is based on hidden capacity and hidden paths, rather than on the number of failures seen, allows runs with much faster stopping times. In particular, there exist runs in which all previous protocols decide after $\lfloor t/k \rfloor + 1$ rounds, and in U-$\mathrm{P}_{\min[k]}$ all processes decide by time 2; see Fig. 4 for an example.

At this point, however, we have been unable to resolve the following.

CONJECTURE 1. *U-$\mathrm{P}_{\min[k]}$ is an unbeatable uniform k-set consensus protocol in the crash failure model.*

6. DISCUSSION

In this paper we have presented two main algorithmic results. The first one, $\mathrm{OPT}_{\min[k]}$, is an unbeatable protocol for nonuniform k-set consensus; this protocol has an extremely concise description. Unbeatability [18, 4] is an optimality criterion that formalizes the intuition that a given protocol cannot be improved upon;[6] this is significantly stronger than

[6]We emphasize that the notion of "improvement" captured by the notion of unbeatability studied in this paper is defined in terms of the times at which processes perform their decisions. This is distinct from their halting times, for example (although a process can safely halt at most one round after it decides). Optimizing decision times can come at a cost

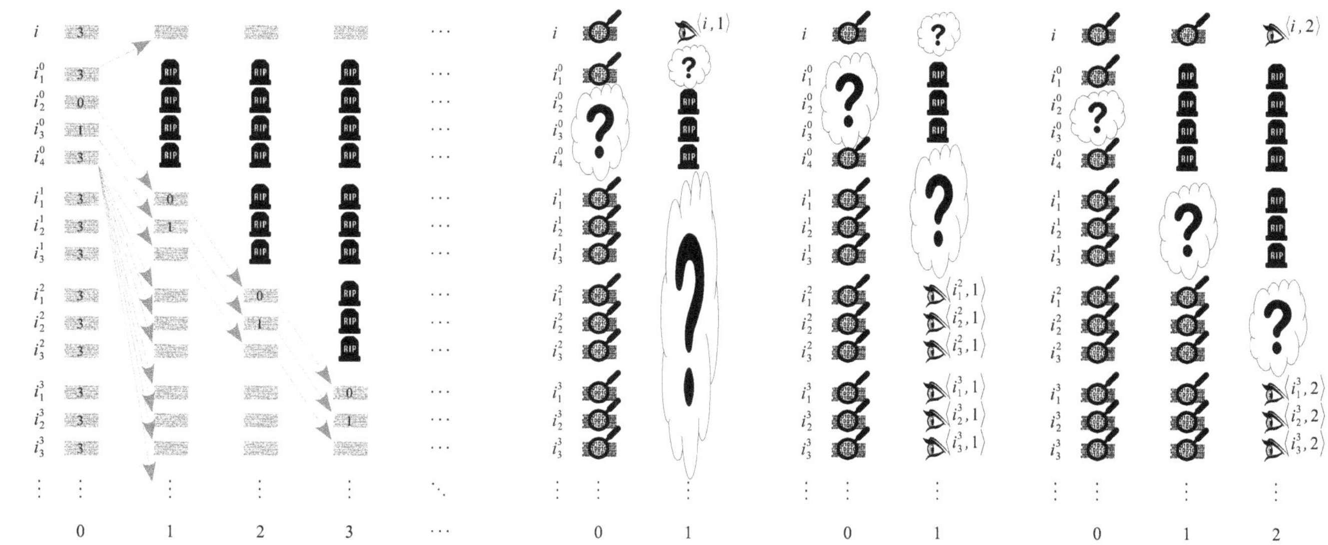

(a) The run r. Messages successfully sent by crashing nodes are marked with an arrow. Starting from time $m = 1$, all processes know $\exists 3$ (i.e., $\exists k$), and so only knowledge of additional values is indicated.

(b) r, as seen by $\langle i, 1\rangle$, which has hidden capacity $k = 3$.

(c) r, as seen by all other nodes that are nonfaulty at time 1. These nodes also have hidden capacity $k = 3$. (These nodes are hidden from one another).

(d) r, as seen by all nodes that are nonfaulty at time 2. All such nodes have hidden capacity $2 < k$, and furthermore know that their min value (i.e., k) will persist; thus, they all decide (on k).

Figure 4: A run (adversary) s.t. in U-P$_{\min[k]}$ all nodes decide by time 2. Nonetheless, in this run, in all previously known protocols (particularly, in the ones of [8, 14, 16, 26]), the correct processes only at time $\lfloor t/k \rfloor + 1$ (assuming $f = t$), as every correct process sees k new failures in each round for the first $\lfloor t/k \rfloor$ rounds. (The figure illustrates the case of $k = 3$ and arbitrarily high t.)

saying that a protocol is worst-case optimal. Our second result is a protocol, U-P$_{\min[k]}$, for uniform k-set consensus that strictly beats all known protocols in the literature [8, 14, 16, 26]; notably, in some executions, processes in our protocol can decide much faster than in those protocols. Whether our uniform k-set consensus protocol is unbeatable remains an open problem. Both protocols are efficiently implementable.

We have presented two distinct proofs for the unbeatability of our nonuniform k-set consensus protocol OPT$_{\min[k]}$. Each proof gives a different perspective of the unbeatability of the protocol. The first proof is fully constructive and combinatorial, while the second relies on Sperner's lemma and is nonconstructive and topological. The topological proof of Lemma 1 is more than just a "trick" to prove the lemma. In a precise sense, the proof shows what a topological analysis of unbeatable protocols is about.

The construction and analysis of both protocols, as well as the unbeatability of OPT$_{\min[k]}$, crucially depends on a new notion hidden capacity. This notion is a generalization of the notion of hidden path introduced in [4], which plays a similar role in the case of (1-set) consensus. Derived from our topological unbeatability proof, we identified a connection between hidden capacity k and local $(k-1)$-connectivity of star subcomplexes of a protocol complex: roughly speaking, hidden capacity at least k implies $(k-1)$-connectivity. Whether the converse is true remains an open problem. This connection sheds light on the open question in [16] asking for extensions to previous topology techniques that deal with optimality of protocols. The full interplay between hidden capacity and topological reasoning (even beyond set consensus) is an interesting direction for future research.

in communication, for example. Finally, of course, one can compare protocols in terms of more global properties such as average decision times (w.r.t. appropriate distributions etc.). Another point to notice when considering unbeatability is that it is based on comparing the performance of different protocols on the same behaviors of the adversary. While we find this a reasonable thing to do in benign failure models such as crash and omission failures, it may be rather tricky in the presence of malicious (Byzantine) failures.

7. ACKNOWLEDGMENTS

Figs. 1–4 include visual elements designed by Freepik.

Armando Castañeda is supported partially by a project PAPIIT-UNAM IA101015. This research was partially done while Armando Castañeda was at the Department of Computer Science of the Technion, supported by an Aly Kaufman post-doctoral fellowship.

Yannai Gonczarowski is supported by the Adams Fellowship Program of the Israel Academy of Sciences and Humanities; his work is supported by the European Research Council under the European Community's Seventh Framework Programme (FP7/2007-2013) / ERC grant agreement no. [249159], by ISF grants 230/10 and 1435/14 administered by the Israeli Academy of Sciences, and by Israel-USA Bi-national Science Foundation (BSF) grant number 2014389.

Yoram Moses is the Israel Pollak chair at the Technion; his work was supported in part by ISF grant 1520/11 administered by the Israeli Academy of Sciences.

8. REFERENCES

[1] D. Alistarh, S. Gilbert, R. Guerraoui, and C. Travers. Of choices, failures and asynchrony: The many faces of set agreement. *Algorithmica*, 62(1-2):595–629, 2012.

[2] E. Borowsky and E. Gafni. Generalized FLP impossibility result for t-resilient asynchronous computations. In *Proc. 25th ACM Symp. on Theory of Computing*, pages 91–100, 1993.

[3] A. Castañeda, Y. A. Gonczarowski, and Y. Moses. Brief announcement: Pareto-optimal solutions to consensus and set consensus. In *Proc. 32nd ACM Symp. on Principles of Distributed Computing*, pages 113–115, 2013.

[4] A. Castañeda, Y. A. Gonczarowski, and Y. Moses. Unbeatable consensus. In *Proc. 28th International Symp. on Distributed Computing*, pages 91–106, 2014. Full version available on arXiv.

[5] A. Castañeda, Y. A. Gonczarowski, and Y. Moses. Unbeatable set consensus via topological and combinatorial reasoning. Available on arXiv.org, 2016.

[6] B. Charron-Bost and A. Schiper. Uniform consensus is harder than consensus. *Journal of Algorithms*, 51(1):15–37, 2004.

[7] S. Chaudhuri. Agreement is harder than consensus: Set consensus problems in totally asynchronous systems. In *Proc. 9th ACM Symp. on Principles of Distributed Computing*, pages 311–324, 1990.

[8] S. Chaudhuri, M. Herlihy, N. A. Lynch, and M. R. Tuttle. Tight bounds for k-set agreement. *Journal of the ACM*, 47(5):912–943, 2000.

[9] B. Coan. A communication-efficient canonical form for fault-tolerant distributed protocols. In *Proc. 5th ACM Symp. on Principles of Distributed Computing*, pages 63–72, 1986.

[10] D. Dolev, R. Reischuk, and H. R. Strong. Early stopping in Byzantine agreement. *Journal of the ACM*, 34(7):720–741, 1990.

[11] P. Dutta, R. Guerraoui, and B. Pochon. Tight bounds on early local decisions in uniform consensus. In *Proc. 17th International Symp. on Distributed Computing*, pages 264–278, 2003.

[12] C. Dwork and Y. Moses. Knowledge and common knowledge in a Byzantine environment: crash failures. *Information and Computation*, 88(2):156–186, 1990.

[13] M. J. Fischer, N. A. Lynch, and M. S. Paterson. Impossibility of distributed consensus with one faulty processor. *Journal of the ACM*, 32(2):374–382, 1985.

[14] E. Gafni, R. Guerraoui, and B. Pochon. The complexity of early deciding set agreement. *SIAM Journal on Computing*, 40(1):63–78, 2011.

[15] R. Guerraoui, M. Herlihy, and B. Pochon. A topological treatment of early-deciding set-agreement. *Theoretical Computer Science*, 410(6-7):570–580, 2009.

[16] R. Guerraoui and B. Pochon. The complexity of early deciding set agreement: How can topology help? *Electr. Notes Theor. Comput. Sci.*, 230:71–78, 2009.

[17] V. Hadzilacos. On the relationship between the atomic commitment and consensus problems. In *Fault-Tolerant Distributed Computing*, pages 201–208, 1986.

[18] J. Y. Halpern, Y. Moses, and O. Waarts. A characterization of eventual Byzantine agreement. *SIAM Journal on Computing*, 31(3):838–865, 2001.

[19] M. Herlihy, D. N. Kozlov, and S. Rajsbaum. *Distributed Computing Through Combinatorial Topology*. Morgan Kaufmann, 2013.

[20] M. Herlihy, Y. Moses, and M. R. Tuttle. Transforming worst-case optimal solutions for simultaneous tasks into all-case optimal solutions. In *Proc. 30th ACM Symp. on Principles of Distributed Computing*, pages 231–238, 2011.

[21] M. Herlihy, S. Rajsbaum, and M. R. Tuttle. Unifying synchronous and asynchronous message-passing models. In *Proc. 17th ACM Symp. on Principles of Distributed Computing*, pages 133–142, 1998.

[22] M. Herlihy and N. Shavit. The topological structure of asynchronous computability. *Journal of the ACM*, 46(6):858–923, Nov. 1999.

[23] I. Keidar and S. Rajsbaum. A simple proof of the uniform consensus synchronous lower bound. *Information Processing Letters*, 85(1):47–52, 2003.

[24] Y. Moses. Relating knowledge and coordinated action: The knowledge of preconditions principle. In *Proc. 15th Conference on Theoretical Aspects of Rationality and Knowledge*, pages 207–216, 2015.

[25] Y. Moses and M. R. Tuttle. Programming simultaneous actions using common knowledge. *Algorithmica*, 3:121–169, 1988.

[26] P. R. Parvédy, M. Raynal, and C. Travers. Early-stopping k-set agreement in synchronous systems prone to any number of process crashes. In *Proc. 8th International Conference on Parallel Computing Technologies*, pages 49–58, 2005.

[27] M. Raynal. Optimal early stopping uniform consensus in synchronous systems with process omission failures. In *Proc. 16th Annual ACM Symp. on Parallelism in Algorithms and Architectures*, pages 302–310. ACM Press, 2004.

[28] M. E. Saks and F. Zaharoglou. Wait-free k-set agreement is impossible: The topology of public knowledge. *SIAM Journal on Computing*, 29(5):1449–1483, 2000.

[29] X. Wang, Y. M. Teo, and J. Cao. A bivalency proof of the lower bound for uniform consensus. *Information Processing Letters*, 96(5):167–174, 2005.

A Polylogarithmic Gossip Algorithm for Plurality Consensus

Mohsen Ghaffari
MIT
ghaffari@mit.edu

Merav Parter
MIT
parter@mit.edu

ABSTRACT

Consider n anonymous nodes each initially supporting an opinion in $\{1, 2, \ldots, k\}$ and suppose that they should all learn the opinion with the largest support. Per round, each node contacts a random other node and exchanges B bits with it, where typically B is at most $O(\log n)$.

This basic distributed computing problem is called the *plurality consensus* problem (in the *gossip* model) and it has received extensive attention. An efficient plurality protocol is one that converges to the plurality consensus as fast as possible, and the standard assumption is that each node has memory at most polylogarithmic in n. The best known time bound is due to Becchetti et al. [SODA'15], reaching plurality consensus in $O(k \log n)$ rounds using $\log(k+1)$ bits of local memory, under some mild assumptions. As stated by Becchetti et al., achieving a poly-logarithmic time complexity remained an open question.

Resolving this question, we present an algorithm that with high probability[1] reaches plurality consensus in $O(\log k \log n)$ rounds, while having message and memory size of $\log k + O(1)$ bits. This even holds under considerably more relaxed assumptions regarding the initial bias (towards plurality) compared to those of prior work. The algorithm is based on a very simple and arguably natural mechanism.

1. INTRODUCTION AND RELATED WORK

Coordination problems in distributed systems require nodes to agree on a common action or value. These problems are referred to as consensus, agreement, or voting and are among the most fundamental problems in distributed computing [Lyn96, Tsi84, TBA86]. In this paper, we consider the following basic agreement problem, often called plurality consensus problem—also known as *proportionate agreement* or *majority agreement* when $k = 2$—in the gossip model:

> There are n nodes each supporting an opinion in $\{1, \ldots, k\}$. Per round each node contacts one random other node and exchanges B bits with it, where typically B is at most $O(\log n)$. Eventually, all nodes should hold the opinion with the largest initial support.

This problem, or close variants of it, come up in computer networks such as sensor networks [AAD[+]06] and peer-to-peer networks [AFJ06], as well as in a wider range of settings that goes much beyond the classical distributed computing settings: e.g., social networks [MS], biological systems [CKFL05, SKJ[+]08, CCN12, BSDDS14], and chemical reaction networks [CDS[+]13, Dot14].

State of the Art: Gossip algorithms for plurality have received extensive attention, see e.g. [BCN[+]14, BCN[+]15a, BCN[+]15b, AAE08, PVV09]. The key performance measures of the algorithms are: (1) *time complexity*, and (2) space measured by the *message size* and *memory size* per node. In the standard regime where message and memory sizes are at most poly($\log n$), the best known algorithm is due to Becchetti et al. [BCN[+]15a], achieving a time complexity of $O(k \log n)$, under some mild assumptions, while having $\log(k+1)$ bit message/memory. A faster solution was known before, however at the expense of a significantly larger message/memory size. Particularly, the general approach of Kempe et al. [KDG03] can be used to obtain a plurality algorithm with $O(\log n)$ time-complexity but with $O(k \log n)$ message/memory size. Also, a number of other fast algorithms are known but all limited to very small k, e.g., $k = 2$ [AAE08, PVV09]. Given that each of the known solutions lacks in one of the dimensions, Bechetti et al. [BCN[+]15a] state:

> *"a major open question for the plurality consensus problem is whether a plurality protocol exists that converges in polylogarithmic time and uses only polylogarithmic local memory."*

Our Result: In this paper, we answer this question in the affirmative. We particularly present an algorithm that has nearly optimal bounds in both dimensions:

Theorem 1.1. *There is a gossip algorithm that solves plurality w.h.p. in $O(\log k \cdot \log n)$ rounds using $\log k + O(1)$ bits of local memory, assuming that the initial bias $p_1 - p_2 =$*

This work was partially funded by the following grants: AFOSR FA9550-13-1-0042, NSF CCF-1461559, CCF-1217506, CCF-0939370.

[1]As standard, *with high probability* (w.h.p.) indicates that an event has probability $1 - 1/n^c$ for a constant $c \geq 2$.

PODC'16, July 25-28, 2016, Chicago, IL, USA
© 2016 ACM. ISBN 978-1-4503-3964-3/16/07...$15.00
DOI: http://dx.doi.org/10.1145/2933057.2933097

$\Omega(\sqrt{\log n/n})$. *Here* p_1 *and* p_2 *are, respectively, the fractions of nodes holding the plurality and second largest opinions.*

This initial bias assumption $p_1 - p_2 = \Omega(\sqrt{\log n/n})$ is due to the concentration considerations[2], and it is at least as relaxed as the assumptions in prior work. In fact under the stronger assumptions of [BCN+15a] (to be stated later), our algorithm converges in $O(\log k \log\log n + \log n)$ rounds.

As we will see, the algorithm is based on a quite simple and intuitive mechanism and one can even argue that dynamics with a similar flavor occur in nature. We also note that the result might be viewed as somewhat surprising, given the indications in the prior work and especially when put in contrast to what Becchetti et al. [BCN+15a] write in their conclusion:

> "*We believe that this distance* [referring to the monochromatic distance, which can be as large as $\Omega(k)$] *might represent a general lower bound on the convergence time of any plurality dynamics which uses only* $\log k + O(1)$ *bits of local memory.*"

A Remark—Measuring Memory Size: We note that because of the practical scenarios in which gossip algorithms are applied, it is more standard to measure the memory size in terms of the *number of states* rater than the *number of bits*. Here we briefly discuss the reasons. One justification for considering the number of states is that many of these dynamics are often viewed as Finite-state Automota, for which minimizing the number of states is a classical optimization objective (see, e.g., [Hop71, Yu05]). In addition, states of nodes have a clear physical interpretation in practical settings such as in molecular programming: in particular, in chemical reaction networks, the encoding of the state is not binary but rather (closer to) unary [CSWB09], and hence minimizing the number of the states is a more sensible objective. Although these two ways of measuring are equivalent when talking about exact bounds—as the number of states is simply exponential in the number of bits—they differ when discussing relaxed notions of optimality. Particularly, a constant factor improvement in the bit complexity, which might be regarded negligible, translates to a polynomial improvement in the number of states, which would be considered significant.

In fact, when presenting our result, we start with a simpler algorithm with $\log k + O(\log\log k)$ bit complexity, and then present a more complex one with bit complexity of $\log k + O(1)$. Our first algorithm converges within $O(\log k \cdot \log n)$ rounds but uses $\log k + O(\log\log k)$ bits. Note that this already gives an answer to the open problem raised by Bechetti et al. [BCN+15a], stated above. Yet, even though the message size of this simple algorithm in terms of the number bits is optimal up to an *additive* $O(\log\log k)$ term, with respect to the *number of states*, its $O(k \log k)$ state complexity bound is an $O(\log k)$ factor off from the trivial lower bound k. In our second algorithm, we improve this to a *state complexity* of $O(k)$, which is optimal up to a constant.

[2]Even when flipping n fair coins, there is a $1/n^{0.1}$ probability that the number of heads is outside $n/2 \pm \Omega(\sqrt{n \log n})$, which means a relative deviation of $\pm\Omega(\sqrt{\log n/n})$. This is essentially why we need to assume $p_1 - p_2 = \Omega(\sqrt{\log n/n})$.

1.1 Our approach, in the context of the previous ones

Plurality protocols can be roughly divided into two main classes: what we call *"reading"* protocols and what we call *plurality amplification* protocols (or amplification protocols, for short).

A natural approach for solving plurality, in fact perhaps the first approach that comes to the mind from a standard algorithm design viewpoint, is to estimate the frequencies of the nodes of each opinion and pick the most frequent one. In a more relaxed definition, in a reading style protocol, for each opinion i, we would have at least one node v that learns some estimation for the frequency of this opinion in the population. Kempe et al. [KDG03] provided a general approach for designing reading type protocols for computing aggregate functions (e.g. sum or average). As noted by Becchetti et al. [BCN+15a], adopting the approach of Kemp et al. to the plurality problem yields an $O(\log n)$ time complexity but with $O(k \log n)$ message/memory size. Generally, it seems implausible that reading style algorithms would lead to a plurality algorithm for the random gossip model with polylogarithmic size messages and polylogarithmic time complexity[3].

The second class of plurality amplification protocols do not try to estimate the initial distribution, but rather attempt to *modify* this initial distribution into another distribution of the same plurality opinion, but with a *larger* bias towards plurality. In other words, throughout the execution of an amplification protocol, there is a shift from the initial distribution (with possibly very weak bias) towards the target configuration (where we have consensus on plurality) by repetitively amplifying the bias towards the plurality opinion via some *positive feedback mechanism*. The standard plurality amplification protocols are based on simple majority rules. For example, Becchetti et al. [BCN+14] consider an update rule where each node polls the opinion of three random nodes and adopts the majority opinion among these. This algorithm uses only $\Theta(\log k)$ bits of local memory, but unfortunately has running time $O(\min\{k \log n, n^{1/3} \cdot \log^{2/3} n\})$. Other known time efficient algorithms exist for small values of k, e.g., $k = 2$ [PVV09, DGM+11]. Recently, Becchetti et al. [BCN+15a] analyzed the well-known *Undecided-State Dynamics*, in which each decided node meeting a node of different opinion becomes undecided (i.e., forgets its opinion) and every undecided node meeting a decided node adopts its opinion. This protocol provides the current best bounds: they showed that the undecided-state dynamics converges within $O(k \log n)$ rounds, using $\log(k+1)$ bits of local memory, assuming[4] $k = O((n/\log n)^{1/6})$ and $p_1 - p_2 = \Omega(1/n^{1/6})$.

The high level idea of our algorithm: We want to create a protocol with a '*strong and fast positive feedback*' so that, roughly speaking, the opinions with larger support get amplified while those with smaller support get attenuated. In more colloquial terms, we seek a (fast) '*rich get richer*' effect. At the high level, our protocol consists of two main

[3]We note however that if the gossip model is relaxed to include non-random meetings, a rather simple "reading" style algorithm would achieve this objective, as shown in the full version.

[4]They assume $p_1 \geq (1+\alpha)p_2$ for some constant α and $k \leq O(n^{1/6})$. This implies $p_1 - p_2 = \Omega(p_1) = \Omega(1/n^{1/6})$.

alternating steps: A *selection* step, and a sequence of *recovery* steps. The selection process imposes a constraint on the system that potentially may lead many nodes to lose their opinion and become undecided. Specifically, a node survives the selection process only if it meets a node of its *own* opinion. By that, we intentionally cut down the number of decided nodes significantly while opinions with larger support survive through this process slightly better. Particularly, the plurality opinion gets slightly less attenuation in comparison to the others, hence the proportion of the plurality opinion to that of any other opinion grows. Since repetitive applications of selections would eventually diminish the decided population, our system evolution incorporates some healing process between two consecutive selections. In the healing phase, the fraction of undecided nodes shrinks back to (almost) 0 but the ratios between the number of nodes holding different opinions is roughly preserved. We repeat through this cycle of selection and healing, thus continually *amplifying the plurality*, till reaching plurality consensus.

Other related work: The plurality problem bears some resemblance to problems studied in some other settings: The restricted case of $k = 2$ has been extensively studied in the setting of population protocols [AAD+06] and many "plurality amplification" type algorithms using small number of states (e.g., 3 or 4) have been suggested [AAE08, DV12, MNRS14, AGV15]. This case of binary consensus ($k = 2$) has been also studied in the voter model [DW83, HP01, WH04, Lig12]. The plurality problem also resembles the *heavy hitters* problem in the streaming model, see e.g. [BICS10].

2. THE ALGORITHM: TAKE 1

We next present a simpler variant of our algorithm, which reaches plurality in $O(\log k \log n)$ rounds, using messages of size $\log k + O(1)$ bits, but with per node memory size of $\log k + \log\log k + O(1)$ bits. Note that this result already answers the open question stated in the introduction.

2.1 The Algorithm Description

The algorithm is an extremely simple and clean dynamics, as follows: Let us call nodes holding one of opinions $\{1, 2, \ldots, k\}$ *decided* while nodes holding no opinion are called *undecided*.

The algorithm works in phases, each having $R = O(\log k)$ rounds, as follows:

- **Round 1 of each phase:** `- Relative Gap Amplification -`
  - a decided node keeps its opinion *only if* it contacts a node with the same opinion,
  - undecided nodes remains undecided.
- **Rounds 2 to R of each phase:** `- Healing -`
  - decided nodes keep their opinion,
  - an undecided node v that contacts a decided node u adopts u's opinion.

When implementing this algorithm, each message has size $\log(k+1)$ bits as it contains only one opinion in $\{0, 1, \ldots, k\}$, where 0 represents being undecided. As for the memory, the only additional thing that a node needs to remember besides its opinion is the round number in the phase, i.e. modulo $R = O(\log k)$, and that takes $\log\log k + O(1)$ bits.

We next provide some intuition for why this dynamic converges to plurality within $O(\log n)$ phases and then the next subsection presents the related formal analysis.

Before that, we note that it was pointed out to us recently that in a simultaneous and independent work, Berenbrink et al. [BFGK16] also present a similar algorithm and analysis as the take 1 protocol presented here. They prove that this algorithm terminates in $O(\log k \log\log_\gamma n + \log\log n)$ rounds, where γ is the relative gap at the beginning between the first and second largest opinions. In the worst case considered in our paper, $\gamma = 1 + \tilde{O}(1/\sqrt{n})$. Thus in this regime, the two complexities match. For larger initial bias, especially when γ is a constant, there is a difference between the two complexities as our statement is $O(\log k \log\log n + \log n)$. However, one can see that the arguments in Lemma 2.8 could be tightened easily to match the same complexity. Since our main interest is in cases with smaller bias, where the problem is more interesting technically, we keep the statements and analysis as they are.

Basic notations: To keep track of the state of the system, we use a vector $\mathbf{p} = (p_1, p_2, \ldots, p_k) \in [0, 1]^k$ where each entry p_i denotes the fraction of the nodes holding opinion $i \in \{1, 2, \ldots, k\}$. Thus, the fraction of undecided nodes is $1 - \sum_{i=1}^{k} p_i$. Without loss of generality, in our analysis, we assume that the opinions are renumbered such that initially $p_1 > p_2 \geq \cdots \geq p_k$.

Convergence intuition: A rough intuition for why the algorithm is designed this way and why it should intuitively converge to plurality consensus fast, based merely on expectations, is as follows. We emphasize that this explanation is provided only for the sake of intuition and it is imprecise. However, it will be made precise in the sequel. Generally, one should be careful in using similar merely expectation-based arguments, as they might lead to incorrect claims.

In the first round of each phase, each node v keeps its opinion only if it contacted a node with the same opinion. Note that this means, even if v contacted an undecided node, v forgets its opinion and becomes undecided. At the end of this round, the fraction of nodes holding an opinion i changes from p_i to p_i^2, in expectation. Thus, the ratio between the plurality opinion and an opinion $i \in \{2, \ldots, k\}$ goes up from $\frac{p_1}{p_i}$ to $(\frac{p_1}{p_i})^2$. This already is the desired *'rich get richer'* effect, in terms of the ratios. However, as a side-effect of this relative *gap amplification*, the fraction of decided nodes has dropped down significantly to about $\sum_{i=1}^{k} p_i^2$, which can be as small as $\Theta(1/k)$. During rounds 2 to R of the phase, we fix this issue by growing the fraction of decided nodes back to about 1. As we will show, during this *healing* period, the ratio between different opinions remains essentially the same. Thus, looking over phases, we can say that the ratio $\frac{p_1}{p_i}$ starts with at least $1+1/n$ and gets essentially squared in each phase. That means, this ratio reaches 2 within $O(\log n)$ phases and from there to n in $O(\log\log n)$ additional phases. Due to the integralities, once the ratio passes n, it actually means that $p_i = 0$. When this happens for all the opinions $i \in \{2, \ldots, k\}$, all of them have been filtered out and only the plurality opinion remains alive[5]. From there, within ad-

[5]One case say this is virtually the same as '*survival of the fittest*' in Herbert Spencer's terminology for describing Dar-

ditional $O(\log n/\log k)$ phases, the system reaches plurality consensus where all nodes hold the plurality opinion.

2.2 Analysis

We next provide the formal analysis, proving that:

Theorem 2.1. *The above algorithm reaches plurality consensus w.h.p. within $O(\log k \cdot \log n)$ rounds, assuming that the initial bias $p_1 - p_2 \geq \sqrt{C \log n/n}$, for a sufficiently large constant C. Furthermore, if initially $p_1/p_2 \geq 1+\delta$ for some constant $\delta > 0$, then the convergence will happen in fact within $O(\log k \log\log n + \log n)$ rounds, w.h.p.*

Let $\mathsf{bias} = p_1 - p_2$ be the difference between the fraction of the plurality opinion and the second largest opinion. Finally, to keep track of the the ratio between the plurality opinion and the second largest opinion, let us define

$$\mathsf{gap} = \min\{\frac{p_1}{\sqrt{10\log n/n}}, \frac{p_1}{p_2}\} \tag{1}$$

Note that when $p_2 \leq \sqrt{10\log n/n}$, there is a large constant gap between p_1 and each of the other opinions as $p_1 \geq \sqrt{C\log n/n}$. Since once all other opinions are below $\sqrt{10\log n/n}$, we will not be able to bound their deviations from expected by an $(1-o(1))$ factor, in such cases, we will try to base the analysis mainly on the fast growth of p_1, rather than the growth of p_1/p_2. The above definition of gap allows us to unify the two statements.

The three main transitions of the protocol: Our protocol can be characterized by three main transitions: The first transition occurs during the first $O(\log n)$ phases, by the end of which, the relative gap between the plurality opinion and the second largest opinion exceeds a 2 factor. The second transition occurs within $O(\log\log n)$ additional phases, where all the non-plurality opinions become extinct. At that point, we will have $p_1 \geq 2/3$ and $\sum_{i\geq 2} p_i = 0$. Finally, the last transition occurs within $O(\log n/\log k)$ additional phases where all nodes hold the plurality opinion. The second and third transitions are proven in Lemma 2.5 to Lemma 2.8.

We begin by showing that in every phase, three conditions hold: two of these are safety conditions guaranteeing that the fraction of decided is sufficiently large and that the initial bias is maintained; the third condition is a progress condition that guarantees the growth of the gap.

Lemma 2.2. *Consider a phase j. Let $\mathbf{p} = (p_1, p_2, \ldots, p_k)$ denote the vector of opinions at the beginning of this phase and $\mathbf{p}^{new}$ to denote the same vector at the end of the phase. Assume that $\sum_{i=1}^{k} p_i \geq 2/3$, $\mathsf{bias} \geq \sqrt{C\log n/n}$ and $p_1 \leq 2/3$. Then, with high probability, we have:*

(S1) $\sum_{i=1}^{k} p_i^{new} \geq 2/3$,

(S2) $\mathsf{bias}^{new} = p_1^{new} - p_2^{new} \geq \sqrt{C\log n/n}$, *and most importantly*

(P) either $p_1^{new} \geq 2/3$ *or* $\mathsf{gap}^{new} \geq \mathsf{gap}^{1.4}$ *where* gap^{new} *is defined as in Eq. (1) with* p_1^{new}, p_2^{new}.

Proof. We begin with (S1). We first claim that due to the gap-amplification step of phase j, the fraction of decided nodes has been dropped down to $\Omega(1/k + \log n/n)$,

win's *natural selection* concept [Spe64]. In our setting, the largest opinion is effectively the fittest.

and then show that this drop is recovered during the $R = O(\log k)$ rounds of the healing step. To see this, note that the expected fraction of decided nodes at the end of the gap amplification round is $\sum_{i=1}^{k} p_i^2$. Since $\sum_{i=1}^{k} p_i \geq 2/3$, we have $\sum_{i=1}^{k} p_i^2 \geq k \cdot ((\sum_{i=1}^{k} p_i)/k)^2 \geq 4/(9k)$. In addition, since $p_1 \geq \sqrt{\log n/n}$, $p_1^2 = \Omega(\log n/n)$. We thus get that $\sum_{i=1}^{k} p_i^2 = \Omega(1/k + \log n/n)$. We now claim that the $\Omega(1/k + \log n/n)$ fraction of decided nodes after the gap-amplification is increased to at least $2/3$ over the R rounds of the healing process. The argument is simple and similar to the usual process of gossiping a rumor. Particularly, in every round $r \in \{2, \ldots, R\}$ of phase j, so long as the fraction of decided nodes is less than $2/3$, this fraction grows in expectation by a factor of at least $4/3$ and hence, it will grow by factor of $6/5$ with high probability. We therefore get that within $O(\log k)$ rounds, the fraction of decided nodes $\sum_{i=1}^{k} p_i$ reaches at least $2/3$ as required. Thus, property (S1) holds.

Next, we prove Claim (P) and then, we reuse some of the arguments to establish (S2). For (P), we distinguish between two cases depending on the magnitude of the second largest opinion p_2.

Case (P.a), when $p_2 \geq \sqrt{10\log n/n}$: After the first gap-amplification round, in expectation, there are np_1^2 nodes with opinion 1 and np_2^2 nodes with opinion 2. We want to show that the ratio between the actual numbers is very close to what we would have according to these expectations, i.e., $(\frac{p_1}{p_1})^2$, and remains so throughout rounds 2 to R. Since we might start with a bias as small as $\mathsf{bias} = \Theta(\sqrt{\log n/n})$, the deviations from expectations should be analyzed carefully. Throughout, we focus on the two leading opinions of this phase and denote by the random variables x_r and y_r, the number of nodes in these two opinions at round $r \in \{1, \ldots, R\}$ of this phase. By Chernoff, it holds that w.h.p.

$$x_1 \in np_1^2\left(1 \pm \frac{\sqrt{5\log n/n}}{p_1}\right) \text{ and } \tag{2}$$
$$y_1 \in np_2^2\left(1 \pm \frac{\sqrt{5\log n/n}}{p_2}\right).$$

We now use this to bound the ratio x_1/y_1:

$$\begin{aligned}\frac{x_1}{y_1} &\geq \left(\frac{p_1}{p_2}\right)^2 \cdot \left(1 + \frac{3\sqrt{5\log n/n}}{p_2}\right)^{-2} \\ &\geq \left(\frac{p_1}{p_2}\right)^2 (1 + \frac{p_1 - p_2}{p_2})^{-0.2} = \left(\frac{p_1}{p_2}\right)^{1.8},\end{aligned} \tag{3}$$

where the last inequality follows because at the start of the phase we have $\mathsf{bias} = p_1 - p_2 \geq \sqrt{C\log n/n}$. We next argue that throughout rounds $r \in \{2, \ldots, R\}$, this ratio between the plurality opinion and the second opinion remains almost the same, except for minimal deviations similar to above which would be tolerable and still leave the gap amplified to at least $(p_1/p_2)^{1.4}$.

First, we provide an initial intuition about the change in the number of decided nodes of each of these opinions throughout rounds $r \in \{2, \ldots, R\}$ and the potential deviations. Let us use (the random variable) q_r to denote the fraction of undecided nodes at the end of round r. For each r, we expect $q_r x_r$ and $q_r y_r$ new nodes to adopt, respectively, the plurality opinion and the second largest opinion. Thus, $\mathbb{E}[x_{r+1}] = x_r(1+q_r)$ and $\mathbb{E}[y_{r+1}] = y_r(1+q_r)$. Here, the expectation is based on the randomness in round $r+1$. If the random variables happen to be sharply around their expectations, the ratio remains essentially preserved. We next argue that this is true even despite the possible deviations.

We break the argument into two parts: Let r^* be the first round in which the fraction of undecided nodes is below $1/2$—i.e., r^* is the minimum r satisfying that $q_r < 1/2$. We first show in Claim 2.3 that the ratio remains essentially preserved by round r^*, and then we use a reasoning with a similar flavor to argue in Claim 2.4 that a similar thing happens even for up to round R.

Claim 2.3. *W.h.p., we have* $\frac{x_{r^*}}{y_{r^*}} \geq (\frac{p_1}{p_2})^{1.7}$.

Proof. For each round $r \in \{1, \ldots, r^*\}$, Chernoff bound shows that the random variables of how many nodes get added to each of the opinions can deviate from their expectations by at most $\pm(\sqrt{5x_r q_r \log n})$ and $(\pm\sqrt{5y_r q_r \log n})$. Here, we have used that $x_r q_r \geq x_1/2 \geq 5\log n$ and $y_r q_r \geq y_1/2 \geq 5\log n$. Hence, we can say w.h.p.,

$$\frac{x_{r+1}}{y_{r+1}} \geq \frac{x_r(1+q_r) - \sqrt{5x_r q_r \log n}}{y_r(1+q_r) + \sqrt{5y_r q_r \log n}} \geq \frac{x_r}{y_r} \cdot \left(\frac{1-\sqrt{5q_r \log n/x_r}}{1+\sqrt{5q_r \log n/y_r}}\right).$$

Let us define $\texttt{DEV}(x_r) = \sqrt{5q_r \log n/x_r}$ and $\texttt{DEV}(y_r) = \sqrt{5q_r \log n/y_r}$. Then, we can write

$$\frac{x_{r^*}}{y_{r^*}} \geq \frac{x_1}{y_1} \prod_{r=1}^{r^*} \left(\frac{1-\texttt{DEV}(x_r)}{1+\texttt{DEV}(y_r)}\right).$$

Recall that we want to argue that despite the deviations of each round $r \in \{1, \ldots, r^*\}$, the ratio remains essentially preserved. For that, we need to analyze the deviation product in the above inequality. Noting that since p_1 and p_2 are both at least $\Omega(\sqrt{\log n/n})$, we know that for each r, $\texttt{DEV}(x_r)$ and $\texttt{DEV}(y_r)$ are both smaller than 0.1. This allows us to write

$$\prod_{r=1}^{r^*} \left(\frac{1-\texttt{DEV}(x_r)}{1+\texttt{DEV}(y_r)}\right) \geq 4^{-2(\sum_{r=1}^{r^*} \texttt{DEV}(x_r) + \sum_{r=1}^{r^*} \texttt{DEV}(y_r))}$$

Thus, we need to upper bound the summations $\sum \texttt{DEV}(x_r)$ and $\sum \texttt{DEV}(y_r)$. For convenience in doing this without repeating the argument, let us use $z \in \{x, y\}$ and consider the z_r for $r \in \{1, \ldots, r^*\}$. We next show that $\sum_r^{r^*} \texttt{DEV}(z_r) = \sum_{r=1}^{r^*} \sqrt{5q_r \log n/z_r} = O(\frac{\sqrt{\log n}}{\sqrt{z_1}})$, with high probability. During rounds $r \in \{2, r^*\}$, in each round we expect z_{r+1} to be $z_r(1+q_r) \geq 3z_r/2$. Since $z_r q_r = \Omega(\log n)$, with high probability, we will indeed have $z_{r+1} \geq 4z_r/3$. Hence, we have $\sum_{r=1}^{r^*} \sqrt{5q_r \log n/z_r} \leq \sum_{r=1}^{r^*} \sqrt{5\log n/z_r} < O(\sqrt{5\log n/z_1})$ where the last inequality holds because, during these rounds, the sum is a geometric series with a constant decay factor. Now we can use the inequality established in the above paragraph to write:

$$\begin{aligned}
\frac{x_{r^*}}{y_{r^*}} &\geq \frac{x_1}{y_1} \prod_{r=1}^{r^*} \left(\frac{1-\texttt{DEV}(x_r)}{1+\texttt{DEV}(y_r)}\right) \\
&\geq \frac{x_1}{y_1} 4^{-2(\sum_{r=1}^{r^*} \texttt{DEV}(x_r) + \sum_{r=1}^{r^*} \texttt{DEV}(y_r))} \\
&\geq \frac{x_1}{y_1} 4^{-O(\sqrt{\log n/x_1} + \sqrt{\log n/y_1})} \\
&\geq \frac{x_1}{y_1} (1 - O(\sqrt{\log n/x_1} + \sqrt{\log n/y_1})) \\
&\geq (\frac{p_1}{p_2})^{1.8} (1 - O(\sqrt{\log n/np_1^2} + \sqrt{\log n/np_2^2})) \\
&\geq (\frac{p_1}{p_2})^{1.8} (1 + (p_1 - p_2)/p_2)^{-0.1} = (\frac{p_1}{p_2})^{1.7}
\end{aligned}$$

□

Claim 2.4. *W.h.p., we have* $\frac{x_R}{y_R} \geq (\frac{p_1}{p_2})^{1.4}$.

Proof. Notice that even in these rounds, it is true that per round r, $\mathbb{E}[x_{r+1}] = x_r(1+q_r)$ and $\mathbb{E}[y_{r+1}] = y_r(1+q_r)$. However, here $x_r q_r$ and $y_r q_r$ might drop below $O(\log n)$, which means every time when we write the additive deviations, we should still add a possible $O(\log n)$ term. Particularly, for each $r \in \{r^*+1, \ldots, R\}$ we can say w.h.p.,

$$\frac{x_{r+1}}{y_{r+1}} \geq \frac{x_r(1+q_r) - (\sqrt{3x_r q_r \log n} + 5\log n)}{y_r(1+q_r) + (\sqrt{5y_r q_r \log n} + 5\log n)} \geq \frac{x_r}{y_r} \cdot \left(\frac{1-(\sqrt{5q_r \log n/x_r} + 5\log n/x_r)}{1+\sqrt{5q_r \log n/y_r} + 5\log n/y_r}\right).$$

Let us define $\texttt{DEV}(x_r) = \sqrt{5q_r \log n/x_r} + 5\log n/x_r$ and $\texttt{DEV}(y_r) = \sqrt{5q_r \log n/y_r} + 5\log n/y_r$, for $r \in \{r^*+1, \ldots, R\}$. Then, we can write

$$\frac{x_R}{y_R} \geq \frac{x_{r^*}}{y_{r^*}} \prod_{r=r^*+1}^{R} \left(\frac{1-\texttt{DEV}(x_r)}{1+\texttt{DEV}(y_r)}\right).$$

Noting that since p_1 and p_2 are both at least $\Omega(\sqrt{\log n/n})$, we know that for each r, $\texttt{DEV}(x_r)$ and $\texttt{DEV}(y_r)$ are both smaller than 0.1. This allows us to write

$$\prod_{r=r^*+1}^{R} \left(\frac{1-\texttt{DEV}(x_r)}{1+\texttt{DEV}(y_r)}\right) \geq 4^{-(\sum_{r=r^*+1}^{R} \texttt{DEV}(x_r) + \sum_{r=r^*+1}^{R} \texttt{DEV}(x_r))}$$

Thus, we need to upper bound the summations $\sum \texttt{DEV}(x_r)$ and $\sum \texttt{DEV}(y_r)$ in the above inequality. Again, for convenience in doing this without repeating the argument, let us use $z \in \{x, y\}$ and consider the z_r for $r \in \{r^*+1, \ldots, R\}$. We next show that w.h.p.,

$$\begin{aligned}
\sum_{r=r^*+1}^{R} \texttt{DEV}(z_r) &= \sum_{r=r^*+1}^{R} \sqrt{5q_r \log n/z_r} + 5\log n/z_r \\
&= O(\frac{\sqrt{\log n}}{\sqrt{z_{r^*}}} + \frac{\log k \log n}{z_{r^*}}).
\end{aligned}$$

First, note that the z_r values cannot decrease in the healing phase, and hence for each for $r' \in \{r^*, \ldots, R\}$, we have

$z_{r'} \geq z_{r^*}$. Thus,

$$\sum_{r=r^*}^{R} (\sqrt{5 \log n q_r / z_r} + 5 \log n / z_r) \leq$$

$$\sqrt{5 \log n / z_{r^*}} \cdot \sum_{r=r^*+1}^{R} (\sqrt{q_r}) + 5R \log n / z_{r^*}.$$

We next bound the term $\sum_{r=r^*+1}^{R}(\sqrt{q_r})$. Note that in round r^*+1, we expect the number of undecided nodes to change from $n/2$ to $n/4$ and with high probability, it will be at most $n/3$. Similarly, so long as $nq_r \geq \Omega(\log n)$, with high probability, we have $q_{r+1} \leq 3q_r/4$. Thus, the summation $\sum_{r=r^*+1}^{R}(\sqrt{q_r})$ is also a summation of a geometric series, so long as $q_r \geq \Omega(\log n/n)$. For rounds where $q_r \leq O(\log n/n)$, the summation of $\sqrt{q_r}$ is at most $O(\log^2 n/n) = o(1)$. Therefore, we get that $\sum_{r=r^*}^{R} \sqrt{q_r} \leq 4q_{r^*} + o(1) \leq 5$. This means: $\sum_{r=r^*+1}^{R}(\sqrt{5 \log n q_r/z_r} + 5\log n/z_r) \leq 10\sqrt{\log n}/\sqrt{z_{r^*}} + 5R \log n/z_{r^*}$.

From the above, it thus follows that the $\sum_{r=r^*+1}^{R} \mathtt{DEV}(x_r) + \sum_{r=r^*+1}^{R} \mathtt{DEV}(x_r) \leq O(\frac{\sqrt{\log n}}{\sqrt{x_{r^*}}} + \frac{\log k \log n}{x_{r^*}}) + O(\frac{\sqrt{\log n}}{\sqrt{y_{r^*}}} + \frac{\log k \log n}{y_{r^*}})$. We know that w.h.p. $x_{r^*} = \Omega(np_1)$ and $y_{r^*} = \Omega(np_2^2/p_1)$. The reason for this is as follows: Note that at round r^*, the total fraction of decided nodes has dropped below $1/2$, which means, ignoring a 2-factor, x_{r^*} is the same as the fraction among decided nodes that have opinion 1. Now, at the end of the gap amplification round, this fraction is w.h.p. $\frac{\Theta(np_1^2)}{\Theta(\sum i=1^k np_i^2)} \geq \frac{\Theta(np_1^2)}{\Theta(np_1)} \geq \Omega(p_1)$. Now, during the rounds $r \in \{1, \ldots, r^*\}$, even in a coarse and pessimistic estimate, this fraction deviates by at most a constant factor, because of the deviation factor analysis that we provided above for rounds $r \in \{1, \ldots, r^*\}$. Hence, in round r^*, about $\Omega(p_1)$ fraction of decided nodes have opinion 1, which since at r^* more than $n/2$ nodes are decided, means $x_{r^*} = \Omega(np_1)$. A similar argument can be used to show that $y_{r^*} = \Omega(n\frac{p_2^2}{\sum i=1^k p_i^2}) = \Omega(np_2^2/(p_1^2 + p_2)) = \Omega(\min\{np_2^2/p_1^2, np_2)\})$.

For simplicity, let us now distinguish between two cases, regarding the value of p_1/p_2. First, we consider the possibly sensitive regime when $p_1/p_2 \in [1, 500]$. In the complementary case, the concentrations we need will be far more relaxed. For the case $p_1/p_2 \in [1, 500]$, from above we get that

$$\begin{aligned}
\frac{x_R}{y_R} &\geq \frac{x_{r^*}}{y_{r^*}} \cdot \prod_{r=r^*+1}^{R} \left(\frac{1 - \mathtt{DEV}(x_r)}{1 + \mathtt{DEV}(y_r)}\right) \\
&\geq \frac{x_{r^*}}{y_{r^*}} \cdot 4^{-(\sum_{r=r^*+1}^{R} \mathtt{DEV}(x_r) + \sum_{r=r^*+1}^{R} \mathtt{DEV}(x_r))} \\
&\geq \frac{x_{r^*}}{y_{r^*}} \cdot 4^{-O(\frac{\sqrt{\log n}}{\sqrt{x_{r^*}}} + \frac{\log k \log n}{x_{r^*}} + \frac{\sqrt{\log n}}{\sqrt{y_{r^*}}} + \frac{\log k \log n}{y_{r^*}})} \\
&\geq \frac{x_{r^*}}{y_{r^*}} \cdot 4^{-O(\frac{\sqrt{\log n}}{\sqrt{np_1}} + \frac{\log k \log n}{np_1} + \frac{\sqrt{\log n}}{\sqrt{np_2}} + \frac{\log k \log n}{np_2})} \\
&\geq \frac{x_{r^*}}{y_{r^*}} \cdot 4^{-O(\frac{\sqrt{\log n}}{\sqrt{np_2}} + \frac{\log k \log n}{np_2})} \geq \frac{x_{r^*}}{y_{r^*}} \cdot 4^{-O(\frac{\sqrt{\log n}}{\sqrt{np_2^2}})} \\
&\geq \frac{x_{r^*}}{y_{r^*}} \cdot (1 - O(\frac{\sqrt{\log n}}{\sqrt{np_2^2}})) \\
&\geq (\frac{p_1}{p_2})^{1.7}(1 + \frac{p_1 - p_2}{p_2})^{-0.3} = (\frac{p_1}{p_2})^{1.4}
\end{aligned}$$

Now suppose that $p_1/p_2 > 500$. Here, it suffices to bound the deviations by a small constant. It is easy to see that w.h.p. $y_R \leq 5y_{r^*} + O(\log^2 n)$, because during these rounds, as discussed above, q_r decays exponentially with r. Thus, $\frac{x_R}{y_R} \geq \frac{x_{r^*}}{y_R} \geq \frac{x_{r^*}}{5y_{r^*} + O(\log^2 n)} \geq \frac{x_{r^*}}{y_{r^*}}/(5+o(1)) > (\frac{p_1}{p_2})^{1.7}/5.1 \geq (\frac{p_1}{p_2})^{1.4}$. This completes the proof of (P3.a). Next, we consider the complementary case where p_2 is small. □

Case (P.b), when $p_2 \leq \sqrt{10 \log n/n}$: Now we come back to the case that $p_2 = \max_{i=2}^{k} p_i \leq \sqrt{10 \log n/n}$. Note that in this case, the multiplicative factor deviations of the opinion 2 from its expected values might be large. Recall the definition $\mathsf{gap} = \min\{\frac{p_1}{\sqrt{10 \log n/n}}, \min_{i=2}^{k} \frac{p_1}{p_i}\}$. Also, note that by the above arguments, the ratio between $\frac{p_1}{p_2}$ will grow to at least $\mathsf{gap}^{1.4}$ because that would happen even if we manually raise the initial p_2 to $\sqrt{10 \log n/n}$, thus allowing us to use the above concentration arguments, and the whole process is clearly monotonic meaning that raising the initial p_2 cannot increase the ratio $\frac{p_1^{new}}{p_2^{new}}$. However, to show that gap_{new} increases to $\mathsf{gap}^{1.4}$, in this regime of $p_2 \leq \sqrt{10 \log n/n}$, the minimizer in the definition of gap is the $\frac{p_1}{\sqrt{10 \log n/n}}$ term which means we should show that p_1 will grow accordingly.

Here, since $p_1 \geq \sqrt{C \log n/n}$, we have $\mathsf{gap} \geq \frac{\sqrt{C \log n/n}}{\sqrt{10 \log n/n}} \gg 20$. On the other hand, by repeating the arguments given above, we know that p_1^{new} will be within at most a $1 \pm o(1)$ factor of its expectation, which is $\frac{p_1^2}{\sum_{i=1}^{k} p_i^2} = \frac{p_1^2}{p_1^2 + \sum_{i=2}^{k} p_i^2} \geq \frac{p_1^2}{p_1^2 + p_{i^*}}$. Thus, the growth factor from p_1 to p_1^{new} is at least $(1 - o(1))\frac{p_1}{p_1^2 + p_2} \geq \frac{1 - o(1)}{p_1 + 1/\mathsf{gap}}$. If $1/\mathsf{gap} \leq 0.45p_1$, then $p_1^{new} > 2/3$. Otherwise, the growth is at least $\frac{1 - o(1)}{3.3/\mathsf{gap}} \geq \mathsf{gap}/4 \geq \mathsf{gap}^{1/2}$, which finishes the proof of case (P.b) and thus also property (P).

Property (S2): Finally, we use the above concentration arguments to prove property (S2), by showing that w.h.p. $\mathsf{bias}^{new} \geq p_1 - p_2$. First suppose that $\frac{p_1}{p_2} < 10$. Then, we know that p_1^{new} and p_2^{new} will be within $1 + o(1)$ factors of their expectations (as analyzed above), which are, respectively, $\frac{p_1^2}{\sum_{j=1}^{k} p_j^2}$ and $\frac{p_1^2}{\sum_{j=1}^{k} p_j^2}$. Thus,

$$\begin{aligned}
p_1^{new} - p_2^{new} &\geq (1 - o(1))\frac{p_1^2}{\sum_{j=1}^{k} p_j^2} - \frac{p_1^2}{\sum_{j=1}^{k} p_j^2} \\
&= (1 - o(1))(p_1 - p_2) \cdot \frac{(p_1 + p_2)}{\sum_{j=1}^{k} p_j^2} \\
&\geq (1 - o(1))(p_1 - p_2) \cdot \frac{(p_1 + p_i)}{p_1 \sum_{j=1}^{k} p_j} \\
&\geq (1 - o(1))(p_1 - p_2) \cdot \frac{(p_1 + p_2)}{p_1} \\
&\geq (1.1 - o(1))(p_1 - p_2).
\end{aligned}$$

On the other hand, when $\frac{p_1}{p_2} > 10$, we know the $\frac{p_1^{new}}{p_2^{new}} \geq \mathsf{gap}^{new} \geq \mathsf{gap}^{1.4} > 2.5\mathsf{gap}$. We also know that w.h.p. p_1 does not decrease in this case. This implies that $\mathsf{bias} = p_1^{new} - p_2^{new}$ also does not decrease, thus proving property (S2).

□

Lemma 2.5. *After $O(\log n)$ phases from the start, we have* $\texttt{gap} \geq 2$. *If initially we had $p_1 > (1+\delta)p_2$ for some constant δ, then in fact within $O(1)$ phases we would have* $\texttt{gap} \geq 2$.

Proof. Initially,

$$\texttt{gap} \geq \min\{\frac{p_1}{\sqrt{10\log n/n}}, \min_{i=2}^{k} \frac{p_1}{p_i}\} \geq \min\{3, \frac{p_1}{p_2}\} > 1 + \frac{1}{\sqrt{n}}.$$

Note that once $p_1 \geq 2/3$, we also have $\texttt{gap} \geq 2$. Define $\gamma = \texttt{gap} - 1$. In every phase that $p_1^{new} \geq 2/3$ does not happen, Lemma 2.2 gives $\texttt{gap}^{new} \geq \texttt{gap}^{1.4}$. This implies $\gamma^{new} \geq (1+\gamma)^{1.4} - 1 \geq 6\gamma/5$. Hence, after $O(\log n)$ phases, γ becomes larger than 1 which means $\texttt{gap} \geq 2$. If initially we had $p_1 > (1+\delta)p_2$, then initially $\texttt{gap} \geq 1+\delta$ and thus it takes it only $O(1)$ phases to reach $\texttt{gap} \geq 2$. □

Lemma 2.6. *If at the start of a phase $p_1 \geq \frac{2}{3}$, then w.h.p. we have $p_1^{new} \geq \frac{2}{3}$ also at the end of it.*

Proof. At the end of the gap amplification round, w.h.p., the fraction of decided nodes of opinion 1 is $(1-o(1))4/9$ and the fraction of decided nodes of all other opinions is at most $(1+o(1))1/9$. That is, w.h.p., the fraction among decided nodes that have opinion 1 is at least $(1-o(1))\frac{4/9}{4/9+1/9} > 3/4$. During each round r of the healing rounds, both the fraction of plurality nodes and the total fraction of decided nodes are expected to grow by $(1+q_r)$, where q_r is the fraction of undecided nodes at the start of that round. Since the number of plurality opinion nodes and also the total number of decided nodes are $\Omega(n)$, the actual growth in the two fractions will be within $1 \pm o(\frac{1}{\log n})$ factor of their expectations. Thus, the fraction among the decided node that have opinion 1 remains preserved up to at most a $1 \pm o(\frac{1}{\log n})$ factor. This means, even after all the $O(\log k)$ rounds of healing, the fraction among the decided nodes that have opinion 1 is at least $(1-o(1/\log n))^{O(\log k)}3/4 = (1-o(1))3/4$. On the other hand, at that point the probability for a node to remain undecided is at most $(1/3)^{O(\log k)} \leq 0.01/k$, which means w.h.p., at least 0.99 fraction of nodes will be decided. Hence, w.h.p., at least $0.98 \times (1-o(1))3/4 > 2/3$ fraction of nodes will have opinion 1. □

Lemma 2.7. *After* $\texttt{gap} \geq 2$, *within $O(\log\log n)$ phases, w.h.p., we have $p_1 \geq 2/3$ and $\sum_{i\geq 2} p_i = 0$.*

Proof. By Lemma 2.2, in each phase j, either we get $p_1 \geq 2/3$ or $\texttt{gap}^{new} \geq \texttt{gap}^{1.4}$. Since we start with a $\texttt{gap} \geq 2$, within $O(\log\log n)$ phases, the latter condition cannot continue to hold which means we would have $p_1 \geq 2/3$. At this point, by Lemma 2.6, it will always remain true that $p_1 \geq 2/3$.

Then, for any other opinion $i \in [2,k]$, in each phase, the change satisfies the following inequality: $\mathbb{E}[p_i^{new}] = \frac{p_i^2}{\sum_{i=1}^{k} p_i^2} \geq \frac{p_i^2}{4/9} = 2.25p_i^2$. Here, the expectation is based only on the randomness of this phase. Hence, within $O(\log\log n)$ phases, we expect p_i to fall below $1/n^c$, for any desirable constant c. By Markov's inequality, this means at that point, we actually have $p_i = 0$ w.h.p. □

We proceed by showing that from that point on, the plurality opinion becomes the consensus.

Lemma 2.8. *After $p_1 \geq 2/3$ and $\sum_{i\geq 2} p_i = 0$, within $O(\log n/\log k)$ phases, w.h.p., $p_1 = 1$.*

Proof. Consider the first phase after we have $p_1 \geq 2/3$ and $\sum_{i\geq 2} p_i = 0$. First note that by Lemma 2.6, w.h.p. $p_1 \geq 2/3$ from now on. Now, let q be the fraction of undecided nodes. Notice that after the first round, q increases slightly to q' where $\mathbb{E}[q'] = 1-(1-q)^2 \leq 2q$. During the next $R-1 = O(\log k)$ rounds of this phase, a node remains undecided only if all nodes that it contacted where undecided and that has probability at most $(5/9)^{R-1} \leq 1/(4k)$. Thus, $\mathbb{E}[q^{new}] \leq \frac{q}{2k}$. This expectation relies only on the randomness of this phase. Thus, the expected value of q after $O(\log n/\log k)$ phases is $1/n^c$—for any arbitrary c, by adjusting the constant in the number of phases. Hence, by Markov's inequality, the probability that $q \neq 0$, which would imply $q \geq 1/n$, is at most $1/n^{c-1}$. Thus, w.h.p., $q = 0$ and $p_1 = 1$. Clearly, from that point onwards, it remains true that $p_1 = 1$. □

We are now ready to complete the proof of Theorem 2.1

Proof of Theorem 2.1. By Lemma 2.5, within $O(\log n)$ phases from the beginning of the execution, $\texttt{gap} \geq 2$. In fact if we initially have $p_1 \geq (1+\delta)p_2$ for a constant δ, this part takes $O(1)$ phases. Then, after additional $O(\log\log n)$ phases, by Lemma 2.5, we have $p_1 \geq 2/3$ and all other nodes are undecided. Finally, by Lemma 2.8, w.h.p., within $O(\log n/\log k)$ phases, plurality achieves totality. □

3. THE ALGORITHM: TAKE 2

In the algorithm presented in the previous section, each node has a memory size of $\log k + \log\log k + O(1)$ bits, where $\log\log k + O(1)$ bits of it are used solely to remember the round number, modulo $R = O(\log k)$. Here, we explain how to remove this $\log\log k$ overhead. Thus, we get a dynamics in which each node has at most $O(k)$ states—i.e., within constant factor of the trivially optimal—instead of the $O(k\log k)$ states of the previous algorithm.

Intuitive Discussions: If we are to reduce the memory from $\log k + \log\log k + O(1)$ to $\log k + O(1)$, we cannot require each node to know both an opinion and the round number modulo R. Nodes not knowing the time create the risk that nodes might not be "*in sync*" in regards to whether at a given point of time, they should be performing *gap amplification* or *healing*. We try to minimize this effect and keep the vast majority of the nodes essentially "*in sync*".

Notice that when we allow memory size of $\log k + O(1)$, we have (in fact far more than) enough space for keeping the time modulo R; we just cannot ask each node to keep both time and an opinion. To overcome this, we simply *split the responsibilities among the nodes*: particularly, at the start, each node tosses a fair random coin and decides to be a *clock-node* or a *game-player*, each with probability 1/2. Clock-nodes forget their initial opinion and instead keep the time (say modulo $4R$, thus needing at most $\log k + O(1)$ bits). On the other hand, the game-players will try to follow the approach of the take 1 algorithm, using the help of the clock-nodes.

There are three subtleties this intuitive idea: First, note that now the *game-players*, who actually play the main role in getting to plurality consensus, do not know the time and

Algorithm 1 The algorithm run at each game-player node v

```
In each round, node v does as follows (assuming u is the node that v contacted):
if u.isClock = true then
    if phase_v ≠ end-game or (phase_v = end-game and phase_u = 0) then
        phase_v ← phase_u;
else
    switch phase_v do
        case 0:                                   - Time Buffer 1-
            sampled ← false; forget ← false;
        case 1:                 - Gap Amplification (Sampling) -
            if sampled = false and v.opinion ≠ u.opinion then forget ← true;
            sampled ← true;
        case 2:                                   - Time Buffer 2-
            if forget = true then v.opinion ← 0; forget ← false;
        case 3:                                        - Healing -
            if v.opinion = 0 then v.opinion ← u.opinion;
                sampled ← false; forget ← false;
        case end-game:                                - End Game -
            if v.opinion ≠ 0 and v.opinion ≠ u.opinion then v.opinion ← 0;
            if v.opinion = 0 then v.opinion ← u.opinion;
```

thus cannot perform the take 1 algorithm *per se*. Furthermore, they cannot really expect to receive the precise time from the clock-nodes and remember it, as that would again require $\log k + \log\log k + O(1)$ memory bits. We will make the clock nodes report the time only in (integer) factors of $R = O(\log k)$, and modulo say $4R$. That is, the reported phase number is always in $\{0, 1, 2, 3\}$. Reporting these numbers and remembering them will thus require only $O(1)$ bits. Second, now the *game-players* do not really know the precise time, and thus they cannot update the phase numbers on their own. They will have to instead rely completely on receiving phase-updates from *clock-nodes*. Third, we want that eventually all the nodes to hold the plurality opinion, including the *clock-nodes*. Hence, each clock-node needs to at some point forget it's *time-keeping responsibilities* and try to learn the plurality opinion. This has to be done in a judicious manner so that the system as a whole has enough time-keepers, so long as they are needed. We next present the algorithm that deals with these challenges.

The Algorithm Description: The algorithm performed by the game-player nodes is described in Algorithm 1 and the algorithm performed by the clock-nodes is presented in Algorithm 2.

We next provide some intuitive explanation for what these algorithms are doing. The algorithm run the by game-player nodes can be viewed as *interpolating* between two algorithms: the protocol presented in the previous section, which we will call hereafter the Gap Amplification (`GA`) protocol, and the Undecided State (`Undecided`) protocol[6] as used in [BCN+15a]. We have the `Undecided` protocol for the time that the number of clock-nodes that are following their time-keeping responsibilities goes down, and thus we cannot follow the `GA` protocol. In reality, as long as p_1 is far from 1, there will be a large population of clock-nodes that are still performing their time-keeping responsibilities, and thus the `GA` protocol will be the dominant part of the system (formalizing this will take some care). Hence, during that time, the system will enjoy the fast gap amplification behavior of `GA`. Once p_1 gets close to 1, the number of active clock-nodes drops and the game-players gradually move to the `Undecided` protocol. At this time, we no longer need the power of the `GA` protocol; regardless of how game-player nodes are split between the two protocol, as we will show, the system evolves almost as good as the `Undecided` protocol and gets to plurality consensus fast.

Let us now discuss the `GA` protocol, which is the core of the algorithm of the game-players, and it is essentially a simulation of the take 1 algorithm. We have a few small changes, in comparison to the take 1 algorithm, which are added to deal with the subtleties described above: Particularly, since the game-player nodes will not be able to know the precise time, to mitigate the effects of asynchrony, we extend the *gap amplification* to a full phase (instead of one round) and we also add some time buffer between the *gap amplification* period and the *healing* period. Thus, now the execution of the algorithm can be broken to intervals made of 4 consecutive phases, which we call a "long-phase". Particularly, a long-phase is made of 4 phases, the two main ones being gap amplification and healing phases, interspersed with two (essentially) time buffer phases. Although the gap amplification period is now one full phase, we still make each node act based on a single sample: that is, in the first round in this phase that the game-player node v contacts another game-player u, node v decides whether to keep its opinion or not, and it remains with this decision. If v decided to forget its opinion, then it remembers this decision (via a Boolean variable called *forget*) and once v sees the next phase (by meeting a clock-node of phase 2), it becomes undecided. With a slight informality, from now on, we will refer to the protocol described by phases $\{0, 1, 2, 3\}$ as the `GA` (gap amplification) protocol. A game-player node goes out of the `GA` protocol only if it meets a clock-node that has moved to the end-game (to be explained while discussing the algorithm of the clock-nodes). Game-players that move out of the `GA` protocol go to the `Undecided` protocol, as described the pseudocode in the `end-game` switch case. However, each such game-player node might come back to the `GA` protocol later on, if it meets a clock-node that reports phase 0.

Let us now discuss the algorithm for the clock-nodes. As mentioned above, an important challenge is for the clock-nodes to recognize that the game-players have reached consensus, so that they can switch to adopt an opinion then. Since the `GA` protocol might take $O(\log n \log k)$ rounds to reach plurality consensus, we cannot require the clock-nodes to keep the precise time until this period has passed, as that would require $\Omega(\log\log n)$ memory bits. Instead, we make the clock-nodes use the existence of undecided nodes as a signal to detect that the game-players still have not reached consensus. Although this is not a perfect check, it will be good enough for our purposes, i.e., so long as p_1 is far from 1. Particularly, note that in the `GA` protocol, so long as we are far from reaching consensus (while p_1 is far from 1), there will be a considerable fraction of undecided nodes (at some point during at least one of the phases). We make the clock-nodes remain active—i.e., keeping time—as long

[6]We note that in fact any other protocol with a minimal plurality amplification behavior would suffice for this part; we choose the `Undecided` protocols just for convenience.

Algorithm 2 The algorithm run at each clock-node v

In each round, node v does as follows (assuming u is the node that v contacted):

switch $v.status$ **do**
  case `counting`: - Time Keeping -
    $v.opinion \leftarrow$ `null`;
    $v.time \leftarrow v.time + 1 \ mod \ 4R$;
    $v.phase \leftarrow \lceil v.time/R \rceil \ mod \ 4$;
    if $u.isClock = false$ and $u.opinion = 0$ **then** $v.consensus \leftarrow false$;
    if $u.isClock = true$ and $u.consensus = false$ **then** $v.consensus \leftarrow false$;
    if $v.time \ mod \ 4R = 0$ **then**
      if $v.consensus = true$ **then** $v.status \leftarrow$ `end-game`;
      $v.consensus \leftarrow true$;
  case `end-game`: - End Game -
    $v.time \leftarrow$ `null`;
    $v.phase \leftarrow$ `end-game`;
    if $u.isClock = false$ **then** $v.opinion \leftarrow u.opinion$
    else if $u.status = 0$ and $u.consensus = false$ **then**
      $v.status \leftarrow$ `counting`;
      $v.opinion \leftarrow$ `null`;
      $v.time \leftarrow u.time$; $v.phase \leftarrow u.phase$; $v.consensus \leftarrow u.consensus$;

as they meet an undecided node directly or indirectly. Here, indirectly means by meeting a clock-node that is aware of the existence of undecided nodes. This information spreading essentially in the usual gossip spreading style and via the boolean variable *consensus*, for which $consensus = false$ indicates that an undecided node still exists, i.e., an indication for that the system has not reached plurality consensus yet. If during a long-phase, a clock-node receives no information about the existence of undecided nodes, it neglects its time keeping task, by forgetting time, and attempts to move to the end-game reporting phase (possibly temporarily). Here, the phase number it reports is a special symbol "end-game". Also, at this time, this clock-node that now has forgotten time adopts an opinion, always remembering the opinion of the last game-player that it met. However, this clock-node that has become "deactivated" from time-keeping by switching to the end-game mode might get reactivated again: particularly, if this "deactivated" clock-node v meets an active clock-node u who is aware of the existence of undecided nodes (has $u.consensus = false$), then v gets reactivated again, keeping track of time, using the clock that it gets from u, and reporting the phase number in $\{0, 1, 2, 3\}$.

The analysis of the algorithm is provided in the full version. We next provide some intuition for the analysis, for the cases in which $k \geq n^{0.1}$. The analysis for the complementary case of $k < n^{0.1}$ also follows a similar outline, roughly speaking, but typically requires more care.

Analysis Intuition, for when $k \geq n^{0.1}$: Here the length of each phase is $R = \Theta(\log k) = \Theta(\log n)$, which allows us to say that some good events happen w.h.p. without needing to keep track of their precise probability, e.g., this is sufficient time for information to spread to the whole system.

Specifically, the first analysis step is to establish that as long as $p_1 \leq 1 - \Theta(\log n/n)$, all clock-nodes will continue to perform their time-keeping responsibilities. Thus, during this period, all game-player nodes will be performing the `GA` protocol without going to the end-game of the `Undecided` protocol. The (formally inductive) argument for why all clock-nodes will remain is roughly as follows: Consider one long-phase (4 consecutive phases). Because game-player nodes are following the `GA` protocol and there are $\Omega(\log n)$ non-plurality nodes, during phase 2 of this long-phase, there will be $\Theta(\log n)$ undecided nodes w.h.p. Thus, w.h.p., there will be clock-nodes that notice this undecided population. This information about the existence of undecided nodes will spread among the clock-nodes following essentially the pattern of a usual rumor spreading. Particularly, w.h.p. within $O(\log n)$ rounds all clock-nodes will be aware of the existence of undecideds and thus, at the end of the long-phase, none of the clock-nodes switches to the end-game mode. Given this, during this time of $p_1 \leq 1 - \Theta(\log n/n)$, all game-players are acting according to the `GA` protocol. This allows us to use the analysis of take 1, modulo minor details, and argue that in $O(\log n)$ phases, w.h.p., we reach $p_1 \geq 1 - \Theta(\log n/n)$.

Once p_1 reaches $1 - \Theta(\log n/n)$, some clock-nodes might start to switch to the end-game mode and thus some game-player nodes might act based on the `Undecided` protocol. However, now that p_1 is very close to 1, we do not need the power of `GA`. Here, even the `Undecided` protocol would be pushing us towards consensus on plurality quickly enough, and we can actually prove that the system (which is an uncontrolled mix of `GA` and `Undecided`) does not behave worse than the worst of them. Particularly, we can first see that w.h.p. the system remains in this regime of p_1 very close to 1, and then use this to establish that non-plurality opinions get filtered out within $O(1)$ phases and that plurality reaches totality among game-players within $O(1)$ phases. By the end of that time, all clock-nodes switch to the end-game, as they will not see undecided game-players anymore. Since clock-nodes in the end-game adopt the opinion of the last game-player they have seen, within $O(1)$ phases, all nodes will hold the plurality opinion.

4. REFERENCES

[AAD+06] Dana Angluin, James Aspnes, Zoë Diamadi, Michael J Fischer, and René Peralta. Computation in networks of passively mobile finite-state sensors. *Distributed computing*, 18(4):235–253, 2006.

[AAE08] Dana Angluin, James Aspnes, and David Eisenstat. A simple population protocol for fast robust approximate majority. *Distributed Computing*, 21(2):87–102, 2008.

[AFJ06] Dana Angluin, Michael J Fischer, and Hong Jiang. Stabilizing consensus in mobile networks. In *Distributed Computing in Sensor Systems*, pages 37–50. Springer, 2006.

[AGV15] Dan Alistarh, Rati Gelashvili, and Milan Vojnovic. Fast and exact majority in population protocols. In *the Proc. of the Int'l Symp. on Princ. of Dist. Comp. (PODC)*, pages 47âĂŞ56, 2015.

[BCN+14] Luca Becchetti, Andrea Clementi, Emanuele Natale, Francesco Pasquale, Riccardo Silvestri, and Luca Trevisan. Simple dynamics for plurality consensus. In *Proceedings of the 26th ACM symposium on Parallelism in algorithms and architectures*, pages 247–256. ACM, 2014.

[BCN+15a] L Becchetti, A Clementi, E Natale, F Pasquale, and R Silvestri. Plurality consensus in the gossip model. In *Pro. of ACM-SIAM Symp. on Disc. Alg. (SODA)*, pages 371–390, 2015.

[BCN+15b] Luca Becchetti, Andrea Clementi, Emanuele Natale, Francesco Pasquale, and Luca Trevisan. Stabilizing consensus with many opinions. *to appear at SODA'16, arXiv preprint arXiv:1508.06782*, 2015.

[BFGK16] Petra Berenbrink, Tom Friedetzky, George Giakkoupis, and Peter Kling. Efficient plurality consensus, or: The benefits of cleaning up from time to time. In *the Pro. of the Int'l Colloquium on Automata, Languages and Programming (ICALP)*, page to appear, 2016.

[BICS10] Radu Berinde, Piotr Indyk, Graham Cormode, and Martin J Strauss. Space-optimal heavy hitters with strong error bounds. *ACM Transactions on Database Systems (TODS)*, 35(4):26, 2010.

[BSDDS14] Ohad Ben-Shahar, Shlomi Dolev, Andrey Dolgin, and Michael Segal. Direction election in flocking swarms. *Ad Hoc Networks*, 12:250–258, 2014.

[CCN12] Luca Cardelli and Attila Csikász-Nagy. The cell cycle switch computes approximate majority. *Scientific reports*, 2, 2012.

[CDS+13] Yuan-Jyue Chen, Neil Dalchau, Niranjan Srinivas, Andrew Phillips, Luca Cardelli, David Soloveichik, and Georg Seelig. Programmable chemical controllers made from DNA. *Nature nanotechnology*, 8(10):755–762, 2013.

[CKFL05] Iain D Couzin, Jens Krause, Nigel R Franks, and Simon A Levin. Effective leadership and decision-making in animal groups on the move. *Nature*, 433(7025):513–516, 2005.

[CSWB09] Matthew Cook, David Soloveichik, Erik Winfree, and Jehoshua Bruck. Programmability of chemical reaction networks. In *Algorithmic Bioprocesses*, pages 543–584. Springer, 2009.

[DGM+11] Benjamin Doerr, Leslie Ann Goldberg, Lorenz Minder, Thomas Sauerwald, and Christian Scheideler. Stabilizing consensus with the power of two choices. In *Proceedings of the twenty-third annual ACM symposium on Parallelism in algorithms and architectures*, pages 149–158. ACM, 2011.

[Dot14] David Doty. Timing in chemical reaction networks. In *Proceedings of the Twenty-Fifth Annual ACM-SIAM Symposium on Discrete Algorithms*, pages 772–784. SIAM, 2014.

[DV12] Moez Draief and Milan Vojnovic. Convergence speed of binary interval consensus. *SIAM Journal on Control and Optimization*, 50(3):1087–1109, 2012.

[DW83] Peter Donnelly and Dominic Welsh. Finite particle systems and infection models. In *Mathematical Proceedings of the Cambridge Philosophical Society*, volume 94, pages 167–182. Cambridge Univ Press, 1983.

[Hop71] John Hopcroft. An $n \log n$ algorithm for minimizing states in a finite automaton. *Theory of Machines and Computations*, pages 189–196, 1971.

[HP01] Yehuda Hassin and David Peleg. Distributed probabilistic polling and applications to proportionate agreement. *Information and Computation*, 171(2):248–268, 2001.

[KDG03] David Kempe, Alin Dobra, and Johannes Gehrke. Gossip-based computation of aggregate information. In *Proc. of the Symp. on Found. of Comp. Sci. (FOCS)*, pages 482–491, 2003.

[Lig12] Thomas Liggett. *Interacting particle systems*, volume 276. Springer Science & Business Media, 2012.

[Lyn96] Nancy A Lynch. *Distributed algorithms.* Morgan Kaufmann, 1996.

[MNRS14] George B Mertzios, Sotiris E Nikoletseas, Christoforos L Raptopoulos, and Paul G Spirakis. Determining majority in networks with local interactions and very small local memory. In *Automata, Languages, and Programming*, pages 871–882. Springer, 2014.

[MS] Elchanan Mossel and Grant Schoenebeck. Reaching consensus on social networks.

[PVV09] Etienne Perron, Dinkar Vasudevan, and Milan Vojnovic. Using three states for binary consensus on complete graphs. In *the Proc. of IEEE INFOCOM*, pages 2527–2535, 2009.

[SKJ+08] David JT Sumpter, Jens Krause, Richard James, Iain D Couzin, and Ashley JW Ward. Consensus decision making by fish. *Current Biology*, 18(22):1773–1777, 2008.

[Spe64] H. Spencer. *The Principles of Biology.* Number v. 1 in Spencer, Herbert: A system of synthetic philosophy. Williams and Norgate, 1864.

[TBA86] J. N. Tsitsiklis, D. P. Bertsekas, and M. Athans. Distributed asynchronous deterministic and stochastic gradient optimization algorithms. *IEEE transactions on automatic control*, 31(9):803–812, 1986.

[Tsi84] John Nikolas Tsitsiklis. Problems in decentralized decision making and computation. Technical report, DTIC Document, 1984.

[WH04] Fang Wu and Bernardo A Huberman. Social structure and opinion formation. *arXiv preprint cond-mat/0407252*, 2004.

[Yu05] Sheng Yu. State complexity: Recent results and open problems. *Fundamenta Informaticae*, 64(1-4):471–480, 2005.

Noisy Rumor Spreading and Plurality Consensus

[Extended Abstract] *

Pierre Fraigniaud†
Laboratoire d'Informatique Algorithmique
CNRS and University Paris Diderot
France
pierref@liafa.univ-paris-diderot.fr

Emanuele Natale‡
Dipartimento di Informatica
Sapienza Università di Roma
Italy
natale@di.uniroma1.it

ABSTRACT

Error-correcting codes are efficient methods for handling *noisy* communication channels in the context of technological networks. However, such elaborate methods differ a lot from the unsophisticated way biological entities are supposed to communicate. Yet, it has been recently shown by Feinerman, Haeupler, and Korman [PODC 2014] that complex coordination tasks such as *rumor spreading* and *majority consensus* can plausibly be achieved in biological systems subject to noisy communication channels, where every message transferred through a channel remains intact with small probability $\frac{1}{2}+\epsilon$, without using coding techniques. This result is a considerable step towards a better understanding of the way biological entities may cooperate. It has nevertheless been established only in the case of 2-valued *opinions*: rumor spreading aims at broadcasting a single-bit opinion to all nodes, and majority consensus aims at leading all nodes to adopt the single-bit opinion that was initially present in the system with (relative) majority. In this paper, we extend this previous work to k-valued opinions, for any constant $k \geq 2$.

Our extension requires to address a series of important issues, some conceptual, others technical. We had to entirely revisit the notion of noise, for handling channels carrying k-*valued* messages. In fact, we precisely characterize the type of noise patterns for which plurality consensus is solvable. Also, a key result employed in the bivalued case by Feinerman et al. is an estimate of the probability of observing the most frequent opinion from observing the mode of a small sample. We generalize this result to the multivalued case by providing a new analytical proof for the bivalued case that is amenable to be extended, by induction, and that is of independent interest.

*A full version of this paper is available at https://arxiv.org/abs/1507.05796v5.

†Additional support from the ANR project DISPLEXITY and from the INRIA project GANG.

‡This work was done in part while the author was visiting the Simons Institute for the Theory of Computing.

PODC'16, July 25-28, 2016, Chicago, IL, USA
© 2016 ACM. ISBN 978-1-4503-3964-3/16/07...$15.00
DOI: http://dx.doi.org/10.1145/2933057.2933089

Keywords

plurality consensus; uniform push model; rumor spreading; noisy communication.

1. INTRODUCTION

1.1 Context and Objective

To guarantee reliable communication over a network in the presence of noise is the main goal of Network Information Theory [18]. Thanks to the achievements of this theory, the impact of noise can often be drastically reduced to almost zero by employing *error-correcting codes*, which are practical methods whenever dealing with artificial entities. However, as observed in [19], the situation is radically different for scenarios in which the computational entities are biological. Indeed, from a biological perspective, a computational process can be considered "simple" only if it consists of very basic primitive operations, and is extremely lightweight. As a consequence, it is unlikely that biological entities are employing techniques like error-correcting codes to reduce the impact of noise in communications between them. Yet, biological signals are subject to noise, when generated, transmitted, and received. This rises the intriguing question of how entities in biological ensembles can cooperate in presence of noisy communications, but in absence of mechanisms such as error-correcting codes.

An important step toward understanding communications in biological ensembles has been achieved recently in [19], which showed how it is possible to cope with noisy communications in absence of coding mechanisms for solving complex tasks such as *rumor-spreading* and *majority consensus*. Such a result provides highly valuable hints on how complex tasks can be achieved in frameworks such as the immune system, bacteria populations, or super-organisms of social insects, despite the presence of noisy communications.

In the case of rumor-spreading, [19] assumes that a source-node initially handles a bit, set to some binary value, called the *correct opinion*. This opinion has to be transmitted to all nodes, in a noisy environment, modeled as a complete network with unreliable links. More precisely, messages are transmitted in the network according to the classical *uniform push model* [14, 24, 29] where, at each round, every node can send one binary opinion to a neighbor chosen uniformly and independently at random and, before reaching the receiver, that opinion is flipped with probability at most $\frac{1}{2} - \epsilon$ with $\epsilon > 0$. It is proved that, even in this very noisy setting, the rumor-spreading problem can be solved quite efficiently. Specifically, [19] provides an algorithm that solves the noisy rumor-spreading problem in $O(\frac{1}{\epsilon^2} \log n)$ communication rounds, with high probability[1] (w.h.p.) in n-node networks, using $O(\log \log n + \log(1/\epsilon))$ bits of memory per node. Again, this algorithm exchanges solely opinions between nodes.

In the case of majority consensus, [19] assumes that some nodes are supporting opinion 0, some nodes are supporting opinion 1, and some other nodes are supporting no opinion. The objective is that all nodes eventually support the initially most frequent opinion (0 or 1). More precisely, let A be the set of nodes with opinion, and let $b \in \{0, 1\}$ be the majority opinion in A. The *majority bias* of A is defined as $\frac{1}{2}(|A_b| - |A_{\bar{b}}|)/|A|$ where A_i is the set of nodes with opinion $i \in \{0, 1\}$. In the very same noisy communication model as above, [19] provides an algorithm that solves the noisy majority consensus problem for $|A| = \Omega(\frac{1}{\epsilon^2} \log n)$ with majority-bias $\Omega(\sqrt{\log n/|A|})$. The algorithm runs in $O(\frac{1}{\epsilon^2} \log n)$ rounds, w.h.p., in n-node networks, using $O(\log \log n + \log(1/\epsilon))$ bits of memory per node. As for the case of rumor spreading, the algorithm exchanges solely opinions between nodes. In fact, the latter algorithm for majority consensus is used as a subroutine for solving the rumor-spreading problem. Note that the majority consensus algorithm of [19] requires that the nodes are initially aware of the size of A.

According to [19], both algorithms are optimal, since both rumor-spreading and majority consensus require $\Omega(\frac{1}{\epsilon^2} \log n)$ rounds w.h.p. in n-node networks.

Our objective is to extend the work of [19] to the natural case of an arbitrary number of opinions, to go beyond a proof of concept. The problem that results from this extension is an instance of the *plurality consensus* problem in the presence of noise, i.e., the problem of making the system converging to the initially most frequent opinion (i.e., the *plurality* opinion). Indeed, the plurality consensus problem naturally arises in several biological settings, typically for choosing between different directions for a flock of birds [10], different speeds for a school of fish [31], or different nesting sites for ants [22]. The computation of the most frequent value has also been observed in biological cells [11].

1.2 Our Contribution

1.2.1 Our Results

We generalize the results in [19] to the setting in which an arbitrary large number k of opinions is present in the system. In the context of rumor spreading, the correct opinion is a value $i \in \{1, \ldots, k\}$, for any constant $k \geq 2$. Initially, one node supports this opinion i, and the other nodes have no opinions. The nodes must exchange opinions so that, eventually, all nodes support the correct opinion i. In the context of (relative) majority consensus, also known as *plurality consensus*, each node u initially supports one opinion $i_u \in \{1, \ldots, k\}$, or has no opinion. The objective is that all nodes eventually adopt the *plurality opinion* (i.e., the opinion initially held by more nodes than any other, but not necessarily by an overall majority of nodes). As in [19], we restrict ourselves to "natural" algorithms [12], that is, algorithms in which nodes only exchange opinions in a straightforward manner (i.e., they do not use the opinions to encode, e.g., part of their internal state). For both problems, the difficulty comes from the fact that every opinion can be modified during its traversal of any link, and switched at random to any other opinion. In short, we prove that there are algorithms solving the noisy rumor spreading problem and the noisy plurality consensus problem for multiple opinions, with the same performances and probabilistic guarantees as the algorithms for binary opinions in [19].

1.2.2 The technical challenges

Generalizing noisy rumor spreading and noisy majority consensus to more than just two opinions requires to address a series of issues, some conceptual, others technical.

Conceptually, one needs first to redefine the notion of noise. In the case of binary opinions, the noise can just flip an opinion to its complement. In the case of multiple opinions, an opinion i subject to a modification is switched to another opinion i', but there are many ways of picking i'. For instance, i' can be picked uniformly at random (u.a.r.) among all opinions. Or, i' could be picked as one of the "close opinions", say, either $i + 1$ or $i - 1$ modulo k. Or, i' could be "reset" to, say, $i = 1$. In fact, there are very many alternatives, and not all enable rumor spreading and plurality consensus to be solved. One of our contributions is to characterize *noise matrices* $P = (p_{i,j})$, where $p_{i,j}$ is the probability that opinion i is switched to opinion j, for which these two problems are efficiently solvable. Similar issues arise for, e.g., redefining the majority bias into a *plurality bias*.

The technical difficulties are manifold. A key ingredient of the analysis in [19] is a fine estimate of how nodes can mitigate the impact of noise by observing the opinions of *many* other nodes, and then considering the mode of such sample. Their proof relies on the fact that for the binary opinion case, given a sample of size γ, the number of 1s and 0s in the sample sum up to γ. Even for the ternary opinion case, the additional *degree of freedom* in the sample radically changes the nature of the problem, and the impact of noise is statistically far more difficult to handle.

Also, to address the multivalued case, we had to cope with the fact that, in the uniform push model, the messages received by nodes at every round are correlated. To see why, consider an instance of the system in which a certain opinion b is held by one node only, and there is no noise at all. In one round, only one other node can receive b. It follows that if a certain node u has received b, no other nodes have received it. Thus, the messages each node receives are not independent. In [19], probability concentration results are claimed for random variables (r.v.) that depend on such messages, using Chernoff bounds. However, Chernoff bounds have been proved to hold only for random variables whose stochastic dependence belongs to a very limited class (see for example [17]). In [20], it is stated that the binary random variables on which the Chernoff bound is applied satisfy the property of being negatively 1-correlated (see Section 1.7 in [20] for a formal definition). In our analysis, we show instead how to obtain concentration of probability in this dependent setting by leveraging Poisson approximation techniques. Our approach has the following advantage: in-

[1]A series of events $\mathcal{E}_n$, $n \geq 1$, hold w.h.p. if $\Pr(\mathcal{E}_n) \geq 1 - O(1/n^c)$ for some $c > 0$.

stead of showing that the Chernoff bound can be directly applied to the specific involved random variables, we show that the execution of the given protocol, on the uniform push model, can be tightly approximated with the execution of the same protocol on a another suitable communication model, that is not affected by the stochastic correlation that affects the uniform push model.

1.3 Other Related work

By extending the work of [19], we contribute to the theoretical understanding of how communications and interactions function in biological distributed systems, from an algorithmic perspective [6, 7, 3, 2, 5, 26]. We refer the reader to [19] for a discussion on the computational aspects of biological distributed systems, an overview of the rumor spreading problem in distributed computing, as well as its biological significance in the presence of noise. In this section, we mainly discuss the previous technical contributions from the literature related to the novelty of our work, that is the extension to the case of several different opinions.

In the context of population protocol, the problem of achieving majority consensus in the binary case has been solved by employing a simple protocol called *undecided state dynamic* [5]. In the uniform push model, the binary majority consensus problem can be solved very efficiently as a consequence of a more general result about computing the median of the initial opinions [15]. Still in the uniform push model, the undecided state dynamic has been analyzed in the case of an arbitrarily large number of opinions, which may even be a function of the number of agents in the system [8]. A similar result has been obtained for another elementary protocol, so-called *3-majority dynamics*, in which, at each round, each node samples the opinion of three random nodes, and adopts the most frequent opinion among these three [9]. The 3-majority dynamics has also been shown to be fault-tolerant against an adversary that can change up to $O(\sqrt{n})$ agents at each round [15, 9]. Other works have analyzed the undecided state dynamics in asynchronous models with a constant number of opinions [16, 23, 28], and the h-majority dynamics (or slight variations of it) on different graph classes in the uniform push model [13, 1]. Note that the above protocols converge to the correct value with high probability. In [4], the tradeoff between deterministic success and convergence speed for protocols solving the binary majority consensus problem in population protocols is investigated.

A general result by Kempe et al. [25] shows how to compute a large class of functions in the uniform push model. However, their protocol requires the nodes to send slightly more complex messages than their sole current opinion, and its effectiveness heavily relies on a potential function argument that does not hold in the presence of noise.

To the best of our knowledge, we are the first considering the plurality consensus problem in the presence of noise.

2. MODEL AND FORMAL STATEMENT OF OUR RESULTS

In this section we formally define the communication model, the main definitions, the investigated problems and our contribution to them.

We do not provide a definition of what is a biologically feasible protocol, since the computational investigation with this respect is still too premature for such an attempt. As discussed in Section 1.1, intuitively we look for protocols that are simple enough to be plausible communication strategies for primitive biological system. As the reader can see in section 2.3 and 3.1, we consider a natural generalization of the protocol given in [20], which is plainly an elementary combination of sampling and majority operations.

2.1 Communication model and definition of the problems

The communication model we consider is essentially the *uniform push model* [14, 24, 29], where in each (synchronous) round each agent can send *(push)* a message to another agent chosen uniformly at random. This occurs without having the sender or the receiver learning about each other's identity. Note that it may happen that several agents push a message to the same node u at the same round. In the latter case we assume that the nodes receive them in a random order; for a detailed discussion regarding this assumption, we refer the reader to the full version [21].

We study the problems of rumor-spreading and plurality consensus. In both cases, we assume that nodes can support opinions represented by an integer in $[k] = \{1, \dots, k\}$. Additionally, there may be *undecided* nodes that do not support any opinion, which represents nodes that are not actively aware that the system has started to solve the problem; thus, undecided nodes are not allowed to send any message before receiving any of them.

- In rumor spreading, initially, one node, called the source, has an opinion $m \in \{1, \dots, k\}$, called the *correct opinion*. All the other nodes have no opinion. The objective is to design a protocol insuring that, after a certain number of communication rounds, every node has the correct opinion m.
- In plurality consensus, initially, for every $i \in \{1, \dots, k\}$, a set A_i of nodes have opinion i. The sets A_i, $i = 1, \dots, k$, are pairwise disjoint, and their union does not need to cover all nodes, i.e., there may be some *undecided* nodes with no opinion initially. The objective is to design a protocol insuring that, after a certain number of communication rounds, every node has the plurality opinion, that is, the opinion m with relative majority in the initial setting (i.e., $|A_m| > |A_j|$ for any $j \neq m$).

Observe that the rumor-spreading problem is a special case of the plurality consensus problem with $|A_m| = 1$ and $|A_j| = 0$ for any $j \neq m$.

Following the guidelines of [19], we work under two constraints:

1. We restrict ourselves to protocols in which each node can only transmit opinions, i.e., every message is an integer in $\{1, \dots, k\}$.
2. Transmissions are subject to noise, that is, for every round, and for every node u, if an opinion $i \in \{1, \dots, k\}$ is transmitted to node u during that round, then node u will receive message $j \in \{1, \dots, k\}$ with probability $p_{i,j} \geq 0$, where $\sum_{j=1}^{k} p_{i,j} = 1$.

The *noisy push model* is the uniform push model together with the previous two constraints. The probabilities $\{p_{i,j}\}_{i,j \in [k]}$

can be seen as a transition matrix, called the *noise matrix*, and denoted by $P = (p_{i,j})_{i,j \in [k]}$. The noise matrix in [19] is simply

$$P = \begin{pmatrix} \frac{1}{2} + \epsilon & \frac{1}{2} - \epsilon \\ \frac{1}{2} - \epsilon & \frac{1}{2} + \epsilon \end{pmatrix}. \quad (1)$$

2.2 Plurality bias, and majority preservation

When time proceeds, our protocols will result in the proportion of nodes with a given opinion to evolve. Note that there might be nodes who do not support any opinion at time t. As mentioned in the previous section, we call such nodes *undecided*. We denote by $a^{(t)}$ the fraction of nodes supporting any opinion at time t and we call the nodes contributing to $a^{(t)}$ *opinionated*. Consequently, the fraction of undecided nodes at time t is $1 - a^{(t)}$. Let $c_i^{(t)}$ be the fraction of opinionated nodes in the system that support opinion $i \in [k]$ at the beginning of round t, so that $\sum_{i \in [k]} c_i^{(t)} = a^{(t)}$. Let $\hat{c}_i^{(t)}$ be the fraction of opinionated nodes which receive at least one message at time $t-1$ and support opinion $i \in [k]$ at the beginning of round t. We write $\mathbf{c}^{(t)} = (c_1^{(t)}, ..., c_k^{(t)})$ to denote the *opinion distribution* of the opinions at time t. Similarly, let $\hat{\mathbf{c}}^{(t)} = (\hat{c}_1^{(t)}, ..., \hat{c}_k^{(t)})$. In particular, if every node would simply switch to the last opinion it received, then

$$\mathbb{E}[\hat{c}_i^{(t+1)} \mid \mathbf{c}^{(t)}] = \sum_{j \in [k]} \Pr[\text{received } i \mid \text{original message is } j] \cdot$$
$$\cdot \Pr[\text{original message is } j] = \sum_{j \in [k]} c_j^{(t)} \cdot p_{j,i}.$$

That is,

$$\mathbb{E}[\hat{\mathbf{c}}^{(t+1)} \mid \mathbf{c}^{(t)}] = \mathbf{c}^{(t)} \cdot P, \quad (2)$$

where P is the noise matrix. In particular, in the absence of noise, we have $P = I$ (the identity matrix), and if every node would simply copy the opinion that it just received, we had $\mathbb{E}[\hat{\mathbf{c}}^{(t+1)} \mid \mathbf{c}^{(t)}] = \mathbf{c}^{(t)}$. So, given the opinion distribution at round t, from the definition of the model it follows that the messages each node receives at round $t+1$ can equivalently be seen as being sent from a system without noise, but whose opinion distribution at round t is $\mathbf{c}^{(t)} \cdot P$.

Recall that m denotes the initially correct opinion, that is, the source's opinion in the rumor-spreading problem, and the initial plurality opinion in the plurality consensus problem. The following definition naturally extends the concept of *majority bias* in [19] to *plurality bias*.

Definition 1. Let $\delta > 0$. An opinion distribution $\mathbf{c}$ *is said to be* δ-biased toward opinion m *if $c_m - c_i \geq \delta$ for all $i \neq m$.*

In [19], each binary opinion that is transmitted between two nodes is flipped with probability at most $\frac{1}{2} - \epsilon$, with[2] $\epsilon = n^{-\frac{1}{4}+\eta}$ for an arbitrarily small $\eta > 0$. Thus, the noise is parametrized by ϵ. The smaller ϵ, the more noisy are the communications. We generalize the role of this parameter with the following definition.

Definition 2. Let $\epsilon = \epsilon(n)$ and $\delta = \delta(n)$ be positive. A noise matrix P is said to be (ϵ, δ)-majority-preserving ((ϵ, δ)-m.p.) with respect to opinion m *if, for every opinion distribution* $\mathbf{c}$ *that is δ-biased toward opinion m, we have $(\mathbf{c} \cdot P)_m - (\mathbf{c} \cdot P)_i > \epsilon\delta$ for all $i \neq m$.*

[2]For a discussion on what happens for other values of ϵ, see Appendix D of the full version [21].

In the rumor-spreading problem, as well as in the plurality consensus problem, when we say that a noise matrix is (ϵ, δ)-m.p., we implicitly mean that it is (ϵ, δ)-m.p. with respect to the initially correct opinion. We defer the discussion on the class of (ϵ, δ)-m.p. noise matrices in Section 4 (including its tightness w.r.t. theorems 1 and 2).

2.3 Our formal results

We show that a natural generalization of the protocol in [19] solves the rumor spreading problem and the plurality consensus problem for an arbitrary number of opinions k. More precisely, using the protocol which we describe in Subsection 3.1, we can establish the following two results, whose proof can be found in Section 3.

THEOREM 1. *Assume that the noise matrix P is (ϵ, δ)-m.p. with $\epsilon = \Omega(n^{-\frac{1}{4}+\eta})$ for an arbitrarily small constant $\eta > 0$ and $\delta = \Omega(\sqrt{\log n / n})$. The noisy rumor-spreading problem with k opinions can be solved in $O(\frac{\log n}{\epsilon^2})$ communication rounds, w.h.p., by a protocol using $O(\log \log n + \log \frac{1}{\epsilon})$ bits of memory at each node.*

THEOREM 2. *Let S with $|S| = \Omega(\frac{1}{\epsilon^2} \log n)$ be an initial set of nodes with opinions in $[k]$, the rest of the nodes having no opinions. Assume that the noise matrix P is (ϵ, δ)-m.p. for some $\epsilon > 0$, and that S is $\Omega(\sqrt{\log n / |S|})$-majority-biased. The noisy plurality consensus problem with k opinions can be solved in $O(\frac{\log n}{\epsilon^2})$ communication rounds, w.h.p., by a protocol using $O(\log \log n + \log \frac{1}{\epsilon})$ bits of memory at each node.*

For $k = 2$, we get the theorems in [19] from the above two theorems. Indeed, the simple 2-dimensional noise matrix of Eq. (1) is ϵ-majority-biased. Note that, as in [19], the plurality consensus algorithm requires the nodes to known the size $|S|$ of the set S of opinionated nodes.

3. THE ANALYSIS

In this section we prove Theorem 1 and Theorem 2 by generalizing the analysis of Stage 1 given in [19] and by providing a new analysis of Stage 2. Note that the proof techniques required for the generalization to arbitrary k significantly depart from those in [19] for the case $k = 2$. In particular, our approach provides a general framework to rigorously deal with many kind of stochastic dependences among messages in the uniform push model.

3.1 Definition of the Protocol

We describe a rumor spreading protocol performing in two *stages*. Each stage is decomposed into a number of *phases*, each one decomposed into a number of *rounds*. During each phase of the two stages, the nodes apply the simple rules given below.

3.1.1 The rule during each phase of Stage 1.

Nodes that already support some opinion at the beginning of the phase push their opinion at each round of the phase. Nodes that do not support any opinion at the beginning of the phase but receive at least one opinion during the phase start supporting an opinion at the end of the phase, chosen u.a.r. (counting multiplicities) from the received opinions[3].

[3]Note that, in the protocol considered in [19], the choice of each node's new opinion in both stages is based on the first

In other words, each node tries to acquire an opinion during each phase of Stage 1, and, as it eventually receives some opinions, it starts supporting one of them (chosen u.a.r.) from the beginning of the next phase. In particular, opinionated nodes never change their opinion during the entire stage.

More formally, let ϕ, β, and s be three constants satisfying $\phi > \beta > s$. The rounds of Stage 1 are grouped in $T + 2$ phases with $T = \lfloor \log(n/(2s/\epsilon^2 \log n))/\log(\beta/\epsilon^2+1) \rfloor$. Phase 0 takes $s/\epsilon^2 \log n$ rounds, phase $T+1$ takes $\phi/\epsilon^2 \log n$ rounds, and each phase j with $1 \le j \le T$ takes β/ϵ^2 rounds. We denote with τ_j the end of the last round of phase j.

Let t_u be the first time in which u receives any opinion since the beginning of the protocol (with $t_u = 0$ for the source). Let j_u be the phase of t_u, and let val(u) be an opinion chosen u.a.r. by u among those that it receives during phase j_u[4]. During the first stage of the protocol each node applies the following rule.

Rule of Stage 1. Each opinionated node u pushes opinion val(u) during each round of every phase $j = j_u + 1, ..., T + 1$.

3.1.2 *The rule during each phase of Stage 2.*

During each phase of Stage 2, every node pushes its opinion at each round of the phase. At the end of the phase, each node that received "enough" opinions takes a random sample[3] of them, and starts supporting the most frequent opinion in that sample (breaking ties u.a.r.).

More formally, the rounds of stage 2 are divided in $T' + 1$ phases with $T' = \lceil \log(\sqrt{n/\log n}) \rceil$. Each phase j, $0 \le j \le T' - 1$, has length 2ℓ with $\ell = \lceil c/\epsilon^2 \rceil$ for some large-enough constant $c > 0$, and phase T' has length $2\ell'$ with $\ell' = O(\epsilon^{-2} \log n)$. For any finite multiset A of elements in $\{1, \ldots, k\}$, and any $i \in \{1, \ldots, k\}$, let occ(i, A) be the number of occurrences of i in A, and let mode(A) $= \{i \in \{1, \ldots, k\} \mid \text{occ}(i, A) \ge \text{occ}(j, A) \text{ for every } j \in \{1, \ldots, k\}\}$. We then define maj($A$) as the most frequent value in A (breaking ties u.a.r.), i.e., maj(A) is the r.v. on $\{1, \ldots, k\}$ such that $\Pr(\text{maj}(A) = i) = \mathbb{1}_{\{i \in \text{mode}(A)\}}/|\text{mode}(A)|$. Let $R_j(u)$ be the multiset of messages received by node u during phase j. During the second stage of the protocol each node applies the following rule.

Rule of Stage 2. During each phase j of length $2L$ of Stage 2 ($L = \ell$ or ℓ'), each node u pushes its current opinion at each round of the phase, and starts drawing a random uniform sample $\mathcal{S}(u)$ of size L from $R_j(u)$. Provided $|R_j(u)| \ge L$, at the end of the phase u changes its opinion to maj($\mathcal{S}(u)$).

Let us remark that the reason we require the use of sampling in the previous rule is that at a given round a node may receive much more messages than $2L$. Thus, if the nodes were to collect all the messages they receive, some of them would need much more memory than our protocol does. Finally, observe that overall both stages 1 and 2 take $O(\frac{1}{\epsilon^2} \log n)$ rounds.

messages received. In [20], in order to relax the synchronicity assumption that nodes share a common clock, they adopt the same sample-based variant of the rule that we adopt here.

[4]Note that, in order to sample u.a.r. one of them, u does not need to collect all the opinions it receives. A natural sampling strategy such as reservoir sampling can be used.

3.2 Pushing Colored Balls into Bins

Before delving into the analysis of the protocol, we provide a framework to rigorously deal with the stochastic dependence that arises between messages in the uniform push model. Let process **O** be the process that results from the execution of the protocol of Subsection 3.1 in the uniform push model. In order to apply concentration of probability results that requires the involved random variables to be independent, we view the messages as balls, and the nodes as bins, and employ Poisson approximation techniques. More specifically, during each phase j of the protocol, let M_j be the set of messages that are sent to random nodes, and N_j be the set of messages sent *after* the noise has acted on them. (In other words, $N_j = \bigcup_u R_j(u)$). We prove that, at the end of phase j, we can equivalently assume that all the messages M_j have been sent to the nodes according to the following process.

Definition 3. The balls-into-bins process **B** associated to phase j is the two-step process in which the nodes represent bins and all messages sent in the phase represent colored balls, with each color corresponding to some opinion. Initially, balls are colored according to M_j. At the first step, each ball of color $i \in \{1, \ldots, k\}$ is re-colored with color $j \in \{1, \ldots, k\}$ with probability $p_{i,j}$, independently of the other balls. At the second step all balls are thrown to the bins u.a.r. as in a balls-into-bins experiment.

CLAIM 1. *Given the opinion distribution and the number of active nodes at the beginning of phase j, the probability distribution of the opinion distribution and the number of active nodes at the end of phase j in process* **O** *is the same as if the messages were sent according to process* **B**.

It is not hard to see that Claim 1 holds in the case of a single round. For more than one round, it is crucial to observe that the way each node u acts in the protocol depends only on the received messages $R_j(u)$, regardless of the order in which these messages are received. As an example, consider the opinion distribution in which one node has opinion 1, one other node has opinion 2, and all other nodes have opinion 3. Suppose that each node pushes its opinion for two consecutive rounds. Since, at each round, exactly one opinion 1 and exactly one opinion 2 are pushed, no node can receive two 1s during the first round and then two 2s during the second round, i.e. no node can possibly receive the sequence of messages "1,1,2,2" in this exact order. Instead, in process **B** such a sequence is possible. A formal proof of Claim 1 can be found in the full version [21].

Now, one key ingredient in our proof is to approximate process **B** using the following process **P**.

Definition 4. Given N_j, process **P** associated to phase j is the one-shot process in which each node receives a number of opinions i that is a random variable with distribution Poisson(h_i/n), where h_i is the number of messages in N_j carrying opinion i, and each Poisson random variable is independent of the others.

Now we provide some results from the theory of Poisson approximation for balls-in-bins experiments. For a nice introduction to the topic, we refer to [27].

LEMMA 1. *Let $\{X_j\}_{j \in [\tilde{n}]}$ be independent r.v. such that $X_j \sim$Poisson(λ_j). The vector $(X_1, ..., X_{\tilde{n}})$ conditional on*

$\sum_j X = \tilde{m}$ *follows a multinomial distribution with* $\tilde{m}$ *trials and probabilities* $(\frac{\lambda_1}{\sum_j \lambda_j}, ..., \frac{\lambda_{\tilde{n}}}{\sum_j \lambda_j})$.

LEMMA 2. *Consider a balls-in-bins experiment in which* h *colored balls are thrown in* n *bins, where* h_i *balls have color* i *with* $i \in \{1, ..., k\}$ *and* $\sum_i h_i = h$. *Let* $\{X_{u,i}\}_{u\in\{1,...,n\},i\in\{1,...,k\}}$ *be the number of* i*-colored balls that end up in bin* u, *let* $f(x_{1,1}, ..., x_{n,1}, x_{n,2}, ..., x_{n,n}, z_1, ..., z_n)$ *be a non-negative function with positive integer arguments* $x_{1,1}, ..., x_{n,1}, x_{n,2}, ..., x_{n,n}, z_1, ..., z_n$, *let* $\{Y_{u,i}\}_{u\in\{1,...,n\},i\in\{1,...,k\}}$ *be independent r.v. such that* $Y_{u,i} \sim$*Poisson*(h_i/n) *and let* $Z_1, ..., Z_n$ *be integer valued r.v. independent from the* $X_{u,i}$*s and* $Y_{u,i}$*s. Then*

$$\mathbb{E}\left[f\left(X_{1,1}, ..., X_{n,1}, X_{n,2}, ..., X_{n,n}, Z_1, ..., Z_n\right)\right]$$
$$\leq e^k \sqrt{\prod_i h_i}\ \mathbb{E}\left[f\left(Y_{1,1}, ..., Y_{n,1}, Y_{n,2}, ..., Y_{n,n}, Z_1, ..., Z_n\right)\right].$$

PROOF. To simplify notation, let $\bar{Z} = (Z_1, ..., Z_n)$, $\bar{X} = (X_{1,1}, ..., X_{n,1}, X_{n,2}, ..., X_{n,n})$, $\bar{Y} = (Y_{1,1}, ..., Y_{n,1}, Y_{n,2}, ..., Y_{n,n})$, $\bar{Y}_{\sum} = (\sum_{u=1}^n Y_{u,1}, ..., \sum_{u=1}^n Y_{u,k})$, $\lambda_i = h_i/n$, $\bar{\lambda} = (\lambda_1, ..., \lambda_k)$ and finally $\bar{x} = (x_1, ..., x_k)$ for any $x_1, ..., x_k$. Observe that, while $X_{u,i}$ and $X_{v,i}$ are clearly dependent, $X_{u,i}$ and $X_{v,j}$ with $i \neq j$ are stochastically independent (even if $u = v$). Indeed, the distribution of the r.v. $\{X_{u,i}\}_{u\in\{1,...,n\}}$ for each fixed i is multinomial with λ_i trials and uniform distribution on the bins. Thus, from Lemma 1 we have that $\{X_{u,i}\}_{u\in\{1,...,n\}}$ are distributed as $\{Y_{u,i}\}_{u\in\{1,...,n\}}$ conditional on $\sum_{u=1}^n Y_{u,i} = \lambda_i$, that is

$$\mathbb{E}\Big[f\left(\bar{Y}, \bar{Z}\right) \Big| \sum_{u=1}^n Y_{u,1} = \lambda_1, ..., \sum_{u=1}^n Y_{u,k} = \lambda_k\Big] = \mathbb{E}\left[f\left(\bar{X}, \bar{Z}\right)\right].$$

Therefore, we have

$$\mathbb{E}\left[f\left(\bar{Y}, \bar{Z}\right)\right] = \sum_{\bar{x}:x_1,...,x_k\geq 0} \mathbb{E}\left[f\left(\bar{Y}, \bar{Z}\right) \middle| \bar{Y}_{\sum} = \bar{x}\right] \Pr\left(\bar{Y}_{\sum} = \bar{x}\right)$$
$$\geq \mathbb{E}\left[f\left(\bar{Y}, \bar{Z}\right) \middle| \bar{Y}_{\sum} = \bar{\lambda}\right] \Pr\left(\bar{Y}_{\sum} = \bar{\lambda}\right)$$
$$= \mathbb{E}\left[f\left(\bar{X}, \bar{Z}\right)\right] \Pr\left(\bar{Y}_{\sum} = \bar{\lambda}\right)$$
$$= \mathbb{E}\left[f\left(\bar{X}, \bar{Z}\right)\right] \prod_i \frac{h_i^{h_i}}{h_i!} e^{-h_i} \geq \mathbb{E}\left[f\left(\bar{X}, \bar{Z}\right)\right] \frac{e^{-k}}{\sqrt{\prod_i h_i}},$$

where, in the last inequality, we use that, by Stirling's approximation, $a! \leq e\sqrt{a}(\frac{a}{e})^a$ for any $a > 0$. □

From Lemma 1 and Lemma 2, we get the following general result which says that if a generic event $\mathcal{E}$ holds w.h.p in process **P**, it also holds w.h.p. in process **O**.

LEMMA 3. *Given the opinion distribution and the number of active nodes at the beginning of a fixed phase* j, *let* $\mathcal{E}$ *be an event that, at the end of that phase, holds with probability at least* $1 - n^{-b}$ *in process* **P**, *for some* $b > (k \log h)/(2 \log n)$ *with* $h = \sum_i h_i$.[5] *Then, at the end of phase* j, $\mathcal{E}$ *holds w.h.p. also in process* **O**.

PROOF. Thanks to Claim 1, it suffices to prove that, at the end of phase j, $\mathcal{E}$ holds w.h.p. in process **B**. Let $\bar{\mathcal{E}}$ be the complementary event of $\mathcal{E}$. Let $h = |M_j|$ be the number of balls that are thrown in process **B** associated to phase j, where h_i balls have color i with $i \in \{1, ..., k\}$ and $\sum_i h_i = h$. Let $\{X_{u,i}\}_{u\in\{1,...,n\},i\in\{1,...,k\}}$ be the number of i-colored balls that end up in bin u, let $\{Y_{u,i}\}_{u\in\{1,...,n\},i\in\{1,...,k\}}$ be the independent r.v. of process **P** such that $Y_{u,i} \sim$Poisson(h_i/n) and let $Z_1, ..., Z_n$ be integer valued r.v. independent from the $X_{u,i}$s and $Y_{u,i}$s.

Fix any realization of N_j, i.e. any re-coloring of the balls in the first step of process **B**. By choosing f in Lemma 2 as the binary r.v. indicating whether event $\bar{\mathcal{E}}$ has occurred, where $\bar{\mathcal{E}}$ is a function of the r.v. $X_{1,1}, ..., X_{n,1}, X_{n,2}, ..., X_{n,n}, Z_1, ..., Z_n$, we get

$$\Pr\left(\bar{\mathcal{E}}\left(X_{1,1}, ..., X_{n,n}, Z_1, ..., Z_n\right) \middle| N_j\right)$$
$$\leq e^k \sqrt{\prod_i h_i}\ \Pr\left(\bar{\mathcal{E}}\left(Y_{1,1}, ..., Y_{n,n}, Z_1, ..., Z_n\right) \middle| N_j\right). \quad (3)$$

Thus, from Eq. (3), the inequality of arithmetic and geometric means and the hypotheses on the probability of $\mathcal{E}$, we get

$$\Pr\left(\bar{\mathcal{E}}\left(X_{1,1}, ..., X_{n,n}, Z_1, ..., Z_n\right) \middle| N_j\right)$$
$$\leq e^k \left(\frac{h}{k}\right)^{\frac{k}{2}} \Pr\left(\bar{\mathcal{E}}\left(Y_{1,1}, ..., Y_{n,n}, Z_1, ..., Z_n\right) \middle| N_j\right)$$

Finally, let $\mathcal{N}$ be the set of all possible realizations of N_j. By the law of total probability over $\mathcal{N}$, we get that

$$\sum_{s\in\mathcal{N}} \Pr\left(\bar{\mathcal{E}}\left(X_{1,1}, ..., X_{n,n}, Z_1, ..., Z_n\right) \middle| N_j = s\right) \Pr\left(N_j = s\right)$$
$$\leq e^k \left(\frac{h}{k}\right)^{\frac{k}{2}} \Pr\left(\bar{\mathcal{E}}\left(Y_{1,1}, ..., Y_{n,n}, Z_1, ..., Z_n\right)\right) \leq n^{-\Theta(1)},$$

where in the first inequality of the last line we used the hypotheses on the probability of $\bar{\mathcal{E}}$. □

We now analyze the two stages of our protocol, starting with Stage 1. Note that, in the following two sections, the statements about the evolution of the process refer to process **O**.

3.3 Stage 1

The rule of Stage 1 is aimed at guaranteeing that, w.h.p., the system reaches a target opinion distribution from which the rumor-spreading problem becomes an instance of the plurality consensus problem. More precisely, we have the following.

LEMMA 4. *Stage 1 takes* $O(\frac{1}{\epsilon^2}\log n)$ *rounds, after which w.h.p. all nodes are active and* $\mathbf{c}^{(\tau_T+1)}$ *is* δ*-biased toward the correct opinion, with* $\delta = \Omega(\sqrt{\log n/n})$.

PROOF. The fact that an undecided node becomes opinionated during a phase only depends on whether it gets a message during that phase, regardless of the value of such messages. Hence, the proof that, w.h.p., $a^{(\tau_T+1)} = 1$ is reduced to the analysis of the rule of Stage 1 as an information spreading process. First, by carefully exploiting the Chernoff bound and Lemma 3, we can establish Claim 2 and Claim 3 below (the proofs are given in the full version [21]).

CLAIM 2. *W.h.p., at the end of phase 0, we have*

$$s/\epsilon^2 \cdot \log n/3n \leq a^{(\tau_0)} \leq s/\epsilon^2 \log n/n.$$

[5]Note that, if N_j is not yet fixed, the parameters h_i of process **P** associated to phase j are random variables. However, if the opinion distribution and the number of active nodes at the beginning of phase j are given, then $h = \sum_i h_i = |N_j| = |M_j|$ is fixed.

CLAIM 3. *W.h.p., at the end of phase j, $1 \leq j \leq T$, we have*

$$(\beta/\epsilon^2 + 1)^j a^{(\tau_0)}/8 \leq a^{(\tau_j)} \leq (\beta/\epsilon^2 + 1)^j a^{(\tau_0)}.$$

From the previous two claims, and by the definition of T we get the following.

LEMMA 5. *W.h.p., at the end of phase T, we have $a^{(\tau_{T+1})} = \Omega((\beta/\epsilon^2 + 1)^T a^{(\tau_0)}) = \Omega(\epsilon^2)$.*

Finally, from Lemma 5, an application of the Chernoff bound gives us the following.

LEMMA 6. *W.h.p., at the end of Stage 1, all nodes are opinionated.*

As for the fact that, w.h.p., $\mathbf{c}^{(\tau+1)}$ is a δ-biased opinion distribution with $\delta = \Omega(\sqrt{\log n/n})$, we can prove the following.

LEMMA 7. *W.h.p., at the end of each phase j of Stage 1, we have an $(\epsilon/2)^j$-biased opinion distribution.*

PROOF. We prove the lemma by induction on the phase number. The case $j = 1$ is a direct application of the Chernoff bound (see Lemma 16 in the full version [21]) to $c_m^{(\tau_1)} - c_i^{(\tau_1)}$ $(i \neq m)$, where the number of opinionated nodes is given by Claim 2, and, where the independence of the r.v. follows from the fact that each node that becomes opinionated in the first phase has necessarily received the messages from the source-node. Now, suppose that the lemma holds up to phase $j - 1 \leq T$. Let $S_j = \{u | \, j_u = j\}$ be the set of nodes that become opinionated during phase j. Recall the definition of M_j and N_j from Subsection 3.2, and observe that $|M_j| = |N_j| = (\tau_j - \tau_{j-1})\, n \cdot a^{(\tau_{j-1})}$, and that the number of times opinion i occurs in M_j is $|M_j|\, c_i^{(\tau_{j-1})}$. Let us identify each message in M_j with a distinct number in $1, ..., |M_j|$, and let $\{X_w(i)\}_{w \in \{1,...,|M_j|\}}$ be the binary r.v. such that $X_w(i) = 1$ if and only if w is i after the action of the noise. The frequency of opinion i in N_j is $\frac{1}{|N_j|}\sum_{w=1}^{|N_j|} X_w(i)$.

Thanks to Lemma 3, it suffices to prove the lemma for process $\mathbf{P}$. By definition, in process $\mathbf{P}$, for each i, the number of messages with opinion i that each node receives conditional on N_j follows a Poisson($\frac{1}{n}\sum_{w=1}^{|N_j|} X_w(i)$) distribution. Each node u that becomes opinionated during phase j gets at least one message during the phase. Thus, from Lemma 1, the probability that u gets opinion i conditional on N_j is

$$\frac{\sum_{w=1}^{|N_j|} X_w(i)}{\sum_{i=1}^{k}\sum_{w=1}^{|N_j|} X_w(i)} = \frac{1}{|N_j|}\sum_{w=1}^{|N_j|} X_w(i).$$

Since opinionated nodes never change opinion during Stage 1, the bias of $\mathbf{c}^{(\tau_j)}$ is at least the minimum between the bias of $\mathbf{c}^{(\tau_{j-1})}$ and the bias among the newly opinionated nodes in S_j. Hence, we can apply the Chernoff bound to the nodes in S_j to prove that the bias at the end of phase j is, w.h.p.[6],

$$\Pr\left(c_m^{(\tau_j)} - c_i^{(\tau_j)} | N_j\right) \geq \frac{1-\tilde{\delta}_j}{|N_j|}\sum_{w=1}^{|N_j|}\left(X_w(m) - X_w(i)\right), \quad (4)$$

where $\tilde{\delta}_j = O(\sqrt{\log n/|S_j|})$.

Moreover, note that

$$\mathbb{E}\Big[\frac{1}{|N_j|}\sum_{w=1}^{|N_j|} X_w(i) \,\Big|\, \mathbf{c}^{(\tau_{j-1})}, a^{(\tau_{j-1})}\Big] = \left(\mathbf{c}^{(\tau_{j-1})} \cdot P\right)_i.$$

Furthermore, (conditional on $\mathbf{c}^{(\tau_{j-1})}$ and $a^{(\tau_{j-1})}$) the r.v. $\{X_w(i)\}_{w \in \{1,...,|N_j|\}}$ are independent. Thus, for each $i \neq m$, from Claim 3, and by applying the Chernoff bound on $\sum_{w=1}^{|N_j|} X_w(m)$, and on $\sum_{w=1}^{|N_j|} X_w(i)$, we get that w.h.p.

$$\frac{1}{|N_j|}\sum_{w=1}^{|N_j|}\left(X_w(m) - X_w(i)\right) \geq (1-\delta_j)\, 2^{-j+1}\epsilon^j, \quad (5)$$

where $\delta_j = O(\sqrt{\log n/|N_j|})$.

From Claim 2 and Claim 3, it follows that $\tilde{\delta}_j, \delta_j \leq \frac{1}{4}$ w.h.p. Thus by putting together Eq. (4) and (5) via the chain rule, we get that w.h.p.

$$c_m^{(\tau_j)} - c_i^{(\tau_j)} \geq \left(1 - \tilde{\delta}_j\right)(1-\delta_j)\, 2^{-j+1}\epsilon^j \geq \left(\frac{\epsilon}{2}\right)^j,$$

concluding the proof. □

Lemma 7 implies that, w.h.p., we get a bias $\epsilon^{T+2} = \Omega(\sqrt{\log n/n})$ at the end of Stage 1, which completes the proof of Lemma 4.

3.4 Stage 2

As proved in the previous section, w.h.p., all nodes are opinionated at the end of Stage 1, and the final opinion distribution is $\Omega(\sqrt{\log n/n})$-biased. Now, we have that the rumor-spreading problem is reduced to an instance of the plurality consensus problem. The purpose of Stage 2 is to progressively amplify the initial bias until all nodes support the plurality opinion, i.e. the opinion originally held by the source node.

During the first T' phases, it is not hard to see that, by taking c large enough, a fraction arbitrarily close to 1 of the nodes receives at least ℓ messages, w.h.p. Each node u in such fraction changes its opinion at the end of the phase. With a slight abuse of notation, let $\mathrm{maj}_\ell(u) = \mathrm{maj}(\mathcal{S}(u))$ be u's new opinion based on the $\ell = |\mathcal{S}(u)|$ randomly sampled received messages. We show that, w.h.p., these new opinions increase the bias of the opinion distribution toward the plurality opinion by a constant factor > 1.

For the sake of simplicity, we assume that ℓ is odd (see Appendix C of the full version [21] for details on how to remove this assumption).

PROPOSITION 1. *Suppose that, at the beginning of phase j of Stage 2 with $0 \leq j \leq T' - 1$, the opinion distribution is δ-biased toward m. In process $\mathbf{P}$, if a node u changes its opinion at the end of the phase, then, for any $i \neq m$, we have*

$$\Pr\left(\mathrm{maj}_\ell(u) = m\right) - \Pr\left(\mathrm{maj}_\ell(u) = i\right) \geq \sqrt{\frac{2\ell}{\pi}}\frac{g(\delta,\ell)}{e^{(k-2)\ln 4}}, \quad (6)$$

[6] We remark that Eq. (4) concerns the value of $\Pr(c_m^{(\tau_j)} - c_i^{(\tau_j)} | N_j)$, which is a random variable.

where

$$g(\delta,\ell)=\begin{cases}\delta(1-\delta^2)^{\frac{\ell-1}{2}} & \text{if } \delta<\frac{1}{\sqrt{\ell}},\\ \sqrt{1/\ell}\,(1-\sqrt{1/\ell})^{\frac{\ell-1}{2}} & \text{if } \delta\geq\frac{1}{\sqrt{\ell}}.\end{cases}$$

First, we prove Eq. (6) for $k=2$. We then obtain the general case by induction. The proof for $k=2$ is based on a known relation between the cumulative distribution function of the binomial distribution, and the cumulative distribution function of the beta distribution. This relation is given by the following lemma.

LEMMA 8. *Given $p\in(0,1)$ and $0\leq j\leq\ell$ it holds*

$$\sum_{j<i\leq\ell}\binom{\ell}{i}p^i(1-p)^{\ell-i}$$
$$=\binom{\ell}{j+1}(j+1)\int_0^p z^j(1-z)^{\ell-j-1}\,dz. \quad (7)$$

Lemma 8 allows us to express the survival function of a binomial sample as an integral. Thanks to it, we can prove Proposition 1 when $k=2$.

LEMMA 9. *Let $\mathbf{c}=(c_1,c_2)$ be a δ-biased opinion distribution during Stage 2. In process $\mathbf{P}$, for any node u, we have* $\Pr(\mathrm{maj}_\ell(u)=m)-\Pr(\mathrm{maj}_\ell(u)=3-m)\geq\sqrt{2\ell/\pi}\cdot g(\delta,\ell)$.

PROOF. Without loss of generality, let $m=1$. Let $X_1^{(\ell)}$ be a r.v. with distribution $Bin(\ell,p_1)$, and let $X_2^{(\ell)}=\ell-X_1^{(\ell)}$. By using Lemma 8, we get

$$\Pr(\mathrm{maj}_\ell(u)=1)-\Pr(\mathrm{maj}_\ell(u)=2)$$
$$=\sum_{\lceil\frac{\ell}{2}\rceil\leq i\leq\ell}\binom{\ell}{i}p_1^ip_2^{\ell-i}-\sum_{\lceil\frac{\ell}{2}\rceil\leq i\leq\ell}\binom{\ell}{i}p_1^{\ell-i}p_2^i$$
$$=\sum_{\lceil\frac{\ell}{2}\rceil\leq i\leq\ell}\binom{\ell}{i}p_1^i(1-p_1)^{\ell-i}-\sum_{\lceil\frac{\ell}{2}\rceil\leq i\leq\ell}\binom{\ell}{i}p_1^{\ell-i}(1-p_1)^i$$
$$=\binom{\ell}{\lceil\frac{\ell}{2}\rceil}\left\lceil\frac{\ell}{2}\right\rceil\left(\int_0^{p_1}z^{\lfloor\frac{\ell}{2}\rfloor}(1-z)^{\lfloor\frac{\ell}{2}\rfloor}dz\right.$$
$$\left.-\int_0^{p_2}z^{\lfloor\frac{\ell}{2}\rfloor}(1-z)^{\lfloor\frac{\ell}{2}\rfloor}dz\right).$$

By setting $t=z-\frac{1}{2}$, and rewriting $p_1=\frac{p_1-p_2}{2}+\frac{1}{2}$ and $p_2=\frac{p_2-p_1}{2}+\frac{1}{2}$ we obtain

$$\Pr(\mathrm{maj}_\ell(u)=1)-\Pr(\mathrm{maj}_\ell(u)=2)$$
$$=\binom{\ell}{\lceil\frac{\ell}{2}\rceil}\left\lceil\frac{\ell}{2}\right\rceil\left(\int_0^{p_1}z^{\lfloor\frac{\ell}{2}\rfloor}(1-z)^{\lfloor\frac{\ell}{2}\rfloor}dz\right.$$
$$\left.-\int_0^{p_2}z^{\lfloor\frac{\ell}{2}\rfloor}(1-z)^{\lfloor\frac{\ell}{2}\rfloor}dz\right)$$
$$=\binom{\ell}{\lceil\frac{\ell}{2}\rceil}\left\lceil\frac{\ell}{2}\right\rceil\left(\int_{-\frac{1}{2}}^{\frac{p_1-p_2}{2}}\left(\frac{1}{4}-t^2\right)^{\lfloor\frac{\ell}{2}\rfloor}dt\right.$$
$$\left.-\int_{-\frac{1}{2}}^{\frac{-p_1-p_2}{2}}\left(\frac{1}{4}-t^2\right)^{\lfloor\frac{\ell}{2}\rfloor}dt\right)$$
$$=\binom{\ell}{\lceil\frac{\ell}{2}\rceil}\left\lceil\frac{\ell}{2}\right\rceil\int_{-\frac{p_1-p_2}{2}}^{\frac{p_1-p_2}{2}}\left(\frac{1}{4}-t^2\right)^{\lfloor\frac{\ell}{2}\rfloor}dt.$$

For any $t\in(-\frac{y}{2},\frac{y}{2})\subseteq(-\frac{p_1-p_2}{2},\frac{p_1-p_2}{2})$, it holds $(\frac{1}{4}-t^2)^{\lfloor\frac{\ell}{2}\rfloor}\geq(\frac{1-y^2}{4})^{\lfloor\frac{\ell}{2}\rfloor}$. Thus, for any $y\in(-p_1+p_2,p_1-p_2)$ we have

$$\int_{-\frac{p_1-p_2}{2}}^{\frac{p_1-p_2}{2}}\left(\frac{1}{4}-t^2\right)^{\lfloor\frac{\ell}{2}\rfloor}dt\geq y\left(\frac{1-y^2}{4}\right)^{\lfloor\frac{\ell}{2}\rfloor}. \quad (8)$$

The r.h.s. of Eq. (8) is maximized w.r.t. $y\in(-p_1+p_2,p_1-p_2)$ when $y=\min\{p_1-p_2,(2\lfloor\frac{\ell}{2}\rfloor+1)^{-\frac{1}{2}}\}=\min\{p_1-p_2,\frac{1}{\sqrt{\ell}}\}$. Hence, for $p_1-p_2<\frac{1}{\sqrt{\ell}}$, we get

$$\int_{-\frac{p_1-p_2}{2}}^{\frac{p_1-p_2}{2}}\left(\frac{1}{4}-t^2\right)^{\lfloor\frac{\ell}{2}\rfloor}dt\geq(p_1-p_2)\left(\frac{1-(p_1-p_2)^2}{4}\right)^{\lfloor\frac{\ell}{2}\rfloor}$$
$$=2^{-\ell+1}(p_1-p_2)\left(1-(p_1-p_2)^2\right)^{\frac{\ell-1}{2}}=2^{-\ell+1}g(p_1-p_2,\ell).$$

For $p_1-p_2\geq\frac{1}{\sqrt{\ell}}$ we get

$$\int_{-\frac{p_1-p_2}{2}}^{\frac{p_1-p_2}{2}}\left(\frac{1}{4}-t^2\right)^{\lfloor\frac{\ell}{2}\rfloor}dt$$
$$\geq\frac{2^{-\ell+1}}{\sqrt{\ell}}\left(1-\frac{1}{\ell}\right)^{\frac{\ell-1}{2}}=2^{-\ell+1}g(p_1-p_2,\ell).$$

Thus, by using the fact that g is a non-decreasing function w.r.t. its first argument, we obtain

$$\Pr(\mathrm{maj}_\ell(u)=1)-\Pr(\mathrm{maj}_\ell(u)=2)$$
$$\geq\binom{\ell}{\lceil\frac{\ell}{2}\rceil}\left\lceil\frac{\ell}{2}\right\rceil2^{-\ell+1}g(\delta,\ell).$$

Finally, by using the bounds $\binom{2r}{r}\geq\frac{2^{2r}}{\sqrt{\pi r}}e^{\frac{1}{9r}}$ (see Lemma 13 in the full version [21]),and $e^x\geq1-x$ together with the identity[7]

$$\binom{\ell}{\lceil\frac{\ell}{2}\rceil}\left\lceil\frac{\ell}{2}\right\rceil=\binom{\ell}{\frac{\ell+1}{2}}\frac{\ell+1}{2}=\binom{\ell-1}{\frac{\ell-1}{2}}\ell,$$

we get

$$\Pr(\mathrm{maj}_\ell(u)=1)-\Pr(\mathrm{maj}_\ell(u)=2)$$
$$\geq\binom{\ell}{\lceil\frac{\ell}{2}\rceil}\left\lceil\frac{\ell}{2}\right\rceil2^{-\ell+1}g(\delta,\ell)\geq\frac{2^{\ell-1}}{\sqrt{\pi\frac{\ell-1}{2}}}e^{\frac{2}{9(\ell-1)}}\ell\,2^{-\ell+1}g(\delta,\ell)$$
$$\geq\sqrt{\frac{2\ell}{\pi}}\left(1-\frac{2}{9(\ell-1)}\right)\left(1-\frac{1}{\ell}\right)^{-\frac{1}{2}}g(\delta,\ell)\geq\sqrt{\frac{2\ell}{\pi}}g(\delta,\ell),$$

concluding the proof. □

Next we show how to lower bound the above difference with a much simpler expression.

LEMMA 10. *In process $\mathbf{P}$, during Stage 2, for any node u*

$$\Pr(\mathrm{maj}_\ell(u)=m)-\Pr(\mathrm{maj}_\ell(u)=3-m)$$
$$\geq\Pr(X_1^{(\ell)}>X_2^{(\ell)},\ldots,X_k^{(\ell)})$$
$$-\Pr(X_i^{(\ell)}>X_1^{(\ell)},\ldots,X_{i-1}^{(\ell)},X_{i+1}^{(\ell)},\ldots,X_k^{(\ell)}),$$

where $\bar{X}^{(\ell)}=(X_1^{(\ell)},\ldots,X_k^{(\ell)})$ follows a multinomial distribution with ℓ trials and probability distribution $\mathbf{c}\cdot P$.

[7]Recall that we are assuming that ℓ is odd.

Intuitively, Lemma 10 (whose proof is deferred in the full version [21]) says that the set of events in which a tie occurs among the most frequent opinions in the node's sample of observed messages does not favor the probability that the node picks the wrong opinion. Thus, by avoiding considering those events, we get a lower bound on $\Pr(\text{maj}_\ell(u) = 1) - \Pr(\text{maj}_\ell(u) = i)$.

Thanks to Lemma 10, the proof of Eq. (6) reduces to proving the following:

LEMMA 11. *For any fixed k, and with $\bar{X}$ defined as in Lemma 10, we have*

$$\begin{aligned}&\Pr(X_1^{(\ell)} > X_2^{(\ell)}, ..., X_k^{(\ell)}) \\ &\quad - \Pr(X_i^{(\ell)} > X_1^{(\ell)}, ..., X_{i-1}^{(\ell)}, X_{i+1}^{(\ell)}, ..., X_k^{(\ell)}) \\ &\geq \sqrt{2\ell/\pi}\, \frac{g(\delta, \ell)}{4^{k-2}}. \end{aligned} \tag{9}$$

Lemma 11 can be proved by an inductive argument based on Lemma 9 (see the full version [21]), concluding the proof of Proposition 1.

By using Proposition 1, we can then prove Lemma 12 (see the full version [21]).

LEMMA 12. *W.h.p., at the end of Stage 2, all nodes support the initial plurality opinion.*

Finally, the time efficiency claimed in Theorem 1 and Theorem 2 directly follows from Lemma 12, while the required memory follows from the fact that in each phase each node needs only to count how many times it has received each opinion, i.e. to count up to at most $O(\frac{1}{\epsilon^2} \log n)$ w.h.p.

4. ON THE NOTION OF (ϵ, δ)-MAJORITY-PRESERVING MATRIX

In this section we discuss the notion of (ϵ, δ)-m.p. noise matrix introduced by Definition 2. Let us consider Eq. (2). The matrix P represents the "perturbation" introduced by the noise, and so $(\mathbf{c} \cdot P)_m - (\mathbf{c} \cdot P)_i$ measures how much information the system is losing about the correct opinion m, in a single communication round. An (ϵ, δ)-m.p. noise matrix is a noise matrix that preserves at least an ϵ fraction of bias, provided the initial bias is at least δ. The (ϵ, δ)-m.p. property essentially characterizes the amount of noise beyond which some coordination problems cannot be solved without further hypotheses on the nodes' knowledge of the matrix P. To see why this is the case, consider an (ϵ, δ)-m.p. noise matrix for which there is a δ-biased opinion distribution $\tilde{\mathbf{c}}$ such that $(\tilde{\mathbf{c}} \cdot P)_m - (\tilde{\mathbf{c}} \cdot P)_i < 0$ for some opinion i. Given opinion distribution $\tilde{\mathbf{c}}$, *from each node's perspective, opinion m does not appear to be the most frequent opinion.* Indeed, the messages that are received are more likely to be i than m. Thus, plurality consensus cannot be solved from opinion distribution $\tilde{\mathbf{c}}$.

Observe that verifying whether a given matrix P is (ϵ, δ)-m.p. with respect to opinion m consists in checking whether for each $i \neq m$ the value of the following linear program is at least $\epsilon\delta$:

$$\begin{aligned} &\text{maximize } (P \cdot \mathbf{c})_m - (P \cdot \mathbf{c})_i \\ &\text{subject to } \sum_j c_j = 1, \\ &\qquad \text{and } \forall j,\ c_j \geq 0, c_m - c_j - \delta \geq 0. \end{aligned}$$

We now provide some negative and positive examples of (ϵ, δ)-m.p. noise matrices. First, we note that a natural matrix property such as being diagonally dominant does not imply that the matrix is (ϵ, δ)-m.p. For example, by multiplying the following diagonally dominant matrix by the δ-biased opinion distribution $\mathbf{c} = (1/2 + \delta, 1/2 - \delta, 0)^\intercal$, we see that it does not even preserve the majority opinion at all when $\epsilon, \delta < 1/6$:

$$\begin{pmatrix} \frac{1}{2} + \epsilon & 0 & \frac{1}{2} - \epsilon \\ \frac{1}{2} - \epsilon & \frac{1}{2} + \epsilon & 0 \\ 0 & \frac{1}{2} - \epsilon & \frac{1}{2} + \epsilon \end{pmatrix}.$$

On the other hand, the following natural generalization of the noise matrix in [19] (see Eq. (1)), is (ϵ, δ)-m.p. for every $\delta > 0$ with respect to any opinion:

$$(P)_{i,j} = p_{i,j} = \begin{cases} \frac{1}{k} + \epsilon & \text{if } i = j, \\ \frac{1}{k} - \frac{\epsilon}{k-1} & \text{otherwise.} \end{cases}$$

More generally, let P be a noise matrix such that

$$(P)_{i,j} = \begin{cases} p & \text{if } i = j, \\ q_l \leq q_{i,j} \leq q_u & \text{otherwise,} \end{cases} \tag{10}$$

for some positive numbers p, q_u and q_l. Since

$$\begin{aligned} &(P\mathbf{c})_m - (P\mathbf{c})_i = pc_m + \sum_{j \neq m} q_{j,m} c_j - pc_i - \sum_{j \neq i} q_{j,i} c_j \\ &\geq p(c_m - c_i) + \sum_{j \neq m} q_l c_j - \sum_{j \neq i} q_u c_j \\ &\geq p(c_m - c_i) + q_l(1 - c_m) - q_u(1 - c_i) \\ &\geq (p - q_u)(c_m - c_i) - (q_u - q_l) \\ &\geq (p - q_u)\delta - (q_u - q_l). \end{aligned} \tag{11}$$

By defining $\epsilon = (p - q_u)/2$, we get that the last line in Eq. (11) is greater than $\epsilon\delta$ iff $(p - q_u)\delta/2 \geq (q_u - q_l)$, which gives a sufficient condition for any matrix of the form given in Eq. (10) for being (ϵ, δ)-m.p.

5. CONCLUSION

In this paper, we solved the general version of rumor spreading and plurality consensus in biological systems. That is, we have solved these problems for an arbitrarily large number k of opinions. We are not aware of realistic biological contexts in which the number of opinions might be a function of the number n of individuals. Nevertheless, it could be interesting, at least from a conceptual point to view, to address rumor spreading and plurality consensus in a scenario in which the number of opinions varies with n. This appears to be a technically challenging problem. Indeed, extending the results in the extended abstract of [20] from 2 opinions to any constant number k of opinions already required to use complex tools. Yet, several of these tools do not apply if k depends on n. This is typically the case of Proposition 1. We let as an open problem the design of stochastic tools enabling to handle the scenario where $k = k(n)$.

6. ACKNOWLEDGMENTS

We thank the anonymous reviewers of an earlier version of this work for their constructive criticisms and comments, which were of great help in improving the results and their presentation.

7. REFERENCES

[1] M. A. Abdullah and M. Draief. Global majority consensus by local majority polling on graphs of a given degree sequence. *Discrete Applied Mathematics*, 180:1–10, 2015.

[2] Y. Afek, N. Alon, Z. Bar-Joseph, A. Cornejo, B. Haeupler, and F. Kuhn. Beeping a maximal independent set. *Distributed computing*, 26(4):195–208, 2013.

[3] Y. Afek, N. Alon, O. Barad, N. Barkai, Z. Bar-Joseph, and E. Hornstein. A biological solution to a fundamental distributed computing problem. *Science*, 331(6014):183–185, 2011.

[4] D. Alistarh, R. Gelashvili, and M. Vojnović. Fast and exact majority in population protocols. In *Proceedings of the 35th ACM Symposium on Principles of Distributed Computing*, pages 47–56. ACM, 2015.

[5] D. Angluin, J. Aspnes, and D. Eisenstat. A simple population protocol for fast robust approximate majority. *Distributed Computing*, 21(2):87–102, 2008.

[6] D. Angluin, J. Aspnes, D. Eisenstat, and E. Ruppert. The computational power of population protocols. *Distributed Computing*, 20(4):279–304, 2007.

[7] J. Aspnes and E. Ruppert. An introduction to population protocols. In *Middleware for Network Eccentric and Mobile Applications*, pages 97–120. Springer, 2009.

[8] L. Becchetti, A. Clementi, E. Natale, F. Pasquale, and R. Silvestri. Plurality consensus in the gossip model. In *Proceedings of the 26th Annual ACM-SIAM Symposium on Discrete Algorithms*, pages 371–390. SIAM, 2015.

[9] L. Becchetti, A. Clementi, E. Natale, F. Pasquale, R. Silvestri, and L. Trevisan. Simple dynamics for plurality consensus. In *Proceedings of the 26th ACM Symposium on Parallelism in Algorithms and Architectures*, pages 247–256. ACM, 2014.

[10] O. Ben-Shahar, S. Dolev, A. Dolgin, and M. Segal. Direction election in flocking swarms. In *Proceedings of the 6th International Workshop on Foundations of Mobile Computing*, pages 73–80. ACM, 2010.

[11] L. Cardelli and A. Csikász-Nagy. The cell cycle switch computes approximate majority. *Scientific Reports*, 2:656–656, 2011.

[12] B. Chazelle. Natural algorithms. In *Proceedings of the 20th Annual ACM-SIAM Symposium on Discrete Algorithms*, pages 422–431. SIAM, 2009.

[13] C. Cooper, R. Elsässer, and T. Radzik. The power of two choices in distributed voting. In *Automata, Languages, and Programming*, volume 8573 of *Lecture Notes in Computer Science*, pages 435–446. Springer, 2014.

[14] A. Demers, D. Greene, C. Hauser, W. Irish, J. Larson, S. Shenker, H. Sturgis, D. Swinehart, and D. Terry. Epidemic algorithms for replicated database maintenance. In *Proceedings of the 6th Annual ACM Symposium on Principles of Distributed Computing*, pages 1–12. ACM, 1987.

[15] B. Doerr, L. A. Goldberg, L. Minder, T. Sauerwald, and C. Scheideler. Stabilizing consensus with the power of two choices. In *Proceedings of the 23th annual ACM symposium on Parallelism in algorithms and architectures*, pages 149–158. ACM, 2011.

[16] M. Draief and M. Vojnovic. Convergence speed of binary interval consensus. *SIAM J. on Control and Optimization*, 50(3):1087–1109, 2012.

[17] D. P. Dubhashi and A. Panconesi. *Concentration of measure for the analysis of randomized algorithms*. Cambridge University Press, 2009.

[18] A. El Gamal and Y.-H. Kim. *Network information theory*. Cambridge University Press, 2011.

[19] O. Feinerman, B. Haeupler, and A. Korman. Breathe before speaking: Efficient information dissemination despite noisy, limited and anonymous communication. In *Proceedings of the 34th ACM Symposium on Principles of Distributed Computing*, pages 114–123. ACM, 2014. Extended abstract of [19].

[20] O. Feinerman, B. Haeupler, and A. Korman. Breathe before speaking: Efficient information dissemination despite noisy, limited and anonymous communication. *Distributed Computing*, pages 1–17, 2015.

[21] P. Fraigniaud and E. Natale. Noisy Rumor Spreading and Plurality Consensus. *arXiv preprint arXiv:1507.05796v5*, 2015.

[22] N. R. Franks, S. C. Pratt, E. B. Mallon, N. F. Britton, and D. J. Sumpter. Information flow, opinion polling and collective intelligence in house–hunting social insects. *Philosophical Transactions of the Royal Society of London B: Biological Sciences*, 357(1427):1567–1583, 2002.

[23] K. Jung, B. Y. Kim, and M. Vojnović. Distributed ranking in networks with limited memory and communication. In *Proceedings of the 2012 IEEE International Symposium on Information Theory*, pages 980–984. IEEE, 2012.

[24] R. Karp, C. Schindelhauer, S. Shenker, and B. Vocking. Randomized rumor spreading. In *Proceedings of the 41st Annual Symposium on Foundations of Computer Science*, pages 565–574. IEEE, 2000.

[25] D. Kempe, A. Dobra, and J. Gehrke. Gossip-based computation of aggregate information. In *Proceedings of the 44st Annual Symposium on Foundations of Computer Science*, pages 482–491. IEEE, 2003.

[26] A. Korman, E. Greenwald, and O. Feinerman. Confidence sharing: an economic strategy for efficient information flows in animal groups. *PLoS computational biology*, 10(10):e1003862–e1003862, 2014.

[27] M. Mitzenmacher and E. Upfal. *Probability and Computing: Randomized Algorithms and Probabilistic Analysis*. Cambridge University Press, 2005.

[28] E. Perron, D. Vasudevan, and M. Vojnovic. Using three states for binary consensus on complete graphs. In *Proc. of 28th IEEE INFOCOM*, 2009.

[29] B. Pittel. On spreading a rumor. *SIAM J. Appl. Math.*, 47(1):213–223, Mar. 1987.

[30] H. Robbins. A remark on stirling's formula. *American Mathematical Monthly*, pages 26–29, 1955.

[31] D. J. Sumpter, J. Krause, R. James, I. D. Couzin, and A. J. Ward. Consensus decision making by fish. *Current Biology*, 18(22):1773–1777, 2008.

Rational Consensus: Extended Abstract

Joseph Y. Halpern
Cornell University
halpern@cs.cornell.edu

Xavier Vilaça
INESC-ID Instituto Superior Técnico
Universidade de Lisboa
xvilaca@gsd.inesc-id.pt

ABSTRACT

We provide a game-theoretic analysis of consensus, assuming that processes are controlled by rational agents and may fail by crashing. We consider agents that *care only about consensus*: that is, (a) an agent's utility depends only on the consensus value achieved (and not, for example, on the number of messages the agent sends) and (b) agents strictly prefer reaching consensus to not reaching consensus. We show that, under these assumptions, there is no *ex post Nash Equilibrium*, even with only one failure. Roughly speaking, this means that there must always exist a *failure pattern* (a description of who fails, when they fail, and which agents they do not send messages to in the round that they fail) and initial preferences for which an agent can gain by deviating. On the other hand, if we assume that there is a distribution π on the failure patterns and initial preferences, then under minimal assumptions on π, there is a Nash equilibrium that tolerates f failures (i.e., π puts probability 1 on there being at most f failures) if $f+1 < n$ (where n is the total number of agents). Moreover, we show that a slight extension of the Nash equilibrium strategy is also a *sequential* equilibrium (under the same assumptions about the distribution π).

Keywords

Consensus; Game Theory; Crash Failures

1. Introduction

Consensus is a fundamental problem in distributed computing; it plays a key role in state machine replication, transaction commitment, and many other tasks where agreement among processes is required. It is well known that consensus cannot be deterministically achieved in asynchronous systems [9], but can be achieved in synchronous systems even if we allow Byzantine failures (see, e.g., [16]). The assumption in all these solutions is that the reason that processes do not follow the protocol is that they have been taken over by some adversary.

PODC'16 July 25–28, 2016, Chicago, IL, USA

ISBN 978-1-4503-3964-3/16/07...$15.00

DOI: http://dx.doi.org/10.1145/2933057.2933088

There has been a great deal of interest recently in viewing at least some of the processes as being under the control of rational agents, who try to influence outcomes in a way that promotes their self interest. Halpern and Teague [13] were perhaps the first to do this. Their focus was on secret sharing and multiparty computation. Following [2, 3, 6, 12], we are interested in applying these ideas to standard problems in game theory. And like [1, 4, 6], we are interested in what happens when there is a mix of rational and faulty agents. For the purposes of this paper, we restrict to crash failures. As we shall see, a number of subtle issues arise even in this relatively simple setting.

We focus on the *fair* consensus problem, where fairness means that the input of every agent is selected with equal probability. Fairness seems critical in applications where we do not want agents to be able to influence an outcome unduly. For instance, when agents must decide whether to commit or abort a transaction, it is useful to ensure that the outcome reflects the preferences of the agents, so that if a majority of agents prefers a particular outcome, it is selected with higher probability. Abraham, Dolev and Halpern [2] present a protocol for fair leader election that even tolerates coalitions of rational agents. That is, in equilibrium, a leader is elected, and each agent is elected with equal probability. Fair leader election can be used to solve fair consensus (for example, once a leader is elected, the consensus value can be taken to be the leader's value). However, the protocol of [2] assumes that there are no faulty agents. Groce et al. [12] directly provide protocols for consensus with rational agents, but again, they do not consider faulty agents and do not require fairness. Afek et al. [3] and Bei, Chen, and Zhang [6] provide protocols for consensus with crash failures and rational agents. However, Afek et al.'s protocol works only under strong assumptions about agents' preferences, such as an agent having a strict preference for outcomes where it learns the input of other agents, while Bei, Chen, and Zhang require that their protocol be robust to deviations (that is, it achieves agreement even if rational agents deviate), a requirement that we view as unreasonably strong (see Section 3). Neither of these protocols satisfy the fairness requirement. Moreover, the protocol proposed by Afek et al. is not even an equilibrium if some agent knows the input of other agents. As we show, this is not an accident.

To explain our result, we need to briefly recall the standard notion of *ex post Nash equilibrium*. In a setting where we have an adversary, a protocol is an ex post equilibrium if no agent has any incentive to deviate no matter what the adversary does. Formally, "no matter what the adversary does" is captured by saying that even if we fix the adversary's choice (so that the agents essentially know what the adversary does), agents have no incentive to deviate. Abraham, Dolev, and Halpern [2] provide protocols for leader election (and hence consensus) that achieve ex post Nash equilibrium if there are no failures. Here, we show that even in synchronous systems, there is no consensus protocol that is an ex post Nash equilibrium if there can be even one crash failure.

In the case of crash failures, the adversary can be viewed as choosing two things: the *failure pattern*—which agents fail, when they fail, and which other agents they send a message to in the round that they fail, and the *initial configuration*—what the initial preference of each of the agents is. Roughly speaking, the reason that we cannot obtain an ex post Nash equilibrium is that if the failure pattern and initial configuration have a specific form, a rational agent i can take advantage of knowing this to increase the probability of obtaining consensus on its preferred value.

There might seem to be an inconsistency here. It is well known that we can achieve consensus in synchronous systems with crash failures, so it seems that we shouldn't have any difficulty dealing with one possibly faulty agent and one rational agent who does not follow the protocol. After all, we can view a rational agent who deviates from the protocol as a faulty agent. But there is no contradiction. When the agent deviates from the purported equilibrium, consensus is still reached, just on a different value. That is, a rational agent may want to deviate so as to bias the decision, although a consensus is still reached.

To get around our impossibility result, rather than trying to achieve ex post Nash equilibrium, we assume that there is some distribution π on *contexts*: pairs $(F, \vec{v})$ consisting of a failure pattern F and an initial configuration $\vec{v}$. We show that under appropriate assumptions about π, if agents *care only about consensus*—specifically, if (a) an agent's utility depends only on the consensus value achieved (and not, for example, on the number of messages the agent sends) and (b) agents strictly prefer reaching consensus to not reaching consensus—then there is a Nash equilibrium that tolerates up to f failures, as long as $f + 1 < n$, where n is the total number of agents. Specifically, we make two assumptions about π, namely, we assume that π *supports reachability* and is *uniform*. Roughly speaking, we say that π supports reachability if it attributes small probability to particular failure patterns that prevent information from one agent reaching an agent that has not crashed by the end of the protocol; we say that π is uniform if it attributes equal probability to equivalent failures of different agents. We believe that these assumptions apply in many practical systems; we discuss this further in Section 4.

Our Nash equilibrium strategy relies on "threats"; the threat that there will be no consensus if an agent deviates (and is caught). There might be some concern that these are empty threats, which will never be carried out. The notion of *sequential equilibrium* [15] is intended to deal with empty threats. Roughly speaking, a strategy is a sequential equilibrium if all agents are best responding to what the others are doing even off the equilibrium path. We generalize sequential equilibrium to our setting, where there might be failures, and show that the strategy that gives a Nash equilibrium can be slightly extended to give a sequential equilibrium that tolerates up to f failures.

The rest of this paper is organized as follows. In Section 2 we discuss the model that we are using. Our main technical results on Nash equilibrium and sequential equilibrium are given in Section 3. We conclude with some discussion of the assumptions in Section 4.

2. Model

We consider a synchronous message-passing system with n agents and reliable communication channels between each pair of agents. Time is divided into synchronous rounds. Each round is divided into a *send phase*, where agents send messages to other agents, a *receive phase*, where agents receive messages sent by other agents in the send phase of that round, and an *update phase*, where agents update the value of variables based on what they have sent and received. We denote by N the set of agents and assume that they have commonly-known identifiers in $\{0, \dots, n-1\}$. Round m takes place between time m and time $m+1$.

We now formalize the notion of run. We take a *round-m history* for agent i to be a sequence of form $(v, t_1, \dots, t_{m-1})$, where v is agent i's initial preference and t_j has the form (s_j, r_j, d_j), where s_j is the set of messages that i sent in round j tagged by who they were sent to, r_j is the set of messages that i received in round j tagged by who they were sent by, and $d_j \in \{\lambda\} \cup V$ is i's decision (where λ denotes that no decision has been made yet and V is the set of decision values). A *global (round-m) history* has the form $(h_1, \dots, h_n)$ where h_i is a round-m history, if j receives a message $\mathbf{m}$ from i in round m' of h_j, then i sends $\mathbf{m}$ to j in round m' in history h_i. A *run* r is a function from time (which ranges over the natural numbers) to global histories such that (a) $r(m)$ is a global round-m history and (b) if $m < m'$, then for each agent i, i's history in $r(m)$ is a prefix of i's history in $r(m')$.

Agents are either correct or faulty in a run. An agent fails only by crashing. If it crashes in round m of run r, then it may send a message to some subset of agents in round m, but from then on, it sends no further messages. We assume that all messages sent are received in the round in which they are sent. Thus, we take a *failure* $\mathbf{f}$ of agent i to be a tuple (i, m, A), where m is a round number (intuitively, the round at which i crashes) and A is a set of agents (intuitively, the set of agents j to whom i can send a message before it fails). We assume that if $m > 1$, then A is non-empty, so that i sends a message to at least one agent in round m if i fails in round m. (Intuitively, if $m > 1$, we are identifying the failure pattern where i crashes in round m and sends no message with the failure pattern where i crashes in round $m-1$ and sends messages to all the agents.) A *failure pattern* F is a set of failures of distinct agents i. A run r *has context* $(F, \vec{v})$ if (a) $\vec{v}$ describes the initial preferences of the agents in r, (b) if $(i, m, A) \in F$, then i sends all messages according to its protocol in each round $m' < m$, sends no messages in each round $m' > m$, and sends messages according to its protocol only to the agents in A in round m, and (c) all messages sent in r are received in the round that they are sent. Let $\mathcal{R}(F, \vec{v})$ consist of all runs r that have context $(F, \vec{v})$. Let $\mathcal{R}(F)$ consist of all runs that have F as the set of failures.

In the consensus problem, we assume that each agent i has an initial preference v_i in some set V. For ease of exposition, we take $V = \{0, 1\}$. (Our results can easily be extended to deal with larger sets of possible values.) A protocol achieves consensus if it satisfies the following properties [9]:

- **Agreement**: No two correct agents decide different values.
- **Termination**: Every correct agent eventually decides.
- **Integrity**: All agents decide at most once.
- **Validity**: If an agent decides v, then v was the initial preference of some agent.

We are interested in one other property: fairness. Note that, once we fix a context, a protocol for the agents generates a probability on *runs*, and hence on outcomes, in the obvious way. Fairness just says that each agent has probability at least $1/n$ of having its value be the consensus value, no matter what the context. More precisely, we have the following condition:

- **Fairness**: For each context $(F, \vec{v})$, if c of the nonfaulty agents in F have initial preference v, then the probability of v being the consensus decision conditional on $\mathcal{R}(F, \vec{v})$ is at least c/n.

It is straightforward to view a consensus problem as a game once we associate a utility function u_i with each agent i, where u_i maps each outcome to a utility for i. Technically, it is an *extensive-form Bayesian game*. In a Bayesian game, agents have *types*, which encode private information. In consensus, an agent's type is its initial preference. A strategy for agent i in this game is just a protocol: a function from information sets to actions. As usual, we view an extensive-form game as being defined by a game tree, with the nodes where an agent i moves into *information sets* where, intuitively, two nodes are in the same information set of agent i if i has the same information at both. In our setting, the nodes in a game tree correspond to global histories, and agent i's information set at a global history is determined by i's history in that global history; that is, we can take i's information set at a global history h to consist of all global histories where i's history is the same as it is at h. Thus, we identify an information set I_i for agent i with a history h_i for agent i. If I_i is the information set associated with history h_i, we denote by $\mathcal{R}(I_i)$ the set of runs r where i has history h_i in $r(m)$.

In game theory, a *strategy* for agent i is a function that associates with each information set I_i for agent i a distribution over the actions that i can take at I_i. In distributed computing, a protocol for agent i is a function that associates with each history h_i for agent i a distribution over the actions that i can take at h_i. Since we are identifying histories for agent i with information sets, it is clear that a protocol for agent i can be identified with a strategy for agent i. In consensus, the actions involve sending messages and deciding on values. We assume that there is a special value $\perp$ that an agent can decide on. By deciding on $\perp$, an agent guarantees that there is no consensus. If we assume that an agent prefers to reach consensus on some value to not reaching consensus at all, in the language of Ben Porath [7], this means that each agent has a *punishment strategy*.

We next want to define an appropriate solution concept for our setting. The standard approach is to say that an equilibrium is a *strategy profile* (i.e., a tuple of strategies, one for each agent) where no agent can do better by deviating. "Doing better" is typically taken to mean "gets a higher expected utility". However, if we do not have a probability on contexts, we cannot compute an agent's expected utility. We thus consider two families of solution concepts. In the first, we take "doing better" to mean that, for each fixed context, no agent can do better by deviating. Once we fix the context, the strategy profile generates a probability distribution on runs, and we can compute the expected utility. In the second approach we assume a distribution on contexts.

A strategy profile $\vec{\sigma}$ is an *ϵ–f-Nash equilibrium* if, for each fixed context $(F, \vec{v})$ where there are at most f faulty agents in F, and all agents i, there is no strategy σ_i' for agent i such that i can improve its expected utility by more than ϵ. Formally, if $u_i(\vec{\tau} \mid \mathcal{R}(F, \vec{v}))$ denotes i's expected utility if strategy profile $\vec{\tau}$ is played, conditional on the run being in $\mathcal{R}(F, \vec{v})$, we require that for all strategies σ_i' for i, $u_i((\sigma_i', \vec{\sigma}_{-i}) \mid \mathcal{R}(F, \vec{v})) \leq u_i(\vec{\sigma} \mid \mathcal{R}(F, \vec{v})) + \epsilon$. An f-Nash equilibrium is a 0–f-Nash equilibrium. The notion of f-Nash equilibrium extends the notion of ex post Nash equilibrium by allowing up to f faulty agents; a 0-Nash equilibrium is an ex post Nash equilibrium.[1]

Given a distribution π on contexts and a strategy profile $\vec{\sigma}$, π and $\vec{\sigma}$ determine a probability on runs denoted $\pi_{\vec{\sigma}}$ in the obvious way. We say that $\vec{\sigma}$ is an *ϵ–π-Nash equilibrium* if, for all agents i and all strategies σ_i' for i, we have $u_i(\sigma_i', \vec{\sigma}_{-i}) \leq u_i(\vec{\sigma}) + \epsilon$, where now the expectation is taken with respect to the probability $\pi_{\vec{\sigma}}$. A π-Nash equilibrium is a 0–π-Nash equilibrium. If π puts probability 1 on there being no failures, then we get the standard notion of (ϵ-) Nash equilibrium.

3. Possibility and Impossibility Results for Consensus

In this section, we consider the consensus problem from a game-theoretic viewpoint. We focus on the case where agents care only about consensus, since this type of utility function seems to capture many situations of interest. For the rest of this section, let β_{0i} be i's utility if its initial preference is decided, let β_{1i} be i's utility if there is consensus, but not on i's initial preference, and let β_{2i} be i's utility if there is no consensus. The assumption that agents care only about consensus means that, for all i, $\beta_{0i} > \beta_{1i} > \beta_{2i}$.

Note that although we assume that agents prefer consensus to no consensus, unlike Bei, Chen, and Zhang. [6], we do not require that our algorithms guarantee consensus when rational agents deviate. Our algorithm does guarantee that there will be consensus if there are no deviations. On the other hand, we allow for the possibility that a deviation by a rational agent will result in there being no consensus. For example, suppose that a rational agent pretends to fail in a setting where there is a bound f on the number of crash failures. That means that if f other agents actually do crash, then some agent will detect that $f + 1$ agents seem to have crashed. Our algorithm requires that if an agent detects such an inconsistency, then it aborts. If the probability that f agents actually crash is low, in our framework, a rational agent may decide that it is worth the risk of pretending to

[1]This definition is in the spirit of the notion of (k, t)-robustness as defined by Abraham et al. [1], where coalitions of size k are allowed in addition to t "faulty" agents, but here we restrict the behavior of the faulty agents to crash failures rather than allowing the faulty agents to follow an arbitrary protocol, and take $k = 1$. We also allow the deviating agents to fail (this assumption has no impact on our results).

crash if the potential gain is sufficiently large. Bei, Chen, and Zhang would not permit this, since they require consensus even if rational agents deviate from the algorithm. This requirement thus severely limits the possible deviations.

3.1 An Impossibility Result

We start by showing that there is no fair consensus protocol that is an f-Nash equilibrium.

THEOREM 1. *If $\vec{\sigma}$ solves fair consensus, agents care only about consensus, and $f \geq 1$, then $\vec{\sigma}$ is not an f-Nash equilibrium*

PROOF. Consider the initial configuration $\vec{v}$ where all agents but i have initial preference 0 and i has initial preference 1. If F^1 is the failure pattern where no agent fails, by Fairness, the agents must decide 1 with positive probability in context $(\vec{v}, F^1)$. It follows that there must be a failure pattern F^2 where only agent i fails but the agents decide 1 with positive probability in context $(\vec{v}, F^2)$. (In F^2, i fails only after a decision has been made in F^1.) If F^0 is the failure pattern where only i fails, and i fails immediately, before sending any messages, then it is clear that no agents can distinguish this context from one where all agents have initial preference 0, so all agents must decide 0, by the Validity requirement.

Put a partial order $\leq$ on failure patterns where only i crashes by taking $F \leq F'$ if either i crashes in an earlier round in F than in F', or i crashes in the same round m in both F and F', but the set of agents to whom i sends a message in F is a subset of the set of agents to whom i sends a message in F'. Clearly $F^0 < F^2$. Thus, there exists a minimal failure pattern F^* such that $F^0 < F^* \leq F^2$, only i fails in F^*, the consensus is on 1 with positive probability in context $(\vec{v}, F^*)$, the consensus is 0 with probability 1 in all contexts $(F, \vec{v})$ where only agent i fails in F and $F < F^*$. We can assume without loss of generality that i sends a message to some agent j in the round m in which i fails. To see this, note that if i crashes in the first round then i must send a message to some agent (otherwise $F^* = F^0$ and the decision is 0 with probability 1). And if i crashes in round $m > 1$, we have assumed that i sends at least one message before crashing (recall that we identify an agent crashing at round $m > 1$ and sending no messages with the agent crashing at round $m-1$ and sending to all agents).

Now suppose that an agent j that receives a message from i in round m pretends not to receive that message. This makes the situation indistinguishable from the context $(F, \vec{v})$ where F is just like F^* except that i does not send a message to j in round m. Since $F^0 \leq F < F^*$, the decision must be 0 with probability 1 in context $(\vec{v}, F)$. Since j has initial preference 0 in $\vec{v}$, j can increase its expected utility by this pretense, so $\vec{\sigma}$ is not an f-Nash equilibrium. □

3.2 Obtaining a π-Nash equilibrium

We now prove a positive result. If we are willing to assume that there is a distribution π on contexts with some reasonable properties, then we can get a fair π-Nash equilibrium. But, as we show below, there are some subtle problems in doing this.

Before discussing these problems, it is useful to recall some results from social choice theory. Consider a setting with n agents where each has a preference order (i.e., a total order) over some set O of outcomes. A *social-choice function* is a (possibly randomized) function that maps a profile of preference orders to an outcome. For example, we can consider agents trying to elect a leader, where each agent has a preference order over the candidates; the social-choice function chooses a leader as a function of the expressed preferences. A social-choice function is *incentive compatible* if no agent can do better by lying about its preferences. The well-known *Gibbard-Satterthwaite* theorem [10, 18] says that if there are at least three possible outcomes, then the only incentive-compatible deterministic social-choice function f is a *dictatorship*; i.e., the function f just chooses a player i and takes the outcome to be i's most-preferred candidate, ignoring all other agents' preferences. Gibbard [11] extends this result to show that if there are at least three outcomes, then the only randomized incentive-compatible social-choice function is a *random dictatorship*, which essentially amounts to choosing some player i according to some probability distribution and then choosing i's value.

Bei, Chen, and Zehang [6] point out that a strategy profile that solves consensus can be viewed as a social-choice function: agents have preferences over three outcomes, 0, 1, and $\perp$, and the consensus value (or $\perp$, if there is no consensus) can be viewed as the outcome chosen by the function. A strategy profile that is a Nash equilibrium is clearly incentive-compatible; no agent has an incentive to lie about its preferences. Thus, it follows from Gibbard's [11] result that a solution to rational consensus must be a randomized dictatorship. And, indeed, our protocols can be viewed as implementing a randomized dictatorship: one agent is chosen at random, and its value becomes the consensus value. However, implementing such a randomized dictatorship in our setting is nontrivial because of the possibility of failures.[2]

A naive protocol.

We start with a protocol that, while not solving the problem, has many of the essential features of our solution, and also helps to point out the subtleties. Consider the following slight variant of one of the early protocols for consensus [8]: In round 1, each agent i broadcasts a tuple $(i, v_i, x_{i0}, \ldots, x_{if})$, where v_i is i's initial preference, and x_{it} is a random element in $\{0, \ldots, n-t\}$. For round $2, \ldots, f+1$, each agent i broadcasts all the tuples $(j, v_j, \vec{x}_j)$ that i received and did not already forward in earlier rounds. At the end of round $f+1$, each agent checks for consistency; specifically, it checks that it has received tuples from at least $n-f$ agents and that it has not received distinct tuples claimed to have been sent by some agent j. If i detects an inconsistency, then i decides $\perp$. Otherwise, suppose that i received tuples from $n-t$ agents. Then i computes the sum mod $n-t$ of the values x_{jt} for each agent j from which it received a tuple. If the sum is S, then i decides on the value of the agent with the $(S+1)$st highest id among the $n-t$ agents from which it received tuples. (Here is where we are implementing the random dictatorship.) Note that the random value x_{jt} is used by i in computing the consensus value if

[2]We remark that Theorem 1 of Bei, Chen, and Zhang [6] claims that, given a fixed failure pattern, a strategy profile for consensus that is a Nash equilibrium must implement a dictatorship, rather than randomized dictatorship. While this is true if we restrict to deterministic strategies, neither we nor Bei, Chen, and Zhang do so. We have not checked carefully whether results of Bei, Chen, and Zhang that depend on their Theorem 1 continue to hold once we allow for randomized dictatorships.

exactly t faulty agents are discovered; the remaining random values sent by agent j in the first round are discarded.

It is straightforward to check that if all nonfaulty agents follow this protocol, then they will all agree on the set of tuples received (see the proof of Theorem 2 for an argument similar in spirit), and so will choose the same decision value, and each agent whose value is considered has an equal chance of having their value determine the outcome. But this will not be in general a π-Nash equilibrium if π *allows up to f failures*, that is, π puts probability 0 on all failure patterns that have more than f failures and $f \geq 2$.

Consider a distribution π that puts positive probability on all contexts with at most f failures, and an initial configuration where agent 1 prefers 1, but all other agents prefer 0. Agent 1 follows the protocol in the first round, and receives a message from all the other agents. We claim that agent 1 may have an incentive to pretend to fail (without sending any messages) at this point. Agent 1 can gain by doing this if one of the other agents, say agent 2, crashed in the first round and sent a message only to agent 1. In this case, if 1 pretends to crash, no other agent will learn 2's initial preference, so 1's initial preference will have a somewhat higher probability (at least $\frac{1}{n-1} - \frac{1}{n}$) of becoming the consensus decision. Of course, there is a risk in pretending to crash: if f agents really do crash, then an inconsistency will be detected, and the decision will be $\perp$. Let $\alpha_{<f}$ be the probability of there being fewer than f failures and at least one agent crashing in the first round who does not send to any agent other than 1 (this is the probability that 1 gains some utility by its action); let $\alpha_{=f}$ be the probability of there being f crashes other than 1 (this is an upper bound on the probability that 1 loses utility by its action). Then 1's expected gain by deviating is at least

$$(\beta_{0i} - \beta_{1i})\left(\frac{1}{n-1} - \frac{1}{n}\right)\alpha_{<f} - (\beta_{0i} - \beta_{2i})\alpha_{=f}.$$

This is a small quantity. However, if f is reasonably large and failures are unlikely, we would expect $\alpha_{=f}$ to be much smaller than $\alpha_{<f}$, so as the number f of failures that the protocol is designed to handle increases, deviating becomes more and more likely to produce a (small) gain.

A π-Nash equilibrium.

There are three problems with the preceding protocol. The first is that, even if 1 pretends to fail, 1's value will be considered a potential consensus value, since everyone received the value before 1 failed. This means that there is little downside in pretending to fail. Roughly speaking, we deal with this problem by taking into consideration only the values of nonfaulty agents when deciding on a consensus value. The second problem is that since agents learn the random values $(x_{i0}, \ldots, x_{if})$ that will be used in determining the consensus value in round 1, they may be able to guess with high probability the value that will be decided on at a point when they can still influence the outcome. To address this problem, agents do not send these random values in the first round; instead, they use secret sharing [19], so as to allow the nonfaulty agents to reconstruct these random values when they need to decide on the consensus value. This prevents agents from being able to guess with high probability what the decision will be too early. The third problem is that in some cases agents can safely lie about the messages sent by other agents (e.g., i can pretend that another agent did not crash). We could solve this by assuming that messages can be signed using unforgeable signatures. We do not need this or any other cryptographic assumption. Instead, we use some randomization to ensure that if an agent lies about a message that was sent, it will be caught with high probability.

Thus, in our algorithm, an agent i generates random numbers for two reasons. The first is that it generates $f+1$ random numbers $(x_{i0}, \ldots, x_{if})$, where x_{it} is used in choosing the consensus value if there are exactly t faulty agents discovered, and then, as we suggested above, shares them using secret sharing, so that the numbers can be reconstructed at the appropriate time (see below). The second is that it generates $n-1$ additional random numbers, denoted $z_{ij}^m[i]$, one for each agent $j \neq i$, in each round m, and sends them to j in round m. Then if agent j claims that it got a message in round m from i, it will have to also provide $z_{ij}^m[i]$ as proof.

In more detail, we proceed as follows. Initially, each agent i generates a random tuple $(x_{i0}, \ldots, x_{if})$, where x_{it} is in $\{0, \ldots, n-t\}$. It then computes $f+1$ random polynomials $q_{i0}, \ldots, q_{if}$, each of degree 1, such that $q_{it}(0) = x_{it}$. It then sends $(q_{i0}(j), \ldots, q_{if}(j))$ to agent j. The upshot of this is that no agent will be able to compute x_{it} given this information (since one point on a degree-1 polynomial q_{it} gives no information regarding $q_{it}(0)$). In addition, in round 1, each agent i sends v_i to each agent j, just as in the naive algorithm; it also generates the random number $z_{ij}^1[i]$ and a special random number z, and sends each agent the vector $z_{ij}^1 = (z_{ij}^1[1], \ldots, z_{ij}^1[n])$, where $z_{ij}^1[j'] = 0$ for $j' \neq i, j$ and $z_{ij}^1[j] = z$. (As we said, these random numbers form a "signature"; their role will become clearer in the proof.) Finally, in round 1, agent i sends a status report SR_i^1; we discuss this in more detail below. In the receive phase of round 1, agent i adds all the values received from other agents to the set ST_i.

In round m with $2 \leq m \leq f$, i again sends a status report SR_i^m and a vector z_{ij}^m. For each agent j, $SR_i^m[j]$ is a tuple of the form (m, x), where m is the first round that i knows that j crashed ($m = \infty$ if i believes that j has not yet crashed), and x is either the vector z_{ji}^{m-1} of random values sent by j in $m-1$ (if i believes that j has not yet crashed) or an agent that told i that j crashed in round m. The tuple z_{ij}^m is computed by setting $z_{ij}^m[l]$ for $l \neq i, j$ to be $z_{li}^{m-1}[l]$, the random number sent by l in the previous round (this will be used to prove that i really got a message from l in the previous round—it is our replacement for unforgeable signatures); again, $z_{ij}^m[i]$ is a random value generated by i. In round $f+1$, i also sends j the secret shares y_{li}^t it received in round 1 from each agent l (i.e., the value $q_l^t(i)$ that it received from l, assuming that l did not lie). This enables j to compute the polynomials q_{it}, and hence the secret $q_{it}(0) = x_{it}$ for $0 \leq t \leq f$.

If i detects an inconsistency in round $m \leq f+1$, then i decides $\perp$, where *i detects an inconsistency in round m* if the messages received by i are inconsistent with all agents following the protocol except that up to f agents may crash. (In the full paper [14], we give an exhaustive list of all the ways that i can detect an inconsistency.)

If agent i does not detect an inconsistency at some round $m \leq f+1$, i proceeds as follows in round $f+1$. For each round $1 \leq m \leq f+1$ in a run r, agent i computes $NC_m(r)$, the set of agents that it believes did not crash up to and including round m. Take $NC_0(r) = N$ (the set of all agents). Say that round m in run r *seems clean* if $NC_{m-1}(r) = NC_m(r)$. As we show (Theorem 2), if no inconsistency is detected in run r, then there must be a round in r that seems clean. Moreover, we show that if m^* is the first round in r that seems clean to a nonfaulty agent i, then all the nonfaulty agents agree that m^* is the first round that seems clean in r, and they agree on the initial preference of all agents in $NC_{m^*}(r)$, and the random numbers sent by these agents in round 1 messages in run r. The agents then use these random numbers to choose an agent j among the agents in $NC_{m^*}(r)$ and take v_j to be the consensus value.

The pseudocode for the strategy (protocol) $\vec{\sigma}^{cons}$ that implements this idea is given in Figure 1. We discuss the algorithm in more detail in the full paper.

We now prove that $\vec{\sigma}^{cons}$ gives a π-Nash equilibrium, under reasonable assumptions about π. We first prove that the protocol satisfies all the properties of fair consensus without making any assumptions about π.

THEOREM 2. *$\vec{\sigma}^{cons}$ solves fair consensus if at most f agents crash, $f+1 < n$, and all the remaining agents follow the protocol.*

The proof of this theorem (and all others) is in the full paper.

It remains to show that $\vec{\sigma}^{cons}$ is a π-Nash equilibrium. We show that $\vec{\sigma}^{cons}$ is a π-Nash equilibrium under appropriate assumptions about π. Specifically, we assume that π *supports reachability* and is *uniform*, notions that we now define. The reachability assumption has three parts. The first two parts consider how likely it is that some information that an agent j has will reach an agent that will decide on a value; the third part is quite similar, and considers how likely it is that a nonfaulty agent becomes aware that an agent j failed in round m. Of course, the answer to these questions depends in part on whether agents are supposed to send messages in every round (as is the case with $\vec{\sigma}^{cons}$). In the formal definition, we implicitly assume that this is the case. (So, effectively, the reachability assumption is appropriate only for protocols where agents send messages in every round.) Given agents i and $j \neq i$, a round-m information set I_i for i, a failure pattern F compatible with I_i, in that $\mathcal{R}(F) \cap \mathcal{R}(I_i) \neq \emptyset$, and $m' \geq m$, say that *a nonfaulty agent $l \neq i$ is reachable from j without i between rounds m' and $f+1$ given F* if there is a sequence $j_{m'}, \ldots, j_{f+1}$ of agents different from i such that $j = j_{m'}$, for $m'' = \{m', \ldots, f\}$, $j_{m''}$ has not failed prior to round m'' according to F, and either does not fail in round m'' or, if $m'' < f+1$, $j_{m''}$ fails in round m'' but sends a message to $j_{m''+1}$ before failing (i.e., if $(j_{m''}, m'', A) \in F$, then $j_{m''+1} \in A$), and $l = j_{f+1}$.

Note that if j is nonfaulty according to F, then a nonfaulty agent is certainly reachable from j without i between rounds m' and $f+1$; just take $j_{m'} = \cdots = j_{f+1} = j$. But even if j fails in round m' according to F, as long j can send a message to a nonfaulty agent other than i, or there is an appropriate chain of agents, then a nonfaulty agent is reachable from j without i by round $f+1$. The probability of there being a failure pattern for which a nonfaulty agent is reachable from j without i depends in part on how many agents are known to have failed in I_i; the more agents are known not to have failed, the more likely we would expect a nonfaulty agent to be reachable from j without i.

We also want this condition to hold even conditional on a set of failure patterns, provided that the set of failure patterns does not favor particular agents failing. To make this precise, we need a few more definitions. Say that an agent j is *known to be faulty in I_i* if j is faulty in all runs in $\mathcal{R}(I_i)$; thus, j is known to be faulty in I_i if j did not send a message to i at round $m-1$ according to I_i. Say that a set $\mathcal{F}$ of failure patterns *satisfies the permutation assumption with respect to a set F of failures and an information set I_i* if, for all permutations g of the agents that keep fixed the agents that fail in F or are known to be faulty in I_i, if $F' \in \mathcal{F}$, then so is $g(F')$, where $g(F')$ is the failure pattern that results by replacing each triple $(j, m'', A) \in F'$ by $(g(j), m'', g(A))$. *$\mathcal{F}$ satisfies the permutation assumption with respect to I_i* if $\mathcal{F}$ satisfies it with respect to the empty set of failures and I_i. Let $\mathcal{R}(\mathcal{F}) = \cup_{F \in \mathcal{F}} \mathcal{R}(F)$.

We say that π *supports reachability* if for all agents i, all time-m information sets I_i such that M agents are not known to be faulty in I_i, failure pattern F, and all sets $\mathcal{F}$ of failure patterns that satisfy the permutation assumption with respect to F and I_i, we have that

1. if $j \neq i$ is not known to be faulty in I_i and is not in F, then

   π(no nonfaulty agent $l \neq i$ is reachable from j without i between rounds m and $f+1 \mid \mathcal{R}(I_i) \cap \mathcal{R}(\mathcal{F}) \cap \mathcal{R}(F)$) $\leq \frac{1}{2M}$;

2. if $j \neq i$ is not known to be faulty in I_i and is not in F, then

   π(no nonfaulty agent $l \neq i$ is reachable from j without i between rounds $m-1$ and $f+1 \mid \mathcal{R}(I_i) \cap \mathcal{R}(\mathcal{F}) \cap \mathcal{R}(F$ $\leq \frac{1}{2M}$;

3. if a message from some agent j not in F was received up to and including round $m-2$ but not in round $m-1$, then

   π(no nonfaulty agent $l \neq i$ is reachable from an agent $j' \neq i$ that did not receive a message from j in round $m-1$ without i between rounds m and $f+1$ $\mid \mathcal{R}(I_i) \cap \mathcal{R}(\mathcal{F}) \cap \mathcal{R}(F)) \leq \frac{1}{2M}$.

The first two requirements essentially say that if i hears from j in round $m-1$, then it is likely that other agents will hear from j as well in a way that affects the decision, even if i does not forward j's information. That is, it is unlikely that j will fail right away, and do so in a way that prevents its information from having an effect. Similarly, the third requirement says that if i does not hear from j in round $m-1$ (as reflected in I_i), then it is likely that other agents will hear that j crashed at or before round $m-1$ even if i does not report this fact.

We next define the notion of uniformity. Given two failure patterns F^1 and F^2, we say that F^1 and F^2 are *equivalent* if there is a permutation g of the agents such that $F^2 = g(F^1)$. We say that π is *uniform* if, for all equivalent failure patterns F^1 and F^2 and vectors $\vec{v}$ of initial preferences, we have $\pi(F^1, \vec{v}) = \pi(F^2, \vec{v})$. Intuitively, if π is uniform, then the probability of each failure pattern depends only on the number of messages omitted by each agent in each round; it does not depend on the identity of faulty agents.

THEOREM 3. *If $f+1 < n$, π is a distribution that supports reachability, is uniform, and allows up to f failures, and agents care only about consensus, then $\vec{\sigma}^{cons}$ is a π-Nash equilibrium.*

PROOF. Fix an agent i and a strategy σ_i. We must show that we have

$$u_i(\vec{\sigma}^{cons}) \geq u_i(\sigma_i, \vec{\sigma}_{-i}^{cons}). \tag{1}$$

Suppose, by way of contradiction, that (1) does not hold. Then i must deviate from σ_i^{cons} at some round m. Consider all the ways that i can deviate in round m that can affect the outcome (we discuss what it means to affect the outcome shortly):

1. i pretends to crash; it does not send messages to some subset of agents in round m (and then does not not send messages from then on).
2. $m = 1$ and i sends $(i, 1 - v_i)$ to some agent $j \neq i$ (i.e., i lies about its initial preference to at least one agent).
3. i sends an incorrectly formatted message to $j \neq i$ (i.e., i sends a message that is different in format from that required by $\vec{\sigma}^{cons}$).
4. $m = 1$ and i sends values y_{ij}^t to an agent $j \neq i$ such that there is no polynomial q_i^t of degree 1 that interpolates them all or does not choose the polynomials q_i^t at random.
5. i does not choose some z_{ij}^m appropriately (as specified by $\vec{\sigma}^{cons}$).
6. $m < f + 1$ and i decides on a value in $\{0, 1\}$ in round m or $m = f + 1$ and i decides on an incorrect value on the equilibrium path.
7. $m = f + 1$ and i sends a value y_{ji}^t to $j' \neq i$ different from the value y_{ji}^t that i received from j in round 1.
8. i does not send a round $m' < m$ message to some agent j that i does not know at round m to have been faulty in round m', and sends a round m message to $j' \neq i$.
9. i lies about j's status to $j' \neq i$; that is, i sends j' a status report $\overline{SR}_i^m$ such that $\overline{SR}_i^m[j] \neq SR_i^m[j]$.

Note that in a deviation of type 8, we did not consider the case where i deviates by not sending a message to j in round m' and then sending a message to j' if i knows that j failed in round m'. In this case, i's deviation is undetectable, and will not affect the outcome. Clearly if i performs only such undetectable deviations, then σ_i is equivalent to σ_i^{cons}, so we do not need to worry about these deviations.

We consider these deviations one by one, and show that none of them makes i better off. More precisely, we show that if σ_i involves only deviations 1–d on the list above for appropriate choices of d, then (1) holds. But even this "brute force" argument requires some care, using a somewhat delicate induction on the number of deviations that i is better off not deviating. We sketch the argument for deviations of type 1 (which turns out to be the hardest case) here, leaving the remaining details to the full paper.

So suppose that σ_i involves only i pretending to crash and that if I_i^* is a time-m^* information set for i, $\mathcal{F}$ is a set of failure patterns that satisfies the permutation assumption relative to I_i^*, $\pi_{\vec{\sigma}^{cons}}(\mathcal{R}(I_i^*) \cap \mathcal{R}(\mathcal{F})) > 0$, and either there are no deviations in runs in $\mathcal{R}(I_i^*)$ or the first deviation in a run in $\mathcal{R}(I_i^*)$ occurs at or after information set I_i^*, then

$$u_i(\vec{\sigma}^{cons} \mid \mathcal{R}(I_i^*) \cap \mathcal{R}(\mathcal{F})) \geq u_i((\sigma_i, \vec{\sigma}_{-i}^{cons}) \mid \mathcal{R}(I_i^*) \cap \mathcal{R}(\mathcal{F})). \tag{2}$$

(1) clearly follows from (2) by taking I_i^* to be the initial information set and letting $\mathcal{F}$ be the set of all failure patterns compatible with I_i^*.

Given a strategy profile $\vec{\sigma}$, let $\mathcal{R}(\vec{\sigma})$ denote the possible runs of $\vec{\sigma}$. If there are no runs in $\mathcal{R}(\sigma_i, \vec{\sigma}_{-i}^{cons}) \cap \mathcal{R}(I_i^*)$ in which i pretends to fail, then conditional on $\mathcal{R}(I_i^*)$, σ_i and σ_i^{osc} agree, so (2) holds. If there are runs in $\mathcal{R}(\sigma_i, \vec{\sigma}_{-i}^{cons}) \cap \mathcal{R}(I_i^*)$ in which i pretends to fail, then we proceed by induction on the number of information sets I_i at or after I_i^* at which i first pretends to crash such that $\pi_{(\sigma_i, \vec{\sigma}_{-i}^{cons})}(\mathcal{R}(I_i^*) \cap \mathcal{R}(\mathcal{F}) \cap \mathcal{R}(I_i)) > 0$. Suppose that i first pretends to crash at some information set I_i that comes at or after I_i^* and $\pi_{(\sigma_i, \vec{\sigma}_{-i}^{cons})}(\mathcal{R}(I_i^*) \cap \mathcal{R}(\mathcal{F}) \cap \mathcal{R}(I_i)) > 0$. Thus, there are no runs in $\mathcal{R}(I_i)$ in which i pretends to crash prior to information set I_i. Let σ_i' be identical to σ_i except that i does not pretend to fail at or after I_i. By (2),

$$u_i(\vec{\sigma}^{cons} \mid \mathcal{R}(I_i^*) \cap \mathcal{R}(\mathcal{F})) \geq u_i((\sigma_i', \vec{\sigma}_{-i}^{cons}) \mid \mathcal{R}(I_i^*) \cap \mathcal{R}(\mathcal{F})).$$

We now show that

$$\begin{aligned} &u_i((\sigma_i', \vec{\sigma}_{-i}^{cons}) \mid \mathcal{R}(I_i^*) \cap \mathcal{R}(\mathcal{F})) \\ &\geq u_i((\sigma_i, \vec{\sigma}_{-i}^{cons}) \mid \mathcal{R}(I_i^*) \cap \mathcal{R}(\mathcal{F})). \end{aligned} \tag{3}$$

(2) follows immediately.

To prove (3), since $\mathcal{R}(I_i^*)$ is the union of all the time-m information sets for i that follow I_i^*, it suffices to prove that for all time-m information sets I_i' for i that follow I_i^*, we have

$$u_i((\sigma_i', \vec{\sigma}_{-i}^{cons}) \mid \mathcal{R}(I_i') \cap \mathcal{R}(\mathcal{F})) \geq u_i((\sigma_i, \vec{\sigma}_{-i}^{cons}) \mid \mathcal{R}(I_i') \cap \mathcal{R}(\mathcal{F})) \tag{4}$$

(provided, of course, that $\pi_{\vec{\sigma}^{cons}}(\mathcal{R}(I_i') \cap \mathcal{R}(\mathcal{F})) > 0$; in the future, we take it for granted that the relevant results apply only if we are conditioning on a set with positive measure). (3) clearly follows from (4), since the time-m information sets for i partition $\mathcal{R}(I_i^*) \cap \mathcal{R}(\mathcal{F})$.

If $I_i' \neq I_i$, then (4) holds trivially, since in that case σ_i' agrees with σ_i at I_i' and all subsequent information sets. Thus, it suffices to prove (4) in the case that $I_i' = I_i$. We can assume without loss of generality that i's actions at and after I_i are deterministic. If i is better off by pretending to fail at I_i with some probability, then i is better off by pretending to fail at I_i with probability 1. Note that (a) whether or not there is a seemingly clean round, (b) which is the first seemingly clean round if there is one, and (c) which agents are considered nonfaulty at that round are completely determined by the failure pattern. Specifically, a particular failure pattern $F' \in \mathcal{F}$ determines the first seemingly clean round m^*. We partition the set $\mathcal{F}$ into four sets, $\mathcal{F}_1, \ldots, \mathcal{F}_4$, and show that conditional on $\mathcal{R}(I_i) \cap \mathcal{R}(F_j)$, agent i does at least as well by using σ_i' as it does by using σ_i, for $j = 1, \ldots, 4$.

- $\mathcal{F}_1$ consists of the failure patterns in $\mathcal{F}$ where with $(\sigma_i, \vec{\sigma}_{-i}^{cons})$ an inconsistency is detected (because $f + 1$ agents seem to fail).
- $\mathcal{F}_2$ consists of the failure patterns $F' \in \mathcal{F} - \mathcal{F}_1$ such that in all runs r' in $\mathcal{R}((\sigma_i', \vec{\sigma}_{-i}^{cons})) \cap \mathcal{R}(I_i) \cap \mathcal{R}(F')$, the first seemingly clean round occurs at some round $m^* < m$.
- $\mathcal{F}_3$ consists of the failure patterns in $\mathcal{F} - \mathcal{F}_1$ that result in m being the first seemingly clean round with both $(\sigma_i, \vec{\sigma}_{-i}^{cons})$ and $(\sigma_i', \vec{\sigma}_{-i}^{cons})$.

- $\mathcal{F}_4$ consists of the failure patterns in $\mathcal{F} - \mathcal{F}_1$ where the first seemingly clean round m^* with $(\sigma_i', \vec{\sigma}_{-i}^{cons})$ comes at or after m while with $(\sigma_i, \vec{\sigma}_{-i}^{cons})$, the first seemingly clean round m^* comes strictly before m or strictly after m.

The arguments in the first three cases is relatively straightforward. To show that, conditional on $\mathcal{R}(I_i) \cap \mathcal{R}(\mathcal{F}_4)$, i's utility is at least as large with $(\sigma_i', \vec{\sigma}_{-i}^{cons})$ as with $(\sigma_i, \vec{\sigma}_{-i}^{cons})$ requires the reachability and uniformity assumptions. We leave details to the full paper. □

3.3 A π-Sequential Equilibrium for Fair Consensus

Our π-Nash equilibrium requires an agent i to decide on $\perp$ whenever i detects a problem. While this punishes the agent that causes the problem, it also punishes i. Would a rational agent actually play such a punishment strategy? Note that the need to punish occurs only off the equilibrium path; if all agents follow $\vec{\sigma}^{cons}$, agents never decide $\perp$. But to get agents to play according to $\vec{\sigma}^{cons}$ requires the threat of playing $\perp$. There might be a concern that this is an empty threat; a rational agent might not be willing to play $\perp$ if it detects a deviation.

The solution concept of *sequential equilibrium* [15] is a refinement of Nash equilibrium that, roughly speaking, requires that agents also make best responses not only on the equilibrium path, but off the equilibrium path as well. We now define *π-sequential equilibrium*, a generalization of sequential equilibrium that allows for faulty agents (where, as before, π is a distribution on failure contexts). We then show that $\vec{\sigma}^{cons}$ is essentially a π-sequential equilibrium.

Defining π-sequential equilibrium.

Roughly speaking, a strategy profile $\vec{\sigma}$ is a sequential equilibrium if, for each agent i and information set I_i for agent i, σ_i is a best response to $\vec{\sigma}_{-i}$ conditional on reaching I_i (i.e. conditional on $\mathcal{R}(I_i)$). The problem is that the probability of $\mathcal{R}(I_i)$ is 0 if I_i is not on the equilibrium path, so we cannot condition on $\mathcal{R}(I_i)$.

Define a *belief system* μ to be a function that associates with each agent i and information set I_i for agent i a probability μ_{I_i} on histories in I_i. Say that a belief system μ is *consistent with $\vec{\sigma}$ and π* if there exists a sequence of *completely mixed* strategy profiles $\vec{\sigma}^1, \vec{\sigma}^2, \ldots$ (where a strategy profile is completely mixed if it gives positive positive probability to every action at every information set) converging to $\vec{\sigma}$ such that

$$\mu_{I_i}(h) = \lim_{M \to \infty} \frac{\pi_{\vec{\sigma}^M}(h)}{\pi_{\vec{\sigma}^M}(I_i)}.$$

Note that μ_{I_i}, π, and $\vec{\sigma}$ together define a probability distribution over runs in $\mathcal{R}(I_i)$. Let $\mu_{I_i,\pi,\vec{\sigma}}$ denote this probability distribution.

A pair $(\vec{\sigma}, \mu)$ is a *π-sequential equilibrium* if μ is a belief system consistent with $\vec{\sigma}$ and π such that, for every agent i, information set I_i, and strategy σ_i', $u_i((\sigma_i, \vec{\sigma}_{-i}) \mid \mathcal{R}(I_i)) \geq u_i((\sigma_i', \vec{\sigma}_{-i}) \mid \mathcal{R}(I_i))$, where now the expected utility is taken with respect to $\mu_{I_i,\pi,\vec{\sigma}}$. (Kreps and Wilson's [15] definition of sequential equilibrium is identical, except that there is no distribution π on failure contexts.)

Extending $\vec{\sigma}^{cons}$ to a π-sequential equilibrium.

We now show that the protocol $\vec{\sigma}^{cons}$ can be extended to a π-sequential equilibrium with minimal changes. In the proof of Theorem 3, we showed that i could not gain by deviating at an information set I_i where there were no deviations of type 1–9 prior to I_i. We did not show that i does not gain from deviating at I_i if an inconsistency is detected at I_i, so that i is expected to decide $\perp$. In fact, if i believes that the inconsistency may go unnoticed by other agents due to crashes and consensus may still be reached on some value in $\{0,1\}$, then i always gains by not deciding $\perp$. However, suppose that μ^{se} is a belief system such that at an information set I_i for i that is off the equilibrium path due to a deviation (or multiple deviations) from $\vec{\sigma}^{cons}$ by agents other than i, i believes that these agents decided $\perp$ when they deviated. (Intuitively, i believes that if the agents were crazy enough to deviate in the first place, then they were also crazy enough to decide $\perp$.) In that case, deciding $\perp$ is also a best response for i.

The belief system μ^{se} is not enough to deal with information sets I_i off the equilibrium path due to i himself having deviated. Agent i cannot believe that it played $\perp$ when it in fact did not. To get a sequential equilibrium, we modify σ_i^{cons} at information sets off the equilibrium path that are reached due only to agent i's deviations. Define the strategy σ_i^{se} so that it agrees with σ_i^{cons} at every information set I_i where agent i has not deviated in the past. Thus, in particular, i decides $\perp$ with σ_i^{se} if i detects an inconsistency at one of these information sets. More generally, say that an information set I_i is *unsalvageable* if i knows at I_i that another agent j deviated or detected an inconsistency at a point when j had not crashed, and thus decided $\perp$. I_i is certainly unsalvageable if reaching I_i requires deviations by agents other than i (for then the agent that performed that deviation decided $\perp$). But even if i is the only agent who deviates at I_i, I_i may be unsalvageable. For example, i does not send a message to j in round m_1, i sends a message to j in round $m_2 > m_1$, and then j sent a message to i in round $m_2 + 1$, the round-(m_2+2) information set where i receives j's message is also unsalvageable. If I_i is unsalvageable, i decides $\perp$. Finally, if I_i is salvageable, then at I_i agent i acts in a way that is most likely to have the other agents think that there has been no inconsistency. In general, there may be more than one failure pattern that will prevent a nonfaulty agent from realizing that there is an inconsistency. For example, if $f = 1$, $n = 3$, and agent 1 did not send a message to agent 2 in round m, but did send a message to agent 3, then i can either not send a message to any agent in round $m+1$, or it can send a message to agent 3. If it is more likely that neither 2 nor 3 failed in round m than agent 2 failed before telling agent 3 that it did not hear from 1, then it would be better for i not to send a message to 2 or 3 in round $m+1$. If there is more than one best response, then i chooses a fixed one according to some ordering on actions. (Note that this means that, unlike $\vec{\sigma}^{cons}$, the behavior of $\vec{\sigma}^{se}$ may depend on π.)

Having defined $\vec{\sigma}^{se}$, we can now define μ^{se} formally. We assume that there are only finitely many actions that i can play at each of its information sets I_i: it can send one of K_{I_i} possible messages and/or decide one of $\perp$, 0, or 1 if it has not yet made a decision, or do nothing. Given an integer $M > 0$, let $\vec{\sigma}^M$ be the strategy profile where at each information set I_i, agent i plays $\sigma_i^{se}(I_i)$ with probability $1 - 1/M$, and divides the remaining probability $1/M$ over all the actions that can be played at I_i as follows: if i has already decided before, then i sends each of the K_{I_i} possible messages with equal probability $\frac{1}{M(K_{I_i}+1)}$ and does nothing with probability $\frac{1}{M(K_{I_i}+1)}$; if i has not yet decided at I_i, then for each of the K_{I_i} messages $\mathbf{m}$ that it can send, it decides $\perp$ and sends $\mathbf{m}$ with probability $\frac{1}{M(K_{I_i}+1)} - \frac{1}{M^2(K_{I_i}+1)}$, decides $\perp$ and sends no message with probability $\frac{1}{M(K_{I_i}+1)} - \frac{1}{M^2(K_{I_i}+1)}$, and performs each of the remaining $3(K_{I_i}+1)$ possible actions with equal probability $\frac{1}{3M^2(K_{I_i}+1)}$. Clearly $\vec{\sigma}^M$ is completely mixed and the sequence $\vec{\sigma}^M$ converges to $\vec{\sigma}^{se}$. Given a round-m information set I_i and global history $h \in I_i$, let

$$\mu^{se}_{I_i}(h) = \lim_{M\to\infty} \frac{\pi_{\vec{\sigma}^M}(h)}{\pi_{\vec{\sigma}^M}(I_i)}.$$

The effect of this definition of $\mu^{se}_{I_i}$ beliefs is that if I_i is off the equilibrium path as a result of some other agent j's deviation, then i believes that j played $\perp$. Moreover, i believes that other agents j have similar beliefs.

THEOREM 4. *If $f+1<n$, π is a distribution that supports reachability, is uniform, and allows up to f failures, and agents care only about consensus, then $(\vec{\sigma}^{se}, \mu^{se})$ is a π-sequential equilibrium.*

4. Discussion

We have provided a strategy for consensus that is a π-Nash equilibrium and can be extended to a π-sequential equilibrium, where π is a distribution on contexts that allows up to f failures and satisfies minimal conditions, as long as $n > f+1$. Although our argument is surprisingly complicated, we have considered only the simplest possible case: synchronous systems, crash failures, and only one player deviating (i.e., no coalitions). A small variant of our strategy also gives a Nash and sequential equilibrium even if coalitions are allowed, but proving this seems significantly more complicated. We are currently writing up the details carefully. Of course, things will get even worse once we allow more general types of failures, such as omission failures and Byzantine failures. But such failure types, combined with rational agents, are certainly of interest if we want to apply consensus in, for example, financial settings of the type considered by Mazières [17]. Consensus is known to be impossible in an asynchronous setting, even with just one failure [9], but algorithms that attain consensus with high probability are well known (e.g., [5]). We may thus hope to get an ϵ–π-Nash equilibrium in the asynchronous setting if we also allow rational agents. We believe that the techniques developed in this paper will be applicable to these more difficult problems.

It is also worth examining our assumptions regarding distributions in more detail. The uniformity assumption implies that no agent is more likely to fail than any other. If all agents can be identified with identical computers, then this seems quite reasonable. But if one agent can be identified with a computer that is known to be more prone to failure, then the uniformity assumption no long holds. Note that the uniformity assumption does allow for correlated failures, just as long as the permutation of a correlated failure is just as likely as the unpermuted version.

Now consider the assumption that π supports reachability. If we are considering Nash equilibrium (where there is only one deviating agent), the assumption says that the probability, conditional on an information set I_i (and some assumptions about failures), that some information (about a message sent by an agent that crashes or about the fact that an agent crashed in a particular round) is quite high, where "quite high" is a function of the number of agents M that are nonfaulty according to I_i. Since the more nonfaulty agents there are, the more likely it is that an agent $l \neq i$ is reachable from j without i.

Our final comment concerns the fairness assumption. While this assumption distinguishes our work from some of the other related work (e.g., [3, 6]), since, as we observed above, a consensus protocol must essentially implement a randomized dictatorship, achieving fairness once we get consensus in the presence of rational and faulty agents is not that difficult; we must simply ensure that the rational agents cannot affect the probability of a particular agent being selected as dictator. We enforce this using appropriate randomization in our protocol. The requirement in [6] that consensus must be achieved no matter what the deviating agents do turns out to have far more impact on the technical results than the fairness requirement.

In any case, we believe that the need for dealing with both rational and faulty agents in consensus protocols is compelling. There is clearly much more to be done on this problem.

Acknowledgments: Joe Halpern's work supported in part by NSF grants IIS-0911036 and CCF-1214844, and by AFOSR grant FA9550-12-1-0040, and ARO grant W911NF-14-1-0017. Xavier Vilaça has been partially supported by Fundação para a Ciência e Tecnologia (FCT) through projects with references PTDC/EEI-SCR/1741/2014 (Abyss), UID/CEC/-50021/2013, and ERC-2012-StG-307732, and through the PhD grant SFRH/BD/79822/2011.

5. References

[1] I. Abraham, D. Dolev, R. Gonen, and J. Y. Halpern. Distributed computing meets game theory: robust mechanisms for rational secret sharing and multiparty computation. In *Proc. 25th ACM Symposium on Principles of Distributed Computing*, pages 53–62, 2006.

[2] I. Abraham, D. Dolev, and J. Y. Halpern. Distributed protocols for leader election: a game-theoretic perspective. In *Proc. 27th International Symposium on Distributed Computing*, pages 61–75, 2013.

[3] Y. Afek, Y. Ginzberg, S. Landau, and M. Sulamy. Distributed computing building blocks for rational agents. In *Proc. 33rd ACM Symposium on Principles of Distributed Computing*, pages 406–415, 2014.

[4] A. S. Aiyer, L. Alvisi, A. Clement, M. Dahlin, J. P. Martin, and C. Porth. BAR fault tolerance for cooperative services. In *Proc. 20th ACM Symposium on Operating Systems Principles (SOSP 2005)*, pages 45–58, 2005.

[5] J. Aspnes. Randomized protocols for distributed consensus. *Distributed Computing*, 16(2–3):165–176, 2003.

[6] X. Bei, W. Chen, and J. Zhang. Distributed consensus resilient to both crash failures and strategic

manipulations. Available at http://arxiv.org/abs/1203.4324; version 3, 2012.

[7] E. Ben-Porath. Cheap talk in games with incomplete information. *Journal of Economic Theory*, 108(1):45–71, 2003.

[8] D. Dolev and H. R. Strong. Polynomial algorithms for multiple processor agreement. In *Proc. 14th ACM Symposium on Theory of Computing*, pages 401–407, 1982.

[9] M. J. Fischer, N. A. Lynch, and M. S. Paterson. Impossibility of distributed consensus with one faulty processor. *Journal of the ACM*, 32(2):374–382, 1985.

[10] A. Gibbard. Manipulation of voting schemes. *Econometrica*, 41:587–602, 1973.

[11] A. Gibbard. Manipulation of schemes that mix voting with chance. *Econometrica*, 45(3):665–681, 1977.

[12] A. Groce, J. Katz, A. Thiruvengadam, and V. Zikas. Byzantine agreement with a rational adversary. In *Proc. 39th Internation Colloquium on Automata, Languages, and Programming, Part II*, pages 561–572, 2012.

[13] J. Y. Halpern and V. Teague. Rational secret sharing and multiparty computation: extended abstract. In *Proc. 36th ACM Symposium on Theory of Computing*, pages 623–632, 2004.

[14] J. Y. Halpern and X. Vilaca. Rational consensus. available at www.cs.cornell.edu/home/halpern/papers/ratconsensus.pdf, 2016.

[15] D. M. Kreps and R. B. Wilson. Sequential equilibria. *Econometrica*, 50:863–894, 1982.

[16] N. A. Lynch. *Distributed Algorithms*. Morgan Kaufmann, San Francisco, 1997.

[17] D. Mazières. The Stellar consensus protocol: a federated model for internet-level consensus. Available at www.stellar.org/papers/stellar-consensus-protocol.pdf, 2015.

[18] M. Satterthwaite. Strategy-proofness and Arrow's conditions: existence and correspondence theorems for voting procedures and social welfare functions. *Journal of Economic Theory*, 10:187–217, 1975.

[19] A. Shamir. How to share a secret. *Communications of the ACM*, 22:612–613, 1979.

Algorithm 1 $\sigma_i^{cons}(v_i)$: i's consensus protocol with initial value v_i

decided $\leftarrow$ *false*
$ST_i \leftarrow \{(i, v_i)\}$
$z \leftarrow$ random in $\{0 \ldots n-1\}$
for all $j \neq i$ **do**
  $SR_i^1[j] \leftarrow (\infty, \bot)$ ▷ All agents are initially active
  for all $l \neq j, i$ **do**
    $z_{ij}^1[l] \leftarrow 0$
  $z_{ij}^1[i] \leftarrow$ random in $\{0 \ldots n-1\}$ ▷ Random number to be used by j in round 2
  $z_{ij}^1[j] \leftarrow z$ ▷ Proves that i sends round 1 message to j
for all $0 \leq t \leq f$ **do**
  $x_i[t] \leftarrow$ random in $\{0, \ldots, n-t-1\}$ ▷ A random number for each possible value of t
  $q_i^t \leftarrow$ random polynomial of degree 1 with $q_i^t(0) = x_i[t]$
  for all $j \neq i$ **do**
    $y_{ij}[t] \leftarrow q_i^t(j)$

for all round $1 \leq m \leq f+1$ such that $\neg$decided **do**
  Phase 1: send phase
    for all $j \neq i$ **do**
      if $m = 1$ **then** Send $\langle v_i, SR_i^m, (y_{ij}^0, \ldots, y_{ij}^f), z_{ij}^m \rangle$ to j
      if $2 \leq m \leq f$ **then** Send $\langle SR_i^m, z_{ij}^m \rangle$ to j
      if $m = f+1$ **then** Send $\langle SR_i^m, (y_{li}^0, \ldots, y_{li}^f)_{l \neq j} \rangle$ to j
  EndPhase

  Phase 2: receive phase
    $SR_i^{m+1} \leftarrow SR_i^m$
    for all $j \neq i$ **do**
      if receive valid message from j **then**
        if $m = 1$ **then** $ST_i \leftarrow ST_i \cup \{(j, v_j)\}$ ▷ ST_i contains all the values that i has seen
        $SR_i^{m+1}[j] \leftarrow (\infty, z_{ji}^m)$ ▷ Note that j is still active
        for all $l \neq i, j$ **do**
          if $SR_j^m[l] = (m', j')$ and $SR_i^m[l] = (m'', j'')$ and $m' < m''$ **then**
            $SR_i^{m+1}[l] \leftarrow (m', j)$ ▷ l crashed earlier than previously thought
            $z_{il}^{m+1}[j] \leftarrow \bot$
          else if $SR_j^m[l] = (\infty, z_j^m)$ **then**
            $z_{il}^{m+1}[j] = z_{ji}^m[j]$
      else if $SR_i^{m+1}[j] = (\infty, z')$ for some z' **then**
        $SR_i^{m+1}[j] \leftarrow (m, i)$ ▷ i detects a crash of j
        for all $l \neq i$ **do**
          $z_{il}^{m+1}[j] \leftarrow \bot$
  EndPhase

  Phase 3: update phase
    if an inconsistency is detected **then**
      Decide$(\bot)$ ▷ Punishment
      decided $\leftarrow$ *true*
    else if $m \leq f$ **then**
      for all $j \neq i$ **do**
        $z_{ij}^{m+1}[i] \leftarrow$ random in $\{0, \ldots, n-1\}$
    else if decided = *false* **then**
      $NC_0 = N$
      for all $1 \leq m' \leq f+1$ **do**
        $NC_{m'} \leftarrow \{j \in N - \{i\} \mid \forall m'' \leq m', l(SR_i^{f+2}[j] \neq (m'', l)) \cup \{i\}$ ▷ Agents that did not crash up to round m'
      $m^* \leftarrow$ first round m' such that $NC_{m'} = NC_{m'-1}$ ▷ First round that seems clean
      $t \leftarrow n - |NC_{m^*}|$ ▷ Number of crashes prior to m^*
      for all $j \in NC_{m^*}$ **do**
        $q_j^t \leftarrow$ unique polynomial interpolating the values y_{jl}^t received ▷ otherwise, an inconsistency was detected
        $x_j[t] \leftarrow q_j^t(0)$
      $S \leftarrow \sum_{j \in NC_{m^*}} x_j[t] \bmod (n-t)$ ▷ Calculate a random number in $0, \ldots, n-t-1$
      Decide(v_j), where j is the $(S+1)$st highest id in NC_{m^*}
  EndPhase

Brief Announcement: A Tight Space Bound for Consensus

Leqi Zhu
Department of Computer Science
University of Toronto
Canada
lezhu@cs.toronto.edu

ABSTRACT

Existing n-process randomized wait-free and obstruction-free consensus protocols from registers all use at least n registers. In 1992, it was proved that such protocols must use $\Omega(\sqrt{n})$ registers. Recently, this was improved to $\Omega(n)$ registers in the anonymous setting, where processes do not have identifiers. We have recently proved that at least $n-1$ registers are needed, even if processes have identifiers.

1. INTRODUCTION

A well-known problem in the theory of distributed computing is the *consensus* problem, in which n processes, each with a local input value, are required to decide upon a single output value.

It is known that deterministically solving consensus in a *wait-free* manner is impossible in an asynchronous shared memory system, where processes can crash and can only communicate by taking *steps* that read from and write to shared memory locations, called *registers* [LAA87]. In particular, every deterministic consensus protocol has an infinite *execution* in which some processes take infinitely many steps, but no decision is ever reached.

On the other hand, there are many *randomized* wait-free consensus protocols, where every process is guaranteed to eventually reach a decision with probability 1 [AC08, AH90, AW96, CIL94]. For such protocols, it is known that $\Theta(n^2)$ total steps, in expectation, are necessary and sufficient to reach a decision [AC08]. There are also a number of *obstruction-free* consensus protocols, where every process is guaranteed to eventually reach a decision, provided no other processes are also taking steps [Bow11, BRS15, Zhu15].

In 1992, Fich, Herlihy, and Shavit proved that every randomized wait-free or obstruction-free consensus protocol uses $\Omega(\sqrt{n})$ registers [FHS98]. However, existing protocols all use at least n registers. Closing this gap has been a long standing open problem.

Recently, we proved that n registers are necessary and sufficient for solving randomized wait-free or obstruction-free consensus in a restricted model, where processes are *anonymous* (i.e. have no identifiers) and *memoryless* (i.e. do not make use of local memory) [Zhu15]. At the same time, using very interesting, different techniques, Gelashvili proved that $\Omega(n)$ registers are necessary, *without* the memoryless assumption [Gel15]. In [Zhu16], we prove that $n-1$ registers are necessary, without any additional assumptions.

PODC'16 July 25-28, 2016, Chicago, IL, USA

ACM ISBN 978-1-4503-3964-3/16/07.
DOI: http://dx.doi.org/10.1145/2933057.2933078

2. PRELIMINARIES

A *configuration* (of a consensus protocol) consists of the state of each process and the contents of each register. An *initial* configuration is determined by the input value of each process. The contents of the registers are the same in all initial configurations.

A step e by a process p is *applicable* at a configuration C if e is the next step of process p given its state in C. If e is applicable at C, then we use Ce to denote the configuration resulting from p taking step e.

A sequence of steps $\alpha = e_1, e_2, \ldots$ is *applicable* at a configuration C if e_1 is applicable at C and, for each $i \geq 1$, e_{i+1} is applicable at $Ce_1 \cdots e_i$. In this case, α is an *execution* from C. If all steps in α are by processes in some set of processes P, then α is a P*-only* execution. If α is finite, then we use $C\alpha$ to denote the configuration reached after applying α to C. A configuration C is *reachable* if $C = I\alpha$, for some initial configuration I and some execution α from I.

Finally, we consider consensus protocols which satisfy *nondeterministic solo termination* [FHS98]. That is: for every process p, and every reachable configuration C, there exists a $\{p\}$-only execution α from C such that p has decided a value (and terminated) in $C\alpha$. Randomized wait-free and obstruction-free consensus protocols both satisfy nondeterministic solo termination.

3. LOWER BOUND

In this section, we give an overview of the proof of our lower bound. Intuitively, the goal is to keep the processes uncertain about which value they should decide. This will allow us to show that they will have to write to more and more registers in order to convince one another. This is formally captured in terms of *valency* and *covering*.

3.1 Valency

The notion of the *valency* of a configuration was introduced by Fischer, Lynch, and Paterson [FLP85]. Informally, they consider the values that can decided by processes from a reachable configuration of a binary consensus protocol.

The configuration is *bivalent* if both 0 and 1 can be decided. Otherwise, the configuration is *univalent*.

We refine their notion of valency by considering the values that specific (non-empty) subsets of the processes can decide from a reachable configuration. In this view, the notion of valency is no longer attached to the entire configuration, but to subsets of processes in the configuration.

Definition 1. Let C be a reachable configuration, and let P be a non-empty set of processes. *P can decide $v \in \{0,1\}$ from C* if there exists a P-only execution from C in which v is decided. If P can decide *both* 0 and 1 from C, then *P is bivalent from C*. If P can decide v, but not $\overline{v}$, from C, then *P is v-univalent from C*.

The fact that a set of processes P is bivalent from a configuration C is not very helpful on its own. It is possible that the exclusion of any particular process in P may suddenly make the remaining processes univalent from C. Our next lemma shows that this problem can be avoided. In fact, repeatedly applying the lemma shows that only a pair of processes in P are needed to guarantee bivalency. For the purposes of our proof, it allows us to do induction arguments on $|P|$. It is one of the reasons why we introduced the notion of valency defined for subsets of processes.

LEMMA 1. *Let C be a reachable configuration and let P be a set of processes with $|P| \geq 3$. If P is bivalent from C, then there exists a P-only execution φ from C and a process $z \in P$ such that $P - \{z\}$ is bivalent from $C\varphi$.*

3.2 Covering

The first covering argument is due to Burns and Lynch [BL93]. Since then, covering arguments have become the main tool for proving space lower bounds in shared memory systems.

The main idea is the following: Suppose there is a set of processes R that are about to write to a set of registers V. Then any process $z \notin R$ which needs the other processes to see its actions must perform a write to a register not in V. Otherwise, as observed in [BL93], the processes in R can "obliterate" the information that z writes (to registers in V) by performing their writes all at once. The next definition formally captures these notions.

Definition 2. Let C be a reachable configuration. A process *covers* a register r in C if it is poised to perform a write to r in C. If every process in a set of processes R covers a register in C, then R is a set of *covering processes* in C and a *block write* by R is an execution in which each process in R performs its write (and nothing else).

Given a set of covering processes R in a configuration C, it is tempting to think that any process $z \notin R$ must write to a register not covered by R before it can decide a value. If this were true, then we could inductively obtain a configuration in which n different registers are covered. Unfortunately, this is not true. For example, if the set of all processes is v-univalent from C, then z does not have to write anything. It can simply decide v and terminate. The next lemma gives us a way to guarantee that a process will write to a register that is not covered. A similar result appears in all existing space lower bounds for consensus [FHS98, Gel15, Zhu15].

LEMMA 2. *Let C be a reachable configuration, let P be a set of processes, let $R \subseteq P$ be a set of covering processes in C, and let β be a block write by R. If P is bivalent from $C\beta$, then, for every $z \notin P$, every deciding $\{z\}$-only execution from C contains a write to a register not covered by R in C.*

A block write by a set of covering processes $R \subseteq P$ can change P from being bivalent to being univalent. The next lemma shows that, as long as the set of remaining processes, $P - R$, is bivalent, it is possible to ensure that P remains bivalent after the block write by R.

LEMMA 3. *Let C be a reachable configuration, let P be a set of processes, let $R \subseteq P$ be a non-empty set of covering processes in C, and let β be a block write by R. If $Q = P - R$ is bivalent from C, then there exists a Q-only execution φ from C and a process $q \in Q$ such that q covers a register not covered by R in $C\varphi$ and $R \cup \{q\}$ is bivalent from $C\varphi\beta$.*

3.3 The Main Result

The next result is the main technical lemma.

LEMMA 4. *Let C be a reachable configuration and let P be a set processes with $|P| \geq 2$. If P is bivalent from C, then there exists a P-only execution α from C and a pair of processes $Q \subseteq P$ such that Q is bivalent from $C\alpha$ and every process in $P - Q$ covers a different register in $C\alpha$.*

Intuitively, this lemma says that, whenever we have a configuration C from which a set of processes P is bivalent, we can reach a nice configuration D from which a *pair* of processes in P is bivalent and in which the remaining processes in P cover distinct registers.

Combined with Lemma 3, this allows us to construct an infinite sequence of nice configurations $D_0, D_1, D_2, \ldots$, where D_{i+1} is reachable from D_i by an execution that contains a block write by a set of that cover different registers in D_i. There are only finitely many registers, so by the pigeonhole principle, there are two distinct configurations D_i and D_j where the covering processes in D_i and D_j cover the same set of registers, V.

Now, suppose that we have a process $z \notin P$. Consider any solo execution by z starting from immediately before the block write to V between D_i and D_{i+1}. By Lemma 2, z writes to a register not in V. If we stop z immediately before its first write to a register not in V, then, after the block write, the processes in P can't detect that z took any steps. Thus, they can perform the same sequence of steps as they did to reach D_j. The resulting configuration is a nice bivalent configuration in which a larger set of processes (that includes z) cover distinct registers.

We use Lemma 1 to do induction on $|P|$ to get successively larger sets of processes covering distinct registers.

To get the $n-1$ lower bound, we note that, by a standard argument, there is an initial configuration from which the set of all processes is bivalent. Thus, Lemma 4 shows that we can reach a configuration D such that there is a pair of processes Q that is bivalent from D and the remaining processes R all cover different registers. In particular, we have a lower bound of $|R| = n - 2$ registers. To get one more register, we apply Lemma 3 to D to get a process in Q to cover a register not covered by R.

4. FUTURE WORK

There are a number of interesting research problems arising from our new lower bound. Of-course, there is the obvious gap of 1 in the lower bound and the best known upper bounds. We conjecture that the true space complexity is n (we have proved this for $n \leq 3$ in the general case and for $n \leq 4$ in the anonymous case).

Another interesting avenue is to see if our techniques can be used to prove an $\Omega(n-k)$ space lower bound for *k-set agreement.* This problem is a generalization of the consensus problem which allows up to k different values to be decided. In particular, consensus is another name for 1-set agreement. The best existing protocols for k-set agreement use $n-k+1$ registers [BRS15].

Finally, the $\Omega(\sqrt{n})$ lower bound in [FHS98] actually holds for *historyless* base objects, such as *swap* objects. It is not clear how to modify our lower bound to work in this case. The difficulty is that, when a process performs swap, it sees the value it overwrote. Thus, it might be able to detect whether some other process has performed a swap on this object since it last accessed this object.

More generally, how does the space complexity change when we have access to more powerful synchronization objects? We have taken a preliminary step in answering this question in [EGSZ16].

5. REFERENCES

[AC08] Hagit Attiya and Keren Censor. Tight bounds for asynchronous randomized consensus. *J. ACM*, 55(5), 2008.

[AE14] Hagit Attiya and Faith Ellen. *Impossibility Results for Distributed Computing.* Morgan & Claypool Publishers, 2014.

[AH90] James Aspnes and Maurice Herlihy. Fast randomized consensus using shared memory. *J. Algorithms*, 11(3):441–461, 1990.

[AW96] James Aspnes and Orli Waarts. Randomized consensus in expected o(n log^2 n) operations per processor. *SIAM J. Comput.*, 25(5):1024–1044, 1996.

[BL93] James E. Burns and Nancy A. Lynch. Bounds on shared memory for mutual exclusion. *Inf. Comput.*, 107(2):171–184, 1993.

[Bow11] Jack R. Bowman. Obstruction-free snapshot, obstruction-free consensus, and fetch-and-add modulo k. Technical Report TR2011-681, Dartmouth College, Computer Science, Hanover, NH, June 2011.

[BRS15] Zohir Bouzid, Michel Raynal, and Pierre Sutra. Brief Announcement: Anonymous Obstruction-free (n, k)-Set Agreement with n–k+1 Atomic Read/Write Registers. In *Proceedings of 29th International Symposium on Distributed Computing (DISC 2015)*, volume 9363 of *LNCS*, pages 668–669. Springer, 2015.

[CIL94] Benny Chor, Amos Israeli, and Ming Li. Wait-free consensus using asynchronous hardware. *SIAM J. Comput.*, 23(4):701–712, 1994.

[EFR08] Faith Ellen, Panagiota Fatourou, and Eric Ruppert. The space complexity of unbounded timestamps. *Distributed Computing*, 21(2):103–115, 2008.

[EGSZ16] Faith Ellen, Rati Gelashvili, Nir Shavit, and Leqi Zhu. A complexity-based hierarchy for multiprocessor synchronization. 2016. To appear in PODC '16.

[FHS98] Faith Ellen Fich, Maurice Herlihy, and Nir Shavit. On the space complexity of randomized synchronization. *J. ACM*, 45(5):843–862, 1998. A preliminary version appeared in PODC '93.

[FLP85] Michael J. Fischer, Nancy A. Lynch, and Mike Paterson. Impossibility of distributed consensus with one faulty process. *J. ACM*, 32(2):374–382, 1985.

[Gel15] Rati Gelashvili. On the optimal space complexity of consensus for anonymous processes. In *Proceedings of 29th International Symposium on Distributed Computing (DISC 2015)*, volume 9363 of *LNCS*, pages 452–466. Springer, 2015.

[GHHW13] George Giakkoupis, Maryam Helmi, Lisa Higham, and Philipp Woelfel. An $O(\sqrt{n})$ space bound for obstruction-free leader election. In *Proceedings of 27th International Symposium on Distributed Computing (DISC 2013)*, volume 8205 of *LNCS*, pages 46–60. Springer, 2013.

[GHHW15] George Giakkoupis, Maryam Helmi, Lisa Higham, and Philipp Woelfel. Test-and-set in optimal space. In *Proceedings of the Forty-Seventh Annual ACM on Symposium on Theory of Computing (STOC 2015)*, pages 615–623, 2015.

[GR05] Rachid Guerraoui and Eric Ruppert. What can be implemented anonymously? In *Proceedings of 19th International Symposium on Distributed Computing (DISC 2005)*, volume 3724 of *LNCS*, pages 244–259. Springer, 2005.

[Her91] Maurice Herlihy. Wait-free synchronization. *ACM Trans. Program. Lang. Syst.*, 13(1):124–149, 1991.

[HHPW14] Maryam Helmi, Lisa Higham, Eduardo Pacheco, and Philipp Woelfel. The space complexity of long-lived and one-shot timestamp implementations. *J. ACM*, 61(1):7:1–7:25, 2014.

[LAA87] Michael C. Loui and Hosame H. Abu-Amara. Memory requirements for agreement among unreliable asynchronous processes. *Advances in Computing Research*, 4:163–183, 1987.

[Zhu15] Leqi Zhu. Brief Announcement: Tight Space Bounds for Memoryless Anonymous Consensus. In *Proceedings of 29th International Symposium on Distributed Computing (DISC 2015)*, volume 9363 of *LNCS*, pages 665–666. Springer, 2015.

[Zhu16] Leqi Zhu. A tight space bound for consensus. 2016. To appear in STOC '16.

Concurrent Data Structures

Faith Ellen
Department of Computer Science
University of Toronto, Canada
faith@cs.toronto.edu

Trevor Brown
Department of Computer Science
University of Toronto, Canada
tabrown@cs.toronto.edu

Data structures are an important component of efficient and well-structured programs. In shared memory distributed computing, correct data structures are difficult to construct because concurrent accesses by different processes can conflict with one another. One simple approach is to use a global lock to restrict access to one process at a time. But this can severely affect performance. This talk will present a survey of some of the interesting techniques that have been developed to build efficient concurrent data structures. It will also discuss how we think concurrent data structures should be evaluated.

1. TECHNIQUES

One natural technique is for a process to only lock a small portion of the data structure that is currently being accessed. This is known as fine grain locking. An example of this is hand-over-hand locking [2, 19]. However, such data structures are not fault tolerant. If a process crashes while holding a lock, part of the data structure may become inaccessible.

Another approach is to build lock-free (non-blocking) or wait-free data structures. These ensure that some processes or all processes can always complete an operation on the data structures, no matter how the processes are scheduled. However, there typically needs to be some way for processes accessing the same part of a data structure to synchronize with one another. For example, nodes that are going to be deleted can be *marked* so that no other processes will later modify these nodes [14] or auxillary nodes can be added between real nodes be prevent conflicts between updates of adjacent nodes [25].

For complicated updates that involve changing multiple pointers, processes must record information about the updates they are performing, so that other processes can help complete the updates, in case the processes are slow or crash. Nodes involved in such an update can be *flagged* and store information in specially dedicated fields or store a pointer to an information node describing the update [12, 10].

PODC'16 July 25-28, 2016, Chicago, IL, USA

ACM ISBN 978-1-4503-3964-3/16/07.
DOI: http://dx.doi.org/10.1145/2933057.2933123

If an operation takes effect by applying a single atomic primitive, there is no need to record information about the update, because it is never interrupted. Atomic multi-word primitives (such as multi-word compare&swap) can simplify the implementation of complicated updates. However, such primitives are typically not available. An alternative is to use lock-free linearizable implementations of more powerful primitives from weaker primitives such as compare&swap [7]. The key is to choose powerful primitives that are well-suited for implementing data structure operations, but are not so powerful that they preclude efficient implementations.

Transactional memory enables concurrent data structures to be built very easily: simply put each operation inside a transaction [16]. However, the high overhead of software transactional memory means that the resulting data structures are inefficient. Using hardware transactional memory reduces the overhead, but does not provide any progress guarantees. Therefore, data structures built using hardware transactional memory must provide a software fallback path. To allow the hardware and software paths to run concurrently (avoiding concurrency bottlenecks), hardware transactions must be instrumented, which adds significant overhead. With two hardware paths, one instrumented and one not, together with a software fallback path, high efficiency can be obtained without introducing concurrency bottlenecks [5].

It is typically easier to implement a data-structure with weak progress guarantees, for example, obstruction-freedom. However, there are techniques that can automatically transform (a class of) implementations to have stronger progress guarantees [11, 13, 24].

Instead of trying to implement an efficient sequential data structure in a concurrent setting, it is sometimes better to implement a version having relaxed structural properties. For example, with lazy deletion, a node is marked to logically delete it from a set and may be physically deleted later [14, 4]. In a chromatic tree, updates (such as rotations), which are used to help rebalance the tree, are decoupled from the insertion and deletion of nodes and can be freely interleaved with other updates [3, 8]. Breaking up a big operation into a number of smaller pieces can be especially beneficial for implementations using hardware transactional memory, because there are capacity limits that cause transactions accessing too many memory locations to fail.

Alternatively, one can relax the definition of the abstract data type to be implemented. A pool (bag) maintains a set which supports an operation that returns an an *arbitrary* element, rather than a specified element (such as the element that was inserted earliest or latest). For some applications where a queue or stack is employed, a pool is sufficient and can be implemented more efficiently [17, 23, 1]. Other examples of relaxed concurrent data types can be found in [22].

An atomic snapshot of a data structure is useful for iterating through the data structure, for example, when performing a range query or for generating a consistent backup copy of the data structure. A *persistent data structure*, in which each update creates a new version of the data structure without destroying previous versions, automatically provides atomic snapshots. However, it can use a lot of space, even when large parts of the data structure are shared by consecutive versions. For example, in a persistent binary search tree, each update creates a copy of all the nodes it changes as well as all ancestors of these nodes. Other implementations are more space efficient [4, 21, 20].

For sequential and lock-based data structures, memory reclamation is easy. For lock-free and wait-free data structures, it can be difficult to determine when a node can safely be freed (and then reused) after it has been deleted from the data structure. Before a process can free a node, it must know that no other process is currently accessing the node or can reach it (by following a sequence of pointers). Hazard pointers [15, 18] provide a very popular memory reclamation scheme for use with concurrent data structures. However, when a deleted node can point to other deleted nodes, as in the chromatic tree, hazard pointers cannot be used. There are alternative memory reclamation schemes for such data structures (surveyed in [6]), but they are significantly more complicated. Because many concurrent data structures involve a lot of copying and, thus, create a lot of garbage, memory reclamation can have a significant impact on their performance. Thus, choosing (or possibly constructing) a good memory reclamation scheme is an important component of building a concurrent data structure.

2. EVALUATION

Papers about concurrent data structures range from the presentation of new algorithmic techniques and the design and analysis of new data structures to experimental comparison of different data structures and algorithmic engineering.

If the focus of the paper is algorithmic, the work must include rigorous proofs of correctness. Researchers should not rely on high level proof sketches. Concurrent data structures can be sensitive to seemingly insignificant reordering of operations and some errors are quite subtle. Unfortunately, there are numerous examples of incorrect concurrent data structures that have been published (or would have been published, but for a dedicated expert reviewer). It is the responsibility of researchers to ensure that their data structures are correct. Verification tools are being developed, but, so far, they are difficult to use and have only been applied to relatively simple concurrent data structures.

Complexity analyses of concurrent data structures should also be provided. For wait-free algorithms, determining the worst-case step complexity is usually straightforward and is often part of the proof of wait-freedom. However, lock-free data structures require an amortized or average-case analysis. This is typically much more involved [9]. As is the case for papers about sequential data structures, an interesting analysis (and, especially, new analytical techniques) can be an important contribution of a paper.

If the focus of the paper is experimental, the experiments should be reproducible and, ideally, vetted (for example, through artifact evaluation, as is done in some systems conferences). It is important that experiments are measuring the right aspects of concurrent data structures. For example, one concurrent data structure may appear to be more efficient than another, but, in reality, the differences can be due to small optimizations, better coding, or a different memory reclamation scheme. Even when two different data structures are evaluated using the same experimental setup, on the same hardware, using the same operating system and the same memory reclamation scheme, there may be significant overhead in the experimental setup that masks substantial differences in their performance. For example, if an operation takes 1 millisecond and another operation takes 1 microsecond, but the overhead is 1 millisecond, then the first operation appears to be only a factor of 2 slower, rather than a factor of 1000 slower. Even more troubling, a set of experiments performed on two concurrent data structures on the same machine can lead to opposite conclusions when performed on a different machine.

When evaluating concurrent data structures, such as balanced search trees, which are designed for good worst-case behaviour, it is insufficient to only consider randomly generated input data. Since binary search trees are likely to remain relatively balanced under random sequences of insertions and deletions, the overhead of rebalancing is wasted. Naturally, unbalanced binary search trees perform significantly better in these experiments.

Even when one wants to compare the average case performance of concurrent data structures, one has to be careful how one chooses the data. For example, for multi-sets (which can contain multiple copies of the same key), using different proportions of insertions and deletions might lead to data structures that become empty or grow without bound. However, this is provably not the case for sets.

Comprehensive experiments that fairly evaluate a variety of concurrent data structures can be very valuable. Experiments should be chosen to not only present the relative performance of different concurrent data structures, but provide some understanding about *why* one performs better than another under various conditions. For example, one might use experiments to determine when it is faster to replace a small subtree with a new copy rather than update information in that subtree. It is also interesting to compare concurrent data structures using real-world data to determine which is best for a particular application or class of applications and which optimizations are useful.

Papers which describe a slightly new concurrent data structure (for example, using known techniques to obtain a small variation of an existing data structure), together with experiments on which it performs better than some other existing data structures, are not worthy of publication in top conferences and journals. Unfortunately, many such papers are submitted.

On the other hand, a paper with a new and interesting algorithmic idea, but with performance results that are comparable to (or slightly worse than) existing data structures (or even with no experiments), should not be automatically rejected "since it isn't practical." Other researchers may be able to build on the approach or combine it with other existing approaches to engineer a very efficient data structure, possibly for a specific application.

Acknowledgments

This work was supported by by the Natural Science and Engineering Research Council of Canada.

3. REFERENCES

[1] Y. Afek, M. Hakimi, and A. Morrison. Fast and scalable rendezvousing. *Distributed Computing*, 26(4):243–269, 2013.

[2] R. Bayer and M. Schkolnick. Concurrency of operations on B-trees. *Acta Inf.*, 9:1–21, 1977.

[3] J. Boyar, R. Fagerberg, and K. S. Larsen. Amortization results for chromatic search trees, with an application to priority queues. *Journal of Computer and System Sciences*, 55(3):504–521, 1997.

[4] N. G. Bronson, J. Casper, H. Chafi, and K. Olukotun. A practical concurrent binary search tree. In *Proc. 15th ACM Symposium on Principles and Practice of Parallel Programming (PPoPP)*, pages 257–268, 2010.

[5] T. Brown. Brief announcement: Faster data structures in transactional memory using three paths. In *Proc. 29th International Symposium on Distributed Computing (DISC)*, pages 671–672, 2015.

[6] T. Brown. Reclaiming memory for lock-free data structures: There has to be a better way. In *Proc. 34rd ACM Symposium on Principles of Distributed Computing (PODC)*, pages 261–270, 2015.

[7] T. Brown, F. Ellen, and E. Ruppert. Pragmatic primitives for non-blocking data structures. In *Proc. 32nd ACM Symposium on Principles of Distributed Computing (PODC)*, pages 13–22, 2013.

[8] T. Brown, F. Ellen, and E. Ruppert. A general technique for non-blocking trees. In *Proc. 19th ACM Symposium on Principles and Practice of Parallel Programming (PPoPP)*, pages 329–342, 2014.

[9] F. Ellen, P. Fatourou, J. Helga, and E. Ruppert. The amortized complexity of non-blocking binary search trees. In *Proc. 33rd ACM Symposium on Principles of Distributed Computing (PODC)*, pages 332–340, 2014.

[10] F. Ellen, P. Fatourou, E. Ruppert, and F. van Breugel. Non-blocking binary search trees. In *Proc. 29th ACM Symposium on Principles of Distributed Computing (PODC)*, pages 131–140, 2010.

[11] F. E. Fich, V. Luchangco, M. Moir, and N. Shavit. Obstruction-free algorithms can be practically wait-free. In *Proc. 19th International Conference on Distributed Computing (DISC)*, pages 78–92, 2005.

[12] M. Fomitchev and E. Ruppert. Lock-free linked lists and skip lists. In *Proc. 23rd ACM Symposium on Principles of Distributed Computing (PODC)*, pages 50–59, 2004.

[13] G. Giakkoupis, M. Helmi, L. Higham, and P. Woelfel. An $O(\sqrt{n})$ space bound for obstruction-free leader election. In *Proc. 27th International Symposium on Distributed Computing (DISC)*, pages 46–60, 2013.

[14] T. L. Harris. A pragmatic implementation of non-blocking linked-lists. In *Proc. 15th International Conference on Distributed Computing (DISC)*, pages 300–314, 2001.

[15] M. Herlihy, V. Luchangco, P. A. Martin, and M. Moir. Nonblocking memory management support for dynamic-sized data structures. *ACM Trans. Comput. Syst.*, 23(2):146–196, 2005.

[16] M. Herlihy and N. Shavit. *The Art of Multiprocessor Programming*. Morgan Kaufmann, 2012.

[17] U. Manber. On maintaining dynamic information in a concurrent environment (preliminary version). In *Proc. 16th Annual ACM Symposium on Theory of Computing (STOC)*, pages 273–278, 1984.

[18] M. Michael. Hazard pointers: Safe memory reclamation for lock-free objects. *IEEE Transactions on Parallel and Distributed Systems*, 15(6):491–504, 2004.

[19] M. Moir and N. Shavit. Concurrent data structures. In *Handbook of Data Structures and Applications*. Chapman and Hall/CRC Press, 2004.

[20] E. Petrank and S. Timnat. Lock-free data-structure iterators. In *Proc. 27th International Symposium on Distributed Computing (DISC)*, pages 224–238, 2013.

[21] A. Prokopec, N. Bronson, P. Bagwell, and M. Odersky. Concurrent tries with efficient non-blocking snapshots. In *Proc. 17th ACM SIGPLAN Symposium on Principles and Practice of Parallel Programming (PPoPP)*, pages 151–160, 2012.

[22] N. Shavit and G. Taubenfeld. The computability of relaxed data structures: Queues and stacks as examples. In *Proc. 22nd International Colloquium on Structural Information and Communication Complexity (SIROCCO)*, pages 414–428, 2015.

[23] N. Shavit and D. Touitou. Elimination trees and the construction of pools and stacks. *Theory Comput. Syst.*, 30(6):645–670, 1997.

[24] S. Timnat and E. Petrank. A practical wait-free simulation for lock-free data structures. In *Proc. ACM SIGPLAN Symposium on Principles and Practice of Parallel Programming (PPoPP)*, pages 357–368, 2014.

[25] J. D. Valois. Lock-free linked lists using compare-and-swap. In *Proc. 14th ACM Symposium on Principles of Distributed Computing (PODC)*, pages 214–222, 1995.

Contention Resolution on a Fading Channel

Jeremy T. Fineman*
Georgetown University
jfineman@cs.georgetown.edu

Seth Gilbert†
Natl. Univ. of Singapore
seth.gilbert@comp.nus.edu.sg

Fabian Kuhn‡
U. of Freiburg, Germany
kuhn@cs.uni-freiburg.de

Calvin Newport§
Georgetown University
cnewport@cs.georgetown.edu

ABSTRACT

In this paper, we study upper and lower bounds for contention resolution on a single hop *fading* channel; i.e., a channel where receive behavior is determined by a signal to interference and noise ratio (SINR) equation. The best known previous solution solves the problem in this setting in $O(\log^2 n/\log\log n)$ rounds, with high probability in the system size n. We describe and analyze an algorithm that solves the problem in $O(\log n + \log R)$ rounds, where R is the ratio between the longest and shortest link, and is a value upper bounded by a polynomial in n for most feasible deployments. We complement this result with an $\Omega(\log n)$ lower bound that proves the bound tight for reasonable R. We note that in the classical *radio network model* (which does not include signal fading), high probability contention resolution requires $\Omega(\log^2 n)$ rounds. Our algorithm, therefore, affirms the conjecture that the spectrum reuse enabled by fading should allow distributed algorithms to achieve a significant improvement on this $\log^2 n$ speed limit. In addition, we argue that the new techniques required to prove our upper and lower bounds are of general use for analyzing other distributed algorithms in this increasingly well-studied fading channel setting.

CCS Concepts

•Networks → Network algorithms; •Theory of computation → Distributed algorithms;

Keywords

contention resolution, leader election, wireless channel, wireless algorithms, SINR model

*Research supported by NSF CCF 1314633
†Research supported by NUS FRC T1 251RES1404
‡Research supported by ERC Grant No. 336495 (ACDC)
§Research supported by NSF CCF 1320279

PODC'16, July 25 - 28, 2016, Chicago, IL, USA

ISBN 978-1-4503-3964-3/16/07...$15.00

DOI: http://dx.doi.org/10.1145/2933057.2933091

1. INTRODUCTION

Contention resolution is one of the oldest and most important problems in distributed computing. In its basic form, an unknown set of nodes are activated and connected to a shared multiple-access channel (MAC). The protocol completes when any active node transmits alone on the channel. This problem (also, in some contexts, called *wake-up* or *leader election*) was introduced in the seminal 1970 paper on the ALOHA radio network [1]. In the decades that followed, researchers have studied it under a wide variety of assumptions concerning the MAC model and algorithm constraints; e.g., [2, 5, 7, 9, 10, 15, 17, 18, 20, 21, 23]. This interest in contention resolution is well-deserved. From a theoretical perspective, the problem reduces to most non-trivial tasks in MAC models, and therefore lower bounds provide fundamental speed limits for distributed computation in these settings. And from a practical perspective, algorithms for contention resolution have been integrated into link-layer implementations for numerous real world systems, including Ethernet, fiber optic, packet-switch radio, and satellite networks.

Our Results. We study contention resolution in a *fading* MAC model—i.e., a model in which radio signal reception is determined by a *signal to interference and noise ratio* (SINR) equation [19] (see Section 2). Signal fading is a characteristic behavior of radio communication. Therefore, by studying contention resolution on a fading MAC, we can probe the possibility of leveraging this property to speed-up distributed computation in the increasingly important radio network setting.

We study randomized algorithms using a fixed transmission power. We develop an algorithm that solves the problem in $O(\log n + \log R)$ rounds, where n is the number of participating nodes, and R describes the ratio between the longest and shortest link in the network. In most feasible deployments, R is upper bounded by a polynomial in n,[1] yielding performance in $O(\log n)$. Our algorithm solves the problem with high probability in n, and does not require any advance knowledge of n. By contrast, the best existing bound requires just under $\log^2 n$ rounds (specifically,

[1]It is, of course, mathematically possible for R to be super-polynomial in n—say, exponential in n—which would cause the $\log^2 n$ bound to dominate. In practice, however, once n grows beyond relatively small numbers, to maintain such a large gap between link distances becomes increasingly infeasible. Even a network size of only 20 nodes, for example, would require that the longest link be on the order of a million times longer than the shortest link.

$O(\log^2 n/\log\log n)$ rounds), and assumes advance knowledge of n [16] (see the related work below).

We then match this upper bound with an $\Omega(\log n)$ lower bound that establishes our result's optimality in most networks. Our lower bound reduces a basic two-player symmetry breaking problem to contention resolution in a carefully constructed large fading network. This technique is potentially applicable to other lower bounds for distributed computation in fading models and is therefore of standalone interest.

Finally, we note that in the standard non-fading *radio network model* [2,3], the lower bound for contention resolution—and therefore for many problems—is $\Omega(\log^2 n)$ rounds. Our result improves this time by a square root, and therefore resolves the long-standing conjecture that the ability to leverage spatial reuse in fading models should allow distributed algorithms to significantly improve on this $\Omega(\log^2 n)$ speed limit.

Our Algorithm. A surprising attribute of our result is the simplicity of the algorithm from which it derives:

> Each participating node starts in an *active* state; at the beginning of each round, each node that is still active broadcasts with a constant probability p (that we fix in our analysis); if an active node receives a message, it becomes inactive.

Arguably, this algorithm represents the simplest possible strategy for reducing contention, and yet it nonetheless implicitly leverages spectrum reuse to provide a time bound that is optimal in a fading model and beats the lower bounds for non-fading models. This outcome was unexpected when we began this investigation, and it is something we find to be pleasingly elegant.

Our Techniques. The simplicity of our algorithm is counterbalanced by the complexity of its analysis. The bulk of this paper is dedicated to showing that it terminates in $O(\log n+\log R)$ rounds. In more detail, a standard approach for analyzing algorithms in a fading model is to divide nodes into *link classes* based on the distance to their nearest neighbors. Existing techniques based on packing arguments prove that nodes in the smallest non-empty link class have limited contention. Our algorithm should then "knock out" a constant fraction of these nodes. These observations yield an $O(\log n \log R)$ bound, i.e., in the worst-case, we spend $\log n$ rounds emptying each of the $\leq \log R$ link classes, in order of smallest to largest.

To break past the $\log n \log R$ threshold, however, we must show that *many* link classes can concurrently experience limited contention. To show this fact requires two analytical innovations that we argue are of general use for the study of distributed algorithms on fading channels. First, we prove that a larger (in terms of link length) link class can have many (though not all) nodes enjoying low contention if there are not *too many* nodes in smaller link classes. We show this in Section 3.2, fully exploiting the geometry of the fading model. Among other tactics, when studying the interference at a receiver from the same (and larger) link classes, we take advantage of the small—but non-trivial—gap between the quadratic growth of interfering nodes as we move away from the receiver, and the super-quadratic fading of signals, as captured by the standard assumption that the fading exponent α is greater than 2. In the space created by this gap, we are able, in some sense, to fit the interference from the bounded number of smaller link class nodes.

Second, we introduce a *fitting strategy* for bounding the fluctuations in link class sizes as the execution proceeds. As described in Section 3.3, we define a sequence of vectors, $q_1, q_2, \ldots$, where each q_t is an upper bound on the link class sizes. These vectors describe, roughly speaking, how these link class sizes would decrease in an ideal execution. We then show that every execution eventually obeys this steady progression. We note that the process of bounding the link class sizes is complicated by two factors in particular: (1) nodes can move between link classes during an execution as their nearest neighbors are deactivated, so progress is not monotonic; and (2) as link class sizes get small (i.e., $o(\log n)$), we can no longer make high probability arguments about their sizes continuing to reduce. We overcome these issues by carefully defining the q vectors, and a careful treatment of probabilities in which we show that the higher error probabilities of small link classes are balanced by the geometrically decreasing error probabilities of the larger classes.

Related Work. The study of contention resolution began with the random access method introduced in the ALOHA paper in 1970 [1], and continued in the 1980's [9,10,17,18, 21,23] (see [6] for a good survey of early work). Over the next decade, there was an increasing interest in the so-called *radio network model* [2,3], which assumes concurrent transmissions are lost at all receivers due to collision and—in a break from earlier work—transmitters do not learn the fate of their transmissions. (Once in this model, the contention resolution problem is now also sometimes called *wake-up* [7].) In this model, high probability contention resolution requires $\Theta(\log^2 n)$ rounds—a bound that improves to $\Theta(\log n)$ if you assume receivers can detect collisions [20]. Given an upper bound N on the network size n, the strategy of [2] can be adapted to yield a solution that solves the problem in $O(\log N)$ expected rounds. (Our algorithm, by contrast, works without any information about n, and with high probability.)

Early in the new millennium came a renewed interest in algorithms for *fading models* of radio networks (sometimes called the *SINR* or *physical* model) which claim to better capture the real behavior of radio communication. The bulk of these initial efforts focused on centralized approximation algorithms for core problems such as link scheduling and capacity maximization. Early on, Moscibroda and Wattenhofer [19] proved that algorithms for fading models can achieve better performance than for the radio network model for certain centralized scheduling problems due to spatial reuse of the spectrum (a capability enabled by super-quadratic signal fading). This result implies that a similar advantage should hold for distributed algorithms as well. As detailed below, although others have studied distributed algorithms in the fading model, our paper is one of the first to validate this conjecture by demonstrating a solution to a fundamental distributed problem that significantly outperforms the relevant radio network model lower bound. (A key caveat to this claim is that we restrict our attention to the standard model for the distributed setting where the transmission power is fixed and provided. Under the assumption of power control, it is sometimes possible to do better; e.g., [11]. Similarly, under the assumption of tunable carrier sensing—a generalization of receiver collision detection—it it is also possible to do better than the radio network model without collision detection; e.g., [22].

Specifically, Jurdziński and Kowalski [13] describe how to create a low-contention backbone in $O(\Delta\text{polylog}(n))$ rounds, for local density bound Δ, Daum et al. [4] show how to solve global broadcast in $O(D \log n \cdot \text{polylog}(R))$ rounds, for network diameter D, while Jurdziński et al. [14] provide a $O(D \log^2 n)$ round broadcast solution, which is more efficient for sufficiently large R. Turning to local communication, Goussevskaia et al. [8] show how to solve local broadcast in $O(\Delta \log^3 n)$ nodes, which Halldorsson and Mitra later improved to $O(\Delta \log n + \log^2 n)$ rounds [12]. All of these results can be used to solve contention resolution in a single-hop fading MAC. None, however, perform better than $\Omega(\log^2 n)$ rounds in this context. Moreover, we also note that each of these distributed algorithms at best matches the best known result for their problem in the non-fading radio network model. It follows that none of these previous results demonstrate the potential to *beat* these bounds in a fading setting—a key contribution of our result.

In a recent breakthrough, Jurdziński and Stachowiak [16] confirmed the permeability of the $\log^2 n$ barrier by showing how to solve contention resolution on a fading MAC in $O(\log^2 n/\log\log n)$ rounds. Their algorithm speeds up a standard $O(\log^2 n)$ strategy from the radio network model to now progress a factor of $\log\log n$ times faster. To compensate for this speed-up, they also add a dampening strategy that takes advantage of the spatial reuse possible on a fading channel to slow down the algorithm *just enough* at the right phase to allow it to succeed with the needed probability. Unlike our algorithm, their solution requires advance knowledge of a (polynomial) upper bound on the network size. On the other hand, their solution is insensitive to R, whereas our algorithm slows as R increases. To the best of our knowledge, our algorithm remains the first to achieve a significant improvement on the $\log^2 n$ bound for the contention resolution problem on a fading channel.

2. MODEL AND PROBLEM

We model randomized algorithms in a synchronous single hop radio network with fading signals. Let V be a set of *nodes* (representing wireless devices) deployed in the two-dimensional Euclidean plane. Time is divided into synchronous rounds, labeled $1, 2, 3, \ldots$. In each round, each node can either (i) transmit at a fixed power P, or (ii) listen. The standard signal to interference and noise ratio (SINR) equation governs which messages are received by listening nodes. That is, node $v \in V$ receives a message transmitted by a node $u \in V$, in a round where the nodes in $I \subseteq V \setminus \{u, v\}$ also transmit, if and only if v is listening and:

$$SINR(u,v,I) = \frac{\frac{P}{d(u,v)^\alpha}}{N + \sum_{w\in I}\frac{P}{d(w,v)^\alpha}} \geq \beta, \qquad (1)$$

where P is the constant transmission power, $d(x,y)$ is the distance between x and y, $\alpha > 2$ is the path-loss exponent, and $N \geq 0$ is the noise. We refer to $\frac{P}{d(w,v)^\alpha}$ as the interference caused by w at v.

Let R be the ratio of the longest to shortest link in the network. To simplify, we assume that link lengths are normalized so that the shortest is 1 and the longest is R. We assume that $\lg R$ is a whole number.

We assume a *single hop* network. In the context of fading models, this means that all node pairs are sufficiently close to communicate in the absence of interference. Formally, the power P must be sufficiently large so that, for every pair $u, v \in V$: $P > c \cdot \beta \cdot N \cdot d(u,v)^\alpha$, for some constant $c > 1$ (for the purposes herein, it is sufficient to assume $c \geq 4$). This assumption that node pairs have a signal strength at least a constant factor larger than β is standard in defining "single hop" in the SINR context. (Allowing node pairs to be placed at distances too near the communication threshold trivially eliminates the possibility of spatial reuse.)

Problem. The *contention resolution* problem assumes an unknown subset of nodes in V are activated. The problem is solved in the first round in which a participating node transmits alone among all participating nodes. (We emphasize that these nodes receive no *a priori* information about the number or identity of the other active nodes.) We study probabilistic solutions that work with *high probability*, i.e., at least $1 - \frac{1}{n}$.

3. UPPER BOUND ANALYSIS

We now analyze the performance of the simple contention resolution algorithm described in the introduction. Our goal is to prove that the algorithm solves the problem in $O(\log n + \log R)$ rounds. After defining some useful notation and assumptions in Section 3.1, we split the analysis into two parts. The first part (Section 3.2) leverages the geometric properties of the model to analyze conditions under which nodes experience bounded contention. The second part (Section 3.3) makes use of this result to bound the number of rounds required for our algorithm to resolve contention. All omitted proofs (along with more detailed calculations) can be found in the full version.

3.1 Preliminaries

For this analysis, we assume R is upper bounded by a polynomial or a quasipolynomial in n—as this is the interesting case for which our $O(\log n + \log R)$ bound beats existing $O(\log^2 n)$ strategies. (For the case where R is larger, one can default to existing results. If R is unknown, then our algorithm can be interleaved with an existing algorithm.) Accordingly, we use $O(\log n)$ and $O(\log R)$ interchangeably in the following.

For a given round, we partition the active nodes into at most $\lg R$ ***link classes***, $d_0, d_1, \ldots, d_{\log R-1}$, where d_i contains all nodes whose nearest neighbor is at a distance in the range $[2^i, 2^{i+1})$. For a given link class d_i, we define V_i to be the set of nodes in link class d_i that are active, and n_i to indicate $|V_i|$. We can replace subscript i with $< i$, $\leq i$, $> i$, and $\geq i$, in defining V and n, as needed. When there is only one node left, it has no closest active neighbor, and therefore it is not in any link class. Once we have emptied all link classes the problem is solved: the broadcast that deactivates the final remaining nodes is a solo broadcast.

3.2 Interference Analysis

Fix a single round of an execution of our contention resolution algorithm. All definitions and claims in this section are defined with respect to this fixed round. In the following, for a fixed distance d, let $B(u,d)$ be the set of active nodes within distance d of u. For two natural numbers i and t, and node $u \in V$, let the ***exponential annulus*** $A_t^i(u)$ be the set of active nodes $B(u, 2^{(t+1)}2^i) \setminus B(u, 2^t 2^i)$.

Good Nodes. We use the definition of an exponential annulus to define the notion of a ***good node***. Intuitively, a good node is one for which each annulus centered on the node does not contain too many other nodes, for a definition of "too many" that grows with distance as a function of α (defined in Equation 1). Formally:

DEFINITION 1. *Fix a node $u \in V_i$ (i.e., it is active and in link class d_i). We say u is* **good** *if for every $t \in \{0, \ldots, \lg R\}$, $|A_t^i(u)| \leq 96 \cdot 2^{t(\alpha-\epsilon)}$, for $\epsilon = \alpha/2 - 1$.*

We want to show that a large fraction of the good nodes have a good probability of receiving a message and becoming inactive—an event we refer to as being "knocked out." To do so, we first identify a subset of the good nodes that are (at the risk of overusing this word) good candidates to be knocked out. In more detail, for a given link class V_i and constant $s > 0$ (that is fixed in Lemma 4), we define $S_i \subseteq V_i$ to be the largest subset of good nodes in V_i such that for every $u, v \in S_i$, the distance $d(u,v) > (s+1)2^i$. That is, every pair of nodes in S_i is sufficiently far apart. Applying a standard circle-packing argument, we note that S_i contains at least a constant fraction of the good nodes in V_i:

LEMMA 2. *If link class d_i contains k good nodes, then $|S_i| = \Theta(k)$.*

Now we bound the expected interference at the nodes in S_i during our fixed round. (It is in this lemma that the probability of broadcast p is fixed.) We begin by bounding the interference from nodes not in S_i. For a given node $u \in S_i$, let its *partner* be the closest active node v to u (breaking ties arbitrarily). We use T_i to be the set of partner nodes of the nodes in S_i. For the purpose of the below lemma, we define *outside interference* for u to be the sum of the signal strengths of all transmitting nodes that are *not* in $S_i \cup T_i$.

LEMMA 3. *For any constant $c > 0$, there exists a choice of constant broadcast probability $p > 0$ and a constant c' (depending only on c and α) such that the following holds: Let d_i be a non-empty link class. Then with probability at least $1 - e^{-c'|S_i|}$, for at least $|S_i|/2$ nodes in S_i, the outside interference at each of these nodes is $\leq cP/2^{i\alpha}$.*

PROOF. The proof proceeds in several steps. We first observe that the collective interference on nodes in S_i is bounded by $c_{max}|S_i|P/2^{i\alpha}$, for some constant c_{max} that depends only on α; similarly, the maximum interference that any single node outside S_i can generate on nodes in S_i is $c_{max}|S_i|P/2^{i\alpha}$, even if they all broadcast at once. (See Claims 1 and 2).

We then use a Chernoff bound to show that the total interference caused by all the nodes outside S_i, since they broadcast with probability p, is at most $c|S_i|P/2^{i\alpha+1}$ with probability at least $1 - e^{-c'|S_i|}$, for some constant c' that depends only on c and c_{max} (i.e., it depends on α). (See Claim 3.) This then immediately implies the lemma.

Claim 1. The total interference experienced by all the nodes in S_i, collectively, is at most $P_{max} = c_{max}|S_i|P/2^{i\alpha}$, for some constant c_{max}.

PROOF OF CLAIM 1. Fix a node $u \in S_i$. We now bound the maximum interference at u. In more detail, to sum the interference at u, we sum the possible outside interference from the nodes in every (potentially) non-empty annulus defined with respect to u and d_i; e.g., $A_0^i(u), A_1^i(u), \ldots, A_{\lg R}^i(u)$. Noting that a node in $A_t^i(u)$ is of distance at least $2^i 2^t$ from u, we bound the maximum interference by:

$$\begin{aligned}
\sum_{t=0}^{\lg R} |A_t^i(u)| \frac{P}{(2^i 2^t)^\alpha} &= \frac{P}{2^{i\alpha}} \sum_{t=0}^{\lg R} \frac{|A_t^i(u)|}{2^{t\alpha}} \\
&\leq \frac{P}{2^{i\alpha}} \sum_{t=0}^{\lg R} \frac{96 \cdot 2^{t(\alpha-\epsilon)}}{2^{t\alpha}} \\
&= \frac{96 \cdot P}{2^{i\alpha}} \sum_{t=0}^{\lg R} \frac{1}{2^{t\epsilon}} \\
&\overset{\epsilon>0}{<} \frac{96 \cdot P}{2^{i\alpha}} \left(\frac{1}{1 - 1/2^\epsilon} \right)
\end{aligned}$$

The final simplification is taken from a geometric series, observing that 2^ϵ is a constant strictly greater than 1 (because $\epsilon = \alpha/2 - 1 > 0$ for $\alpha > 2$).

Setting $c_{max} = 96(1/(1-1/2^\epsilon))$, we conclude that the total interference at u is at most $c_{max}P/2^{i\alpha}$, and hence the total interference experienced by all the nodes in S_i, collectively, is at most $c_{max}|S_i|P/2^{i\alpha}$. □

Notice that if $c \geq c_{max}$, then we are already done, since we have shown in the proof of Claim 1 that the total interference at each node $u \in S_i$ is at most $c_{max}P/2^{i\alpha}$. For the remainder of the proof, we assume that $c < c_{max}$.

Next, we focus on the nodes broadcasting. For each node u *not* in S_i, let $int(u)$ be the sum total possible interference generated by node u at nodes in S_i, i.e., $int(u) = \sum_{v \in S_i} P/d(u,v)^\alpha$.

Claim 2. For all $u \notin S_i$, $int(u) \leq c_{max}P/2^{i\alpha}$, for constant c_{max}.

PROOF OF CLAIM 2. Notice that this is actually almost identical to Claim 1, except the symmetric opposite: we are quantifying the interference caused by u instead of the interference caused at u. This claim again follows by summing the possible interference by u in each of the exponential annuli, as before.

However, we cannot depend on node u being good. Instead, we conclude that there cannot be too many nodes in S_i in an annulus because the nodes in S_i are at least distance 2^i apart.

More specifically, for each node in S_i, we can draw a circle of radius 2^{i-1} around it such that no two circles intersect. That is, each point occupies an area of $\pi 2^{2(i-1)}$. The annulus A_t^i has outer radius $2^{t+1}2^i$ and inner radius $2^t 2^i$. Some of the circles drawn around points in S_i may be near the edge of the annulus, and hence we increase its outer radius and decrease its inner radius by 2^{i-1} to account for this. Thus, all the points in S_i in A_t^i are contained in area:

$$\begin{aligned}
\pi(2^{t+1}2^i + 2^{i-1})^2 - \pi(2^t 2^i - 2^{i-1})^2 &\leq \pi(2^{t+1}2^i + 2^{i-1})^2 \\
&\leq \pi(2^{t+1}2^{i+1})^2 \\
&\leq \pi 2^{2(t+i+2)}
\end{aligned}$$

(Note that this is a loose approximation that ignores the inner part that is subtracted off, but it is sufficient.) Since each point occupies $\pi 2^{2(i-1)}$ space, we conclude that there are at most $2^{2(t+3)}$ points in S_i in the annulus A_t^i.

$$\begin{aligned}\sum_{t=0}^{\lg R} |A_t^i(u)\cap S_i| \frac{P}{(2^i 2^t)^\alpha} &= \frac{P}{2^{i\alpha}} \sum_{t=0}^{\lg R} \frac{|A_t^i(u)\cap S_i|}{2^{t\alpha}} \\ &\le \frac{P}{2^{i\alpha}} \sum_{t=0}^{\lg R} \frac{2^{2t+6}}{2^{t\alpha}} \\ &= \frac{64P}{2^{i\alpha}} \sum_{t=0}^{\lg R} \frac{1}{2^{t(\alpha-2)}} \\ &\overset{\alpha-2>0}{<} \frac{64\cdot P}{2^{i\alpha}}\left(\frac{1}{1-1/2^{\alpha-2}}\right)\end{aligned}$$

Since $(\alpha-2) \ge (\alpha/2-1) = \epsilon$ (and $64 < 96$), we conclude that the maximum interference by any node not in S_i is bounded by $c_{max}P/2^{i\alpha}$. □

We now proceed to show that, with high probability (with respect to $|S_i|$), the total interference when nodes broadcast with some probability p is not too large, i.e., is no greater than $c|S_i|P/2^{i\alpha+1}$.

Claim 3. The total interference caused by outside nodes is $c|S_i|P/2^{i\alpha+1}$ with probability at least $1-e^{-c'|S_i|}$, for some constant c' that depends only on c and c_{max}.

PROOF OF CLAIM 3. First, if the total interference, even if all the outside nodes broadcast, is already $\le c|S_i|P/2^{i\alpha+1}$, then we are done. For the remainder of the proof, we assume the maximum total interference created by outside nodes is at least $c|S_i|P/2^{i\alpha+1}$, that is, $\sum_{u\notin S_i\cup T_i} int(u) \ge c|S_i|P/2^{i\alpha+1}$.

We have shown in Claim 2 that for all $u \notin S_i$, $int(u) \le c_{max}P/2^{i\alpha}$. We define the random variable x_u that equals $int(u)2^{i\alpha}/(c_{max}P)$ when u broadcasts with probability p, and 0 otherwise. Notice that $x_u \in [0,1]$.

We now fix the probability p that a node broadcasts: choose $p = c/(4c_{max})$ (where the constant c is that given in the statement of Lemma 3). Recall that $c < c_{max}$ (or we would have been done after Claim 1), and so we know that $p \in [0, 1/4]$.

Recall, from Claim 1, we know that $\sum_{u\notin S_i\cup T_i} int(u) \le c_{max}|S_i|P/2^{i\alpha}$. Hence, we can bound the expected value of the sum of x_u as follows:

$$\begin{aligned}\mathbb{E}\left[\sum_{u\notin S_i\cup T_i} x_u\right] &= \sum_{u\notin S_i} p\cdot int(u)2^{i\alpha}/(c_{max}P) \\ &= p \sum_{u\notin S_i\cup T_i} int(u)2^{i\alpha}/(c_{max}P) \\ &\le p\cdot(c_{max}|S_i|P/2^{i\alpha})(2^{i\alpha})/(c_{max}P) \\ &\le p|S_i| \\ &\le c|S_i|/(4c_{max}) \ .\end{aligned}$$

By the same logic, since we have assumed that $\sum_{u\notin S_i} int(u) \ge c|S_i|P/2^{i\alpha+1}$, we can lower bound the expected value of the sum of x_u:

$$\begin{aligned}\mathbb{E}\left[\sum_{u\notin S_i\cup T_i} x_u\right] &= \sum_{u\notin S_i} p\cdot int(u)2^{i\alpha}/(c_{max}P) \\ &= p \sum_{u\notin S_i\cup T_i} int(u)2^{i\alpha}/(c_{max}P) \\ &\ge p\cdot(c|S_i|P/2^{i\alpha+1})(2^{i\alpha})/(c_{max}P) \\ &\ge p(c/2c_{max})|S_i| \\ &\ge (c^2/8c_{max}^2)|S_i| \ .\end{aligned}$$

We now rely on the standard Chernoff bound which states that for any set of independent random variables $x_1,\ldots,x_n$ where $x_i \in [0,1]$, we know that $\Pr(\sum_{i=1}^n x_i \ge 2\mu) \le e^{-\mu/3}$, where $\mu = \mathbb{E}\left[\sum_{i=1}^n x_i\right]$.

Let $\mu = \mathbb{E}\left[\sum_{u\notin S_i\cup T_i}(x_u)\right]$. Then we conclude that:

$$\begin{aligned}\Pr\left(\sum_{u\notin S_i} x_u \ge 2\mu\right) &\le e^{-\mu/3} \\ &\le e^{-\left(\frac{c^2}{24c_{max}^2}\right)|S_i|}\end{aligned}$$

Here, we set $c' = \left(\frac{c^2}{24c_{max}^2}\right)$, and conclude that the probability of failure is at most $e^{-c'|S_i|}$, for some constant c' that depends only on c and c_{max}, as stipulated by the claim.

Finally, we observe that when this failure does not occur, i.e., $\sum_{u\notin S_i\cup T_i} x_u < 2\mu$, this implies that the total interference caused by nodes not in S_i can be bounded by:

$$\begin{aligned}\sum_{u\notin S_i\cup T_i} x_u\cdot c_{max}P/2^{i\alpha} &\le (c_{max}P/2^{i\alpha})\cdot(2c|S_i|/(4c_{max})) \\ &\le c|S_i|P/2^{i\alpha+1}\end{aligned}$$

This concludes the proof of the claim. □

From Claim 3, we immediately derive the desired conclusion for Lemma 3: it cannot be the case that there are $|S_i|/2$ nodes in S_i that are subject to more than $cP/2^{i\alpha}$ interference each from outside nodes, since that requires total interference from outside nodes of more than $c|S_i|P/2^{i\alpha+1}$. □

We next consider the interference caused by nodes *in* the set $S_i \cup T_i$ and show that it too is bounded. By leveraging the fact that nodes in S_i are not too close to each other (by definition), we can prove the strong bound that even if all nodes in $S_i \cup T_i$ transmit, the interference this causes at each node in the set is low.

LEMMA 4. *For any constant $c > 0$, there exists a choice of constant $s > 0$ such that the following holds: Let $u \in S_i$ be a good node in S_i, let $v \in T_i$ be u's partner, and let d_i be the link class of u. Then the sum of interference at u from nodes in $S_i \cup T_i \setminus \{v\}$ is no more than $cP/2^{i\alpha}$.*

PROOF. Let $S_t^i(u) = (S_i \cup T_i \setminus \{v\}) \cap A_t^i(u)$ be the set of nodes in S_i in the annulus $A_t^i(u)$. We calculate the interference from the nodes in $S_i \cup T_i \setminus \{v\}$ by summing over each annulus. Every node in S_i is at distance at least $(s+1)2^i$ away from u; hence every node in $S_i \cup T_i$ is at distance at least $s2^i$ away from u, and the smallest non-empty annulus $A_i^t(u)$ is $t = \log s$. Note that nodes in annulus $A_t^i(u)$ are at distance at least $2^i 2^t$ away from u, we rely on the notion of "good" to bound the interference from $S_i \cup T_i \setminus \{v\}$:

$$\sum_{t=\log s}^{\lg R} |A_t^i(u)| \frac{P}{(2^i 2^t)^\alpha} \frac{96 \cdot P}{2^{i\alpha}} \left(\frac{1/s^\epsilon}{1 - 1/2^\epsilon} \right)$$

Setting $s = \left(\frac{96}{c(1-1/2^\epsilon)}\right)^{1/\epsilon}$ we get our needed total interference of $cP/2^{i\alpha}$. □

At this point, we have proved that for each d_i, the set S_i (consisting of well-spaced good nodes) contains many nodes that expect low total interference (both internal and external). We now leverage this property to prove the key corollary: with high probability in $|S_i|$, a constant fraction of the nodes in S_i are knocked out.

COROLLARY 5. *Let d_i be a non-empty link class. There exists a constant broadcast probability $p > 0$ and constant $c > 0$, such that with probability at least $1 - e^{-c|S_i|}$: at least a constant fraction of the nodes in S_i become inactive.*

PROOF. By Lemmas 3 and 4, for any constant c', with probability at least $1 - e^{-|S_i|/c''}$ (for some c''), there exists a subset of nodes $S \subseteq S_i$ such that: S contains at least $|S_i|/2$ nodes and for each node $u \in S$ with partner node $v \in T_i$, even if all nodes in $S_i \cup T_i \setminus \{u, v\}$ broadcast, the interference at node u is upper bounded by $\leq 2c'P/2^{i\alpha}$. For now, assume these two properties hold for S.

Next, consider a node $u \in S$, and let v be its partner. The interference bounds derived in Lemmas 3 and 4 are independent of whether u and v broadcast. Hence, conditioned on S satisfying the above two properties, with probability $p(1-p)$, node v transmits and node u listens.

If this event (v transmits and u listens) occurs, we argue that node u receives this message and becomes inactive: the strength of the signal from v at u is at least least $P/2^{\alpha(i+1)}$, and the total interference at u is at most $2c'P/2^{i\alpha}$, for an arbitrary choice of c'. Thus the condition for u to receive the message from v is:

$$\frac{P/2^{\alpha(i+1)}}{2c'P/2^{i\alpha} + N} > \beta \ .$$

We see that the condition is satisfied as long as: (i) $c' \leq 1/(2^{\alpha+2}\beta)$ (as determined in Lemma 3 by choice of the constant), and (ii) $P > 4BNd(u,v)^\alpha \geq 2\beta N 2^{\alpha(i+1)}$ (as required by the assumption in Section 2 that the network is connected).

Let $S' \subseteq S$ be the subset of S that is knocked out. Each node in S succeeds independently with probability $p(1-p)$ (since no two nodes share the same partner, by the definition of S_i), and hence the expected number of successes is $p(1-p)|S|$. A standard Chernoff bound then implies that: $\mathbb{P}[|S'| < p(1-p)|S|/2] \leq e^{-p(1-p)|S|/8}$. Thus, with probability at least $1 - e^{-|S_i|/16}$, our above two properties on S hold, and with an additional probability $1 - e^{-p(1-p)|S|/8}$ we know that S' is at least a constant fraction of S (and therefore is a constant fraction of S_i). The corollary follows from a union bound of these two error probabilities. □

Bounding the Number of Good Nodes. So far, we have shown that a constant fraction of the good nodes in a given link class will be knocked out with high probability (w.r.t. the number of such nodes in the class). We now prove that we expect there to be *enough* good nodes, in general, that these knock outs can add up to something significant. The remainder of this section is dedicated to proving a single lemma that takes on this challenge. In particular, it argues that if some link class d_i has more nodes than all smaller link classes combined (by some constant factor), then at least a constant fraction of the nodes in d_i are good. Combining this lemma with Corollary 5 implies that big link classes shrink quickly (see Corollary 7 below). This observation is the club that Section 3.3 will later wield to subdue our algorithm's time complexity.

LEMMA 6. *There exists a constant fraction δ, $0 < \delta < 1$, such that for every link class d_i, if $n_{<i} \leq \delta \cdot n_i$, then at least half the nodes in V_i are good.*

PROOF. There are two types of nodes found in the annuli of a node in d_i those in link classes d_i or larger, and those from smaller link classes. We deal with each case separately. Before doing so, we introduce an extra definition. We define a node u to be ***extra good*** with respect to $V_{\geq i}$ (or $V_{<i}$), if the number of these nodes that fall within each $A_t^i(u)$ is at least a factor of 2 smaller than required simply to be *good* (i.e., replace the 96 with a 48 in the earlier definition). If a node is extra good with respect to *both* $V_{<i}$ and $V_{\geq i}$ simultaneously, then the node is good as per the original definition. We will show: (1) every node in V_i is extra good with respect to $V_{\geq i}$, and (2) at least half the nodes are extra good with respect to $V_{<i}$.

Step #1: Nodes in $V_{\geq i}$. Fix any node $u \in d_i$ and any annulus $A_t^i(u)$. We will show that the number of nodes from larger link classes $V_{\geq i}$ falling within this annulus satisfies the definition of extra good. By the definition of the link class, no disk of radius $2^i/4$ can contain more than one such node. A straightforward packing argument bounds the number of such disks that fit in the annulus, showing that there are at most $48 \cdot 2^{2t} \leq 48 \cdot 2^{t(\alpha-\epsilon)}$ node from link classes $V_{\geq i}$ in $A_t^i(u)$.

Step #2: Nodes in $V_{<i}$. We now consider the more difficult case. Fix an annulus distance t. We will sum $|A_t^i(u) \cap V_{<i}|$ over every $u \in V_i$. To do so, we leverage the first key technical insight in this argument: $\sum_{u \in V_i} |A_t^i(u) \cap V_{<i}| = \sum_{v \in V_{<i}} |A_t^i(v) \cap V_i|$ (i.e., just switch the endpoint from which we consider each relevant link). This insight is important because the latter sum is counting nodes from V_i, which allows us to deploy the same style of density bound that proved useful in the large link class case. In more detail, let Γ_t^i indicate the above sum. We bound this parameter as:

$$\begin{aligned} \Gamma_t^i &= \sum_{u \in V_i} |A_t^i(u) \cap V_{<i}| = \sum_{v \in V_{<i}} |A_t^i(v) \cap V_i| \\ &\leq n_{<i} \cdot 48 \cdot 2^{2t} \leq n_i \cdot \delta \cdot 48 \cdot 2^{2t}. \end{aligned}$$

This derivation uses the following properties: (1) $|A_t^i(v) \cap V_i| \leq 48 \cdot 2^{2t}$, as we established in our argument above for larger link classes; and (2) $n_{<i} \leq \delta \cdot n_i$, as assumed by the lemma statement.

The second key technical insight in this argument is to note that the average number of nodes in $A_t^i(u) \cap V_{<i}$ for a node $u \in V_i$ is $O(2^{2t})$. This amount is asymptotically less than the number of nodes allowed in this annulus for the definition of extra good. (Recall, a good node can tolerate up to $O(2^{t(\alpha-\epsilon)})$ nodes in this annulus, and because $\epsilon =$

$\alpha/2-1$ and $\alpha > 2$, this simplifies to $2^{t(\alpha/2+1)} = \omega(2^{2t})$). It follows the number of nodes in V_i that violate the definition of (extra) good for this annulus distance must be *less* than a constant fraction. To be more precise, suppose that $n_i \cdot \gamma \cdot \frac{1}{2^{t(\alpha-\epsilon-2)}}$ nodes violate the extra good definition for this annulus, for a constant fraction γ, $0 < \gamma < 1$, which we will fix later. At a minimum, these nodes contribute more than the following number of nodes to Γ_t^i:

$$n_i \cdot \gamma \cdot \frac{1}{2^{t(\alpha-\epsilon-2)}} \cdot 48 \cdot 2^{t(\alpha-\epsilon)} = n_i \cdot \gamma \cdot 48 \cdot \frac{2^{t(\alpha-\epsilon)}}{2^{t(\alpha-\epsilon-2)}} = n_i \cdot \gamma \cdot 48 \cdot 2^{2t}.$$

If we fix $\delta < \gamma$, then this sum is already larger than Γ_t^i. It follows, therefore, that the fraction of nodes that are not extra good in this annulus must be less than $\gamma \cdot \frac{1}{2^{t(\alpha-\epsilon-2)}}$.

We now sum up the total number of nodes that might violate the definition of extra good over all $\lg R$ annulus distances. We note that:

$$\sum_{t=0}^{\lg R} n_i \cdot \gamma \frac{1}{2^{t(\alpha-\epsilon-2)}} = \sum_{t=0}^{\lg R} n_i \cdot \gamma \frac{1}{2^{t\epsilon}} = n_i \cdot \gamma \sum_{t=0}^{\lg R} \frac{1}{c^t},$$

for constant $c = 2^\epsilon > 1$.[2] The fact that $c > 1$ is important as this casts the sum as a converging geometric series. In particular, we know that: $\sum_{t=0}^{\lg R} \frac{1}{c^t} < \sum_{t=0}^{\infty} \frac{1}{c^t} \le \frac{1}{1-(1/c)}$.

To achieve our final lemma, however, we need our sum over all annuli to be upper bounded by $n_i/2$. Unfortunately, $1/(1-1/c)$ may be much larger than $1/2$, i.e., if c is close to 1. Fixing $\gamma = (1-1/c)/2$, we recast our above upper bound sum of the number of *not* extra good nodes overall as:

$$\sum_{t=0}^{\lg R} n_i \cdot \gamma \frac{1}{2^{\epsilon t}} \le n_i \cdot \gamma \cdot \frac{1}{1-1/c} = n_i/2,$$

as needed. Having fixed γ, we set $\delta = \gamma/2$. □

Combining the main result of both parts of this analysis section we conclude with the final corollary:

COROLLARY 7. *There exists a constant broadcast probability $p > 0$, constant δ, $0 < \delta < 1$, and constant $c > 0$ such that for every link class d_i, if V_i is non-empty, and $n_{<i} \le \delta \cdot n_i$, then with probability at least $1 - e^{-c|V_i|}$, at least a constant fraction of the active nodes in V_i become inactive.*

PROOF. If we fix δ as required by Lemma 6, we know by this same lemma that (at least) half the nodes in V_i are good. By Lemma 2, we know that S_i contains at least a constant fraction of the good nodes in V_i. By Corollary 5, we know that there exists a broadcast probability p such that with probability at least $1 - e^{-c'|S_i|}$, for a constant $c' > 0$, a constant fraction of the nodes in S_i, and therefore a (smaller) constant fraction of V_i, receive a message and become inactive. The constant factor c in the probability in our corollary statement is simply the constant needed to satisfy the equality $c'|S_i| = c|V_i|$. □

3.3 Round Complexity Analysis

We now leverage the analysis of interference in a single round from Section 3.2 to bound the behavior of our algorithm over multiple rounds. We will conclude with our main result: our algorithm solves contention resolution in $O(\log n + \log R)$ rounds, with high probability. Our strategy is to first define a series of variables that capture the evolution of link class sizes in an ideal execution. We will then prove that these size bounds provide an upper bound (of sorts) on these sizes in all executions.

[2]To establish that $c > 1$, note that $2^\epsilon = 2^{\alpha/2-1}$. Because $\alpha > 2$, c is defined as 2 raised to some small value greater than 0, which implies $c > 1$.

Definitions. We begin by extracting key constants from Corollary 7. In the following, assume the algorithm uses a broadcast probability no larger than the necessary probability identified by this corollary. Let γ be the constant fraction, also provided by the corollary, that describes an upper bound on the fraction of nodes in a link class d_i that will remain (i.e., not be knocked out), with high probability in the link class size $|V_i| = n_i$, given that the size of smaller link classes sum to something sufficiently small; i.e., $n_{<i} \le \delta \cdot n_i$.

Building on these values, let γ_{slow}, where $\gamma < \gamma_{slow} < 1$, be a constant fraction larger than γ that we will define later. Let $\rho < 1$ be another positive constant that we will define later, and let $\ell = \lceil \log_{\gamma_{slow}} \rho \rceil$. In the following, let $m = \lg R$. Recall, we assumed for simplicity that m is a whole number.

Class Bounds Vectors. We now define a series of m-vectors, $q_0, q_1, q_2, \ldots$, that we call ***class bound vectors***. These vectors will later be used to provide a sequence of upper bounds on the sizes of the link classes. To define these vectors, we first define a *start step* s_i for each $i \in [m]$ as $s_i = i \cdot \ell$. That is, $s_0 = 0$, $s_1 = \ell$, $s_2 = 2\ell$, and so on. Prior to round s_i, we do not require any progress to be made in link class d_i. For each $i \in [m]$, we define the corresponding position in our class bound vector as follows:

$$\forall t \ge 0 : q_t(i) = \begin{cases} n & \text{if } t \le s_i, \\ \lfloor q_{t-1}(i) \cdot \gamma_{slow} \rfloor & \text{if } t > s_i \end{cases}$$

In other words, the size of each link class reduces by a factor of γ_{slow} in each phase. The smallest link class, $i = 0$, begins this reduction immediately. For each $i > 0$, the reduction begins an additional ℓ rounds later. Viewed differently, because link class $i-1$ has undergone ℓ more reductions in size than class i whenever $t \ge s_i$, we have $q_t(i-1) = \gamma_{slow}^{\ell} q_t(i) \le \rho q_t(i)$. That is, ρ can be interpreted as (approximately) the constant ratio in size between two consecutive link classes. Given that γ_{slow} and ℓ are both constants, it is straightforward to bound the smallest t for which all positions in the vector q_t are 0:

CLAIM 8. *Let T be the smallest phase number where $\forall i \in [m], q_T(i) = 0$. Then $T = \Theta(\log n + \log R)$.* □

Link Class Size Behavior. To establish progress, we want to identify a time when a given link class bound is achieved. That is, for each position t (equiv., *step t*) in our sequence of class bound vectors, we want to find an execution round such that in this round, for every link class d_i: $n_i \le q_t(i)$. This task, however, is complicated by the observation that a link class can both shrink *and* grow (i.e., when a node u's nearest neighbor is knocked out, u's next nearest neighbor might upgrade it to a larger link class). Therefore, we refine our goal, seeking a round such that for that round, *and all following rounds*, the link class sizes are bounded by q_t. With this in mind, we define an auxiliary class bound vector that captures an important threshold of link size that implies performance. Specifically, for each step t and class d_i we define:

$$\widehat{q_{t+1}}(i) = q_t(i)\gamma_{slow} - q_t(i)\rho/(1-\rho).$$

In other words, $\widehat{q_{t+1}}(i)$ is a more aggressive bound on $q_{t+1}(i)$ that subtracts an additional factor of $q_t(i)\rho/(1-\rho)$ from the number of nodes allowed in a class. Intuitively, this bound implies permanence. To make this argument more precise, we need the following claim about the original class bound vector definitions, which follows from the fact that $q_t(i)$ decreases geometrically in t:

LEMMA 9. *If $q_{t+1}(i) < n$ for some step t and link class i, then $q_t(< i) = \sum_{j=0}^{i-1} q_t(j) \le q_t(i)\left(\frac{\rho}{1-\rho}\right)$.*

Now assume that in round r, for link class d_i and step t, two things are true: (1) for all $j < i$, $n_j \le q_t(j)$; and (2) $n_i \le \widehat{q_{t+1}(i)}$. Then n_i will remain less than $q_{t+1}(i)$ for all future rounds. To see why, observe that even if all the at most $q_t(< i)$ nodes in smaller link classes jumped to link class d_i, by the definition of $\widehat{q_{t+1}(i)}$, the size of d_i would still be bounded by $q_{t+1}(i)$. (And no node can join a smaller link class.)

With our auxiliary definitions in place, we can continue our effort to bound the evolution of link class sizes with respect to our class bound vectors. To this end, we define event $r(t)$, for step t, to be the earliest point in the execution where, for every size class d_i, $n_i \le q_t(i)$, and this bound holds for the remainder of the execution. That is, $r(t)$ is the point where the link class sizes *permanently* fall below q_t.

To analyze these events, we divide the execution into *segments* each consisting of a constant number of rounds (we will fix the constant in the proof). Conditioned on the fact that event $r(t)$ occurred by the end of segment $k-1$, we calculate the probability that event $r(t+1)$ happens by the end of segment k. We will show that this probability is constant. To do so, we emphasize that success in each round (and therefore also each multi-round segment) is independent, as they consist of nodes making independent random choices.

LEMMA 10. *Consider a segment and assume that by the beginning of the segment, event $r(t)$ has occurred, for some step $t \ge 0$. Then event $r(t+1)$ occurs by the end of this segment, with constant probability.*

PROOF SKETCH. By assumption, at the beginning of the segment, the vector q_t bounds all size classes. We examine each round in the segment and calculate the probability that by the end of the round, q_{t+1} is a permanent upper bound on all link classes. To do so, we will show the stronger property that the link classes sizes drop below the $\widehat{q_{t+1}}$ sizes. We begin by fixing class d_i and focus on a single round r in the segment.

One round analysis: There are three cases for this class in this round. The first two cases are easy to dispose of: if $q_t(i) = 0$ or if $q_{t+1}(i) = n$, then it is easily observed that the condition is satisfied $q_{t+1}(i)$.

The third case is that $q_{t+1}(i) < n$. First we fix γ_{slow} and ρ. Specifically, we choose: $\gamma_{slow} = \gamma + \rho/(1-\rho)$, and we choose ρ sufficiently small that $\frac{\rho}{1-\rho} < \gamma\delta$, where δ is the constant derived in Corollary 7.

We now focus on round r in the current segment, and calculate the probability that n_i falls below $\widehat{q_{t+1}}(i)$. Assume that prior to round r, $n_i \ge \widehat{q_{t+1}}(i)$. (Otherwise, we are already done.) In order to apply Corollary 7, our main tool for reducing link class sizes, we need that $n_{<i} \le \delta n_i$. By assumption $n_{<i} \le q_t(< i)$, and by Lemma 9, $q_t(< i) \le q_t(i)\,(\rho/(1-\rho))$. We also assumed: $n_i > \widehat{q_{t+1}}(i) = q_t(i)\gamma_{slow} - q_t(i)\rho/(1-\rho)$. Therefore, solving for $q_t(i)$ in the $\widehat{q_{t+1}}(i)$ definition and substituting into our $q_t(< i)$ equation, we get $n_{<i} \le \left(\frac{\rho}{1-\rho}\right)\frac{n_i}{\gamma_{slow}-\rho/(1-\rho)}$. To bound $n_{<i}$, therefore, we need to show the following inequality:

$$n_{<i} \le \left(\frac{\rho}{1-\rho}\right)\frac{n_i}{\gamma_{slow}-\rho/(1-\rho)} < \delta n_i \ .$$

By the manner in which we fixed γ_{slow} and ρ, this inequality is true.

We can now apply Corollary 7 to class i and obtain the following result: with probability at least $1-e^{-cn_i}$, a constant fraction of nodes in n_i are knocked out, i.e., after round r, the number of remaining active nodes (not counting new nodes that migrate to d_i from smaller link classes) is at most

$$\gamma n_i \le (\gamma_{slow} - \rho/(1-\rho))q_t(i) = \widehat{q_{t+1}}(i) \ .$$

That is, with probability at least $1-e^{-c|n_i|}$, link class d_i falls below $\widehat{q_{t+1}(i)}$, and by our above arguments, will therefore remain bounded by $q_{t+1}(i)$ permanently—regardless of migrations from smaller link classes.

Concluding: To this point, we have shown that in every round in our fixed segment, with probability at least $1-e^{-cn_i}$, the size of link class d_i drops permanently below the threshold $q_{t+1}(i)$ (i.e., as indicated by dropping below $\widehat{q_{t+1}(i)}$). Until we meet this threshold, this is true independently in each round independently of what happened in previous rounds, as each round's outcome is based on the independent broadcast choices made during the round.

Fix the segment length to $\max\{(2\tau)/(c(1-\gamma_{slow})), 2\tau\} = \Theta(1)$ rounds, where $\tau > 1$ is the constant that satisfies $q_{t+1}(i) = \tau\widehat{q_{t+1}}(i)$. Notice that

$$\tau \le q_{t+1}(i)/\left(q_t(i)\left[\gamma_{slow} - \rho/(1-\rho)\right]\right) \le \gamma_{slow}/\gamma.$$

The probability of class d_i *not* dropping below the threshold is therefore at most:

$$\begin{aligned} e^{-2\tau n_i/(1-\gamma_{slow})} &\le (1-\gamma_{slow})/(2\tau n_i) \\ &\le (1-\gamma_{slow})/(2\tau\widehat{q_{t+1}}(i)) \\ &= (1-\gamma_{slow})/(2q_{t+1}(i)). \end{aligned}$$

Since n_i has not yet dropped below our target threshold, we can substitute n_i with the value $\widehat{q_{t+1}}(i)$.

We then take a union bound over all the link classes d_j where $q_t(j) > 0$ and $q_{t+1}(j) < n$, calculating the probability that even one of them does not drop permanently below the threshold $q_{t+1}(\cdot)$:

$$\sum(1-\gamma_{slow})/(2n_j) \le \frac{(1-\gamma_{slow})}{2}\sum_{j=0}^{j=\infty}\gamma_{slow}^j \le \frac{1}{2}$$

This follows from the geometrically decreasing values of $q_t(\cdot)$, which bounds the n_j. We conclude that, with probability $\ge 1/2$, by the end of the segment, every link class irrevocably crosses the threshold of q_{t+1}. □

We can now conclude the analysis with our main result:

THEOREM 11. *Our algorithm solves contention resolution in $O(\log n + \log R)$ rounds, with high probability.*

PROOF SKETCH. In each segment, with constant probability, the system advances from $r(t)$ to $r(t+1)$ by Lemma 10. Since segments are independent, we conclude by a Chernoff bound that the process completes with high probability in $\Theta(T)$ segments, that is, (via Claim 8) in $\Theta(\log n + \log R)$ rounds. □

4. LOWER BOUND

By leveraging spatial reuse, the algorithm described above can solve high probability contention resolution in $O(\log n)$ rounds in networks of size n with $O(\log n)$ link classes.[3] Here we prove this bound near tight by establishing a $\Omega(\log n)$ lower bound for the contention resolution problem under these assumptions:

THEOREM 12. *Let $\mathcal{A}$ be an algorithm that guarantees to solve contention resolution in $f(n)$ rounds, with probability at least $1 - \frac{1}{n}$, when run in a network of size n with $O(\log n)$ link classes. It follows that $f(n) \in \Omega(\log n)$.*

We emphasize that our lower bound places no restrictions on the behavior of the algorithms we lower bound; e.g., as compared to many lower bounds in the MAC setting that require the assumption that the algorithm can be described as a fixed sequence of broadcast probabilities (see [20] for more discussion). The algorithms we bound, for example, can correlate behavior in one round with the outcome of random choices in a previous round, or have nodes that have successfully communicated correlate their behavior. As noted in the introduction, there are not many non-trivial lower bounds known for distributed computing in fading models, rendering this general strategy—which connects fading to combinatorial hitting games—of standalone interest.

We now continue with the proof details.

Restricted k-Hitting. We begin by introducing an abstract hitting game that was defined and bounded in [20]. We will use this existing result below to generate our bound for the related problem of two-player symmetry breaking. In more detail, the *restricted k-hitting* game is defined for an integer $k > 1$. It is played between a *player* and a *referee.* At the beginning of the game, the referee chooses a target set $T \subseteq \{1, 2, ..., k\}$ such that $|T| = 2$. The game proceeds in rounds. In each round, the player proposes a set $P \subseteq \{1, 2, ..., k\}$. If $|P \cap T| = 1$, the player wins. Otherwise, it moves to the next round, learning no information except that its proposal did not win. We can lower bound solutions to this game as follows:

LEMMA 13 (FROM [20]). *Fix some player $\mathcal{P}$ that guarantees, for all $k > 1$, to solve the restricted k-hitting game in $f(k)$ rounds, with probability at least $1 - \frac{1}{k}$. It follows that $f(k) \in \Omega(\log k)$.*

[3]When we say a network has ℓ link classes, we mean there are ℓ link classes that contain at least one of the $\binom{n}{2}$ possible links in the network. It is straightforward to show that the algorithm analyzed in this paper solves contention resolution in $O(\log n + \ell)$ rounds.

Two-Player Contention Resolution. Consider a *two-player* variant of the contention resolution problem that we parameterize with an integer $k > 1$, and that requires the players to break symmetry with probability at least $1 - \frac{1}{k}$. Notice, with two players, the fading behavior of the channel does not matter as with only two nodes there is no opportunity for spatial reuse. The game is won the first time one player transmits while the other listens: in all previous rounds, no messages are received.

We now lower bound this problem by reducing k-hitting to it and then applying Lemma 13.

LEMMA 14. *Let $\mathcal{A}$ be an algorithm that solves two-player contention resolution in $f(k)$ rounds with probability $1 - \frac{1}{k}$, for every parameter $k > 1$. It follows that $f(k) \in \Omega(\log k)$.*

PROOF. Fix some algorithm $\mathcal{A}$ that solves two-player contention resolution in $f(k)$ rounds with probability $1 - \frac{1}{k}$, for every parameter k. We use $\mathcal{A}$ to construct a player $\mathcal{P}_{\mathcal{A}}$ for the restricted k-hitting game that works in this same time with this same probability. It will then follow, by the direct application of Lemma 13, that $f(k) \in \Omega(\log k)$.

In more detail, our player simulates $\mathcal{A}$ on k nodes with unique ids from $\{1, 2, ..., k\}$. Each simulated round corresponds to a round of the restricted hitting game as follows: first, the player proposes the set containing the id of every node that broadcast in the current simulated round; then second, the player completes its simulation of the round by simulating all k nodes receiving nothing.

Let $T = \{i, j\}$ be the target set (unknown to the player) chosen for this instance of the restricted hitting game. Although the player is simulating k processes, we only care about its simulation of the processes with ids i and j. Notice, in each round of its simulation, these processes (like all others in the simulation) receive nothing. We want to argue that this behavior is consistent with an execution where only two nodes, with ids i and j, are present in the network. To see why this is true, notice that there are two relevant cases for what happens in a given round. The first case is that exactly one of the pair broadcasts. Here, it would be incorrect to subsequently simulate both receiving nothing (as in an execution with just i and j, the silent node would hear from the broadcaster). In this case, however, the player's proposal would win the restricted hitting game *before* the player is required to simulate the receive behavior for the current simulated round. The second case is that both nodes are silent or both broadcast. Here, the player is correct to simulate them receiving nothing, as this is consistent with what would happen in an execution with just i and j present, during a round where both did the same behavior.

Because the states of simulated nodes i and j are consistent with an execution in which only nodes i and j are present, it follows that $\mathcal{A}$ must solve two-player contention resolution with respect to these two nodes in $f(k)$ rounds, with probability at least $1 - \frac{1}{k}$. It follows, therefore, that our player solves the restricted hitting game in this same time with this same probability—as required by our argument. □

Reducing Two-Player to General Contention Resolution (sketch). To prove Theorem 12, we will prove that an algorithm that solves contention resolution in $f(n)$

rounds, with probability $1 - \frac{1}{n}$, when executed in a network of size n (for any $n > 1$), can be used to solve two-player contention resolution in $f(k)$ rounds, for any parameter k. The high-level idea is to have the two players—whom we will call Alice and Bob in this argument—each simulate the general contention resolution algorithm on half the nodes in a network of size k. In each round, if any of Alice's (resp. Bob's) simulated nodes transmit, then Alice (resp. Bob) transmits. Assuming Alice and Bob keep their local simulations valid, eventually exactly one node in the full simulated network transmits, meaning exactly one of the two simulators transmits—winning the two-player version of the problem.

The tricky part of this argument is defining the network simulated by Alice and Bob in such a way that they can keep their local simulations valid, even though they do not always know the behavior of the nodes simulated by the other player. Recall that we need this network to still maintain the strong assumptions that the network is single hop (for every (a, b), $SINR(a, b, \emptyset) \geq c \cdot \beta$, for some fixed constant $c \geq 1$) and that there are only $O(\log n)$ link classes (recall, our theorem statement only makes assumptions about the algorithm's behavior when the link class count is bounded, therefore the network we use in our simulation must bound the link classes). Our strategy is to carefully construct a network (e.g., identify node positions and valid model parameter values) in which interference from Bob cannot change the outcome of receive behaviors among Alice's nodes, and vice versa. The details of this network construction and the final proof for Theorem 12 are deferred to the full version.

5. REFERENCES

[1] N. Abramson. The ALOHA System: Another Alternative for Computer Communications. In *Proceedings of the Fall Joint Computer Conference*, 1970.

[2] R. Bar-Yehuda, O. Goldreich, and A. Itai. On the Time Complexity of Broadcast in Radio Networks: an Exponential Gap Between Determinism and Randomization. In *Proceedings of the International Symposium on Principles of Distributed Computing*, 1987.

[3] I. Chlamtac and S. Kutten. On Broadcasting in Radio Networks: Problem Analysis and Protocol Design. In *Proceedings of the Conference on Computer Communication*, 1985.

[4] S. Daum, S. Gilbert, F. Kuhn, and C. Newport. Broadcast in the Ad Hoc SINR Model. In *Proceedings of the International Symposium on Distributed Computing*, 2013.

[5] S. Daum, F. Kuhn, and C. Newport. Efficient Symmetry Breaking in Multi-Channel Radio Networks. In *Proceedings of the International Symposium on Distributed Computing*, 2012.

[6] R. Gallager. A Perspective on Multiaccess Channels. *IEEE Transactions on Information Theory*, 31(2):124–142, 1985.

[7] L. Gasieniec, A. Pelc, and D. Peleg. The Wakeup Problem in Synchronous Broadcast Systems. *SIAM Journal on Discrete Mathematics*, 14(2):207–222, 2001.

[8] O. Goussevskaia, T. Moscibroda, and R. Wattenhofer. Local Broadcasting in the Physical Interference Model. In *Proceedings of the International Workshop on the Foundations of Mobile Computing*. ACM, 2008.

[9] A. Greenberg and S. Winograd. A Lower Bound on the Time Needed in the Worst Case to Resolve Conflicts Deterministically in Multiple Access Channels. *Journal of the ACM*, 32(3):589–596, 1985.

[10] B. Hajek and T. van Loon. Decentralized Dynamic Control of a Multiaccess Broadcast Channel. *IEEE Transactions on Automatic Control*, 27(3):559–569, 1982.

[11] M. M. Halldorsson and P. Mitra. Distributed Connectivity of Wireless Networks. In *Proceedings of the ACM Conference on Distributed Computing*, 2012.

[12] M. M. Halldorsson and P. Mitra. Towards Tight Bounds for Local Broadcasting. In *Proceedings of the International Workshop on the Foundations of Mobile Computing*. ACM, 2012.

[13] T. Jurdzinski and D. Kowalski. Distributed Backbone Structure for Algorithms in the SINR Model of Wireless Networks. In *Proceedings of the International Conference on Distributed Computing*, 2012.

[14] T. Jurdzinski, D. R. Kowalski, M. Rozanski, and G. Stachowiak. On the impact of geometry on ad hoc communication in wireless networks. In *Proceedings of the ACM Conference on Distributed Computing*, 2014.

[15] T. Jurdziński and G. Stachowiak. Probabilistic Algorithms for the Wakeup Problem in Single-Hop Radio Networks. In *Algorithms and Computation*, pages 535–549. Springer, 2002.

[16] T. Jurdzinski and G. Stachowiak. The cost of synchronizing multiple-access channels. In *Proceedings of the ACM Conference on Distributed Computing*, 2015.

[17] M. Kaplan. A Sufficient Condition for Non-Ergodicity of a Markov Chain. *IEEE Transactions on Information Theory*, IT-25:470–471, July 1979.

[18] J. Komlos and A. Greenberg. An Asymptotically Nonadaptive Algorithm for Conflict Resolution in Multiple-Access Channels. *IEEE Transactions on Information Theory*, 31(2):302–306, 1985.

[19] T. Moscibroda and R. Wattenhofer. The Complexity of Connectivity in Wireless Networks. In *Proceedings of the IEEE International Conference on Computer Communications*, 2006.

[20] C. Newport. Radio Network Lower Bounds Made Easy. In *Proceedings of the International Symposium on Distributed Computing*, 2014.

[21] L. G. Roberts. ALOHA Packet System with and Without Slots and Capture. *ACM SIGCOMM Computer Communication Review*, 5(2):28–42, 1975.

[22] C. Scheideler, A. Richa, and P. Santi. An $O(\log n)$ Dominating Set Protocol for Wireless Ad-Hoc Networks under the Physical Interference Model. In *Proceedings of the International Symposium on Mobile Ad Hoc Networking and Computing*, 2008.

[23] D. Willard. Log-logarithmic selection resolution protocols in a multiple access channel. *SIAM Journal on Computing*, 15(2):468–477, 1986.

Reliable Communication over Highly Connected Noisy Networks

Noga Alon*
Tel Aviv University
nogaa@tau.ac.il

Mark Braverman†
Princeton University
mbraverm@cs.princeton.edu

Klim Efremenko‡
Tel-Aviv University
klimefrem@gmail.com

Ran Gelles
Princeton University
rgelles@cs.princeton.edu

Bernhard Haeupler
Carnegie Mellon University
haeupler@cs.cmu.edu

ABSTRACT

We consider the task of multiparty computation performed over networks in the presence of random noise. Given an n-party protocol that takes R rounds assuming noiseless communication, the goal is to find a coding scheme that takes R' rounds and computes the same function with high probability even when the communication is noisy, while maintaining a constant asymptotic *rate*, i.e., while keeping $\liminf_{n,R\to\infty} R/R'$ positive.

Rajagopalan and Schulman (STOC '94) were the first to consider this question, and provided a coding scheme with rate $O(1/\log(d+1))$, where d is the maximal degree in the network. While that scheme provides a constant rate coding for many practical situations, in the worst case, e.g., when the network is a complete graph, the rate is $O(1/\log n)$, which tends to 0 as n tends to infinity.

We revisit this question and provide an efficient coding scheme with a constant rate for the interesting case of fully connected networks. We furthermore extend the result and show that if a (d-regular) network has mixing time m, then there exists an efficient coding scheme with rate $O(1/m^3 \log m)$. This implies a constant rate coding scheme for any n-party protocol over a d-regular network with a constant mixing time, and in particular for random graphs with n vertices and degrees $n^{\Omega(1)}$.

*Sackler School of Mathematics and Blavatnik School of Computer Science, Tel Aviv University, Tel Aviv 69978, Israel and School of Mathematics, Institute for Advanced Study, Princeton, NJ 08540. Research supported in part by a USA-Israeli BSF grant, by an ISF grant, by the Israeli I-Core program and by the Oswald Veblen Fund.

†Research supported in part by an NSF CAREER award (CCF-1149888), a Turing Centenary Fellowship, a Packard Fellowship in Science and Engineering, and the Simons Collaboration on Algorithms and Geometry.

‡Research supported in part by: European Communitys Seventh Framework Programme (FP7/2007-2013) under grant agreement number 257575.

PODC'16, July 25 - 28, 2016, Chicago, IL, USA

ISBN 978-1-4503-3964-3/16/07...$15.00

DOI: http://dx.doi.org/10.1145/2933057.2933085

1. INTRODUCTION

The field of coding for interactive communication, initiated by Schulman in the early 90's [40, 41, 42], aims at performing arbitrary distributed computations when the communication channels between the different nodes suffer from noise. For the case where two parties communicate over a discrete memoryless channel (say, the binary symmetric channel that flips every bit with an independent probability of ε, denoted BSC_ε), the scheme of [42] provides an efficient coding with good parameters: the coding of an R-round (noiseless) protocol takes only $O(R)$ rounds, and gives the correct outputs with probability $1-2^{-\Omega(R)}$ over the noisy network.

In 1994, Rajagopalan and Schulman [39] extended the result to the multiparty case. Here we are given a network with n nodes of some arbitrary topology, where each communication link is an independent BSC_ε, where at every step of the protocol each party sends one bit through each one of the channels it is connected to (possibly sending different bits to different parties). In this case, any protocol of R rounds over the noiseless network can be coded into a resilient protocol that takes $O(R\log(d+1)+\log n)$ rounds and succeeds with probability $1-2^{-\Omega(R)}$. The parameter d is the maximum degree of any node in the network, i.e., the maximal number of links connected to a single party. Although the scheme of [39] is not efficient, Gelles, Moitra and Sahai [24, 25] showed that it can be extended to a fully efficient (randomized) scheme. The coding scheme of [39] has good parameters for any constant number of parties, however it may not work as well when the number of parties is large. Indeed, in highly connected networks, and in particular when the topology is a complete graph on n vertices, the redundancy added by the coding becomes $\Theta(\log n)$. In other words, the *rate*, the length of the noiseless protocol divided by the length of the encoded protocol, is vanishing, being $O(1/\log n)$.

We revisit the question of coding for multiparty interactive communication, and ask whether it is possible to find efficient coding schemes with rate $O(1)$ for the case where the network is highly connected, for example, when the topology is a complete graph.

We answer the above in the affirmative.

THEOREM 1.1 (CODING OVER COMPLETE GRAPHS). *For any n-party protocol π that takes R-rounds over the fully-connected (noiseless) network, and for any constant $\varepsilon < 1/2$, there exists a resilient protocol Π that simulates π over a fully connected network in which every link is a BSC_ε. The simulation is computationally efficient, takes $O_\varepsilon(R)$ rounds and succeeds with probability $1 - 2^{-\Omega(\sqrt{n}R)}$.*

This result sheds some light on the differences between the case where each pair of parties share a separate (noisy) channel, and the case where all the parties share a joint (noisy) broadcast channel. It was previously shown that if the users share a noisy *broadcast channel* then certain tasks, such as computing the parity of all the inputs, or learning the input bit of all the parties can be done in $O(n \log\log n)$ noisy-broadcast rounds [21], while assuming a noiseless broadcast channel, these tasks trivially take n rounds. Furthermore, these tasks cannot be done with fewer rounds when the channel is noisy, i.e., the $O(\log\log n)$ blowup is tight [29]. On the other hand, as implied by Theorem 1.1, such a blowup no longer holds in a setting where any two connected parties use a separate noisy channel.

In order to prove Theorem 1.1, we show a coding that simulates a single round of the noiseless protocol. Consider the *neighborhood connectivity* task in which each party holds one bit designated to each one of its neighbors. It is easy to verify that sending each bit directly requires $\Omega(\log n)$ rounds in order to be decoded correctly with high probability. However, we show a coding protocol that solves the neighborhood-connectivity task over a noisy network with high probability in $O(1)$ rounds. Instead of transmitting each bit directly, we relay each bit through large portions of the network using an appropriate (Shannon) error correcting code [43]. To illustrate this simple idea, consider a very simplified case in which some source s wishes to send a single bit to a target node t, over the noisy network. In order to complete this task in $O(1)$ rounds, s can relay its bit to all its $n-1$ neighbors, and then they will send their (noisy) copy to t. Thus, in two rounds the target node t receives $n-1$ independent estimations of the bit, where each estimation is correct with probability $(1-\varepsilon)^2 + \varepsilon^2$; this allows t to correctly decode the bit with high probability by taking the majority of the estimations.

With the above relaying technique in mind, we can design a coding scheme for the neighborhood connectivity in $O(1)$ rounds. Here is an outline. We describe the neighborhood connectivity task as an $n \times n$ matrix where each row and column describes a specific party and the (i, j) entry is the amount of bits the i-th party wants to communicate to the j-th party (in particular, the matrix is all-ones in the case of a complete graph). We first divide the n parties into subsets of size $\sqrt{n}$. This division can be seen as splitting the above matrix into n blocks of size $\sqrt{n}$ by $\sqrt{n}$. Next, we associate each such block with a specific party, or more accurately, we associate this party with the n-bits of information defined by that block in the matrix. The coding will work in two symmetric parts. First, each party (each row in the matrix) will encode each of the $\sqrt{n}$ bits that belong to a specific block and send it to the party associated with it. After this step, each party knows all the n bits of the block associated to it. Next, each associated party of a specific block will encode the $\sqrt{n}$ bits designated to a specific party (that is, the bits that lie in a column of the matrix), and send them to that party. Since both parts encode the bits prior to sending them, they will be decoded correctly with high probability.

Note that using the above relaying technique, it is possible to send each of the encodings (of length $O(\sqrt{n})$) in a constant number of rounds. In fact, we can parallelize their transmissions and communicate all the necessary information in a constant number of rounds.

Coding over Highly-Connected Topologies.

In addition to the complete graph topology, we also consider highly-connected networks whose topology is a d-regular graph with a small mixing time m (see Definition 5.1). We show a coding scheme with rate $O(1/(m^3 \log m))$ that succeeds with high probability.

THEOREM 1.2 (CODING OVER d-REGULAR GRAPHS). *Assume a network topology G of a d-regular graph with mixing time m, and assume $d > \log^{1+\Omega(1)} n$. For any n-party protocol π that takes R rounds over the noiseless network and for any $\varepsilon < 1/2$, there exists a resilient protocol Π that simulates π over the network G where every link is a BSC_ε. The simulation is computationally efficient, takes $O_\varepsilon(R \cdot m^3 \log m)$ rounds and succeeds with probability $1 - 2^{-\Omega(d^{\Omega(1)} \cdot R)} > 1 - n^{-\omega(1)R}$.*

For the case of $m = O(1)$, e.g., for random graphs with $d = n^\alpha$ for some constant $\alpha > 0$, Theorem 1.2 implies a coding scheme with a constant rate $\Theta(1)$, and a success probability of $1 - 2^{-n^{\Omega(1)}R}$. Note that the rate obtained by the coding scheme of [39] for such networks is $O(1/\log n^\alpha) = o(1)$.

Similar to the case of complete graphs, it suffices to solve the neighborhood-connectivity task in $O(1)$ rounds in order to obtain a constant rate scheme over a d-regular graph, assuming a constant mixing time $m = O(1)$. However, the challenge here is bigger than in the complete graph case, as every node is connected to a relatively small number of nodes, and it is not clear how to relay bits using arbitrary portions of the network. Nevertheless, we show a way for large subsets of nodes to talk with each other simultaneously without disturbing each other, in a reliable way. Specifically, assume we have a list of (distinct) source-target pairs where each source node aims to send a total amount of $O(d)$ bits, and so that each node appears at most $O(d/\Lambda)$ times in the list, for some parameter Λ. First we encode each chunk of information using a standard error correcting code that has failure probability $2^{-\Omega(\Lambda)}$ over a BSC_ε, and define a new list where each source-target pair appears with multiplicity which equals the number of bits to be transferred from that source to the target after the encoding. Note that in the transformed list, each node may appear up to $O(d)$ times. Next we show that it is possible to choose a set of short paths, such that for every element in the list there is a unique path connecting the source with the target (i.e., with parallel paths between multiple occurrences of the same source and target), and yet these paths are *jointly edge-disjoint*. This implies that we can deliver all the codewords to their destinations in constant number of rounds, and successfully decode each codeword with high probability. Choosing a set of edge-disjoint paths applies a variant of the methods used in the papers about finding edge-disjoint paths in expander graphs and in particular [12], see also [4] and the references therein. However, in our case we need all the paths to be of constant length $O(m)$, and we do not restrict the list of source-target pairs to be disjoint. Our approach applies the Lovász Local Lemma, where the basic combinatorial statement applied is the fact, first proved in [2], that given any family of pairwise disjoint sets of vertices in a graph, each of size somewhat larger than the maximum degree in the graph, there is always an independent set containing a vertex from each of these sets. Moreover, such an independent set can be found efficiently.

The above reliable coding is not enough to complete the proof: since we are restricted to source-target lists where each node appears at most $O(d/\Lambda)$ times, we cannot apply this method directly to the neighborhood-connectivity task. Indeed, each party begins with one bit to send to each of its d neighbors, and the $O(d/\Lambda)$ restriction cannot hold.

Still, using the above coding we show how to perform a sequence of relays where each causes the communication to be more "local". In other words, each relay splits the network into disjoint subsets where the communication is guaranteed to occur only between parties of the same subset. Each such a relay reduces the subset size by a factor of $\frac{\Lambda}{d}$ and increases the communication by only a constant factor. Since a mixing time m implies $d > n^{1/m}$, after $O(m) = O(1)$ relays (with the right choice of Λ), each subset is of size at most $O(d/\Lambda)$ while each party needs to communicate at most $O(d)$ bits. Now the communication demand satisfies the conditions of the coding scheme (i.e., every node appears at most $O(d/\Lambda)$ times in the induced source-target list) and we can employ the coding one last time to complete the task.

Related Work.

As mentioned above, the task of coding for interactive communication in the two party case, assuming random noise, was first considered by Schulman [40, 41, 42]. These constructions either have non-constant rate, or they utilize a data structure named *tree-code* for which no efficient construction is known. Later, Gelles, Moitra and Sahai [24, 25] provided a randomized relaxation for the tree code which can be constructed efficiently, thus solving the task efficiently when the noise model is random.

Another interesting model for the two-party interactive communication task is when the noise is not random but rather adversarial, where the only limit is on the total fraction of bit flips allowed. The maximal noise that can be tolerated, and efficient schemes that tolerate a constant fraction of noise (up to the possible limit) were considered in [10, 11, 6, 7, 27, 8]. A long sequence of works consider two-party interactive communication for various models and assumptions, e.g. when the parties are allowed to share a (private) random string [19, 20], the case of adaptive protocols [28, 1], the case of erasure channels and channels with feedback [20, 23, 17], and the case of private computations [14, 26]. The capacity (the maximal rate) of interactive protocols in the two-party case was considered by [34, 37, 31, 23]. See [22] for a survey.

Despite a large body of work on the two-party case, not too much is known for the multiparty case, beyond the aforementioned result of Rajagopalan and Schulman [39], and its efficient extension [24, 25]. Subsequent to the appearance of a preliminary version of this work, it was shown that a rate of $O(1)$ *cannot* be achieved for certain topologies, e.g., a star [9].

For the adversarial noise model, Jain, Kalai and Lewko [33] consider the case of multiparty interaction and show a tight $\Theta(1/n)$ bound on the fraction of noise, for star topology networks in the asynchronous model. Hoza and Schulman [32] show a coding scheme that applies to any network topology in the synchronous model, and resists a maximal noise level of $O(1/n)$ with rate $O(n/(E\log n))$, where E is the number of edges in the network. In addition, they provide a coding scheme, along with tight bounds on the permissible level of noise, for the interesting case where the noise level *per edge* is bounded.

2. PRELIMINARIES

Notations.

Let us fix some notations used throughout. Let $\mathbb{N} = \{0, 1, 2, \ldots\}$ denote the natural numbers (including zero), and for any integer $n \geq 1$, put $[n] = \{1, 2, 3, \ldots, n\}$. We say that a function $f(n)$ is *negligible* in n, if $f(n) \leq n^{-\omega(1)}$; We will usually want our constructions to fail with at most negligible probability in the number of parties. All logarithms throughout the paper are in base 2.

Noisy Networks and Protocols.

Given an undirected graph $G = (V, E)$ we assume a network with $n = |V|$ parties, where $u, v \in V$ share a communication channel if $(u, v) \in E$. In the case of a noisy network, each such link is assumed to be a BSC_ε.

DEFINITION 2.1. *A binary symmetric channel with error probability ε, is a binary channel $\mathsf{BSC}_\varepsilon : \{0,1\} \to \{0,1\}$ such that for any $b \in \{0,1\}$, it holds that $\Pr[\mathsf{BSC}_\varepsilon(b) \neq b] = \varepsilon$ independently for each instantiation of the channel.*

A single *round* of communication in the network means the simultaneous transmission of $2|E|$ bits: for any $(u, v) \in E$, u sends a bit to v and receives a bit from v. A protocol of length m that computes $f(x_1, \ldots, x_n) = (y_1, \ldots, y_n)$ is a distributed algorithm where each p_i begins the protocol with an input x_i, and after m rounds of communication each p_i outputs y_i.

In order to ease notations we usually assume G contains self loops and that a party can "send" a bit to itself. Concretely for a complete graph, each node has n neighbors rather than $n - 1$.

Finally, we will be using a standard error correction code, implied by the work of Shannon. Formally,

LEMMA 2.2 (SHANNON CODING THEOREM [43]). *For any discrete memoryless channel T with capacity C and any k, there exists a code $\mathsf{ECC} : \{0,1\}^k \to \{0,1\}^n$ and $\mathsf{ECC}^{-1} : \{0,1\}^n \to \{0,1\}^k$ with $n = O(\frac{1}{C}k)$ such that for any $m \in \{0,1\}^k$ it holds that,*

$$\Pr\left[\mathsf{ECC}^{-1}(T(\mathsf{ECC}(m))) \neq m\right] < 2^{-\Omega(n)}.$$

For a BSC_ε channel, the capacity C is given by $1 - H(\varepsilon) = 1 + \varepsilon\log\varepsilon + (1-\varepsilon)\log(1-\varepsilon)$. We note that one can efficiently construct codes with the above parameters (and efficiently encode and decode them), see, e.g., [44, 30].

3. THE NEIGHBORHOOD CONNECTIVITY TASK AND INTERACTIVE PROTOCOLS

A trivial observation is that any R-round multiparty interactive protocol can be split into R basic steps, in each of which every party has a single bit to send to any of its neighbors. We define this task as the *neighborhood connectivity* task.

Formally, for any network with n nodes, the neighborhood connectivity task is defined by

DEFINITION 3.1. *Let $\vec{a}_i = (a_{i,1}, \dots, a_{i,d_i})$ where for any $i \in [n], j \in [d_i]$ the bit $a_{i,j} \in \{0,1\}$ is to be interpreted as the input of party i which is designated to its j-th neighbor. The* Neighbor *function is defined as:*

$$\mathsf{Neighbor}(\vec{a}_1, \vec{a}_2, \dots, \vec{a}_n) = (\vec{b}_1, \vec{b}_2, \dots, \vec{b}_n).$$

where $\vec{b}_i$ consists of the d_i bits designated to party i by its d_i neighbors.

We say that some protocol computes the Neighbor task over a BSC_ε, if it fails with a negligible probability in n. Note that a successful computation of the Neighbor task implies that *all* parties have received the correct output; this is different from the standard successful transmission which usually accounts for only a single party, or a single bit transmission.

Composing R rounds of neighborhood connectivity immediately gives a coding scheme for any R-round protocol, yet with a success probability that decreases with R.

CLAIM 3.2. *For any network G and any R-round multiparty protocol π, if the neighborhood connectivity task over G can be performed in k rounds with probability $1 - n^{-\omega(1)}$, then there exists a coding Π that simulates π with $O(kR)$ rounds and succeeds with probability $1 - R \cdot n^{-\omega(1)}$.*

However in general the number of rounds R can be very large. We claim that even in this case, obtaining a coding protocol that succeeds with high probability is possible. To this end we use a result by Rajagopalan and Schulman [39] who showed an efficient coding scheme that succeeds to simulate any protocol over a memoryless noisy channel as long as the probability of correctly decoding a single transmission is at least $1 - (d+1)^{-\Omega(1)}$, where d is the maximal degree of a node in the network.

THEOREM 3.3 ([39]). *For any R round protocol π over any network G, there exists a coding scheme Π, that takes $O(R)$ rounds and succeeds with probability $1-n(2(d+1)p)^{\Omega(R)}$ given that any symbol transmitted in the network is correctly received with probability $1-p$ where d is the maximal degree of nodes in G.*

Sketch of proof. The theorem is an immediate consequence of the analysis of [39]. Although not written explicitly there, it easily follows from the analysis of Lemmas 5.1.1 and 5.1.2 in [39]; see also the detailed analysis in [38, Section 3]. We omit the details here. □

To bring the decoding probability of a single transmission to the required level of $p < (2(d+1))^{-\Omega(1)}$, Rajagopalan and Schulman simply use a Shannon code of length $O(\log(d+1))$, thus obtaining a similar overhead (see Lemma 5.1.2 in [39]). However, if we replace the Shannon code used in [39] with $O(1)$ rounds[1] of the neighborhood connectivity task, we effectively reduce the probability of a failed transmission to $p < n^{-\omega(1)} \ll (d+1)^{-\Omega(1)}$. This immediately implies the following.

[1]Each transmission in [39] is of a symbol taken from a small finite alphabet. Hence, each such symbol can be communicated with $O(1)$ rounds of (bit) neighborhood connectivity.

COROLLARY 3.4. *For any network G and any R-round multiparty protocol π, if the neighborhood connectivity task over G can be performed in k rounds with probability $1-p$ where $p = n^{-\omega(1)}$, then there exists a coding Π that simulates π with $O(kR)$ rounds and succeeds with probability $1 - p^{\Omega(R)}$.*

4. RESILIENT COMMUNICATION OVER COMPLETE GRAPHS

In this section we show a coding scheme for the neighborhood connectivity task that takes $O(1)$ rounds assuming the network has an underlying topology of a complete graph. Consider n parties where each two are connected via a BSC_ε for some constant $\varepsilon < 1/2$. The neighborhood connectivity task in the case of complete-graph networks can be described by giving each p_i the n input bits $\vec{a}_i \equiv (a_{i,1}, a_{i,2}, \dots, a_{i,n})$ where the i-th bit should be sent to the i-th party. Then,

$$\mathsf{Neighbor}(\vec{a}_1, \vec{a}_2, \dots, \vec{a}_n) = (\vec{a}_1^\mathsf{T}, \vec{a}_2^\mathsf{T}, \dots, \vec{a}_n^\mathsf{T}),$$

where $\vec{a}_j^\mathsf{T} \equiv (a_{1,j}, a_{2,j}, \dots, a_{n,j})$.

Our main theorem in this section is a coding scheme that solves the Neighbor task in $O(1)$ rounds over complete graph noisy networks.

THEOREM 4.1. *For any constant $\varepsilon < 1/2$, the* Neighbor *task for n-parties can be efficiently computed with probability $1 - 2^{-\Omega(\sqrt{n})}$ in $O(1)$ communication rounds over a fully-connected network, where each channel is a BSC_ε.*

The above theorem along with Corollary 3.4 give a constant rate coding scheme for any multiparty protocol over complete graphs, establishing Theorem 1.1.

Before we prove the theorem, let us begin by showing that any specific party can reliably transfer a large amount of information to a single party, using $O(1)$ rounds of communication. Assume p_1 wishes to send n bits to p_2. Obviously, p_1 can send the information to p_2 bit by bit, yet this would take them n rounds. A different approach would be to relay the bits using the entire network. That is, on the first round, p_1 sends one bit of its input to all the other parties (e.g., the i-th bit is sent to the i-th party). On the second round, all the parties relay the bit they have received at the first round back to p_2. This way, p_2 gets all the n bits, where each bit is flipped with probability $2\varepsilon(1-\varepsilon)$. In order to send the information reliably, p_1 can use a code ECC using Lemma 2.2. Such an encoding increases the amount of information to be communicated to $c \cdot n$ bits for some constant $c > 1$, and thus requires repeating the above process $c = O(1)$ times. We name the above approach *two-steps transfer*.

An interesting observation is that during each round, we utilize only n links of the entire networks (that has n^2 links). This means that we can perform the above two-steps transfer n times *in parallel* as long as no two instantiations have the same sender or the same receiver (this is a special case of the routing scheme by [16, 35]). Using this observation, we can complete the proof of Theorem 4.1. See Appendix A for full details.

5. RESILIENT COMMUNICATION OVER HIGHLY CONNECTED GRAPHS

In this section we generalize the above result, to the case where the underlying network is a d-regular graph, rather than a complete graph. The overhead of the coding scheme in this case depends on the mixing time of the network graph.

DEFINITION 5.1. *Let $\hat{A}$ be the normalized adjacency matrix*[2] *of a d-regular graph $G = (V, E)$ with n nodes. Let $\vec{u} = (1/n, 1/n, \ldots, 1/n)$. The graph G has* mixing time *m if, for any probability vector $\vec{p}$,*

$$\left\| \hat{A}^m \vec{p} - \vec{u} \right\|_\infty \leq \frac{1}{2n}.$$

We note that if a d-regular graph has a mixing time m, then $d > n^{\frac{1}{m}}$. Also we note that a random graph with $d \geq \Omega((n \log n)^{\frac{1}{m}})$ has mixing time at most m.

As before, we aim to solve the neighborhood connectivity task. That is, each party now begins with d bits designated to his neighbors, and the goal is to reliably transfer all these $n \cdot d$ bits to their destinations, in a number of rounds that only depends on m.

THEOREM 5.2. *For any constant $\varepsilon < 1/2$, the* Neighbor *task can be efficiently computed with probability $1 - mn^2 2^{-d^{\Omega(1)}}$ in $O(m^3 \log m)$ communication rounds over any d-regular graph network with a mixing time m, assuming each link is a BSC_ε.*

For any graph with a constant mixing time $m = O(1)$ (and thus, with $d \geq n^\alpha$, for some constant $\alpha > 0$), Theorem 5.2 determines that we can solve the neighborhood connectivity task in $O(1)$ rounds and success probability $1 - 2^{-n^{\Omega(1)}}$. By Corollary 3.4 the above implies a constant rate coding scheme that succeeds with subexponentially high probability for any multiparty interactive protocol over G with the same parameters. In the general case, as long as $d > \log^{1+\Omega(1)} n$, Theorem 5.2 and Corollary 3.4 prove Theorem 1.2.

The proof of Theorem 5.2 is composed of two main parts. First, in Section 5.1 we show that for any not-too-large list of pairs of nodes $\{(s_i, t_i)\}$, it is possible to find *disjoint* paths between any s_i and t_i, such that the length of each such path is $2m$. Then, in Section 5.2 we use these disjoint paths (along with some standard coding) to reliably relay large chunks of information between any two parties.

5.1 Finding Disjoint Paths

In this subsection we show how to find short edge disjoint paths for any list $\{(s_i, t_i)\}$ of source nodes and target nodes, such that no node appears more than $O(d/m)$ times in the list. It is important that the paths are edge disjoint so that the coding scheme could send messages from each source s_i to its target t_i without colliding with a message sent from some other s_j to t_j.

More precisely, note that we do not need the paths to be fully disjoint. Assume all the paths are of the same length, say ℓ. Sending a message from s_i to t_i would take ℓ rounds, where at the k-th round $1 \leq k \leq \ell$ the k-th link in the path is utilized, and the others are not. Therefore, it suffices that every two paths are disjoint in their k-th edge, for all $k \in [1, \ell]$. We denote such paths, whose k-th edges are disjoint (for all $k \in [1, \ell]$), as *time-multiplexed* edge disjoint.

[2]The adjacency matrix of a graph $G = (V, E)$ is defined by $A(i, j) = 1$ if $(i, j) \in E$ and zero otherwise. In d-regular graphs, the normalized matrix is given by $\hat{A} = \frac{1}{d} A$.

THEOREM 5.3. *Let $G = (V, E)$ be a d-regular graph with mixing time m. Let $\mathcal{L} = \{(s_i, t_i)\}$ be a list of pairs of nodes, $s_i, t_i \in V$, such that every $u \in V$ appears at most $\frac{d}{1600m}$ times in the list. Then, one can efficiently construct a set of* time-multiplexed edge disjoint *paths of length $2m$, connecting each $(s_i, t_i) \in \mathcal{L}$.*

PROOF. Fix a pair (s_i, t_i). We count the number of paths of length $2m$ connecting these two nodes. For any two nodes u, v define $\mathsf{P}_{u,v}(m)$ to be the set of all paths of length m connecting u and v. Note that the paths are not necessarily simple, and are allowed to intersect themselves or even repeat edges.

CLAIM 5.4. *For any $u, v \in V$,*

$$\frac{1}{2n} d^m \leq |\mathsf{P}_{u,v}(m)| \leq \frac{2}{n} d^m.$$

PROOF. Recall that G has a mixing time of m. Therefore, beginning at any node u, the probability to reach v after m (uniformly random) steps is $\frac{1}{n} \pm \frac{1}{2n}$. Since there are d^m different paths of length m starting at u, the claim follows. □

Now, set $\tilde{\mathsf{P}}_{s_i,t_i}(2m) = \bigcup_{v \in V} \mathsf{P}_{s_i,v}(m) \times \mathsf{P}_{v,t_i}(m)$ to be the set of all the paths of size $2m$ composed as an m-long path from s_i to some middle point v concatenated to an m-long path from v to t_i. Clearly,

$$\frac{1}{4n} d^{2m} \leq |\tilde{\mathsf{P}}_{s_i,t_i}(2m)| \leq \frac{4}{n} d^{2m}.$$

Next, we would like to choose, for each i, one path out of $\tilde{\mathsf{P}}_{s_i,t_i}(2m)$ so that the collection of joint paths are time-multiplexed edge disjoint. This can be done using the combinatorial result from [2], see also [5], Propostion 5.5.3, applied to the coincidence graph H described below. It is also similar to the approach of [12]. For completeness, we describe the argument, which proceeds by bounding the dependency between the events of two paths sharing an edge, and then by using the Lovász Local Lemma to prove there exists a set of paths that are jointly time-multiplexed edge disjoint. The details follow.

Define the following coincidence graph $H = (V', E')$. For every i, every path in $\tilde{\mathsf{P}}_{s_i,t_i}(2m)$ becomes a node in H, that is,

$$V' = \{p_{i,j} \mid p_{i,j} \text{ is the } j\text{-th path in } \tilde{\mathsf{P}}_{s_i,t_i}(2m)\}.$$

The edges E' are defined as follows. For any i and $i' \neq i$, we connect the node $p_{i,j}$ with $p_{i',j'}$ if, for some $1 \leq k \leq 2m$, these two paths share the k-th edge. We say that such paths are *k-time-colliding*.

CLAIM 5.5. *The degree of each node in H is at most $\frac{d^{2m}}{400n}$.*

PROOF. In the following we will fix a path p^* (i.e., a node in H) and bound the number of paths that k-time-collide with p^*, for some $k \in [1, 2m]$. Denote $p^* = (e_1, e_2, \ldots, e_{2m})$, and consider the k-th edge, e_k. Let us assume that $k \leq m$ (the other case is symmetric). First, we note that there are exactly d^{m-1} paths of length m, in which e_k is the k-th edge. Denote them as,

$$P(e_k, k) \triangleq \left\{ (e_1', \ldots, e_{k-1}', e_k, e_{k+1}', \ldots, e_m') \mid e_j' \in E \right\}.$$

If we fix a specific $p \in P(e_k, k)$, and assume its end nodes are (u, v), we can ask how many nodes in H have p as their first half. Since fixing p fixes a specific starting node u and this node can appear at most $d/1600m$ times in $\mathcal{L}$, it follows that p is the first half of at most

$$\frac{d}{1600m} \times \frac{2}{n} d^m$$

paths in H. Summing over all possible p's, the number of paths (nodes in H) whose first half is some path in $P(e_k, k)$ is bounded by $\frac{d^{2m}}{800nm}$. This is also the number of paths that k-time-collide with p^*. Summing over all $k \in [1, 2m]$ completes the claim. □

Given the bound on the degree of each node in H, we can use the Lovász Local Lemma ([18], cf. also [5], Chapter 5) to show that we can pick, for every i, one node $p_{i,j} \in V'$ so that we obtain an independent set. Such an independent set implies non-colliding paths in G.

Lemma 5.6 (Lovász Local Lemma [18]). *Let $\{A_i\}$ be a finite set of events. If,*

(1) $\forall i$, $\Pr[A_i] \le p$,

(2) $\forall i$, *A_i is mutually independent of all other events but at most d, and*

(3) $e(d+1)p < 1$,

then, $\Pr[\overline{A_1} \wedge \overline{A_2} \wedge \cdots] > 0$.

Assume that for each (s_i, t_i) we choose one of the paths in $P_{s_i,t_i}(2m)$ at random. For any two time colliding paths $p_{i,j}$, $p_{i',j'}$ denote by $A_{ij,i'j'}$ the bad event that we choose $p_{i,j}$ for (s_i, t_i) and $p_{i',j'}$ for $(s_{i'}, t_{i'})$, thus

$$\Pr[A_{ij,i'j'}] \le \frac{1}{|\tilde{\mathsf{P}}_{s_i,t_i}(2m)|} \cdot \frac{1}{|\tilde{\mathsf{P}}_{s_{i'},t_{i'}}(2m)|} \le \frac{16n^2}{d^{4m}}.$$

Each such a bad event is independent of all other events $A_{ab,cd}$ besides those with either $a = i$ or $c = i'$ (note that $A_{ab,cd}$ is the same as $A_{cd,ab}$). Since each path collides with at most $\frac{d^{2m}}{400n}$ other paths (Claim 5.5), each such bad event is independent of all but at most

$$\deg(A_{ij,i'j'}) \le \left(|\tilde{\mathsf{P}}_{s_i,t_i}(2m)| + |\tilde{\mathsf{P}}_{s_{i'},t_{i'}}(2m)|\right) \cdot \frac{d^{2m}}{400n} \le \frac{d^{4m}}{50n^2}$$

others. It is easy to verify that the conditions of Lemma 5.6 are satisfied,

$$e \cdot \Pr[A_{ij,i'j'}] \cdot (\deg(A_{ij,i'j'}) + 1) < 1,$$

which implies we can pick paths that connect all pairs in $\mathcal{L}$ such that no two paths are time-colliding. We note that finding such a set in our case can be done with high probability in quasilinear time $\tilde{O}(n)$, via the algorithm of Moser and Tardos [36]. A deterministic construction with polynomial time is possible as well, as mentioned in [3], see also [13].

5.2 The Coding Scheme

The ability to find many time-multiplexed edge disjoint paths allows us to communicate large chunks of information by relaying them through intermediate points in a way that resembles the approach of Section 4. Specifically, if each party sends and receives $O(d)$ bits from at most $O(d/\Lambda)$ different parties the communication can be done in a reliable way, except with probability $n^2 2^{-\Omega(\Lambda)}$.

Definition 5.7. *A communication demand for a network with n parties, is a matrix $A \in \mathbb{N}^{n \times n}$ such that $a_{i,j}$ describes the amount of bits party i wishes to send to party j.*

Proposition 5.8. *Consider a d-regular graph G with mixing time m. Let A be a communication demand matrix, and assume that for any j, $\sum_i a_{i,j} \le d$ and for any i, $\sum_j a_{i,j} \le d$. Furthermore assume that every row and column in A has at most $O(d/\Lambda)$ non-zero elements, for some parameter $\Lambda > 1$. Then, for any $\varepsilon < 1/2$, there exists a communication protocol that fulfills the demand A in $O(m^2 \log m)$ rounds, and succeeds with probability $1 - n^2 2^{-\Omega(\Lambda)}$, over a network G where each link is a BSC_ε.*

Proof. The idea of the coding scheme is to send each chunk of information (i.e., each $a_{i,j}$ bits defined by the demand A), via $O(d)$ disjoint paths given by Theorem 5.3. However, note that each path given by that theorem consists of $2m$ cascaded BSC_ε. Such a cascade flips each bit with probability $(1-(1-2\varepsilon)^{2m})/2$, and thus has a capacity $C \le (1-2\varepsilon)^{4m}$, see e.g., [15, Chapter 7]. To overcome this error we can use a standard error correction, yet this will incur a blowup of $2^{O(m)}$ which we can substantially reduce by adding another layer of (trivial) encoding/decoding per BSC_ε link. Indeed, in the following assume that each bit we communicate through a BSC_ε is first encoded to length $O(\log m)$, sent over the network in $O(\log m)$ rounds and then decoded at the other side of the link. Effectively, this reduces the error at each link to $1/m$, so each link can be seen as $\mathsf{BSC}_{1/m}$. Cascading $2m$ such channels is equivalent to BSC_γ with $\gamma = (1-(1-2/m)^{2m})/2 \approx (1-e^{-4})/2$, that is, the error level is bounded by some constant independent of m.

The protocol for reliably delivering the communication demand A goes as follows. For any given i, j, the i-th party encodes its $a_{i,j}$ bits targeted to the j-th party, using a Shannon error correction code that succeeds with probability $1-2^{-\Omega(\Lambda)}$ assuming a BSC_γ. Using Lemma 2.2, there exists such a code that encodes $a_{i,j}$ bits into $\tilde{a}_{i,j} = O(a_{i,j} + \Lambda)$ bits. Observe that after this encoding, each party i holds $\sum_j \tilde{a}_{i,j} = \sum_j O(a_{i,j}+\Lambda) = O(d)$ bits to communicate, since it is guaranteed that the i-th party has at most $O(d/\Lambda)$ parties j for which $a_{i,j} \neq 0$, and that $\sum_j a_{i,j} \le d$. Let $\tilde{A}$ be the communication demand defined by the above $\tilde{a}_{i,j}$.

Next, define $O(m)$ matrices $\{B_k\}$ such that any row and column in B_k sums up to at most $d/1600m$ and such that $\sum_k B_k = \tilde{A}$. This can be done (efficiently) by König's Theorem, using any efficient algorithm for edge coloring bipartite graphs. Communicating $\tilde{A}$ is equivalent to communicating all the demands $\{B_k\}$, which we will do in a sequential manner. Each such B_k defines a list $\mathcal{L}_k$ in which the pair (i,j) appears exactly $(b_{i,j})_k$ times in $\mathcal{L}_k$. Since the sum of each row and column in B_k is bounded by $d/1600m$, the list satisfies the conditions of Theorem 5.3. Thus, the demand described by B_k can be transmitted by a sequence of $2m$ bit-transmissions over the noisy network. Moreover, since there are at most $O(m)$ many B_k's, transmitting all of them sequentially (i.e., unreliably fulfilling the communication demand defined by $\tilde{A}$) can be done in $O(m^2)$ bit-transmissions. Recall that each bit-transmission consists of $O(\log m)$ rounds of communication, and we get that the entire process takes $O(m^2 \log m)$ rounds.

Last, we show that the entire process implies a reliable communication of the demand A. Recall that each chunk of information in $\tilde{A}$ is encoded to resist the noise γ, that is, the noise induced by transferring each bit through the path of $2m$ consecutive independent $\mathsf{BSC}_{1/m}$ links. It follows that each encoded chunk (i.e., each $\tilde{a}_{i,j}$) is decoded correctly with probability $1-2^{-\Omega(\Lambda)}$. A union bound on all the ($< n^2$) different encoded transmissions $\{\tilde{a}_{i,j}\}$ gives the claimed success probability. □

As a corollary of the above theorem, note that the same result holds for any communication demand A in which each row and column sums up to $K \cdot d$ rather than d, in $O(K \cdot m^2 \log m)$ rounds. In that case, after encoding each chunk we get the demand $\tilde{A}$ in which the sum of each row or column is $O(Km^2)$, and thus it can be transmitted in $O(Km^2 \log m)$ rounds.

We are now ready to complete the proof of Theorem 5.2.

PROOF. (*Theorem 5.2*). Let A_0 be the communication demand induced by the neighborhood connectivity, thus for any j, $\sum_i a_{i,j} = d$ and for any i, $\sum_j a_{i,j} = d$, since the network's graph is d-regular. The number of non-zero elements in every row or column is d, so we cannot apply Proposition 5.8 directly. Instead, we perform a sequence of relays[3], using Proposition 5.8, that converts the initial communication demand A_0 into one that satisfies the conditions of Proposition 5.8, i.e., where each party has at most d bits to send to at most $O(d/\Lambda)$ different destinations. Specifically, there is a sequence of ℓ matrices $A_0, A_1, \ldots, A_\ell$ such that for any $l \in [\ell]$ we convert A_{l-1} into A_l in $O(m^2 \log m)$ rounds, and where it holds that (1) each A_l is a block-diagonal matrix with block size at most $n(d/\Lambda)^{-l}$; (2) the sum of each column in A_l is d; and (3) the sum of each row in A_l is at most $4d$.

LEMMA 5.9. *Let the communication demand $A_l \in \mathbb{N}^{n\times n}$ be block diagonal with block size b, and assume that $\sum_i (a_{i,j})_l \leq d$ and $\sum_j (a_{i,j})_l \leq 4d$. Then, it is possible to reliably relay information by $O(m^2 \log m)$ rounds of communication, so that $A_{l+1} \in \mathbb{N}^{n\times n}$ describing the communication demand after the relay is block diagonal with block size at most $b\frac{\Lambda}{d}$, and it holds that $\sum_i (a_{i,j})_{l+1} \leq d$ and $\sum_j (a_{i,j})_{l+1} \leq 4d$. The coding succeeds with probability at least $1 - n^2 2^{-\Omega(\Lambda)}$.*

PROOF. Consider the r-th block of A_l, that is, the submatrix that contains the communication between parties $P_r \equiv \{(r-1)b+1, (r-1)b+2, \ldots, rb\}$; note that these parties wish to send information only between themselves due to the block diagonal form of A_l. Therefore, we can treat each such block independently.

Split P_r into d/Λ disjoint subsets $P_{r,1}, \ldots, P_{r,d/\Lambda}$ of equal size, in an arbitrary way. For any $j = 1, \ldots, d/\Lambda$, each $p_i \in P_r$ will send *all* the information directed to parties in $P_{r,j}$, i.e. $\sum_{u\in P_{r,j}} a_{i,u}$ bits, to a single party of $P_{r,j}$. The recipient can be chosen in a "greedy" way: order the parties of $P_{r,j}$ in some order, say $p'_1, p'_2, \ldots$; iterate over all $p_i \in P_r$ in an increasing order of the demand $\sum_{u\in P_{r,j}} a_{i,u}$, and determine the recipient as the first $p' \in P_{r,j}$ that (i) is currently scheduled to receive bits from less than $2d/\Lambda$ different parties, and (ii) will receive at most $4d$ bits (including the $\sum_{u\in P_{r,j}} a_{i,u}$ bits held by p_i). Under these restrictions, we can use Proposition 5.8 to perform the relay in $O(m^2 \log m)$ rounds in a reliable way (with high probability).

To see that the greedy algorithm succeeds in accommodating the demand of all $p_i \in P_r$, split P_r into parties for which $\sum_{u\in P_{r,j}} a_{i,u} \leq \Lambda$, denoted as the subset $P_< \subseteq P_r$, and the other parties, denoted $P_>$. Parties in $P_<$ are aggregated in groups of size $2d/\Lambda$. Note that the joint demand of each such group never exceeds $2d$ bits. We need $|P_<|/(2d/\Lambda) \leq b\Lambda/2d$ parties $p' \in P_{r,j}$ to accommodate all these groups. Parties from $P_>$ are aggregated until adding an additional party causes the demand to exceed $4d$ bits of information. Since we order the parties according to an increasing order of demand, each assigned p' (maybe, except one) accommodates at least $2d$ bits of demand (and at most $4d$ bits). Also note that the total amount of bits to be sent by parties in $P_>$ (to a specific $P_{r,j}$) is at most $b\Lambda$, since each column in A_l sums up to at most d bits, and there are at most $b/(d/\Lambda)$ columns to be considered here. Thus, in order to accommodate all $P_>$ we need at most $b\Lambda/2d$ different parties $p' \in P_{r,j}$. Summing these two parts, the total number of parties in $P_{r,j}$ needed to accommodate both $P_<$ and $P_>$, is bounded by $b\Lambda/d \leq |P_{r,j}|$.

The above is being performed, in parallel, for each block of A_l. Recall that the block-diagonal form of A_l implies a partition of the parties into disjoint sets $\{P_r\}$ corresponding to each block, where each relay happens only within the block. Moreover, within each block each party communicates at most $O(d)$ bits and at most $O(d/\Lambda)$ different parties. Thus the joint communication demand satisfies the conditions of Proposition 5.8, and we can perform the relay in $O(m^2 \log m)$ rounds, reliably. At the end of this process, each block of size b is transformed into d/Λ disjoint blocks of size at most $b\Lambda/d$. Note that all the parties reliably receive the information relayed to them, except with a probability of $n^2 2^{-\Omega(\Lambda)}$. □

We perform the above process of Lemma 5.9 recursively, starting from A_0 being the incidence matrix of the the underlying network (i.e., the demands induced by the Neighbor task). If we set $\Lambda = d^c$ for some constant $c < 1$, then after $\ell = m/(1-c) - O(1)$ steps we reach a matrix A_ℓ that is block diagonal with block size at most

$$n(d/\Lambda)^{-\ell} = nd^{-m}\frac{d}{\Lambda} \leq d/\Lambda.$$

Specifically, each column in A_ℓ sums up to d, each row sums to $4d$, and at each row/column there are $O(d/\Lambda)$ non-zero element. We can now use Proposition 5.8 one last time to fulfill the communication demand A_ℓ and complete the proof. The entire scheme takes $O((\ell+1)\cdot m^2 \log m) = O(m^3 \log m)$ rounds, and succeeds with probability $1 - mn^2 2^{-\Omega(\Lambda)} = 1 - mn^2 2^{-\Omega(d^c)}$. To succeed with high probability we require $d > \log^{1+\alpha} n$, for some $\alpha > 0$ and $c > 1/(1+\alpha)$.

It can be easily verified that each step of the protocol is computationally efficient, which makes the entire simulation efficient.

[3]In *relay* we mean that if party i wants to send a bit to party j, it can send that bit to some party k who will later relay that bit to j. Thus, after sending the bit to k, the communication demand changes so that $a_{i,j} = 0$ and $a_{k,j}$ increases by one.

6. REFERENCES

[1] S. Agrawal, R. Gelles, and A. Sahai. Adaptive protocols for interactive communication. In *2016 IEEE International Symposium on Information Theory (ISIT)*, 2016.

[2] N. Alon. The linear arboricity of graphs. *Israel J. Math.*, 62(3):311–325, 1988.

[3] N. Alon. A parallel algorithmic version of the local lemma. In *32nd Annual Symposium on Foundations of Computer Science (San Juan, PR, 1991)*, pages 586–593, 1991.

[4] N. Alon and M. Capalbo. Finding disjoint paths in expanders deterministically and online. In *48th Annual Symposium on Foundations of Computer Science, 2007)*, pages 518–524, 2007.

[5] N. Alon and J. H. Spencer. *The Probabilistic Method.* Wiley-Interscience Series in Discrete Mathematics and Optimization. John Wiley & Sons, Inc., Hoboken, NJ, third edition, 2008. With an appendix on the life and work of Paul Erdős.

[6] Z. Brakerski and Y. T. Kalai. Efficient interactive coding against adversarial noise. *Proceedings of the IEEE Symposium on Foundations of Computer Science*, pages 160–166, 2012.

[7] Z. Brakerski and M. Naor. Fast algorithms for interactive coding. In *Proceedings of the 24th Annual ACM-SIAM Symposium on Discrete Algorithms*, SODA '13, pages 443–456, 2013.

[8] M. Braverman and K. Efremenko. List and unique coding for interactive communication in the presence of adversarial noise. In *Proceedings of the IEEE Symposium on Foundations of Computer Science*, FOCS '14, pages 236–245, 2014.

[9] M. Braverman, K. Efremenko, R. Gelles, and B. Haeupler. Constant-rate coding for multiparty interactive communication is impossible. In *Proceedings of the 48th Annual ACM Symposium on Theory of Computing*, STOC '16, 2016.

[10] M. Braverman and A. Rao. Towards coding for maximum errors in interactive communication. In *Proceedings of the 43rd annual ACM symposium on Theory of computing*, STOC '11, pages 159–166, 2011.

[11] M. Braverman and A. Rao. Toward coding for maximum errors in interactive communication. *Information Theory, IEEE Transactions on*, 60(11):7248–7255, Nov 2014.

[12] A. Broder, A. Frieze, and E. Upfal. Existence and construction of edge-disjoint paths on expander graphs. *SIAM Journal on Computing*, 23(5):976–989, 1994.

[13] K. Chandrasekaran, N. Goyal, and B. Haeupler. Deterministic algorithms for the lovász local lemma. *SIAM Journal on Computing*, 42(6):2132–2155, 2013.

[14] K.-M. Chung, R. Pass, and S. Telang. Knowledge-preserving interactive coding. In *Proceedings of the 54th annual IEEE Symposium on Foundations of Computer Science (FOCS)*, pages 449–458, 2013.

[15] T. M. Cover and J. A. Thomas. *Elements of Information Theory (2nd edition).* John Wiley & Sons, 2006.

[16] D. Dolev, C. Lenzen, and S. Peled. "Tri, Tri Again": Finding triangles and small subgraphs in a distributed setting. In M. Aguilera, editor, *Distributed Computing*, volume 7611 of *Lecture Notes in Computer Science*, pages 195–209, 2012.

[17] K. Efremenko, R. Gelles, and B. Haeupler. Maximal noise in interactive communication over erasure channels and channels with feedback. In *Proceedings of the 6th Conference on Innovations in Theoretical Computer Science*, ITCS '15, pages 11–20, 2015.

[18] P. Erdős and L. Lovász. Problems and results on 3-chromatic hypergraphs and some related questions. *Infinite and finite sets*, 10:609–627, 1975.

[19] M. Franklin, R. Gelles, R. Ostrovsky, and L. J. Schulman. Optimal coding for streaming authentication and interactive communication. In *Advances in Cryptology – CRYPTO 2013*, volume 8043 of *LNCS*, pages 258–276, 2013.

[20] M. Franklin, R. Gelles, R. Ostrovsky, and L. J. Schulman. Optimal coding for streaming authentication and interactive communication. *Information Theory, IEEE Transactions on*, 61(1):133–145, Jan 2015.

[21] R. Gallager. Finding parity in a simple broadcast network. *Information Theory, IEEE Transactions on*, 34(2):176–180, Mar 1988.

[22] R. Gelles. Coding for interactive communication: A survey, 2015.

[23] R. Gelles and B. Haeupler. Capacity of interactive communication over erasure channels and channels with feedback. In *Proceedings of the Twenty-Sixth Annual ACM-SIAM Symposium on Discrete Algorithms*, SODA '15, pages 1296–1311, 2015.

[24] R. Gelles, A. Moitra, and A. Sahai. Efficient and explicit coding for interactive communication. In *Proceeding of the IEEE Symposium on Foundations of Computer Science*, FOCS '11, pages 768–777, 2011.

[25] R. Gelles, A. Moitra, and A. Sahai. Efficient coding for interactive communication. *Information Theory, IEEE Transactions on*, 60(3):1899–1913, March 2014.

[26] R. Gelles, A. Sahai, and A. Wadia. Private interactive communication across an adversarial channel. In *Proceedings of the 5th Conference on Innovations in Theoretical Computer Science*, ITCS '14, pages 135–144, 2014.

[27] M. Ghaffari and B. Haeupler. Optimal Error Rates for Interactive Coding II: Efficiency and List Decoding. In *Proceedings of the IEEE Symposium on Foundations of Computer Science*, FOCS '14, pages 394–403, 2014.

[28] M. Ghaffari, B. Haeupler, and M. Sudan. Optimal error rates for interactive coding I: Adaptivity and other settings. In *Proceedings of the 46th Annual ACM Symposium on Theory of Computing*, STOC '14, pages 794–803, 2014.

[29] N. Goyal, G. Kindler, and M. Saks. Lower bounds for the noisy broadcast problem. *SIAM Journal on Computing*, 37(6):1806–1841, 2008.

[30] V. Guruswami and P. Indyk. Linear-time encodable/decodable codes with near-optimal rate. *IEEE Trans. on Information Theory*, 51(10):3393–3400, 2005.

[31] B. Haeupler. Interactive Channel Capacity Revisited. In *Proceedings of the IEEE Symposium on Foundations of Computer Science*, FOCS '14, pages 226–235, 2014.

[32] W. M. Hoza and L. J. Schulman. The adversarial noise threshold for distributed protocols. In *Proceedings of*

the Twenty-Seventh Annual ACM-SIAM Symposium on Discrete Algorithms, pages 240–258, 2016.

[33] A. Jain, Y. T. Kalai, and A. Lewko. Interactive coding for multiparty protocols. In *Proceedings of the 6th Conference on Innovations in Theoretical Computer Science, ITCS '15*, pages 1–10, 2015.

[34] G. Kol and R. Raz. Interactive channel capacity. In *STOC '13: Proceedings of the 45th annual ACM Symposium on theory of computing*, pages 715–724, 2013.

[35] C. Lenzen. Optimal deterministic routing and sorting on the congested clique. In *Proceedings of the 2013 ACM Symposium on Principles of Distributed Computing*, PODC '13, pages 42–50, 2013.

[36] R. A. Moser and G. Tardos. A constructive proof of the general lovász local lemma. *J. ACM*, 57(2):11:1–11:15, Feb. 2010.

[37] D. Pankratov. On the power of feedback in interactive channels. [Online:] http://people.cs.uchicago.edu/~pankratov/papers/feedback.pdf, 2013.

[38] S. Rajagopalan. *A Coding Theorem for Distributed Computation.* PhD thesis, University of California at Berkeley, 1994. UMI Order No. GAX95-29464.

[39] S. Rajagopalan and L. Schulman. A coding theorem for distributed computation. In *STOC '94: Proceedings of the twenty-sixth annual ACM symposium on Theory of computing*, pages 790–799, 1994.

[40] L. J. Schulman. Communication on noisy channels: a coding theorem for computation. *Foundations of Computer Science, Annual IEEE Symposium on*, pages 724–733, 1992.

[41] L. J. Schulman. Deterministic coding for interactive communication. In *STOC '93: Proceedings of the twenty-fifth annual ACM symposium on Theory of computing*, pages 747–756, 1993.

[42] L. J. Schulman. Coding for interactive communication. *IEEE Transactions on Information Theory*, 42(6):1745–1756, 1996.

[43] C. E. Shannon. A mathematical theory of communication. *ACM SIGMOBILE Mobile Computing and Communications Review*, 5(1):3–55, 2001. Originally appeared in *Bell System Tech. J.* 27:379–423, 623–656, 1948.

[44] D. A. Spielman. Linear-time encodable and decodable error-correcting codes. In *Proceedings of the twenty-seventh annual ACM symposium on Theory of computing*, STOC '95, pages 388–397, 1995.

APPENDIX

A. MISSING PROOFS

We give here the detailed proof of Theorem 4.1.

PROOF. Consider the n^2 bits $\{a_{i,j}\}$ that have to be sent as the $n \times n$ matrix A. Let $k = \sqrt{n}$, and split the matrix A into n disjoint sub-matrices $B_{t,l}$, each of size $k \times k$. Specifically,

$$A = \begin{pmatrix} B_{1,1} & B_{1,2} & \cdots & B_{1,k} \\ B_{2,1} & B_{2,2} & \cdots & B_{2,k} \\ & & \ddots & \\ B_{k,1} & B_{k,2} & \cdots & B_{k,k} \end{pmatrix},$$

where for any $t, l \in [k]$ we let

$$B_{t,l} = \begin{pmatrix} a_{(t-1)k+1,(l-1)k+1} & a_{(t-1)k+1,(l-1)k+2} & \cdots & a_{(t-1)k+1,lk} \\ a_{(t-1)k+2,(l-1)k+1} & a_{(t-1)k+2,(l-1)k+2} & \cdots & a_{(t-1)k+2,lk} \\ \vdots & & \ddots & \vdots \\ a_{tk,(l-1)k+1} & a_{tk,(l-1)k+2} & \cdots & a_{tk,lk} \end{pmatrix}.$$

Associate each block $B_{t,l}$ with a responsible party $f(t,l) \in [n]$ in a bijective way, without loss of generality, we can take $f(t,l) = k(t-1) + l$. The protocol proceeds in two steps, each of which takes $O(1)$ rounds. In the first step, each party $f(t,l)$ learns all the bits that belong to $B_{t,l}$ with high probability. In the second step, each such party distributes the bits of the appropriate matrix $B_{t,l}$ to their destinations.

The protocol uses an error correcting code $\mathsf{ECC} : \{0,1\}^k \to \{0,1\}^{k'}$ that, assuming a BSC_ε, fails with probability at most $2^{-\Omega(k)}$; note that $k' = O_\varepsilon(k)$ (see Lemma 2.2).

To explain the first step suppose, first, that we do not use the code and each party i wishes to send the bit $a_{i,j}$ to party j. This can be done in two rounds as follows. In the first round, party i sends the bit $a_{i,j}$ to party $(ki+j) (\text{mod } n)$. Note that here, crucially, each party i sends exactly one bit to each other party, and that for each block $B_{t,l}$, no two bits of $B_{t,l}$ reach the same party. Thus the bits of $B_{t,l}$ reach all the n parties, each getting exactly one bit. In the second step, each party sends the unique bit from $B_{t,l}$ that it received to the responsible party $f(t,l)$. Clearly after these two steps, $f(t,l)$ receives all bits of the block $B_{t,l}$. A similar routing technique appears in [16, 35].

In the actual realization of the first step, each party i applies the code from Lemma 2.2 to the k bits in each block in its row before transmitting them. Thus the bits $a_{i,(l-1)k+1}, a_{i,(l-1)+2}, \ldots, a_{i,lk}$ are first encoded to get k' bits, which are sent using the above procedure, simulating each of the two rounds by $\lceil k'/k \rceil$ rounds. Once the party $f(t,l)$ gets the bits of the encoded rows of the block $B_{t,l}$, he can decode them, using the error correcting code, and get all the bits of the block $B_{t,l}$ correctly, with high probability.

The second step is performed in the same way, reversing the directions. Ignoring the encoding, this can be done in two rounds as follows. In the first round, each party $f(t,l)$ responsible to the bits in the block $B_{t,l}$ sends the bit $a_{i,j}$ of this block to party number $(i + kj)(mod\ n)$. Note that no two bits of the block have to be sent to the same destination, and hence this can indeed be performed in one round. In the second round the party that got the bit $a_{i,j}$ sends it to its destination: party number j. Since for distinct i, i', $(i + kj)(mod\ n)$ is not equal to $(i' + kj)(mod\ n)$ this can also be done in one round. To ensure that with high probability no errors will occur, the party $f(t,l)$ encodes each column of its block $B_{t,l}$ before sending the bits of the encoded message. As before, after the encoding each of these two rounds can be simulated by a constant number of rounds. This completes the proof. □

Contention Resolution on Multiple Channels with Collision Detection

Jeremy T. Fineman
Georgetown University
Washington, DC, USA
jf474@georgetown.edu

Calvin Newport
Georgetown University
Washington, DC, USA
cn248@georgetown.edu

Tonghe Wang
Georgetown University
Washington, DC, USA
tw473@georgetown.edu

ABSTRACT

In this paper, we consider the classical *contention resolution* problem in which an unknown subset of n possible nodes are activated and connected to a shared channel. The problem is solved in the first round that an active node transmits alone (thus breaking symmetry). Contention resolution has been an active research topic for over four decades. Accordingly, tight upper and lower bounds are known for most major model assumptions. There remains, however, an important case that is unresolved: contention resolution with multiple channels and collision detection. (Tight bounds are known for contention resolution with multiple channels, and contention resolution with collision detection, but not for the combination of *both* assumptions.) Recent work [14] proved the first non-trivial lower bound for randomized solutions to this problem in this setting. The optimality of this lower bound was left an open question. In this paper, we answer this open question by describing and analyzing new contention resolution algorithms that match, or come within a $\log\log\log n$ factor of matching, this bound for all relevant parameters. By doing so, we help advance our understanding of an important longstanding problem. Of equal importance, our solutions introduce a novel new technique in which we leverage a distributed structure we call *coalescing cohorts* to simulate a well-known parallel search strategy from the structured PRAM CREW model [16] in our unstructured distributed model. We conjecture that this approach is relevant to many problems in the increasingly important setting of distributed computation using multiple shared channels.

Keywords

contention resolution; collision detection; symmetry breaking

1. INTRODUCTION

The contention resolution problem assumes an unknown subset of n possible nodes that are *activated* and connected to a shared multiple-access channel (MAC). The problem is solved in the first round that one of these *active* nodes transmits alone on the shared channel. Contention resolution (which is also sometimes called *leader election* or *wake-up*, depending on the model assumptions and context) is one of the longest studied problems in the theory of distributed algorithms. It was first identified in the 1970 paper on the ALOHA radio network and variations have been extensively explored by theoretical computer scientists and mathematicians ever since; e.g., [15, 12, 10, 13, 9, 5, 2, 8, 11, 4, 14]. In this paper, we advance an important open case regarding this problem, and in doing so also introduce a novel algorithmic technique potentially applicable to many other problems in this setting.

An Open Problem. Contention resolution has been studied under many different model variations. Two of the most important assumptions concern collision detection and number of available channels. Tight bounds are known for contention resolution on a single channel with and without collision detection [5, 11, 6, 14], and for contention resolution on multiple channels without collision detection [3, 14]. (See Section 2 for details). Until recently, however, little was known about the remaining case of multiple channels with collision detection. In 2014 [14], progress was made with a new lower bound that established $\Omega\left(\frac{\log n}{\log \mathcal{C}} + \log\log n\right)$ rounds are needed to solve contention resolution with collision detection and $\mathcal{C} \geq 1$ channels (with high probability in n). This bound holds *even* if we consider the easier restricted case where only two nodes out of the n possible will be activated. In [14], the question of this bound's optimality was left as an open problem—though it was suspected to be *not tight* because it followed from the limits of a specific proof technique and had no connection to a particular upper bound intuition.

Our Solution. In this paper, we resolve this open problem. In more detail, we show (perhaps surprisingly) that the lower bound from [14] *is tight* or within a $\log\log\log n$ factor of tight for all relevant values of n and $\mathcal{C}$. To do so, we describe and analyze two new contention resolution algorithms for MACs with collision detection and $\mathcal{C} > 1$ channels. The first algorithm (presented in Section 4) solves the problem in an optimal $O\left(\frac{\log n}{\log \mathcal{C}} + \log\log n\right)$ rounds in the restricted case where only two nodes are activated—exactly matching the lower bound from [14], which applies to this restricted case. The second algorithm (presented in

PODC'16, July 25–28, 2016, Chicago, IL, USA
© 2016 ACM. ISBN 0-89791-88-6/97/05...$15.00
DOI: http://dx.doi.org/10.1145/2933057.2933110

Section 5) solves the problem in a near optimal $O\Big(\frac{\log n}{\log \mathcal{C}} + (\log\log n)(\log\log\log n)\Big)$ rounds for the general case where any number of nodes are activated—coming within a $\log\log\log n$ factor of the existing bound for large $\mathcal{C}$ (i.e., when the $\log\log n$ term dominates) and otherwise matching the bound.

Our Techniques. Our two-node algorithm works in two phases. The first phase renames the two active nodes with unique ids from the range $\{1, 2, ..., \mathcal{C}\}$ instead of $\{1, 2, ..., n\}$ (for the case where $\mathcal{C} > n$, we use only the first n channels). Notice, with a single channel, renaming (with high probability in n) would require $\Omega(\log n)$ rounds, as it takes this many rounds to even just break symmetry between two nodes with respect to their transmit/receive behavior. In our setting, however, we can leverage the presence of $\mathcal{C}$ channels and collision detection to speed up this process to require only $O(\log n/\log \mathcal{C})$ rounds (with high probability).

Once the two nodes have renamed themselves in a smaller id space, we consider the binary tree with the leaves labeled with this smaller set of $\mathcal{C}$ possible ids. Let i and j be the unique ids of the renamed nodes. Let P_i and P_j be the two paths in our tree from the root to the leaves labelled i and j, respectively. In our second phase, we associate a channel with each node in this tree. We use these channels to perform a binary search over the tree's $O(\log \mathcal{C})$ levels to identify the level where P_i and P_j first diverge. Once we identify this key divergence, the node associated with the path that splits to the *left* (by some fixed labeling of the child orientations) is the *winner* and can go transmit alone on the primary channel[1] to solve the problem. This second stage requires $O(\log\log \mathcal{C}) = O(\log\log n)$ rounds and is deterministic.

Our general algorithm, which works for any number of nodes, builds on a similar structure, but requires more complex analysis and the introduction of novel algorithmic strategies to overcome the issues introduced by larger sets of active nodes. In more detail, this general algorithm deploys three steps. The first step reduces the number of active nodes to a count in $O(\log n)$ in $O(\log\log n)$ rounds using an aggressive knock out strategy. This preliminary reduction serves to simplify analysis in the remaining steps.

The second step renames the remaining nodes with unique IDs from the space $[\mathcal{C}/2]$. As with the two node algorithm, this renaming leverages the presence of multiple channels. Each active node chooses a channel from 1 to $\mathcal{C}/2$ with uniform randomness, then transmits using its collision detector to determine if it is alone. If *any* node is alone on its channel, it can adopt the channel label as its unique ID and notify the nodes that have not yet adopted a new ID to become inactive. To handle the case where $\mathcal{C}$ is small compared to $\log n$, we interleave these renaming attempts with continued attempts to reduce the active nodes using a knock out strategy. Analysis of the reduction rounds in this phase is complicated by the fact that we need to achieve reductions to active node counts (potentially) much smaller than $\log n$ with high probability in n. The analysis of the renaming attempts deploys a custom balls-in-bins argument that treats the nodes as balls and the channels they choose as bins.

[1]The definition of contention resolution with multiple channels fixes one channel to play the role of the *primary* channel. The problem is solved when an active node broadcasts alone on the primary channel.

When the renaming completes, we proceed to the third step which elects a leader and features the primary algorithmic contributions of this paper. For this step, we once again consider a binary tree with one leaf for each possible id in our reduced space, and focus on the paths from the root to the *occupied* leaves corresponding to the ids of active nodes. As in the two node algorithm, in $O(\log\log n)$ rounds we can complete a binary search that finds the level closest to the root in which all paths occupy unique tree nodes. Also as in the two node algorithm, we can use the identification of this level to reduce the number of active nodes by a factor of at least 2. After our first step, we have at most $O(\log n)$ nodes, so we would need $O(\log\log n)$ such searches. The resulting time complexity for this strategy, however, is too large. To optimize this process to our desired $(\log\log n)(\log\log\log n)$ rounds, we need to speed up the time required by these searches.

To accomplish this speed up, we introduce a new technique called ***coalescing cohorts***. The idea is that when we first enter this step, the active nodes are not coordinated. As we proceed with our basic strategy of conducting searches to reduce active nodes, however, we *coalesce* coordinated groups of nodes that we call *cohorts*. A key guarantee of these cohorts is that after each search, they each have the same size p and their members have unique IDs from a known set of size p. (We cannot immediately solve leader election from this property, however, because the total number of cohorts in the system is unknown.) This structure allows us to simulate a CREW PRAM parallel search algorithm [16] that has p processes work in parallel to perform a $(p+1)$-ary search. After each search, this cohort size p doubles, and therefore the search time decreases rapidly enough that the sum of the rounds spent to conduct $O(\log\log n)$ search/reductions is in $O\Big((\log\log n)(\log\log\log n)\Big)$.

Impact. These results generate both specific and general impacts. The specific impact is that they close a long-standing open question regarding a classical distributed algorithm problem. The general impact comes from the new techniques we developed to prove our results. In particular, our *coalescing cohorts* strategy provides a method to quickly build large collections of coordinated nodes in distributed multiple channel models. In this paper, we use the structure in these groups to simulate efficient strategies from the parallel algorithms literature. We conjecture that this strategy can be combined with a variety of well-known parallel algorithms to speed up computation in our distributed model. Even without parallel algorithm simulation, however, we note that the structure provided by these cohorts still provides a powerful algorithmic tool that can potentially be leveraged in developing efficient solutions for many problems.

2. RELATED WORK

The study of contention resolution developed out of the network random access method introduced in the ALOHA paper in 1970 [1]. Early work on this problem focused on the *stability* of contention resolution algorithms for different packet arrival rates; e.g., [15, 12, 10] (see [7] for a good survey). By the mid-1980's, however, the literature split, with an increasingly number of mathematicians and computer scientists studying a one-shot version of the problem where a single set of packets arrives at the beginning of the execution, and the problem is solved once the first packet is successfully delivered e.g., [13, 9, 5]. This is the version of the problem we study in this paper.

As mentioned, contention resolution has been considered under many model assumptions. The two assumptions relevant to this paper are collision detection capability and the number of available channels. Many of the original papers on contention resolution (e.g., [13, 9, 5]) assume *collision detection*, which they define (as do we) such that *all* nodes learn of a collision during any round with two or more transmitters.[2] A straightforward algorithm solves contention resolution in $O(\log n)$ rounds in this setting with probability 1: active nodes use collisions to guide a descent through a binary search tree over the n possible ids to identify the smallest id of an active node. This solution is optimal for solving this problem with high probability in n [14]. Without collision detection, by contrast, contention resolution can be solved with high probability in $O(\log^2 n)$ rounds. Jurdzinkski et al. [11] proved this near optimal for uniform[3] algorithms and Colton et al. [6] eliminated the remaining gap. Recently, Newport [14] proved this bound optimal for all algorithms.

Providing nodes additional channels also speeds up contention resolution. Daum et al. [3] show how to solve contention resolution with high probability in $O\Big(\log^2 n/\mathcal{C} + \log n\Big)$ rounds with $\mathcal{C} \geq 1$ channels—achieving a linear speed up in $\mathcal{C}$ until reaching the lower limit of $\Omega(\log n)$. In [3], this bound was proved near tight for uniform algorithms. Newport [14] subsequently proved it tight for all algorithms. This same paper proved that solving contention resolution with high probability with collision detection and multiple channels requires $\Omega\Big(\frac{\log n}{\log \mathcal{C}} + \log\log n\Big)$ rounds for all algorithms, even if we consider the restricted case where only two nodes are activated. At the time, the best known upper bound for these assumptions required $O(\log n)$ rounds (i.e., the optimal algorithm for collision detection on a single channel). Finally, we note the parallel binary search strategy we leverage in our new upper bound for general network size came from Snir's classic 1985 paper on parallel searching [16].

3. THE CONTENTION RESOLUTION PROBLEM

We parameterize our model with integers $\mathcal{C} > 0$ and $n \geq 2$. We assume a set V consisting of n *nodes* each executing a randomized algorithm, and a collection of $\mathcal{C}$ multiple-access channels (called *channels* for short in the following), labelled $1, 2, ..., \mathcal{C}$. Our algorithms do not require nodes to have unique ids (though the lower bounds in [14] hold even if they do).

At the beginning of an execution, some arbitrary subset $A \subset V$ of the n possible nodes are designated as *active*. (When specified, we sometimes consider a *restricted* case in which $|A|$ must equal 2.) The active nodes are the only nodes that participate in the execution. Time then proceeds in synchronous rounds. In each round, each node in A must make two decisions: (1) it must choose a single channel from 1 to $\mathcal{C}$ on which to participate; and (2) it must decide whether to *transmit* a message or *receive*. Each individual channel behaves like a standard MAC with (strong) collision detection. In more detail, fix some node $u \in A$ that chooses to participate on channel i in round r. If no node transmits on i in this round, u detects silence. If exactly one node transmits on i in this round, u receives this message. If two or more nodes transmit on i, u receives a collision notification. Notice, as in [14], we assume the classical definition of collision detection (common in much of the original work on this problem), where both transmitters and receivers learn about message collisions on their channel in a given round.

The *contention resolution* problem is solved in the first round in which a single node transmits on channel 1. We assume all nodes start during the same round. It is easy to transform a solution that works in this model to a solution that works in the harder model where nodes can start during different rounds, at the cost of a factor of 2 in time complexity. In nonsimultaneous wake-up case, we can have each node listen for two rounds on channel 1. If both rounds are silent, it starts running a modified version of the protocol where node broadcasts in the odd rounds (on channel 1) and runs the protocol in the even. If the node instead hears a collision or message in the first two rounds, it just stop participating in the algorithm.

In this paper, we consider results that hold with high probability in n (the maximum number of nodes that might be activated), which we define to mean probability at least $1 - 1/n^c$ for some fixed constant $c \geq 1$. We define the notation $[i, j]$, for integers $i \leq j$, to denote the range $\{i, i+1, ..., j\}$, and define $[i]$, for integer $i > 0$, to denote $[1, i]$.

4. CONTENTION RESOLUTION FOR TWO NODES

We begin by considering the restricted case where exactly two nodes are activated. Under this assumption, we describe and analyze an algorithm that solves contention resolution in $O\Big(\frac{\log n}{\log \mathcal{C}} + \log\log n\Big)$ rounds, with high probability. This algorithm matches the lower bound from [14], which holds for this two node assumption. This algorithm is also useful as it isolates and highlights some of the general ideas leveraged by the more involved general algorithm that follows.

In the following we assume that $\mathcal{C}$ is a power of 2 (the strategies are easily modified to handle other values). We also assume $\mathcal{C} \leq n$. Notice, no optimality is lost by this latter assumption.[4]

The TwoActive Algorithm. The algorithm executes in two steps. The first step implements an ID reduction strategy that renames the two active nodes with unique ids from the range $[\mathcal{C}]$. The two nodes each choose a channel from the $\mathcal{C}$ available channels and then transmit and use their

[2]In more recent years, some papers also assume *receiver collision detection*, in which the transmitters involved in the collision do not directly learn about the collision (as would be the case with half-duplex transmitters).

[3]This is one of several terms used to describe a restriction common in many contention resolution lower bounds: the transmission probabilities used by the algorithm are fixed at each node in advance. This restriction forbids, for example, nodes to base their transmission probability in one round on coin flips from an earlier round.

[4]The lower bound for $\mathcal{C} > n$ is $\Omega(\log\log n)$, and our algorithm executes in $O(\log\log n)$ rounds when run on n channels.

TwoActive (for node $i \in A$)

(Step #1: ID Reduction)
do
Choose ID_i from $[1, \mathcal{C}]$ with uniform randomness
Transmit on channel ID_i
until i is alone on channel ID_i

(Step #2: Symmetry Breaking)
$L \leftarrow$ SplitCheck$(0, \lg \mathcal{C}, ID_i)$
if the node at level L in $T_{\mathcal{C}}$ on P_i is left child of parent at level $L-1$
then transmit on channel 1

SplitCheck(l, r, id)
(return the level where P_i and P_j split)

if $l \geq r$, **then**,
return l
else
$m = \lfloor (l+r)/2 \rfloor$
Transmit on channel $\lceil id/2^{\lg \mathcal{C} - m} \rceil$
if collision is detected **then**
return SplitCheck$(m+1, r, id)$
else
return SplitCheck(l, m, id)

Figure 1: The TwoActive Algorithm

collision detectors to see if they are alone. (This step leverages the strong collision detection assumption that allows transmitters to detect collisions.) The nodes repeat this random channel selection strategy until they detect they are on unique channels: at which point, each node then adopts the label of its selected channel as its new unique id. This step requires $O(\log n / \log \mathcal{C})$ rounds (with high probability).

The second step makes use of these new IDs to efficiently break symmetry among the two nodes. To do so, the nodes consider a canonical full binary tree $T_{\mathcal{C}}$, with $\mathcal{C}$ leaves labelled with the values in $[\mathcal{C}]$. Note that $T_{\mathcal{C}}$ has a height of $h = \lg \mathcal{C}$. Let i and j be the two active nodes, and let ID_i and ID_j be their ids selected in the previous step. Node i considers the unique simple path in $T_{\mathcal{C}}$ from the root to the leaf labelled ID_i, and j does the same with respect to ID_j. We call these paths P_i and P_j, respectively. Notice that these paths begin together at the root and split at some point by the time they reach their respective leaves. This second step conducts a binary search over the h levels of the tree to find the smallest level at which the two paths diverge. This search requires an assignment of a unique channel to each node at the tree level being checked at a given step of the algorithm; that is, the multiple channel assumption is necessary for this step as well. Once we have found this level—which we call ℓ in this exposition—breaking symmetry is simple: the single node that is a left child of its parent at $\ell - 1$ (on its path from the root) *wins* and transmits on channel 1 to solve the problem. This step requires $O(\log h) = O(\log \log \mathcal{C}) = O(\log \log n)$ rounds.

Analysis. We are now ready to state our main correctness theorem:

Theorem 1. *In a network with 2 active nodes (out of n possible nodes) and $\mathcal{C}$ channels,* TwoActive *solves contention resolution in $O\left(\frac{\log n}{\log \mathcal{C}} + \log \log n\right)$ rounds, with high probability.*

The correctness of our theorem is a direct consequence of the following two lemmas.

Lemma 2. *With high probability: nodes i and j conclude Step #1 with $ID_i \neq ID_j$, during the same round $r \in O\left(\frac{\log n}{\log \mathcal{C}}\right)$.*

Proof. Fix $t = \lg n / \lg \mathcal{C}$. The probability that nodes i and j select the same channel for t consecutive rounds in the ID reduction phase is bounded as:

$$\prod_{r=1}^{t} Pr\{ID_i = ID_j \text{ for round } r\} = \prod_{r=1}^{t} (1/\mathcal{C})$$

$$= (2^{-\lg \mathcal{C}})^t = 2^{-\lg n} = \frac{1}{n},$$

which is sufficiently small for our lemma statement. (Notice, we can easily adjust this result for probability $1/n^c$, for constant $c > 1$, by simply increasing t by a factor of c.) □

Lemma 3. *Assuming that nodes i and j begin Step #2 during the same round with $ID_i \neq ID_j$, then this step will go on to solve contention resolution in an additional $O(\log \log n)$ rounds.*

Proof. Consider a binary array $B \in \{0,1\}^{\lg \mathcal{C}+1}$, defined such that for each $m \in [0, \lg \mathcal{C}]$, $B[m] = 1$ iff P_i and P_j pass through the same node in level m of $T_{\mathcal{C}}$. Notice that $B[0] = 1$, $B[\lg \mathcal{C}] = 0$, and the array, when read from small to large indices starts with 1's then changes over to 0's. The SplitCheck subroutine implements a standard binary search logic on B to identify $\ell = \min\{m : B[m] = 0\}$. The correctness of this search depends on the correctness of the logic SplitCheck uses to test whether a given position is 1 or 0. This correctness follows from how the algorithm assigns i and j to channels when testing a given level m. The formula used—$\lceil id/2^{\lg \mathcal{C} - m} \rceil$—assigns i and j to the same channel iff their paths share a node at that level of $T_{\mathcal{C}}$ (that is, if $B[m] = 1$). The nodes then use collision detection to determine whether or not they share the same channel for a given check.

Once we have established that the nodes effectively set $L = \ell$ with their call to SplitCheck, the correctness of the whole routine follows. By definition, i and j share a parent at level $\ell - 1$ in $T_{\mathcal{C}}$ and therefore only one these two nodes is the common parent's left child—the node that will go on to transmit alone on channel 1 and solve the problem.

Finally, we note that the time required to complete this search is in $O(\log h) = O(\log \log \mathcal{C}) = O(\log \log n)$, where the final step follows from our assumption that $\mathcal{C} \leq n$. □

5. CONTENTION RESOLUTION FOR ANY NUMBER OF NODES

We now present our main algorithm which solves contention resolution for any number of active nodes. The algorithm consists of three steps that are executed one after another in a synchronized manner. The first step leverages a straightforward *knock out* strategy to reduce the number of active nodes to a count in $O(\log n)$. (This preliminary reduction will simplify the steps that follow.) The second step reassigns active nodes unique ids from the space $[\mathcal{C}/2]$ (further reducing the number of active nodes if needed to enable this task). The third step leverages the guarantees of the two that precede it to solve the contention resolution problem.

REDUCE (for active node v)

$\hat{n} \leftarrow n, r \leftarrow 1$
do
  repeat twice:
    v broadcasts on channel 1 with probability $1/\hat{n}$
    if v broadcasts without collision
      v become leader and terminates
    else if v receives and does not hear silence
      v becomes inactive and terminates
  $r \leftarrow r+1$
  $\hat{n} \leftarrow \sqrt{\hat{n}}$
while $r \leq \lceil \lg \lg n \rceil$

Figure 2: The Reduce Algorithm

Our main theorem follows directly from Theorems 5, 6, and 17:

THEOREM 4. *In a network with up to $n \geq 1$ possible active nodes and $\mathcal{C} \geq 1$ channels, our algorithm solves contention resolution in $O\Big(\frac{\log n}{\log \mathcal{C}} + (\log\log n)(\log\log\log n)\Big)$ rounds, with high probability.*

5.1 Step #1: Reduce to $O(\log n)$ Active Nodes

The first step of our leader election algorithm is to reduce the number of active nodes to $O(\log n)$. This reduction will prove helpful to both of the steps that follow. We note that with collision detection, reducing a set of no more than n nodes to less than $O(\log n)$ nodes does not require multiple channels. Accordingly, the algorithm we deploy for this purpose only uses channel 1. Our algorithm REDUCE uses a standard knock out strategy and reduces the active node count to $O(\log n)$ in $O(\log\log n)$ rounds. We formalize this result with the following theorem which can be shown using standard techniques from the single channel setting:

THEOREM 5. *There exists a constant $\alpha \geq 1$, such that for any constant $\beta \geq 1$, when Algorithm* REDUCE *terminates the number of active nodes is between 1 and $\alpha\beta\log n$, with probability at least $1 - n^{-\beta}$.*

5.2 Step #2: Reduce the Unique ID Space from $[n]$ to $[\mathcal{C}/2]$

Our goal in this second step is to continue to reduce the set of active nodes as needed until we succeed in reassigning nodes unique IDs from $[\mathcal{C}/2]$. We accomplish this task with an algorithm we call IDREDUCTION, which guarantees to complete the needed reduction/renaming in $O(\log n/\log \mathcal{C})$ rounds, with high probability. We describe and analyze the algorithm below.

The IDReduction Algorithm. This algorithm alternates between *renaming* and *reduction* phases. The renaming phase is implemented by a pair of rounds. During the first round of the pair, all nodes that are still active at the beginning of the renaming phase choose a channel from the range $[\mathcal{C}/2]$ with uniform randomness and transmit. If a node detects it is alone on some channel i, it adopts i as its unique id. In the next round of the pair all nodes go to channel 1. Any node that adopted a unique id in the preceding round transmits. If there are any transmissions, the algorithm is over, and only those nodes who transmitted remain active (with their recently adopted ids as their new unique id).

The reduction phase requires only a single round. During a reduction phase round, all nodes that are still active transmit with probability $1/k$ on channel 1, where $k = \sqrt{\mathcal{C}}/144$. Nodes that do not transmit receive on channel 1. If there is at least one transmission, then any active node that did not transmit becomes inactive. Otherwise, the set of active nodes does not change in this round.

Analysis. In the following, we use the notation A_r to represent the set of active nodes in the beginning of the rth round of IDREDUCTION. Note that $\ldots \subseteq A_{r+1} \subseteq A_r \subseteq \ldots \subseteq A_1 = A$. In the following, we assume $\mathcal{C}$ is a sufficiently large such that $k = \sqrt{\mathcal{C}}/144 \geq 3$. (Spread throughout this analysis are several other places where we similarly assume $\mathcal{C}$ is larger than some fixed constant.) We note that we are always safe to fix a constant lower bound for $\mathcal{C}$, as when $\mathcal{C} = O(1)$, the lower bound simplifies to $\Omega(\log n)$, which we can match with the well-known $O(\log n)$ contention resolution algorithm that is optimal for the single channel case. Finally, to simplify notation, the theorem, lemma, and corollary statements that follow, when we claim a result holds *with high probability*, we mean that it holds with probability at least $1 - n^{-\beta}$, where $\beta \geq 1$ is a constant that increases along with the constants hidden within the asymptotic time complexity.

We begin our analysis by stating the main theorem. Its correctness follows directly from Corollary 8 and Lemma 10 which we describe and prove below.

THEOREM 6. *Assume $|A| = O(\log n)$. With high probability:* IDREDUCTION *terminates in $O(\log n/\log \mathcal{C})$ rounds with no more than $\mathcal{C}/2$ active nodes, each with a unique ID from $[\mathcal{C}/2]$.*

Our analysis proceeds in two pieces. In more detail, first we show that the reduction rounds reduce the number of active nodes below $\mathcal{C}/6$ within $O(\log n/\log \mathcal{C})$ rounds. Second, we show that once we have less than $\mathcal{C}/6$ participants, the renaming rounds will succeed within an additional $O(\log n/\log \mathcal{C})$ rounds. The below lemma addresses the first piece. The main idea is to note that when the number of active nodes is large compared to a target of $\approx k\log k$ (where k comes from the knock probability $1/k$ used in the reduction rounds in IDREDUCTION) the reduction rounds achieve big reductions with high probability after only a small number of rounds. As the active node count approaches the target, the number of rounds required for high probability increases. We show that this count falls fast enough that the total number of rounds spent reducing does not sum to something too large.

LEMMA 7. *Assume $|A| = O(\log n)$. There exists a round $\hat{r} = O(\log n/\log k)$, such that with high probability: $|A_{\hat{r}}| \leq 24k\log k$.*

PROOF. Let $c_1 = 24$ be the constant from the lemma statement; i.e., our goal can be stated as achieving $|A_{\hat{r}}| \leq c_1 k \log k$. By assumption, $|A| \leq c'\log n$ for some constant $c' \geq 0$. Therefore, it clearly follows that $|A| \leq \gamma\log n$ for $\gamma = \max\{24, c'\}$. We also assume $k < n$. If this was not true, then the assumption that $|A| = O(\log n)$ would imply that $|A| \leq c'\log k$ which is smaller than $24k\log k$ for any constant

c' once $\mathcal{C}$ is a sufficiently large constant, which would make the lemma trivially true. We also assume $\mathcal{C}$ is a sufficiently large constant that $k \geq 3$. An immediate corollary from this assumption is that $|A| \leq \gamma k \log n$. Because the set of active nodes can never increase as the execution continues, this upper bound always holds.

To begin our proof argument, we note that in each round r for which we have not yet sufficiently reduced the number of active nodes, we know: $c_1 k \log k < |A_r| \leq \gamma k \log n$. For each such round r, therefore, we can express $|A_r|$ as the quantity $\gamma k(\log n / q(r))$, for some value $q(r)$ that is from the range 1 to $T = (\gamma \log n)/(c_1 \log k)$. (We know $T > 1$ because $\gamma \geq c_1$ and $n > k$.) Furthermore, we know the sequence $q(1), q(2), q(3), \ldots$, is strictly non-decreasing, as the active node count can never grow.

Fix some reduction round r such that we are not yet done. Let X_r be the number of nodes that choose to transmit during this round. We know: $E(X_r) = |A_r|/k = \gamma(\log n / q(r))$.

Because the transmission decisions are independent, we can express X_r as the sum of independent indicator variables describing the nodes' transmission decisions, and can therefore apply a Chernoff bound to achieve concentration. We use the following special form:

$$\Pr[|X_r - E(X_r)| \geq E(X_r)/2] < 2e^{-E(X_r)/12}.$$

Notice, if $|X_r - E(X_r)| < E(X_r)/2$, then because $k \geq 3$ and $E(X_r) \geq 2$, it holds that we have reduced the set of active nodes by at least a factor of 2; i.e., $|A_r|/|A_{r+1}| \geq 2$. (The former assumption ensures $(3/2)E(X_r)$ is not too large, and the latter ensures that $(1/2)E(X_r) \geq 1$.)

We want to bound the probability that $|A_r|/|A_{r+x}| < 2$, for some $x \geq 1$. That is, we want to bound the probability that after x rounds we still have not yet reduced the active node count at the start of the interval by at least a factor of 2. To bound this probability, we instead consider the *harder* model where if a round is not good, then no node becomes inactive. In this harder model, the probability that we have x reduction rounds in a row that are *not good* is less than:

$$\left(2\exp\left\{-\frac{E(X_r)}{12}\right\}\right)^x < \left(\exp\left\{-\tfrac{E(X_r)}{24}\right\}\right)^x = \exp\left\{-\tfrac{x\gamma \log e \ln n}{24q(r)}\right\},$$

where the first inequality loosely holds so long as we assume that $E(X_r) \geq 24$ (for all values of $q(r)$ from 1 to T the expectation is greater than this value). Next notice for that for $x \geq \frac{q(r)c_2 24}{\gamma \log e}$, defined for any constant $c_2 \geq 1$, this probability is less than n^{-c_2}. Put another way, starting from any given round r, with high probability, after $\Theta(q(r))$ reduction rounds we have reduced the active node count by a factor of at least 2. (And as we increase the constant c_2 hidden in the $\Theta(q(r))$ term, the exponent on the failure probability increases as well.)

We next partition reduction rounds into intervals, where the first interval starts in the first reduction round, and the start of interval $i+1$, for $i \geq 1$, corresponds to the first round after which the number of active nodes is at least a factor of 2 smaller than at the start of interval i. Let r_i be the reduction round at the start of interval i. Let $\hat{i}$ be the latest interval before we fall below our target threshold of $c_1 k \log k$.

Consider the sequence of $q(r)$ values associated with the size of the active node sets during these intervals' start rounds: $q(r_1), q(r_2), \ldots, q(r_{\hat{i}})$. We note two things about this sequence. First, by our definition of an interval, for each i, $q(r_i) \leq q(r_{i+1})/2$. That is, the values at least double between intervals, corresponding to the node set size reducing by at least a factor of 2. We also note that by definition: $q(r_{\hat{i}}) = O(T) = O(\log n / \log k)$.

Leveraging our above probabilistic analysis, we note that for each interval i, with high probability, it takes only $O(q(r_i))$ rounds to get to interval $i+1$. Therefore, by a union bound, this is true of all intervals, also with high probability. Under this assumption, we can upper bound the number of rounds required to get through all $O(T)$ intervals with the summation $c + 2c + 4c + \ldots + T$, for some constant $c \geq 1$. This time complexity simplifies to $O(T) = O(\log n / \log k)$—as needed. □

Our goal is to get the number of active nodes below $\mathcal{C}/6$. Notice, however, that for our definition $k = \sqrt{\mathcal{C}}/144$, the $\leq 24k \log k$ nodes guaranteed by Lemma 7 reduces to no more than:

$$\begin{aligned} 24k \log k &= 24(\sqrt{\mathcal{C}}/144)\log(\sqrt{\mathcal{C}}/144) < 24(\sqrt{\mathcal{C}}/144)\log(\sqrt{\mathcal{C}}) \\ &\leq (1/6)\sqrt{\mathcal{C}}\log(\sqrt{\mathcal{C}}) < \mathcal{C}/6. \end{aligned}$$

The following corollary is a direct implication of Lemma 7 and the above inequality and the fact $O\left(\frac{\log n}{\log k}\right) = O\left(\frac{\log n}{\log \mathcal{C}}\right)$:

COROLLARY 8. *Assume* $|A| = O(\log n)$. *There exists a round* $\hat{r} = O\left(\frac{\log n}{\log \mathcal{C}}\right)$, *such that with high probability:* $|A_{\hat{r}}| < \mathcal{C}/6$.

We are left now to show that if the number of active nodes reduces below $\mathcal{C}/6$, renaming becomes likely to succeed. Before making our main argument to this effect, we first isolate a useful balls-in-bins claim that the argument will leverage.

LEMMA 9. *Assume you throw b balls into m bins such that $b = m/\beta$, where $3 \leq \beta < m$. The probability that* no *ball ends up alone in a bin is less than* $\frac{1}{2^{b/2}}$.

PROOF. To achieve our bound we will bound the probability that $(m - m/(2\beta))$ of m bins are empty. Notice, this event must hold if no ball ends up alone, as if more than $m/(2\beta)$ bins are full, then by a straightforward counting argument, at least one ball must end up alone.

Continuing with our calculation, consider a fixed set of $(m - m/(2\beta))$ empty bins. For each ball, the probability that the ball misses these empty bins and falls into one of the $m/(2\beta)$ *free* bins it is allowed to occupy, is $1/(2\beta)$. The probability that *all* balls land in a free bin is therefore $1/(2\beta)^{m/\beta}$. This probability concerns only a single set of empty bins. We now consider all such sets. In more detail, there are $\binom{m}{m-m/(2\beta)}$ different ways to select our $(m - m/(2\beta))$ empty bins. Taking a union bound over these different selections, we derive that the probability that there is at least one selection of $(m - m/(2\beta))$ empty bins that remains empty after throwing m/β balls, is upper bounded as follows:

$$\frac{\binom{m}{m-\frac{m}{2\beta}}}{(2\beta)^{\frac{m}{\beta}}} = \frac{\binom{m}{\frac{m}{2\beta}}}{(2\beta)^{\frac{m}{\beta}}} \leq \frac{(2\beta e)^{\frac{m}{2\beta}}}{(2\beta)^{\frac{m}{\beta}}} = \left(\frac{e}{2\beta}\right)^{\frac{m}{2\beta}} < \frac{1}{2^{\frac{m}{2\beta}}},$$

where the last step holds because we assume $\beta \geq 3 > e \Rightarrow e/(2\beta) < (1/2)$. To achieve the bound stated in the lemma our final step is to substitute the definition $b = m/\beta$. □

We now leverage Lemma 9 to argue that renaming will succeed once the number of active nodes is small enough for the above balls-in-bins argument to give us a sufficiently high probability of success. The probability we seek is something at least $(1 - (1/\mathcal{C}))$. If we succeed with this probability, then the probability we fail $O(\log n/\log \mathcal{C})$ times in a row becomes small in n,

LEMMA 10. *Fix a round r such that $|A_r| \leq \mathcal{C}/6$. With high probability, renaming succeeds and the algorithm terminates within $O(\log n/\log \mathcal{C})$ rounds.*

PROOF. In renaming rounds, active nodes each select a channel with uniform randomness. If any node is alone on its chosen channel the algorithm terminates. We will prove here that once we fall below $\mathcal{C}/6$ nodes, this will occur with high probability after the stated number of attempts. To do so, fix some renaming round t. Let $n' = |A_t|$ be the number of nodes still active during this round. Assume $1 < n' \leq \mathcal{C}/6$ (the lower bound is safe to assume as if $n' = 1$ it is trivial to show we will terminate in this round). Let $\hat{\mathcal{C}} = \mathcal{C}/2$. We consider two cases concerning the size of n', and will show for each that the probability we do *not* terminate in t is less than $1/2^{\log \hat{\mathcal{C}}/2}$. We will then show this probability is sufficiently low to terminate within the time claimed by the lemma statement with high probability.

The first case for the size of n' is when $n' \leq \sqrt{\hat{\mathcal{C}}}$. Fix any node $i \in A_t$. Let x be the channel it selects in this round. The probability that some other $j \in A_t$ also chooses x is $1/\hat{\mathcal{C}}$. By a union bound, the probability that at least one node in A_t chooses x is less than: $n'/\hat{\mathcal{C}} \leq 1/\sqrt{\hat{\mathcal{C}}} = 1/2^{\lg(\sqrt{\hat{\mathcal{C}}})} = 1/2^{\lg \hat{\mathcal{C}}/2}$, as needed.

The second case is when $n' > \sqrt{\hat{\mathcal{C}}}$. Here we can apply Lemma 9 to the problem of throwing n' balls in $\hat{\mathcal{C}}$ bins (which requires our assumption that $1 < n' \leq \mathcal{C}/6$ which implies $n' \leq \hat{\mathcal{C}}/3$). This lemma tells us that the probability that *no* ball is alone is less than $\frac{1}{2^{n'/2}}$. Given our assumption that $n' > \sqrt{\hat{\mathcal{C}}}$, it follows that $1/2^{n'/2} < 1/2^{\sqrt{\hat{\mathcal{C}}}/2} < 1/2^{\log \hat{\mathcal{C}}/2}$. This final step requires the assumption that $\log \hat{\mathcal{C}} \leq \sqrt{\hat{\mathcal{C}}}$, which is always true for $\hat{\mathcal{C}} \geq 16$. Given that we assumed $\mathcal{C} \geq 32$ at the beginning of this section, it follows that $\hat{\mathcal{C}} \geq 16$.

We have just shown that in every round (once the number of active nodes is sufficiently small), we fail to terminate with probability less than $1/2^{\log \hat{\mathcal{C}}/2}$. The probability that we fail to terminate for $T = (c \log n)/\log \hat{\mathcal{C}}$ renaming rounds in a row (for a fixed constant $c \geq 1$), therefore, is less than:

$$\left(\left(\frac{1}{2}\right)^{\frac{\log \hat{\mathcal{C}}}{2}}\right)^{T} = \left(\left(\frac{1}{2}\right)^{\frac{\log \hat{\mathcal{C}}}{2}}\right)^{\frac{c \log n}{\log \hat{\mathcal{C}}}} = \left(\frac{1}{2}\right)^{\frac{c \log n}{2}} = \left(\frac{1}{2}\right)^{\frac{c}{2}}.$$

Because $T = O(\log n/\log \mathcal{C})$, it follows that the probability we fail to terminate in $T = O(\log n/\log \mathcal{C})$ rounds is polynomially small in n (with an exponent that increases with the constant c in T). □

5.3 Step #3: Elect a Leader

The result of the first and second step of our algorithm is that we now have $x \leq \mathcal{C}/2$ active nodes with unique IDs in $[\mathcal{C}/2]$, and in addition $x = O(\log n)$ with high probability. These nodes participate in the third and final step of our algorithm, which we call LEAFELECTION. This algorithm *deterministically* elects a leader using a tree of channels (i.e., a tree with $\leq \mathcal{C}$ nodes for which we have assigned a unique channel for each tree node). This algorithm runs in $O(\log h \log \log x)$ rounds, where x is the starting number of active nodes and $h = \lg \mathcal{C}$ is the height of the tree of channels. As before, we shall assume without loss of generality that $\mathcal{C}$ is a power of 2.

Algorithm Description. Before describing the algorithm mechanics (see Figure 3 for pseudocode), we first discuss the tree of channels (equiv., channel tree) the algorithm uses. As in Section 4 (the two node algorithm), we map channels to a complete binary tree T with $\mathcal{C}/2$ leaves, with channels identified in the same canonical fashion as before. In certain rounds, it will also be convenient to choose a single channel to represent each level (or row) in the tree; to do so, we choose the leftmost tree node at that level to act as the level's representative channel.

The core behavior of our algorithm is to *coalesce* active nodes into larger and larger groups we call *cohorts* such that every node in the same cohort has a distinct ID from a known ID space the same size as the cohort. Eventually, only one cohort remains, and the distinct IDs can be used to identify the leader for the whole network. The main point of the cohorts is to accelerate the binary searches used to identify key levels in the channel tree.

More precisely, the main algorithm LEAFELECTION consists of a sequence of iterations or *phases*. Initially, all active nodes belong to their own cohorts of size 1. We associate with each cohort a distinct tree node *cNode*, which is the least common ancestor of all active nodes in the cohort. Initially, therefore, the cohorts are associated with the leaves of the channel tree. The algorithm maintains the invariant that at the start of the ith phase all active cohorts have exactly 2^{i-1} active nodes, and each active node in a particular cohort has a distinct *cID* (or cohort ID) from $[2^{i-1}]$. We call the node with $cID = 1$ in the cohort the *cohort master*.

Each phase begins by testing whether more than one cohort exists by having the cohort masters broadcast on the root channel. If there is more than one cohort, then the phase must guarantee that (1) at least one cohort exists at the end of the phase, and (2) all cohorts become twice as large. We achieve this goal by pairing together some cohorts and having others become inactive. In particular, we employ SPLITSEARCH to identify the level ℓ closest to the root such that all cohorts have a different level-ℓ ancestor. Since we choose the smallest such level, there exists at least one pair (and possibly many pairs) of cohorts that have the common level-$(\ell - 1)$ ancestor. To identify these pairs, each cohort master broadcasts on the channel for its level-$(\ell - 1)$ ancestor (and all other members of the cohort listen). If there is a collision, then this cohort can be paired; otherwise, it becomes inactive. To pair the cohorts, we observe that one cohort is in the ancestor's left subtree, whereas the other must be in the right subtree, so we increase the *cIDs* of nodes in the right subtree by the cohort size. Finally, the cohort tree node *cNode* can be updated to this ancestor.

```
LEAFELECTION (for active node v)
cSize ← 1              // size of all active cohorts
cNode ← v's leaf       // the subtree for v's cohort
cID ← 1                // v's distinct id within its cohort
repeat
  if cID = 1
    v broadcasts on root's channel
  else v listens on root's channel
  if there was no collision
    the lone broadcaster is the leader
  else let ℓ_max = cNodes's level
    ℓ ← SPLITSEARCH(0, ℓ_max, cSize, cNode, cID)
    if cID = 1
      v broadcasts on a_{ℓ-1}(v)'s channel
    else v listens on a_{ℓ-1}(v)'s channel
    if collision at a_{ℓ-1}(v)
      if v in right subtree of a_{ℓ-1}(v)
        cID ← cID + cSize
      cSize ← 2cSize
      cNode ← a_{ℓ-1}(v)
    else v becomes inactive
until leader declared

SPLITSEARCH(ℓ_min, ℓ_max, cSize, cNode, cID) for active v
// return level closest to root where all subtrees
  have ≤ 1 cohort
if ℓ_max = ℓ_min + 1 return ℓ_max
else let probedist = ⌈(ℓ_max − ℓ_min)/cSize⌉
  let k be smallest value such that
  ℓ_min + k · probedist ≥ ℓ_max
  for i < k, define ℓ_i as ℓ_i = ℓ_min + i · probedist
  define ℓ_k = ℓ_max
  if cID < k
    CHECKLEVEL(ℓ_cID)
    CHECKLEVEL(ℓ_{cID+1})
  else do nothing for 4 rounds
  if cID = 1 and the first check returned "no collision"
    announce 0 on channel cNode and set i ← 0
  else if cID < k and only the first check returned
  "collision"
    announce cID on channel cNode and set i ← cID
  else listen to cNode and set i to the announced value
  return SPLITSEARCH(ℓ_i, ℓ_{i+1}, cSize, cNode, cID)

CHECKLEVEL(ℓ) for active node v
broadcast on a_ℓ(v)
if a collision occurred on a_ℓ(v)
  broadcast on the channel for row ℓ
else listen on the channel for row ℓ
if the channel for row ℓ was silent
  return "no collision"
else return "collision"
```

Figure 3: The Algorithm LeafElection. The notation $a_\ell(v)$ refers to v's level-ℓ (i.e., depth-ℓ) ancestor in the tree of channels.

The SPLITSEARCH routine is similar to SPLITCHECK in Section 4, with the exception of two key differences. First, the paths down to active cohorts may diverge at different points, but we wish to identify the smallest level ℓ globally where all have diverged. We thus employ a slightly more complicated test, called CHECKLEVEL to test whether any nodes share an ancestor at level ℓ. The test consists of two rounds. During the first round, one node per cohort broadcasts on its level-ℓ ancestor. Some nodes may observe a collision, whereas others may not. To arrive at the same conclusion, any collisions are announced on the row channel for level-ℓ.

The second key difference in SPLITSEARCH is that we exploit the large size of cohorts to accelerate the search. In particular, let p be the size of cohorts. Then the search is a $(p+1)$-ary search, instead of a binary search, adapted from Snir's [16] CREW parallel search. The search takes as input a range of levels $(\ell_{\min}, \ell_{\max}]$ to search. This range is then subdivided into $p+1$ subranges of roughly the same size, given by $(\ell_0 = \ell_{\min}, \ell_1], (\ell_1, \ell_2], (\ell_2, \ell_3], \ldots, (\ell_{k-1}, \ell_k = \ell_{\max}]$. (Usually $k = p+1$, except within one recursion of the base case where k can be smaller.) The observation is that each subrange can be tested independently—if there is a collision at level ℓ_i but no collision at level ℓ_{i+1}, then $(\ell_i, \ell_{i+1}]$ is the subrange to search. Thus, we can test the subranges in parallel by assigning one node per cohort to each range according to *cID*s. Once the correct subrange has been identified by one node per cohort, that node announces the range to its comrades on the cohort tree node *cNode*. Note that this step requires listeners to read and interpret the message, not just listen for collisions. In this way, all nodes know which subrange to recurse in, and the size of the range has been reduced by roughly a $p+1$ factor.

Analysis. To prove correctness, we will argue that the following structural properties are invariant across phases. Assuming the properties hold for each iteration, we first prove that subroutines operate correctly (Lemmas 12 and 13). We then inductively argue that Property 11 indeed holds with Lemma 14.

PROPERTY 11. *Let i be the phase number of* LEAFELECTION*:*

- *All active nodes belong to a cohort.*
- *Each cohort has exactly $cSize = 2^{i-1}$ active nodes as members.*
- *Each member of a particular cohort has a distinct identifier $cID \in [2^{i-1}]$.*
- *The cohort node is the treenode that is the least common ancestor of all members (which correspond to leaves). All cohort nodes occur at distinct nodes in the same level of the tree. Moreover, all members of a cohort correctly identify their cohort node with cNode.*

LEMMA 12. *Suppose that Property 11 holds and that exactly one node in each active cohort performs* CHECKLEVEL(ℓ)*. Then the return value is "no collision" if and only if all cohorts have distinct level-ℓ ancestors.*

PROOF. By assumption, all cohort nodes occur at the same level. If ℓ is a descendent level (i.e., ℓ is at least the level of cohort nodes), then CHECKLEVEL correctly returns "no collision"—by Property 11, each participating node is a descendent of a distinct cohort node, so they broadcast on different channels.

Suppose instead that ℓ is smaller than the cohort nodes' level. If two cohorts share an ancestor at level ℓ, then by Property 11 all members of those cohorts also share that ancestor. Thus, the first broadcast observes a collision, which is advertised to all other cohorts in the second broadcast. If no cohorts share an ancestor at that level, then no collision is observed by anyone. □

LEMMA 13. *Suppose that Property 11 holds when* SPLITSEARCH *is called from* LEAFELECTION. *Then* SPLITSEARCH *correctly returns the smallest level ℓ (nearest to root) such that all cohorts have distinct level-ℓ ancestors.*

PROOF. The proof is by induction over the recursive calls. The hypothesis is that on each call 1) all concurrent calls are synchronized and use the same values of $\ell_{\min}$ and $\ell_{\max}$, 2) $\ell_{\min} < \ell$, and 3) $\ell \leq \ell_{\max}$. Assuming the hypothesis, the search only terminates if the correct value is identified. It is easy to verify that the search eventually terminates because the range gets strictly smaller on each recursive call.

For the base case, (1) follows from the fact that all cohort nodes have the same level, and hence all active nodes agree on $\ell_{\max}$. (3) is true trivially since all cohort nodes are distinct nodes at level $\ell_{\max}$. Since the search only executes if there was a collision at the root, we know $0 < \ell$ and hence (2) holds.

For the inductive step, it is easy to verify that $\ell_{\min} = \ell_0 < \ell_1 < \cdots \ell_k = \ell_{\max}$. Moreover, due to distinct *cIDs* (Property 11), CHECKLEVEL(ℓ_i) is performed by exactly one node in each cohort at a time. Thus, by Lemma 12 these calls perform the correct answers, with the corresponding nodes in each cohort observing the same answers. Moreover, CHECKLEVEL(ℓ_i) returns "collision" for all $\ell_i < \ell$ and "no collision" for $\ell_i \geq \ell$, so only one subrange can be identified for the recursive search and hence only one node per cohort makes an announcement. (This is essentially the same argument as Section 4 as well as the parallel search [16].) Finally, we must verify that the range is announced without collision and that all nodes in the cohort listen, which follows from the assumption that each cohort has a different *cNode*. □

LEMMA 14. *Property 11 holds at the start of the ith phase of* LEAFELECTION.

PROOF. The proof is by induction. By assumption that each active node is a separate leaf of the tree, the property holds trivially initially with all cohorts consisting of a single active node.

Suppose the property holds at the start of the ith phase. Then we must show that it holds at the start of the next iteration. Since SPLITSEARCH returns the correct answer (Lemma 13), we know that (1) all cohorts have distinct level-ℓ ancestors, (2) at least one level-$(\ell - 1)$ treenode has multiple descendent cohorts, and (3) all such level-$(\ell - 1)$ treenodes have exactly two descendent cohorts, one in the left and one in the right subtree. Since exactly one node per cohort broadcasts on its level-$(\ell - 1)$ ancestor, the cohorts observe a collision if and only and only if they share a level-$(\ell - 1)$ ancestor with another cohort. Thus, cohorts remain active if and only if they can be paired with another cohort, thereby doubling the size of the cohort. Since the *cIDs* for a cohort are by inductive assumption distinct values from [*cSize*], adding *cSize* to the IDs of one of the paired cohorts preserves distinctness. Moreover, the new *cNode* is indeed the least common ancestor of both cohorts, and hence of all nodes therein. □

We are now ready to bound the performance of LEAFELECTION. We first bound the number of phases as a direct corollary of Property 11. Then we bound the cost of the searches.

COROLLARY 15. *If* LEAFELECTION *begins with x active nodes assigned to distinct leaves of the channel tree, then it correctly identifies a leader in $O(\log x)$ phases.*

PROOF. By Lemma 14, Property 11 holds, and hence at the start of the ith phase all cohorts have size 2^{i-1}. Thus, there cannot be more than $\lg x + 1$ phases. □

LEMMA 16. *During the ith phase,* SPLITSEARCH *completes in $O((1/i) \log h)$ rounds, where $h = \lg \mathcal{C}$ is the height of the channel tree.*

PROOF. With each recursive call, the size of the level subrange to search becomes $\lceil (\ell_{\max} - \ell_{\min})/cSize \rceil$, i.e., reducing by at least a $\Theta(cSize) = \Theta(2^i) + 1$ factor. Thus, the number of recursive calls is $O(\log_{2^i+1} h) = O(\log h/ \log 2^i) = O((1/i) \log h)$. Noting that each call is a constant number (specifically 5) of rounds completes the proof. □

Finally, we have our main theorem for this step of leader election:

THEOREM 17. *If* LEAFELECTION *begins with x active nodes assigned to distinct leaves of the channel tree, then it correctly identifies a leader in $O(\log h \log \log x)$ phases, where $h = \lg \mathcal{C}$ is the height of the channel tree.*

PROOF. Correctness follows from the Lemma 14. To prove the performance, we observe that the work of each of the $\lg x$ phases is dominated by the SPLITSEARCH. Applying Corollary 15 and Lemma 16, we conclude that the total number of rounds is $\sum_{i=1}^{O(\log x)} O((1/i) \log h) = O\left(\log h \sum_{i=1}^{O(\log x)} (1/i)\right) = O(\log h \log \log x)$. □

Recall that if the previous steps are successful, then $x = O(\log n)$, and hence this bound reduces to:

$$O(\log \log \mathcal{C} \cdot \log \log \log n) = O(\log \log n \cdot \log \log \log n).$$

6. CONCLUSION

In this paper, we study the classical *contention resolution* problem, in which an unknown subset of n possible nodes are activated and connected on shared channels with the goal of breaking symmetry. We considered, in particular, the case where nodes have access to multiple channels and collision detectors. We described and analyzed new algorithms that match the relevant lower bound for the restricted case of two active nodes, and for the general case come within a factor of $\log \log n$. These results help advance one of the few remaining major open cases for the longstanding study of contention resolution.

The obvious next step is to tackle this final small gap between lower and upper bounds. We predict that the lower bound is in fact tight. Proving this (somewhat tentative) assertion, however, will require more advanced algorithmic techniques. Another open problem is to tackle contention resolution in this setting with respect to expected time of termination. Not much is known about expected time solutions in this case. One reason for this omission is that even *without* collision detection, the best expected time solutions are really fast, reaching $O(1)$ expected complexity with as few as $\log n$ channels. This leaves only a small band of parameters for which the addition of collision detection might possibly improve performance.

7. ACKNOWLEGEMENTS

The research in this paper has been supported by NSF grants CCF 1320279 and CCF 1314633.

8. REFERENCES

[1] N. Abramson. The ALOHA System: Another Alternative for Computer Communications. In *Proceedings of the Fall Joint Computer Conference*, 1970.

[2] R. Bar-Yehuda, O. Goldreich, and A. Itai. On the Time Complexity of Broadcast in Radio Networks: an Exponential Gap Between Determinism and Randomization. In *Proceedings of the International Symposium on Principles of Distributed Computing*, 1987.

[3] S. Daum, S. Gilbert, F. Kuhn, and C. Newport. Leader Election in Shared Spectrum Networks. In *Proceedings of the International Symposium on Principles of Distributed Computing*, 2012.

[4] S. Daum, F. Kuhn, and C. Newport. Efficient Symmetry Breaking in Multi-Channel Radio Networks. In *Proceedings of the International Symposium on Distributed Computing*, 2012.

[5] W. D.E. Log-logarithmic selection resolution protocols in a multiple access channel. *SIAM Journal on Computing*, 15(2):468–477, 1986.

[6] M. Farach-Colton, R. J. Fernandes, and M. A. Mosteiro. Lower Bounds for Clear Transmissions in Radio Networks. In *Proceedings of the Latin American Symposium on Theoretical Informatics*, 2006.

[7] R. Gallager. A Perspective on Multiaccess Channels. *IEEE Transactions on Information Theory*, 31(2):124–142, 1985.

[8] L. Gasieniec, A. Pelc, and D. Peleg. The Wakeup Problem in Synchronous Broadcast Systems. *SIAM Journal on Discrete Mathematics*, 14(2):207–222, 2001.

[9] A. Greenberg and S. Winograd. A Lower Bound on the Time Needed in the Worst Case to Resolve Conflicts Deterministically in Multiple Access Channels. *Journal of the ACM*, 32(3):589–596, 1985.

[10] B. Hajek and T. van Loon. Decentralized Dynamic Control of a Multiaccess Broadcast Channel. *IEEE Transactions on Automatic Control*, 27(3):559–569, 1982.

[11] T. Jurdziński and G. Stachowiak. Probabilistic Algorithms for the Wakeup Problem in Single-Hop Radio Networks. In *Algorithms and Computation*, pages 535–549. Springer, 2002.

[12] M. Kaplan. A Sufficient Condition for Non-Ergodicity of a Markov Chain. *IEEE Transactions on Information Theory*, IT-25:470–471, July 1979.

[13] J. Komlos and A. Greenberg. An Asymptotically Nonadaptive Algorithm for Conflict Resolution in Multiple-Access Channels. *IEEE Transactions on Information Theory*, 31(2):302–306, 1985.

[14] C. Newport. Radio Network Lower Bounds Made Easy. In *Proceedings of the International Symposium on Distributed Computing*, 2014.

[15] L. G. Roberts. ALOHA Packet System with and Without Slots and Capture. *ACM SIGCOMM Computer Communication Review*, 5(2):28–42, 1975.

[16] M. Snir. On Parallel Searching. *SIAM Journal on Computing*, 14(3):688–708, 1985.

How Asynchrony Affects Rumor Spreading Time*

George Giakkoupis
INRIA Rennes
France
george.giakkoupis@inria.fr

Yasamin Nazari
University of Calgary
Canada
ynazari@ucalgary.ca

Philipp Woelfel
University of Calgary
Canada
woelfel@ucalgary.ca

ABSTRACT

In standard randomized (push-pull) rumor spreading, nodes communicate in synchronized rounds. In each round every node contacts a random neighbor in order to exchange the rumor (i.e., either push the rumor to its neighbor or pull it from the neighbor). A natural asynchronous variant of this algorithm is one where each node has an independent Poisson clock with rate 1, and every node contacts a random neighbor whenever its clock ticks. This asynchronous variant is arguably a more realistic model in various settings, including message broadcasting in communication networks, and information dissemination in social networks.

In this paper we study how asynchrony affects the rumor spreading time, that is, the time before a rumor originated at a single node spreads to all nodes in the graph. Our first result states that the asynchronous push-pull rumor spreading time is asymptotically bounded by the standard synchronous time. Precisely, we show that for any graph G on n-nodes, where the synchronous push-pull protocol informs all nodes within $T(G)$ rounds with high probability, the asynchronous protocol needs at most time $O(T(G) + \log n)$ to inform all nodes with high probability. On the other hand, we show that the expected synchronous push-pull rumor spreading time is bounded by $O(\sqrt{n})$ times the expected asynchronous time.

These results improve upon the bounds for both directions shown recently by Acan et al. (PODC 2015). An interesting implication of our first result is that in regular graphs, the weaker push-only variant of synchronous rumor spreading has the same asymptotic performance as the synchronous push-pull algorithm.

*This research was undertaken, in part, thanks to funding from the Canada Research Chairs program, the Discovery Grants program of NSERC, the INRIA Associate Team RADCON, Alberta Innovates Technology Futures, and MITACS.

PODC'16, July 25 - 28, 2016, Chicago, IL, USA

ISBN 978-1-4503-3964-3/16/07...$15.00

DOI: http://dx.doi.org/10.1145/2933057.2933117

Keywords

randomized rumor spreading; push/pull; asynchronous vs synchronous models

1. INTRODUCTION

Broadcasting information in large networks is a fundamental and well-studied problem. Desirable properties of broadcasting algorithms are efficiency, simplicity, decentralization, and tolerance to changes in the network topology. The classical abstraction is the randomized (synchronous) rumor spreading protocol [7, 22]: Initially, a piece of information, called rumor, is injected at a random or arbitrarily chosen node. After that, nodes communicate in synchronous rounds to inform each other of the rumor. In every round, each node calls a uniformly random neighbor and establishes a communication with its callee in order to possibly exchange the rumor: In the *push* protocol, an informed caller pushes the rumor to its callee, while in the *pull* protocol, a non-informed caller receives the rumor from its callee, if the callee is informed. The *push-pull* protocol combines the push and pull communication and allows a bi-directional rumor exchange in each round between each caller and its callee.

Besides being of fundamental interest, rumor spreading protocols have many direct applications, such as in the maintenance of distributed replicated database systems [7, 13], failure detection [26], resource discovery [20], and data aggregation [4]. As such, the rumor spreading time, i.e., the number of rounds until all nodes in a network have received the rumor (either in expectation or with high probability), has been studied intensively. A large body of research work deals with the question how the rumor spreading time is influenced by the network topology (e.g., [8, 12, 15, 16]), network parameters such as expansion [5, 6, 17–19, 25], or the communication modes push, pull, and push-pull (e.g., [24]).

The synchrony assumption, according to which all nodes establish connections simultaneously in a round-by-round fashion, has been criticized for not being plausible in many scenarios [9–11]. Real networks typically do not have a centralized clock, and individual links are affected by frequent changes in communication speed. Moreover, decentralization has been emphasized as one of the main advantages of the rumor spreading protocol, but this contradicts the model assumption of a centralized clock. More recently the performance of rumor spreading protocols in a natural asynchronous setting, initially proposed by Boyd, Ghosh, Prabhakar, and Shah [4], has been considered. Here, nodes establish communications with their neighbors at times determined by independent Poisson processes, rather than at fixed unit times. More precisely, each node is equipped with an independent Poisson clock with rate 1, and whenever a node's clock ticks, the node exchanges the rumor with a uniformly random neighbor (using push, pull, or push-pull communication).

On the hypercube, the asynchronous push-pull protocol corresponds to Richardson's model for the spread of a disease, and has been investigated in the study of first-passage percolation [3, 14]. But only recently has asynchronous rumor spreading found the interest of researchers in the area of networks, initially in order to understand information spread in social networks. It was observed that on common network topologies modelling social networks, such as Chung-Lu power law graphs [16] or preferential attachment graphs [9], the push-pull protocol spreads the rumor to a large fraction of the nodes significantly faster in the asynchronous than in the synchronous model. There are even graph topologies for which the asynchronous push-pull protocol has poly-logarithmic rumor spreading time, whereas the synchronous protocol requires a polynomial number of rounds [1]. On the other hand, there are simple networks, where synchrony allows for faster rumor spreading than asynchrony [1]: In an n-vertex star, it takes at most 2 rounds of the synchronous push-pull protocol to spread the rumor to all nodes (it takes at most one round for the centre node to get informed by push, and another round for all remaining nodes to pull the rumor from the center); whereas in the asynchronous model it takes with high probability $\Theta(\log n)$ time until sufficiently many different Poisson clocks have ticked for all nodes to get informed. Finally, for various classical graph topologies such as the hypercube, random graphs, and random regular graphs, both protocols have the same rumor spreading times within constant factors [2, 14, 21, 23].

These results raise the question how big the gap between the asynchronous and the synchronous rumor spreading times can be. In the following discussion we restrict ourselves to push-pull communication for graphs with n vertices, unless mentioned otherwise. Acan, Collevecchio, Mehrabian, and Wormald [1] showed that for any graph the high-probability rumor spreading time in the asynchronous model is at most a multiplicative $O(\log n)$ factor larger than that of the synchronous model. While this result is tight for the n-vertex star, it may not be tight for graphs that have super-constant synchronous rumor spreading time. In fact, Acan et al. conjectured that the high-probability asynchronous rumor spreading time can be at most by an additive $O(\log n)$ term larger than the synchronous one. Our first main result proves that this conjecture is true up to a constant factor.

THEOREM 1. *Let G be a connected graph with n vertices, u be a vertex of G, and $T_{1/n}$ be the number of synchronous push-pull rounds before the rumor spreads from u to all other nodes with high probability (i.e., with probability $1 - 1/n$). Then the time in the asynchronous push-pull protocol before the rumor spreads from u to all other nodes is at most $O(T_{1/n} + \log n)$ with high probability.*

This bound is asymptotically tight, and in particular it shows that for most graphs, namely those that have at least logarithmic high-probability rumor spreading time, the asynchronous rumor spreading time is not asymptotically larger than the synchronous one. Further, it implies that several known upper bounds that have been shown to hold for the synchronous push-pull protocol carry over to the asynchronous, such as known bounds with graph expansion parameters [17, 18].

Acan et al. [1] showed also that the high-probability rumor spreading time in the synchronous model can be at most by a factor of $O(n^{2/3})$ larger than in the asynchronous model. They conjecture that this factor can be improved to $n^{1/2} \cdot (\log n)^{O(1)}$. Our second main result is a proof of this conjecture.

THEOREM 2. *Let G be a connected graph with n vertices, u be a vertex of G, and T be the number of synchronous push-pull rounds before the rumor spreads from u to all other nodes. Then the time in the asynchronous push-pull protocol before the rumor spreads from u to all other nodes has expectation $\Omega(\mathrm{E}[T]/\sqrt{n})$.*

Using this theorem, the conjecture of Acan et al. follows from the fact that with high probability the synchronous rumor spreading time T is at most by a multiplicative $O(\log n)$ factor larger than its expectation; i.e., $T = O(\mathrm{E}[T] \cdot \log n)$ with high probability. We currently do not know if the above bound is tight. Acan et al. [1] described a graph in which the asynchronous push-pull protocol has logarithmic running time, whereas synchronous push-pull has a running time of $\Theta(n^{1/3})$. This implies that the lower bound of Theorem 2 may be smaller than the best possible bound by at most a factor of $\Theta(n^{1/6})$.

In the synchronous model, the push-pull protocol can be significantly faster than the push(-only) protocol (but clearly it cannot be slower). For example, for an n-vertex star it takes with high probability $\Theta(n \log n)$ synchronous rounds to inform all nodes using the push protocol, while it takes at most two rounds using the push-pull protocol, as discussed earlier. Theorem 1 has the interesting consequence that push-pull communication can only have performance benefits over push on *non-regular* graphs. This is immediate from the following observations: (1) For the push protocol, Sauerwald [24] showed that for any graph, the high-probability synchronous rumor spreading time is bounded by the asynchronous rumor spreading time within a constant multiplicative factor. (2) It is not hard to see that on regular graphs, the asynchronous rumor spreading time of the push protocol has the same distribution as twice the asynchronous rumor spreading time of the push-pull protocol (see the full version of the paper for details). Last, (3) Theorem 1 implies that on regular graphs, the high-probability asynchronous push-pull rumor spreading time is bounded by the synchronous push-pull rumor spreading time within a constant multiplicative factor.[1] To summarize, we obtain the following, informally stated relations for the asymptotic high-probability rumor spreading times on any regular graph:[2]

$$\text{synchronous push} \overset{(1)}{\leq} \text{asynchronous push} \overset{(2)}{\leq} \text{asynchronous push-pull} \overset{(3)}{\leq} \text{synchronous push-pull}.$$

COROLLARY 3. *Let G be a connected regular graph with n vertices, u be a vertex of G, and $T_{p,1/n}, T_{pp,1/n}$ be the*

[1]The logarithmic additive term in the bound of Theorem 1 can be omitted as the synchronous push-pull rumor spreading time is with high probability at least $\Omega(\log n)$ on any regular graph.

[2]Here, '$\leq$' reads as 'has with high probability smaller or equal rumor spreading time, modulo constant factors.'

number of synchronous push, respectively, push-pull rounds before the rumor spreads from u to all other nodes with high probability. Then $T_{p,1/n} = \Theta(T_{pp,1/n})$.

2. DEFINITIONS

Let $G = (V, E)$ be a connected undirected graph with $|V| = n$ nodes. For each node $u \in V$, $\deg_G(u)$ denotes the degree of u, and $\Gamma_G(u)$ is the set of neighbors of u in G; we will omit subscript G when there is no ambiguity.

Rumor Spreading Algorithms

We consider two randomized rumor spreading algorithms on graph G. The first is the standard *synchronous push-pull* algorithm, or simply *push-pull*, which proceeds in synchronized rounds; we will write *pp* to denote this algorithm. Initially, in round 0, a source node $u \in V$ generates a rumor. In each subsequent round $r = 1, 2, \ldots$, every node $v \in V$ initiates a communication channel with a uniformly random neighbor $w \in \Gamma(v)$ (we say v *contacts* w), and if before the round exactly one of v, w knows the rumor (is *informed*), then the other node gets informed in round r as well. In particular, if node v is informed before the round and w is not, we say that v *pushes* the rumor to w in round r, while if v is not informed and w is, we say that v *pulls* the rumor from w. Note that each node contacts exactly one other node, but may be contacted by several nodes in the same round. In this case, we assume that the communications take place in parallel and independently. In the analysis, we will represent the pairwise communications that take place in a round by a set $\{(v, w_v)\}_{v\in V}$ of n pairs, denoting that each node v contacts node w_v in the round.

The second algorithm we consider is the *asynchronous push-pull* algorithm, denoted *pp-a*. In this algorithm, each node $v \in V$ has its own independent Poisson clock with rate $\lambda = 1$, and each time v's clock ticks, v contacts a uniformly random neighbor $w \in \Gamma(v)$. As before, if only one of v, w knows the rumor before the communication takes place, then the other node gets informed as well. We refer to this communication as a *step* of the algorithm, and say that node v *takes* or *executes* this step. We will represent a step by a pair (v, w), denoting that node v contacts w in the step.

We will consider a couple of alternative, but equivalent views of asynchronous push-pull. Rather than assuming a Poisson clock with rate 1 on each node, we can assume that we have an independent Poisson clock for each (ordered) pair of adjacent nodes (v, w) with rate $1/\deg(v)$, and each time this clock ticks, v contacts w. A second alternative is to assume that we have a single Poisson clock with rate n, and each time this clock ticks, a uniformly random node is chosen to take a step, i.e., contact a random neighbor. The equivalence of these descriptions is immediate from the properties of the superposition of independent Poisson processes and the memoryless property of exponential random variables.

Rumor Spreading Time

Next we define the time complexity measures we will use. For a rumor spreading algorithm α, we define the *rumor spreading time of* α *on* $G = (V, E)$ *for source* $u \in V$, denoted $T(\alpha, G, u)$, to be the "time" before a rumor originated at node u spreads to all nodes in G using algorithm α. The notion of time is different for synchronous and asynchronous algorithms. For the former, time is measured in terms of *rounds*, while for asynchronous algorithms time is measured in terms of *time units*.[3] For $0 < q < 1$, we define

$$T_q(\alpha, G, u) = \min\{t\colon \Pr[T(\alpha, G, u) \le t] \ge 1 - q)\},$$

i.e., the time before all nodes are informed with probability $1 - q$. We will be particularly interested in $T_{1/n}(\alpha, G, u)$, the *high-probability rumor spreading time* of α.

Other Notation

We write $X \sim Y$ to denote that random variables X and Y have the same distribution, and $X \preccurlyeq Y$ to denote that Y stochastically dominates X.

Unif(A) denotes the uniform distribution over the set A; Geom(p) is the geometric distribution with success probability p; Exp(λ) is the exponential distribution with rate λ; NegBin(k, p) is the negative-binomial distribution, i.e., the distribution of the sum of k i.i.d. geometric random variables with probability parameter p; and Erl(k, λ) is the Erlang distribution, i.e., the distribution of the sum of k i.i.d. exponential random variables with rate λ.

For any function $f(x)$, we define the set $\operatorname{argmin}_x f(x) = \{x\colon \forall\, y, f(x) \le f(y)\}$. In case this set is a singleton set $\{a\}$, we will write $\operatorname{argmin}_x f(x) = a$.

3. ANALYSIS OVERVIEW

Below we highlight the main ideas and techniques used in the analysis of our main results: the upper bound of Theorem 1, and the lower bound of Theorem 2.

Upper Bound

Our proof of Theorem 1 relies on a new coupling argument. This argument can be viewed as an extension of a basic coupling technique first used in [24] to relate the rumor spreading time of the asynchronous push algorithm (denoted *push-a*) with that of synchronous *push*. The following simple coupling was proposed there: Once it gets informed, each node v contacts its neighbors in the exact same order in both algorithms *push* and *push-a*. I.e., if r_v is the round when v gets informed in *push*, t_v is the time when v gets informed in *push-a*, and $t_{v,i}$ is the i-th time that v's clock ticks after time t_v, then v pushes the rumor to the same node in round $r_v + i$ of *push*, and at time $t_{v,i}$ in *push-a*. Consider a path $v_0 = u, v_1, \ldots, v_l = v$ through which v receives the rumor in *push*, where u is the initially informed node and node v_{i+1} learns the rumor from v_i, for $0 \le i < l$; let also $d_i = r_{v_{i+1}} - r_{v_i}$. The time before v gets informed is then $r_v = \sum_i d_i$. Consider now the same path in *push-a* and let $\tau_i = t_{v_{i+1}} - t_{v_i}$; then $t_v = \sum_i \tau_i$. The coupling implies that in *push-a*, v_{i+1} learns the rumor no later than in time t_{v_i,d_i}, when v_i pushes the rumor to it (but it may learn the rumor sooner, from another neighbor). And since for any j we have in expectation that $t_{v,j} - t_v = j$, it follows that $\mathrm{E}[\tau_i \mid d_i] \le d_i$, and thus $\mathrm{E}[t_v] \le \mathrm{E}[r_v]$. This expectation bound can be turned into a high-probability bound, but we do not discuss the details here.

The above simple technique does not work for push-pull as there is no obvious way to couple pull operations. In fact, as

[3] An alterative measure for the asynchronous rumor spreading time would be the total number of *steps* before all nodes get informed. The ratio of this number of steps over n is equal in expectation to the number of time units before all nodes get informed.

far as we know, there is no coupling technique in the rumor spreading literature that achieves such a coupling between pull operations. Our analysis does exactly that: it provides a method to couple pull operations to achieve the same effect as the above natural coupling between push operations.

The coupling we propose and, especially, its analysis are somewhat involved, so we give the high-level ideas first. For each node v and each neighbor w of v we consider an independent exponential random variable $Y_{v,w}$ with rate $\lambda_v = 1/\deg(v)$. In *pp-a*, we set to be equal to $Y_{v,w}$ the time between the point t_w when w gets informed, and the point when v contacts w for the first time after t_w in order to pull the rumor, provided that v is still not informed by that time. For *pp*, we would like to set equal to $Y_{v,w}$ (precisely, to $\lceil Y_{v,w} \rceil$) the number of rounds after r_w, when v pulls the rumor from w, provided v is still not informed by that round. Doing so, however, results in a number of issues

(1) The probability for v to pull the rumor from any specific informed neighbor in a round of *pp* is $1 - e^{-1/\deg(v)}$ under this coupling, which is slightly smaller than $1/\deg(v)$. For this reason we set $\lambda_v = 2/\deg(v)$ (while we use $2Y_{v,w} \sim \text{Exp}(1/\deg(v))$ rather than $Y_{v,w}$ in *pp-a*).

(2) Node v may have to contact more than one informed node in a round. However, this is not a real issue as it suffices to pull from just one of them to get informed.

(3) The overall probability that v succeeds in pulling the rumor in a given round is not exactly the right one: if fewer than some constant fraction of v's neighbors are informed then the probability is larger that it should be, otherwise it is smaller. Consider for example the two extreme cases: if v has only one informed neighbor the probability of pulling from it is $1 - e^{-2/\deg(v)} \approx 2/\deg(v)$ instead of $1/\deg(v)$; while if all of v's neighbors are informed, the probability of pulling from (at least) one of them is $1 - e^{-2}$, which is smaller than the correct value of 1. The former is not an actual problem, as it just speeds up *pp* which only makes our result stronger. The latter however is a problem. To solve it, we impose that as soon as v has at least $\deg(v)/2$ informed neighbors (and is still not informed), it pulls the rumor in the next round r^* with probability 1.

This last modification requires some subtle handing in order to work: Among all its (at least $\deg(v)/2$) informed neighbors, we let v pull the rumor from the neighbor w^* that minimizes the quantity $t_w + Y_{v,w}$. We show that this implies that the value of $r_{w^*} + Y_{v,w^*}$ is not much larger than r^*, in particular, $r_{w^*} + Y_{v,w^*} = r^* + O(1)$ in expectation. Hence, this case is not very different from the setting without the last modification, i.e., the setting in which v pulls the rumor from w in a round r such that $r_w + \lceil Y_{v,w} \rceil = r$. The intuition why we have $r_{w^*} + Y_{v,w^*} - r^* = O(1)$ in expectation is simple: for each of the at least $\deg(v)/2$ informed neighbors w of v, the difference $r_w + Y_{v,w} - r^*$ is an independent exponential random variable with rate $2/\deg(v)$, and $r_{w^*} + Y_{v,w^*} - r^*$ is the minimum of them. This implies that $r_{w^*} + Y_{v,w^*} - r^*$ is exponentially distributed with a rate of at least 1, thus its expectation is at most 1.

The detailed analysis is given in Section 4

Lower Bound

Our proof of Theorem 2 can be viewed as a refinement of the analysis technique used in [1] to prove a lower bound of $\Omega(n^{-2/3})$ on the ratio of asynchronous over synchronous push-pull rumor spreading times. However, our analysis introduces several new ideas, in order to improve the lower bound to $\Omega(n^{-1/2})$.

We use a coupling argument which, roughly speaking, allows us to divide the sequence of steps in *pp-a* into *blocks*, and map each block to one or more consecutive rounds of *pp*, so that the set of informed nodes in *pp-a* after each block of steps is a subset of the set of informed nodes in *pp* after the last round corresponding to that block. The rounds mapped to a block contain all pairwise communications of the steps in the block. *On average* a block contains $\Theta(\sqrt{n})$ steps and is mapped to $O(1)$ rounds of *pp* (even though some blocks may be much smaller and mapped to a larger number of rounds as discussed below). Since the expected time between consecutive steps is $1/n$, the desired bound follows.

We have two types of blocks: *normal* and *special* blocks. A normal block consists of at most $\sqrt{n}$ steps and is mapped to a single round of *pp*, while a special block consists of a single step and may be mapped to more than one round. Let $S_1 = (x_1, y_1), S_2 = (x_2, y_2), \ldots$ be the sequence of steps in *pp-a*, where $S_i = (x_i, y_i)$ denotes that node x_i contacts node y_i in step i. The first of the blocks into which the sequence of S_i is partitioned is a normal block (starting from S_1). A normal block B starting from S_i consists of the steps $S_i, \ldots, S_{j-1}$, where $j > i$ is the smallest index for which some of the following three conditions hold:

(1) $j - i = \sqrt{n}$, i.e., B contains the maximum allowed number, $\sqrt{n}$, of steps.

(2) $x_j = x_k$ or $x_j = y_k$ for some $k \in \{i, \ldots, j-1\}$, i.e., in some of the steps i up to $j-1$, node x_j either contacted or was contacted by a node. We say that S_j is *left-incompatible* with $(S_i, \ldots, S_{j-1})$.

(3) Node y_j got informed in one of the steps i up to $j-1$. We say that S_j is *right-incompatible* with $(S_i, \ldots, S_{j-1})$.

Conditions (2) and (3) above ensure that all steps of a normal block can be mapped to a single round of *pp*. In particular, (2) implies that no node contacts more than one neighbor in a single block, while (2) and (3) together prevent the following undesirable scenario: a node v gets informed by some neighbor (via push or pull), and then during the same block a non-informed neighbor of v pulls the rumor from v. Clearly, this scenario cannot take place in just one round of *pp*. The single round of *pp* that corresponds to a normal block contains all the pairwise communications of the steps in that block.

If a normal block $B = (S_i, \ldots, S_{j-1})$ ends because condition (1) or (2) is met, then the next block is also normal. If this is not the case, and thus $S_j = (x_j, y_j)$ is right-incompatible with B, then the next block is a special block. The reason why we have to treat this case differently is the following. We want to ensure that in each round of *pp*, the neighbor that each node contacts is chosen independently of all other choices (in the same or previous rounds). If r is the round that corresponds to block B, treating the next block as normal despite knowing that S_j is right-incompatible with B would imply that (with probability 1) some of the nodes that got informed in round r will be contacted by at least one node in round $r+1$. And this could introduce dependencies between nodes' random choices in round $r+1$ and the past. Note that knowing instead that S_j is *left*-incompatible with B does not cause the same problems, because each round contains one communication pair (v, v') for *every* node v (and thus for node x_j).

We handle a special block as follows: We run a number of rounds in *pp* (independent of the sequence of steps so far) until we have a round that contains at least one communication pair (a, b) that is right-incompatible with the normal block B which is before the special block; these rounds will be the rounds of *pp* that correspond to the special block. Moreover we "discard" the right-incompatible pair S_j, and replace it by pair (a, b) in *pp-a*. If more than one such pair (a, b) exists in the round, then we choose one of them at random, from some appropriate distribution.

Establishing that the above coupling is a proper coupling is a bit technical. But once we have done so, proving the desired lower bound is not difficult. The proof goes roughly as follows. We argue that t steps of *pp-a* are mapped to at most $O(t/\sqrt{n} + \sqrt{n})$ rounds of *pp* in expectation: At most $t/\sqrt{n}$ rounds correspond to blocks of size exactly $\sqrt{n}$. Further, at most $t/\sqrt{n}$ rounds in expectation corresponding to blocks that end because a left-incompatible pair is encountered; the reason is that such a pair is encountered with probability $O(1/\sqrt{n})$ in a step, given that the block size is at most $\sqrt{n}$. It remains to bound the number of rounds corresponding to special blocks. By (3), a node v can result in a special block only if the following scenario occurs: v gets informed during a step in some block B, and after that, v is contacted by some neighbor before $\sqrt{n}$ additional steps are taken (otherwise B finishes due to (1)). Let $\pi(v)$ denote the probability that v is contacted in a random step (this probability depends on the degrees of v's neighbors). The probability that v causes a special block is then bounded by $\sqrt{n} \cdot \pi(v)$. Moreover, if that special block exists, the expected number of rounds mapped to the block is upper bounded by the expected number of rounds until v is contacted by some neighbor. The probability that v is contacted by at least one neighbor in a round can be easily shown to be $q_v \geq 1 - e^{-n\pi(v)}$. So, the expected number of rounds corresponding to the special block is at most $1/q_v$. It follows that the expected total number of special blocks is at most $\sum_v \frac{\sqrt{n}\cdot\pi(v)}{1-e^{-n\pi(v)}}$, which is easily shown to be $O(\sqrt{n})$.

Applying the above result, that t steps of *pp-a* are mapped to at most $O(t/\sqrt{n}+\sqrt{n})$ rounds of *pp* in expectation, to the total number of steps before all nodes get informed in *pp-a* (thus $t \geq n-1$), and using that the expected time between two consecutive steps is $1/n$, gives that the expected total number of rounds in *pp* is by at most a factor of $O(\sqrt{n})$ larger than the expected time in *pp-a*.

The detailed analysis can be found in Section 5.

4. UPPER BOUND ANALYSIS

We prove that on any graph, the high-probability rumor spreading time of asynchronous push-pull is bounded by the high-probability rumor spreading time of synchronous push-pull plus a logarithmic term.

THEOREM 4. *For any connected n-node graph* $G = (V, E)$, *and any vertex* $u \in V$ *of* G, *we have* $T_{1/n}(pp\text{-}a, G, u) = O(T_{1/n}(pp, G, u) + \log n)$.

The proof is based on a coupling argument. For the sake of comprehension, we define two auxiliary rumor spreading processes, *ppx* and *ppy*, and present the coupling in three steps: first we couple *pp* with *ppx*, then *ppx* with *ppy*, and finally *ppy* with *pp-a*.

Processes *ppx* and *ppy* are very similar to *pp*, except that they use different rules to decide from which neighbor a non-informed node tries to pulls the rumor in a round. We point out that *ppx* and *ppy* are not realistic rumor spreading algorithms, as they assume that at any time, a node knows the set of its informed neighbors; we introduce these processes just to facilitate our analysis. We describe process *ppx* first.

DEFINITION 5 (PROCESS *ppx*). *Process ppx is the following synchronous rumor spreading algorithm: For each round* r *and* $v \in V$, *(1) if* v *is informed before round* r, *then in round* r, v *pushes the rumor to a random neighbor; (2) if* v *is not informed before round* r *and has* k *informed neighbors at that time, then with probability*

$$p = \begin{cases} 1 - e^{-2k/\deg(v)}, & \text{if } k < \deg(v)/2; \\ 1, & \text{if } k \geq \deg(v)/2, \end{cases}$$

v *pulls the rumor from a random informed neighbor in round* r, *while with the remaining probability,* $1-p$, v *does not pull the rumor in this round.*

The rumor spreading time for *ppx* is dominated by that for *pp*. The proof (which can be found in the full version of the paper) relies on the observation that, for the same set of informed nodes, a non-informed node is more likely to pull the rumor in *ppx* than in *pp* in the next round.

LEMMA 6. $T(ppx, G, u) \preccurlyeq T(pp, G, u)$.

The second auxiliary process we introduce, *ppy*, is identical to *ppx* except for the probability with which a node pulls the rumor in a round.

DEFINITION 7 (PROCESS *ppy*). *Process ppy is the following synchronous rumor spreading algorithm: For each round* r *and* $v \in V$, *(1) if* v *is informed before round* r, *then in round* r, v *pushes the rumor to a random neighbor; (2) if* v *is not informed before round* r *and has* k *informed neighbors at that time, then with probability*

$$p = 1 - e^{-2k/\deg(v)},$$

v *pulls the rumor from a random informed neighbor in round* r, *while with the remaining probability,* $1-p$, v *does not pull the rumor in this round.*

In Lemma 9 below, we bound the rumor spreading time for *ppy* in terms of the rumor spreading time for *ppx*. First we provide a technical lemma that we will need. This lemma computes the conditional distribution of the minimum of a collection of independent exponential random variables, given some limited information about them. (The proof can be found in the full version of the paper)

LEMMA 8. *Let* $Z_1, \ldots, Z_k$ *be i.i.d. random variables with* $Z_i \sim Exp(\lambda)$, *and let* $J = \operatorname{argmin}_i Z_i$. *For* $\alpha_1, \ldots, \alpha_k$ *arbitrary non-negative integers, let* $Z = \min_i\{Z_i - \alpha_i\}$, *and let* $\mathcal{A}$ *be the event:* $\forall i, Z_i > \alpha_i$. *Then* $(Z \mid J = j, \mathcal{A}) \sim Exp(k\lambda)$, *i.e., for any* $t \geq 0$, $\Pr[Z \leq t \mid J = j, \mathcal{A}] = 1 - e^{-k\lambda t}$.

We remark that from the memoryless property of exponential distribution it is immediate that $(Z \mid \mathcal{A}) \sim \text{Exp}(k\lambda)$. The lemma above says that conditioning also on J does not add any information. We now proceed to the main lemma.

LEMMA 9. $T_\delta(ppy, G, u) = O\big(T_\delta(ppx, G, u) + \log(n/\delta)\big)$, *for any* $0 < \delta \leq 1/2$.

PROOF. We define a coupling of the random choices in *ppx* and *ppy*. In this coupling, let r_v and r'_v denote the rounds in which node v gets informed in *ppx* and *ppy*, respectively (for the source u, $r_u = r'_u = 0$). We will show that for any $v \in V$, with probability at least $1 - \delta/2n$ we have $r'_v \le 2r_v + O(\log(n/\delta))$. A union bound then completes the proof.

To facilitate the coupling we define the following collection of random variables. For each $v \in V$, $i \ge 1$, and $w \in \Gamma(v)$, let $X_{v,i}$ and $Y_{v,w}$ be random variables with $X_{v,i} \sim \mathrm{Unif}(\Gamma(v))$ and $Y_{v,w} \sim \mathrm{Exp}(\lambda_v)$, with $\lambda_v = 2/\deg(v)$ (i.e., $X_{v,i}$ is a random neighbor of v, and $Y_{v,w}$ is an exponential random variable with rate λ_v). We assume that all these random variables are mutually independent.

For *push* operations, the coupling states that each node pushes the rumor to the same neighbor in both processes, in the i-th round after the node gets informed. Precisely, for each $v \in V$ and $i \ge 1$, v pushes the rumor to node $X_{v,i}$ in round $r_v + i$ of *ppx*, and in round $r'_v + i$ of *ppy*.

For *pull* operations, the coupling is more involved. For *ppy*, for each pair of adjacent nodes v, w, if w gets informed before v (i.e., $r'_w < r'_v$), and v is still not informed before round $r'_w + \lceil Y_{v,w} \rceil$, then we let v pull the rumor from w in round $r'_w + \lceil Y_{v,w} \rceil$. The formal definition takes also into account the possibility that $r'_w + \lceil Y_{v,w} \rceil = r'_x + \lceil Y_{v,x} \rceil$ for two distinct neighbors w, x of u, in which case the tie is broken based on the actual values of $Y_{v,w}$ and $Y_{v,x}$ (rather than their rounded up values). Precisely, for any $v \in V \setminus \{u\}$, if v does not get informed by a push operation before round $t = \min_{w \in \Gamma(v)} \{r'_w + \lceil Y_{v,w} \rceil\}$, then in round t, v pulls the rumor from node $\mathrm{argmin}_{w \in \Gamma(v)} \{r'_w + Y_{v,w}\}$, i.e., the neighbor w that minimizes $r'_w + Y_{v,w}$.[4] Clearly, for this neighbor w, $r'_w + \lceil Y_{v,w} \rceil = t$.

For *ppx*, we use a similar coupling rule except that we need to enforce that, as soon as half of v's neighbors get informed, v will pull the rumor in the next round with probability 1, if it is not already informed. The neighbor w from which v pulls the rumor in this case is the (currently informed) neighbor that minimizes $r_w + Y_{v,w}$. Precisely, for any $v \in V \setminus \{u\}$, if $t = \min_{w \in \Gamma(v)} \{r_w + \lceil Y_{v,w} \rceil\}$ and z is the first round by the end of which at least $\deg(v)/2$ of v's neighbors have been informed, we distinguish the following two cases:

(i) If $t \le z$ and v does not get informed by a push operation before round t, then in round t, v pulls the rumor from node $\mathrm{argmin}_{w \in \Gamma(v)} \{r_w + Y_{v,w}\}$. So, in this case the rule is the same as for *ppy*.

(ii) If $t > z$ and v does not get informed by a push operation before round $z + 1$, then in round $z + 1$, v pulls the rumor from node $\mathrm{argmin}_{w \in \Gamma(v):\, r_w \le z} \{r_w + Y_{v,w}\}$.

It is not hard to verify that the above coupling is valid, in the sense that the marginal distributions of the two processes are the correct ones: For push operations there is nothing to argue about, so we focus on pull operations. In *ppy*, if before round r node v is still not informed, and its set of informed neighbors is S with $|S| = k$, then the probability that v pulls the rumor in round r is the same as the conditional probability that $\min_{w \in S} \{r'_w + Y_{v,w}\} \le r$, given that $\min_{w \in S} \{r'_w + Y_{v,w}\} > r - 1$. Since $Y_{v,w} \sim \mathrm{Exp}(\lambda_v)$, from the memoryless property of the exponential distribution and the independence between random variables $Y_{v,w}$, it follows that the above conditional probability is

$$1 - \big(1 - \Pr[r'_w + Y_{v,w} > r \mid r'_w + Y_{v,w} > r - 1]\big)^k = 1 - e^{-k\lambda_v} = 1 - e^{-2k/\deg(v)},$$

which is the right probability according to Definition 7. Moreover, if v *does* pull the rumor in round r, then it is equally likely to pull it from any of its informed neighbors in S, as the conditional random variables $(r'_w + Y_{v,w} \mid r'_w + Y_{v,w} > r - 1)$, for $w \in S$, have the same distribution and are independent. A very similar argument shows that our coupling yields the correct distribution for the pull operations in *ppx*, as well.

Next we show that with probability at least $1 - \delta/2n$, $r'_v \le 2r_v + O(\log(n/\delta))$.

Let π_v be a path through which the rumor reaches node $v \in V \setminus \{u\}$ in *ppx*. Formally, $\pi_v = v_0 v_1 \ldots v_l$, where $v_0 = u$, $v_l = v$, and for each $0 \le i < l$, v_i is a node from which v_{i+1} receives the rumor for the first time (i.e., in round $r_{v_{i+1}}$). We express r_v and r'_v as

$$r_v = \sum_{0 \le i < l} (r_{v_{i+1}} - r_{v_i}), \quad r'_v = \sum_{0 \le i < l} (r'_{v_{i+1}} - r'_{v_i}).$$

(Note that these equations hold for any collection of v_i, not just for the specific definition of π_v.) For $0 \le i < l$, let $d_i = r_{v_{i+1}} - r_{v_i}$ and $d'_i = r'_{v_{i+1}} - r'_{v_i}$. We will show that the difference $d'_i - d_i$ is dominated by a geometric random variable with constant expectation. We distinguish three cases, depending on how v_{i+1} gets the rumor from v_i in *ppx*.

Case 1: v_i pushes the rumor to v_{i+1}, in round $r_{v_{i+1}}$ of *ppx*. In this case, we have $r_{v_{i+1}} = r_{v_i} + \min\{j \colon X_{v_i,j} = v_{i+1}\}$, and thus $d_i = \min\{j \colon X_{v_i,j} = v_{i+1}\}$. Similarly, in *ppy*, v_i pushes the rumor to v_{i+1} in round $r'_{v_i} + \min\{j \colon X_{v_i,j} = v_{i+1}\}$. Thus v_{i+1} gets informed in *ppy* no later than in this round, i.e., $r'_{v_{i+1}} \le r'_{v_i} + \min\{j \colon X_{v_i,j} = v_{i+1}\}$, and so, $d'_i \le \min\{j \colon X_{v_i,j} = v_{i+1}\} = d_i$.

Case 2: v_{i+1} pulls the rumor from v_i, in round $r_{v_{i+1}}$ of *ppx*, and before that round fewer than half of v_{i+1}'s neighbors are informed. In this case, $r_{v_{i+1}} = r_{v_i} + \lceil Y_{v_{i+1},v_i} \rceil$, thus $d_i = \lceil Y_{v_{i+1},v_i} \rceil$. Similarly, in *ppy*, v_{i+1} gets informed no later than in round $r'_{v_i} + \lceil Y_{v_{i+1},v_i} \rceil$, because if v_{i+1} is still not informed before that round, it will pull the rumor in round $r'_{v_i} + \lceil Y_{v_{i+1},v_i} \rceil$ (from v_i or some other informed neighbor). It follows that $d'_i \le \lceil Y_{v_{i+1},v_i} \rceil = d_i$.

Case 3: v_{i+1} pulls the rumor from v_i, in round $r_{v_{i+1}}$ of *ppx*, and before that round at least half of v_{i+1}'s neighbors are informed. This case is more involved. As in case 2, we have $d'_i \le \lceil Y_{v_{i+1},v_i} \rceil$, but now it is possible that $d_i < \lceil Y_{v_{i+1},v_i} \rceil$. We will use Lemma 8 to bound $d'_i - d_i$.

Let z be the first round in *ppx* after which at least half of the neighbors of v_{i+1} are informed, and let S be the set of those informed neighbors (so $|S| \ge \deg(v_{i+1})/2$). Then $r_{v_{i+1}} = z + 1$. Also, from the coupling (case (ii)), $v_i = \mathrm{argmin}_{w \in S} \{r_w + Y_{v_{i+1},w}\}$, thus $r_{v_i} + Y_{v_{i+1},v_i} < r_w + Y_{v_{i+1},w}$ for all $w \in S \setminus \{v_i\}$. Notice that it is possible to have $r_{v_i} + Y_{v_{i+1},v_i} > z + 1$, which implies $d_i < Y_{v_{i+1},v_i}$.

Let us fix the pairwise communications that occur in *all* rounds of *ppx*, and for each $w \in S$, let $Z_w = r_w + Y_{v_{i+1},w} - z$. The set $\{Z_w\}_{w \in S}$ is then a collection of i.i.d. random variables with distribution $\mathrm{Exp}(\lambda_{v_{i+1}})$, and we know that $\mathrm{argmin}_{w \in S} \{Z_w\} = v_i$.

[4]Since $r'_w + Y_{v,w}$ is a continuous random variable, the probability this quantity is the same for two distinct w is 0.

Consider now process *ppy*. To simplify exposition we shift all round numbers in *ppy* by an appropriate offset, so that the round number in which v_i gets informed in *ppy* is the same as the one in *ppx*. E.g., if v gets informed after k rounds in *ppx* and after ℓ rounds in *ppy*, we add an offset of $(k-\ell)$ to all round numbers in *ppy*. So, the i-th round in *ppx* has number $i+(k-\ell)$, and the round when v gets informed is $r'_{v_i} = k = r_{v_i}$.

If $r'_{v_{i+1}} \le z$, then $d'_i = r'_{v_{i+1}} - r'_{v_i} = r'_{v_{i+1}} - r_{v_i} \le z - r_{v_i}$, and since $d_i = (z+1) - r_{v_i}$, we have $d'_i < d_i$. In the following we assume that $r'_{v_{i+1}} > z$, and bound the quantity $d'_i - d_i + 1 = r'_{v_{i+1}} - z$ using Lemma 8.

Let us fix all random communications in the first z rounds of *ppy*, in a way that respects our coupling (recall we have already fixed the communications in all rounds of *ppx*). Revealing these random choices in *ppy* discloses additional information about variables $Y_{v_{i+1},w}$, and thus also about the variables $Z_w = r_w + Y_{v_{i+1},w} - z$. Precisely, the additional information is that for each $w \in S$, $r'_w + Y_{v_{i+1},w} - z > 0$, which follows from the assumption $r'_{v_{i+1}} > z$. Therefore, $Z_w > r_w - r'_w$, and since it is also $Z_w > 0$ (from *ppx*), we have that for any $w \in S$, $Z_w > \alpha_w$, where $\alpha_w = \max\{0, r_w - r'_w\}$.

To summarize, we have that random variables Z_w, $w \in S$, are independent with distribution $\mathrm{Exp}(\lambda_{v_{i+1}})$, and we know that $\mathrm{argmin}_{w\in S}\{Z_w\} = v_i$ and $Z_w > \alpha_w = \max\{0, r_w - r'_w\}$. Letting $Z = \min_{w\in S}\{Z_w - \alpha_w\}$, we can apply Lemma 8 to obtain for $t \ge 0$,

$$\Pr[Z \le t] = 1 - e^{-|S|\lambda_{v_{i+1}} t} \ge 1 - e^{-t},$$

because $|S| \ge \deg(v_{i+1})/2$ and $\lambda_{v_{i+1}} = 2/\deg(v_{i+1})$.

We can now argue that $r'_{v_{i+1}} - z \le \lceil Z \rceil$, and use the result above to bound the distribution of $r'_{v_{i+1}} - z$.

$$\begin{aligned} Z &= \min_{w\in S}\{Z_w - \alpha_w\} \\ &= \min_{w\in S}\{(r_w + Y_{v_{i+1},w} - z) - \max\{0, r_w - r'_w\}\} \\ &= \min_{w\in S}\{\min\{r_w + Y_{v_{i+1},w},\, r'_w + Y_{v_{i+1},w}\}\} - z \\ &= \min\{r_{v_i} + Y_{v_{i+1},v_i},\, \min_{w\in S}\{r'_w + Y_{v_{i+1},w}\}\} - z \\ &= \min_{w\in S}\{r'_w + Y_{v_{i+1},w}\} - z, \end{aligned}$$

where the last equation holds because $r_{v_i} = r'_{v_i}$. Since $\min_{w\in S}\{r'_w + \lceil Y_{v_{i+1},w}\rceil\} \ge \min_{w\in\Gamma(v_{i+1})}\{r'_w + \lceil Y_{v_{i+1},w}\rceil\} = r'_{v_{i+1}}$, the equation above yields $\lceil Z \rceil \ge r'_{v_{i+1}} - z$. From this and the bound $\Pr[Z \le t] \ge 1 - e^{-t}$ shown earlier, it follows that for any *integer* t, $\Pr[r'_{v_{i+1}} - z \le t] \ge 1 - e^{-t}$.

Finally, substituting $d'_i = r'_{v_{i+1}} - r'_{v_i} = r'_{v_{i+1}} - r_{v_i}$ and $d_i = (z+1) - r_{v_i}$, yields that for any integer $t \ge 0$,

$$\Pr[d'_i - d_i + 1 \le t] \ge 1 - e^{-t}.$$

This completes the analysis of Case 3.

In each of the above cases, 1–3, we have showed that either (1) $d'_i \le d_i$, or (2) given all communications that take place in every round of *ppx*, and in the first $z = r'_{v_i} + d_i - 1$ rounds of *ppy*, we have $d'_i - d_i + 1 \le t$ with probability at least $1 - e^{-t}$, for any integer $t \ge 0$. Note that (1) implies (2).

Let us fix all random communications that take place in *ppx* (and thus all d_i). From (2) it follows that

$$\Pr[d'_i - d_i + 1 \le t \mid d'_1 \dots d'_{i-1}] \ge 1 - e^{-t}.$$

This says that random variable $Z_i = d'_i - d_i + 1$ is dominated by $\mathrm{Geom}(1/e)$, independently of $Z_1 \dots Z_{i-1}$. Using that $r_v = \sum_{0\le i<l} d_i$ and $r'_v = \sum_{0\le i<l} d'_i$, we obtain $r'_v - r_v + l = \sum_{0\le i<l}(d'_i - d_i + 1)$, and applying Lemma 15 (in the appendix) for the sum of the (dependent) random variables Z_i, $0 \le i < l$, we obtain that $r'_v - r_v + l \preccurlyeq \mathrm{NegBin}(l, 1 - 1/e)$. From this, it follows that with probability at least $1 - \delta/2n$, $r'_v - r_v + l \le 2l + O(\log(n/\delta))$, and thus $r'_v \le 2r_v + O(\log(n/\delta))$, as $l \le r_v$.

Taking the union bound over all v, gives that with probability at least $1 - \delta/2$, we have for all v simultaneously that $r'_v \le 2r_v + O(\log(n/\delta))$. And since by definition, with probability $1 - \delta/2$, for all v we have $r_v \le T_{\delta/2}(ppx, G, u)$, another union bound gives that with probability at least $1 - \delta$, we have for all v that $r'_v \le 2T_{\delta/2}(ppx, G, u) + O(\log(n/\delta))$. This means $T_\delta(ppy, G, u) \le 2T_{\delta/2}(ppx, G, u) + O(\log(n/\delta))$. Finally, observing that $T_{\delta/2}(ppx, G, u) \le 2T_\delta(ppx, G, u)$ for $\delta \le 1/2$, concludes the proof of Lemma 9. □

It remains to couple process *ppy* with the asynchronous push-pull rumor spreading algorithm, *pp-a*.

LEMMA 10. *$T_\delta(pp\text{-}a, G, u) = O(T_\delta(ppy, G, u) + \log(n/\delta))$, for any $0 < \delta \le 1/2$.*

PROOF. The structure of the proof is similar to that for Lemma 9. The coupling is similar as well, even though the details and the justification are simpler in this case. Essentially, the coupling captures the intuition that *ppy* is just a discretized version of *pp-a*.

In this coupling, for each $v \in V$, let t_v be the *time* in which v gets informed in *pp-a*, and let r_v be the *round* in which v gets informed in *ppy*. We will show that for any $v \in V$, with probability at least $1 - \delta/2n$, $t_v \le 4r_v + O(log(n/\delta))$. A union bound then completes the proof.

We define the same random variables as for the coupling in the proof of Lemma 9: For any $v \in V$, $i \ge 1$, and $w \in \Gamma(v)$, let $X_{v,i}$ and $Y_{v,w}$ be random variables with $X_{v,i} \sim \mathrm{Unif}(\Gamma(v))$ and $Y_{v,w} \sim \mathrm{Exp}(\lambda_v)$, where $\lambda_v = 2/\deg(v)$; all these random variables are mutually independent. For *ppy*, we use the same coupling rules as in the proof of Lemma 9, and for *pp-a* we use a continuous-time version of those rules.

Precisely, for *push* operations the coupling is as follows. For each $v \in V$ and $i \ge 1$, v pushes the rumor to node $X_{v,i}$ in round $r_v + i$ of *ppy*, and similarly v pushes the rumor to $X_{v,i}$ at time $t_{v,i}$ in *pp-a*, where $t_{v,i}$ is the time at which v takes its i-th step after time t_v.

For *pull* operations, the coupling is as follows. In *ppy*, for each $v \in V \setminus \{u\}$, if v does not get informed by a push operation before round $r = \min_{w\in\Gamma(v)}\{r_w + \lceil Y_{v,w}\rceil\}$, then in round r, v pulls the rumor from node $\mathrm{argmin}_{w\in\Gamma(v)}\{r_w + Y_{v,w}\}$. In *pp-a*, for each $v \in V \setminus \{u\}$, if v does not get informed by a push operation before time $t = \min_{w\in\Gamma(v)}\{t_w + 2Y_{v,w}\}$, then at time t, v pulls the rumor from node $\mathrm{argmin}_{w\in\Gamma(v)}\{t_w + 2Y_{v,w}\}$ (the factor 2 is justified below).

The above coupling yields the correct marginal distribution for the two processes: For *ppy* the same argument applies as in the proof of Lemma 9, so we just argue about *pp-a*. The distribution of the push operations is clearly the right one, so we just need to argue about pull operations. For that, it is convenient to consider the view of *pp-a* in which for each (ordered) pair v, w of adjacent nodes, there is an independent poisson clock $C_{v,w}$ with rate $1/\deg(v)$, and for each time t at which the clock ticks, if right before the tick

v is still not informed and w is informed, then v pulls the rumor from w at time t. Our coupling sets the length L_w of the interval between time t_w and the next tick of clock $C_{v,w}$ to be $L_w = 2Y_{v,w}$. Since $Y_{v,w} \sim \text{Exp}(2/\deg(v))$ it follows that $2Y_{v,w} \sim \text{Exp}(1/\deg(v))$, and this is the correct distribution for L_w.

Next we show that with probability at least $1 - \delta/2n$, $t_v \leq 4r_v + O(log(n/\delta))$.

Let π_v be a path through which the rumor reaches node $v \in V \setminus \{u\}$ in *ppy*. Formally, $\pi_v = v_0 v_1 \ldots v_l$, where $v_0 = u$, $v_l = v$, and for each $0 \leq i < l$, v_i is a node from which v_{i+1} receives the rumor for the first time (i.e., in round $r_{v_{i+1}}$). In line with the proof of Lemma 9, we compare the random variables $d_i = r_{v_{i+1}} - r_{v_i}$ and $\tau_i = t_{v_{i+1}} - t_{v_i}$. We have two cases:

Case 1: v_{i+1} pulls the rumor from v_i in round $r_{v_{i+1}}$ of *ppy*. In this case, $r_{v_{i+1}} = r_{v_i} + \lceil Y_{v_{i+1},v_i} \rceil$, thus $d_i = \lceil Y_{v_{i+1},v_i} \rceil$. Similarly, in *pp-a*, v_{i+1} gets informed no later than in time $t_{v_i} + 2Y_{v_{i+1},v_i}$, because if v_{i+1} is still not informed by that time, it will pull the rumor from v_i. It follows that $\tau_i = t_{v_{i+1}} - t_{v_i} \leq 2Y_{v_{i+1},v_i} \leq 2d_i$.

Case 2: v_i pushes the rumor to v_{i+1} in round $r_{v_{i+1}}$ of *ppy*. In this case, $r_{v_{i+1}} = r_{v_i} + x$, where $x = \min\{j \colon X_{v_i,j} = v_{i+1}\}$, thus $d_i = x$. Similarly in *pp-a*, v_i pushes the rumor to v_{i+1} at time $t_{v_i,x}$ (i.e., in its x-th step after it gets informed). Thus, $t_{v_{i+1}} \leq t_{v_i,x}$, and $\tau_i \leq t_{v_i,x} - t_{v_i}$. Given the random communications in every round of *ppy*, and the steps in *pp-a* up to time t_{v_i}, we have $(t_{v_i,x} - t_{v_i}) \sim \text{Erl}(x, 1)$, [5] and thus $\tau_i \preccurlyeq \text{Erl}(x, 1)$.

To summarise, in each case above, either (1) $\tau_i \leq 2d_i$, or (2) given the communications in every round of *ppy*, and the steps in *pp-a* up to time t_{v_i}, we have $\tau_i \preccurlyeq \text{Erl}(d_i, 1)$. Hence in both cases it holds $\tau_i - 2d_i \preccurlyeq \text{Erl}(d_i, 1)$, given all communications in *ppy*, and the steps in *pp-a* up to time t_{v_i}.

Let us fix all communications in *ppy* (and thus all d_i). Using the result above, and a similar reasoning as in the proof of Lemma 9 to tackle dependencies between variables $\tau_i - 2d_i$ for different i, we obtain that $\sum_i (\tau_i - 2d_i)$ is dominated by the sum $\sum_i Z_i$ of independent random variables $Z_i \sim \text{Erl}(d_i, 1)$, for $0 \leq i < l$. It follows $\sum_i (\tau_i - 2d_i) \preccurlyeq \text{Erl}\big(\sum_i d_i,\ 1\big)$. Substituting $\sum_i \tau_i = t_v$ and $\sum_i d_i = r_v$ we obtain that $t_v - 2r_v \preccurlyeq \text{Erl}(r_v, 1)$. Using that $\text{Erl}(k, \lambda) \preccurlyeq \text{NegBin}(k, 1 - e^{-\lambda})$, yields $t_v - 2r_v \preccurlyeq \text{NegBin}(r_v, 1 - 1/e)$. From this, it follows that $t_v \leq 4r_v + O\big(\log(n/\delta)\big)$, with probability at least $1 - \delta/2n$. Using now the union bound as in the end of the proof of Lemma 9, we finish the proof of Lemma 10. □

PROOF OF THEOREM 4. Combining Lemma 10, Lemma 9, and Lemma 6, we obtain that for any $0 < \delta \leq 1/2$,

$$\begin{aligned} T_\delta(\textit{pp-a}, G, u) &= O\big(T_\delta(\textit{ppy}, G, u) + \log(n/\delta)\big) \\ &= O\big(T_\delta(\textit{ppx}, G, u) + \log(n/\delta)\big) \\ &= O\big(T_\delta(\textit{pp}, G, u) + \log(n/\delta)\big). \end{aligned}$$

Setting $\delta = 1/n$, yields the statement of the theorem. □

5. LOWER BOUND ANALYSIS

We prove that the expected rumor spreading time of asynchronous push-pull is at least $\Omega(1/\sqrt{n})$ times the expected rumor spreading time of synchronous push-pull.

[5]Recall, $\text{Erl}(k, \lambda)$ is the distribution of the sum of k independent exponential random variables with rate λ.

THEOREM 11. *For any connected n-node graph $G = (V, E)$, and any vertex $u \in V$ of G, we have* $\text{E}[T(\textit{pp-a}, G, u)] = \Omega\big((1/\sqrt{n}) \cdot \text{E}[T(\textit{pp}, G, u)]\big)$.

The proof is based on a coupling between *pp-a* and *pp*.

Let $H = ((u_i, v_i))_{1 \leq i \leq k}$ be a sequence of k pairs of adjacent nodes, and let $I \subseteq V$ be a set of nodes. We say that a pair (x, y) of adjacent nodes is *left-incompatible* with H, if $x \in \{u_i\}_{1 \leq i \leq k} \cup \{v_i\}_{1 \leq i \leq k}$. We say that (x, y) is *right-incompatible* with H and I, if the next two conditions hold:

(1) The pair (x, y) is *not* left-incompatible with H.

(2) If k steps of *pp-a* are executed such that in the i-th step node u_i contacts node v_i, and before the first of these steps the set of informed nodes is I, then node y gets informed in one of those steps (note, this implies $y \notin I$).

We say that H is *incompatible-free* with I if no pair (u_i, v_i) in H is left-incompatible with $H_{i-1} = ((u_j, v_j))_{1 \leq j < i}$, or right-incompatible with H_{i-1}, I.

REMARK 12. *Suppose that H is incompatible-free with I, and we execute the pairwise push-pull communications described in H, assuming that at the beginning the set of informed nodes is I. Then the final set of informed nodes is the same whether these communications take place sequentially (as in pp-a), or in parallel (as in a round of pp).*

Let S denote a random variable that is a pair (x, y) with $x \sim \text{Unif}(V)$ and $(y \mid x) \sim \text{Unif}(\Gamma(x))$, i.e., x is a random node and y a random neighbor of x. Let R denote a random variable that is an n-set of pairs $\{(v, z_v)\}_{v \in V}$, with one pair per node, such that $z_v \sim \text{Unif}(\Gamma(v))$ and the random variables z_v, $v \in V$, are independent.

For the coupling of *pp* and *pp-a* we will use the following notation. For $t \geq 1$, let a_t denote the node that takes the t-th step in *pp-a*, and let b_t be the neighbor that a_t contacts in that step. For $r \geq 1$ and $v \in V$, let $c_{r,v}$ denote the neighbor that node v contacts in round r of *pp*. The coupling must ensure that $(a_t, b_t) \sim S$ and $\{(v, c_{r,v})\}_{v \in V} \sim R$. We define also the following random variables, which will facilitate the coupling. For $i, j \geq 1$, let $S_i = (x_i, y_i) \sim S$ and $R_{i,j} = \{(v, z_{i,j,v})\}_{v \in V} \sim R$. We assume that all variables $S_i, R_{i,j}$ are mutually independent.

We partition the sequence $(S_i)_{i \geq 1}$ into *blocks* of consecutive elements. Each block corresponds to a number of steps of *pp-a* equal to the size of the block, and to one or more rounds on *pp*. We distinguish between *normal* and *special* blocks. The first block starts with element S_1 and is normal. A normal block B starting from S_i consists of the elements $S_i, \ldots, S_{j-1}$, where $j > i$ is the smallest index for which at least one of the following conditions holds:

(1) $j - i = \sqrt{n}$;

(2) S_j is left-incompatible with $H = (S_i, \ldots, S_{j-1})$;

(3) S_j is right-incompatible with H and the set I of nodes that are informed before the i-th step in *pp-a*.

Note that normal block B is incompatible-free with I, and contains at most $\sqrt{n}$ elements. If $|B| = \sqrt{n}$, or the element S_j after the last element of B is left-incompatible with B, then the next block is a normal block as well. Otherwise, S_j is *right*-incompatible with B, I, and the next block is a special block; this special block contains just the single pair S_j. The block right after a special block is always normal.

We describe now the steps in *pp-a* and the rounds in *pp* that correspond to each block. Let $(B_k)_{k \geq 1}$ be the sequence of blocks in which $(S_i)_{i \geq 1}$ is partitioned, as described above.

Suppose that $B_k = (S_i, \ldots, S_{j-1})$ is a normal block. Then we set $(a_t, b_t) = S_t$, for all $i \le t < j$, i.e., the steps in *pp-a* are described precisely by the sequence of pairs in the block. In *pp* we have a single round r corresponding to B_k, and for this round we set $c_{r,x_t} = y_t$ for all $i \le t < j$; for the remaining nodes $v \in V \setminus \{x_i, \ldots, x_{j-1}\}$, we can assume that they do not contact any node in the round, as this can only increase the rumor spreading time of *pp*.

Suppose now that $B_k = (S_i)$ is a special block, thus S_i is right-incompatible with B_{k-1} and the set I of informed nodes in *pp-a* before the first step in block B_{k-1}. In this case, the step (a_i, b_i) in *pp-a* that corresponds to B_k may be different than S_i, and we may have more than one rounds in *pp*; the communications in those rounds are described by the sets $R_{i,j}$, $j \ge 1$. Let j^* be the smallest j such that $R_{i,j}$ contains at least one element that is right-incompatible with B_{k-1}, I. Then for block B_k we will have j^* rounds in *pp*: if r is the index of the round corresponding to the previous block B_{k-1}, then for $1 \le j \le j^*$, we set $\{(v, c_{r+j,v})\}_{v\in V} = R_{i,j}$. For *pp-a* we set (a_i, b_i) to be a pair from R_{i,j^*} that is right-incompatible with B_{k-1}, I. If more than one such pair exists, we choose one as follows. Let A be the set containing all possible pairs of adjacent nodes that are right-incompatible with B_{k-1}, I. We set (a_i, b_i) to be an element of the set $D = A \cap R_{i,j^*}$ selected at random according to a distribution $\mu_{A|D}$ with the following property: Let

$$\mu_A(a,b) = \sum_{C \subseteq A} \Big(\mu_{A|C}(a,b) \cdot \Pr[A \cap R = C \mid A \cap R \neq \emptyset]\Big);$$

then

$$\forall (a,b) \in A, \quad \mu_A(a,b) = \Pr[S = (a,b) \mid S \in A]. \quad (1)$$

I.e., $\mu_{A|D}$ is such that the pair (a,b) chosen has the same distribution as the pair S in a random step of *pp-a*, given that S is right-incompatible with B_{k-1}, I (μ_A averages over all possible rounds containing at least one right-incompatible pair.)

In the full version of the paper, we show that the above probability distributions $\mu_{A|D}$ exist, and establish that the coupling is valid, i.e., the marginal distribution of each process is the right one. In the full version, we also prove the next simple lemma. For $k \ge 0$, let $I_k(\text{pp-a})$ be the set of informed nodes in *pp-a* after the steps corresponding to the first k blocks, and let $I_k(\text{pp})$ be the set of informed nodes in *pp* after the rounds corresponding to the first k blocks.

LEMMA 13. *For any $k \ge 0$, $I_k(\text{pp-a}) \subseteq I_k(\text{pp})$.*

Next we bound the expected number of rounds in *pp* that correspond to the steps in *pp-a* before all nodes get informed. Let I_t be the set of informed nodes in *pp-a* after the first t steps, and let $\tau = \min\{t \colon I_t = V\}$ be the number of steps before all nodes get informed. Let ρ_t be the number of rounds in *pp* that correspond to the first k blocks, where k is the index of the block containing S_t.

LEMMA 14. $\mathrm{E}[\rho_\tau] = O\left(\mathrm{E}[\tau]/\sqrt{n} + \sqrt{n}\right)$.

PROOF. Let $B_1, \ldots, B_{k_t}$ denote the blocks into which the sequence $S_1, \ldots, S_t$ is partitioned. We decompose ρ_t into the following four terms:

The number $\rho_{t,full}$ of rounds corresponding to (normal) blocks B_k, $k \le k_t$, with $|B_k| = \sqrt{n}$.

The number $\rho_{t,left}$ of rounds corresponding to normal blocks $B_k = (S_i, \ldots, S_{j-1})$, with $k \le k_t$ and $|B_k| < \sqrt{n}$, such that S_j is left-incompatible with B_k.

The number $\rho_{t,right}$ of rounds corresponding to normal blocks $B_k = (S_i, \ldots, S_{j-1})$, with $k \le k_t$ and $|B_k| < \sqrt{n}$, such that S_j is right-incompatible with B_k and the set I of informed nodes in *pp-a* before step i.

The number $\rho_{t,special}$ of rounds corresponding to special blocks.

We have $\rho_t = \rho_{t,full} + \rho_{t,left} + \rho_{t,right} + \rho_{t,special}$. Since $\rho_{t,full} \le \frac{t}{\sqrt{n}}$, and $\rho_{t,right} \le \rho_{t,special} + 1$, we have that $\rho_t \le \frac{t}{\sqrt{n}} + \rho_{t,left} + 2\rho_{t,special} + 1$. Letting $t = \tau$ and taking the expectation of both sides yields

$$\mathrm{E}[\rho_\tau] = O\left(\mathrm{E}[\tau]/\sqrt{n} + \mathrm{E}[\rho_{\tau,left}] + \mathrm{E}[\rho_{\tau,special}] + 1\right).$$

We show $\mathrm{E}[\rho_{\tau,left}] \le 2\mathrm{E}[\tau]/\sqrt{n}$ and $\mathrm{E}[\rho_{\tau,special}] \le 2\sqrt{n}$. Substituting these above yields the claim.

The bound on $\rho_{\tau,left}$ is based on the following observation. For any $t \ge 1$, and any way of fixing the first $t-1$ steps of *pp-a*, the probability that $S_t = (x_t, y_t)$ is left-incompatible with $(S_i, \ldots, S_{t-1})$, where S_i is the first element in the block containing S_{t-1}, is at most $\frac{2(t-i)}{n} \le \frac{2}{\sqrt{n}}$. The reason is that x_t is chosen uniformly at random among all n nodes, and at most $2(t-i)$ distinct nodes appear in the pairs $S_i, \ldots, S_{t-1}$, while the number of those pairs is $t - i \le \sqrt{n}$.

For $t \ge 0$, define $Z_t = \rho_{t,left} - \frac{2t}{\sqrt{n}}$. The sequence $(Z_t)_{t\ge 0}$ is a supermartingale with respect to $(X_t)_{t\ge 1}$, where $X_t = (a_t, b_t)$, because: (1) $\rho_{t,left}$ (and thus Z_t) is a function of $X_1, \ldots, X_t$, as this sequence completely determines the collection of normal blocks into which $S_1, \ldots, S_t$ are divided; and (2) for $t \ge 1$, $\mathrm{E}[Z_t - Z_{t-1} \mid X_1 \ldots X_{t-1}] = \Pr[\rho_{t,left} - \rho_{t-1,left} = 1 \mid X_1 \ldots X_{t-1}] - \frac{2}{\sqrt{n}} \le 0$, as we argued above.

We use the optional stopping theorem for this supermartingale sequence and stopping time τ. Since for any $t \ge 1$, $|Z_t - Z_{t-1}| \le 1$, and $\mathrm{E}[\tau]$ is finite (bounded by $n^2 \log n$), the optional stopping theorem yields $\mathrm{E}[Z_\tau] \le \mathrm{E}[Z_0]$. Substituting $Z_\tau = \rho_{\tau,left} - \frac{2\tau}{\sqrt{n}}$ and $Z_0 = 0$, yields $\mathrm{E}[\rho_{\tau,left}] \le \frac{2\mathrm{E}[\tau]}{\sqrt{n}}$.

Next we bound $\rho_{\tau,special}$. The $O(\sqrt{n})$ bound we will show holds for any t, not just for $t = \tau$. For each node v, we bound the expected number of rounds that correspond to special blocks (S_t) with $y_t = v$, and then sum these expectations over all v to obtain a bound on $\mathrm{E}[\rho_{\tau,special}]$. For each v, there is at most one special block (S_t) with $y_t = v$, as this block must immediately follow the block in which v gets informed in *pp-a*. To prove the bound we just use a weaker fact: If t_v denotes the step when v gets informed in *pp-a*, and (S_t) is a special block with $y_t = v$, then it must be $t \le t_v + \sqrt{n}$, as the maximum block size is $\sqrt{n}$.

Let us fix $X_1, \ldots, X_{t-1}$, for some $t_v < t \le t_v + \sqrt{n}$, and let S_i be the first element in the block containing S_{t_v}. The probability that (S_t) is a special block with $y_t = v$, is the probability that v is contacted in the step by one of its neighbors in $\Gamma_t(v) = \Gamma(v) \setminus \{x_i, \ldots, x_{t-1}\} \cup \{y_i, \ldots, y_{t-1}\}$, and this probability is $\pi_t(v) = \frac{1}{n}\sum_{w\in\Gamma_t(v)} \frac{1}{\deg(w)}$ (we do not take into account v's neighbors that have already appeared in a pair in $(S_i, \ldots, S_{t-1})$, as S_t should not be left-incompatible). Given now that (S_t) is a special block with $y_t = v$, the expected number of rounds that correspond to this block is at most $1/q_t(v)$, where $q_t(v)$ is the probability that v is contacted by a neighbor from $\Gamma_t(v)$ in a given round. We have

$$\begin{aligned} q_t(v) &= 1 - \prod_{w\in\Gamma_t(v)} (1 - 1/\deg(w)) \\ &\ge 1 - e^{-\sum_{w\in\Gamma_t(v)} \frac{1}{\deg(w)}} = 1 - e^{-n\pi_t(v)}. \end{aligned}$$

Therefore, the expected number of rounds as a result of the possibility that (S_t) is a special block with $y_t = v$, is at most

$$\frac{\pi_t(v)}{q_t(v)} \leq \frac{\pi_t(v)}{1 - e^{-n\pi_t(v)}} = \frac{1}{n} \cdot \frac{n\pi_t(v)}{1 - e^{-n\pi_t(v)}}$$
$$\leq \frac{1}{n} \cdot (1 + n\pi_t(v)) = \frac{1}{n} + \pi_t(v) \leq \frac{1}{n} + \pi(v),$$

where $\pi(v) = \frac{1}{n}\sum_{w\in\Gamma(v)} \frac{1}{\deg(w)}$, and the first inequality in the last line is obtained using that $e^{-x} \leq \frac{1}{1+x}$, for $x \geq 0$. Summing over all $t_v < t \leq t_v + \sqrt{n}$, and over all v, we obtain

$$\mathrm{E}[\rho_{\tau,special}] \leq \sqrt{n}\sum_{v\in V}\left(\tfrac{1}{n} + \pi(v)\right) = \sqrt{n} + \sqrt{n}\sum_{v\in V}\pi(v)$$
$$= 2\sqrt{n}.$$

This completes the proof of Lemma 14. □

From Lemmas 13 and 14, it follows that the expected number of rounds before all nodes get informed in *pp* is $\mathrm{E}[T(pp, G, u)] \leq \mathrm{E}[\rho_\tau] = O(\mathrm{E}[\tau]/\sqrt{n} + \sqrt{n})$. The expected time in *pp-a* until all nodes get informed is $\mathrm{E}[T(pp\text{-}a, G, u)] = \mathrm{E}[\tau]/n$, because the expected time between two consecutive steps is $1/n$, and the times between steps are independent and also independent of τ. It follows that $\mathrm{E}[T(pp, G, u)] = O(\sqrt{n} \cdot \mathrm{E}[T(pp\text{-}a, G, u)] + \sqrt{n})$, which implies the bound of Theorem 11.

6. REFERENCES

[1] H. Acan, A. Collevecchio, A. Mehrabian, and N. Wormald. On the push&pull protocol for rumour spreading. In *Proc. 34th PODC*, pp. 405–412, 2015.

[2] H. Amini, M. Draief, and M. Lelarge. Flooding in weighted sparse random graphs. *SIAM J. Discrete Math.*, 27(1):1–26, 2013.

[3] B. Bollobás and Y. Kohayakawa. On Richardson's Model on the hypercube. In *Combinatorics, Geometry and Probability*, pp. 129–138. Cambridge University Press, 1997.

[4] S. P. Boyd, A. Ghosh, B. Prabhakar, and D. Shah. Randomized gossip algorithms. *IEEE Trans. Inf. Theory*, 52(6):2508–2530, 2006.

[5] K. Censor-Hillel and H. Shachnai. Fast information spreading in graphs with large weak conductance. In *Proc. 22nd SODA*, pp. 440–448, 2011.

[6] F. Chierichetti, S. Lattanzi, and A. Panconesi. Almost tight bounds for rumour spreading with conductance. In *Proc. 42nd STOC*, pp. 399–408, 2010.

[7] A. Demers, D. Greene, C. Hauser, W. Irish, J. Larson, S. Shenker, H. Sturgis, D. Swinehart, and D. Terry. Epidemic algorithms for replicated database maintenance. In *Proc. 6th PODC*, pp. 1–12, 1987.

[8] B. Doerr, M. Fouz, and T. Friedrich. Social networks spread rumors in sublogarithmic time. In *Proc. 43rd STOC*, pp. 21–30, 2011.

[9] B. Doerr, M. Fouz, and T. Friedrich. Asynchronous rumor spreading in preferential attachment graphs. In *Proc. 13th SWAT*, pp. 307–315, 2012.

[10] B. Doerr, M. Fouz, and T. Friedrich. Experimental analysis of rumor spreading in social networks. In *Proc. 1st MedAlg*, pp. 159–173, 2012.

[11] B. Doerr, T. Friedrich, M. Künnemann, and T. Sauerwald. Quasirandom rumor spreading: An experimental analysis. *ACM Journal of Experimental Algorithmics*, 16, 2011.

[12] R. Elsässer and T. Sauerwald. Broadcasting vs. mixing and information dissemination on Cayley graphs. In *Proc. 24th STACS*, pp. 163–174, 2007.

[13] U. Feige, D. Peleg, P. Raghavan, and E. Upfal. Randomized broadcast in networks. *Random Struct. Algorithms*, 1(4):447–460, 1990.

[14] J. Fill and R. Pemantle. Percolation, first-passage percolation and covering times for Richardson's Model on the n-cube. *The Annals of Applied Probability*, 3(2):593–629, 1993.

[15] N. Fountoulakis and K. Panagiotou. Rumor spreading on random regular graphs and expanders. In *Proc. 14th RANDOM*, pp. 560–573, 2010.

[16] N. Fountoulakis, K. Panagiotou, and T. Sauerwald. Ultra-fast rumor spreading in social networks. In *Proc. 23rd SODA*, pp. 1642–1660, 2012.

[17] G. Giakkoupis. Tight bounds for rumor spreading in graphs of a given conductance. In *Proc. 28th STACS*, pp. 57–68, 2011.

[18] G. Giakkoupis. Tight bounds for rumor spreading with vertex expansion. In *Proc. 25th SODA*, pp. 801–815, 2014.

[19] G. Giakkoupis and T. Sauerwald. Rumor spreading and vertex expansion. In *Proc. 23rd SODA*, pp. 1623–1641, 2012.

[20] M. Harchol-Balter, T. Leighton, and D. Lewin. Resource discovery in distributed networks. In *Proc. 18th PODC*, pp. 229–237, 1999.

[21] S. Janson. One, two and three times $\log(n)/n$ for paths in a complete graph with random weights. *Combinatorics, Probability & Computing*, 8(4):347–361, 1999.

[22] R. Karp, C. Schindelhauer, S. Shenker, and B. Vöcking. Randomized rumor spreading. In *Proc. 41st FOCS*, pp. 565–574, 2000.

[23] K. Panagiotou and L. Speidel. Asynchronous rumor spreading on random graphs. In *Proc. 24th ISAAC*, pp. 424–434, 2013.

[24] T. Sauerwald. On mixing and edge expansion properties in randomized broadcasting. *Algorithmica*, 56(1):51–88, 2010.

[25] T. Sauerwald and A. Stauffer. Rumor spreading and vertex expansion on regular graphs. In *Proc. 22nd SODA*, pp. 462–475, 2011.

[26] R. van Renesse, Y. Minsky, and M. Hayden. A gossip-style failure detection service. In *Proc. 15th Middleware*, pp. 55–70, 1998.

APPENDIX

A. A DOMINATION LEMMA

LEMMA 15. *Let $Z_1, \ldots, Z_k$ be random variables such that for each $1 \leq i \leq k$ and $j \geq 0$, $\Pr[Z_i \leq j \mid Z_1 \ldots Z_{i-1}] \geq 1 - q^j$, for some $0 < q < 1$. Then $\sum_i Z_i \preccurlyeq$ NegBin$(k, 1-q)$.*

PROOF. A standard coupling argument shows that $\sum_i Z_i$ is dominated by the sum of k independent random variables $Z'_1, \ldots, Z'_k$ with $Z'_i \sim \mathrm{Geom}(1-q)$. The claim then follows because $\sum_i Z'_i \sim \mathrm{NegBin}(k, 1-q)$. □

Brief Announcement: An Exponential Separation Between Randomized and Deterministic Complexity in the LOCAL Model*

Yi-Jun Chang
University of Michigan
Ann Arbor, MI
cyijun@umich.edu

Tsvi Kopelowitz
University of Michigan
Ann Arbor, MI
tsvi@umich.edu

Seth Pettie
University of Michigan
Ann Arbor, MI
pettie@umich.edu

ABSTRACT

Over the past 30 years numerous algorithms have been designed for symmetry breaking problems in the LOCAL model, such as maximal matching, MIS, vertex coloring, and edge-coloring. For most problems the best randomized algorithm is at least exponentially faster than the best deterministic algorithm. In this paper we prove that these exponential gaps are *necessary* and establish numerous connections between the deterministic and randomized complexities in the LOCAL model. Each of our results has a very compelling take-away message:

1. **Fast Δ-coloring of trees requires random bits.** Building on the recent randomized lower bounds of Brandt et al. [6], we prove that the randomized complexity of Δ-coloring a tree with maximum degree Δ is $\Theta(\log_\Delta \log n)$, for any $\Delta \geq 55$, whereas its deterministic complexity is $\Theta(\log_\Delta n)$ for any $\Delta \geq 3$.[1] This also establishes a large separation between the deterministic complexity of Δ-coloring and $(\Delta+1)$-coloring trees.

2. **Randomized lower bounds imply deterministic lower bounds.** We prove that any deterministic algorithm for a natural class of problems that runs in $O(1) + o(\log_\Delta n)$ rounds can be transformed to run in $O(\log^* n - \log^* \Delta + 1)$ rounds. If the transformed algorithm violates a lower bound (even allowing randomization), then one can conclude that the problem requires $\Omega(\log_\Delta n)$ time deterministically. (This gives an alternate proof that deterministically Δ-coloring a tree with small Δ takes $\Omega(\log_\Delta n)$ rounds.)

3. **Deterministic lower bounds imply randomized lower bounds.** We prove that the randomized complexity of any natural problem on instances of size n is at least its deterministic complexity on instances of size $\sqrt{\log n}$. This shows that a *deterministic* $\Omega(\log_\Delta n)$ lower bound for any problem (Δ-coloring a tree, for example) implies a *randomized* $\Omega(\log_\Delta \log n)$ lower bound. It also illustrates that the *graph shattering* technique employed in recent randomized symmetry breaking algorithms is *absolutely essential* to the LOCAL model. For example, it is provably impossible to improve the $2^{O(\sqrt{\log\log n})}$ terms in the complexities of the best MIS and $(\Delta+1)$-coloring algorithms without *also* improving the $2^{O(\sqrt{\log n})}$-round Panconesi-Srinivasan algorithms.

Keywords

Coloring; distributed algorithm; symmetry breaking

1. INTRODUCTION

One of the central problems of theoretical computer science is to determine the value of *random bits*. If the distinction is between computable vs. incomputable functions, random bits are provably useless in centralized models (Turing machines). However, this is not true in the distributed world! The celebrated Fischer-Lynch-Patterson theorem [10] states that asynchronous deterministic agreement is impossible with one unannounced failure, yet it is possible to accomplish with probability 1 using randomization [4].

In this paper we examine the value of random bits in Linial's [16] LOCAL model, which, for the sake of clarity, we bifurcate into two models RandLOCAL and DetLOCAL. In both models the input graph $G = (V, E)$ and communications network are identical. Each vertex hosts a processor and all vertices run the same algorithm. Each edge supports communication in both directions. The computation proceeds in synchronized *rounds*. In a round, each processor performs some computation and sends a message along each incident edge, which is delivered before the beginning of the next round. Each vertex v is initially aware of its degree $\deg(v)$ and certain global parameters such as $n \stackrel{\text{def}}{=} |V|$, $\Delta = \Delta(G) \stackrel{\text{def}}{=} \max_{v\in V} \deg(v)$, and possibly others.[2] In the LOCAL model the only measure of efficiency is the number

*A more detailed version of this paper appears in [7]. This work is supported by NSF grants CCF-1217338, CNS-1318294, and CCF-1514383.

[1]For simplicity, here we suppress any $\log^* n$ additive term in $\Theta(\cdot)$.

PODC'16 July 25-28, 2016, Chicago, IL, USA

ACM ISBN 978-1-4503-3964-3/16/07.
DOI: http://dx.doi.org/10.1145/2933057.2933079

[2]The assumption that global parameters are common knowledge can sometimes be removed; see Korman, Sereni, and Viennot [14].

of rounds. *All local computation is free and the size of messages is unbounded.* Henceforth "time" refers to the number of rounds.

DetLOCAL: In order to avoid trivial impossibilities, all vertices are assumed to hold unique $\Theta(\log n)$-bit IDs. Except for the registers holding $\deg(v)$ and $\mathrm{ID}(v)$, the initial state of v is identical to every other vertex. The algorithm executed at each vertex is deterministic.

RandLOCAL: In this model each vertex may locally generate an unbounded number of independent truly random bits. (There are no globally shared random bits.) Except for the register holding $\deg(v)$, the initial state of v is identical to every other vertex. Algorithms in this model operate for a specified number of rounds and have some probability of *failure*, the definition of which is problem specific. We usually only consider algorithms whose global probability of failure is at most $1/\mathrm{poly}(n)$.

Observe that the lack of IDs in RandLOCAL is not a practical limitation. Before the first round each node can locally generate a random $O(\log n)$-bit ID, which is unique with probability $1/\mathrm{poly}(n)$.

Early work in the LOCAL models suggested that randomness is of limited help. Naor [17] showed that Linial's $\Omega(\log^* n)$ lower bound [16] for 3-coloring the ring holds even in RandLOCAL, and Naor and Stockmeyer [18] proved that the class of problems solvable by $O(1)$-round algorithms is the same in RandLOCAL and DetLOCAL. However, in the intervening decades we have seen dozens of examples of symmetry breaking algorithms for RandLOCAL that are substantially faster than their counterparts in DetLOCAL; see [3] for a survey of three archetypal problems: maximal independent set (MIS), maximal matching, and $(\Delta+1)$-coloring.

Graph Shattering.

Randomized symmetry breaking algorithms are typically exponentially faster *in two ways.* Their dependence on Δ is exponentially faster and their dependence on n is usually identical to the best deterministic complexity, but for $\mathrm{poly}(\log n)$-size instances, for example, $2^{O(\sqrt{\log n})}$ becomes $2^{O(\sqrt{\log\log n})}$. This second phenomenon is no coincidence! It is a direct result of the *graph shattering* approach to symmetry breaking used in [3] and further in [11, 13]. The idea is to apply some randomized procedure that fixes some fragment of the output (e.g., part of the MIS is fixed, part of the coloring is fixed, etc.), thereby effectively removing a large fraction of the vertices from further consideration. If it can be shown that the connected components in the subgraph still under consideration have size $\mathrm{poly}(\log n)$, one can revert to the best available *deterministic* algorithm and solve the problem on each component of the "shattered" graph in parallel.

Lower Bounds in the LOCAL *Model.*

Until recently, the main principle used to prove lower bounds in the LOCAL model was *indistinguishability.* The first application of this principle was by Linial [16] himself, who argued that any algorithm for coloring degree-Δ trees either uses $\Omega(\Delta/\log\Delta)$ colors or takes $\Omega(\log_\Delta n)$ time. The proof is as follows (i) in $o(\log_\Delta n)$ time, a vertex *cannot always distinguish* whether the input graph G is a tree or a graph with girth $\Omega(\log_\Delta n)$, (ii) for all Δ and all n, there exists a degree-Δ graph with girth $\Omega(\log_\Delta n)$ and chromatic number $\chi=\Omega(\Delta/\log\Delta)$, hence[3] (iii) any $o(\log_\Delta n)$-time algorithm for coloring trees could also color such a graph, and therefore must use at least χ colors. A more subtle indistinguishability argument was used by Kuhn, Moscibroda, and Wattenhofer [15], who showed that $O(1)$-approximate vertex cover, maximal matching, MIS, and several other problems have $\Omega(\min\{\log\Delta/\log\log\Delta, \sqrt{\log n/\log\log n}\})$ lower bounds. Recently, Bar-Yehuda, Censor-Hillel, and Schwartzman [1] showed that a $(2+\epsilon)$-approximate vertex cover can be found in $O(\log\Delta/\epsilon\log\log\Delta)$ time, matching the above lower bound. By its nature, indistinguishability is not very good at separating randomized and deterministic complexities. Recently, Brandt et al. [6] developed a lower bound technique that explicitly incorporates error probabilities and proved that several problems on graphs with constant Δ take $\Omega(\log\log n)$ time in RandLOCAL (with error probability $1/\mathrm{poly}(n)$) such as *sinkless orientation*, *sinkless coloring*, and Δ-coloring. Since the existence of a sinkless orientation can be proved with the Lovász local lemma (LLL), this gave $\Omega(\log\log n)$ lower bounds on distributed algorithms for the constructive LLL. See [8, 11] for upper bounds on the distributed LLL.

2. NEW RESULTS

We exhibit an exponential separation between RandLOCAL and DetLOCAL for several *specific* symmetry breaking problems. More generally, we give new connections between the randomized and deterministic complexities of all *locally checkable labeling* (LCL) problems, a class that includes essentially any natural symmetry breaking problem.

Separation of RandLOCAL *and* DetLOCAL.

We extend Brandt et al.'s [6] randomized lower bound as follows: on degree-Δ graphs, Δ-coloring takes $\Omega(\log_\Delta\log n)$ time in RandLOCAL and $\Omega(\log_\Delta n)$ time in DetLOCAL. The hard graphs in this lower bound have girth $\Omega(\log_\Delta n)$, so by the indistinguishability principle, these lower bounds also apply to Δ-coloring trees. On the upper bound side, Barenboim and Elkin [2] showed that for $\Delta\geq 3$, Δ-coloring trees takes $O(\log_\Delta n+\log^* n)$ time in DetLOCAL. We give an elementary proof that for $\Delta\geq 55$, Δ-coloring trees can be done in $O(\log_\Delta\log n+\log^* n)$ time in RandLOCAL, matching Brandt et al.'s [6] lower bound up to the $\log^* n$. A more complicated algorithm for Δ-coloring trees could be derived from [20], for $\Delta>\Delta_0$ and some very large constant Δ_0.[4]

Randomized lower bounds imply deterministic lower bounds.

We give a second, more generic proof that Δ-coloring trees

[3]Linial [16] actually only used the existence of Δ-regular graphs with high girth and chromatic number $\Omega(\sqrt{\Delta})$. See [5] for constructions with chromatic number $\Omega(\Delta/\log\Delta)$.

[4]The reason we are interested in minimizing the $\Delta_0\leq\Delta$ for which the algorithm works is somewhat technical. It seems as if Δ-coloring trees is a problem whose character makes a *qualitative* transition when Δ is a small enough constant. Using our technique (graph shattering) we may be able to replace 55 with a smaller constant, *but not too small.* Any algorithm that 3-colors 3-regular trees, for example, will need to be qualitatively very different in its design.

takes $\Omega(\log_\Delta n)$ time. The proof shows that any $f(\Delta) + o(\log_\Delta n)$ time algorithm for an LCL problem can be transformed in a black box way to run in $O((1 + f(\Delta))(\log^* n - \log^* \Delta + 1))$ time. Thus, on bounded-degree graphs, there are no "natural" deterministic time bounds between $\omega(\log^* n)$ and $o(\log n)$. Any $\omega(\log^* n)$ lower bound for bounded degree graphs (in either RandLOCAL or DetLOCAL) *immediately* implies an $\Omega(\log n)$ lower bound in DetLOCAL. This reduction can be parameterized in many different ways. Under a different parametrization it shows that any $O(\log^{1-\frac{1}{k+1}} n)$-time DetLOCAL algorithm for an LCL problem can be transformed to run in $O(\log^k \Delta(\log^* n - \log^* \Delta + 1))$-time. For example, if one were to develop a deterministic $O(\sqrt{\log n})$-time MIS or maximal matching algorithm—almost matching one of the KMW [15] lower bounds—it would immediately imply an $O(\log \Delta(\log^* n - \log^* \Delta + 1))$-time MIS/maximal matching algorithm, which almost matches the *other* KMW lower bound, for $\Delta > \log^{O(1)} n$. By some strange coincidence, [3] gave an analogous reduction for MIS/maximal matching in bounded arboricity graphs, but for RandLOCAL and in the *reverse direction*. Specifically, any $O(\log^k \Delta + f(n))$-time RandLOCAL MIS/maximal matching algorithm can be transformed into an $O(\log^{1-\frac{1}{k+1}} n + f(n))$-time RandLOCAL algorithm for bounded arboricity graphs.

Deterministic lower bounds imply randomized lower bounds.

We prove that for any LCL problem, its RandLOCAL complexity on instances of size n is at least its DetLOCAL complexity on instances of size $\sqrt{\log n}$. This *reverses* the implication proved above. For example, if we begin with a proof that Δ-coloring takes $\Omega(\log_\Delta n)$ time in DetLOCAL, then we conclude that it must take $\Omega(\log_\Delta \log n)$ time in RandLOCAL. This result has a very clear take-away message: the *graph shattering* technique applied by recent randomized symmetry breaking algorithms [3, 11] is *inherent* to the RandLOCAL model and every optimal RandLOCAL algorithm for instances of size n must, in some way, encode an optimal DetLOCAL algorithm on poly$(\log n)$-size instances. It is therefore impossible to improve the $2^{O(\sqrt{\log \log n})}$ terms in the RandLOCAL MIS and coloring algorithms of [3, 11, 13, 9] without also improving the $2^{O(\sqrt{\log n})}$-time DetLOCAL algorithms of Panconesi and Srinivasan [19], and it is impossible to improve the $O(\log^4 \log n)$ term in the RandLOCAL maximal matching algorithm of [3] without also improving the $O(\log^4 n)$ DetLOCAL maximal matching algorithm of [12].

3. REFERENCES

[1] R. Bar-Yehuda, K. Censor-Hillel, and G. Schwartzman. A distributed $(2 + \epsilon)$-approximation for vertex cover in $O(\log \Delta/\epsilon \log \log \Delta)$ rounds. In *Proceedings 35th Annual ACM Symposium on Principles of Distributed Computing (PODC)*, 2016.

[2] L. Barenboim and M. Elkin. Sublogarithmic distributed MIS algorithm for sparse graphs using Nash-Williams decomposition. *Distributed Computing*, 22(5-6):363–379, 2010.

[3] L. Barenboim, M. Elkin, S. Pettie, and J. Schneider. The locality of distributed symmetry breaking. *J. ACM*, 2016. to appear.

[4] M. Ben-Or. Another advantage of free choice: Completely asynchronous agreement protocols. In *Proceedings of the 2nd ACM SIGACT-SIGOPS Symposium on Principles of Distributed Computing (PODC)*, pages 27–30, 1983.

[5] B. Bollobás. Chromatic number, girth and maximal degree. *Discrete Mathematics*, 24(3):311–314, 1978.

[6] S. Brandt, O. Fischer, J. Hirvonen, B. Keller, T. Lempiäinen, J. Rybicki, J. Suomela, and J. Uitto. A lower bound for the distributed Lovász local lemma. In *Proceedings 48th ACM Symposium on the Theory of Computing (STOC)*, 2016.

[7] Y.-J. Chang, T. Kopelowitz, and S. Pettie. An exponential separation between randomized and deterministic complexity in the local model. *CoRR*, abs/1602.08166, 2016.

[8] K.-M. Chung, S. Pettie, and H.-H. Su. Distributed algorithms for the Lovász local lemma and graph coloring. In *Proceedings 33rd ACM Symposium on Principles of Distributed Computing (PODC)*, pages 134–143, 2014.

[9] M. Elkin, S. Pettie, and H. H. Su. $(2\Delta - 1)$-edge coloring is much easier than maximal matching in the distributed setting. In *Proceedings 26th ACM-SIAM Symposium on Discrete Algorithms (SODA)*, pages 355–370, 2015.

[10] M. J. Fischer, N. A. Lynch, and M. Paterson. Impossibility of distributed consensus with one faulty process. *J. ACM*, 32(2):374–382, 1985.

[11] M. Ghaffari. An improved distributed algorithm for maximal independent set. In *Proceedings 27th Annual ACM-SIAM Symposium on Discrete Algorithms (SODA)*, pages 270–277, 2016.

[12] M. Hańćkowiak, M. Karoński, and A. Panconesi. On the distributed complexity of computing maximal matchings. *SIAM J. Discrete Mathematics*, 15(1):41–57 (electronic), 2001.

[13] D. Harris, J. Schneider, and H.-H. Su. Distributed $(\Delta + 1)$-coloring in sublogarithmic rounds. In *Proceedings 48th ACM Symposium on Theory of Computing (STOC)*, 2016.

[14] A. Korman, J.-S. Sereni, and L. Viennot. Toward more localized local algorithms: removing assumptions concerning global knowledge. *Distributed Computing*, 26(5–6):289–308, 2013.

[15] F. Kuhn, T. Moscibroda, and R. Wattenhofer. Local computation: Lower and upper bounds. *J. ACM*, 63(2):17:1–17:44, 2016.

[16] N. Linial. Locality in distributed graph algorithms. *SIAM J. Comput.*, 21(1):193–201, 1992.

[17] M. Naor. A lower bound on probabilistic algorithms for distributive ring coloring. *SIAM J. Discrete Mathematics*, 4(3):409–412, 1991.

[18] M. Naor and L. J. Stockmeyer. What can be computed locally? *SIAM J. Comput.*, 24(6):1259–1277, 1995.

[19] A. Panconesi and A. Srinivasan. On the complexity of distributed network decomposition. *J. Algor.*, 20(2):356–374, 1996.

[20] S. Pettie and H.-H. Su. Distributed algorithms for coloring triangle-free graphs. *Information and Computation*, 243:263–280, 2015.

Brief Announcement: Data Dissemination in Unified Dynamic Wireless Networks

Magnús M. Halldórsson
ICE-TCS, School of Computer Science, Reykjavik University
Reykjavik, Iceland
mmh@ru.is

Tigran Tonoyan
ICE-TCS, School of Computer Science, Reykjavik University
Reykjavik, Iceland
ttonoyan@gmail.com

Yuexuan Wang
College of Comp. Sci. & Tech.
Zhejiang University
Hangzhou, P.R. China
amywang@hku.hk

Dongxiao Yu
SCTS-CGCL, School of Comp. Sci. & Tech.,
Huazhong University of Science and Technology
Wuhan, P.R. China
dxyu@hust.edu.cn

1. INTRODUCTION

We address in this paper core information dissemination problems – *local broadcast* and (global) *broadcast* – in dynamic distributed networks, under very weak assumptions on the communication. To this end, we propose a communication model with significant flexibility that allows for adversarial control, generalizing essentially all known analytic wireless models. It allows for more general interference relationships than treated before. The network can experience adversarial dynamic behavior, both edge changes (change of signal strengths) and node insertions/deletions.

Our Contributions. We obtain generalized and improved algorithms for two of the most fundamental dissemination problems, in some cases improving the best results known in static settings. The local broadcast algorithm runs in time $O(\hat{\Delta}+\log n)$, and the broadcast algorithm runs in time $O(\hat{D}\log n)$, where $\hat{\Delta}$ and $\hat{D}$ are generalizations of the maximum degree and diameter of the communication graph, respectively, suitable for the dynamic setting. Beyond these specific results, we identify the following technical contributions:

1. *Unified model of wireless networks.* The model proposed appears to be the first that allows for the development of pan-model distributed dissemination algorithms. This hopefully prompts further studies crossing the artificial boundary between graph- and fading-based models.
2. *Dynamic networks under interference.* This appears to be the first work to address dynamic networks in the presence of comprehensive interference.
3. *Uniform algorithms.* Our algorithms in the static spontaneous setting appear to be the first in fading models that work independent of instance parameters (number of nodes, max. degree).
4. *Primitives for carrier-sense.* We introduce several primitives or *capabilities* that can be implemented using environmental sensing, and propose to study the power of such primitives.
5. *Stabilization mechanisms.* We identify contention adaptation as a fundamental ability in wireless networks, that appears to be of crucial value to implement other distributed tasks.

A full version of the paper is available as [1].

PODC'16 July 25-28, 2016, Chicago, IL, USA

ACM ISBN 978-1-4503-3964-3/16/07.
DOI: http://dx.doi.org/10.1145/2933057.2933065

2. SETTING AND MODEL

Nodes are distributed and autonomous. There is no built-in structure and the nodes have no information besides bounds on model parameters and an upper bound on the number of nodes. Communication is locally synchronous, but there is no global clock.

Nodes are located in space, with separation between points given by the relative decrease in strength of signal (or interference) sent between the points. This induces a quasi-metric space, when these decays are raised to the appropriate power. For distributed computation to be possible, the quasi-metric must have *bounded independence* which is strictly weaker than the Euclidean metric assumption.

Nodes may arrive and leave the network at any time. We say a node is *alive* at some point in time if it is present in the network. We assume the total number of nodes in the network is polynomially bounded by a number n in each round. *Edge changes* can occur, with some restrictions, which are changes in the signal strength between the pair of points.

We assume all nodes use the same transmission power P for communication in all rounds, which implies that they have equal *transmission distance* R. The *communication radius* is defined as a fraction of the transmission distance: $R_B = (1-\epsilon)R$, where ϵ is a precision parameter.

The rule for when communication is successful is only partially pre-specified: transmission succeeds on a "clear channel". That is, if a sender is within the communication radius from the receiver, if no other node transmits within a (larger) radius, and if the combined interference from all other transmitting nodes is (quite) small, then the transmission succeeds. Otherwise, success is up to the adversary, or it can be further specified by the particular model assumptions desired. This captures essentially all known algorithmic wireless models (including quasi-unit disc graphs, unit-ball graphs, bounded-independence graphs, k-hop extensions, and SINR). The only exception is the radio network model with general graphs, which cannot be extended to involve comprehensive interference without a major hit in time complexity.

The *neighborhood* of a node in round t is $N_t(u,\epsilon) = \{v \in V : d(u,v) \leq R_B\}$, describing who u can communicate with directly, where d is the metric distance. The basic operation of interest is when u broadcasts a message to its neighbors $N_t(u)$. The *communication graph* is a directed graph $G_t(V,E)$, where $(u,v) \in E$ if and only if $v \in N_t(u)$. Thus, the sequence $G_0, G_1, \ldots$ defines a *dynamic graph.*

We say that a node u *mass-delivers* in round t if it transmits and all its neighbors ($N_t(u)$) receive the message.

- In the *Local Broadcast* problem, given a node u, it is required to minimize the time from the beginning of the algorithm until node u mass-delivers at least once, assuming it stays alive during that time.
- In the *(global) Broadcast* problem, given a distinguished *source* node that initially holds a message, the goal is to minimize the time needed to deliver the message to every node in the network through multihop transmissions.

We consider randomized algorithms of the following form: in each round t, node v makes a transmission with probability $p_t(v)$, independent of other nodes' transmissions in that round. In the run of such an algorithm, we account for the interference at a node in two ways: the *contention* captures the expected interference from the nodes' *close neighbors*, while the *total interference* integrates also the interference from nodes further away.

More formally, the contention in round t in a ball $B(v)$ around node v is $P_t(v) = \sum_{w \in B(v)} p_t(w)$. We will be particularly interested in the contention in the *close neighborhood* of v – a fraction of the neighborhood, and in the larger *vicinity* of v – a larger ball that includes the neighborhood. Bounding contention in each close neighborhood helps us to bound the *expected interference* in the network.

A crucial component of our algorithms is the use of *carrier sense* to detect the cumulative amount of signals in the air. Since it is supplied by the cheapest available hardware today as, for instance, RSS (received signal strength) readings, we posit that carrier-sense capability should be the default assumption in wireless algorithmics. As carrier-sense indicators can provide fine-grained information, we identify several *primitives* that carrier-sense can supply, restrict the algorithm to use only a subset of the primitives, and examine which of these are truly necessary.

Thus, we assume the nodes are able to detect high and low contention in their vicinity, detect (under some conditions) whether their transmission in a given round succeeded and detect a single very near transmission. We show that *all* these primitives can be implemented with environment sensing[1] and possibly also with other means.

Contention Detection (CD). For each node v and round t:

- if contention among close neighbors is higher than ϕ then they *all* detect BUSY channel in round t with probability that decreases with increasing ϕ
- if the contention in the larger vicinity of v is below a (fixed) threshold *and* the interference on v from outside its vicinity is below a threshold then v detects IDLE channel in round t with constant probability.

Successful Transmission Detection (ACK). If a node u has the ACK=ACK(ϵ) primitive (depending on the precision parameter ϵ) then: if u transmits in round t, the interference at u is below a threshold and the transmission is received by all nodes in $N_t(u,\epsilon)$, then the outcome of ACK is 1. If the transmission is not received by a node $v \in N_t(u,\epsilon)$ then the outcome is 0. Otherwise, the outcome is 0 or 1, adversarially.

Near Transmission Detection (NTD). With NTD=NTD(ϵ) primitive, a node is able to detect if a transmitter is very close (on the order of ϵR_B), assuming that it receives the transmitted message.

3. RESULTS

The key algorithmic technique is a natural randomized *contention balancing* procedure, where a node continuously adjusts its transmission probability based on the interference that it senses. It allows nodes to stabilize quickly from any initial conditions, or after waking up. This routine is a variation on an old story, a simple backoff procedure to manage local contention.

> TRY&ADJUST: Each node v maintains transmission probability $p_t(v) \leq p_{max}$ in each round t, initialized as $p_t(v) = p_{min}$ when v enters the network. In round $t+1$, v does (using CD primitive):
> 1. Transmit with probability $p_t(v)$, and
> 2. Set $p_{t+1}(v) = \begin{cases} \max\{\frac{p_t(v)}{2}, p_{min}\} & \text{if BUSY,} \\ \min\{2p_t(v), p_{max}\}, & \text{otherwise.} \end{cases}$

Our main technical contribution is to show logarithmic-round convergence of this method to a steady state of nearly balanced contention, from an arbitrary starting configuration and in the presence of network changes. The higher level algorithms are then built on top of this primitive.

Namely, we show that for each node v, during any sequence of $\gamma \log n$ rounds with constant γ, which is called a *phase*, in most of the rounds (i.e. a $1-\sigma$ fraction, where $\sigma < 1$ is smaller if γ is larger), the contention in the vicinity of v is bounded by some constant and the average interference from the nodes outside the vicinity is below a threshold, w.h.p. Such rounds are called *good rounds.* Thus, a good round has *bounded contention* and *small interference*, and there are mostly good rounds in any phase. It is worth mentioning that in order to ensure this property in dynamic networks, we set p_{min} sufficiently small, depending on n. However, in *static spontaneous* networks, when all nodes start the algorithm simultaneously, p_{min} can be any constant: the contention balance property holds in any phase except, perhaps, the first one.

[1]Note that the ACK primitive is implemented in this version as a sender-side primitive, but the algorithms will also work with receiver-side sensing and explicit acknowledgment messages.

Local Broadcast. The local broadcast algorithm simply runs the contention balancing procedure, with nodes bowing out when they are sure to have completed their transmission (using the ACK primitive).

We measure the performance of the algorithm using the notion of *dynamic degree* $\hat{\Delta}_v(t,t')$ for node v and rounds t, t' with $t' > t$, which is the number of nodes that have appeared in the vicinity of node v during the time interval $[t,t']$.

We essentially prove that if there are not too many node insertions in the neighborhood of a node v, then v mass-delivers in time comparable to its dynamic degree.

THEOREM 3.1. *Each node v performing the local broadcast algorithm in a time interval $T = [t,t']$ of length $t' - t = \Omega(\hat{\Delta}_v(t,t') + \log n)$ mass-delivers, w.h.p.*

The idea behind the analysis is to use the property of TRY&ADJUST that most rounds in any phase are good. The phases in the interval $[t,t']$ can be classified as *low contention* or *high contention*, depending if the contention in most rounds is lower than a specific threshold, or there are significant number of rounds where the contention is high. In a low contention phase, v is likely to mass-deliver, as it will detect IDLE many times and increase its transmission probability and this will probably happen during good rounds (as they are many), where the chances of success are higher. In a higher contention phase, on the other hand, there will be many nodes in the vicinity of v mass-delivering, which, after a sufficiently many phases, leads to a mostly low contention phase.

Implications for Static Networks. In static networks, we have that $\hat{\Delta}_v(t,t') = O(\Delta)$, where Δ is the maximum degree. Thus, we obtain that in static asynchronous networks the local broadcast algorithm runs in $O(\Delta + \log n)$ rounds, w.h.p., which is optimal (up to constant factors) for static networks, as Δ and $\log n$ are lower bounds even when running in the spontaneous mode [3].

In the special case when the nodes can start executing the algorithm simultaneously, i.e. in the *spontaneous mode*, the nodes need not know an upper bound on the size of the network. In this case, we obtain a *uniform algorithm*.

Broadcast. The broadcast algorithms are based on sparsifying the instance, so that only nodes of constant density actually participate in the global broadcast action. This takes $O(\hat{D})$ rounds, where $\hat{D}$ is a dynamic diameter.

The outline of the algorithm is as follows. Each round consists of two slots. The idea is to use the first slot of each round for disseminating the message with TRY&ADJUST and the second slot for notifying nodes that have no uninformed neighbors. The latter is accomplished by using a higher precision ACK primitive, namely ACK($\epsilon/2$), when executing TRY&ADJUST. This helps to detect a transmission that is successfully received by all nodes in a slightly extended neighborhood $N(v, \epsilon/2)$ of a node v. Upon detecting such a transmission (using ACK primitive), node v re-sends the message in the second slot, in order to inform nodes u that are very near (e.g. at distance at most $\epsilon R_B/2$) that their neighborhood ($N(u,\epsilon)$) has been covered. Such nodes can detect that the message is intended to them by using the NTD primitive.

In order to evaluate the progress of the algorithm, we use a notion of *stable s-v path*, where s is the source node. This is essentially a *temporal* $s - v$ path where each edge stays active for an interval of at least $O(\log n)$ rounds, after the corresponding intervals of previous edges. The minimum time-length of a stable s-v path is then called the *stable* $s - v$ *distance* $\hat{D}(s,v)$. Note that a stable path need not be connected at any fixed point in time. Moreover, most of the nodes might be missing at any given point in time.

THEOREM 3.2. *Each node v receives the message in $O(\hat{D}(s,v))$ rounds of the broadcast algorithm, w.h.p.*

The core idea behind the analysis of the theorem is similar to the case of local broadcast: we show that as soon as a neighbor u of a node v has the message and u and v keep being neighbors for $O(\log n)$ rounds, v will receive a transmission of u during those rounds.

Implications for Static Networks. When the network is static, Theorem 3.2 can be reformulated in terms of hop-distance $dist_G(s,v)$ in the communication graph: we have that $\hat{D}(s,v) = O(\log n) \cdot dist_G(s,v)$ for any node v. Thus, when running the broadcast algorithm in a static non-spontaneous network with source s, each node v receives the message in $O(\log n) \cdot dist_G(s,v)$ rounds w.h.p. When the communication graph is strongly connected, the broadcast from any source node is completed in $O(\log n) \cdot D_G$ rounds, where D_G is the diameter of the communication graph.

In the spontaneous mode, the bound above can be further improved to $O(D_G + \log n)$. This is based on finding a constant-density dominating set in $O(\log n)$ time [2] and simultaneously propagating along the dominators in $O(D_G + \log n)$ time. We can therefore extend the approach based on [2] to uniform algorithms in bounded-independence metrics.

These results are close to best possible. We show that in order to obtain bounds of that magnitude, it is necessary to have the NTD primitive.

4. ACKNOWLEDGMENTS

This work was partially supported by Iceland Research Foundation grants 120032011 and 152679-051, National Natural Science Foundation of China grants 61073174, 61373027, 61402461, 61433019 and HKU Small Project.

5. REFERENCES

[1] M. M. Halldórsson, T. Tonoyan, Y. Wang, and D. Yu. Data dissemination in unified dynamic wireless networks. *arXiv preprint 1605.02474*, 2016.

[2] C. Scheideler, A. Richa, and P. Santi. An $O(\log N)$ Dominating Set Protocol for Wireless Ad-hoc Networks Under the Physical Interference Model. In *MobiHoc '08*, pages 91–100, 2008.

[3] D. Yu, Q.-S. Hua, Y. Wang, and F. Lau. An $O(\log n)$ Distributed Approximation Algorithm for Local Broadcasting in Unstructured Wireless Networks. In *DCOSS '12*, pages 132–139, 2012.

Brief Announcement: Reliable Message Transmission under Partial Knowledge and General Adversaries*

Aris Pagourtzis
School of Electrical and Computer Engineering
Nat. Tech. Univ. of Athens
pagour@cs.ntua.gr

Giorgos Panagiotakos
Department of Informatics and Telecommunications
University of Athens
g.panagiotakos@di.uoa.gr

Dimitris Sakavalas
School of Electrical and Computer Engineering
Nat. Tech. Univ. of Athens
sakaval@corelab.ntua.gr

ABSTRACT

We address the problem of *Reliable Message Transmission* (RMT), in the general adversary model of Hirt and Maurer [2], which subsumes earlier models such as the global or local threshold adversaries. We employ the recently introduced *Partial Knowledge Model* [8], which captures any case of initial players' topology knowledge. Our main contribution is the determination of a necessary and sufficient condition for achieving RMT in the partial knowledge model with a general adversary. We propose the RMT-Partial Knowledge Algorithm (RMT-PKA), which solves RMT whenever this is possible, therefore it is a *unique* algorithm, as defined in [10]. To the best of our knowledge, this is the first unique protocol for RMT against general adversaries in the partial knowledge model.

1. INTRODUCTION

The *Reliable Message Transmission* problem (RMT) is the problem of achieving correct delivery of a message m from a *dealer* (sender) D to a receiver R, in a possibly incomplete network, even if some of the intermediate nodes are corrupted and do not relay the message as agreed. In this work, we study RMT in the presence of a *Byzantine adversary* which is able to make some nodes deviate from the protocol arbitrarily.

The study of RMT was initiated in [1] in the context of the (global) threshold adversary model. The more realistic *t-locally bounded adversary* model, was introduced by Koo [4] in order to study the closely related *Reliable Broadcast* problem in networks of specific topology. Our approach stems from a line of work ([3, 6]) initiated by Pelc and Peleg [10] which studied the solvability of the problem in generic networks under the t-locally bounded adversary model. Studies of the RMT problem in the *general adversary model* were initiated in [5]. In this model, introduced by Hirt and Maurer [2], the adversary may corrupt any player-set among a given family of all possible corruption sets (*adversary structure*); it subsumes all known adversary models.

Regarding topology knowledge, the recently introduced *Partial Knowledge Model* [8] assumes that each player only has knowledge over some arbitrary subgraph of the network. It encompasses all previous topology knowledge models including the extensively studied full knowledge and unknown topology (*ad hoc*) models. The motivation for partial knowledge considerations comes from large scale networks where topologically local estimation of the power of the adversary may be possible, while global estimation may be hard to obtain due to physical constraints. Additionally, proximity in social networks is often correlated with an increased amount of available information, further justifying the relevance of the model. Here, we focus on Perfectly Reliable Message Transmission under partial knowledge and general adversaries; he strength of our approach lies in the combination of these two quite general models, forming the most general setting we have encountered so far within the synchronous deterministic model.

1.1 Our results

We focus on the feasibility of RMT under partial knowledge and general adversaries. We prove a necessary and sufficient condition for achieving RMT in this setting, and present the RMT-PKA algorithm, which achieves RMT whenever this condition is met. In terminology of [10, 8] this is a *unique* RMT algorithm, in the sense that whenever any algorithm achieves RMT in a certain instance so does our algorithm. This settles an open question of [8] and is, to the best of our knowledge, the first algorithm with this property.

A key notion that we define and use is the *joint adversary structure* of (a set of) players which corresponds to the worst case adversary structure that conforms to each player's initial knowledge; this notion is crucial in obtaining the tight condition mentioned above since it provides a way to safely utilize the maximal valid information from all the messages exchanged. We also make use of the local pair-cut technique concept, introduced by Pelc and Peleg [10] and extended in [8]; our adaptation of the latter yields a new pair-cut notion which provides the first exact characterization of the classes of graphs for which RMT is possible for any level of topology knowledge and type of corruption distribution.

1.2 Model and definitions

We assume a synchronous network represented by a graph $G = (V, E)$ consisting of the player (node) set $V(G)$ and edge set $E(G)$ which represents undirected authenticated channels between players. The set of neighbors of a player v

*The full version of this paper is available in [9].

PODC'16 July 25-28, 2016, Chicago, IL, USA

ACM ISBN 978-1-4503-3964-3/16/07.
DOI: http://dx.doi.org/10.1145/2933057.2933080

is denoted with $\mathcal{N}(v)$. In our study we will often make use of node-cuts (separators) which separate the receiver R from the dealer, hence, node-cuts that do not include the dealer. From here on we will simply use the term *cut* to denote such a separator. The problem definition follows.

Reliable Message Transmission. We assume the existence of a designated player $D \in V$, called the *dealer*, who wants to propagate a certain value $x_D \in X$, where X is the initial message space, to a designated player R, called the receiver. We say that a distributed protocol achieves (or solves) RMT if by the end of the protocol the receiver R has *decided on* x_D, i.e. if it has been able to output the value x_D originally sent by the dealer.

The Adversary Model. The *general adversary model* was introduced by Hirt and Maurer in [2]. It assumes the *adversary structure*, that is, a family of subsets of the players; the adversary is able to corrupt one of these subsets. More formally, a structure $\mathcal{Z}$ for the set of players V is a monotone family of subsets of V, i.e. $\mathcal{Z} \subseteq 2^V$, where all subsets of a set Z are in $\mathcal{Z}$ if $Z \in \mathcal{Z}$.

The Partial Knowledge Model [8]. In this setting each player v only has knowledge of the topology of a certain subgraph G_v of G which includes v. Namely if we consider the family $\mathcal{G}$ of subgraphs of G we use the *view function* $\gamma : V(G) \to \mathcal{G}$, where $\gamma(v)$ represents the subgraph over which player v has knowledge of the topology. We extend the domain of γ by allowing as input a set $S \subseteq V(G)$. The output will correspond to the *joint view* of nodes in S. More specifically, if $\gamma(v) = G_v = (V_v, E_v)$ then $\gamma(S) = G_S = (\bigcup_{v \in S} V_v, \bigcup_{v \in S} E_v)$. Considering the partial knowledge model under the existence of a general adversary, we assume that given the actual adversary structure $\mathcal{Z}$ each player v only knows the possible corruption sets in his view $\mathcal{Z}_v = \{A \cap V(\gamma(v)) \mid A \in \mathcal{Z}\}$ (*local adversary structure*).

Protocol Properties. We say that an RMT protocol is *resilient* for an instance $\mathcal{I} = (G, \mathcal{Z}, \gamma, D, R)$ if it achieves RMT on $\mathcal{I}$ for any possible corruption set and any admissible behavior of the corrupted players. We say that an RMT protocol is *safe* if it never causes the receiver R to decide on an incorrect value on any instance. An algorithm A is unique (for RMT) among algorithms in family $\mathcal{A}$ if the existence of an algorithm of family $\mathcal{A}$ which achieves RMT in an instance $\mathcal{I}$ implies that A also achieves RMT in $\mathcal{I}$.

2. PARTIAL KNOWLEDGE AND GENERAL ADVERSARIES

Considering two players who have partial knowledge of the adversary, we define an operation to calculate their joint knowledge about the adversary. For an adversary structure $\mathcal{E}$ and a node set A let $\mathcal{E}^A = \{Z \cap A \mid Z \in \mathcal{E}\}$. The joint adversary structure from two restricted adversary structures can be obtained through the $\oplus$ operator[1].

Joint Adversary Structure. Let $\mathbb{T}^A = 2^{2^A}$ denote the space of adversary structures on a set of nodes A. For any node sets A, B and adversary structures $\mathcal{E}, \mathcal{F}$, the operation $\oplus : \mathbb{T}^A \times \mathbb{T}^B \to \mathbb{T}^{(A \cup B)}$, is defined as follows:

$$\mathcal{E}^A \oplus \mathcal{F}^B = \{Z_1 \cup Z_2 | (Z_1 \in \mathcal{E}^A) \wedge (Z_2 \in \mathcal{F}^B) \wedge (Z_1 \cap B = Z_2 \cap A)\}$$

[1]We define the operation on two possibly different structures $\mathcal{E}, \mathcal{F}$ so that the operation is well defined even if a corrupted player falsely reports a different structure than the real one.

Informally, the $\mathcal{E}^A \oplus \mathcal{F}^B$ operation unites possible corruption sets from $\mathcal{E}^A$ and $\mathcal{F}^B$ that 'agree' on $A \cap B$. The $\oplus$ operation is commutative, associative and idempotent. The next theorem shows a property of the $\oplus$ operation which is important for our study.

THEOREM 1. *For any adversary structure $\mathcal{Z}$ and node sets A, B: $\mathcal{Z}^{(A \cup B)} \subseteq \mathcal{Z}^A \oplus \mathcal{Z}^B$.*

What Theorem 1 tells us is that the $\oplus$ operation gives the maximal (w.r.t inclusion) possible adversary structure that is indistinguishable by two agents that know $\mathcal{Z}^A$ and $\mathcal{Z}^B$ respectively, i.e., it coincides with their knowledge of the adversary structures on sets A and B respectively. This allows us to define the combined knowledge of a set of nodes B about the adversary structure $\mathcal{Z}$ given a view function γ:

$$\mathcal{Z}_B = \bigoplus_{v \in B} \mathcal{Z}^{V(\gamma(v))}$$

Note that $\mathcal{Z}_B$ exactly captures the maximal adversary structure possible, restricted in $\gamma(B)$, relative to the initial knowledge of players in B. Also notice that using Theorem 1 we get $\mathcal{Z}^{V(\gamma(B))} \subseteq \mathcal{Z}_B$. This means that, what nodes in B conceive as the worst case adversary structure indistinguishable to them, always contains the actual adversary structure in their scenario.

2.1 Reliable message transmission in the partial knowledge model

To analyze feasibility of RMT we introduce the notion of *RMT-cut*: Let $(G, \mathcal{Z}, \gamma, D, R)$ be an RMT instance and $C = C_1 \cup C_2$ be a cut in G, partitioning $V \setminus C$ in two sets $A, B' \neq \emptyset$ where $D \in A$ and $R \in B'$. Let $B \subseteq B'$ be the node set of the connected component that R lies in. Then C is a *RMT-cut* iff $C_1 \in \mathcal{Z}$ and $C_2 \cap V(\gamma(B)) \in \mathcal{Z}_B$.

Non-existence of an RMT-cut proves to be a necessary condition to safely achieve RMT. The proof combines ideas from [10, 8] with the $\oplus$ operation and is presented in [9].

THEOREM 2 (NECESSITY). *Let $(G, \mathcal{Z}, \gamma, D, R)$ be an RMT instance. If there exists a RMT-cut in G then no safe and resilient RMT algorithm exists for $(G, \mathcal{Z}, \gamma, D, R)$.*

2.2 The RMT Partial Knowledge Algorithm (RMT-PKA)

We next present the *RMT Partial Knowledge Algorithm* (RMT-PKA), an RMT protocol which succeeds whenever the necessary condition of Theorem 2 is met, rendering it a tight condition on when RMT is possible. In RMT-PKA there are two type of messages exchanged. *Type 1 messages* are used to propagate the dealer's value and are of the form (x, p) where $x \in X$ and p is a path. *Type 2 messages* of the form $((v, \gamma(v), \mathcal{Z}_v), p)$ are used for every node v to propagate its initial information $\gamma(v), \mathcal{Z}_v$ throughout the graph. Let M denote a subset of the messages of type 1 and 2 that the receiver node R receives at some round of the protocol on $(G, \mathcal{Z}, \gamma, D, R)$. We will say that *value*$(M) = x$ if and only if all the type 1 messages of M report the same dealer value x, i.e., for every such message (y, p), it holds that $y = x$, for some $x \in X$. Observe that M may consist of messages which contain contradictory information. We next define the form of a message set M which contains no contradictory information in our setting (a valid set M).

Valid set M. A set M of both type 1 and type 2 messages *corresponds to a valid scenario*, or more simply is *valid*, if
(a) $\exists x \in X$ s.t. $value(M) = x$. That is, all type 1 messages relay the same x as dealer's value.
(b) $\forall m_1, m_2 \in M$ of type 2, their first component is the same when they refer to the same node. That is, if $m_1 = ((v, \gamma(v), \mathcal{Z}_v), p)$ and $m_2 = (((v', \gamma'(v), \mathcal{Z}'_v), p')$, then $v = v'$ implies that $\gamma(v) = \gamma'(v)$ and $\mathcal{Z}_v = \mathcal{Z}'_v$.

For every valid M we can define the pair (G_M, x_M) where $x_M = value(M)$. To define G_M let V_M be the set of nodes u for which the information $\gamma(u), \mathcal{Z}_u$ is included in M, namely $V_M = \{v \mid ((v, \gamma(v), \mathcal{Z}_v), p) \in M$ for some path $p\}$. Then, G_M is the node induced subgraph of graph $\gamma(V_M)$ on node set V_M. Therefore, a valid message set M uniquely determines the pair (G_M, x_M). We next propose two notions that we use to check if a valid set M contains correct information.

A *full message set* M is a valid set M that contains all the D-R paths which appear in G_M as part of type 1 messages.

An *adversary cover* of message set M is a set $C \subseteq V_M$ with following property: C is a cut between D, R on G_M and if B is the node set of the connected component that R lies in, it holds that $(C \cap V(\gamma(B))) \in \mathcal{Z}_B$.

Protocol 1: *RMT-PKA*

Input (for each node v): dealer's label D, $\gamma(v)$, $\mathcal{Z}_v$.
Additional input for D : value $x_D \in X$ (message space).

Code for D: send messages $(x_D, \{D\})$ and $((D, \gamma(D), \mathcal{Z}_D), \{D\})$ to all neighbors and terminate.

Code for $v \notin \{D, R\}$: send message $((v, \gamma(v), \mathcal{Z}_v), \{v\})$ to all neighbors.
  upon reception of type 1 or type 2 message (a, p) from node u `do`: `if` $(v \in p) \vee (tail(p) \neq u)$[2] `then discard` (a, p) `else send` $(a, p||v)$ [3] to all neighbours.

Code for R: upon reception of (x, p) from node u `do`:
  `if decision` $\neq \bot$ `then output decision` and terminate.

Subroutine `decision`
  (* *dealer propagation rule* *)
  `if` $R \in \mathcal{N}(D)$ and R receives $(x_D, \{D\})$ `then return` x_D.
  (* *full message set propagation rule* *)
  `if` R receives a full set M with $value(M) = x$ and $\nexists$ an adversary cover for M
    `then return` x `else return` $\bot$.

RMT-PKA proves, somewhat counterintuitively, to be safe (cf. [9]), i.e., that the receiver will never decide on an incorrect value despite the increased adversary's attack capabilities, which includes reporting fictitious nodes and false local knowledge. More importantly, it achieves RMT whenever the necessary condition presented in Theorem 2 is met and thus is unique among safe algorithms.

THEOREM 3 (SUFFICIENCY). *Let $(G, \mathcal{Z}, \gamma, D, R)$ be an RMT instance. If no RMT-cut exists, then RMT-PKA achieves reliable message transmission.*

[2]We use $tail(p)$ to denote the last node of path p. Checking whether $tail(p) \neq u$ we ensure that at least one corrupted node will be included in a faulty propagation path.
[3]$p||v$ is the concatenation of path p with node v.

The proofs of safety and correctness of RMT-PKA combine techniques from [8] with the novel notions of full message set M, adversary cover of M and corresponding graph G_M.

3. CONCLUSIONS

The RMT-PKA protocol employs topology information exchange between players. Although topology discovery was not our motive, techniques used here (e.g. the $\oplus$ operation) may be applicable to that problem under a Byzantine adversary (e.g. [7]). A comparison with the techniques used in this field might give further insight on how to efficiently extract information from maliciously crafted topological data.

We have shown that RMT-PKA protocol is unique for the partial knowledge model; this only addresses the feasibility issue. A natural question is whether and when we can devise a unique and also efficient algorithm for this setting. The techniques used so far to reduce the communication complexity (e.g. [5]) do not seem to be directly applicable to this model. So, this direction seems particularly meaningful.

It would also be interesting to argue about protocol uniqueness with respect to efficiency for RMT in the partial knowledge model. A first step towards this direction is provided in [9] for the *ad hoc* case. There, we propose the *ad hoc* RMT algorithm $\mathcal{Z}$-CPA, and prove that if it is not fully polynomial, then no fully polynomial RMT protocol exists.

4. REFERENCES

[1] D. Dolev, C. Dwork, O. Waarts, and M. Yung. Perfectly secure message transmission. *J. ACM*, 40(1):17–47, Jan. 1993.

[2] M. Hirt and U. M. Maurer. Complete characterization of adversaries tolerable in secure multi-party computation (extended abstract). In *PODC '97*, pages 25–34. ACM, 1997.

[3] A. Ichimura and M. Shigeno. A new parameter for a broadcast algorithm with locally bounded byzantine faults. *Inf. Process. Lett.*, 110(12-13):514–517, 2010.

[4] C.-Y. Koo. Broadcast in radio networks tolerating byzantine adversarial behavior. In *PODC '04*, pages 275–282. ACM, 2004.

[5] M. V. N. A. Kumar, P. R. Goundan, K. Srinathan, and C. P. Rangan. On perfectly secure communication over arbitrary networks. In *PODC '02*, pages 193–202, New York, NY, USA, 2002. ACM.

[6] C. Litsas, A. Pagourtzis, and D. Sakavalas. A graph parameter that matches the resilience of the certified propagation algorithm. In *ADHOC-NOW*, volume 7960 of *LNCS*, pages 269–280. Springer, 2013.

[7] M. Nesterenko and S. Tixeuil. Discovering network topology in the presence of byzantine faults. *IEEE Trans. Parallel Distrib. Syst.*, 20(12):1777–1789, 2009.

[8] A. Pagourtzis, G. Panagiotakos, and D. Sakavalas. Reliable broadcast with respect to topology knowledge. In *DISC '14*, pages 107–121. Springer, 2014.

[9] A. Pagourtzis, G. Panagiotakos, and D. Sakavalas. Reliable message transmission under partial knowledge and general adversaries. *IACR Cryptology ePrint Archive*, 2015:243, 2015.

[10] A. Pelc and D. Peleg. Broadcasting with locally bounded byzantine faults. *Inf. Process. Lett.*, 93(3):109–115, 2005.

Brief Announcement: Self-Stabilizing Clock Synchronization with 3-bit Messages *

Lucas Boczkowski[†]
Institut de Recherche en Informatique Fondamentale
CNRS and University Paris Diderot
France
lucas.boczkowski@irif.fr

Amos Korman[†]
Institut de Recherche en Informatique Fondamentale
CNRS and University Paris Diderot
France
amos.korman@irif.fr

Emanuele Natale[‡]
Dipartimento di Informatica
Sapienza Università di Roma
Italy
natale@di.uniroma1.it

ABSTRACT

This paper is motivated by the aspiration to identify the weakest computational models that allow for efficient, robust distributed computation. We focus on one of the most fundamental building-blocks in distributed computing, namely, Broadcast. In this problem, a unique source agent s needs to disseminate a bit b to the rest of the population. To account for unpredictability issues that may result from uncoordinated executions, we consider a *self-stabilizing* setting, in which a correct configuration must be reached eventually, despite processors starting the execution with arbitrary initial states (that do not violate the requirement for the existence of a unique source). Similarly to many works on broadcast, we consider a synchronous communication model on a complete anonymous network, in which in each round, each agent can extract information from two other agents, chosen uniformly at random. Our focus is on identifying the smallest message size that is required in order to achieve fast self-stabilizing broadcast. We first observe that with an extra bit added to the message-size and a small additive penalty to the running time, the self-stabilizing broadcast problem can be reduced to a self-stabilizing clock-synchronization problem, where agents aim to synchronize their clocks modulo some integer T. Our main technical contribution lies in solving the latter problem in poly-logarithmic time using only 3 bits per interaction. This allows for a self-stabilizing broadcast protocol that uses only 4 bits per interaction and converges in $\tilde{\mathcal{O}}(\log n)$ time.

*A full version of this paper is available at [4]

†This work has received funding from the European Research Council (ERC) under the European Union's Horizon 2020 research and innovation programme (grant agreement No 648032).

‡This work was done in part while the author was visiting the Simons Institute for the Theory of Computing.

PODC'16, July 25-28, 2016, Chicago, IL, USA
ACM 978-1-4503-3964-3/16/07.
http://dx.doi.org/10.1145/2933057.2933075

1. INTRODUCTION

Chaotic distributed systems composed of limited agents that interact in an unpredictable fashion to jointly perform computational tasks are common in the natural world as well as in engineered systems [3].

From an algorithmic perspective, these systems share a number of computational challenges. Indeed, they all perform collectively in dynamically changing environments despite being composed of individuals with little computational power, that communicate through unpredictable, unreliable, and limited interactions. Recently, there has been significant interest in understanding the computational limitations that are inherent to such systems, by abstracting some of their ingredients as simple distributed computing models, and analyzing the models algorithmically [2, 9, 8]. These models, often grouped under the term *population protocols*, are usually defined as a collection of anonymous agents which are restricted in their memory and communication capacities, and which interact in pairs according to a uniform probabilistic scheduler.

By now, our understanding of the computational power of population protocols is rather advanced. It is important to note, however, that most of this progress has been made assuming non-faulty scenarios. As indicated by these works, when memory and communication are limited in capacity, efficient cooperation is difficult to achieve even in non-faulty systems with perfect communication. However, things may potentially become much worse under faulty or dynamic conditions. To have a better understanding of chaotic systems such as the ones mentioned above, it is therefore desirable to identify the weakest computational models that allow for both efficient as well as robust performances. This paper takes a step in this challenging direction by studying population protocols that operate under conditions of increased uncertainty, where the memories of agents are initially inconsistent with each other and information flows across the system are unreliable.

We focus our attention on the *broadcast* problem [5], one of the most fundamental primitives in distributed computing. In this problem, a single piece of information initially residing at some source processor (agent) is to be disseminated to the rest of the population. A classical example considers the uniform synchronous PUSH/PULL communication model, where a message (*e.g.*, a bit) can be propagated to all agents in $\mathcal{O}(\log n)$ rounds, by simply letting each uninformed agent copy it whenever it sees an informed agent [10]. The correctness of this protocol relies on the memory of agents being non-corrupt, and in particular, on the agents' ability to detect if they themselves are informed with the correct bit. However, such certainly conditions are difficult to achieve in unpredictable scenarios. For example, if the source is sensitive to an unstable environment, or when its ability to learn the environment is limited, it may change its mind several times before stabilizing to its final opinion. Meanwhile, it may have already initiated several consecutive executions of the protocol with contradicting initial values, which may in turn "infect" other agents with the wrong opinion. If agents do not share a common time notion, it is unclear how to let infected agents distinguish their current wrong opinion from the more "fresh", correct opinion. Indeed, running a broadcast protocol under such unpredictability circumstances may result in a complex configuration of internal states by the time the source has stabilized, which could be difficult to overcome.

Self-stabilization with small messages.
To address the aforementioned difficulties, we study the broadcast problem in the context of *self-stabilization* [6], where the system must converge to a correct configuration regardless of the initial states of the agents. More specifically, we consider a network of n agents with a designated *source* agent s. We assume that at the beginning of the execution, the states of all agents are arbitrary, except that it is guaranteed that there is precisely one source agent. The source holds an *output bit* b that is to be disseminated to the rest of the population. That is, it is required that all agents set their output bit to b eventually.

Similarly to many works on broadcast, we consider a random meeting pattern on a complete graph [10]. Specifically, we study the synchronous PULL model of communication, in which at each round, each agent can "observe" few other agents, chosen uniformly at random. Agents can use the synchronous setting to count rounds and hold clocks. Note however, that although agents share a notion of a "pulse" (a round), they do not necessarily agree on a common time notion since the initial configuration may consist of corrupted clock values.

Our main challenge is to identify the minimal *message size*, namely, the number of bits revealed in each interaction, that allows to solve the self-stabilizing broadcast problem in poly-logarithmic time. Indeed, it is important to note that stochastic communication patterns are inherently sensitive to congestion issues, and in such models it is unclear how to simulate a protocol that uses large messages while using only small size messages. For example, the straightforward strategy of breaking a large message into small pieces and sequentially sending them one after another does not work, since one typically cannot make sure that the small messages reach the same destination. Hence, reducing the message size may have a profound impact on the running time, and perhaps even on the solvability of the problem at hand.

A main difficulty behind the self-stabilizing broadcast problem lies in the fact that nodes do not necessarily share a common time notion. Indeed, it is straightforward to see that if all agents share the same clock, then convergence can be achieved in $\mathcal{O}(\log n)$ time with high probability and using only 2 bits per interaction (see [4] for a detailed discussion). Still under the assumption that all agents share the same clock, the following trick shows how to obtain convergence in $\mathcal{O}(\log n)$ time and using only a single bit per message, namely, the output bit. Essentially, agents divide time into phases of some prescribed length $T = \mathcal{O}(\log n)$, each of them being further subdivided into 2 subphases of length $T/2$. In the first subphase of each phase, non-source agents are *sensitive* to opinion 0. This means that whenever they see a 0 in the output bit of another agent, they turn their output bit to 0, but if they see 1 they ignore it. Then, in the second phase of each phase, they do the opposite, namely they switch their output bit to 1 as soon as they see a 1. Of course, the source agent does not apply this rule. Consider the first phase starting after the time the output bit of the source has stabilized to some b. If $b = 0$ then within one complete subphase $[0, T/2 - 1]$, every output bit is 0 and remains there forever. Otherwise, if $b = 1$, when all agents go over a subphase $[T/2, T - 1]$ all output bits are set to 1 and remain 1 forever.

This observation indicates that the self-stabilizing broadcast problem is highly related to the self-stabilizing *clock synchronization* problem, where each agent internally stores a counter modulo $T = \mathcal{O}(\log n)$, which is incremented at every round, and that all agents should converge on having the same value in their counter values, despite arbitrary initial states. Indeed, given such a self-stabilizing clock-synchronization protocol, we can obtain a self-stabilizing broadcast protocol by running this protocol in parallel to the aforementioned broadcast protocol (that relies on synchronized clocks). This parallel execution costs only an additional bit to the message size and an additional $\mathcal{O}(\log n)$ additive factor to the time complexity over the corresponding message size and time complexities of the clock-synchronization protocol.

To synchronize clocks modulo T in a self-stabilizing manner, one could use the self-stabilizing consensus protocol in [7], by displaying all the bits of the clocks in each message, and synchronizing on each of them separately and in parallel while incrementing the clocks. Unfortunately, this approach is wasteful in terms of message size, as it requires to reveal $\log T$ bits per interaction. As another approach, one could aim at sequentially synchronizing clocks bit after bit. That is, first display and synchronize the first bit; then, once agents "know" that the first bit has been synchronized, display and synchronize the second bit, etc. This approach is problematic in the context of self-stabilization, since, first, it requires agents to "know" when a bit is synchronized, and second, it requires agents to agree on the bit index that they currently aim to synchronize. Both of these require clocks to be synchronized to begin with.

1.1 Our Results

We focus on the randomized PULL model of communication as assumed in [7], in which in each round, each agent contacts two agents chosen uniformly at random among all agents (including itself, with replacement). Our main technical contribution is the construction of a time efficient self-stabilizing clock synchronization protocol that employs only 3 bits per interaction, and synchronizes clocks modulo T, where T is a power of 2. Relying on this clock synchronization algorithm, and using an additional bit in each message, we solve the self-stabilizing broadcast problem using only 4 bits of communication per message. Formally, we prove the following.

Theorem 1.1. *Let T be a power of 2. There exists a self-stabilizing clock synchronization algorithm that synchronizes clocks modulo T and uses only 3 bits per interaction. The protocol converges in $\tilde{\mathcal{O}}(\log^3 T \log n)$ rounds w.h.p.*

Theorem 1.2. *Assume that agents know n. There exists a self-stabilizing broadcast protocol that uses 4-bit messages, converges in $\tilde{\mathcal{O}}(\log n)$ rounds w.h.p., and afterwords remains in a legal configuration indefinitely.*

Intuition behind the synchronization algorithm.

Our technique for obtaining the clock synchronization protocol is based on a compact simulation of the stabilizing consensus protocol proposed by Doerr et al. [7]. We first describe a simple protocol called SYNC-SIMPLE that uses $O(\log T)$ bits per message. Essentially, each agent u maintains a clock $C_u \in [0, T-1]$. At each round, each agent u displays the value of its clock, pulls 2 uniform other such clock values, and updates its clock as the bitwise majority of the two clocks it pulled, and its own. Then the clock C_u is incremented. Since this protocol essentially amounts to running the protocol of Doerr et al. on each bit separately and in parallel, it is relatively easy to see that protocol SYNC-SIMPLE self-stabilizes in $\mathcal{O}(\log T \log n)$ rounds w.h.p. We want to apply a similar strategy to SYNC-SIMPLE, while using only $O(1)$ many bits per interaction. At a high level, agents keep a clock internally which they write using $\log T$ bits. This time, instead of displaying the full clock, we would like them to display the first bit of their clock all at the same time, then the second bit etc. They could do that, if they had a clock, which is precisely what we are trying to achieve. To handle this difficulty, we use a recursive approach, by which agents maintain several clocks, of larger and larger sizes, and use the already synchronized clocks to decide which bit of the next (bigger) clock to display (and synchronize on). More precisely, the recursion is initialized by synchronizing a small clock $C^{(1)}$ of 2 bits (thus running modulo 4). This is done in the same way as SYNC-SIMPLE. The small clock in fact corresponds to the first two bits of the clock C to be synchronized. The third bit displayed gives the value at some index of the (binary expansion) of C. As time progresses, this third bit traverses all indices. Initially, the traversals are not synchronized, and agents are not displaying the same index in each round necessarily. The traversals are designed in a self improving way, making them more and more synchronized, as the protocol progresses.

The clock-synchronization protocol.

Agents want to synchronize a big clock C. They divide the bits used to write C into blocks of increasing sizes $C^{(1)}, \ldots, C^{(k)}$, so the clock C can be written as the concatenation of all the $C^{(i)}$'s: $C = (C^{(k)}, \ldots, C^{(1)})$. We refer to these blocks as *sub-clocks*. In fact, when $C^{(i)} \neq 0$ we view $C^{(i)}$ as an *index* of the binary representation of $C^{(i+1)}$. Otherwise, if $C^{(i)} = 0$, we interpret $C^{(i)}$ differently.

Let m_i denote the number of bits in the binary representation of $C^{(i)}$. Subclock $C^{(i)}$ thus represents an integer between 0 and $2^{m_i} - 1$. The sequence $(m_i)_{i\in\mathbb{N}}$ is chosen as follows: $m_1 = 2$; $\forall i \leq k-2, m_{i+1} = 2^{m_i} - 1$; $m_k = \log T - m_1 - \ldots - m_{k-1}$.

Note the parameter k is a function of T. The last element of the sequence $m_k \in [1, \log T]$ is the only one whose value depends on T. Each agent displays 3 bits. The first two correspond to $C^{(1)}$, a clock modulo 4. We call the third one the *rabbit-hole* bit. It corresponds to the value of some bit of some clock $C^{(i)}$ for some $i \leq k$. The index of this bit is given by a procedure called FETCH, which we define next. The procedure takes as input a clock $C \in [0, T-1]$ and returns an index in $[1, \log T]$. To decide what is the fetched index, consider the minimal index $i \leq k-1$ such that $C^{(i)} \neq 0$, which we denote by i^*. If all first $k-1$ clocks are 0, then i^* is set to 1. The fetched index is the $C^{(i^*)}$th bit of the subclock $C^{(i^*+1)}$, where the index is taken modulo m_{i^*+1}. The modulo operation aims to take care of a boundary affect. Indeed, note that for all values of $i \leq k-2$ the value of $C^{(i+1)}$ is written on $m_{i+1} = 2^{m_i} - 1$ bits, and the value of $C^{(i)}$ never exceeds $2^{m_i} - 1$. Hence taking the modulo m_{i^*+1} does not change anything for $i^* \leq k-2$. It only makes a difference in the case where $i^* = k-1$.

Now that we have specified what agents store and display. We next describe how they use the 2×3 bits they collect at each round, to update their clock. Suppose agent u sampled u_1, u_2 and collected $M_{u_1} = (C^{(1)}_{u_1}, b_{u_1})$ and $M_{u_2} = (C^{(1)}_{u_2}, b_{u_2})$. First, the clock $C^{(1)}_u$ is updated by applying a bitwise majority to $(C^{(1)}_u, C^{(1)}_{u_1}, C^{(1)}_{u_2})$.

The location where the third bit "comes from" is updated by replacing it with the majority of the three corresponding bits b_u, b_{u_1}, b_{u_2}). The last step is incrementing the clock C by one. This step potentially affects all clocks $C^{(k)}, \ldots, C^{(1)}$.

2. REFERENCES

[1] D. Alistarh and R. Gelashvili. Polylogarithmic-time leader election in population protocols. *ICALP'15, pages 479–491.*

[2] D. Angluin, J. Aspnes, Z. Diamadi, M. J. Fischer, and R. Peralta. Computation in networks of passively mobile finite-state sensors. *Distributed Computing*, 18(4):235–253, 2006.

[3] D. Angluin, M. J. Fischer, and H. Jiang. Stabilizing consensus in mobile networks. In *Distributed Computing in Sensor Systems*, pages 37–50. 2006.

[4] L. Boczkowski, A. Korman, and E. Natale. Self-stabilizing clock synchronization with 3-bit messages. *arXiv preprint arXiv:1602.04419*, 2016.

[5] A. J. Demers, D. H. Greene, C. Hauser, W. Irish, J. Larson, S. Shenker, H. E. Sturgis, D. C. Swinehart, and D. B. Terry. Epidemic algorithms for replicated database maintenance. *Operating Systems Review*, 22(1):8–32, 1988.

[6] E. W. Dijkstra. Self-stabilizing systems in spite of distributed control. *Commun. ACM*, 17(11):643–644, 1974.

[7] B. Doerr, L. A. Goldberg, L. Minder, T. Sauerwald, and C. Scheideler. Stabilizing consensus with the power of two choices. *SPAA'11, pages 149–158.*

[8] D. Doty and D. Soloveichik. Stable leader election in population protocols requires linear time. *CoRR*, abs/1502.04246, 2015.

[9] Y. Emek and R. Wattenhofer. Stone age distributed computing. *PODC'13, pages 137–146.*

[10] R. M. Karp, C. Schindelhauer, S. Shenker, and B. Vöcking. Randomized rumor spreading. *FOCS'00, pages 565–574.*

Distributed Strong Diameter Network Decomposition

[Extended Abstract] *

Michael Elkin†
Department of Computer Science,
Ben-Gurion University of the Negev,
Beer-Sheva, Israel.
elkinm@cs.bgu.ac.il

Ofer Neiman‡
Department of Computer Science,
Ben-Gurion University of the Negev,
Beer-Sheva, Israel.
neimano@cs.bgu.ac.il

ABSTRACT

For a pair of positive parameters D, χ, a partition $\mathcal{P}$ of the vertex set V of an n-vertex graph $G = (V, E)$ into disjoint clusters of diameter at most D each is called a (D, χ) *network decomposition*, if the supergraph $\mathcal{G}(\mathcal{P})$, obtained by contracting each of the clusters of $\mathcal{P}$, can be properly χ-colored. The decomposition $\mathcal{P}$ is said to be *strong* (resp., *weak*) if each of the clusters has strong (resp., weak) diameter at most D, i.e., if for every cluster $C \in \mathcal{P}$ and every two vertices $u, v \in C$, the distance between them in the induced graph $G(C)$ of C (resp., in G) is at most D.

Network decomposition is a powerful construct, very useful in distributed computing and beyond. It was introduced by Awerbuch *et. al.* [AGLP89] in the end of the eighties. These authors showed that strong $(2^{O(\sqrt{\log n \log\log n})}, 2^{O(\sqrt{\log n \log\log n})})$ network decompositions can be computed in $2^{O(\sqrt{\log n \log\log n})}$ distributed time. Their result was improved at the beginning of nineties by Panconesi and Srinivasan [PS92], who showed that $2^{O(\sqrt{\log n \log\log n})}$ in all the three expressions can be replaced by $2^{O(\sqrt{\log n})}$. Around the same time Linial and Saks [LS93] devised an ingenious randomized algorithm that constructs *weak* $(O(\log n), O(\log n))$ network decompositions in $O(\log^2 n)$ time. Awerbuch *et. al.* [ABCP96] devised a randomized algorithm that builds a strong $(O(\log n), O(\log n))$ network decomposition in $O(\log^4 n)$ time, using very large messages and heavy local computations. It was however open till now if *strong* network decompositions with both parameters $2^{o(\sqrt{\log n})}$ can be constructed in distributed $2^{o(\sqrt{\log n})}$ time using short messages, or if a result of [LS93] can be strengthened to provide a strong $(O(\log n), O(\log n))$ network decomposition within $O(\log^2 n)$ time (even using large messages).

In this paper we answer these long-standing open questions in the affirmative, and show that strong $(O(\log n), O(\log n))$ network decompositions can be computed in $O(\log^2 n)$ time. We also present a tradeoff between parameters of our network decomposition. Our work is inspired by and relies on the "shifted shortest path approach", due to Blelloch *et. al.* [BGK+14], and Miller *et. al.* [MPX13]. These authors developed this approach for PRAM algorithms for padded partitions. We adapt their approach to network decompositions in the distributed model of computation.

Keywords

Network decompositions; Distributed Model

1. INTRODUCTION

1.1 Definitions and Motivation

Consider an unweighted undirected n-vertex graph $G = (V, E)$, and suppose that it models a communication network. Each vertex hosts a processor with a distinct identity number from the range $\{1, \ldots, n\}$, and these processors communicate with one another via the edges of G in synchronous rounds. If messages are of unbounded length, the model is called *LOCAL*. If each message has size $O(1)$ words (or, equivalently, $O(\log n)$ bits), then the model is called *CONGEST*. The running time of an algorithm in this model is the number of rounds of distributed communication.

In the coloring problem one wishes to compute a proper coloring φ of G that employs a small number of colors. A coloring φ is said to be *proper* if for every edge $(u, v) \in E$, we have $\varphi(u) \neq \varphi(v)$. In a seminal paper [AGLP89], Awerbuch *et. al.* introduced a generalization of vertex coloring, in which one can cluster vertices of G into clusters of small diameter. A partition $\mathcal{P}$ of G into disjoint clusters induces a supergraph $\mathcal{G}(\mathcal{P}) = (\mathcal{P}, \mathcal{E})$, where

$$\mathcal{E} = \{(C, C') \mid C, C' \in \mathcal{P}, C \neq C', \exists (v, v') \in E \cap (C \times C')\} .$$

A partition $\mathcal{P}$ is called a *strong* (respectively, *weak*) *network decomposition* of G with parameters D and χ, or shortly, (D, χ) *network decomposition*, if all clusters of $\mathcal{P}$ have strong (resp., weak) diameter at most D, and the supergraph $\mathcal{G}(\mathcal{P})$ can be properly colored with at most χ colors. Note that an

*A full version of this paper is available at `http://arxiv.org/abs/1602.05437`

†This research was supported by the ISF grant 724/15.

‡Supported in part by ISF grant No. (523/12) and by the European Union Seventh Framework Programme (FP7/2007-2013) under grant agreement $n^\circ 303809$.

PODC'16, July 25-28, 2016, Chicago, IL, USA

© 2016 ACM. ISBN 978-1-4503-3964-3/16/07...$15.00

DOI: http://dx.doi.org/10.1145/2933057.2933094

ordinary proper χ-coloring can be viewed as a $(0,\chi)$ network decomposition.

The *strong* (respectively, *weak*) *diameter* of a cluster C is defined by $Diam(C) = \max_{v,v' \in C} d_{G(C)}(v,v')$ (resp., $WeakDiam(C) = \max_{v,v' \in C} d_G(v,v')$). The notation d_G (respectively, $d_{G(C)}$) denotes the distance function in G (resp., in the induced subgraph $G(C)$ of C). The strong (resp., weak) diameter of a partition $\mathcal{P}$ is the maximum strong (resp., weak) diameter of its clusters.

Network decomposition is a very powerful construct in distributed computing. The original motivation of [AGLP89] was symmetry breaking problems, such as maximal independent set, maximal matching and $(\Delta+1)$-vertex-coloring, where Δ is the maximum degree of the input graph. Given a (D,χ) network decomposition $\mathcal{P}$ along with a χ-coloring of the induced supergraph $\mathcal{G}(\mathcal{P})$, each of these problems can be solved within $O(D\cdot\chi)$ time. This is done by solving them in parallel on each of the clusters of color class 1, then extending the solution to each of the clusters of color class 2, etc. Since clusters within each color class are at least 2 apart one from another, computations within the same color class can be conducted in parallel. Moreover, since the maximum clusters' diameter is bounded by D, one can perform each of these χ phases within $O(D)$ time by a naive algorithm. (The naive algorithm collects the entire cluster's topology into a central vertex, solves the problem locally, and disseminates the solution to all vertices of the given cluster.)

Later additional applications of network decompositions were discovered. Dubhashi *et. al.* [DMP+05] used network decompositions for computing sparse spanners and linear-size skeletons. Barenboim *et. al.* [Bar12, BEG15] devised distributed approximation algorithm for the graph coloring and minimum dominating set problems, which employ network decompositions. Network decompositions are also closely related to *neighborhood covers*, which are used extensively for routing [AP92] and synchronization [Awe85, APPS92]. The relationship between neighborhood covers and network decompositions was explored in [ABCP96]. The latter authors [ABCP94] also devised an NC PRAM algorithm for computing network decompositions. Barenboim *et. al.* [BEG15] have also showed that network decompositions can be used to build low-intersecting partitions, which are, in turn, used for computing universal Steiner trees [BDR+12].

To summarize, network decompositions have numerous applications in distributed computing and beyond. They also constitute a very appealing combinatorial construct, well worth studying on its own right.

1.2 Previous and Our Results

Awerbuch *et. al.* [AGLP89] devised a deterministic algorithm with running time $2^{O(\sqrt{\log n \log\log n})}$, that computes a strong $(2^{O(\sqrt{\log n \log\log n})}, 2^{O(\sqrt{\log n \log\log n})})$ network decomposition. This result was improved by Panconesi and Srinivasan [PS92], whose algorithm has running time $2^{O(\sqrt{\log n})}$, and both parameters of the decomposition of [PS92] are $2^{O(\sqrt{\log n})}$ as well. In another seminal work, titled "Low Diameter Graph Decompositions", Linial and Saks [LS93] conducted a systematic investigation of network decompositions. They showed that for any $k \leq \log n$, every n-vertex graph admits a strong $(2k-2, 2n^{1/k}\log n)$ network decomposition, and for any $\lambda \leq \log n$, it admits a strong $(2n^{1/\lambda}\log n, \lambda)$ network decomposition, and that these bounds are nearly tight. They have also devised a randomized distributed algorithm for computing *weak* network decompositions in expected time $O(k\cdot n^{1/k}\cdot\log n)$, with essentially the same parameters. In particular, and most notably, for $k = \log n$, their algorithm produces a *weak* $(O(\log n), O(\log n))$ network decomposition in $O(\log^2 n)$ time.

The algorithms of [AGLP89] and [LS93] work in the CONGEST model. Awerbuch *et. al.* [ABCP96] devised a distributed reduction from strong network decompositions to weak ones. Their reduction introduces an overhead of $O(\log^2 n)$ in the running time. Also, it employs very large messages, and heavy local computations. By composing the algorithm of [LS93] with the reduction of [ABCP96] one obtains a randomized algorithm in the LOCAL model that computes an $(O(\log n), O(\log n))$ network decomposition in $O(\log^4 n)$ time.

Remarkably, quarter a century after the SODA'91 publication of Linial and Saks' paper, their algorithm is still the only algorithm whose running time is at most polylogarithmic in n, and which produces a network decomposition with both parameters being at most polylogarithmic in n. Moreover, so far it was not known if such a result can be achieved for *strong* network decompositions in the CONGEST model.

In this paper we resolve this long-standing open question in the affirmative. We devise a randomized algorithm with running time $O(\log^2 n)$ that computes a *strong* $(O(\log n), O(\log n))$ network decomposition in the CONGEST model. Moreover, similarly to Linial and Saks [LS93], we can also trade between the parameters. Specifically, for any $k \leq \log n$, our randomized algorithm has running time $O(n^{1/k}\cdot k^2)$ and computes a *strong* $(2k-2, O(k\cdot n^{1/k}))$ network decomposition. In the other regime, for any $\lambda \leq \log n$, in time $O(\lambda\cdot n^{1/\lambda}\cdot\log n)$ we compute a strong $(O(n^{1/\lambda}\log n), \lambda)$ network decomposition. Note that the number of colors and running time are slightly better than those of [LS93] in the first regime. As in [LS93], all messages sent in our algorithm consist of $O(1)$ words. Note, however, that even for the LOCAL model, our result improves the previous state-of-the-art running time $O(\log^4 n)$ of [ABCP96] to $O(\log^2 n)$.

The main technique that made our result possible is the "shifted shortest path approach", due to Blelloch *et. al.* [BGK+14], and Miller *et. al.* [MPX13]. These authors developed this approach for computing padded partitions in the PRAM model. Specifically, Miller *et. al.* [MPX13] devised a PRAM algorithm for computing a *strong padded partition*, i.e., a partition with strong diameter at most $O(\log n)/\beta$, for a parameter $\beta \leq 1/2$, and such that the fraction of edges that cross between different clusters of the partition is at most β.

It is known that padded partitions are related to network decompositions. This relationship was exploited by Bartal [Bar96], who showed that the approach of Linial and Saks [LS93] for constructing network decompositions can be used to build padded partitions. In this work we exploit this relationship in the opposite direction, and show that Miller's *et. al.* [MPX13] approach for constructing padded partitions can be used for building network decompositions. Our algorithm is similar in spirit to the algorithm of [LS93], in which every vertex v samples a radius r_v from a geometric (or exponential, in our case) distribution, and broadcasts this to its r_v-neighborhood. The main difference is in determining the clusters: While in [LS93] a vertex x decides to join a cluster centered at v if v has the minimal ID among broadcasts that reached x, and furthermore r_v is strictly larger than the distance $d(x,v)$ (this is the distance in the current graph). In our algorithm, we do not use IDs, we let x compare the shifted random variables $r_v - d(x,v)$ for all vertices v whose broadcast reached it, and decide according to the difference between the largest and the second largest values. This idea is inspired by [MPX13], who use a similar comparison in the *analysis* of their algorithm for padded partitions. However, the fact that this algorithm yields a strong diameter is somewhat more involved in our setting.

1.3 Related Work

Barenboim *et. al.* [BEG15] devised a randomized constant time algorithm for constructing strong $(O(1), n^{\epsilon})$ network decompositions, for an arbitrarily small constant $\epsilon > 0$. Kutten *et. al.* [KNPR14] extended the algorithm of Linial and Saks [LS93] for constructing network decompositions to hypergraphs. A long line of research developed network decompositions for graphs of bounded growth, see, e.g., [GV07, KMW05, SW08]. Miller *et. al.* [MPVX15] built upon the ideas of [MPX13] to devise efficient parallel algorithms for constructing spanners and hopsets.

2. DISTRIBUTED ALGORITHM FOR STRONG DIAMETER NETWORK DECOMPOSITION

Here we prove our main result. For a more accessible presentation, we first show a simpler version, and improve the number of colors in Section 2.1.

THEOREM 1. *For any unweighted graph $G = (V,E)$ on n vertices, and parameters $1 \le k \le \ln n$, $3 < c$, our randomized distributed algorithm computes, with probability at least $1-3/c$, a strong $(2k-2, (cn)^{1/k}\cdot\ln(cn))$ network decomposition of G. The number of rounds required is $k(cn)^{1/k}\cdot\ln(cn)$, and each message consists of $O(1)$ words.*

Note that taking $c = 2^k$ does not affect the number of blocks and rounds by more than a constant factor. Following [LS93], we form the partition by carving blocks. A *block* $W \subseteq V$ is a set of vertices, and the connected components of $G(W)$ are clusters. Clearly, these clusters form an independent set in $\mathcal{G}(\mathcal{P})$, and thus can be colored with a single color. So the chromatic number of $\mathcal{G}(\mathcal{P})$ is bounded by the number of blocks our algorithm generates.

Construction.

The algorithm is a subtle modification of the [LS93] algorithm, inspired by the recent methods of [MPX13]. Let $\beta = \ln(cn)/k$. The algorithm consists of phases $t = 1, 2, \ldots, \lambda$, for $\lambda = (cn)^{1/k}\cdot\ln(cn)$. Let $G_1 = G$. In each phase t we carve a block W_t out of the current graph G_t, and let $G_{t+1} = G_t \setminus W_t$.

To implement the t-th phase, every vertex $v \in V(G_t)$ chooses independently in parallel a value $r_v^{(t)}$ (we shall omit the superscript whenever it is clear from context), by sampling from the exponential distribution with parameter β, denoted $\mathcal{EXP}(\beta)$, which has density

$$f(x) = \begin{cases} \beta\cdot e^{-\beta x} & x \ge 0 \\ 0 & \text{otherwise.} \end{cases}$$

For $v \in V$, let $\mathcal{E}_v$ be the event that at some phase t, $r_v^{(t)} \ge k+1$. We will later prove the following lemma.

LEMMA 1. *With probability at least $1 - 2/c$, none of the events $\mathcal{E}_v$ hold.*

Every vertex v will broadcast the value r_v to every vertex of G_t within distance $R_v := \lfloor r_v \rfloor$ from it. Note that assuming Lemma 1, $R_v \le k$. Each vertex y in G_t records the values of r_v for vertices v whose broadcast reached y, and also the distances in G_t to these vertices. Then y orders these vertices $v_1, \ldots, v_s$ in non-increasing order according to $m_i = r_{v_i} - d_{G_t}(y, v_i)$. We declare that y is added to W_t iff $m_1 - m_2 > 1$. Observe that all m_i are nonnegative, since y will hear the broadcast of v_i only if $d_{G_t}(y, v_i) \le R_{v_i}$, the latter is at most r_{v_i}. If $s = 1$, i.e. there is no second broadcast that reached y, define $m_2 = 0$ (observe m_1 is well defined as y also broadcasts). If indeed y joins W_t, then we say that y *chose* the center v_1.

We begin by analyzing the strong diameter of the blocks.

OBSERVATION 2. *If y chose v_1 as a center at phase t, then $d_{G_t}(v_1, y) < r_{v_1} - 1$.*

PROOF. If $d_{G_t}(v_1, y) \ge r_{v_1} - 1$, then $m_1 \le 1$, which implies that $m_1 - m_2 \le 1$, contradicting the fact that y is added to W_t. □

CLAIM 3. *If a vertex $y \in V(G_t)$ chose v at phase t, then every vertex x on a shortest path from v to y in G_t must have chosen v at phase t as well.*

PROOF. Since $d_{G_t}(v,x) \le d_{G_t}(v,y)$, the broadcast of v at phase t must have reached x as well, so x records the value $m = r_v - d_{G_t}(x,v)$. Seeking contradiction, assume x did not choose v, then there exists v' for which x records the value $m' = r_{v'} - d_{G_t}(x,v')$ with $m' \ge m - 1$ (if there is no such v', then x would have joined W_t with v as center). In particular,

$$d_{G_t}(x, v') \le r_{v'} - r_v + d_{G_t}(x,v) + 1 \ . \tag{1}$$

It follows that

$$\begin{aligned} d_{G_t}(y,v') &\le d_{G_t}(y,x) + d_{G_t}(x,v') \\ &\overset{(1)}{\le} d_{G_t}(y,x) + r_{v'} - r_v + d_{G_t}(x,v) + 1 \\ &= (d_{G_t}(y,v) - r_v + 1) + r_{v'} \qquad (2) \\ &< r_{v'} \qquad (3) \end{aligned}$$

where the last inequality uses Observation 2. Thus $d_{G_t}(y,v') \le R_{v'}$, so the broadcast of v' will reach y, and y will record a corresponding value of

$$r_{v'} - d_{G_t}(y,v') \overset{(2)}{\ge} r_v - d_{G_t}(y,v) - 1 \ ,$$

that is, it is within 1 of the value y stored for v, which contradicts the fact that y chose v. □

LEMMA 4. *For every $1 \le t \le \lambda$, the block W_t has strong diameter at most $2k-2$.*

PROOF. Fix any cluster C which is a connected component of $G(W_t)$. We first argue that if all vertices in C chose the same center v, then its strong diameter is at most $2k-2$. To see this, note that by Observation 2 all vertices $y \in C$ are within $r_v - 1$ distance from v, since the graph is unweighted, this is at most $R_v - 1 \le k - 1$ (assuming the event of Lemma 1 holds). By Claim 3, every vertex on a shortest path from v to y (in G_t) is also included in C, so the strong diameter is at most $2k-2$.

Consider now the case that there are two vertices $y, z \in C$ that chose different centers v, u. We will show that this assumption must lead to a contradiction. Note we may assume that y, z are adjacent, since for any two non-adjacent y', z' who chose different centers, we can simply walk on the path in C (which is connected) from y' to z' until we find adjacent vertices with a center change occurring. W.l.o.g assume y is the vertex which recorded the larger value, that is,

$$r_v - d_{G_t}(y,v) \geq r_u - d_{G_t}(z,u) \ . \tag{4}$$

By the triangle inequality and Observation 2 we see that $d_{G_t}(z,v) \leq d_{G_t}(y,v)+1 < r_v$, which implies $d_{G_t}(z,v) \leq R_v$, so that the broadcast of v will reach z. The value z obtains from v is

$$r_v - d_{G_t}(z,v) \geq r_v - (d_{G_t}(y,v)+1) \overset{(4)}{\geq} r_u - d_{G_t}(z,u) - 1 \ ,$$

which contradicts the assumption that z chose u. □

We next show that λ phases suffice to exhaust the graph, which gives this bound on the number of blocks. To this end, we use the following result from [MPX13, Lemma 4.4] on the order statistics of shifted exponential random variables.

LEMMA 5 ([MPX13]). *Let $d_1 \leq \ldots \leq d_q$ be arbitrary values and let $\delta_1, \ldots, \delta_q$ be independent random variables picked from $\mathcal{EXP}(\beta)$. Then the probability that the largest and the second largest values of $\delta_j - d_j$ are within 1 of each other is at most $1-e^{-\beta}$.* [1]

We use this result to prove the following:

CLAIM 6. *For any $y \in V$, and $1 \leq t' \leq \lambda$,*

$$\Pr[y \in G_{t'+1}] \leq (1-(cn)^{-1/k})^{t'} \ .$$

PROOF. Fix any $1 \leq t \leq t'$, and any possible graph G_t such that $y \in V(G_t)$. Let $v_1, \ldots, v_q$ be the vertices of G_t that are in the same connected component of G_t with y. Let $d_j = d_{G_t}(v_j, y)$, and $\delta_j = r_{v_j}$ (where each r_{v_j} is sampled independently from $\mathcal{EXP}(\beta)$). Recall that $y \in W_t$ iff the maximum value among $\delta_j - d_j$ is larger than the second largest by more than 1 (additively). Applying Lemma 5, we conclude that the probability a vertex $y \in V(G_t)$ joins W_t is at least $e^{-\beta} = (cn)^{-1/k}$ (this holds even in the event that no other broadcast reached y, by definition of $\mathcal{EXP}(\beta)$). Since this bound holds regardless of the outcome of previous phases,

$$\begin{aligned}\Pr[y \in G_{t'+1}] &= \Pr\left[\bigcap_{t=1}^{t'} \{y \notin W_t\}\right] \\ &= \prod_{t=1}^{t'} \Pr[y \notin W_t \mid y \notin W_1, \ldots, y \notin W_{t-1}] \\ &\leq (1-(cn)^{-1/k})^{t'}\end{aligned}$$

□

COROLLARY 7. *With probability at least $1-1/c$, $G_{\lambda+1}$ is empty.*

[1] We state here a special case of their result. The assertion in [MPX13] gives the bound $O(\beta)$, but their proof in fact yields the stronger bound given here.

PROOF. Using Claim 6 with $t' = \lambda = (cn)^{1/k} \cdot \ln(cn)$, we see that the probability a vertex y did not join any block is at most $(1-(cn)^{-1/k})^{\lambda} \leq 1/(cn)$. Applying the union bound on the n vertices, we get that with probability $1-1/c$, within λ phases the graph is indeed exhausted. □

We are now ready to prove Lemma 1.

PROOF OF LEMMA 1. Fix any $v \in V$. Since each r_v is sampled independently from $\mathcal{EXP}(\beta)$, we have for any $1 \leq t \leq \lambda$, $\Pr[r_v^{(t)} \geq k+1] = e^{-\beta(k+1)}$. By using Claim 6 with $t' = i \cdot (cn)^{1/k}$ (for some $0 \leq i \leq \ln(cn)$), we obtain $\Pr[v \in G_{t'+1}] \leq e^{-i}$. Now,

$$\begin{aligned}&\Pr[\mathcal{E}_v] \\ &\leq \sum_{t=1}^{\lambda} \Pr[r_v^{(t)} \geq k+1 \mid v \in G_t] \cdot \Pr[v \in G_t] \\ &\leq \sum_{i=0}^{\ln(cn)} \sum_{t=1}^{(cn)^{1/k}} \Pr[r_v^{(i\cdot(cn)^{1/k}+t)} \geq k+1 \mid v \in G_{i\cdot(cn)^{1/k}+t}] \\ &\qquad \cdot \Pr[v \in G_{i\cdot(cn)^{1/k}+1}] \\ &\leq \sum_{i=0}^{\ln(cn)} e^{-i} \cdot \sum_{t=1}^{(cn)^{1/k}} e^{-\beta(k+1)} \\ &= \sum_{i=0}^{\ln(cn)} e^{-i} \cdot (cn)^{1/k} \cdot (cn)^{-1-1/k} \\ &\leq 2/(cn) \ .\end{aligned}$$

The lemma follows from a union bound over the n vertices. □

We conclude by analyzing the running time and messages size. Note that there are $\lambda = (cn)^{1/k} \cdot \ln(cn)$ phases, and each phase requires k rounds (assuming Lemma 1), so the total number of rounds is as promised. We claim that our algorithm can in fact be implemented efficiently also in the CONGEST model, where messages must be of size at most $O(\log n)$ bits. This follows since at every round, every vertex can sort the values m_i it has so far, and send to its neighbors only the top two from its list. This is because the values $\lfloor m_i \rfloor$ determine the remaining range the message of v_i needs to be forwarded to, and clustering decisions are based only on the largest two values, so the third and onward values in v's list will not be used by any other vertex.

2.1 Improved Number of Blocks

Here we show how to improve the bound on the number of colors to $O(k \cdot n^{1/k})$, and prove the following.

THEOREM 2. *For any unweighted graph $G = (V,E)$ on n vertices, and parameters $1 \leq k \leq \ln n$, $5 < c$, a variant of our randomized distributed algorithm computes, with probability at least $1-5/c$, a strong $(2k-2, 4k(cn)^{1/k})$ network decomposition of G. The number of rounds required is $O(k^2(cn)^{1/k})$, and each message consists of $O(1)$ words.*

The main difference from the previous construction is that the parameter β of the exponential distribution will change at certain points. There will be $\ln n$ stages, each stage consists of a certain number of phases in which we use the same value of β. The first stage lasts $s_0 = 2(cn)^{1/k}$ phases in which we use $\beta_0 = \ln(cn)/k$. The next stage lasts $s_1 =$

$2(cn/e)^{1/k}$ phases, in which we use $\beta_1 = \ln(cn/e)/k$. In general, the i-th stage lasts $s_i = 2(cn/e^i)^{1/k}$ phases, and we use $\beta_i = \ln(cn/e^i)/k$ in these phases. For $0 \le i \le \ln n$, denote by J_i the set of phases in the i-th stage, that is, $J_i = \{\sum_{j=0}^{i-1}(s_j) + 1, \ldots, \sum_{j=0}^{i} s_j\}$.

The total number of phases, which bounds the number of colors needed, is thus

$$\sum_{i=0}^{\ln n} s_i = 2\sum_{i=0}^{\ln n}(cn/e^i)^{1/k} \le 2(cn)^{1/k}\sum_{i=0}^{\infty} e^{-i/k} \le 4k(cn)^{1/k} .$$

The strong diameter bound of Lemma 4 holds regardless of which β we use, as long as an analogue of Lemma 1 holds. Decreasing the parameter β of the exponential distribution increases the probability that a vertex joins a block (so we need less blocks). However, the radius of blocks tend to increase as β gets smaller. The following claim implies that the graph is exhausted with high probability.

CLAIM 8. *For any vertex $y \in V$, $0 \le i \le \ln n$, and $t \in J_i$,*

$$\Pr[y \in G_t] \le e^{-2i} . \tag{5}$$

PROOF. In order to be included in G_t, y must not be selected to a block in any phase of any of the stages $0, 1, \ldots, i-1$. By Lemma 5, the probability that y did not join a block in a certain phase of stage j is at most $(1 - e^{-\beta_j})$ (even conditioning on anything that happened in previous phases), thus the probability it survived until stage i is at most

$$\begin{aligned}\prod_{j=0}^{i-1}(1-e^{-\beta_j})^{s_j} &= \prod_{j=0}^{i-1}\left(1-\left(\frac{cn}{e^j}\right)^{-1/k}\right)^{2(cn/e^j)^{1/k}} \\ &\le \prod_{j=0}^{i-1} e^{-2} = e^{-2i} .\end{aligned}$$

□

The claim implies (by the union bound), that with probability at least $1 - 1/n$, there are no remaining vertices after stage $\ln n$. It remains to prove an analogue of Lemma 1, and argue that with probability at least $1 - 4/c$, none of the events $\mathcal{E}_v$ took place. We calculate,

$$\begin{aligned}\Pr[\mathcal{E}_v] &\le \sum_{i=0}^{\ln n}\sum_{t\in J_i}\Pr[r_v^{(t)} \ge k+1 \mid v \in G_t]\cdot\Pr[v \in G_t] \\ &\le \sum_{i=0}^{\ln n}\sum_{t\in J_i} e^{-\beta_i(k+1)}\cdot e^{-2i} \\ &= \sum_{i=0}^{\ln n} 2\left(\frac{cn}{e^i}\right)^{1/k}\cdot\left(\frac{e^i}{cn}\right)^{1+1/k}\cdot e^{-2i} \\ &= \frac{1}{n}\sum_{i=0}^{\ln n}\frac{2}{c\cdot e^i} \\ &\le \frac{4}{cn} .\end{aligned}$$

So by the union bound, with probability at least $1 - 4/c$, none of events $\mathcal{E}_v$ occurred, as desired.

2.2 High Radius Regime

Note that in Theorem 1 and Theorem 2 the number of blocks is $\Omega(\log n)$ for any choice of k. In the regime that k, the parameter governing the radius, is larger than $\ln n$, we can get fewer than $\ln n$ blocks. Concretely, by Claim 6 we have that the probability that a vertex y is not in any of the first λ blocks is at most $(1 - (cn)^{-1/k})^\lambda \le (\ln(cn)/k)^\lambda$ (here we use the estimate $1 - e^{-x} \le x$, which is useful when x is small). We would like this probability to be at most $1/cn$, so that the graph will be empty after λ phases with probability at least $1 - 1/c$. To this end, we need

$$\lambda = \frac{\ln(cn)}{\ln(k/\ln(cn))} .$$

In other words, if the number of blocks we want is λ, then we need to take $k = (cn)^{1/\lambda}\cdot\ln(cn)$, exactly the inverse tradeoff of Theorem 1.

THEOREM 3. *For any unweighted graph $G = (V, E)$ on n vertices, and parameters $1 \le \lambda \le \ln n$, $c > 3$, our randomized distributed algorithm computes, with probability at least $1-3/c$, a strong $(2(cn)^{1/\lambda}\cdot\ln(cn), \lambda)$ network decomposition of G. The number of rounds required is $\lambda(cn)^{1/\lambda}\cdot\ln(cn)$, and each message consists of $O(1)$ words.*

3. ACKNOWLEDGEMENT

We are grateful to Nati Linial for discussions that initiated this work. We would also like to thank an anonymous reviewer of PODC'16 and Mohsen Ghaffari for pointing out to us the result of [ABCP96]. We are particularly grateful to Mohsen for explaining us the algorithm and the proof of [ABCP96].

4. REFERENCES

[ABCP94] Baruch Awerbuch, Bonnie Berger, Lenore Cowen, and David Peleg. Low-diameter graph decomposition is in NC. *Random Struct. Algorithms*, 5(3):441–452, 1994.

[ABCP96] Baruch Awerbuch, Bonnie Berger, Lenore Cowen, and David Peleg. Fast distributed network decompositions and covers. *J. Parallel Distrib. Comput.*, 39(2):105–114, 1996.

[AGLP89] Baruch Awerbuch, Andrew V. Goldberg, Michael Luby, and Serge A. Plotkin. Network decomposition and locality in distributed computation. In *30th Annual Symposium on Foundations of Computer Science, Research Triangle Park, North Carolina, USA, 30 October - 1 November 1989*, pages 364–369, 1989.

[AP92] B. Awerbuch and D. Peleg. Routing with polynomial communication-space tradeoff. *SIAM J. Discrete Mathematics*, 5:151–162, 1992.

[APPS92] Baruch Awerbuch, Boaz Patt-Shamir, David Peleg, and Michael E. Saks. Adapting to asynchronous dynamic networks (extended abstract). In *Proceedings of the 24th Annual ACM Symposium on Theory of Computing, May 4-6, 1992, Victoria, British Columbia, Canada*, pages 557–570, 1992.

[Awe85] B. Awerbuch. Complexity of network synchronization. *J. ACM*, 4:804–823, 1985.

[Bar96] Yair Bartal. Probabilistic approximations of metric spaces and its algorithmic applications. In *FOCS*, pages 184–193, 1996.

[Bar12] Leonid Barenboim. On the locality of some NP-complete problems. In *Automata, Languages, and Programming - 39th International Colloquium, ICALP 2012, Warwick, UK, July 9-13, 2012, Proceedings, Part II*, pages 403–415, 2012.

[BDR+12] Costas Busch, Chinmoy Dutta, Jaikumar Radhakrishnan, Rajmohan Rajaraman, and Srinivasagopalan Srivathsan. Split and join: Strong partitions and universal steiner trees for graphs. In *53rd Annual IEEE Symposium on Foundations of Computer Science, FOCS 2012, New Brunswick, NJ, USA, October 20-23, 2012*, pages 81–90, 2012.

[BEG15] Leonid Barenboim, Michael Elkin, and Cyril Gavoille. A fast network-decomposition algorithm and its applications to constant-time distributed computation - (extended abstract). In *Structural Information and Communication Complexity - 22nd International Colloquium, SIROCCO 2015, Montserrat, Spain, July 14-16, 2015, Post-Proceedings*, pages 209–223, 2015.

[BGK+14] Guy E. Blelloch, Anupam Gupta, Ioannis Koutis, Gary L. Miller, Richard Peng, and Kanat Tangwongsan. Nearly-linear work parallel SDD solvers, low-diameter decomposition, and low-stretch subgraphs. *Theor. Comp. Sys.*, 55(3):521–554, October 2014.

[DMP+05] Devdatt P. Dubhashi, Alessandro Mei, Alessandro Panconesi, Jaikumar Radhakrishnan, and Aravind Srinivasan. Fast distributed algorithms for (weakly) connected dominating sets and linear-size skeletons. *J. Comput. Syst. Sci.*, 71(4):467–479, 2005.

[GV07] Beat Gfeller and Elias Vicari. A randomized distributed algorithm for the maximal independent set problem in growth-bounded graphs. In *Proceedings of the Twenty-Sixth Annual ACM Symposium on Principles of Distributed Computing, PODC 2007, Portland, Oregon, USA, August 12-15, 2007*, pages 53–60, 2007.

[KMW05] Fabian Kuhn, Thomas Moscibroda, and Roger Wattenhofer. On the locality of bounded growth. In *Proceedings of the Twenty-Fourth Annual ACM Symposium on Principles of Distributed Computing, PODC 2005, Las Vegas, NV, USA, July 17-20, 2005*, pages 60–68, 2005.

[KNPR14] Shay Kutten, Danupon Nanongkai, Gopal Pandurangan, and Peter Robinson. Distributed symmetry breaking in hypergraphs. In *Distributed Computing - 28th International Symposium, DISC 2014, Austin, TX, USA, October 12-15, 2014. Proceedings*, pages 469–483, 2014.

[LS93] N. Linial and M. Saks. Decomposing graphs into regions of small diameter. *Combinatorica*, 13:441–454, 1993.

[MPVX15] Gary L. Miller, Richard Peng, Adrian Vladu, and Shen Chen Xu. Improved parallel algorithms for spanners and hopsets. In *Proceedings of the 27th ACM on Symposium on Parallelism in Algorithms and Architectures, SPAA 2015, Portland, OR, USA, June 13-15, 2015*, pages 192–201, 2015.

[MPX13] Gary L. Miller, Richard Peng, and Shen Chen Xu. Parallel graph decompositions using random shifts. In *25th ACM Symposium on Parallelism in Algorithms and Architectures, SPAA '13, Montreal, QC, Canada - July 23 - 25, 2013*, pages 196–203, 2013.

[PS92] Alessandro Panconesi and Aravind Srinivasan. Improved distributed algorithms for coloring and network decomposition problems. In *Proceedings of the 24th Annual ACM Symposium on Theory of Computing, May 4-6, 1992, Victoria, British Columbia, Canada*, pages 581–592, 1992.

[SW08] Johannes Schneider and Roger Wattenhofer. A log-star distributed maximal independent set algorithm for growth-bounded graphs. In *Proceedings of the Twenty-Seventh Annual ACM Symposium on Principles of Distributed Computing, PODC 2008, Toronto, Canada, August 18-21, 2008*, pages 35–44, 2008.

Optimal Dynamic Distributed MIS

Keren Censor-Hillel*
Department of Computer Science, Technion
ckeren@cs.technion.ac.il

Elad Haramaty†
College of Computer and Information Science, Northeastern University
eladh@cs.technion.ac.il

Zohar Karnin
Yahoo Labs
zkarnin@ymail.com

ABSTRACT

Finding a maximal independent set (MIS) in a graph is a cornerstone task in distributed computing. The local nature of an MIS allows for fast solutions in a static distributed setting, which are logarithmic in the number of nodes or in their degrees. The result trivially applies for the dynamic distributed model, in which edges or nodes may be inserted or deleted. In this paper, we take a different approach which exploits locality to the extreme, and show how to update an MIS in a dynamic distributed setting, either *synchronous* or *asynchronous*, with only *a single adjustment* and in a single round, in expectation. These strong guarantees hold for the *complete fully dynamic* setting: Insertions and deletions, of edges as well as nodes, gracefully and abruptly. This strongly separates the static and dynamic distributed models, as super-constant lower bounds exist for computing an MIS in the former.

Our results are obtained by a novel analysis of the surprisingly simple solution of carefully simulating the greedy *sequential* MIS algorithm with a random ordering of the nodes. As such, our algorithm has a direct application as a 3-approximation algorithm for correlation clustering. This adds to the important toolbox of distributed graph decompositions, which are widely used as crucial building blocks in distributed computing.

Finally, our algorithm enjoys a useful *history-independence* property, meaning the output is independent of the history of topology changes that constructed that graph. This means the output cannot be chosen, or even biased, by the adversary in case its goal is to prevent us from optimizing some objective function.

1. INTRODUCTION

Dynamic environments are very common in distributed settings, where nodes may occasionally join and leave the network, and communication links may fail and be restored. This makes solving tasks in a dynamic distributed setting of fundamental interest.

Solutions for problems from the static distributed setting translate nicely into the dynamic distributed setting, by running them in response to topology changes, in order to adjust the output [6,7,46]. This can be quite efficient especially for *local* problems, such as finding a maximal independent set (MIS) in the network graph. The cornerstone MIS problem admits fast distributed solutions whose complexities are logarithmic in the size of the graph or in the degrees of the nodes [2,28,36,49].

In this paper, we exploit locality to the extreme and present an MIS algorithm for the dynamic distributed setting, which surprisingly requires in expectation only *a single adjustment* and a single round. The adjustment measure of an algorithm is the number of nodes that need to change their output in response to the topology change. These strong guarantees hold for both *synchronous* or *asynchronous* models, and for the *complete fully dynamic* setting, i.e., we handle all cases of *insertions* and *deletions*, of *edges* as well as *nodes*, *gracefully* and *abruptly*.[1] This is a strong separation between the static model and dynamic distributed model under an oblivious adversary, as super-constant lower bounds exist for the static setting [43,48]. We further prove that for any deterministic algorithm, there is a topology change that requires n adjustments in the worst case, with n being the number of nodes, thus we also strongly separate randomized and deterministic solutions. Below, we overview the challenge we face, our technique for overcoming it, and the applications of our result.

1.1 Is This Not Trivial?

Indeed, the local structure of an MIS allows the nodes to easily detect whether it has suffered from a topology change. At a first glance, it may seem trivial to fix an MIS after a single topology change, as described next[2].

Suppose a new node is inserted into the graph. The node simply has to check whether it is connected to any MIS node and enter the MIS if and only if the answer is no. In particular, no other node needs to change its output. Similarly, it is an easy exercise to check that if an edge $\{u, v\}$ is deleted, at most one node needs to change its output.

Despite being simple, these two examples are misleading as they do not capture what happens in case of other topol-

*Supported in part by ISF grant 1696/14.
†Supported in part by NSF grant CCF-1319206. Part of this work was done while the author was at Yahoo Labs.

PODC'16, July 25-28, 2016, Chicago, IL, USA
© 2016 ACM. ISBN 978-1-4503-3964-3/16/07...$15.00
DOI: http://dx.doi.org/10.1145/2933057.2933083

[1]See definitions of topology changes in Section 2.
[2]The cautious reader should remain suspicious.

ogy changes. Suppose an MIS node v is deleted from the graph. All of the nodes who were previously neighbors of v, i.e., who were in $N(v)$, now need to check whether they still have MIS neighbors. This can be a large number of nodes who may need to change their output. This alone is still not a problem from the communication perspective, since no other node needs to change its output, and the nodes who were in $N(v)$ detect this immediately along with detecting the topology change. However, the crucial difficulty here is that these nodes need to coordinate their decisions. If two nodes in $N(v)$ are connected by an edge, then only one of them can enter the MIS. In general, the induced subgraph $N(v) \setminus \{v\}$ can have any structure, and deciding which nodes enter the MIS (among those who now do not have a neighbor in the MIS) is equivalent to *constructing* an MIS on the induced subgraph $N(v) \setminus \{v\}$ from scratch. As this graph can be linear in the size of the original graph, this would lead to fixing the MIS being asymptotically as expensive as structuring it from scratch.

1.2 Our Contribution

Our approach is surprisingly simple: We simulate the greedy *sequential* algorithm for solving MIS. The greedy sequential algorithm orders the nodes and then inspects them by increasing order. A node is added to the MIS if and only if it does not have a lower-order neighbor already in the MIS. We consider *random greedy*, the variant of greedy in which the order is chosen uniformly at random. Consider simulating random greedy in a dynamic environment with the following template (ignoring the model of computation/communication for the moment). Each node needs to maintain the invariant that its state depends only on the states of its neighbors with lower order, such that it is in the MIS if and only if none of its lower order neighbors are in the MIS. When a change occurs in the graph, nodes may need to change their output, perhaps more than once, until they form a new MIS. Our key technical contribution is in proving:

Theorem 1 For any *arbitrary* change in the graph, the expectation over all random orders, of the number of nodes that change their output in the above random greedy template is at most 1.

The Challenge: We denote by π the random order of nodes, we denote by v^* the only node (if any) for which the above invariant does not hold after the topology change, and we denote by S the set of nodes that need to be changed in order for the invariant to hold again at all nodes. We look at S', the set of nodes that would have needed to be changed if the order was as in π, except for pushing v^* to be the first node in that order. The definition of S' does not depend on the real order of v^* in π. Therefore, we can prove that S can either be equal to S' if the order of v^* in π is minimal in S', and empty otherwise. Now the question is, what is the probability, given S', that v^* is indeed its minimal order node? The answer is that if S' were deterministic, i.e. independent of π, the probability would be $1/|S'|$. However, S' is a random set and having knowledge of its members restricts π to be non-uniform, which in turn requires a careful analysis of the required probability. To overcome this issue, we prove that the information that S' gives about π is either about the order between nodes not in S', or about the order within $S' \setminus \{v^*\}$, which both do not affect the probability that v^* is the minimal in S'.

Distributed Implementation: This powerful statement of $\mathbb{E}[|S|] \leq 1$ directly implies that a *single* adjustment is sufficient for maintaining an MIS in a dynamic setting. A direct distributed implementation of our template implies that in expectation also a single round is sufficient. This applies both to the synchronous and asynchronous models, where the number of rounds in the asynchronous model is defined as the longest path of communication.

Obtaining $O(1)$ Broadcasts and Bits: In fact, in the synchronous model, it is possible to obtain an expected number of $O(1)$ *broadcasts* and *bits*. Here the number of broadcasts is the total number of times, over all nodes, that any node sends a $O(\log n)$-bit broadcast message (to all of its neighbors)[3]. Moreover, since we only need a node to know the order between itself and its neighbors, using a similar technique to that of [51], we obtain that in expectation, a node only needs to send a constant number of bits in each broadcast. The above holds for edge insertions and deletions, graceful node deletion, and node *unmuting* (which is defined formally in Section 2), while for an abrupt deletion of a node v^* we will need $O(\min\{\log(n), d(v^*)\})$ broadcasts, and for an insertion of a node v^* we will need $O(d(v^*))$ broadcasts, in expectation.

This is done with a careful dynamic distributed implementation (Section 4) which guarantees that each node that changes its output does so at most $O(1)$ times, as opposed to the direct distributed implementation [4]. Hence, obtaining these broadcast and bit complexities comes at a cost of increasing the round complexity, but it remains constant (albeit not 1).

Matching Lower Bounds: We claim that any deterministic algorithm requires n adjustments in the worst case, which can be seen through the following example. Let A be a dynamic deterministic MIS algorithm. Let G_0 be the complete bipartite graph over two sets of nodes of size k. We denote by L the side of G_0 that is chosen to be the MIS by A, and we denote the other side by R. For every $i \in [k]$ let G_i be the graph obtained after deleting i nodes from L, and consider executing A on $G_0, G_1, ..., G_k$. For every i, since G_i is a complete bipartite graph, one of the sides has to be the MIS. Since G_k contains only disconnected nodes of R then R is the only MIS of G_k. This implies that after some specific change along the sequence, the side of the MIS changes from L to R. In this topology change, *all* of the nodes change their output.

This gives a strong separation between our result and deterministic algorithms. Moreover, it shows that (1) the expected adjustment complexity of any algorithm must be at least 1, as we have a sequence of k topology changes that lead to at least k adjustments, and (2) it is impossible to achieve high probability bounds that improve upon a simple Markov bound. Specifically, this explains why we obtain our result in expectation, rather than with high probability.

[3]We emphasize that the term broadcast is used here to indicate the more restricted setting of not being able to send different messages to different neighbors in the same round. It does not refer to a wireless setting of communication.

[4]This bears some similarity to the method in [60], where the number of *moves* is reduced in an MIS self-stabilizing algorithm by adding a possible *wait* state to the standard *in MIS* and *not in MIS* states.

This is because the example can be inserted into any larger graph on n nodes, showing that *for every* value of k, there exists an instance for which at least $\Omega(k)$ adjustments are needed with probability at least $1/k$.

Approximate Correlation Clustering: In addition to the optimal complexity guarantees, the fact that our algorithm simulates the random greedy sequential algorithm has a significant application to correlation clustering. Correlation clustering requires the nodes to be partitioned into clusters in a way that minimizes the sum of the number of edges outside clusters and the number of non neighboring pairs of nodes within clusters (that is, missing edges within clusters). Ailon et al. [1] show that random greedy obtains a 3-approximation for correlation clustering[5], by having each MIS node inducing a cluster, and each node not in the MIS belonging to the cluster induced by the smallest random ID among its MIS neighbors. This directly translates to our model, by having the nodes know that random ID of their neighbors. Graph decompositions play a vital role in distributed computing (see, e.g., [54]), and hence the importance of obtaining a 3-approximation for correlation clustering.

History Independence: Finally, our algorithm has a useful property, which we call *history independence* (in full version [16]) , which means that the structure output by the algorithm (e.g., the MIS) depends only on the current graph, and does not depend on the history of topology changes. This means that the output cannot be chosen, or even biased, by the adversary, in case its goal is to prevent us from optimizing some objective function. Moreover, history independent algorithms compose nicely, which allows us to obtain history independent coloring and matching algorithms, using standard reductions.

1.3 Previous Work

A strongly related previous work is that of König and Wattenhofer [39], where they also show that the above can be obtained in a single round. However, their setting differs crucially from ours, by two major aspects. In their solution, an MIS node that needs to be removed from the MIS (following a topology change) already has a "last will" for it in the local states of its neighbors, which tells each of them whether it should enter the MIS or not. This constitutes the first huge difference: our algorithm updates only a *single state* in expectation. But even more critical is that in order to compute this last will, each node must be aware of the edges between its neighbors. This is an enormous amount of information, which can be quadratic in the size of the network, and is therefore ruled out in our setting as an unacceptable amount of information to be sent in a single round. Our algorithms send only a constant number of bits in each message.

In fact, [39] argues that without a "last will" it is impossible to fix an MIS in constant time. This because a node v that is in the MIS can be deleted, and its neighborhood $N(v)$ can be arbitrarily connected, which reduces the problem of fixing the solution to that of finding an MIS in $N(v)$. Since $N(v)$ can have linear size, and since lower bounds on finding an MIS are super-constant [43,48], this implies that some mechanism is required in order to be able to fix an MIS in a constant number of rounds.

However, notice that the above argument only holds under the implicit assumption that the MIS and the topology change can be arbitrary, i.e., controlled by an adaptive adversary. Our contribution is exactly in making sure that such a bad example does not occur. For this, we make the standard assumption of an *oblivious* non-adaptive adversary. This means that the topology changes do not depend on the randomness of the algorithm. This is the standard assumption in dynamic settings (see literature about sequential dynamic computing, e.g., [18] and references therein), where typically an adaptive adversary that can choose the topology changes based on the status of the data structure that the algorithm maintains is too strong and renders most problems unsolvable in any reasonable complexity measure. An oblivious adversary is natural also for our setting, as, for example, an adaptive adversary can always choose to delete MIS nodes and thereby force worst-case behavior in terms of the number of adjustments.

1.4 Additional Related Work

Distributed MIS: Finding an MIS is a central theme in the classical distributed setting. The classic algorithms [2,36,49] complete within $O(\log n)$ rounds, with high probability. More recently, a beautiful line of work reduced the round complexity to depend on Δ, the maximal degree in the graph. These include the $O(\Delta + \log^* n)$-round and $O(\log^2 \Delta + 2^{O(\sqrt{\log \log n})})$-round algorithms of [10], the $O(\log \Delta \sqrt{\log n})$-round algorithm of [11], and the very recent $O(\log \Delta) + 2^{O(\sqrt{\log \log n})}$-round algorithm of [28]. An excellent source for additional background and relations to coloring can be found in [9].[6]

Distributed dynamic MIS: The problem of finding a fast dynamic distributed MIS algorithm appears as an open problem in [24], which studies the problem of maintaining a sparse spanner a dynamic setting. Additional problems in a dynamic setting are also addressed in [12], and in slightly different settings in [5,17,37,41]. One standard approach for maintaining an MIS is running distributed algorithms that are designed for the static setting. This can be done for any distributed algorithm, sometimes using a corresponding *compiler*, e.g., when applied to an asynchronous dynamic setting [6,7,46].

One important exception is the aforementioned solution shown by König and Wattenhofer [39], which as in our algorithm, requires a constant number of rounds, but as opposed to our algorithm, has the following two very expensive properties: (1) the number of updates following a topology change can be linear in the number of nodes and (2) the size of messages can be almost quadratic in the number of nodes. The only way to overcome item (2) is to pay the cost of that information in terms of round complexity rather

[5]In the same paper, they also provide a 2.5 approximation based on rounding a solution of a linear program. We do not elaborate on the details of this algorithm, nor the history of the correlation clustering problem as it is outside the scope of our paper.

[6]As in all of these static MIS algorithms, we also do not maintain a Lexicographic MIS (LexMIS). One could argue that our algorithm maintains an MIS that corresponds to the random permutation over the nodes. This, however, by itself is not as powerful as maintaining a LexMIS with respect to any *given* order, say, of node IDs. In fact, any MIS can be seen as an MIS that is induced by *some* order of the nodes, so only an MIS corresponding to a specific given order should be considered as LexMIS.

than message complexity, a solution that is very expensive as well. We are unaware of any other work in this setting about maintaining an MIS.

Additional distributed dynamic algorithms: Indeed, because of its extreme importance, dynamic distributed computing is a widely studied area of research. However, different assumptions on the setting have a significant influence on what can be done.

A huge amount of literature is devoted to devising different algorithms in a self-stabilizing setting (see, e.g., [20, 21, 29, 57] and references therein). This setting is inherently different from ours since it is asynchronous, and considers the *time* that it takes an algorithm to stabilize as the number of asynchronous rounds until the set of outputs satisfies the problem specifications and all of the nodes are quiet (it is typically not possible to actually detect this state and terminate). An asynchronous round requires that each node communicates with all of its neighbors, and hence inherently implies a lot of communication (broadcasts). In our work, we do not assume that the topology ever stops changing, and just assume that enough time is given in order to recover from a change. This is why it is crucial to obtain an algorithm that requires only a constant (in fact, even a single) update and round in order to recover.

An MIS-based clustering algorithm for the asynchronous model that appeared in [23] also uses a random node order for recovering after a change. However, their self-stabilizing setting differs from ours in several aspects, such as assuming a bounded degree graph and discussing corrupted states of multiple nodes and topology changes. In addition, our techniques and analysis are completely different. In particular, the clustering obtained there may not be an approximation to correlation clustering. Furthermore, the number of rounds required by [23] is $O(\log(n))$ as opposed to our single round (in expectation) algorithm.

Related, but not identical, notions of error confinement, fault local and fault amendable algorithms have been studied in [8, 44, 45], where the internal memory of a node may change. Another property that self-stabilizing algorithms should aim for is super-stabilization [22], which means that they are self-stabilizing (eventually output the required structure) and also recover extremely fast from a single topology change. Super-stabilization requires also a small adjustment measure, which is the maximum number of nodes that have to change their output. Our MIS algorithm recovers from a single topology change in a constant number of rounds, and has an adjustment measure of exactly 1, in expectation.

Other studied models are of more severe graph changes, whether arbitrary [42] or evolving randomly [4]. In such models, one typically addresses problems of gathering information rather than maintaining graph structures, as the latter is intuitively unattainable. In contrast, in this paper, we consider a dynamic distributed setting which is in the same spirit of the literature on *sequential dynamic algorithms* [18].

Simulating the sequential greedy algorithm: Simulating random greedy has been used before in order to obtain fast solutions for sequential local computation algorithms (LCA). In this setting, the algorithm does not have access to the entire graph, but rather an oracle access using queries about nodes or edges, and needs to provide an approximate solution for various problems, among which are the problems considered in this paper. We emphasize that the models are inherently different, and hence is our technical analysis. While we bound the size of the set of nodes that may change their output after a topology change, studies in the local computation literature [3, 47, 50, 52, 61] bound the size of the set of nodes that need to be recursively queried in order to answer a *random* node query. In some sense, these sets are opposite: We begin with a single node v changing its state due to a topology change, and look at the set of nodes that change their state *due* to the change of v. Local computation algorithms begin with a single node v and look at the set of nodes whose states *determine* the state of v.

In [15], the DAG of *all* nodes is considered, according to the same random order we consider here. The paper analyzes its depth (rather than its size, which is n) and obtains a bound of $O(\log^2 n)$, w.h.p. This translates to a bound on the performance of the parallel random greedy algorithm for finding an MIS. It also implies that w.h.p., our algorithm finishes to update after at most $O(\log^2 n)$ steps.

2. DYNAMIC DISTRIBUTED COMPUTATIONS

The distributed setup is a standard message passing model. The network is modeled by an undirected graph $G = (V, E)$ where the node set is V, and E consists of the node pairs that have the ability to directly communicate. We assume a broadcast setting where a message sent by a node is heard by all of its neighbors. Also, we assume a synchronous communication model, where time is divided into rounds and in each round any willing node can broadcast a message to its neighbors. We restrict the size of each message to be $O(\log(n))$ bits, with $n = |V|$ being the size of the network[7]. The computational task is to maintain a graph structure, such as a maximal independent set (MIS) or a node clustering. That is, each node has an output, such that the set of outputs defines the required structure.

Our focus is on a dynamic network, where the graph changes over time. As a result, nodes may need to communicate in order to adjust their outputs. The system is *stable* is when the structure defined by the outputs satisfies the problem requirements.

A graph topology change can be with respect to either an edge or a node. In both cases we address both deletions and insertions, both of which are further split into two different types. For deletions we discuss both a *graceful deletion* and an *abrupt deletion*. In the former, the deleted node (edge) may be used for passing messages between its neighbors (endpoints), and retires completely only once the system is stable again. In the latter, the neighbors of the deleted node simply discover that the node (edge) has retired but it cannot be used for communication. For insertions, we distinguish between a *new node insertion* and an *unmuting* of a previously existing node. In the former, a new node is inserted to the graph, possibly with multiple edges. In the latter, a node that was previously invisible to its neighbors

[7]This is the standard assumption in a distributed setting. In our dynamic setting where the size of the graph may change we assume knowledge of some upper bound $N \geq n$, with $N = n^{O(1)}$, and restrict the message length to $O(\log(N)) = O(\log(n))$.

but heard their communication, becomes visible and enters the graph topology[8].

We assume that the system is always stable before a change occurs. Since our algorithm requires in expectation only an extremely short single time unit to recover, this even allows topology changes that are more frequent compared to other models. Specifically, many previous work in dynamic models, whether sequential [18] or distributed [30,32,40,53], assume that the topology does not change too fast, so that there is only a single topology change at a time with sufficient recovery time in between changes. Since our algorithm runs in expectation in a super-fast constant time which is completely independent on the size of the network, we can in fact tolerate more changes.

We consider the performance of an algorithm according to three complexity measures. The first is the *adjustment-complexity*, measuring the number of nodes that change their output as a result of the recent topology change. The second is the *round-complexity*, which is the number of rounds required for the system to become stable. Finally, the third, more harsh, score is the *broadcast-complexity*, measuring the total number of broadcasts.

Our algorithms are randomized and thus our results apply to the expected values of the above measures, where the expectation is taken over the randomness of the nodes. We emphasize that this is the only randomness discussed; specifically, the result is not for a random node in the graph nor a random sequence of changes, but rather applies to any node and any sequence of changes. It holds for *every* change in the graph, not only amortized over all changes.

In what follows we discuss the problem of computing an MIS. Here, the outputs of the nodes define a set M, where any two nodes in M are not connected by an edge, and any node not in M has a neighbor in M. The second problem we discuss is that of *correlation clustering*. Here, the objective is to find a partitioning $\mathcal{C}$ of the node set V, where we favor partitions with a small number of "contradicting edges". That is, we aim to minimize the sum $\sum_{C\in\mathcal{C}}\sum_{u,v\in C}\mathbb{1}_{[(u,v)\notin E]} + \sum_{C_1\neq C_2\in\mathcal{C}}\sum_{u\in C_1,v\in C_2}\mathbb{1}_{[(u,v)\in E]}$.

3. A TEMPLATE FOR MAINTAINING A MAXIMAL INDEPENDENT SET

In this section we describe a template for maintaining a maximal independent set (MIS). Initially, we are given a graph $G=(V,E)$ along with an MIS that satisfies certain properties, and after a topology change occurs in the graph, applying the template results in an MIS that satisfies the same properties. That is, the template describes what we do after a single topology change, and if one considers a long-lived process of topology changes, then this would correspond to having initially an empty graph and maintaining an MIS as it evolves. We emphasize that the template describes a process that is not in any particular model of computation, and later in Section 4 we show how to implement it efficiently in our dynamic distributed setting. This also means that there are only four topology changes we need to consider: edge-insertion, edge-deletion, node-insertion and node-deletion. For example, the notions of abrupt and graceful node deletions are defined with respect to the dynamic distributed setting because they affect communication, and therefore the implementation of the template will have to address this distinction, but the template itself is only concerned with a single type of node deletion, not in any particular computation model.

[8]The distinction is only relevant for nodes insertions, as there is no knowledge associated with an edge.

Throughout, we assume a uniformly random permutation π on the nodes $v\in V$. We define two *states* in which each node can be: M for an MIS node, and $\bar{M}$ for a non-MIS node. We abuse notations and also denote by M and $\bar{M}$ the sets of all MIS and non-MIS nodes, respectively. Our goal is to maintain the following *MIS invariant*: A node v is in M if and only if all of its neighbors $u\in N(v)$ which are ordered before it according to π, i.e., for which $\pi(u)<\pi(v)$, are not in M. It is easy to verify that whenever the MIS invariant is satisfied, it holds that the set M is a maximal independent set in G. Furthermore, it is easy to verify that this invariant simulates the greedy sequential algorithm, as defined in the introduction.

When any of the four topology changes occurs, there is at most a single node for which the MIS invariant no longer holds, as we explain next and in Footnote 9. We denote this node by $v^*=v^*(G_{\text{old}},G_{\text{new}},\pi)$, where G_{old} and G_{new} are the graphs before and after the topology change. For an edge insertion or deletion, v^* is the endpoint with the larger order according to π. For a node insertion or deletion, v^* is that node[9]. In case the topology change is an edge change, we will need also to take into consideration its other endpoint. We denote it by $v^{**}=v^{**}(G_{\text{old}},G_{\text{new}},\pi)$, and notice that by our notation, it must be the case that $\pi(v^{**})<\pi(v^*)$. In order to unify our proofs for all of the four possible topology changes, we talk about a node v^{**} also for node changes. In this case we define v^{**} to be v^* itself, and we have that $\pi(v^{**})=\pi(v^*)$. Therefore, for any topology change, it holds that $\pi(v^{**})\leq\pi(v^*)$.

To describe our template, consider the case where a new edge is inserted and it connects two nodes $\pi(v^{**})<\pi(v^*)$, where both nodes are in M. As a result, v^* must now be deleted from the MIS and hence we need to change its state. Notice that as a result of the change in the state of v^*, additional nodes may need their state to be changed, causing multiple state changes in the graph. An important observation is that it is possible that during this process of propagating local corrections of the MIS invariant, we change the state of a node more than once. As a simple example, consider the case in which v^* has two neighbors, u_1 and u_2, for which $\pi(v^*)<\pi(u_1),\pi(u_2)$, and that u_1 and u_2 are connected by a path (u_1,w_1,w_2,u_2), with $\pi(u_1)<\pi(w_1)<\pi(w_2)<\pi(u_2)$. Now, when we change the state of v^* to $\bar{M}$, both u_1 and u_2 need to be changed to M, for the MIS invariant to hold. This implies that w_1 needs to be changed to $\bar{M}$ and w_2 needs to be changed to M. In this case, since $\pi(w_2)<\pi(u_2)$, the node u_2 needs to be changed back to state $\bar{M}$.

The above observation leads us to define a set of *influenced* nodes, denoted by $S=S(G_{\text{old}},G_{\text{new}},\pi)$, containing

[9]For a node deletion, we slightly abuse the definition of v^* in order to facilitate the presentation, and consider it to be the deleted node. This means that here we consider an intermediate stage of having v^* still belong to the graph w.r.t. the MIS invariant of all the other nodes, but for v^* the MIS invariant no longer holds. This is in order to unify the four cases, otherwise we would have to consider all of the neighbors of a deleted node as nodes for which the MIS invariant no longer holds after the topology change.

v^* in the scenario where we need to change its state, and all other nodes whose state we must subsequently change as a result of the state change of v^*. To formally define the set S we introduce some notations. The notations rely on the graph structure of G_{new} unless the change is a node deletion in which case they rely on G_{old}. For each node u, we define $I_\pi(u) = \{v \in N(u) \mid \pi(v) < \pi(u)\}$, the set of neighbors of u that are ordered before it according to π. These are the nodes that can potentially *influence* the state of u according to the MIS invariant. The definition of S is recursive, according to the ordering induced by π. If immediately after the topology change, in the new graph G with the order π it holds that the MIS invariant still holds for v^*, then we define $S = \emptyset$. (This is motivated by the fact that no node is influenced by this change.) Otherwise, we denote $S_0 = \{v^*\}$, and inductively define

$$\begin{aligned} S_i &= \{u \mid u \in M, \text{ and } S_{i-1} \cap I_\pi(u) \neq \emptyset\} \quad (1)\\ &\cup \{u \mid u \in \bar{M}, \text{ and every } v \in I_\pi(u) \cap M \text{ is in } \cup_{j=0}^{i-1} S_j\}. \end{aligned}$$

The set S is then defined as $S = \bigcup_i S_i$.[10] Notice that a node u can be in more than one set S_i, as is the case for u_2 in the example above, which is in both S_1 and S_4. The impact of a node u being in more than one S_i is that in order to maintain the MIS invariant, we need to make sure that we update the state of u after we update that of w, for any w such that $w \in I_\pi(u)$. Instead of updating the state of u twice, we can simply wait and update it only after the state of every such w is updated. For this, we denote by $i_u = \max\{i \mid u \in S_i\}$ the maximal index i for which u is in S_i.

Algorithm 1 A Template for MIS.

Initially, $G = (V, E)$ satisfies the MIS invariant.
On topology change at node v^* do:
1. Update state of v^* if required for MIS to hold
2. For $i \leftarrow 1$, until $S_i = \emptyset$, do:
3. For every $u \in S_i$ such that $i = i_u$:
4. Update state of u
5. $i \leftarrow i + 1$

We formally describe our template in Algorithm 1. By construction, the updated states after executing Algorithm 1 satisfy the MIS invariant. In addition, the crucial property that is satisfied by the above template is that in expectation, the size of the set S is 1. The remainder of this section is devoted to proving the following, which is our main technical result.

THEOREM 1. $\mathbb{E}_\pi\left[|S(G_{\text{old}}, G_{\text{new}}, \pi)|\right] \leq 1$.

Outline of the proof.

In order to prove that $\mathbb{E}[|S|] \leq 1$, instead of analyzing the set S directly, we analyze the set $S' = S'(G_{\text{old}}, G_{\text{new}}, \pi, v^*)$, which is defined via recursion similarly to S with three modifications: (1) It is always the case that $S'_0 = \{v^*\}$ (2) The graph according to which S' is defined is G_{old} in the case of a node deletion or an edge insertion, and G_{new} otherwise. (3) For any permutation π' that is identical to π on all pairs not containing v^*, $S'(G_{\text{old}}, G_{\text{new}}, \pi, v^*)$ remains the same set. In other words, having knowledge of S' does not provide information regarding the location of v^* in π.

In Lemma 2, we prove that if $\pi(v^*) \neq \min\{\pi(u) \mid u \in S'\}$ then $S = \emptyset$, and otherwise $S = S'$ (in fact, it would be enough that $S \subseteq S'$). Then, in Lemma 3, we prove that for any set $P \subseteq V$, given the event that $S' = P$, the probability, over the random choice of π, that $\pi(v^*) = \min\{\pi(u) \mid u \in P\}$ is $1/|P|$. This leads to the required result of Theorem 1. Lemma 3 would be trivial if there was no dependency between π and S'. However, the trap we must avoid here is that S' is defined according to π, and therefore when analyzing its size we cannot treat π as a *uniformly* random permutation. To see why, suppose we know that inside $S' \setminus \{v^*\}$ we have nodes with large order in π. Then the probability that the order of v^* in π is smaller than all nodes in $S' \setminus \{v^*\}$, is much larger than $1/|S'|$, and can in fact be as large as $1 - o(1)$. In other words, S' gives some information over π. Nevertheless, we show that for our particular definition of S' this information is either about the order between nodes outside of S', or about the order between nodes within $S' \setminus \{v^*\}$. Both types of restrictions on π do not affect the probability that v^* is the minimal of S'.

We now formally prove our result as outlined above. Throughout we use the notation $u \in M$ or $u \in \bar{M}$. This applies only to nodes u for which we are guaranteed that their states remain the same despite the topology change.

LEMMA 2. *If* $\pi(v^*) \neq \min\{\pi(u) \mid u \in S'\}$ *then* $S = \emptyset$. *Otherwise,* $S \subseteq S'$.

PROOF. First, assume that $\pi(v^*) \neq \min\{\pi(u) \mid u \in S'\}$. We show that the MIS invariant still holds after the topology change, and so $S = \emptyset$. Consider the node w, for which $\pi(w) = \min\{\pi(u) \mid u \in S'\}$. Notice that $w \notin S$, because $\pi(w) < \pi(v^*)$ and by the definition of S it can contain only nodes whose order in π is larger than that of v^*. We claim that $w \in M$. Assume, towards a contradiction, that $w \in \bar{M}$. This implies that w has a neighbor $u \in M$ such that $\pi(u) < \pi(w)$. For this node u we must have $u \notin S'$ due to the minimality of $\pi(w)$. It follows, according to the construction of S' that w cannot be an element of S', leading to a contradiction.

We have that $w \in M$ and due to the minimality of $\pi(w)$, it must be that $w \in S'_1$, which implies that w is a neighbor of v^*. But then, when considering S, v^* has a neighbor other than v^{**} (since v^* and v^{**} cannot be neighbors in the graph defining S') which is ordered before it according to π which is in M. In the case of an edge insertion or deletion, this means that v^* remains in $\bar{M}$ despite the topology change meaning that $S = \emptyset$. In the case of a node deletion, v^* was not in M prior to the change hence $S = \emptyset$. In the case of a node insertion, v^* does not enter M hence again, $S = \emptyset$.

Next, assume that $\pi(v^*) = \min\{\pi(u) \mid u \in S'\}$. We show that either $S = \emptyset$ or $S = S'$. If there is no need to change the state of v^* as a result of the topological change then $S_0 = \emptyset$, and so $S = \emptyset$ and the claim holds. It remains to analyze the case where $S_0 = S'_0 = \{v^*\}$. If $u \in S'_1$ then $\pi(v^*) < \pi(u)$ hence according to its definition $u \in S_1$. If $u \notin S'_1$ then u must have a neighbor $w \in M$ with $\pi(w) < \pi(u)$ meaning that $u \notin S_1$. We have that $S_1 = S'_1$ and similarly $S_i = S'_i$ for all $i > 1$. We conclude that $S' = S$ as required. □

The following lemma shows that the probability of having

[10] All states above refer to the time at which the topology change occurs. The times of actual updates will in fact be captured by the indexes i of the sets S_i to which a node belongs.

$S = S'$ is $1/|S'|$, which immediately lead to Theorem 1 as the only other alternative is $S = \emptyset$.

LEMMA 3. *For any set of nodes $P \subseteq V$, it holds that* $\Pr[\pi(v^*) = \min\{\pi(u) \mid u \in P\} \mid S' = P$ *and* $\pi(v^{**}) \leq \pi(v^*)] = \frac{1}{|P|}$.

To prove this lemma we focus on S'. Notice that the events we considered in the previous lemma depend only on the ordering implied by π and hold for any configuration of states for the nodes that satisfy the MIS invariant. Roughly speaking, the lemma will follow from the fact that the event $S' = P$ does not give any information about the order implied by π between nodes in P and nodes in $V \backslash P$. To this end, for every permutation τ on V, we define $S'(\tau) = S'(G_{\text{old}}, G_{\text{new}}, \tau, v^*)$ as the set corresponding to S' under the ordering induced by τ. We denote by Π_P the set of all permutations τ for which it holds that $S'(\tau) = P$. We first need to establish the following about permutations in Π_P: If π and σ are two permutations on V such that $\pi|_P = \sigma|_P$ and $\pi|_{V \backslash P} = \sigma|_{V \backslash P}$, then $\sigma \in \Pi_P$ if and only if $\pi \in \Pi_P$.

CLAIM 4. *Let $P \subseteq V$ be a set of nodes, and let π and σ be two permutations such that $\pi|_P = \sigma|_P$ and $\pi|_{V \backslash P} = \sigma|_{V \backslash P}$. Assume $\pi \in \Pi_P$. We have that $V \backslash P \subseteq V \setminus S'(\sigma)$ and every $u \in V \backslash P$ has the same state according to π and σ.*

PROOF. Let $u \in V \backslash P$. We prove that $u \in V \setminus S'(\sigma)$ and that its state under σ is the same as it is under π by induction on the order of nodes in $V \backslash P$ according to π (which is equal to their order according to σ).

For the base case, assume that u has the minimal order in $V \backslash P$. We claim that u cannot have a neighbor in P. Assume, towards a contradiction, that u has a neighbor $w \in P$. Since $w \in P$ then it is possible that after the updates, w will be in M. In particular, w cannot have a neighbor in M, otherwise w would not be in P, since two nodes in M cannot be neighbors and $u \notin P$. Hence, u must be in $\bar{M}$ according to π. In this case there is a node $z \in I_\pi(u) \cap V \backslash P$ that is in M according to π. But this cannot occur due to the minimality of $\pi(u)$ in $V \backslash P$. Therefore, u has no neighbors in P as required.

We have that all of the neighbors of u are in $V \backslash P$ and that u is the minimal among its neighbors according to π. Since $\pi|_{V \backslash P} = \sigma|_{V \backslash P}$ we have that u has the minimal order among its neighbors according to σ. This translates into u having a state of M under σ and in particular, u is not an element of $S'(\sigma)$, thus proving our base case.

For the induction step, consider a node $u \in V \backslash P$, and assume the claim holds for every $w \in V \backslash P \cap I_\pi(u)$. We consider two cases, depending on whether u has a neighbor in P or not.

Case 1: u does not have any neighbor in P. If $u \in \bar{M}$, then there is a node $z \in I_\pi(u) \cap V \backslash P$ that is in M according to π. By the induction hypothesis, $z \in V \setminus S'(\sigma)$ and $z \in M$ also according to σ. Since $\pi|_{V \backslash P} = \sigma|_{V \backslash P}$, we have that u is in $\bar{M}$ according to σ too. Otherwise, if $u \in M$, then every $w \in I_\pi(u)$ (which is also $V \backslash P$) is in $\bar{M}$ according to π. Any node $w \in I_\sigma(u)$ is also in $w \in I_\pi(u)$, since it is not in P and $\pi|_{V \backslash P} = \sigma|_{V \backslash P}$. The induction hypothesis on w gives that it is also in $V \setminus S'(\sigma)$ (otherwise it would be in $S'_\pi = P$ in contradiction to the assumption of case 1), and its state according to σ is $\bar{M}$. Hence, u must be in $V \setminus S'(\sigma)$ as well, and in state M according to σ.

Case 2: Assume u has a neighbor $w \in P$. Since $w \in P$, it is possible that after the updates, w will be in M. Since two nodes in M cannot be neighbors and $u \notin P$, then u must be in $\bar{M}$ according to π. In this case there is a node $z \in I_\pi(u) \backslash P$ that is in M according to π. By the induction hypothesis, $z \in V \setminus S'(\sigma)$ and $z \in M$ also according to σ. Since $\pi|_{V \backslash P} = \sigma|_{V \backslash P}$, then u is in $\bar{M}$ and in $V \setminus S'(\sigma)$ according to σ too. □

CLAIM 5. *Let $P \subseteq V$ be a set of nodes, and let π and σ be two permutations such that $\pi|_P = \sigma|_P$ and $\pi|_{V \backslash P} = \sigma|_{V \backslash P}$. Assume $\pi \in \Pi_P$. We have that $P \subseteq S'(\sigma)$.*

The proof of Claim 5 appears in the full version [16]. Claims 4 and 5 combined imply that if $\pi|_P = \sigma|_P$ and $\pi|_{V \backslash P} = \sigma|_{V \backslash P}$ then $\sigma \in \Pi_P$ if and only if $\pi \in \Pi_P$. This is used in the full version [16] to prove Lemma 3. Lemmas 2 and 3 immediately lead to Theorem 1. As an immediate corollary of Theorem 1 we get:

COROLLARY 6. *A direct distributed implementation of Algorithm 1 has, in expectation, both a single adjustment and round, in both the synchronous and asynchronous models.*

4. A CONSTANT BROADCAST IMPLEMENTATION

Theorem 1 promises that the expected number of nodes that need to change their output according to our template algorithm is 1. However, a direct implementation of the template in Algorithm 1 in a dynamic distributed setting may require a much larger broadcast complexity because it may be the case that a node needs to change its state several times until the MIS invariant holds at all nodes. This is because a node can be in more than a single set S_i, as discussed in the previous section. In such a case, despite the fact that the expected number of nodes in S is a constant, it may be that the expected number of state changes is much larger. Specifically, in a naive implementation, the number of broadcasts may be as large as $|S|^2$. Hence, although $\mathbb{E}[|S|] = 1$, the expected number of broadcasts may be as large as n.

We thus take a different approach for implementing the template in Algorithm 1, in the *synchronous* setting, where each node waits until it knows the maximal i for which it belongs to S_i, and changes it state only once. This allows to obtain, for almost all of the possible topology changes a constant broadcast complexity at the cost of a constant, rather than single, round complexity.

In order to implement the random permutation π we assume each node $v \in V$ has a uniformly random and independent ID $\ell_v \in [0, 1]$. We will maintain the property that each node has knowledge of its ℓ value and those of its neighbors. We describe our algorithm in Algorithm 2. This directly applies to the following topology changes: edge-insertion, graceful-edge-deletion, abrupt-edge-deletion, graceful-node-deletion and node-unmuting. An extension of the analysis is provided in the full version [16] for the case of an abrupt node deletion, and a slight modification is provided there for the case of node-insertion. The following summarizes the guarantees of our implementation, and is proven in Lemma 9 and in the full version [16].

THEOREM 7. *There is a complete fully dynamic distributed MIS algorithm which requires in expectation a single adjustment and $O(1)$ rounds for all topology changes. For edge insertions and deletions, graceful node deletion, and node unmuting, the algorithm requires $O(1)$ broadcasts, for an abrupt deletion of a node v^* it requires $O(\min\{\log(n), d(v^*)\})$ broadcasts, and for an insertion of a node v^* it requires $O(d(v^*))$ broadcasts, in expectation.*

In the algorithm a node may be in one of four states: M for an MIS node, $\bar{M}$ for a non-MIS node, C for a node that may need to change from M to $\bar{M}$ or vice-versa, and R for a node that is ready to change. We will sometimes abuse notation and consider a state as the set of nodes which are in that state. Our goal is to maintain the MIS invariant.

Algorithm 2 MIS Algorithm for node v

1: $v \in M$: If some $u \in I_\pi(v)$ changes to state C, change state to C.
2: $v \in \bar{M}$: If some $u \in I_\pi(v)$ changes to state C and all other $w \in I_\pi(v)$ are not in M, change state to C.
3: $v \in C$: If (1) all neighbors u with $\pi(v) < \pi(u)$ are not in state C and (2) v changed to state C at least 2 rounds ago, change state to R.
4: $v \in R$: If all $u \in I_\pi(v)$ are in states $\bar{M}$ or M, change state to M if all $u \in I_\pi(v)$ are in $\bar{M}$, and change state to $\bar{M}$ otherwise.

Any change of state of a node is followed by a broadcast of the new state to all of its neighbors. We now define our implementation as a sequence of state changes. When a topology change occurs at node v^*, if the MIS invariant still holds then v^* does not change its state and algorithm consists of doing nothing. Otherwise, v^* changes its state to C.

From states M or $\bar{M}$, a node changes to state C when it discovers it is in the set S of influenced nodes, as defined in Equation (1). From state C, a node v changes to state R when (1) none of its neighbors u for which $\pi(v) < \pi(u)$ are in state C and (2) v changed its state to C at least two rounds ago. Finally, from state R a node v returns to states M or $\bar{M}$ when all of its neighbors u for which $\pi(u) < \pi(v)$ are in states M or $\bar{M}$. In order to bound the complexity of the algorithm we first show that every node can change from state R to either M or $\bar{M}$ at most once.

LEMMA 8. *In Algorithm 2, a node u changes its state from R to another state at most once.*

PROOF. First, note that every $u \notin S$ never changes its state. Consider a node u changing its state from R to either M or $\bar{M}$. Since u changes from state R, if $u \neq v^*$ then it must have a neighbor $w \in I_\pi(u)$ that was in state C, changed to state R and then changed to M or $\bar{M}$. It follows that v^* must be the first node to change its state from R to M or $\bar{M}$. This event occurs only when all neighbors u of v^* are not in C, which in turn can happen only when all neighbors of each such u with higher π value have changed from C to R at least once. But, since no node could have changed its state from R to another state before v^* has done so, we have that when v^* changes its state from R to another, all $u \in S$ are in state R.

In particular, we have that at the round of the first change of a node from R to another state, there are no nodes in state C. Since a node can only change to state C due to a neighbor at state C we have that any node changing its state from R to M or $\bar{M}$ will not change its state again, thus proving our claim. □

LEMMA 9. *For edge-insertion, graceful-edge-deletion, abrupt-edge-deletion, graceful-node-deletion and node-unmuting, Algorithm 2 requires in expectation a single adjustment, $O(1)$ rounds, and $O(1)$ broadcasts.*

PROOF. Since only nodes in S can change their outputs, the number of adjustments is bounded by $|S|$, and hence is 1 in expectation, by Theorem 1. According to Lemma 8, if a node changes its state then it does so exactly three times. First it changes from either M or $\bar{M}$ to C, then it changes to R, and finally it changes to either M or $\bar{M}$ again. Since only nodes in S change their states and since the round and broadcast complexities are clearly bounded by the number of state changes plus 1 (due to the forced waiting round before changing from C to R), the claim follows. □

The cases of node insertion and abrupt node deletion are addressed in the full version [16].

5. DISCUSSION

This paper studies computing an MIS in a distributed dynamic setting. The strength of our analysis lies in obtaining that for an algorithm that simulates the sequential random greedy algorithm, the size of the set of nodes that need to change their output is in expectation 1. This brings the locality of the fundamental MIS problem to its most powerful setting.

We are able to extend our analysis to show that our algorithm can cope with any number k of topology changes that overlap. The required time for updating the MIS naturally depends on k, but remains constant if k is constant. For clarity of presentation, we defer this extension to a future extended version of this paper.

The expected update time required for our algorithm is with respect to a random order of nodes. One might argue that once we have a network in a fixed state then this order is given, and so an interesting question is whether our algorithm can perform well for this particular given order, even with possibly relaxing the topology changes to be random. However, a simple counter-example shows that this is not the case: consider a path with the nodes ordered from left to right $(v_1, \dots, v_n)$. The greedy MIS consists of all v_i for odd i. Any topology change of removing v_i causes $n-i$ nodes to change their state. This means that in expectation we will suffer a linear number of changes.

Our work sets the ground for more research in this crucial setting. First, there are many additional problems that can be addressed in the dynamic distributed setting, especially in the synchronous case. We believe that our contribution can find applications in solving many additional dynamic distributed tasks.

A major open question is whether our techniques can be adapted to sequential dynamic graph algorithms, which constitutes a major area of research in the sequential setting [13, 14, 19, 25–27, 31, 33–35, 38, 55, 56, 58, 59]. A formal definition and description of typical problems can be found in, e.g., [18]. Notice that our algorithms are *fully dynamic*, which means that they handle both insertions and deletions (of edges and nodes). Although our template for finding an MIS can be easily implemented in a sequential dynamic setting, it would come with a cost of at least $O(\Delta)$ for the update complexity in a direct implementation. This is because we would have to access neighbors of the set of nodes analyzed in Theorem 1. Our distributed implementation avoids this by having them simply not respond since they do not need to change their output, and hence they do not contribute to the communication. Nevertheless, we believe that our approach may be useful for designing an MIS algorithm for the dynamic sequential setting, and leave this for future research.

Acknowledgements.
We thank Reuven Bar-Yehuda, Mohsen Ghaffari, and Boaz Patt-Shamir for interesting discussions.

6. REFERENCES

[1] N. Ailon, M. Charikar, and A. Newman. Aggregating inconsistent information: Ranking and clustering. *J. ACM*, 55(5), 2008.

[2] N. Alon, L. Babai, and A. Itai. A fast and simple randomized parallel algorithm for the maximal independent set problem. *J. Algorithms*, 7(4):567–583, 1986.

[3] N. Alon, R. Rubinfeld, S. Vardi, and N. Xie. Space-efficient local computation algorithms. In *Proceedings of the Twenty-Third Annual ACM-SIAM Symposium on Discrete Algorithms, SODA*, pages 1132–1139, 2012.

[4] C. Avin, M. Koucký, and Z. Lotker. How to explore a fast-changing world (cover time of a simple random walk on evolving graphs). In *Proceedings of the 35th International Colloquium on Automata, Languages and Programming, ICALP*, pages 121–132, 2008.

[5] B. Awerbuch, I. Cidon, and S. Kutten. Communication-optimal maintenance of replicated information. In *31st Annual Symposium on Foundations of Computer Science, FOCS*, pages 492–502, 1990.

[6] B. Awerbuch and M. Sipser. Dynamic networks are as fast as static networks (preliminary version). In *29th Annual Symposium on Foundations of Computer Science, FOCS*, pages 206–220, 1988.

[7] B. Awerbuch and G. Varghese. Distributed program checking: a paradigm for building self-stabilizing distributed protocols (extended abstract). In *32nd Annual Symposium on Foundations of Computer Science, FOCS*, pages 258–267, 1991.

[8] Y. Azar, S. Kutten, and B. Patt-Shamir. Distributed error confinement. *ACM Trans. Algorithms*, 6(3):48:1–48:23, July 2010.

[9] L. Barenboim and M. Elkin. *Distributed Graph Coloring: Fundamentals and Recent Developments.* Synthesis Lectures on Distributed Computing Theory. Morgan & Claypool Publishers, 2013.

[10] L. Barenboim, M. Elkin, and F. Kuhn. Distributed (delta+1)-coloring in linear (in delta) time. *SIAM J. Comput.*, 43(1):72–95, 2014.

[11] L. Barenboim, M. Elkin, S. Pettie, and J. Schneider. The locality of distributed symmetry breaking. In *53rd Annual IEEE Symposium on Foundations of Computer Science, FOCS*, pages 321–330, 2012.

[12] S. Baswana, S. Khurana, and S. Sarkar. Fully dynamic randomized algorithms for graph spanners. *ACM Transactions on Algorithms*, 8(4):35, 2012.

[13] A. Bernstein and C. Stein. Fully dynamic matching in bipartite graphs. In *Proceedings of the 42nd International Colloquium on Automata, Languages, and Programming ICALP*, pages 167–179, 2015.

[14] S. Bhattacharya, M. Henzinger, and G. F. Italiano. Deterministic fully dynamic data structures for vertex cover and matching. In *Proceedings of the Twenty-Sixth Annual ACM-SIAM Symposium on Discrete Algorithms, SODA*, pages 785–804, 2015.

[15] G. E. Blelloch, J. T. Fineman, and J. Shun. Greedy sequential maximal independent set and matching are parallel on average. In *24th ACM Symposium on Parallelism in Algorithms and Architectures, SPAA*, pages 308–317, 2012.

[16] K. Censor-Hillel, E. Haramaty, and Z. S. Karnin. Optimal dynamic distributed MIS. *CoRR*, abs/1507.04330, 2015.

[17] S. Cicerone, G. D. Stefano, D. Frigioni, and U. Nanni. A fully dynamic algorithm for distributed shortest paths. *Theor. Comput. Sci.*, 297(1-3):83–102, 2003.

[18] C. Demetrescu, D. Eppstein, Z. Galil, and G. F. Italiano. Dynamic graph algorithms. In M. J. Atallah and M. Blanton, editors, *Algorithms and Theory of Computation Handbook*, chapter 9. Chapman & Hall/CRC, 2010.

[19] C. Demetrescu and G. F. Italiano. Fully dynamic transitive closure: Breaking through the $o(n^2)$ barrier. In *41st Annual Symposium on Foundations of Computer Science, FOCS*, pages 381–389, 2000.

[20] E. W. Dijkstra. Self-stabilizing systems in spite of distributed control. *Commun. ACM*, 17(11):643–644, 1974.

[21] S. Dolev. *Self-Stabilization.* MIT Press, 2000.

[22] S. Dolev and T. Herman. Superstabilizing protocols for dynamic distributed systems. *Chicago J. Theor. Comput. Sci.*, 1997, 1997.

[23] S. Dolev and N. Tzachar. Empire of colonies: Self-stabilizing and self-organizing distributed algorithm. *Theor. Comput. Sci.*, 410(6-7):514–532, 2009.

[24] M. Elkin. A near-optimal distributed fully dynamic algorithm for maintaining sparse spanners. In *Proceedings of the Twenty-Sixth Annual ACM Symposium on Principles of Distributed Computing, PODC*, pages 185–194, 2007.

[25] D. Eppstein, Z. Galil, G. F. Italiano, and A. Nissenzweig. Sparsification - a technique for speeding up dynamic graph algorithms. *J. ACM*, 44(5):669–696, 1997.

[26] S. Even and Y. Shiloach. An on-line edge-deletion problem. *J. ACM*, 28(1):1–4, 1981.

[27] G. N. Frederickson. Data structures for on-line updating of minimum spanning trees, with applications. *SIAM J. Comput.*, 14(4):781–798, 1985.

[28] M. Ghaffari. An improved distributed algorithm for maximal independent set. In *Proceedings of the Twenty-Seventh Annual ACM-SIAM Symposium on Discrete Algorithms, SODA*, pages 270–277, 2016.

[29] N. Guellati and H. Kheddouci. A survey on self-stabilizing algorithms for independence, domination, coloring, and matching in graphs. *J. Parallel Distrib. Comput.*, 70(4):406–415, 2010.

[30] T. P. Hayes, J. Saia, and A. Trehan. The forgiving graph: a distributed data structure for low stretch under adversarial attack. *Distributed Computing*, 25(4):261–278, 2012.

[31] M. Henzinger, S. Krinninger, and D. Nanongkai. Dynamic approximate all-pairs shortest paths: Breaking the O(mn) barrier and derandomization. In *54th Annual IEEE Symposium on Foundations of Computer Science, FOCS*, pages 538–547, 2013.

[32] M. Henzinger, S. Krinninger, and D. Nanongkai. Sublinear-time maintenance of breadth-first spanning tree in partially dynamic networks. In *Proceedings of the 40th International Colloquium on Automata, Languages, and Programming ICALP*, pages 607–619, 2013.

[33] M. R. Henzinger and V. King. Fully dynamic biconnectivity and transitive closure. In *36th Annual Symposium on Foundations of Computer Science FOCS*, pages 664–672, 1995.

[34] M. R. Henzinger and V. King. Randomized fully dynamic graph algorithms with polylogarithmic time per operation. *J. ACM*, 46(4):502–516, 1999.

[35] J. Holm, K. de Lichtenberg, and M. Thorup. Poly-logarithmic deterministic fully-dynamic algorithms for connectivity, minimum spanning tree, 2-edge, and biconnectivity. In *Proceedings of the Thirtieth Annual ACM Symposium on the Theory of Computing, Dallas, Texas, USA, May 23-26, 1998*, pages 79–89, 1998.

[36] A. Israeli and A. Itai. A fast and simple randomized parallel algorithm for maximal matching. *Inf. Process. Lett.*, 22(2):77–80, 1986.

[37] G. F. Italiano. Distributed algorithms for updating shortest paths (extended abstract). In *Proceedings of the 5th International Workshop on Distributed Algorithms, WDAG*, pages 200–211, 1991.

[38] B. M. Kapron, V. King, and B. Mountjoy. Dynamic graph connectivity in polylogarithmic worst case time. In *Proceedings of the Twenty-Fourth Annual ACM-SIAM Symposium on Discrete Algorithms, SODA*, pages 1131–1142, 2013.

[39] M. König and R. Wattenhofer. On local fixing. In *Proceedings of the 17th International Conference on Principles of Distributed Systems, OPODIS*, pages 191–205, 2013.

[40] A. Korman. Improved compact routing schemes for dynamic trees. In *Proceedings of the Twenty-Seventh Annual ACM Symposium on Principles of Distributed Computing, PODC*, pages 185–194, 2008.

[41] A. Korman and D. Peleg. Labeling schemes for weighted dynamic trees. In *Proceedings of the 30th International Colloquium on Automata, Languages and Programming ICALP*, pages 369–383, 2003.

[42] F. Kuhn, N. A. Lynch, and R. Oshman. Distributed computation in dynamic networks. In *Proceedings of the 42nd ACM Symposium on Theory of Computing, STOC*, pages 513–522, 2010.

[43] F. Kuhn, T. Moscibroda, and R. Wattenhofer. What cannot be computed locally! In *Proceedings of the Twenty-Third Annual ACM Symposium on Principles of Distributed Computing, PODC*, pages 300–309, 2004.

[44] S. Kutten and D. Peleg. Fault-local distributed mending. *J. Algorithms*, 30(1):144–165, 1999.

[45] S. Kutten and D. Peleg. Tight fault locality. *SIAM J. Comput.*, 30(1):247–268, 2000.

[46] C. Lenzen, J. Suomela, and R. Wattenhofer. Local algorithms: Self-stabilization on speed. In *Proceedings of the 11th International Symposiumon Stabilization, Safety, and Security of Distributed Systems SSS*, pages 17–34, 2009.

[47] R. Levi, R. Rubinfeld, and A. Yodpinyanee. Local computation algorithms for graphs of non-constant degrees. *CoRR*, abs/1502.04022, 2015.

[48] N. Linial. Locality in distributed graph algorithms. *SIAM J. Comput.*, 21(1):193–201, 1992.

[49] M. Luby. A simple parallel algorithm for the maximal independent set problem. *SIAM J. Comput.*, 15(4):1036–1053, 1986.

[50] Y. Mansour, A. Rubinstein, S. Vardi, and N. Xie. Converting online algorithms to local computation algorithms. In *Proceedings of the 39th International Colloquium on Automata, Languages, and Programming ICALP*, pages 653–664, 2012.

[51] Y. Métivier, J. M. Robson, N. Saheb-Djahromi, and A. Zemmari. An optimal bit complexity randomized distributed MIS algorithm. *Distributed Computing*, 23(5-6):331–340, 2011.

[52] H. N. Nguyen and K. Onak. Constant-time approximation algorithms via local improvements. In *49th Annual IEEE Symposium on Foundations of Computer Science, FOCS*, pages 327–336, 2008.

[53] G. Pandurangan and A. Trehan. Xheal: a localized self-healing algorithm using expanders. *Distributed Computing*, 27(1):39–54, 2014.

[54] D. Peleg. *Distributed Computing: A Locality-sensitive Approach.* Society for Industrial and Applied Mathematics, Philadelphia, PA, USA, 2000.

[55] L. Roditty and U. Zwick. On dynamic shortest paths problems. *Algorithmica*, 61(2):389–401, 2011.

[56] L. Roditty and U. Zwick. Dynamic approximate all-pairs shortest paths in undirected graphs. *SIAM J. Comput.*, 41(3):670–683, 2012.

[57] M. Schneider. Self-stabilization. *ACM Comput. Surv.*, 25(1):45–67, 1993.

[58] R. E. Tarjan. Efficiency of a good but not linear set union algorithm. *J. ACM*, 22(2):215–225, 1975.

[59] M. Thorup. Near-optimal fully-dynamic graph connectivity. In *Proceedings of the Thirty-Second Annual ACM Symposium on Theory of Computing STOC*, pages 343–350, 2000.

[60] V. Turau. Linear self-stabilizing algorithms for the independent and dominating set problems using an unfair distributed scheduler. *Inf. Process. Lett.*, 103(3):88–93, 2007.

[61] Y. Yoshida, M. Yamamoto, and H. Ito. Improved constant-time approximation algorithms for maximum matchings and other optimization problems. *SIAM J. Comput.*, 41(4):1074–1093, 2012.

A Local Constant Factor MDS Approximation for Bounded Genus Graphs

Saeed Amiri*
TU Berlin, Germany
saeed.amiri@tu-berlin.de

Stefan Schmid
Aalborg University, Denmark
& TU Berlin, Germany
schmiste@cs.aau.dk

Sebastian Siebertz*
TU Berlin, Germany
sebastian.siebertz@tu-berlin.de

ABSTRACT

The Minimum Dominating Set (MDS) problem is not only one of the most fundamental problems in distributed computing, it is also one of the most challenging ones. While it is well-known that minimum dominating sets cannot be approximated locally on general graphs, over the last years, several breakthroughs have been made on computing local approximations on *sparse graphs*.

This paper presents a deterministic and local constant factor approximation for minimum dominating sets on bounded genus graphs, a large family of sparse graphs. Our main technical contribution is a new analysis of a slightly modified variant of an existing algorithm by Lenzen et al. Interestingly, unlike existing proofs for planar graphs, our analysis does not rely on direct topological arguments. We believe that our techniques can be useful for the study of local problems on sparse graphs beyond the scope of this paper.

CCS Concepts

•Theory of computation → Distributed computing models; Distributed algorithms; •Networks → *Network algorithms;*

Keywords

Distributed Algorithms, LOCAL Model, Sparse Graphs, Minimum Dominating Sets

1. INTRODUCTION

This paper attends to the Minimum Dominating Set (MDS) problem, arguably one of the most intensively studied graph theoretic problems in computer science in general, as well as in distributed computing.

A dominating set D in a graph G is a set of vertices such that every vertex of G either lies in D or is adjacent to a vertex in D. Finding a minimum dominating set is NP-complete, even on planar graphs, however, the problem can be approximated well on planar graphs [1].

In this paper, we study the *distributed* time complexity of finding small dominating sets, in the classic *LOCAL model* of distributed computing [4, 11, 13, 14]. It is known that finding small dominating sets locally is hard: Kuhn et al. [7] show that in r rounds the MDS problem on an n-vertex graphs of maximum degree Δ can only be approximated within factor $\Omega(n^{c/r^2})$ and $\Omega(\Delta^{c'/r})$, where c and c' are constants. This implies that, in general, to achieve a constant approximation ratio, every distributed algorithm requires at least $\Omega(\sqrt{\log n})$ and $\Omega(\log \Delta)$ communication rounds. The currently best results for general graphs are by Kuhn et al. [7] who present a $(1+\epsilon)\ln\Delta$-approximation in $\mathcal{O}(\log(n)/\epsilon)$ rounds for any $\epsilon > 0$, and by Barenboim et al. [2] who present a deterministic $\mathcal{O}((\log n)^{k-1})$-time algorithm that provides an $\mathcal{O}(n^{1/k})$-approximation, for any integer parameter $k \geq 2$.

For sparse graphs, the situation is more promising. For graphs of arboricity a, Lenzen and Wattenhofer [10] present a forest decomposition algorithm achieving a factor $\mathcal{O}(a^2)$ approximation in randomized time $\mathcal{O}(\log n)$, and a deterministic $\mathcal{O}(a \log \Delta)$ approximation algorithm requiring time $\mathcal{O}(\log \Delta)$ rounds. Graphs of bounded arboricity include all graphs which exclude a fixed graph as a (topological) minor and in particular, all planar graphs and any class of bounded genus. Czygrinow et al. [3] show that given any $\delta > 0$, $(1+\delta)$-approximations of a maximum independent set, a maximum matching, and a minimum dominating set, can be computed in $\mathcal{O}(\log^* n)$ rounds in planar graphs, which is asymptotically optimal [9]. Lenzen et al. [8] proposed a constant factor approximation on planar graphs that can be computed locally in a constant number of communication rounds. A finer analysis of Wawrzyniak [16] showed that the algorithm of Lenzen et al. in fact computes a 52-approximation of a minimum dominating set with small message size. Wawrzyniak [15] also showed that message sizes of $\mathcal{O}(\log n)$ suffice to give a (slightly worse) constant factor approximation on planar graphs. In terms of lower bounds, Hilke et al. [6] show that there is no deterministic local algorithm (constant-time distributed graph algorithm) that finds a $(7-\epsilon)$-approximation of a minimum dominating set on planar graphs, for any positive constant ϵ.

*The research of Saeed Amiri and Sebastian Siebertz has been supported by the European Research Council (ERC) under the European Union's Horizon 2020 research and innovation programme (ERC consolidator grant DISTRUCT, agreement No 648527).

PODC'16, July 25 - 28, 2016, Chicago, IL, USA

ISBN 978-1-4503-3964-3/16/07...$15.00

DOI: http://dx.doi.org/10.1145/2933057.2933084

1.1 Our Contributions

The main contribution of this paper is a deterministic and local constant factor approximation for MDS on graphs that we call *locally embeddable graphs.* A locally embeddable graph G excludes the complete bipartite graph $K_{3,t}$ ($t \geq 3$) as a depth-1 minor, that is, as a minor obtained by star contractions, and furthermore satisfies that all depth-1 minors of G have constant edge density. The most prominent locally embeddable graph classes are classes of bounded genus. Concretely, our result implies that MDS can be $\mathcal{O}(g)$-approximated locally and deterministically on graphs of (both orientable or non-orientable) genus g. This result generalizes existing constant factor approximation results for planar graphs to a significantly larger graph family. Prior works by Lenzen et al. [8] and Wawrzyniak [16] heavily depend on topological properties of planar graphs: For example, their analyses exploit the fact that each cycle in a planar graph defines an "inside" and an "outside" region, without any edges connecting the two; this facilitates a simplified accounting and comparison to the optimal solution. In the case of locally embeddable graphs, such global, topological properties do not exist. In contrast, in this paper we leverage the inherent local properties of our low-density graphs, which opens a new door to approach the problem.

Our main *technical* contribution is a new analysis of a sligthly modified variant of the elegant algorithm by Lenzen et al. [8] for planar graphs. As we will show, with a slight modification, the algorithm also works for locally embeddable graphs.

A second interesting technique developed in this paper is based on *preprocessing*: we show that the constants involved in the approximation can be further improved by a local preprocessing step.

We believe that our new analysis and techniques can be useful also for the study of other local problems and on more general sparse graphs, beyond the scope of this paper.

An interesting side contribution of our modified algorithm is that it is *first-order definable.* In particular, the algorithm can again be modified such that it does not rely on any *maximum* operations, such as finding the neighbor of maximal degree. The advent of sub-microprocessor devices, such as biological cellular networks or networks of nano-devices, has recently motivated the design of very simple, "stone-age" distributed algorithms [5], and we believe that our work nicely complements the finite-state machine model assumed in related work, and opens an interesting field for future research.

1.2 Organization

The remainder of this paper is organized as follows. We introduce some preliminaries in Section 2. Our basic local approximation result is presented in Section 3, and the improved approximation, using preprocessing, is presented in Section 4. After discussing a logic perspective on our work in Section 5, we conclude in Section 6.

2. PRELIMINARIES

Graphs. We consider finite, undirected, simple graphs. Given a graph G, we write $V(G)$ for its vertices and $E(G)$ for its edges. Two vertices $u, v \in V(G)$ are adjacent or neighbors in G if $\{u, v\} \in E(G)$. The degree $d_G(v)$ of a vertex $v \in V(G)$ is its number of neighbors in G. We write $N(v)$ for the set of neighbors and $N[v]$ for the closed neighborhood $N(v) \cup \{v\}$ of v. We let $N^1[v] := N[v]$ and $N^{i+1}[v] := N[N^i[v]]$ for $i > 1$. If $E' \subseteq E$, we write $N_{E'}(v)$ for the set $\{u \in V(G) : \{u, v\} \in E'\}$. For $A \subseteq V(G)$, we write $N[A]$ for $\bigcup_{v \in A} N[v]$. The edge density of G is $\epsilon(G) = |E(G)|/|V(G)|$. For $A \subseteq V(G)$, the graph $G[A]$ induced by A is the graph with vertex set A and edge set $\{\{u, v\} \in E(G) : u, v \in A\}$. For $B \subseteq V(G)$ we write $G - B$ for the graph $G[V(G) \setminus B]$. A graph H is a subgraph of a graph G if $V(H) \subseteq V(G)$ and $E(H) \subseteq E(G)$.

Depth-1 minors and local embeddable graphs. A graph H is a minor of a graph G, written $H \preceq G$, if there is a set $\{G_v : v \in V(H)\}$ of pairwise disjoint connected subgraphs $G_v \subseteq G$ such that if $\{u, v\} \in E(H)$, then there is an edge between a vertex of G_u and a vertex of G_v. We say that G_v is contracted to the vertex v and we call $G[\bigcup_{v \in V(H)} V(G_v)]$ a *minor model* of H in G.

A star is a connected graph G such that at most one vertex of G, called the center of the star, has degree greater than one. H is a *depth*-1 *minor* of G if H is obtained from a subgraph of G by star contractions, that is, if there is a set $\{G_v : v \in V(H)\}$ of pairwise disjoint stars $G_v \subseteq G$ such that if $\{u, v\} \in E(H)$, then there is an edge between a vertex of G_u and a vertex of G_v.

We write $K_{t,3}$ for the complete bipartite graph with partitions of size t and 3, respectively. A graph G is a *locally embeddable graph* if it excludes $K_{3,t}$ as a depth-1 minor for some $t \geq 3$ and if $\epsilon(H) \leq c$ for some constant c and all depth-1 minors H of G.

Dominating set. Let G be a graph. A set $M \subseteq V(G)$ *dominates* G if all vertices of G lie either in M or are adjacent to a vertex of D, that is, if $N[M] = V(G)$. A minimum dominating set M is a dominating set of minimum cardinality (among all dominating sets). The size of a minimum dominating set of G is denoted $\gamma(G)$.

f-Approximation. Let $f : \mathbb{N} \rightarrow \mathbb{R}^+$. Given an n-vertex graph G and a set D of G, we say that D is an f-approximation for the dominating set problem if D is a dominating set of G and $|D| \leq f(n) \cdot \gamma(G)$. An algorithm computes an f-approximation for the dominating set problem on a class $\mathcal{C}$ of graphs if for all $G \in \mathcal{C}$ it computes a set D which is an f-approximation for the dominating set problem.

Bounded genus graphs. The (orientable, resp. non-orientable) genus of a graph is the minimal number ℓ such that the graph can be embedded on an (orientable, resp. non-orientable) surface of genus ℓ. We write $g(G)$ for the orientable genus of G and $\tilde{g}(G)$ for the non-orientable genus of G. Every connected planar graph has orientable genus 0 and non-orientable genus 1. In general, for connected G, we have $\tilde{g}(G) \leq 2g(G) + 1$. On the other hand, there is no bound for $g(G)$ in terms of $\tilde{g}(G)$. As all our results apply to both variants, for ease of presentation, and as usual in the literature, we will not mention them explicitly in the following. We do not make explicit use of any topological arguments and hence refer to [12] for more background on graphs on surfaces. We will use the following facts about bounded genus graphs.

Graphs of genus g are closed under taking subgraphs and edge contraction.

LEMMA 1. *If $H \preceq G$, then $g(H) \leq g(G)$ and $\tilde{g}(H) \leq \tilde{g}(G)$.*

One of the arguments we will use is based on the fact that bounded genus graphs exclude large bipartite graphs as minors (and in particular as depth-1 minors). The lemma follows immediately from Lemma 1 and from the fact that $g(K_{m,n}) = \left\lceil \frac{(m-2)(n-2)}{4} \right\rceil$ and $\tilde{g}(K_{m,n}) = \left\lceil \frac{(m-2)(n-2)}{2} \right\rceil$ (see e.g. Theorem 4.4.7 in [12]).

LEMMA 2. *If $g(G) = g$, then G excludes $K_{4g+3,3}$ as a minor and if $\tilde{g}(G) = \tilde{g}$, then G excludes $K_{2\tilde{g}+3,3}$ as a minor.*

Graphs of bounded genus do not contain many disjoint copies of minor models of $K_{3,3}$: this is a simple consequence of the fact that the orientable genus of a connected graph is equal to the sum of the genera of its blocks (maximal connected subgraphs without a cut-vertex) and a similar statement holds for the non-orientable genus, see Theorem 4.4.2 and Theorem 4.4.3 in [12].

LEMMA 3. *G contains at most* $\max\{g(G), 2\tilde{g}(G)\}$ *disjoint copies of minor models of $K_{3,3}$.*

Finally, note that graphs of bounded genus have small edge density.

LEMMA 4. *We have $|E(G)| \leq 3 \cdot |V(G)| + 6g(G) - 6$ and $|E(G)| \leq 3 \cdot |V(G)| + 3\tilde{g}(G) - 3$*

Distributed complexity. We consider the standard *LOCAL* model of distributed computing [11, 13], see also [14] for a recent survey. A distributed system is modeled as a graph G. At each vertex $v \in V(G)$ there is an independent agent/host/processor with a unique identifier $id(v)$. Initially, each agent has no knowledge about the network, but only knows its own identifier. Information about other agents can be obtained through message passing, i.e., through repeated interactions with neighboring vertices, which happens in synchronous communication rounds. In each round the following operations are performed: (1) Each vertex performs a local computation (based on information obtained in previous rounds). (2) Each vertex v sends one message to each of its neighbors. (3) Each vertex v receives one message from each of its neighbors. The *distributed complexity* of the algorithm is defined as the number of communication rounds until all agents terminate. We call a distributed algorithm r-local, if its output depends only on the r-neighborhoods $N^r[v]$ of its vertices.

3. THE LOCAL MDS APPROXIMATION

Let us start by revisiting the MDS approximation algorithm for planar graphs by Lenzen et al. [8], see Algorithm 1. The algorithm works in two phases. In the first phase, it adds all vertices whose (open) neighborhood cannot be dominated by a small number of vertices to a set D. It has been shown in [8] that the set D is small in planar graphs. In the second phase, it defines a dominator function *dom* which maps every vertex v that is not dominated yet by D to its dominator. The dominator $dom(v)$ of v is chosen arbitrary among those vertices of $N[v]$ which dominate the maximal number of vertices not dominated yet.

We now propose the following small change to the algorithm. As additional input, we require an integer c which bounds the edge density of depth-1 minors of G from below and we replace the condition $|A| \leq 6$ in Line 5 by the condition $|A| \leq 2c$. In the rest of this section, we show that the modified algorithm computes a constant factor approximation on any locally embeddable class of graphs. Note that

Algorithm 1 Dominating Set Approximation Algorithm for Planar Graphs

1: Input: Planar graph G
2: (∗ *Phase 1* ∗)
3: $D \leftarrow \emptyset$
4: **for** $v \in V$ (in parallel) **do**
5: **if** there does not exist a set $A \subseteq V(G) \setminus \{v\}$ such that $N(v) \subseteq N[A]$ and $|A| \leq 6$ **then**
6: $D \leftarrow D \cup \{v\}$
7: **end if**
8: **end for**
9: (∗ *Phase 2* ∗)
10: $D' \leftarrow \emptyset$
11: **for** $v \in V$ (in parallel) **do**
12: $d_{G-D}(v) \leftarrow |N[v] \setminus N[D]|$
13: **if** $v \in V \setminus N[D]$ **then**
14: $\Delta_{G-D}(v) \leftarrow \max_{w \in N[v]} d_{G-D}(w)$
15: choose any $dom(v)$ from $N[v]$ with $d_{G-D}(dom(v)) = \Delta_{G-D}(v)$
16: $D' \leftarrow D' \cup \{dom(v)\}$
17: **end if**
18: **end if**
19: **end for**
20: **return** $D \cup D'$

the algorithm does not have to compute the edge density of G, which is not possible in a local manner. Rather, we leverage Lemma 4 which upper bounds $\epsilon(G)$ for any fixed class of bounded genus graphs: this upper bound can be used as an input to the local algorithm.

We first show that the set D computed in Phase 1 of the algorithm is small. The following lemma is a straightforward generalization of Lemma 6.3 of [8], which in fact uses no topological arguments at all.

LEMMA 5. *Let G be a graph and let M be a minimum dominating set of G. Assume that for some constant c all depth-1 minors H of G satisfy $\epsilon(H) \leq c$. Let*

$$D := \{v \in V(G) : \text{ there is no set } A \subseteq V(G) \setminus \{v\} \text{ such that } N(v) \subseteq N[A] \text{ and } |A| \leq 2c\}.$$

Then $|D| \leq (c+1) \cdot |M|$.

PROOF. Let H be the graph with $V(H) = M \cup N[D \setminus M]$ and where $E(H)$ is a minimal subset of $E(G[V(H)])$ such that all edges with at least one endpoint in $D \setminus M$ are contained in $E(H)$ and such that M is a dominating set in H. By this minimality condition, every vertex $v \in V(H) \setminus (D \cup M)$ has exactly one neighbor $m \in M$, no two vertices of $V(H) \setminus (M \cup D)$ are adjacent, and no two vertices of M are adjacent.

We construct a depth-1 minor $\tilde{H}$ of H by contracting the star subgraphs G_m induced by $N_H[m] \setminus D$ for $m \in M \setminus D$ to a single vertex v_m. Let $w \in D \setminus M$. As $N_G(w)$ cannot be covered by less than $(2c+1)$ elements from $V(G) \setminus \{w\}$ (by definition of D), w also has at least $(2c+1)$ neighbors in $\tilde{H}$. On the other hand, $\tilde{H}$ has at most $c \cdot |V(\tilde{H})|$ edges, and also the subgraph $\tilde{H}[D \setminus M]$ has at most $c \cdot |D \setminus M|$ edges (by assumption on $\epsilon(\tilde{H})$).

Hence

$$
\begin{aligned}
&(2c+1)\cdot|D\setminus M| - c\cdot|D\setminus M| \\
&\le \sum_{w\in D\setminus M} d_{\tilde{H}}(w) - |E(\tilde{H}[D\setminus M])| \\
&\le |E(\tilde{H})| \\
&\le c\cdot|V(\tilde{H})| \\
&= c\cdot(|D\setminus M| + |M|),
\end{aligned}
$$

and hence $|D\setminus M| \le c\cdot|M|$, which implies the claim. □

ASSUMPTION 6. *For the rest of this section, we assume that G satisfies that for all depth-1 minors H of G, $\epsilon(H)\le c$ for some constant c, and we fix M and D as in Lemma 5. We furthermore assume that for some $t\ge 3$, G excludes $K_{t,3}$ as depth-1 minor.*

Let us write R for the set $V(G)\setminus N[D]$ of vertices which are not dominated by D. The algorithm defines a dominator function $dom : R\to N[R]\subseteq V(G)\setminus D$. The set D' computed by the algorithm is the image $dom(R)$, which is a dominating set of vertices in R. As R contains the vertices which are not dominated by D, $D'\cup D$ is a dominating set of G. This simple observation proves that the algorithm correctly computes a dominating set of G. Our aim is to find a bound on $|dom(R)|$.

We fix an ordering of M as $m_1,\ldots,m_{|M|}$ such that the vertices of $M\cap D$ are first in the ordering and inductively define a minimal set $E'\subseteq E(G)$ such that M is a dominating set with respect to E'. For this, we add all edges $\{m_1,v\}\in E(G)$ with $v\in N(m_1)\setminus M$ to E'. We then continue inductively by adding for $i>1$ all edges $\{m_i,v\}\in E(G)$ with $v\in N(m_i)\setminus(M\cup N_{E'}(m_1,\ldots,m_{i-1}))$.

For $m\in M$, let G_m be the star subgraph of G with center m and all vertices v with $\{m,v\}\in E'$. Let H be the depth-1 minor of G which is obtained by contracting all stars G_m for $m\in M$. This construction is visualized in Figure 1. In the figure, solid lines represent edges from E', lines from $E(G)\setminus E'$ are dashed. We want to count the *endpoints* of directed edges, which represent the dominator function *dom*.

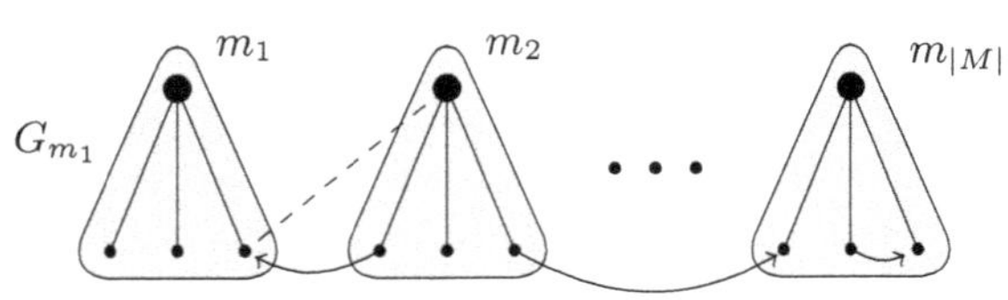

Figure 1: The graphs G_m. Solid lines represent edges from E', directed edges represent the dominator function *dom*.

In the following, we call a directed edge which represents the function *dom* a *dom-edge*. We did not draw *dom*-edges that either start or end in M. When counting $|dom(R)|$, we may simply add a term $2|M|$ to estimate the number of endpoints of those edges. We also did not draw a *dom*-edge starting in G_{m_1}. In the figure, we assume that the vertex m_1 belongs to $M\cap D$. Hence every vertex v from $N[m_1]$ is dominated by a vertex from D and the function is thus not defined on v.

H has $|M|$ vertices and by our assumption on the density of depth-1 minors of G, it has at most $c|M|$ edges.

Our analysis proceeds as follows. We distinguish between two types of *dom*-edges, namely those which go from one star to another star and those which start and end in the same star. By the star contraction, all edges which go from one star to another star are represented by a single edge in H. We show in Lemma 7 that each edge in H does not represent many such *dom*-edges with distinct endpoints. As H has at most $c|M|$ edges, we will end up with a number of such edges that is linear in $|M|$. On the other hand, all edges which start and end in the same star completely disappear in H. In Lemma 11 we show that these star contractions "absorb" only few such edges with distinct endpoints.

We first show that an edge in H represents only few *dom*-edges with distinct endpoints. For each $m\in M\setminus D$, we fix a set $C_m\subseteq V(G)\setminus\{m\}$ of size at most $2c$ which dominates $N_{E'}(m)$, note that existence of C_m follows from the definition of the set D. Recall that we assume that G excludes $K_{t,3}$ as depth-1 minor.

LEMMA 7. *Let $1\le i<j\le |M|$. Let $N_i := N_{E'}(m_i)$ and $N_j := N_{E'}(m_j)$.*

1. *If $m_j\notin D$, then*
$$|\{u\in N_j : \text{ there is } v\in N_i \text{ with } \{u,v\}\in E(G)\}| \le 2ct.$$
2. *If $m_i\notin D$ (and hence $m_j\notin D$), then*
$$|\{u\in N_i : \text{ there is } v\in N_j \text{ with } \{u,v\}\in E(G)\}| \le 4ct.$$

PROOF. By definition of E', it holds that $m_i\notin C_{m_j}$. Let $c\in C_{m_j}$ be arbitrary. Then there are at most $t-1$ distinct vertices $u_1,\ldots,u_{t-1}\in(N_j\cap N(c))$ such that there are $v_1,\ldots,v_{t-1}\in N_i$ (possibly not distinct) with $\{u_k,v_k\}\in E(G)$ for all k, $1\le k\le t-1$. Otherwise, we can contract the star with center m_i and branch vertices $N(m_i)\setminus\{c\}$ and thereby find $K_{t,3}$ as depth-1 minor, a contradiction. See Figure 2 for an illustration in the case of an excluded $K_{3,3}$. Possibly, $c\in N_j$ and it is connected to a vertex of N_i, hence we have at most t vertices in $N_j\cap N[c]$ with a connection to N_i. As $|C_{m_j}|\le 2c$, we conclude the first item.

Regarding the second item, let $c\in C_{m_i}$ be arbitrary. If $c\ne m_j$, we conclude just as above, that there are at most $t-1$ distinct vertices $u_1,\ldots,u_{t-1}\in(N_i\cap N(c))$ such that there are $v_1,\ldots,v_{t-1}\in N_j$ (possibly not distinct) with $\{u_k,v_k\}\in E(G)$ for all k, $1\le k\le t-1$ and hence at most t vertices in $N_i\cap N[c]$ with a connection to N_j. Now assume $c=m_j$. Let $c'\in C_{m_j}$. There are at most $t-1$ distinct vertices $u_1,\ldots,u_{t-1}\in(N_i\cap N_E(m_j))$ such that there are vertices $v_1,\ldots,v_{t-1}\in N_j\cap N(c)$ (possibly not distinct) with $\{u_k,v_k\}\in E(G)$ for all k, $1\le k\le t-1$. Again, considering the possibility that $c'\in N_i$, there are at most t vertices in $N_i\cap N_E(m_j)$ with a connection to $N_j\cap N(c)$. As $|C_{m_j}|\le 2c$, we conclude that in total there are at most $2ct$ vertices in $N_i\cap N_E(m_j)$ with a connection to N_j. In total, there are hence at most $(2c-1)t+2ct\le 4ct$ vertices of the described form. □

We write Y for the set of all vertices $\{u\in N_{E'}(m_i) : m_i\notin D \text{ and there is } v\in N_{E'}(m_j), j\ne i \text{ and } \{u,v\}\in E(G)\}$.

COROLLARY 8. $|Y|\le 6c^2t|M|$.

PROOF. Each of the $c|M|$ many edges in H represents edges between N_i and N_j, where N_i and N_j are defined as

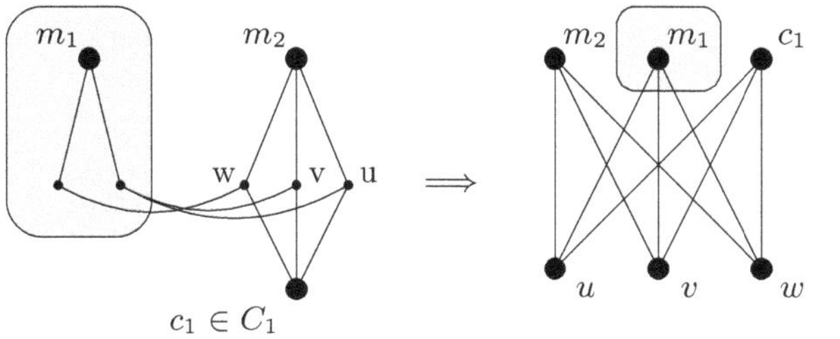

Figure 2: Visualisation of the proof of Lemma 7 in the case of excluded $K_{3,3}$

above. By the previous lemma, if $i < j$, there are at most $2ct$ vertices in $N_i \cap Y$ and at most $4ct$ vertices in $N_j \cap Y$, hence in total, each edge accounts for at most $6ct$ vertices in Y. □

We continue to count the edges which are inside the stars. First, we show that every vertex has small degree inside its own star.

LEMMA 9. *Let $m \in M \setminus D$ and let $v \in N_{E'}(m) \setminus C_m$. Then*

$$|\{u \in N_{E'}(m) : \{u,v\} \in E(G)\}| \leq 2c(t-1).$$

PROOF. Let $c \in C_m$. By the same argument as in Lemma 7, there are at most $t-1$ distinct vertices $u_1, \ldots, u_{t-1} \in (N_{E'}(m) \cap N(c))$ such that $\{u_k, v\} \in E(G)$ for all k, $1 \leq k \leq t-1$. □

Let $C := \bigcup_{m \in M \setminus D} C_m$. There are only few vertices which are highly connected to $M \cup C$. Let $Z := \{u \in N_{E'}(M \setminus D) : |N(u) \cap (M \cup C)| > 4c\}$.

LEMMA 10.

$$|Z| < |M \cup C|.$$

PROOF. Assume that $|Z| > |M \cup C|$. Then the subgraph induced by $Z \cup M \cup C$ has more than $\frac{1}{2}4c|Z|$ edges and $|Z \cup M \cup C|$ vertices. Hence its edge density is larger than $2c|Z|/(|Z \cup M \cup C|) > 2c|Z|/(2|Z|) = c$, contradicting our assumption on the edge density of depth-1 minors of G (which includes its subgraphs). □

Finally, we consider the image of the *dom*-function inside the stars.

LEMMA 11.

$$\left| \bigcup_{m \in M \setminus D} \{u \in N_{E'}(m) : dom(u) \in (N_{E'}(m) \setminus (Y \cup Z))\} \right|$$
$$\leq (2(t-1)+4)c|M|.$$

PROOF. Fix some $m \in M \setminus D$ and some $u \in N_{E'}(m)$ with $dom(u) \in N_{E'}(m) \setminus (Y \cup Z)$. Because $dom(u) \notin Y$, $dom(u)$ is not connected to a vertex of a different star, except possibly for vertices from M. Because $dom(u) \notin Z$, it is however connected to at most $4c$ vertices from $M \cup C$. Hence it is connected to at most $4c$ vertices from different stars. By Lemma 9, $dom(u)$ is connected to at most $2c(t-1)$ vertices from the same star. Hence the degree of $dom(u)$ is at most $4c + 2c(t-1)$. Because u preferred to choose $dom(u) \in N_{E'}(m)$ over m as its dominator, we conclude that m has at most $4c + 2c(t-1)$ E'-neighbors. Hence, in total there can be at most $(2(t-1)+4)c|M|$ such vertices. □

We are now ready to put together the numbers.

LEMMA 12. *If all depth-1 minors H of G have edge density at most c and G excludes $K_{t,3}$ as depth-1 minor, then the modified algorithm computes a $6c^2t + (2t+5)c + 4$ approximation for the minimum dominating set problem on G.*

PROOF. The set D has size at most $(c+1)|M|$ according to Lemma 5. Since M is a dominating set also with respect to the edges E', it suffices to determine $|\{dom(u) : u \in (N_{E'}[M \setminus D] \setminus N[D])\}|$. According to Corollary 8, the set $Y = \{u \in N_{E'}(m_i) :$ there is $v \in N_{E'}(m_j)$, $i \neq j$ and $\{u,v\} \in E(G)\}$ has size at most $6c^2t|M|$. In particular, there are at most so many vertices $dom(u) \in N_{E'}(m_i)$ with $u \in N_{E'}(m_j)$ for $i \neq j$. Clearly, $|dom(R) \cap M| \leq |M|$ and $|dom(M)| \leq |M|$. Together, this bounds the number of endpoints of *dom*-edges that go from one star to another star. According to Lemma 10, there are only few vertices which are highly connected to $M \cup C$, that is, the set $Z = \{u \in N_{E'}(M \setminus D) : |N(u) \cap (M \cup C)| > 4c\}$ satisfies $|Z| < |M \cup C|$. We have $|C| \leq 2c|M|$, as each C_m has size at most $2c$. It remains to count the image of *dom* inside the stars which do not point to Y or Z. According to Lemma 11, this image has size at most $(2(t-1)+4)c|M|$. In total, we hence find a set of size

$$(c+1)|M| + 6c^2t|M| + 2|M| + (2c+1)|M| +$$
$$(2(t-1)+4)c|M| \leq (6c^2t + (2t+5)c + 4)|M|.$$

□

Our theorem for bounded genus graphs is now a corollary of Lemma 2 and 12.

THEOREM 13. *Let $\mathcal{C}$ be a class of graphs of orientable genus at most g (non-orientable genus at most $\tilde{g}$ resp.). The modified algorithm computes an $\mathcal{O}(g)$-approximation ($\mathcal{O}(\tilde{g})$-approximation resp.) for the dominating set in $\mathcal{O}(g)$ ($\mathcal{O}(\tilde{g})$ resp.) communication rounds.*

For the special case of planar graphs, our analysis shows that the algorithm computes a 199-approximation. This is not much worse than Lenzen et al.'s original analysis (130), however, off by a factor of almost 4 from Wawrzyniak's [16] improved analysis (52).

4. IMPROVING THE APPROXIMATION FACTOR WITH PREPROCESSING

We now show that the constant approximation factors related to the genus g, derived in the previous section, can be improved, using a local preprocessing step.

Given a graph G and a vertex $v \in V(G)$. Let $K = \{K_1, \ldots, K_j\}$ denote the set of minimal subgraphs of G such that for all $1 \leq i \leq j$, $K_{3,3}$ is a depth-1 minor of K_i. Let $K_h \in K$ be the one with lexicographically smallest identifiers in K, we say K_h is the v-canonical subgraph of G and we denote it by K_v. If $K = \emptyset$ we set $K_v := \emptyset$.

Algorithm 2 Dominating Set Approximation Algorithm for Graphs of Genus $\leq g$

Input: Graph G of genus at most g
Run Phase 1 of Algorithm 1
(* *Preprocessing Phase* *)
for $v \in V - D$ (in parallel) **do**
    compute K_v **in** $G - D$ **(see Lemma 14)**
for $i = 1..g$ **do**
  for $v \in V - D$ (in parallel) **do**
    if $K_v \neq \emptyset$ **then**
      chosen : = true
      for all $u \in N^{12}(v)$
        if $K_u \cap K_v \neq \emptyset$ **and** $u < v$ **then chosen := false**
      if (chosen = true) then $D := D \cup V(K_v)$
Run Phase 2 of Algorithm 1

LEMMA 14. *Given a graph G and a vertex $v \in V(G)$. The v-canonical subgraph of G (K_v) can be computed locally in at most 6 communication rounds. Furthermore, K_v has at most 24 vertices.*

PROOF. The proof is constructive. As $K_{3,3}$ has diameter 2, every minimal subgraph of G containing $K_{3,3}$ as a depth-1 minor has diameter at most 6 (every edge may have to be replaced by a path of length 3). Therefore, it suffices to consider the subgraph $H = G[N^6(v)]$ and find the lexicographically minimal subgraph which contains $K_{3,3}$ as depth-1 minor in H which includes v as a vertex. If this is the case, we output it as K_v; otherwise we output the empty set. Furthermore, $K_{3,3}$ has 9 edges and hence a minimal subgraph containing it as depth-1 minor has at most 24 vertices (again, every edge is subdivided at most twice and $2 \cdot 9 + 6 = 24$). □

To improve the approximation factor, we propose the following modified algorithm, see Algorithm 2.

THEOREM 15. *Algorithm 2 provides a $24g + \mathcal{O}(1)$ MDS approximation for graphs of genus at most g, and requires $12g + \mathcal{O}(1)$ communication rounds.*

PROOF. The resulting vertex set is clearly a legal dominating set. Moreover, as Phase 1 is unchanged, we do not have to recalculate D.

In the preprocessing phase, if for two vertices $u \neq v$ we choose both K_u, K_v, then they must be disjoint. Since the diameter of any depth-1 minor of $K_{3,3}$ is at most 6, if two such canonical subgraphs intersect, the distance between u, v can be at most 12. On the other hand, by Lemma 3, there are at most g disjoint such models. So in the *preprocessing* phase, we can remove at most g disjoint subgraphs K_v (and add their vertices to the dominating set) and thereby select at most $24g$ extra vertices for the dominating set. Once the *preprocessing* phase is finished, the remaining graph is locally embeddable.

In order to compute the size of the set in the third phase, we can use the analysis of Lemma 12 for $t = 3$, which together with the first phase and preprocessing phase, results in a $24g + \mathcal{O}(1)$-approximation guarantee.

To count the number of communication rounds, note that the only change happens in the second phase. In that phase, in each iteration, we need 12 communication rounds to compute the 12-neighbourhood. Therefore, the number of communication rounds is $12g + \mathcal{O}(1)$. □

This significantly improves the approximation upper bound of Theorem 13: namely from $4(6c^2 + 2c)g + \mathcal{O}(1)$, which, since $c \leq 3.01$ can be as high as $241g + \mathcal{O}(1)$ in sufficiently large graphs, to $24g + \mathcal{O}(1)$, at the price of $12g$ extra communication rounds.

5. A LOGICAL PERSPECTIVE

Interestingly, as we will elaborate in the following, a small modification of Algorithm 1 can be interpreted both from a distributed computing perspective, namely as a local algorithm of constant distributed time complexity, as well as from a logical perspective.

First order logic has atomic formulas of the form $x = y, x < y$ and $E(x, y)$, where x and y are first-order variables. The set of first order formulas is closed under Boolean combinations and existential and universal quantification over the vertices of a graph. To define the semantics, we inductively define a satisfaction relation $\models$, where for a graph G, a formula $\phi(x_1, \dots, x_k)$ and vertices $v_1, \dots, v_k \in V(G)$, $G \models \phi(v_1, \dots, v_k)$ means that G satisfies ϕ if the free variables $x_1, \dots, x_k$ are interpreted as $v_1, \dots, v_k$, respectively. The free variables of a formula are those not in the scope of a quantifier, and we write $\phi(x, \dots, x_k)$ to indicate that the free variables of the formula ϕ are among $x_1, \dots, x_k$. For $\phi(x_1, x_2) = x_1 < x_2$, we have $G \models \phi(v_1, v_2)$ if $v_1 < v_2$ with respect to the ordering $<$ of $V(G)$ and for $\phi(x_1, x_2) = E(x_1, x_2)$ we have $G \models \phi(v_1, v_2)$ if $\{v_1, v_2\} \in E(G)$. The meaning of the equality symbol, the Boolean connectives, and the quantifiers is as expected.

A first-order formula $\phi(x)$ with one free variable naturally defines the set $\phi(G) = \{v \in V(G) : G \models \phi(v)\}$. We say that a formula ϕ defines an f-approximation to the dominating set problem on a class $\mathcal{C}$ of graphs, if $\phi(G)$ is an f-approximation of a minimum dominating set for every graph $G \in \mathcal{C}$.

Observe that first-order logic is not able to count, in particular, no fixed formula can determine a neighbor of maximum degree in Line 14 of the algorithm. Observe however, that the only place in our analysis that refers to the dominator function d explicitly is Lemma 11. The proof of the lemma in fact shows that we do not have to choose a vertex of maximal residual degree, but that it suffices to choose a vertex of degree greater than $4c + 2c(t - 1)$ if such a vertex exists, or any vertex, otherwise. For every fixed class of bounded genus, this number is a constant, however, we have to address how logic should choose a vertex among the candidate vertices. For this, we assume that the graph is equipped with an order relation such that the formula can simply choose the smallest candidate with respect to the order. It is now easy to see that the solution computed by the algorithm is first-order definable.

6. CONCLUSION

This paper presented the first constant round, constant factor local MDS approximation algorithm for locally embeddable graphs, a class of graphs which is much more general than planar graphs. Our proofs are purely combinatorial and avoid any topological arguments. For the family of bounded genus graphs, topological arguments helped to improve the obtained approximation ratio in a preprocessing step. We believe that this result constitutes a major step forward in the quest for understanding for which graph families such local approximations exist. Besides the result itself, we believe that our analysis introduces several new techniques which may be useful also for the design and analysis of local algorithms for more general graphs, and also problems beyond MDS.

Moreover, this paper established an interesting connection between distributed computing and logic, by presenting a local approximation algorithm which is first-order logic definable. This also provides an interesting new perspective on the recently introduced notion of stone-age distributed computing [5]: distributed algorithms making minimal assumptions on the power of a node.

It remains open whether the local constant approximation result can be generalized to sparse graphs beyond bounded genus graphs. Also, it will be interesting to extend our study of first-order definable approximations.

7. REFERENCES

[1] Baker, B. S. Approximation algorithms for np-complete problems on planar graphs. *J. ACM 41*, 1 (Jan. 1994), 153–180.

[2] Barenboim, L., Elkin, M., and Gavoille, C. A fast network-decomposition algorithm and its applications to constant-time distributed computation. In *Proc. SIROCCO*. 2014, pp. 209–223.

[3] Czygrinow, A., Hańćkowiak, M., and Wawrzyniak, W. Fast distributed approximations in planar graphs. In *Proc. 22nd International Symposium on Distributed Computing (DISC)* (2008), pp. 78–92.

[4] Elkin, M. An overview of distributed approximation. *ACM SIGACT News Distributed Computing Column 35*, 4 (Mar. 2004), 40–57.

[5] Emek, Y., and Wattenhofer, R. Stone age distributed computing. In *Proc. ACM Symposium on Principles of Distributed Computing (PODC)* (2013), pp. 137–146.

[6] Hilke, M., Lenzen, C., and Suomela, J. Brief announcement: local approximability of minimum dominating set on planar graphs. In *Proc. ACM Symposium on Principles of Distributed Computing (PODC)* (2014), pp. 344–346.

[7] Kuhn, F., Moscibroda, T., and Wattenhofer, R. Local computation: Lower and upper bounds. *arXiv preprint arXiv:1011.5470* (2010).

[8] Lenzen, C., Pignolet, Y. A., and Wattenhofer, R. Distributed minimum dominating set approximations in restricted families of graphs. *Distributed Computing 26*, 2 (2013), 119–137.

[9] Lenzen, C., and Wattenhofer, R. Leveraging linial's locality limit. In *Distributed Computing*, vol. 5218 of *Lecture Notes in Computer Science*. 2008, pp. 394–407.

[10] Lenzen, C., and Wattenhofer, R. Minimum dominating set approximation in graphs of bounded arboricity. In *Distributed Computing*, vol. 6343. 2010, pp. 510–524.

[11] Linial, N. Locality in distributed graph algorithms. *SIAM J. Comput. 21*, 1 (Feb. 1992), 193–201.

[12] Mohar, B., and Thomassen, C. *Graphs on Surfaces*. Johns Hopkins University Press, 2001.

[13] Peleg, D. *Distributed Computing: A Locality-sensitive Approach*. Society for Industrial and Applied Mathematics, Philadelphia, PA, USA, 2000.

[14] Suomela, J. Survey of local algorithms. *ACM Comput. Surv. 45*, 2 (Mar. 2013), 24:1–24:40.

[15] Wawrzyniak, W. Brief announcement: a local approximation algorithm for mds problem in anonymous planar networks. In *Proceedings of the 2013 ACM symposium on Principles of distributed computing* (2013), ACM, pp. 406–408.

[16] Wawrzyniak, W. A strengthened analysis of a local algorithm for the minimum dominating set problem in planar graphs. *Proc. Information Processing Letters (IPL) 114*, 3 (2014), 94 – 98.

On Efficient Distributed Construction of Near Optimal Routing Schemes

[Extended Abstract] *

Michael Elkin[†]
Department of Computer Science,
Ben-Gurion University of the Negev,
Beer-Sheva, Israel.
elkinm@cs.bgu.ac.il

Ofer Neiman[‡]
Department of Computer Science,
Ben-Gurion University of the Negev,
Beer-Sheva, Israel.
neimano@cs.bgu.ac.il

ABSTRACT

Given a distributed network represented by a weighted undirected graph $G = (V, E)$ on n vertices, and a parameter k, we devise a distributed algorithm that computes a routing scheme in $O(n^{1/2+1/k}+D)\cdot n^{o(1)}$ rounds, where D is the hop-diameter of the network. The running time nearly matches the lower bound of $\tilde{\Omega}(n^{1/2} + D)$ rounds (which holds for any scheme with polynomial stretch). The routing tables are of size $\tilde{O}(n^{1/k})$, the labels are of size $O(k \log^2 n)$, and every packet is routed on a path suffering stretch at most $4k-5+o(1)$. Our construction nearly matches the state-of-the-art for routing schemes built in a centralized sequential manner. The previous best algorithms for building routing tables in a distributed small messages model were by [LP13a, STOC 2013] and [LP15, PODC 2015]. The former has similar properties but suffers from substantially larger routing tables of size $O(n^{1/2+1/k})$, while the latter has sub-optimal running time of $\tilde{O}(\min\{(nD)^{1/2} \cdot n^{1/k}, n^{2/3+2/(3k)} + D\})$.

Keywords

Routing; CONGEST model

1. INTRODUCTION

A routing scheme in a distributed network is a mechanism that allows packets to be delivered from any node to any other node. The network is represented as a weighted undirected graph, and each node should be able to forward incoming data by using local information stored at the node, and the (short) packet's header. The local routing information is often referred to as a routing table. The routing scheme has two main phases: in the preprocessing phase, each node is assigned a routing table and a short label. In the routing phase, each node receiving a packet should make a local decision, based on its own routing table and the packet's header (which contains the label of the destination), to which neighbor forward the packet to. The *stretch* of a routing scheme is the worst ratio between the length of a path on which a packet is routed, to the shortest possible path.

Designing efficient routing schemes is a central problem in the area of distributed networking, and was studied intensively [ABLP90, Cow01, EGP03, GP03, AGM04, PU89, TZ01, Che13]. In [TZ01], Thorup and Zwick presented the following compact routing scheme: Given a weighted graph G on n vertices and a parameter $k \geq 1$, the scheme has routing tables of size $\tilde{O}(n^{1/k})$,[1] labels of size $O(k \log n)$ and stretch $4k-5$. (Assuming that port numbers may be assigned by the routing process, otherwise the label size increases by a factor of $\log n$.)[2] The state-of-the-art is a scheme of [Che13], which is based on [TZ01], and improves the stretch to $3.68k$.

All the results above assume that the preprocessing phase can be computed in a sequential centralized manner. However, as the problem of designing a compact routing scheme is inherently concerned with a distributed network, constructing the scheme efficiently in a distributed manner is a very natural direction. We focus on the standard CONGEST model [Pel00a]. In this model, every vertex initially knows only the edges touching it, and communication between vertices occurs in synchronous *rounds*. On every round, each vertex may send a small message to each of its neighbors. Every message takes a unit time to reach the neighbor, regardless of the edge weight. The time complexity is measured by the number of rounds it takes to complete a task (we assume local computation does not cost anything). Often the time depends on n, the number of vertices, and D, the *hop-diameter* of the graph. The hop-diameter is the

*A full version of this paper is available at `http://arxiv.org/abs/1602.02293`

†This research was supported by the ISF grant 724/15.

‡Supported in part by ISF grant No. (523/12) and by the European Union Seventh Framework Programme (FP7/2007-2013) under grant agreement $n^\circ 303809$.

PODC'16, July 25-28, 2016, Chicago, IL, USA

© 2016 ACM. ISBN 978-1-4503-3964-3/16/07…$15.00

DOI: http://dx.doi.org/10.1145/2933057.2933098

[1]The $\tilde{O}$ hides $\log^{O(1)} n$ factors.

[2]They also presented stretch $2k-1$, assuming "handshaking": allowing the source and destination to communicate before the routing phase begins, but it is often desirable to avoid handshaking.

maximum hop-distance between two vertices, where the hop-distance is the minimal number of edges on a path between the vertices (regardless of the weights). The hop diameter is not to be confused with the *shortest path diameter* S, which is the maximal number of hops a shortest path uses (assuming shortest paths are unique). We always have $D \leq S$, and typically D is small while S could be as large as $\Omega(n)$. We also assume, as common in the literature [LP13a, Nan14, KP98, GK13, HKN16], that edge weights are integers and at most polynomial in n (so that they could be sent in a single message).[3]

A rich research thread concerns with finding efficient distributed (approximation) algorithms for classical graph problems (e.g., minimum spanning tree, minimum cut, shortest paths), in sub-linear time [GKP98, PR00, Elk06a, SHK+12, HKN16]. There are several results obtaining running times of the form $\tilde{O}(\sqrt{n}+D)$, e.g. for MST, connectivity, minimum cut, approximate shortest path tree, etc. These results are often accompanied by a (nearly) matching lower bounds. The lower bound of [SHK+12], based on [PR00, Elk06b], implies that devising a routing scheme with any polynomial stretch, requires $\tilde{\Omega}(\sqrt{n}+D)$ rounds.

The first result on computing a routing scheme in a distributed manner within $o(n)$ rounds (for general graphs with $D = o(n)$), was shown by Lenzen and Patt-Shamir [LP13a].[4] Their algorithm, given a graph on n vertices and a parameter k, provides routing tables of size $\tilde{O}(n^{1/2+1/k})$, labels of size $O(\log n \cdot \log k)$, stretch at most $O(k \log k)$, and has a nearly optimal running time of $\tilde{O}(n^{1/2+1/k}+D)$ rounds. Note that the routing tables are of size $\Omega(\sqrt{n})$ for any value of k, which could be prohibitively large (the routing scheme of [TZ01] supports stretch 3 with $\tilde{O}(\sqrt{n})$ table size). They also show implications for related problems, such as approximate diameter, generalized Steiner forest, and distance estimation. In a follow-up paper, [LP15] showed how to improve the stretch of the above scheme to roughly $3k/2$ (for any k divisible by 4). They also exhibited a different tradeoff, that overcame the issue of large routing tables. They devised an algorithm that produced routing tables of size $\tilde{O}(n^{1/k})$, labels of size $O(k \log^2 n)$ and stretch $4k-3+o(1)$,[5] but the number of rounds increases to $\tilde{O}(\min\{(nD)^{1/2} \cdot n^{1/k}, n^{2/3+2/(3k)}+D\})$. Note that for moderately large hop-diameter $D \approx n^{1/3}$, the number of rounds is bounded by only $\approx n^{2/3}$ for any value of k. (They also show a variant where the number of rounds is $\tilde{O}(S+n^{1/k})$, but as was mentioned above, S might be much larger than D.)

In the *distance estimation* problem (also known as sketching, or distance labeling), we wish to compute a small *sketch* for each vertex, so that given any two sketches, one can efficiently compute the (approximate) distance between the vertices. This problem was introduced in [Pel00b], who provided initial existential results. In [SDP15], a distributed (randomized) algorithm running in $\tilde{O}(S \cdot n^{1/k})$ rounds was shown, that computes sketches of size $O(kn^{1/k} \log n)$ with stretch at most $2k-1$. While this essentially matches the best sequential algorithm of [TZ05], the number of rounds could be $\Omega(n)$, even when D is small. In [LP13a], a running time of $\tilde{O}(n^{1/2+1/k}+D)$ rounds was presented, at the cost of significantly increasing the stretch to $O(k^2)$.[6]

Our contribution.

We devise a randomized distributed algorithm running in $(n^{1/2+1/k}+D) \cdot \min\{(\log n)^{O(k)}, 2^{\tilde{O}(\sqrt{\log n})}\}$ rounds[7], that with high probability, computes a compact routing scheme with routing tables of size $O(n^{1/k} \log^2 n)$, labels of size $O(k \log^2 n)$, and stretch at most $4k-5+o(1)$. Note that our result nearly matches the construction of [TZ01], up to logarithmic terms in the size and $o(1)$ additive term in the stretch. This is even though the latter is computed in a sequential centralized manner. Observe that our running time nearly matches the lower bound of [SHK+12], and is substantially better than that of [LP15] whenever $D \geq n^{\Omega(1)}$ (which achieved similar size-stretch tradeoff). The previous result obtaining near optimal running time [LP13a], suffers from excessive routing table size.

As a corollary, we show a distance estimation scheme, whose computation can be done in $(n^{1/2+1/k}+D) \cdot \min\{(\log n)^{O(k)}, 2^{\tilde{O}(\sqrt{\log n})}\}$ rounds, providing sketches of size $O(n^{1/k} \log n)$ with stretch $2k-1+o(1)$. Each distance estimation takes only $O(k)$ time. Our result combines the improved running time of [LP13a] (up to lower order terms), with the near optimal size-stretch tradeoff of [SDP15].

When preparing this submission, we learnt that concurrently and independently of us [LPP16] came up with a distributed algorithm running in $(n^{1/2+1/k}+D) \cdot 2^{\tilde{O}(\sqrt{\log n})}$ rounds, that with high probability, computes a routing scheme with routing tables of size $\tilde{O}(n^{1/k})$, labels of size $O(k \log n)$, and stretch at most $4k-3+o(1)$. Full details of [LPP16] algorithm and analysis are not currently available to us.

1.1 Overview of Techniques

Let us first briefly sketch the Thorup-Zwick construction of a routing scheme. First they designed a routing scheme for trees, with constant routing tables and logarithmic label size. For a general graph $G = (V, E)$ on n vertices, they randomly sample a collection of sets $V = A_0 \supseteq A_1 \cdots \supseteq A_k = \emptyset$, where for each $0 < i < k$, each vertex in A_{i-1} is chosen independently to be in A_i with probability $n^{-1/k}$. The *cluster* of a vertex $u \in A_i \setminus A_{i+1}$ is defined as

$$C(u) = \{v \in V \ : \ d_G(u,v) < d_G(v, A_{i+1})\} \ . \qquad (1)$$

They proved that each cluster $C(x)$ can be viewed as a tree rooted at x, and showed an efficient procedure that given a pair $u, v \in V$, finds a vertex x so that routing in the tree $C(x)$ has small stretch. So each vertex u maintains in its routing table the routing information for all trees $C(x)$ containing it, while the label of u consists of the tree-labels

[3]We shall not consider *name-independent* routing, in which the label of a vertex is its ID, because [LP13a] showed a strong lower bound: any such scheme with stretch ρ (even average stretch ρ) must take $\tilde{\Omega}(n/\rho^2)$ rounds to compute in this model.

[4]We remark that for the class of k-chordal graphs, [NRS12] showed a construction of a routing scheme that could be computed efficiently in a distributed manner.

[5]The paper [LP15] claimed label size $O(k \log n)$, but in [LP16] it was communicated to us that the actual size is $O(k \log^2 n)$.

[6]In fact, they showed a scheme in which it suffices to have a sketch of one vertex, and a $O(k \log n)$ size label of the other vertex, to derive the distance estimation. Our result has a similar flavor.

[7]In fact, for odd k the number of rounds becomes $(n^{1/2+1/(2k)}+D) \cdot \min\{(\log n)^{O(k)}, 2^{\tilde{O}(\sqrt{\log n})}\}$.

	Number of Rounds	Table size	Label size	Stretch
[TZ01, Che13]	$O(m)$	$\tilde{O}(n^{\frac{1}{k}})$	$O(k\log n)$	$3.68k$
[LP15]	$\tilde{O}(S+n^{\frac{1}{k}})$	$\tilde{O}(n^{\frac{1}{k}})$	$O(k\log n)$	$4k-3$
[LP13a, LP15]	$\tilde{O}(n^{\frac{1}{2}+\frac{1}{4k}}+D)$	$\tilde{O}(n^{\frac{1}{2}+\frac{1}{4k}})$	$O(\log n)$	$6k-1+o(1)$
[LP15]	$\tilde{O}(\min\{(nD)^{\frac{1}{2}}\cdot n^{\frac{1}{k}}, n^{\frac{2}{3}+\frac{2}{3k}}+D\})$	$\tilde{O}(n^{\frac{1}{k}})$	$O(k\log^2 n)$	$4k-3+o(1)$
This paper	$(n^{1/2+1/k}+D)\cdot\min\{(\log n)^{O(k)}, 2^{\tilde{O}(\sqrt{\log n})}\}$	$\tilde{O}(n^{\frac{1}{k}})$	$O(k\log^2 n)$	$4k-5+o(1)$

Figure 1: Comparison of compact routing schemes for graphs with n vertices, m edges, hop-diameter D, and shortest path diameter S.

for a few special trees. They also show that (with high probability) every vertex is contained in at most $\tilde{O}(n^{1/k})$ trees.

The first difficulty we must deal with, is that the routing scheme of Thorup-Zwick for a tree could take a linear number of rounds. We thus develop a variation on that scheme, that can be implemented efficiently in a distributed network. The basic idea is inspired by [KP98] (and also used in [Nan14]), which is to select $\approx\sqrt{n}$ vertices that partition the tree into bounded depth subtrees. We then apply the TZ-scheme locally in every subtree. The subtler part is to design a global routing scheme for the virtual tree[8] induced on the sampled vertices, which must incorporate the local routing information.

Approximate Clusters.

Once we have a distributed algorithm for routing in trees, we set off to apply the TZ-scheme for general graphs. Unfortunately, it is not known how to compute the exact clusters efficiently in a distributed manner. Even for a single shortest path tree (SPT), no algorithm running in $o(n)$ rounds is known. In order to circumvent this barrier, we introduce the notion of *approximate clusters*. An approximate cluster is a subset of a cluster, that may exclude vertices that are "near" the boundary. (Slightly more formally, we may omit vertices for which the inequality (1) becomes false if we multiply the left hand side by a $1+\epsilon$ factor, for a small $\epsilon>0$.) Our main technical contributions are: exhibiting a procedure that computes these approximate clusters, and showing that these are sufficient for constructing a routing scheme, with nearly matching size and stretch as in [TZ01].

The construction of clusters $C(u)$ for $u\in A_i\setminus A_{i+1}$ where $i<k/2$, can be done in a straightforward manner (within the allotted number of rounds), since the depth of the corresponding tree is $\tilde{O}(\sqrt{n})$ with high probability, and since the *overlap* (the number of clusters containing a fixed vertex) is only $\tilde{O}(n^{1/k})$. The main challenge is computing the approximate clusters in the large scales, for $i\geq k/2$. To this end, we employ several tools. The first is *approximate multi-source hop-bounded distance computation*, which appeared recently in [Nan14] (a certain variation appeared also in [LP13b]). This enables us to compute approximations for B-hops shortest paths (paths that use at most B edges), from a given m sources to every vertex, in $\tilde{O}(B+m+D)$ rounds. The second tool we use is *hopsets*. The notion of hopsets was introduced by [Coh00] in the context of parallel approximate shortest path algorithms, and it has found applications in dynamic and distributed settings as well [Ber09, HKN14, HKN16]. A (β,ϵ)-hopset is a (small) set of edges F, so that every shortest path has a corresponding β-hops path, whose weight is at most $1+\epsilon$ larger.

We compute the approximate clusters in the large scales as follows. First we sample $\approx\sqrt{n}$ vertices (those in $A_{k/2}$), and compute approximate $\sqrt{n}$-hops shortest paths from all the sampled vertices. Next we apply a (β,ϵ)-hopset on the graph induced by these sampled vertices, where $\beta\leq 2^{\tilde{O}(\sqrt{\log n})}$ and $\epsilon\approx 1/k^4$. An efficient distributed algorithm to construct such hopsets is given by [HKN16, EN16]. We shall use the construction of [EN16], since it facilitates much smaller β, whenever k is small. This enables us to compute the approximate clusters on the sampled vertices, since we need only β steps of exploration from each source u, using again that the overlap is small. Finally we extend each approximate cluster to the other vertices, by initiating an exploration from each sampled vertex to hop-distance $\approx\sqrt{n}$ in the original graph (in fact, one can use the multi-source hop-bounded distance computation of [Nan14]). The correctness follows since with high probability, every vertex that should be included in some approximate cluster $\tilde{C}(u)$, has either u or a sampled vertex within $\approx\sqrt{n}$ hops on the shortest path to it. The thresholds for entering an approximate cluster must be set carefully, so that every vertex on that shortest path will also join $\tilde{C}(u)$, in order to guarantee that the trees will indeed be connected (which is clearly crucial for routing), and on the other hand, to make sure that no vertex participates in too many trees. Unlike the exact TZ clusters, approximate clusters generally do not have to be connected.

The fact that our clusters are only approximate induces increased stretch. The analysis is similar to that of [TZ05], which consists of k iterations of searching for the "right" tree. We must pay a factor of $1+O(\epsilon)$ in every one of these iterations, but fortunately, the hopset construction allows us to take sufficiently small ϵ, so that all the additional stretch accumulates to an additive $o(1)$.

From a high level, our approach is similar to those of [LP13a, LP15]. In [LP15], they also use a variant of the TZ-routing scheme, which allows small errors in the distance estimations. The main difference is in handling the large scales. In [LP13a], the idea was to build a spanner on a sample of $\approx\sqrt{n}$ vertices, which helps by reducing the number of edges, so a routing scheme could be efficiently computed on the spanner, and then extended to the entire graph. This approach inherently suffers from large storage requirement, since every vertex needs to know all the spanner edges. In [LP15] the idea was to "delay" the start of large scales from $k/2$ to roughly $l_0=(k/2)\cdot(1+\log D/\log n)$. Then they apply a distance estimation on the sampled ver-

[8] By a virtual tree we mean a tree whose edges are not present in the network.

tices at scale l_0 (those in A_{l_0}) to construct the routing tables for all higher scales, and extend these to the remainder of the graph. However, the exploration in the graph on A_{l_0} may need to be of $\approx n^{1-l_0/k}$ hops, which induces a factor of $D \cdot n^{1-l_0/k} = (nD)^{1/2}$ to the number of rounds. The use of hopsets allows us to avoid the large memory requirement, since the routing is oblivious to the hopset, while significantly shortening the exploration range, enabling fast running time.

1.2 Organization

After stating in Section 2 some of the tools we shall apply, in Section 3 we describe the notion of approximate clusters, and show how to compute these efficiently in a distributed manner. The proof of correctness is deferred to the full version. Then in Section 4, we demonstrate how these approximate clusters could be used for a routing scheme in general graphs. In Section 5 we show the distance estimation scheme. Our distributed tree routing is deferred to the full version.

2. PRELIMINARIES

Let $G = (V, E, w)$ be a weighted graph on n vertices. We assume that $w : E \to \{1, \dots, \text{poly}(n)\}$ (without this assumption, there will be a logarithmic dependence on the aspect ratio in the data structures size and running times). Let D be the *hop-diameter* of G, that is, the diameter of G if all weights were 1. Denote by d_G the shortest path metric on G. Let $d_G^{(t)}$ be the *t-hops* shortest path distance (abusing notation, since this is not a metric). That is, $d_G^{(t)}(u, v)$ is the shortest length of a path from u to v, that has at most t edges (set $d_G^{(t)}(u, v) = \infty$ if every path from u to v has more than t edges). For each $u, v \in V$, define $h_G(u, v)$ as the number of hops on the shortest path in G between u and v. We shall always use this notation with respect to the input graph G, and thus will omit the subscript. A (dominating) *virtual graph* on G is a graph $G' = (V', E', w')$ with $V' \subseteq V$, and for every $u, v \in V'$ we have that $d_{G'}(u, v) \geq d_G(u, v)$. Every vertex in V' should know all the edges of E' touching it. Throughout the paper, we measure the size of the labels and routing tables in machine *words*, where a word consists of $\Theta(\log n)$ bits. The following lemma formalizes the broadcast ability of a distributed network (see, e.g., [Pel00a]).

LEMMA 1. *Suppose every $v \in V$ holds m_v messages, each of $O(1)$ words, for a total of $M = \sum_{v \in V} m_v$. Then all vertices can receive all the messages within $O(M + D)$ rounds.*

2.1 Tools

We first state our theorem on distributed tree routing, which is proven in the full version of this paper.

THEOREM 1. *Fix a graph $G = (V, E)$ on n vertices with hop-diameter D. For any tree T which is a subgraph of G, there is a routing scheme with stretch 1, routing tables of size $O(\log n)$ and labels of size $O(\log^2 n)$, that can be computed in a distributed manner within $\tilde{O}(\sqrt{n} + D)$ rounds.*

We also note we can compute efficiently many trees in parallel, if no vertex participates in too many of them.

REMARK 1. *If we are given n trees, each a subgraph of $G = (V, E)$, so that each vertex $v \in V$ participates in at most s trees, then routing schemes for all the trees can be computed in $\tilde{O}(\sqrt{n} \cdot s + D)$ rounds.*

Computing hop-bounded distances from multiple sources.

We will make use of the following theorem due to [Nan14, Theorem 3.6], which shows how to compute hop-bounded distances from a given set of sources, efficiently in a distributed manner.

THEOREM 2 ([NAN14]). *Given a weighted graph $G = (V, E, w)$ of hop-diameter D, a set $V' \subseteq V$, and parameters $B \geq 1$ and $0 < \epsilon < 1$, there is a (randomized) distributed algorithm that w.h.p runs in $\tilde{O}(|V'| + B + D)/\epsilon$ rounds, so that every $u \in V$ will know values $\{d_{uv}\}_{v \in V'}$ satisfying*[9]

$$d_G^{(B)}(u, v) \leq d_{uv} \leq (1 + \epsilon) d_G^{(B)}(u, v) \ , \tag{2}$$

REMARK 2. *While not explicitly stated in [Nan14], the proof also provides that each $u \in V$ knows, for every $v \in V'$, a vertex $p = p_v(u)$ which is a neighbor of u satisfying*

$$d_{uv} \geq w(u, p) + d_{pv} \ . \tag{3}$$

The following notion of hopsets was introduced by [Coh00].

DEFINITION 1 (HOPSETS). *A set of (weighted) edges F is a (β, ϵ)-hopset for a graph $G = (V, E)$, if in the graph $H = (V, E \cup F)$, for every $u, v \in V$,*

$$d_G(u, v) \leq d_H(u, v) \leq d_H^{(\beta)}(u, v) \leq (1 + \epsilon) d_G(u, v) \ . \tag{4}$$

We will need the following *path-reporting* property from our hopset. This property will be crucial for the connectivity of the trees corresponding to the approximate clusters.

PROPERTY 1. *A hopset F for a graph G is called* path-reporting, *if for every hopset edge $(u, v) \in F$ of weight b, there exists a corresponding path P in G between u and v of length b. Furthermore, every vertex x on P knows $d_P(x, u)$ and $d_P(x, v)$, and its neighbors on P.*

The following result is from our companion paper [EN16], which provides a path-reporting hopset. We remark that the original hopset construction of [Coh00] could be made path-reporting. Also, in [HKN16, Theorem 4.10], a distributed algorithm constructing a hopset is provided, which possibly could be made to be path-reporting, however, it inherently cannot provide a better hopbound than $2^{\tilde{O}(\sqrt{\log n})}$.

THEOREM 3 ([EN16]). *Let G be a weighted graph on n vertices with hop-diameter D, let $0 < \epsilon < 1$, and let G' be a virtual graph on G with m vertices. Let $0 < \rho < 1/2$ be a parameter, and write $\beta = \left(\frac{\log m}{\epsilon \cdot \rho}\right)^{O(1/\rho)}$. Then there is a randomized distributed algorithm that w.h.p computes in $\tilde{O}(m^{1+\rho} + D) \cdot \beta^2$ rounds, a path-reporting (β, ϵ)-hopset F for G'.*

We remark that in many applications the size of the hopset is important. However, here we only care about the size to the extent that it affects the number of rounds required to compute the hopset.

[9]The computed values are symmetric, that is, $d_{uv} = d_{vu}$ whenever $u, v \in V'$.

Approximate Shortest Path Tree (SPT).

Very recently, [HKN16] obtained an efficient distributed algorithm for computing an approximate SPT, which we shall use. Let us first define the problem formally. Let $G = (V, E, w)$ be a weighted graph. Given a set of vertices $A \subseteq V$, computing an $(1+\epsilon)$-approximate SPT rooted at A, means that every vertex $u \in V$ will know a value $\hat{d}(u)$ satisfying

$$d_G(u, A) \leq \hat{d}(u) \leq (1+\epsilon) d_G(u, A) \ , \tag{5}$$

and that u will know a vertex $\hat{z}(u) \in A$ so that $d_G(u, \hat{z}(u)) \leq \hat{d}(u)$. The following theorem is shown in [HKN16].[10]

THEOREM 4 ([HKN16]). *Let $G = (V, E, w)$ be a weighted graph on n vertices with hop-diameter D. Given a set $A \subseteq V$ of size $|A| \leq 2\sqrt{n} \ln n$, and $\frac{1}{\text{polylog } n} < \epsilon < 1$, there is a distributed algorithm that computes an $(1+\epsilon)$-approximate SPT rooted at A in $\tilde{O}(\sqrt{n} + D) \cdot 2^{\tilde{O}(\sqrt{\log n})}$ rounds.*

We remark that using the hopsets of [EN16], one can obtain an approximate SPT as in Theorem 4 within $(n^{1/2+1/k} + D) \cdot \min\{(\log n)^{O(k)}, 2^{\tilde{O}(\sqrt{\log n})}\}$ rounds. (This holds for any $1 \leq k \leq \log n$. Choosing $k = \sqrt{\log n}$ captures the bound in the theorem.)

3. DISTRIBUTED ROUTING SCHEME

In this section we define the notions of approximate pivots and approximate clusters, and describe an efficient distributed algorithm that computes these. Let us first recall the basic definitions from [TZ05].

Let $G = (V, E, w)$ be a weighted graph, fix $k \geq 1$. Sample a collection of sets $V = A_0 \supseteq A_1 \cdots \supseteq A_k = \emptyset$, where for each $0 < i < k$, each vertex in A_{i-1} is chosen independently to be in A_i with probability $n^{-1/k}$. A point $z \in A_i$ is called an i-pivot of v, if $d_G(v, z) = d_G(v, A_i)$. The cluster of a vertex $u \in A_i \setminus A_{i+1}$ is defined as

$$C(u) = \{v \in V \ : \ d_G(u, v) < d_G(v, A_{i+1})\} \ . \tag{6}$$

We quote a claim from [TZ05], which provides a bound on the overlap of clusters.

CLAIM 2. *With high probability, each vertex is contained in at most $4n^{1/k} \log n$ clusters.*

The following claim shows that (with high probability) the sets A_i have favorable properties.

CLAIM 3. *With high probability the following holds for every $0 \leq i \leq k-1$: (1) $|A_i| \leq 4n^{1-i/k} \ln n$, and (2) For every $u, v \in V$ such that $h(u, v) > 4n^{i/k} \ln n$, there exists a vertex of A_i on the shortest path between u and v.*

PROOF. Fix i. The first assertion holds by a simple Chernoff bound, since every vertex is chosen to be in A_i independently with probability $n^{-i/k}$, and the expected size of A_i is $n^{1-i/k}$. For the second assertion, let u, v be such that $h(u, v) > 4n^{i/k} \ln n$ (recall that $h(u, v)$ is the number of hops on the shortest path from u to v in G). The probability that none of the vertices on the u to v shortest path is included in A_i is at most

$$\left(1 - n^{-i/k}\right)^{4n^{i/k} \ln n} \leq n^{-4} \ .$$

Taking a union bound on the k possible values of i and $\binom{n}{2}$ pairs completes the proof. $\square$

From now on assume that all the events in the claims above hold, which yields the following corollary.

COROLLARY 4. *For any $0 \leq i < k-1$, $u \in A_i \setminus A_{i+1}$ and $v \in C(u)$, it holds that $h(u, v) \leq 4n^{(i+1)/k} \ln n$.*

PROOF. If it were the case that $h(u, v) > 4n^{(i+1)/k} \ln n$, then Claim 3 would imply that there exists a vertex of A_{i+1} on the shortest path from v to u. In particular, $d_G(v, u) > d_G(v, A_{i+1})$, which contradicts (6). $\square$

3.1 Approximate Clusters and Pivots

Since we do not know how to compute efficiently in a distributed manner the pivots and clusters, we settle for an approximate version, which is formally defined in this section. Fix the parameter $\epsilon = \frac{1}{48k^4}$. For each $v \in V$ and $0 \leq i \leq k-1$, a point $\hat{z} \in A_i$ is called an *approximate i-pivot* of v if

$$d_G(v, \hat{z}) \leq (1+\epsilon) d_G(v, A_i) \ . \tag{7}$$

Now we define for each $0 \leq i \leq k-1$ and each vertex $u \in A_i \setminus A_{i+1}$, a set of vertices which we call an *approximate cluster*. The approximate cluster is a subset of the cluster $C(u)$, and it is allowed to exclude vertices of $C(u)$ which are "close" to the boundary. First define the vertices that are far from the boundary (with respect to ϵ), as

$$C_\epsilon(u) = \{v \in V \ : \ d_G(u, v) < \frac{d_G(v, A_{i+1})}{1+\epsilon}\}. \tag{8}$$

The approximate cluster $\tilde{C}(u)$ will be a set that satisfies the following:

$$C_{6\epsilon}(u) \subseteq \tilde{C}(u) \subseteq C(u) \ . \tag{9}$$

Each approximate cluster $\tilde{C}(u)$ we compute, will be stored as a tree rooted at u, that is, each vertex $v \in \tilde{C}(u)$ will store a pointer to its parent in the tree. This tree (abusing notation, we call this tree $\tilde{C}(u)$ as well) has the property that distances to the root u are approximately preserved, that is, for any $v \in \tilde{C}(u)$ we have that

$$d_G(u, v) \leq d_{\tilde{C}(u)}(u, v) \leq (1+\epsilon)^4 d_G(u, v) \ . \tag{10}$$

REMARK 3. *Since $\tilde{C}(u) \subseteq C(u)$, Claim 2 implies that with high probability, each vertex is contained in at most $4n^{1/k} \log n$ approximate clusters.*

In the remainder of this section we devise an efficient distributed algorithm for computing the approximate pivots and the trees built from approximate clusters, and show the following.

THEOREM 5. *Let $G = (V, E)$ be a weighted graph with n vertices and hop-diameter D, and let $k \geq 1$ be an integer. Set $\epsilon = 1/(48k^4)$. Then there is a randomized distributed algorithm that w.h.p computes all approximate pivots and approximate clusters (with respect to ϵ) within $(n^{1/2+1/k} + D) \cdot \min\{(\log n)^{O(k)}, 2^{\tilde{O}(\sqrt{\log n})}\}$ rounds.*[11]

[10] In fact, [HKN16] shows this theorem for a single root and for $\epsilon = 1/\log n$, but an inspection of their proof gives the claimed result.

[11] For odd k the number of rounds becomes $(n^{1/2+1/(2k)} + D) \cdot \min\{(\log n)^{O(k)}, 2^{\tilde{O}(\sqrt{\log n})}\}$.

Computing Pivots.

We first compute the pivots for $0 \le i \le \lceil k/2 \rceil$. For these values of i we can compute the exact pivots. We conduct $4n^{i/k} \cdot \ln n$ iterations of Bellman-Ford rooted in the vertex set A_i. As a result, every $v \in V$ learns the exact value $\hat{d}_i(v) = d_G(v, A_i)$ and a pivot $\hat{z}_i(v) \in A_i$. Indeed, for any $v \in V$, if $u \in A_i$ is a vertex such that $d_G(v,u) = d_G(v, A_i)$, then Claim 3 implies that $h(v,u) \le 4n^{i/k} \cdot \ln n$, so the exploration will detect this shortest path. As every message consists of $O(1)$ words (every vertex sends to its neighbors the name of the vertex in A_i and the current distance to it), the total number of rounds is $\sum_{i=0}^{\lceil k/2 \rceil} O(n^{i/k} \cdot \ln n) \le \tilde{O}(n^{1/2+1/(2k)})$.

For $\lceil k/2 \rceil < i \le k-1$ we can only compute *approximate* pivots $\hat{z}_i(v)$ for each $v \in V$. For each such i, apply Theorem 4 with root set A_i and the parameter ϵ (indeed by Claim 3, $|A_i| \le 4n^{1-(\lceil k/2 \rceil+1)/k} \ln n \le 2\sqrt{n} \ln n$, and $\epsilon = \Omega(1/k^4) \ge \Omega(1/\log^4 n)$). This will take $(n^{1/2+1/(2k)} + D) \cdot \min\{(\log n)^{O(k)}, 2^{\tilde{O}(\sqrt{\log n})}\}$ rounds (see the remark after Theorem 4). At the end, every vertex $v \in V$ will know its approximate pivot $\hat{z}_i(v)$, and the (approximate) distance $\hat{d}_i(v)$, as returned by the algorithm. By (5), $\hat{z}_i(v)$ satisfies the requirement from an approximate pivot (see (7)).

3.2 Building the Small Trees

For $0 \le i < \lceil k/2 \rceil$, we can compute the trees $C(u)$ corresponding to the actual clusters. We need to find such a tree for every $u \in A_i \setminus A_{i+1}$, and it is done in the following manner. For each such u in parallel, we initiate a bounded-depth Bellman-Ford exploration for $4n^{(i+1)/k} \ln n$ iterations. By bounded-depth we mean the following: each $v \in V$ that receives a message originated at u, and computes that its (current) distance to u is $b_v(u)$, will join $C(u)$ and broadcast the message to its neighbors in G iff

$$b_v(u) < d_G(v, A_{i+1}) \; . \tag{11}$$

(Recall that for $i \le \lceil k/2 \rceil$, each vertex stores the distance to the exact i-th pivot $\hat{d}_i(v) = d_G(v, A_i)$.) The vertex v will also store the name of its parent in $C(u)$, the neighbor $p \in V$ that sent v the message which last updated $b_v(u)$.

We now argue that if $v \in C(u)$, then v will surely receive a message from u and will have $b_v(u) = d_G(u,v)$. Let P be the shortest path in G between u and v. Note that every vertex y on P has $y \in C(u)$, because

$$\begin{aligned} d_G(y,u) &= d_G(v,u) - d_G(v,y) \\ &\overset{(6)}{<} d_G(v, A_{i+1}) - d_G(v,y) \le d_G(y, A_{i+1}) \; . \end{aligned}$$

It follows by a simple induction that every such y will receive a message with the exact distance $b_y(u) = d_G(y,u)$ and thus will send it onwards, after at most $h(u,y)$ steps of the algorithm. In particular, distances to the root u in $C(u)$ are preserved exactly. Corollary 4 asserts that for all $v \in C(u)$ we have that $h(u,v) \le 4n^{(i+1)/k} \ln n$. So there are enough Bellman-Ford iterations to reach all vertices of $C(u)$.

The middle level.

When k is odd, the level $i = (k-1)/2$ will induce large running time $\tilde{O}(n^{1/2+3/(2k)})$ (see the upcoming paragraph on running-time analysis). To overcome this, we use a different method for this level. We apply Theorem 2 on the set of sources $S = A_{(k-1)/2} \setminus A_{(k+1)/2}$, with $B = 4n^{(i+1)/k} \cdot \ln n$ and ϵ, each vertex $v \in V$ will get a distance estimate $b_v(u)$ for each $u \in S$. Indeed, if $v \in C(u)$ then $h(u,v) \le B$, so that the distance estimate returned by the theorem is a $1+\epsilon$ approximation to $d_G(u,v) = d_G^{(B)}(u,v)$.

We say that v joins the (approximate) cluster $\tilde{C}(u)$ of $u \in S$ if the following holds

$$b_v(u) < d_G(v, A_{(k+1)/2})$$

(recall that v knows the exact distance to the pivot of level $(k+1)/2$). The parent p of v in the tree induced by $\tilde{C}(u)$ will be the parent given by Remark 2. We must show that p will join $\tilde{C}(u)$ as well. This holds because

$$\begin{aligned} b_p(u) &\overset{(3)}{\le} b_v(u) - w(v,p) < d_G(v, A_{(k+1)/2}) - d_G(v,p) \\ &\le d_G(p, A_{(k+1)/2}) \; . \end{aligned}$$

Finally, we note that this is an approximate cluster; since $d_G(u,v) \le b_v(u)$ it follows that $\tilde{C}(u) \subseteq C(u)$, while if $v \in C_\epsilon(u)$ then

$$b_v(u) \overset{(2)}{\le} (1+\epsilon) d_G(u,v) \overset{(8)}{<} d_G(v, A_{(k+1)/2}) \; ,$$

so $\tilde{C}(u) \supseteq C_\epsilon(u)$, satisfying (9). (We remark that the middle level is the only one in which one may use Theorem 2. In all other levels, either the number of sources $|A_i| \approx n^{1-i/k}$ or the required depth $B \approx n^{(i+1)/k}$ will be larger than $n^{1/2+1/k}$.)

Running time.

By Claim 2, every vertex can belong to at most $\tilde{O}(n^{1/k})$ clusters. Hence, the congestion at every Bellman-Ford iteration is at most $\tilde{O}(n^{1/k})$. Thus the number of rounds required to implement each of the $4n^{(i+1)/k} \ln n$ iterations of Bellman-Ford is $\tilde{O}(n^{1/k})$. When k is even, the total running time is $\sum_{i=0}^{k/2-1} \tilde{O}(n^{(i+2)/k}) = \tilde{O}(n^{1/2+1/k})$. When k is odd, the middle level $(k-1)/2$ will take time $\tilde{O}(|S| + B + D) = \tilde{O}(n^{1/2+1/(2k)} + D)$, while the lower levels will take $\sum_{i=0}^{(k-3)/2} \tilde{O}(n^{(i+2)/k}) = \tilde{O}(n^{1/2+1/(2k)})$. So for odd k the total running time is $\tilde{O}(n^{1/2+1/(2k)} + D)$.

3.3 Building the Large Trees

Building the trees $\tilde{C}(u)$ for $u \in A_i \setminus A_{i+1}$ when $i \ge \lceil k/2 \rceil$ is more involved, since the number of iterations for the simple Bellman-Ford style approach grows like $\approx n^{(i+1)/k}$. We will use the fact that there are only few roots, and divide the computation into two phases. In the first phase we compute virtual trees only on $\approx \sqrt{n}$ vertices, and in the second phase we extend the trees to all the graph. Before we turn to the two-phase construction, we describe the preprocessing stage, in which we build structures that are later used in both phases.

3.3.1 *Preprocessing*

Let $V' = A_{\lceil k/2 \rceil}$, and set $B = 4\mathbb{E}[n/|V'|] \cdot \ln n$. That is, for even k we set $B = 4n^{1/2} \cdot \ln n$, while for odd k, $B = 4n^{1/2+1/(2k)} \cdot \ln n$. Apply Theorem 2 to G with the set V' and parameters B and $\epsilon/2$. By Claim 3 we may assume $|V'| \le 4n^{1/2} \ln n$, and since $1/\epsilon \le 48 \log^4 n$, the number of rounds required is w.h.p $\tilde{O}(n^{1/2+1/(2k)} + D)$. From now on assume that (2) indeed holds (which happens w.h.p). Let $G' = (V', E', w')$ be a (virtual) graph on G, and for each $u, v \in V'$ with $d_{uv} < \infty$, set the weight of the edge connecting them to be $w'(u,v) = d_{uv}$ (where d_{uv} is the value computed in Theorem 2). Following [Nan14], it can be shown that for any $u, v \in V'$,

$$d_G(u,v) \le d_{G'}(u,v) \le (1+\epsilon/2)d_G(u,v) . \qquad (12)$$

Apply Theorem 3 on G' with parameters $\epsilon/3$ and $\rho = \max\{1/k, \log\log n/\sqrt{\log n}\}$. We obtain a $(\beta, \epsilon/3)$-hopset F with $\beta = \min\{2^{\tilde{O}(\sqrt{\log n})}, (\log n)^{O(k)}\}$. The number of rounds is

$$\begin{aligned}&\tilde{O}(|V'|^{1+\rho} + D) \cdot \beta^2 \\ &= \tilde{O}(n^{1/2+1/(2k)} + D) \cdot \min\{2^{\tilde{O}(\sqrt{\log n})}, (\log n)^{O(k)}\} .\end{aligned}$$

Let $G'' = (V', E' \cup F, w'')$ be the graph obtained from G' by adding all the hopset edges. (Note that some edges may have their weight replaced. In the case of conflict, the weights w'' agree with the weights of F.) By (4) and (12) we have that G'' is indeed a virtual graph since $d_{G''}(u,v) \ge d_{G'}(u,v) \ge d_G(u,v)$. On the other hand,

$$\begin{aligned} d^{(\beta)}_{G''}(u,v) &\le (1+\epsilon/3)d_{G'}(u,v) \le (1+\epsilon/2)(1+\epsilon/3)d_G(u,v) \\ &\le (1+\epsilon)d_G(u,v) .\end{aligned}$$

We conclude that the graph G'' satisfies the following property: for every $u, v \in V'$,

$$d_G(u,v) \le d^{(\beta)}_{G''}(u,v) \le (1+\epsilon)d_G(u,v) , \qquad (13)$$

3.3.2 Construction

Fix $\lceil k/2 \rceil \le i \le k-1$. We build the trees $\tilde{C}(u)$ for all $u \in A_i \setminus A_{i+1}$ in parallel, in two main phases.

Phase 1.

For each such u, conduct β iterations of depth-bounded Bellman-Ford in the graph G''.[12] (Since this is a virtual graph, all the messages will be collected at the root of some BFS tree via pipelined convergecast, and then broadcast to the entire graph G via pipelined broadcast. See Lemma 1.) If $v \in V'$ receives a message originated at u with (current) distance to u which is $b_v(u)$, it will join the approximate cluster of u and forward the message to its neighbors in G'' iff

$$b_v(u) < \frac{\hat{d}_{i+1}(v)}{(1+\epsilon)^3} . \qquad (14)$$

(Recall that $\hat{d}_{i+1}(v)$ is the approximate distance from v to the its (approximate) level i pivot.) The vertex v will also store its *virtual* parent, the neighbor $p \in V'$ that sent v the message which last updated $b_v(u)$. For each $u \in A_i \setminus A_{i+1}$, we have a (virtual) tree $\tilde{C}'(u)$ on the vertices of V' that received a message originated at u and satisfy (14).

Phase 1.5.

The purpose of this additional step is to guarantee that every vertex which was added to the (virtual) tree being built for some $u \in A_i \setminus A_{i+1}$, will have an appropriate parent in G (through which it will route later on). The issue is that hopset edges are not equipped with parents in G, unlike the edges of G', for which Remark 2 provides parents. We deal with this by using the path-reporting property of hopset edges – each such edge is realized by a path in G', so we

[12]See (14) below for the required condition.

ensure the vertices of this path join the tree as well, and set parents accordingly. We now describe this formally.

When the first phase ends after β iterations, for every hopset edge $(x,y) \in F$ such that x is the virtual parent of y we do the following. Let P be the path in G' realizing this edge. Each $v \in P \setminus \{x\}$ that has $b_v(u)$ value at least $b_x(u) + d_P(x,v)$, updates its distance estimate $b_v(u) = b_x(u) + d_P(x,v)$, joins $\tilde{C}'(u)$ (if it hasn't already), and sets its virtual parent as v', where v' is the neighbor of v on P closer to x (recall Property 1, which guarantees that v knows the relevant information).

Finally, set the *real* parents: for each vertex $v \in \tilde{C}'(u)$ with a virtual parent v', set $p(v) = p_{v'}(v)$ (recall Remark 2).

Phase 2.

Here we extend each virtual tree $\tilde{C}'(u)$ to the vertices of V. For all $u \in A_i \setminus A_{i+1}$, every vertex $v \in \tilde{C}'(u)$ broadcasts to the entire graph its value $b_v(u)$ (and the name of u). A vertex $y \in V$ will add itself to $\tilde{C}(u)$ if

$$d_{yv} + b_v(u) < \frac{\hat{d}_{i+1}(y)}{1+\epsilon} , \qquad (15)$$

where d_{yv} is the value computed in Theorem 2. Also y will set $p(y) = p_v(y)$ as its parent in $\tilde{C}(u)$ for the v minimizing $b_y(u) = d_{yv} + b_v(u)$ (breaking ties arbitrarily). We remark that the condition of (15) is less stringent than that of (14). Thus vertices of V' who did not join $\tilde{C}'(u)$, may now be included in $\tilde{C}(u)$.

We defer the proof that every $\tilde{C}(u)$ is indeed an approximate cluster, that it corresponds to a tree in G, and the running time analysis, to the full version.

4. ROUTING BASED ON APPROXIMATE CLUSTERS

In this section we show that approximate pivots and approximate clusters suffice for a compact routing scheme, and prove our main result.

THEOREM 6. *Let $G = (V, E)$ be a weighted graph with n vertices and hop-diameter D, and let $k \ge 1$ be a parameter. Then there exists a routing scheme with stretch at most $4k - 5 + o(1)$, labels of size $O(k \log^2 n)$ and routing tables of size $O(n^{1/k} \log^2 n)$, that can be computed in a distributed manner within $(n^{1/2+1/k} + D) \cdot \min\{(\log n)^{O(k)}, 2^{\tilde{O}(\sqrt{\log n})}\}$ rounds.*

Construction.

Apply Theorem 5 on G to obtain approximate pivots and approximate clusters for all vertices. For each $0 \le i \le k-1$ and each $u \in A_i \setminus A_{i+1}$, construct the routing scheme for trees given by Theorem 1 on $\tilde{C}(u)$. Recall that in each tree, every vertex stores a table of size $O(\log n)$ and has a label of size $O(\log^2 n)$. The routing table of each $v \in V$ consists of all the tree-routing tables, for every $u \in V$ such that $v \in \tilde{C}(u)$. The label of v consists of the tree-labels for the (at most) k trees $\tilde{C}(\hat{z}_0(v)), \ldots, \tilde{C}(\hat{z}_{k-1}(v))$, where $\hat{z}_i(v)$ is the approximate i-pivot of v (note that it could be that v does not belong to some of these trees, the label of v will mark these as missing). By Remark 3 there are at most $O(n^{1/k} \log n)$ trees containing v, and as each tree-table is of size $O(\log n)$, the routing table size is as promised. Since each tree-label is of size $O(\log^2 n)$, the label size also obeys the given bound.

Finding a Tree.

Assume we would like to route from vertex u to vertex v. The routing protocol will find a vertex $w = \hat{z}_i(v)$ for some $0 \le i \le k-1$, such that the stretch of the (unique) path from u to v in the tree $\tilde{C}(w)$ is at most $4k - 5 + o(1)$. The algorithm to find such a vertex appears in Algorithm 1.

Algorithm 1 `Find-tree`(u, v)

$i \leftarrow 0$;
while $|\{u, v\} \cap \tilde{C}(\hat{z}_i(v))| < 2$ **do**
  $i \leftarrow i + 1$;
end while
return $\hat{z}_i(v)$;

We note that our algorithm differs slightly from that of [TZ05], since it could be the case that v does not belong to the cluster centered at the pivot of v at level i. For this reason we keep searching until we find a cluster containing both u, v.

First we claim that the algorithm is correct. Note that (9) implies that $\tilde{C}(x) = V$ for every $x \in A_{k-1}$ (this holds since the distance to A_k is defined as ∞). Therefore when $i = k-1$ it must be that both $u, v \in \tilde{C}(\hat{z}_{k-1}(v))$, and the algorithm indeed halts. The tree $\tilde{C}(w)$ contains both u, v (where $w = \hat{z}_i(v)$ is the vertex returned by the algorithm) by definition. Finally, the information from the label of v indicates which of these trees contain it, and the routing table of u also lists the names of all trees containing it, so we can run the algorithm from u knowing the label of v.

Once u computes the root w, it appends w to the message header along with the label of v. From this point on the header does not change, and we route in the tree $\tilde{C}(w)$. Since this routing is exact, it remains to bound the stretch incurred by using the tree.

Bounding Stretch.

We distinguish between two types of iterations i that algorithm did not stop at. Let $I_u = \{0 \le i \le k-1 \;:\; u \notin \tilde{C}(\hat{z}_i(v))\}$ be the iterations in which $\{u, v\} \cap \tilde{C}(\hat{z}_i(v))$ is empty or contains just v, and let $I_v = \{0 \le i \le k-1 \;:\; \{u, v\} \cap \tilde{C}(\hat{z}_i(v)) = \{u\}\}$ be the remaining iterations that did not halt. For any $i \in I_u$, by (9) it holds that $C_{6\epsilon}(\hat{z}_i(v)) \subseteq \tilde{C}(\hat{z}_i(v))$. Hence, we have $u \notin C_{6\epsilon}(\hat{z}_i(v))$, which suggests that

$$\begin{aligned} d_G(u, \hat{z}_{i+1}(u)) &\overset{(7)}{\le} (1+\epsilon) d_G(u, A_{i+1}) \\ &\overset{(8)}{\le} (1+\epsilon)(1+6\epsilon) d_G(u, \hat{z}_i(v)) \\ &\le (1+8\epsilon) d_G(u, \hat{z}_i(v)) \;. \end{aligned} \tag{16}$$

Similarly for $i \in I_v$,

$$\begin{aligned} d_G(v, \hat{z}_{i+1}(v)) &\le (1+\epsilon) d_G(v, A_{i+1}) \\ &\le (1+\epsilon)(1+6\epsilon) d_G(v, \hat{z}_i(v)) \\ &\le (1+8\epsilon) d_G(v, \hat{z}_i(v)) \;. \end{aligned} \tag{17}$$

Define the following values $y_0 = d_G(u, v)$, $x_0 = 0$, and for $0 < i \le k-1$ define recursively $y_i = (1+10\epsilon)[y_0 + x_{i-1}]$, and $x_i = (1+\epsilon)[y_0 + y_i]$. Assume that the algorithm halted at iteration i', then for each $0 \le i \le i'$ we claim that

$$d_G(v, \hat{z}_i(v)) \le x_i \;. \tag{18}$$

We verify the validity of (18) by induction, the base case trivially holds since $\hat{z}_0(v) = v$ and $x_0 = 0$. Fix $0 < i \le i'$. The algorithm did not halt at iteration $i-1$. If it is the case that $i - 1 \in I_u$, then we have that

$$\begin{aligned} d_G(u, \hat{z}_i(u)) &\overset{(16)}{\le} (1+8\epsilon) d_G(u, \hat{z}_{i-1}(v)) \\ &\le (1+8\epsilon)[d_G(u, v) + d_G(v, \hat{z}_{i-1}(v))] \\ &\overset{(18)}{\le} (1+8\epsilon)[y_0 + x_{i-1}] \\ &\le y_i \;. \end{aligned} \tag{19}$$

The other case is that $i-1 \in I_v$. Since $\hat{z}_i(u) \in A_i$ we obtain

$$\begin{aligned} d_G(u, \hat{z}_i(u)) &\overset{(7)}{\le} (1+\epsilon) d_G(u, A_i) \\ &\le (1+\epsilon) d_G(u, \hat{z}_i(v)) \\ &\le (1+\epsilon)[d_G(u, v) + d_G(v, \hat{z}_i(v))] \\ &\overset{(17)}{\le} (1+\epsilon)[d_G(u, v) + (1+8\epsilon) d_G(v, \hat{z}_{i-1}(v))] \\ &\le (1+10\epsilon)[y_0 + x_{i-1}] \\ &= y_i \end{aligned} \tag{20}$$

We conclude that in both cases,

$$\begin{aligned} d_G(v, \hat{z}_i(v)) &\le (1+\epsilon) d_G(v, A_i) \\ &\le (1+\epsilon) d_G(v, \hat{z}_i(u)) \\ &\le (1+\epsilon)[d_G(u, v) + d_G(u, \hat{z}_i(u))] \\ &\overset{(19)\wedge(20)}{\le} (1+\epsilon)[y_0 + y_i] \\ &= x_i \;. \end{aligned} \tag{21}$$

We now have a recurrence $x_i = (1+\epsilon)(2+10\epsilon)y_0 + (1+\epsilon)(1+10\epsilon)x_{i-1}$. Solving it, yields

$$x_i = (1+\epsilon)(2+10\epsilon)y_0 \sum_{j=0}^{i-1} [(1+\epsilon)(1+10\epsilon)]^j \;.$$

We use the fact that for any real $x \ge 0$ and positive integer r such that $xr \le 1/2$, the following holds $(1+x)^r \le 1 + 2xr$. Now we may bound x_i by

$$\begin{aligned} x_i &\le (2+13\epsilon)y_0 \sum_{j=0}^{i-1} (1+12\epsilon)^j \\ &\le (2+13\epsilon)y_0 \sum_{j=0}^{i-1} (1+24\epsilon j) \\ &\le (2+13\epsilon)y_0 (i + 12\epsilon i^2) \\ &\le (2+13\epsilon)y_0 (i + 1/(4k^2)) \;, \end{aligned} \tag{22}$$

where in the last inequality we use that $\epsilon = \frac{1}{48k^4} \le \frac{1}{48k^2 i^2}$. Finally, using that $i' \le k-1$ and that $w = \hat{z}_{i'}(v)$, the stretch is given by

$$
\begin{aligned}
& d_{\tilde{C}(w)}(u,w) + d_{\tilde{C}(w)}(w,v) \\
& \overset{(10)}{\leq} \quad (1+\epsilon)^4[d_G(u,w) + d_G(v,w)] \\
& \overset{(18)}{\leq} \quad (1+5\epsilon)[d_G(u,v) + 2x_{i'}] \\
& \overset{(22)}{\leq} \quad (1+5\epsilon)[1+(4+26\epsilon)(k-1+1/(4k^2))]\cdot d_G(u,v) \\
& \leq \quad (4k-3+o(1))\cdot d_G(u,v)\ .
\end{aligned}
$$

In order to improve the stretch to the promised $4k-5+o(1)$, we use same trick as in [TZ01]. Each vertex $u \in A_0 \setminus A_1$ will store in its routing table all the labels for vertices in $C(u)$, which enables to save an additive term of $d_G(u,v)$ in both x_i and y_i. We refer the reader to [TZ01] for the details.

Running time.

By Theorem 5, the time required to compute the approximate pivots and the trees $\tilde{C}(u)$ for every $u \in A_i \setminus A_{i+1}$ is $(n^{1/2+1/k}+D)\cdot\min\{(\log n)^{O(k)}, 2^{\tilde{O}(\sqrt{\log n})}\}$. By Claim 2 each vertex participates in at most $\tilde{O}(n^{1/k})$ trees, so Remark 1 implies that it will take only $\tilde{O}(n^{1/2+1/k}+D)$ rounds to compute the routing tables for all trees in parallel. We conclude that the total number of rounds is $(n^{1/2+1/k}+D)\cdot\min\{(\log n)^{O(k)}, 2^{\tilde{O}(\sqrt{\log n})}\}$.

5. DISTANCE ESTIMATION

In this section we sketch how the routing tables can be used for distance estimation, and prove the following.

THEOREM 7. *Let $G=(V,E)$ be a weighted graph with n vertices and hop-diameter D, and let $k \geq 1$ be a parameter. Then there exists a distance estimation scheme, that assigns a sketch of size $O(n^{1/k}\log n)$ for each node, and has stretch $2k-1+o(1)$, that can be computed by a randomized distributed algorithm within $(n^{1/2+1/k}+D)\cdot\min\{(\log n)^{O(k)}, 2^{\tilde{O}(\sqrt{\log n})}\}$ rounds (whp). Furthermore, the distance computation can be done in time $O(k)$.*

Apply Theorem 5, which computes all the approximate pivots and approximate clusters. Each vertex $v \in V$ include in its sketch for every $u \in V$ so that $v \in \tilde{C}(u)$, the pair $(u, b_v(u))$, where $b_v(u)$ is the approximate distance to u computed in Section 3. Also for every $0 \leq i \leq k-1$, add $(\hat{z}_i(v), \hat{d}_i(v))$, which is the approximate i-pivot and distance to it. By Remark 3 every sketch is of size $O(n^{1/k}\log n)$. The algorithm that computes the distance estimation given two sketches is similar to that of [TZ05]. We state it formally in Algorithm 2.

Algorithm 2 Dist(u,v)

```
i ← 0;
w ← u;
while v ∉ C̃(w) do
    i ← i + 1;
    (u, v) ← (v, u);
    w ← ẑ_i(u);
end while
return d̂_i(u) + b_v(w);
```

Observe that the sketch contains all the relevant information for executing Algorithm 2. When the while loop terminates $v \in \tilde{C}(w)$, so it has the estimate $b_v(w)$, while u stores the approximate distance $\hat{d}_i(u)$ to every one of its approximate pivots. The stretch analysis is a variation of the analysis of [TZ05], similar in spirit to that of Section 4. Roughly speaking, on the stretch $2k-1$ achieved by [TZ05], we pay a multiplicative factor of $(1+O(\epsilon))^k$ due to the fact that distances are approximated, but this boils down to an $o(1)$ additive term, since $\epsilon = \frac{1}{48k^4}$. We leave the details to the reader.

6. REFERENCES

[ABLP90] Baruch Awerbuch, Amotz Bar-Noy, Nathan Linial, and David Peleg. Improved routing strategies with succinct tables. *J. Algorithms*, 11(3):307–341, 1990.

[AGM04] Ittai Abraham, Cyril Gavoille, and Dahlia Malkhi. Routing with improved communication-space trade-off. In *Distributed Computing, 18th International Conference, DISC 2004, Amsterdam, The Netherlands, October 4-7, 2004, Proceedings*, pages 305–319, 2004.

[Ber09] Aaron Bernstein. Fully dynamic (2 + epsilon) approximate all-pairs shortest paths with fast query and close to linear update time. In *50th Annual IEEE Symposium on Foundations of Computer Science, FOCS 2009, October 25-27, 2009, Atlanta, Georgia, USA*, pages 693–702, 2009.

[Che13] Shiri Chechik. Compact routing schemes with improved stretch. In *ACM Symposium on Principles of Distributed Computing, PODC '13, Montreal, QC, Canada, July 22-24, 2013*, pages 33–41, 2013.

[Coh00] Edith Cohen. Polylog-time and near-linear work approximation scheme for undirected shortest paths. *J. ACM*, 47(1):132–166, 2000.

[Cow01] Lenore Cowen. Compact routing with minimum stretch. *J. Algorithms*, 38(1):170–183, 2001.

[EGP03] Tamar Eilam, Cyril Gavoille, and David Peleg. Compact routing schemes with low stretch factor. *J. Algorithms*, 46(2):97–114, 2003.

[Elk06a] Michael Elkin. A faster distributed protocol for constructing a minimum spanning tree. *J. Comput. Syst. Sci.*, 72(8):1282–1308, 2006.

[Elk06b] Michael Elkin. An unconditional lower bound on the time-approximation trade-off for the distributed minimum spanning tree problem. *SIAM J. Comput.*, 36(2):433–456, 2006.

[EN16] Michael Elkin and Ofer Neiman. Hopsets with constant hopbound, and applications to approximate shortest paths. *CoRR*, abs/1605.04538, 2016.

[GK13] Mohsen Ghaffari and Fabian Kuhn. Distributed minimum cut approximation. In *Distributed Computing - 27th International Symposium, DISC 2013, Jerusalem, Israel, October 14-18, 2013. Proceedings*, pages 1–15, 2013.

[GKP98] Juan A. Garay, Shay Kutten, and David Peleg. A sublinear time distributed algorithm for minimum-weight spanning trees. *SIAM J. Comput.*, 27(1):302–316, 1998.

[GP03] Cyril Gavoille and David Peleg. Compact and localized distributed data structures. *Distributed Computing*, 16(2-3):111–120, 2003.

[HKN14] Monika Henzinger, Sebastian Krinninger, and Danupon Nanongkai. Decremental single-source shortest paths on undirected graphs in near-linear total update time. In *55th IEEE Annual Symposium on Foundations of Computer Science, FOCS 2014, Philadelphia, PA, USA, October 18-21, 2014*, pages 146–155, 2014.

[HKN16] Monika Henzinger, Sebastian Krinninger, and Danupon Nanongkai. An almost-tight distributed algorithm for computing single-source shortest paths. 2016. To appear in STOC'16.

[KP98] Shay Kutten and David Peleg. Fast distributed construction of small k-dominating sets and applications. *J. Algorithms*, 28(1):40–66, 1998.

[LP13a] Christoph Lenzen and Boaz Patt-Shamir. Fast routing table construction using small messages. In *Symposium on Theory of Computing Conference, STOC'13, Palo Alto, CA, USA, June 1-4, 2013*, pages 381–390, 2013.

[LP13b] Christoph Lenzen and David Peleg. Efficient distributed source detection with limited bandwidth. In *ACM Symposium on Principles of Distributed Computing, PODC '13, Montreal, QC, Canada, July 22-24, 2013*, pages 375–382, 2013.

[LP15] Christoph Lenzen and Boaz Patt-Shamir. Fast partial distance estimation and applications. In *Proceedings of the 2015 ACM Symposium on Principles of Distributed Computing, PODC 2015, Donostia-San Sebastián, Spain, July 21 - 23, 2015*, pages 153–162, 2015.

[LP16] Christoph Lenzen and Boaz Patt-Shamir. Personal communication, 2016.

[LPP16] Christoph Lenzen, Boaz Patt-Shamir, and David Peleg. Distributed distance computation and routing with small messages. 2016.

[Nan14] Danupon Nanongkai. Distributed approximation algorithms for weighted shortest paths. In *Symposium on Theory of Computing, STOC 2014, New York, NY, USA, May 31 - June 03, 2014*, pages 565–573, 2014.

[NRS12] Nicolas Nisse, Ivan Rapaport, and Karol Suchan. Distributed computing of efficient routing schemes in generalized chordal graphs. *Theor. Comput. Sci.*, 444:17–27, 2012.

[Pel00a] David Peleg. *Distributed Computing: A Locality-sensitive Approach.* Society for Industrial and Applied Mathematics, Philadelphia, PA, USA, 2000.

[Pel00b] David Peleg. Proximity-preserving labeling schemes. *J. Graph Theory*, 33(3):167–176, March 2000.

[PR00] David Peleg and Vitaly Rubinovich. A near-tight lower bound on the time complexity of distributed minimum-weight spanning tree construction. *SIAM J. Comput.*, 30(5):1427–1442, 2000.

[PU89] David Peleg and Eli Upfal. A trade-off between space and efficiency for routing tables. *J. ACM*, 36(3):510–530, 1989.

[SDP15] Atish Das Sarma, Michael Dinitz, and Gopal Pandurangan. Efficient distributed computation of distance sketches in networks. *Distributed Computing*, 28(5):309–320, 2015.

[SHK+12] Atish Das Sarma, Stephan Holzer, Liah Kor, Amos Korman, Danupon Nanongkai, Gopal Pandurangan, David Peleg, and Roger Wattenhofer. Distributed verification and hardness of distributed approximation. *SIAM J. Comput.*, 41(5):1235–1265, 2012.

[TZ01] Mikkel Thorup and Uri Zwick. Compact routing schemes. In *Proceedings of the Thirteenth Annual ACM Symposium on Parallel Algorithms and Architectures*, SPAA '01, pages 1–10, New York, NY, USA, 2001. ACM.

[TZ05] Mikkel Thorup and Uri Zwick. Approximate distance oracles. *J. ACM*, 52(1):1–24, 2005.

Brief Announcement: Deterministic Graph Connectivity in the Broadcast Congested Clique

Pedro Montealegre
Université d'Orléans
INSA Centre Val de Loire, LIFO EA 4022
Orléans, France
pedro.montealegre@univ-orleans.fr

Ioan Todinca
Université d'Orléans
INSA Centre Val de Loire, LIFO EA 4022
Orléans, France
ioan.todinca@univ-orleans.fr

ABSTRACT

We present deterministic constant-round protocols for the graph connectivity problem in the model where each of the n nodes of a graph receives a row of the adjacency matrix, and broadcasts a single sublinear size message to all other nodes. Communication rounds are synchronous. This model is sometimes called the broadcast congested clique. Specifically, we exhibit a deterministic protocol that computes the connected components of the input graph in $\lceil 1/\epsilon \rceil$ rounds, each player communicating $\mathcal{O}(n^\epsilon \cdot \log n)$ bits per round, with $0 < \epsilon \leq 1$.

We also provide a deterministic one-round protocol for connectivity, in the model when each node receives as input the graph induced by the nodes at distance at most $r > 0$, and communicates $\mathcal{O}(n^{1/r} \cdot \log n)$ bits. This result is based on a d-pruning protocol, which consists in successively removing nodes of degree at most d until obtaining a graph with minimum degree larger than d. Our technical novelty is the introduction of deterministic sparse linear sketches: a linear compression function that permits to recover sparse Boolean vectors deterministically.

Keywords

broadcast congested clique; graph connectivity; spanning forest; deterministic protocol

1. INTRODUCTION

This paper proposes the first (to our knowledge) constant-round deterministic protocol that computes a spanning forest[1] in the *broadcast congested clique* model with *sub-linear* message size.

The *congested clique* model is a message-passing model of distributed computation where n nodes communicate with each other in synchronous rounds over a *complete network* [1, 2, 4, 5]. The joint input of the n nodes is an undirected graph G on the same set of nodes, with node v receiving the list of its neighbors in G. Nodes have pairwise distinct identities, which are numbers upper bounded by some polynomial in n. Moreover, all nodes know this upper bound. At the end of a protocol, each node must produce the same output. In the *broadcast congested clique* (denoted $\text{BC}\textsc{lique}[f(n)]$) each node broadcasts, in each round, a single $\mathcal{O}(f(n))$-sized message[2] along each of its $n-1$ communication links, while in the *unicast congested clique* (denoted $\text{UC}\textsc{lique}[f(n)]$) nodes are allowed to send *different* $\mathcal{O}(f(n))$-size messages through different links.

There exists a basic $\mathcal{O}(\log n)$-round connectivity protocol in the $\text{BC}\textsc{lique}[\log n]$ model. Each node successively sends a neighbor outside its current cluster (initially the clusters consist in single nodes), and at each round the adjacent clusters are merged. The protocol can be adapted to compute a maximum weight spanning forest. Despite its simplicity, only few results exist improving the basic connectivity protocol.

On one hand, Lotker *et al.* [8] proposed the first improvement in the unicast congested clique, namely a $\mathcal{O}(\log \log n)$-round protocol for maximum weight spanning forest in the $\text{UC}\textsc{lique}[\log n]$ model, which also runs in $\mathcal{O}(1/\epsilon)$ rounds in $\text{UC}\textsc{lique}[n^\epsilon]$, for any constant $\epsilon > 0$. Later, Hegeman *et al.* [6] improved the number of rounds to $\mathcal{O}(\log \log \log n)$, also in $\text{UC}\textsc{lique}[\log n]$, but in a randomized protocol, which outputs a maximum weight spanning forest with high probability. On the other hand, in the broadcast congested clique, a one-round randomized protocol for graph connectivity in $\text{BC}\textsc{lique}[\log^3 n]$ was proposed by Ahn *et al.* [1], using an elegant techinque called *linear sketches*.

Our results. First, we observe that the basic connectivity protocol can be used to produce, for each $0 < \epsilon \leq 1$ a $\mathcal{O}(1/\epsilon)$-round protocol that computes a spanning forest in the $\text{BC}\textsc{lique}[n^\epsilon \cdot \log n]$ model.

We also propose a one-round connectivity protocol, this time the $\text{BC}\textsc{lique}_r[n^{1/r} \log n]$ model. This corresponds to the broadcast congested clique model, when each node receives as input the graph induced by the nodes at distance at most r (one may think of this model as the one where vertices are allowed to perform r unrestricted *local* communications, and then some congested *global* communications).

Our main tool is a protocol to *prune* a graph. The *d-pruning* of graph G, for $d > 0$, consists of finding a sequence of nodes $(x_1, \ldots, x_p)$, together with their incident edges, such that each vertex x_i has degree at most d in the

[1]In this paper a spanning forest designs a maximal one.

[2]Some authors consider that in the *congested clique* model only $\mathcal{O}(\log n)$-size messages are allowed. In our case the *congestion* refers to sublinear capacity communication channels.

PODC'16 July 25-28, 2016, Chicago, IL, USA

ACM ISBN 978-1-4503-3964-3/16/07...$15.00

DOI: http://dx.doi.org/10.1145/2933057.2933066

graph obtained by removing vertices $\{x_1, \ldots, x_{i-1}\}$ from G, and the graph obtained by removing the whole sequence has minimum degree strictly larger than d.

Becker *et al.* [4] provide a one-round deterministic protocol for d-pruning a graph in $\text{BCLIQUE}[d^2 \cdot \log n]$. They actually work on the reconstruction of d-degenerate graphs, i.e., graphs for which the pruning sequence is the whole vertex set.

We give a new protocol for d-pruning, which also runs in one round, but improves the message size to $\mathcal{O}(d \cdot \log n)$. Our protocol is optimal since the number of d-degenerate graphs is $2^{\Omega(nd \log n)}$. This new protocol is inspired by the *fingerprint* technique, which uses the Schwartz-Zippel Lemma for equality testing in randomized communication complexity [7]. The protocol is based on a derandomized version of fingerprints to compute *sparse linear sketches*: a linear compression function that permits to recover d-sparse Boolean vectors deterministically. This technique has its own interest and we believe that can be used in other applications.

2. PRUNING AND CONNECTIVITY

THEOREM 1. *Let $0 < \epsilon \leq 1$. There is a $\lceil 1/\epsilon \rceil$-round deterministic protocol that computes the connected components of the input graph in the $\text{BCLIQUE}[n^\epsilon \cdot \log n]$ model. The protocol returns a spanning forest of the input graph.*

Proof sketch. Let $G = (V, E)$ the input graph. The protocol is very similar to the basic connectivity protocol described in the introduction. First, denote $\hat{V}$ the set of *supernodes*, which initially are the n singletons $\{\{u\} | u \in V\}$. At each round, every node sends n^ϵ arbitrary neighbors in pairwise different supernodes (if it sees less than n^ϵ supernodes, then it sends one neighbor for each of them). At the end of each round adjacent supernodes are merged.

A supernode of round $t > 1$ is called *active* if it contains at least n^ϵ supernodes of round $t-1$, and otherwise is called *inactive*. Note that at any round $t > 0$, an inactive supernode corresponds to a connected component of G. The protocol finishes when every supernode is inactive. Let n_t be the number of active supernodes at round $t \geq 0$. Since the number of active nodes at round $t+1$ at most n_t/n^ϵ, the protocol stops in at most $\lceil 1/\epsilon \rceil$ rounds. □

We remark that when $\epsilon \leq 1/(\log n)$ our protocol matches de basic one. When $\epsilon = 1/2$, we obtain a sublinear, two-round protocol for connectivity. To our knowledge, there are no nontrivial lower bounds for deterministic protocols solving graph connectivity in the broadcast congested clique, even restricted to one-round protocols. However, even in the powerful unicast congested clique, there are no known sublinear one-round deterministic protocols. In the following, we propose a one-round deterministic protocol for graph connectivity in the BCLIQUE_r model.

THEOREM 2. *There exists a deterministic protocol in the $\text{BCLIQUE}[d \cdot \log n]$ model that computes a d-pruning in one round.*

Let $d > 0$. We say that a vector is d-sparse if it has at most d nonzero coordinates. We show that there exists a linear function compressing integer vectors, and such that if the compressed vector is Boolean and d-sparse, the vector can be recovered. We emphasize that the recovery property does not work over all d-sparse integer vectors, but only on Boolean ones. In the following $\mathbb{F}_p$ denotes the field of integers *modulo* p, where $p > 0$ is prime.

LEMMA 1. *Let $n, d > 0$. There exists a function $f : \mathbb{Z}^n \to \mathbb{F}_p$, for some prime number $p = 2^{\mathcal{O}(d \cdot \log n)}$, such that: (1) f is linear, and (2) f is injective when restricted to d-sparse Boolean inputs.*

Proof sketch. Let $\mathcal{B} = \{b \in \{0,1\}^n : \sum_{i=1}^n b_i \leq d\}$ be the family of d-sparse Boolean vectors of dimension n, and $\mathcal{T} = \{t \in \{-1, 0, 1\}^n : \exists \text{ distinct } b, b' \in \mathcal{B}, t = b - b'\}$. Call $p = p(n, d)$ the smallest prime number greater than $(1+n)^{2d} \cdot n$. Let $P(\mathcal{T})$ be the family of polynomials over the field $\mathbb{F}_p$ associating to each $t \in \mathcal{T}$ the polynomial $P(t, X) = \sum_{i=1}^n t_i X^{i-1}$ (values are taken modulo p). Let $\overline{x} = \overline{x}(n, d)$ be the minimum integer in $\mathbb{F}_p$ which is not a root of any polynomial in $P(\mathcal{T})$; $\overline{x}$ exists because there are at most $|\mathcal{T}|$ polynomials in $P(\mathcal{T})$, each polynomial has at most n roots in $\mathbb{F}_p$, and $p > |\mathcal{T}| \cdot n$. We define then for each $v \in \mathbb{Z}^n$ the function $f(v) = P(v, \overline{x})$. Clearly f is linear, and by definition of $\overline{x}$, for any distinct $b, b' \in \mathcal{B}$, we have $f(b) = P(b, \overline{x}) \neq P(b', \overline{x}) = f(b')$. □

Proof sketch of Theorem 2. In the d-pruning protocol, each player i sends the message $M_i = (M_i^1, M_i^2) = (d_i, f(a_i))$, where d_i is its degree, a_i is the row of the adjacency matrix corresponding to node i, and f is the function of Lemma 1. The number of communicated bits is $\mathcal{O}(d \log n)$. Call $M(G) = (M_1, \ldots, M_n)$ the *messages vector* of G. The nodes use $M(G)$ to prune the graph as follows. First they look for a node k such that $M_k^1 \leq d$. Using the injectivity property of f they can obtain the neighborhood of k in G. Then, using the linearity of f they compute the messages vector of $G - \{k\}$ updating $M_j = (M_j^1 - 1, M_j^2 - f(e_k))$ for each j neighbor of k, where e_k is the Boolean vector having a unique one in the k-th coordinate. The process is reiterated (with no extra communication) until there is no more node of degree at most d. □

We use our d-pruning protocol to produce a one-round connectivity protocol, this time in the $\text{BCLIQUE}_r[n^{1/r} \cdot \log n]$ model. Our protocol is based in the following propositions respectively found in [3], and [5]. Let $G = (V, E)$ be a graph, $r > 0$, and σ some total ordering of E. For each cycle of length at most $2r$ pick the maximum edge of the cycle according to σ. Call $\tilde{E}$ the set of picked edges, and call $\tilde{G} = (V, E - \tilde{E})$. Note that $\tilde{G}$ has no cycles of length at most $2r$.

PROPOSITION 1 ([3]). *G is connected if and only if $\tilde{G}$ is connected, and any spanning forest of $\tilde{G}$ is a spanning forest of G.*

The following proposition shows that $\tilde{G}$ has *sublinear* degeneracy. Recall that the girth of a graph is the length of a shortest cycle.

PROPOSITION 2 ([5]). *Let G be a graph of girth at least $2r$. Then G is $\mathcal{O}(n^{1/r})$-degenerate.*

THEOREM 3. *There is a one-round deterministic protocol that computes the connected components of the input graph in the $\text{BCLIQUE}_r[n^{1/r} \cdot \log n]$ model. The protocol returns a spanning forest of the input graph.*

PROOF. Choose an ordering of the edges of G, for example if we denote the edges $e = (u, v)$ with $u < v$, then $(u_1, v_1) < (u_2, v_2)$ if either $u_1 < u_2$ or $u_1 = u_2$ and $v_1 < v_2$.

In the protocol, a node v looks for all cycles of length at most $2r$ in G that contain it. Notice that nodes do this without any communication since they see all neighbors at distance at most r. For each such cycle, v picks the maximum edge according to the edge ordering, obtaining the row of the adjacency matrix of $\tilde{G}$ corresponding to v. Then each node can simulate the s-pruning protocol when the input graph is $\tilde{G}$, where $s = \mathcal{O}(n^{1/r})$ is the degeneracy of graphs of girth at least $2r$, obtained from Proposition 2. Each node then reconstructs $\tilde{G}$ and computes a spanning forest of $\tilde{G}$. □

3. DISCUSSION

We have shown that, in the BCLIQUE$[n^\epsilon \cdot \log n]$ model, $\mathcal{O}(1/\epsilon)$ rounds are enough to decide connectivity deterministically. If nodes see the graph induced by the nodes at distance at most r, then connectivity can be decided by a deterministic one-round protocol, with messages of size $\mathcal{O}(n^{1/r} \cdot \log n)$.

These results rely on a deterministic protocol for d-pruning, which in particular reconstructs d-degenerate graphs. We believe that this protocol, and the sketch function it is based on, might be of interest for further applications.

Like Ahn *et al.*'s results [1], our connectivity protocol can be transformed into protocols to detect if the input graph is bipartite. Moreover, the d-pruning protocol can be implemented as a $\mathcal{O}(nd \log n)$-space protocol in the *dynamic graph streaming* model.

To wrap up, let us recall that the existence of a one-round deterministic protocol for connectivity, in the broadcast congested clique with sublinear message size, is still open. We might as well ask whether the problem could be solved by randomized protocols using only *private coins*.

4. ACKNOWLEDGMENTS

We thank F. Becker and I. Rapaport for fruitful discussions on the subject, and the anonymous referees for useful suggestions. P. Montealegre would like to thank the support of Conicyt Becas Chile-72130083.

5. REFERENCES

[1] K. J. Ahn, S. Guha, and A. McGregor. Analyzing graph structure via linear measurements. In *Proc. of the 23rd Annual ACM-SIAM Symposium on Discrete Algorithms*, SODA '12, pages 459–467, 2012.

[2] K. J. Ahn, S. Guha, and A. McGregor. Graph sketches: Sparsification, spanners, and subgraphs. In *Proc. of the 31st Symposium on Principles of Database Systems*, PODS '12, pages 5–14, 2012.

[3] B. Awerbuch, O. Goldreich, R. Vainish, and D. Peleg. A trade-off between information and communication in broadcast protocols. *J. ACM*, 37(2):238–256, Apr. 1990.

[4] F. Becker, A. Kosowski, M. Matamala, N. Nisse, I. Rapaport, K. Suchan, and I. Todinca. Allowing each node to communicate only once in a distributed system: shared whiteboard models. *Distributed Computing*, 28(3):189–200, 2015.

[5] A. Drucker, F. Kuhn, and R. Oshman. The communication complexity of distributed task allocation. In *Proc. of the 2012 ACM Symposium on Principles of Distributed Computing*, PODC '12, pages 67–76, 2012.

[6] J. W. Hegeman, G. Pandurangan, S. V. Pemmaraju, V. B. Sardeshmukh, and M. Scquizzato. Toward optimal bounds in the congested clique: Graph connectivity and mst. In *Proceedings of the 2015 ACM Symposium on Principles of Distributed Computing*, PODC '15, pages 91–100, New York, USA, 2015. ACM.

[7] E. Kushilevitz and N. Nisan. *Communication Complexity*. Cambridge University Press, New York, USA, 1997.

[8] Z. Lotker, B. Patt-Shamir, E. Pavlov, and D. Peleg. Minimum-weight spanning tree construction in O(log log n) communication rounds. *SIAM Journal on Computing*, 35(1):120–131, 2005.

Space Bounds for Reliable Storage: Fundamental Limits of Coding*

Alexander Spiegelman†
Viterbi EE Department
Technion, Haifa, Israel
sashas@tx.technion.ac.il

Yuval Cassuto
Viterbi EE Department
Technion, Haifa, Israel
ycassuto@ee.technion.ac.il

Gregory Chockler
CS Department
Royal Holloway, London, UK
gregory.chockler@rhul.ac.uk

Idit Keidar
Viterbi EE Department
Technion, Haifa, Israel
idish@ee.technion.ac.il

ABSTRACT

We study the inherent space requirements of reliable storage algorithms in asynchronous distributed systems. A number of recent works have used codes in order to achieve a better storage cost than the well-known replication approach. However, a closer look reveals that they incur extra costs in certain scenarios. Specifically, if multiple clients access the storage concurrently, then existing asynchronous code-based algorithms may store a number of copies of the data that grows linearly with the number of concurrent clients. We prove here that this is inherent. Given three parameters, (1) the data size – D bits, (2) the concurrency level – c, and (3) the number of storage node failures that need to be tolerated – f, we show a lower bound of $\Omega(min(f,c) \cdot D)$ bits on the space complexity of asynchronous distributed storage algorithms. Intuitively, this implies that the asymptotic storage cost is either as high as with replication, namely $O(fD)$, or as high under concurrency as with the aforementioned code-based algorithms, i.e., $O(cD)$.

We further present a technique for combining erasure codes with replication so as to obtain the best of both. We present an adaptive $f-tolerant$ storage algorithm whose storage cost is $O(min(f,c) \cdot D)$. Together, our results show that the space complexity of providing reliable storage in asynchronous distributed systems is $\Theta(min(f,c) \cdot D)$.

*This work was supported in part by the Israel Science Foundation and Royal Society International Exchanges Grant IE130802.

†Alexander Spiegelman is grateful to the Azrieli Foundation for the award of an Azrieli Fellowship.

PODC'16, July 25 - 28, 2016, Chicago, IL, USA

ISBN 978-1-4503-3964-3/16/07...$15.00

DOI: http://dx.doi.org/10.1145/2933057.2933104

1. INTRODUCTION

In recent years we have seen an exponential increase in storage capacity demands, creating a need for big data storage solutions. In this era, distributed storage plays a key role. Data is typically stored on a collection of nodes accessed asynchronously by clients over a network. By storing redundant information, data remains available following failures. The most common approach to achieve this is via replication [4]; in asynchronous settings, $2f+1$ replicas are needed in order to tolerate f failures [4]. Given the immense size of data, the storage cost of replication is significant. Previous works have attempted to mitigate this cost via the use of erasure codes [3, 5, 11, 7, 18, 10].

Indeed, codes can reduce the storage cost as long as data is not accessed concurrently by multiple clients. For example, if the data size is D bits and a single failure needs to be tolerated, erasure-coded storage ideally requires $(k+2)D/k$ bits for some parameter $k > 1$ instead of the $3D$ bits needed for replication. But as concurrency grows, the cost of erasure-coded storage grows with it: when c clients access the storage concurrently, existing asynchronous code-based algorithms [5, 11, 7, 10] store $O(cD)$ bits in storage nodes or communication channels. Intuitively, this occurs because coded data cannot be reconstructed from a single storage node. Therefore, writing coded data requires coordination – old values cannot be deleted before ensuring that sufficiently many blocks of the new value are in place. This is in contrast to replication, where written values can always be read coherently from a single copy, and so old values may be safely overwritten without coordination.

In this work we prove that this extra cost is inherent: Given three problem parameters: f, c, and D, where f is the number of storage node failures tolerated (client failures are unrestricted), c is the concurrency allowed by the algorithm, and D is the data size, we prove that the storage complexity is $\Theta(min(f,c) \cdot D)$. Asymptotically, this means either a storage cost as high as that of replication, or as high as keeping as many versions of the data as the concurrency level.

Lower bound.

Our results are proven for emulations of a lock-free multi-reader multi-writer regular register [14, 16]; see Section 2 for definitions. (Interestingly, the lower bound does not hold for the weaker safe register semantics; see our technical report [17] for details). We consider algorithms that use (arbitrary) *black-box* encoding schemes, i.e., produce and manipulate code blocks of a given value independently of other values and meta-data; as formalized in Section 3. The storage consists of such code blocks, in addition to possibly unbounded data-independent meta-data, (e.g., timestamps), which we do not count as part of the storage cost. Our black-box assumption excludes storage-reduction techniques like de-duplication, which do require data-dependent meta-data. In Section 4 we survey how this assumption holds in related work on popular storage algorithms [3, 5, 11, 7, 10, 12], and compare it with assumptions made in proving other lower bounds [6]. Yet, the question whether there is a more storage-efficient algorithm that circumvents our result by taking stored values into consideration remains open; see further discussion in Section 7.

We prove the bound in Section 5: we first use a fundamental pigeonhole argument to show that as long as no ongoing write operation contributes code blocks consisting of D or more bits to the storage, no write operation can complete. We then define a parameter $0 < \ell \leq D$. For a given ℓ, we devise a particular adversary behavior, which we prove drives the storage to a state where either (1) $f+1$ storage nodes hold at least ℓ bits each, or (2) the storage holds more than $D - \ell + 1$ bits in distinct code blocks for each of c different operations. Now, picking $\ell = D/2$ implies our lower bound.

Algorithm.

To prove our bound tight, we present in Section 6 a reliable storage algorithm whose storage cost is $O(min(f, c) \cdot D)$. We achieve this by combining the advantages of replication and erasure coding. Our algorithm does not assume any a priori bound on concurrency; rather, it uses erasure codes when concurrency is low and adaptively switches to replication when it is high.

2. COMPUTATION MODEL

We consider an asynchronous fault-prone shared memory system [2, 1, 13] consisting of set $B = \{bo_i, \ldots, bo_n\}$ of n base objects (typically residing at distinct storage nodes) supporting arbitrary atomic *read-modify-write* (RMW) access by clients from some infinite set Π (see Figure 1). Any f out of n base objects and any number of clients may fail by crashing, for some predefined $f < n/2$.

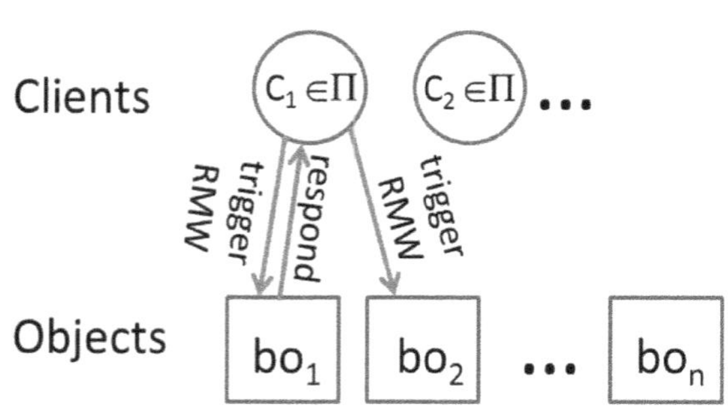

Figure 1: Clients and base objects.

We study algorithms that emulate a shared *register* [14], which stores a value v from some domain $\mathbb{V}$, where $D = \log_2 |\mathbb{V}|$. Initially, the register holds some initial value $v_0 \in \mathbb{V}$. Clients interact with the emulated register via high-level *read* and *write operations*. A client that performs a write operation is called a *writer*, and a client performing a read is a *reader*.

To distinguish the high-level emulated operations from low-level base object access, we refer to the latter as *RMWs*. We say that RMWs are *triggered* and *respond*, whereas operations are *invoked* and *return*. A (high-level) operation is emulated via a series of trigger and respond *actions* on base objects, starting with the operation's invocation and ending with its return. In the course of an operation, a client triggers RMWs separately on each $bo_i \in B$. The state of each $bo_i \in B$ changes atomically, according to the RMW triggered on it, at some point after the time when the RMW is triggered but no later than the time when the matching response occurs. To distinguish incomplete invocations to the emulated register from incomplete RMWs triggered on base objects, we refer to the former as *outstanding* operations and to the latter as *pending* RMWs.

A parameter c defines the write concurrency level, that is, at most c write operations are outstanding at a given time. We assume that $c < |\mathbb{V}|/2 = 2^{D-1}$. We use standard definitions of algorithms, runs, etc, which, for completeness, appear in Appendix A. The emulated register must satisfy the following two properties:

Lock-freedom If at some point in a fair run there is an outstanding operation of a correct client, then *some* operation eventually returns.

Regularity Our safety requirement is regularity, which is weaker than atomicity. There are a number of ways to extend Lamport's notion of regularity [14] to multi-writer registers [16]; we use the weakest one for our lower bound and the strongest for our algorithm, (called MWRegWeak and MWRegWO in [16], resp.), as defined in Appendix A. Intuitively, regularity means that a read rd returns a value written by either (1) the last write w that completes before rd is invoked, or (2) some write that is concurrent to rd or to w, or (3) v_0 if no value is written before rd.

3. STORAGE ALGORITHM MODEL AND ASSUMPTIONS

We first give a formal model for coded storage algorithms, then define the notion of storage cost in this model, and finally state our assumptions that the encoding is symmetric and algorithms use it as a black-box.

We consider algorithms that use (arbitrary) encoding schemes, which produce code blocks in some domain $\mathcal{E}$, so that each value is coded independently of other values. The coding scheme is based on two functions: The encoding function $\mathbb{E} : \mathbb{V} \times \mathbb{N} \rightarrow \mathcal{E}$ maps value/natural number pairs to code blocks. We denote the number of bits in block $e \in \mathcal{E}$ as $|e|$. The decoding function $\mathbb{D} : 2^{\mathcal{E}} \rightarrow \mathbb{V} \cup \{\perp\}$ takes as a parameter a set of code blocks and returns a value in $\mathbb{V}$, or $\perp$ in case no value can be decoded. For example, in a replication approach, each block e can be a full value v, so $\mathbb{D}(\{e\})$ simply returns v. Another example is *k-of-n* erasure codes, where for any value v and any subset S of size k of the set $\{e_i \mid e_i = E(v, i), 1 \leq i \leq n\}$, $\mathbb{D}(S) = v$. We capture rateless codes [15], in which an encoder can generate a

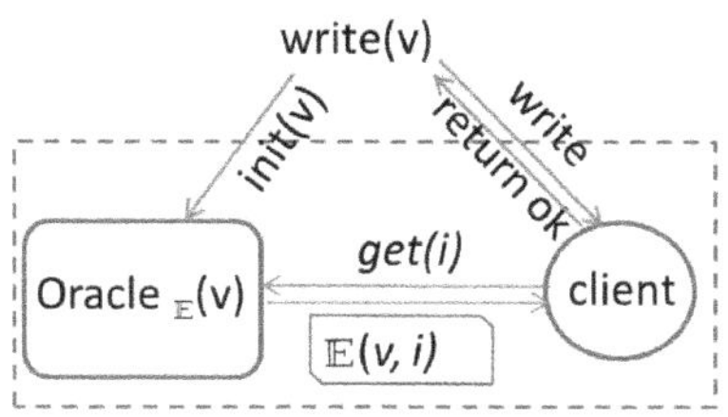

(a) A writer and its oracle.

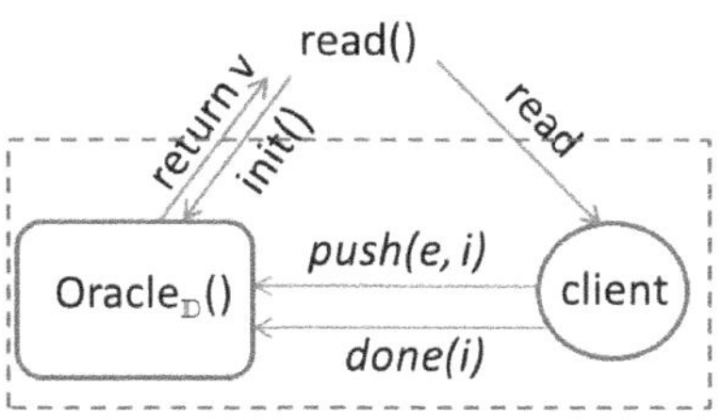

(b) A reader and its oracle.

Figure 2: A model for code-based storage. Encoding and decoding are captured by oracles.

limit-less sequence of blocks, by using $\mathbb{N}$ as the domain for block numbers.

We encapsulate the encoder and decoder into two oracles, $oracle_{\mathbb{E}}$ and $oracle_{\mathbb{D}}$ as illustrated in Figure 2. The interaction with these oracles is as follows:

Definition 1 (Encoding/Decoding Oracles)**.** A w=*write(v)* (*read()*) invocation at a client c_k initializes an $oracle_{\mathbb{E}}(c_k, w)$ ($oracle_{\mathbb{D}}(c_k, w)$, resp.), which expires when w completes. $oracle_{\mathbb{E}}(c_k, w)$ exposes a $get(i)$ operation, which returns $\mathbb{E}(v, i)$ for $i \in \mathbb{N}$; and $oracle_{\mathbb{D}}(c_k, w)$ exposes two operations, $push(e, i)$ and $done(i)$, such that for all $i \in \mathbb{N}$, if c_i calls $done(i)$, then its read operation completes and returns $\mathbb{D}(\{e \mid push(e, i) \text{ previously occurred}\})$. We omit the parameters c_k, w when they are clear from the context.

Writers produce code blocks via $oracle_{\mathbb{E}}$ and store them in the storage, whereas readers try to obtain enough blocks to decode legal values via $oracle_{\mathbb{D}}$. In addition to code blocks, clients and base objects can store unbounded meta-data, e.g., program counters and timestamps. But to avoid trivializing the problem, the meta-data must be data-independent, as formally defined below.

Information is represented as list of code blocks and meta-data, $\langle e_1, e_2, \ldots, e_k; m\rangle$, where $\forall i$, $e_i \in \mathcal{E}$ and the meta-data m is from some arbitrary domain. The *state of a client* that has an outstanding operation consists of the information stored at the client as well the parameters of its pending RMWs that have not yet taken effect. The state of a client with no outstanding operation is empty. A *base object's state* consists of the information stored at the base object and all the responses of pending RMWs that took effect on it. For a base object bo_i (client c_i), we denote the list of code blocks in bo_i's (c_i's) state at time t in run r as $bo_i^r(t)$ (resp. $c_i^r(t)$).

Let $\mathcal{S}$ be an ordered set including all base objects and clients, i.e., $B \cup \Pi$ ordered in some arbitrary way. For $S = \{bo_1, \ldots, bo_k, c_1, \ldots\} \subseteq \mathcal{S}$, $S^r(t)$ is the list of lists $bo_1^r(t), \ldots, bo_k^r(t), c_1^r(t), \ldots$ sorted according to their order in $\mathcal{S}$. A *block instance* $b \in \mathcal{S}^r(t)$ is a triple $\langle i, j, e\rangle$ so that e is stored in the jth position in the ith list in S. We refer to the block contents as $b.e$.

Storage cost.

We count the number of bits stored in blocks in base objects as well as in clients, and neglect meta-data size. Note that oracle states are not counted as part of the storage cost, since we wish to measure the additional space required for making the data available for shared access, beyond its (trivial) existence at its sources and readers.

Definition 2 (Storage Cost)**.** The *storage cost at time t in a run r* is $\Sigma_{b \in \mathcal{S}^r(t)} |b.e|$. The *storage cost of an algorithm A* is the maximum storage cost at any point t in any run r of A.

Assumptions.

To make sure that the encoding does not leak information using block sizes, we assume *symmetry*, in the sense that output block sizes do not depend on input values. (Otherwise, we could for example, represent three values 0, 1, and 10 using a single coded block e_1 of size at most 1 bit by having $|e_1| = 0$ encode 10). Formally:

Definition 3 (Symmetric Encoding)**.** An encoding function $\mathbb{E}$ is *symmetric* if for every $v, v' \in \mathbb{V}$ and for all $i \in \mathbb{N}$, $|\mathbb{E}(v, i)| = |\mathbb{E}(v', i)|$. We denote $size(i) \triangleq |\mathbb{E}(v, i)|$.

Note that different block numbers (of all values) may have different sizes.

We next state our assumption that the storage treats the coding as a black-box. First, we define the notion of a source function, which we shall use to prohibit generation of code blocks by any source other than $oracle_{\mathbb{E}}$:

Definition 4 (Source Function)**.** A function is a *source function* for a run r if it maps every (b, t) s.t. $b \in \mathcal{S}^r(t)$ to a pair $\langle w, i\rangle$ s.t. $b.e$ was returned by $get(i)$ in $oracle_{\mathbb{E}}(w)$.

We use a source function to trace blocks in the storage to operations that produced them. To capture the restriction that the algorithm's decision what to store does not rely on block contents, we stipulate that we can replace the value written by a write operation w in a run r by an arbitrary value v, yielding the same sequence of states and actions, except that all stored block instances whose source is $\langle w, i\rangle$ are replaced with $\mathbb{E}(v, i)$. For clarity, we refer to the operation as w in both runs (see Figure 3).

Definition 5 (Black-Box Coding)**.** An algorithm A is *black-box coding* if for every run r there is a source function $source^r$ s.t. for every $w = write(u)$ operation in r, $\forall u \in \mathbb{V}$, there is run r_v satisfying the following:

1. r_v has the same sequences of invocations and returns as r except that $w = write(v)$ (possibly with no change) and return values of read operations may be different; and

2. client and base object states at every time t in r_v are the same as at time t in r except that the contents of every $b \in \mathcal{S}^r(t)$ s.t. $source^r(b, t) = \langle w, i\rangle$ for some i is replaced by $e' = \mathbb{E}(v, i)$.

In the following, we will only consider source functions satisfying Definition 5. In case multiple such source functions for r exist, we fix an arbitrary one and refer to it as $source^r$.

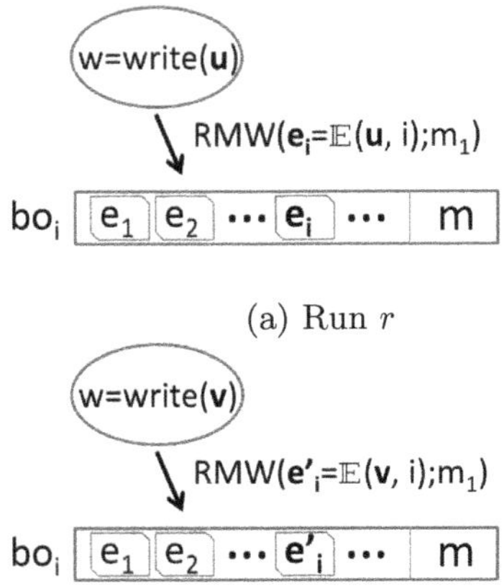

(a) Run r

(b) Run r_v

Figure 3: Black-box coding. Runs r and r_v have the same trace except that write w is invoked with u in r and with v in r_v; and each base object bo_i's state (blocks and meta-data) is identical at all times in both runs, except that blocks produced by w's oracle in r are replaced in r_v by the corresponding blocks of v.

4. RELATED WORK

Our model captures numerous existing distributed storage algorithms, including ones that use replication [4], and erasure codes [3, 5, 11, 7, 10, 12]. We note that some of them report a storage cost below $O(cD)$ [3, 5, 18, 10]. This is sometimes achieved by assuming periods of synchrony [3]. Other works shift the cost from storage nodes to the network and keep unbounded information in channels [10, 5]. However, since we define parameters and responses of pending RMWs to be part of clients' and base objects' states, information in channels is counted in our storage cost model and hence these algorithms are subject to our bound. The only non-black-box storage algorithm we are aware of is [18], where multiple values are encoded jointly, saving space, but also forfeiting regular register semantics. It is as of now unclear whether lifting the black-box assumption suffices in order to circumvent our result.

An earlier version of this work [17] showed a special case of the result in this paper for infinite concurrency. Cadambe et al. [6] prove closely related lower bounds for coded storage algorithms. First, they show that asynchronous fault-tolerant storage algorithms require strictly more storage than synchronous erasure-coded algorithms. Second, similarly to this paper, they extend the result given in our earlier version to show that the storage cost must grow linearly with $\min(f, c)$, but their result is proven under a different set of assumptions than ours. In particular, while both papers make certain "black box" assumptions about the storage, [6] does not rule out joint coding as we do, but instead restricts protocol actions in a way that forbids them from depending on a written value in more than one communication round; this affords the protocol more freedom than our model in one communication round, and less freedom in all other rounds. On the face of it, the two sets of assumptions appear to be incomparable, though they both achieve the same end result, as we discuss in Section 7 below. Additionally, our bound allows algorithms to use unbounded (data-independent) meta-data and is proven for lock-free register emulations, whereas the bound in [6] includes meta-data and is shown for wait-free registers.

Another tradeoff between the number of writers and space complexity of reliable register emulations has been recently studied in [8]. Inspired by our adversary structure, they show that the number of fault-prone read/write registers needed to emulate a reliable multi-writer register grows linearly with the number of clients that can write to the register (even in sequential runs). Here, on the other hand, we consider storage nodes supporting fully general read-modify-write, for which that lower bound does not apply.

The challenge of providing a lower bound on stored data when meta-data is potentially unbounded was also previously addressed in the context of byzantine storage [9]. That paper has shown that certain storage algorithms cannot be "amnesic", i.e., cannot "forget" values written to them. Like our black-box assumption, the notion of amnesia was defined in terms of runs. However, it did not yield explicit bound on storage cost.

5. STORAGE LOWER BOUND

We now show a lower bound of $O(min(f, c) \cdot D)$ bits on the storage cost of any lock-free algorithm that uses symmetric black-box coding to simulate a regular register:

Theorem 1. *Consider a lock-free algorithm A that uses symmetric black-box coding to simulate a regular register. The storage cost of A is $\Omega(min(f, c) \cdot D)$.*

For the sake of our proof, we quantify the number of bits in blocks contributed by client c_i's operation w to base objects and clients other than c_i.

Definition 6. Let $S \subset \mathcal{S}$, and consider a time t and an operation w by client c_j in a run r. We define $S^r(t, w) \triangleq \{i \in \mathbb{N} \mid \exists b \in (S \setminus \{c_j\})^r(t)\colon source^r(b, t) = \langle w, i\rangle\}$, and $||S^r(t, w)|| \triangleq \Sigma_{i \in S^r(t,w)} size(i)$.

For $I \subseteq \mathbb{N}$, we say that two values $v' \neq v''$ in $\mathbb{V}$ are *I-colliding* if $\forall i \in I$, $\mathbb{E}(v', i) = \mathbb{E}(v'', i)$. We next use the pigeonhole argument and the assumption of symmetric black-box coding in order to show that write operations cannot return until some write stores enough bits in different blocks in every set of $n - f$ base objects.

Claim 1. *Let w be a write operation invoked in a run r of A, and t be a point in r. Consider a set of values $U \subset \mathbb{V}$, $|U| < 2^{D-1}$, and a set of base objects $S \subset \mathcal{S}$. If $||S^r(t, w)|| < D$, then there are two $S^r(t, w)$-colliding values $u \neq u'$ in $\mathbb{V} \setminus U$.*

Proof. Since $|\mathbb{V} \setminus U| > 2^{D-1}$ and $||S^r(t, w)|| < D$, the claim follows from the pigeonhole argument. □

Lemma 1. *Consider a run r of algorithm A that begins with the invocation of c concurrent write operations. Let S be a set of at least $n - f$ base objects and assume that at every time t in r for every operation w in r, $||S^r(t, w)|| < D$. Then no write operation returns in r.*

Proof. Let $W_{ops} = \{w_1, \ldots, w_c\}$ be the set of c concurrent writes invoked in r. Assume by contradiction that there exists a complete write in W_{ops}. Let w be the first such write, and t be the time when it returns. Next we inductively build a sequence of sets of values $U_0, U_1, \ldots, U_c$, where $|U_i| = i$:

- $U_0 = \{\}$

- $\forall i \in \{0, \ldots, c-1\}$, we use U_i to build U_{i+1}. By the lemma premise, $||S^r(t, w_{i+1})|| < D$. Now since $|U_i| < c < 2^{D-1}$, by Claim 1, there are two $S^r(t, w_{i+1})$-*colliding* values $u_{w_{i+1}} \neq u'_{w_{i+1}}$ in $\mathbb{V} \setminus U_i$. We let $U_{i+1} = U_i \cup \{u_{w_{i+1}}\}$.

The set U_c contains exactly c (different) values s.t. for every operation $w_i \in W_{ops}$ there is a value $u_{w_i} \in U_c$ that has a $S^r(t, w_i)$-*colliding* value $u'_{w_i} \in \mathbb{V}$. By applying Definition 5 (c times), there is a run r' that begins with the invocation of c concurrent write operations, in which every operation $w_i \in W_{ops}$ writes u_{w_i} s.t. w returns at time t, and for every operation $w_i \in W_{ops}$, $S^r(t, w_i) = S^{r'}(t, w_i)$. Next, let clients with outstanding operations and all base objects in $B \setminus S$ fail at time t in r' (note that by assumption $|S| \geq n - f$, so $|B \setminus S| \leq f$), and let some client c_j invoke a solo read operation at time $t+1$. By lock-freedom, c_j's read operation completes, and by regularity, it returns a value $u \in U_c$ at some time $t' > t$.

Let w' be the operation that writes u in r'. Since u has a $S^r(t, w')$-*colliding* value u' and since $S^r(t, w') = S^{r'}(t, w')$, u and u' are $S^{r'}(t, w')$-*colliding*. By Definition 5, there is a run r'' with the same operations as in r' except that w' writes u' (instead of u) s.t. every client's and base object's state at time t in r' is identical to its state at time t in r'' (note that clients with outstanding operations and all base objects in $B \setminus S$ fail at time t) except that for every block instance $b \in \mathcal{S}^{r'}(t)$ s.t. $source^{r'}(b, t) = \langle w', i \rangle$, $b.e$ is replaced with a block $\mathbb{E}(u', i)$. In particular, states of base objects in S at time t are identical to their states at time t in r' except that for every block instance $b \in S^{r'}(t)$ s.t. $source^{r'}(b, t) = \langle w', i \rangle$, $b.e$ is replaced with a block $\mathbb{E}(u', i)$.

Now since u and u' are $S_{r'}(t, w')$-*colliding*, states of base objects in S at time t in r'' are identical to their states at time t in r'. In addition, since clients with outstanding operations and all base objects in $B \setminus S$ fail at time t, the solo reader c_j cannot distinguish between r' and r'', and thus, it pushes the same blocks to its oracle and calls *done* with the same number in r'' as in r', and therefore, its read operation returns u at time t'' in run r''. However, since the clients invoke write operations with different values in r', u is not written in r''. A contradiction to regularity. $\square$

Having shown a condition under which write operations cannot complete, we define an (unfair) adversary behavior that takes advantage of this in order to prevent progress. We introduce some notation, and then use it in order to define the adversary. We define a parameter $0 < \ell \leq D$, and for any time t in a run r of algorithm A we define the following sets, as illustrated in Figure 4. For convenience, from now on we omit the superscript r.

- $C(t)$: the set of outstanding write operations at time t.

- $C_\ell^-(t) = \{w \in C(t) \mid ||\mathcal{S}(t, w)|| \leq D - \ell\}$: The set of write operations each of which has at most $D-\ell$ bits in blocks, produced by its oracle with different numbers, in the storage (excluding the client performing it) at time t.

- $C_\ell^+(t) = C(t) \setminus C_\ell^-(t)$.

- $F_\ell(t) = \{bo_i \in B \mid \Sigma_{b \in \{bo_i\}(t)} |b.e| \geq \ell\}$. Base objects that store blocks that consist (together) of more than ℓ bits at time t. These are base objects that we will "freeze" in our counter-example because they are already "full", i.e., consume enough space for our lower bound.

We fix the parameter ℓ throughout the proof and omit subscript ℓ from the notation. The next observation on storage cost immediately follows from the definitions.

Observation 1. *At any point t in every run r of A, the storage cost is at least $|C^+(t)|(D - \ell + 1)$.*

We next define a particular adversary behavior that schedules actions in a way that prevents progress. Note that the adversary controls the scheduling of client actions and RMW responses.

Definition 7. (*Ad*) At any time t, *Ad* schedules an action as follows:

1. If there is a pending RMW on a base object in $B \setminus F(t)$ by a client performing an operation in $C^-(t)$, then choose the longest pending of these RMWs, allow it to take effect on the corresponding base object, and schedule its response.

2. Else, choose in a fair order an operation by a client $c_i \in \Pi$ and schedule its action (trigger RMW, call its oracle, get response from its oracle, or return), without allowing it to affect the base object yet. By fair order we mean any order in which every client is chosen infinitely often (e.g., $c_1, c_1, c_2, c_1, c_2, c_3 \ldots$).

In other words, *Ad* delays RMWs triggered by operations in $C^+(t)$ (for which the storage already holds $D - \ell$ bits) as well as RMWs on "frozen" base objects in $F(t)$ (which store at least ℓ bits), and fairly schedules all other actions. We demonstrate *Ad*'s behavior in Figure 4. Though this behavior may be unfair, in every infinite run of *Ad*, every correct client gets infinitely many opportunities to take steps. We use *Ad* to build an unfair run with no progress (no write returns), and then build an indistinguishable fair run to contradict lock-freedom. The following observation immediately follows from the adversary's freezing of base objects in F.

Observation 2. *Assume run r of algorithm A in which the environment behaves like Ad. For each base object bo, if $bo \in F(t)$ at some time t, then $bo \in F(t')$ for all $t' > t$ in r.*

Another consequence of *Ad*'s behavior is captured by the following:

Lemma 2. *Consider a run r of algorithm A. If the adversary behaves like Ad, then for every time t and for every write operation w in r, $||(\mathcal{S} \setminus F(t))(t, w)|| < D$.*

Proof. Assume by way of contradiction that there is time t and write operation w performed by client c_j s.t. $||(\mathcal{S} \setminus F(t))(t, w)|| \geq D$. The definition of $(\mathcal{S} \setminus F(t))(t, w)$ takes into account only blocks returned by w's oracle that are stored outside of $c_j(t)$. Thus, w triggered at least one RMW that has a matching response before time t in r. Let $t' \leq t$ be the

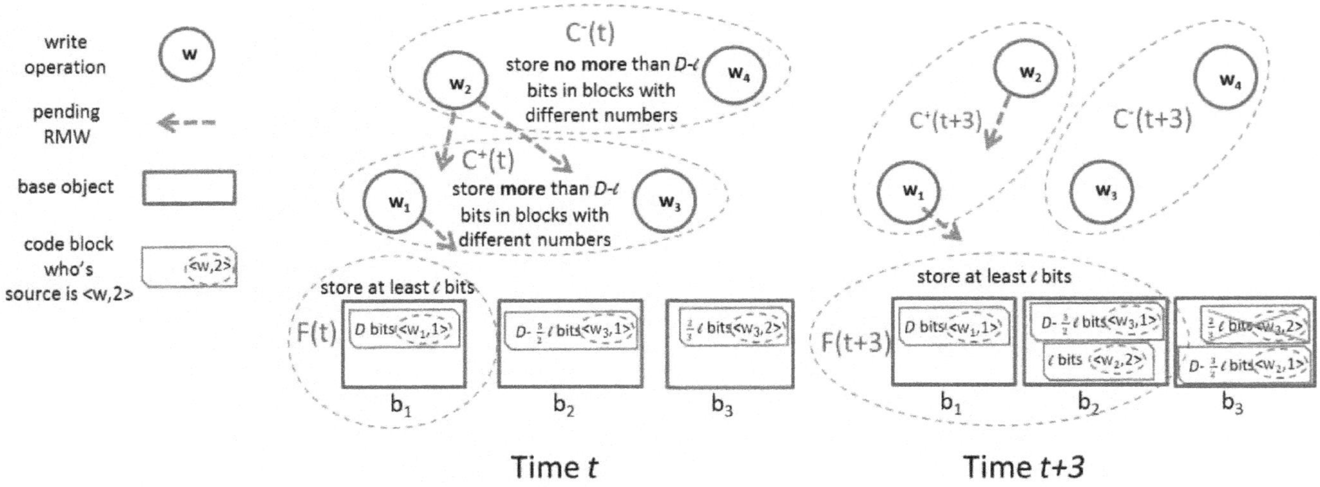

Figure 4: Example scenario in run of a storage algorithm with adversary Ad. In this example, $2D/5 < \ell < D$. At time t, only w_2 and w_4 are in $C^-(t)$, where w_4 has no pending RMWs and w_2 has one triggered RMW on $b_1 \in F(t)$ and one triggered RMW on $b_3 \notin F(t)$. Therefore, by the first rule, Ad schedules the response on the RMW triggered by w_2 on b_3. In this example w_2 overwrites w_3's block in b_3, thus w_3 moves from C^+ to C^-. Then, at time $t+1$, no response can be scheduled by rule 1 (no operation in $C^-(t+1)$ has a pending RMW on a base object in $N \setminus F(t+1)$), so by rule 2, Ad chooses w_2 and lets it trigger an RMW on base object b_2. Now since w_2 is the only operation that has a pending RMW on a base object not in $F(t+2)$, Ad schedules the response on the RMW triggered by w_2 on b_2 at time $t+2$. In this example w_2 adds a block with ℓ bits to b_2. Thus, c_2 is included in $C^+(t+3)$. In addition, b_2 stores more than ℓ bits at time $t+3$, so it belongs to $F(t+3)$.

time when the last RMW triggered by w responded, and denote this RMW by rmw and the base object on which rmw was triggered by bo. By Ad, $w \in C^-(t'-1)$, and therefore, by definition, $||(\mathcal{S} \setminus F(t'-1))(t'-1, w)|| \leq D - \ell$. Now consider two cases:

- First, rmw adds blocks (possibly overwriting other blocks) with less than ℓ bits to bo. In this case, since bo is the only storage component that changed at time t', $|(\mathcal{S} \setminus F(t'))(t', w)| < D$.
- Second, rmw adds blocks (possibly overwriting other blocks) with at least ℓ bits to bo. In this case, $bo \in F(t')$. Now since $||(\mathcal{S} \setminus F(t'-1))(t'-1, w)|| \leq D$, by Observation 2, $F(t'-1) \subseteq F(t')$, and given $bo \in F(t')$ and it is the only storage component that changed at time t', we get $||(\mathcal{S} \setminus F(t'))(t', w)|| \leq ||(\mathcal{S} \setminus F(t'-1))(t'-1, w)|| < D$.

So far we showed that $||(\mathcal{S} \setminus F(t'))(t', w)|| < D$. By Observation 2, and since no RMW by w takes effect after time t', $(\mathcal{S} \setminus F(t''))(t'', w) \subseteq (\mathcal{S} \setminus F(t'))(t', w)$, $\forall t'' \geq t'$. Therefore, we get $||(\mathcal{S} \setminus F(t))(t, w)|| < D$. A contradiction.

□

The next corollary uses Lemmas 1 and 2 in order to conclude that Ad can prevent progress of write operations.

Corollary 1. *Consider a run r of algorithm A that begins with the invocation of c concurrent write operations. If the adversary behaves like Ad and $|F(t)| \leq f$ for all t in r, then no write operation returns in r.*

Proof. By Lemma 2, for every time t for every write operation w in r, $||(\mathcal{S} \setminus F(t))(t, w)|| < D$. And since $B \subset \mathcal{S}$, for every time t for every write operation w in r, $||(B \setminus F(t))(t, w)|| < D$. Now since $|F(t)| \leq f$ for every time t in r, $|B \setminus F(t)| \geq n - f$. Therefore, by Lemma 1, no write operation returns in r.

□

We have shown that Ad can prevent completion of write operations in algorithms that store ℓ bits in less than $f+1$ base objects. However, this does not directly imply a storage bound, since Ad is not fair. In the next lemma we close this gap by showing a fair run in which lock-freedom must be satisfied , i.e., operations invoked by correct clients must eventually complete, in order to blow up the storage. We show that for every algorithm, we can build a run where at some point the algorithm either stores ℓ bits in each of $f+1$ base objects (namely, $\exists t : |F(t)| > f$), or there are c concurrent operations each of which adds at least $D - \ell + 1$ bits to the storage cost (i.e., $|C^+(t)| = c$).

Lemma 3. *There is a run r of A and a time t in r when $|C^+(t)| = c$ or $|F(t)| > f$.*

Proof. Assume by way of contradiction that there is no such run of algorithm A. We first build a run r of A with c clients that concurrently write different values, in which the environment behaves like adversary Ad. By the contradiction assumption, $|C^+(t)| < c$ and $|F(t)| \leq f$ for all t in r. We start with the invocation of c concurrent write operations, and allow the run to proceed indefinitely according to Ad. We say that a client c, which performs write operation w, is *stuck* in r if there is a time t in r s.t. for all $t' \geq t$, $w \in C^+(t')$ (and so no RMWs triggered by c take effect after time t). By Observation 2 and the assumption that $|F(t)| \leq f$ for all t, there is a time t_1 in r s.t. for every time $t_2 \geq t_1$, $F(t_1) = F(t_2)$.

Now we build a run r' that is identical to r but every base object $bo \in F(t_1)$ fails at time t_1 ($|F(t_1)| \leq f$), and every stuck client fails after its last RMW takes effect. Since by Ad, RMWs do not take effect on base objects in $F(t_1)$ after time t_1, runs r and r' are indistinguishable to all correct clients and base objects. Now notice that by Ad's behavior, each correct client in r' gets infinitely many opportunities to trigger RMWs. In addition, since (1) for every correct client c_i in r' there are infinitely many times t when $c_i \in C^-(t)$, (2) Ad picks responses from base objects not in $F(t)$ in the order they are triggered, and (3) there are no correct base objects in $F(t')$ for all $t' > t_1$, every RMW triggered by a correct client on a correct base object has a matching response in r'. Therefore, run r' is fair.

By the contradiction assumption $|C^+(t)| < c$ for all t in r. Therefore, there is at least one client that is not stuck in r, and thus, there is at least one client that is correct in r'. Hence, by lock-freedom, some client eventually completes its write operation in r'. Now since r and r' are indistinguishable to all clients that are correct in both, the same is true in r. However, by Corollary 1, no write operation completes in r. A contradiction.

□

So far we have shown that every algorithm has a run where at some point either ℓ bits are stored in $f+1$ base objects, or there are c concurrent operations each of which adds at least $D - \ell + 1$ bits to the storage cost. We now combine this result with Observation 1 to conclude our lower bound:

Proof (Theorem 1). Let $\ell = D/2$. By Lemma 3, there is a run r of A and a time t in r when $|C^+(t)| = c$ or $|F(t)| > f$. If $|F(t)| > f$, then the storage cost at time t in r is $(f+1)\ell = (f+1)D/2 = \Omega(fD)$. Otherwise, $|C^+(t)| = c$, and so by Observation 1, the storage cost at time t in r is at least $c(D - \ell) = cD/2 = \Omega(cD)$. The theorem follows.

□

By picking $\ell = D$, we get a second conclusion from Lemma 3 and Observation 1. The following corollary proves that any coding scheme short of full replication must exhibit storage growth linear in the concurrency.

Corollary 2. *The storage cost of any algorithm that uses a black-box coding scheme to simulate a regular lock-free register, and does not store D bits (enough to represent a full replica) in $f+1$ base objects, grows linearly with the concurrency.*

6. ADAPTIVE REGULAR REGISTER

We present a storage algorithm that combines full replication with erasure coding in order to achieve the advantages of both. A k-of-n erasure code takes a value from $\mathbb{V}$ and produces a set S of n blocks from $\mathcal{E}$ s.t. the value can be restored from any subset of S that contains no less than k different blocks. We assume that the size of each block is D/k. $Oracle_{\mathbb{E}}$ and $Oracle_{\mathbb{D}}$ are encapsulated by two functions *encode* and *decode*, respectively: *encode* gets a value $v \in \mathbb{V}$ and returns a set of n ordered elements $W = \{\langle e_1, 1\rangle, \ldots, \langle e_n, n\rangle\}$, where $e_1, \ldots, e_n \in \mathcal{E}$, and *decode* gets a set $W' \subset \mathcal{E} \times \mathbb{N}$ and returns $v' \in \mathbb{V}$ s.t. if $|W'| \geq k$ and $W' \subseteq W$, then $v = v'$. We use $k = n - 2f$. Note that when $k = 1$, we get full replication.

The main idea behind our algorithm is to have base objects store blocks from at most k different *writes*, and then turn to store full replicas. Our algorithm satisfies strong regularity and FW-termination, which is a stronger liveness property than lock-freedom (see Appendix A). In the technical report [17], we prove the following:

Theorem 2. *There is an FW-terminating algorithm that simulates a regular register, whose storage cost is $min((c+1)(2f+k)D/k, (2f+k)2D)$ bits. Moreover, in a run with a finite number of writes, if all the writers are correct, the storage is eventually reduced to $(2f+k)D/k$ bits.*

Notice that k is a parameter of the algorithm, and if we pick $k = f$, then asymptotically the storage cost of our algorithm is $O(min(cD, fD)) = O(min(c, f) \cdot D)$.

The algorithm's pseudocode appears in Algorithms 1-3. The algorithm uses a set of n shared base objects $bo_1, \ldots, bo_n$ each of which holds three fields V_p, V_f, and $storedTS$.

Algorithm 1 Definitions.

1: $TimeStamps = \mathbb{N} \times \Pi$, with selectors num and c, ordered lexicographically.
2: $Pieces = (\mathcal{E} \times \mathbb{N})$
3: $Chunks = Pieces \times TimeStamps$, with selectors val, ts
4: $encode : \mathbb{V} \rightarrow 2^{\mathcal{E} \times \{1,2,\ldots,n\}}$, $decode : 2^{\mathcal{E} \times \{1,2,\ldots,n\}} \rightarrow \mathbb{V}$ s.t. $\forall v \in \mathbb{V}$, $encode(v) = \{\langle *, 1\rangle, \ldots, \langle *, n\rangle\} \wedge \forall W \in 2^{\mathcal{E} \times \mathbb{N}}$, if $W \subseteq encode(v) \wedge |W| \geq k$, then $decode(W) = v$

5: **base objects:**
6: $\forall i \in \{1, \ldots, n\}$, $bo_i = \langle storedTS, V_p, V_f\rangle$ s.t. $V_f, V_p \subset Chunks$, and $storedTS \in TimeStamps$, initially $\langle\langle 0,0\rangle, \{\langle\langle 0,0\rangle, \langle v_{0_i}, i\rangle\rangle\}, \{\}\rangle$.

The V_p field holds a set of timestamped code blocks so that the ith block of a value can be stored in the V_p field of object bo_i. The V_f field stores a timestamped replica of a *single* value, (represented as a set of k code blocks). And $storedTS$ holds a timestamp, as explained below.

Write operation and storage efficiency.

The write operation (lines 3–14) consists of 3 sequentially executed rounds: *read timestamp*, *update*, and *garbage collection*; and, the read consists of one or more sequentially executed *read* rounds. At each round, the client invokes RMWs on all base objects in parallel, and awaits responses from at least $n - f$ base objects. The read rounds of both write and read rely on the readValue routine (lines 21–28) to collect the contents of the V_p and V_f, fields from $n - f$ base objects, as well as to determine the highest $storedTS$ known to these objects. The implementations of the update and garbage collection rounds are given by the update (lines 29–36) and GC (lines 37–42) routines, respectively.

The write implementation starts by encoding v into k code blocks (line 4) and invoking the read round where the client uses the combined contents of the V_p, V_f and $storedTS$ fields returned by readValue to determine the timestamp ts to be stored alongside v's code blocks on the base object; ts is set to be higher than all returned timestamps thus ensuring that the order of the timestamps associated with the stored values is compatible with the order of their corresponding writes, (which is essential for regularity).

The client then proceeds to the update round where it attempts to store the ith code block $\langle e, i\rangle$ of v in $bo_i.V_p$ if the size of $bo_i.V_p$ is less than k (lines 33), or its full replica in $bo_i.V_f$ if ts is higher than the timestamp associated with the value currently stored in $bo_i.V_f$ (line 35). Storing $\langle e, i\rangle$ in $bo_i.V_p$ coincides with an attempt to reduce its size by removing stale code blocks of values whose timestamps are smaller than $storedTS$ (line 33). This guarantees that the size of V_p never exceeds the number of concurrent writes, which is a key for achieving our adaptive storage bound. Lastly, the client updates $bo_i.storedTS$ so as its new value is at least as high as the one returned by the readValue routine. This allows the timestamp associated with the latest complete update to propagate to the base object being written, in order to prevent future writes of old blocks into this base object.

In the write's garbage collection round, the client attempts to further reduce the storage usage by (1) removing all code blocks associated with timestamps lower than ts from both $bo_i.V_p$ and $bo_i.V_f$ (lines 38–39), and (2) replacing a full replica (if it exists) of its written value v in $bo_i.V_f$ with its ith code block $\langle e, i\rangle$ (line 41). It is safe to remove the full replica and values with older timestamps at this point, since once the update round has completed, it is ensured that the written value or a newer written value is restoreable from any $n - f$ base objects. This mechanism ensures that all code blocks except the ones comprising the value written with the highest timestamp are eventually removed from all objects' V_p and V_f sets, which reduces the storage to a minimum in runs with finitely many writes, which all complete. The garbage collection round also updates the $bo_i.storedTS$ field to ensure its value is at least as high as ts.

Algorithm 2 regular register emulation. Algorithm for client c_j.

```
1: local variables:
2:      storedTS, ts ∈ TimeStamp, WriteSet ∈ Pieces

3: operation Write(v) do
4:      WriteSet ← encode(v)
        ▷ round 1: read timestamps
5:      ⟨storedTS, ReadSet⟩ ← readValue()
6:      tmp ← max(storedTS.num,
            max{tmp' | ⟨⟨tmp', ∗⟩, ∗⟩ ∈ ReadSet})
7:      ts ← ⟨n + 1, j⟩
        ▷ round 2: update
8:      || for i = 1 to n
9:          update(bo_i, WriteSet, ts, storedTS, i)
10:     wait for n − f responses
        ▷ round 3: garbage collect
11:     || for i = 1 to n
12:         GC(bo_i, WriteSet, ts, i)
13:     wait for n − f responses
14:     return "ok"

15: operation Read() do
16:     ⟨storedTS, ReadSet⟩ ← readValue()
17:     while ∄ts ≥ storedTS s.t.
            |{⟨ts, v⟩ | ⟨ts, v⟩ ∈ ReadSet}| ≥ k do
18:         ⟨storedTS, ReadSet⟩ ← readValue()
19:     ts' ← max_{ts ≥ storedTS} (|{⟨ts, v⟩ | ⟨ts, v⟩ ∈ ReadSet}| ≥ k)
20:     return decode({v | ⟨ts', v⟩ ∈ ReadSet})
```

Key Invariant and read operation.

The write implementation described above guarantees the following key invariant: at all times, a value written by either the latest complete write or a newer write is available from every set consisting of at least $n-f$ base objects (either in the form of k code blocks in the objects' V_p fields, or in full from one of their V_f fields). Therefore, a read will always be able to reconstruct the latest completely written or a newer value provided it can successfully retrieve k matching blocks of this value. However, a read round may sample different base objects at different times (that is, it does not necessarily obtain an atomic snapshot of the base objects), and the number of blocks stored in V_p is bounded. Thus, the read may be unable to see k matching blocks of any single new value, as long as new values continue to be written concurrently with the read.

Nevertheless, for FW-Termination, the reads are only required to return in runs where a finite number of writes are invoked. Our implementation of read (lines 15–20) proceeds by invoking consecutive rounds of RMWs on the base objects via the readValue routine. After each round, the reader examines the collection of returned values and timestamps to determine if any value has k code blocks and is also associated with a timestamp that is at least as high as $storedTS$ (line 17). If any such value is found, the one associated with the highest timestamp is returned (line 20). Otherwise, the reader proceeds to invoke another round of base object accesses. Note that returning values associated with older timestamps may violate regularity, since they may have been written earlier than the write with timestamp $storedTS$, which in turn may have completed before the read was invoked.

Algorithm 3 Functions used in regular register emulation.

```
21: procedure readValue()
22:     ReadSet ← {}, T ← {}
23:     || for i=1 to n
24:         tmp ← read(bo_i)
25:         ReadSet ← ReadSet ∪ tmp.V_f ∪ tmp.V_p
26:         T ← T ∪ {tmp.storedTS}
27:     wait for n − f responses
28:     return ⟨max(T), ReadSet⟩

29: update(bo, WriteSet, ts, storedTS, i) ≜
30:     if ts ≤ bo.storedTS
31:         return
32:     if |bo.V_p| < k
            ▷ write a piece and remove old pieces
33:         bo.V_p ← bo.V_p \ {⟨ts', v⟩ ∈ bo.V_p | ts' < storedTS}
                ∪{⟨ts, ⟨e, i⟩⟩ | ⟨e, i⟩ ∈ WriteSet}
34:     else if bo.V_f = {} ∨ ∃ts' < ts : ⟨ts', ∗⟩ ∈ bo.V_f
            ▷ write a piece and remove old pieces
35:         bo.V_f ← {⟨ts, ⟨e, j⟩⟩ | ⟨e, j⟩ ∈ WriteSet
                ∧j ∈ {1, . . . , k}}
36:     bo.storedTS ← max(bo.storedTS, storedTS)

37: GC(bo, WriteSet, ts, i) ≜
        ▷ keep only new pieces
38:     bo.V_p ← {⟨ts', v⟩ ∈ bo.V_p | ts' ≥ ts}
39:     bo.V_f ← {⟨ts', v⟩ ∈ bo.V_f | ts' ≥ ts}
40:     if ⟨ts, ∗⟩ ∈ bo.V_f
            ▷ V_f holds a full replica of my write
            ▷ V_f keep only one piece of it
41:         bo.V_f ← {⟨ts, ⟨e, i⟩⟩ | ⟨e, i⟩ ∈ WriteSet}
42:     bo.storedTS ← max(bo.storedTS, ts)
```

7. DISCUSSION

We studied the inherent space requirements of reliable storage in asynchronous distributed settings. We proved an asymptotic bound of $\Omega(min(f, c) \cdot D)$ for any storage algorithm using a symmetric black-box coding scheme, which produces code blocks of values independently of other values. We then presented an algorithm that combines replication and erasure codes, whose storage cost is $O(min(f, c) \cdot D)$.

Our work leaves open questions for future work. First, it is unclear whether the same lower bound still applies when stored bits are allowed to depend on multiple concurrent write values. The main requirement for extending our proof to general coding is a model that correctly accounts for the information stored in the base objects and clients when the clients code jointly. Our black-box assumption rules out such joint coding. Whereas in principle, [6] allows stored information to depend on multiple input values, their assumption that only one round of the protocol depends on the written value essentially forces clients to "forget" the value they used in such joint coding. For example, if the algorithm stores $v_1 + v_2$ instead of either v_1 or v_2, it cannot reproduce the original values, rendering such joint coding useless. Second, while asymptotically optimal, the constants in our bound are not tight, and it could be interesting to close this gap. Finally, we believe that our model and adversary definitions can yield additional lower bounds.

Acknowledgements

We thank Dahlia Malkhi, Yoram Moses, and Rotem Oshman for insightful comments.

References

[1] Ittai Abraham, Gregory Chockler, Idit Keidar, and Dahlia Malkhi. Byzantine disk paxos: optimal resilience with byzantine shared memory. *Distributed Computing*, 18(5), 2006.

[2] Yehuda Afek, Michael Merritt, and Gadi Taubenfeld. Benign failure models for shared memory. In *Distributed Algorithms*. Springer, 1993.

[3] Marcos Kawazoe Aguilera, Ramaprabhu Janakiraman, and Lihao Xu. Using erasure codes efficiently for storage in a distributed system. In *Dependable Systems and Networks, 2005. DSN 2005. Proceedings. International Conference on*. IEEE, 2005.

[4] Hagit Attiya, Amotz Bar-Noy, and Danny Dolev. Sharing memory robustly in message-passing systems. *Journal of the ACM (JACM)*, 42(1), 1995.

[5] Christian Cachin and Stefano Tessaro. Optimal resilience for erasure-coded byzantine distributed storage. In *Dependable Systems and Networks, 2006. DSN 2006. International Conference on*. IEEE, 2006.

[6] Viveck Cadambe, Zhiying Wang, and Nancy Lynch. Information-theoretic lower bounds on the storage cost of shared memory emulation. In *PODC*, 2016.

[7] Viveck R Cadambe, Nancy Lynch, Muriel Medard, and Peter Musial. A coded shared atomic memory algorithm for message passing architectures. In *Network Computing and Applications (NCA), 2014 IEEE 13th International Symposium on*. IEEE, 2014.

[8] Gregory Chockler, Dan Dobre, Alexander Shraer, and Alexander Spiegelman. Space bounds for reliable multi-writer data store: Inherent cost of read/write primitives. *arXiv preprint arXiv:1508.03762*, 2015.

[9] Gregory Chockler, Rachid Guerraoui, and Idit Keidar. Amnesic distributed storage. In *Distributed Computing*. Springer, 2007.

[10] Partha Dutta, Rachid Guerraoui, and Ron R. Levy. Optimistic erasure-coded distributed storage. In *Proceedings of the 22Nd International Symposium on Distributed Computing*, DISC '08, Berlin, Heidelberg, 2008. Springer-Verlag.

[11] Garth R Goodson, Jay J Wylie, Gregory R Ganger, and Michael K Reiter. Efficient byzantine-tolerant erasure-coded storage. In *Dependable Systems and Networks, 2004 International Conference on*. IEEE, 2004.

[12] James Hendricks, Gregory R Ganger, and Michael K Reiter. Low-overhead byzantine fault-tolerant storage. In *ACM SIGOPS Operating Systems Review*, volume 41. ACM, 2007.

[13] Prasad Jayanti, Tushar Deepak Chandra, and Sam Toueg. Fault-tolerant wait-free shared objects. *Journal of the ACM (JACM)*, 45(3), 1998.

[14] Leslie Lamport. On interprocess communication. *Distributed computing*, 1(2), 1986.

[15] Heverson Borba Ribeiro and Emmanuelle Anceaume. Datacube: A p2p persistent data storage architecture based on hybrid redundancy schema. In *Parallel, Distributed and Network-Based Processing (PDP), 2010 18th Euromicro International Conference on*. IEEE, 2010.

[16] Cheng Shao, Jennifer L Welch, Evelyn Pierce, and Hyunyoung Lee. Multiwriter consistency conditions for shared memory registers. *SIAM Journal on Computing*, 40(1), 2011.

[17] Alexander Spiegelman, Yuval Cassuto, Gregory Chockler, and Idit Keidar. Space bounds for reliable storage: Fundamental limits of coding. *arXiv preprint arXiv:1507.05169*, 2015.

[18] Zhiying Wang and Viveck Cadambe. Multi-version coding in distributed storage. In *Information Theory (ISIT), 2014 IEEE International Symposium on*. IEEE, 2014.

APPENDIX

A. FORMAL DEFINITIONS

An *algorithm* defines the behavior of clients as deterministic state machines, where state transitions are associated with actions such as RMW trigger/response. A *configuration* is a mapping to states from system components, i.e., clients and base objects. An *initial configuration* is one where all components are in their initial states.

A *run* of algorithm A is a (finite or infinite) alternating sequence of configurations and actions, beginning with some initial configuration, such that configuration transitions occur according to A. For a run r, *trace(r)* is the subsequence of r consisting of all the operation invocation and returns in r. We use the notion of time t during a run r to refer to the configuration reached after the tth action in r. A *run fragment* is a contiguous subsequence of a run starting and ending with a configuration. We assume that runs are *well-formed*, in that each client's first action is an invocation, and a client has at most one outstanding operation at any time.

We say that a base object or client is *faulty* in a run r if it fails any time in r, and otherwise, it is *correct*. A run is *fair* if (1) for every RMW triggered by a correct client on a correct base object, there is eventually a matching response, (2) every correct client gets infinitely many opportunities to trigger RMWs.

Liveness There is a range of possible liveness conditions, which need to be satisfied in fair runs. A *wait-free* object is one that guarantees that every correct client's operation completes, regardless of the actions of other clients. A *lock-free* object guarantees progress: if at some point in a run there is an outstanding operation of a correct client, then *some* operation eventually completes. An *FW-terminating* [1] register is one that has wait-free *write* operations, and in addition, if there are finitely many *write* invocations in a run, then every *read* operation completes.

Safety In order to define regularity, we first introduce some terminology: Operation op_i *precedes* operation op_j in a run r, denoted $op_i \prec_r op_j$, if op_i's return occurs before op_j's invoke in r. Operations op_i and op_j are *concurrent* in a run r if neither one precedes the other. A run with no concurrent operations is *sequential*. Two runs are *equivalent* if every client performs the same sequence of operations in both, where operations that are outstanding in one can either be included in or excluded from the other. A *linearization* of a run r is an equivalent sequential run that preservers r's operation precedence relation and the object's sequential specification. The sequential specification for a register is as follows: A read returns the latest written value, or v_0 if none was written. A *write* w in a run r is *relevant* to a *read* rd in r [16] if $rd \not\prec_r w$; *rel-writes*(r, rd) is the set of all *writes* in r that are relevant to rd.

Following Lamport [14], we consider a hierarchy of safety notions. Lamport [14] defines *regular* and *safe* single-writer registers. Shao et al. [16] extend Lamport's notion of regularity to MWMR registers, and give four possible definitions. Here we use two of them. The first is the weakest definition, and we use it in our lower bound proof. The second, which we use for our algorithm, is the strongest definition that is satisfied by ABD [4] in case readers do not change the storage (no *write-back*):

A MWMR register is *weakly regular*, (called *MWRegWeak* in [16]), if for every run r and *read* rd that returns in r, there exists a linearization of the subsequence of r consisting of rd and the writes in r. A MWMR register is *strongly regular*, (called *MWRegWO* in [16]), if it satisfies weak regularity and the following condition: For all *reads* rd_1 and rd_2 that return in r, for all writes w_1 and w_2 in *rel-writes*$(r, rd_1) \cap$ *rel-writes*(r, rd_2), it holds that $w_1 \prec_{L_{rd_1}} w_2$ if and only if $w_1 \prec_{L_{rd_2}} w_2$.

We extend the safe register definition and say that a MWMR register is *strongly safe* if there exists a linearization σ_w of the subsequence of r consisting of the *write* operations in r, and for every *read* operation rd that has no concurrent *writes* in r, it is possible to add rd at some point in σ_w so as to obtain a linearization of the subsequence of r consisting

Specification and Complexity of Collaborative Text Editing

Hagit Attiya
Technion

Sebastian Burckhardt
Microsoft Research

Alexey Gotsman
IMDEA Software Institute

Adam Morrison
Technion

Hongseok Yang
University of Oxford

Marek Zawirski*
Inria & Sorbonne Universités,
UPMC Univ Paris 06, LIP6

ABSTRACT

Collaborative text editing systems allow users to concurrently edit a shared document, inserting and deleting elements (e.g., characters or lines). There are a number of protocols for collaborative text editing, but so far there has been no precise specification of their desired behavior, and several of these protocols have been shown not to satisfy even basic expectations. This paper provides a precise specification of a replicated *list* object, which models the core functionality of replicated systems for collaborative text editing. We define a *strong* list specification, which we prove is implemented by an existing protocol, as well as a *weak* list specification, which admits additional protocol behaviors.

A major factor determining the efficiency and practical feasibility of a collaborative text editing protocol is the space overhead of the metadata that the protocol must maintain to ensure correctness. We show that for a large class of list protocols, implementing *either the strong or the weak list specification* requires a metadata overhead that is at least *linear* in the number of elements deleted from the list. The class of protocols to which this lower bound applies includes all list protocols that we are aware of, and we show that one of these protocols almost matches the bound.

Keywords

Collaborative text editing; eventual consistency

1. INTRODUCTION

Collaborative text editing systems, like Google Docs [7, 8], Apache Wave [1], or wikis [16], allow users at multiple sites to concurrently edit the same document. To achieve high responsiveness and availability, such systems often replicate the document in geographically distributed sites or on user devices. A user can modify the document at a nearby replica, which propagates the modifications to other replicas asynchronously. This propagation can be done either via a *centralized server* or *peer-to-peer*. An essential feature of a collaborative editing system is that all changes eventually propagate to all replicas and get incorporated into the document in a consistent way. In particular, such systems aim to guarantee *eventual consistency*: if users stop modifying the document, then the replicas will eventually converge to the same state [29,30].

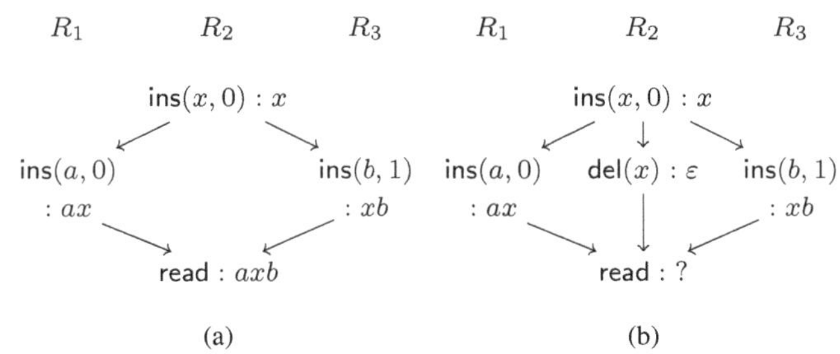

Figure 1: Example scenarios of collaborative text editing. Events are presented in format "operation : return value". An arrow from an event e' to an event e expresses that the effects of e' get incorporated at e's replica before e executes.

Figure 1(a) gives an example scenario of a document edited at several replicas. First, replica R_2 inserts x at the first position (zero-indexed) into the empty list. This insertion then propagates to replica R_1, which inserts a to the left of x, and to R_3, which inserts b to the right of x. Later the modifications made by R_1 and R_3 propagate to all other replicas, including R_2; when the latter reads the list, it observes axb. In this scenario, the desired system behavior is straightforward, but sometimes this is not the case. To illustrate, consider the scenario in Figure 1(b), where R_2 deletes x from the list before the insertions of a and b propagate to it. One might expect the read by R_2 to return ab, given the orderings ax and xb established at other replicas. However, some implementations allow ba as a response; e.g., this is the case in a Jupiter protocol [20], used in public collaboration systems [31].

There have been a number of proposals of highly available collaborative editing protocols, using techniques such as *operation transformations* [13, 23, 27, 28] and *replicated data types* (aka CRDTs) [22, 24, 32]. However, specifications of their desired behavior [17,28] have so far been informal and imprecise, and several of the protocols have been shown not to satisfy even the basic expectation of eventual consistency [14]. To address this problem, we introduce a precise specification of a replicated list object, which allows its clients to insert and delete elements into the list at different replicas and thereby captures the core aspects of collaborative text editing [13] (Section 3). Our specification has two flavors. The *strong* specification ensures that orderings relative to deleted elements hold even after the deletion, thereby disallowing the response ba for the read in Figure 1(b). The *weak* specification provides no such guarantee, while still requiring the ordering between elements

*Now at Google.

PODC'16, July 25–28, 2016, Chicago, IL, USA.

ISBN 978-1-4503-3964-3/16/07...$15.00

DOI: http://dx.doi.org/10.1145/2933057.2933090

that are not deleted to be consistent across the system. We show that both of these specifications ensure eventual consistency.

We prove that the strong specification is correctly implemented by a variant of an existing RGA (Replicated Growable Array) protocol [24], which is in the style of replicated data types [22] (Section 4). The protocol represents the list as a tree, with read operations traversing the tree in a deterministic order. Inserting an element a right after an element x (as in Figure 1(b)) adds a as a child of x in the tree. Deleting an element x just marks it as such; the node of x is left in the tree, creating a so-called *tombstone*. Keeping the tombstone enables the protocol to correctly incorporate insertions of elements received from other replicas that are ordered right after x (e.g., that of b in Figure 1(b)).

The simplicity of handling deletions via tombstones in the RGA protocol comes with a high space overhead. More precisely, the *metadata overhead* [5] of a list implementation is the ratio between the size of a replica's state (in bits) and the size of the user-observable content of the state, i.e., the list that will be read in this state. As we show, the metadata overhead of the RGA protocol is $O(D \lg k)$, where D is the number of deletions issued by clients and k is the total number of operations (Section 4). The number of deletions can be high. For example a 2009 study [32] indicates that the "George W. Bush" Wikipedia page has about 500 lines. However, since modifications are usually handled as deleting the original line and then inserting the revised line, the page had accumulated about 1.6 million deletions.[1]

Our main result is that this overhead is, in some sense, inherent. We prove that any protocol from a certain class which implements the list specification for $n \geq 3$ replicas incurs a metadata overhead of $\Omega(D)$, where D is the number of deletions. This result holds even for the *weak* list specification and even if the network guarantees causal atomic broadcast [10]. The result holds for all *push-based* protocols, where each replica propagates list updates to its peers as soon as possible, and merges remote updates into its state as soon as they arrive (we give a precise definition in Section 5). This assumption captures the operation of all highly available protocols that we are aware of.

We establish our lower bound for the peer-to-peer model. However, using the fact that it holds for a network with causal atomic broadcast, we extend it to show that, in a push-based client/server list protocol, the metadata overhead at the clients is still $\Omega(D)$.

We prove our lower bound using an information-theoretic argument. For every $d \approx D/2$-bit string w, we construct a particular execution α_w of the protocol such that, at its end, the user-observable state σ_w of some replica is a list of size $O(1)$ bits. We then show that, given σ_w, we can decode w by exercising the protocol in a black-box manner. This implies that all states σ_w must be distinct and, since there are 2^d of them, one of these states must take at least d bits. The procedure that decodes w from σ_w is nontrivial and represents the key insight of our proof. It recovers w one bit at a time using a "feedback loop" between two processes: one performs a black-box experiment on the protocol to recover the next bit of w, and the other reconstructs the corresponding steps of the execution α_w; the messages sent in the reconstructed part of α_w then form the basis for the experiment to decode the next bit of w.

2. SYSTEM MODEL

We are concerned with highly available implementations of a replicated object [3, 5], which supports a set of operations Op. Such an implementation consists of *replicas* that receive and respond to user operations on the object and use message passing to communicate changes to the object's state. The *high availability* property sets this model apart from standard message-passing models: we require that replicas respond to user operations *immediately*—without performing any communication—so that user operations complete regardless of network latency and network partitions (e.g., device disconnection).

Replicas. We model a replica as a state machine $R = (Q, M, \Sigma, \sigma_0, E, \Delta)$, where Q is a set of *internal states*, M is a set of possible *messages*, $\Sigma = Q \times (M \cup \{\bot\})$ is a set of *replica states*, $\sigma_0 = (q_0, \bot) \in \Sigma$ is the *initial state*, E is a set of possible *events*, and $\Delta : \Sigma \times E \rightharpoonup \Sigma$ is a (partial) *transition function*. Note that a replica state explicitly includes a *send buffer*, containing the message pending transmission or $\bot$, which indicates that no message is pending. If $\Delta(\sigma, e)$ is defined, we say that event e is *enabled* in state σ. Transitions determined by Δ describe local steps of a replica in which it interacts with users and other replicas. These interactions are modeled by three kinds of events:

- $do(op, v)$: a user invokes an operation $op \in \mathsf{Op}$ on the replicated object and immediately receives a response v from the replica;
- $send(m)$: the replica broadcasts a message $m \in M$; and
- $receive(m)$: the replica receives a message $m \in M$.

A *protocol* is a collection $\mathcal{R}$ of replicas.

We require that a $send(m)$ event is enabled in state σ if and only if $\sigma = (q, m)$ for $m \neq \bot$, and in this case $\Delta((q, m), send(m)) = (q', \bot)$ for some q'. We further require that a replica can execute any operation with its return values computed deterministically: for any operation $op \in \mathsf{Op}$, exactly one $do(op, v)$ event is enabled in σ. We also require that a replica can accept any message: for any message m, $receive(m)$ is enabled in σ. We assume that messages are unique and that a message's sender is uniquely identifiable (e.g., messages are tagged with the sender id and a sequence number). We also assume that a replica broadcasts messages to all replicas, including itself[2]; replicas can implement point-to-point communication by ignoring messages for which they are not the intended recipient.

Executions. An *execution* of a protocol $\mathcal{R}$ is a (possibly infinite) sequence of events occurring at the replicas in $\mathcal{R}$.[3] For each event e, we let $\mathsf{repl}(e) \in \mathcal{R}$ be the replica at which it occurs, and for each *do* event $e = do(op, v)$ we let $\mathsf{op}(e) = op$ and $\mathsf{rval}(e) = v$. A (finite or infinite) sequence of events $e_1, e_2, \ldots$ occurring at a replica $R = (Q, M, \Sigma, \sigma_0, E, \Delta)$ is *well-formed* if there is a sequence of states $\sigma_1, \sigma_2, \ldots$ such that $\sigma_i = \Delta(\sigma_{i-1}, e_i)$ for all i. If the sequence is of length n, we refer to σ_n as the *state of R at the end of the sequence.*

We consider only *well-formed* executions, in which for every replica $R \in \mathcal{R}$: (1) the subsequence of events at R, denoted $\alpha|_R$, is well-formed; and (2) every $receive(m)$ event at R is preceded by a $send(m)$ event in α.

Let α be an execution. Event $e \in \alpha$ *happens before* event $e' \in \alpha$ [15] (written $e \xrightarrow{\mathsf{hb}(\alpha)} e'$, or simply $e \xrightarrow{\mathsf{hb}} e'$ if the context is clear) if one of the following conditions holds: *(1) Thread of execution:* $\mathsf{repl}(e) = \mathsf{repl}(e')$ and e precedes e' in α. *(2) Message delivery:* $e = send(m)$ and $e' = receive(m)$. *(3) Transitivity:* There is an event $f \in \alpha$ such that $e \xrightarrow{\mathsf{hb}} f$ and $f \xrightarrow{\mathsf{hb}} e'$.

[1] Wikipedia stores this information also to track the document's edit history.

[2] The latter is used to support atomic broadcast [10], defined later.

[3] Formally, an execution consists of events instrumented with unique event ids and replicas. In the paper we do not use this more accurate formulation so as to avoid clutter.

Network model. To ensure that every operation *eventually* propagates to all the replicas, we require that the network does not remain partitioned indefinitely. A replica R *has a message pending in event* e *of execution* α if R's has a $send(m)$ event enabled in the state at the end of $\alpha'|_R$, where α' is the prefix of α ending with e.

DEFINITION 1. *The network is* sufficiently connected *in an infinite well-formed execution* α *of a protocol* $\mathcal{R}$ *if the following conditions hold for all replicas* $R \in \mathcal{R}$*:* (1) Eventual transmission: *if* R *has a message pending infinitely often in* α*, then* R *also sends a message infinitely often in* α*, and* (2) Eventual delivery: *if* R *sends a message* m*, then every replica* $R' \neq R$ *eventually receives* m*.*

Collaborative editing protocols generally assume causal message delivery [24,27]. We model this by considering only executions that satisfy *causal broadcast* [6]:

DEFINITION 2. *An execution* α *of a protocol* $\mathcal{R}$ *satisfies* causal broadcast *if for any messages* m, m'*, whenever* $send(m) \xrightarrow{\mathsf{hb}} send(m')$*, any replica* R *can receive* m' *only after it receives* m*.*

In fact, our results hold even under a more powerful *atomic broadcast* [10] model, which delivers all messages to all replicas in the exact same order.

DEFINITION 3. *An execution* α *of protocol* $\mathcal{R}$ *satisfies* causal atomic broadcast *if the following conditions hold:* (1) Causal broadcast: α *satisfies causal broadcast.* (2) No duplicate delivery: *each* $send(m)$ *event in* α *is followed by at most one* $receive(m)$ *event per replica* $R' \in \mathcal{R}$*.* (3) Consistent order: *if* R *receives* m *before* m'*, then any other replica* R' *receives* m *before* m'*.*

These broadcast primitives can be implemented when not provided by the network [6]; by providing them "for free," we strengthen our lower bounds and ensure their independence from the complexity of implementing the broadcast primitive.

3. COLLABORATIVE TEXT EDITING

Following Ellis and Gibbs [13], we model the collaborative text editing problem (henceforth, simply collaborative editing) as the problem of implementing a highly available replicated list object whose elements are from some universe U. Users can insert elements, remove elements and read the list using the following operations, which form Op:

- $\mathsf{ins}(a, k)$ for $a \in U$ and $k \in \mathbb{N}$: inserts a at position k in the list (starting from 0) and returns the updated list. For k exceeding the list size, we assume an insertion at the end. We assume that users pass identifiers a that are globally unique.
- $\mathsf{del}(a)$ for $a \in U$: deletes the element a and returns the updated list. We assume that users pass only identifiers a that appear in the return value of the preceding operation on the same replica.
- read: returns the contents of the list.

The definition above restricts user behavior to simplify our technical development. Note that these restrictions are insignificant from a practical viewpoint, because they can be easily enforced: (1) identifiers can be made unique by attaching replica identifiers and sequence numbers; and (2) before each deletion, we can read the state of the list and skip the deletion if the deleted element does not appear in it.

3.1 Preliminaries: Replicated Data Types

We cannot specify the list object with a standard sequential specification, since replicas may observe only subsets of operations executed in the system, as a result of remote updates being delayed by the network. We address this difficulty by specifying the response of a list operation based on operations that are *visible* to it. Intuitively, these are the prior operations executed at the same replica and remote operations whose effects have propagated to the replica through the network. Formally, we use a variant of a framework by Burckhardt et al. [5] for specifying replicated data types [26]. We specify the list object by a set of *abstract executions*, which record the operations performed by users (represented by *do* events) and visibility relationships between them. Since collaborative editing systems generally preserve causality between operations [27], here we consider only *causal* abstract executions, where the visibility relation is transitive.

DEFINITION 4. *A* causal abstract execution *is a pair* (H, vis)*, where* H *is a sequence of do events*[4]*, and* $\mathsf{vis} \subseteq H \times H$ *is an acyclic visibility relation (with* $(e_1, e_2) \in \mathsf{vis}$ *denoted by* $e_1 \xrightarrow{\mathsf{vis}} e_2$*) such that: (1) if* e_1 *precedes* e_2 *in* H *and* $\mathsf{repl}(e_1) = \mathsf{repl}(e_2)$*, then* $e_1 \xrightarrow{\mathsf{vis}} e_2$*; (2) if* $e_1 \xrightarrow{\mathsf{vis}} e_2$*, then* e_1 *precedes* e_2 *in* H*; and (3)* vis *is transitive (if* $e_1 \xrightarrow{\mathsf{vis}} e_2$ *and* $e_2 \xrightarrow{\mathsf{vis}} e_3$*, then* $e_1 \xrightarrow{\mathsf{vis}} e_3$*).*

Figure 1 graphically depicts abstract executions, where vis is the transitive closure of arrows in the figure and H is the result of some topological sort of vis. An abstract execution $A' = (H', \mathsf{vis}')$ is a *prefix* of abstract execution A if: (1) H' is a prefix of H; and (2) $\mathsf{vis}' = \mathsf{vis} \cap (H' \times H')$. A *specification* of an object is a prefix-closed set of abstract executions. A protocol correctly implements a specification when the outcomes of operations that it produces in any (concrete) execution can be justified by some abstract execution allowed by the specification.

DEFINITION 5. *An execution* α *of a protocol* $\mathcal{R}$ complies with *an abstract execution* $A = (H, \mathsf{vis})$ *if for every replica* $R \in \mathcal{R}$*,* $H|_R = \alpha|_R^{do}$*, where* $\alpha|_R^{do}$ *denotes the subsequence of do events by replica* R *in* α*.*

DEFINITION 6. *A protocol* $\mathcal{R}$ satisfies *a specification* $\mathcal{S}$ *if every execution* α *of* $\mathcal{R}$ *complies with some abstract execution* $A \in \mathcal{S}$*.*

3.2 Specifying the List Object

We present two list specifications: strong and weak. Conceptually, the *strong* specification ensures that orderings relative to deleted elements hold even after the deletion, thereby disallowing the response *ba* for the read in Figure 1(b). The *weak* specification does not guarantee this property, allowing both *ba* and *ab* as responses.

We denote by $\mathsf{elems}(A)$ the set of all elements inserted into the list in an abstract execution $A = (H, \mathsf{vis})$:

$$\mathsf{elems}(A) = \{a \mid do(\mathsf{ins}(a, \_), \_) \in H\}.$$

Recall that we assume all inserted elements to be unique, and so there is a one-to-one correspondence between inserted elements and insert operations. For brevity, we write $e_1 \leq_{\mathsf{vis}} e_2$ for $e_1 = e_2 \vee e_1 \xrightarrow{\mathsf{vis}} e_2$.

DEFINITION 7. *An abstract execution* $A = (H, \mathsf{vis})$ *belongs to the* strong list specification $\mathcal{A}_{\mathsf{strong}}$ *if and only if there is a relation* $\mathsf{lo} \subseteq \mathsf{elems}(A) \times \mathsf{elems}(A)$*, called the* list order*, such that:*

[4]Formally, H consists of *do* events instrumented with unique event ids and replicas, as in the case of an execution α. To avoid clutter, we do not use this more accurate presentation.

1. *Each event* $e = do(op, w) \in H$ *returns a sequence of elements* $w = a_0 \dots a_{n-1}$, *where* $a_i \in \mathsf{elems}(A)$, *such that*
   (a) *w contains exactly the elements visible to e that have been inserted, but not deleted:*
   $$\forall a.\, a \in w \iff (do(\mathsf{ins}(a, \_), \_) \leq_{\mathsf{vis}} e) \wedge \neg(do(\mathsf{del}(a), \_) \leq_{\mathsf{vis}} e).$$
   (b) *The order of the elements is consistent with the list order:* $\forall i, j.\ (i < j) \implies (a_i, a_j) \in \mathsf{lo}$.
   (c) *Elements are inserted at the specified position: if* $op = \mathsf{ins}(a, k)$, *then* $a = a_{\min\{k, n-1\}}$.
2. *The list order* lo *is transitive, irreflexive and total, and thus determines the order of all insert operations in the execution.*

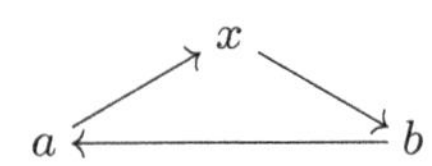

For example, the strong list specification is satisfied by the abstract execution in Figure 1(a) and the one in Figure 1(b) with the read returning ab; this is justified by the list order $a \to x \to b$. On the other hand, the specification is not satisfied by the execution in Figure 1(b) with the read returning ba: for the outcomes of operations in this execution to be consistent with item 1 of Definition 7, the list order would have to be as shown above; but this order contains a cycle, contradicting item 2. In Section 4 we prove that the strong specification is implemented by an existing protocol, RGA [24]. However, some protocols, such as Jupiter [20], provide weaker guarantees and, in particular, allow the outcome ba in Figure 1(b). We therefore introduce the following weak list specification, to which our lower bound result applies (Section 6)[5].

DEFINITION 8. *An abstract execution* $A = (H, \mathsf{vis})$ *belongs to the* weak list specification $\mathcal{A}_{\mathsf{weak}}$ *if and only if there exists a relation* $\mathsf{lo} \subseteq \mathsf{elems}(A) \times \mathsf{elems}(A)$ *such that:*

1. *Condition 1 in Definition 7 is satisfied.*
2. lo *is irreflexive and, for all events* $e = do(op, w) \in H$, *it is transitive and total on* $\{a \mid a \in w\}$.

Unlike the strong specification, the weak one allows the list order lo to have cycles; the order is required to be acyclic only on the elements returned by some operation. In particular, the weak specification allows the execution in Figure 1(b) with the read returning ba, which is justified using the above cyclic list order. Since at the time of the read, x is deleted from the list, the specification permits us to decide how to order a and b without taking into account the orderings involving x: $a \to x$ and $x \to b$.

Eventual consistency. A desirable property of highly available replicated objects is *eventual consistency*. Informally, this guarantees that, if users stop issuing update requests, then the replicas will eventually converge to the same state [29, 30]. Our specifications imply a related *convergence* property: in an abstract execution satisfying $\mathcal{A}_{\mathsf{strong}}$ or $\mathcal{A}_{\mathsf{weak}}$, two read operations that see the same sets of list updates return the same response. This is because such operations will return the same elements (Definition 7, item 1a) and in the same order (Definition 7, item 1b). From the convergence property we can establish that our specifications imply eventual consistency for a class of protocols that guarantee the following property of *eventual visibility*.

DEFINITION 9. *An abstract execution* $A = (H, \mathsf{vis})$ *satisfies* eventual visibility *if for every event* $e \in H$, *there are only finitely many events* $e' \in H$ *such that* $\neg(e \xrightarrow{\mathsf{vis}} e')$.

[5]We conjecture that Jupiter satisfies the weak specification.

DEFINITION 10. *A protocol* $\mathcal{R}$ *satisfying the weak (resp., strong) list specification* guarantees eventual visibility *if every execution* α *of* $\mathcal{R}$ *complies with some abstract execution* $A \in \mathcal{A}_{\mathsf{weak}}$ *(respectively,* $A \in \mathcal{A}_{\mathsf{strong}}$*) that satisfies eventual visibility.*

Informally, eventual consistency holds for a protocol guaranteeing eventual visibility because: in an abstract execution with finitely many list updates, eventual visibility ensures that all but finitely many reads will see all the updates; then convergence ensures that they will return the same list. To guarantee eventual visibility, a protocol would rely on the network being sufficiently connected (Definition 1).

3.3 Metadata Overhead

In addition to the user-observable list contents, the replica state in a list protocol typically contains user-unobservable metadata that is used internally to provide correct behavior. The metadata overhead is the proportion of metadata relative to the user-observable list content.

Formally, let the *size* of an internal replica state q or a list $w \in U^*$ be the number of bits required to represent it in a standard encoding; we denote the size of x by $|x|$. The *metadata overhead* [5] of a state $\sigma = (q, m)$ is $|q|/|w|$ for the unique w such that $do(\mathsf{read}, w)$ is enabled in σ; here w represents the user-observable contents of σ. Note that the contents of the send buffer is not part of the metadata.

DEFINITION 11 ([5]). *The* worst-case metadata overhead *of a protocol over a given subset of its executions is the largest metadata overhead of the state of any replica in any of these executions.*

4. AN IMPLEMENTATION OF THE STRONG LIST SPECIFICATION

We now present an implementation of the list object, which is a reformulation of the RGA (Replicated Growable Array) protocol [24], and prove that it implements the strong list specification.

4.1 Timestamped Insertion Trees

Our representation of the list at a replica uses a *timestamped insertion (TI) tree* data structure. It stores both the list content and timestamp metadata used for deterministically resolving the order between elements concurrently inserted at the same position.

Formally, a tree is a finite set N of *nodes*, each corresponding to an element inserted into the list. A node is a tuple $n = (a, t, p)$, where $a \in U$ is the element, $t \in C$ is a *timestamp* for the insertion, and $p \in (C \cup \{\circ\})$ is either the parent node (identified by its timestamp) or the symbol $\circ$ representing the tree root. We define the set C of timestamps and a total order on them later (Section 4.2). For a node $n = (a, t, p)$ we let $n.a = a$, $n.t = t$, and $n.p = p$. For two nodes n, n' with $n'.p = n.t$, we say n is the parent of n' and write $n \xrightarrow{\mathsf{pa}} n'$.

DEFINITION 12. *A set of nodes* N *is a* TI tree *if (1) timestamps uniquely identify nodes:* $\forall n, n' \in N : n.t = n'.t \implies n = n'$; *(2) all parents are present: if* $n \in N$ *and* $n.p \neq \circ$, *then* $n' \xrightarrow{\mathsf{pa}} n$ *for some* $n' \in N$; *and (3) parents are older than their children:* $n \xrightarrow{\mathsf{pa}} n' \implies n.t < n'.t$.

Figure 2 shows an example of a TI tree and illustrates the read and insert operations explained below.

Read. To read the list, we traverse the tree N by depth-first search, starting at the root. We assemble the visited elements into a sequence $s(N)$ using prefix order (the parent precedes its children) and visit the children in decreasing timestamp order.

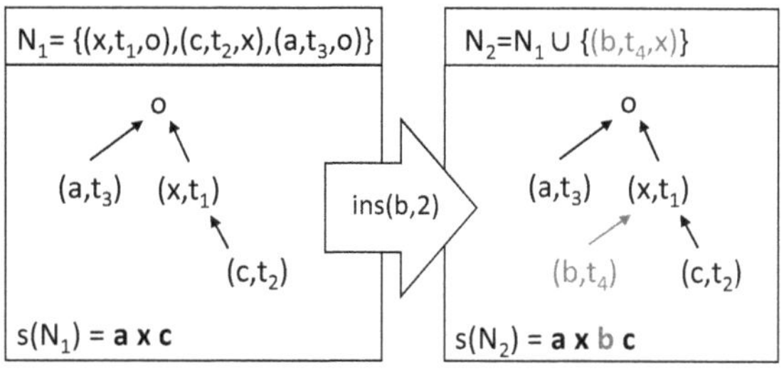

Figure 2: Illustration of TI trees. Each box shows a tree, with the set of nodes that define it, its graphical representation, and the sequence of elements it denotes. The tree on the right results from an insert operation for element b at position 2. The order on the timestamps is $t_1 < t_2 < t_3 < t_4$.

Insert. To insert a new element a at position k into the list, let $s(N) = a_0 \dots a_{n-1}$ and pick a new timestamp t that is larger than any of the timestamps appearing in N. Then let p be the element to the left of the insertion position: $p = a_{k-1}$ (if $k > 0$) or $p = \circ$ (if $k = 0$). We now add a new node (a, t, p) to N. Note that a newly inserted node is the child of the immediately preceding element with the highest timestamp. Thus, it is visited immediately after that element during a read, which makes it appear at the correct position in the list.

4.2 The RGA Protocol

We now define the RGA protocol $\mathcal{R}^n_{\text{rga}}$ for n replicas. Each replica stores a TI tree, as well as a set of elements that represent *tombstones*, used to handle deletions (Section 1). Insertions and deletions are recorded in a send buffer, which is periodically transmitted to other replicas by causal broadcast.

State and messages. Timestamps are pairs (x, i), where $x \in \mathbb{N}$ and $i \in \{1, \dots, n\}$ is a replica identifier. They are ordered lexicographically:

$$(x, i) < (x', i') \iff (x < x') \vee ((x = x') \wedge (i < i')).$$

Messages are of the form (A, K), where A is a set of nodes (representing insert operations) and K is a set of elements (representing delete operations), and either A or K is non-empty. The state of a replica is $(N, T, (A, K))$, where: N is a TI tree, representing the replica-local view of the list; $T \subseteq U$ is the set of tombstones; and (A, K) is a send buffer, containing the message to send next. A pair $(\emptyset, \emptyset)$ indicates that no message is pending (thus corresponding to $\perp$ in Section 2). The initial state is $(\emptyset, \emptyset, (\emptyset, \emptyset))$.

do **transitions.** To execute an insert operation at a replica i in a state $(N, T, (A, K))$, we construct a node as described in the "Insert" procedure of Section 4.1 and add it to both N and A. As the timestamp of the node we take $((1 + (\text{the largest timestamp in } N)), i)$, or $(1, i)$ if $N = \emptyset$. This timestamp is guaranteed to be globally unique. To execute a delete operation, we add the deleted element to both T and K. All operations return the local view of the list, which is obtained by traversing N as described in the "Read" procedure of Section 4.1, and then removing all elements belonging to T.

send **transition** is enabled whenever either A or K is nonempty. It sends (A, K) as the message and sets both A and K to empty.

receive **transition** for a message (A_m, K_m) adds A_m to N and K_m to T. The protocol relies on causal delivery of messages, which ensures that no parents can be missing from N. In particular, N stays well-formed after adding A_m.

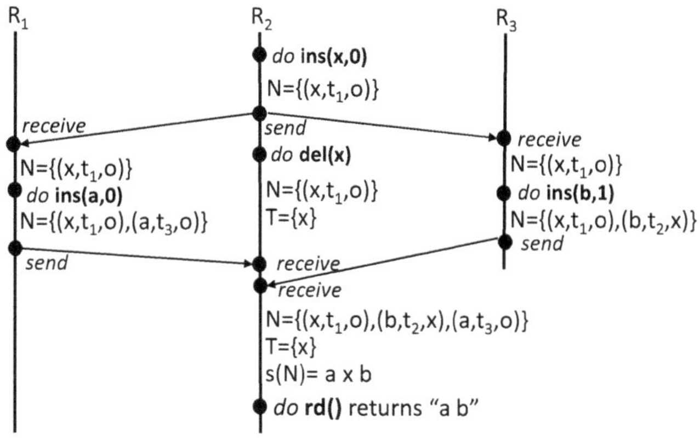

Figure 3: Illustration of an RGA execution, with time proceeding from top to bottom. Bullets show the transitions of the replicas R_1, R_2, and R_3, and in some places we indicate the current state of the tree N and the tombstone set T. The order on the timestamps is $t_1 < t_2 < t_3$.

We show an example execution in Figure 3, which matches the example in Figure 1(b) and complies with the strong list specification.

4.3 Guarantees

The following theorems state the correctness and asymptotic complexity bounds of RGA. We provide full proofs in [2, §A] and discuss the key insights (convergence and stability) below.

THEOREM 1. *The protocol $\mathcal{R}^n_{\text{rga}}$ satisfies the strong list specification.*

THEOREM 2. *The worst-case metadata overhead of $\mathcal{R}^n_{\text{rga}}$ over executions with k operations and D deletions is $O(D \lg k)$.*

Convergence. Each replica maintains a TI tree that grows over time, meaning that nodes are added to the set, but never modified or removed. Because set union is associative and commutative, the order in which nodes are added does not matter. For example, changing the order of message delivery to R_2 in Figure 3 does not change the final tree. As a consequence, if the same set of nodes is delivered to any two replicas in any order, their trees are guaranteed to match, which ensures convergence.

Stability. The following lemma (proved in [2, §A]) shows that when we add more elements to a TI tree, the order of existing elements remains stable. This implies the strong list specification, because all replicas order all insertions the same way at all times.

LEMMA 3. *Let A, B be two TI trees such that $A \subseteq B$. Then $s(A)$ is a subsequence of $s(B)$.*

Trees vs. Lists. In the standard RGA implementation [25], TI trees are represented as lists (corresponding to the tree traversal). We show in [2, §A] that these representations are functionally equivalent. Lists are convenient to implement, but offer little insight as to why the algorithm guarantees convergence. Not surprisingly, the reason why RGA actually works has been a bit of a mystery, and we are not aware of any prior correctness proofs.

5. PUSH-BASED PROTOCOLS

Our lower bound results hold for *push-based* protocols, a class of protocols that contains the protocols of several collaborative editing systems [20, 22, 24, 27], including the RGA protocol of Section 4. Informally, a replica in a push-based protocol propagates list updates to its peers as soon as possible and merges remote updates into its state as soon as they arrive (as opposed to using a more sophisticated mechanism, such as a consensus protocol). We define this class of protocols assuming that the network provides causal broadcast; when this is not the case, a protocol may need to delay merging arriving updates to enforce casuality. Formally, we require that in a push-based protocol, every operation observe all operations that happen before it, that list insertions always generate a message, and that a deletion—which, unlike an insertion, may not be unique—generates a message if it does not already observe another deletion of the same element.

DEFINITION 13. *A protocol $\mathcal{R}$ satisfying the weak (strong) list specification is* push-based *if the following hold:*

- *For any execution α of $\mathcal{R}$ and $e = do(\mathsf{ins}(a, \_), \_) \in \alpha$, replica $\mathsf{repl}(e)$ has a message pending after e.*
- *For any execution α of $\mathcal{R}$ and $e = do(\mathsf{del}(a), \_) \in \alpha$, if there does not exist event $e' = do(\mathsf{del}(a), \_) \in \alpha$ that happens before e, then replica $\mathsf{repl}(e)$ has a message pending after e.*
- *For every execution α of $\mathcal{R}$ there exists an abstract execution $A = (H, \mathsf{vis}) \in \mathcal{A}_{\mathsf{weak}}$ ($A \in \mathcal{A}_{\mathsf{strong}}$) that α complies with, such that $\forall e', e \in H.\, e' \xrightarrow{\mathsf{vis}} e \iff e' \xrightarrow{\mathsf{hb}} e$.*

The class of push-based protocols contains both *op-based* protocols [5], in which a message carries a description of the latest operations that the sender has performed (e.g., RGA), and *state-based* [5] protocols, in which a message describes all operations the sender knows about (i.e., its state). We also show ([2, §B]) that the class of push-based protocols contains eventually consistent write-propagating protocols [3]—which model many deployed highly available eventually consistent protocols [4, 5, 9, 11, 12, 18, 26, 33]—under the natural assumption that sending a message does not affect the state of the list at the sending replica.

6. LOWER BOUNDS ON METADATA OVERHEAD

Here we show a lower bound on the worst-case metadata overhead (Definition 11) of a push-based protocol satisfying the weak or strong list specification.

THEOREM 4. *Let $\mathcal{R}$ be a push-based protocol that satisfies the weak or strong list specification for $n \geq 3$ replicas. Then the worst-case metadata overhead of $\mathcal{R}$ over executions with D deletions is $\Omega(D)$.*

This follows from the following theorem, because any execution consistent with the strong list specification is also consistent with the weak one.

THEOREM 5. *Let $\mathcal{R}$ be a push-based protocol that satisfies the weak list specification for $n \geq 3$ replicas. Then for every integer $D \geq 4$, there exists an execution α_D of $\mathcal{R}$ with D deletions such that: (1) the metadata overhead of some state σ of some replica R in α_D is $\Omega(D)$; (2) α_D satisfies causal atomic broadcast; and (3) R does not receive any message before σ in α_D.*

PROOF. Let $d = \lfloor (D-2)/2 \rfloor$. We show that there exists an execution of $\mathcal{R}$ with D deletions that satisfies the desired conditions, in which the user-observable contents of some internal state is a list with a single element, and yet the size of this state is at least d bits. It follows that the metadata overhead of this state is $\Omega(D)$.

We show the existence of this execution using an information-theoretic argument. Namely, for every d-bit string w we construct an execution α_w that satisfies causal atomic broadcast and in which: (1) replica R_1 performs D deletions and receives no messages; (2) at the end of α_w, the user-observable list at R_1 contains the single element "$*$" and R_1 has no messages pending; and yet (3) we can decode w given only σ_w, the state of R_1 at the end of α_w (this decoding process exercises the protocol $\mathcal{R}$ in a black-box manner). Hence, all states σ_w must be distinct. Since there are 2^d of them, one of these states σ_{w_0} must take at least d bits. Since this state has no messages pending, its metadata overhead is $\Omega(D)$, and thus, α_{w_0} is the desired execution.

Encoding w. Given a d-bit string $w = w_1 \dots w_d$, we construct an execution α_w of $\mathcal{R}$ that builds a list encoding the path from the root of a binary tree of height d to the w-th leaf (when w is interpreted as the binary representation of an integer). Figure 4(a) details the construction: it shows pseudocode which, as it executes, constructs the execution; instructions of the form e_i correspond to a state transition e at replica R_i. We abuse notation by writing op instead of $do(op, \_)$, by specifying inserts of whole strings instead of element by element, and by specifying positions relative to prior insertions rather than with integers. Figure 5(a) depicts α_w for $w = 10$.

Only replica R_1 participates in the encoding execution α_w. We start by inserting the string $[_0\,]_0$ (i.e., the root). Because $\mathcal{R}$ is a push-based protocol, R_1 has a message m_1 pending following these insertions. We then proceed with a series of steps, for $i = 1, \dots, d$. Each step i begins with R_1 in state σ_i having a message m_i pending. R_1 first broadcasts m_i. We then insert the string $[_i\,]_i$ immediately to the left or to the right of $[_{i-1}\,]_{i-1}$, depending on whether the i-th bit of w is set. Because $\mathcal{R}$ is a push-based protocol, R_1 has a message pending following these insertions, and we proceed to step $i+1$. When we are done, we broadcast the current pending message and insert the element $*$ between $[_d$ and $]_d$, and broadcast the message m_{d+2} that is pending following this insertion. For example, if $w = 10$, the state of the list at R_1 at this point is $[_0\,]_0\, [_2 *]_2\, [_1\,]_1$. We then delete all the $[_i$ and $]_i$ elements, for $i = 0, \dots, d$, and if D is odd, we insert and delete an additional element, so that the number of deletions in α_w is exactly D. Because $\mathcal{R}$ is a push-based protocol, R_1 has a message pending following these deletions, which we broadcast to empty R_1's send buffer. Finally, we read the list at R_1, observing that it is $*$. This follows because for any abstract execution $A = (H, \mathsf{vis})$ that the encoding execution α_w complies with, all ins and del events are visible to the read, due to Condition (1) of Definition 4. The read's response must thus be $*$, since by assumption one of such executions A is consistent with the weak list specification.

The output of the encoding procedure is σ_w, the state of R_1 at the end of the encoding execution α_w. It is easy to check that α_w is well-formed; furthermore, it vacuously satisfies causal atomic broadcast.

Decoding w from σ_w. We reconstruct w one bit at a time by "replaying" the execution α_w. To replay iteration i of α_w, we rely on a procedure Recover() that recovers w_i from σ_w and $m_1, \dots, m_i$. (We describe Recover() in the next paragraph; for now, assume it is an oracle.) Knowing w_i, in turn, determines the next event of R_1 in α_w, and hence provides us with m_{i+1}. The decoding process thus only uses messages from R_1 that it reconstructs with the bits of w already known. Figure 4(b) shows the pseudocode which, as it executes, decodes w. We start with R_1 in its initial state and recon-

```
Input: w = w_1, ..., w_d
// R_1 starts in its initial state σ_0.
ins_1([_0 ]_0, 0)
for i = 1, ..., d
  // The state of R_1 here is σ_i.
  send_1(m_i)
  if w_i = 1 then
    ins_1([_i ]_i just after ]_{i-1})
  else
    ins_1([_i ]_i just before [_{i-1})
  // The state of R_1 here is σ_{i+1}.
send_1(m_{d+1})
ins_1(* between [_d and ]_d)
send_1(m_{d+2})
for i = 0, ..., d
  del_1([_i)
  del_1(]_i)
if D = 2(d+1) + 1 then
  ins_1(b, 0)
  del_1(b)
send_1(m_{d+3})
read_1 = *
// The state of R_1 here is σ_w.
```

(a) Execution α_w, at the end of which the state of R_1 encodes w

```
Input: σ_w
// R_1 starts in its initial state σ_0,
// which does not depend on w.
ins_1([_0 ]_0, 0)
for i = 1, ..., d
  // We now know σ_i,
  // so can generate m_i.
  send_1(m_i)
  w_i ← Recover(σ_w, m_1, ..., m_i)
  if w_i = 1 then
    ins_1([_i ]_i just after ]_{i-1})
  else
    ins_1([_i ]_i just before [_{i-1})
  // We now know σ_{i+1}.
output w
```

(b) Decoding w given σ_w

```
Input: σ_w, m_1, ..., m_i
// We perform the state transitions
// below on copies of the state
// machines, with R_2 starting in its
// initial state and R_1 in state σ_w.
// The replica state in the outer
// decoding procedure is unaffected.
for j = 1, ..., i
  receive_2(m_j)
  receive_1(m_j)
read_2 = ... [_{i-1} ]_{i-1} ...
ins_2(x between [_{i-1} and ]_{i-1})
send_2(m_x)
receive_2(m_x)
receive_1(m_x)
if read_1 = x *
  return 1
else // read_1 = * x
  return 0
```

(c) Recover($\sigma_w, m_1, \ldots, m_i$)

Figure 4: Encoding and decoding procedures. Events are subscripted with the id of their replica.

struct m_1, which does not depend on w. We then proceed in steps, for $i = 1, \ldots, d$. In step i we know $m_1, \ldots, m_i$, and we recover bit w_i from σ_w and $m_1, \ldots, m_i$. Having recovered w_i, we replay the insertion that R_1 performs at step i of the encoding and reconstruct m_{i+1}.

Recovering w_i from σ_w and $m_1, \ldots, m_i$. The Recover() procedure determines w_i by performing state transitions on fresh copies of R_1 and R_2; the transitions that an execution of Recover() performs have no effect on the state of the replicas in the "replayed" execution constructed by the decoding process, or on other Recover() executions. Figure 4(c) shows these state transitions, and Figures 5(b)–5(c) illustrate the overall decoding of $w = 10$ (the use of the replica R_3 is explained below). We start off with R_2 in its initial state and R_1 in state σ_w. We deliver the messages $m_1, \ldots, m_i$ to both replicas in the same order. We then read at R_2 and receive response v^i_w; we will show that $[_{i-1}\,]_{i-1} \in v^i_w$. Next, R_2 inserts element x between $[_{i-1}$ and $]_{i-1}$ and broadcasts a message m_x, which we deliver to both replicas. Finally, we read at R_1 and observe the list in state y^i_w. We will show that y^i_w contains only x and $*$, and if x precedes $*$ then $w_i = 1$; otherwise, $w_i = 0$.

Validity of Recover($\sigma_w, m_1, \ldots, m_i$) state transitions. Assuming that $m_1, \ldots, m_i$ are the first i messages sent by R_1 in α_w, we show that the state transitions performed by an execution of Recover($\sigma_w, m_1, \ldots, m_i$) in Figure 4(c) occur in an extension β^i_w of α_w of the form:

$$\beta^i_w = \alpha_w \; receive_2(m_1)\, receive_1(m_1) \ldots receive_2(m_i)\, receive_1(m_i)\; do_2(\mathsf{read}_2, v^i_w)\, do_2(\mathsf{ins}_2(x, k^i_w), \_)\, send_2(m_x)\; receive_2(m_x)\, receive_1(m_x)\, do_1(\mathsf{read}_1, y^i_w),$$

where k^i_w is the position at which R_2 inserts x into the list. In the following, we prove that the execution β^i_w is well-formed (Claim 6), that it satisfies causal atomic broadcast (Claim 7), that $[_{i-1}\,]_{i-1} \in v^i_w$ (Claim 8), and that $y^i_w = x*$ or $y^i_w = *x$ (Claim 9). To this end, we exploit the fact that σ_w is R_1's state at the end of α_w, which allows Recover() to perform the same state transitions at R_1 that occur in β^i_w, without having access to the entire execution α_w that leads R_1 to state σ_w.

CLAIM 6. *Execution β^i_w is well-formed.*

PROOF. By assumption, Recover() is passed the first i messages sent by R_1 in α_w. The claim thus follows from the following: (1) α_w is well-formed; (2) at the end of α_w, R_1 is in state σ_w; (3) because R_2 does not participate in α_w, the state of R_2 at the end of α_w is its initial state; (4) a replica always accepts any sent message (by definition); and (5) $\mathcal{R}$ is push-based, and so R_2 has a message pending following its ins operation. □

CLAIM 7. *Execution β^i_w satisfies causal atomic broadcast.*

PROOF. Immediate from inspection of the message delivery order in β^i_w. □

CLAIM 8. $[_{i-1}\,]_{i-1} \in v^i_w$.

PROOF. For $j = 1, \ldots, d+1$, let $e_j, f_j \in \alpha_w$ be the *do* events in which R_1 inserts $[_{j-1}$ and $]_{j-1}$ into the list. Let $r \in \beta^i_w$ be the *do* event at which R_2 reads v^i_w. Because $\mathcal{R}$ is a correct push-based protocol and β^i_w satisfies causal atomic broadcast, by Definition 13, β^i_w complies with some abstract execution $A = (H, \mathsf{vis}) \in \mathcal{A}_{\mathsf{weak}}$ such that $e_j \xrightarrow{\mathsf{vis}} r$ and $f_j \xrightarrow{\mathsf{vis}} r$ if and only if $j \leq i$, and no del operation is visible to r. This holds because in β^i_w, R_2 receives only the messages $m_1, \ldots, m_i$ before r, and each m_j is the first message sent by R_1 after e_j and f_j. It thus follows from the definition of the weak list specification (Definition 8) that $v^i_w = \ldots [_{i-1}\,]_{i-1} \ldots$. □

CLAIM 9. $y^i_w = x*$ *or* $y^i_w = *x$.

PROOF. Let $f \in \beta^i_w$ be the *do* event at which R_2 inserts x into the list, and $r \in \beta^i_w$ be the *do* event at which R_1 reads y^i_w. Because

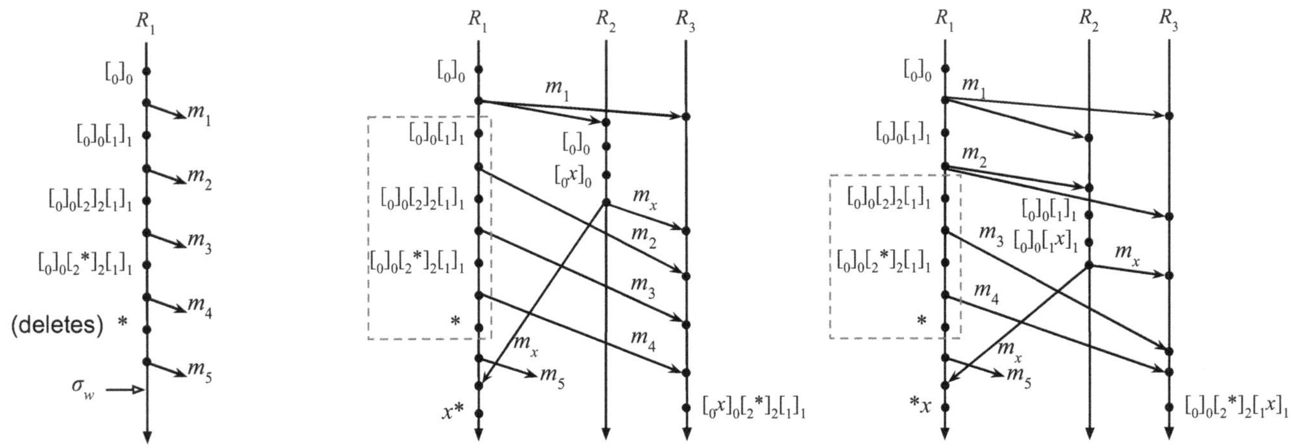

(a) Encoding $w = 10$: execution α_w, at the end of which the state of R_1 is σ_w.

(b) Decoding $w_1 = 1$ given σ_w and m_1. (We do not show replicas receiving their own messages.)

(c) Decoding $w_2 = 0$ given σ_w, m_1 and m_2. (We do not show replicas receiving their own messages.)

Figure 5: Examples of the encoding and decoding procedures from Theorem 5 applied to $w = 10$. Figure 5(a) shows the execution α_w constructed by the encoding procedure, whose output is σ_w, the state of R_1 at the end of α_w. Figure 5(b) shows the first step of decoding w from σ_w. The decoding procedure performs the state transitions of the events at R_1 that are outside of the dashed rectangle and of the events at R_2; these transitions are valid because they occur in the depicted execution, in which the events inside the dashed rectangle lead R_1 to state σ_w. The relative order of x and $*$ read at R_1 therefore recovers bit $w_1 = 1$. Figure 5(c) shows the second step of decoding w: Recovering $w_1 = 1$ allows the decoding procedure to perform the state transitions by R_1 in α_w that depend on w_1.

$\mathcal{R}$ is a correct push-based protocol, β_w^i compiles with some abstract execution $A = (H, \mathsf{vis}) \in \mathcal{A}_{\mathsf{weak}}$ such that $f \xrightarrow{\mathsf{vis}} r$. Now, let $e \in \beta_w^i$ be the *do* event at which R_1 inserts $*$ into the list. Then $e \xrightarrow{\mathsf{vis}} r$ by definition of an abstract execution (Definition 4). Because all other elements inserted in β_w^i are deleted by R_1 before r, but x and $*$ are not deleted in β_w^i, the claim follows. □

Correctness of recovering w_i. Having shown that the state transitions performed by Recover() yield the lists $y_w^i = x*$ or $y_w^i = *x$, it remains to show that we correctly recover w_i from y_w^i: $(y_w^i = x*) \iff (w_i = 1)$.

In principle, the weak list specification allows R_1's read to order x and $*$ arbitrarily, since $[_{i-1}$ and $]_{i-1}$ are deleted from the list by the time the read occurs. We show, however, that R_1 cannot do this, because it cannot rule out the possibility that another replica has already observed $[_{i-1}\, x\,]_{i-1}$ and $*$ together, and therefore their order is fixed. Consider the following extension of β_w^i, in which R_3 receives the messages generated after each insertion and then reads the list (it is easy to see that this execution satisfies causal atomic broadcast):

$$\gamma_w^i = \beta_w^i\ \mathit{receive}_3(m_1)\ \ldots\ \mathit{receive}_3(m_i)\ \mathit{receive}_3(m_x)$$
$$\mathit{receive}_3(m_{i+1})\ \ldots\ \mathit{receive}_3(m_{d+2})\ \mathit{do}_3(\mathsf{read}_3, z_w^i).$$

We show that the list z_w^i contains $*$ after x if and only $w_i = 1$. Informally, this follows because every element inserted from iteration i onwards in the encoding procedure (and hence in γ_w^i), including $*$, goes after $]_{i-1}$ if and only if $w_i = 1$, and no del events are visible to R_3, so its read response must order x before $]_{i-1}$ before $*$.

Formally, consider the following events in γ_w^i: w_*, the ins of $*$ by R_1; w_x, the ins of x by R_2; and r_z, the read by R_3, whose response is z_w^i. Because $\mathcal{R}$ is a correct push-based protocol and γ_w^i satisfies causal broadcast, by Definition 13, γ_w^i complies with some abstract execution $A = (H, \mathsf{vis}) \in \mathcal{A}_{\mathsf{weak}}$ such that for any $e, e' \in H$, $e' \xrightarrow{\mathsf{vis}} e$ if and only if $e' \xrightarrow{\mathsf{hb}} e$. Therefore, no del event is visible to w_*, w_x or r_z. Let lo be a list order that A is consistent with (Definition 8). We proceed to show that $(x, *) \in \mathsf{lo}$ if and only if $w_i = 1$. Observe that if $w_i = 1$, every element inserted from iteration i onwards of the encoding process is inserted after $]_{i-1}$, and if $w_i = 0$, every element inserted from iteration i onwards is inserted before $[_{i-1}$. Therefore, the response of w_* establishes that $(]_{i-1}, *) \in \mathsf{lo}$ if and only if $w_i = 1$. The response of w_x establishes that $([_{i-1}, x) \in \mathsf{lo}$ and $(x,]_{i-1}) \in \mathsf{lo}$. It follows that $(x, *) \in \mathsf{lo}$ if and only if $w_i = 1$, since $[_{i-1}, x,]_{i-1}, * \in z_w^i$ and lo is total and transitive on $\{a \mid a \in \mathsf{rval}(r_z) = z_w^i\}$.

We conclude by noting that $y_w^i = x*$ or $y_w^i = *x$ (Claim 9); recall that y_w^i is the response to the read at R_1 performed by Recover(). Since $(x, *) \in \mathsf{lo}$ if and only if $w_i = 1$, then $y_w^i = x*$ if and only if $w_i = 1$.

6.1 Extension to a Client/Server Model

In a *client/server protocol*, replicas communicate only with a central server and not directly with each other. (The motivation is to maintain state on the server instead of on the replicas, and so the server usually does more than merely relay messages between replicas [20].) To model such protocols in our framework, which assumes a broadcast transport, we require replicas to process only messages to/from the server:

DEFINITION 14. *A protocol* $\mathcal{R} = \{R_1, \ldots, R_n, S\}$ *is a* client/server protocol *if for every replica* $R_i = (Q^i, M, \Sigma^i, \sigma_0^i, E, \Delta^i)$, *and* $\sigma \in \Sigma^i$, *if* $\Delta^i(\sigma, \mathit{receive}(m)) \neq \sigma$, *then* m *was sent by* S. *We call* S *the* server.

In practice, users do not interact directly with the server, and so we consider only executions in which *do* events do not occur at the server.

Assuming atomic broadcast, a broadcast protocol can *simulate* a client/server protocol using state machine replication [15].

PROPOSITION 10. *Let* $\mathcal{R} = \{R_1, \ldots, R_n, S\}$ *be a client/server protocol. Then there exists a protocol* $\mathcal{R}' = \{R'_1, \ldots, R'_n\}$

State	Event e	New state
$((r,s),m)$	$do(op,v)$	$((r',s),m')$, where $(r',m') = \Delta^i((r,m),e)$
$((r,s),m)$	$send(m)$	$((r',s),\bot)$, where $(r',\bot) = \Delta^i((r,m),e)$
$((r,s),m)$	$receive(m)$	$((r',s'),m')$, where if $\Delta^S((s,\bot),e) = (s^*,\bot)$, then $s' = s^*$ and $(r',m') = (r,m) = \Delta^i((r,m), receive(m))$; and if $\Delta^S((s,\bot),e) = (s^*,m^*)$, then $(s',\bot) = \Delta^S((s^*,m^*), send(m^*))$, $(r',m') = \Delta^i((\hat{r},\hat{m}), receive(m^*))$, where $(\hat{r},\hat{m}) = (r,m) = \Delta^i((r,m), receive(m))$

Figure 6: State machine of replica $R_i' \in \mathcal{R}'$ simulating replica $R_i = (Q^i, M, \Sigma^i, \sigma_0^i, E, \Sigma^i) \in \mathcal{R}$. The initial internal state is (q_0^i, q_0^S), where q_0^i and q_0^S are the initial internal states of R_i and of S, respectively.

that simulates $\mathcal{R}$ *in the following sense: (1) for any execution* α' *of* $\mathcal{R}'$ *that satisfies causal atomic broadcast, there exists an execution* α *of* $\mathcal{R}$ *such that* $\alpha|^{do}_{R_i} = \alpha'|^{do}_{R_i'}$ *for* $i = 1..n$*; (2) the set of internal states of each* R_i' *is* $Q^i \times Q^S$*, where* Q^i *and* Q^S *are respective sets of* R_i *and* S*; and (3) until* R_i' *receives a message, its state is* $(\_, q_0^S)$*, where* $(q_0^S, \bot)$ *is the initial state of* S.

PROOF. For $1 = 1..n$, replica $R_i' \in \mathcal{R}'$ maintains two state machines, of R_i and of S. R_i' broadcasts exactly the messages broadcast by the replica R_i it is simulating. We use the fact that messages are delivered to all replicas in $\mathcal{R}'$ in the same order to simulate the server S using state machine replication.

Figure 6 shows the state machine of replica $R_i' \in \mathcal{R}'$. Upon a do event, R_i' performs the corresponding transition on R_i's state machine and broadcasts any message m' that R_i would send to S. Upon receiving a message m, R_i' delivers m to the two state machines it maintains. (However, because m corresponds to a message sent by some R_j, the R_i state machine ignores it, by Definition 14.) If, as a result of receiving m, S broadcasts a message m^*, then R_i' (locally) delivers m^* to R_i's state machine and broadcasts any message m' that R_i sends as a result of receiving m^*.

In any execution α' of $\mathcal{R}'$ that satisfies causal atomic broadcast, all messages are delivered to all replicas in the same order. Therefore, each replica R_i' performs the same state transitions at S, and (locally) delivers the same messages from S to its R_i state machine. The claim follows. □

Client/server lower bound. Since the executions constructed in the proof of Theorem 5 satisfy causal atomic broadcast, they can also be viewed as executions of a protocol simulating a push-based client/server protocol (Proposition 10). We therefore obtain

COROLLARY 11. *Let* $\mathcal{R}$ *be a push-based client/server protocol that satisfies the weak or strong list specification for* $n \geq 3$ *replicas. Then the worst-case metadata overhead of* $\mathcal{R}$ *on the clients over executions with* D *deletions is* $\Omega(D)$.

PROOF. Let $\mathcal{R}$ be a push-based client/server protocol that satisfies the weak or strong list specification. Let $\mathcal{R}'$ be the protocol simulating $\mathcal{R}$ from Proposition 10. Take $D \geq 4$. By Theorem 5, there exists an execution α_D of $\mathcal{R}'$ with D deletions such that: (1) the metadata overhead of some state σ of some replica $R' \in \mathcal{R}'$ is $\Omega(D)$; (2) α_D satisfies causal atomic broadcast; and (3) R' does not receive any message before σ. Because $\mathcal{R}'$ simulates $\mathcal{R}$, we have that $\sigma = ((q^R, q^S), \_)$, where q^R and q^S are, respectively, internal states of the replica $R \in \mathcal{R}$ that R' is simulating and of the server. Moreover, it follows from Proposition 10 that q^S is the initial internal state of the server. Therefore, $|(q^R, q^S)| = O(|q^R| + |q^S|) = O(|q^R|)$, because $|q^S|$ is a constant. Since the user-observable content at R' and R is the same, it follows that the metadata overhead at R is $\Omega(D)$. □

7. RELATED WORK

Previous attempts at specifying the behavior of replicated list objects [17, 28] have been informal and imprecise: they typically required the execution of an operation at a remote replica to *preserve the effect* of the operation at its original replica, but they have not formally defined the notions of the effect and its preservation.

Burckhardt et al. [5] have previously proposed a framework for specifying replicated data types (on which we base our list specifications) and proved lower bounds on the metadata overhead of several data types. In contrast to us, they handle much simpler data types than a list. Thus, our specifications have to extend theirs with an additional relation, defining the order of elements in the list. Similarly, their proof strategy (and its extension in [3]) for establishing lower bounds would not be applicable to lists; obtaining a lower bound in this case requires a more delicate decoding argument, recovering information incrementally.

There are more protocols implementing a highly available replicated list than the RGA protocol we considered. Treedoc [22] and Logoot [32] are other implementations of the strong list specification using the approach of replicated data types [26]. As in RGA, the state of a replica can be viewed as a tree, where a deterministic traversal defines the order of the list. The replication protocol represents position of a node in the tree as a sequence of edge labels on the path from the root of the tree (in RGA, it is a relative position to an existing node). Like RGA, these protocols have worst-case metadata overhead linear in the number of deletions. WOOT [21] is a graph-based list implementation: its main component is a representation of a partial list order, i.e., ordering restrictions inferred at the time user performs operations. The total list order is computed as a view of the graph based on a non-declarative specification of intended ordering.

Another class of protocols is based on operational transformations (OT) [13], which apply certain transformation functions to pairs of concurrent updates. If applying the transformation function allows commuting two operations (TP1) and three operations (TP2) then OT ensures that the list state converges, regardless of the order in which the operations are received [23]. However, it was shown [14] that several OT protocols do not satisfy TP1 and TP2 and do not converge. OT protocols store a log of updates at each replica, so their metadata overhead is also at least linear in the number of updates.

8. CONCLUSION

This paper provides a precise specification of the list replicated object, which models the core functionality of collaborative text editing systems. We define a *strong* list—and show that it is implemented by an existing system [24]—as well as a *weak* list, which we conjecture describes the behavior of the Jupiter protocol [20], underlying public collaboration systems [31].

We prove a lower bound of $\Omega(D)$, where D is the number of deletions, on the metadata overhead of push-based list protocols, which model the implementation of all highly available list protocols that we are aware of. Our lower bound applies for both weak and strong semantics. Exploring client/server systems in future research is therefore of practical interest, as some client/server systems do not implement the strong semantics, and our results suggest that this might not offer a complexity advantage.

We also show a simple list protocol whose metadata overhead is $O(D \lg k)$, where k is the number of operations. Closing the gap between the upper and lower bound is left for future work, as is the question of relaxing the restriction to push-based protocols.

Our work is a first step towards specifying and analyzing general collaborative editing systems, providing more features than those captured by the list object. This includes systems for sharing structured documents, such as XML [19]. While our lower bound would hold for more general systems, it is possible that the additional features induce additional complexity.

Acknowledgments

We would like to thank Marc Shapiro and Pascal Urso for comments that helped improve the paper. Attiya and Morrison were supported by the Israel Science Foundation (grant 1749/14) and by Yad Hanadiv Foundation. Gotsman was supported by an EU project ADVENT. Yang was supported by an Institute for Information & Communication Technology Promotion (IITP) grant funded by the Korea government (MSIP, No. R0190-15-2011). Zawirski was supported by an EU project SyncFree.

9. REFERENCES

[1] Apache Wave. https://incubator.apache.org/wave/.

[2] H. Attiya, S. Burckhardt, A. Gotsman, A. Morrison, H. Yang, and M. Zawirski. Specification and Complexity of Collaborative Text Editing (Extended Version). Available from http://www.software.imdea.org/~gotsman.

[3] H. Attiya, F. Ellen, and A. Morrison. Limitations of Highly-Available Eventually-Consistent Data Stores. In *PODC*, 2015.

[4] P. Bailis, A. Ghodsi, J. M. Hellerstein, and I. Stoica. Bolt-on Causal Consistency. In *SIGMOD*, 2013.

[5] S. Burckhardt, A. Gotsman, H. Yang, and M. Zawirski. Replicated Data Types: Specification, Verification, Optimality. In *POPL*, 2014.

[6] C. Cachin, R. Guerraoui, and L. Rodrigues. *Introduction to Reliable and Secure Distributed Programming*. Springer Publishing Company, Incorporated, 2nd edition, 2011.

[7] J. Day-Richter. What's different about the new Google Docs: Conflict resolution. http://googledrive.blogspot.com/2010/09/whats-different-about-new-google-docs_22.html, 2010.

[8] J. Day-Richter. What's different about the new Google Docs: Making collaboration fast. http://googledrive.blogspot.com/2010/09/whats-different-about-new-google-docs.html, 2010.

[9] G. DeCandia, D. Hastorun, M. Jampani, G. Kakulapati, A. Lakshman, A. Pilchin, S. Sivasubramanian, P. Vosshall, and W. Vogels. Dynamo: Amazon's Highly Available Key-value Store. In *SOSP*, 2007.

[10] X. Défago, A. Schiper, and P. Urbán. Total Order Broadcast and Multicast Algorithms: Taxonomy And Survey. *ACM CSUR*, 36(4), 2004.

[11] J. Du, S. Elnikety, A. Roy, and W. Zwaenepoel. Orbe: Scalable Causal Consistency Using Dependency Matrices and Physical Clocks. In *SoCC*, 2013.

[12] J. Du, C. Iorgulescu, A. Roy, and W. Zwaenepoel. Closing The Performance Gap between Causal Consistency and Eventual Consistency. In *PaPEC*, 2014.

[13] C. A. Ellis and S. J. Gibbs. Concurrency Control in Groupware Systems. In *SIGMOD*, 1989.

[14] A. Imine, M. Rusinowitch, G. Oster, and P. Molli. Formal Design and Verification of Operational Transformation Algorithms for Copies Convergence. *TCS*, 351(2), 2006.

[15] L. Lamport. Time, Clocks, and the Ordering of Events in a Distributed System. *CACM*, 21(7), 1978.

[16] B. Leuf and W. Cunningham. *The Wiki Way: Quick Collaboration on the Web*. Addison-Wesley Longman Publishing Co., Inc., Boston, MA, USA, 2001.

[17] D. Li and R. Li. Preserving Operation Effects Relation in Group Editors. In *CSCW*, 2004.

[18] W. Lloyd, M. J. Freedman, M. Kaminsky, and D. G. Andersen. Don't Settle for Eventual Consistency. *CACM*, 57(5), 2014.

[19] S. Martin, P. Urso, and S. Weiss. Scalable XML collaborative editing with undo. In *OTM*, 2010.

[20] D. A. Nichols, P. Curtis, M. Dixon, and J. Lamping. High-latency, low-bandwidth windowing in the Jupiter collaboration system. In *UIST*, 1995.

[21] G. Oster, P. Urso, P. Molli, and A. Imine. Data consistency for P2P collaborative editing. In *CSCW*, 2006.

[22] N. Preguiça, J. M. Marquès, M. Shapiro, and M. Leţia. A commutative replicated data type for cooperative editing. In *ICDCS*, 2009.

[23] M. Ressel, D. Nitsche-Ruhland, and R. Gunzenhäuser. An integrating, transformation-oriented approach to concurrency control and undo in group editors. In *CSCW*, 1996.

[24] H.-G. Roh, M. Jeon, J.-S. Kim, and J. Lee. Replicated abstract data types: Building blocks for collaborative applications. *JPDC*, 71(3), 2011.

[25] M. Shapiro, N. Preguiça, C. Baquero, and M. Zawirski. A Comprehensive study of Convergent and Commutative Replicated Data Types. Technical Report RR-7506, INRIA, Jan. 2011.

[26] M. Shapiro, N. Preguiça, C. Baquero, and M. Zawirski. Conflict-free Replicated Data Types. In *SSS*, 2011.

[27] C. Sun and C. Ellis. Operational transformation in real-time group editors: issues, algorithms, and achievements. In *CSCW*, 1998.

[28] C. Sun, X. Jia, Y. Zhang, Y. Yang, and D. Chen. Achieving convergence, causality preservation, and intention preservation in real-time cooperative editing systems. *ACM TOCHI*, 5(1), 1998.

[29] D. B. Terry, M. M. Theimer, K. Petersen, A. J. Demers, M. J. Spreitzer, and C. H. Hauser. Managing Update Conflicts in Bayou, a Weakly Connected Replicated Storage System. In *SOSP*, 1995.

[30] W. Vogels. Eventually Consistent. *CACM*, 52(1), 2009.

[31] D. Wang, A. Mah, and S. Lassen. Google Wave Operational Transformation. https://wave-protocol.googlecode.com/hg/whitepapers/operational-transform/operational-transform.html, 2010.

[32] S. Weiss, P. Urso, and P. Molli. Logoot: A Scalable Optimistic Replication Algorithm for Collaborative Editing on P2P Networks. In *ICDCS*, 2009.

[33] M. Zawirski, N. Preguiça, S. Duarte, A. Bieniusa, V. Balegas, and M. Shapiro. Write fast, read in the past: Causal consistency for client-side applications. In *Middleware*, 2015.

Optimal Mobile Byzantine Fault Tolerant Distributed Storage

[Extended Abstract]

Silvia Bonomi
DIAG - University of Rome "La Sapienza"
Rome, Italy
bonomi@dis.uniroma1.it

Antonella Del Pozzo
DIAG - University of Rome "La Sapienza"
Rome, Italy
Sorbonne Universités, UPMC, LIP6-CNRS 7606
Paris, France
delpozzo@dis.uniroma1.it

Maria Potop-Butucaru
Sorbonne Universités, UPMC, LIP6-CNRS 7606
Paris, France
maria.potop-butucaru@lip6.fr

Sébastien Tixeuil
Sorbonne Universités, UPMC, LIP6-CNRS 7606
Paris, France
sebastien.tixeuil@lip6.fr

ABSTRACT

We present an optimal emulation of a server based regular read/write storage in a synchronous round-free message-passing system that is subject to mobile Byzantine failures and prove that the problem is impossible to solve in asynchronous settings. In a system with n servers implementing a regular register, our construction tolerates faults (or attacks) that can be abstracted by agents that are moved (in an arbitrary and unforeseen manner) by a computationally unbounded adversary from a server to another in order to deviate the server's computation. When a server is infected by an adversarial agent, it behaves arbitrarily until the adversary decides to "move" the agent to another server. We investigate the case where the movements of the mobile Byzantine agents are decided by the adversary and are completely decoupled from the message communication delay. Our emulation spans two awareness models: servers with and without self-diagnosis mechanism. In the first case servers are aware that the mobile Byzantine agent has left and hence they can stop running the protocol until they recover a correct state while in the second case, servers are not aware of their faulty state and continue to run the protocol using an incorrect local state. Our results, proven optimal with respect to the threshold of the tolerated mobile Byzantine faults in the first model, are significantly different from the round-based synchronous models. Another interesting side result of our study is that, contrary to the round-based synchronous consensus implementation for systems prone to mobile Byzantine faults, our storage emulation does not rely on the necessity of a core of correct processes all along the computation. That is, every server in the system can be compromised by the mobile Byzantine agents at some point in the computation. This leads to another interesting conclusion: storage is easier than consensus in synchronous settings, when the system is hit by mobile Byzantine failures.

PODC'16, July 25 - 28, 2016, Chicago, IL, USA

ISBN 978-1-4503-3964-3/16/07...$15.00
DOI: http://dx.doi.org/10.1145/2933057.2933100

1. INTRODUCTION

Byzantine fault tolerance is at the core of Distributed Computing and a fundamental building block in any reasonably sized distributed system. Byzantine failures encompass all possible cases that can occur in practice (even unforeseen ones) as the impacted process may simply exhibit arbitrary behavior. Specifically targeted attacks to compromise processes and/or virus infections can indeed cause malicious code execution.

In classical Byzantine fault-tolerance, attacks and infections are typically abstracted as an upper bound f on the number of Byzantine processes that a given set of n processes should be able to tolerate. Such bounds permit to characterize the solvable cases for benchmarking problems in Distributed Computing (*e.g.* Agreement and Register Emulation). However, this abstraction fails the reality test of long-lived distributed services. With new exploits being publicized daily and hackers offering services at amazingly low prices, *every* process is bound to be compromised in a long lasting execution. On the light side, dedicated cure and software rejuvenation techniques increase the possibility that a compromised node *does not remain compromised forever*, and may be aware about its previously compromised status [16]. To integrate both aspects, Mobile Byzantine Failures (MBF) models have been introduced. Then, faults are represented by Byzantine agents that are managed by a powerful omniscient adversary that "moves" them from a process to another. Mobile Byzantine failures that have been investigated so far consider round-based computations, and can be classified according to Byzantine mobility constraints: *(i)* Byzantines with constrained mobility [6] may only move from one process to another when protocol messages are sent (similarly to how viruses would propagate), while *(ii)* Byzantines with unconstrained mobility [1, 3, 7, 12, 13, 14] may move independently of protocol messages.

Buhrman *et al.* [6] studied the problem of Agreement when Byzantines have constrained mobility. In the case of unconstrained mobility, several variants were investigated, still for the Agreement problem [1, 3, 7, 12, 13, 14]. Reischuk [13] considers that malicious agents are stationary for a given period of time. Ostrovsky and Yung [12] introduce the notion of mobile viruses and define the adversary as an entity that can inject and distribute faults. Garay [7], and more recently Banu *et al.* [1], and Sasaki *et al.* [14] or Bonnet *et al.* [3] consider that processes execute synchronous rounds composed of three phases: *send*, *receive*, and *compute*. Between two consecutive such synchronous rounds, Byzantine agents can move from one node to another. Hence the set of faulty processes at any given time has a bounded size, yet its membership may evolve from one round to the next. The main difference between the aforementioned four works [1, 3, 7, 14] lies in the knowledge that processes have about their previous infection by a Byzantine agent. In Garay's model [7], a process is able to detect its own infection after the Byzantine agent left it. More precisely, during the first round following the leave of the Byzantine agent, a process enters a state, called *cured*, during which it can take preventive actions to avoid sending messages that are based on a corrupted state. Garay [7] proposed, in this model, an algorithm that solves Mobile Byzantine Agreement provided that $n > 6f$. This bound was later dropped to $n > 4f$ by Banu *et al.* [1]. Sasaki *et al.* [14] investigated the same problem in a model where processes do not have the ability to detect when Byzantine agents move, and show that the bound raises to $n > 6f$. Finally, Bonnet *et al.* [3] considers an intermediate setting where cured processes remain in *control* on the messages they send (in particular, they send the same message to all destinations, and they do not send obviously fake information, *e.g.* fake id); this subtle difference on the power of Byzantine agents has an important impact on the bounds for solving agreement: the bound becomes $n > 5f$ and is proven tight.

Traditional solutions to build a Byzantine tolerant storage service (*a.k.a.* register emulation) can be divided into two categories: *replicated state machines* [15], and *Byzantine quorum systems* [2, 9, 11, 10]. Both approaches are based on the idea that the current state of the storage is replicated among processes, and the main difference lies in the number of replicas that are simultaneously involved in the state maintenance protocol. Recently, Bonomi *et al.* [4] proposed optimal self-stabilizing atomic register implementations for round-based synchronous systems under the four Mobile Byzantine models described in [1, 3, 7, 14].

Our Contribution. The main motivation for our work comes from realizing that the hypothesis that Byzantine agent moves are tightly synchronized with protocol rounds is not a realistic assumption, when Byzantine agents are driven by an adversary that can make use of out of band resources for coordinating them. Indeed, infection and cure are independent from the protocol that is executed on the servers, and typically result from external actions.

Our first contribution (Section 3) is to propose and formalize a general mobile Byzantine model, where Byzantine agent movements are decoupled from the protocol computation steps (in particular, movements of the Byzantine agents are no more related to messages that are exchanged through the protocol). We explore the fundamental implications of the relaxed hypothesis about Byzantine agent movements, and nevertheless retain the dimension related to process awareness about its failure state.

The second contribution of the paper is a protocol to emulate a regular register in our general mobile Byzantine model. We first explore (Section 4) the instances of the model where this problem is solvable (*e.g.* we provide impossibility results for the asynchronous setting), and in the solvable cases, we present and prove a protocol (Section 5) whose resilience is optimal with respect to the number of Byzantine agents.

2. SYSTEM MODELS

We consider a distributed system composed of an arbitrary large set of client processes $\mathcal{C}$ and a set of n server processes $\mathcal{S} = \{s_1, s_2 \dots s_n\}$. Each process in the distributed system (*i.e.*, both servers and clients) is identified by a unique identifier. Servers run a distributed protocol emulating a shared memory abstraction and such protocol is totally transparent to clients (i.e., clients do not know the protocol executed by servers). The passage of time is measured by a fictional global clock (*e.g.*, that spans the set of natural integers). Processes in the system do not have access at the fictional global time. At each time t, each process (either client or server) is characterized by its *internal state* i.e., by the set of all its local variables and the corresponding values. We assume that an arbitrary number of clients may crash while up to f servers are affected, at any time t, by *Mobile Byzantine Failures*. The Mobile Byzantine Failure adversarial model considered in this paper (and described in details below) is stronger than any other adversary previously considered in the literature [1, 3, 6, 7, 12, 13, 14].

No agreement abstraction is assumed to be available at each process (i.e. processes are not able to use consensus or total order primitives to agree upon the current values). Moreover, we assume that each process has the same role in the distributed computation (i.e., there is no special process acting as a coordinator).

Communication model. Processes communicate trough message passing. In particular, we assume that: *(i)* each client $c_i \in \mathcal{C}$ can communicate with every server trough a broadcast() primitive, *(ii)* each server can communicate with every other server trough a broadcast() primitive, and *(iii)* each server can communicate with a particular client trough a send() unicast primitive. We assume that communications are authenticated (*i.e.*, given a message m, the identity of its sender cannot be forged) and reliable (*i.e.*, spurious messages are not created and sent messages are neither lost nor duplicated).

Timing Assumptions. We consider two types of systems: *(i)* asynchronous (see Section 4.2), and *(ii)* round-free synchronous (see Section 5).

The system is *asynchronous* in the sense that there not exists any upper bound on communication and computation latencies. As a consequence, messages are delivered but it is not possible do compute any upper bounds on their delivery time. The system is *round-free synchronous* if: *(i)* the processing time of local computations (except for wait statements) are negligible with respect to communication delays, and are assumed to be equal to 0, and *(ii)* messages take time to travel to their destination processes. In particular, concerning point-to-point communications, we assume that if a process sends a message m at time t then it is delivered by time $t + \delta_p$ (with $\delta_p > 0$). Similarly, let t be the time at which a process p invokes the broadcast(m) primitive, then there is a constant δ_b (with $\delta_b \geq \delta_p$) such that all servers have delivered m at time $t + \delta_b$. For the sake of presentation, in the following we consider a unique message delivery delay δ (equal to $\delta_b \geq \delta_p$), and assume δ is known to every process.

Computation model. Each process of the distributed system executes a distributed protocol $\mathcal{P}$ that is composed by a set of distributed algorithms. Each algorithm in $\mathcal{P}$ is represented by a finite state automata and it is composed of a sequence of computation and communication steps. A computation step is represented by the computation executed locally to each process while a communication step is represented by the sending and the delivering events of a message. Computation steps and communication steps are generally called *events*.

DEFINITION 1 (EXECUTION HISTORY). *Let $\mathcal{P}$ be a distributed protocol. Let H be the set of all the events generated by $\mathcal{P}$ at any process p_i in the distributed system and let $\rightarrow$ be the happened-before relation. An execution history $\hat{H} = (H, \rightarrow)$ is a partial order on H satisfying the relation $\rightarrow$.*

DEFINITION 2 (VALID STATE AT TIME t). *Let $\hat{H} = (H, \rightarrow)$ be an execution history of a generic computation and let $\mathcal{P}$ be the corresponding protocol. Let p_i be a process and let $state_{p_i}$ be the state of p_i at some time t. $state_{p_i}$ is said to be valid at time t if it can be generated by executing $\mathcal{P}$ on $\hat{H}$.*

3. ADVERSARY MODEL

The Mobile Byzantine Failure (MBF) models considered so far in literature [1, 3, 6, 7, 12, 13, 14] assume that faults, represented by Byzantine agents, are controlled by a powerful external adversary that "moves" them from a server to another. Note that the term "mobile" does not necessary mean that a Byzantine agent physically moves from one process to another but it rather captures the phenomenon of a progressive infection, that alters the code executed by a process and its internal state.

3.1 Mobile Byzantine Models for round-based computations

In all the above cited works the system evolves in synchronous rounds. Every round is divided in three phases: *(i) send* where processes send all the messages for the current round, *(ii) receive* where processes receive all the messages sent at the beginning of the current round, and *(iii) computation* where processes process received messages and prepare those that are to be sent in the next round. Concerning the assumptions on agent movements and servers awareness on their *cured* state the Mobile Byzantine Models defined in [3, 7, 6, 14] are summarized as follows:

- *Garay's model* [7]. In this model, agents can move arbitrarily from a server to another at the beginning of each round (i.e. before the send phase starts). When a server is in the *cured* state it is aware of its condition and thus can remain silent for a round to prevent the dissemination of wrong information.
- *Bonnet et al.'s model* [3] and *Sasaki et al.'s model* [14]. As in the previous model, agents can move arbitrarily from a server to another at the beginning of each round (i.e. before the send phase starts). Differently from the Garay's model, in both models it is assumed that servers do not know if they are correct or cured when the Byzantine agent moved. The main difference between these two models is that in the [14] model a cured process still acts as a Byzantine one extra round.
- *Buhrman's model* [6]. Differently from the previous models, agents move together with the message (i.e., with the send or broadcast operation). However, when a server is in the *cured* state it is aware of that.

Most of the previously cited models [1, 3, 6, 7, 14] consider that the Byzantine agents mobility is related to the round-based synchronous system communication. That is, processes execute synchronous rounds composed of three phases: send, receive, compute. Only between two consecutive rounds, Byzantine agents are allowed to move from one node to another. In the sequel we formalize and generalize the MBF model. Our generalization is twofold: *(i)* we decouple the Byzantine agents movement from the structure of the computation making it round-free and hence suitable for any distributed application, and *(ii)* we model the infection diffusion in relation with the detection/recovery capabilities of servers.

Informally, in the MBF model, when a Byzantine agent is hosted by a process, the adversary takes the entire control of the process making it Byzantine faulty (i.e., it can corrupt the process's local variables, forces the process to send arbitrary messages etc...). Then, the Byzantine agent moves away and it leaves the process with a possible corrupted state (i.e., in cured state). Such movement abstracts, for example, a virus that has been detected and putted in quarantine or a software update/patching of the machine.

As in the case of round-based MBF models [1, 3, 6, 7, 14], we assume that any process previously infected by a mobile Byzantine agent has access to a tamper-proof memory storing the correct protocol code. However, a healed (cured) server may still have a corrupted internal state and cannot be considered correct. As a consequence, the notions of correct and faulty process need to be redefined when dealing with Mobile Byzantine Failures.

DEFINITION 3 (CORRECT PROCESS AT TIME t). *Let us denote by $\hat{H} = (H, \rightarrow)$ an execution history and let $\mathcal{P}$ be the protocol generating $\hat{H}$. A process is said to be* correct *at time t if* (i) *it is correctly executing its protocol $\mathcal{P}$, and* (ii) *its state is a valid state at time t. We denote as $Co(t)$ the set of correct processes at time t while, given a time interval $[t, t']$. We denote as $Co([t, t'])$ the set of all the processes that are correct during the whole interval $[t, t']$ (i.e., $Co([t, t']) = \bigcap_{\tau \in [t,t']} Co(\tau)$).*

DEFINITION 4 (FAULTY PROCESS AT TIME t). *Let $\hat{H} = (H, \rightarrow)$ be an execution history and let $\mathcal{P}$ be the protocol generating $\hat{H}$. A process is said to be* faulty *at time t if it is controlled by a mobile Byzantine agent and it is not executing correctly its protocol $\mathcal{P}$ (i.e., it is behaving arbitrarily).*

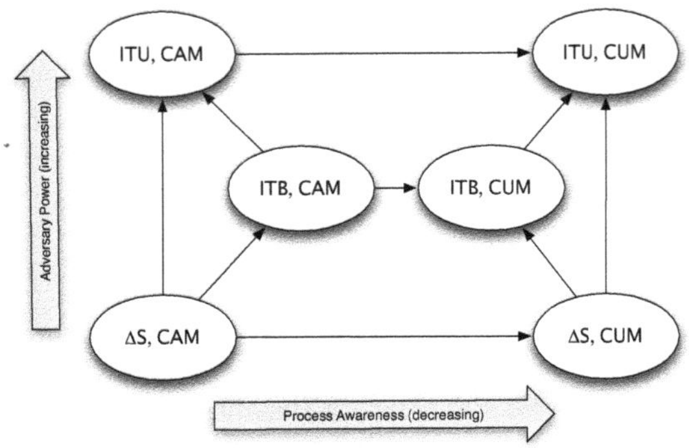

Figure 1: MBF model instances for round-free computations and their relations.

We denote as $B(t)$ the set of faulty processes at time t while, given a time interval $[t, t']$. We denote as $B([t, t'])$ the set of all the processes that are faulty during the whole interval $[t, t']$ (i.e., $B([t, t']) = \bigcap_{\tau \in [t,t']} B(\tau)$).

DEFINITION 5 (CURED PROCESS AT TIME t). *Let $\hat{H} = (H, \rightarrow)$ be an execution history and let $\mathcal{P}$ be the protocol generating $\hat{H}$. A process is said to be* cured *at time t if* (i) *it is correctly executing its protocol $\mathcal{P}$, and* (ii) *its state is not a valid state at time t. We denote as $Cu(t)$ the set of cured processes at time t while, given a time interval $[t, t']$. We denote as $Cu([t, t'])$ the set of all the processes that are cured during the whole interval $[t, t']$ (i.e., $Cu([t, t']) = \bigcap_{\tau \in [t,t']} Cu(\tau)$).*

3.2 Mobile Byzantine Models for round-free computations

We now discuss further how the MBF model for round-free computations introduced informally in the previous section is able to abstract different attack scenarios mentioned in Section 1. In addition, we classify its six possible instances (see Figure 1) according to the adversary power (from the weakest adversary model $(\Delta S, CAM)$ to the strongest one (ITU, CUM)) showing the relationships between them.

Our model takes into account two different attack dimensions: *(i)* how the external adversary can coordinate the movement of the Byzantine agents, and *(ii)* the process awareness about their current failure state. The first point abstracts the capability of the external adversary to propagate the infection with respect to the detection and recovery capability of processes while the second point distinguishes between detection and proactive recovery capabilities. Thus, any instance of our MBF model is characterized by a pair (X, Y), where X represents the coordination aspect (i.e., one among ΔS, ITB and ITU) and Y represents the process awareness (i.e., CAM vs. CUM).

The coordination dimension allows to characterize the infection spreading from a time point of view. In particular:

- $(\Delta S, *)$ allows to consider coordinated attacks where the external adversary needs to control a subset of machines. In this case, compromising new machines takes almost the same time as the time needed to detect the attack or the time necessary to rejuvenate. This may represent scenarios with low diversity where compromising time depends only on the complexity of the exploit and not on the target server. More formally, the external adversary moves all the f mobile Byzantine Agents at the same time t and movements happen periodically (i.e., movements happen at time $t_0 + \Delta$, $t_0 + 2\Delta$, ..., $t_0 + i\Delta$, with $i \in \mathbb{N}$).

- $(ITB, *)$ slightly relaxes the assumption about the time of the infection propagation. In particular, in this case the Byzantine agents may affect different servers for different periods of time. This abstracts in some way the possible different complexities of various attack steps (each mobile agent can do a set of exploits and each exploit may take different time to succeed and then to be detected). As a consequence, we are able to capture possible differences in the detection and the rejuvenation times that are now different from server to server. More formally, each of the f Mobile Byzantine Agent ma_i is forced to remain on a process for at least a period Δ_i. Given two mobile Byzantine Agents ma_i and ma_j, their movement periods Δ_i and Δ_j may be different.

- $(ITU, *)$ further relaxes the coordination assumption and allows to consider extremely fast infection and detection/rejuvenation processes. More formally, each Mobile Byzantine agent ma_i is free to move at any time (i.e., it may occupy a process for one time unit, corrupt its state and then leave). This case can be seen as a particular case of ITB where $\Delta_i = 1$ for each mobile agent ma_i.

Let us note that, obviously, $(\Delta S, *)$ is the more restrictive coordination case with respect to the adversary power while $(ITU, *)$ represents the maximum freedom (from the coordination point of view) for the external adversary.

Example of $(\Delta S, *)$ coordination, $(ITB, *)$ coordination and $(ITU, *)$ coordination are shown respectively in Figure 2, Figure 3 and Figure 4 (where ma_i denotes the mobile Byzantine agents).

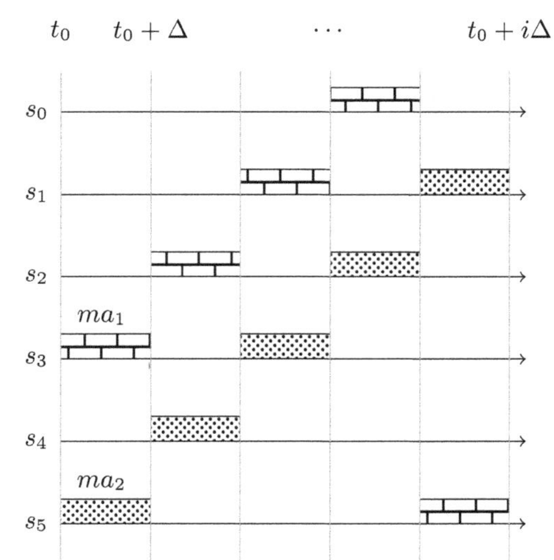

Figure 2: Example of a $(\Delta S, *)$ run with $f = 2$.

The awareness dimension allows to distinguish between servers under continuous monitoring from the non-monitored

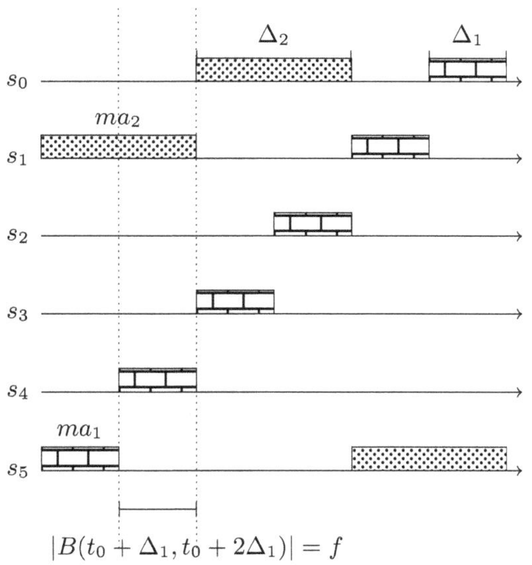

Figure 3: Example of a $(ITB, *)$ run with $f = 2$.

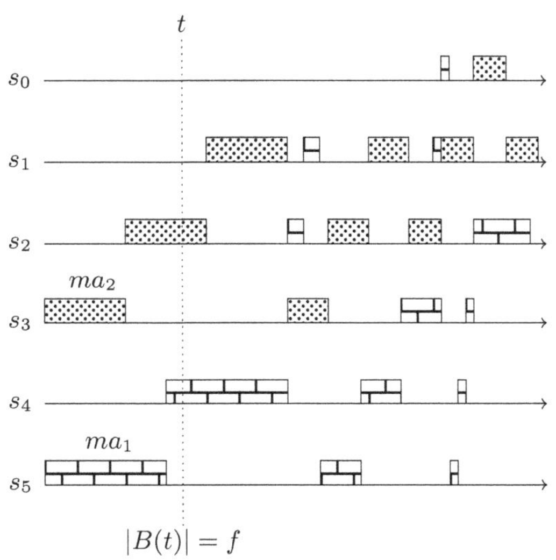

Figure 4: Example of a $(ITU, *)$ run with $f = 2$.

ones. Monitored systems are, in fact, characterized by detection and reaction capabilities that enable them to detect their failure state and to act accordingly. On the contrary, non-monitored servers have no self-diagnosis capabilities but they can try to prevent infections by adopting pessimistic strategies that include proactive rejuvenation. In particular:

- $(*, CAM)$ is able to capture scenarios where servers are aware of a past infection as they abstract environments characterized by the presence of monitors (e.g., antivirus, Intrusion Detection System etc...) that are able to detect the infection and notify the server when the threat is no more affecting the server.

- $(*, CUM)$ represents situations where the server is not aware of a possible past infection. This scenario is typical of distributed systems subject to periodic maintenance and proactive rejuvenation. In this systems, there is a schedule that reboots all the servers and reloads correct versions of the code to prevent infections to be propagated in the whole network. However, this happens independently from the presence of a real infection and implies that there could be periods of time where the server execute the correct protocol however its internal state is not aligned with non compromised servers.

It is easy to prove that CAM is a stronger awareness condition with respect to CUM and thus represents a restriction over the adversary power.

Combining together a type of movement and one of the two awareness conditions, we obtain six different instances of our MBF model for round-free computations, see Figure 1. The instance $(\Delta S, CAM)$ is the strongest one as it is the more restrictive for the external adversary and it provides cured processes with the highest awareness while the instance (ITU, CUM) represents the weakest model as it considers the most powerful adversary and provides no awareness to cured processes.

As in the round-based models, we assume that the adversary can control at most f Byzantine agents at any time (i.e., Byzantine agents are not replicating themselves while moving).

In our work, only servers can be affected by the mobile Byzantine agents[1]. It follows that, at any time t $|B(t)| \leq f$. However, during the system life, all servers may be affected by a Byzantine agent (i.e., none of the server is guaranteed to be correct forever). In order to abstract the knowledge a server has on its state (i.e. *cured* or *correct*), we assume the existence of a cured_state oracle. When invoked via report_cured_state() function, the oracle returns, in the CAM model, true to *cured* servers and false to others. Contrarily, the cured_state oracle returns always false in the CUM model. The implementation of the oracle is out of scope of this paper and the reader may refer to [12] for further details.

4. REGISTERS IN MBF MODEL

4.1 Register Specification

A register is a shared variable accessed by a set of processes (i.e., clients) through two operations, namely read() and write(). Informally, the write() operation updates the value stored in the shared variable while the read() obtains the value contained in the variable (*i.e.*, the last written value). The register state is maintained by the set of servers S. Every operation issued on a register is, generally, not instantaneous and it can be characterized by two events occurring at its boundaries: an *invocation* event and a *reply* event. These events occur at two time instants (i.e., invocation time and the reply time) according to the fictional global time.

An operation *op* is *complete* if both the invocation event and the reply event occurred (*i.e.*, the client issuing the operation does not crash between the invocation time and the

[1]It is trivial to prove that in our model when clients are Byzantine it is impossible to implement deterministically even a safe register. The Byzantine client always introduce a corrupted value. A server cannot distinguish between a correct client and a Byzantine one.

reply time). Then, an operation op is *failed* if it is invoked by a process that crashes before the reply event occurs.

Given two operations op and op', their invocation times ($t_B(op)$ and $t_B(op')$) and reply times ($t_E(op)$ and $t_E(op')$), we say that *op precedes op'* ($op \prec op'$) if and only if $t_E(op) < t_B(op')$. If op does not precede op' and op' does not precede op, then op and op' are *concurrent* (noted $op||op'$). Given a write(v) operation, the value v is said to be written when the operation is complete.

In this paper, we consider a single-writer/multi-reader regular register (SWMR) [8] specified as follows:

— **Termination**: if a correct client invokes an operation, it eventually returns from that operation (i.e., every operation issued by a correct client eventually terminates).

— **Validity**: A read() operation returns the last value written before its invocation (*i.e.* the value written by the latest completed write() preceding it), or a value written by a concurrent write() operation.

Our impossibility results (reported in the next section) are proven for the case of safe register (weaker than the regular register in the Lamport's hierarchy [8]). A read operation on a safe register concurrent with a write operation may return any value in the register domain.

We consider in the sequel only execution histories related to the register computation. In particular, the set of relevant computation events H are defined by the set of all the operations issued on the register and the happened-before relation is substituted by the precedence relation $\prec$ between operations. Thus, we consider a *register execution history* specified as $\hat{H}_R = (H, \prec)$.

From the specification above, we can define the notion of *valid value at time t* as follow:

DEFINITION 6 (VALID VALUE AT TIME t). *Let us denote by $\hat{H}_R = (H, \prec)$ a register execution history of a regular register $\mathcal{R}$.* A valid value at time t *is any value returned by a fictional* read() *operation on the register $\mathcal{R}$ executed instantaneously at time t.*

A protocol $\mathcal{P}_{reg}$ is a collection of distributed algorithms implementing basic register operations. In the sequel, we consider $\mathcal{P}_{reg} \subseteq \{\mathcal{A}_R, \mathcal{A}_W\}$, where $\mathcal{A}_R$ is the algorithm implementing the read() operation and $\mathcal{A}_W$ is the algorithm implementing the write() operation. We say that $\mathcal{P}_{reg}$ *is correct with respect to its specification* if it implements a register satisfying the specification.

4.2 Impossibility results

In this section we prove that, contrary to the static Byzantine tolerant implementations of registers, in the case of MBF tolerant implementations a new operation, namely maintenance(), must be implemented to prevent servers from losing the current register value. Then, we show that in an asynchronous system and in the presence of single Mobile Byzantine Agent, there is no protocol $\mathcal{P}_{reg}$ implementing a safe register and consequently a regular register. Due to the lack of space, we report here only the statement of the main Theorems. Complete proofs can be found in [5].

THEOREM 1. *Let n be the number of servers emulating a safe register and let f be the number of Mobile Byzantine Agents affecting servers. Let $\mathcal{A}_R$ and $\mathcal{A}_W$ be respectively the algorithms implementing the* read() *and the* write() *operation assuming no communication between servers. If $f > 0$ then there exists no protocol $\mathcal{P}_{reg} = \{\mathcal{A}_R, \mathcal{A}_W\}$ implementing a safe register in any of the MBF models for round-free computations.*

From Theorem 1 it follows that, in presence of Mobile Byzantine Agents, a new operation must be defined to allow cured servers to restore a valid state and avoid the loss of the register value.

DEFINITION 7 (maintenance AND $\mathcal{A}_M$). *Let us define a* maintenance() *operation as an operation that, when executed by a process p_i, terminates at some time t leaving p_i with a valid state at time t (i.e., it guarantees that p_i is correct at time t). A maintenance algorithm $\mathcal{A}_M$ is an algorithm that implements the* maintenance() *operation.*

As a consequence, any correct protocol $\mathcal{P}_{reg}$ must include one more algorithm implementing the maintenance() operation[2]. That is, if $f > 0$ then any correct protocol $\mathcal{P}_{reg}$ implementing a register in the round-free Mobile Byzantine Failure model must include an algorithm $\mathcal{A}_M$ (i.e., $\mathcal{P}_{reg} = \{\mathcal{A}_R, \mathcal{A}_W, \mathcal{A}_M\}$).

The next theorem proves that the safe register and consequently the regular register cannot be implemented in asynchronous settings in MBF model. The basic intuition is that, even considering the weakest adversary ($\Delta S, CAM$) and a single mobile Byzantine agent the maintenance() operation is not implementable and the agent may be able to compromise every server before the maintenance() completion.

THEOREM 2. *Let n be the number of servers emulating the register and let f be the number of Byzantine agents in the ($\Delta S, CAM$) Mobile Byzantine Failure model. If $f > 0$, then there exists no protocol $\mathcal{P}_{reg} = \{\mathcal{A}_R, \mathcal{A}_W, \mathcal{A}_M\}$ implementing a safe register in an asynchronous system.*

4.3 Lower bounds

In the following we present lower bounds with respect to the number of correct servers to implement a safe register in the ($\Delta S, CAM$) model, the extension to the ($\Delta S, CUM$) model is presented in [5]. In particular we consider different cases depending on the relationship between Δ and δ. Due to lack of space, the corresponding theorems and proofs are delegated to [5].

- If $\delta \leq \Delta < 2\delta$ and $n \leq 5f$, then there exists no protocol $\mathcal{P}_{reg}$ that implements the safe register abstraction in the ($\Delta S, CAM$) model.
- If $2\delta \leq \Delta < 3\delta$ and $n \leq 4f$, then there exists no protocol $\mathcal{P}_{reg}$ that implements the safe register abstraction in the ($\Delta S, CAM$) model.

5. IMPLEMENTING AN OPTIMAL REGULAR REGISTER

In this section, we present an optimal protocol $\mathcal{P}_{reg}$ that implements a SWMR Regular Register in a round-free synchronous system for ($\Delta S, CAM$) instance of the proposed MBF model. The same protocol with small modifications

[2]Let us note that such an operation can also be embedded in the other algorithm. However, for the sake of clarity, we consider here only protocols where valid state recovery is managed by a specific operation.

implements a SWMR Regular Register in the $(\Delta S, CUM)$ model. This extension is proposed in [5]).

Our solution is based on the following three key points: (1) we implement a maintenance() operation that is executed periodically at each $T_i = t_0 + i\Delta$ time. In this way, the effect of a Byzantine agent on a server disappears in a bounded period of time; (2) we implement read() and write() operations following the classical quorum-based approach. The size of the quorum needed to carry on the operations, and consequently the total number of servers required by the computation, is computed by taking into account the time to terminate the maintenance() operation, δ and Δ; (3) we define a forwarding mechanism to avoid that READ() and WRITE() messages are "lost" by some server s_i due to a concurrent movement of the Byzantine agent during such operations. Note that even though communication channels are reliable, we may have the following situation: a message is sent by a client at time t and the Byzantine agents move at some $t' < t + \delta$. As a consequence, some faulty servers may receive the message in the interval $[t, t']$ and then agents move leaving cured servers without any trace of the message.

Interestingly, we found that the number of replicas needed to tolerate f Byzantine agents does not depend only on f but also on the Δ and δ relationship (see Table 1).

5.1 $\mathcal{P}_{reg}$ Detailed Description

The protocol $\mathcal{P}_{reg}$ for the $(\Delta S, CAM)$ model is described in Figures 5 - 7, which present the maintenance(), write(), and read() operations, respectively.

Local variables at client c_i. Each client c_i maintains a set $reply_i$ that is used during the read() operation to collect the three tuples $\langle j, \langle v, sn\rangle\rangle$ sent back from servers. Additionally, c_i also maintains a local sequence number csn that is incremented each time it invokes a write() operation and is used to timestamp such operations.

Local variables at server s_i. Each server s_i maintains the following local variables (we assume these variables are initialized to zero, false or empty sets according their type):

- V_i: an ordered set containing tree tuples $\langle v, sn\rangle$, where v is a value and sn the corresponding sequence number. Such tuples are ordered incrementally according to their sn values. The function insert($V_i, \langle v_k, sn_k\rangle$) places the new value in V_i according to the incremental order and, if there are more than three values, it discards from V_i the value associated to the lowest sn.
- $cured_i$: boolean flag updated by the cured_state oracle. In particular, while considering the CAM model, such variable is set to true when s_i becomes aware of its cured state and it is reset during the algorithm when s_i becomes correct.
- $echo\_vals_i$ and $echo\_read_i$: two sets used to collect information propagated trough ECHO messages. The first one stores tuple $\langle j, \langle v, sn\rangle\rangle$ propagated by servers just after the mobile Byzantine agents moved, while the second stores the set of concurrently reading clients in order to notify cured servers and expedite termination of read().
- fw_vals_i: set variable storing a triple $\langle j, \langle v, sn\rangle\rangle$ meaning that server s_j forwarded a write message with value v and sequence number sn.
- $pending\_read_i$: set variable used to collect identifiers of the clients that are currently reading.

In order to simplify the code of the algorithm, let us define the following functions:

- select_three_pairs_max_sn($echo\_vals_i$): this function takes as input the set $echo\_vals_i$ and returns, if they exist, three tuples $\langle v, sn\rangle$, such that there exist at least $2f+1$ occurrences in $echo\_vals_i$ of such tuple. If more than three of such tuple exist, the function returns the tuples with the highest sequence numbers. Otherwise if there are two tuples, the third tuple returned is $\langle \bot, 0\rangle$.
- select_value($reply_i$): this function takes as input the $reply_i$ set of replies collected by client c_i and returns the pair $\langle v, sn\rangle$ occurring at least $\#reply_{CAM}$ times (see Table 1). If there are more pairs satisfying such condition, it returns the one with the highest sequence number.

The maintenance() operation. Such operation is executed by servers periodically at any time $T_i = t_0 + i\Delta$.

If a server s_i is not in a cured state then it broadcasts an ECHO message carrying the set V_i and the set $pending\_read_i$ (it contains identifiers of clients that are currently running a read() operation). Moreover if in V_i there are no $\langle \bot, 0\rangle$ values then it empties the fw_vals_i and $echo\_vals_i$ sets, meaning that it is not trying to retrieve a value lost because s_i was affected by a Byzantine agent while such value has been written.

Otherwise, if a server s_i is in a cured state it first cleans its local variables and then, after δ time units, tries to update its state by checking the number of occurrences of each pair $\langle v, sn\rangle$ received with ECHO messages. In particular, it updates V_i invoking the select_three_pairs_max_sn($echo\_vals_i$) function that populates V_i with three or at least two tuples $\langle v, sn\rangle$. If there are only two tuple $\langle v, sn\rangle$, it means that there exists a concurrent write() operation that is updating the register value concurrently with the maintenance() operation. Thus, s_i considers $\langle \bot, 0\rangle$ as the pair associated to the value that is concurrently written. Finally, it assigns false to $cured_i$, meaning that it is now correct and starts replying to clients that are currently reading.

The write() operation. When the writer wants to write a value v, it increments its sequence number csn and propagates v and csn to all servers. Then it waits for δ time units (the maximum message transfer delay) before returning.

When a server s_i delivers a WRITE, it updates its local variables and forwards the message, trough a WRITE_FW(i, $\langle v, csn\rangle$), to others servers. This prevents the message loss in case servers deliver such message while they are affected by mobile Byzantine agents. In addition, it also sends a REPLY() message to all clients that are currently reading (clients in $pending\_read_i$) to allow them to terminate their read() operation.

When s_i delivers a WRITE_FW($j, \langle v, csn\rangle$) message, it stores such message in fw_vals_i set. Such set is constantly monitored together with $echo\_vals_i$ set to find a couple $\langle v, sn\rangle$ occurring at least $\#reply_{CAM}$ times. This continuous check

Table 1: Parameters for $\mathcal{P}_{Rreg}$ Protocol.

	n_{CAM}	$\#reply_{CAM}$
$k\Delta \geq 2\delta$, $k \in \{1,2\}$	$\geq (k+3)f+1$	$(k+1)f+1$
$k=1$	$4f+1$	$2f+1$
$k=2$	$5f+1$	$3f+1$

```
operation maintenance() executed every T_i = t_0 + Δ_i :
    cured_i ← report_cured_state();
    if (cured_i) then
        V_i ← ∅; echo_vals_i ← ∅; echo_read_i ← ∅;
        wait(δ);
        insert(V_i, select_three_pairs_max_sn(echo_vals_i));
        cured_i ← false;
        for each (j ∈ (pending_read_i ∪ echo_read_i)) do
                send REPLY (i, V_i) to c_j;
        endFor
    else
            broadcast ECHO(i, V_i, pending_read_i);
            if(∄⟨⊥, 0⟩ ∈ V_i)then
                fw_vals_i ← ∅; echo_vals_i ← ∅;
            endif
endif
---------------------------------------------------------------
when ECHO (j, V_j, pr) is received:
    echo_vals_i ← echo_vals_i ∪ V_j;
    echo_read_i ← echo_read_i ∪ pr;
```

Figure 5: $\mathcal{A}_M$ algorithm implementing the maintenance() operation (code for server s_i) in the $(\Delta S, CAM)$ model.

enables servers in a cured state to store the new value and reply to a reading client as soon as possible even in case they delivered such value when affected by mobile Byzantine agents.

The read() operation. When a client wants to read, it broadcasts a READ() request to all servers and waits 2δ time (i.e., one round trip delay) to collect replies. When it is unblocked from the wait statement, it selects a value v invoking the select_value function on $reply_i$ set, sends an acknowledgement message to servers to inform that its operation is now terminated and returns v as result of the operation.

When a server s_i delivers a READ(j) message from client c_j it first puts its identifier in the set $pending\_read_i$ to remember that c_j is reading and needs to receive possible concurrent updates, then s_i checks if it is in a cured state and if not, it sends a reply back to c_j. Note that, the REPLY() message carries the set V_i, which contains three tuples $\langle value, ts\rangle$ or two tuples $\langle value, ts\rangle$ and one $\langle \bot, 0\rangle$.

The last case occurs if s_i was affected by a Byzantine agent when the last write() operation occurred so that s_i is still retrieving such value. As soon as s_i retrieve such value through the fw_vals_i and $echo\_vals_i$ sets, such value is sent back to c_j.

In any case, s_i forwards a READ_FW message to inform other servers about c_j read request. This is useful in case some server missed the READ(j) message as it was affected by mobile Byzantine agent when such message has been delivered.

When a READ_FW(j) message is delivered, c_j identifier is added to $pending\_read_i$ set, as when the read request is just received from the client.

When a READ_ACK(j) message is delivered, c_j identifier is removed from both $pending\_read_i$ and $echo\_read_i$ sets as it does not need anymore to receive updates for the current read() operation.

```
operation read():
    reply_i ← ∅;
    broadcast READ(i);
    wait (2δ);
    ⟨v, sn⟩ ← select_value(reply_i);
    broadcast READ_ACK(i);
    return v;
---------------------------------------------------------------
when REPLY (j, V_j) is received:
    for each (⟨v, sn⟩ ∈ V_j) do
            reply_i ← reply_i ∪ {⟨j, ⟨v, sn⟩⟩};
    endFor
```

(a) Client code (code for client c_i).

```
when READ (j) is received:
    pending_read_i ← pending_read_i ∪ {j};
    if (¬cured_i)
      then send REPLY (i, V_i);
    endif
    broadcast READ_FW(j);
---------------------------------------------------------------
when READ_FW (j) is received:
    pending_read_i ← pending_read_i ∪ {j};
---------------------------------------------------------------
when READ_ACK (j) is received:
    pending_read_i ← pending_read_i \ {j};
    echo_read_i ← echo_read_i \ {j};
```

(b) Server code (code for server s_i).

Figure 7: $\mathcal{A}_R$ algorithm implementing the read() operation in the $(\Delta S, CAM)$ model.

5.2 Correctness Proofs

We report here only the statement of the main Lemmas and Theorems. Complete proofs can be found in [5].

LEMMA 1. *If a correct client c_i invokes* write(v) *operation at time t then this operation terminates at time $t+\delta$.*

LEMMA 2. *If a correct client c_i invokes* read() *operation at time t then this operation terminates at time $t+2\delta$.*

```
operation write(v):
  csn ← csn + 1;
  broadcast WRITE(v, csn);
  wait (δ);
  return write_confirmation;
```

(a) Client code (code for client c_i).

```
when WRITE(v, csn) is received:
  insert(V_i, ⟨v, csn⟩);
  for each j ∈ (pending_read_i ∪ echo_read_i) do
      send REPLY (i, {⟨v, csn⟩});
  endFor
  broadcast WRITE_FW(i, ⟨v, csn⟩);
---------------------------------------------------------------
when WRITE_FW(j, ⟨v, csn⟩) is received:
  fw_vals_i ← fw_vals_i ∪ {⟨j, ⟨v, csn⟩⟩};
---------------------------------------------------------------
when ∃⟨j, ⟨v, sn⟩⟩ ∈ (fw_vals_i ∪ echo_vals_i) occurring at least #reply_CAM times:
  insert(V_i, ⟨v, sn⟩);
  ∀j : fw_vals_i ← fw_vals_i \ {⟨j, ⟨v, ts⟩⟩};
  ∀j : echo_vals_i ← echo_vals_i \ {⟨j, ⟨v, ts⟩⟩};
  for each (j ∈ (pending_read_i ∪ echo_read_i)) do
          send REPLY (i, {⟨v, sn⟩}) to c_j;
  endFor
```

(b) Server code (code for server s_i).

Figure 6: $\mathcal{A}_W$ algorithm implementing the write(v) operation in the $(\Delta S, CAM)$ model.

THEOREM 3 (TERMINATION). *If a correct client c_i invokes an operation, c_i returns from that operation in finite time.*

LEMMA 3. *Let op be a* write(v) *operation invoked by a correct client at time t. Any $s_j \in Co([t, t+\delta])$ has v in V_j at time $t+\delta$.*

LEMMA 4. *If* (i) $k\Delta \geq 2\delta$ *(with $k \in \{1,2\}$), and* (ii) $n_{CAM} \geq (k+3)f+1$ *, then at time $T_2 - 1$ (where $T_2 - 1 = t_0 + 2\Delta - 1$) there exists at least $(k+1)f+1$ correct servers storing locally a valid value v (i.e., $v \in VVS(T_2 - 1)$).*

LEMMA 5. *If* (i) $k\Delta \geq 2\delta$ *(with $k \in \{1,2\}$), and* (ii) $n_{CAM} \geq (k+3)f+1$ *, then at time $T_i - 1$ (where $T_i - 1 = t_0 + i\Delta - 1$) there exists at least $(k+1)f+1$ correct servers storing locally a valid value v (i.e., $v \in VVS(T_i - 1)$).*

COROLLARY 1. *If* (i) $k\Delta \geq 2\delta$ *(with $k \in \{1,2\}$), and* (ii) $n_{CAM} \geq (k+3)f+1$ *, then there always exist at least $(k+1)f+1$ correct servers storing locally a valid value v (i.e., $v \in VVS(T_i - 1)$).*

COROLLARY 2. *If* (i) $k\Delta \geq 2\delta$ *(with $k \in \{1,2\}$), and* (ii) $n_{CAM} \geq (k+3)f+1$ *, then each server that became cured at T_i, at $T_i + \delta$ has at least one valid value.*

LEMMA 6. *Let op be a* read() *operation issued at time t and terminating at time $t+2\delta$. Let $Max\tilde{B}(t, t+2\delta)$ be the maximum number of servers that can be faulty for at least one time unit in the interval $[t, t+2\delta]$. If* (i) $k\Delta \geq 2\delta$ *(with $k \in \{1,2\}$), and* (ii) $n_{CAM} \geq (k+3)f+1$*, then $|Co(t+\delta)| > Max\tilde{B}(t, t+2\delta)$.*

COROLLARY 3. *Let op be a* read() *operation issued at time t and terminating at time $t+2\delta$. The number of replies carrying valid values at some time $\tau \in [t, t+2\delta]$ is always greater than the number of replies carrying non valid values.*

THEOREM 4 (VALIDITY). *If* (i) $k\Delta \geq 2\delta$ *(where $k \in \{1,2\}$), and* (ii) $n_{CAM} \geq (k+3)f+1$*, then any* read() *operation returns the last value written before its invocation, or a value written by a* write() *operation concurrent with it.*

THEOREM 5. *Let n be the number of servers emulating the register and let f be the number of Byzantine agents in the $(\Delta S, CAM)$ round-free Mobile Byzantine Failure model. Let δ be the upper bound on the communication latencies in the synchronous system. If* (i) $k\Delta \geq 2\delta$ *(with $k \in 1, 2$), and* (ii) $n \geq (k+3)f+1$*, then $\mathcal{P}_{reg}$ implements a SWMR Regular Register in the $(\Delta S, CAM)$ round-free Mobile Byzantine Failure model.*

6. CONCLUSION

This paper addressed the problem of emulating multi-reader regular registers under the MBF adversarial model for round-free computations. We first formalized MBF adversarial model in order to capture dynamic failures in generic (round-free) distributed computations and then we studied solvability issues raised by this powerful adversary. In particular, we proved that in the presence of mobile Byzantine agents a new operation, namely *maintenance*() must be defined. Then, we proved that in asynchronous distributed systems it is not possible to emulate a safe or regular register even in the presence of one Byzantine agent governed by the weakest $(\Delta S, CAM)$ adversary. We then considered the case of round-free synchronous systems and we proved that an emulation of an optimal regular register is possible against $(\Delta S, CAM)$ adversary provided that, $n_{CAM} \geq 4f+1$ if $2\delta \leq \Delta < 3\delta$ and $n_{CAM} \geq 5f+1$ if $\delta \leq \Delta < 2\delta$. The extension of the current reported results to the $(\Delta S, CUM)$ model is provided in [5]. We currently are investigating the solvability of other distributed building blocks under the proposed models.

Acknowledgements

The authors would like to thank Francois Bonnet and Marc Shapiro for their comments and suggestions on a previous version of this paper. For Italian authors, this work is partially supported by the Ateneo 2015 project (grant n. C26A157FBX) and by the EURASIA project.

7. REFERENCES

[1] N. Banu, S. Souissi, T. Izumi, and K. Wada. An improved byzantine agreement algorithm for synchronous systems with mobile faults. *International Journal of Computer Applications*, 43(22):1–7, April 2012.

[2] Rida A. Bazzi. Synchronous byzantine quorum systems. *Distributed Computing*, 13(1):45–52, January 2000.

[3] François Bonnet, Xavier Défago, Thanh Dang Nguyen, and Maria Potop-Butucaru. Tight bound on mobile byzantine agreement. In *Distributed Computing - 28th International Symposium, DISC 2014, Austin, TX, USA, October 12-15, 2014. Proceedings*, pages 76–90, 2014.

[4] Silvia Bonomi, Antonella Del Pozzo, and Maria Potop-Butucaru. Tight self-stabilizing mobile byzantine-tolerant atomic register. In *Proceedings of the 17th International Conference on Distributed Computing and Networking*, ICDCN '16, pages 6:1–6:10, Singapore, January 2016. ACM.

[5] Silvia Bonomi, Antonella Del Pozzo, Maria Potop-Butucaru, and Sébastien Tixeuil. Optimal mobile byzantine fault tolerant distributed storage. *(Available on line on arXiv)*, 2016.

[6] H. Buhrman, J. A. Garay, and J.-H. Hoepman. Optimal resiliency against mobile faults. In *Proceedings of the 25th International Symposium on Fault-Tolerant Computing (FTCS'95)*, pages 83–88, 1995.

[7] J. A. Garay. Reaching (and maintaining) agreement in the presence of mobile faults. In *Proceedings of the 8th International Workshop on Distributed Algorithms*, volume 857, pages 253–264, 1994.

[8] Leslie Lamport. On interprocess communication. part i: Basic formalism. *Distributed Computing*, 1(2):77–85, 1986.

[9] Dahlia Malkhi and Michael Reiter. Byzantine quorum systems. *Distributed Computing*, 11(4):203–213, October 1998.

[10] Jean-Philippe Martin, Lorenzo Alvisi, and Michael Dahlin. Minimal byzantine storage. In *Proceedings of the 16th International Conference on Distributed Computing*, DISC '02, pages 311–325, London, UK, UK, 2002. Springer-Verlag.

[11] Jean-Philippe Martin, Lorenzo Alvisi, and Michael Dahlin. Small byzantine quorum systems. In *Dependable Systems and Networks, 2002. DSN 2002. Proceedings. International Conference on*, pages 374–383. IEEE, 2002.

[12] R. Ostrovsky and M. Yung. How to withstand mobile virus attacks (extended abstract). In *Proceedings of the 10th Annual ACM Symposium on Principles of Distributed Computing (PODC'91)*, pages 51–59, 1991.

[13] R. Reischuk. A new solution for the byzantine generals problem. *Information and Control*, 64(1-3):23–42, January-March 1985.

[14] T. Sasaki, Y. Yamauchi, S. Kijima, and M. Yamashita. Mobile byzantine agreement on arbitrary network. In *Proceedings of the 17th International Conference on Principles of Distributed Systems (OPODIS'13)*, pages 236–250, December 2013.

[15] Fred B. Schneider. Implementing fault-tolerant services using the state machine approach: A tutorial. *ACM Computing Surveys*, 22(4):299–319, December 1990.

[16] Paulo Sousa, Alysson Neves Bessani, Miguel Correia, Nuno Ferreira Neves, and Paulo Verissimo. Highly available intrusion-tolerant services with proactive-reactive recovery. *IEEE Transactions on Parallel & Distributed Systems*, (4):452–465, 2009.

A Markov Chain Algorithm for Compression in Self-Organizing Particle Systems *

Sarah Cannon[†]
Georgia Institute of Technology
Atlanta, GA, USA
sarah.cannon@gatech.edu

Joshua J. Daymude[‡]
Arizona State University
Tempe, AZ, USA
jdaymude@asu.edu

Dana Randall[§]
Georgia Institute of Technology
Atlanta, GA, USA
randall@cc.gatech.edu

Andréa W. Richa[‡]
Arizona State University
Tempe, AZ, USA
aricha@asu.edu

ABSTRACT

We consider programmable matter as a collection of simple computational elements (or *particles*) with limited (constant-size) memory that self-organize to solve system-wide problems of movement, configuration, and coordination. Here, we focus on the *compression* problem, in which the particle system gathers as tightly together as possible, as in a sphere or its equivalent in the presence of some underlying geometry. More specifically, we seek fully distributed, local, and asynchronous algorithms that lead the system to converge to a configuration with small perimeter. We present a Markov chain based algorithm that solves the compression problem under the *geometric amoebot model*, for particle systems that begin in a connected configuration with no holes. The algorithm takes as input a bias parameter λ, where $\lambda > 1$ corresponds to particles favoring inducing more lattice triangles within the particle system. We show that for all $\lambda > 5$, there is a constant $\alpha > 1$ such that at stationarity with all but exponentially small probability the particles are α-*compressed*, meaning the perimeter of the system configuration is at most $\alpha \cdot p_{min}$, where p_{min} is the minimum possible perimeter of the particle system. We additionally prove that the same algorithm can be used for *expansion* for small values of λ; in particular, for all $0 < \lambda < \sqrt{2}$, there is a constant $\beta < 1$ such that at stationarity, with all but an exponentially small probability, the perimeter will be at least $\beta \cdot p_{max}$, where p_{max} is the maximum possible perimeter.

Keywords

Self-organizing Particles; Compression; Markov Chains

1. INTRODUCTION

Many programmable matter systems have recently been proposed and realized—modular and swarm robotics, synthetic biology, DNA tiling, and smart materials form an incomplete list—and each is often tailored toward a specific task or physical setting. In our work on self-organizing particle systems, we abstract away from specific settings and instead describe programmable matter as a collection of simple computational elements (to be referred to as *particles*) with limited computational power that each perform fully distributed, local, asynchronous algorithms to solve system-wide problems such as movement, configuration, and coordination. Here we present an algorithm for *compression*, in which the particle system gathers as tightly together as possible, as in a sphere or its equivalent in the presence of some underlying geometry. This phenomenon is often found in natural systems: fire ants form floating rafts by gathering in such a manner, and honey bees communicate foraging patterns within their hives. While each individual ant or bee cannot view the group as a whole when soliciting information, it can take cues from its immediate neighbors to achieve cooperation. It is with this motivation that we present a distributed algorithm for compression in the amoebot model derived from a Markov chain process.

In the (geometric) amoebot model, more formally defined in Section 2.1, particles with limited computational power move among the vertices of the triangular lattice Γ (Figure 1(a)) by traveling along the edges of Γ. The *compression problem* seeks to reorganize the configuration of a particle system (via movements of particles) such that the system converges to a configuration with small perimeter, where we measure the perimeter of a configuration by the length of the walk along its boundary. We say a particle system is α-*compressed*, for $\alpha > 1$, if the perimeter of the particle configuration is at most α times the minimum possible perimeter for those particles.

---

*A full version of this paper, including omitted proofs, is available at www.arxiv.org/abs/1603.07991.

†Supported in part by NSF DGE-1148903 and a grant from the Simons Foundation (#361047 to Sarah Cannon)

‡Supported in part by NSF awards CCF-1353089, CCF-1422603, and REU-026935.

§Supported in part by NSF grant CCF-1526900.

PODC'16, July 25-28, 2016, Chicago, IL, USA
© 2016 ACM. ISBN 978-1-4503-3964-3/16/07...$15.00
DOI: http://dx.doi.org/10.1145/2933057.2933107

1.1 Our results and techniques

We present a *Markov chain* $\mathcal{M}$ for particle compression under the geometric amoebot model that can be directly translated into a *fully distributed, local, asynchronous compression algorithm* $\mathcal{A}$. Both $\mathcal{A}$ and $\mathcal{M}$ take as input a *bias parameter* λ (where $\lambda > 1$ makes induced lattice triangles more favorable) and start from an arbitrary initial configuration for the particles that is connected and has no holes.

Markov chain $\mathcal{M}$ is carefully designed according to the distributed and local nature of the system, so that the particles always stay connected and no holes form. Furthermore, we prove $\mathcal{M}$ is *reversible and ergodic*, meaning many of the standard tools of Markov chain analysis can be applied. While most of these proofs rely only on first principles, we emphasize they are far from trivial; working in a distributed setting necessitated carefully defined protocols for local moves that made proofs challenging.[1]

When the particles execute the local moves of $\mathcal{M}$ (by running $\mathcal{A}$) for long enough, the configuration of the particles converges to the stationary distribution of $\mathcal{M}$. We prove for all large enough λ there is a constant $\alpha = \alpha(\lambda) > 1$ such that at stationarity, with all but exponentially small probability, the particles are *α-compressed*, meaning the perimeter of the particle configuration is at most α times the minimum perimeter (which is $\Theta(\sqrt{n})$ for systems of n particles). We additionally show the counterintuitive result that $\lambda > 1$ is not enough to guarantee compression. In fact, for all $0 < \lambda < \sqrt{2}$, there is a constant $\beta < 1$ such that at stationarity with all but exponentially small probability the perimeter is at least a β fraction of the maximum perimeter, which is $\Theta(n)$ for systems of n particles. We call such a configuration *β-expanded*. This implies that for any $0 < \lambda < \sqrt{2}$, the probability that the particles are α-compressed is exponentially small for any constant α.

The motivation underlying the design of this Markov chain is from statistical physics, where ensembles of particles reminiscent of our amoebot model are used to study physical systems. Like a spring relaxing, systems tend to favor configurations that minimize energy. The energy function is determined by a *Hamiltonian* $H(\sigma)$; each configuration σ has weight $w(\sigma) = e^{-B \cdot H(\sigma)}/Z$, where where $B = 1/T$ is inverse temperature and $Z = \sum_{\tau} e^{-B \cdot H(\tau)}$ is the normalizing constant known as the *partition function*.

In our amoebot model, we assign each configuration σ a Hamiltonian $H(\sigma) = -t(\sigma)$, where $t(\sigma)$ is the number of triangles in σ, i.e., the number of faces of the triangle lattice Γ with all three vertices occupied by particles. Setting $\lambda = e^B$, we get $w(\sigma) = \lambda^{t(\sigma)}$. As λ gets larger (by increasing B, effectively lowering temperature), we favor configurations with a large number of occupied triangles, causing increasingly compressed configurations. Favoring edges with both endpoints occupied is an alternative metric we could consider, but we prove for connected configurations on Γ without holes the two measures are equivalent. Likewise, favoring shorter perimeter is a third equivalent representation.

The key tool used to establish compression is a careful *Peierls argument*, used in statistical physics to study nonuniqueness of limiting Gibbs measures and determining the presence of phase transitions (see, e.g., [9]), and in computer science to establish slow mixing of Markov chains (see, e.g., [2]). For standard Peierls arguments, configurations typically are not required to be connected and can have holes. Here, we focus on the connected a0nd hole-free model to show compression can be achieved, even in an asynchronous distributed system where particles have constant-size memory and use only local information.

1.2 Related Work

Our algorithm is derived from a carefully designed Markov chain, enabling us to provide provable guarantees of its behavior. Random particle processes on the grid with hard constraints (e.g., *simple exclusion processes* where no two particles can occupy the same location) have been studied in statistical physics, but we want results under the further constraints of distributed computing. Our work exploits the memoryless, stochastic nature of Markov chains to accomplish particle compression in the amoebot model, just one of many distributed physical systems where compression-type problems have been studied.

When considering physical systems and models, one can differentiate between active and passive systems. Particles in passive systems have no explicit control over their movements, and in some cases do not have any computational power. One example is the DNA self-assembly work described in [19], where strands of DNA gather together to form larger structures with certain patterns.

In active systems, particles have control over their behavior and—depending on the model—can achieve some directed locomotion. *Swarm robotics* is one example; different variations of shape formation and collection problems have been studied (e.g. [11, 17]), but always with more computational power or global knowledge of the system. Similarly, pattern formation and creation of convex structures has been studied in the *cellular automata* domain (e.g. [4, 8]), but differs from our model by assuming more powerful computational capabilities. The *nubot* model [20] addresses a framework for biomolecular-inspired models which—although allowing some non-local movements—provides additional ways to create two dimensional shapes in polylogarithmic time.

Nature offers a variety of examples in which gathering and cooperative behavior is apparent. For example, social insects often exhibit compression-like characteristics in their collective behavior: fire ants form floating rafts [15], cockroach larvae perform self-organizing aggregation [13, 16], and honey bees choose hive locations based on a decentralized process of swarming and recruitment [3].

The rendezvous (or gathering) problem seeks to gather mobile agents together on some node of a graph (see e.g. [1] and the references within). In comparison, our particles follow the exclusion principle, and hence would not be able to gather at a single node, and are computationally simpler than the mobile agents considered.

Lastly, in [5, 6], algorithms for hexagon shape formation in the amoebot model were presented. Although a hexagon satisfies a compressed configuration as we define here, the Markov chain-based algorithm we present takes a fully decentralized and local approach. This is naturally self-stabilizing, forgoing the need for a seed particle that may coordinate or initiate some underlying organization of the set of particles, as required in [5] and even more critically in [6].

[1]Due to length constraints some proofs were omitted.

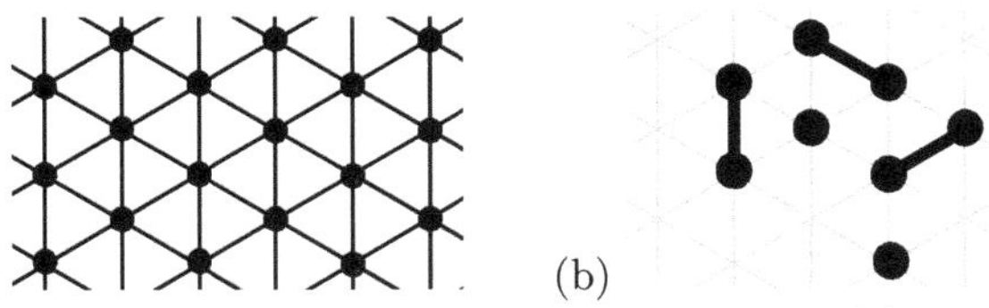

Figure 1: (a) A section of the triangular lattice Γ; (b) expanded particles (each denoted by its two occupied adjacent locations in Γ and a thick line in between) and contracted particles (occupying one location).

2. BACKGROUND AND MODEL

We begin with the geometric amoebot model for programmable matter. We then define some properties of particle systems and discuss what it means for a particle system to be compressed. We conclude with an overview of Markov chains, which form the basis for our algorithm for compression to be presented in Section 3.

2.1 The Amoebot Model

In the *amoebot model* [7], programmable matter consists of particles whose properties we now detail. An infinite undirected graph $G = (V, E)$ represents the set of relative locations that the particles can occupy (given by V) and the set of all possible atomic transitions between locations in V (given by E) [7]. We further assume the *geometric* variant of the amoebot model, which imposes an underlying geometric structure $G = \Gamma$, where Γ is the *triangular lattice* shown in Figure 1(a) (also called the infinite regular triangular grid graph, and denoted by G_{eqt} in earlier work).

Each particle occupies either a single location (i.e., it is *contracted*) or a pair of two adjacent locations on the graph (i.e., it is *expanded*); Figure 1(b) illustrates expanded and contracted particles on Γ. Each location can be occupied by at most one particle. Particles achieve movement via a series of *expansions* and *contractions*: a contracted particle may expand into an adjacent unoccupied location to become expanded, and completes its movement by contracting to once again occupy only one location.

Two particles occupying adjacent nodes are said to be connected by a bond (and hence induce an *edge* in the particle system), and we refer to them as *neighbors*. Particles are *anonymous*, but can uniquely identify each one of their (six) possible bonds and check which bonds lead to nodes occupied by neighboring particles. Additionally, the particles do not share any global orientation or coordinate system.

Every particle has a constant-size, shared, local memory which both it and its neighbors can read and write to for communication. Because of the limitation on memory size, particles cannot know neither the total size of the system nor an estimate of it. Particles execute a sequence of *atomic actions*, in each of which they do some local computation (in our case, those may involve checking which of its adjacent locations are occupied with particles) and an expansion or contraction. We assume a fully asynchronous system, where particles perform atomic actions concurrently and at different, possibly variable speeds; conflicts, which in our context arise when two particles attempt to expand into the same location, are resolved in an arbitrary manner. In order to analyze such systems, we use the standard asynchronous model from distributed computing, allowing us to evaluate the progress of the system through a sequential series of individual *particle activations*, where every time a particle is activated, it performs an atomic action.

2.2 Terminology for Particle Systems

First, we introduce notation and terminology that will be used throughout this paper. We call the collection of locations in Γ that are occupied by particles an *arrangement*; note two arrangements are the same even if particles occupy different locations within the arrangement. We can define an equivalence relation on arrangements, where two arrangements are equivalent if one is a translation of the other. We define a *configuration* to be an equivalence class of arrangements. If configuration σ is a rotation of configuration τ, we still consider σ and τ to be distinct configurations. That is, for the purpose of monitoring the particle system we maintain a global orientation of the particles, even though each individual particle has no sense of global orientation.

We will let capital letters refer to particles and lower case letters refer to locations on the triangular lattice Γ, e.g., "particle P at location ℓ." For a particle P (resp., location ℓ), we use $N(P)$ (resp., $N(\ell)$) to denote the set of particles adjacent to P (resp., to ℓ), where by *adjacent* we mean connected by a lattice edge. Similarly, for a particle P (resp., location ℓ), we will use $n(P)$ (resp., $n(\ell)$) to denote the six locations in the neighborhood of P (resp., of ℓ). For locations ℓ and ℓ', by $N(\ell \cup \ell')$ we mean $(N(\ell) \cup N(\ell')) \setminus \{\ell, \ell'\}$; the same holds for $n(\ell \cup \ell')$.

By an *edge* or *triangle* of a configuration σ we mean, respectively, an edge or face of Γ such that all (respectively, two or three) incident vertices are occupied by particles. The number of edges of σ is $e(\sigma)$ and the number of triangles is $t(\sigma)$. Throughout, by a *path* or a *cycle* we mean a path or cycle in the underlying graph Γ where all vertices are occupied by particles, and in the case of a cycle, at least one location inside the cycle is unoccupied. Two particles are *connected* if there exists a path between them, and a configuration is *connected* if all pairs of particles are. A *hole* in a configuration is a maximal finite component of adjacent unoccupied locations. We specifically consider connected configurations with no holes, and our algorithm, if starting at such a configuration, will maintain these properties.

2.3 Compression of Particle Systems

Our objective is to find a solution to the particle compression problem. There are many ways to formalize what it means for a particle system to be *compressed*. For example, one could try to minimize the diameter of the system, maximize the number of edges, or maximize the number of triangles. We choose to define compression in terms of minimizing the *perimeter*. We prove for connected configurations with no holes, minimizing perimeter, maximizing the number of edges, and maximizing the number of triangles are all equivalent and are stronger notions of compression than minimizing the diameter.

For a connected configuration σ of n particles with no holes, the *perimeter* of σ, denoted $p(\sigma)$, is the length of the walk around the (single external) boundary of the particles. In an abuse of notation, we use the term *perimeter* to refer both to the length $p(\sigma)$ of this walk and the walk itself. We assume any walk $\mathcal{W}$ along the perimeter of a configuration is in the clockwise direction. For a walk $\mathcal{W}$ in Γ with some notion of direction, we say location ℓ is *left* of edge $e = \overrightarrow{st} \in \mathcal{W}$ traversed from s to t if ℓ, s and t are the vertices of a triangular face of Γ with ℓ the next vertex counterclockwise around this face from t. With this terminology, every edge traversed in a clockwise walk $\mathcal{W}$ along the perimeter of σ has an unoccupied location to its left. Specifically, for any consecutive particles A, B, C in $\mathcal{W}$, the locations in the clockwise span of $n(B)$ from A to C are always unoccupied and there is at least one of them. Note an edge may appear twice in a perimeter walk $\mathcal{W}$; in this case, its length is counted twice in $p(\sigma)$. For a connected configuration of n particles without holes, the perimeter ranges from a maximum value of $2n-2$ when the particles are in their least compressed state (a tree with no induced triangles) to some minimum value $p_{min}(n) = \Theta(\sqrt{n})$ when the particles are in their most compressed state. It is easy to see $p_{min}(n) \leq 4\sqrt{n}$, and we now prove any configuration σ of n particles has $p(\sigma) \geq \sqrt{n}$; this bound is not tight but suffices for our proofs.

LEMMA 2.1. *A connected configuration with $n \geq 2$ particles and no holes has perimeter at least $\sqrt{n}$.*

PROOF. We argue by induction on n. A particle system with two particles necessarily has perimeter $2 \geq \sqrt{2}$, as claimed. Let σ be any particle configuration with n particles where $n > 2$, and suppose the lemma holds for all configurations with less than n particles.

First, suppose there is a particle $Q \in \sigma$ not incident to any triangles of σ. This implies Q has one, two, or three neighbors, none of which are adjacent. If Q has one neighbor, removing Q from σ yields a configuration σ' with $n-1$ particles and, by induction, perimeter at least $\sqrt{n-1}$. Thus

$$p(\sigma) = p(\sigma') + 2 \geq \sqrt{n-1} + 2 \geq \sqrt{n}.$$

If Q has two neighbors, removing Q from σ produces two connected particle configurations σ_1 and σ_2, where σ_1 has n_1 particles, σ_2 has n_2 particles, and $n_1 + n_2 = n - 1$. Thus

$$p(\sigma) \geq \sqrt{n_1} + \sqrt{n_2} + 4 > \sqrt{n-1} + 4 > \sqrt{n}.$$

Similarly, if Q has three neighbors its removal produces three particle configurations with n_1, n_2, and n_3 particles where $n_1 + n_2 + n_3 = n - 1$ and we conclude

$$p(\sigma) \geq \sqrt{n_1} + \sqrt{n_2} + \sqrt{n_3} + 6 > \sqrt{n}.$$

Now, suppose every particle in σ is incident to some triangle of σ, implying there are at least $n/3$ triangles in σ. An equilateral triangle with side length 1 has area $\sqrt{3}/4$, so the perimeter of σ encloses an area of at least $A = \sqrt{3}n/12$. By the isoperimetric inequality, the minimum perimeter way of enclosing this area, without regard to lattice constraints, is with a circle of radius r and perimeter p, where

$$r = \sqrt{\frac{A}{\pi}} = \sqrt{\frac{n\sqrt{3}}{12\pi}}, \quad p = 2\pi r = \sqrt{\frac{\pi n}{\sqrt{3}}} > \sqrt{n}.$$

As the perimeter of σ also encloses an area of at least $\sqrt{3}n/12$, it is of length at least $\sqrt{n}$. □

When n is clear from context we omit it and refer to $p_{min} = p_{min}(n)$ and $p_{max} = p_{max}(n)$. We now define what it means for a particle system to be compressed.

DEFINITION 2.2. *For any $\alpha > 1$, a connected configuration σ with no holes is α-compressed if $p(\sigma) \leq \alpha \cdot p_{min}$.*

We prove in Section 4 that our algorithm, when executed for a sufficiently long time, achieves α-compression with all but exponentially small probability for any constant $\alpha > 1$, provided n is sufficiently large. We note α-compression implies the diameter of the particle system is also $O(\sqrt{n})$, so our definition of α-compression is stronger than defining compression in terms of diameter.

In order to minimize perimeter using only simple local moves, we exploit the following relationship.

LEMMA 2.3. *For a connected particle configuration σ with no holes, $t(\sigma) = 2n - p(\sigma) - 2$.*

PROOF. We count particle-triangle incidences, of which there are $3t(\sigma)$. Counting another way, every particle has six incident triangles, except for those on the perimeter. Consider any traversal $\mathcal{W}$ of the perimeter; at each particle, the exterior angle is 120, 180, 240, 300, or 360 degrees. These correspond to the particle "missing" 2, 3, 4, 5, or 6 of its possible six incident triangles, or *degree*/60 missing triangles. If $\mathcal{W}$ visits the same particle multiple times, count the appropriate exterior angle at each visit. The sum of exterior angles along $\mathcal{W}$ is $180p(\sigma)+360$, so in total particles on the perimeter are missing $3p(\sigma)+6$ triangles. This implies $6n-3p(\sigma)-6$ particle-triangle incidences, so $3t(\sigma) = 6n - 3p(\sigma) - 6$. □

Minimizing perimeter is also equivalent to maximizing edges, as we now show.

LEMMA 2.4. *For a connected particle configuration σ with no holes, $e(\sigma) = 3n - p(\sigma) - 3$.*

PROOF. The proof is nearly identical to that of Lemma 2.3, counting particle-edge incidences instead. □

COROLLARY 2.5. *For a connected particle configuration σ with no holes, $t(\sigma) = e(\sigma) - (n-1)$.*

COROLLARY 2.6. *A connected particle configuration σ with no holes and minimum perimeter is also a configuration with the maximum number of triangles (and edges).*

2.4 Markov chains

The distributed protocol for particle compression we present is based on a Markov chain, i.e., a memoryless stochastic process defined on a finite set of states Ω. The transition matrix P on $\Omega \times \Omega \to [0,1]$ is defined so that $P(x,y)$ is the probability of moving from state x to state y in one step, for any pair $x, y \in \Omega$. The t-step transition probability $P^t(x,y)$ is the probability of moving from x to y in exactly t steps.

A Markov chain is *ergodic* if it is *irreducible*, i.e., for all $x, y \in \Omega$, there is a t such that $P^t(x,y) > 0$, and *aperiodic*, i.e., for all $x, y \in \Omega$, g.c.d.$\{t : P^t(x,y) > 0\} = 1$. Any finite, ergodic Markov chain converges to a unique distribution π, i.e., for all $x, y \in \Omega$, $\lim_{t\to\infty} P^t(x,y) = \pi(y)$. In fact, for any distribution π' such that $\pi'(x)P(x,y) = \pi'(y)P(y,x)$ (the *detailed balance condition*) and $\sum_{x\in\Omega} \pi'(x) = 1$, π' is the unique stationary distribution of $\mathcal{M}$ (see, e.g., [10]).

Given a desired stationary distribution π on Ω, the celebrated Metropolis-Hastings algorithm [12] defines appropriate transition probabilities. Starting at state x, pick a neighbor y in Ω uniformly with probability $1/(2\Delta)$, where Δ is the maximum number of neighbors of any state, and move to y with probability $\min(1, \pi(y)/\pi(x))$; with the remaining probability stay at x and repeat. Using detailed balance, one can verify if the state space is connected then π must be the stationary distribution. While calculating $\pi(x)/\pi(y)$ seems to require global knowledge, this ratio can often be calculated using only local information when many terms cancel out. In our case, the Metropolis probabilities are simply $\min(1, \lambda^{|t(y)-t(x)|})$; this difference is just the change in the number of triangles incident to the moving particle, which can be calculated with only local information.

3. ALGORITHMS FOR COMPRESSION

Our objective is to demonstrate how stochastic algorithms can provably achieve compression, focusing on self-organizing particle systems on the triangular lattice Γ. Our algorithm is based on Markov chain principles that will enable us to prove rigorous results about the algorithm's behavior. Remarkably, it does not even require the particles to communicate more than one bit of information to each other, even though the amoebot model allows for such exchanges; at any activation, a particle only needs to know which of its neighboring locations are occupied and if any of those neighbors are expanded.

Our algorithm carefully maintains several critical properties throughout its execution. First, the particle system stays connected and no holes form, even while particles decide where to move based only on local information. Additionally, any moves made are reversible: if a particle moves to a new location, there is a nonzero probability that during the next step, it moves back to its previous location. Finally, the moves allowed by the algorithm (and respective Markov chain) suffice to transform any configuration of particles into any other configuration. These conditions are essential so certain tools from Markov chain analysis can be applied.

In addition to the precise conditions needed to ensure connectivity and reversibility, our algorithm achieves compression by making particles more likely to move into a position where they form more triangles with their neighbors. Specifically, a bias parameter λ controls how strongly the particles favor being incident to triangles; $\lambda > 1$ corresponds to favoring triangles, while $\lambda < 1$ corresponds to disfavoring triangles. As Lemma 2.3 shows, locally favoring more triangles is equivalent to globally favoring a shorter perimeter; this is the relationship we exploit to obtain particle compression.

3.1 The Local Algorithm $\mathcal{A}$

We start with two key properties that enable a particle to move from location ℓ to location ℓ'. If ℓ and ℓ' are neighboring locations on Γ, let $\mathbb{S} = N(\ell) \cap N(\ell')$ be the set of particles adjacent to both ℓ and ℓ' (i.e., $|\mathbb{S}| = 0, 1,$ or 2).

PROPERTY 1. *$|\mathbb{S}| = 1$ or 2 and every particle in $N(\ell \cup \ell')$ is connected to a particle in $\mathbb{S}$ by a path through $N(\ell \cup \ell')$.*

PROPERTY 2. *$|\mathbb{S}| = 0$; ℓ and ℓ' each have at least one neighbor; all particles in $N(\ell) \setminus \{\ell'\}$ are connected by paths within this set; and all particles in $N(\ell') \setminus \{\ell\}$ are connected by paths within this set.*

These properties capture precisely the structure required to maintain particle connectivity and prevent holes from forming. Additionally, both are symmetric for ℓ and ℓ', necessary for reversibility. However, they are not so restrictive as to limit the movement of particles and prevent compression from occurring; we will see moves satisfying these properties suffice to transform any configuration into any other.

We now present the local asynchronous algorithm that each particle runs. Later we show how to view this algorithm through the lens of our Markov chain $\mathcal{M}$. Both $\mathcal{A}$ and $\mathcal{M}$ take as an input a bias parameter $\lambda > 1$, and begin in an arbitrary starting configuration σ_0 of contracted particles that is connected and has no holes.

Algorithm $\mathcal{A}$: Algorithm for compression run by particle P

If P is contracted:

1: Let ℓ denote P's current location.
2: Particle P chooses neighboring location ℓ' uniformly at random from the six possible choices, and generates a random number $q \in (0, 1)$.
3: **if** ℓ' is unoccupied and P has no expanded neighboring particle at ℓ **then**
4: P expands to simultaneously occupy ℓ and ℓ'.
5: **if** there are no expanded particles adj. to ℓ or ℓ' **then**
6: P sets $flag = TRUE$ in its local memory
7: **else** P sets $flag = FALSE$.

If P is expanded:

8: Let t be the number of triangles formed by P when it was contracted at its original location ℓ, and let t' be the number of triangles formed by P if it contracts at the location it expanded into, ℓ'.
9: **if** (1) location ℓ does not have five neighboring particles, (2) locations ℓ and ℓ' satisfy Property 1 or Property 2, (3) $q < \lambda^{t'-t}$, and (4) $flag = TRUE$ **then**
10: P contracts to ℓ'.
11: **else** P contracts back to ℓ.

Each particle P continuously runs Algorithm $\mathcal{A}$, executing Steps 1–7 if P is contracted, and Steps 8–11 if P is expanded. Note a constant number of random bits suffice to generate q, as only a constant precision is required (given that $t' - t$ is an integer in $[-6, 6]$ and λ is a constant). In Step 9, Condition (1) ensures no holes form; Condition (2) ensures the particles stay connected and the corresponding Markov chain $\mathcal{M}$ is reversible; Condition (3) ensures the moves happen with probabilities such that $\mathcal{M}$ converges to the desired distribution; and Condition (4) ensures P is the only particle in its neighborhood potentially moving to a new position, ℓ', since P last expanded. The claims regarding Conditions (1)–(3) pertain to the underlying Markov process and will be formalized in the next subsections. To understand why Condition (4) suffices to ensure P is the only particle (potentially) moving to a new location in its immediate neighborhood, note that once P expands, any other particle P' expanding into a position adjacent to P will contract back to its original position, since P' will set its own flag to FALSE in Step 7. We assume any conflicts arising from two particles attempting to concurrently move into the same location are resolved arbitrarily. Hence, any concurrent movements will cover pairwise disjoint neighborhoods and the respective actions will be mutually independent.

Following the classical asynchronous model [14], for any starting configuration σ_0, we have that for any concurrent execution of $\mathcal{A}$ that reaches a configuration σ, there is a sequential execution of the same atomic actions that also reaches σ, for all σ.

3.2 The Markov Chain $\mathcal{M}$

We now make explicit the Markov chain $\mathcal{M}$ corresponding to Algorithm $\mathcal{A}$. The state space of $\mathcal{M}$ is the set of all connected configurations of n contracted particles and no holes.

Transitions between states happen subject to the rules and probabilities we now present.

Beginning at any connected, hole-free configuration σ_0 of contracted particles, repeat:

1. Select particle P uniformly at random from among all particles; let ℓ be its location. Choose, uniformly at random, $\ell' \in n(\ell)$ and $q \in (0, 1)$.

2. **If** ℓ' is unoccupied, **then** P expands to simultaneously occupy ℓ and ℓ'; **Else** return to Step 1.

3. Let t be the number of triangles formed by P in position ℓ, and let t' be the number of triangles formed by P in position ℓ'.

4. **If** (1) location ℓ does not have five neighboring particles, (2) locations ℓ and ℓ' satisfy Property 1 or Property 2, and (3) $q < \lambda^{t'-t}$ **then** contract P to ℓ'.

5. **Else** contract P back to ℓ.

In $\mathcal{M}$, we have paired up the consecutive actions that a particle will take according to Algorithm $\mathcal{A}$ when contracted and then expanded into one state transition, so that a transition corresponds to the complete movement of exactly one (contracted) particle into a new (adjacent) location. Let P be a particle that eventually moves from location ℓ to ℓ' at some time t' according to an execution of $\mathcal{A}$. Condition (4) in Step 9 and the condition in Step 3 of $\mathcal{A}$ ensure that if P was activated and expanded at time t before being activated once again and contracting to occupy ℓ' at time $t' > t$, even if other particles are activated between t and t' no movement to a new location will occur in the neighborhood of P in that time interval. Hence all activations of other particles in the neighborhood of P in the interval (t, t') can be ignored, justifying the pairing of actions in the Markov chain $\mathcal{M}$.

For every sequential execution of atomic actions that leads to configuration σ' in $\mathcal{A}$, there exists a sequence of transitions in $\mathcal{M}$ that reaches a configuration σ such that σ can be obtained from σ' by preserving the locations of all contracted particles in σ' and by letting every expanded particle in σ' contract according to the rules of $\mathcal{A}$, for all corresponding pairs (σ', σ). Conversely, every sequence of transitions in $\mathcal{M}$ that reaches a configuration σ directly corresponds to a sequence of atomic actions in $\mathcal{A}$ also leading to $\sigma' = \sigma$. The perimeter of the respective σ' and σ differs by at most a constant factor, and hence proving α-compression for σ also implies α'-compression for σ', and vice-versa, for constants α and α'. Hence, we can use $\mathcal{M}$, and respective Markov chain tools and techniques, in order to analyze the correctness of algorithm $\mathcal{A}$.

We note that, under the assumptions of the asynchronous model of distributed computing, one cannot typically assume the next particle to be activated is equally likely to be any particle, as we assume in Step 1 of the description of $\mathcal{M}$. We make this assumption in order to be able to explicitly calculate the stationary distribution of $\mathcal{M}$ so that we can provide rigorous guarantees about its structure, but do not expect the behavior of the system would be substantially different if this requirement was relaxed.

To justify this random activation assumption, we note that random sequences of particle activations can be approximated using Poisson clocks with mean 1.[2] That is, each particle activates, and executes Algorithm $\mathcal{A}$, at a random real time drawn from the exponential distribution e^{-t}. After each action, the particle then computes another random time drawn from the same distribution e^{-t} and executes again after that amount of time has elapsed. The exponential distribution is unique in that, if particle P has just activated, it is equally likely that any particle will be the next particle to activate, including particle P (see, e.g., [10]). Moreover, the particles update without requiring knowledge of any of the other particles' clocks. Similar Poisson clocks are commonly used to describe physical systems that perform updates in parallel in continuous time.

3.3 Invariants for Markov chain $\mathcal{M}$

We begin by showing $\mathcal{M}$ maintains certain invariants. We prove Conditions (1) and (2) in Step 4 of Markov chain $\mathcal{M}$ ensure the particles remain in a connected configuration with no holes, provided they start in such a configuration.

LEMMA 3.1. *If the particles are initially connected, during the execution of Markov chain $\mathcal{M}$ they remain connected.*

PROOF. Consider one iteration of $\mathcal{M}$ where a particle P moves from location ℓ to location ℓ'. Let σ be the configuration before this move, and σ' the configuration after. We show if σ is connected, then so is σ'.

A move of particle P from ℓ to ℓ' occurs only if ℓ and ℓ' are adjacent and satisfy Property 1 or Property 2. First, suppose they satisfy Property 1. Let $P_1, P_2 \neq P$ be particles, and let $\mathcal{Q}$ be a path connecting them in σ. If $P \notin \mathcal{Q}$, then P_1 and P_2 remain connected by $\mathcal{Q}$ in σ'. If $P \in \mathcal{Q}$, let N_1 and N_2 be the two particles on path $\mathcal{Q}$ before and after P, respectively. By Property 1, there exist paths in $N(\ell \cup \ell')$ from N_1 to a particle $S_1 \in \mathbb{S}$ and from N_2 to a particle $S_2 \in \mathbb{S}$, possibly with $S_1 = S_2$. A (not necessarily simple) path from P_1 to P_2 in σ' is the union of $\mathcal{Q}$ from P_1 to N_1; the path from N_1 to S_1 in $N(\ell \cup \ell')$; if $S_1 \neq S_2$, the path from S_1 to P at location ℓ' to S_2; the path from S_2 to N_2 in $N(\ell \cup \ell')$; and $\mathcal{Q}$ from N_2 to P_2. As P is connected to $S_1 \in \mathbb{S}$ and by the above argument S_1 is connected to all other particles, we conclude P is connected to every other particle and thus σ' is connected.

Next, assume locations ℓ and ℓ' satisfy Property 2. Let $P_1, P_2 \neq P$ be particles; we show they are connected by a path not containing P. Path $\mathcal{Q}$ connecting P_1 and P_2 in σ exists, and suppose it contains P. Let N_1 and N_2 be the vertices on $\mathcal{Q}$ before and after P, respectively. Both N_1 and N_2 are neighbors of ℓ, and by Property 2 all neighbors of ℓ are connected by a path in $N(\ell)$. Thus $\mathcal{Q}$ can be augmented to form a (not necessarily simple) walk $\mathcal{Q}'$ by replacing P with a path from N_1 to N_2 in $N(\ell)$. As $P \notin \mathcal{Q}'$, this walk also connects P_1 and P_2 in σ'. Additionally, because ℓ' has at least one neighbor by Property 2, P remains connected to all other particles in σ' and thus σ' is connected. ☐

LEMMA 3.2. *If the particles begin in a connected configuration with no holes, during the execution of Markov chain $\mathcal{M}$ they will never form a configuration with a hole.*

PROOF. Recall we assume a *cycle* in σ encircles at least one unoccupied location; note a configuration has a hole if

[2]The analysis can be modified to accommodate each clock having its own constant mean; however, for the sake of ease of presentation, we assume here that they are all i.i.d.

and only if it has a cycle encircling that hole. Let σ be a particle configuration with particle P at location ℓ, and σ' the same configuration with P at neighboring location ℓ'. We assume σ has no cycles (i.e., no holes) and prove σ' has no cycles (i.e., no holes).

We first show if a cycle is introduced in σ', then P must be on that cycle. Suppose this is not the case and σ' has a cycle $\mathcal{C}$ with $P \notin \mathcal{C}$. If P is removed from location ℓ', $\mathcal{C}$ still exists. If P is then placed at ℓ, yielding σ, then $\mathcal{C}$ still exists unless it had enclosed exactly one unoccupied location, ℓ. However, this is not possible as any cycle in $\sigma' \setminus P$ encircling ℓ would also necessarily encircle neighboring unoccupied location ℓ'. This implies $\mathcal{C}$ is present in σ, a contradiction, so we conclude any cycle in σ' must contain P.

By the conditions in Step 4 of Markov chain $\mathcal{M}$ that must be met before a move occurs, particle P necessarily has fewer than five neighbors in σ and locations ℓ and ℓ' satisfy Property 1 or Property 2. First, suppose they satisfy Property 2. While P might momentarily create a cycle when it expands to occupy both locations ℓ and ℓ', it will then contract to location ℓ'. Suppose P is part of some cycle $\mathcal{C}$ in σ'. Before and after P on $\mathcal{C}$ are some neighbors N_1 and N_2 of P. By Property 2, N_1 and N_2 are connected by a path in $N(\ell')$, which doesn't contain P. Replacing path $N_1 - P - N_2$ in cycle $\mathcal{C}$ by this path in $N(\ell')$ yields a (not necessarily simple) cycle $\mathcal{C}'$ in σ' not containing P, a contradiction.

Suppose ℓ and ℓ' satisfy Property 1; recall location ℓ has less than five neighbors in σ. Suppose there exists a cycle $\mathcal{C}$ in σ', which by definition encircles at least one unoccupied location. If ℓ is unoccupied inside $\mathcal{C}$, then so is at least one of its neighbors; we conclude $\mathcal{C}$ encircles some unoccupied location $\ell'' \neq \ell$. Let N_1 and N_2 be the particles on cycle $\mathcal{C}$ before and after P. If there exists a path between N_1 and N_2 in $N(\ell')$, the argument in the previous paragraph applies, so we suppose this is not the case. It must be, without loss of generality, that $|\mathbb{S}| = 2$ and there exist paths in $N(\ell \cup \ell')$ from N_1 to $S_1 \in \mathbb{S}$ and from N_2 to $S_2 \in \mathbb{S}$, with $S_1 \neq S_2$. There then exists cycle $\mathcal{C}'$ in σ, obtained from $\mathcal{C}$ by replacing path $N_1 - P - N_2$, where P is in location ℓ', with the path $N_1 - ... - S_1 - P - S_2 - ... - N_2$, where P is in location ℓ. This is a valid (not necessarily simple) cycle in σ, as it still encircles unoccupied location $\ell'' \neq \ell$. This is also a contradiction, so in all cases we find σ' has no cycles. □

3.4 Ergodicity of Markov chain $\mathcal{M}$

We next show the carefully-defined moves of $\mathcal{M}$ suffice to move from any configuration σ to any other configuration τ, necessary for showing $\mathcal{M}$ is ergodic and thus has a unique stationary distribution.

We emphasize the details of this proof are far from trivial, and occupy ten pages in the full version of this paper*. Figure 2 illustrates one difficulty. It depicts a particle configuration for which there exist no valid moves satisfying Property 1; the only valid moves satisfy Property 2. Thus if moves satisfying Property 2 are not included, the state space of $\mathcal{M}$ is not connected. Our approach relies critically on moves satisfying Property 2.

Here we outline and explain our approach to proving $\mathcal{M}$ is ergodic. At a high level, we prove for any configuration σ there exists a sequence of valid particle moves transforming σ into a straight line, and then prove $\mathcal{M}$ is reversible, implying for any other configuration τ there exists a sequence of valid particle moves transforming that straight line into τ.

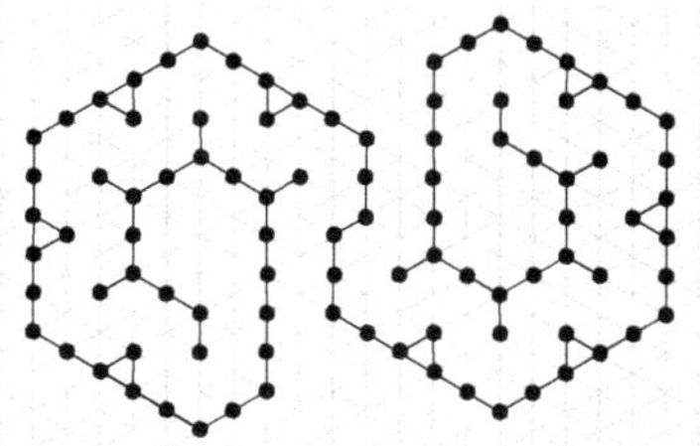

Figure 2: A particle configuration for which all valid moves of Markov chain $\mathcal{M}$ satisfy Property 2; no particle has a valid move satisfying Property 1 (darker lines represent induced edges of the system). This demonstrates the subtlety of the Markov chain rules we have defined.

Given a particle configuration σ with lowest leftmost particle S, we find a sequence of moves transforming σ into a line of particles stretching down and left from S; particle S never moves. We traverse the perimeter of σ, starting at S, finding particles which we can *eliminate*, or move to this line. We begin with a crucial definition.

Definition 3.3. *An unoccupied location ℓ in Γ is a gap of configuration σ if placing an additional particle P at ℓ results in a hole in configuration $\sigma \cup P$.*

Lemma 3.4. *There exists a sequence of particle moves transforming any configuration σ into a straight line.*

Proof. Traverse the perimeter of σ starting from lowest leftmost particle S. When possible, particles encountered move via a sequence of valid particle moves backwards along the perimeter to S, and then into a line stretching down and left from S, eliminating them. This is possible precisely when particles can move along the perimeter to S without ever occupying a gap location. We prove if $\mathcal{W}$ is the longest clockwise walk around the perimeter of σ starting at S that is not adjacent to any gaps, then it is possible to either eliminate one particle or execute a valid sequence of particle moves that lengthens walk $\mathcal{W}$. In fewer than $2n^2$ iterations, all particles are eliminated: a particle must be eliminated at least once every $2n$ steps, as the length of $\mathcal{W}$ can increase at most $p(\sigma) < 2n$ times in a row. After this, all particles form a straight line stretching down and left from S. □

We present one more lemma before proving $\mathcal{M}$ is irreducible. Recall $P(\sigma, \tau)$ is the probability of moving from configuration σ to state τ in one step of $\mathcal{M}$.

Lemma 3.5. *For any two configurations σ and τ in Ω, if $P(\sigma,\tau) > 0$, then $P(\tau,\sigma) > 0$.*

Proof. Let $\sigma, \tau \in \Omega$ be any two configurations such that $P(\sigma,\tau) > 0$. This means σ and τ differ by one particle P at location ℓ in σ and at adjacent location ℓ' in τ.

Note in τ, particle P at location ℓ' has at most four neighbors. This is because $l \in n(\ell')$ is unoccupied as particle P is instead at ℓ', and at least one other location in $n(\ell')$ is unoccupied as otherwise ℓ' would have been a hole in σ, impossible by Lemma 3.2. Because $P(\sigma,\tau) > 0$, Property 1 or Property 2 must hold for ℓ and ℓ'. Both properties are symmetric with regard to the role played by ℓ and ℓ'. If Markov chain $\mathcal{M}$, in state τ, selects in Step 1 particle P, location $\ell \in n(P)$, and a sufficiently small probability q, then because Conditions 1, 2, and 3 are necessarily satisfied, particle P moves to location ℓ. This proves $P(\tau,\sigma) > 0$. □

Lemma 3.6. *Markov chain $\mathcal{M}$ connects the state space of all connected configurations without holes.*

Proof. Let σ and τ be any two connected configurations of n particles with no holes. By Lemma 3.4, there exists a sequence of moves transforming σ into a line with slope $1/\sqrt{3}$. By Lemmas 3.4 and 3.5, there exists a sequence of valid moves transforming this line into τ. $\square$

Corollary 3.7. *$\mathcal{M}$ is ergodic.*

Proof. By Lemma 3.6, the state space is connected. $\mathcal{M}$ is aperiodic as at each iteration there is a probability of at least $1/6$ that no move is made. Therefore $\mathcal{M}$ is ergodic. $\square$

3.5 The stationary distribution π of $\mathcal{M}$

We now know the Markov chain $\mathcal{M}$ is ergodic and finite, so its stationary distribution is unique.

Lemma 3.8. *The stationary distribution π of $\mathcal{M}$ is*

$$\pi(\sigma) = \lambda^{t(\sigma)}/Z,$$

where $Z = \sum_\sigma \lambda^{t(\sigma)}$ is the normalizing constant.

Proof. We confirm π is the stationary distribution by detailed balance. Let σ and τ be configurations in Ω with $\sigma \neq \tau$ such that $P(\sigma, \tau) > 0$. By Lemma 3.5, also $P(\tau, \sigma) > 0$. Suppose particle P moves from location ℓ in σ to neighboring location ℓ' in τ. Let t be the number of triangles on which Q is incident when it is in location ℓ, and let t' be that number when P is in location ℓ'. This implies $t(\sigma) - t(\tau) = t - t'$. Without loss of generality, let $t' < t$. We see

$$P(\sigma,\tau) = \frac{1}{n} \cdot \frac{1}{6} \cdot \lambda^{t'-t} \quad \text{and} \quad P(\tau, \sigma) = \frac{1}{n} \cdot \frac{1}{6} \cdot 1.$$

We now show σ and τ satisfy the detailed balance condition:

$$\pi(\sigma) P(\sigma,\tau) = \frac{\lambda^{t(\sigma)}}{Z} \frac{\lambda^{t'-t}}{6n} = \frac{\lambda^{t(\tau)}}{Z \cdot 6n} = \pi(\tau) P(\tau, \sigma).$$

We conclude π is the stationary distribution of $\mathcal{M}$. $\square$

While it is natural to assume maximizing the number of triangles in a particle configuration results in more compression, here we formalize this. We prove π can also be expressed in terms of perimeter, which implies $\mathcal{M}$ converges to a distribution weighted by the perimeter of configurations, a global characteristic, even though the probability of any particle move is determined only by local information.

Corollary 3.9. *The stationary distribution π of $\mathcal{M}$ is*

$$\pi(\sigma) = \lambda^{-p(\sigma)}/Z,$$

where $Z = \sum_\sigma \lambda^{-p(\sigma)}$ is the normalizing constant.

Proof. We use Lemma 2.3 and Lemma 3.8:

$$\pi(\sigma) = \frac{\lambda^{t(\sigma)}}{\sum_\sigma \lambda^{t(\sigma)}} = \frac{\lambda^{2n-p(\sigma)-2}}{\sum_\sigma \lambda^{2n-p(\sigma)-2}} = \frac{\lambda^{2n-2}}{\lambda^{2n-2}} \cdot \frac{\lambda^{-p(\sigma)}}{\sum_\sigma \lambda^{-p(\sigma)}} = \frac{\lambda^{-p(\sigma)}}{\sum_\sigma \lambda^{-p(\sigma)}}. \quad \square$$

The stationary distribution of $\mathcal{M}$ can also be expressed in terms of edges.

Corollary 3.10. *The stationary distribution π of $\mathcal{M}$ is*

$$\pi(\sigma) = \lambda^{e(\sigma)}/Z,$$

where $Z = \sum_\sigma \lambda^{e(\sigma)}$ is the normalizing constant.

Proof. This follows from Lemma 2.4 and Corollary 3.9:

$$\pi(\sigma) = \frac{\lambda^{-p(\sigma)}}{\sum_\sigma \lambda^{-p(\sigma)}} = \frac{\lambda^{-(3n-e(\sigma)-3)}}{\sum_\sigma \lambda^{-(3n-e(\sigma)-3)}} = \frac{\lambda^{-3n+3}}{\lambda^{-3n+3}} \cdot \frac{\lambda^{e(\sigma)}}{\sum_\sigma \lambda^{e(\sigma)}} = \frac{\lambda^{e(\sigma)}}{\sum_\sigma \lambda^{e(\sigma)}}. \quad \square$$

3.6 Convergence Time of Markov Chain $\mathcal{M}$

We prove in Section 4 that when $\lambda > 5$, if Markov chain $\mathcal{M}$ has converged to its stationary distribution, then with all but exponentially small probability the particle system will be compressed. However, we do not give explicit bounds on the time required for this to occur; we give experimental evidence of convergence times in Section 6, but believe proving rigorous bounds will be challenging.

A common measure of convergence time of a Markov chain is the *mixing time*, the number of iterations until the distribution is within total variation distance ε of the stationary distribution, starting from the worst initial configuration. Bounding the mixing time of a Markov chain achieving compression is likely to be challenging because of the similarity to physical systems such as the Ising and Potts models, common models for ferromagnetism. Algorithms that perform local updates are known to require exponential time for many of these models precisely because of a type of compression of the systems [18]. However, mixing time most likley is not the correct measure of our algorithm's convergence. Even if it takes exponential time for $\mathcal{M}$ to converge to its stationary distribution, which is certainly plausible, it may be true that the particles achieve α-compression after only a polynomial number of steps. In fact, based on simulations, it appears compression occurs in polynomial time; doubling the number of particles consistently results in a ten-fold increase in iterations until compression starting from a straight line of n particles, so we conjecture the number of iterations until compression occurs is close to $O(n^{3.3})$.

4. ACHIEVING COMPRESSION

If $\mathcal{M}$ executes long enough, it will converge to its stationary distribution π; we will use the expression of π given in Corollary 3.9. To simplify notation, we define the *weight* of a configuration σ to be $w(\sigma) = \lambda^{-p(\sigma)}$. For a set $S \subseteq \Omega$, we define $w(S)$ as the sum of the weights of all configurations in S. We now show that, provided λ and n are large enough, with all but exponentially small probability if $\mathcal{M}$ is at stationarity then the particles are in an α-compressed configuration. Constant $\alpha > 1$ can be as close to 1 as desired, though smaller α requires larger λ. We begin with a crucial counting lemma.

Lemma 4.1. *The number of connected configurations with no holes and perimeter k is at most 5^k.*

Proof. Consider any configuration σ. Let $\mathcal{W}$ be a clockwise traversal of its perimeter, beginning at the lowest leftmost particle of σ; for every edge e traversed in $\mathcal{W}$, the location left of e is unoccupied. At each step of $\mathcal{W}$, the perimeter can continue straight, turn left by 60 degrees, turn right by 60 degrees, turn right by 120 degrees, or turn right by 180 degrees; the perimeter can never turn left by 120 or 180 degrees. Thus, at any point there are at most five possible locations for the next particle on $\mathcal{W}$. We conclude that there are fewer than 5^k configurations of perimeter k, each specified by the directions of the turns on $\mathcal{W}$. $\square$

We note this bound is not tight; see the full version* for stronger bounds, which lead directly to lower values of λ^* below. We now prove our main result.

THEOREM 4.2. *For any $\alpha > 1$, there exists $\lambda^* = 5^{\frac{\alpha}{\alpha-1}}$, $n^* \geq 0$, and $\gamma < 1$ such that for all $\lambda > \lambda^*$ and $n > n^*$, the probability that a random sample σ drawn according to the stationary distribution π of $\mathcal{M}$ is not α-compressed is exponentially small:*

$$\mathbb{P}\left(p(\sigma) \geq \alpha \cdot p_{min}\right) < \gamma^{\sqrt{n}}.$$

PROOF. Let S_α be the set of configurations of perimeter at least $\alpha \cdot p_{min}$. Let σ_{min} be a configuration of n particles achieving the minimum perimeter p_{min}. We show

$$\pi(S_\alpha) = \frac{w(S_\alpha)}{Z} < \frac{w(S_\alpha)}{w(\sigma_{min})} \leq \gamma^{\sqrt{n}}.$$

The first equality is the definition of π; the next inequality follows from the definitions of Z and w. We focus on the last inequality. Using Lemma 4.1 and noting the weight of any σ with $p(\sigma) = k$ is $\lambda^{-p(\sigma)} = \lambda^{-k}$, we sum over S_α:

$$\frac{w(S_\alpha)}{w(\sigma_{min})} \leq \frac{\sum_{k=\lceil \alpha \cdot p_{min}\rceil}^{2n-2} 5^k \lambda^{-k}}{\lambda^{-p_{min}}}$$
$$= \sum_{k=\lceil \alpha \cdot p_{min}\rceil}^{2n-2} 5^{(1-\log_5 \lambda)k + (\log_5 \lambda)p_{min}}.$$

Using the inequality $p_{min} \leq k/\alpha$, it follows that

$$\frac{w(S_\alpha)}{w(\sigma_{min})} \leq \sum_{k=\lceil \alpha \cdot p_{min}\rceil}^{2n-2} 5^{(1-\log_5 \lambda)k + (\log_5 \lambda)(k/\alpha)}$$
$$= \sum_{k=\lceil \alpha \cdot p_{min}\rceil}^{2n-2} 5^{(1-(1-1/\alpha)\log_5 \lambda)k}.$$

As $\lambda > \lambda^* = 5^{\frac{\alpha}{\alpha-1}}$, then $-c_1 := 1 - (1-1/\alpha)\log_5 \lambda < 0$. Also $k \geq \alpha \cdot p_{min}$, and by Lemma 2.1, $p_{min} > \sqrt{n}$, so

$$\frac{w(S_\alpha)}{w(\sigma_{min})} \leq \sum_{k=\lceil \alpha \cdot p_{min}\rceil}^{2n-2} 5^{-c_1 \cdot 2\alpha\sqrt{n}} \leq 2n\left(5^{-2\alpha c_1}\right)^{\sqrt{n}}.$$

There exists $\gamma < 1$ and n^* such that for all $n \geq n^*$,

$$\mathbb{P}\left(p(\sigma) \geq \alpha \cdot p_{min}\right) = \pi(S_\alpha) \leq \frac{w(S_\alpha)}{w(\sigma_{min})}$$
$$\leq 2n\left(5^{-2\alpha c_1}\right)^{\sqrt{n}} < \gamma^{\sqrt{n}}. \quad \square$$

COROLLARY 4.3. *For any $\lambda > 5$, there exists a value $\alpha = \log_5 \lambda / (\log_5 \lambda - 1)$, $n^* \geq 0$, and $\gamma < 1$ such that for all $n > n^*$, a random sample σ drawn according to the stationary distribution π of $\mathcal{M}$ satisfies*

$$\mathbb{P}\left(p(\sigma) \geq \alpha \cdot p_{min}\right) < \gamma^{\sqrt{n}}.$$

5. USING $\mathcal{M}$ FOR EXPANSION

A nice feature of our algorithm is that it also provably achieves particle expansion for different values of bias parameter λ. We say a configuration σ is *β-expanded* for some $\beta < 1$ if $p(\sigma) > \beta \cdot p_{max}$, where $p_{max} = 2n-2$. We note as $p_{max} = \Theta(n)$ and $p_{min} = \Theta(\sqrt{n})$ for a system of n particles, β-expansion and α-compression for any constants β and α are mutually exclusive for sufficiently large n. We show that, provided n is large enough, for all $0 < \lambda < \sqrt{2}$ there is a constant β such that with all but exponentially small probability, if $\mathcal{M}$ is at stationarity then the particles are β-expanded. This is notable because it implies, counter-intuitively, that $\lambda > 1$ is not sufficient to guarantee particle compression as one might first guess.

THEOREM 5.1. *For all $0 < \beta < 1$, there exists $\lambda^* = \lambda^*(\beta) < \sqrt{2}$, $n^* \geq 0$, and $\gamma < 1$ such that for all $\lambda < \lambda^*$ and $n > n^*$, the particles achieve β-expansion with all but exponentially small probability: for a configuration σ drawn at random according to stationary distribution π,*

$$\mathbb{P}\left(p(\sigma) < \beta \cdot p_{max}\right) \leq \gamma^{\sqrt{n}}.$$

PROOF. We let

$$\lambda < \lambda^* = 5^{\frac{\beta - \frac{\log_5 2}{2}}{\beta - 1}} < 5^{\frac{0 - \frac{\log_5 2}{2}}{0-1}} = \sqrt{2}.$$

Let S_β be the set of configurations σ with $p(\sigma) \leq \beta \cdot p_{max}$. Let σ_{max} be a configuration achieving maximum perimeter $p_{max} = 2n-2$. Note the number N of configurations achieving this maximum is at least $2^{n-1} = 2^{p_{max}/2}$; this is the number of paths where every step is up or up-right, which have no triangles and thus maximum perimeter. We show

$$\pi(S_\beta) = \frac{w(S_\beta)}{Z} < \frac{w(S_\beta)}{N \cdot w(\sigma_{max})} \leq \gamma^{\sqrt{n}}.$$

We focus on proving the last of the inequalities above. Applying Lemma 4.1, we see

$$\frac{w(S_\beta)}{N \cdot w(\sigma_{max})} \leq \frac{\sum_{k=p_{min}}^{\lfloor \beta \cdot p_{max}\rfloor} 5^k \lambda^{-k}}{2^{p_{max}/2} \cdot \lambda^{-p_{max}}}$$
$$= \sum_{k=p_{min}}^{\lfloor \beta \cdot p_{max}\rfloor} 5^k \lambda^{-k} \left(\frac{\lambda}{\sqrt{2}}\right)^{p_{max}}.$$

Recalling that $\lambda < \sqrt{2}$ and $k < \beta \cdot p_{max}$, we see

$$\frac{w(S_\beta)}{N \cdot w(\sigma_{max})} \leq \sum_{k=p_{min}}^{\lfloor \beta \cdot p_{max}\rfloor} 5^k \lambda^{-k} \left(\frac{\lambda}{\sqrt{2}}\right)^{\frac{k}{\beta}}$$
$$= \sum_{k=p_{min}}^{\lfloor \beta \cdot p_{max}\rfloor} 5^{k\left(1 - \log_5 \lambda + \frac{\log_5 \lambda}{\beta} - \frac{\log_5 2}{2\beta}\right)}.$$

Let c_3 be such that

$$-c_3 = 1 - \log_5 \lambda + \frac{\log_5 \lambda}{\beta} - \frac{\log_5 2}{2\beta}.$$

We want $-c_3 < 0$, so we solve for λ and see $-c_3 < 0$ precisely when $\lambda < \lambda^*$, a condition we know to hold. It follows that

$$\frac{w(S_\beta)}{N \cdot w(\sigma_{max})} \leq \sum_{k=p_{min}}^{\lfloor \beta \cdot p_{max}\rfloor} 5^{-c_3 k}$$
$$\leq \sum_{k=p_{min}}^{\lfloor \beta \cdot p_{max}\rfloor} 5^{-c_3 \cdot 2\sqrt{n}} \leq 2n5^{-2c_3\sqrt{n}}.$$

Hence there exists $n^* \geq 0$ and $\gamma < 1$ such that for all $n \geq n^*$,

$$\mathbb{P}\left(p(\sigma) \leq \beta \cdot p_{max}\right) = \pi(S_\beta) \leq \frac{w(S_\beta)}{N \cdot w(\sigma_{max})}$$
$$\leq 2n5^{-c_3 \cdot 2 \cdot \sqrt{n}} < \gamma^{\sqrt{n}}. \quad \square$$

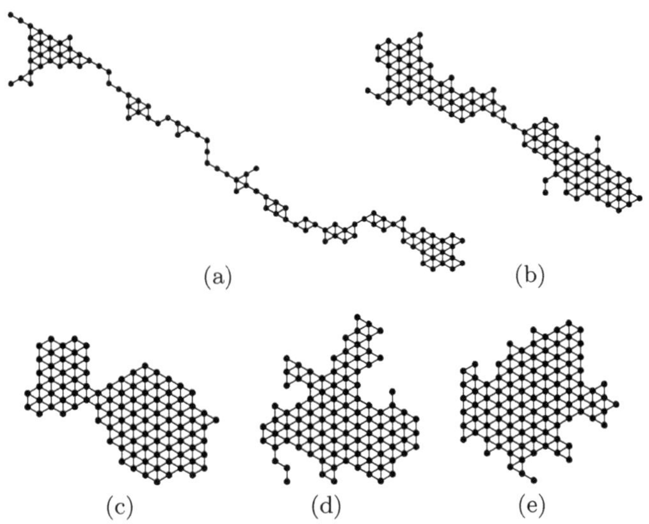

Figure 3: 100 particles in a line with occupied edges drawn, after (a) 1 million, (b) 2 million, (c) 3 million, (d) 4 million, and (e) 5 million iterations of $\mathcal{M}$ with bias $\lambda = 4$.

Corollary 5.2. *For all $\lambda < \sqrt{2}$, there exists a constant $0 < \beta < 1$ such that with all but exponentially small probability a sample drawn according to stationary distribution π of $\mathcal{M}$ is β-expanded.*

Proof. This follows immediately from the previous theorem; for $\lambda < \sqrt{2}$, there exists β such that $\lambda < \lambda^*(\beta)$. □

6. SIMULATIONS

In practice, Markov chain $\mathcal{M}$ yields good compression, even beyond the values of λ for which our proofs apply. We simulated $\mathcal{M}$ for $\lambda = 4$ on 100 particles that began in a line; the configurations after 1, 2, 3, 4, and 5 million steps of $\mathcal{M}$ are shown in Figure 3.

In contrast, $\lambda = 2$, while still favoring particles forming triangles, does not appear to yield compression; see Figure 4, where even after 20 million simulated steps of $\mathcal{M}$, the particles have not compressed. We conjecture there is a phase transition in λ, i.e., a critical value λ_c such that for all $\lambda < \lambda_c$ the particles do not compress and for all $\lambda > \lambda_c$ they do compress. Such phase transitions exist for similar statistical physics models (e.g., [2]). Our proofs indicate if λ_c exists, then $\sqrt{2} \leq \lambda_c \leq 5$; simulations suggest $2 < \lambda_c < 4$.

7. REFERENCES

[1] E. Bampas, J. Czyzowicz, L. Gąsieniec, D. Ilcinkas, and A. Labourel. Almost optimal asynchronous rendezvous in infinite multidimensional grids. In *Distributed Comp.: 24th Int. Symp., DISC 2010*, pages 297–311, 2010.

[2] C. Borgs, J.T. Chayes, A. Frieze, J.H. Kim, P. Tetali, E. Vigoda, and V.H. Vu. Torpid mixing of some MCMC algorithms in statistical physics. In *40th IEEE Symp. on Found. of Comp. Sci.*, FOCS 1999, pages 218–229, 1999.

[3] S. Camazine, K.P. Visscher, J. Finley, and S.R. Vetter. House-hunting by honey bee swarms: Collective decisions and individual behaviors. *Insectes Sociaux*, 46:348–360.

[4] A. Chavoya and Y. Duthen. Using a genetic algorithm to evolve cellular automata for 2D/3D computational development. In *Genetic and Evolut. Comp. Conf., GECCO 2006*.

[5] Z. Derakhshandeh, R. Gmyr, A.W. Richa, C. Scheideler, and T. Strothmann. An algorithmic framework for shape formation problems in self-organizing particle systems. In *Proc. of the 2nd Ann. Int. Conf. on Nanoscale Computing and Comm., NANOCOM' 15*, pages 21:1–21:2, 2015.

[6] Z. Derakhshandeh, R. Gmyr, A.W. Richa, C. Scheideler, and T. Strothmann. Universal shape formation for programmable matter. In *To appear, 28th ACM Symp. on Parallelism in Alg. and Arch., SPAA '16*, 2016. To appear.

[7] Z. Derakhshandeh, R. Gmyr, T. Strothmann, R.A. Bazzi, A.W. Richa, and C. Scheideler. Leader election and shape formation with self-organizing programmable matter. In *21st DNA Comp. and Molec. Prog., DNA 21*, pages 117–132, 2015.

[8] A. Deutsch and S. Dormann. *Cellular Automaton Modeling of Biological Pattern Formation: Characterization, Applications, and Analysis*. Modeling and Simulation in Science, Eng. and Technology. Birkhäuser Boston, 2007.

[9] R.L. Dobrushin. The problem of uniqueness of a gibbsian random field and the problem of phase transitions. *Functional Analysis and Its Applications*, 2:302–312, 1968.

[10] W. Feller. *An Introduction to Probability Theory and Its Applications*, volume 1. Wiley, 1968.

[11] P. Flocchini, G. Prencipe, N. Santoro, and P. Widmayer. Arbitrary pattern formation by asynchronous, anonymous, oblivious robots. *Theoretical Computer Science*, 407:412–447, 2008.

[12] W. K. Hastings. Monte carlo sampling methods using markov chains and their applications. *Biometrika*, 57:97–109, 1970.

[13] R. Jeanson, C. Rivault, J.L. Deneubourg, S. Blanco, R. Fournier, C. Jost, and G. Theraulaz. Self-organized aggregation in cockroaches. *Animal Behaviour*, 69:169 – 180, 2005.

[14] N. Lynch. *Distributed Algorithms*. Morgan Kauffman, 1996.

[15] N.J. Mlot, C.A. Tovey, and D.L. Hu. Fire ants self-assemble into waterproof rafts to survive floods. *Proc. of the National Academy of Sci.*, 108:7669–7673, 2011.

[16] C. Rivault and A. Cloarec. Cockroach aggregation: Discrimination between strain odours in Blattella germanica. *Animal Behaviour*, 55:177–184, 1998.

[17] M. Rubenstein, A. Cornejo, and R. Nagpal. Programmable self-assembly in a thousand-robot swarm. *Science*, 345:795–799, 2014.

[18] L.E. Thomas. Bounds on the mass gap for finite volume stochastic Ising models at low temperature. *Comm. Math. Phys.*, 126:1–11, 1989.

[19] E. Winfree, F. Liu, L.A. Wenzler, and N.C. Seeman. Design and self-assembly of two-dimensional DNA crystals. *Nature*, 394(6693):539–544, 1998.

[20] D. Woods, H.L. Chen, S. Goodfriend, N. Dabby, E. Winfree, and P. Yin. Active self-assembly of algorithmic shapes and patterns in polylogarithmic time. In *Proc. of the 4th Conf. on Innovations in Theoretical Computer Science*, pages 353–354, 2013.

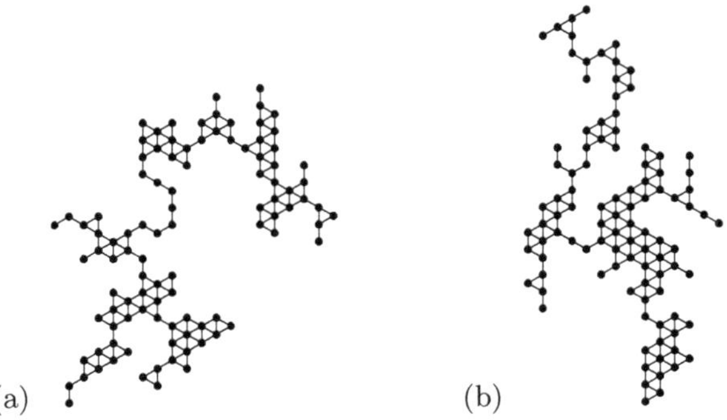

Figure 4: 100 particles after (a) 10 million and (b) 20 million iterations of $\mathcal{M}$ with bias $\lambda = 2$, starting with all particles in a diamond shape of side lengths 10.

A Complexity-Based Hierarchy for Multiprocessor Synchronization

[Extended Abstract]

Faith Ellen
University of Toronto
faith@cs.toronto.edu

Rati Gelashvili
MIT
gelash@mit.edu

Nir Shavit
MIT
shanir@csail.mit.edu

Leqi Zhu
University of Toronto
lezhu@cs.toronto.edu

ABSTRACT

For many years, Herlihy's elegant computability based Consensus Hierarchy has been our best explanation of the relative power of various types of multiprocessor synchronization objects when used in deterministic algorithms. However, key to this hierarchy is treating these instructions as distinct objects, an approach that is far from the real-world, where multiprocessor programs apply synchronization instructions to collections of arbitrary memory locations. We were surprised to realize that, when considering instructions applied to memory locations, the computability based hierarchy collapses. This leaves open the question of how to better captures the power of various synchronization instructions.

In this paper, we provide an approach to answering this question. We present a hierarchy of synchronization instructions, classified by their space complexity in solving obstruction-free consensus. Our hierarchy provides a classification of combinations of known instructions that seems to fit with our intuition of how useful some are in practice, while questioning the effectiveness of others. We prove an essentially tight characterization of the power of buffered read and write instructions. Interestingly, we show a similar result for multi-location atomic assignments.

1. INTRODUCTION

Herlihy's Consensus Hierarchy [Her91] assigns a consensus number to each object, namely, the number of processes for which there is a wait-free binary consensus algorithm using only instances of this object and read-write registers. It is simple, elegant and, for many years, has been our best explanation of synchronization power.

Robustness says that, using combinations of objects with consensus numbers at most k, it is not possible to solve wait-free consensus for more than k processes [Jay93]. The implication is that modern machines need to provide objects with infinite consensus number. Otherwise, they will not be universal, that is, they cannot be used to implement all objects or solve all tasks in a wait-free (or non-blocking) manner for any number of processes [Her91, Tau06, Ray12, HS12]. Although there are ingenious non-deterministic constructions that prove that Herlihy's Consensus Hierarchy is not robust [Sch97, LH00], it is known to be robust for deterministic one-shot objects [HR00] and deterministic read-modify-write and readable objects [Rup00]. It is unknown whether it is robust for general deterministic objects.

In adopting this explanation of computational power, we failed to notice an important fact: multiprocessors do not compute using synchronization objects. Rather, they apply synchronization instructions to locations in memory. With this point of view, Herlihy's Consensus Hierarchy no longer captures the phenomena we are trying to explain.

For example, consider two simple instructions:

- *fetch-and-add*(2), which returns the number stored in a memory location and increases its value by 2, and
- *test-and-set*(), which returns the number stored in a memory location and sets it to 1 if it contained 0[1].

Objects that support only one of these instructions as an operation have consensus number 2 and cannot be combined to solve wait-free consensus for 3 or more processes. However, a system that supports both instructions can solve wait-free binary consensus for any number of processes. The protocol uses a single memory location initialized to 0. Processes with input 0 perform *fetch-and-add*(2), while processes with input 1 perform *test-and-set*(). If the value returned is odd, the process decides 1. If the value 0 was returned from *test-and-set*(), the process also decides 1. Otherwise, the process decides 0.

Another example considers three instructions:

- *read*(), which returns the number stored in a memory location,
- *decrement*(), which decrements the number stored in a memory location and returns nothing, and

[1]This definition of *test-and-set* is slightly stronger than the standard one, which simply always sets the location to 1. However, they have the same consensus number and they behave identically if the values are always binary.

PODC'16, July 25-28, 2016, Chicago, IL, USA
© 2016 ACM. ISBN 978-1-4503-3964-3/16/07...$15.00
DOI: http://dx.doi.org/10.1145/2933057.2933113

- *multiply*(x), which multiplies the number stored in a memory location by x and returns nothing.

A similar situation arises: Objects that support *read* and one of *decrement* and *multiply* have consensus number 1 and cannot be combined to solve wait-free consensus for 2 or more processes. However, a system that supports all three instructions can solve wait-free binary consensus for any number of processes. The protocol uses a single memory location initialized to 1. Processes with input 0 perform *decrement*(), while processes with input 1 perform *multiply*(n). The second operation by each process is *read*(). If the value returned is positive, then the process decides 1. If it is negative, then the process decides 0.

For randomized computation, Herlihy's Consensus Hierarchy also collapses: randomized wait-free binary consensus among any number of processes can be solved using only read-write registers, which have consensus number 1. Fich, Herlihy, and Shavit [FHS98] proved that $\Omega(\sqrt{n})$ historyless objects, which support only trivial operations, such as *read*, and historyless operations, such as *write*, *test-and-set*, and *swap*, are necessary to solve this problem. They noted that, in contrast, only one fetch-and-increment or fetch-and-add object suffices for solving this problem. Yet, these objects and historyless objects are similarly classified in Herlihy's Consensus Hierarchy (i.e. they all have consensus number 1 or 2). They suggested that the number of instances of an object needed to solve randomized wait-free consensus among n processes might be another way to classifying its power.

Motivated by these observations, we consider a classification of instruction sets based on the number of memory locations needed to solve *obstruction-free n-valued* consensus among $n \geq 2$ processes. Obstruction freedom is a simple and natural progress measure. Some state-of-the-art synchronization operations, for example hardware transactions [Int12], do not guarantee more than obstruction freedom. Obstruction freedom is also closely related to randomized computation. In fact, any (deterministic) obstruction free algorithm can be transformed into a randomized wait-free algorithm that uses the same number of memory locations (against an oblivious adversary) [GHHW13]. Obstruction-free algorithms can also be transformed into wait-free algorithms in the unknown-bound semi-synchronous model [FLMS05].

1.1 Our Results

For various instruction sets $\mathcal{I}$, we provide upper and lower bounds on $\mathcal{SP}(\mathcal{I}, n)$, the number of memory locations (supporting $\mathcal{I}$) needed to solve obstruction-free n-valued consensus among $n \geq 2$ processes (abbreviated as *n-consensus*). The results are summarized in Table 1.

We begin, in Section 3, by considering the instructions

- *multiply*(x), which multiplies the number stored in a memory location by x and returns nothing, and
- *add*(x), which adds x to the number stored in a memory location and returns nothing.

We show that one memory location supporting *read*() and one of these instructions can be used to solve n-consensus. The idea is to show that these instruction sets can implement n counters in a single location. We can then use a *racing counters* algorithm.

Next, we consider *max-registers* [AAC09], which are memory locations supporting

- *read-max*(), which reads the number stored in a memory location, and
- *write-max*(x), which stores the number x in a memory location, provided it contains a value less than x, and returns nothing.

In Section 4, we prove that two max registers are necessary and sufficient for solving n-consensus.

In Section 5, we prove that a single memory location supporting {*read*(), *write*(x), *fetch-and-increment*()} cannot be used to solve n-consensus, for $n \geq 3$. We also present an algorithm for solving n-consensus using $O(\log n)$ such memory locations.

In Section 6, we introduce a family of instructions $\mathcal{B}_\ell$, for $\ell \geq 1$, and show how to solve n-consensus using $\lceil \frac{n}{\ell} \rceil$ memory locations supporting these instructions. Extending Zhu's $n-1$ lower bound [Zhu16], we also prove that $\lceil \frac{n-1}{\ell} \rceil$ such memory locations are necessary, which is tight except when $n-1$ is divisible by ℓ.

Our main technical contribution is in Section 7, where we show that the preceding lower bound holds within a factor of two even in the presence of atomic multiple assignment. Multiple assignment can be implemented by simple transactions, so our result implies that such transactions cannot significantly reduce space complexity. The proof further extends the techniques of [Zhu16] via a nice combinatorial argument, which we hope will be of independent interest.

There are algorithms that solve n-consensus using n registers [AH90, BRS15, Zhu15]. The best-known lower bound is $n-1$ registers [Zhu16]. A modification of the anonymous algorithm for n-consensus in [Zhu15] allows us to use only $n-1$ memory locations supporting {*read*(), *swap*(x)}. It is presented in Section 8. We also explain how to adapt the lower bound in [Zhu16] to get a simpler proof that $\Omega(\sqrt{n})$ memory locations, which support only trivial and historyless instructions, are necessary to solve n-consensus.

Finally, in Section 9, we show that an unbounded number of memory locations supporting {*read*(), *write*(*1*)} or, more generally, {*read*(), *test-and-set*()}, are necessary and sufficient to solve n-consensus, for $n \geq 3$. Furthermore, we show how to reduce the number of memory locations to $O(n \log n)$ when *write*(0) is also available.

2. MODEL

Our model bears similarities to the standard asynchronous shared memory model, albeit with a few important differences. We consider a system of $n \geq 2$ processes that *supports* some set of deterministic synchronization *instructions*, $\mathcal{I}$, on a set of identical memory locations. The processes take steps at arbitrary, possibly changing, speeds and may crash at any time. Each step is an atomic invocation of some instruction on some memory location. Scheduling is controlled by an adversary.

The processes can use instructions on the memory locations to *simulate* (or *implement*) various objects. An object provides a set of operations which processes can call. Although a memory location together with the supported instructions can be viewed as an object, we do not do so, to emphasize the *uniformity requirement* that the same set of instructions is supported on all memory locations.

Instructions $\mathcal{I}$	$\mathcal{SP}(\mathcal{I}, n)$
$\{read(), test\text{-}and\text{-}set()\}$, $\{read(), write(1)\}$	∞
$\{read(), test\text{-}and\text{-}set(), reset()\}$, $\{read(), write(1), write(0)\}$	$n-1$ (lower), $O(n \log n)$ (upper)
$\{read(), write(x)\}$	$n-1$ (lower), n (upper)
$\{read(), swap(x)\}$	$\Omega(\sqrt{n})$ (lower), $n-1$ (upper)
$\{\ell\text{-}buffer\text{-}read(), \ell\text{-}buffer\text{-}write(x)\}$	$\lceil \frac{n-1}{\ell} \rceil$ (lower), $\lceil \frac{n}{\ell} \rceil$ (upper)
$\{read(), write(x), increment()\}$ $\{read(), write(x), fetch\text{-}and\text{-}increment()\}$	2 (lower), $O(\log n)$ (upper)
$\{read\text{-}max(), write\text{-}max(x)\}$	2
$\{compare\text{-}and\text{-}swap(x, y)\}$ $\{read(), add(x)\}$, $\{read(), multiply(x)\}$ $\{fetch\text{-}and\text{-}add(x)\}\}$, $\{fetch\text{-}and\text{-}multiply(x)\}$	1

Table 1: Space Hierarachy

We consider the problem of solving *obstruction-free m-valued consensus* in such a system. Here, each of the n processes has an input from $\{0, 1, \dots, m-1\}$ and is supposed to output the same input value (called a *decision*). Obstruction-free means that every process can eventually decide a value if no other process is taking steps at the same time. When $m = n$, we will refer to this problem as *n-consensus*.

In some of our algorithms, we let the processes take snapshots of all memory locations. If the system supports *read*(), or a similar instruction, then processes can implement an atomic snapshot in an obstruction-free way by using the double collect algorithm in [AAD+93]: i.e. they repeatedly collect the values of all locations until they observe two adjacent collects whose values agree in each location.

In our lower bound proofs, we consider solving n-consensus when each process starts with an input in $\{0, 1\}$ (i.e. binary consensus). We say that a process p is *poised* to perform a specific instruction on a memory location r at a configuration C if p's next step in configuration C is to perform that instruction to r. Since we consider deterministic algorithms, the next step of a process is uniquely defined at every configuration C.

3. ARITHMETIC INSTRUCTIONS

Consider a system that supports only *read*() and either *add*(x) or *multiply*(x). We show how to solve n-consensus using a single memory location in such systems. The idea is to show that we can simulate certain collections of objects that can solve n-consensus.

A *counter* object supports two operations, *read*() and *increment*(), where *read*() returns the current value of the counter and *increment*() increments the value of the counter by 1. In the next lemma, we present a *racing counters* protocol that bears some similarity to the consensus protocol of Aspnes and Herlihy [AH90].

LEMMA 1. *It is possible to solve obstruction-free m-valued consensus among any number of processes using m counter objects.*

PROOF. We associate a separate counter c_v for each possible input value v. Processes that *promote* a particular value v increment c_v. (Initially each process promotes its input value.) After performing an increment, a process takes an atomic snapshot of all m counters and promotes the value associated with a counter with the maximum value (breaking ties arbitrarily). When a process observes that some counter c_v is more than n larger than all other counters, it returns the value v associated with c_v. This works because all other processes will increment some counter at most once before next taking a snapshot, where c_v will still be the only maximum. From there on, all processes will promote value v and keep incrementing c_v, which will shortly become large enough for all processes to return v. Obstruction-freedom follows because a process running on its own will continue to increment the same counter and, thus, eventually be able to return. □

The counters may grow arbitrarily large in the preceding protocol. The next lemma shows that it is possible to overcome this limitation when the counter objects additionally support a *decrement*() operation, which simply decrements the value of the counter object by 1. We call such counter objects *decrementable*.

LEMMA 2. *It is possible to solve obstruction-free m-valued consensus among any number of processes using m decrementable counter objects, each of which only takes on values in the range* $\{0, 1, \dots, 3n-1\}$.

PROOF. We modify the construction in Lemma 1 slightly by changing what a process does when it wants to increment c_u after performing a snapshot to promote the value u. Let c_v be a counter with the largest value among the other counters (i.e. excluding c_u, which has the largest value). If $c_v < n$, it increments c_u, as before. If $c_v \geq n$, then, instead of incrementing c_u, it decrements c_v.

A counter with value 0 is never decremented. This is because, after the last time some process observed it to have value at least n, each process will decrement the counter at most once before reading its value again. Similarly, a counter c_u never becomes larger than $3n-1$. After the last time some process observed it to have value less than $2n$, each process can increment c_u at most once before reading its value again. If $c_u \geq 2n$, then either the largest value of the other counters is less than n, in which case the process returns without incrementing c_u, or it is at least n, in which case the process decrements a counter with this value, instead of incrementing c_u. □

In the following theorem, we show how to n simulate counters and n decrementable counters.

THEOREM 3. *It is possible to solve n-consensus using a single memory location that supports only read() and either multiply(x) or add(x).*

PROOF. We first give an obstruction-free implementation n counters using a single location in a system with *read*() and *multiply*(x) instructions, which proves the claim for this set of instructions, by Lemma 1. The location is initialized with 1. For a value v, let p_v be the $(v+1)$'st prime number. A process increments a counter corresponding to v by performing *multiply*(p_v). A *read*() instruction returns the value x currently stored in the memory location, which gives a snapshot of all counter values: The value of the counter c_v is the exponent of p_v in the prime decomposition of x.

A similar construction does not work in a system with *read*() and *add*(x) instructions. For example, suppose one counter is incremented by calling *add*(a) and another counter is incremented by calling *add*(b). Then the value ab can be obtained by incrementing the first counter b times or incrementing the second counter a times. However, we can use a single memory location that supports $\{read(), add(x)\}$ to implement n different decrementable counters which always have values in $\{0, 1, \ldots, 3n-1\}$, which is also sufficient for solving consensus by Lemma 2. We initialize the location with 0. We view the value stored in the location as a number written in base $3n$ and interpret its i'th least significant digit as the value of counter c_{i-1}. To increment c_i, we perform $add((3n)^i)$, to decrement c_i, we perform $add(-(3n)^i)$, and *read*() provides an atomic snapshot of all n counters. □

4. MAX-REGISTERS

A *max-register* object [AAC09] supports two operations, *write-max*(x) and *read-max*(). The *write-max*(x) operation sets the value of the max-register to x if x is larger than the current value and *read-max*() returns the current value of the max-register (which is the largest amongst all values previously written to it). We show that 2 max-registers are necessary and sufficient for solving n-consensus.

THEOREM 4. *It is not possible to solve n-consensus using a single max-register.*

PROOF. Consider a solo execution α of the first process that returns 0, and a solo execution β of the second process that returns 1. We show how to interleave these two executions so that the resulting execution is indistinguishable to both processes from their respective solo executions. Hence, both values will be returned, violating the agreement property of consensus.

To build the interleaved execution, run both processes until there are first poised to perform *write-max*. Suppose the first process is poised to perform *write-max*(a) and the second process is poised to perform *write-max*(b). If $a \leq b$, let the first process take steps until it is next poised to perform *write-max* or until the end of α, if it performs no more *write-max* operations. Otherwise, let the second process take steps until it is next poised to perform *write-max* or until the end of β. Repeat this until one of the processes reaches the end of its execution and then let the other process finish. □

THEOREM 5. *It is possible to solve n-consensus using two max registers.*

5. INCREMENT

Consider a system that supports only *read*, *write*(x), and either *fetch-and-increment*() or *increment*(). We prove that it is not possible to solve n-consensus in the first (stronger) case using a single memory location and we provide an algorithm in the second (weaker) case, which uses $O(\log n)$ memory locations.

THEOREM 6. *It is not possible to solve n-consensus using a single memory location that supports only read(), write(x), and fetch-and-increment().*

PROOF. Suppose there is a binary consensus algorithm for two processes, p and q, using only 1 memory location. Consider solo executions α and β by p with input 0 and input 1, respectively. Let α' be the longest prefix of α that does not contain a *write* and define β' analogously. Without the loss of generality, assume that β' performs at least as many *fetch-and-increment* instructions as α'. Let C be the configuration that results from performing α' starting from the initial configuration in which p has input 0 and the other process, q has input 1.

Consider the shortest prefix β'' of β' in which p performs the same number of fetch-and-increments as it performs in α'. Let C' be the configuration that results from performing β'' starting from the initial configuration in which both p and q have input 1. Then q must decide 1 in its solo execution γ starting from configuration C'. However, C and C' are indistinguishable to process q, so it must decide 1 in γ starting from configuration C. Thus, p cannot have decided yet in configuration C, otherwise both 0 and 1 would have been decided.

Therefore, p is poised to perform a *write* in configuration C. Let α'' be the remainder of α, so $\alpha = \alpha'\alpha''$. The configurations resulting from performing this *write* starting from C and $C\gamma$ are indistinguishable to p, so p also decides 0 starting from $C\gamma$. But in this execution, both 0 and 1 are decided. This is a contradiction. □

The following well-known construction converts any algorithm for solving binary consensus to an algorithm for solving n-valued consensus [HS12].

LEMMA 7. *Consider a system that supports a set of instructions that includes read() and write(x). If it is possible solve obstruction-free binary consensus among n processes using only c memory locations, then it is possible to solve n-consensus using only $(c+2) \cdot \lceil \log_2 n \rceil - 2$ locations.*

By Lemma 1, n processes can solve obstruction-free binary consensus using two counter objects and, hence, in this system, using two memory locations. The next result then follows from Lemma 7.

THEOREM 8. *It is possible to solve n-consensus using only $O(\log n)$ memory locations that support only read(), write(x), and increment().*

6. ℓ-BUFFERS

In this section, we consider the instructions *ℓ-buffer-read*() and *ℓ-buffer-write*(x), for $\ell \geq 1$, which generalize read and write, respectively. Specifically, an *ℓ-buffer-read*() instruction returns the last ℓ inputs to *ℓ-buffer-write* instructions previously applied on the memory location, in order from least recent to most recent.

We consider a system that supports the instruction set $\mathcal{B}_\ell = \{\ell\text{-}buffer\text{-}read(), \ell\text{-}buffer\text{-}write(x)\}$, for some $\ell \geq 1$.

We call each memory location in such a system an *ℓ-buffer*. Note that a 1-buffer is simply a register. For $\ell > 1$, an ℓ-buffer essentially maintains a buffer of the ℓ most recent writes to that location and allows them to be read.

In Section 6.1, we show that a single ℓ-buffer can be used to simulate a powerful *history* object that can be updated by at most ℓ processes. This will immediately allow us to simulate Aspnes and Herlihy's algorithm for n-consensus [AH90] and, hence, solve n-consensus, using only $\lceil n/\ell \rceil$ ℓ-buffers. In Section 6.2, we prove that $\lceil (n-1)/\ell \rceil$ ℓ-buffers are necessary, which matches the upper bound whenever $n-1$ is not a multiple of ℓ.

6.1 Simulations Using ℓ-Buffers

A *history* object H supports two operations, *get-history*() and *append*(x), where *get-history*() returns the sequence of all values appended to H by prior *append* operations, in order. We first show that, using a single ℓ-buffer B, we can simulate a history object H that supports at most ℓ different appenders, but arbitrarily many readers.

LEMMA 9. *A single ℓ-buffer can simulate a history object on which at most ℓ different processes can perform append(x) and any number of processes can perform get-history().*

PROOF. Without loss of generality, assume that no value is appended to H more than once. This can be achieved by having a process include its process identifier and a sequence number along with the value that it wants to append.

In our implementation, B is initially $\perp$ and each value written to B is of the form $(\mathbf{h}, x)$, where $\mathbf{h}$ is a history of appended values and x is a single appended value.

To *get-history*() from H, a process simply performs an *ℓ-buffer-read* of B to obtain a vector $(a_1, \ldots, a_\ell)$. The operation is linearized at this step. If $(a_1, \ldots, a_\ell) = (\perp, \ldots, \perp)$, then the empty sequence is returned. Otherwise, let k be the smallest integer such that $a_k \neq \perp$. It follows that, for $k \leq i \leq \ell$, $a_i = (\mathbf{h}_i, x_i)$, where $\mathbf{h}_i$ is a history and x_i is an appended value. If $k > 1$, then $(x_k, x_{k+1}, \cdots, x_\ell)$ is returned. Now suppose $k = 1$. Let $\mathbf{h}$ be the longest history amongst $\mathbf{h}_1, \ldots, \mathbf{h}_\ell$. If $\mathbf{h}$ contains x_1, then $\mathbf{h}' \cdot (x_1, \ldots, x_\ell)$ is returned, where $\mathbf{h}'$ is the prefix of $\mathbf{h}$ up to, but not including, x_1. If $\mathbf{h}$ does not contain x_1, then $\mathbf{h} \cdot (x_1, \ldots, x_\ell)$ is returned.

To *append*(x) to H, a process first performs a *get-history*() on H to obtain a history $\mathbf{h}$ and then performs *ℓ-buffer-write* on B with value $(\mathbf{h}, x)$. The operation is linearized at this *ℓ-buffer-write* step.

We claim that every *get-history*() operation X returns the sequence of inputs to all *append* operations on H linearized before the linearization point of X, in order from least recent to most recent. The proof is by induction on the number of *append* operations on H linearized before X. Let R be the *ℓ-buffer-read* step in X, which is the linearization point of X, and let $(a_1, \ldots, a_\ell)$ be the vector returned by R.

If there are no *append* operations linearized before R, then there are no *ℓ-buffer-write* steps before R. It follows that $(a_1, \ldots, a_\ell) = (\perp, \ldots, \perp)$ and X returns the empty sequence, as required.

Now, suppose that there is at least one *append* operation linearized before R. Let k be the smallest integer such that $a_k \neq \perp$. For $k \leq i \leq \ell$, $a_i = (\mathbf{h}_i, x_i)$, where $\mathbf{h}_i$ is a history returned by a *get-history*() operation X_i on H which had strictly fewer *append* operations linearized before it than X.

If $k > 1$, then there are only $\ell - k + 1$ occurrences of *ℓ-buffer-write* before R. Since each *append* operation is linearized at its *ℓ-buffer-write*, only $\ell - k + 1$ *append* instructions are linearized before X and $x_k, \ldots, x_\ell$ are the values appended by these $\ell - k + 1$ *append* operations, in order from least recent to most recent. In this case, $(x_k, x_{k+1}, \ldots, x_\ell)$ is returned, as required.

Now suppose $k = 1$. Let $\mathbf{h}$ be the longest history amongst $\mathbf{h}_1, \ldots, \mathbf{h}_\ell$, let m be such that $\mathbf{h}_m = \mathbf{h}$, and let W be the *ℓ-buffer-write* which wrote x_1 to B. There are two cases to consider.

Case 1: $\mathbf{h}$ *contains* x_1. By the induction hypothesis, X_m returns the history of all values appended to H by *append* operations linearized before X_m, in order from least recent to most recent. By definition, $x_1, \ldots, x_\ell$ are the last ℓ values appended to H prior to R, in order. Since $\mathbf{h}$ contains x_1, it must also contain all values appended to H prior to x_1. It follows that $\mathbf{h}' \cdot (x_1, \ldots, x_\ell)$ is the correct return value, where $\mathbf{h}'$ is the prefix of $\mathbf{h}$ up to, but not including, x_1.

Case 2: $\mathbf{h}_1$ *does not contain* x_1. Since $\mathbf{h}_i$ is a prefix of $\mathbf{h}$, it does not contain x_1, either. By the induction hypothesis, W occurs after $X_1, \ldots, X_\ell$. Thus, the *append* operations which performed $X_1, \ldots, X_\ell$ are all concurrent. In particular, W occurs in each of their execution intervals. It follows that these *append* operations are all by different processes. Since there are at most ℓ updating processes, there is no *append* operation linearized between X_m and W. Therefore, $\mathbf{h}$ contains all values appended to H prior to W. It follows that $\mathbf{h} \cdot (x_1, \ldots, x_\ell)$ is the correct return value. □

In fact, this lemma allows us to simulate *any* object that supports at most ℓ updating processes using only a single ℓ-buffer. This is because the state of an object is determined by the history of the non-trivial operations performed on it. In particular, we can simulate an array of ℓ single-writer registers using a single ℓ-buffer.

LEMMA 10. *A single ℓ-buffer can simulate ℓ single-writer registers.*

Thus, we can use $\lceil \frac{n}{\ell} \rceil$ ℓ-buffers to simulate n single-writer registers. This, in turn, allows us to simulate the n-consensus algorithm of Aspnes and Herlihy [AH90].

THEOREM 11. *It is possible to solve n-consensus using only $\lceil n/\ell \rceil$ ℓ-buffers.*

6.2 A Lower Bound

In this section, we show a lower bound on the number of memory locations necessary for solving obstruction-free binary consensus among $n \geq 2$ processes.

A location r is *covered* by a process p in some configuration, if p is poised to perform *ℓ-buffer-write* on r. An ℓ-buffer is *k-covered* by a set of processes $\mathcal{P}$ in some configuration, if there are exactly k processes in $\mathcal{P}$ that cover it. A configuration is *at most k-covered* by $\mathcal{P}$, if no ℓ-buffer in the system is k'-covered by $\mathcal{P}$ in this configuration, for any $k' > k$.

Let $\mathcal{Q}$ be a set of processes, each of which is poised to perform *ℓ-buffer-write* in some configuration C. A *block write* by $\mathcal{Q}$ *from* C is an execution, starting at C, in which each process in $\mathcal{Q}$ takes exactly one step. If a block write is performed that includes ℓ different *ℓ-buffer-write* instructions to some ℓ-buffer, then any process that performs *ℓ-buffer-read* on that ℓ-buffer immediately afterwards, gets the same result (and ends up in the same state) regardless of the value of that ℓ-buffer in C.

We say that a set of processes $\mathcal{P}$ *can decide* $v \in \{0,1\}$ *from* a configuration C if there exists a $\mathcal{P}$-only execution from C in which v is decided. If $\mathcal{P}$ can decide both 0 and 1 from C, then $\mathcal{P}$ is *bivalent* from C. If $\mathcal{P}$ can decide v, but not $\bar{v}$, from C, then $\mathcal{P}$ is v-univalent from C. Note that, because the system is deterministic, each process p has only one solo execution starting from C that decides a value. Thus $\{p\}$ is either 0-univalent or 1-univalent from C.

To obtain the lower bound, we extend the proof of the $n-1$ lower bound on the number of registers required for solving n-process consensus [Zhu16], borrowing intuition about reserving executions from the $\Omega(n)$ lower bound for anonymous consensus [Gel15]. The following auxiliary lemmas are largely unchanged from [Zhu16]. The main difference is that we only perform block writes on ℓ-buffers that are ℓ-covered by $\mathcal{P}$.

LEMMA 12. *There is an initial configuration from which the set of all processes in the system is bivalent.*

LEMMA 13. *Let R be a set of locations that are ℓ-covered by $\mathcal{P}$ in C, let $\mathcal{Q} \subseteq \mathcal{P}$ be the set of the $\ell \cdot |R|$ processes that cover R, and let β be a block write from C by $\mathcal{Q}$. Suppose some process $q \in \mathcal{Q}$ can decide some value $v \in \{0,1\}$ from configuration $C\beta$ and γ is a p-only execution from C by a process $p \notin \mathcal{Q}$ in which $\bar{v}$ is decided. Let γ' be the longest prefix of γ such that q can decide v from $C\gamma'\beta$. Then, in configuration in $C\gamma'$, p covers a location not in R and $\{p,q\}$ is bivalent from $C\gamma'\beta$.*

The next result says that if a set of processes is bivalent in some configuration, then it is possible to reach a configuration from which some process can decide 0 and another process can decide 1. It does not depend on what instructions are supported by the memory.

LEMMA 14. *Suppose a set U of at least two processes is bivalent from configuration C. Then it is possible to reach, via a U-only execution from C, a configuration C' in which there are processes $p_0, p_1 \in U$, such that for each $v \in \{0,1\}$, p_v can decide v from C'.*

An induction similar to [Zhu16] allows the processes to reach a configuration that is at most ℓ-covered by a set of processes $\mathcal{R}$, while another process $z \notin \mathcal{R}$ covers a location that is not ℓ-covered by $\mathcal{R}$. This implies that the configuration is also at most ℓ-covered by $\mathcal{R} \cup \{z\}$, allowing the inductive step to go through.

LEMMA 15. *Let C be a configuration and let $\mathcal{P}$ be a set of $n \geq 2$ processes. If $\mathcal{P}$ is bivalent from C, then there is a $\mathcal{P}$-only execution α and a pair of processes $\mathcal{Q} \subseteq \mathcal{P}$ such that $\mathcal{Q}$ is bivalent from $C\alpha$ and $C\alpha$ is at most ℓ-covered by the remaining processes $\mathcal{P} - \mathcal{Q}$.*

Finally, we can prove the main theorem.

THEOREM 16. *Consider a memory consisting of ℓ-buffers. Then any algorithm for solving obstruction-free binary consensus for n processes uses at least $\lceil (n-1)/\ell \rceil$ locations.*

PROOF. Consider an obstruction-free binary consensus algorithm. Let C be an initial configuration from which the set of all n processes, $\mathcal{P}$, is bivalent. Such a configuration exists by Lemma 12. Lemma 15 implies there is a reachable configuration C and a pair of processes $\mathcal{Q} \subseteq \mathcal{P}$ that are bivalent from C. Furthermore, C is at most ℓ-covered by the remaining processes $\mathcal{R}$. By the pigeonhole principle, $\mathcal{R}$ covers at least $\lceil (n-2)/\ell \rceil$ different locations. If $\lceil (n-2)/\ell \rceil < \lceil (n-1)/\ell \rceil$, then $n-2$ is a multiple of ℓ and every location covered by $\mathcal{R}$ is in fact ℓ-covered by $\mathcal{R}$. By Lemma 13, since $\mathcal{Q}$ is bivalent from C, we can use a process in $\mathcal{Q}$ to cover a location not ℓ-covered by $\mathcal{R}$. Hence, there are at least $\lceil (n-2)/\ell \rceil + 1 = \lceil (n-1)/\ell \rceil$ locations. □

The lower bound can be easily generalized to consensus algorithms that satisfy nondeterministic solo termination [FHS98]. It can also be extended to a *heterogeneous setting*, where memory locations need not be identical, for example, ℓ-buffers for possibly different values of ℓ. For this, we need to extend the definition of at most ℓ-covered to, instead, require each ℓ-buffer to be covered by at most ℓ processes, for all values of ℓ. Then we consider block writes to a set of locations containing ℓ different *ℓ-buffer-write* operations to each ℓ-buffer in the set. The general result is that, for any algorithm which solves consensus for n processes and satisfies non-deterministic solo termination, the sum of capacities of all buffers must be at least $n-1$.

The lower bound also applies to systems in which the output of every non-trivial instruction on a memory location does not depend on the value of that location and the output of any trivial instruction is a function of the sequence of the preceding ℓ non-trivial instructions performed on the location. This is because such instructions can be implemented by *ℓ-buffer-read* and *ℓ-buffer-write* instructions.

7. MULTIPLE ASSIGNMENT

With m-register multiple assignment, we can atomically write to m locations. This plays an important role in [Her91], as m-register multiple assignment can used to solve wait-free consensus for $2m-2$ processes, but not for $2m-1$ processes.

In this section, we explore whether multiple assignment could improve the space complexity of solving obstruction-free consensus. A practical motivation to this question is that obstruction-free multiple assignment can be easily implemented using s simple transaction.

We prove a lower bound that is similar to the lower bound in Section 6.2. Suppose *ℓ-buffer-read*() and *ℓ-buffer-write*(x) instructions are supported on every memory location in a system and, for any subset of locations, we are allowed to atomically perform one *ℓ-buffer-write* instruction per location. Then $\lceil n/2\ell \rceil$ locations are necessary for n processes to solve obstruction-free consensus. As in Section 6.2, this result can be generalized to nondeterministic solo termination, different sets of instructions, and heterogeneous settings.

The main difficulty in this lower bound is proving an analogue of Lemma 13. In the absence of multiple assignment, if β is a block *ℓ-buffer-write* to a set of ℓ-covered locations R and δ is an *ℓ-buffer-write* to a location not in R, then β and δ trivially commute (in the sense that the resulting configurations are indistinguishable to all processes). However, a multiple assignment δ may now atomically *ℓ-buffer-write* to many locations, including some in R. Thus, it is now possible for processes to distinguish between $\beta\delta$ and $\delta\beta$. Using a careful combinatorial argument, we show how to perform a block of multiple assignments $\beta^1\beta^2$, such that, in β^i, *ℓ-buffer-write* is invoked exactly ℓ times for each location in R, and is never invoked for any location not in R. Given this, we can show that $\beta^1\delta\beta^2$ and $\delta\beta^1\beta^2$ are indistinguishable to all processes, which is enough to prove an analogue of Lemma 13.

First, we define the notion of covering in this setting. We say that a process p *covers* location r in a configuration C, when the next step of p in C is a multiple assignment that involves an *ℓ-buffer-write* to r. The next definition is key to our proof. *A k-packing* of a set of processes $\mathcal{P}$ in some configuration C is a function π mapping each process in $\mathcal{P}$ to some memory location it covers such that no location r has more than k processes mapped to it (i.e., $|\pi^{-1}(r)| \leq k$). When $\pi(p) = r$ we say that π *packs* p in r. A k-packing may not always exist, or there may be many, depending on the configuration, the set of processes, and the value of k. A location r is *fully k-packed* by $\mathcal{P}$ in configuration C, if a k-packing of $\mathcal{P}$ exists in C and all such k-packings pack exactly k processes in r.

Suppose that, in some configuration, there are two k-packings of the same set of processes such that the first packs more processes in some location r than the second. We show there is a location r' in which the first packing packs fewer processes than the second and a k-packing that pack one less process to location r, one more process to location r' and the same number of processes to all other locations, as compare to the first packing. This iterative procedure has some resemblance to cuckoo hashing [PR01]. The proof relies on existence of a certain Eulerian path in a multigraph that we build to represent these two k-packings.

LEMMA 17. *Suppose g and h are two k-packings of the same set of processes $\mathcal{P}$ in some configuration C and r_1 is a location such that g packs more processes in r_1 than h does (i.e., $|g^{-1}(r_1)| > |h^{-1}(r_1)|$). Then, there exists a sequence of locations $r_1, r_2, \ldots, r_t$ and a sequence of distinct processes $p_1, p_2, \ldots, p_{t-1}$, such that h packs more processes in r_t than g, (i.e., $|h^{-1}(r_t)| > |g^{-1}(r_t)|$) and, for $1 \leq i \leq t-1$, $g(p_i) = r_i$ and $h(p_i) = r_{i+1}$.*

PROOF. Consider a multigraph with one node for each memory location in the system and one directed edge labelled by p, from node $g(p)$ to node $h(p)$, for each process $p \in \mathcal{P}$. Therefore, the in-degree of a node v is equal to $|h^{-1}(v)|$, which is the number of processes that are packed into memory location v by h, and the out-degree of node v is equal to $|g^{-1}(v)|$, which is the number of processes that are packed in v by g.

Now, consider any maximal Eulerian path in this multigraph starting from node r_1. This path follows a sequence of edges for as long as possible without repeating any edge. Let $r_1, \ldots, r_t$ be the sequence of nodes visited (which may contain repetitions) and let p_i be the labels of the traversed edges, in order. Then $g(p_i) = r_i$ and $h(p_i) = r_{i+1}$ for $1 \leq i \leq t-1$. Since the path is Eulerian, the labels of the edges are distinct, which, in turn, guarantees that these sequences are finite. Finally, by maximality, the last node in the sequence must have more incoming than outgoing edges, so $|h^{-1}(r_t)| > |g^{-1}(r_t)|$. $\square$

COROLLARY 18. *Let the k-packings g and h and the sequences r_i and p_i be defined as in Lemma 17. For $1 \leq j < t$, there exists a k-packing g', such that g' packs one less process than g in r_j, one more process than g in r_t, and the same number of processes as g in all other locations.*

PROOF. We construct g' from g by re-packing each process p_i from r_i to r_{i+1} for all $j \leq i < t$. Then $g'(p_i) = r_{i+1}$ for $j \leq i < t$ and $g'(p) = g(p)$ for all other processes p. Notice that p_i covers r_{i+1}, since $h(p_i) = r_{i+1}$ and h is a k-packing.

As compared to g, g' packs one less process in r_j, one more process in r_t, and the same number of processes in every other location. Since h is a k-packing, it packs at most k processes in r_t. Because g is a k-packing that packs less processes in r_t, g' is also a k-packing. $\square$

Let $\mathcal{Q}$ be a set of processes, each of which is poised to perform a multiple assignment in some configuration C. A *block multi-assignment* by $\mathcal{Q}$ from C is an execution interval starting at C, in which each process in $\mathcal{Q}$ takes exactly one step. Consider some configuration C, a set of processes $\mathcal{P}$, and a 2ℓ-packing π of $\mathcal{P}$ in C. Let R be the set of all locations that are fully 2ℓ-packed by $\mathcal{P}$ in C. By definition, π packs exactly 2ℓ processes from $\mathcal{P}$ in each location $r \in R$.

Suppose $\mathcal{Q}_1, \mathcal{Q}_2 \subseteq \mathcal{P}$ is a partition of all processes that are packed in R by π, such that for each location $r \in R$, exactly ℓ packed processes belong to $\mathcal{Q}_1$ and the remaining ℓ packed processes belong to $\mathcal{Q}_2$. Let β_i be a block multi-assignment by $\mathcal{Q}_i$ for $i \in \{1, 2\}$.

Notice that, for any location $r \in R$, after β_1 or β_2, the outcome of any subsequent *ℓ-buffer-read* on r does not depend on multiple assignments that occurred prior to the block multi-assignment. Moreover, we can prove the following crucial property about these block multi-assignments to fully packed locations.

LEMMA 19. *Neither β_1 nor β_2 involves an ℓ-buffer-write to a location outside of R.*

PROOF. Assume the contrary. Let $q \in \mathcal{Q}_1 \cup \mathcal{Q}_2$ be a process with $\pi(q) \in R$, such that q also covers some location $r_1 \notin R$ in C. It must be the case that π packs exactly 2ℓ processes in r_1 ($|\pi^{-1}(r_1)| = 2\ell$). Otherwise, re-packing q in r_1 instead of $\pi(q)$ leads to another 2ℓ-packing that does not pack exactly 2ℓ processes in $\pi(q) \in R$, contradicting the definition of a fully 2ℓ-packed location.

Since R is the set of all fully 2ℓ-packed locations, there exists a 2ℓ-packing h, which packs strictly less than 2ℓ processes in r_1. Applying Lemma 17 for 2ℓ-packings π and h, we get a sequence of locations $r_1, \ldots, r_t$ and a sequence of processes $p_1, \ldots p_{t-1}$. $|\pi^{-1}(r_t)| < |h^{-1}(r_t)|$, and since h is a 2ℓ-packing, we must have that $|\pi^{-1}(r_t)| < 2\ell$, i.e. π packs strictly less than 2ℓ processes in r_t in C. We consider two cases.

First, assume that q does not occur in the sequence, i.e. $\forall i : p_i \neq q$. We know that $|\pi^{-1}(r_1)| = 2\ell$ and $|\pi^{-1}(r_t)| < 2\ell$, implying that the locations r_1 and r_t must be different. This allows us to apply Corollary 18 for the whole sequence with $j = 1$. We get a 2ℓ-packing π' that packs less than 2ℓ processes in r_1, and exactly 2ℓ processes in each of the fully 2ℓ-packed locations R, including $\pi(q)$. Moreover, we did not re-pack process q, so $\pi'(q) = \pi(q)$. Hence, modifying π' by re-packing q in r_1 instead of $\pi'(q)$ again leads to a 2ℓ-packing that does not pack exactly 2ℓ processes in a location in R, a contradiction.

Now, assume that $q = p_s$, for some s. By the properties of our sequences, we know $r_s = \pi(p_s) = \pi(q) \in R$, and since this location is fully 2ℓ-packed in configuration C we have $|\pi^{-1}(r_s)| = 2\ell$. Similar to the first case, since $|\pi^{-1}(r_t)| < 2\ell$ in C, locations r_s and r_t must be different and we now apply Corollary 18 with $j = s$. We get a 2ℓ-packing π'' that packs less than 2ℓ processes in location $r_s \in R$. This is a contradiction with the definition of a fully 2ℓ-packed location, completing the proof. □

We can now prove a lemma that replaces Lemma 13 in the main argument.

LEMMA 20. *Suppose $C\beta^1\beta^2$ is v-deciding for $\mathcal{Q}_1 \cup \mathcal{Q}_2$ for some $v \in \{0,1\}$. If γ is a solo execution from C by a process $p \notin \mathcal{Q}_1 \cup \mathcal{Q}_2$ in which $\overline{v}$ is decided, and γ' is the longest prefix of γ such that $C\gamma'\beta^1\beta^2$ is v-deciding for $\mathcal{Q}_1 \cup \mathcal{Q}_2$, then p is poised to perform a multiple assignment which contains an ℓ-buffer-write to a location not in R in $C\gamma'$ and the configuration $C\gamma'\beta^1$ is bivalent for $\mathcal{Q}_1 \cup \mathcal{Q}_2 \cup \{p\}$.*

PROOF. Let δ be the next step by p in γ after γ'. Since $C\gamma'\beta^1\beta^2$ is v-deciding for $\mathcal{Q}_1 \cup \mathcal{Q}_2$, but $C\gamma'\delta\beta^1\beta^2$ is $\overline{v}$-univalent for $\mathcal{Q}_1 \cup \mathcal{Q}_2$, δ must be a multiple assignment which includes an *ℓ-buffer-write* to a location not in R. (If δ is a read, the resulting configurations would be indistinguishable. Similarly, if δ is a multiple assignment containing only *ℓ-buffer-write*'s to locations in R, then no process in $\mathcal{Q}_1 \cup \mathcal{Q}_2$ can observe a difference due to the block writes $\beta^1\beta^2$.)

We claim that the configuration $C\gamma'\beta^1\delta\beta^2$ is indistinguishable from $C\gamma'\delta\beta^1\beta^2$ to $\mathcal{Q}_1 \cup \mathcal{Q}_2$. Indeed, for each location $r \in R$, since $|\pi^{-1}(r) \cap \mathcal{Q}_i| = \ell$ (that is, r is covered by exactly ℓ processes in $\mathcal{Q}_i$), the contents in location r is the same in $C\gamma'\delta\beta^1\beta^2$ as it is in $C\gamma'\beta^1\delta\beta^2$. On the other hand, for each location $r \notin R$, by Lemma 19, neither β^1 nor β^2 performs an *ℓ-buffer-write* to r, thus, the contents in location r is the same in $C\gamma'\delta\beta^1\beta^2$ as it is in $C\gamma'\beta^1\delta\beta^2$.

Therefore, $C\gamma'\beta^1\delta\beta^2$ is $\overline{v}$-univalent for $\mathcal{Q}_1 \cup \mathcal{Q}_2$, hence $C\gamma'\beta^1$ is $\overline{v}$-deciding for $\mathcal{Q}_1 \cup \mathcal{Q}_2 \cup \{p\}$. Moreover, $C\gamma'\beta^1\beta^2$ is v-deciding for $\mathcal{Q}_1 \cup \mathcal{Q}_2$ by definition of γ', thus $C\gamma'\beta^1$ is v-deciding for $\mathcal{Q}_1 \cup \mathcal{Q}_2 \cup \{p\}$. We have thus established the desired bivalency of $C\gamma'\beta^1$, completing the proof. □

Using these tools, we can prove the following analogue of Lemma 15:

LEMMA 21. *Let C be a configuration and let $\mathcal{P}$ be a set of $n \geq 2$ processes. If $\mathcal{P}$ is bivalent from C, then there is a $\mathcal{P}$-only execution α and a pair of processes $\mathcal{Q} \subseteq \mathcal{P}$ such that $\mathcal{Q}$ is bivalent from $C\alpha$ and there is a 2ℓ-packing π of the remaining processes $\mathcal{P} - \mathcal{Q}$ in $C\alpha$.*

We can now prove the main theorem.

THEOREM 22. *Consider a memory consisting of ℓ-buffers. If the processes can atomically ℓ-buffer-write to any subset of the ℓ-buffers, then any algorithm for solving obstruction consensus for n processes needs at least $\lceil (n-1)/2\ell \rceil$ space.*

PROOF. Consider an obstruction-free binary consensus algorithm. Let C be an initial configuration from which the set of all n processes, $\mathcal{P}$, is bivalent. Such a configuration exists by Lemma 12. Lemma 21 implies there is a reachable configuration C and a pair of processes $\mathcal{Q} \subseteq \mathcal{P}$ that are bivalent from C. Furthermore, there is a 2ℓ-packing π of the remaining processes $\mathcal{R} = \mathcal{P} - \mathcal{Q}$ in C. Let R be the set of all locations that are covered by $\mathcal{R}$. By the pigeonhole principle, $|R| \geq \lceil (n-2)/2\ell \rceil$ different locations. If $|R| < \lceil (n-1)/2\ell \rceil$, then $|R| = \lceil (n-2)/2\ell \rceil$, $n-2$ is a multiple of 2ℓ, and every location in R is fully 2ℓ-packed by $\mathcal{R}$. By Lemma 20, since $\mathcal{Q}$ is bivalent from C, we can use a process in $\mathcal{Q}$ to cover a location not fully 2ℓ-packed by $\mathcal{R}$. Hence, there are at least $\lceil (n-2)/2\ell \rceil + 1 = \lceil (n-1)/2\ell \rceil$ locations. □

8. SWAP AND READ

It is possible to solve n-consensus using $n-1$ memory locations that support only *read*() and *swap*(x) The idea is to modify the anonymous algorithm of [Zhu15], which uses n locations supporting *read*() and *write*(x). In that algorithm, processes obtain a snapshot of all n values by repeatedly performing collect. If all n memory locations have the same (non-$\bot$) contents, the process returns the value each of them contains. Otherwise, it overwrites one location and repeats the same sequence of steps again. After some process p returns, each of the remaining $n-1$ processes may overwrite one location before taking a snapshot. This ensures that that the value p decided is not lost, since it is contained in at least one location.

In the modified algorithm, instead of collecting the contents from n locations, a process collects the contents from $n-1$ locations and also uses the result of its last *swap*. After some process p returns, if all $n-1$ remaining processes perform *swap* on different locations, the result of each of their *swap* operations is the contents of each location seen by p in its last snapshot. Otherwise, as in the original algorithm, the value p decided is contained in at least one location.

A lower bound of $\Omega(\sqrt{n})$ locations when the system only supports *swap* and*read* instructions appears in [FHS98]. We can also adapt the recent proof of [Zhu16], which corresponds to our proof for buffered read-write instructions with capacity $\ell = 1$, to get a simpler proof of the $\Omega(\sqrt{n})$ lower bound

Only the proof of Lemma 15 needs to change. It must change because the processes perform block swaps instead of block writes, and can detect the steps by process z. To account for this, in the inductive step from i to $i+1$ locations, we consider a set Z of $i+1$ processes instead of the single process z. We still perform the block swaps and reach new configurations. If, in any such configuration, two processes in Z cover the same location. then steps are allocated to one of them, until it covers a location not covered by any other process in Z. This is repeated until all processes in Z cover $i+1$ different locations. Counting the number of extra processes used in the argument leads to the lower bound of $\Omega(\sqrt{n})$ locations.

9. TEST-AND-SET AND READ

Consider a system that supports only *test-and-set*() and *read*(). If there are only 2 processes, then it is possible to solve wait-free consensus using a single memory location. However, we claim that any algorithm for solving obstruction-free binary consensus among $n \geq 3$ processes must use an unbounded number of memory locations. The key is to prove the following analogue of Lemma 13.

LEMMA 23. *Let P be a set of at least 3 processes and let C be a configuration. If P is bivalent from C, then, for every $k \geq 0$, there exists a P-only execution α_k from C such that P is bivalent from $C\alpha_k$ and at least k locations have been set to 1 in $C\alpha_k$.*

PROOF. By induction on k. The base case is when $k = 0$ and is trivial. Given α_k, we show how to construct α_{k+1}. By Lemma 14, there is a P-only execution φ from $C\alpha_k$ and a pair of processes, p_0 and p_1, that can decide 0 and 1, respectively, from $C\alpha_k\varphi$. Pick $z \in P - \{p_0, p_1\}$. Since $\{p_0, p_1\}$ is bivalent from $C\alpha_k\varphi$, we may run z until it first performs a *test-and-set*() on a memory location, call it r, that had not been set to 1. Let β denote this execution. If $C\alpha_k\varphi\beta$ is bivalent from $\{p_0, p_1\}$, then we are done with $\alpha_{k+1} = \alpha_k\varphi\beta$. So, without loss of generality, suppose $\{p_0, p_1\}$ is 0-univalent from $C\alpha_k\varphi\beta$. Let ψ be the longest prefix of p_1's solo terminating execution from $C\alpha_k\varphi$ such that $C\alpha_k\varphi\psi\beta$ is 0-univalent for $\{p_0\}$. It follows that, in configuration $C\alpha_k\varphi\psi$, the set β' that p_1 is poised to perform is a *test-and-set*() on an unset memory location. Note that this location is not r, since, otherwise, $C\alpha_k\varphi\psi\beta'\beta$ is indistinguishable from $C\alpha_k\varphi\psi\beta$ to p_0. Therefore, $C\alpha_k\varphi\psi\beta\beta'$ is indistinguishable from $C\alpha_k\varphi\psi\beta'\beta$ to p_0. Let $\alpha_{k+1} = \alpha_k\varphi\psi\beta$. It follows that $\{p_0, p_1\}$ is bivalent from $C\alpha_{k+1}$. Furthermore, β includes a *test-and-set*() to a location that was not already set to 1 and $C\alpha_k$ had at least k locations set to 1, $C\alpha_{k+1}$ has at least $k + 1$ locations set to 1. □

By Lemma 12, there is an initial configuration from which the set of all processes in the system is bivalent. It follows that we may repeatedly apply the preceding lemma to show that any binary consensus algorithm for $n \geq 3$ processes uses an unbounded number of locations.

THEOREM 24. *For $n \geq 3$, it is not possible to solve n-consensus using a bounded number of memory locations supporting only read() and test-and-set().*

There is an algorithm for obstruction-free binary consensus that uses an unbounded number of binary registers, initially all set to 0, and only performs *write*(1) [GR05]. The idea is to simulate a counter using an unbounded number of binary registers and then to run the racing counters algorithm presented in Lemma 1. In their algorithm, there are two unbounded tracks on which processes (with preference 0 and 1, respectively) race, flipping 0's to 1's one by one on their respective tracks to indicate progress. A process changes its preference if it sees that the number of 1's on its side is less than the number of 1's on the other side. Once a process sees that its side is at least 2 ahead of the other side, it decides its current preference.

It is possible to generalize this algorithm to solve n-valued consensus by having n race tracks, where register j is used for track k whenever $j \equiv k \bmod n$. Since *test-and-set*() is at least as powerful as *write*(1), we get the following result.

THEOREM 25. *It is possible to solve n-consensus using only an unbounded number of memory locations supporting only read() and either write(1) or test-and-set().*

Now, suppose we can also *reset*() a memory location from 1 to 0 or perform *write*(0). Then we can solve n-consensus using only $O(n \log n)$ locations by combining an existing binary consensus algorithm that uses only $2n$ binary registers [Bow11] with Lemma 7. There is a slight subtlety in that we don't have *write*(x). However, in the proof of Lemma 7, it suffices to use n binary locations in each layer that are initialized to 0, instead of 2 registers. The idea is that a process sets the i'th location to 1 to indicate that it had value $i - 1$.

THEOREM 26. *It is possible to solve n-consensus using only $O(n \log n)$ memory locations supporting only read(), write(1) or test-and-set(), and write(0) or reset().*

10. CONCLUSIONS AND FUTURE WORK

In this paper, we defined a hierarchy based on the space complexity of solving consensus. We used consensus because it is a well-studied, general problem that seems to capture a fundamental difficulty of multiprocessor synchronization. Moreover, consensus is *universal*: any sequentially defined object can be implemented in a wait-free way using only consensus objects and registers [Her91].

We did not address the issue of universality within our hierarchy. One history object can be used to implement any sequentially defined object. Consequently, it may make sense to consider defining a hierarchy on sets of instructions based on their ability to implement a history object, a compare-and-swap object, or a repeated consensus object shared by n processes. However, the space complexity of solving n-consensus is the same as the space complexity of implementing these long-lived objects, for many of the instruction sets that we considered. (It appears that this may not be true for $\{$*read*, *increment*$\}$.)

It may be that a truly accurate complexity-based hierarchy would have to take time complexity into consideration. However it is even unclear which definition of time to use. Exploring this may be an important future direction.

There are several other interesting open problems. To the best of our knowledge, all existing space lower bounds rely on a combination of covering and indistinguishability arguments. However, when the covering processes apply *swap*(x), as opposed to *write*(x), they can observe differences between executions, so they can no longer be reused to maintain indistinguishability. This means that getting a tighter space lower bound for $\{$*swap*(x), *read*()$\}$ would most likely require a completely novel approach. An algorithm that uses less than $n-2$ space would be even more surprising, as the processes would necessarily have to adapt their access patterns to the memory locations based on the swapped values, in order to circumvent the argument from [Zhu16]. The authors are unaware of any such algorithm.

We conjecture that, for sets of instructions, $\mathcal{I}$, which contain only *read*(), *write*(x), and either *fetch-and-increment*() or *increment*(), $\mathcal{SP}(\mathcal{I}, n) \in \Theta(\log n)$. We have a similar conjecture for $\mathcal{I} = \{read(), write(0), write(1)\}$: we believe that $\mathcal{SP}(\mathcal{I}, n) \in \Theta(n \log n)$. Proving this is likely to require techniques that depend on the number of values, such as in the lower bound for m-valued adopt-commit objects in [AE14].

We would like to understand the properties of sets of instructions at certain levels in the hierarchy. For instance, what properties enable a collection of instructions to solve n-consensus using a single location? Is there an interesting characterization of the sets of instructions $\mathcal{I}$ for which $\mathcal{SP}(\mathcal{I}, n)$ is constant?

How do subsets of a set of instructions relate to one another in terms of their locations in the hierarchy? Alternatively, what combinations of sets of instructions decrease the amount of space needed to solve consensus? For example, using only *read*(), *write*(x), and either *increment*() or *decrement*(), more than one memory location is needed to solve binary consensus. But with both *increment*() and *decrement*() a single location suffices. Are there general properties governing these relations?

11. ACKNOWLEDGMENTS

Support is gratefully acknowledged from the Natural Science and Engineering Research Council of Canada, the National Science Foundation under grants CCF-1217921, CCF-1301926, and IIS-1447786, the Department of Energy under grant ER26116/DE-SC0008923, and Oracle and Intel corporations.

The authors would like to thank Michael Coulombe, Dan Alistarh, Yehuda Afek, Eli Gafni and Philipp Woelfel for helpful conversations and feedback.

12. REFERENCES

[AAC09] James Aspnes, Hagit Attiya, and Keren Censor. Max registers, counters, and monotone circuits. In *Proc. 28th ACM Symposium on Principles of Distributed Computing*, pages 36–45, 2009.

[AAD+93] Yehuda Afek, Hagit Attiya, Danny Dolev, Eli Gafni, Michael Merritt, and Nir Shavit. Atomic snapshots of shared memory. *Journal of the ACM*, 40(4):873–890, 1993.

[AE14] James Aspnes and Faith Ellen. Tight bounds for adopt-commit objects. *Theory Comput. Syst.*, 55(3):451–474, 2014.

[AH90] James Aspnes and Maurice Herlihy. Fast randomized consensus using shared memory. *Journal of Algorithms*, 11(3):441–461, 1990.

[Bow11] Jack R. Bowman. Obstruction-free snapshot, obstruction-free consensus, and fetch-and-add modulo k. Technical Report TR2011-681, Computer Science Department, Dartmouth College, 2011. http://www.cs.dartmouth.edu/reports/TR2011-681.pdf.

[BRS15] Zohir Bouzid, Michel Raynal, and Pierre Sutra. Brief announcement: Anonymous obstruction-free (n, k)-set agreement with $n - k + 1$ atomic read/write registers. In *Proc. 29th International Symposium on Distributed Computing (DISC)*, page 669, 2015.

[FHS98] Faith Ellen Fich, Maurice Herlihy, and Nir Shavit. On the space complexity of randomized synchronization. *Journal of the ACM*, 45(5):843–862, 1998.

[FLMS05] Faith Ellen Fich, Victor Luchangco, Mark Moir, and Nir Shavit. Obstruction-free algorithms can be practically wait-free. In *Proc. 19th International Conference on Distributed Computing (DISC)*, pages 78–92, 2005.

[Gel15] Rati Gelashvili. On the optimal space complexity of consensus for anonymous processes. In *Proc. 29th International Symposium on Distributed Computing (DISC)*, pages 452–466, 2015.

[GHHW13] George Giakkoupis, Maryam Helmi, Lisa Higham, and Philipp Woelfel. An $\mathcal{O}(\sqrt{n})$ space bound for obstruction-free leader election. In *Proc. 27th International Symposium on Distributed Computing (DISC)*, pages 46–60, 2013.

[GR05] Rachid Guerraoui and Eric Ruppert. What can be implemented anonymously? In *Proc. 19th International Symposium on Distributed Computing (DISC)*, pages 244–259, 2005.

[Her91] Maurice Herlihy. Wait-free synchronization. *ACM Transactions on Programming Languages and Systems (TOPLAS)*, 13(1):124–149, 1991.

[HR00] Maurice Herlihy and Eric Ruppert. On the existence of booster types. In *Proc. 41st IEEE Symposium on Foundations of Computer Science (FOCS)*, pages 653–663, 2000.

[HS12] Maurice Herlihy and Nir Shavit. *The Art of Multiprocessor Programming.* Morgan Kaufmann, 2012.

[Int12] Intel. *Transactional Synchronization in Haswell*, 2012. http://software.intel.com/en-us/blogs/2012/02/07/transactional-synchronization-in-haswell.

[Jay93] Prasad Jayanti. On the robustness of herlihy's hierarchy. In *Proc. 12th ACM Symposium on Principles of Distributed Computing (PODC)*, pages 145–157, 1993.

[LH00] Wai-Kau Lo and Vassos Hadzilacos. All of us are smarter than any of us: Nondeterministic wait-free hierarchies are not robust. *SIAM Journal on Computing*, 30(3):689–728, 2000.

[PR01] Rasmus Pagh and Flemming Friche Rodler. Cuckoo hashing. In *Proc. 9th Annual European Symposium on Algorithms (ESA)*, pages 121–133, 2001.

[Ray12] Michel Raynal. *Concurrent programming: algorithms, principles, and foundations.* Springer Science & Business Media, 2012.

[Rup00] Eric Ruppert. Determining consensus numbers. *SIAM Journal on Computing*, 30(4):1156–1168, 2000.

[Sch97] Eric Schenk. The consensus hierarchy is not robust. In *Proc. 16th ACM Symposium on Principles of Distributed Computing (PODC)*, page 279, 1997.

[Tau06] Gadi Taubenfeld. *Synchronization algorithms and concurrent programming.* Pearson Education, 2006.

[Zhu15] Leqi Zhu. Brief announcement: Tight space bounds for memoryless anonymous consensus. In *Proc. 29th International Symposium on Distributed Computing (DISC)*, page 665, 2015.

[Zhu16] Leqi Zhu. A tight space bound for consensus. In *Proc. 48th ACM Symposium on Theory of Computing (STOC)*, 2016. To appear.

Brief Announcement: Asynchronous Coordination with Constraints and Preferences

Armando Castañeda
Instituto de Matemáticas
UNAM
Mexico City, Mexico
castaneda@unam.mx

Pierre Fraigniaud
IRIF, CNRS
University Paris Diderot
Paris, France
fraigniaud@irif.fr

Eli Gafni
CS Dept.
UCLA
Los Angeles, CA, USA
eli@ucla.edu

Sergio Rajsbaum
Instituto de Matemáticas
UNAM
Mexico City, Mexico
rajsbaum@unam.mx

Matthieu Roy
LAAS-CNRS
Université de Toulouse, CNRS
Toulouse, France
roy@laas.fr

ABSTRACT

Adaptive renaming can be viewed as a coordination task involving a set of asynchronous agents, each aiming at grabbing a single resource out of a set of resources totally ordered by their desirability. We consider a generalization of adaptive renaming to take into account scenarios in which resources are not independent.

We model constraints between resources as an undirected graph: nodes represent the ressources, and an edge between two ressources indicates that these two ressources cannot be used simultaneously. In such a setting, the sets of resources that processes may use simultaneously form independent sets. In this note, we focus on this task in a model where such independent sets are computed by wait-free processes.

1. ASYNCHRONOUS COORDINATION AND RENAMING

Adaptive Renaming

In distributed computing, several *tasks* have an *adaptive* version in which the quality of the solution must depend only on the number of processes that participate in a given execution, and not on the total number of processes that may be involved in this task (this number may even be unbounded). A typical example of an adaptive task is *adaptive renaming* [3]: processes acquire distinct *output names* in the space $[1, r]$, where r depends only on the number k of participating processes. In the asynchronous setting with crash-prone processes and read/write registers (the wait-free case), the optimal value for the range is known to be $r = 2k - 1$ [4, 5].

Interestingly, adaptive renaming can also be viewed as a task in which name i is preferred to name j whenever $i < j$. Hence, adaptive renaming can be thought as an abstraction of the problem in which asynchronous *agents* are competing for *resources* totally ordered by their desirability. In other words, adaptive renaming is an abstraction of a problem of *coordination* between agents under *preferences*. Coordination between agents under preferences has been recently investigated in [1, 2] where the *musical chairs* game has been formally defined and solved. In this game, a set of players (modeling the agents) must coordinate so that each player eventually picks one of the available chairs (modeling the resources). Each player initially comes with an a priori *preference* for one chair. In absence of conflict with other players, the player can pick the desired chair, otherwise the conflicting players must coordinate so that they pick different chairs. It has been proven that the smallest number r of chairs for which musical chairs with k players has a solution is $r = 2k - 1$.

Dealing with Constraints on Resources

We foresee that neither adaptive renaming nor musical chairs fully capture typical scenarios of agents competing for resources.

It is often the case that resources are not independent: the literature on scheduling, partitioning or resource allocation — to cite a few— provide several examples in which resources are inter-dependent, causing some resource a not being allowed to be used simultaneously with resource b. That is, using one possibly resource disables others.

In this work, we consider the case in which constraints are modeled as an indirected graph whose nodes are resources, and every edge $\{a, b\}$ indicates that resources a and b cannot be both simultaneously acquired, i.e., acquiring a node disables all its neighbors. In other words, the sets of resources that are allowed are those which form *independent sets* in the constraints graph.

Following this framework, renaming as well as musical chairs tasks correspond to cases where the constraints graph is a stable graph (i.e., a graph with no edges). We address an extension of renaming and musical chairs, targeting an abstraction of a problem of coordination between agents under *preferences* and *constraints.*

PODC'16 July 25-28, 2016, Chicago, IL, USA

ACM ISBN 978-1-4503-3964-3/16/07.
DOI: http://dx.doi.org/10.1145/2933057.2933081

Problem Statement

DEFINITION 1. *In the* coordination with constraints and preferences task CCP, *given an n-node graph $G = (V, E)$ modeling the constraints between the resources in E,*

- *an input is a multiset M of k elements in V, representing the preferences of k processes $p_1, \ldots, p_k$,*
- *an output is an* independent set $I = \{u_1, \ldots, u_k\}$ *of G, of size k, representing the fact that process p_i acquires u_i, for $i = 1, \ldots, k$.*
- *if the input is an independent set of k elements in V, then every process should output its initial preference.*

Seminal papers on renaming [4] and musical chairs [2] showed that in an asynchronous system in which the processes are subject to crash failures, the CCP task is not solvable for k larger than some bound, even for the stable graph G (the value of the bound on k for the stable graph is roughly half the number of nodes of the graph n). Indeed, we are interested in understanding how the addition of constraints may affect the computability of this task.

More precisely, given a graph G, we want to determine the largest k for which the coordination with constraints and preferences task on G is solvable, for any preference multiset M of size at most k. Regarding the computation model, we focus here on *wait-free* systems, in which any subset of processes may fail by crashing, all processes are asynchronous, and communication is performed using read and write operations in shared memory, where each process has its own private registers.

2. LOWER BOUNDS, ALGORITHMS AND OPEN PROBLEMS

A Tight Lower Bound for Paths

Let us first consider the problem for an n-node path P_n. This particular case will enable us to prove a lower bound on the size of Hamiltonian graphs for which the coordination with constraints and preferences task is solvable. Interestingly, this lower bound is almost twice as large as the $2k-1$ bound without constraints resulting from renaming or musical chairs. Specifically, we establish the following:

THEOREM 1. *Let k be a positive integer. The smallest integer n for which the coordination with constraints and preferences task in the line of n nodes P_n is solvable for k processes satisfies $n = 4k - 3$. As a consequence, if the coordination with constraints and preferences task in an n-node Hamiltonian graph G is solvable for k processes then $n \geq 4k - 3$.*

The lower bound on n follows from reduction of CCP on a $4k-4$ line to musical chairs with $2k-2$ chairs, i.e., $2k-2$ renaming with initial preference, which is impossible [2]. As sketched in Figure 1, the reduction proceeds by assigning one edge over two to a chair. In the line, each vertex is connected to exactly one bold edge. Bold edges are labelled $1..2k-2$ and correspond to the vertex labelling of the empty graph, and arrows represent the reduction.

The upper bound on n comes from a wait-free algorithm, inspired from the optimal adaptive renaming algorithm in [3], whose main lines are: (1) fix a maximum independent set

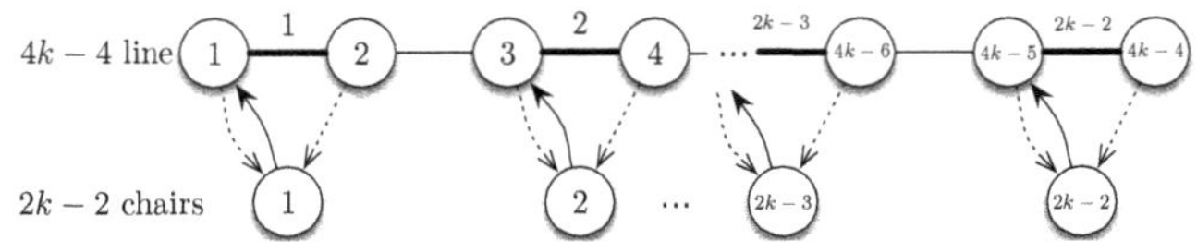

Figure 1: Reduction of CCP task on a $4k-4$ line to renaming on $2k-2$ names.

I in P_n, (2) index the vertices of I from 1 to $2k-1$, and (3) p_i checks if there is no conflict with its initial preference; if p_i is not in conflict, the it decides its initial preference, otherwise it runs an optimal (adaptive) renaming algorithm on these indexes. This algorithm is *static* in the sense that I is predetermined in advance and not during an execution. Algorithm 1 describes such a generic static algorithm.

From this preliminary result on P_n, one may think that solving the coordination with constraints and preferences task in a graph G boils down to classical renaming once a maximum independent set in G is fixed. We show that this is *not* the case. In fact, even for an instance as simple as the n-node ring C_n, the problem becomes highly non trivial.

Rings: the Case of the Pentagon

THEOREM 2. *Let k be a positive integer. The smallest n for which the coordination with constraints and preferences task in C_n is solvable for k processes satisfies $4k - 3 \leq n \leq 4k - 2$.*

The lower bound is a consequence of Theorem 1 since C_n is Hamiltonian. A quite intriguing fact is that the wait-free algorithm derived from an adaptation of an optimal algorithm for classical renaming run on a maximum independent set of C_n does not match the lower bound, and is off by an additive factor $+1$.

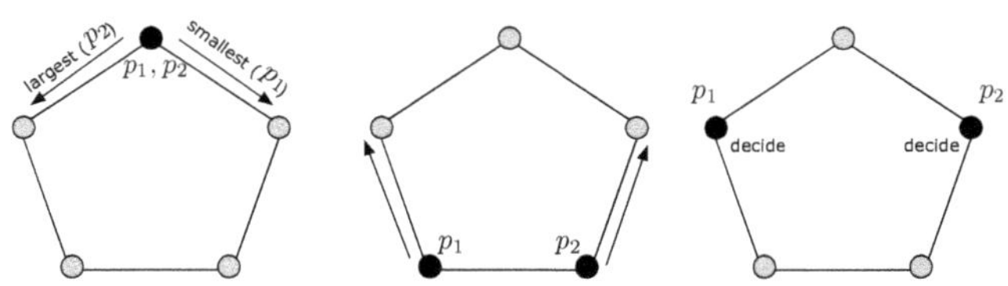

Figure 2: Optimal algorithm for two processes in the pentagon: rules when two processes are executing

The algorithm for two processes in the pentagon C_5 is depicted on Figure 2, which represents the snapshot of a process, and the action to take (represented as arrows) based on this snapshot when 2 processes participate. There are three cases, depending on whether the two processes are currently occupying nodes at distance 0, 1, or 2. Notice that if the snapshot reveals that the process is alone, then it decides the node that it currently occupies, i.e., its preferred node. If the snapshot reveals that the two processes occupy the same node, then the action depends on the ID: going clockwise for the process with smallest ID, and counterclockwise otherwise. If the snapshot reveals that the two processes occupy two neighboring nodes, then the action is: going away from the other node. Finally, if the snapshot reveals that the two processes occupy two nodes at distance 2, then the action is to decide the currently occupied node.

We believe that the difference of 1 between the lower and upper bounds for C_n is certainly not anecdotal, but is the witness of a profound phenomenon that is not yet understood, with potential impact on classical renaming and musical chairs. The main outcome of this paper is probably the observation that *static* algorithms, i.e., algorithms based on *fixed* precomputed positions in the graph of constraints, might be sub-optimal by allocating less resources than the optimal. The optimal algorithm for coordinating two processes in the pentagon is not static, and the set of allocated resources output by this algorithm spans *all possible* independent sets. The design of optimal *dynamic* (i.e., non static) algorithms for solving the coordination with constraints and preferences task appears to be a challenge, even in the specific case of the cycle C_n.

The Inherent Difficulty of the General Case

The inherent difficulty for asynchronous crash-prone processes to coordinate under constraints and preferences, even in graphs with arbitrarily large independent sets, can also be illustrated by the complete bipartite graph $K_{x,y}$ with $n = x + y$ nodes. We show that, although $K_{x,y}$ has very large independent sets (of size at least $\min\{x, y\}$), processes cannot coordinate *at all* in this graph.

THEOREM 3. *Let x, y be positive integers. Coordination with constraints and preferences in the complete bipartite graph $K_{x,y}$ is unsolvable for more than one process.*

A Suboptimal Static Algorithm for General Graphs

Finally, on the positive side, given any graph G, we can design a static algorithm ALG solving the coordination with constraints and preferences task in G —recall that static, in this case, means that ALG is based on a statically defined independent set I, a priori known to processes.

More precisely, ALG requires a *k-admissible* independent set: given $G = (V, E)$, an independent set I of G is k-admissible if for every $W \subseteq V$ of size at most $k - 1$, we have $|I \setminus N[W]| \geq |I \cap W| + 1$ where $N[W]$ denotes the set of nodes at distance at most 1 from a node in W ($N[w] = \{w\} \cup \{v \in V : \{v, w\} \in E\}$, and $N[W] = \cup_{w \in W} N[w]$). Figure 3 provides a sketch of k-admissibility.

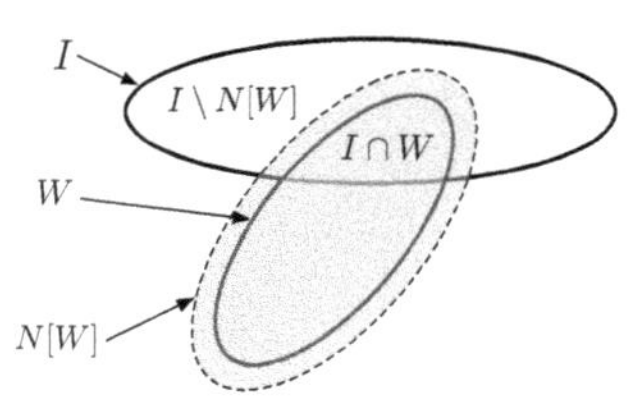

Figure 3: k-admissibility : $|I \setminus N[W]| \geq |I \cap W| + 1$, if $|W| \leq k - 1$

We can prove that among static algorithms, ALG is optimal, which completely closes the problem for static algorithms.

THEOREM 4. *Let G be a graph, and k be a positive integer. Let I be a k-admissible independent set in G. Then,* ALG *instantiated with I solves the coordination with constraints and preferences task in G with k processes. Moreover, if G has no $(k + 1)$-admissible independent set, then no static algorithm can solve the coordination with constraints and preferences task in G with more than k processes.*

Algorithm 1 $G = (V, E)$ is a graph, and I is an ordered independent set in G. Code for p_i.

```
function CoordinationConstraints(u_i ∈ V: initial preference)
  cur_i ← u_i
  loop
     write(cur_i)
     snapshot memory to get view = {cur_j1, ..., cur_jr}
     view' ← view \ {cur_i}                ▷ remove cur_i from view
     if view' ∩ N[cur_i] = ∅ then           ▷ check for conflicts
        return cur_i                        ▷ no conflict ⇒ decide cur_i
     else                         ▷ conflict ⇒ compute a new position
        free ← I \ N[view']            ▷ rule out conflicts from I
        ℓ ← |{s : cur_js ∈ I and j_s < i}| + 1          ▷ ranking
        cur_i ← ℓ^th element in free              ▷ next proposal
     end if
  end loop
```

Algorithm 1 is the pseudocode of ALG. The algorithm uses a shared array *view*, accessed with write and snapshot operations, where each entry is initially $\perp$. The local variable cur_i stores the current proposal of process p_i. Algorithm 1 is a rewriting of a textbook renaming algorithm for shared memory [4], adapted to take into account the statically fixed independent set I and the constraint that no two process may end up in connected vertices.

Conclusion

In this note, we introduced the coordination with constraints and preferences task, a task that models a set of processes competing for interdependent resources. We sketched a lower bound for Hamiltonian graphs, and provided an optimal algorithm for 2 processes on a pentagon. If processes agree beforehand on a given maximal independent set, we describe a *static* algorithm for solving this problem. Static algorithms are in general sub-optimal, as illustrated on the pentagon.

Hence, the design of optimal *dynamic* algorithms for solving the coordination with preferences and constraints tasks in graphs appears to be a challenging open problem, even for the relatively simple case of rings.

3. REFERENCES

[1] Y. Afek, Y. Babichenko, U. Feige, E. Gafni, N. Linial, and B. Sudakov. Oblivious collaboration. In D. Peleg, editor, *Distributed Computing*, volume 6950 of *Lecture Notes in Computer Science*, pages 489–504. Springer Berlin Heidelberg, 2011.

[2] Y. Afek, Y. Babichenko, U. Feige, E. Gafni, N. Linial, and B. Sudakov. Musical chairs. *SIAM Journal on Discrete Mathematics*, 28(3):1578–1600, 2014.

[3] H. Attiya, A. Bar-Noy, D. Dolev, D. Peleg, and R. Reischuk. Renaming in an asynchronous environment. *Journal of the ACM*, 37(3):524–548, 1990.

[4] H. Attiya and J. Welch. *Distributed Computing Fundamentals, Simulations, and Advanced Topics, Second Edition.* John Wiley and Sons, Inc., 2004.

[5] E. Gafni, A. Mostéfaoui, M. Raynal, and C. Travers. From adaptive renaming to set agreement. *Theoretical Computer Science*, 410(14):1328 – 1335, 2009. Structural Information and Communication Complexity (SIROCCO 2007).

How Emerging Memory Technologies Will Have You Rethinking Algorithm Design

Phillip B. Gibbons
Carnegie Mellon University
gibbons@cs.cmu.edu

ABSTRACT

We are on the cusp of the emergence of a new wave of non-volatile memory technologies that are projected to become the dominant type of main memory in the near future. A key property of these new memory technologies is their asymmetric read-write costs: Writes can be an order of magnitude or more higher energy, higher latency, and lower (per-module) bandwidth than reads. This high cost for writes motivates a rethinking of algorithm design towards "write-efficient" algorithms and data structures that reduce their number of writes [1, 2, 3, 4, 5, 6]. Many popular techniques for sequential, distributed, and parallel algorithms are tuned to the setting where reads and writes cost the same, and hence need to be revisited. Prior work on reducing writes to *contended* cache lines in shared memory algorithms can be useful here, but with the new technologies, even writes to *uncontended* memory is costly. Moreover, the new technologies are unlikely to replace the fastest cache memory, motivating the study of a multi-level memory hierarchy comprised of smaller symmetric level(s) and a larger asymmetric level. Lower bounds, too, need to be revisited in light of asymmetric costs.

This talk provides background on these emerging memory technologies, highlights the progress to date on these exciting research questions, and touches on a few of the many open problems.

CCS Concepts

•Theory of computation → Models of computation; Design and analysis of algorithms; •Hardware → Emerging technologies; Memory and dense storage;

Keywords

write-efficient algorithms; asymmetric read-write cost; persistent memory; NVRAM; shared memory algorithms; memory hierarchies; models of computation

PODC '16 July 25-28, 2016, Chicago, IL, USA

ACM ISBN 978-1-4503-3964-3/16/07.

DOI: http://dx.doi.org/10.1145/2933057.2933124

SPEAKER BIO

Phillip Gibbons is a Professor in the Computer Science Department and the Electrical & Computer Engineering Department at Carnegie Mellon University. He received his Ph.D. in Computer Science from the University of California at Berkeley. Prior to joining CMU, Gibbons was a researcher at Bell Laboratories and Intel Research Pittsburgh, and co-director of the Intel Science and Technology Center for Cloud Computing. His research areas include big data, parallel computing, distributed systems, databases, and computer architecture. His publications span systems and theory, and have been cited 15,000+ times with an h-index of 63. He is founding Editor-in-Chief for the *ACM Transactions on Parallel Computing*, an Associate Editor for the *Journal of the ACM*, and has served as program/area chair for a number of conferences in parallel/distributed computing, sensor networks, and databases. Gibbons is both an ACM and IEEE Fellow.

Acknowledgments. This research was supported by NSF grants CCF-1314590, CCF-1314633 and CCF-1533858, the Intel Science & Technology Center for Cloud Computing, and the Miller Institute for Basic Research in Science.

REFERENCES

[1] N. Ben-David, G. E. Blelloch, J. T. Fineman, P. B. Gibbons, Y. Gu, C. McGuffey, and J. Shun. Parallel algorithms for asymmetric read-write costs. In *ACM SPAA*, 2016.

[2] G. E. Blelloch, J. T. Fineman, P. B. Gibbons, Y. Gu, and J. Shun. Efficient algorithms under asymmetric read and write costs. *arXiv:1511.01038*, 2015.

[3] G. E. Blelloch, J. T. Fineman, P. B. Gibbons, Y. Gu, and J. Shun. Sorting with asymmetric read and write costs. In *ACM SPAA*, 2015.

[4] E. Carson, J. Demmel, L. Grigori, N. Knight, P. Koanantakool, O. Schwartz, and H. V. Simahdri. Write-avoiding algorithms. In *IEEE IPDPS*, 2016.

[5] S. Chen, P. B. Gibbons, and S. Nath. Rethinking database algorithms for phase change memory. In *CIDR*, 2011.

[6] S. D. Viglas. Write-limited sorts and joins for persistent memory. *Proc. VLDB Endowment*, 7(5), 2014.

Information-Theoretic Lower Bounds on the Storage Cost of Shared Memory Emulation

Viveck R. Cadambe
EE Department
Pennsylvania State University
University Park, PA, USA
viveck@engr.psu.edu

Zhiying Wang
CPCC Center,
University of California, Irvine
Irvine, CA, USA
zhiying@uci.edu

Nancy Lynch
Department of EECS
MIT
Cambridge, MA, USA
lynch@csail.mit.edu

ABSTRACT

The focus of this paper is to understand storage costs of emulating an atomic shared memory over an asynchronous, distributed message passing system. Previous literature has developed several shared memory emulation algorithms based on replication and erasure coding techniques, and analyzed the storage costs of the proposed algorithms. In this paper, we present the first known information-theoretic lower bounds on the storage costs incurred by shared memory emulation algorithms. Our storage cost lower bounds are universally applicable, that is, we make no assumption on the structure of the algorithm or the method of encoding the data.

We consider an arbitrary algorithm A that implements an atomic multi-writer-single-reader (MWSR) shared memory variable whose values come from a finite set $\mathcal{V}$ over a system of N servers connected by point-to-point asynchronous links. We require that in every fair execution of algorithm A where the number of server failures is smaller than a parameter f, every operation invoked at a non-failing client terminates. We define the storage cost of a server in algorithm A as the logarithm (to base 2) of the number of states it can take on; the total storage cost of algorithm A is the sum of the storage cost of all servers. Previously, it was known that the storage cost cannot be smaller than $\frac{N}{N-f}\log_2|\mathcal{V}|$. We develop three new lower bounds on the storage cost of algorithm A.

- In our first lower bound, we show that if algorithm A does not use server gossip, then the total storage cost is lower bounded by $2\frac{N}{N-f+1}\log_2|\mathcal{V}| - o(\log_2|\mathcal{V}|)$.
- In our second lower bound we show that the total storage cost is at least $2\frac{N}{N-f+2}\log_2|\mathcal{V}| - o(\log_2|\mathcal{V}|)$ even if the algorithm uses server gossip.
- In our third lower bound, we consider algorithms where the write protocol sends information about the value in at most one phase. For such algorithms, we show that the total storage cost is at least $\nu^*\frac{N}{N-f+\nu^*-1}\log_2(|\mathcal{V}|) - o(\log_2(|\mathcal{V}|)$, where ν^* is the minimum of $f+1$ and the number of active write operations of an execution.

Our first and second lower bounds are approximately twice as strong as the previously known bound of $\frac{N}{N-f}\log_2|\mathcal{V}|$. Furthermore, our first two lower bounds apply even for regular, single-writer-single-reader (SWSR) shared memory emulation algorithms. Our third lower bound is much larger than our first and second lower bounds, although it is applicable to a smaller class of algorithms where the write protocol has certain restrictions. In particular, our third bound is comparable to the storage cost achieved by most shared memory emulation algorithms in the literature, which naturally fall under the class of algorithms studied. Our proof ideas are inspired by recent results in coding theory.

PODC'16, July 25-28, 2016, Chicago, IL, USA

DOI: http://dx.doi.org/10.1145/2933057.2933118

CCS Concepts

•Mathematics of computing → Information theory; Coding theory; •Information systems → Storage management; •Theory of computation → Distributed algorithms;

Keywords

Atomic Memory; Distributed Storage; Shared Memory Emulation; Storage Cost

1. INTRODUCTION

The emulation of a consistent, fault-tolerant read-write shared memory in a distributed, asynchronous, storage system has been an active area of research in distributed computing theory. In their celebrated paper [3], Attiya, Bar-Noy, and Dolev devised a fault-tolerant algorithm for emulating a shared memory that achieves atomic consistency (linearizability) [17, 16]. Consider a distributed system with server nodes, write client and read client nodes, all of which are connected by point-to-point asynchronous links. The ideas of [3] can be used to design server, write and read protocols that implement an atomic shared memory even if the write and read operations are invoked concurrently with the following guarantee: every read or write operation invoked at a non-failing client terminates so long as the set of servers that fail is restricted to a minority. The algorithm of [3] used a replication-based storage scheme at the servers to attain fault tolerance. Following [3], several papers [15, 13, 1, 4, 21, 12, 5, 2] have developed algorithms that use *erasure coding* instead of replication for fault tolerance, with the goal of improving upon the storage efficiency of [3].

In erasure coding[1] which is studied in classical coding theory, each server stores a function of the value called a codeword symbol. A decoder that is able to access a sufficient number of codeword symbols recovers the value. The number of bits used to represent a codeword symbol is typically much smaller than the number of bits used to represent the value. As a consequence, erasure coding is well known to lead to smaller storage costs as compared to replication in the classical coding-theoretic set-up (See, for example, [11, 19, 8]). Here, we aim to understand storage costs of shared memory emulation, where in contrast with the classical coding-theoretic setup, multiple versions of the data object are to be stored in a consistent manner.

When erasure coding is used for shared memory emulation, new challenges arise. Since, in erasure coding, each server stores a codeword symbol and not the entire value, a read operation has to obtain a sufficient number of codeword symbols to decode the value being stored. When a write operation begins to write a new version of the data object, the old version cannot be deleted from the servers until a sufficient number of codeword symbols corresponding to the new version have been propagated to the servers. As a consequence, servers have to store codeword symbols corresponding to multiple versions of the data object to ensure that a reader can decode an atomically consistent version. Previous erasure coding based shared memory emulation algorithms [15, 13, 1, 4, 21, 12, 5] have noted that the number of versions to be stored at a server can be large if there are a large number of ongoing or failed write operations whose codeword symbols have not been propagated sufficiently. Because servers store codeword symbols corresponding to multiple versions, the storage cost of using erasure coding can be large, even if the number of bits in each codeword symbol is small compared to the number of bits used to represent the value.

Despite the vast amount of literature in the study of storage costs of shared memory emulation, some compelling and fundamental questions remain unanswered. Since a server can store an arbitrary function of all the symbols it receives, can we develop a sophisticated storage strategy that somehow compresses multiple versions at the servers and thereby results in smaller storage costs? If we add multiple phases to read and write protocols or include other algorithmic novelties, can we reduce the storage cost of shared memory emulation? In our paper, we obtain insights into these questions by developing novel impossibility results that lower bound the storage cost of an arbitrary atomic shared memory emulation algorithm.

2. SUMMARY OF RESULTS AND COMPARISONS WITH RELATED WORK

In this section, we first summarize the shared memory emulation and the classical coding theory set-ups. We then describe our storage cost lower bounds in Theorems 4.1 and 5.1. Then, we describe our storage cost lower bound of Theorem 6.5. Finally we compare our results to previously derived storage cost lower bounds.

[1]Server failures are modeled as erasures of codeword symbols; hence the term, erasure coding.

2.1 Set up

Shared Memory Emulation Set-up: We consider an arbitrary algorithm A that implements, over a network of N servers connected by point-to-point asynchronous links, an atomic multi-writer-single-reader (MWSR) shared memory variable whose values come from a finite set $\mathcal{V}$. The algorithm A is required to ensure that all operations terminate so long as the number of server failures is no larger than a parameter f. The storage cost of a server in algorithm A is measured as the logarithm of the number of possible states of the server, and the storage cost of algorithm A is the total storage cost over all the servers.

Classical Coding Theory Set-up: Consider a system with N servers, where a single version of a data object whose values come from a finite set $\mathcal{V}$ is to be stored. The value of the data object must be recoverable, so long as the number of server failures is no larger than a parameter f. The classical *Singleton bound* [18, 20] in coding theory implies that the total storage cost is at least $\frac{N \log_2 |\mathcal{V}|}{N-f}$ bits[2]. The lower bound of $\frac{N \log_2 |\mathcal{V}|}{N-f}$ on the storage cost is known to be tight in the classical coding-theoretic set-up for large values of $|\mathcal{V}|$ [20, 18].

The power of erasure coding is transparent when we want to design a storage system that tolerates failures of f server nodes and the number of server nodes N can be chosen freely. If we use replication, every server stores $\log_2 |\mathcal{V}|$ bits. Since we need at least $f+1$ servers to tolerate f server failures, the total storage cost of the system is at least $(f+1)\log_2 |\mathcal{V}|$ bits. In contrast, if we use erasure coding, the total storage cost of the system is $\frac{N \log_2 |\mathcal{V}|}{N-f}$, which approaches $\log_2 |\mathcal{V}|$ as N increases. If N is sufficiently large, the storage cost of replication is approximately $f+1$ times the storage cost of erasure coding.

2.2 Motivation and Summary - Theorems 4.1 and 5.1

Motivation: The classical coding-theoretic model does not model clients or channels, and therefore differs significantly from the shared memory emulation model. However, the storage cost lower bound of $\frac{\log_2 |\mathcal{V}|}{N-f}$ described by the Singleton bound is, in fact, applicable in the context of shared memory emulation as well. We provide the first formal proof of the lower bound in the extended paper [7]; in particular, we show that for any SWSR regular shared memory emulation algorithm that implements a read write data object whose values come from a set $\mathcal{V}$, the total storage cost is at least $\frac{N \log_2 |\mathcal{V}|}{N-f}$. The natural lower bound of $\frac{N \log_2 |\mathcal{V}|}{N-f}$ inspires the following question.

> **Question 1:** Does there exist an atomic shared memory emulation algorithm whose storage cost is equal to $\frac{N}{N-f} \log_2 |\mathcal{V}|$?

Summary of Theorems 4.1 and 5.1: In this paper, we answer the above question in the negative by proving storage cost lower bounds that are stronger than $\frac{N}{N-f} \log_2 |\mathcal{V}|$. In Theorems 4.1 and 5.1 we show that the total-storage cost of single-writer-single-reader (SWSR) *regular* shared memory emulation algorithm is at least $\frac{2N}{N-f+2} \log_2 |\mathcal{V}| -$

[2]For the sake of the discussion here, we assume that $|\mathcal{V}|$ is a power of 2. We refer the reader to [18, 6] for more details about erasure coding.

$o(\log_2 |\mathcal{V}|)$. In particular, if f is fixed and N is chosen freely, the total-storage cost lower bound of Theorems 4.1 and 5.1 approach $\frac{2N}{N-f} \log_2 |\mathcal{V}| - o(|\log_2 |\mathcal{V}|)$ as N increases; therefore the bounds of Theorems 4.1 and 5.1 are twice as large as the previously known lower bound. Recall that regularity [17] is a weaker consistency model as compared with atomicity. Since Theorems 4.1 and 5.1 apply for regular SWSR shared memory emulation algorithm, they automatically apply for atomic MWSR shared memory emulation algorithms. Theorem 4.1 describe a storage cost lower bound for algorithms which do not use server gossip. Theorem 5.1 describes a lower bound for *any* shared memory emulation algorithm, including algorithms that use server gossip. Our storage cost lower bounds are universal in nature, that is, we make no assumption on the structure of the protocols or the method of data storage. Because we answer Question 1 in the negative, an important implication is that there is an unavoidable price, in terms of storage cost, to ensure regularity in a shared memory emulation system. We next discuss the tightness of Theorems 4.1 and 5.1 in the context of previously derived storage cost upper bounds.

2.3 Motivation and Summary - Theorem 6.5

In the sequel, we define the number of active write operations at point P of an execution as the number of write operations which have begun before the point P but not yet terminated or failed at point P. The number of active write operations of an execution is the supremum, over all points of the execution, of the number of active write operations at the points of the execution.

Motivation: There is a growing body of literature related to erasure coding based shared memory emulation algorithms [15, 13, 1, 4, 21, 12, 6, 5, 2, 22]. These algorithms differ in their structure, liveness conditions on operation termination, and their communication costs. A common insight that applies to all the algorithms of [15, 13, 1, 4, 21, 12, 6, 5, 2, 22] is that, among the class of all executions with at most ν active write operations, the worst case storage cost of implementing an atomic shared memory object whose values come from a finite set $\mathcal{V}$ is *at least* $\nu \frac{N \log_2 |\mathcal{V}|}{N-f}$. In fact, references [13, 5, 2, 4] conduct a formal analysis of the incurred storage cost and show that the storage cost incurred[3] is approximately $\nu \frac{N \log_2 |\mathcal{V}|}{N-f}$. While the prior works highlight the benefit of erasure coding when the number of active writes is small, the storage cost benefits of erasure coding vanish as the number of active writes increases. In particular, for a sufficiently large value of ν, erasure coding based algorithms can even have a higher storage cost as compared to replication based algorithms [3, 14], which incur a storage cost of $\Theta(f) \log_2 |\mathcal{V}|$ irrespective of the number of active writes.

In contrast with the storage cost upper bounds in literature, our lower bounds of Theorem 4.1 and 5.1 do not depend on the number of active writes. Furthermore, if f is proportional to N, then storage cost lower bounds of Theorem 4.1 and 5.1 are both $o(f) \log_2 |\mathcal{V}| + o(\log_2 |\mathcal{V}|)$. Prior literature in conjunction with our results of Theorems 4.1 and 5.1 motivates the following question:

[3]There are subtle differences in the storage cost incurred by the algorithms of [6, 5, 2, 4, 13]. Nonetheless, $\nu \frac{N}{N-f} \log_2 |\mathcal{V}|$ is a lower bound on the cost incurred by these algorithms in the *worst case*, among executions where the number of active writes is bounded by ν.

> **Question 2:** Can we develop an algorithm whose storage cost, when f is proportional to N, is as small as $o(f) \log_2 |\mathcal{V}|$ and does not grow with the number of active writes?

Summary of Theorem 6.5: We provide partial answer to Question 2 in our lower bound presented in Theorem 6.5. The lower bound states that the answer to Question 2 is negative, if the write protocol of the algorithm satisfies certain technical conditions described in Section 6. Informally speaking, the technical conditions in Section 6 imply that the write operation is executed in phases, and a message containing information about the value is sent to the servers in at most one phase per write operation. For any atomic MWSR algorithm that ensures that all operations terminate in every execution where the active number of write operations is at most ν and the number of server failures is at most f, Theorem 6.5 shows that if the write protocol satisfies the conditions stated in Section 6, then the storage cost cannot be smaller than $\nu^* \frac{\log_2 |\mathcal{V}|}{N-f+\nu^*-1} - o(\log |\mathcal{V}|)$, where ν^* is the minimum of $\{f+1, \nu\}$.

Theorem 6.5 is interesting from a conceptual viewpoint since it captures the dependence of the storage cost on the degree of concurrency that has been noticed in the upper bounds of [13, 6, 5, 2, 4]. In particular, the bound of Theorem 6.5 can be much larger than the bounds of Theorems 4.1 and 5.1, if the parameters ν and f are sufficiently large. If the number of active write operations exceeds $(f+1)$, then our storage cost lower bound of Theorem 6.5, which equals $(f+1) \log_2 |\mathcal{V}| - o(\log_2 |\mathcal{V}|)$, implies that replication based algorithms are approximately optimal in the class of algorithms described in the theorem.

The class of algorithms that satisfy the conditions stated in Section 6 include a majority of the algorithms in literature [13, 1, 4, 21, 12, 5]. We refer the reader to Section 6 for a more detailed justification. Theorem 6.5, in the stated form, does not apply to a few algorithms [2, 15] because these protocols send messages related to the value of the write operation in two phases; one phase is used to send a hash of the value for client verification purposes, and a second phase is used to send codeword symbols corresponding to the value.

We provide sketches of proofs in this paper. Full proofs of our results are provided in the extended version of our paper [7].

2.4 Comparison with Prior Storage Cost Lower Bounds

We refer the reader to the extended version of the paper [7] for a comparison with some related works [9, 10, 14, 23, 24]. Here we discuss reference [22], which describes interesting, non-trivial lower bounds on shared memory emulation algorithms where the server and client storage schemes satisfy certain restrictions. Reference [22] assumed that every bit stored in the system is associated uniquely with a write operation, and showed that under such a storage scheme, the worst case total storage cost of the system is at least $\Omega(\min(f, \nu) \log |\mathcal{V}|)$. The implication of [22] is that in the worst case, if the degree of concurrency is infinite and the server storage scheme is restricted in a particular manner, then the replication based algorithms of [3, 14] are approximately optimal.

The assumption of [22] that every bit stored is associated with a unique write operation is restrictive and does not apply to all possible storage methods. To see this, consider a scenario where $\mathcal{V}$ is a finite field. Let $v_1, v_2 \in \mathcal{V}$ be values corresponding to two different write operations. Suppose in some algorithm A, at some point of an execution, a server stores $v_1 + v_2$, where $+$ denotes the addition operator over the field. Then a bit stored by the server cannot be uniquely associated with any of the write operations in an unambiguous way. Therefore, the proof technique and the result of [22] fails to provide any insight on the storage cost of the algorithm A. Put differently, the storage method of [22] does not allow for server storage techniques that potentially compress the values of different versions together (See extended paper [7] for more details). In contrast, the results of Theorems 4.1, 5.1 are universal and would automatically apply to algorithm A. The result of Theorem 6.5 does not impose any structure on the storage method, and could also apply to algorithm A if its write protocol satisfies the appropriate restrictions. In our concluding section, Section 7, we provide a summary of the state of the art based on the main results of our paper and of [22].

3. PRELIMINARIES

We study the emulation of a shared atomic memory in an asynchronous message passing network. Our setting consists of a set of N server nodes and a possibly infinite set of client nodes. Without loss of generality, we let the set of server nodes be $\{1, 2, \ldots, N\}$. We denote the set of client nodes as $\mathcal{C}$. We assume a multi-writer single-reader (MWSR) setting, that is, we assume that $\mathcal{C}$ has a single read client; the remaining clients in $\mathcal{C}$ are write clients, denoted by $\mathcal{C}_w$. If $\mathcal{C}$ has exactly one write client and one read client, we refer to the setting as a single-writer-single-reader (SWSR) setting. Each client node is connected to all the server nodes, and the servers are connected to each other via point-to-point reliable asynchronous channels. Read clients receive read requests (invocations) from some external source and respond with object values. Write clients receive write-requests and respond with acknowledgements. Every new invocation at a client waits for a response of a preceding invocation at the same client. The goal of a shared memory emulation algorithm A studied in this paper is to design the client and server protocols that implement a read-write register of a data object which can take values from a finite set $\mathcal{V}$, with the following safety and liveness properties.

Safety Properties: The algorithms must emulate a SWSR regular registers [17]. Informally a regular shared memory object requires that every read operation returns either the value written by the latest write operation that terminates before the invocation of the read operation, or the value of a write operation that overlaps with the read operation. In Section 6 we further consider multi-writer single-reader algorithms, and we require the algorithm to be atomic [17]. Informally, in an atomic algorithm, the observed external behavior of every execution looks like the execution of a serial variable type. Recall that SWSR execution of an atomic shared memory emulation is also regular, so our lower bounds for regular algorithms in Theorems 4.1 and 5.1 also apply to atomic emulation algorithms.

Liveness Properties: An operation of a non-failed client must terminate in a fair execution, so long as the number of server failures in the execution is bounded by a parameter f. We consider algorithms with weaker liveness properties as well in Section 6, where we ensure termination of operations in executions if the number of *active* write operations is bounded. A formal statement of the weaker liveness properties is provided in Section 6.

Storage Cost Definition: Informally speaking, the *storage cost* of an algorithm is the total number of bits stored by the servers. In general, for an algorithm where the state of server node $i \in \{1, 2, \ldots, N\}$ can take values from a set $\mathcal{S}_i$, we define the storage cost of the server to be equal to $\log_2 |\mathcal{S}_i|$ bits. The *total-storage cost* of the algorithm is defined to be $TotalStorage(A) = \sum_{i=1}^{N} \log_2 |\mathcal{S}_i|$ bits.

4. STORAGE COST LOWER BOUND FOR ALGORITHMS WITHOUT GOSSIP

Our main result of this section is a storage cost lower bound, assuming that servers do not gossip. Specifically, in this section, we assume that every message is sent from a client to a server, or from a server to a client. We state Theorem 4.1, provide an informal description of the proof, followed by a more detailed description.

THEOREM 4.1. *Let A be a single-writer-single-reader shared memory emulation algorithm that implements a regular read-write object whose values come from a finite set $\mathcal{V}$. Suppose that in A, every message is sent from a server to a client, or from a client to a server. Suppose that the algorithm A satisfies the following liveness property: In a fair execution of A, if the number of server failures is no bigger than f, $f \geq 2$, then every operation invoked at a non-failing client terminates. Then, for every subset $\mathcal{N} \subset \{1, 2, \ldots, N\}$ where $|\mathcal{N}| = N - f$,*

$$\sum_{n \in \mathcal{N}} \log_2 |\mathcal{S}_i| + \max_{n \in \mathcal{N}} \log_2 |\mathcal{S}_i| \\ \geq \log_2 |\mathcal{V}| + \log_2 (|\mathcal{V}| - 1)) - \log_2 (N - f). \qquad (1)$$

$$TotalStorage(A) \\ \geq \frac{N(\log_2 |\mathcal{V}| + \log_2(|\mathcal{V}| - 1) - \log_2(N - f))}{N - f + 1}. \qquad (2)$$

Informal Proof Sketch: We show in the extended paper [7] that inequality (2) is a simple consequence of (1). Here we prove (1). Informally speaking, our lower bound argument is as follows. For every subset $\mathcal{N} \subset \{1, 2, \ldots, N\}$ where $|\mathcal{N}| = N - f$, we construct an execution where the servers in $\{1, 2, \ldots, N\} - \mathcal{N}$ fail at the beginning of the execution. The execution has two write operations for values v_1 and v_2, where $v_1 \neq v_2 \in \mathcal{V}$. The second write operation which writes value v_2 begins after the termination of the first write operation, which has value v_1.

In this execution, after the point of termination of the first write, a reader can return v_1 because of regularity. Similarly, after the termination of the second write operation, a reader can return v_2. Therefore, the value v_1 is returnable from the servers at a point before the invocation of the second write operation and v_2 is returnable from the servers at a point after the completion of second write operation. Furthermore, at every point in the interval of the second write operation, at least one of v_1 or v_2 are returnable. This implies that, in the interval of the second write operation, there are two consecutive points P and P' such that v_1 must be returnable from the non-failing servers at point P and v_2 must be returnable from the non-failing servers at point P'. Since (v_1, v_2) can be any ordered pair of distinct values from $\mathcal{V}$, there must be a one-to-one mapping between the set $\{(v_1, v_2) : (v_1, v_2) \in \mathcal{V} \times \mathcal{V}, v_1 \neq v_2\}$ and the set of possible configurations of server states at points P and P'. This implies that the number of possible server states at points P and P' is at least $(|\mathcal{V}|)(|\mathcal{V}|-1)$. Since P and P' are consecutive, at most one non-failing server changes its state between these two points. At least $N-f-1$ non-failing servers have the same state at point P as at point P'. We use this fact to show that the number of elements in the set of possible server states at two consecutive points is at most $\prod_{n\in\mathcal{N}} |\mathcal{S}_i| \times \max_{n\in\mathcal{N}} |\mathcal{S}_n| \times (N-f)$. Therefore, we get $\prod_{n\in\mathcal{N}} |\mathcal{S}_i| \times \max_{n\in\mathcal{N}} |\mathcal{S}_n| \times (N-f) \geq (|\mathcal{V}|)(|\mathcal{V}|-1)$, which implies the lower bound.

4.1 Formal Proof of Theorem 4.1

Consider an arbitrary subset $\mathcal{N} \subset \{1, 2, \ldots, N\}$ such that $|\mathcal{N}| = N - f$. We construct $|\mathcal{V}| \times (|\mathcal{V}| - 1)$ executions of the algorithm A. In particular, for every tuple $(v_1, v_2) \in \mathcal{V} \times \mathcal{V}$ where $v_1 \neq v_2$, we create an execution $\alpha^{(v_1,v_2)}$ of algorithm A. In our proof, we first describe execution $\alpha^{(v_1,v_2)}$ in Section 4.1.1. Then we present some properties of execution $\alpha^{(v_1,v_2)}$ in Section 4.1.2. We use the results of Section 4.1.2 to prove Theorem 4.1 in Section 4.1.3.

4.1.1 Execution $\alpha^{(v_1,v_2)}$

In execution $\alpha^{(v_1,v_2)}$ the reader and the channels from and to the reader do not perform any actions. Among the set of write clients $\mathcal{C}_w$, only one write client takes actions. The f servers in $\{1, 2, \ldots, N\} - \mathcal{N}$ fail at the beginning of the execution. No further server failures occur in the execution. A write π_1 is invoked at a write client with value v_1. All the components of the system except the reader, and the channels from and to the reader, take turns in a fair manner until the completion of π_1. Immediately after the termination of π_1, a write operation π_2 with value v_2 begins. All the components of the system except the reader and the channels from and to the reader take turns in a fair manner until the completion of π_2. The execution $\alpha^{(v_1,v_2)}$ ends after the termination of π_2.

4.1.2 Properties of Execution $\alpha^{(v_1,v_2)}$

Let $P_0^{(v_1,v_2)}, P_1^{(v_1,v_1)}, P_2^{(v_1,v_2)}, \ldots, P_M^{(v_1,v_2)}$ be the adjacent points (or points after successive steps) of the constructed execution $\alpha^{(v_1,v_2)}$, where $P_0^{(v_1,v_2)}$ is an arbitrary point after the termination of π_1 and before the invocation of π_2 and $P_M^{(v_1,v_2)}$ is an arbitrary point after the point of termination of π_2, and M is a positive integer. By the liveness property, we can choose M to be finite. For $i \in \{0, 1, 2, \ldots, M\}$, we denote by $\alpha_i^{(v_1,v_2)}$, the execution between the initial point of $\alpha^{(v_1,v_2)}$ and point $P_i^{(v_1,v_2)}$. We next define the notions of 1-valent and 2-valent points.

DEFINITION 4.2 (k-VALENT, $k \in \{1, 2\}$). *For $i \in \{0, 1, 2, \ldots, M\}$, a point $P_i^{(v_1,v_2)}$ in execution $\alpha_i^{(v_1,v_2)}$ is said to be k-valent if we can extend $\alpha_i^{(v_1,v_2)}$ to an execution β as follows: After $P_i^{(v_1,v_2)}$ in β, all the messages from and to the writer are delayed indefinitely. A read operation starts at point $P_i^{(v_1,v_2)}$ and all the components, except the writer and the channels from and to the writer, perform actions until the read operation terminates. The read operation returns v_k.*

It should be noted that a point of an execution can be both 1-valent and 2-valent.

LEMMA 4.3. *For $i \in \{0, 1, 2, \ldots, M\}$, a point $P_i^{(v_1,v_2)}$ that is not 1-valent is 2-valent.*

Lemma 4.3 is a natural consequence of Lemma 4.4 which informally states that a reader that begins after the termination of the write π_1 should return v_1 or v_2.

LEMMA 4.4. *Consider an execution β which is an extension of $\alpha_i^{(v_1,v_2)}$. In β, after point $P_i^{(v_1,v_2)}$, the writer stops taking steps and all messages from and to the writer are delayed indefinitely. A read operation begins at some point after point $P_i^{(v_1,v_2)}$ and terminates in β. Then, the read operation returns either v_1 or v_2.*

The lemma is a natural consequence of the regularity of algorithm A.

LEMMA 4.5. *There exists some integer $i \in \{0, 2, \ldots, M-1\}$ such that $P_i^{(v_1,v_2)}$ is 1-valent and $P_{i+1}^{(v_1,v_2)}$ is not 1-valent.*

We can show by regularity that (i) Point $P_0^{(v_1,v_2)}$ is 1-valent, and (ii) point $P_M^{(v_1,v_2)}$ is not 1-valent. Among all the numbers in $\{0, 1, 2, \ldots, M\}$, let i denote the largest number such that $P_i^{(v_1,v_2)}$ is 1-valent. If (i) is true, we note that the number i exists. If (ii) is true, then $i < M$. Since i is the largest number such that $P_i^{(v_1,v_2)}$ is 1-valent, we infer that $P_i^{(v_1,v_2)}$ is 1-valent, but $P_{i+1}^{(v_1,v_2)}$ is not 1-valent. The point $P_i^{(v_1,v_2)}$ therefore satisfies the statement of the lemma. Next, we present the definition of a *pair of critical points* of execution $\alpha^{(v_1,v_2)}$.

DEFINITION 4.6 (CRITICAL POINTS). *Let Q_1, Q_2 be two points in execution $\alpha^{(v_1,v_2)}$. The pair of points (Q_1, Q_2) is defined to be a pair of critical points if there exists a number i in $\{0, 2, \ldots, M-1\}$ such that $Q_1 = P_i^{(v_1,v_2)}$, $Q_2 = P_{i+1}^{(v_1,v_2)}$, Q_1 is 1-valent, and Q_2 is not 1-valent.*

Lemma 4.5 implies that every execution $\alpha^{(v_1,v_2)}$ has at least one pair of critical points. Lemma 4.3 implies that if (Q_1, Q_2) is a pair of critical points in $\alpha^{(v_1,v_2)}$, then point Q_2 is 2-valent in $\alpha^{(v_1,v_2)}$. We need the following lemma before proceeding to prove Theorem 4.1.

LEMMA 4.7. *Let (Q_1, Q_2) be a pair of critical points of execution $\alpha^{(v_1,v_2)}$. Then, the reader, and the channels between the reader and the servers, are all in the same state at point Q_2 as at point Q_1. Also, there is at most one non-failing server s such that its state at Q_1 is different from its state at Q_2.*

4.1.3 Proof of Theorem 4.1

For given (v_1, v_2), fix $(Q_1^{(v_1,v_2)}, Q_2^{(v_1,v_2)})$ to be a pair of critical points in execution $\alpha^{(v_1,v_2)}$. From Lemma 4.7, we note that there is at most one non-failing server that changes state between $Q_1^{(v_1,v_2)}$ and $Q_2^{(v_1,v_2)}$. Let s denote the server which changes state between points $Q_1^{(v_1,v_2)}$ and $Q_2^{(v_1,v_2)}$, if there is one; if not, let s denote an arbitrary non-failing server. If $s' \in \mathcal{N}, s' \neq s$, the state of the server s' is the same at points $Q_1^{(v_1,v_2)}$ and $Q_2^{(v_1,v_2)}$.

Let $\vec{S}^{(v_1,v_2)}$ be an element of $\prod_{n\in\mathcal{N}} \mathcal{S}_n \times \mathcal{N} \times \cup_{n\in\mathcal{N}}\mathcal{S}_n$ as follows. The first $N-f$ components of $\vec{S}^{(v_1,v_2)}$ denote the states of the $N-f$ servers in $\mathcal{N}$ at point $Q_1^{(v_1,v_2)}$. The $(N-f+1)$st component of $\vec{S}^{(v_1,v_2)}$ denote the server index s, and the $(N-f+2)$nd component is the state of server s at point $Q_2^{(v_1,v_2)}$. Note that the number of elements in the set $\bigcup_{(v_1,v_2)\in\mathcal{V}\times\mathcal{V}, v_1\neq v_2} \{\vec{S}^{(v_1,v_2)}\}$ is at most $\prod_{i\in\mathcal{N}} |\mathcal{S}_i| \times (N-f) \times \max_{i\in\mathcal{N}} |\mathcal{S}_i|$.

To prove Theorem 4.1, we show that, if (v_1, v_2) and (v_1', v_2') are two *distinct* elements of the set $\{(x,y) : (x,y) \in \mathcal{V}\times\mathcal{V}, x \neq y\}$, then $\vec{S}^{(v_1,v_2)} \neq \vec{S}^{(v_1',v_2')}$. If we show this, then it implies that the number of elements in the set

$$\bigcup_{(v_1,v_2)\in\mathcal{V}\times\mathcal{V}, v_1\neq v_2} \{\vec{S}^{(v_1,v_2)}\}$$

is at least equal to the number of elements in the set $\{(x,y) : (x,y) \in \mathcal{V}\times\mathcal{V}, x\neq y\}$, which is equal to $(|\mathcal{V}|)\times(|\mathcal{V}|-1)$. This implies the following inequality:

$$\prod_{n\in\mathcal{N}} |\mathcal{S}_n| \times (N-f) \times \max_{n\in\mathcal{N}} |\mathcal{S}_n| \geq (|\mathcal{V}|)\times(|\mathcal{V}|-1)$$

which implies the theorem. Suppose, for contradiction, there are two distinct tuples (v_1,v_2) and (v_1',v_2') in $\{(x,y) : (x,y) \in \mathcal{V}\times\mathcal{V}, x\neq y\}$ and $\vec{S}^{(v_1,v_2)} = \vec{S}^{(v_1',v_2')}$.

Let i denote an integer such that $Q_1^{(v_1,v_2)}$ is the point $P_i^{(v_1,v_2)}$ in $\alpha^{(v_1,v_2)}$. Because the point $Q_1^{(v_1,v_2)}$ is 1-valent, there is an execution $\beta_1^{(v_1,v_2)}$ that extends $\alpha_i^{(v_1,v_2)}$ such that, after point $Q_1^{(v_1,v_2)}$ in $\beta_1^{(v_1,v_2)}$, all the messages from and to the writer are delayed indefinitely, and a read operation begins and returns v_1. Similarly, because the point $Q_2^{(v_1,v_2)}$ is 2-valent, there is an execution $\beta_2^{(v_1,v_2)}$ that extends $\alpha_{i+1}^{(v_1,v_2)}$ such that, after point $Q_2^{(v_1,v_2)}$, all the messages from and to the writer are delayed indefinitely, and a read operation begins and returns v_2. The following lemma describes a useful property of executions $\beta_1^{(v_1,v_2)}$ and $\beta_2^{(v_1,v_2)}$.

LEMMA 4.8. *Let $\vec{S}^{(v_1,v_2)} = \vec{S}^{(v_1',v_2')}$. Consider the composite automaton $\mathcal{A}$ formed by the servers, the reader and the channels between the reader and servers. For $k \in \{1,2\}$, every component of the automaton $\mathcal{A}$ has the same state at point $Q_k^{(v_1,v_2)}$ in $\beta_k^{(v_1,v_2)}$ as at point $Q_k^{(v_1',v_2')}$ in execution $\beta_k^{(v_1',v_2')}$.*

We now use Lemma 4.8 to obtain a contradiction. Because (v_1,v_2) and (v_1',v_2') are distinct ordered pairs, there are only two possibilities: (I) $v_1' \neq v_1, v_1' \neq v_2$, (II) $v_2' \neq v_1, v_2' \neq v_2$, or $v_2' = v_1, v_1' = v_2$, both of which imply that $v_2' \neq v_2$. We handle these possibilities separately.

Case (I): $v_1' \neq v_1, v_1' \neq v_2$. We create an execution γ of the algorithm A which contradicts Lemma 4.4. Let i be an integer such that $Q_1^{(v_1,v_2)} = P_i^{(v_1,v_2)}$ in execution $\alpha^{(v_1,v_2)}$. The execution γ extends execution $\alpha_i^{(v_1,v_2)}$, that is, it follows execution $\alpha^{(v_1,v_2)}$ until point $Q_1^{(v_1,v_2)}$. After point $Q_1^{(v_1,v_2)}$, the writer, and the channels from and to the writers do not perform any actions, After point $Q_1^{(v_1,v_2)}$, the servers, reader and the channels between the servers and reader in γ follow the same steps as the corresponding components in $\beta_1^{(v_1',v_2')}$. Lemma 4.8 implies that γ is an execution of algorithm A. In particular, γ is an extension of $\alpha_i^{(v_1,v_2)}$, where, after point $P_i^{(v_1,v_2)}$, the writer and channels from and to the writer do not perform any actions, a read begins and terminates returning v_1'. However, according to Lemma 4.4, the read operation in γ should return either v_1 or v_2,. Since $v_1 \neq v_1', v_2 \neq v_1'$, this is a contradiction.

Case (II): $v_2' \neq v_2$. We create an execution γ of the algorithm A that leads to a contradiction as follows. The execution γ extends execution $\alpha_{i+1}^{(v_1,v_2)}$, that is, it follows execution $\alpha^{(v_1,v_2)}$ until point $Q_2^{(v_1,v_2)}$. After point $Q_2^{(v_1,v_2)}$, the writer does not take any steps, and the messages from and to the writer are delayed indefinitely. After point $Q_2^{(v_1,v_2)}$, the servers, reader and the channels between the servers and reader in γ follow the same steps as the corresponding components in $\beta_2^{(v_1',v_2')}$. Lemma 4.8 implies that γ is an execution of algorithm A. Since γ follows $\beta_2^{(v_1',v_2')}$ from point $Q_2^{(v_1,v_2)}$, a read operation begins in γ and returns v_2'. However, according to Lemma 4.3 and the fact that $Q_2^{(v_1,v_2)}$ is not 1-valent, $Q_2^{(v_1,v_2)}$ is 2-valent, and the read operation in γ should return v_2. This is a contradiction. $\square$

5. UNIVERSAL STORAGE COST LOWER BOUND

Our main result of this section is a storage cost lower bound that is applicable to any regular SWSR shared memory emulation algorithm, even if it uses server gossip.

THEOREM 5.1. *Let A be a single-writer-single-reader shared memory emulation algorithm that implements a regular read-write object whose values come from a finite set $\mathcal{V}$. Suppose that the algorithm A satisfies the following liveness property: In a fair execution of A, if the number of server failures is no bigger than f, then every operation invoked at a non-failing client terminates. Then, for every subset $\mathcal{N} \subset \{1,2,\ldots,N\}, |\mathcal{N}| = N-f$,*

$$2\max_{n\in\mathcal{N}} \log_2 |\mathcal{S}_i| + \sum_{n\in\mathcal{N}} \log_2 |\mathcal{S}_i| \geq \log_2 |\mathcal{V}| + \log_2(|\mathcal{V}|-1) - 2\log_2(N-f), \tag{3}$$

$$TotalStorage(A) \geq \frac{N(\log_2 |\mathcal{V}| + \log_2 |\mathcal{V}-1| - 2\log_2(N-f))}{N-f+2}. \tag{4}$$

Informal Proof Sketch: The proof of Theorem 5.1 shares many common elements with the proof of Theorem 4.1. The main difference is that, here, we need to carefully handle the actions performed by the channels between servers. Like our proof of Theorem 4.1, for every subset $\mathcal{N} \subset \{1,2,\ldots,N\}$ where $|\mathcal{N}| = N-f$, we construct an execution $\alpha^{(v_1,v_2)}$ where the servers in $\{1,2,\ldots,N\} - \mathcal{N}$ fail at the beginning of the execution. The execution has two write operations for distinct values v_1 and v_2. The second write operation which writes value v_2 begins after the termination of the first write operation, which has value v_1.

After the point of termination of the first write, if we let the channels between servers deliver all the gossip messages, and begin a read operation after the delivery of these messages, the read can return v_1. Similarly, after the termination of the second write operation, if we let the channels between servers deliver all the gossip messages, a read can return v_2. This implies that, in the interval of the second write operation, there are two consecutive points Q_1 and Q_2 as follows: for $i \in \{1,2,\}$, if at point Q_i we stop the writers and the channels from the writers and let the channels between servers deliver all the gossip messages to arrive at point Q_i, then v_i must be returnable by a read operation that begins at point Q_i. By ensuring that gossip messages are delivered in the same order after Q_i, we can ensure that after the delivery of the messages, at most 2 servers differ in their states. We use this fact to show that the number of elements in the set of possible server states after the delivery of the gossip messages is at most $\prod_{n \in \mathcal{N}} |\mathcal{S}_i| \times \max_{n \in \mathcal{N}} |\mathcal{S}_n| \times \max_{n \in \mathcal{N}} |\mathcal{S}_n| \times (N-f)^2$. Therefore, we get $\prod_{n \in \mathcal{N}} |\mathcal{S}_i| \times (\max_{n \in \mathcal{N}} |\mathcal{S}_n|)^2 \times (N-f)^2 \geq (|\mathcal{V}|)(|\mathcal{V}|-1)$, which implies the lower bound.

5.1 Detailed Proof Sketch of Theorem 5.1

We provide a proof sketch of Theorem 5.1 here. Omitted details can be found in [7].

5.1.1 Execution $\alpha^{(v_1,v_2)}$

Let $\mathcal{N}$ be an arbitrary subset of $\{1,2,\ldots,N\}$ with $N-f$ elements. Like the proof of Theorem 4.1, for every tuple $(v_1,v_2) \in \mathcal{V} \times \mathcal{V}$ where $v_1 \neq v_2$, we create an execution $\alpha^{(v_1,v_2)}$ of algorithm A. The f servers in $\{1,2,\ldots,N\} - \mathcal{N}$ fail at the beginning of $\alpha^{(v_1,v_2)}$. The execution $\alpha^{(v_1,v_2)}$ has two complete write operations π_1 and π_2 with values v_1 and v_2, with π_2 being invoked after the termination of π_1.

Let $P_0^{(v_1,v_2)}, P_1^{(v_1,v_1)}, P_2^{(v_1,v_2)}, \ldots, P_M^{(v_1,v_2)}$ be a sequence of consecutive points in execution $\alpha^{(v_1,v_2)}$, where $P_0^{(v_1,v_2)}$ is an arbitrary point after the termination of π_1 and before the invocation of π_2, and $P_M^{(v_1,v_2)}$ is an arbitrary point after the point of termination of π_2. We denote by $\alpha_i^{(v_1,v_2)}$, the execution between the initial point of $\alpha^{(v_1,v_2)}$ and point $P_i^{(v_1,v_2)}$.

5.1.2 Properties of Execution $\alpha^{(v_1,v_2)}$

The definition of k-valent points are similar to Definitions 4.2, $k=1,2$, with the exception that we allow the channels the servers to deliver their messages before the invocation of the read operation.

DEFINITION 5.2 (k-VALENT, $k \in \{1,2\}$). *For $i \in \{0,1,2,\ldots,M\}$, a point $P_i^{(v_1,v_2)}$ in the constructed $\alpha_i^{(v_1,v_2)}$ is said to be k-valent if we can extend $\alpha_i^{(v_1,v_2)}$ to an execution β as follows: After $P_i^{(v_1,v_2)}$ all the messages from and to the writer are delayed indefinitely. At $P_i^{(v_1,v_2)}$ all the channels between the servers act, delivering all their messages. After the delivery of the messages in the channels between the servers, a read operation starts and all the components, except the writer and the channels from and to the writer, execute their protocols until the read operation terminates. The read operation returns v_k.*

We inherit the definition of critical points from Definition 4.6. The only change is that the terms k-valent points use the modified definition. Results analogous to Lemmas 4.3, 4.4 and 4.5 in the Section 4 hold, with the modified definition of k-valent points. Lemma 4.7 requires some minor modifications as follows.

LEMMA 5.3 (ANALOGOUS TO LEMMA 4.7). *Let (Q_1,Q_2) be a pair of critical points of execution $\alpha^{(v_1,v_2)}$. Then, (i) the readers, and the channels between the readers and the servers, are all in the same state at point Q_2 as at point Q_1; (ii) there is at most one non-failing server such that its state at Q_1 is different from its state at Q_2; (iii) among all the channels between the servers, there is at most one channel whose state at Q_1 is different from its state at Q_2.*

5.1.3 Proof of Theorem 5.1

From Lemma 5.3, we note that there is at most one non-failing server and one channel that changes its state between a pair of critical points $Q_1^{(v_1,v_2)}$ and $Q_2^{(v_1,v_2)}$. Let s denote the non-failing server which changes state between points $Q_1^{(v_1,v_2)}$ and $Q_2^{(v_1,v_2)}$, if there is one; if not, let s denote an arbitrary non-failing server. Let s' be a non-failing server such that the channel from s'' to s' change its state between $Q_1^{(v_1,v_2)}$ and $Q_2^{(v_1,v_2)}$, for some server s'', if there is such a server [4]; let s' be an arbitrary non-failing server if there is not.

We next present constructions of two executions, $\beta_1^{(v_1,v_2)}$ and $\beta_2^{(v_1,v_2)}$. We know that $Q_1^{(v_1,v_2)}$ is the point $P_i^{(v_1,v_2)}$ for some $i \in \{0,1,\ldots,M-1\}$. Create $\beta_1^{(v_1,v_2)}$ as an extension of $\alpha_i^{(v_1,v_2)}$. At point $P_i^{(v_1,v_2)}$, the writer and channels from the writer stop performing actions, the channels between the servers deliver all their messages. Denote this point by $R_1^{(v_1,v_2)}$. A read operation begins after $R_1^{(v_1,v_2)}$ and returns v_1. Such an execution exits because $Q_1^{(v_1,v_2)}$ is 1-valent.

The execution $\beta_2^{(v_1,v_2)}$ follows $\alpha^{(v_1,v_2)}$ until point $Q_2^{(v_1,v_2)}$. At point $Q_2^{(v_1,v_2)}$, all the channels between the servers act delivering all their messages. For a server j in $\{1,2,\ldots,N-f\} - \{s,s'\}$, the channels with destination j are at the same state at $Q_2^{(v_1,v_2)}$ as they are at $Q_1^{(v_1,v_2)}$; these channels act and deliver their messages in the same order as they do after point $Q_1^{(v_1,v_2)}$ in $\beta_1(v_1,v_2)$. At point $Q_2^{(v_1,v_2)}$, server $j \in \mathcal{N} - \{s,s''\}$ is at the same state as it was at point $Q_1^{(v_1,v_2)}$. Also, at point $Q_2^{(v_1,v_2)}$, server j receives messages in the same order as it does at point $Q_1^{(v_1,v_2)}$ in $\beta_1^{(v_1,v_2)}$; on receiving each message, server j takes the same action in $\beta_2^{(v_1,v_2)}$ as it does in $\beta_1^{(v_1,v_2)}$. The channels with destinations s or s' deliver messages in some arbitrary order, and servers s and s' perform actions based on the protocol specified by algorithm A. We denote this point as $R_2^{(v_1,v_2)}$. It is worth noting that at point $R_2^{(v_1,v_2)}$, all the channels are empty, and every server in $\mathcal{N}-\{s,s'\}$ is at the same state as it is at point $R_1^{(v_1,v_2)}$ in $\beta_1^{(v_1,v_2)}$. At $R_2^{(v_1,v_2)}$, a read operation begins, all the components except the writer and the channels from and to the writer act in a fair manner until the read returns. Because the point $Q_2^{(v_1,v_2)}$ is 2-valent but not 1-valent, the read returns v_2 in $\beta_2^{(v_1,v_2)}$.

[4] Between $Q_1^{(v_1,v_2)}, Q_2^{(v_1,v_2)}$, if there is a server s that changes its state, and a channel between two servers s'' and s' that changes its state, it is easy to show that $s \in \{s',s''\}$. We nonetheless use distinct notation for servers s,s',s'' since it simplifies presentation.

Let $\vec{S}^{(v_1,v_2)}$ be an element of $\prod_{n\in\mathcal{N}} \mathcal{S}_n \times \mathcal{N} \times \cup_{n\in\mathcal{N}}\mathcal{S}_n \times \mathcal{N} \times \cup_{n\in\mathcal{N}}\mathcal{S}_n$ as follows. The first $N-f$ components of $\vec{S}^{(v_1,v_2)}$ denote the states of the $N-f$ servers in $\mathcal{N}$ at point $R_1^{(v_1,v_2)}$. The $(N-f+1)$st component of $\vec{S}^{(v_1,v_2)}$ denotes the server index s and $(N-f+2)$nd component denotes the state of server s at point $R_2^{(v_1,v_2)}$ in $\alpha^{(v_1,v_2)}$. The $(N-f+3)$nd component denotes the server index s' and the $(N-f+4)$th component denotes the state of server s' at point $R_2^{(v_1,v_2)}$ in execution $\beta_2^{(v_1,v_2)}$. Note that the number of elements in the set $\bigcup_{(v_1,v_2)\in\mathcal{V}\times\mathcal{V},v_1\neq v_2} \{\vec{S}^{(v_1,v_2)}\}$ is at most $\prod_{i\in\mathcal{N}} |\mathcal{S}_i| \times (N-f)^2 \times (\max_{i\in\mathcal{N}} |\mathcal{S}_i|)^2$.

To prove Theorem 5.1, we show that, if (v_1,v_2) and (v_1',v_2') are two *distinct* elements of the set $\{(x,y) : (x,y) \in \mathcal{V} \times \mathcal{V}, x \neq y\}$, then $\vec{S}^{(v_1,v_2)} \neq \vec{S}^{(v_1',v_2')}$. If we show this, then it implies that the number of elements in the set

$$\bigcup_{(v_1,v_2)\in\mathcal{V}\times\mathcal{V},v_1\neq v_2} \{\vec{S}^{(v_1,v_2)}\}$$

is at least equal to the number of elements in the set $\{(x,y) : (x,y) \in \mathcal{V}\times\mathcal{V}, x\neq y\}$, which is equal to $(|\mathcal{V}|) \times (|\mathcal{V}|-1)$. This leads to the following inequality:

$$\prod_{n\in\mathcal{N}} |\mathcal{S}_n| \times (N-f)^2 \times (\max_{n\in\mathcal{N}} |\mathcal{S}_n|)^2 \geq (|\mathcal{V}|) \times (|\mathcal{V}|-1)$$

which implies the theorem.

The following lemma is analogous to Lemma 4.8.

LEMMA 5.4. *Let $\vec{S}^{(v_1,v_2)} = \vec{S}^{(v_1',v_2')}$. Consider the composite automaton formed by the servers, the readers, the channels between the servers, and the channels between the readers and servers. For $k \in \{1,2\}$, every component of this system at point $R_k^{(v_1,v_2)}$ in $\beta_k^{(v_1,v_2)}$ is identical to the state of the corresponding component at point $R_k^{(v_1',v_2')}$ in execution $\beta_k^{(v_1',v_2')}$.*

Using the above lemma and similar arguments as in Theorem 4.1, we can prove that for two distinct tuples (v_1,v_2) and (v_1',v_2') in $\{(x,y) : (x,y) \in \mathcal{V}\times\mathcal{V}, x\neq y\}$, we have $\vec{S}^{(v_1,v_2)} \neq \vec{S}^{(v_1',v_2')}$. Therefore, the proof of Theorem 5.1 is completed.

6. STORAGE LOWER BOUND FOR A RESTRICTED CLASS OF ALGORITHMS

In this section, we study a restricted class of MWSR algorithms where the write protocols have specific structure. In our restricted class, the write protocols consist of a fixed number of phases. During an operation the writer performs *black-box* actions that handle objects obliviously, without regard to the actual value. We assume that there is only one phase where a message containing information about the actual value is sent to the servers. The formal statement of our assumptions on the write protocol in Section 6.1 is somewhat technically involved. However the write protocols of most previous algorithms [13, 1, 4, 21, 12, 6, 5] satisfy our assumptions. After stating our assumptions, we state in Theorem 6.5 in Section 6.2, a storage cost lower bound that applies to the class of algorithms that we study. The lower bound of Theorem 6.5 is much larger than the bound of Theorems 4.1 and 5.1, and is close to the costs of previously developed algorithms.

6.1 Protocol Assumptions

Assumption 1: *The state of a write client during a write operation is of the form $(v, m, h(v,m))$ where $v \in \mathcal{V}$ is the value of the write operation, m is an element of a set $\mathcal{M}$, and $h(m,v)$ is the value of function h whose domain is $\mathcal{V}\times\mathcal{M}$ and range is a finite set.*

The set $\mathcal{M}$ is referred to as the metadata set of the write protocol of the algorithm. The function $h(m,v)$ can contain components of the send buffers that depend on the value, and hashed values used for verification to handle Byzantine adversaries [2, 15, 12]. To describe Assumption 2, we first define the notion of a quorum system and a phase. A quorum system $\mathcal{Q}$ is a collection of subsets of $\{1,2,\ldots,N\}$.

DEFINITION 6.1 (PHASE). *For an arbitrary subset $\mathcal{N} \subseteq \{1,2,\ldots,N\}$ and a quorum system $\mathcal{Q}$, a $(\mathcal{N},\mathcal{Q})$-phase consists of a sequence of actions at a write client as follows: (i) Send message m_n to server node n for* every *$n \in \mathcal{N}$. (ii) Wait for responses from least one subset of servers in the collection $\mathcal{Q}$. (iii) Perform internal actions, and finish the phase.*

DEFINITION 6.2 (DECOMPOSABLE INTO PHASES). *We say a write protocol is* decomposable into phases *if, on the invocation of a write operation, it invokes a phase, and on the termination of a phase, it either invokes another phase, or terminates the write operation.*

Assumption 2: *The write protocol is decomposable into phases.*

Before we state Assumption 3, we state the notion of the black-box action. Informally, actions treat the data object obliviously without regard to the actual value of the object. Recall that the write protocol is specified as a set of transitions (old-state, action, new-state).

DEFINITION 6.3 (BLACK-BOX ACTION). *An internal or output action σ performed by a write client is said to be a black-box action if the following holds:* ***if****, for some value $v \in \mathcal{V}$, the action σ is enabled when the client's state is $(m, v, h(m,v))$ for some $m \in \mathcal{M}$, and can result in the transition of the client's state from $(m,v,h(m,v))$ to $(m',v, h(m,v))$ for some $m' \in \mathcal{M}$,* ***then****, for every value $v' \in \mathcal{V}$, the action σ is enabled when the client's state is $(m, v', h(m,v'))$, and can result in the transition of the client's state from $(m,v',h(m,v'))$ to $(m',v',h(m',v'))$.*

A write client's output actions are send and return. Send actions are categorized as below.

DEFINITION 6.4 (VALUE-DEPENDENT SEND ACTIONS). *A black-box send action σ that is enabled during a write operation is said to be value-independent if the message sent does not depend on the value of the operation. A send action that is not a value-independent send action is referred to as a value-dependent send action.*

Messages sent by value-dependent and value-independent send actions are respectively referred to as value-dependent and value-independent messages.

Assumption 3: (a) *All write client actions are black-box actions,* and **(b)** *in a write operation π in an execution α, if there is a phase where at least one value-dependent send action is performed, then every send action in every subsequent phase of the write operation π is a value-independent send action.*

In particular, Assumption 3(b) implies that there is at most one phase where the writer sends value-dependent messages on behalf of a write operation in any execution.

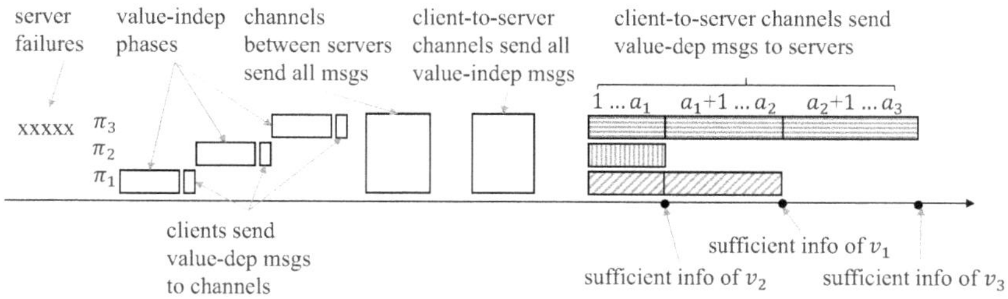

Figure 1: Pictorial description of the execution for $\nu = 3$. $b_1 = 2, b_2 = 1, b_3 = 3$.

6.2 Main Result

In an execution α, a write operation π is said to be active at point P if the point P is after the point of invocation but before the point of termination of π.

THEOREM 6.5. *Let A be a multi-writer-single-reader shared memory emulation algorithm that implements an atomic read-write object whose values come from a finite set $\mathcal{V}$. Suppose algorithm A satisfies Assumptions 1, 2, and 3 stated in Section 6.1, and following liveness property: In a fair execution of A, if the number of server failures is no bigger than f and the number of active write operations is no bigger than ν, then every operation invoked at a non-failing client terminates. Let $\nu^* = \min(\nu, f+1)$. Then, for every subset $\mathcal{N} \subseteq \{1, 2, \ldots, N\}, |\mathcal{N}| = \min(N - f + \nu - 1, N)$,*

$$\sum_{n \in \mathcal{N}} \log_2 |\mathcal{S}_n|$$

$$\geq \log_2 \binom{|\mathcal{V}| - 1}{\nu^*} - \log_2(\nu^*!) - \nu^* \log_2(N - f + \nu^* - 1),$$

$$TotalStorage(A) \geq \frac{\nu^* N}{N - f + \nu^* - 1} \log |\mathcal{V}| - o(\log |\mathcal{V}|).$$

Informal Proof Sketch: For simplicity of exposition, assume $\mathcal{N} = \{1, 2, \ldots, N - f + 2\}$. For our informal description, we set the parameter $\nu = 3$, and $f \geq \nu - 1 = 2$. Our proof of Theorem 6.5 constructs an execution where the servers in $\{N - f + 3, N - f + 4, \ldots, N\}$ fail at the beginning of the execution. The execution has $\nu = 3$ write operations π_1, π_2, π_3 with distinct values v_1, v_2, v_3 respectively invoked at distinct clients C_1, C_2, C_3. We assume that at the beginning of the execution before the invocation of any write operation, a default initial value v_0 can be returned by any read operation, and that values v_1, v_2, v_3 are distinct from the default initial value v_0.

Operations π_1, π_2, π_3 execute their protocols in a fair manner until they reach their respective phases where they send the value-dependent messages (refer to Assumption 3). The 3 clients send the value-dependent messages onto the channels, but the channels do not yet deliver the value-dependent messages.

Now allow the channels from the clients to the servers to deliver all the value-dependent messages to the first $N - f$ servers. It must be the case that the first $N - f$ servers store "sufficient information" to return at least one of the values v_1, v_2 or v_3. This is because there are no additional phases where value-dependent messages are sent, so the servers cannot receive any additional information related to v_1, v_2 or v_3. Furthermore, if we let at least one of the operations π_1, π_2, π_3 complete by performing the remaining phases, then, by safety property, at least one of the values v_1, v_2 or v_3 must be returnable from the first $N - f$ servers after the completion of the operation. So it must be the case that the servers store sufficient information to return one of v_1, v_2 or v_3. Let a_1 be the smallest number such that, if the channels between the clients and the first a_1 servers deliver all their messages, then the first a_1 servers store sufficient information of value v_{b_1} for some $b_1 \in \{1, 2, 3\}$. Note that $1 \leq a_1 \leq N - f$, and sufficient information of any *one* of v_1, v_2 or v_3 is not contained from any of the first $a_1 - 1$ servers.

Now allow the channels from clients $\{C_1, C_2, C_3\} - \{C_{b_1}\}$ deliver their value-dependent messages to servers in $\{a_1 + 1, a_1 + 2, \ldots, N - f + 1\}$. After the delivery of the messages, sufficient information of one of the values v_{b_2} must be available in the first $N - f + 1$ servers for some $b_2 \in \{1, 2, 3\} - \{b_1\}$. This is because, if, after the delivery of the value-dependent messages, server a_1 stops taking actions, and clients $\{C_1, C_2, C_3\} - \{C_{b_1}\}$, and the first $N - f + 1$ servers apart from server a_1 take actions in a fair manner, then one of the operations π_1, π_2, π_3 completes; safety property implies that one of the values v_1, v_2, v_3 is returnable from the first $N - f + 1$ servers. However, note that sufficient information related to v_{b_1} is not contained in the first $a_1 - 1$ servers. As a consequence, v_{b_1} cannot be returnable from the first $N - f + 1$ servers if server a_1 does not take actions and we do not allow the value-dependent messages from client C_{b_1} to be delivered to any one of the servers $\{a_1 + 1, a_1 + 2, \ldots, N - f + 1\}$; therefore a value $v_{b_2} \neq v_{b_1}$ must be returnable from the first $N - f + 1$ servers. Let a_2 be a number with $a_1 < a_2 \leq N - f + 1$ such that, if all the channels deliver their value-dependent messages to the first a_1 servers and the channels from clients in $\{C_1, C_2, C_3\} - \{C_{b_1}\}$ deliver their value-dependent messages to the servers in $\{a_1 + 1, a_1 + 2, \ldots, a_2\}$, then sufficient information about value v_{b_2} is contained in the first a_2 servers for some $b_2 \neq b_1, b_2 \in \{1, 2, 3\}$.

Similarly, if we let the channels from remaining client in $\{C_1, C_2, C_3\} - \{C_{b_1}, C_{b_2}\}$ deliver their value-dependent messages to the servers in $\{a_2 + 1, a_2 + 2, \ldots, N - f + 2\}$, then sufficient information about the value in $\{v_1, v_2, v_3\} - \{v_{b_1}, v_{b_2}\}$ is contained from the first $N - f + 2$ servers after the delivery of the messages. At this point, sufficient information about all 3 values is contained in the first $N - f + 2$ servers. We can show that this implies that there is a one-to-one mapping from the states of the first $N - f + 2$ servers to the values in $(\mathcal{V} - \{v_0\})^3$, where v_0 is the initial value. This implies that the storage cost must be at least $\frac{3}{N-f+2} \log_2 |\mathcal{V}| + o(\log_2 |\mathcal{V}|)$.

Our proof involves developing an appropriate notion of *sufficient information of a value* that is applicable even when each server stores some arbitrary function of the values of the different versions it receives. In particular, we cannot directly borrow from other work [22], whose notion of sufficient information of a value is tied to the storage scheme imposed by the model studied.

7. CONCLUSION

This paper was motivated by open questions, Question 1 and Question 2 in Section 2. We resolved Question 1 in the paper in the negative. Although Question 2 remains open, we obtain the following insights via our results in conjunction with the result of [22]: If there is an algorithm whose storage cost is $g(\nu, N, f)\log_2|\mathcal{V}| + o(\log_2|\mathcal{V}|)$, where $g(\nu, N, f)$ is some real-valued function of parameters ν, N, f then $g(\nu, N, f) \geq \frac{2N}{N-f+2}$, and

- if $g(\nu, N, f) < \frac{\min(\nu, f+1)N}{N-f+\min(\nu,f+1)-1}$, then a write operation sends information about the value of the operation in multiple phases to the servers;
- if, for given values of parameters N, f, we have $g(\nu, N, f) < f+1$ for all values of ν, then, in certain executions, the servers store symbols which somehow compress values across different versions.

8. ACKNOWLEDGMENTS

This work is supported by the National Science Foundation (NSF) under grant numbers CCF-1553248, CCF-1464336, CCF-0939370, CCF-1217506, CCF-1566587, and by the Air Force Office of Scientific Research (AFOSR) under grant number FA9550-14-1-0403.

9. REFERENCES

[1] M. K. Aguilera, R. Janakiraman, and L. Xu. Using erasure codes efficiently for storage in a distributed system. In *Dependable Systems and Networks, 2005. DSN 2005. Proceedings. International Conference on*, pages 336–345. IEEE, 2005.

[2] E. Androulaki, C. Cachin, D. Dobre, and M. Vukolić. Erasure-coded Byzantine storage with separate metadata. In *Principles of Distributed Systems*, pages 76–90. Springer, 2014.

[3] H. Attiya, A. Bar-Noy, and D. Dolev. Sharing memory robustly in message-passing systems. In *Proceedings of the ninth annual ACM symposium on principles of distributed computing*, PODC '90, pages 363–375. ACM, 1990.

[4] C. Cachin and S. Tessaro. Optimal resilience for erasure-coded Byzantine distributed storage. In *Dependable Systems and Networks, 2006. DSN 2006. International Conference on*, pages 115–124. IEEE, 2006.

[5] V. Cadambe, N. Lynch, M. Medard, and P. Musial. A coded shared atomic memory algorithm for message passing architectures. In *2014 IEEE 13th International Symposium on Network Computing and Applications (NCA),*, pages 253–260, 2014.

[6] V. R. Cadambe, N. Lynch, M. Medard, and P. Musial. A coded shared atomic memory algorithm for message passing architectures. 2014. MIT CSAIL Technical Report MIT-CSAIL-TR-2014-015, http://hdl.handle.net/1721.1/88551; Also available on http://arxiv.org/abs/1407.4167.

[7] V. R. Cadambe, Z. Wang, and N. Lynch. Information-theoretic lower bounds on the storage cost of shared memory emulation. 2016. arxiv pre-print, available on http://arxiv.org/abs/1605.06844.

[8] Y. Cassuto. What can coding theory do for storage systems? *ACM SIGACT News*, 44(1):80–88, 2013.

[9] G. Chockler, D. Dobre, A. Shraer, and A. Spiegelman. Space bounds for reliable multi-writer data store: Inherent cost of read/write primitives. 2015. arXiv pre-print, available on http://arxiv.org/abs/1508.03762.

[10] G. Chockler, R. Guerraoui, and I. Keidar. Amnesic distributed storage. In *Distributed Computing*, pages 139–151. Springer, 2007.

[11] A. G. Dimakis, P. Godfrey, Y. Wu, M. J. Wainwright, and K. Ramchandran. Network coding for distributed storage systems. *IEEE Transactions on Information Theory*, 56(9):4539–4551, 2010.

[12] D. Dobre, G. Karame, W. Li, M. Majuntke, N. Suri, and M. Vukolić. PoWerStore: proofs of writing for efficient and robust storage. In *Proceedings of the 2013 ACM SIGSAC conference on Computer & communications security*, pages 285–298. ACM, 2013.

[13] P. Dutta, R. Guerraoui, and R. R. Levy. Optimistic erasure-coded distributed storage. In *Distributed Computing*, pages 182–196. Springer, 2008.

[14] R. Fan and N. Lynch. Efficient replication of large data objects. In *In Proceedings of the 17th International Symposium on Distributed Computing (DISC)*, pages 75–91, 2003.

[15] J. Hendricks, G. R. Ganger, and M. K. Reiter. Low-overhead Byzantine fault-tolerant storage. *ACM SIGOPS Operating Systems Review*, 41(6):73–86, 2007.

[16] M. P. Herlihy and J. M. Wing. Linearizability: a correctness condition for concurrent objects. *ACM Trans. Program. Lang. Syst.*, 12:463–492, July 1990.

[17] L. Lamport. On interprocess communication. Part I: basic formalism. *Distributed Computing*, 2(1):77–85, 1986.

[18] S. Lin and D. J. Costello. *Error control coding, Second edition.* Prentice-Hall, Inc., 2004.

[19] D. A. Patterson, G. Gibson, and R. H. Katz. *A case for redundant arrays of inexpensive disks (RAID)*, volume 17. ACM, 1988.

[20] R. Roth. *Introduction to coding theory.* Cambridge University Press, 2006.

[21] Y. Saito, S. Frølund, A. Veitch, A. Merchant, and S. Spence. FAB: building distributed enterprise disk arrays from commodity components. *ACM SIGOPS Operating Systems Review*, 38(5):48–58, 2004.

[22] A. Spiegelman, Y. Cassuto, G. Chockler, and I. Keidar. Space bounds for reliable storage: Fundamental limits of coding. In *Proceedings of the 2016 ACM symposium on principles of distributed computing*, PODC '16. ACM, 2016.

[23] Z. Wang and V. R. Cadambe. Multi-version coding - an information theoretic perspective of consistent distributed storage. arxiv pre-print, available on http://arxiv.org/abs/1506.00684.

[24] Z. Wang and V. R. Cadambe. Multi-version coding in distributed storage. In *2014 IEEE International Symposium on Information Theory (ISIT)*, 2014.

On the Complexity of Reader-Writer Locks*

[Extended Abstract]

Danny Hendler
Department of Computer Science
Ben-Gurion University of the Negev
Beer-Sheva, Israel
hendlerd@cs.bgu.ac.il

ABSTRACT

A *reader-writer lock* [7] is a widely-used variant of the mutual exclusion lock abstraction [10]. It is shared by n readers and m writers, whose accesses of the Critical Section (CS) must satisfy the following requirement: reader processes are allowed to be in the CS simultaneously but each writer process requires exclusive access. We study the (worst-case) remote memory reference (RMR) complexity of reader-writer locks in the cache-coherent (CC) read/write model [2].

The tight logarithmic RMRs lower bound on mutual exclusion locks [6, 11] implies an $\Omega(\log m)$ lower bound on the RMR complexity of writers. But how does the RMR complexity of reader-writer locks depend on n, the number of readers? This is the question that we address in this work.

We establish an $\Omega(\log n)$ RMR complexity lower bound that holds even for single-writer reader-writer locks. It is derived from the following complexity tradeoff that we prove: if the number of RMRs incurred by the entry section of the writer is $O(f(n))$, then the RMR complexity of the reader's exit section is $\Omega(\log \frac{n}{f(n)})$. The tradeoff holds even if processes may use the compare-and-swap (CAS) operation in addition to reads and writes. We present a family of reader-writer lock algorithms that establishes that the tradeoff is asymptotically tight for any function f(n).

Keywords

Reader-writer lock; Remote memory references; Compare and swap

1. INTRODUCTION

Over the last 20 years, shared-memory mutual exclusion research has investigated the *remote memory references* (RMR) complexity of local-spin mutual exclusion algorithms [2]; much of this work has focused on read/write mutual exclusion [10] (see [1, 3, 4, 8, 16, 17, 19, 21] for some examples).

A reader-writer lock [7] is a widely-used variant of the mutual exclusion lock abstraction. It is shared by n reader processes and m writer processes. While readers are allowed to be in the Critical Section (CS) simultaneously, no process is allowed in the CS concurrently with a writer. Reader-writer locks must also satisfy the *Concurrent Entering* requirement [13, 18]: if all writers are in the remainder section, a reader must be able to enter the CS in a bounded number of its own steps.

There exist read/write mutual exclusion algorithms that incur only a logarithmic number of RMRs per *passage* (entry and corresponding exit of the critical section) [21] and a matching lower bound established that this is optimal [6, 11].[1] Less is known about the RMR complexity of reader-writer lock algorithms. The logarithmic RMRs lower bound on mutual exclusion locks [6, 11] implies an $\Omega(\log m)$ lower bound on the RMR complexity of writers. But how does the RMR complexity of reader-writer locks depend on n, the number of readers? This is the question that we address in this work.

We prove the following RMR complexity tradeoff for reader-writer locks: If the number of RMRs incurred by the entry section of the writer is $O(f(n))$, then the RMR complexity of the reader's exit section is $\Omega(\log \frac{n}{f(n)})$. The tradeoff holds even if processes may use the compare-and-swap (CAS) operation in addition to reads and writes and even for single-writer reader-writer locks. It implies that at least one of these complexities must be asymptotically logarithmic in n. In turn, this implies that the RMR complexity of reader-writer locks is $\Omega\big(max(\log n, \log m)\big)$.

We also present a family A_f of reader-writer lock algorithms, using read, write and CAS operations, that is parameterized on f — the number of RMRs performed by writers. For all $f(n)$, the RMR complexities of writers and readers executing a passage of A_f are $\Theta(f(n))$ and $\Theta(\log(n/f(n)))$, respectively. This establishes that the tradeoff is tight for all $f(n)$.

The rest of this paper is organized as follows. In Section 2, we describe the model and define the reader-writer lock problem. We present our complexity tradeoff in Section 3. This is followed by Section 4, where the algorithms matching

*Supported in part by the Israel Science Foundation (grant 1749/14) and by the Lynne and Wiliam Frankel Center for Computer Science.

PODC'16, July 25-28, 2016, Chicago, IL, USA
© 2016 ACM. ISBN 978-1-4503-3964-3/16/07...$15.00
DOI: http://dx.doi.org/10.1145/2933057.2933099

[1]The lower bound of [6] applies also to mutual exclusion algorithms that may use *comparison* primitives, such as compare-and-swap, in addition to reads and writes.

the tradeoff are described. We prove the correctness of the algorithms in Section 5. We conclude, in Section 6, with a short discussion of related work and directions for future research.

2. MODEL

We assume a standard model of an asynchronous shared memory system, where a set $\mathbf{P} = \{R_1, \ldots, R_n, W_1, \ldots, W_m\}$ of n reader processes and m writer processes communicate via a set $\mathbf{V}$ of shared variables. In each *step* s, a process applies a read, write, or compare-and-swap (CAS) operation to a shared-memory variable v, and returns some response *res*. *CAS(v,expected,new)* changes the value of variable v to *new* only if its value just before it is applied is *expected*; it returns the value of v prior to its application.

We say that step s *accesses* v. If s applies a read or CAS operation to v, we say that s is a *reading step*. If s applies a write or a CAS operation to v, we say that s is a *writing step*. Thus, a CAS step is both a reading and a writing step. We say that a step is *trivial*, if it does not change the value of the variable which it accesses. If a step is not trivial, we say it is *non-trivial*.

An *execution fragment* E is a sequence of steps taken by processes as they perform their algorithms starting from some configuration C. We say that E is permissable from C and denote its execution from C by $C \hookrightarrow E$. We let CE denote the configuration reached after executing fragment E starting from C. An *execution* is an execution fragment that starts from the initial configuration, denoted by C_{init}. We let $\perp$ denote the empty execution fragment.

We consider the *cache-coherent* (CC) shared-memory model. In the CC model, each processor maintains copies of shared variables inside its private cache, whose consistency is ensured by a coherence protocol. Our results apply to both the *write-through* and *write-back* CC coherence protocols [20]. Quoting from [12]: "In a write-through protocol, to read a variable v a process p must have a (valid) cached copy of v. If it does, p reads that copy without causing an RMR; otherwise, p causes an RMR that creates a cached copy of v. To write v, p causes an RMR that invalidates (i.e., effectively deletes) all other cached copies of v and writes v to main memory. In a write-back protocol, each cached copy is held in either *shared* or *exclusive* mode. To read a variable v, a process p must hold a cached copy of v in either mode. If it does, p reads that copy without causing an RMR. Otherwise, p causes an RMR that: (a) eliminates any copy of v held in exclusive mode, typically by downgrading the status to shared and, if the exclusive copy was modified, writing v back to memory; and (b) creates a cached copy of v held in shared mode. To write v, p must have a cached copy of v held in exclusive mode. If it does, p writes that copy without causing RMRs. Otherwise, p causes an RMR that: (a) invalidates all other cached copies of v and writes any modified copy held in exclusive mode back to memory; and (b) creates a cached copy of v held in exclusive mode."

2.1 Reader-Writer Locks

A *reader-writer lock* allows concurrent access of the critical section for read-only operations, while write operations require exclusive access. It is a relaxation of a *mutual exclusion* lock, which only allows a single process in the critical section at any given time. Each process sharing the read-write lock is labeled a *reader* or a *writer*. A reader-writer lock algorithm consists of an *entry section* and an *exit section* that surround a *critical section* (CS). A single execution of the entry, critical and exit section is called a *passage*. When a process is not in the midst of performing a passage, we say that it is in the *remainder section*. In C_{init}, the initial configuration, all processes are in their remainder section and all shared variables store their initial values. We say that a configuration C is *quiescent* if all processes are in the remainder section in C.

We say that a process p *fail-stops* in an infinite execution E, if p enters the CS and does not subsequently exit from it or if p has an incomplete passage in E and executes only a finite number of steps in E. We make the standard assumption that processes do not fail-stop outside the remainder section.

We now state the properties required from a reader-writer lock.

- **Mutual Exclusion**: If a writer is in the CS at any given time, then no other process is in the CS at that time.
- **Bounded Exit**: A process completes the exit section in a bounded number of its own steps.
- **Deadlock Freedom**: Infinitely many passages complete in any execution in which processes perform infinitely many steps.
- **Concurrent Entering**: Let C be a configuration in which all writers are in the remainder section and let $C \hookrightarrow E$ be an execution fragment in which no writers take steps. Then there is a constant b such that any reader that executes at most b steps in $C \hookrightarrow E$ in the course of its entry section enters the CS.

3. A COMPLEXITY TRADEOFF FOR READER-WRITER LOCKS

In executions in which only writer processes participate, a read-write lock algorithm functions as a mutual-exclusion lock. Consequently, read-write locks from read, write and CAS operations are subject to the logarithmic RMR lower bound of Attiya et al. [6]. This implies a lower bound on RMR complexity of writer processes that is logarithmic in m — the number of writers.

In this section, we prove an $\Omega(\log n)$ RMR complexity lower bound that holds even for single-writer read-write locks. In fact, we prove a more general complexity tradeoff between the number of RMRs incurred by the exit section of a reader and the number of RMRs incurred by the entry section of a writer. This tradeoff implies that at least one of these complexities must be asymptotically logarithmic in n, the number of readers.

3.1 High-Level Proof Overview

We now provide a high-level overview of our proofs. We construct an execution whose structure is depicted by Figure 1. It is comprised of 3 execution fragments. In fragment E_1, all readers execute their entry section and enter the CS. In fragment E_2, all readers return to the remainder section. Finally, in fragment E_3, a single writer, say W_1, enters the CS.

The key intuition behind our complexity tradeoff is the following. Before entering the CS, the writer must verify that the CS is empty. In order to do so, it must "become aware" of all the readers that participated in E_2. If the writer accesses at most $f(n)$ shared variables in its entry section, then the value of each such variable must, on average, "inform" the writer about at least $n/f(n)$ readers that completed their exit section. Say the writer reads value v, then it follows that v must have been written by a reader that (on average) "became aware" of $\Theta(n/f(n))$ other readers that exited the CS. To obtain our tradeoff, we schedule reader steps in E_2 so that they collect this "awareness" relatively slowly.

Our proofs require a formalization of the notion of knowledge. Attiya and Hendler defined the concepts of process awareness sets and variable familiarity sets [5]. The *awareness set* of process p quantifies the number of processes that p may be aware of in an execution. The *familiarity set* of variable v quantifies the number of processes a process may become aware of by reading v.

We extend this formalism in two ways. First, we define the new notion of an *expanding step* — a step that expands the awareness set of the executing process; we prove that each such step incurs an RMR. Second, we generalize these notions so that we can argue about the number of readers that a reader becomes aware of during its exit section only, that is, after it "forgets", in a sense, the information it collected during its entry section. Technically this is done by defining the awareness/familiarity sets of execution fragments rather than of executions only.

Execution $E_2 = \sigma_0\sigma_1 \ldots \sigma_r$, for some $r \geq 0$, is constructed in $r+1$ iterations. Each iteration $i \in \{1, \ldots, r\}$ begins with expanding steps executed by all the readers not yet in the remainder section (see Figure 1). To establish the tradeoff, we prove that $r \in \Theta(\log(n/f(n)))$ must hold.

3.2 Detailed Proofs

We start by formalizing a notion of knowledge. Let $C \hookrightarrow E$ be an execution fragment. We quantify the knowledge that processes and variables hold regarding which processes take steps in E. The *awareness set* of process p after $C \hookrightarrow E$, denoted $AW(p, C \hookrightarrow E)$, is the set of processes of whose participation in $C \hookrightarrow E$ p may become aware via its reading steps in E. Similarly, the *familiarity set* of variable v after $C \hookrightarrow E$, denoted $F(v, C \hookrightarrow E)$, is the set of processes whose participation in $C \hookrightarrow E$ may be inferred by reading v. The following two (mutually recursive) definitions formalize these notions.

Definition 1 *Let $C \hookrightarrow E$ be an execution fragment and v be a variable. If no non-trivial steps were applied to v in $C \hookrightarrow E$, then we let $F(v, C \hookrightarrow E) = \emptyset$. Otherwise let s be the last such step, executed by process p, and let $E = E_1 s E_2$. The familiarity set of v after $C \hookrightarrow E$, denoted $F(v, C \hookrightarrow E)$, is defined as follows.*

1. *If s is a write step, we let $F(v, C \hookrightarrow E) = AW(p, C \hookrightarrow E_1)$.*
2. *If s is a CAS step, we let $F(v, C \hookrightarrow E) = AW(p, C \hookrightarrow E_1) \cup F(v, C \hookrightarrow E_1)$.*

Definition 1 implies that the familiarity set of a variable v depends on the last non-trivial step s that accesses v. If s is a write step, executed by some process p, then v's familiarity set becomes the awareness set of p (when it applies it), since s overwrites v. If s is a CAS step, then v's familiarity set is *extended* by p's awareness set. This is because a successful CAS step applied to a variable increases, in general, the knowledge that may be inferred from reading that variable. The familiarity set of a variable to which no non-trivial steps were applied is empty.

Definition 2 *Let $C \hookrightarrow E$ be an execution fragment and p be a process. The awareness set of p after $C \hookrightarrow E$, denoted $AW(p, C \hookrightarrow E)$, is defined as follows.*

1. *If E contains no reading steps by p, we let $AW(p, C \hookrightarrow E) = \{p\}$.*
2. *Otherwise, let s be the last reading step by p, v be the variable accessed by s and $E = E_1 s E_2$. We let $AW(p, C \hookrightarrow E) = AW(p, C \hookrightarrow E_1) \cup F(v, C \hookrightarrow E_1)$.*

We say that process p is $C \hookrightarrow E$-aware of process q if $q \in AW(p, C \hookrightarrow E)$ holds.

Intuitively, a process p is aware of the participation of another process q in an execution fragment if there is (either direct or indirect) information flow from q to p in that fragment via shared memory. Thus, whenever p executes a reading step (a read or a CAS) to some variable v, the processes in f's familiarity set (if any) are added to p's awareness set. Notice that the awareness-set of a process can only grow as an execution fragment unfolds.

The following observations are immediate from Definition 1 and 2.

Observation 1 *Let $C \hookrightarrow E$ and $C \hookrightarrow F$ be two execution fragments. If E is a prefix of F, then $AW(p, C \hookrightarrow E) \subseteq AW(p, C \hookrightarrow F)$ for all $p \in \boldsymbol{P}$.*

Observation 2 *Let $C \hookrightarrow E$ be an execution fragment and v be a variable. Assume there were non-trivial steps applied to v in $C \hookrightarrow E$ and let s be the last such step, applied by some process p. Also let $E = E_1 s E_2$. Then $F(v, C \hookrightarrow E_1 s) = AW(p, C \hookrightarrow E_1 s)$.*

PROOF. If s is a write step, this follows from the first condition of Definition 1. If s is a CAS step, this follows from the second condition in Definitions 1 and 2 and the fact that a CAS step is both a reading and a writing step. □

Our proofs use the notion of *expanding steps*, which are steps that expand the awareness sets of processes. This is formalized by the following definition.

Definition 3 *Let $C \hookrightarrow E$ be an execution fragment, where $E = E_1 s E_2$. We say that s is a $C \hookrightarrow E$ expanding step, if there exists a process p such that $|AW(p, C \hookrightarrow E_1)| < |AW(p, C \hookrightarrow E_1 s)|$.*

Fact 1 *Let $C \hookrightarrow E$ be an execution fragment, where $E = E_1 s E_2$, and assume that s is a $C \hookrightarrow E$ expanding step, applied by some process p, that accesses some variable v, then: $|AW(q, C \hookrightarrow E_1)| < |AW(q, C \hookrightarrow E_1 s) \Rightarrow s$ is a reading step and $q = p$.*

We now show that every expanding step is an RMR.

Lemma 1 *Let s be a $C \hookrightarrow E$ expanding step by some process p, then p incurs an RMR when it executes s.*

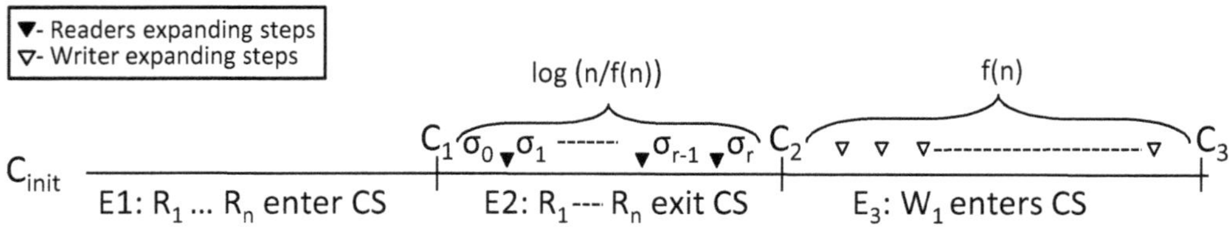

Figure 1: Structure of execution constructed for complexity tradeoff.

PROOF. Let $E = E_1 s E_2$. Since s is a $C \hookrightarrow E$ expanding step, there is a process q such that $|AW(q, C \hookrightarrow E_1)| < |AW(q, C \hookrightarrow E_1 s)|$. From Fact 1, s is a reading step and $q = p$. If p does not have a valid copy of v in its cache immediately after $C \hookrightarrow E_1$, then p incurs an RMR when it executes s. Assume otherwise towards a contradiction. Let s' be the last step previously executed by p (either in E or in the execution leading to C), before which there was no valid copy of v in p'th cache. Let t' and t respectively denote the times when s' and s are executed. Thus, p's cache has a valid copy of v all throughout $(t', t]$. Since t is an expanding step, from Definitions 1-3, there must be a process $q \neq p$ that writes to v during (t_1, t_2). However, in both the write-through and write-back CC models, the write by q invalidates p's copy of v. This is a contradiction. □

We require the following two technical lemmas.

Lemma 2 *Let $C \hookrightarrow E$ be an execution fragment. Let $\mathcal{M}(C \hookrightarrow E) = \max_{p \in P} |AW(p, C \hookrightarrow E)|$ be the maximum size of all process awareness sets after $C \hookrightarrow E$. Let S be the set of steps that processes are about to execute after $C \hookrightarrow E$ in the course of performing their entry or exit section. Then, there is an ordering σ of these steps such that $\mathcal{M}(C \hookrightarrow E\sigma) \leq 3 \cdot \mathcal{M}(C \hookrightarrow E)$.*

PROOF. We now describe how to construct σ. First, we order all read, trivial CAS and trivial write steps in an arbitrary order. Let σ_1 denote the resulting sequence of steps. No step in $CE \hookrightarrow \sigma_1$ changes the value of the variable to which it is applied, hence:

$$\forall v \in V : F(v, C \hookrightarrow E\sigma_1) = F(v, C \hookrightarrow E) \leq \mathcal{M}(\mathcal{C} \hookrightarrow \mathcal{E}), \tag{1}$$

where the last inequality follows from Definition 1 and Observations 1 and 2.

Moreover, for every $p \in P$ that has a step in σ_1 accessing variable v_p:

$$\begin{aligned} AW(p, C \hookrightarrow E\sigma_1) &\leq AW(p, C \hookrightarrow E) + F(v, C \hookrightarrow E) \\ &\leq 2 \cdot \mathcal{M}(C \hookrightarrow E). \end{aligned} \tag{2}$$

We next order all remaining write steps (in an arbitrary order) and let σ_2 denote the resulting sequence of steps. Consider all the steps of σ_2 that access a specific variable v and let the last of them be denote by l_v. Let p_l be the process that executes l_v. From Definition 1:

$$F(v, C \hookrightarrow E\sigma_1\sigma_2) = AW(p_l, C \hookrightarrow E) \leq \mathcal{M}(C \hookrightarrow E). \tag{3}$$

Moreover, for every $p \in P$ that takes a step in σ_2:

$$AW(p, C \hookrightarrow E\sigma_1\sigma_2) = AW(p, C \hookrightarrow E) \leq \mathcal{M}(C \hookrightarrow E). \tag{4}$$

Finally, we schedule all remaining CAS steps (in an arbitrary order) and denote the resulting sequence by σ_3. We also let $\sigma = \sigma_1\sigma_2\sigma_3$. Consider all steps of σ_3 that access a specific variable v, if there are any. Let s_f be the first of these steps and let p_f be a process that executes s_f. There are two cases to consider.

1. If v was written to in σ_2, then its value after $E\sigma_1\sigma_2$ differs from the expected parameter of s_f and of all the other CAS steps of σ_3. Thus, all these steps are trivial, hence:

$$F(v, C \hookrightarrow E\sigma) = F(v, C \hookrightarrow E\sigma_1\sigma_2) \leq \mathcal{M}(C \hookrightarrow E), \tag{5}$$

where the last inequality follows from Inequality 3. Moreover, for every $p \in \mathbf{P}$ that takes a step in σ_3:

$$\begin{aligned} AW(p, C \hookrightarrow E\sigma) &\leq AW(p, C \hookrightarrow E) + F(v, C \hookrightarrow E\sigma_1\sigma_2) \\ &\leq 2 \cdot \mathcal{M}(C \hookrightarrow E), \end{aligned} \tag{6}$$

where the last inequality follows again from Inequality 3.

2. If v was not written in σ_2, then s_f is non-trivial and does change the value of v, making all subsequent CAS steps in σ_3 trivial. Hence:

$$\begin{aligned} F(v, C \hookrightarrow E\sigma) &= F(v, C \hookrightarrow E\sigma_1) + AW(p_f, C \hookrightarrow E) \\ &\leq 2 \cdot \mathcal{M}(C \hookrightarrow E). \end{aligned} \tag{7}$$

Moreover, for every $p \in \mathbf{P}$ that takes a step in σ_3:

$$\begin{aligned} AW(p, C \hookrightarrow E\sigma) \leq & AW(p, C \hookrightarrow E) + \\ & F(v, C \hookrightarrow E) + \\ & AW(p_f, C \hookrightarrow E) \leq 3 \cdot \mathcal{M}(C \hookrightarrow E). \end{aligned} \tag{8}$$

The lemma now follows from Inequalities 2, 4, 6 and 8. □

Lemma 3 *Let $C \hookrightarrow E$ be an execution fragment and let $p \in \mathbf{P}$ be a process that executes steps in E. Let E' be a sequence of steps obtained from E by removing from it all the steps in E that are either by p or that are executed by other processes when they are aware of p. Then $C \hookrightarrow E'$ is an execution fragment.*

PROOF. Let $s_q \in E'$ be a step by process q such that $E' = E'_1 s_q E'_2$. Since $s_q \in E$ we can write $E = E_1 s_q E_2$. If $|E'_1| = k$ we denote E_1 by σ_k and E'_1 by σ'_k. By induction on $k = 1, \cdots |E'|$, we prove that $C \hookrightarrow \sigma'_k$ is an execution fragment. For the base case, $\sigma'_0 = \bot$ and $C \hookrightarrow \bot$ is an execution fragment.

Assume now that $C \hookrightarrow \sigma'_k$ is an execution fragment and let $\sigma'_{k+1} = \sigma'_k s_q$, we prove that $C \hookrightarrow \sigma'_{k+1}$ is an execution fragment. Assume otherwise towards a contradiction. From Observation 1, E' is obtained from E by removing the suffixes of some processes' steps in E. If σ'_k is an execution but σ'_{k+1} is not, it must be that s_q is a reading event from some variable v that returns some response res (the value it returns in $C \hookrightarrow E$) but v's value after $C \hookrightarrow E\sigma'_k$ is some $res' \neq res$. This implies in turn that there is a writing event w that writes res to v in $C \hookrightarrow E$ before v is read by s_q, and w is removed from E. It follows that w was executed by a process that was aware of p when it executed w. From Definitions 1 and 2, this implies that s_q should have been removed from E as well. This is a contradiction. □

Let $\mathcal{A}$ be a reader-writer lock algorithm. Our proofs construct an execution $E = E_1E_2E_3$ of $\mathcal{A}$ defined as follows. In E_1, all reader processes, $R_1, \ldots, R_n$, leave the remainder section, execute the entry section and enter the critical section. Let C_1 be the resulting configuration. In execution fragment $C_1 \hookrightarrow E_2$, all the readers execute the exit section and return to the remainder section. Let C_2 denote the resulting configuration. Finally, in execution fragment $C_2 \hookrightarrow E_3$, writer process W_1 performs its entry section and enters the critical section.

Observation 3 *Execution E is a finite, well-defined execution and W_1 is in the critical section after E.*

PROOF. Since all writers are in the remainder section in C_{init}, Concurrent Entering ensures that $R_1, \ldots, R_n$ each complete its entry section in a bounded number of steps, so E_1 is finite. Bounded Exit ensures that $R_1, \ldots, R_n$ each complete its exit section in a bounded number of steps, so $C_{init}E_1 \hookrightarrow E_2$ is finite. From construction, C_2 is quiescent, so Deadlock Freedom ensures that $C_{init}E_1E_2 \hookrightarrow E_3$ is finite and W_1 is in the CS after E. □

We now show that while W_1 performs its entry section, it must become aware of steps executed by all the readers as they performed their exit section.

Lemma 4 $\{R_1, \ldots, R_n\} \subset AW(W_1, C_1 \hookrightarrow E_2E_3)$.

PROOF. From Observation 3, E is well-defined and finite. Assume towards a contradiction that there is a process $R_i \notin AW(W_1, C_1 \hookrightarrow E_2E_3)$. We construct from E_2E_3 a sequence of events E' as follows: We remove from E_2E_3 all the steps executed by R_i as well as all the steps executed by other processes when they are aware of R_i. From Lemma 3, $C_1 \hookrightarrow E'$ is an execution.

Since R_i is in the critical section in C_1 and since it takes no steps in $C_1 \hookrightarrow E'$, it is in the critical section also after $C_1 \hookrightarrow E'$. W_1 is in the critical section after E. Since W_1 is not aware of R_i at the end of E, none of its steps is removed from E_1E_2. Hence it is inside the critical also at the end of $C_1 \hookrightarrow E'$, together with R_i. This violates Mutual Exclusion. □

Theorem 5 *Let $\mathcal{A}$ be a reader-writer lock algorithm for n readers and a single writer, using read, write and CAS operations. If the RMR complexity of the writer's entry code is $O(f(n))$, then the RMR complexity of the reader's exit code is $\Omega(\log \frac{n}{f(n)})$.*

PROOF. Let E_1 be an execution in which all reader processes, $R_1, \ldots, R_n$, leave the remainder section, execute the entry section and enter the critical section. Let C_1 be the resulting configuration. We iteratively construct execution fragment $C_1 \hookrightarrow E_2$, $E_2 = \sigma_0\sigma_1, \ldots, \sigma_r$, in which all readers execute their exit code and return to the remainder section. For $j \in \{0, \ldots, r\}$, we let $E'_j = \sigma_0, \sigma_1, \ldots, \sigma_j$, so $E_2 = E'_r$. Our construction maintains the following two invariants for all $j \in \{1, \ldots, r\}$:

1. $\forall v \in \mathbf{V} : |F(v, C_1 \hookrightarrow E'_j)| \leq 3^j \wedge \forall p \in \mathbf{P} : |AW(p, C_1 \hookrightarrow E'_j)| \leq 3^j$;
2. All readers not in their remainder section after $C_1 \hookrightarrow E'_j$ are about to execute an expanding step.

For the base case, from $C_1 \hookrightarrow \perp$, we let all readers execute their steps until they are either about to perform an expanding step or they return to the remainder section. We let σ_0 denote the resulting execution fragment and $E'_0 = \sigma_0$. From Bounded Exit, σ_0 is finite. The second invariant follows immediately from construction. As for the first invariant, we have $\forall v \in \mathbf{V} : |F(v, C_1 \hookrightarrow \perp)| = 0$ and $\forall p \in \{R_1, \ldots, R_n\} : |AW(p, C_1 \hookrightarrow \perp)| = 1$, so $\max_{p \in P} |AW(p, C_1 \hookrightarrow \perp)| = 1$. Since none of the steps in σ_0 is expanding, $\forall p \in \{R_1, \ldots, R_n\} : |AW(p, C_1 \hookrightarrow \sigma_0)| = 1$ hence, from Observation 2, $\forall v \in \mathbf{V} : |F(v, C_1 \hookrightarrow \sigma_0)| \leq 1$ and so the invariant holds.

Assume we have constructed E'_j. Let $\mathcal{R}_j$ denote the set of readers that did not complete their exit section during $C_1 \hookrightarrow E'_j$. If $\mathcal{R}_j = \phi$, the construction of E_2 terminated and so $r = j$. Otherwise, we construct E'_{j+1} as follows. From the second invariant applied to E'_j, each of the readers of $\mathcal{R}_j$ is about to perform an expanding step. From Lemma 2, there is an ordering σ'_{j+1} of these steps, such that:

$$\max_{p \in P} |AW(p, C_1 \hookrightarrow E'_j\sigma'_{j+1}| \leq 3 \max_{p \in P} |AW(p, C_1 \hookrightarrow E'_j) \leq 3^{j+1},$$

where the last inequality follows from the first invariant applied to E'_j. Next, we let all the readers of $\mathcal{R}_j$ take steps until they either return to the remainder section or are about to perform another expanding step. We denote the resulting execution fragment by σ''_{j+1}. From Bounded Exit, σ''_{j+1} is finite. We let $\sigma_{j+1} = \sigma'_{j+1}\sigma''_{j+1}$ and $E'_{j+1} = E'_j\sigma_{j+1}$. The second invariant follows immediately from the construction of σ''_{j+1}. Since none of the steps of σ''_{j+1} is expanding, none of the awareness sets grows during σ''_{j+1} so the first invariant also holds.

We proceed with the construction of E_2 until either all readers return to the remainder section or until we complete $\log_3(n/f(n))$ iterations (that is, until we construct $E'_{\log_3(n/f(n))}$), whatever occurs first. We let C_2 denote the configuration immediately after $C_1 \hookrightarrow E_2$.

Next, we show that $r = \Omega\big(\log_3(n/f(n))\big)$. Assume otherwise towards a contradiction, then $r \in o\big(\log_3(n/f(n))\big)$ holds. From construction and the second invariant applied to E'_r:

$$\forall v \in \mathbf{V} : |F(v, C_1 \hookrightarrow E_2)| \leq 3^r = o\big(n/f(n)\big). \qquad (9)$$

Let $C_2 \hookrightarrow E_3$ be an execution fragment in which writer W_1 enters its critical section as it runs solo starting from C_2. E_3 is finite, since all the readers are in the remainder section in C_2 and from Deadlock Freedom. From assumption, the number of RMRs incurred by W_1 in the course of its entry section is $O\big(f(n)\big)$. From Lemma 1, this implies that W_1 executes $O\big(f(n)\big)$ expanding steps. From Equation 9, this implies in turn that $|AW(W_1, C_1 \hookrightarrow E_2E_2)| < n$. This contradicts Lemma 4.

We have shown that $r = \Omega\big(\log_3(n/f(n))\big)$. Let R_i be a reader that did not complete its exit section in the course of E'_{r-1}. There must be such a reader, as otherwise the construction would have stopped before iteration r. From construction, R_i executes exactly r expanding events during $C_1 \hookrightarrow E_2$ as it exits the critical section. The theorem now follows from Lemma 1. □

Corollary 6 *Let $\mathcal{A}$ be a reader-writer lock algorithm for n readers and and a single writer, using read, write and CAS operations. Then either the RMR complexity of the writer's entry code is $\Omega\big(\log n\big)$ or the RMR complexity of the reader's exit code is $\Omega\big(\log n\big)$.*

Corollary 7 *Let $\mathcal{A}$ be a reader-writer lock algorithm for n readers and and m writers, using read, write and CAS operations. Then its RMR complexity is $\Omega\big(max(\log m, \log n)\big)$.*

4. A FAMILY OF ALGORITHMS MATCHING THE TRADEOFF

In this section, we show that the complexity tradeoff we presented in Section 3 is tight. We do so by presenting a family A_f of reader-writer lock algorithms, using read, write and CAS operations, that is parameterized on f — the number of RMRs performed by writers. For all $f(n)$, the RMR complexities of writers and readers executing a passage of A_f are $\Theta(f(n))$ and $\Theta(\log(n/f(n)))$, respectively. This establishes that the tradeoff is tight for all (non super-linear) $f(n)$.

The pseudo-code is given in Algorithm 1. We start by describing the shared variables used by it. We (statically) partition the readers to groups of size $K = \lceil n/f(n) \rceil$ each, according to their ID. The processes in each of these $f(n)$ groups consolidate information using K-process counter objects (see line **1**). A *counter* supports atomic *add* and *read* operations. Jayanti [15] presented an f-array based counter implementation from read, write and load link / store conditional (LL/SC) operations, where add and read operations perform logarithmic and constant numbers of steps, respectively. Jayanti's construction is easily modified to use CAS instead of LL/SC [14]. Thus, in our algorithm a reader performs an add operation in $O(\log K)$ steps and a writer may read all group counters in $O(f(n))$ steps.

The i'th readers group (for $i \in \{0, \ldots, f(n) - 1\}$) uses counters $C[i]$ and $W[i]$. $C[i]$ counts the number of readers that are currently in a passage; it is incremented in line **31** when a reader starts a passage and decremented in line **40** in the exit section. $W[i]$ counts the number of readers that observed a writer and are waiting to be signalled by it. A group-i reader increments $W[i]$ in line **34** after it observes the writer (in line **32**)and decrements $W[i]$ in line **37** after it it signalled by the writer and stops waiting.

Writers ensure mutual exclusion among themselves by using WL (see line **2**) — an m-process starvation-free read/write mutual exclusion lock algorithm satisfying Bounded Exit. There are such algorithms with logarithmic per-passage RMR complexity (e.g. [21]). Each passage by a writer process is associated with a unique sequence number. This sequence

Pseudo-code for reader-writer algorithm A_f.

```
1  const K = ⌈n/f(n)⌉ , shared C[f(n)], W[f(n)]:
   K-process Counter init [0,...,0] ;
2  shared WL: m-process mutex lock ;
3  shared WSEQ: int init 0 ;
4  shared WSIG[f(n)]: int init < 0,⊥ > , RSIG: int
   init < 0, NOP > ;
5  Procedure WriterPassage(){ ;
6  WL.Enter() ;
7  for i ∈ {0,...,f(n) − 1} do
8  |  WSIG[i] ←< WSEQ,⊥ > ;
9  end
10 ;
11 RSIG ←< WSEQ, PREENTRY > ;
12 for i ∈ {0,...,f(n) − 1} do
13 |  if C[i].read() > 0 then
14 |  |  await (WSIG[i] =< WSEQ, PROCEED >) ;
15 |  end
16 |  WSIG[i] ←< WSEQ, WAIT > ;
17 end
18 RSIG ←< WSEQ, WAIT > ;
19 for i ∈ {0,...,f(n) − 1} do
20 |  if C[i].read() > 0 then
21 |  |  await (WSIG[i] =< WSEQ, CS >) ;
22 |  end
23 end
24 Critical Section ;
25 WSEQ ← WSEQ + 1 ;
26 RSIG ←< WSEQ, NOP > ;
27 WL.Exit() ;
28 }
29 Procedure ReaderPassage_p(){ ;
30 local i: int init ⌊p/f(n)⌋ ;
31 C[i].add(1) ;
32 < seq, op >← RSIG ;
33 if op = WAIT then
34 |  W[i].add(1) ;
35 |  HelpWCS(seq );
36 |  await RSIG ≠< seq, WAIT > ;
37 |  W[i].add(-1) ;
38 end
39 Critical Section;
40 C[i].add(−1) ;
41 < seq', op' >← RSIG ;
42 if op'=PREENTRY then
43 |  if C[i].read()=0 then
44 |  |  WSIG[i].CAS(< seq',⊥ >,
45 |  |  < seq', PROCEED >) ;
46 |  end
47 else if op = WAIT then
48 |  HelpWCS(seq') ;
49 } ;
50 Procedure HelpWCS(int seq) {;
51 if C[i].read() = W[i].read() then
52 |  WSIG[i].CAS(< seq, WAIT >,< seq, CS >) ;
53 end
54 }
```

number is stored in variable $WSEQ$ (line **3**), which is incremented by a writer before it returns to the remainder section. Readers and writers synchronize by signalling each other. A writer uses variable $RSIG$ (line **4**) to signal readers and group-i readers use $WSIG[i]$ (line **4**) to signal the writer. $RSIG$ holds a pair of values. The first is a sequence number identifying a writer process passage. The second is either NOP — indicating that no writer currently holds WL, or an opcode signalling the readers that they may need to perform an operation on behalf of the writer that holds WL. We now provide a detailed description of the algorithm, in which the usage of these variables is also explained.

Writers pseudo-code

Writers perform procedure *WriterPassage* (lines **5**–**28**) to execute a passage. After capturing WL in line **6**, process q initializes the variables it uses for synchronizing with concurrent readers. First, it sets variable $WSIG[i]$, for $i \in \{0, \ldots, f(n)-1\}$, used by by group-$i$ readers to signal the writer, to values-pair $< WSEQ, \perp >$ (lines **7**–**9**). This is the initial state of $WSIG[i]$ for signalling the writer performing the passage identified by sequence number $WSEQ$. Then, it sets $RSIG$ to a pair of values $<$*WSEQ,PREENTRY*$>$ (line **11**). The second value — $PREENTRY$, is an opcode instructing a reader-i process that reads 0 from $C[i]$ to notify q (via $WSIG[i]$). The purpose of the $PREENTRY$ command, as well as that of the loop of lines **12**–**17**, is to verify that no readers are already waiting (for previous writer passages), before w instructs concurrent readers to wait for its current passage. This is done as follows. For each readers-group $i \in \{0, \ldots, f(n)-1\}$, q reads $C[i]$ (line **13**). If it is positive, q busy-waits to be signalled on $WSIG[i]$ (line **14**). As we prove, in this case, one of the readers that read 0 from $W[i]$ is guaranteed to successfully CAS $WSIG[i]$ to values-pair $<$*wseq,PROCEED*$>$ (in line **45**), where $wseq$ is the current value of $WSEQ$. At the end of the i'th loop iteration, w ensures that $WSIG[i]$ has value $<$*WSEQ,PROCEED*$>$, in preparation for issuing a new command.

Having verified that no readers are waiting, q must ensure that readers in their passage either exit or will observe it and will wait until it completes its current CS entry. It does by setting *RSIG*$=<$*WSEQ, WAIT*$>$ in line **18**. Now, any reader that reads $RSIG$ in line **32** must busy-wait on it (in line **36**) until its value is changed by q. Next, q ensures that all the readers that did not observe it in their entry section clear the CS (lines **19**–**23**). For each readers-group i, it reads $C[i]$ (line **20**) and, if non-zero, busy-waits (line **21**) until some group-i reader signals it (in line **52**). This completes the entry section.

In its exit section, writer q increments WSEQ (in line **25**) and initializes RSIG for the next writer CS entry (in line **26**); The latter operation signals to readers that already started waiting that they may proceed to the CS. Finally, w releases the writers lock (line **27**).

Readers pseudo-code

Readers perform procedure *ReaderPassage* (lines **29**–**49**) to execute a passage. A group-i reader p first indicates it starts a passage by incrementing $C[i]$ (line **31**). It then reads $RSIG$ - the variable using which the writer that holds WL signals the readers, returning a pair of values to local variables *seq* and *op* (line **32**). To ensure that readers wait for it, a writer writes the $WAIT$ command (along with the sequence number associated with its passage) in line **18**. If $op \neq WAIT$, p may safely enter the CS. Otherwise, let q be the writer holding lock WL, then p must wait for q, so it increments the number of group-i waiting processes (line **34**). It then calls the *HelpWCS* procedure (line **35**). *HelpWCS* (lines **50**–**54**) reads counters $C[i]$ and $W[i]$. If both reads return the same value then, as we prove, it is safe for q to enter the CS (if it is not there already), so p attempts to signal q that it may do so (line **52**) by CAS'ing $WSIG[i]$. It may be the case that multiple readers attempt to signal q. As we prove, the semantics of CAS and the fact that value written by it must match the sequence number *seq* associated with w'th passage ensure that exactly one reader succeeds in signalling q. After *HelpWCS* returns, p waits until it is signalled on variable $RSIG$ that q completed this passage (line **36**). As we prove, it is now safe for p to enter the CS. Before it does, p decrements $W[i]$ in line **37**.

In its exit section, reader p first decrements $C[i]$ in line **40**. Then, it reads $RSIG$ once again in line **41**. If the *op* field equals $PREENTRY$, then a writer w' whose passage sequence number is seq' previously requested (in line **11**) to be signalled when counter $C[i]$ becomes 0. In this case, p checks if $C[i]$ equals 0 (in line **43**) and, if so, attempts to signal w' (in line **45**) that it may proceed in its entry section. Otherwise, if *op* equals $WAIT$, then p calls the *HelpWCS* procedure (described previously) in line **48**, in case w' should be signalled to enter to the CS (in its passage associated with the sequence number seq').

5. ALGORITHM CORRECTNESS PROOFS

In this section, we show that algorithms A_f are correct and provide the following properties: Mutual Exclusion, Bounded Exit, Deadlock Freedom and Concurrent Entering. We also prove that readers do not starve. We start by introducing some notation. For process p and integer N, we write $pc_p = N$ if the next line that p is about to execute is line number N. We write $pc_p \in [N_1, N_2]$, if the next line that p will execute is some line $N, N_1 \leq N \leq N_2$. If $pc_p \in \{\mathbf{35}, \mathbf{48}\}$, then p is about to invoke procedure *HelpWCS*. Thus, if $pc_p \in [N_1, N_2]$ and $\mathbf{35} \in [N_1, N_2]$ or $\mathbf{48} \in [N_1, N_2]$, then $pc_p \in [\mathbf{51} - \mathbf{54}] \cup [N_1, N_2]$ is implicity assumed (that is, the body of procedure $HWCS$ is part of the lines-range). For local variable v and process p, we let $val_p(v)$ denote the value of the p's local instance of v. For shared variable V, we let $val(V)$ denote V's value.

Definition 4 *We say that* reader r is waiting, *if* $pc(r) \in [34, 36]$. *We say it is* waiting for writer passage seq, *if it is waiting after reading values-par* $< seq, X >$ *from RSIG in line* **32**.

Definition 5 *We say that* writer w is waiting, *if* $pc(w) = 14$ *or* $pc(w) = 21$.

Observation 4 *Mutual exclusion between writer processes is maintained.*

PROOF. Immediate from the fact that writer processes start their entry section by capturing an m-process mutual exclusion lock (in line **6**) and end it by releasing it (in line **27**). □

Lemma 8 *If a writer is in the CS, then no reader is in the CS.*

PROOF. Assume towards a contradiction that some writer w is in the CS together with a group-i reader r. Assume w is executing writer passage u. Consider the i'th iteration of the loop of lines **19**–**23** performed by w before it entered the CS. Assume first that w reads 0 from $C[i]$ in line **20**, then r did not yet execute line **31** in its entry section and so it will read a *WAIT* opcode from *WSIG* (in line **32**) and must busy-wait (in line **36**) until w exits the CS.

So assume that w reads a positive value from $C[i]$ in time t and thus has to busy-wait in line **21**. Since w eventually manages to proceed to the CS, it must eventually read values-pair *<seq,CS>* from *WSIG*$[i]$, where *seq* is the sequence number of its passage. This values-pair can only be written in line **52** of the *HelpWCS* procedure. Thus, from line **52**, there is a time $t' < t$ in which all readers that incremented $C[i]$ and did not yet decrement it (if any) are waiting, and therefore may not enter the CS before w exits the CS and executes line **26**. Moreover, any group-i reader that increments $C[i]$ after t' and before w exits the CS must read a *WAIT* opcode from *WSIG* (in line **32**) and will also need to wait. This is a contradiction. □

Lemma 9 *Algorithms A_f satisfy Mutual Exclusion.*

PROOF. Follows immediately from Observation 4 and Lemma 8. □

Lemma 10 *Algorithms A_f satisfy Bounded Exit.*

PROOF. The exit code of readers (lines **40**–**54**) contains no await instructions or other loops. The same is true for the exit code of writers (lines **25**–**28**), so the only place where the Bounded Exit property may be violated is the body of *WL.exit*, but this is not the case as *WL* is a lock that provides Bounded Waiting. □

Observation 5 *Let C be a configuration in which all writers are in the remainder section, then the opcode stored in variable RSIG is* NOP.

PROOF. The claim holds in the initial configuration since *RSIG* is initialized to *<0,NOP>*. Since all writers are in the remainder section, the last writer passage (if there were any) was completed and so *RSIG* was set to *<seq,NOP>* (for some sequence number *seq*) in line **26**. □

Lemma 11 *Let w be a writer in its entry section. If $pc(w) =$ **18**, then there are no waiting readers.*

PROOF. From the code, reader processes only wait for a writer after reading an opcode of *WAIT* from the *RSIG* variable in line **32**. Clearly from the code and from Observation 5, when $pc(w) \in [\mathbf{6}, \mathbf{18}]$ holds, the opcode stored by *RSIG* is not *WAIT*. Thus, no reader starts to wait when $pc(w) \in [\mathbf{6}, \mathbf{18}]$. It therefore suffices to show that any reader that waits when w starts its entry section no longer waits when $pc(w) = \mathbf{18}$.

Assume towards a contradiction that this is not the case and let r be such a reader. So, denoting by t_1 the time when w starts its entry section and by t_2 the time when it finishes the loop of lines **12**–**17**, r is waiting all throughout $[t_1, t_2]$. Let i be the readers group to which r belongs, it follows that w evaluates the condition of line **13** in the i'th loop iteration as true and proceeds to busy-wait in line **14**. Since we assume that w reaches line **18**, it must be that some group-i reader r' wrote values-pair *<seq,PROCEED>* to *WSIG*$[i]$, where *seq* is the sequence number identifying w's current passage. Moreover, since *WSEQ* is incremented only in the writers exit section, it must be that r' read *RSIG* after w wrote it in line **11** of its current passage. Thus, r' read 0 from $C[i]$ at some time $t \in (t_1, t_2]$, implying that r was no longer waiting in time t hence it is not waiting when $pc(w) = \mathbf{18}$. This is a contradiction. □

Lemma 12 *Algorithms A_f satisfy Concurrent Entering.*

PROOF. Let C be a configuration in which all writers are in the remainder section and let $C \hookrightarrow E$ be an execution fragment in which only readers take steps. Let r be a process that executes steps in its entry section in the course of E. If r executes line **32** in E then, from Observation 5, it reads a *NOP* opcode from *RSIG* in line **32** and so enters the CS in a constant number of its steps. This is true also if r read a non-*WAIT* opcode in line **32** before C. So assume that r read a *<seq, WAIT>* values-pair from *RSIG* before C and that r is waiting in C. From Lemma 11, *seq* is the sequence number of the last writer passage, as otherwise the last writer cannot arrive at line **18**. It follows that *RSIG* =< *seq*, *NOP* > all throughout $C \hookrightarrow E$ and so r executes line **36** at most once in E and enters the CS in a constant number of its steps. □

Observation 6 *For all $i \in \{0, \dots f(n)-1\}$, $C[i] > 0$ if and only if there is a group-i reader r such that $pc_r \in [\mathbf{32}, \mathbf{40}]$.*

PROOF. Follows from lines **31**, **40** and their order. □

Lemma 13 *Let w be a writer process executing writer passage seq and let C be a configuration in which $pc_w \in [\mathbf{12}, \mathbf{17}]$. Let $C \hookrightarrow E$ be an execution fragment from C in which, for each $i \in \{0, \dots, f(n)-1\}$, $C[i]$ equals 0 in at least one configuration reached in the course of $C \hookrightarrow E$ (not necessarily all in the same configuration), leading to configuration C'. Then there is a (possibly empty) finite solo execution fragment of w, $C' \hookrightarrow E'$, during which WSIG[i]=<seq, WAIT> holds for all $i \in \{0, \dots, f(n)-1\}$.*

PROOF. Consider w's execution of iteration i of lines **12**–**17**. If $C[i]$*.read*() returns 0 in line **13**, then w proceeds to write *<seq, WAIT>* to *WSIG*$[i]$ in line **16** before C or during $C \hookrightarrow EE'$.

Otherwise, $C[i]$*.read*() returns a positive value so w becomes waiting. Assume this occurs in time t and let $t_2 > t$ be the time when $C \hookrightarrow E$ completes. From line **11**, *RSIG*=< *WSEQ,PREENTRY*> holds in t and so *RSIG* continues to assume this value as long as w does not execute line **18**. Also, from assumptions, there is a time t_1, $t < t_1 < t2$, during the execution of $C \hookrightarrow E$ in which $C[i]$ becomes 0. Thus, there is at least one reader that performs a CAS in line **45** during $C \hookrightarrow E$ and at least one successful CAS is applied to *WSIG*$[i]$, setting it to values-pair *<seq,PROCEED>*. Then w stops waiting and proceeds to write *<seq, WAIT>* to *WSIG*$[i]$ in line **16**. □

Lemma 14 *Let w be a writer process executing writer passage seq and let C be a configuration in which $pc_w \in [\mathbf{19}, \mathbf{23}]$. Let $C \hookrightarrow E$ be an infinite execution fragment from C. Then there is a finite prefix E' of E so that w is in the CS after $C \hookrightarrow E'$.*

PROOF. Let t be the time when w sets *RSIG* $\leftarrow$ *<seq, WAIT>* in line **18** and configuration C is reached. From lines **12**–**17**, *WSIG*[i]=*<seq,PROCEED>* holds for all $i \in \{0, \ldots, f(n)-1\}$ in t. Let r be a group-i reader and consider the value of its program counter in t. There are two cases to consider.

1. If $pc_r > \mathbf{32}$ then r will not wait for w; from Lemma 11, r is not waiting for any other writer passage in C. Consequently, from Lemmas 10 and 12, r eventually returns to the remainder section. Before it does, it decrements $C[i]$ in line **40** at which point it is not counted by either $C[i]$ or $W[i]$.

2. Otherwise $pc_r \leq \mathbf{32}$, so r eventually reads values-pair *<seq, WAIT>* from *RSIG* in *line* **32**. It then increments $W[i]$ in line **34** at which point it is counted by both $C[i]$ or $W[i]$ before it proceeds to busy-wait in line **36**.

It follows from the above that before all group-i readers return to the remainder section or start to busy-wait in line **36**, $W[i] = C[i]$ holds. Also, in both of the above cases, r calls the *HelpWCS* procedure. Thus, there is at least one group-i reader that performs a CAS in line **52** and at least one successful CAS is applied to *WSIG*[i], setting it to values-pair *<seq,CS>*. It follows that eventually writer w stops busy-waiting and may proceed to the CS.

□

Lemma 15 *Algorithms A_f satisfy Deadlock Freedom.*

PROOF. Assume towards a contradiction that the algorithm has an infinite execution fragment $C \hookrightarrow E$ in which no process enters the CS. The following cases exist.

- $C \hookrightarrow E$ is a fragment in which all writers are in the remainder section. This contradicts Lemma 12.

- Otherwise, since the writers synchronize on the *WL* lock, in $C \hookrightarrow E$ there is a single writer process w such that $pc_w \in [\mathbf{7}-\mathbf{27}]$. If w evaluates the conditions of line **13** and line **20** as false for all i then it enters the CS in a finite number of steps. This is a contradiction. Assume, then, that w is waiting forever in C, so $pc_w = \mathbf{14}$ or $pc_w = \mathbf{21}$. In the first case, from Lemma 13, there is a (possibly empty) prefix of $C \hookrightarrow E$ after which $WSIG[i] =< seq, WAIT >$ for all $i \in \{0, \ldots, f(n)-1\}$. As only w itself may write this value to $WSIG[i]$, it must be that w stops busy-waiting. Otherwise, w is waiting forever in **21**. This, however, is a contradiction to Lemma 14.

□

We next prove that readers do not starve.

Lemma 16 *There is no reader starvation in Algorithms A_f.*

PROOF. Assume towards a contradiction that there is an infinite execution E in which some reader r is forever in the entry section. It must be that r busy-waits in line **36**. Let t be the time when r executes line **32**. Since r waits, it reads in time t values-pair *<seq, WAIT>*, where *seq* is some sequence number associated with a passage of some writer w. This implies that w already executed line **18** in the passage associated with *seq*, so $pc_w > \mathbf{18}$ in t. From Lemma 14, there is a finite prefix E' of E so that w is in the CS after E'. From Lemma 10, w returns to the reminder in a bounded number of steps after that. Thus, w eventually increments *WSEQ* in line **25**. Since the value of *WSEQ* is non-decreasing, eventually r reads in line **36** a values-pair that is different from *<seq, WAIT>* and so proceeds to the CS. This is a contradiction. □

Lemma 17 *The RMR complexities incurred by writer and reader processes as they perform a passage in algorithm A_f are $O(f(n))$ and $O(\log(n/f(n)))$, respectively.*

PROOF. A writer process q performs $f(n)$ iterations in the loops of lines **7**–**9**, lines **12**–**17**, and lines **19**–**23**. In each iteration line, possibly except for the lines in which q awaits, it incurs a constant number of RMRs per iteration. It therefore remains to show that q incurs only a constant number of RMRs in each await line. We now consider these lines.

In line **14**, q busy-waits on $WSIG[i]$, until it reads the PROCEED code. Before waiting, it initializes $WSIG[i]$ to *<val(WSEQ),⊥ >* in line **8**. From the code of the readers and the semantics of the CAS operation, the value of *WSIG*[i] can now be changed only by line **45** to *<val(WSEQ),PROCEED>*. It follows that q incurs at most a single RMR in line **14**.

Process q busy waits also in line **21**. Before busy-waiting, q sets $WSIG[i]$ to *<val(WSEQ), WAIT>* in line **16**. From the code of the readers and the semantics of CAS, the value of *WSIG*[i] can now be changed only by line **52** to *<val(WSEQ),CS>*. It follows that q incurs at most a single RMR in line **21**. This concludes the proof for the writers.

A reader process r incurs $O(\log n/f(n))$ RMRs whenever it applies an add operations on a counter object, in lines **31**, **34**, **37** or **40**. In all non-await lines, it only incurs a constant number of RMRs. It remain to consider line **36**, which is the single await line in the reader's code.

In line **36**, r waits until it reads a value of *RSIG* other than $< val_p(seq), WAIT >$ and, once it does, stops waiting. Since the value of *WSEQ* is incremented whenever a writer passage ends, the same value is never written twice to *RSIG*, so r incurs at most two RMRs in line **36**.

□

Theorem 18 *Algorithms A_f guarantee there is no reader starvation and satisfy the following properties: Mutual Exclusion, Bounded Exit, Deadlock Freedom and Concurrent Entering. The RMR complexity of a writer passage is $O(f(n))$ and the RMR complexity of a reader passage is $O(\log n/f(n))$.*

PROOF. Follows from Lemmas 9, 10, 12, 15, 16 and 17. □

6. DISCUSSION

Hendler and Khait [14] presented complexity tradeoffs between read and update operations for several concurrent objects and use a proof technique similar to ours.

The key differences between our lower bound proof technique and theirs are the following. First, whereas their proofs consider obstruction-free implementations and use the step complexity metric, ours consider blocking ones and use RMR complexity. Additionally, in order to capture the knowledge accumulated by readers in their exit section only, our notion of knowledge must be applied to execution fragments rather than to executions (starting from the initial configuration).

A lower bound of Danek and Hadzilacos [9] implies an $\Omega(n)$ RMRs lower bound on Distributed Shared Memory (DSM) [2] reader-writer locks. This linear bound does not apply to the CC model, however.

Hadzilacos and Danek [9] presented a 2-session group mutual exclusion algorithm for the CC model that can be easily transformed to a reader-writer lock algorithm with $\Omega(max(\log n, \log m))$ RMR complexity. The algorithm uses *fetch-and-add* and *compare-and-swap* operations, in addition to reads and writes. Our reader-writer algorithms attain the same complexity using read, write, and compare-and-swap operations only; they also allow choosing one of many optimal tradeoff points between the reader and writer complexities.

Bhatt and Jayanti presented a constant-RMRs reader-writer lock algorithm for the CC model, using *fetch-and-add*, read and write operations.

Our algorithms use compare-and-swap, in addition to read and write. An interesting open question is whether there is an algorithm with the same properties and RMR complexity using read and write operations only.

Our algorithms guarantee that readers do not starve. Writers, however, may starve if there are always readers performing passages. Finding a family of reader-writer algorithms (implemented from the same operations) that match our complexity tradeoff and provide better fairness is left for future work.

7. REFERENCES

[1] J. Anderson and Y.-J. Kim. An improved lower bound for the time complexity of mutual exclusion. *Distributed Computing*, 15(4):221–253, 2002.

[2] J. H. Anderson, Y. Kim, and T. Herman. Shared-memory mutual exclusion: major research trends since 1986. *Distributed Computing*, 16(2-3):75–110, 2003.

[3] J. H. Anderson and Y.-J. Kim. Adaptive mutual exclusion with local spinning. In *DISC '00: Proceedings of the 14th International Conference on Distributed Computing*, pages 29–43, London, UK, 2000. Springer-Verlag.

[4] J. H. Anderson and Y.-J. Kim. Nonatomic mutual exclusion with local spinning. In *PODC '02: Proceedings of the twenty-first annual symposium on Principles of distributed computing*, pages 3–12, New York, NY, USA, 2002. ACM.

[5] H. Attiya and D. Hendler. Time and space lower bounds for implementations using k-cas. *IEEE Trans. Parallel Distrib. Syst.*, 21(2):162–173, 2010.

[6] H. Attiya, D. Hendler, and P. Woelfel. Tight RMR lower bounds for mutual exclusion and other problems. In *STOC*, pages 217–226, 2008.

[7] P. Courtois, F. Heymans, and D. L. Parnas. Concurrent control with "readers" and "writers". *Commun. ACM*, 14(10):667–668, 1971.

[8] R. Danek and W. M. Golab. Closing the complexity gap between FCFS mutual exclusion and mutual exclusion. In *DISC*, pages 93–108, 2008.

[9] R. Danek and V. Hadzilacos. Local-spin group mutual exclusion algorithms. In *Distributed Computing, 18th International Conference, DISC 2004, Amsterdam, The Netherlands, October 4-7, 2004, Proceedings*, pages 71–85, 2004.

[10] E. W. Dijkstra. Solution of a problem in concurrent programming control. *Commun. ACM*, 8(9):569, 1965.

[11] R. Fan and N. Lynch. An $\Omega(n \log n)$ lower bound on the cost of mutual exclusion. In *PODC*, pages 275–284, 2006.

[12] W. M. Golab, V. Hadzilacos, D. Hendler, and P. Woelfel. Constant-RMR implementations of CAS and other synchronization primitives using read and write operations. In *Proceedings of the Twenty-Sixth Annual ACM Symposium on Principles of Distributed Computing, PODC 2007*, pages 3–12, 2007.

[13] V. Hadzilacos. A note on group mutual exclusion. In *Proceedings of the Twentieth Annual ACM Symposium on Principles of Distributed Computing, PODC 2001, Newport, Rhode Island, USA, August 26-29, 2001*, pages 100–106, 2001.

[14] D. Hendler and V. Khait. Complexity tradeoffs for read and update operations. In *ACM Symposium on Principles of Distributed Computing, PODC '14*, pages 186–195, 2014.

[15] P. Jayanti. *f*-arrays: implementation and applications. In *PODC*, pages 270–279, 2002.

[16] P. Jayanti. Adaptive and efficient abortable mutual exclusion. In *PODC '03: Proc. of the 22nd annual symposium on Principles of distributed computing*, pages 295–304, New York, NY, USA, 2003. ACM Press.

[17] P. Jayanti, S. Petrovic, and N. Narula. Read/write based fast-path transformation for FCFS mutual exclusion. In *SOFSEM*, pages 209–218, 2005.

[18] Y. Joung. Asynchronous group mutual exclusion. *Distributed Computing*, 13(4):189–206.

[19] Y.-J. Kim and J. Anderson. A time complexity bound for adaptive mutual exclusion. In *DISC '01: Proc. of the 15th International Conference on Distributed Computing*, pages 1–15, London, UK, 2001. Springer-Verlag.

[20] D. A. Patterson and J. L. Hennessy. *Computer Organization & Design: The Hardware/Software Interface.* Morgan Kaufmann, 1994.

[21] J.-H. Yang and J. Anderson. A fast, scalable mutual exclusion algorithm. *Distributed Computing*, 9(1):51–60, 1995.

An Algorithm for Replicated Objects with Efficient Reads (Extended Abstract)

Tushar D. Chandra
Google
Mountain View, CA, USA

Vassos Hadzilacos
University of Toronto
Toronto, ON, Canada

Sam Toueg
University of Toronto
Toronto, ON, Canada

1. INTRODUCTION

The problem. We consider the problem of implementing a consistent replicated object in a partially synchronous message passing distributed system susceptible to process and communication failures. The object is a generic shared resource, such as a data structure, a file, or a lock. The processes implementing the replicated object access it by applying operations to it at unpredictable times and potentially concurrently.[1] The object should be linearizable: it should behave as if each operation applied to it takes effect at a distinct instant in time during the interval between its invocation and its response.

The main reason for replicating an object is fault tolerance; if a copy of the object becomes inaccessible, the object can still be accessed through the other copies. Another reason for replicating an object is performance; a process that requires the object can access its local copy. The benefit of accessing a local copy, however, must be weighed against the cost of keeping the copies consistent.

Many objects support *read operations*, i.e., operations that return a function of the object's state without changing that state. In practice, read operations often vastly outnumber *read-modify-write (RMW) operations*, i.e., operations that modify the state and return a value that, in general, depends on the object's old state. It is in such instances that replication can be leveraged for performance, in addition to fault tolerance.

In this paper we present a fault-tolerant algorithm to implement a linearizable replicated object that handles read operations very efficiently and RMW operations about as efficiently as existing implementations of linearizable replicated objects. In our algorithm, every read operation is local, i.e., it does not generate messages. In addition, eventually every read operation is non-blocking, i.e., it can be completed in a constant number of local steps by the process that issued it, unless there is a "pending" RMW operation that conflicts with this read. Furthermore, there is a process for which eventually every read operation is non-blocking, regardless of conflicting RMW operations. We use the "shifting executions" technique [2,13,14,19] to prove that the blocking exhibited by our algorithm is, in some sense, optimal: every algorithm that implements linearizable objects has a run in which read operations of all processes but one block in the presence of conflicting RMW operations.

Model sketch. We assume a distributed system in which a fixed set of n processes communicate by exchanging messages. Messages sent are not corrupted and no spurious messages are generated. Processes are subject to crash failures only, and a majority of them are non-faulty.

The system is *partially synchronous*: it is initially asynchronous and after some unknown point in time, called the *system stabilization time*, it becomes synchronous [7]. In addition we assume that processes are equipped with approximately synchronized clocks. We refer to the values of process clocks as *local time*, to distinguish it from real time. We make the following assumptions on clocks, process speeds, and message delays.

Clocks. Each process p has a local clock denoted $ClockTime_p$. Local clocks are non-negative integers that are monotonically increasing with respect to real time, and they are *always* synchronized within a *known* constant ϵ of each other.[2] (This is satisfied if local clocks are within $\epsilon/2$ of *real* time.)

Processes. There is a known lower bound on the speed of processes (as measured on any local clock) that holds forever after some unknown real time.

Messages. There is a known upper bound δ on message delays (as measured on any local clock) that holds forever after some unknown real time.

Note that the clock properties are perpetual, while the process speed and message delay properties are eventual. Before these eventual properties hold, processes can be arbitrarily slow, and messages can take arbitrarily long to arrive and can even be lost.

Local and non-blocking reads and the properties of our algorithm. An object is defined by specifying a set of states Σ, a set of operations Ops, a set of responses Res. The effect of an operation $op \in Ops$ applied to state $s \in \Sigma$ is given by a transition function $\Delta : \Sigma \times Ops \to \Sigma \times Res$; if $\Delta(s, op) = (s', v)$ then the new state of the object is s' and the response of the operation is v. An operation op is a

[1]In practice these operations are generated by applications that wish to use the object. We assume that there is a mechanism, outside the scope of our algorithm, that allows applications to locate processes that implement the object.

[2]Many present-day devices are equipped with GPS, which can be used to provide highly synchronized clocks.

PODC'16 July 25-28, 2016, Chicago, IL, USA

ACM ISBN 978-1-4503-3964-3/16/07.
DOI: http://dx.doi.org/10.1145/2933057.2933111

read operation if, for every $s \in \Sigma$, $\Delta(s, op) = (s, v)$ for some $v \in Res$; op is a *read-modify-write (RMW)* operation if it is not a read operation.

A read operation R *conflicts with* a RMW operation W if there is an object state s such that if we execute R and W starting from s, R reads different values depending on whether it executes before or after W. More precisely, R and W conflict if there exist $s, s' \in \Sigma$ and $v \neq v' \in Res$ such that $\Delta(s, W) = (s', -)$, $\Delta(s, R) = (s, v)$, and $\Delta(s', R) = (s', v')$.

We say that reads are *local* if read operations do not result in messages being sent. More precisely, reads are local if the number of messages sent during the execution of the algorithm does not depend on the number of reads performed in the execution. We say that an instance of a read operation issued by process p in an execution is *non-blocking* if it completes within a constant number of steps of p, without waiting for a message to arrive or for the process's clock to reach a certain value.

In this paper we present an algorithm for implementing linearizable replicated objects in which read operations are always local and, in certain circumstances, non-blocking. Specifically, after the system stabilizes, reads at one process (the "leader") are always non-blocking; and at any other process p, a read blocks only if p is aware of an on-going RMW operation that conflicts with the read. In many practical settings, this means that with our algorithm most reads are indeed non-blocking. Even a read that blocks because of conflicting RMW operations, blocks only for a short period, namely for at most 3δ time (after the system stabilizes).

Our algorithm is quite robust, in that it retains important properties even when the assumptions of the model do not hold. If a majority of processes crash or the bounds on process speed or message delay never hold, only liveness is compromised — i.e., operations applied to the object may not terminate, but they will never return incorrect results. If clocks are not synchronized, the object remains consistent in the sense that the sub-execution consisting of the RMW operations (i.e., the execution excluding the read operations) is still linearizable, but reads may stall or return stale object states. Once clock synchrony is restored, however, reads will again return the current object state.

Roadmap. The rest of the paper is organized as follows. Our algorithm requires a leader election service, which we describe in Section 2; this service may be of wider interest than its use in our algorithm. In Section 3 we describe the algorithm. In Section 4 we show that in any algorithm reads exhibit blocking similar to that of our algorithm. We conclude in Section 5 with a discussion of related work.

2. ENHANCED LEADER SERVICE

We assume that each process has access to a procedure *leader*(), which returns the name of a process such that there is a nonfaulty process ℓ and a real time after which every call to *leader*() returns ℓ. In other words, the procedure *leader*() is the well-known Ω failure detector [5]. There are efficient implementations of *leader*(), even under weaker assumptions than those required for our algorithm [1, 18].

Note that with *leader*() multiple processes can consider themselves to be leaders at the same (local or real) time. For our implementation of replicated objects we need a leader election algorithm with a stronger property; namely, that at all *local* times, at most one process considers itself to be leader. We present an algorithm that transforms (as a "black box") any simple leader service *leader*() to one that satisfies this stronger property. The resulting service, called *enhanced leader service*, provides to each process a procedure $AmLeader(t_1, t_2)$. Roughly speaking, this procedure returns TRUE if the process that invoked it has been the leader *continuously* at all local times t such that $t_1 \le t \le t_2$, and returns FALSE otherwise. More precisely, the procedure $AmLeader(-, -)$ satisfies the following properties:

(EL1) If the calls $AmLeader(t_1, t_2)$ and $AmLeader(t'_1, t'_2)$ by *distinct* processes both return TRUE, where $t_1 \le t_2$ and $t'_1 \le t'_2$, then the intervals $[t_1, t_2]$ and $[t'_1, t'_2]$ are disjoint. (Hence, it is not possible for two different processes to be leaders at the same local time.)

(EL2) There is a nonfaulty process ℓ and a local time t^* such that for all local times $t_2 \ge t_1 \ge t^*$, the procedure $AmLeader(t_1, t_2)$ (i) returns TRUE if called by ℓ at any local time $t \ge t_2$; and (ii) returns FALSE if called by any process $p \ne \ell$ at any local time. (Hence, eventually some correct process ℓ is permanently the leader.)

The basic idea of our leader election enhancer is as follows. Each process p periodically calls *leader*() to determine what it believes is the current leader ℓ. It then sends to ℓ a leader-lease message that contains an interval of *local* time during which p "supports" ℓ as the leader. The leader-lease message also contains a counter c of the number of times p has observed the leader changing. Each process p collects all the leader-lease messages sent to it. To determine whether it has been *continuously* leader from local time t_1 to local time t_2, p checks that there is a majority of processes M such that for each $q \in M$, p has received from q a message m_1 with an interval that covers t_1 and a message m_2 (possibly the same as m_1) that covers t_2 *with the same counter* c *as* m_1. In other words, q was continuously supporting p as the leader throughout an interval that includes both t_1 and t_2. Detailed pseudocode for the enhanced leader service is shown in Appendix B.

3. THE ALGORITHM

We describe the algorithm in English, with comments to provide some intuition why the algorithm is correct. Detailed pseudocode is given in Appendix A. A detailed proof of the algorithm's correctness, and that of the enhanced leader service, will appear in the full paper.

Our algorithm uses the procedure $AmLeader(t_1, t_2)$ to effectively divide local time (i.e., the range of values of local clocks) into a sequence of maximal non-overlapping intervals, during each of which at most one process is continuously the leader, and the last of which is infinite and has a nonfaulty leader ℓ.

The leader has two functions: (i) to linearize the RMW operations using a consensus-like mechanism, and (ii) to issue "read leases", the mechanism the algorithm uses to execute read operations efficiently. These two functions, though not independent of each other, are well separated. To highlight this, we present the pseudocode in Appendix A in two colours: code in black implements the consensus-like mechanism that handles RMW operations; code in red implements the read-lease mechanism that handles read operations. (In black-and-white printing the red code appears in lighter gray.) If we ignore the special property of read operations and submit them as generic RMW operations, the red code could be simply stripped away, and the resulting algorithm would be a linearizable implementation of replicated objects. The red code can be treated as an add-on, built on top of the black code. This modularity makes reasoning about correctness of the algorithm cleaner, and may make improvements to our algorithm easier to conceive and to prove correct. We consider this clean separation of the two functions an important feature of the algorithm.

For the first function, the leader collects into *batches* the RMW operations submitted by processes (including itself), and then attempts to commit each batch by a two-phase protocol: first, the leader attempts to *notify* all processes about the batch; when it determines that a majority of processes, including itself, have been notified, the leader informs the processes that the batch is *committed*. Each leader ensures that all nonfaulty processes agree on the same sequence of batches, *across all changes of leadership*: It is important to ensure that a batch left incomplete by a leader that was demoted (say because it crashed or was very slow), with some processes notified of the batch and others not, is handled consistently by the demoted leader's successors. Each process applies to its local replica the committed batches in sequence, and applies the operations in each batch in some pre-determined order, the same for all processes. When a process applies one of its own RMW operations to its replica, it determines the response of that operation. Since all processes apply the same sequence of RMW operations in the same order, the execution of RMW operations applied to the object is linearizable.

The second function of the leader is to periodically issue read leases. A read lease is a pair (j, t_s) where j is the sequence number of the latest batch committed by the leader, and t_s is the local time when the leader issued this lease. The end of the lease is $t_s + \mathit{LeasePeriod}$, where *LeasePeriod* is a suitably defined parameter. Intuitively, the read lease (j, t_s) held by a process p is a promise by the leader to p that no batch $j' > j$ of RMW operations will be committed (by *any* leader, current or future) before local time $t_s + \mathit{LeasePeriod}$ according to p's clock, *unless p has been notified of batch j'*. We will explain later how the leader makes good on this promise and how processes use the leases to read.

Key data structures. If a leader that has notified other processes of batch k receives acknowledgements from $\lfloor n/2 \rfloor$ other processes that they have received the notification, we say that batch k is *committed*. If a batch is committed, its RMW operations have been applied, or are sure to be applied in the future, by all nonfaulty processes to their replicas. Each process p maintains three key pieces of information:

- An array *Batch* of *committed* batches that p knows about. Initially, $\mathit{Batch}[j] = \emptyset$ for each batch j. If $\mathit{Batch}[j] = O \neq \emptyset$, then p has been informed that the j-th batch has been committed and consists of the operations in set O.
- A triple $(\mathit{Ops}, \mathit{ts}, k)$, which is called p's *estimate* and indicates the "freshest" batch of which p has been *notified* (but which is not necessarily committed). *Ops* is the set of RMW operations in that batch, and the pair (ts, k) uniquely identifies the batch and indicates its freshness: *ts* is the local time when the process that sent the notification to p became leader, and k is the sequence number of the batch. The larger this pair (in lexicographic ordering), the fresher the batch.
- An array *PendingBatch* such that $\mathit{PendingBatch}[j] = O \neq \emptyset$ at p if O is the most recent batch with number j for which p has received a notification.

The algorithm satisfies the following invariants:

(I1) If a process has $\mathit{Batch}[j] = O \neq \emptyset$, then the value of $\mathit{Batch}[j]$ at that process remains O thereafter and if some other process has $\mathit{Batch}[j] = O' \neq \emptyset$ then $O = O'$. Furthermore, if $j \neq j'$, $\mathit{Batch}[j] \cap \mathit{Batch}[j'] = \emptyset$. That is, once assigned, the value of a batch is stable in each process, processes agree on the sequence of committed batches, and no operation is included in two different batches.

(I2) If p's estimate is (O, t, j), then p has $\mathit{Batch}[j-1] \neq \emptyset$; i.e., the previous batch of p's estimate is committed and p knows that batch.

(I3) If process p has $\mathit{Batch}[j] \neq \emptyset$, then for each i, $1 \leq i < j$, a majority of processes have $\mathit{Batch}[i] \neq \emptyset$; i.e., all previous batches are committed and each is known by a majority of processes.

Overall structure of the algorithm. Each process p is structured as three parallel threads:

- Thread 1 handles the RMW operations (lines 2–6) and read operations (lines 7–19) submitted to p.
- Thread 2 (lines 20–23) is an infinite loop in which p repeatedly checks to see if it is the leader at the present local time t. If so, it launches procedure $\mathit{LeaderWork}(t)$, described below, in which it performs the two tasks of a leader outlined above: committing the batches of RMW operations and issuing read leases. The process p remains in this procedure until it discovers that it is no longer the leader. While p is not a leader, its Thread 2 simply handles certain types of messages sent to it.
- Thread 3 (line 24) handles the messages received by p other than those handled in Thread 2.

Procedure *LeaderWork*. A demoted leader may leave its last batch in an indeterminate state, with some processes notified of this batch and others not. Thus, when a process p becomes leader at local time t and launches the procedure $\mathit{LeaderWork}(t)$ (line 22), its first order of business is to (i) commit a batch that may have been left half-done by a previous leader or ensure that this batch will not be committed, even if traces of it remain in the system — e.g., some process still has an estimate with that batch, and (ii) determine the state of the object after all committed batches. This initialization of a new leader (lines 26–36) is done as follows. (We note that throughout the description below the variable t refers to the local time when process p determined that it is the new leader.)

The new leader p first tries to find the most recent estimate that any process has (lines 26–30). It does so by sending $\langle \text{ESTREQ}, t \rangle$ messages to the other processes, requesting their current estimates, and waiting for $\lfloor n/2 \rfloor$ responses (lines 99—101) so that, together with its own, it has estimates from a majority of processes. To tolerate message loss, p sends ESTREQ messages periodically, all the while ensuring it is still the leader and exiting the procedure $\mathit{LeaderWork}(t)$ if it is not (line 29).

Once p has estimates from a majority of processes, it selects the "freshest" estimate $(\mathit{Ops}^*, \mathit{ts}^*, k^*)$ (line 31). The set of operations Ops^* of estimate $(\mathit{Ops}^*, \mathit{ts}^*, k^*)$ is not necessarily committed as batch k^*, but batch $k^* - 1$ is committed and p knows this batch. To see this recall that, by Invariant (I2) of the algorithm, the process q that sent estimate (Ops^*, ts^*, k^*) to p knew batch k^*-1; q included that batch in its reply to p's ESTREQ message (line 101), and p assigned it to its $Batch[k^*-1]$ variable when it received q's estimate (line 90). Also, by Invariant (I3) of the algorithm, since q has $Batch[k^*-1] \neq \emptyset$, each of batches $1, 2, \dots, k^*-2$ is known by a majority of processes, and therefore by at least one nonfaulty process. Thus, p can find any of these batches that it is missing from one of its nonfaulty peers. This is done by calling procedure $FindMissingBatches(k^*-2)$ (line 33).

Once the new leader p has batches $1..k^*-1$, it determines the state of the object after all operations in these batches have been applied. This is done by calling the procedure $ExecuteUpToBatch(k^*-1)$ (line 34). In catching up to the latest state of the object, the leader does not apply all these operations from scratch, but picks up from the most recent state it has computed. The leader now attempts to commit Ops^* as batch number k^* by calling the procedure $DoOps(Ops^*, t, k^*)$ (line 35), which we will describe shortly. If this call fails, p has ceased being leader and exits $LeaderWork(t)$. Otherwise, p initiates a single operation NOOP (that has no effect on the state of the object) as a RMW operation via Thread 1. This ensures the liveness of reads even if no process ever submits a RMW operation again. (Initiating this NOOP is unnecessary if processes keep submitting RMW operations.) At this point, p has successfully completed its initialization as leader, and proceeds with the leader's continuing tasks: granting read leases and committing new batches of RMW operations. To do so, p enters a loop (lines 39–51) in which it records the current local time t', verifies that it has been continuously the leader since local time t by calling $AmLeader(t, t')$ (line 40), and

- if it is time to renew the read leases, it sends a new read lease (k, t') to all other processes, where k is the number of the latest batch committed (line 44),
- if it has received requests for a set $NextOps$ of new RMW operations, it tries to commit this as the next batch of operations by calling the procedure $DoOps(NextOps, t, k+1)$ (line 49), and
- it sends the last committed batch to all other processes (line 51). This can be done "lazily"; its only purpose is to safeguard against message loss.

The leader repeats these actions until it ceases being leader, in which case it exits $LeaderWork(t)$ (lines 41 and 50).

Procedure *DoOps*. Next we describe the procedure $DoOps(O, t, j)$, by which a process p that became leader at local time t attempts to commit O as the j-th batch of RMW operations, and succeeds in doing so unless it crashes or loses its role as leader during the procedure's execution.

Process p first checks whether it has previously sent its estimate to a process that became leader later than it (line 52); if so, it abdandons its attempt to commit batch j and abdicates. Otherwise, p adopts (O, t, j) as its current estimate (line 53). It then notifies other processes of this new batch by sending $\langle \text{PREPARE}, O, t, j, B\rangle$ to all other processes repeatedly (to safeguard against message loss), where B is p's current value of $Batch[j-1]$, until it receives acknowledgments from $\lfloor n/2 \rfloor$ processes (lines 54–58). When a process q receives this $\langle \text{PREPARE}, O, t, j, B\rangle$ message, it sets its $Batch[j-1]$ variable to B, and if (O, t, j) is not outdated, it adopts (O, t, j) as its estimate and sets $PendingBatch[j]$ to O. If q's estimate is (O, t, j), q sends an acknowledgement to p.

Note that, because of the initialization step, and the fact that a leader commits batches in sequence, when p sends the above $\langle \text{PREPARE}, O, t, j, B\rangle$ message, the set B is the previously committed batch $j-1$. So if a process q adopts (O, t, j) it also knows batch $j-1$, ensuring Invariant (I2). Thus, when the leader has received $\lfloor n/2 \rfloor$ acknowledgements to its PREPARE messages it knows that a majority of processes (including itself) have adopted estimate (O, t, j), and know batch $j-1$. This ensures Invariant (I3).

Having received $\lfloor n/2 \rfloor$ acknowledgements to its PREPARE messages, the leader p next checks that all processes potentially holding read leases have acknowledged; if not, it waits until the last read lease that it (or a previous leader) issued has expired (lines 59–62). This step is critical to ensure that processes do not read stale states, and we will describe it in more detail in the next subsection.

Finally, p verifies that it has continuously remained the leader from local time t (when it became leader) until the current local time t'; if not, p abandons $DoOps$ and abdicates (lines 63–64). If p is still the leader, it commits O as the j-th batch: it stores O in its $Batch[j]$ variable, applies the operations in O to the object's state (this is done by calling procedure $ExecuteBatch(j)$), and sends COMMIT messages to all other processes to inform them that batch j is now committed (lines 65–70).

The leaseholder mechanism. Suppose a process p with a lease, other than the leader, crashes or becomes temporarily disconnected from the leader. The leader attempting to commit a batch will be delayed by p's failure or disconnection: it will not receive an acknowledgement to the PREPARE message it sent to p, and so it must wait for the read lease of p to expire. Our algorithm incorporates a mechanism, described below, that prevents a crashed or disconnected process from delaying RMW operations more than once.

The leader keeps track of a set of processes that it considers to be the current "leaseholders", i.e., the processes potentially holding a valid lease issued by this (or a previous) leader. The leader includes this set in each read-lease message that it sends periodically to all processes (line 44). A process q that receives such a message updates its lease only if it belongs to the set of leaseholders contained in that message (lines 113–116). If q is not in the set of leaseholders, it sends a LEASEREQUEST message to the leader (lines 114–116); when the leader receives that message, it reintegrates q by adding it to the set of leaseholders (line 46).

The leader p initializes the set of leaseholders to be all processes other than itself (line 25), and it maintains this set as follows. After receiving $\lfloor n/2 \rfloor$ acknowledgements to the PREPARE message for some batch j, p waits for one of two conditions: (i) to receive acknowledgements from *all* current leaseholders, or (ii) for 2δ local time units to elapse since it started sending the PREPARE messages (line 59).[3] If this waiting ends because of condition (i), it is safe for p to commit batch j right away. If, however, some current leaseholder fails to acknowledge within the maximum round-trip delay of 2δ, p delays committing the new batch until it is certain that all read leases it (or a previous leader) has issued have become invalid. More precisely, in this case, if

[3]Recall that δ is the worst-case delay of a message after the system stabilizes. For simplicity, we assume that the time β to process and reply to a PREPARE message is negligible compared to δ and in fact is 0. Alternatively, p should wait for $2\delta + \beta$.

$(-, t_s)$ is the last read lease it issued and t is the local time when p became leader, p waits until its clock shows local time after $\max(t, t_s) + \mathit{LeasePeriod} + \epsilon$ (lines 60–61). The term $\max(t, t_s)$ ensures that p waits until the last lease it *or a previous leader* issued has expired. The term ϵ ensures that the lease has expired even at processes whose clocks are slow compared to p's clock.Thus, p makes sure that any process q that was not notified of the new batch j no longer has a valid lease for any previous batch, and so q will not read a stale state of the object. At this point, p updates the set of leaseholders to be the set of processes that acknowledged the PREPARE messages for the new batch j (line 62), and is ready to commit this batch. Hence, processes that did not acknowledge batch j in a timely manner cease being leaseholders, and p will no longer wait for their acknowledgements until they become leaseholders again.

Processing RMW operations. A process p that wishes to execute a RMW operation o, creates a unique ID (p, i) for that operation consisting of its name and a counter i, and sends $(o, (p, i))$ to the process it believes is the leader. (It does so repeatedly to deal with transient message loss and with the possible initial uncertainty about who the leader is (lines 2–5).) The leader will include this operation in some batch of operations, and will commit that batch using the *DoOps* procedure described earlier (lines 47–51). When p receives the COMMIT message for that batch, say $\langle \text{COMMIT}, O, j \rangle$, it stores O in $\mathit{Batch}[j]$, gets from its peers any batches smaller than j that it is missing (see Invariant (I3)), and applies the operations in O to its replica (lines 109–112). In doing so, it executes the RMW operation $(o, (p, i))$, which is one of the operations in O, and returns its response (line 6).

Processing read operations. A process p that wishes to execute a read operation R, waits until it has a read lease (k^*, t^*) that is valid, i.e., $t' < t^* + \mathit{LeasePeriod}$, where t' is the local time at p (lines 10–13). Process p then determines the batch $\hat{k}$ after which the read operation R should be linearized, i.e., the batch after which R should read the state of the object. A batch j is *pending* at p if p has received a PREPARE but not a COMMIT message for batch j. Process p uses its array *PendingBatch* to compute $\hat{k}$ as follows: if there is no batch $j > k^*$ that is pending at p and contains operations that conflict with R, then p sets $\hat{k} = k^*$ (the batch number for which p holds a valid lease); otherwise, $\hat{k}$ is the maximum number of a batch that is pending at p and contains an operation that conflicts with R (line 15). Note that $\hat{k} \geq k^*$. After determining $\hat{k}$, p waits until it knows all batches up to $\hat{k}$ (line 16), computes the corresponding state of the object if it has not already done so, and applies the read operation to that state.

Non-blocking reads. Consider the behaviour of read operations at a process p after the system stabilizes. After this occurs, p will always hold some valid read lease (k^*, t^*), so p does not wait in lines 10–13. Furthermore, p will already have batches $1, 2, \ldots, k^*$ in its *Batches* array. So if p has no pending batch $j > k^*$ with operations that conflict with R, then $\hat{k} = k^*$ and p does not wait in line 16. Thus p executes a read operation R without blocking unless p has a pending RMW operation that conflicts with R. It turns out that even if R blocks at p, it does so for at most 3δ local time units. Finally, since the permanently elected leader has no pending operations, it can always read without blocking.

Locality of reads. Consider the set of messages sent by the algorithm. If we exclude those sent by (and necessary to) the consensus mechanism used to linearize RMW operations, there are only two types of messages left, namely, those that are sent by the read-lease mechanism (the red code): LEASEGRANT messages to renew read leases and LEASEREQUEST messages to rejoin the set of leaseholders. Some time after the system stabilizes, only LEASEGRANT messages are sent. Furthermore, the frequency with which the permanent leader sends LEASEGRANT messages is fixed and independent of the number of read operations. In fact, the code that a process executes to do a read (lines 7–19) does not trigger the sending of *any* message. Thus, read operations are always local.

Properties of the algorithm. In the full paper we prove that our algorithm satisfies the following properties:

- The execution of the operations applied to the object is linearizable.
- Any operation issued by a correct process eventually terminates.
- Read operations are local.
- There is a time after which every read operation *op* issued by any process p is non-blocking unless p has a pending RMW operation that conflicts with *op*. A read operation that blocks, does so for at most 3δ local time units. Moreover, eventually no read operation by the leader blocks.

4. NECESSITY OF BLOCKING

In our algorithm all read operations are local and, after the system stabilizes, they never block at the leader, and they block at other processes only if there are pending RMW operations that conflict with the reads. We now prove that, in some sense, this is the best that can be done: Even under strong assumptions, any algorithm has runs in which read operations at $n-1$ processes block. Our proof uses the shifting executions technique introduced in [13]. This technique is used in [2, 14, 19] to determine, for each type of operation, a lower bound on the worst-case time of an instance of that operation in a run. Here we use it to show a lower bound on the *number of distinct processes* with a read operation that blocks in a run (as well as on the time during which these operations block). To do so we exploit the ability of each process to apply multiple operations concurrently. We also discuss a version of our result for the case that each process can apply operations only sequentially. Consider the following distributed system S:

Clocks. Each process p has a local clock denoted $\mathit{ClockTime}_p$. Local clocks are non-negative *real numbers* that are monotonically increasing, and they are *always* synchronized within a *known* constant, $\epsilon/2$ with respect to *real time*. (Hence, clocks are synchronized within ϵ of each other.)

Messages. There is a known upper bound δ on message delays (as measured in *real time*) that *always* holds.

Processes. Processes never crash. Each process can start multiple operations concurrently, and can start successive operations within γ real time of each other.

The parameter γ is a reflection of minimum process speed. In practice γ is much smaller than δ or ϵ; henceforth we assume that γ is negligible.

Consider any object O that has at least two states s_0 and s_1, a RMW operation W that changes the state from s_0 to s_1, and a read operation that returns v_0 in s_0 and v_1 in s_1, for some $v_0 \neq v_1$.

THEOREM 4.1. *Any algorithm $\mathcal{A}$ that implements a linearizable object O in system S has a run r with a single instance of W in which each of $n-1$ processes executes a read operation that takes at least $\alpha = \min(\epsilon, \delta/2) - 2\gamma \approx \min(\epsilon, \delta/2)$ real time to complete.*

Since α depends on the synchrony of clocks ϵ and the delay of messages δ, and not on the rate at which a process executes its own steps, the $n-1$ read operations in the run r of Theorem 4.1 are blocked.

PROOF OF THEOREM 4.1. If *op* is an operation that appears in a run r, $start_r(op)$ and $end_r(op)$ denote, respectively, the real times when *op* starts and ends in r.

We build a run r of algorithm $\mathcal{A}$ as follows. All processes' clocks run exactly $\epsilon/2$ ahead of real time. All messages take exactly $\delta/2$ real time to be received. The object O is initially in state s_0. Each process invokes multiple read operations on O repeatedly and concurrently *as fast as it can.* We first let every process complete at least one read that returns the initial value s_0. We then let one process complete an instance of a W operation; this changes the state of O to s_1. All processes continue to start read operations until every process completes at least one operation that returns s_1. We now let all ongoing operations complete without starting any new ones. Note that in run r, any two successive reads by the same process start within 2γ real time units of each other (this is because each process starts an operation every γ, and there is at most one non-read operation, namely W, between any two successive reads of that process).

We claim that in r there are $n-1$ processes each of which executed a read operation that took at least $\alpha = \min(\epsilon, \delta/2) - 2\gamma$ real time. Assume, for contradiction, that there are two processes p and q all read operations of which took less than α time in r. Let R_p^0 and R_q^0 be the last read operations (by start time) of p and q, respectively, that returned v_0 in r. Without loss of generality, assume that R_p^0 starts at the same real time or later than R_q^0. Since R_q^0 and R_q^1 are consecutive reads of q, $start_r(R_q^1) \leq start_r(R_q^0) + 2\gamma$. Since R_q^1 completed in less than α real time, $end_r(R_q^1) < start_r(R_q^1) + \alpha \leq start_r(R_q^0) + \alpha + 2\gamma \leq start_r(R_p^0) + \alpha + 2\gamma$; so, $end_r(R_q^1) < start_r(R_p^0) + \alpha + 2\gamma$ (*).

Now consider another run r' of $\mathcal{A}$ that is indistinguishable from r to all processes, in which, intuitively we delay the execution of process p by $\alpha + 2\gamma$ real time units. More precisely, the clocks of all processes other than p run exactly as in r, i.e., $\epsilon/2$ ahead of real time; p's clock is slower by $\alpha+2\gamma$ than in r; all messages to p take $\delta/2+\alpha+2\gamma$ real time, i.e., an additional $\alpha + 2\gamma$ compared to r; and all messages from p take $\delta/2-(\alpha+2\gamma)$ real time, i.e., $\alpha+2\gamma$ less than in r. Since $\alpha+2\gamma = \min(\epsilon, \delta/2)$, in run r', the clock of p is within $\epsilon/2 - \min(\epsilon, \delta/2)$ of real time, i.e., it is at most $\epsilon/2$ behind real time; the messages to p take $\delta/2+\min(\epsilon, \delta/2) \leq \delta$ time; and the messages from p take $\delta/2 - \min(\epsilon, \delta/2) \geq 0$ time. So r' is a legitimate run of $\mathcal{A}$ in system S.

Since $start_{r'}(R_p^0) = start_r(R_p^0) + \alpha + 2\gamma$, and $end_{r'}(R_q^1) = end_r(R_q^1)$, (*) implies $start_{r'}(R_p^0) > end_{r'}(R_q^1)$. So in r', R_p^0, which returns 0, starts after the completion of R_q^1, which returns v_1. This violates linearizability. □

In the preceding proof, the run r we constructed requires each process to invoke multiple concurrent read operations on O. If each process can apply operations on O only sequentially, we can obtain a similar result, using a similar proof, by taking the value of α to be roughly half of that in Theorem 4.1, i.e., $\alpha \approx \min(\epsilon/2, \delta/4)$.

After the system stabilizes, in our algorithm a read may block for at most 3δ. Thus, if δ is within a constant factor of ϵ, our algorithm's blocking behaviour is within a constant factor of the lower bound. In the case when $\epsilon \ll \delta$, ongoing work suggests that there is an extension of our algorithm such that reads block on only $n-1$ processes, only for $\Theta(\epsilon)$ time, and only if there are conflicting RMW operations.

5. RELATED WORK

The problem of implementing linearizable objects was also studied for systems that are *reliable and synchronous* in the following sense: processes do not crash, messages are never lost, and there is a known bound on the maximum message delay (including processing time) that holds *always*, not only eventually [2, 13, 14, 19]. These assumptions greatly simplify the task of implementing linearizable objects. Because large-scale, geo-replicated distributed systems are subject to process and communication failures, and they experience intermittent periods of asynchrony, most of the literature has focused on implementations that tolerate this behaviour.

The literature on fault-tolerant replication algorithms is vast. Those algorithms that implement linearizable replicated objects typically follow Lamport's "state machine approach", whereby processes use an agreement algorithm to order the operations that they apply to their local copies of the object [10]. Our algorithm uses such an agreement algorithm for the RMW operations only, and uses a different mechanism, based on leases, to process reads efficiently. This should lead to better performance in settings where read operations outnumber RMW operations, which is common in many applications. The idea of supplementing a consensus mechanism with read leases was suggested in [4].

Our agreement algorithm that orders the RMW operations uses techniques that are commonly found in agreement algorithms [6, 7, 11, 12, 16], such as electing a leader to coordinate decisions and ensure progress, and intersecting majorities to ensure that later leaders' decisions are consistent with those of earlier ones. It also incorporates novel elements, especially in relation to the role and properties of the leader, that expedite the handling of failures and dovetail with the read-lease mechanism we use to process reads efficiently. We will highlight these elements as we contrast our algorithm with previous related work, specifically the replication algorithms used in Megastore [9], Spanner [8], and Paxos Quorum Leases [15], which come closest to our algorithm's aim of efficient reads; as well as with Viewstamped Replication [12,16] and Raft [17], two replication algorithms that do not make special provisions for reads.

Megastore and Spanner. Megastore [9] and Spanner [8] are systems developed to support globally distributed databases in Google's data centers. Both systems provide many functionalities in addition to replication, such as support for transactions, that are beyond the scope of our algorithm. Here we focus only on these systems' replication mechanisms. These systems rely on various pieces of Google's software infrastructure and are described in the above-cited papers at a high level, and without correctness proofs.

Megastore implements a replicated log that records updates to a distributed database. Processes append new entries to this log and read the most recently committed entry of the log. To agree on the sequence of log entries, processes use a version of the Paxos consensus algorithm [11]. In Megastore, with each agreement on a log entry, processes also agree on the leader that will coordinate the decision for the next entry, namely the process expected to generate the next write operation (this choice expedites the processing of the next write). If the prediction for the next leader is wrong (e.g., because the chosen leader crashes or because the next write is actually generated at another process), Megastore provides a mechanism to change the leader, but this mechanism is vulnerable to livelock. An exponential back-off scheme can provide a probabilistic defence against this vulnerability. In contrast, our algorithm makes a deterministic guarantee of progress.

In Megastore, before the leader commits a write operation, it must receive acknowledgements that all processes have been notified of the write. If the leader does not receive an acknowledgement from some process p, it must delay the write until it is certain that p has marked its replica as out-of-date, preventing it from being read. This looks similar to our read leases, but the mechanism that Megastore uses relies on a specific piece of Google's software infrastructure, the lock service Chubby [3]. If the leader loses contact with Chubby while other processes maintain contact with it, writes can be left blocked forever. The authors of [9] note that they observed this problem "only a handful of times", and that it requires manual intervention by an operator to fix. Our algorithm is not subject to such vulnerabilities.

Spanner, a more recent system, relies on a different piece of Google's software infrastructure, the "TrueTime" service that provides processes with highly accurate clocks. TrueTime clocks expose the (small) uncertainty with which they track real time by returning the endpoints of a short *interval*, instead of an instant; the guarantee is that the real time when a clock reading is taken lies within the interval returned by the clock. Spanner uses TrueTime to implement a leader election service that guarantees that no two processes are leaders at the same *real* time. This is in contrast to our enhanced leader election service, which guarantees *only* that no two processes are leaders at the same *local* time. This seemingly innocuous difference has important consequences, discussed shortly.

Spanner assigns to each write and read operation a timestamp, which is an instant in time (the high endpoint of the interval returned by a clock). Write operations are linearized in timestamp order using the Paxos consensus algorithm [11], and a read operation with timestamp t returns a value based on the state of the object produced by the write operation with the largest timestamp not exceeding t. Write operation timestamps are generated by the leader, which delays the commit of a write until it is certain that the current real time is after the timestamp it generated. Thus, in Spanner all write operations pay the price of clock skew.[4] In contrast, in our algorithm, the real time to commit a batch of RMW operations does not depend on the clock skew ϵ after the system stabilizes.

[4] In the words of [8], "[i]f the [clock] uncertainty is large, Spanner slows down to wait out that uncertainty". To be fair, this waiting is tempered because it can be overlaid with other waiting due to the agreement algorithm. The extent of its effect depends on the clock skew.

To satisfy the timestamp ordering requirement for read operations in Spanner, a non-leader process that issues a read operation has three options: (a) have the read operation executed by the leader, which always has the most up-to-date state of the object; (b) use the current time as its timestamp and wait until it receives a write with a higher timestamp; or (c) use the maximum timestamp of any write operation it knows of. Option (a) means that reads are not local; it also concentrates load on the leader for each read, instead of distributing it among the replicas. Option (b) causes reads to block for an unbounded amount of time, even if there are no conflicting write operations. Option (c) may result in reading stale values, violating linearizability. In contrast, our algorithm ensures that all reads are local, they block only if there are conflicting pending writes (and only for 3δ time), and they never return stale values.

Paxos Quorum Leases. The Paxos Quorum Leases algorithm (PQL) [15] addresses a shortcoming of Megastore that affects the performance of write operations. As we mentioned earlier, in Megastore, before committing a write operation, the leader must receive acknowledgements that *all* processes have been notified of the write. To reduce the waiting time for writes, PQL maintains a set of leaseholders and waits only for the processes in this set to acknowledge notification of the write, as we do in our algorithm. The two algorithms, however, differ in important ways.

First, each lease renewal requires $\Theta(n^2)$ messages in PQL, as compared to $\Theta(n)$ in our algorithm. This is because in our algorithm only the leader renews leases by sending a lease-grant message to each process. In contrast, in PQL, a lease renewal involves a majority of processes, called *grantors*, sending a message to each leaseholder.

Second, in PQL every lease renewal interaction between each of the $\Theta(n^2)$ grantor-leaseholder pairs requires four rounds of communication (two round trips). In our algorithm, each of the $\Theta(n)$ leader-process pairs requires a single message (one way). This is because PQL uses timers (that measure elapsed time) instead of synchronized clocks. As a result, it requires a clever but expensive four-round protocol for grantors to know when a lease has expired at a leaseholder.

A third difference between our algorithm and PQL is that in PQL each change in the set of leaseholders (removing an unresponsive process or adding one that was isolated for a while) triggers the use of a consensus algorithm (Paxos, in PQL) for the processes to agree on the new set. Our algorithm manages the set of leaseholders in a much simpler way (see the discussion of the leaseholder mechanism in Section 3).

Finally, in PQL a pending write will cause all reads to block, even those with which it does not conflict. Furthermore, a steady stream of write operations can cause leases to be perpetually revoked, permanently disabling local reads. In contrast, even when faced with a steady stream of conflicting RMW operations, in our algorithm *all* reads are local, and after the system stabilizes, each read completes within at most 3δ time. This is because our algorithm *never* revokes read leases. Presented with a read operation while there are conflicting pending RMW operations, our algorithm determines the linearization point for the read (see the calculation of $\hat{k}$, line 15) and services the read from the local replica as soon as all RMW operations up to that point are committed.

Viewstamped Replication. Viewstamped Replication (VR) [12, 16] uses a leader-based mechanism for processes to agree on the sequence of operations to apply to their replicas, as in the state machine approach. It differs from our algorithm primarily in (a) the leader election mechanism that it employs, and (b) treating all operations (reads and RMW alike) in the same way. We elaborate on these differences below.

In VR, the period during which the same leader is in charge of committing operations is called a *view*. Processes take turns as leaders of successive views, based on the order of their IDs. In contrast, in our algorithm the leader is determined by the underlying Ω leader service, and that choice can be based on dynamic criteria such as the leader being well-connected to other processes, or being a process where the majority of RMW operations originate (to expedite their processing) [1, 9, 18]. With a static leader election scheme, if the next several processes to become leaders based on the IDs are partitioned away from the majority of processes, the system will cycle through a succession of ineffective views before it reaches one whose leader can commit operations.

VR treats read operations like all others, and it is not clear how to incorporate a read lease mechanism to it. The problem is that in a leader-based read-lease granting mechanism only one leader must issue leases at any time. Otherwise, an "old" leader unaware of its demotion can issue leases "behind the back" of the new leader, allowing processes to read a stale state. In VR, an old leader is unable to commit operations after it ceases being leader. If, however, in addition to trying to commit operations, an isolated old leader is also granting leases, these can cause trouble by allowing an also isolated recipient to read a stale state.

Raft. Raft [17] is an algorithm to implement a replicated log. A design choice that distinguishes it from other leader-based consensus algorithms is that information about the log entries flows only in one direction, *from* the leader *to* the other processes (the "followers"). Thus, a newly elected leader does not try to find out the latest log entries committed (or pre-committed) by its predecessor(s); rather, it imposes its own copy as the current state of the log. To prevent this from undoing previously committed log entries, Raft uses a specially-crafted leader-election algorithm that allows only a process with the most recent committed copy of the log to be elected leader. As noted in our discussion of VR, restricting the choice of leader has significant drawbacks. In addition, Raft's mechanism by which a newly elected leader imposes its copy of the log on the followers can be costly: It takes up to k message exchanges with each follower, where k is the total number of previous leaders. As a result of these message exchanges, a follower may be forced to successively return to its initial state. Raft also differs from our algorithm in the way it handles read operations. In fact, reads are not local and they always block: each read operation is sent to the current leader, and when the leader receives a read request it exchanges "heartbeat messages with a majority of the cluster before responding" to ensure that it is still the leader. The possibility of using a "form of lease" is briefly mentioned in [17], but no details are given. In contrast to our paper, [17] explains how to dynamically change the set of processes in charge of the replication, and it describes an implementation and performance evaluation.

6. REFERENCES

[1] Marcos K. Aguilera, Carole Delporte-Gallet, Hugues Fauconnier, and Sam Toueg. On implementing Omega in systems with weak reliability and synchrony assumptions. *Dist. Comp.*, 21(4):285–314, 2008.

[2] Hagit Attiya and Jennifer Welch. Sequential consistency versus linearizability. *ACM TOCS*, 12(2):91–122, 1994.

[3] Mike Burrows. The Chubby lock service for loosely-coupled distributed systems. In *OSDI '06*, pages 335–350, 2006.

[4] Tushar D. Chandra, Robert Griesemer, and Joshua Redstone. Paxos made live: An engineering perspective. In *PODC '07*, pages 398–407, 2007.

[5] Tushar D. Chandra, Vassos Hadzilacos, and Sam Toueg. The weakest failure detector for solving consensus. *JACM*, 43(4):685–722, 1996.

[6] Tushar D. Chandra and Sam Toueg. Unreliable failure detectors for reliable distributed systems. *JACM*, 43(2):225–267, 1996.

[7] Cynthia Dwork, Nancy A. Lynch, and Larry Stockmeyer. Consensus in the presence of partial synchrony. *JACM*, 35(2):288–323, 1988.

[8] James Corbett et al. Spanner: Google's globally-distributed database. In *OSDI '12*, pages 261–264, 2012.

[9] Jason Baker et al. Megastore: Providing scalable, highly available storage for interactive services. In *CIDR '11*, pages 223–234, 2011.

[10] Leslie Lamport. Time, clocks, and the ordering of events in a distributed system. *CACM*, 21(7):558–565, 1978.

[11] Leslie Lamport. The part-time parliament. *ACM TOCS*, 16(2):133–169, 1998.

[12] Barbara Liskov and James Cowling. Viewstamped replication revisited. *Technical Report MIT-CSAIL-TR-2012-021*, 2012.

[13] Jennifer Lundelius and Nancy Lynch. An upper and lower bound for clock synchronization. *Information and Control*, 62(2/3):190–204, 1984.

[14] Marios Mavronicolas and Dan Roth. Linearizable read/write objects. *TCS*, 220(1):267–319, 1999.

[15] Iulian Moraru, David Anderson, and Michael Kaminsky. Paxos quorum leases: Fast reads without sacrificing writes. In *SoCC '14*, pages 1–13, 2014.

[16] Brian Oki and Barbara Liskov. Viewstamped replication: A new primary copy method to support highly-available distributed systems. In *PODC '88*, pages 8–17, 1988.

[17] Diego Ongaro and John Ousterhout. In search of an understandable consensus algorithm. In *USENIX ATC'14*, pages 305–320, 2014. An extended version of this paper is in *http://ramcloud.stanford.edu/raft.pdf*.

[18] Nicolas Schiper and Sam Toueg. A robust and lightweight stable leader election service for dynamic systems. In *DSN '08*, pages 207–216, 2008.

[19] Jiaqi Wang, Edward Talmage, Hyunyoung Lee, and Jennifer Welch. Improved time bounds for linearizable implementations of abstract data types. In *IPDPS '14*, pages 691–701, 2014.

APPENDIX

A. REPLICATED OBJECT ALGORITHM

Length and renewal frequency of read leases. To ensure that eventually every correct process has a valid read lease at all times, each LEASEGRANT lease renewal message sent by a leader p must be received before the lease granted by the previous LEASEGRANT message has expired. The leader p is scheduled to send a LEASEGRANT message every *LeaseRenewalPeriod* time units, but this sending may be delayed by up to α local time units, for some small constant α.[5] In addition, the LEASEGRANT message can be delayed by up to δ time units on p's clock, and the recipient's local clock can be up to ϵ time units ahead of p's clock. So, we need $LeaseRenewalPeriod + \alpha + \delta + \epsilon < LeasePeriod$ to ensure that each LEASEGRANT message is received before the read lease granted by the previous LEASEGRANT message has expired.

Simplifying assumptions. We assume that at every process p, p's clock $ClockTime_p$ increases by at least one time unit between any two successive readings of this clock by p. This can be enforced by delaying each clock reading until the clock value exceeds the previously read value. We also assume that the communication links are eventually FIFO. This can be achieved without violating the upper bound δ on message delays that holds after the system stabilizes.

Notation. The two segments of code enclosed by square brackets $[\cdots]$, namely lines 11–12 and 63–66, are uninterruptible — i.e., steps within such a block cannot be interleaved with steps of another thread.

CODE FOR PROCESS p:

```
variables:
Π = set of all processes
(Ops, ts, k) = (∅, −1, 0)                        /* current estimate */
Batch[0, 1, 2, ...] = [∅, ∅, ∅, ...] /* currently known batches */
MaxPendingBatch = 0         /* max pending batch number */
PendingBatch[0, 1, 2, ...] = [∅, ∅, ∅, ...] /* pending batches */
MaxPendingBatch = 0         /* max pending batch number */
state[−1, 0, 1, 2, ...] = [s0, s0, ⊥, ⊥, ...]
            /* object state after each batch; s0 = init state */
reply(op) = ⊥ /* response to RMW operation op, init ⊥ */
                              /* for every operation op */
cntr = 0              /* number of operations issued by p */
OpsRequested = ∅           /* RMW operations requested */
OpsDone = ∅                 /* RMW operations executed */
LastBatchDone = 0   /* max batch number up to which */
                        /* all RMW operations are executed */
t_max = −1   /* max t s.t. p sent ⟨ESTREPLY, t, −, −, −⟩ */
est_replied[t] = ∅            /* responders to ⟨ESTREQ, t⟩ */
est_replies[t] = ∅              /* responses to ⟨ESTREQ, t⟩ */
P-acked[t, j] = ∅   /* responders to ⟨PREPARE, −, t, j, −⟩ */
LeaseHolders = Π − {p}
  /* processes other than p possibly holding valid leases */
LeasePeriod                          /* length of read lease */
LeaseRenewalPeriod  /* frequency of read lease renewal */
lease = (0, −∞)                  /* current lease held by p */
       /* lease has two fields: lease.batch and lease.start */
```

[5]This delay is because up to α time units may elapse between two consecutive checks of whether it is time for p to send a LEASEGRANT message; the full paper contains a more detailed explanation and computation of what α is in our algorithm.

```
cobegin
// THREAD 1:          /* issue read or RMW operations */
1   while TRUE do
2     if p wants to execute a RMW operation o then
3       cntr := cntr + 1
4       op := (o, (p, cntr))
5       while reply(op) = ⊥ do send ⟨OPREQ, op⟩ to leader()
6       return reply(op)
7     if p wants to execute a read operation o then
8       cntr := cntr + 1
9       op := (o, (p, cntr))
10      repeat
11        [ t′ := ClockTime
12          (k*, t*) := lease ]
13      until t′ < t* + LeasePeriod
14      u := MaxPendingBatch
15      k̂ := max{j | j = k* or (k* < j ≤ u and
              o conflicts with an operation in PendingBatch[j])}
16      wait for (for all j, 1 ≤ j ≤ k̂, Batch[j] ≠ ∅)
17      ExecuteUpToBatch(k̂)
18      (−, reply) := Δ(state[k̂], o)
19      return reply
// THREAD 2:
20  while TRUE do
21    t := ClockTime
22    if AmLeader(t, t) = TRUE then LeaderWork(t)
23    ProcessClientMessages()
// THREAD 3:
24  ProcessMessages()
coend

procedure LeaderWork(t):
    /* New leader initialization: find latest batch and (re)do */
25  LeaseHolders := Π − {p}
26  repeat
27    send ⟨ESTREQ, t⟩ to Π − {p}
28    t′ := ClockTime
29    if AmLeader(t, t′) = FALSE then return
30  until |est_replied[t]| ≥ ⌊n/2⌋
31  (Ops*, ts*, k*) := tuple in est_replies[t] ∪ {(Ops, ts, k)} with
                            maximum (ts*, k*)
32  if ts* ≥ t then return
33  FindMissingBatches(k* − 2)
34  ExecuteUpToBatch(k* − 1)
35  outcome := DoOps(Ops*, t, k*)
36  if outcome = FAILED then return
37  initiate a NOOP as a RMW operation via Thread 1
    /* Grant read leases and process new batches */
38  NextSendTime := ClockTime
39  while TRUE do
40    t′ := ClockTime
41    if AmLeader(t, t′) = FALSE then return
42    if t′ ≥ NextSendTime then
43      lease := (k, t′)
44      send ⟨LEASEGRANT, lease, LeaseHolders⟩ to Π − {p}
45      NextSendTime := t′ + LeaseRenewalPeriod
46    if received ⟨LEASEREQUEST⟩ from q then
        LeaseHolders := LeaseHolders ∪ {q}
47    NextOps := OpsRequested − OpsDone
48    if NextOps ≠ ∅ then
49      outcome := DoOps(NextOps, t, k + 1)
50      if outcome = FAILED then return
51    send ⟨COMMIT, Ops, k⟩ to Π − {p}
```

procedure *DoOps*(O, t, j):
52 **if** $t < t_{max}$ **then return** FAILED
53 $(Ops, ts, k) := (O, t, j)$
54 **repeat**
55 **send** $\langle$PREPARE, $O, t, j, Batch[j-1]\rangle$ **to** $\Pi - \{p\}$
56 $t' := ClockTime$
57 **if** $AmLeader(t, t') =$ FALSE **then return** FAILED
58 **until** $|P\text{-}acked[t, j]| \geq \lfloor n/2 \rfloor$
59 **wait until** $LeaseHolders \subseteq P\text{-}acked[t, j]$ **or** 2δ local time has elapsed since p first executed line 55
60 **if** $\neg(LeaseHolders \subseteq P\text{-}acked[t, j])$ **then**
61 **wait until** $ClockTime > max(t, lease.start) + LeasePeriod + \epsilon$
62 $LeaseHolders := P\text{-}acked[t, j]$
63 [$t' := ClockTime$
64 **if** $AmLeader(t, t') =$ FALSE **then return** FAILED
65 $(Batch[j], lease) := (O, (j, t'))$
66 $ExecuteBatch(j)$]
67 $OpsDone := OpsDone \cup Batch[j]$
68 $LastBatchDone := \max(LastBatchDone, j)$
69 **send** $\langle$COMMIT, $O, j\rangle$ **to** $\Pi - \{p\}$
70 **return** DONE

procedure *FindMissingBatches*(k'):
71 **repeat**
72 $Gaps := \{j \mid 1 \leq j \leq k'$ and $Batch[j] = \emptyset\}$
73 **if** $Gaps \neq \emptyset$ **then** **send** $\langle$MISSINGBATCHES, $Gaps\rangle$ **to** $\Pi - \{p\}$
74 **until** $Gaps = \emptyset$
75 **return**

procedure *ExecuteBatch*(j'):
76 $s := state[j'-1]$
77 let $op^1, op^2, \ldots, op^m$ be the operations in $Batch[j']$ listed in operation id order
78 **for** $i = 1$ **to** m **do** /* apply operation i of $Batch[j']$ */ $(s, reply(op^i)) := \Delta(s, op^i.type)$
79 $state[j'] := s$
80 **return**

procedure *ExecuteUpToBatch*(j'):
81 **for** $j = LastBatchDone + 1$ **to** j' **do**
82 $ExecuteBatch(j)$
83 $OpsDone := OpsDone \cup Batch[j]$
84 $LastBatchDone := \max(LastBatchDone, j)$
85 **return**

procedure *ProcessMessages*():
86 **while** TRUE **do**
87 **if received** $\langle$OPREQ, $op\rangle$ **from** q **then**
88 $OpsRequested := OpsRequested \cup \{op\}$
89 **if received** $\langle$ESTREPLY, $t, O', t', j', B'\rangle$ **from** q **then**
90 $Batch[j'-1] := B'$
91 $est\_replied[t] := est\_replied[t] \cup \{q\}$
92 $est\_replies[t] := est\_replies[t] \cup \{(O', t', j')\}$
93 **if received** $\langle$P-ACK, $t, j\rangle$ **from** q **then**
94 $P\text{-}acked[t, j] := P\text{-}acked[t, j] \cup \{q\}$
95 **if received** $\langle$MISSINGBATCHES, $Gaps'\rangle$ **from** q **then**
96 **for all** $j \in Gaps'$ such that $Batch[j] \neq \emptyset$ **do** **send** $\langle$BATCH, $j, Batch[j]\rangle$ **to** q
97 **if received** $\langle$BATCH, $j, O\rangle$ **from** a process q **then**
98 $Batch[j] := O$

procedure *ProcessClientMessages*():
99 **if received** $\langle$ESTREQ, $t\rangle$ **from** q **then**
100 $t_{max} := \max(t_{max}, t)$
101 **send** $\langle$ESTREPLY, $t, Ops, ts, k, Batch[k-1]\rangle$ **to** q
102 **if received** $\langle$PREPARE, $O, t, j, B\rangle$ **from** q **then**
103 $Batch[j-1] := B$
104 **if** $t \geq t_{max}$ **and** $(t, j) > (ts, k)$ **then**
105 $(Ops, ts, k) := (O, t, j)$
106 $PendingBatch[k] := Ops$
107 $MaxPendingBatch := \max(MaxPendingBatch, k)$
108 **if** $(Ops, ts, k) = (O, t, j)$ **then send** $\langle$P-ACK, $t, j\rangle$ **to** q
109 **if received** $\langle$COMMIT, $O, j\rangle$ **from** some process **then**
110 $Batch[j] := O$
111 $FindMissingBatches(j-1)$
112 $ExecuteUpToBatch(j)$
113 **if received** $\langle$LEASEGRANT, $lease', LeaseHolders'\rangle$ **from** q **th**
114 **if** $p \in LeaseHolders'$ **then**
115 **if** $lease' > lease$ **then** $lease := lease'$
116 **else send** $\langle$LEASEREQUEST$\rangle$ **to** q
117 **return**

B. LEADER ENHANCER ALGORITHM

Length and renewal frequency of leader leases. To ensure that a permanent leader is eventually elected, each LEADERLEASE renewal message must be received before the lease granted by the previous LEADERLEASE message has expired. So we need $LeaderLeaseRenewalPeriod + \alpha + \delta + \epsilon < LeaderLeasePeriod$ for a small constant α, as explained in connection with read leases in Appendix A.

CODE FOR PROCESS p:

variables:
$t_s = t_e = 0$ /* $[t_s, t_e)$ is lease period for next leader */
$L = L_{prev} = \bot$ /* current and previous leader votes */
$c = 0$ /* number of times p changed its leader vote */
$LeaderLeases = \emptyset$ /* set of leader lease periods received */
$Supporters = \emptyset$ /* processes that continuously vote for p */
$LeaderLeasePeriod$ /* length of leader lease */
$LeaderLeaseRenewalPeriod$ /* lease renewal frequency */

1 **repeat every** $LeaderLeaseRenewalPeriod$
/* vote for leader of next period */
2 $t := ClockTime$
3 $L := leader()$
4 **if** $L \neq L_{prev}$ **then** /* if leader changed */
5 $c := c + 1$ /* increment the vote change counter */
6 $L_{prev} := L$
7 $t_s := t_e$ /* next lease starts when previous ends */
8 $t_e := t + LeaderLeasePeriod$ /* end of next lease */
9 $P := [t_s, t_e)$ /* next lease period */
10 **send** $\langle$LEADERLEASE, $P, c\rangle$ **to** L

upon receipt of $\langle$LEADERLEASE, $P', c'\rangle$ **from** process q:
11 $LeaderLeases := LeaderLeases \cup \{(P', q, c')\}$

procedure *AmLeader*(t_1, t_2):
12 $Supporters := \{q \mid LeaderLeases$ contains tuples $(P_1, q, i), (P_2, q, i)$ (not necessarily distinct, but with the same third component i) such that P_1 covers t_1 and P_2 covers $t_2\}$
13 **if** $|Supporters| > n/2$ **then** return TRUE
14 **else** return FALSE

Are Shared Objects Composable under an Oblivious Adversary? *

Oksana Denysyuk and Philipp Woelfel
Department of Computer Science, University of Calgary, Canada
{oksana.denysyuk,woelfel}@ucalgary.ca

ABSTRACT

Linearizability [5] of a concurrent object ensures that operations on that object appear to execute atomically. It is well known that linearizable implementations are composable: in an algorithm designed to work with atomic objects, replacing any atomic object with a linearizable implementation preserves the correctness of the original algorithm. However, replacing atomic objects with linearizable ones in a randomized algorithm can break the original probabilistic guarantees [3]. With an *adaptive* adversary, this problem is solved by using *strongly linearizable* [3] objects in the composition. How about with an *oblivious* adversary?

In this paper, we ask the fundamental question of what property makes implementations composable under an oblivious adversary. It turns out that the property depends on the entire collection of objects used in the algorithm. We show that the composition of every randomized algorithm with a collection of linearizable objects $\mathcal{OL}$ is sound if and only if $\mathcal{OL}$ satisfies a property called *library homogeneity*. Roughly, this property says that, for each process, every operation on $\mathcal{OL}$ has the same length and linearization point. This result has several important implications. First, for an oblivious adversary, there is nothing analogous to "strong linearizability" to ensure that the atomic objects of an algorithm can be replaced with their implementations. Second, in general, algorithms cannot use implemented objects alongside atomic objects provided by the system, such as registers. These results show that, with an oblivious adversary, it is much harder to implement reusable object types than previously believed.

Categories and Subject Descriptors

C.2.4 [**Computer Systems Organization**]: Computer-Communication Networks, Distributed Systems

*This research was undertaken, in part, thanks to funding from the Canada Research Chairs program and from the Discovery Grants program of the Natural Sciences and Engineering Research Council of Canada (NSERC).

PODC'16, July 25-28, 2016, Chicago, IL, USA
© 2016 ACM. ISBN 978-1-4503-3964-3/16/07...$15.00
DOI: http://dx.doi.org/10.1145/2933057.2933115

Keywords

Distributed algorithms; randomized algorithms; shared memory; linearizability.

1. INTRODUCTION

Much of distributed computing is concerned about defining interesting shared objects (stacks, queues, snapshots, etc), and then finding suitable implementations of those objects that can then be used in other higher-level algorithms. One expects that, if a high-level algorithm A uses (atomic) objects, then we can replace the objects in A with their implementations such that the resulting algorithm $\tilde{A}$ remains correct. $\tilde{A}$ is called a *composition* of A with the object implementations. Correct composition requires the object implementations to satisfy a suitable property.

For deterministic algorithms, the required property is *linearizability*. In fact, it is well known that if A uses atomic objects, then A remains correct if it is composed with linearizable implementations of those objects. This fact is so engrained that atomic and linearizable objects are sometimes used interchangeably [7].

More recently, it was shown that if A is randomized, then the above does not hold: if we compose A with linearizable implementations of its objects, then the composed $\tilde{A}$ may not ensure the same probabilistic guarantees as A. If the adversary (scheduler) is adaptive, the required property for composition in this case is a property called *strong linearizability* [3].

In this paper, we study composability of randomized algorithms under a weaker *oblivious adversary*. Randomized algorithms are designed to work under different types of adversaries, which differ in their power to schedule processes. An adaptive adversary can dynamically pick the schedule based on everything it observes from the past. An oblivious adversary cannot do that: it must pick the entire schedule ahead of time at the beginning of the execution. We are interested in the latter adversary, which is weaker than an adaptive one.

We ask a fundamental question: what property must object implementations satisfy so that randomized algorithms can compose with them under an oblivious adversary?

It might appear that the answer is strong linearizability: if the object implementations are strongly linearizable, then they compose under an adaptive adversary, therefore they ought to compose under an oblivious adversary, as an oblivious adversary is less powerful. This exact intuition has been evoked before in a recent FOCS paper [1].

In turns out that this intuition is wrong. We show, perhaps surprisingly, that if A works under an oblivious adversary, and the object implementations are strongly linearizable, then $\tilde{A}$ may fail under an oblivious adversary. The problem with the intuition is that it requires A to work under an adaptive adversary[1], but this may not be the case since A may have been designed to work only under an oblivious adversary.

What is, then, the right property that object implementations must satisfy to compose under an oblivious adversary? We first show that the entire implementation library (all implementations used in A) must satisfy an abstract property that we call *uniform linearizability*. In fact, uniform linearizability is necessary and sufficient to ensure that, for every randomized A, the composition $\tilde{A}$ is sound under an oblivious adversary (Theorem 1). Roughly, uniform linearizability requires that for every A, if two executions of $\tilde{A}$ have the same schedule but different coins, then both executions can be linearized in essentially the same way. More precisely, for every nonnegative integer k, the k-th operation belongs to the same process in both linearizations. That is, if we drop the operation and leave just the process ids, the linearizations are the same.

An implication of this property is that it is impossible to define independent properties, such as linearizability or strong linearizability, on the individual object implementations to guarantee composition. Instead, the entire library of object implementations must satisfy a property that binds all implementations together.

To satisfy uniform linearizability, we show that it is necessary and sufficient for the object library[2] to satisfy a property that we call *library homogeneity* (Theorem 2). Thus, linearizability with library homogeneity is necessary and sufficient for object implementations to properly compose under an oblivious adversary. Roughly speaking, library homogeneity requires that (1) all object implementations—even for objects of different types—must execute the same number ℓ_p of steps for each operation of the same process p, and (2) all operations of a process p must linearize in the same k_p-th step (e.g., the third step).

Library homogeneity is a strong but necessary requirement on the implemented objects for composability. For example, libraries with trivial implementations that execute just one step per operation are homogeneous, but libraries that mix such implementations with non-trivial ones (that take more than one step) are not. An implication is that non-atomic objects are generally not composable alongside atomic ones.

We conclude the paper with a brief discussion of how one might design an object library that satisfies homogeneity, but we leave a more elaborate study as an open research direction.

2. OVERVIEW

The main result of this paper is that, to properly compose under an oblivious adversary, object implementations must satisfy linearizability and a property called *library homogeneity*. Roughly, this property constraints all objects in the library to behave similarly, by having, for each process, the same number of steps and the same linearization point. More specifically, suppose $\mathcal{OL}$ denotes the set of all objects used by a randomized algorithm A. Library homogeneity requires two things. First, there is a length requirement: for each process p, there is ℓ_p such that all operations of p of any object in $\mathcal{OL}$ takes exactly ℓ_p steps of p. Second, there is a linearization requirement: for each p, there is $k_p \leq \ell_p$ such that all operations by p can be linearized in the k_p-th step by p.

2.1 Intuition

We now give examples of what could go wrong if library homogeneity does not hold. These examples give an intuition of why library homogeneity is necessary. Figure 1 shows an algorithm A for two processes p_1 and p_2, which uses a counter object C. Process p_1 flips a coin, and depending on the outcome, it either increments or decrements C. Process p_2 reads C.

Consider first an execution of A with an atomic counter (operations take one step) and let us consider what value p_2 might read from C. If p_2 executes first, it reads 0, the initial value of C. If p_1 executes first, then p_2 reads -1 or $+1$ with probability $1/2$ each.

Now, consider the algorithm $\tilde{A}$ obtained by composing A with an implementation of C in which the increment and read operations take one step, while the decrement operation takes two steps and gets linearized in the second step.[3] This violates the length requirement of library homogeneity. Let us consider what values p_2 can read from R. If p_2 executes first, it reads 0. If p_1 executes one step before p_2, then p_2 reads 0 or $+1$ with probability $1/2$ each. If p_1 executes two steps before p_2 (p_1 finishes the algorithm and executes a no-op step), then p_2 reads -1 or $+1$ with probability $1/2$ each. We see that $\tilde{A}$ has an outcome that is impossible with A, namely, reading 0 or $+1$ with probability $1/2$ each, which could be a correctness violation. For instance, A ensures that p_2 reads 0 in expectation in all schedules; in contrast, in $\tilde{A}$, there are schedules where p_2 reads $1/2$ in expectation.

We now examine what might happen if the object library satisfies the length requirement but violates the linearization point requirement. Consider again the algorithm in Figure 1, but now compose it with an implementation of the counter where all operations take two steps, except that increment and read are linearized in the first step, while decrement is linearized in the second step. As before, a simple analysis reveals that $\tilde{A}$ has probability distribution outcomes that are impossible in A.

We would like to find conditions on the implementations that guarantee the same probabilistic outcomes in A and $\tilde{A}$. Specifically, given a randomized algorithm A, note that each schedule of A can cause many possible executions of A according to the coin flips. In fact, each schedule of A determines a probability distribution on the runs of A. Similarly, each schedule of $\tilde{A}$ determines a probability distribution on the runs of $\tilde{A}$. We want those probability distributions to be a subset of the distributions on the runs of A, so that any probabilistic properties satisfied by A (e.g., expectation of a random variable) are also satisfied by $\tilde{A}$. We show that library homogeneity is exactly the property necessary and sufficient for that to hold.

[1]In this case, $\tilde{A}$ also works under an adaptive adversary and therefore it works under an oblivious adversary.

[2]We assume that at least some objects (e.g., registers) in the object library are obstruction-free.

[3]This implementation is strongly linearizable, as the linearization points of operations are fixed.

Code of p_1: **if** *flip_coin*() = heads **then** C.increment()
else C.decrement()

Code of p_2: $v \leftarrow C$.read()

Figure 1: An algorithm A that uses a counter object C.

2.2 Implications

Our main result has several interesting implications.

First, it is impossible to define a property local to an object implementation to provide composability under an oblivious adversary. By local we mean a property that the object implementation can satisfy irrespective of other object implementations. This is unfortunate, because it means that objects cannot be designed separately of one another (e.g., by different teams) and then used together in the same algorithm. Instead, one must develop the entire object library together.

Second, mutual exclusion alone does not help in implementing the objects. Mutual exclusion (or locks) is a common way to deal with concurrency and it is one of the main techniques used today to develop shared objects. Unfortunately, mutual exclusion does not ensure library homogeneity.

Third, composability of object implementations under an oblivious adversary require a property stronger than linearizability or strong linearizability. This is perhaps counterintuitive, because an oblivious adversary is often regarded as easier to tackle than an adaptive adversary. The intuition goes astray here, as we pointed out before.

3. MODEL

We consider an asynchronous shared memory system where an unbounded number of processes $p_1, p_2, \ldots$ can access a set of (atomic shared) objects called *base objects*. We assume that processes have access to random bits by executing coin flip operations, which return uniformly distributed random values from some countable domain. Processes execute a distributed algorithm, which consists of an infinite state machine per process and a set of used objects. If the used objects are a subset of the base objects, the system can execute the algorithm. Execution proceeds in steps of two types: regular and no-op. In a regular step, a process possibly flips a coin, chooses an operation on a base object, invokes it, obtains a result, and changes state.

In a no-op step, the process does nothing. After a no-op step, the process may execute only no-op steps. We use no-op steps to define schedules irrespective of the algorithm: the schedule may require a process to take a step even after it is done.

If the algorithm uses objects not available as base objects, it must be composed with implementations of those objects before it is executed. By composition, we mean replacing the object invocations with steps of the implementations. To simplify the presentation, we assume without loss of generality that composition replaces *all* objects with their implementations, even base objects: these objects can use a trivial pass-through implementation.

Object implementations are deterministic and independent. Independent means that different implementations share no objects. This is sensible because objects are typically implemented by a generic algorithm for their type, instantiated once per object.

Object library. An object library $\mathcal{OL}$ is a set of object implementations. We are concerned with object libraries that provide a superset of the objects used by an algorithm. We assume that $\mathcal{OL}$ has an unbounded supply of objects of each type in the library, and that $\mathcal{OL}$ has a special no-op object with a no-op operation that simply executes (one or more) no-op steps. Given an algorithm A and an object library $\mathcal{OL}$, $A_{\mathcal{OL}}$ denotes the composition of A with $\mathcal{OL}$. In $A_{\mathcal{OL}}$, a process that is finished actually continues executing the no-op operation on the no-op object in $\mathcal{OL}$ forever.

Updatable objects. Intuitively, *updatable objects* can be changed from their initial state by any process, and these changes are visible to other processes. More precisely, an updatable object o supports at least two operations, o.`read`() and o.`update`(). Operation o.`read`() does not change the object's state and returns a value, and operation o.`update`() may or may not return a value. The only requirement that an o.`read`() operation executed when o is in its initial state, returns a different value than an o.`read`() operation that follows an o.`update`() executed in the initial state of o. (This has to be true no matter which processes are executing those operations.) Updatable objects include essentially all natural objects, such as registers, and test-and-set, snapshot, fetch-and-increment, or compare-and-set objects. We assume that $\mathcal{OL}$ contains an unbounded number of updatable objects (possibly of the same type), but not every object in $\mathcal{OL}$ need be updatable. For the ease of description (but w.l.o.g.) we assume throughout that an o.`read`() operation on any updatable object o returns $\perp$ if it is executed when o is in its initial state.

Executions and more. A schedule σ is a finite or infinite sequence of processes, indicating the order in which processes take steps. An execution $E = (\mathrm{A}, \sigma, \vec{c})$ consists of an algorithm A, a schedule σ, and a coin flip vector $\vec{c} = (c_1, c_2, \ldots)$, where each c_i is a sequence of coin flips for process p_i. An execution E has a trace $\tau = \mathit{Tr}(E)$, which is a sequence of steps $(p, c, \mathtt{op}, \mathit{note})$, where p is a process, c is a coin flip or $\perp$, $\mathtt{op}$ is an operation invocation and response on a base object or a special "no-op" value, and *note* is an annotation. The annotation is used in composed algorithms to indicate when the algorithm invokes an operation of an implemented object or obtains a response. More precisely, an annotation is empty, or it contains an invocation or response of an implemented object. A history is a sequence of invocations and responses to shared objects, satisfying well-formedness conditions (e.g, a response of an object occurs only after an invocation to that object). Given a trace τ of an execution, we define its low-level history $h(\tau)$ by extracting the invocations and responses of each base object in the trace, and placing a response right after the corresponding invocation. If τ is an execution of a composed algorithm, we define the high-level history $H(\tau)$ by extracting the invocations and responses in the annotations in τ, corresponding to operations on the implemented objects. We say that operation $\mathtt{op}$ happens before operation $\mathtt{op}'$ in $\hbar$, denoted $\mathtt{op} \prec \mathtt{op}'$, if the response of $\mathtt{op}$ occurs before the invocation of $\mathtt{op}'$ in $\hbar$.

Given a high- or low-level history $\hbar$, $\hbar|p$ is the subsequence of $\hbar$ containing just invocations and responses of process p. Similarly, $\tau|p$ is the subsequence of τ containing just steps by p. A sequential history is one in which an invocation is immediately followed by its response. Low-level histories are sequential histories.

For any sequence α (a schedule or trace), $\alpha[k]$ denotes its prefix with k elements. We denote by $\sigma(\tau)$ the schedule of trace τ. We say that *coin flip vector $\vec{c}$ observes trace τ* if the coin flips in $\vec{c}$ match the coin flips in τ. More precisely, for every i and j, the j'th coin flip of c_i equals the j'th coin flip of process p_i in τ.

Obstruction-Freedom and Linearizability. Some of our results refer to obstruction-freedom or linearizability. Obstruction-freedom [6] requires that if a process takes sufficiently many solo steps, it terminates.

Linearizability [5] roughly requires that each operation appears to take place instantaneously between its invocation and response:

Definition 1 (Linearizability) *A history $\hbar$ is linearizable, if for some history $\hbar_S$ resulting from appending to $\hbar$ responses of some operations pending in $\hbar$, there exists a sequential history L such that: (1) L is a valid history of operations on atomic objects; and (2) the order of operations in L preserves the happens-before order of operations in $\hbar_S$. Such a history L is called* linearization *of $\hbar$.*

Note that a concurrent history may have many linearizations. We say that two histories $\hbar$ and $\hbar'$ are equivalent, denoted $\hbar \simeq \hbar'$, if $\hbar$ and $\hbar'$ have a common linearization.

Object o is linearizable if all histories that can arise from executions of the operations on o are linearizable.

Oblivious Adversary. In randomized algorithms, the adversary model captures how the schedule can depend on the coin flips. We consider an oblivious adversary, which cannot observe coin flips or operations: it chooses ahead of execution the entire schedule σ.

4. COMPOSABILITY

We now define what it means to correctly compose an algorithm A with an object library $\mathcal{OL}$. In this definition, we must reconcile two apparently contradictory goals. First, we want to make sure that the adversary (scheduler) gains no power going from the original algorithm A to the composed algorithm $A_{\mathcal{OL}}$. Second, we must allow the schedule to change going from original to composed algorithm, because the latter algorithm may have many more steps. To resolve this impasse, the key idea is that *the function that maps the original schedule to the composed schedule cannot depend on the coin flips.* If it could, the adversary would be able to schedule the composed algorithm adaptively, which would potentially allow it to change the probability distributions of the executions. These intuitions are captured precisely as follows:

Definition 2 (Sound composition in the oblivious adversary model) *Let A be an algorithm, $\mathcal{OL}$ be an object library that covers the objects used in A, and $A_{\mathcal{OL}}$ the composition of A with $\mathcal{OL}$. We say that $A_{\mathcal{OL}}$ is sound if, for all schedules σ, there exists a schedule σ' such that for all coin flip vectors $\vec{c}$, $h(Tr(A,\sigma',\vec{c})) \simeq H(Tr(A_{\mathcal{OL}},\sigma,\vec{c}))$.*

Note above, in particular, that in the traces of A and $A_{\mathcal{OL}}$, the schedule can change but the coin flip vector $\vec{c}$ is the same.

We define a composable object library as one that can be soundly composed with every algorithm:

Definition 3 (Composable object library) *An object library $\mathcal{OL}$ is composable if, for every algorithm A that uses a subset of objects in $\mathcal{OL}$, the composition of A and $\mathcal{OL}$ is sound.*

5. UNIFORM LINEARIZABILITY

Given an algorithm A and an object library $\mathcal{OL}$, we first prove that the composition $A_{\mathcal{OL}}$ of A with $\mathcal{OL}$ is sound (see Definition 2) if and only if $A_{\mathcal{OL}}$ satisfies *uniform linearizability.* To define uniform linearizability, we first define isomorphic sequential histories, which are two sequential histories where processes appear in the same order.

Definition 4 (Isomorphic histories) *Sequential histories L_1 and L_2 are isomorphic, denoted $L_1 \overset{iso}{\sim} L_2$, if for every positive integer i, the i'th operations in both, L_1 and L_2, are executed by the same process.*

Intuitively, uniform linearizability requires that all histories of executions of $A_{\mathcal{OL}}$ under the same schedule have essentially the same linearization even though different coin flips can yield different operations.

Definition 5 (Uniform linearizability) *The composition $A_{\mathcal{OL}}$ of algorithm A with object library $\mathcal{OL}$ satisfies uniform linearizability if there exists a function L that maps each trace τ of an execution of $A_{\mathcal{OL}}$ to a linearization of $H(\tau)$, such that for any two traces τ_1, τ_2 with $\sigma(\tau_1) = \sigma(\tau_2)$, $L(\tau_1) \overset{iso}{\sim} L(\tau_2)$.*
We say that $\mathcal{OL}$ satisfies uniform linearizability if, for every algorithm A, the composition of A with $\mathcal{OL}$ satisfies uniform linearizability.

Uniform linearizability is a technical property that can be used to prove soundness of the composition of a given randomized algorithm with some object implementations. Moreover, as we will see in the following section, proving that the entire library $\mathcal{OL}$ satisfies uniform linearizability can be done by reasoning about implementation properties, such as operation lengths and linearization points.

5.1 Uniform Linearizability is Sufficient

We show that if $A_{\mathcal{OL}}$ satisfies uniform linearizability, then $A_{\mathcal{OL}}$ is sound under an oblivious adversary. Intuitively, we can take the isomorphic linearizations L_1 and L_2 of any two histories of $A_{\mathcal{OL}}$ under some schedule σ, and simulate (low-level) histories of A (with the same coin flips), under schedule σ', such that σ' is the order of processes in both L_1 and L_2.

LEMMA 6. *If $A_{\mathcal{OL}}$ satisfies uniform linearizability, then $A_{\mathcal{OL}}$ is sound.*

PROOF. Consider some arbitrary schedule σ. We will determine a schedule σ' such that for every coin flip vector $\vec{c}$, histories $H\big(Tr(A_{\mathcal{OL}},\sigma,\vec{c})\big)$ and $h\big(Tr(A,\sigma',\vec{c})\big)$ have a common linearization.

Let $\mathcal{T}_\sigma$ be the set of traces of the executions of $A_{\mathcal{OL}}$ under σ for all possible coin flips. Since $A_{\mathcal{OL}}$ satisfies uniform linearizability, there exists a function L that maps each trace τ in $\mathcal{T}_\sigma$ to a linearization of $H(\tau)$, such that for all τ_1, τ_2 in $\mathcal{T}_\sigma$, $L(\tau_1) \overset{iso}{\sim} L(\tau_2)$. Let $\mathcal{L}$ be the set of all such linearizations $L(\tau)$ for each τ in $\mathcal{T}_\sigma$. By construction, all histories in $\mathcal{L}$ are sequential. We take an arbitrary history L' in $\mathcal{L}$ and let schedule σ' be the sequence of processes that execute operations in L'. By uniform linearizability, this sequence is the same for every history in $\mathcal{L}$.

Now, consider some coin flip vector $\vec{c}$ and execution $E = (A_{\mathcal{OL}}, \sigma, \vec{c})$. Then in $L\big(Tr(E)\big) \in \mathcal{L}$, processes execute operations in the order determined by σ'. Consider the sequential execution $E_{\sigma'}$ of $A_{\mathcal{OL}}$ with the coin flip vector $\vec{c}$, where processes execute their high level-operations in the order determined by σ'. Recall that $\mathcal{OL}$ is deterministic and thus coin flips are outside the object implementations. Thus, by construction,

$$L\big(Tr(E)\big) = H(E_{\sigma'}). \tag{1}$$

Now, consider execution $E' = (A, \sigma', \vec{c})$ of the non-composed algorithm A. The operations on atomic objects in E' are the same as the operations on implemented objects in $E_{\sigma'}$. This implies that $h\big(Tr(E')\big) = H(E_{\sigma'})$, and thus $h\big(Tr(E')\big) = L\big(Tr(E)\big)$ by eq. (1). Thus, this sequential history is a common linearization of the histories of executions $E = (A_{\mathcal{OL}}, \sigma, \vec{c})$ and $E' = (A, \sigma', \vec{c})$, for the coin flip vector $\vec{c}$. Since the choice of $\vec{c}$ is arbitrary, this is true for every execution of $A_{\mathcal{OL}}$ under σ and A under σ'. □

5.2 Uniform Linearizability is Necessary

We show that if composition $A_{\mathcal{OL}}$ is sound under an oblivious adversary, then $A_{\mathcal{OL}}$ satisfies uniform linearizability. We show this by constructing, for any schedule σ, a mapping from all traces of $A_{\mathcal{OL}}$ under σ to linearizations that are isomorphic. First, note that the histories of all executions under the same schedule are isomorphic. Second, by composability, there exists σ' such that each history h of A under σ' and each history H of $A_{\mathcal{OL}}$ under σ have the same linearization S, i.e., $h = S$.

LEMMA 7. *If $A_{\mathcal{OL}}$ is sound, then $A_{\mathcal{OL}}$ satisfies uniform linearizability.*

PROOF. Assume that composition $A_{\mathcal{OL}}$ of A with $\mathcal{OL}$ is sound. Take some schedule σ and all traces of $A_{\mathcal{OL}}$ under σ for all possible coin flips. From Definition 2, it follows that there exists σ' such that the low-level histories of A under σ' have common linearizations with the high-level histories of $A_{\mathcal{OL}}$ under σ. Let $\mathcal{L}$ be the set of all such linearizations.

By the definition of isomorphism, all low-level histories under σ' are isomorphic: each entry in the low-level history corresponds to an entry of the schedule. Moreover, every (low-level) history of A under σ' is equal to its linearization in $\mathcal{L}$. Therefore, all histories in $\mathcal{L}$ are isomorphic among them.

We define function L so that it maps each trace of $A_{\mathcal{OL}}$ under σ to the linearization of its history in $\mathcal{L}$. Note that the choice of σ is arbitrary. By the definition of uniform linearizability (Definition 5), the existence of such mapping for all traces under any σ implies that $A_{\mathcal{OL}}$ satisfies uniform linearizability. □

From Lemmas 7 and 6, it follows that composition $A_{\mathcal{OL}}$ is sound under an oblivious adversary if and only if $A_{\mathcal{OL}}$ satisfies uniform linearizability. From this result and the definition of composable library:

THEOREM 1. *Object library $\mathcal{OL}$ satisfies composability under an oblivious adversary if and only if $\mathcal{OL}$ satisfies uniform linearizability.*

6. OPERATIONS LENGTHS AND LINEARIZATION POINTS

We now give necessary and sufficient conditions for an object library $\mathcal{OL}$ to satisfy uniform linearizability. By Theorem 1, this yields necessary and sufficient conditions for $\mathcal{OL}$ to satisfy composability.

Throughout this section we assume that the updatable objects in $\mathcal{OL}$ are obstruction-free. We show that $\mathcal{OL}$ satisfies uniform linearizability if and only if $\mathcal{OL}$ satisfies a property called *library homogeneity*, which requires that for each process p, all operations by p on $\mathcal{OL}$ have the same length (in atomic shared memory steps) and linearization points. Intuitively, a linearization point of operation op is a step in the trace where op appears to take effect. Note that operations may be assigned different but equivalent linearization points, and the points are only meaningful relative to each other. Library homogeneity requires that there be at least one way to assign the points uniformly across operations of a process. We call k_p a linearization point of process p if every history has a linearization in which each operation op by p is linearized at the k_p'th step of op.

Given a vector $\vec{K} = (k_1, k_2, \dots)$ of positive integers, indexed by process ids, the *$\vec{K}$-ordering* of a trace τ is a sequential history obtained as follows: For each process p and each operation op by p in τ, let lin(op) be point in time when p executes its k_p-th step of op; if operation op consists of fewer than k_p steps, then lin(op) $= \infty$. Then order the operations in τ by their lin(op) values, omitting all operations op with lin(op) $= \infty$.

We now define library homogeneity.

DEFINITION 8. *Object library $\mathcal{OL}$ satisfies* library homogeneity, *if:*

- *For every process p, there exists a positive integer ℓ_p, such that in every trace τ, ℓ_p is the length (in atomic shared memory steps) of every complete operation by p on objects in $\mathcal{OL}$.*
- *There exists a vector $\vec{K} = (k_1, k_2, \dots)$ of positive integers, such that for every trace τ, the $\vec{K}$-ordering of τ is a linearization of $H(\tau)$.*

The proof that uniform linearizability implies *library homogeneity* is divided into two parts. We first look at the length of operations on $\mathcal{OL}$ by each process p, and show that every such op must have the same length. We then show that, in addition to the same length, the operations must have the same linearization points.

In the proofs, without stating explicitly, we only consider executions where all shared objects are from $\mathcal{OL}$. The main proof technique is the following: to prove the properties of some trace τ of algorithm $A_{\mathcal{OL}}$ under schedule σ, we *(i)* find an algorithm $A'_{\mathcal{OL}}$ such that the order of operations in some trace τ' of $A'_{\mathcal{OL}}$ under σ is known in all linearizations; then, *(ii)* we compose $A_{\mathcal{OL}}$ and $A'_{\mathcal{OL}}$ by making processes flip coins to choose between $A_{\mathcal{OL}}$ and $A'_{\mathcal{OL}}$; finally, *(iii)* we use uniform linearizability to find a linearization of $H(\tau)$ that is isomorphic to $H(\tau')$.

Observe that by construction, traces register only shared memory steps. Thus, in trace τ of an execution under schedule σ, every entry in τ corresponds to an entry of σ; thus, prefix $\tau[k]$ is the trace of the execution under prefix $\sigma[k]$.

OBSERVATION 9. *If $\sigma(\tau_1) = \sigma(\tau_2)$, then for every positive integer k, $\sigma(\tau_1[k]) = \sigma(\tau_2[k])$.*

We now state an auxiliary claim: if one process is reading and another is updating some updatable object (as defined in Section 3) concurrently, then there exists a critical step, such that the `update` becomes visible to the reader.

PROPOSITION 10. *Take any two processes p and q, any linearizable (obstruction-free) updatable object o, such that o is in the initial state. Let p execute o.`update`(), and q execute o.`read`(). Then, there is a positive integer k such that, for any non-negative integer $k' < k$:*

- *in the execution under schedule $(p)^{k'}(q)^{\infty}$, `read` returns $\perp$; and*
- *in the execution under schedule $(p)^{k}(q)^{\infty}$, `read` returns a value different from $\perp$.*

PROOF. By obstruction-freedom, for any integer m in execution under schedule $(p)^m(q)^{\infty}$, q completes its `read`. By assumption, p has not started its `update`, so in the execution under schedule $(q)^{\infty}$, the `read` returns the initial value $\perp$. Moreover, by obstruction-freedom, there exists some positive integer ℓ such that under schedule $(p)^{\ell}$, p completes its `update`, and thus under $(p)^{\ell}(q)^{\infty}$, the `read` returns a value $y \neq \perp$. We then take the smallest value $k \in \{1, \ldots, m\}$ such that under $(p)^{k-1}(q)^{\infty}$ the `read` returns $\perp$ and under $(p)^{k}(q)^{\infty}$ the read returns $y \neq \perp$. □

6.1 Operations Lengths

We show that if object library $\mathcal{OL}$ satisfies uniform linearizability, then each process p executes the same number of shared memory steps to complete each operation on $\mathcal{OL}$. The high-level idea of the proof is as follows. Whenever the operations lengths vary in two executions under the same schedule, we create two executions, such that the order of some i'th operation by p and some j'th operation by q is switched, which violates uniform linearizability. To avoid this, operations by the same process must start and finish in lock-step in any two executions.

We first show that the i'th operations of some process p must be aligned in any two executions under the same schedule σ. We assume, by contradiction, there are two traces τ_1 and τ_2 under σ, such that the last steps of the i'th operations by p are not aligned. We then make process p update object o after its i'th operations; then q reads o. Under the same schedule, for some coin flips, p takes enough steps executing `update` and q returns a new value; for some other coin flips, q misses p's `update`. Thus, p's `update` precedes q's `read` in all linearizations of the former history, and q's `read` precedes p's `update` in all linearizations of the latter history. This violates uniform linearizability.

LEMMA 11. *Assume $\mathcal{OL}$ satisfies uniform linearizability. Consider any: composed algorithm $A_{\mathcal{OL}}$, schedule σ, process p, positive integer i, and two vectors of coin-flips $\vec{c}_1$ and $\vec{c}_2$; and let:*

- *op_1 be the i'th operation by p in trace $\tau_1 = Tr(A_{\mathcal{OL}}, \sigma, \vec{c}_1)$;*
- *op_2 be the i'th operation by p in trace $\tau_2 = Tr(A_{\mathcal{OL}}, \sigma, \vec{c}_2)$.*

Then, for any positive integer k, op_1 responds in $\tau_1[k]$ if and only if op_2 responds in $\tau_2[k]$.

PROOF. Suppose by contradiction there exists some composed algorithm $A_{\mathcal{OL}}$ and schedule σ where, for some positive integer k' and different vectors of coin-flips $\vec{c}_1$ and $\vec{c}_2$, for some i, the i'th operations by p are op_1 and op_2, op_1 responds in $\tau_1[k']$, and op_2 does not respond in $\tau_2[k']$ (op_2 either has not been invoked or is pending in $\tau_2[k']$). Let $k \leq k'$ be the smallest integer such that op_1 responds in $\tau_1[k]$ (i.e., the k'th entry in τ_1 is a step by p annotated with a response tag). Now consider schedule $\sigma[k]$.

Let P be the set of processes executing $A_{\mathcal{OL}}$. We take a new updatable object o (as defined in Section 3), in its initial state. We then create an algorithm A' as follows: every process $r \in P \setminus \{p\}$ executes $A_{\mathcal{OL}}$; p executes the modified $A_{\mathcal{OL}}$, in which after op_1 and op_2 we insert o.`update`(); moreover, a process q not in P executes o.`read`(). Since by assumption $\mathcal{OL}$ satisfies uniform linearizability, the composition $A'_{\mathcal{OL}}$ (of A' with $\mathcal{OL}$) also satisfies uniform linearizability.

Recall that objects in $\mathcal{OL}$ are independent. By Proposition 10, if for object o in its initial state, process p executes o.`update`() and q executes o.`read`(), there exists a positive integer ℓ such that

for any non-negative integer $m < \ell$ in the execution under schedule $(p)^m(q)^{\infty}$, q's `read` returns $\perp$ (2)

and

in the execution under $(p)^{\ell}(q)^{\infty}$, q's `read` returns a value $y \neq \perp$. (3)

Consider the traces of the following two executions.

Trace τ_1**:** Let $\tau_1[k]$ be the trace of execution $(A'_{\mathcal{OL}}, \sigma[k], \vec{c}_1)$. By construction, in $(A'_{\mathcal{OL}}, \sigma[k], \vec{c}_1)$ all processes execute the same steps as in $(A_{\mathcal{OL}}, \sigma[k], \vec{c}_1)$. Moreover, by the choice of k we know that in $\tau_1[k]$, process p has completed op_1 and its next operation is o.`update`(). Also, recall that q executes only o.`read`() in $A'_{\mathcal{OL}}$, and object o is still in its initial state in $\tau_1[k]$. We continue the execution under schedule $(p)^{\ell}(q)^{\infty}$. Then by (3), the `read` returns $y \neq \perp$. Take the resulting trace $\tau_1 = Tr(A'_{\mathcal{OL}}, \sigma[k](p)^m(q)^{\infty}, \vec{c}_1)$. Then,

in every linearization of $H(\tau_1)$, p's operation o.`update`() precedes q's operation o.`read`(). (4)

Trace τ_2**:** Let $\tau_2[k]$ be the trace of execution $(A'_{\mathcal{OL}}, \sigma[k], \vec{c}_2)$. By construction, in execution $(A'_{\mathcal{OL}}, \sigma[k], \vec{c}_2)$ all processes execute the same steps as in $(A_{\mathcal{OL}}, \sigma[k], \vec{c}_2)$. Moreover, by assumption, process p has not completed op_2 in $\tau_2[k]$. We continue the execution under schedule $(p)^{\ell}(q)^{\infty}$: process p takes fewer than ℓ steps executing o.`update`(), which by (2) implies that operation o.`read`() by q returns $\perp$. Take the resulting trace $\tau_2 = Tr(A'_{\mathcal{OL}}, \sigma[k](p)^{\ell}(q)^{\infty}, \vec{c}_2)$. Then

in every linearization of $H(\tau_2)$, q's operation o.`read`() precedes p's operation o.`update`(). (5)

Since by assumption $\mathcal{OL}$ satisfies uniform linearizability and both τ_1 and τ_2 have the same schedule, there exist isomorphic linearizations L_1 and L_2 of $H(\tau_1)$ and $H(\tau_2)$, respectively. From (4) and (5) we know that in every linearization of $H(\tau_1)$ the $(i{+}1)$'th operation by p precedes the first operation by q, and in every linearization of $H(\tau_2)$ the first operation by q precedes the $(i{+}1)$'th operation by p. This is a contradiction. □

We now use induction to show that all operations by p are aligned in any two traces under σ.

LEMMA 12. *Assume $\mathcal{OL}$ satisfies uniform linearizability. Then, for any composed algorithm $A_{\mathcal{OL}}$, any process p, any schedule σ, and any positive integer i, there exists an integer ℓ_i such that in every trace of $A_{\mathcal{OL}}$ under schedule σ process p completes its i'th operation in exactly ℓ_i steps.*

PROOF. The proof is by induction on i.

Base case: $i = 1$. By contradiction, assume there exist some traces τ_1 and τ_2 of the executions of $A_{\mathcal{OL}}$ under σ such that for some ℓ_1, after ℓ_1 steps p has completed its first operation in τ_1, but has not completed its first operation in τ_2. Take the smallest k such that p takes ℓ_1 steps in $\tau_1[k]$. Since both traces have the same schedule σ, p takes the same number ℓ_1 of steps in both $\tau_1[k]$ and $\tau_2[k]$ (Observation 9). Thus, p completes its first operation in $\tau_1[k]$, but not in $\tau_2[k]$. This contradicts Lemma 11.

Inductive hypothesis: the claim holds for every positive integer $j < i$. By contradiction, assume every j'th operation by p takes ℓ_j steps, and there exists some τ_1 and τ_2 of the executions of $A_{\mathcal{OL}}$ under σ such that for some positive integer ℓ_i, after ℓ_i steps p completes its i'th operation in τ_1, but does not complete its i'th operation in τ_2. Take k' such that p takes $\ell_1 + \ldots + \ell_i$ steps in schedule $\tau_1[k']$. By Observation 9, p also takes $\ell_1 + \ldots + \ell_i$ steps in $\tau_2[k']$. Thus, p completes its i'th operation in $\tau_1[k']$, but not in $\tau_2[k']$. This contradicts Lemma 11. □

Finally, we show that every operation by process p has the same length, in every execution.

LEMMA 13. *If $\mathcal{OL}$ satisfies uniform linearizability, then for any process p there exists an integer ℓ_p such that ℓ_p is the length of all complete operations by p in all executions.*

PROOF. Take some algorithm $A_{\mathcal{OL}}$ and schedule σ and let P be the set of processes executing $A_{\mathcal{OL}}$.

We then take a new object o with some operation `op`. We create algorithm $A'_{\mathcal{OL}}$ as follows: Each process $q \in P \setminus \{p\}$ executes $A_{\mathcal{OL}}$. Process p executes a modified version of algorithm $A_{\mathcal{OL}}$: Before each (high-level) operation of $A_{\mathcal{OL}}$, if p has not executed o.`op` already, with probability 1/2 p executes o.`op`, and with probability 1/2 it executes the next high-level operation of $A_{\mathcal{OL}}$ instead. If p has already executed o.`op`, then it simply executes the next high-level operation of $A_{\mathcal{OL}}$.

For some coin flips, there are traces $\tau'_1, \tau'_2, \ldots$ of executions of $A'_{\mathcal{OL}}$ under σ, such that the i'th operation by p in τ'_i is o.`op`. In all such traces, the execution on object o is exactly the same. Since objects in $\mathcal{OL}$ are independent, there exists some integer ℓ_p such that in all traces $\tau'_1, \tau'_2, \ldots$, process p takes exactly ℓ_p (shared memory) steps to complete `op`. And by Lemma 12, for every positive integer k, the length of each k'th operation in every $\tau'_1, \tau'_2, \ldots$ is the same. Since the choice of o and `op` is arbitrary, the claim follows, for every o and `op`. Moreover, since the initial choice of $A_{\mathcal{OL}}$ and σ is arbitrary, the claim follows for every $A_{\mathcal{OL}}$ and σ.

It remains to show that for two different composed algorithms $A^1_{\mathcal{OL}}$ and $A^2_{\mathcal{OL}}$, the value ℓ_p is the same. We can easily combine $A^1_{\mathcal{OL}}$ and $A^2_{\mathcal{OL}}$ into one algorithm $A_{\mathcal{OL}}$ by letting each process in the beginning choose at random whether it will execute $A^1_{\mathcal{OL}}$ or $A^2_{\mathcal{OL}}$. Then in $A_{\mathcal{OL}}$ all complete operations by process p have the same length ℓ_p (for any schedule σ). For each $i \in \{1,2\}$, with positive probability all processes execute $A^i_{\mathcal{OL}}$, so in $A^i_{\mathcal{OL}}$ all complete operations by p have length ℓ_p in all executions. □

6.2 Linearization Points

Recall that operations may have several linearization points. We will show that if $\mathcal{OL}$ satisfies uniform linearizability, then for each process p, there exists a common linearization point of all operations by p. In particular, we show that for some vector $\vec{K}$ and every trace τ, $H(\tau)$ linearizes to the $\vec{K}$-ordering of τ. The main idea of the proof is to show that for every trace τ we can find a trace τ' of an execution under the same schedule, such that all linearizations of $H(\tau')$ are $\vec{K}$-orderings of τ' (with a possible exception of linearizations containing, at the end, pending operations that have not taken effect[4]). By uniform linearizability and the fact that operations have same length in both τ and τ', some linearization of $H(\tau)$ is also a $\vec{K}$-ordering of τ.

We already proved in Lemma 13 that, if $\mathcal{OL}$ satisfies uniform linearizability, then for every process p there exists an integer ℓ_p, such that all operations by p complete in exactly ℓ_p steps. We call ℓ_p the *operation length* of p.

We will show that for each process p there is an integer k_p such that all operations by p linearize with the k_p'th step by p.

We start by taking, for each processes p, a value k from Proposition 10, for some process q and some updatable object o (roughly, k is such that, after k steps, `update` by p on object o becomes visible to q). We will show that, for process p, k is the same for every updatable object o and reader q. Then, we will show that k is also the same for every operation by p on any object in $\mathcal{OL}$, not just `update`.

We first take processes p, q and updatable object o, insert two `read` operations by q, one before and one after the k-th step of an `update` by p, and show that the first `read` by q "sees" an old value and the second `read` by q "sees" a new value.

In the proofs, we use subscript to label an operation with the id of the process that executes it, and superscript to indicate the order of operation by the same process (e.g., $\texttt{read}_p^2$ denotes the second `read` by process p).

LEMMA 14. *Assume that $\mathcal{OL}$ satisfies uniform linearizability. Consider any two distinct processes, p and q, and let ℓ_p and ℓ_q, respectively, be their operation lengths. Take any updatable object o in its initial state. Let p execute o.`update`(), and q execute o.`read`(); o.`read`(). Then there exists a non-negative integer k, such that in the execution under schedule $(p)^{k-1}(q)^{\ell_q}(p)(q)^{\ell_q}$, the two `read` operations by q return different values.*

PROOF. Let $A^1_{\mathcal{OL}}$ be the algorithm, where p executes $o.\texttt{update}_p()$, and q executes $o.\texttt{read}_q^1(); o.\texttt{read}_q^2()$. Take process q and integer k from Proposition 10 for p, q and o. Recall

[4]Recall that linearizability always allows adding pending operations that have not taken effect at the end of a linearized history.

that $\texttt{read}_q^1$ completes in exactly ℓ_q steps. Thus, by Proposition 10:

in the execution of $A^1_{\mathcal{OL}}$ under schedule $(p)^{k-1}(q)^{\ell_q}$, $\texttt{read}_q^1$ returns $\bot$; and, in the execution of $A^1_{\mathcal{OL}}$ under $(p)^k(q)^{\ell_q}$, $\texttt{read}_q^1$ returns a value $y \neq \bot$. (6)

Consider history H of the execution of $A^1_{\mathcal{OL}}$ under schedule $\sigma{=}(p)^{k-1}(q)^{\ell_q}(p)(q)^{\ell_q}$. From (6),

$$\texttt{read}_q^1 \text{ returns } \bot \text{ in } H. \quad (7)$$

Now let $A^2_{\mathcal{OL}}$ be the algorithm, where q executes $o'.\texttt{read}_q^1(); o.\texttt{read}_q^2()$ for some new updatable object $o' \neq o$ from $\mathcal{OL}$. Let $A_{\mathcal{OL}}$ be the algorithm, where p executes $A^1_{\mathcal{OL}}$, and q flips a coin and based on the result executes either $A^1_{\mathcal{OL}}$ or $A^2_{\mathcal{OL}}$, each with probability 1/2. Consider the following histories of the executions of $A_{\mathcal{OL}}$ under σ:

- History H_1, in which q executes $A^1_{\mathcal{OL}}$. By construction, $H = H_1$ as the executions are identical except for the initial coin flip by q.
- History H_2, in which q executes $A^2_{\mathcal{OL}}$. Consider the projection of H_2 on object o: p executes k steps of its $o.\texttt{update}_p$ operation, then q executes $o.\texttt{read}_q^2()$. From (6), $o.\texttt{read}_q^2()$ returns $y \neq \bot$.

Thus,

$$\text{in all linearizations of } H_2,\ o.\texttt{update}_p \prec o.\texttt{read}_q^2. \quad (8)$$

Since $\mathcal{OL}$ satisfies uniform linearizability, H_1 and H_2 have isomorphic linearizations L_1 and L_2. From (8), $\texttt{update}_p$ precedes $\texttt{read}_q^2$ in L_2, and by $L_1 \overset{iso}{\sim} L_2$ the same is true for L_1. Hence, $\texttt{read}_q^2$ "sees" $o.\texttt{update}_p()$ and returns y. Recall that $H_1 = H$. Thus in H, $\texttt{read}_q^2$ also returns y. Together with (7), this implies the claim. □

We now show that the value of k is independent of updatable object o and reader q. Intuitively, we show this by composing algorithms so that p flips coins to choose an object for its $\texttt{update}$; and readers q and r flip coins to choose an object for their reads. Then, by the return values of the reads on different objects, we establish the isomorphic order of the operations in the original execution.

LEMMA 15. *Assume that $\mathcal{OL}$ satisfies uniform linearizability. For every process p there exists an integer k_p such that for every updatable object o (in its initial state) and every process $r \neq p$ the following is true: If p executes $o.\texttt{update}()$, and r executes $o.\texttt{read}(); o.\texttt{read}()$, then in the execution under schedule $(p)^{k_p-1}(r)^{\ell_r}(p)(r)^{\ell_r}$, the two $\texttt{read}$ operations by r return different values.*

PROOF. Let $o_1 \neq o$ be an updatable object in its initial state, and let $o_2 = o$. Let $q \notin \{p, r\}$ be a process, and let ℓ_q and ℓ_r, respectively, be the operation lengths of q and r. For $i \in \{1,2\}$ let algorithm $A^i_{\mathcal{OL}}$ be defined as follows: p executes $o_i.\texttt{update}()$, q executes $o_i.\texttt{read}_q^1(); o_i.\texttt{read}_q^1()$, and r executes $o_i.\texttt{read}_r^1(); o_i.\texttt{read}_r^2()$. We create algorithm $A_{\mathcal{OL}}$, in which each of the processes p, q, and r flips a coin and, depending on the result, executes either $A^1_{\mathcal{OL}}$ or $A^2_{\mathcal{OL}}$.

By Lemma 14 there exists an integer k_p such that

in the execution of $A^1_{\mathcal{OL}}$ under schedule $(p)^{k_p-1}(q)^{\ell_q}(p)(q)^{\ell_q}$ the two $\texttt{read}$ operations by q return different values. (9)

Let

$$\sigma = (p)^{k_p-1}(r)^{\ell_r}(q)^{\ell_q}(p)(q)^{\ell_q}(r)^{\ell_r}.$$

We consider three traces obtained by processes executing $A_{\mathcal{OL}}$ according to schedule σ, that differ only in the random choices processes make (i.e., the object processes choose to execute their operations on):

- In τ_1 all processes choose o_1;
- in τ_2 processes p and q choose o_1, and r chooses o_2;
- in τ_3 process q chooses o_1, and p and r choose o_2.

Since $\mathcal{OL}$ satisfies uniform linearizability, there is a mapping L that maps each of the traces τ_j, $j \in \{1,2,3\}$, to a linearization $L(\tau_j)$ of history $H(\tau_j)$, and all those linearizations are isomorphic.

In σ' processes r and q always execute exactly ℓ_r respectively ℓ_p uninterrupted steps, and therefore their operations do not overlap. Hence,

$$\text{in } L(\tau_1): \quad o_1.\texttt{read}_r^1 \prec o_1.\texttt{read}_q^1 \prec o_1.\texttt{read}_q^2 \prec o_1.\texttt{read}_r^2. \quad (10)$$

Now consider the projected trace $\tau_2|o_1$. Since only p and q choose o_1, that projected trace is obtained from $A^1_{\mathcal{OL}}$ under schedule $(p)^{k_p-1}(q)^{\ell_q}(p)(q)^{\ell_q}$, and thus by (9) the two $\texttt{read}$ operations by q return different values. Therefore, in all linearizations of $H(\tau_2|o_1)$ the $\texttt{update}$ operation by p is sandwiched between the two $\texttt{read}$ operations by q. Then the same is also true for all linearizations of $H(\tau_2)$, and in particular

$$\text{in } L(\tau_2): \ o_1.\texttt{read}_q^1 \prec o_1.\texttt{update}_p \prec o_1.\texttt{read}_q^2.$$

The same is true for $L(\tau_1)$, because $L(\tau_1)$ and $L(\tau_2)$ are isomorphic, and p and q both access o_1 in τ_1. Thus, from (10) we obtain

$$\text{in } L(\tau_1): \ o_1.\texttt{read}_r^1 \prec o_1.\texttt{read}_q^1 \prec o_1.\texttt{update}_p \prec o_1.\texttt{read}_q^2 \prec o_1.\texttt{read}_r^2. \quad (11)$$

Then by isomorphism, in all linearizations $L(\tau_j)$, $j \in \{1,2,3\}$, processes appear in the following order:

$$r\,q\,p\,q\,r.$$

In particular, in all traces τ_j, $j \in \{1,2,3\}$, process r returns different values in its two $\texttt{read}$ operations.

Now consider the projected trace $\tau_3|o_2$. Only p and r choose o_2 in τ_3, and so $\tau_3|o_2$ follows the schedule $(p)^{k_p-1}(r)^{\ell_r}(p)(r)^{\ell_r}$. Since $o = o_2$, and the two $\texttt{read}$ operations by r return different values in $\tau_3|o_2$, the lemma follows. □

LEMMA 16. *Suppose $\mathcal{OL}$ satisfies uniform linearizability. For any process p let ℓ_p be the operation length of p and let k_p be as in Lemma 15. Then $k_p \leq \ell_p$.*

PROOF. For the purpose of a contradiction suppose $k_p > \ell_p$. Let o be any updatable object in its initial state, and consider the trace τ obtained from the schedule $(p)^{k_p-1}(r)^{\ell_r}(p)(r)^{\ell_r}$, where p executes $o.\texttt{update}()$, and process $r \neq p$ executes $o.\texttt{read}(); o.\texttt{read}()$. Since $k_p > \ell_p$, process p's $o.\texttt{update}()$ completes before r's first $o.\texttt{read}()$ gets invoked. Thus, $H(\tau)$ can only linearize to the sequential history, in which first p executes $o.\texttt{update}$, and then r executes its two o.**read**() operations. But then the two o.**read**() operations by r must return the same value, which contradicts Lemma 15. □

We now show that uniform linearizability implies that there is a vector $\vec{K}$ such that the $\vec{K}$-ordering of every trace is a linearization of the history of that trace. Let τ be the trace of an arbitrary execution under some schedule σ; then, create new trace τ' by augmenting τ with some reads by a new process q of a new object o, placing the reads by q before and after each "linearization point" specified by the $\vec{K}$-ordering of τ. We take another trace $\tau_{i,p}$ under the same schedule, in which process p replaces its i-th operation with o.**update**(). By Lemma 15, the two o.**read** operations that q performs before and after the k_p'th step of p's o.**update**, must return different values. Doing this for all processes p and all operations yields several isomorphic linearizations in which the linearization points of each operation are restricted to those determined by $\vec{K}$. As a result, we obtain a linearization of $H(\tau)$ that is the $\vec{K}$-ordering of τ.

LEMMA 17. *Suppose $\mathcal{OL}$ satisfies uniform linearizability. Then there exists a vector $\vec{K} = (k_1, k_2, \dots)$ of positive integers, such that for every trace τ, the $\vec{K}$-ordering of τ is a linearization of $H(\tau)$.*

PROOF. Let $\vec{K} = (k_1, k_2, \dots)$, where for every process p, k_p is the value from Lemma 15. Further, let ℓ_p be the operation length of process p (see Lemma 13).

Take an arbitrary trace τ of some algorithm $A_{\mathcal{OL}}$, where $A_{\mathcal{OL}}$ is the composition of $\mathcal{OL}$ with some algorithm A. Let P be the set of processes executing $A_{\mathcal{OL}}$. Let σ be the schedule of τ and $\vec{c}$ be the coin-flip vector that observes τ. We first assume that in τ every process p executes at least k_p steps in each of its operations; later we will explain how to accommodate the proof if this is not the case.

Let q be a process that is not in P, and o an updatable object in $\mathcal{OL}$ that is not used in $A_{\mathcal{OL}}$. Consider a new algorithm $A'_{\mathcal{OL}}$ defined as follows: Process q repeatedly executes o.**read**() in an infinite loop. Each process $p \in P$ chooses a non-negative integer i_p at random (according to an arbitrary distribution that assigns each non-negative integer a positive probability). Then, p executes $A_{\mathcal{OL}}$, but if $i_p > 0$, then p replaces its i_p-th operation with o.**update**(). (If p performs fewer than i_p operations, then p executes $A_{\mathcal{OL}}$.)

By uniform linearizability, there is a mapping L that maps traces of $A'_{\mathcal{OL}}$ to the linearizations of their histories, such that for any two traces μ and μ' obtained by an execution of $A_{\mathcal{OL}}$ with the same schedule, the linearizations $L(\mu)$ and $L(\mu')$ are isomorphic.

We now create a new schedule σ' from σ by inserting ℓ_q steps by q immediately before and after each k_p-th step that any process p executes during each of its operations on an object in $\mathcal{OL}$. Let $\vec{c}$ be the coin-flip vector, where each process $p \in P$ chooses $i_p = 0$. Further, let $\tau' = \mathit{Tr}(A'_{\mathcal{OL}}, \sigma', \vec{c})$. Then in τ' all processes in P execute $A_{\mathcal{OL}}$ in the same order as in τ. Hence, τ and τ' differ only by the added steps by the new process q executing operations on the new object o. Thus the projection of trace τ' on P is exactly the same as trace τ, i.e.,

$$\tau = \tau'|P. \tag{12}$$

For each positive integer i and each process $p \in P$ let $\vec{c}_{i,p}$ be the coin-flip vector where process p chooses $i_p = i$, and each other process $p' \in P \setminus \{p\}$ chooses $i_{p'} = 0$. Let $\tau_{i,p} = \mathit{Tr}(A'_{\mathcal{OL}}, \sigma', \vec{c}_{i,p})$. For each process $p \in P$ let $\mathtt{op}_{i,p}$ denote the i-th operation by p in $H(\tau')$. Recall that by assumption in τ (and thus in τ' and in $\tau_{i,p}$) every operation by p consists of at least k_p steps.

Let $\mathtt{read}^1_{i,p}$ and $\mathtt{read}^2_{i,p}$ denote the two o.**read**() operations by q that are executed immediately before respectively after p's k_p-th step of $\mathtt{op}_{i,p}$ in τ'. Then in $\tau_{i,p}$, $\mathtt{read}^1_{i,p}$ and $\mathtt{read}^2_{i,p}$ are executed immediately before respectively after p's k_p-th step of p's o.**update**() that p executes instead of $\mathtt{op}_{i,p}$ in this trace. Since no other process accesses o in $\tau_{i,p}$, the schedule of $\tau_{i,p}|o$ has the prefix $(p)^{k_p-1}(q)^{\ell_q}(p)q^{\ell_q}$, and in $H(\tau_{i,p}|o)$ process p executes o.**update**() and q executes two o.**read**() operations. Hence, by Lemma 15, operations $\mathtt{read}^1_{i,p}$ and $\mathtt{read}^2_{i,p}$ by q return different values in $H(\tau_{i,p}|o)$, and thus also in $H(\tau_{i,p})$. This means that in every linearization of $H(\tau_{i,p})$, p's o.**update**() appears between these two o.**read** operations. In particular,

$$\text{In } L(\tau_{i,p}): \mathtt{read}^1_{i,p} \prec o.\mathtt{update} \prec \mathtt{read}^2_{i,p}. \tag{13}$$

Since $\tau_{i,p}$ and τ' observe the same schedule σ', $L(\tau_{i,p})$ and $L(\tau')$ are isomorphic. Recall that the only difference between $H(\tau_{i,p})$ and $H(\tau')$ is that the i-th operation by p is o.**update**() in the former history, and it is $\mathtt{op}_i$ in the latter. Therefore by (13),

$$\text{in } L(\tau'): \mathtt{read}^1_{i,p} \prec \mathtt{op}_{i,p} \prec \mathtt{read}^2_{i,p}. \tag{14}$$

By construction, the $\vec{K}$-ordering of τ' observes exactly the same relation, because p executes its k_p-th step of $\mathtt{op}_{i,p}$ between the response of $\mathtt{read}^1_{i,p}$ and the invocation of $\mathtt{read}^2_{i,p}$. Recall that we chose i and p arbitrarily, so relation (14) is true for every process p and every operation $\mathtt{op}_{i,p}$ in τ'. Since all o.**read**() operations by q appear in the same order in $L(\tau')$ as in the $\vec{K}$-ordering of τ', we obtain that $L(\tau')$ is the $\vec{K}$-ordering of τ'.

By (12), $H(\tau) = H(\tau')|P$. Hence, the $\vec{K}$-ordering of τ is the projection of the $\vec{K}$-ordering of τ' on P, i.e., it is $L(\tau')|P$. Now note that in $H(\tau')$ process q (which is not in P) only accesses object o, and no process in P accesses object o. Hence, $L(\tau')|P$ is the same as $L(\tau')$ projected to all objects other than o. By composability of linearizability, this is a linearization of $H(\tau')$ projected to all objects other than o, i.e., it is a linearization of $H(\tau)$. Hence, we proved that the $\vec{K}$-ordering of τ is a linearization of $H(\tau)$.

It remains to consider the case that τ contains for some process p operations that contain fewer than k_p steps. By Lemma 16, $\ell_p \geq k_p$, and so those operations do not complete. We construct τ^* by letting each incomplete operation in τ run to completion in an arbitrary order. More precisely, for each process p let z_p be the number of steps process p executes in its last operation in τ. Then we obtain τ^* by appending for each process p the sequence $(p)^{\ell_p - z}$ to τ. As a result, each operation by a process p consists of $\ell_p \geq k_p$ steps (in particular, all operations complete). We showed above that the $\vec{K}$-ordering L^* of τ^* is a linearization of $H(\tau^*)$.

Let $\mathtt{op}'_1, \dots, \mathtt{op}'_m$ be the operations in τ such that each $\mathtt{op}'_i$, $1 \leq i \leq m$, is performed by some process p which executes fewer than k_p steps of $\mathtt{op}'_i$. Then by construction, in L^* (which is the $\vec{K}$-ordering of τ^*), operations $\mathtt{op}'_1, \dots, \mathtt{op}'_m$ appear at the end. Hence, removing $\mathtt{op}'_1, \dots, \mathtt{op}'_m$ from L^* yields a linearization L of $H(\tau)$. (Recall that $\mathtt{op}'_1, \dots, \mathtt{op}'_m$

do not complete in $H(\tau)$, so they can be removed to obtain a linearization.) Moreover, we can obtain the $\vec{K}$-ordering of τ from the $\vec{K}$-ordering of τ^* by removing $\mathsf{op}'_1, \ldots, \mathsf{op}'_m$ (because by definition each operation by a process p that contains fewer than k_p steps in τ is not part of the $\vec{K}$-ordering of τ). Hence, L is the $\vec{K}$-ordering of τ. Since it is a linearization of $H(\tau)$, this completes the proof. □

6.3 Proof of Sufficiency

We show that if an object library $\mathcal{OL}$ satisfies library homogeneity (Definition 8), then $\mathcal{OL}$ satisfies uniform linearizability. The intuition is that since all operations of the same process have the same length, $\vec{K}$-orderings of all traces, under the same schedule, are isomorphic.

LEMMA 18. *If an object library $\mathcal{OL}$ satisfies library homogeneity, then $\mathcal{OL}$ satisfies uniform linearizability.*

PROOF. Since $\mathcal{OL}$ satisfies library homogeneity, there exists a vector $\vec{K}$, and for each process p accessing $\mathcal{OL}$ there exists an integer ℓ_p such that, in every trace τ, each operation by p completes in ℓ_p steps, and the $\vec{K}$-ordering of τ is a linearization of $H(\tau)$. Let L be the mapping that maps each trace τ to its $\vec{K}$-ordering.

Consider traces τ_1 and τ_2 of any two executions of algorithm $A_{\mathcal{OL}}$ under the same schedule σ. We will show that $L(\tau_1)$ and $L(\tau_2)$ are isomorphic.

Since, for every process p, all operations take ℓ_p shared memory steps, for every positive integer i, every process starts and finishes its i'th operation at exactly the same position in both τ_1 and τ_2. Moreover, if in τ_j, $j \in \{1, 2\}$, we assign each operation by process p the linearization point that is the k_p-th step of that operation, then we obtain the linearization $L(\tau_j)$ of $H(\tau_j)$. In this assignment, the linearization point of the i-th operation by p in τ_1 appears at exactly the same position as the linearization point of the i-th operation by p in τ_2. As a result, for every process p and every i, the i-th operation by p appears at the same position in $L(\tau_1)$ as in $L(\tau_2)$. Therefore, $L(\tau_1)$ and $L(\tau_2)$ are isomorphic. Since the choice of $A_{\mathcal{OL}}$, σ, τ_1 and τ_2 are arbitrary, it follows from Definition 5 that $\mathcal{OL}$ satisfies uniform linearizability. □

We thus prove that library homogeneity (Definition 8) is both necessary (Lemmas 13 and 17) and sufficient (Lemma 18) for uniform linearizability of any object library $\mathcal{OL}$ that contains obstruction-free updatable objects.

THEOREM 2. *Any object library $\mathcal{OL}$ that contains obstruction-free updatable objects satisfies uniform linearizability if and only if $\mathcal{OL}$ satisfies* library homogeneity.

It follows from Theorems 1 and 2:

COROLLARY 1. *Any object library $\mathcal{OL}$ that contains obstruction-free updatable objects satisfies composability if and only if $\mathcal{OL}$ satisfies* library homogeneity.

7. DISCUSSION

We have shown that, to be usable in randomized algorithms under an oblivious adversary, an object library must satisfy library homogeneity, a strong property. We leave it as an open research direction how to implement such libraries. One idea is that, if the implementations in $\mathcal{OL}$ have no loops (all operations take a constant number of steps), then we can pad each operation with appropriately placed "no-op" steps to ensure library homogeneity. In practice, however, many data structures require executing an unbounded number of steps (e.g., depending on the size of the structure). These implementations cannot satisfy library homogeneity. In fact, we conjecture that many data types can never satisfy this property. For instance, library homogeneity implies *strong linearizability* and therefore we can apply the impossibility results shown for strong linearizability [3, 4, 2]. As future work, we would like to study object implementations that are randomized, and try to use randomization to design object libraries that hide the length and linearization points of operations.

Acknowledgements

We thank Lisa Higham for the insightful discussions and Marcos Aguilera for the helpful feedback on earlier drafts of the paper.

8. REFERENCES

[1] Michael Bender and Seth Gilbert. Mutual exclusion with $O(\log^2 \log n)$ amortized work. In *Proceedings of the 52nd Annual IEEE Symposium on Foundations of Computer Science (FOCS)*, pages 728–737, 2011.

[2] Oksana Denysyuk and Philipp Woelfel. Wait-freedom is harder than lock-freedom under strong linearizability. In *Distributed Computing: 29th International Symposium, DISC 2015, Proceedings*, pages 60–74, 2015.

[3] Wojciech Golab, Lisa Higham, and Philipp Woelfel. Linearizable implementations do not suffice for randomized distributed computation. In *Proceedings of the 43rd Annual ACM Symposium on Theory of Computing (STOC)*, pages 373–382, 2011.

[4] Maryam Helmi, Lisa Higham, and Philipp Woelfel. Strongly linearizable implementations: possibilities and impossibilities. In *Proceedings of the 31st SIGACT-SIGOPS Symposium on Principles of Distributed Computing (PODC)*, pages 385–394, 2012.

[5] M. Herlihy and J. M. Wing. Linearizability: A correctness condition for concurrent objects. *ACM Transactions on Programming Languages and Systems*, 12(3):463–492, 1990.

[6] Maurice Herlihy, Victor Luchangco, and Mark Moir. Obstruction-free synchronization: Double-ended queues as an example. In *International Conference on Distributed Computing Systems (ICDCS)*, pages 522–529, May 2003.

[7] Nancy A. Lynch. *Distributed Algorithms*. Morgan Kaufmann Publishers Inc., 1996.

Brief Announcement: A Family of Leaderless Generalized-Consensus Algorithms

Giuliano Losa
ECE, Virginia Tech
glosa@vt.edu

Sebastiano Peluso
ECE, Virginia Tech
peluso@vt.edu

Binoy Ravindran
ECE, Virginia Tech
binoy@vt.edu

1. INTRODUCTION

Most distributed command-ordering algorithms inspired by Paxos and MultiPaxos [4] rely on a unique leader process which enforces an ordering on commands during fault-free periods. In practice, the leader has more work to do than other nodes, causing a *load balancing problem* and forming a performance bottleneck. Moreover, in geo-replicated systems, where bandwidth and latency vary considerably, requiring every node to contact a unique leader results in uneven performance across sites, causing a *fairness problem.*

Recent ordering algorithms like S-Paxos [1] and Mencius [5] address the load-balancing problem: S-Paxos decouples payload distribution, which can be done without any undue burden on the leader, from ordering, while Mencius periodically rotates the role of leader among nodes. However, S-Paxos and Mencius do not solve the fairness problem because nodes have to contact other predetermined nodes independently of the quality of communication links.

To solve the fairness problem, a node must be allowed to choose which other nodes to communicate with based on the performance of its network links, as in the EPaxos [6] and Alvin [7] algorithms, both of which do not employ a unique leader, and allow any node to choose the closest (in terms of latency) set of nodes to reach agreement. EPaxos and Alvin are based on a novel but intricate algorithmic idea first introduced in EPaxos, which is difficult to generalize to devise other algorithms with different performance characteristics.

In this paper we show that the core idea underlying EPaxos can be captured in a *generic leaderless generalized-consensus algorithm* that uses two new abstractions: a *dependency-set algorithm*, which suggests dependencies for commands, and a *map-agreement algorithm*, which ensures that, for each submitted command, processes agree on a dependency set. Both abstractions are easily implemented without a unique leader and while letting nodes choose which set of nodes to communicate with for command ordering. Our generic algorithm gives rise to a family of algorithms whose members are obtained by using concrete dependency-set and map-agreement algorithms.

PODC'16 July 25-28, 2016, Chicago, IL, USA

ACM ISBN 978-1-4503-3964-3/16/07.

DOI: http://dx.doi.org/10.1145/2933057.2933072

On top of enabling modular correctness proofs of algorithms like EPaxos, we expect that the modular structure of our generic leaderless algorithm will allow a principled theoretical and empirical evaluation of the trade-offs that can be achieved by different implementations of our two abstractions. For example, some implementations may perform better in a cluster, while others in a wide area network; similarly, implementations of our abstractions may be optimized for different metrics, such as agreement latency, impact of failures or conflicts, tolerance to slow processes, load balancing, quorum size, etc. A formalization of our work in TLA+ is available at http://losa.fr/research/leaderless.

2. LEADERLESS GENERALIZED-CONSENSUS ALGORITHMS

We consider a set of processes P which are subject to crash-stop faults and which communicate by message-passing in an asynchronous network. Processes in P must solve the Generalized Consensus problem [3], in which each process receives proposals for commands of the form $\mathsf{GC\text{-}propose}(c)$, must produce decisions of the form $\mathsf{GC\text{-}decide}(\sigma)$, where σ is a *c-struct*, and the sequence of calls observed must satisfy the non-triviality, consistency, stability, and liveness properties of generalized consensus. We consider a set C whose members we call c-structs, including the c-struct $\bot$, with an operator $\bullet$, for appending commands to a c-struct, such that any c-struct is of the form $\bot \bullet cs$ for some sequence of commands cs. Intuitively, a c-struct represents a set of sequences of commands that are all equivalent up to the ordering of commutative commands. We say that two commands *commute* when $\sigma \bullet c_1 \bullet c_2 = \sigma \bullet c_2 \bullet c_1$, for every c-struct σ. C-structs are partially ordered: $\sigma_1 \sqsubseteq \sigma_2$ if and only if there exists a sequence of commands s such that $\sigma_2 = \sigma_1 \bullet s$. Moreover, $\bot \sqsubseteq \sigma$ for any σ. A c-struct contains a command c when it is of the form $\bot \bullet cs$ where c appears in the sequence of commands cs. Two c-structs are compatible when they have a common upper bound that is constructible from the commands contained in the two c-structs. The *non-triviality* property of generalized consensus requires that any decided c-struct be of the form $\bot \bullet \mathcal{D}$, where $\mathcal{D}$ is a sequence of proposed commands; *consistency* requires that any two decided c-structs σ_1 and σ_2 be compatible; *stability* requires that when a process p decides a c-struct σ_1 at time t_1 and σ_2 at time t_2, then $t_1 \leq t_2$ imply that $\sigma_1 \sqsubseteq \sigma_2$; finally, *liveness* requires that if a command keeps being proposed, then a c-struct σ containing the command be eventually decided. We refer the reader to Lamport [3] for a thorough discussion of c-structs and generalized consensus.

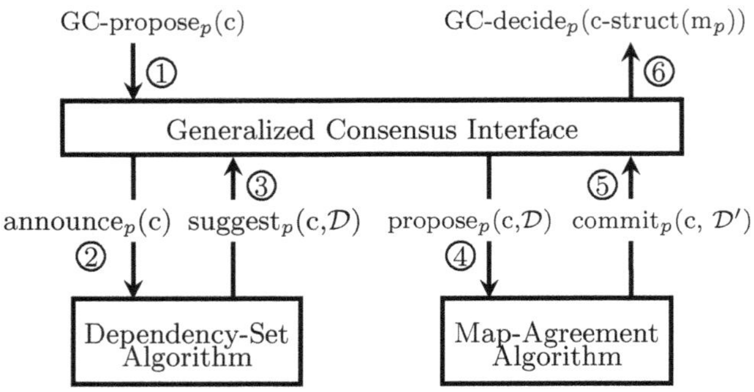

Figure 1: Control flow of a process p using our abstractions; numbers describe the order of events.

Our leaderless generalized consensus algorithm orchestrates a dependency-set algorithm and map-agreement algorithm to implement Generalized Consensus, as shown in fig. 1. A process p maintains a local variables m_p, which is a map from commands to sets of commands. Upon receiving a command c, p proceeds in three phases. First, it calls the *dependency-set* algorithm (Section 2.1) to determine a set of commands $\mathcal{D}$ on which the command c may depend. Second, p proposes the mapping $c \mapsto \mathcal{D}$ to the *map-agreement* algorithm (Section 2.2); when the map-agreement algorithm commits a mapping $c \mapsto \mathcal{D}'$ for c, p inserts the mapping $c \mapsto \mathcal{D}'$ in m_p, and we say that $\mathcal{D}'$ is the dependency set of c. We say that c is *executable* in m_p when every command associated to c in the transitive closure of m_p is in the domain of m_p. Finally, when c is executable in m_p, then p may *locally* run the *graph-processing* algorithm described in Section 2.3 on m_p, obtaining a c-struct σ, and then call $\mathsf{GC\text{-}decide}(\sigma)$.

Any other process can run the three phases for the same command in parallel with the initial proposer of the command, and eventually execute the command, so that a command will be eventually included in a decided c-struct despite failures.

2.1 Computing Potential Dependency Sets

A dependency-set algorithm exposes the following interfaces at each process p: the input interface $\mathsf{announce}_p(c)$, to announce a command c; the output interface $\mathsf{suggest}_p(c, \mathcal{D})$, to suggest a set of dependencies $\mathcal{D}$ for c; and the input interface $\mathsf{commit}(c, \mathcal{D})$, to observe which command is committed by the map-agreement abstraction. Moreover, a dependency-set algorithm must ensure the following properties:

- Safety: (S1), for any call $\mathsf{suggest}_p(c, \mathcal{D})$, every command in $\{c\} \cup \mathcal{D}$ must have been announced before; (S2), for any two calls $\mathsf{suggest}_p(c_1, \mathcal{D}_1)$ and $\mathsf{suggest}_q(c_2, \mathcal{D}_2)$, if c_1 and c_2 do not commute, then $c_1 \in \mathcal{D}_2 \lor c_2 \in \mathcal{D}_1$.
- Liveness: (L1) If a call $\mathsf{announce}_p(c)$ was made, then eventually a suggestion $\mathsf{suggest}(c, \mathcal{D})_p$ is made, and (L2), if a suggestion $\mathsf{suggest}_p(c, \mathcal{D})$ has been made and no input $\mathsf{commit}_q(c, \mathcal{D}')$ is observed, then eventually a new suggestion $\mathsf{suggest}_r(c, \mathcal{D}'')$ for $r \neq p$ is made.

2.2 Agreeing on Dependency Sets

A map-agreement algorithm exposes the following interface at each process p: the input interface $\mathsf{propose}_p(c, \mathcal{D})$, to propose a set of dependencies $\mathcal{D}$ for a command c; the output interface $\mathsf{commit}_p(c, \mathcal{D})$, to commit $\mathcal{D}$ for c. Moreover, a map-agreement algorithm must ensure that:

- Safety: (S3), for any commit $\mathsf{commit}_p(c, \mathcal{D})$, then $\mathcal{D}$ has been proposed for c at an earlier time; (S4), for any two calls $\mathsf{commit}_p(c, \mathcal{D}_1)$ and $\mathsf{commit}_q(c, \mathcal{D}_2)$, $\mathcal{D}_1$ is equal to $\mathcal{D}_2$.
- Liveness: (L3) if a proposal $propose_p(c, \mathcal{D})$ is made, then eventually a decision $\mathsf{commit}_p(c, \mathcal{D})$ is made.

```
upon init_p()
    cmds_p ← ∅
    ∀c, deps_p[c] ← ∅
    ∀c, heard_p[c] ← ∅
    ∀c, suggested_p[c] ← false
upon announce_p(c)
    cmds_p ← cmds_p ∪ {c}
    ∀q ∈ P send ⟨cmd | c⟩ to q
upon receive ⟨cmd | c⟩ from q
    D ← {d : d ∈ cmds_p ∧ d ≠ c ∧ d ≍ c}
    cmds_p ← cmds_p ∪ {c}
    send ⟨deps | c, D⟩ to q
upon receive ⟨deps | c, D⟩ from q
    deps_p[c] ← deps_p[c] ∪ D
    heard_p[c] ← heard_p[c] ∪ {q}
upon ∃c : heard_p[c] ∈ quorums
        ∧ suggested_p[c] = false
    suggested_p[c] ← true
    call suggest_p(c, deps_p[c])
```

Figure 2: Example of dependency-set algorithm implementation.

2.3 Local Dependency-Graph Processing

The graph processing algorithm is executed locally by a process when a new command becomes executable. Based on the map m_p, it computes a c-struct σ that is then used to call $\mathsf{GC\text{-}decide}(\sigma)$. The map m_p defines a directed graph describing dependencies among commands, but it may contain cycles. The graph processing algorithm breaks cycles so as to obtain a partially ordered set of commands that uniquely determines a c-struct. Relying on the properties of the dependency-set and map-agreement algorithm expressed in Lemma 2, the graph processing algorithm ensures the non-triviality, consistency, and stability properties of Generalized Consensus.

For each set of commands $\mathcal{D}$, we assume that processes initially agree on a total order $<_{\mathcal{D}}$ on $\mathcal{D}$. In practice, if each commands is attached a unique identifier taken from a totally ordered set, it is easy to defined and compute $<_{\mathcal{D}}$.

The local variable m_p denotes a directed graph g_p whose set of vertices $V(g_p)$ is the executable commands of m_p and whose edges $E(g_p)$ are such that there is an edge from c_1 to c_2 if and only if $c_2 \in m_p[c_1]$ (i.e., c_1 depends on c_2). For example, if $m_p = [c_1 \mapsto \{c_2, c_4\}, c_2 \mapsto \{c_3\}, c_3 \mapsto \{c_2\}]$ then $V(g_p) = \{c_2, c_3\}$ and $E(g_p) = \{(c_2, c_3), (c_3, c_2)\}$.

A directed graph g *induces a partial order* $\preceq_g$ on its vertices defined such that $c_1 \preceq_g c_2$ if and only if there is a path from c_2 to c_1 and none from c_1 to c_2. For example, consider h where $V(h) = \{c_1, c_2, c_3, c_4\}$ and $E(h) = \{(c_1, c_2), (c_2, c_1), (c_1, c_3)\}$. We have that $\preceq_h = \{(c_3, c_1)\}$. We say that a total order $\ll$ on $V(g)$ is a *linearization* of g when for every $c_1, c_2 \in V(g)$, $c_1 \preceq_g c_2$ implies $c_1 \ll c_2$, and if c_1 and c_2 belong to the same strongly connected component $\mathcal{D}$ and $c_1 <_{\mathcal{D}} c_2$ hold, then $c_1 \ll c_2$. For example, assuming that $c_1 <_{\{c_1, c_2\}} c_2$, the linearizations of h are $\langle c_3, c_1, c_2, c_4\rangle$, $\langle c_3, c_1, c_4, c_2\rangle$, $\langle c_3, c_4, c_1, c_2\rangle$, and $\langle c_4, c_3, c_1, c_2\rangle$.

Let us define graph intersection such that $V(g_1 \cap g_2) = V(g_1) \cap V(g_2)$ and $E(g_1 \cap g_2) = E(g_1) \cap E(g_2)$, and graph union such that $V(g_1 \cup g_2) = V(g_1) \cup V(g_2)$ and $E(g_1 \cup g_2) = E(g_1) \cup E(g_2)$. Then, we say that g is a vertex-induced subgraph of g' if and only if $V(g) \subseteq V(g')$, and for every $e \in E(g')$, if both endpoints of e are in $V(g)$, then $e \in E(g)$. Define two graphs g_1 and g_2 as *compatible* if and only if $g_1 \cap g_2$ is a vertex-induced subgraph of $g_1 \cup g_2$.

Lemma 1. *Assume that l_1 and l_2 are linearizations of two compatible dependency graphs g_1 and g_2, respectively, and that, for every $g \in \{g_1, g_2\}$, if $c_1, c_2 \in V(g)$ are a pair of non-commutative commands, then either $(c_1, c_2) \in E(g)$ or $(c_2, c_1) \in E(g)$. Then we have that: (a), $\bot \bullet l_1$ and $\bot \bullet l_2$ are compatible c-structs; (b), if $g_1 = g_2$ then $\bot \bullet l_1 = \bot \bullet l_2$.*

Definition 1. *Let $\mathsf{c\text{-}struct}(m_p)$ be a c-struct such that $\mathsf{c\text{-}strut}(m_p) = \bot \bullet l$, for every linearization l of g_p. By lemma 1(b), if l_1 and l_2 are linearizations of g_p, then $\bot \bullet l_1 = \bot \bullet l_2$; therefore, $\mathsf{c\text{-}struct}(m_p)$ is well-defined.*

2.4 Correctness

Lemma 2. *For every processes p and q and every two points t_1 and t_2 in an execution of the abstract leaderless algorithm, let g_p^1 be the graph g_p at any time t_1 and g_q^2 be the graph g_q at any time t_2. Then, g_p^1 and g_q^2 are compatible.*

Theorem 1. *The consistency property of generalized consensus always holds.*

From lemma 2 and property S2, for every two points t_1 and t_2 in an execution, g_p^1 (g_p at time t_1) and g_q^2 (g_q at time t_2) satisfy the premises of lemma 1. Therefore we get that $\mathsf{c\text{-}struct}(\mathsf{m_p})$ at time t_1 and $\mathsf{c\text{-}struct}(m_q)$ at time t_2 are compatible, satisfying the consistency property of generalized consensus.

Theorem 2. *If a command c is GC-proposed infinitely often, then a c-struct containing c is eventually decided.*

The properties L1 and L2 ensure that dependency sets are repeatedly proposed for c to the map-agreement algorithm as long as a commit is not observed. Moreover, the map-agreement algorithm ensures that when dependency sets are repeatedly proposed for c, then a dependency set will eventually be committed for c. Similarly, any dependency of c is eventually committed and c becomes executable, at which points it is included in the next decided c-struct.

2.5 Implementing the Abstractions

Both the dependency-set and map-agreement abstractions are well suited for leaderless implementations.

The Dependency-Set Abstraction. The dependency-set abstraction can be implemented as shown in fig. 2. Due to space constraints, our example focuses on satisfying the safety property only. A process p announcing a command c asks all the processes for the set of commands c' that they have seen so far and that do not commute with c (noted $c' \asymp c$). Then, it suggests the union of the dependency sets received from a *quorum* of processes. Quorums are sets of processes such that the intersection of any two quorums is not empty. Since p receives sets of commands seen by other processes, the implementation ensures S1. Moreover, consider two suggestions $\mathsf{suggest}(c_1, \mathcal{D}_1)$ and $\mathsf{suggest}(c_2, \mathcal{D}_2)$ where $c_1 \asymp c_2$. There are two quorums Q_1 and Q_2 such that $\mathcal{D}_1$ was computed from Q_1 and $\mathcal{D}_2$ was computed from Q_2. By the definition of quorums, there is a process q belonging to both Q_1 and Q_2. This process q received either c_1 before c_2, in which case $c_1 \in \mathcal{D}_2$, or c_2 before c_1, in which case $c_2 \in \mathcal{D}_1$. Therefore, property S2 holds.

The Map-Agreement Abstraction. The MultiPaxos algorithm can implement the map-agreement algorithm by uniquely associating commands with positions in its sequence of consensus instances. However, MultiPaxos provides unnecessary guarantees on the ordering among instances. Instead, one can uniquely associate one incarnation of MultiPaxos with each process, which is initially the leader of its MultiPaxos incarnation. We assume that a command is associated with a unique natural number $\mathsf{id}(c)$ and with the process who first received c, noted $\mathsf{pid}(c)$. A process receiving a proposal $\mathsf{propose}_p(c, \mathcal{D})$ proposes $c \mapsto \mathcal{D}$ in instance $\mathsf{id}(c)$ of the MultiPaxos incarnation of process $\mathsf{pid}(c)$. Upon a MultiPaxos decision $c \mapsto \mathcal{D}'$, p calls $\mathsf{commit}_p(c, \mathcal{D}')$. Note that the initial proposer of a command, being the MultiPaxos leader of its MultiPaxos incarnation, is free to choose any quorum of processes to reach agreement with on a dependency set. Therefore, in a geo-replication setting, the initial proposer can choose a quorum of processes excluding those nodes that are too far away. In a failure-free case, a command is committed in one round-trip with the chosen quorum.

EPaxos improves upon this scheme by using an algorithm similar to Fast Paxos [2] instead of MultiPaxos, and by combining the dependency-set algorithm of fig. 2 (except that it uses larger quorums), with a fast round of Fast Paxos: the reception of identical dependency sets from a fast quorum of processes (after an $\mathsf{announce}_p(c)$) acts as a single-round-trip decision of Fast Paxos.

Acknowledgments

This material is based upon work supported by the National Science Foundation under grant CNS-1523558, and by the US Air Force Office of Scientific Research under grant FA9550-15-1-0098.

References

[1] Martin Biely et al. “S-Paxos: Offloading the Leader for High Throughput State Machine Replication”. In: *SRDS*. IEEE Computer Society, 2012, pp. 111–120.

[2] Leslie Lamport. “Fast Paxos”. In: *Distributed Computing* 19.2 (2006), pp. 79–103.

[3] Leslie Lamport. *Generalized Consensus and Paxos.* https://research.microsoft.com/en-us/um/people/lamport/pubs/pubs.html#generalized. 2005.

[4] Leslie Lamport. “Paxos made simple”. In: *ACM Sigact News* 32.4 (2001), pp. 18–25.

[5] Yanhua Mao et al. “Mencius: Building Efficient Replicated State Machine for WANs”. In: *OSDI*. Ed. by Richard Draves and Robbert van Renesse. USENIX Association, 2008, pp. 369–384.

[6] Iulian Moraru et al. “There is more Consensus in Egalitarian Parliaments”. In: *SOSP*. Ed. by Michael Kaminsky and Mike Dahlin. ACM, 2013, pp. 358–372.

[7] Alexandru Turcu et al. “Be General and Don’t Give Up Consistency in Geo-Replicated Transactional Systems”. In: *OPODIS*. Ed. by Marcos K. Aguilera et al. Vol. 8878. LNCS. Springer, 2014, pp. 33–48.

Brief Announcement: Computing in the Presence of Weak Crash Failures*

Gadi Taubenfeld
The Interdisciplinary Center, P.O.Box 167, Herzliya 46150, Israel
tgadi@idc.ac.il

ABSTRACT

We consider an asynchronous shared memory system of n processes where processes may experience *weak* crash failures. A *crash m-failure* is a crash failure of a process that may occurs only while the point contention is at most m. It is known that there is no consensus algorithm for n processes using registers that can tolerate even a single crash n-failure. Is there a consensus algorithm for n processes using registers that can tolerate a single crash $(n-1)$-failure? It is known that there is no k-set consensus algorithm for $n > k$ processes using registers that can tolerate k crash n-failures. How may crash $(n-\ell)$-failures can a k-set consensus algorithm using registers tolerate, as a function of n, k and ℓ? Answers to these questions follow from our results regarding the ability to tolerate weak crash failures.

1. INTRODUCTION

An important meeting of the cabinet is about to take place. In order to prevent information leakage from the deliberations, the following rules has been agreed upon. The participants upon arrival must first notify the secretary of their arrival and only then can enter the meeting room. As long as the meeting has not started yet, participants may leave the room, but in such a case they are not allowed to return and attend the meeting. Once all the the invited participants have notified the secretary of their arrival, the doors are closed, nobody is allowed to leave the room and the meeting starts.

When considering a virtual meeting which corresponds to such a physical meeting, we may think of a participa nt as a process and of an event of leaving the room, as a crash failure. However, such a failure is *weaker* than the traditional crash failure: once the point contention is n – i.e., all the participants have arrived – no process may fail thereafter. This motivates the definition of weak crash failures.

A process is participating in an algorithm if it has executed at least one statement of that algorithm. The *point contention* of an algorithm at given time is the maximal number of (correct and faulty) processes simultaneously participating in the algorithm at a given time. The point contention is clearly bounded by the total number of processes. A *crash m-failure* is a failure of a process that (1) after it has failed the process executes no more steps, and (2) it may occur only while the point contention is at most m. That is, failures may not occur once a certain predefined threshold on the level of point contention is reached.

We derive possibility and impossibility results for solving the well-known problems of consensus and k-set consensus in the presence of weak crash failures. The k-set consensus problem is to design an algorithm for n processes, where each process starts with an input value from some domain, and must choose some participating process input as its output. All n processes together may choose no more than k distinct output values. The 1-set consensus problem, is the familiar consensus problem.

It is known that there is no consensus algorithm for n processes using registers that can tolerate even a single crash n-failure [2, 4]. We show that there is a consensus algorithm for n processes, using registers, that can tolerate a single crash $(n-1)$-failure, for every $n > 1$. We show that there is no consensus algorithm for n processes, using registers, that can tolerate *two* crash $(n-1)$-failures, for every $n > 2$.

It is known that there is no k-set consensus algorithm for $n > k$ processes using registers that can tolerate k crash n-failures [1, 3, 5]. We show that for every $\ell \geq 1$, $k \geq 1$ and $n \geq 2\ell + k - 2$, there is a k-set consensus algorithm for n processes, using registers, that can tolerate $\ell + k - 2$ crash $(n-\ell)$-failures. We show that, there is no k-set consensus algorithm that can tolerate $\ell + k$ crash $(n-\ell)$-failures.

Solving consensus with a single crash $(n-1)$-failure using only registers is a deceptive problem. At first glance, it may seem simple to solve. For that reason, we suggest the readers to try to solve the problem themselves.

The new failure model establishes a link between point contention and failures, which enables us to better understand the known impossibility result of consensus and its generalizations. When facing a failure related impossibility result, one is often tempted to use a solution which guarantees no resiliency at all. We point out that there is a middle ground: tolerating weak crash failures, enables to tolerate failures some of the time. Also traditional t-resilient algorithms tolerate failures only some of the time (i.e., as long as the number of failures is at most t). Afterall, something is better than nothing.

*The full version of this work can be found in [7].

PODC'16 July 25-28, 2016, Chicago, IL, USA

ACM ISBN 978-1-4503-3964-3/16/07.
DOI: http://dx.doi.org/10.1145/2933057.2933058

2. COMPUTATIONAL MODEL

Our model of computation consists of an asynchronous collection of n deterministic processes that communicate via atomic read/write registers. In the sequel, by *registers* we mean *atomic* registers. A process executes correctly its algorithm until it possibly crashes. After it has crashed it executes no more steps. A process that crashes is said to be *faulty*, otherwise it is *correct*.

In a model where participation is required, every correct process must eventually become active and execute its code. Another situation is one in which participation is not required, as is usually assumed when solving the mutual exclusion or k-exclusion problems. All the known impossibility results for consensus and k-set consensus hold even when participating is required. Unless explicitly stated otherwise we will assume that *participation is required*.

3. POSSIBILITY OF CONSENSUS

We show that it is possible to solve consensus with a single crash $(n-1)$-failure.

THEOREM 3.1. *There is a consensus algorithm for n processes, using registers, that can tolerate a single crash $(n-1)$-failure, for every $n \geq 1$.*

In Section 5, it is shown that there does not exist a consensus algorithm for n processes, using registers, that can tolerate *two* crash $(n-1)$-failures, for any $n > 2$.

The algorithm

A CONSENSUS ALGORITHM WHICH CAN TOLERATE A SINGLE CRASH $(n-1)$-FAILURE: Program for process $i \in \{1, ..., n\}$ with a none negative input in_i.

Shared: *state*$[1..n]$: array of registers, ranges over $\{0, 1, 2, 3\}$, initially all entries are 0
input$[1..n]$: arrays of registers, initial values immaterial
decision: register, initially $\perp$
Local: *counter, max, round, j*: initial values immaterial

```
1  input[i] := in_i;
2  for round = 1 to 3 do
3    counter := 0; max := 0;
4    for j = 1 to n do
5      if state[j] ≥ round then counter := counter + 1;
6        if max < input[j] then max := input[j] fi fi od;
7    if counter = n − 1
     then decision := max; decide(decision) fi;
8    state[i] := round;
9    repeat
10     counter := 0;
11     for j = 1 to n do
12       if state[j] ≥ round
         then counter := counter + 1 fi od;
13   until (counter ≥ n − 1 or decision ≠ ⊥)
14   if decision ≠ ⊥ then decide(decision) fi;
15 od;
16 if counter = n − 1 then counter := 0; max := 0;
17   for j = 1 to n do
18     if state[j] ≥ 2 then counter := counter + 1;
19       if max < input[j] then max := input[j] fi fi od;
20   if counter = n − 1
     then decision := max; decide(decision) fi fi;
21 for j = 1 to n do
22   await (state[j] = 3 or decision ≠ ⊥);
23   if decision ≠ ⊥ then decide(decision) fi;
24   if max < input[j] then max := input[j] fi od;
25 decision := max; decide(max).
```

Each process can be in one of four states, 0,1,2 or 3, as recorded in its *state* register. A process participates in three rounds (lines 2–15). At each round $round \in \{1, 2, 3\}$, the process first checks whether all the other $n-1$ processes have already written the round number r into their *state* registers (lines 4–6). In case of a positive answer, the process sets the *decision* register to the maximum input value among the input values of the other $n-1$ processes, decides on that maximum value and terminates (line 7). Otherwise, it writes the value of *round* into its *state* register (line 8), and waits until either a decision is made or until at least $n-1$ processes, including itself, have written the round number *round* into their single-write *state* registers, whatever comes first (lines 9–13). In the former case, it adopts the decision value (line 14), in the later case it completes the current round and moves on.

After completing three rounds, the process checks if there exists a process, say process j, that has not written the value 2 into its state register (lines 16–19). In case of a positive answer, it concludes that process j will never be able to reach round three, and thus, j will never set its state register to 3. This is so, because j will notice that $n-1$ other processes have already set their state registers to 3, and will decide (line 7) before incrementing it state register (line 8). Thus, the process sets the *decision* register to the maximum input value among all the processes, excluding process j, decides on that maximum value and terminates (line 20).

Otherwise, if all the n processes have written the value 2 into their state registers, the process concludes that all the n processes are still active and are guaranteed not to fail. It waits until either a decision is made or until all the processes complete round three, whatever comes first (lines 21–24). In the former case, it adopts the decision value (line 23), in the later case it decides on maximum input value among the input values of all the n processes and terminates (line 25).

4. POSSIBILITY OF SET CONSENSUS

The possibility result presented below *does not* imply the result stated in Theorem 3.1.

THEOREM 4.1. *For every $\ell \geq 1$, $k \geq 1$ and $n \geq 2\ell + k - 2$, there is a k-set consensus algorithm for n processes, using registers, that can tolerate $\ell + k - 2$ crash $(n-\ell)$-failures.*

The following algorithm solves k-set consensus and tolerates $\ell + k - 2$ crash $(n-\ell)$-failures. In Section 5, we show that there there is no k-set consensus algorithm that can tolerate $\ell + k$ crash $(n-\ell)$-failures.

The algorithm

In the implementation below we use a shared object called *atomic snapshot* which can be wait-free implemented from registers. A snapshot object consists of a set of $m > 1$ components, each capable of storing a value. Processes can perform two different types of operations: UPDATE any individual component or instantaneously (atomically) SCAN the entire collection to obtain the values of all the components. So, for an atomic snapshot object S, $S.update(i, v)$ writes v to the ith component, and $S.scan$ returns a snapshot of all m components.

A *single-writer* atomic snapshot object is a restricted version in which there are the same number of processes as components and only process $i \in \{1, ..., n\}$ can UPDATE the ith component. Let $A[1..n]$ be an arrays of n registers and S be a single-writer atomic snapshot object. Then, the assignment $A := S.scan$ atomically sets $A[i]$ to the value of the ith component of S, for each $i \in \{1, ..., n\}$. It is often easier to design fault-tolerant algorithms for asynchronous systems and prove them correct if one can think of the shared memory as a snapshot object, rather than as a collection of individual registers.

The algorithm also makes use of a single one-shot mutual exclusion objects, and a single one-shot $(k-1)$-exclusion object. We assume that the reader is familiar with the k-exclusion problem. The simpler *one-shot* version assumes that a process may try to access its critical section at most once. It is well known that, for any $k \geq 1$, k-exclusion and can be solved using registers only, even when it is assumed that participation is *not* required [6].

A k-SET CONSENSUS ALGORITHM WHICH CAN TOLERATE $\ell + k - 2$ CRASH $(n-\ell)$-FAILURES: `Program for process` $i \in \{1, ..., n\}$ `with a none negative input` in_i.

Constants: ℓ, k: positive integers
Shared: $Flag$: single-writer atomic snapshot object, ranges over $\{0, 1\}$, initially all entries are 0
  decision: register, initially $\perp$
  $EX[1]$: one-shot mutual exclusion object
  $EX[2]$: one-shot $(k-1)$-exclusion object
Local: $lflag[1..n]$: array of variables, ranges over $\{0, 1\}$, initial values immaterial
  $counter, group, j$: variables, initial values immaterial

1 $Flag.update(i, 1)$;
2 **repeat**
3   $lflag := Flag.scan$; $counter := 0$;
4   **for** $j = 1$ **to** n **do if** $lflag[j] = 1$
    then $counter := counter + 1$ **fi od**;
5 **until** $counter \geq n - \ell - k + 2$;
6 **if** $counter \leq n - \ell$ **then** $group := 2$ **else** $group := 1$ **fi**
7 **participate** in $EX[group]$ and in parallel
    continuously check if $decision \neq \perp$
8   **if** at any point $decision \neq \perp$ **then** $decide(decision)$ **fi**;
9   **if** you enter the critical section of $EX[group]$
10 **then** $decision := in_i$; $decide(in_i)$ **fi**.

The first step of each process i is to set the ith component *Flag* to 1 (line 1). Then, process i repeatedly takes a snapshot of the *Flag* object (line 3) and each time it takes a snapshot, it sets *counter* to the number of Flag components which are set to 1 (line 4). Processes i continues to take snapshots until $counter \geq n - \ell - k + 2$ (line 5). Since at most $\ell + k - 2$ processes may fail, each correct process must eventually notice that $counter \geq n - \ell - k + 2$. Next, process i participates in either $EX[1]$ or $EX[2]$ depending on the current value of *group* (line 7). If, at any point, process i notices that $decision \neq \perp$ it decides on the value of *decision* (line 8). If it enters its critical section it sets *decision* to its input value and decides on that value.

5. IMPOSSIBILITY RESULTS

An *initial failure* of a given process is a failure which happens before the process has taken any steps.

THEOREM 5.1. *For every $\ell \geq 0$, $k \geq 1$ and $n > \ell + k$, there is no k-set consensus algorithm for n processes, using registers, that can tolerate k crash $(n-\ell)$-failures and ℓ initial failures.*

COROLLARY 5.2. *For every $\ell \geq 0$, $k \geq 1$ and $n > 2\ell + k$, there is no k-set consensus algorithm for n processes, using registers, that can tolerate $\ell + k$ crash $(n-\ell)$-failures.*

COROLLARY 5.3. *For every $0 \leq \ell < n/2$, there is no consensus algorithm for n processes, using registers, that can tolerate $\ell + 1$ crash $(n-\ell)$-failures.*

6. DISCUSSION

We consider new types of weak failures, where failures may occur only until a certain predefined threshold on the level of contention is reached. To illustrate the utility of the new definitions, we have derived possibility and impossibility results for the well-known basic problems of consensus and k-set consensus. The definitions together with our technical results, indicate that there is an interesting area of fault tolerance that deserve further investigation.

Two specific interesting open problems are: (1) Is the following generalization of Theorem 3.1 correct: There is a k-set consensus algorithm for n processes, using registers, that can tolerate k crash $(n-1)$-failures, for every $n > k \geq 1$; (2) Is the following generalization of Theorem 4.1 correct: For every $\ell \geq 0$, $k \geq 1$ and $n \geq 2\ell + k - 1$, there is a k-set consensus algorithm for n processes, using registers, that can tolerate $\ell + k - 1$ crash $(n-\ell)$-failures.

The full version includes detailed proofs, detailed explanations, additonal open problems and aditonal references [7].

7. REFERENCES

[1] E. Borowsky and E. Gafni. Generalized FLP impossibility result for t-resilient asynchronous computations. In *Proc. 25th ACM Symp. on Theory of Computing*, pages 91–100, 1993.

[2] M.J. Fischer, N.A. Lynch, and M.S. Paterson. Impossibility of distributed consensus with one faulty process. *Journal of the ACM*, 32(2):374–382, 1985.

[3] M. P. Herlihy and N. Shavit. The topological structure of asynchronous computability. *Journal of the ACM*, 46(6):858–923, July 1999.

[4] M.C. Loui and H. Abu-Amara. Memory requirements for agreement among unreliable asynchronous processes. *Advances in Computing Research*, 4:163–183, 1987.

[5] M. Saks and F. Zaharoglou. Wait-free k-set agreement is impossible: The topology of public knowledge. *SIAM Journal on Computing*, 29, 2000.

[6] G. Taubenfeld. *Synchronization Algorithms and Concurrent Programming*. Pearson / Prentice-Hall. ISBN 0-131-97259-6, 423 pages, 2006.

[7] G. Taubenfeld. Computing in the presence of weak crash failures, 2016. The full version is avaliable at: http://www.faculty.idc.ac.il/gadi/Publications.htm.

Brief Announcement: Oh-RAM! One and a Half Round Read/Write Atomic Memory *

Theophanis Hadjistasi † Nicolas Nicolaou ‡ Alexander A. Schwarzmann †

ABSTRACT

Emulating atomic read/write shared objects in a message-passing system is a fundamental problem in distributed computing. Considering that network communication is the most expensive resource, efficiency is measured first of all in terms of the communication needed to implement read and write operations. It is well known that two communication round-trip phases involving in total four message exchanges are sufficient to implemented atomic operations. In this work we present a comprehensive treatment of the question of when and how it is possible to implement atomic memory where read and write operations complete in three message exchanges, i.e., we aim for *One and half Round Atomic Memory*, hence the name Oh-RAM! We present algorithms that allow operations to complete in three communication exchanges without imposing any constraints on the number of readers and writers. We present an implementation for the single-writer/multiple-reader (SWMR) setting, where reads complete in *three* communication exchanges and writes complete in *two* exchanges. Then we pose the question of whether it is possible to implement multiple-writer/multiple-reader (MWMR) memory where operations complete in at most three communication exchanges. We answer this question in the negative by showing that an atomic memory implementation is impossible if both read and write operations take *three* communication exchanges, even when assuming two writers, two readers, and a single replica server failure. Motivated by this impossibility result, we provide a MWMR atomic memory implementation where reads involve *three* and writes involve *four* communication exchanges. In light of our impossibility result these algorithms are optimal in terms of the number of communication exchanges.

†University of Connecticut, Storrs CT, USA. Email: theophanis.hadjistasi@uconn.edu, aas@engr.uconn.edu

‡IMDEA Networks Institute, Madrid, Spain. Email: nicolas.nicolaou@imdea.org

*The work of the second author is fully supported by FP7-PEOPLE-2013-IEF grant ATOMICDFS No:629088.

PODC'16, July 25–28, 2016, Chicago, IL, USA.

ACM ISBN 978-1-4503-3964-3/16/07.

DOI: http://dx.doi.org/10.1145/2933057.2933073

1. INTRODUCTION

For more than two decades a series of solutions sought to provide efficient implementations of the shared memory abstraction for distributed settings where crash-prone asynchronous processors communicate by exchanging messages. To cope with processor failures, distributed object implementations use *redundancy* by replicating the object at multiple network locations (replica servers). Replication introduces the problem of consistency due to the fact that read and write operations may access different object replicas, some of which may contain obsolete object values. Atomicity [7] (or linearizability [6]) is the most intuitive consistency semantic for read/write objects as it provides the illusion of a single-copy object that serializes all accesses such that each read operation returns the value of the latest preceding write operation.

The seminal work of Attiya, Bar-Noy, and Dolev [1] provided the first algorithm, colloquially referred to as ABD, that implements single-writer/multiple-reader (SWMR) atomic objects. The ordering of operations is accomplished with the help of logical *timestamps* associated with each value. Here each operation is guaranteed to terminate as long as some majority of replica servers do not crash. Each write operation takes one communication round-trip phase, or round, involving *two* message exchanges and each read operation takes two rounds involving in total *four* message exchanges. Subsequently, [8] showed how to implement multi-writer/multiple-reader (MWMR) atomic memory where both read and write operations involve two communication round trips involving in total four message exchanges.

The work by Dutta et al. [2] introduced a SWMR implementation where both reads and writes involve a single round consisting of *two* communication exchanges. It was shown that this is possible only when the number of readers r is bounded with respect to the number of servers s and the server failures f, specifically by $r < \frac{s}{f} - 2$, and when there is only a single writer in the system. An interesting observation made in [2] is that atomic memory may be implemented (using a max/min technique) so that each read and write operation complete in *three* communication exchanges. The authors however did not elaborate further on the inherent limitations that such a technique may impose on the distributed system.

Subsequent works, e.g., [4], focused in relaxing the bound on the number of readers and writers in the service by proposing hybrid approaches where some operations complete in *one* and others in *two* rounds. In addition, [3] provides tight bounds on the number of rounds that *read* and *write* operations require in the MWMR model.

Contributions. We address the gap between one-round and two-round implementations by considering implementations that take "one and a half rounds," i.e., where operations complete in *three* message exchanges, and that do not impose constraints on the number of readers. Table 1 summarizes our complexity results. Additional details follow.

Algorithm	Read Ex.	Write Ex.	Read Com.	Write Com.
ABD (SWMR) [1]	4	2	$4\|\mathcal{S}\|$	$2\|\mathcal{S}\|$
Oh-SAM	3	2	$\|\mathcal{S}\|^2+2\|\mathcal{S}\|$	$2\|\mathcal{S}\|$
ABD (MWMR) [1]	4	4	$4\|\mathcal{S}\|$	$4\|\mathcal{S}\|$
Oh-MAM	3	4	$\|\mathcal{S}\|^2+2\|\mathcal{S}\|$	$4\|\mathcal{S}\|$

Table 1: Summary of complexity results.

(1) We present a new SWMR algorithm for atomic objects in the asynchronous message-passing model with processor crashes. The write operation takes *two* communication exchanges and it is similar to the write operation of ABD. Read operations take *three* communication exchanges. A key idea of the algorithm is that the reader returns the value that is associated with the *minimum* timestamp (cf. the observation in [2]). The read operations in this algorithm are optimal in terms of communication exchanges.

(2) A major part of our contribution is to show the impossibility of MWMR implementations where both write and read operations take *three* communication exchanges. We show that atomicity is violated even in a system that consists of two readers, two writers, and is subject to a single server failure.

(3) Motivated by the impossibility result, we revise the SWMR algorithm to yield a MWMR algorithm. The existence of multiple writers complicate the write operations, and in the new algorithm writes take *four* communication exchanges (cf. [8]). Read operations complete again in *three* communication exchanges.

Both of our algorithms are *optimal* in terms of communication exchanges for the settings without constraints on the number of participants. The algorithms improve latency in a trade-off for communication complexity.

2. SYSTEM MODEL AND EFFICIENCY

The system consists of a collection of failure-prone, asynchronous processes with unique identifiers from a totally-ordered set $\mathcal{I}$. The set $\mathcal{I}$ consists of three disjoint sets: set $\mathcal{W}$ of writer identifiers, set $\mathcal{R}$ of reader identifiers, and a set $\mathcal{S}$ of replica servers identifiers with each *server* process maintaining a copy of the object. Processes communicate by exchanging messages via asynchronous point-to-point reliable channels; messages may be reordered in transit. For convenience we use *broadcast* as a shorthand for sending point-to-point messages to multiple destinations. Any subset of writers and readers, and any minority of the servers $\mathcal{S}$ may crash in any execution.

Efficiency of implementations is assessed in terms of (i) *message complexity*, i.e. the worst-case number of messages exchanged during an operation, and (ii) *operation latency*, that is determined by the *computation time* and the *communication delays*. Computation time accounts the computation steps that the algorithm performs in each read or write operation.

Communication delays are measured in terms of *communication exchanges*. The protocol implementing each operation involves a sequence of sends (or broadcasts) of typed messages and the corresponding receives. *Communication exchange* within an execution of an operation is the collection of sends and receives for a specific message type within the protocol. Traditional implementations, such as ABD, are structured in terms of *rounds*, where each round consists of two message exchanges; (i) a broadcast initiated by the process executing an operation; and (ii) a convergecast that consists of responses to the initiator.

3. SWMR ALGORITHM Oh-SAM

We first present the SWMR algorithm Oh-SAM: *One and a half Round Single writer Atomic Memory*. The write operation takes *two* communication exchanges (similarly to ABD). Read operations take *three* communication exchanges: (1) the reader sends message to servers, (2) each server that receives the request, *relays* the request to all servers, and (3) once a server receives the relay for a particular read from a majority of servers, it replies to the reader. The read completes once it collects a majority of these replies. A key idea of the algorithm is that the reader returns the value associated with the *minimum* timestamp.

Messages. There are five types of messages. The *readRequest* and *writeRequest* messages define a request from a process p to servers either for reading or writing respectively. The *readAck* and *writeAck* are messages sent from a server to a process p as an acknowledgement for a read or a write operation respectively. Servers relay a read request to all servers using *readRelay* messages.

Writer Protocol. Writer w increments its timestamp and broadcasts a *writeRequest* message to all servers $s \in \mathcal{S}$. It terminates when $|\mathcal{S}|/2+1$ *writeAck* messages are collected.

Read Protocol. Reader r creates a *readRequest* message and broadcasts it to all the servers. Once "fresh" messages are collected from a majority, then reader returns the value associated with the *minimum* timestamp among the replies.

Server Protocol. (1) Upon receiving *readRequest* message the server uses the information enclosed in the received message along with its local information to create a *readRelay* message which it broadcasts to all servers $s \in \mathcal{S}$.

(2) Upon receiving *readRelay* message server s compares the incoming with its local information and updates accordingly. Next, server s checks if the received *readRelay* message declares a new read operation and updates its local information. Finally, when the server collects *readRelay* messages from a majority of servers, then it creates a *readAck* message which it sends to the reader r.

(3) Upon receiving *writeRequest* message server s compares the incoming with its local information and updates accordingly. Finally, the server sends an acknowledgement message to the requesting writer w.

Correctness. We prove correctness of algorithm Oh-SAM by showing that *liveness* is satisfied with respect to our failure model, and *atomicity* is satisfied with respect to the order imposed by the *timestamps* used by each operation.

THEOREM 1. *Algorithm* Oh-SAM *implements an atomic SWMR read/write register.*

Complexity. The analysis of performance of Oh-SAM is straightforward and the results are given in Table 1.

4. IMPOSSIBILITY RESULT

Next we examine if it is possible to implement MWMR atomic read/write objects in an asynchronous, message-passing system with crash-prone processors where read and write operations take *three* communication exchanges. We consider algorithms that implement a write operation invoked by process p according to the following three-phase scheme: (1) the invoker p sends a message to a set of servers; (2) each server that receives the message from p sends a certain relay message to a set of servers; and (3) once a server receives "enough" relay messages it replies to p. Each phase involves a communication exchange.

We briefly explain why it is reasonable to use such a three-phase scheme. First of all, the servers cannot know about a write operation unless writer contacts them, thus it must be the writer who initiates phase (1). Moreover, since asynchrony makes it impossible to distinguish slow servers from crashed servers, the writer must include all servers in this phase. In phase (3) it must be the servers who inform the writer about the status/completion of the write operation. Otherwise, either the third phase is unnecessary for the writer, or the writer will wait indefinitely. From the above reasoning, phase (2) must be the transitional phase for the servers to move from phase (1) to phase (3). Hence, phase (2) must facilitate the dissemination of the information regarding any write operation to the rest of the servers. Given this communication scheme we obtain the following result.

THEOREM 2. *It is not possible to obtain an atomic read/ write register implementation, where all operations perform 3 communication exchanges, when* $|\mathcal{W}| = |\mathcal{R}| = 2$, $|\mathcal{S}| \geq 3$ *and* $f = 1$.

5. MWMR ALGORITHM Oh-MAM

Motivated by the impossibility result, we sought a solution that involves three or four communications exchanges per operation. We now present our MWMR algorithm Oh-MAM: *One and a half Round Multiple writer Atomic Memory*. Compared with the SWMR setting, we need to impose an ordering on the values that are concurrently written by multiple writers. Since writers may have the same local timestamp, we differentiate them by associating each value with a *tag* consisting of a pair of a timestamp ts and the *id* of the writer. We use lexicographic comparison to order tags (cf. [8]). The read protocol is identical to the SWMR setting, thus in Algorithm Oh-MAM we present only the protocols for the writer and server processes.

Messages. In this algorithm, two additional types of messages are taking place. A *discover* message defines a request from a process p to servers in order to discover the latest tag. Servers response is enclosed in a *discoverAck* message.

Writer Protocol. This protocol is similar to ABD (as given in [8]). Writer w broadcasts a *discover* message to all servers. It then waits to collect $|\mathcal{S}|/2 + 1$ *discoverAck* messages. Once the *discoverAck* messages are collected, writer w determines the maximum timestamp from the tags, increases it, creates a new *writeRequest* message and broadcasts it to all servers. It then waits for $|\mathcal{S}|/2 + 1$ *writeAck* messages to terminate.

Server Protocol. Servers react to messages from the readers exactly as in algorithm Oh-SAM. Here we describe server actions for *discover* and *writeRequest* messages.

(1) Upon receiving *discover* message server s attaches its local information in a new *discoverAck* message that it sends to writer w_i.

(2) Upon receiving *writeRequest* message the server compares the received with its local information and updates accordingly. Server acknowledges this operation to writer w_i by sending a *writeAck* message.

Correctness. We prove correctness of algorithm Oh-MAM by showing that *liveness* is satisfied with respect to our failure model, and *atomicity* is satisfied with respect to the lexicographical order imposed by the *tags* used by each operation.

THEOREM 3. *Algorithm* Oh-MAM *implements an atomic MWMR read/write register.*

Complexity. The performance of Oh-MAM appears in Table 1, in comparison to Oh-SAM and ABD (MWMR) [1].

6. CONCLUSIONS

In this work, we focused on the problem of emulating atomic read/write shared objects in message-passing setting using *three* communication exchanges, i.e., the equivalent of one-and-a-half traditional rounds. We presented an algorithm for the SWMR setting that allows each read operation to complete in *three* and each write operation in *two* communication exchanges. We showed that it is impossible to implement an MWMR atomic object when both read and write operations complete in *three* communication exchanges. Motivated by this, we presented the first algorithm for the MWMR setting that allows each read operation to complete in *three* and each write operation in *four* communication exchanges. In the full paper [5] we rigorously reasoned about the correctness of our algorithms. We note that the algorithms do not impose any constrains on the number of readers (SWMR and MWMR) or the writers (MWMR) participating in the service. Both algorithms are optimal in terms of communication exchanges when no bounds are imposed on participation.

7. REFERENCES

[1] ATTIYA, H., BAR-NOY, A., AND DOLEV, D. Sharing memory robustly in message passing systems. *Journal of the ACM 42(1)* (1996), 124–142.

[2] DUTTA, P., GUERRAOUI, R., LEVY, R. R., AND CHAKRABORTY, A. How fast can a distributed atomic read be? In *Proceedings of the 23rd ACM symposium on Principles of Distributed Computing (PODC)* (2004), pp. 236–245.

[3] ENGLERT, B., GEORGIOU, C., MUSIAL, P. M., NICOLAOU, N., AND SHVARTSMAN, A. A. On the efficiency of atomic multi-reader, multi-writer distributed memory. In *Proceedings 13th International Conference On Principle Of DIstributed Systems (OPODIS 09)* (2009), pp. 240–254.

[4] GEORGIOU, C., NICOLAOU, N. C., AND SHVARTSMAN, A. A. Fault-tolerant semifast implementations of atomic read/write registers. *Journal of Parallel and Distributed Computing 69*, 1 (2009), 62–79.

[5] HADJISTASI, T., NICOLAOU, N., AND SCHWARZMANN, A. A. Oh-ram! one and a half round read/write atomic memory. www.arxiv.com, 2016.

[6] HERLIHY, M. P., AND WING, J. M. Linearizability: a correctness condition for concurrent objects. *ACM Transactions on Programming Languages and Systems (TOPLAS) 12*, 3 (1990), 463–492.

[7] LAMPORT, L. How to make a multiprocessor computer that correctly executes multiprocess program. *IEEE Trans. Comput. 28*, 9 (1979), 690–691.

[8] LYNCH, N. A., AND SHVARTSMAN, A. A. Robust emulation of shared memory using dynamic quorum-acknowledged broadcasts. In *Proceedings of Symposium on Fault-Tolerant Computing* (1997), pp. 272–281.

Brief Announcement: Space-Time Tradeoffs for Distributed Verification*

Mor Baruch
School of Electrical Engineering
Tel Aviv University
Tel Aviv, Israel
mor@eng.tau.ac.il

Rafail Ostrovsky†
Departments of Computer Science and Mathematics
UCLA
Los Angeles, CA 90095
rafail@cs.ucla.edu

Will Rosenbaum
Department of Mathematics
UCLA
Los Angeles, CA 90095-1555
wrosenbaum@math.ucla.edu

ABSTRACT

Verifying that a network configuration satisfies a given boolean predicate is a fundamental problem in distributed computing. Many variations of this problem have been studied, for example, in the context of proof labeling schemes (PLS) [12], locally checkable proofs (LCP) [10], and non-deterministic local decision (NLD) [8]. In all of these contexts, verification time is assumed to be constant. Korman, Kutten and Masuzawa [11] presented a proof-labeling scheme for MST, with poly-logarithmic verification time, and logarithmic memory at each vertex.

In this paper we introduce the notion of a t-PLS, which allows the verification procedure to run for super-constant time. Our work analyzes the tradeoffs of t-PLS between time, label size, message length, and computation space. We construct a universal t-PLS and prove that it uses the same amount of total communication as a known one-round universal PLS, and t factor smaller labels. In addition, we provide a general technique to prove lower bounds for space-time tradeoffs of t-PLS. We use this technique to show an optimal tradeoff for testing that a network is acyclic (cycle free). Our optimal t-PLS for acyclicity uses label size and computation space $O((\log n)/t)$. We further describe a recursive $O(\log^* n)$ space verifier for acyclicity which does not assume previous knowledge of the run-time t.

Keywords

Distributed algorithms, proof-labeling schemes, space-time tradeoffs.

*A full version of this manuscript can be found on the arXiv [5].

†Supported in part by NSF grants 09165174, 1065276, 1118126 and 1136174, US-Israel BSF grant 2008411, OKAWA Foundation Research Award, IBM Faculty Research Award, Xerox Faculty Research Award, B. John Garrick Foundation Award, Teradata Research Award, and Lockheed-Martin Corporation Research Award.

PODC'16 July 25–28, 2016, Chicago, IL, USA.

ACM ISBN 978-1-4503-3964-3/16/07.
DOI: http://dx.doi.org/10.1145/2933057.2933071

1. INTRODUCTION

The problem of determining if a network configuration satisfies some predicate has been studied in the context of checking the ouptut of a distributed algorithm [3, 9], designing self-stabilizing algorithms [1, 2, 6, 11], and complexity theory [7, 8, 9]. A network configuration is represented by an underlying graph, where each vertex represents a processor, edges represent communication links between processors, and each vertex has a state. For example, the state of every vertex can be a color, and the predicate signifies that the coloring is proper. Processors learn about the network by exchanging messages along the edges. Some properties are local by nature and easy to verify, yet many natural problems—for example, testing if the network contains cycles—cannot be tested in less than diameter time, even if message size and local computational power are unbounded.

In order to cope with strong time lower bounds, Korman, Kutten, and Peleg introduced in [12] a computational model, called ***proof-labeling schemes*** (PLS), where vertices are given auxiliary global information in the form of ***labels***. This auxiliary information may allow vertices to verify that a property is satisfied more efficiently than could be achieved without the aid of labels. Specifically, a PLS consists of two components: a ***prover*** and a ***verifier***. The prover is an oracle which assigns labels to vertices. The verifier is a distributed algorithm which runs on the labeled configuration and outputs TRUE or FALSE at each vertex as a function of its state, its label, and the labels it receives. A PLS is ***complete*** if for every legal configuration (satisfying the predicate), prover can assign labels such that all vertices output TRUE. The PLS is ***sound*** if for every illegal configuration (which does not satisfy the predicate) for every labeling, some vertex outputs FALSE.

1.1 Our Contributions

In this brief announcement we consider proof-labeling schemes with super-constant verification time t, and analyze tradeoffs between time, label size, message size, and computation space. Our main contributions are as follows:

- A ***universal scheme*** which can verify any predicate $\mathcal{P}$ on a network.
- A general technique for proving label size lower bounds for t-round schemes.
- Tight lower and upper bounds for testing if a network is cycle free.
- A cycle-free verifier which uses space $O(\log^* n)$.

2. MODEL AND DEFINITIONS

2.1 Computational Framework

A ***graph configuration*** G_s consists of an underling graph $G = (V, E)$, and a state assignment function $\varphi : V \to S$, where S is a state space. The state of a vertex includes all of its local information. It may include the vertex's identity (in an ID based configuration), the weight of its adjacent edges (in a weighted configuration), or the result of an algorithm executed on the graph.

In a proof-labeling scheme, an oracle assigns labels $\ell : V \to L$. Verification is performed by a distributed algorithm on the labeled configuration in synchronous rounds. In each round every vertex receives messages from all of its neighbors, performs local computations, and sends a message to all of its neighbors. At the beginning of each round, a vertex scans its messages in a streaming fashion. The ***computational space*** is the maximum space required by a vertex in its local computation. Each vertex may send different messages to different neighbors in a round. When a vertex halts, it outputs TRUE or FALSE. If the vertex labels contain unique identifiers, then we require that an algorithm has the same output for all legal assignments of unique IDs.

Given a family $\mathcal{F}$ of configurations, and a boolean predicate $\mathcal{P}$ over $\mathcal{F}$, a PLS for $(\mathcal{F}, \mathcal{P})$ is a mechanism for deciding $\mathcal{P}(G_s)$ for every $G_s \in \mathcal{F}$. A PLS consists of a ***prover*** $\mathbf{p}$, and a ***verifier*** $\mathbf{v}$. The prover is an oracle which, given any configuration $G_s \in \mathcal{F}$, assigns a bit string $\ell(v)$ to each vertex v, called the ***label*** of v. The verifier $\mathbf{v}$ at each vertex outputs a boolean value. If the outputs are TRUE at all vertices, $\mathbf{v}$ is said to ***accept*** the configuration. If $\mathbf{v}$ outputs FALSE in at least one vertex, $\mathbf{v}$ is said to ***reject*** the configuration. For correctness, a proof-labeling scheme $(\mathbf{p}, \mathbf{v})$ for $(\mathcal{F}, \mathcal{P})$ must be (1) ***complete*** and (2) ***sound***. Formally, $(\mathbf{p}, \mathbf{v})$ is ***complete*** if $\mathcal{P}(G_s) =$ TRUE then, using the labels assigned by $\mathbf{p}$, the verifier $\mathbf{v}$ accepts G_s. The scheme is ***sound*** if $\mathcal{P}(G_s) =$ FALSE then, for every label assignment, the verifier $\mathbf{v}$ rejects G_s.

The ***verification complexity*** of a proof-labeling scheme $(\mathbf{p}, \mathbf{v})$ is the maximal label size—the maximal length of a label assigned by the prover $\mathbf{p}$ on a legal configuration (satisfying $\mathcal{P}$). Here, we introduce proof-labeling schemes with more than one verification round. In particular the runtime t of $\mathbf{v}$ can be super-constant. We define the ***message size*** of the scheme $(\mathbf{p}, \mathbf{v})$ to be the largest message a vertex sends during the execution of $\mathbf{v}$ on a legal configuration with the labels assigned by $\mathbf{p}$. We denote a proof-labeling scheme with t-round verification by t-PLS.

3. UNIVERSAL SCHEME

A ***universal scheme*** is a PLS that verifies any sequentially decidable property. In this section we assume that each vertex has a unique identifier. A single round 1-PLS can be obtained by having the labels encode a proposed description of the network (along with the states of each vertex). The labeling can be verified in a single round by each vertex ensuring that each of its neighbors' labels are consistent with its label [12, 10, 4]. For $t > 1$, we obtain the following gerenalization a universal scheme.

THEOREM 1. *Let $\mathcal{F}$ be a family of configurations with state set S and diameter at least D. Let $\mathcal{P}$ be a boolean predicate over $\mathcal{F}$. Suppose that every state in S can be represented using s bits. For every $t \in \Omega(D)$ there exists a t-PLS for $(\mathcal{F}, \mathcal{P})$ with label and message size $O((ns + \min\{n^2, m \log n\})/t)$ where n is the number of vertices, and m is the number of edges in the graph.*

For $t = 1$ Theorem 1 reduces to the well-known universal scheme. For larger values of t, labels are significantly smaller, and the total communication is the same as the one round scheme. The idea of the proof of Theorem 1 is to break the labels of the 1-round scheme into $O(t)$ "shares." In t communication rounds, the verifier $\mathbf{v}$ reconstructs the original 1-round labels, which are then accepted or rejected as in the 1-round PLS. We refer to this technique as ***label sharing***.

4. LOWER BOUND TECHNIQUE

The main tool we use for proving lower bounds for t-PLS is Theorem 5. Towards proving Theorem 5, will will find it useful to consider orientated edges in the network. We denote the head and tail of a directed edge e by $H(e)$ and $T(e)$, respectively.

DEFINITION 2 (EDGE CROSSING). *Let $G = (V, E)$ be a graph, and $e_1, e_2 \in E$ be two directed edges. The **edge crossing** of e_1 and e_2 in G, denoted by $C(e_1, e_2, G)$, is the graph obtained from G by replacing e_1 and e_2, by the edges $(T(e_1), H(e_2))$ and $(T(e_2), H(e_1))$.*

Edge crossings were formalized as a tool for proving lower bounds of verification complexity in [4]. We now show how to use edge crossing in order to prove lower bounds for label size of t-PLS.

DEFINITION 3 (EDGE k-NEIGHBORHOOD). *Let $G = (V, E)$ be a graph, and $e = (u, v) \in E$. The **k-neighborhood** of e in G, denoted by $N_k(e, G)$, is the subgraph (V', E') of G satisfying (1) $w \in V'$ if and only if $w \in V$ and $\min(\text{dist}(w, u), \text{dist}(w, v))$ k, and (2) $e' \in E'$ if and only if $e' \in E \cap (V' \times V')$.*

PROPOSITION 4. *Let $(\mathbf{p}, \mathbf{v})$ be a deterministic t-PLS for $(\mathcal{F}, \mathcal{P})$ with label size $|\ell|$. Suppose that there is a configuration $G_s \in \mathcal{F}$ which satisfies $\mathcal{P}$ and contains r directed edges $e_1, \ldots, e_r$, whose t-neighborhoods $N_t(e_1, G_s), \ldots, N_t(e_r, G_s)$ are pairwise disjoint, contain q vertices each, and there exist r state preserving isomorphisms $\sigma_i : V(N_t(e_1, G_s)) \to V(N_t(e_i, G_s))$ for $i = 1, \ldots, r$ such that $\sigma_i(H(e_1)) = H(e_i)$ and $\sigma_i(T(e_1)) = T(e_i)$. If $|\ell| < (\log r)/q$, then there exist i, j with $1 \le i < j \le r$ such that every connected component of $C(e_i, e_j, G_s)$ is accepted by $(\mathbf{p}, \mathbf{v})$.*

The main result of this section follows from Proposition 4.

THEOREM 5. *Let $\mathcal{F}$ be a family of configurations, and let $\mathcal{P}$ be a boolean predicate over $\mathcal{F}$. Suppose that there is a configuration $G_s \in \mathcal{F}$ which satisfies*

1. *$\mathcal{P}(G_s) =$ TRUE,*
2. *G_s contains r directed edges $e_1, \ldots, e_r$, whose t-neighborhoo $N_t(e_1, G_s), \ldots, N_t(e_r, G_s)$ are pairwise disjoint, contain q vertices each, and there exist r state preserving isomorphisms $\sigma_i : V(N_t(e_1, G_s)) \to V(N_t(e_i, G_s))$ for $i = 1, \ldots, r$ such that $\sigma_i(H(e_1)) = H(e_i)$ and $\sigma_i(T(e_1)) = T(e_i)$, and*
3. *for every $i \neq j$, there exists a connected component H_s of $C(e_i, e_j, G_s)$ such that $\mathcal{P}(H_s) =$ FALSE.*

Then the label size of any t-PLS for $(\mathcal{F}, \mathcal{P})$ is $\Omega((\log r)/q)$.

5. ACYCLICITY

In this section we focus on the acyclicity property, and give tight t-PLS lower and upper bounds. The lower bounds hold in computational model where vertices have unique identifiers, and the labels are allowed to depend on the ID of a vertex. The upper bounds apply even in a weaker computational model where vertices do not have unique IDs.

DEFINITION 6 (ACYCLICITY). *Let $\mathcal{F}$ be the family of all connected graphs. Given a graph configuration $G_s \in \mathcal{F}$, $\text{ACYCLIC}(G_s) = \text{TRUE}$ if and only if the underling graph G is cycle free.*

THEOREM 7. *Every scheme which verifies* ACYCLIC *in t communication rounds requires labels of size $\Omega((\log n)/t)$.*

The proof of Theorem 7 is an applicaiton of Theorem 5 to a network consisting of a path. The result follows by observing that any edge-crossing of a path contains a cycle.

THEOREM 8. *Suppose $G = (V, E)$ is a graph with diameter D. For every $t \leq \min\{\log n, D\}$, there exists an $O(t)$-PLS for* ACYCLIC *with labels and messages of size $O((\log n)/t)$. Further, the verifier $\mathbf{v}$ uses space of size $O((\log n)/t)$.*

The upper bound of Theorem 8 is obtained by applying label sharing to a well-known 1-PLS. In the 1-PLS, the labels consist of an integer between 0 and $n-1$. A unique "root" is assigned label 0, while each other label is a vertex's distance from the root. Each vertex then verifies that either (1) its label is 0 and all its neighbors have label 1, or (2) its label is $\ell > 0$, and it has a unique neighbor with label $\ell - 1$, while all other neighbors have label $\ell + 1$. Theorem 8 follows by breaking the 1-PLS labels into $\Theta(t)$ shares of size $\Theta((\log n)/t)$. Each vertex then verifies that the corresponding 1-PLS labeling is correct by examining the labels in its t-neighborhood.

The scheme from Theorem 8 gives asymptotically optimal label size for $t \leq \log n$. Further, the communication per round and local memory usage is linear in the label size. However, the scheme above crucially requires each vertex to be given a truthful representation of the parameter t, the runtime of the verification. This may be undesirable as for $t \sim \log n$, the labels are of size $O(1)$, yet any representation of t is significantly larger ($\Omega(\log\log n)$). We describe a verifier for ACYCLIC that only assumes that the space provided to each processor is $O(\log^* n)$. The tradeoff is that our algorithm runs in time which may be linear in n in the worst case.

THEOREM 9. *There exists an $O(n)$-PLS for* ACYCLIC *which uses labels and space of size $O(\log^* n)$. In each round, the communication per-edge is $O(1)$.*

The $O(\log^* n)$ space scheme of Theorem 9 combines the ideas of label sharing with recursion. At the top level of recursion, we simulate the 1-PLS for acyclicity. Shares of the labels are stored in paths emanating from the proposed root, which we refered to as ***blocks***. Each block has size $O(\log n)$, and stores its distance from the purported root, where each node's share consists of a single bit. The correctness of the block labels are verified recursively using sub-blocks of size $O(\log\log n)$. After $O(\log^* n)$ levels of recursion, the blocks have constant size, and the correctness of the labeling can be trivially verified.

While verification time in Theorem 9 is $O(n)$ in the worst case, the actual time depends on the labels given to the vertices. In particular, for every acyclic graph G, with diameter D, there exists a correct labeling which will be accepted in time $O(\log D)$. Thus there is a tradeoff between the runtime of the algorithm and the amount of truthful information about D given to the vertices.

6. REFERENCES

[1] Y. Afek, S. Kutten, and M. Yung. The local detection paradigm and its application to self-stabilization. *Theor. Comput. Sci.*, 186(1-2):199–229, 1997.

[2] B. Awerbuch and R. Ostrovsky. Memory-efficient and self-stabilizing network reset (extended abstract). In *Proceedings of the Thirteenth Annual ACM Symposium on Principles of Distributed Computing*, PODC '94, pages 254–263, New York, NY, USA, 1994. ACM.

[3] B. Awerbuch, B. Patt-Shamir, and G. Varghese. Self-stabilization by local checking and correction. In *32nd Symposium on Foundations of Computer Science (FOCS)*, pages 268–277. IEEE, 1991.

[4] M. Baruch, P. Fraigniaud, and B. Patt-Shamir. Randomized proof-labeling schemes. In *Proceedings of the 2015 ACM Symposium on Principles of Distributed Computing, PODC*, pages 315–324, 2015.

[5] M. Baruch, R. Ostrovsky, and W. Rosenbaum. Space-time tradeoffs for local verification. Manuscript, available at www.arxiv.org, 2016.

[6] L. Blin, P. Fraigniaud, and B. Patt-Shamir. On proof-labeling schemes versus silent self-stabilizing algorithms. In *16th Int. Symp. on Stabilization, Safety, and Security of Distributed Systems (SSS)*, LNCS, pages 18–32. Springer, 2014.

[7] A. Das Sarma, S. Holzer, L. Kor, A. Korman, D. Nanongkai, G. Pandurangan, D. Peleg, and R. Wattenhofer. Distributed verification and hardness of distributed approximation. *SIAM J. Comput.*, 41(5):1235–1265, 2012.

[8] P. Fraigniaud, A. Korman, and D. Peleg. Towards a complexity theory for local distributed computing. *J. ACM*, 60(5):35, 2013.

[9] P. Fraigniaud, S. Rajsbaum, and C. Travers. Locality and checkability in wait-free computing. *Distributed Computing*, 26(4):223–242, 2013.

[10] M. Göös and J. Suomela. Locally checkable proofs. In *30th ACM Symp. on Principles of Distributed Computing (PODC)*, pages 159–168, 2011.

[11] A. Korman, S. Kutten, and T. Masuzawa. Fast and compact self stabilizing verification, computation, and fault detection of an MST. In *30th Annual ACM Symposium on Principles of Distributed Computing (PODC)*, pages 311–320, 2011.

[12] A. Korman, S. Kutten, and D. Peleg. Proof labeling schemes. *Distributed Computing*, 22(4):215–233, 2010.

A Faster Distributed Radio Broadcast Primitive (Extended Abstract)

Bernhard Haeupler
Carnegie Mellon University
haeupler@cs.cmu.edu

David Wajc
Carnegie Mellon University
wajc@cs.cmu.edu

ABSTRACT

We present a faster distributed broadcasting primitive for the classical radio network model.

The most basic distributed radio network broadcasting primitive - called Decay - dates back to a PODC'87 result of Bar-Yehuda, Goldreich, and Itai. In any radio network with some informed source nodes, running Decay for $O(d \log n + \log^2 n)$ rounds informs all nodes at most d hops away from a source with high probability. Since 1987 this primitive has been the most important building block for implementing many other functionalities in radio networks. The only improvements to this decades-old algorithm are slight variations due to [Czumaj, Rytter; FOCS'03] and [Kowalski and Pelc, PODC'03] which achieve the same functionality in $O(d \log \frac{n}{d} + \log^2 n)$ rounds. To obtain a speedup from this, d and thus also the network diameter need to be near linear, i.e., larger than $n^{1-\epsilon}$.

Our new distributed primitive spreads messages for d hops in $O(d \frac{\log n \log \log n}{\log d} + \log^{O(1)} n)$ rounds with high probability. This improves over Decay for any super-polylogarithmic $d = \log^{\omega(1)} n$ and achieves near-optimal $O(d \log \log n)$ running time for $d = n^{\epsilon}$. This also makes progress on an open question of Peleg.

CCS Concepts

•**Theory of computation** → **Distributed algorithms;** *Graph algorithms analysis;*

Keywords

radio networks; broadcast; d-hop broadcast problem; decay

PODC'16, July 25 - 28, 2016, Chicago, IL, USA

ACM 978-1-4503-3964-3/16/07...$15.00
DOI: http://dx.doi.org/10.1145/2933057.2933121

1. INTRODUCTION

This paper presents a faster distributed broadcasting routine for the classical radio network setting.

The Radio Network Setting.

In the classical radio network setting [3] a multi-hop wireless network is modeled by an undirected graph G. Communication operates in synchronous rounds in which each node can either listen or broadcast some message to all of its neighbors, typically consisting of $O(\log n)$ bits. This message can be received by all listening neighboring nodes, unless multiple transmissions interfere at a receiver. This is modeled by stipulating that a listening node will receive a message sent by a neighboring node if and only if no other neighbor sends at the same time.

The radio network model thus captures both the inherent broadcast nature of wireless transmissions as well as the additional intricacies caused by half-duplex media access and interference. The question of how to coordinate and schedule transmissions in radio networks to most efficiently disseminate information is an interesting and important one. Of particular interest are distributed solutions in which nodes do not need to know the network topology. The 2007 survey of Peleg, "Time-Efficient Broadcasting in Radio Networks"[16], gives an excellent summary and overview of the intense study of this question over the last decades.

The fundamental broadcast problem we study in this paper is the following.

Definition 1.1 (d-hop broadcast)**.** *The d-hop broadcast problem consists of a network $G = (V, E)$ and a subset of nodes $S \subseteq V$ which are informed about a message M. The goal is to transmit M to all nodes in the d-hop neighborhood of S.*

Decay: A Basic Broadcasting Routine.

The first and most basic distributed broadcasting primitive for the radio network setting is a simple algorithm of Bar-Yehuda, Goldreich and Itai published in 1987 called *Decay* [2]. In a network with some informed nodes, Decay uses a simple exponential backoff strategy to neighbors of informed nodes. In particular, in round $i = 0, 1, \ldots, \log_2 n - 1$ every informed node broadcasts independently with probability 2^{-i}. A simple two-line proof shows that after $\log n$ such rounds any node neighboring an informed node will be informed with constant probability. Repeating the above $O(d + \log n)$ times gives the following guarantee:

Lemma 1.1 (Decay [2])**.** *Decay solves the d-hop broadcast problem in the radio network model in $O(d \log n + \log^2 n)$ rounds with high probability.*

Table 1: d-hop broadcast problem

Algorithm	Rounds	Reference
Decay	$O(d \log n + \log^2 n)$	[2]
Modified Decay	$O(d \log \frac{n}{d} + \log^2 n)$	[5, 11]
Divide and Chatter	$O(d \frac{\log n \log\log n}{\log d} + \log^{O(1)} n)$	**This work**

Table 2: One-to-all broadcast problem

Bound	Notes	Reference
$\Omega(D + \log^2 n)$	holds even for offline schedule computation	[1]
$\Omega(D \log \frac{n}{D})$	assuming conditional wake-up	[13]
$O(D \log n + \log^2 n)$		[2]
$O(D \log \frac{n}{D} + \log^2 n)$		[5, 11]
$O(D + \log^2 n)$	assuming known topology	[12, 10]
$O(D + \log^6 n)$	assuming collision detection	[10]
$O(D \frac{\log n \log\log n}{\log D} + \log^{O(1)} n)$		**This work**

Over the last 29 years, work on multi-hop radio network settings has extensively used this basic primitive. Many algorithms implementing higher functionalities, for example, leader election [2, 9] repeatedly run Decay as the most basic communication subroutine for various values of d. One important property of the Decay algorithm is its distributed nature. In particular, nodes do not need to know anything about the topology to be able to execute it.

Related Work: Upper and Lower Bounds.

Subsequent work by Alon et al.[1] showed that Decay's additive polylogarithmic overhead of $\Theta(\log^2 n)$ is necessary and thus optimal even if d is constant and the network topology is known and nodes know which other nodes are already informed. On the positive side, both [5] and [11] showed in 2003 that one can achieve a small improvement over the $d \log n$ term. In particular, by choosing slightly different broadcast probabilities a running time of $O(d \log \frac{n}{d} + \log^2 n)$ rounds suffices to solve the d-hop broadcast problem. For $d \leq n^{1-\epsilon}$ this results in the same $O(d \log n)$ running time as Decay but for near-linear diameters and values of $d = n^{1-\omega(1)}$ this improves over Decay all the way to a linear $O(d)$ running time for linear diameter networks and $d = \Theta(n)$. A lower bound by Kushilevitz and Mansour [13] for the wake-up problem shows this to be tight if one makes the extra assumption that uninformed nodes are not allowed to communicate (until they are informed). Without this assumption only the trivial $\Omega(d)$ lower bound exists and there is nothing that precludes an $O(d + \log^2 n)$ distributed algorithm for the d-hop broadcast problem. On the other hand, except for near-linear d, no improvement on the classical Decay procedure has been put forward over the last three decades. In fact, no better solution than Decay is known for the d-hop broadcast problem, even if one just asks about the existence of a centralized schedule which can utilize the full knowledge of the topology.

Our Result: A Faster d-hop Broadcasting Routine.

In this work we give a new distributed broadcasting routine which solves the d-hop broadcast problem faster than Decay:

Theorem 1.2. *There is a randomized algorithm which solves the d-hop broadcast problem in the radio network model in $O(d \cdot \frac{\log n \log\log n}{\log d}) + \log^{O(1)} n$ rounds with high probability.*

This improves over Decay for any d which is only super-polylogarithmic, i.e., $d = \log^{\omega(1)} n$. It also achieves a near optimal $O(d \log\log n)$ running time for any $d \geq n^{\epsilon}$. As the Decay protocol, our algorithm is a randomized distributed routine succeeding with high probability and operating with $\log n$ bit messages and without collision detection. That is, a node which is broadcast to by several neighbors receives no message, nor does it receive indication of having been broadcast to by multiple neighbors.

The one-to-all broadcast problem.

Beyond providing a faster solution for the (distributed) d-hop broadcast problem, which can be used to replace the Decay type protocols [2, 5, 11] as a communication primitive, our result also makes progress on an open question asked in the survey of Peleg [16]. Peleg asked about the round complexity of informing all nodes of a network about a message which initially starts in a single node. This can be seen as a simple special case of the d-hop broadcast problem where d is set to equal the diameter D of the network and where a single source node is initially informed. A long line of work [7, 6, 8, 12, 4] resulted in a tight bound of $\Theta(D+\log^2 n)$ for the complexity of this problem (and efficient deterministic algorithms for constructing these schedules) for the case that the topology is known. A similar $O(D + \log^6 n)$ bound was proven more recently [10] for distributed algorithms in which nodes can detect collisions. If one disallows collision detection and adds the requirement that nodes need to be woken up first (by receiving a message) before they can take part in the communications, then the $\Theta(D \log \frac{n}{D} + \log^2 n)$ bound of the modified Decay protocol is tight. This line of research leaves the standard distributed setting without collision detection and without wake-up requirement as the only as-of-yet unresolved setting. Our solution is the first to show that the $O(D \log \frac{n}{D} + \log^2 n)$ complexity of Decay is not tight for this setting and can be improved. The exact complexity however remains open. Tables 1 and 2 outline our results and prior work.

Our Approach and Technical Contributions.

Our algorithm differs significantly from Decay.

From the wake-up lower bound of [13] we know nodes cannot efficiently coordinate if they only start acting after receiving a message. On the other hand, the results of [10] and [4] suggest that significantly better schedules can be constructed around a node if it knows a bit more about its neighborhood.

Our high-level idea is thus very simple. We first compute a suitable clustering of the network which can be done locally and thus in sub-diameter many rounds (more generally, $O(d)$ time). Within each cluster we then compute the fast schedules of [10], which can be done in sub-diameter time if cluster diameters are small. The final schedule is then a fully-oblivious schedule which simply interleaves the fast intra-cluster schedules with the Decay routine to allow for crossing between clusters. Low-diameter decompositions are particularly attractive clusterings in this context because they guarantee that: as their name suggest, the clusters they output have small diameter, and each shortest path does not pass through too many clusters, leading to a negligible overhead for the Decay cost of crossing between clusters.

While this approach sounds nice and easy there are several technical difficulties in making it work:

1) The low-diameter decomposition algorithm needs to work in the radio network model, which is much more restrictive than the usual CONGEST setting. The low-diameter decomposition furthermore needs to produce connected clusters with strong diameter guarantees.

2) When using and constructing intra-cluster schedules in all clusters simultaneously, neighboring transmissions from other clusters can cause interference. One thus needs to obtain clusters with few neighboring clusters and somehow coordinate between clusters to avoid these collisions.

3) For low-diameter decompositions which cut an edge with probability β, the cluster diameter can be as high as $\frac{\log n}{\beta}$. As we demonstrate in Section 2.2 this leads to an overall logarithmic slowdown and thus an $O(d \log n + \log^{O(1)} n)$ running time - crushing the attempt to break this barrier. This logarithmic term in the cluster diameters is furthermore known to be necessary in certain settings.

Nonetheless, we overcome these difficulties! Our main technical contributions are:

- We adapt a new low-diameter decomposition of Miller et al. [15] to the radio network model, providing good bounds on the number of neighboring clusters which can interfere with transmissions from an entry point to the cluster center and back. Random backoff together with these properties allow us to solve problems 1 and 2 above.
- We present a refined analysis of distance properties of this low-diameter decomposition. Most importantly, for decompositions cutting edges with probability β, we prove a bound on the expected distance of a node v to its cluster center of roughly $\frac{\log k}{\beta}$, where k is the ratio of the size of balls of radius $\frac{\log n}{\beta}$ and $\frac{1}{\beta}$ around v. This is the first such guarantee for a low-diameter decomposition with strong diameter. This bound then implies that for a randomly-chosen scale a better clustering can be obtained on average, leading to $\frac{\log n \log \log n}{\log d}$ type bounds reflected in our result. We expect these properties of this low-width decomposition to be of further independent interest.

2. THE Divide and Chatter FRAMEWORK

In this section we outline our algorithm's framework, starting with the main radio network broadcast subroutines it relies on. We then give a simplified variant of our algorithm and discuss some of its shortcomings. Finally, we present our algorithm. As our obtained bounds improve prior bounds only when $d = \log^{\omega(1)} n$, we assume throughout our analysis that d is some sufficiently large $\log^{\Omega(1)} n$.

2.1 Radio Network Primitives

In addition to Decay, we rely on two other algorithms as primitives for our d-hop broadcast algorithm. We will rely on these algorithms in a black-box manner. The following two lemmas state our assumptions of these subroutines.

For our first primitive, we rely on the algorithm of [10], which on a network of diameter D and n, in $O(D \cdot \log^{O(1)} n)$ rounds, computes efficient, collision-free schedules for future transmissions. The algorithm of [10] assumes collision detection for its preprocessing stage, but we can simulate collision detection at an extra multiplicative $O(\log^2 n)$ blowup, by having each node which transmits during this stage transmit the same message for $O(\log^2 n)$ Decay rounds. A node transmit to by several neighbors will detect such a collision with high probability, since with high probability it will receive $\Omega(\log n)$ messages, and each of these transmitted message is equally likely to originate at any of its transmitting neighbors. This observation allows us to use the algorithm of [10] in a black box manner, given below.

Lemma 2.1 (Broadcast with Preprocessing, [10]). *A network of diameter D and n nodes can be preprocessed in $O(D \cdot \log^{O(1)} n)$ rounds, yielding a schedule which allows for one-to-all broadcast of k messages in $O(D + k \log n + \log^6 n)$ rounds with high probability. This schedule satisfies the following properties:*

- *For some prescribed node r, the schedule transmits messages to and from nodes at distance ℓ from r in $O(\ell + \log^6 n)$ rounds w.h.p.*
- *The schedule is periodic of period $O(\log n)$: it can be thought of as restarting every $O(\log n)$ steps.*

A further primitive we will need is low-diameter graph decompositions. In Section 3.1, we show how to implement the algorithm of Miller et al. [15] in a distributed setting, giving us the following lemma. In Section 3.2 we will prove some additional useful properties of this partitioning subroutine which will prove crucial for our algorithm and might be of independent interest.

Lemma 2.2. *For any $0 < \beta \leq 1$, a graph on n nodes can be partitioned into clusters each with strong diameter $O(\frac{\log n}{\beta})$ with high probability, and every edge cut by this partition with probability $O(\beta)$. This algorithm can be implemented in the radio network setting in $O(\frac{\log^3 n}{\beta})$ rounds.*

2.2 The Algorithm - General Approach

Given the above subroutines, we can outline a simplified variant of our algorithm which solves the d-hop broadcast problem in $O(d \cdot \log n + \log^{O(1)} n)$ rounds in expectation. This variant is presented below. For simplicity, we describe the algorithm as though d attempting to inform nodes at distance $\Theta(d)$. Doubling d, running the algorithm for $d = 2^i$ with $i = 1, 2, \ldots, \log_2 n$, yields the same guarantees as a function of d for all possible d simultaneously.

Our Algorithm – Take One.
(1) Compute the partition implied by Lemma 2.2 with parameter $\beta = \frac{1}{\log^{\Omega(1)} n}$.
(2) In each part of the decomposition, in tandem, run the preprocessing stage implied by Lemma 2.1.
(3) Alternate between steps of the precomputed schedules of step (2) and Decay.

An important point to note is the possibility of different clusters' schedules interfering with each other in steps (2) and (3). We ignore this issue for now and address it in Section 4.

Proposition 2.3. *Assuming no collision between different clusters' broadcasts, the above algorithm solves the d-hop broadcast problem in $O(d \cdot \log n + \log^{O(1)} n)$ rounds in expectation (though not with high probability).*

Proof. First, as each part has diameter $O(\frac{\log n}{\beta})$ with high probability, by Lemmas 2.1 and 2.2 the preprocessing of steps (1) and (2) can be done in $\log^{O(1)} n$ rounds. Now, consider a path p of length d from an informed source to some other node. By Lemma 2.2 the partitioning subroutine cuts an expected $O(d\beta)$ of the edges of this path. In addition each of the parts of the partition has diameter $O(\frac{\log n}{\beta})$ with high probability. Thus, the algorithm of Lemma 2.1 allows us to transmit a message within each part of the partition in $O(\frac{\log n}{\beta} + \log^6 n)$ rounds. Upon reaching the farthest node of p in some part, within $O(\log^2 n)$ Decay steps, this message will proceed to the next part which p traverses. Overall, the message will reach t after $O((d\beta + 2) \cdot (\frac{\log n}{\beta} + \log^6 n)) = O(d \cdot \log n + \log^{O(1)} n)$ rounds in expectation. □

As stated above the obtained bounds are weaker (and the algorithm more involved) than Decay. In the next section we present our full algorithm, together with intuition driving its design.

2.3 The Divide and Chatter Algorithm

In order to improve upon the bound given in the previous section, for our final algorithm we will effectively rely on a new useful property of PARTITION(β). Informally, this property states that picking $\beta \in [d^{0.001}, d^{0.01}]$ at random, the expected distance of a node to its "cluster center" is $O(\frac{\log n}{\beta} \cdot \frac{\log \log n}{\log d})$. In each cluster, we take the cluster center to be the prescribed node r which the algorithm of Lemma 2.1 allows transmission to and from in time proportional to the distance to r. Consequently, following the above analysis of our algorithm's simplified variant, we would expect that the time to transmit a message to the end of a path of length d be

$$O\left((d\beta + 2) \cdot \left(\frac{\log n}{\beta} \cdot \frac{\log \log n}{\log d} + \log^{O(1)} n\right)\right)$$

$$= O\left(d \cdot \frac{\log n \log \log n}{\log d} + \log^{O(1)} n\right)$$

Of course, we cannot simply naïvely multiply the expected number of cut edges by the distance to the cluster center, and we are sweeping a lot of technical detail under the rug in this description, including the aforementioned issue of potential collisions, but this high-level idea will guide us in the design and analysis of our algorithm.

The above approach entails a few technical difficulties – most prominently how to decide in a centralized manner on a/several random choice(s) of β, as reaching consensus among the nodes of the graph seems tantamount to the all to one broadcast problem. The solution we suggest to this problem involves a two-tiered approach – we first partition the graph into coarse-grained clusters within which the multi-message properties of the algorithm of Lemma 2.1 allow us to transmit the random choices of β for later, finer-grained partitions, with these messages transmitted at a logarithmic rate which will prove to be a lower-order term for the overall algorithm. Our final algorithm is given below.

Algorithm Divide and Chatter.
(1) Compute a coarse-grained clustering by running PARTITION(β) with $\beta = d^{-0.5}$.
(2) Compute a schedule in each cluster of step (1).
(3) Using these schedules, transmit within each cluster $d^{0.3}$ randomly-chosen values $I = \{i_j \mid j \in [d^{0.3}]\}$ with $(2\log n)^i \in [d^{0.001}, d^{0.01}]$ for all $i \in I$.
(4) Obtain $d^{0.3}$ finer clusterings with $\beta = (2\log n)^{-i}$ for each $i \in I$ within the coarse clusterings.
(5) For each of the $d^{0.3}$ clusters in each finer-grained clustering of step (4), compute schedules.
(6) Repeat $\Theta(d^{0.9})$ times - use schedules of fine clusterings of the different i in round-robin order, running for $O(d^{0.1} \frac{\log n \log \log n}{\log n})$ rounds with each i.

Our main result, which we prove in Section 5, is this.

Theorem 2.4. *Running Divide and Chatter on an n-node radio network for $O(d \cdot \frac{\log n \log \log n}{\log d} + \log^{O(1)} n)$ rounds solves the d-hop broadcast problem with high probability.*

A corollary of Lemmas 2.1 and 2.2 is that steps (1)-(5) can be implemented in $O(d)$ rounds. (We elaborate on this in Section 4). Given the running time of step (6), the running time follows. The remainder of the paper will be dedicated to providing implementations of steps (1)-(6) overcoming collisions and allowing this algorithm to succeed with high probability. In Section 3 we discuss our radio network implementation of the low-diameter graph decomposition subroutine and prove some useful properties its output satisfies. In Section 4 we discuss the issue of possible collisions and how to overcome them. Finally, in Section 5 we prove our main result.

3. PARTITIONING THE GRAPH

In [15] Miller et al. gave a parallel algorithm for partitioning a graph's node set, such that for a chosen β each edge is cut (has its endpoints in distinct parts) with probability at most β and each cluster has strong diameter $O(\frac{\log n}{\beta})$ with high probability. This algorithm picks for each node v a random shift value δ_v distributed exponentially with parameter β, and every node u belongs to a cluster $\mathcal{C}_v$ of a node v (which we term the *cluster center* of the cluster $\mathcal{C}_v$) which minimizes the shifted distance to u. That is, u belongs to $\mathcal{C}_v$ for $v = \arg\min_v \{d(u, v) - \delta_v\}$. This is algorithm PARTITION(β), implied by Lemma 2.2 and presented below. An equivalent way to think of PARTITION(β) is as follows: each node v starts growing a cluster at "time" $-\delta_v$ (one hop per step), and every node joins the first cluster to reach it. The algorithm as stated is sequential, but can be readily parallelized, as we discuss in the next subsection.

Algorithm partition(β) [[15]]
For every node v, pick a value $\delta_v \sim Exp(\beta)$. Assign every node u to the cluster of the node v minimizing $d(u,v) - \delta_v$.

3.1 Radio Network Model Implementation

In order to parallelize the above algorithm, Miller et al. [15] presented an equivalent algorithm, wherein each node v is assigned a starting time $\max_u \delta_u - \delta_v$, followed by ball growing around nodes unclustered at their start time. However, this implementation requires reaching consensus among the nodes regarding the maximum shift value, which we cannot afford in our model. Nonetheless, as the maximum possible shift value is bounded by $\max_u \delta_u \leq \frac{2\log n}{\beta}$ with high probability, the following is an implementation of PARTITION(β) in the radio network model, as we shall see in Lemma 3.1.

Algorithm partition(β)
(radio network implementation).
For every node v, pick $\delta_v \sim Exp(\beta)$. Let v's start time be $start_v \leftarrow \frac{2\log n}{\beta} - \lfloor \delta_v \rfloor$. For $\frac{2\log n}{\beta}$ epochs of length $O(\log^2 n)$ each, do the following: Upon start of epoch number t, for every node v not yet in any cluster with starting time $start_v = t$, assign v to its own cluster, with v its cluster center. During an epoch, all nodes not in any cluster at epoch start, listen. All nodes in a cluster at epoch start broadcasting their cluster center name using algorithm Decay. Any listening node receiving a cluster center name joins the first such cluster center's cluster.

Lemma 3.1. *The above radio network implementation of* PARTITION(β) *outputs a partition of the nodes, with every cluster having strong diameter $O(\frac{\log n}{\beta})$ with high probability. It terminates in $O(\frac{\log^3 n}{\beta})$ rounds.*

Proof. First, as Decay solves the 1-hop broadcast problem in $O(\log^2 n)$ steps with high probability, any node neighboring a clustered node at the beginning of an epoch will join a cluster during this epoch with high probability and so clusters are connected and have diameter at most $\frac{2\log n}{\beta}$. Next, as all δ_u are distributed exponentially with parameter β, the probability of any δ_u being greater than $\frac{2\log n}{\beta}$ is $\exp\left(-\frac{2\log n}{\beta}\cdot\right) = \frac{1}{n^2}$, and so with high probability $\frac{2\log n}{\beta} \geq \max_u \delta_u$.[1] Consequently, with high probability every node either joins a cluster before its start time or becomes its own cluster center, as its start time lies in the range $[0, \frac{2\log n}{\beta}]$. Finally, the running time is immediate from the algorithm's description. □

The sequential implementation of PARTITION(β) has every cluster $\mathcal{C}$ grow by one hop per round after $\mathcal{C}$'s inception. Our radio network implementation exhibits the same behavior, in that every cluster grows by one hop per epoch, as every epoch relies on Decay to solve 1-hop, and thus succeeds with high probability. Throughout our analysis, we condition on this high probability event occurring.

[1]This is precisely the reason clusters output by the sequential version of PARTITION(β) have small diameter.

In the following section we prove that our radio network implementation of PARTITION(β) inherits the useful properties of its sequential and parallel counterparts stated in Lemma 2.2. Moreover, we prove several additional useful properties of this algorithm which will prove important in obtaining our main result.

3.2 Partitioning the Graph - Analysis

In this section we state and prove multiple properties of PARTITION(β) useful in the analysis of Divide and Chatter. We start with a definition which will lead our analysis.

Definition 3.1. *For a given node v denote by $N_i = N_i(v) = \mathcal{B}(v, (2\log n)^i)$ the set of nodes at distance $(2\log n)^i$ from v, and by $k_i(v) = \frac{|N_{i+1}|-|N_i|}{|N_i|}$ the ratio of number of nodes at distance in the range $((2\log n)^i, (2\log n)^{i+1}]$ to the number of nodes at distance $(2\log n)^i$ or less from v.*

The expected cost of our protocol will depend on $k_i(v)$. We start by showing these $k_i(v)$ are small on average.

Lemma 3.2. *If we pick an $i \in [s,t]$ uniformly at random for $t - s = \Theta(\log_{\log n} d)$, then $\mathbb{E}[\log k_i(v)] = O\left(\frac{\log n \cdot \log\log n}{\log d}\right)$.*

Proof. As $|N_{i+1}| \geq |N_i|$ for all $i \in [s,t]$ by definition and $|N_1| \geq 1$ and $|N_{t+1}| \leq n$ we have

$$\prod_{i=s}^{t} k_i(v) = \prod_{i=s}^{t} \frac{|N_{i+1}| - |N_i|}{|N_i|} \leq \prod_{i=s}^{t} \frac{|N_{i+1}|}{|N_i|} \leq \frac{|N_{t+1}|}{|N_1|} \leq n$$

Taking out logs we obtain $\sum_{i=s}^{t} \log k_i(v) \leq \log n$. So, if we denote by $\delta \triangleq t - s + 1$, then as $\delta = \Theta(\frac{\log d}{\log\log n})$, we have

$$\mathbb{E}[\log k_i(v)] = \frac{1}{\delta} \cdot \sum_{i=s}^{t} \log k_i(v) = O\left(\frac{\log n \cdot \log\log n}{\log d}\right) \square$$

The range of i considered in Lemma 3.2 will prove useful later, as we will require $(2\log n)^i \in [d^a, d^b]$ for $a, b = \Theta(1)$.

The following simple observation will allow us to show that rounding the δ_v doesn't change the probability space by much compared to the version of algorithm PARTITION(β) in which the δ_v are not rounded down.

Observation 3.3. *For any pair of distances $d(u,v)$ and $d(u,w)$ and shift values δ_v, δ_w, we have*

$$\Pr[d(u,v) - \lfloor\delta_v\rfloor - (d(u,w) - \lfloor\delta_w\rfloor) \leq d]$$
$$\leq \Pr[d(u,v) - \delta_v - (d(u,w) - \delta_w) \leq d + 1]$$

Next, we bound the probability of a node to be another node's cluster center, which will prove crucial in bounding the expected distance of a node to its cluster center.

Lemma 3.4. *Let $\beta = (2\log n)^{-i}$, $i \geq 0$. Then, for any two nodes u and v at distance $d = d(u,v) > \frac{1}{\beta}$, the probability of u being v's cluster center after running* PARTITION(β) *is at most $\frac{\exp(-d\beta+2)}{|N_i|}$.*

Proof. For u to be v's cluster center, we must have in particular that u's cluster reached N_i before the start time of all nodes in N_i; i.e., u's start time must be at least $d - \frac{1}{\beta}$ smaller than the start time of all nodes $w \in N_i$, and so its shift value δ_u must be greater than the shift values of all nodes $w \in N_i$ by at least $d - \frac{1}{\beta} - 1$. (The minus one term is due to the rounding of the shift values, as discussed in Observation 3.3.)

That is, if we denote by $\Delta = \max_{w \in N_i} \delta_w$ the maximum shift value of any node in N_i, we find that the probability of u being v's cluster center is at most $\Pr\left[\delta_u \geq \Delta + d - \frac{1}{\beta} - 1\right]$. But as $d - \frac{1}{\beta} - 1 \geq 0$, this probability is equal to

$$\Pr\left[\delta_u \geq \Delta + d - \frac{1}{\beta} - 1 \,\middle|\, \delta_u \geq \Delta\right] \cdot \Pr\left[\delta_u \geq \Delta\right]$$

By memorylessness of the exponential distribution we have

$$\Pr\left[\delta_u \geq \Delta + d - \frac{1}{\beta} - 1 \,\middle|\, \delta_u \geq \Delta\right] = \Pr\left[\delta_u \geq d - \frac{1}{\beta} - 1\right] \leq \exp(-d\beta + 2)$$

On the other hand, as the random shifts are i.i.d we have that $\Pr\left[\delta_u \geq \Delta\right] = \Pr\left[\delta_u \geq \max_{w \in N_i} \delta_w\right] = \frac{1}{|N_i|+1} \leq \frac{1}{|N_i|}$. Combining both bounds, we find that the probability of u being v's cluster center is at most $\frac{\exp(-d\beta+2)}{|N_i|}$ □

The following corollary, while insufficient for our needs, hints at the usefulness of the random choice of $\beta = (2\log n)^{-i}$, given our prior bound on the expectation of $\log k_i(v)$.

Corollary 3.5. *Denote by $CC(v)$ the cluster center of node v and by $DCC(v) = d(v, CC(v))$ its distance to v. Then, if we run* PARTITION*(β) with $\beta = (2\log n)^{-i}$,*

$$\mathbb{E}[DCC(v)] = O\left(\frac{\log k_i(v) + 1}{\beta}\right)$$

Proof. By definition, $\mathbb{E}[DCC(v)] = \sum_u d(u,v) \cdot \Pr[u = CC(v)]$. To show that $\sum_u d(u,v) \cdot \Pr[u = CC(v)] = O(\frac{\log k_i(v)+1}{\beta})$, we consider three distance ranges. First, the nodes at distance at most $d(u,v) \leq \frac{\log k_i(v)+1}{\beta}$ from v clearly contribute at most $\frac{\log k_i(v)+1}{\beta}$ to this expectation. Next, we consider nodes at distance greater than $\frac{2\log n}{\beta}$ from v. For a node u at distance $d(u,v) \geq \frac{2\log n}{\beta}$ from v to be v's cluster center requires in particular that $\lfloor \delta_u \rfloor \geq \lfloor \delta_v \rfloor + d(u,v) \geq \frac{2\log n}{\beta}$. But as $\Pr[\max_u \delta_u \geq \frac{2\log n}{\beta} - 1] = O(\frac{1}{n})$, we find the contribution of all nodes at distance at least $\frac{2\log n}{\beta}$ from v to this expectation is at most $O(n \cdot \frac{1}{n}) = O(1)$.

Finally, we direct our attention to nodes u at distance between $\frac{\log k_i(v)+1}{\beta}$ and $\frac{2\log n}{\beta}$ from v. By N_i's definition, there are at most $|N_{i+1}| - |N_i|$ such nodes. By Lemma 3.4, for any $d \in [\frac{\log k_i(v)+1}{\beta}, \frac{2\log n}{\beta}]$ the probability of a given node at distance d from v being v's cluster center is at most $\frac{\exp(-d\beta+2)}{|N_i|}$, and so u's contribution to $\mathbb{E}[DCC(v)]$ is at most $d \cdot \frac{\exp(-d\beta+2)}{|N_i|}$. As this expression is monotone decreasing in d, we can upper bound it by assuming all nodes at distance $d \in [\frac{\log k_i(v)+1}{\beta}, \frac{2\log n}{\beta}]$ from v are at distance precisely $d' = \frac{\log k_i(v)+1}{\beta}$ from v, and so the total contribution of such nodes to this expectation is at most $\left(|N_{i+1}| - |N_i|\right) \cdot d' \cdot \frac{\exp(-d'\beta+2)}{|N_i|}$, which is precisely

$$= \frac{\log k_i(v) + 1}{\beta} \cdot k_i(v) \cdot \frac{e^2}{k_i(v)+1} = O\left(\frac{\log k_i(v) + 1}{\beta}\right)$$

Summing the above three contributions to the expectation, the lemma follows. □

As we shall see in Corollary 3.7, the probability of an edge to be cut by PARTITION(β) is at most $O(\beta)$. So, for an edge $e = (u,v)$, if we denote by $\mathbb{1}_e$ an indicator random variable for the event that the edge e is cut and denote by $DCC(v)$ the distance of v to its cluster center, given the above bound $\mathbb{E}[DCC(v)] = O(\frac{\log k_i(v)+1}{\beta})$, we might expect $\mathbb{E}[\mathbb{1}_e \cdot DCC(v)] \leq O(\log k_i(v)+1)$. As we shall see in Lemma 3.11, this is indeed the case. As our algorithm will cost $\mathbb{1}_{(u,v)} \cdot (DCC(u) + DCC(v))$ per edge (u,v) along a path from an informed node to an uninformed node (plus a global additive $O(d)$ term), this will imply our main result. But first, we proceed to prove our main technical lemma, which implies an equivalent of Lemma 2.2 for our radio network implementation of PARTITION(β), as well as several other useful properties of PARTITION(β) which we will rely on.

3.2.1 Key Lemma and Corollaries

The following lemma generalizes Lemma 4.4 in [15] for PARTITION(β). Observation 3.3 implies the same asymptotic properties hold for our partitioning with the random shifts rounded down. The lemma is implied by the proof of Lemma 2.2 in [14], though its statement is strictly stronger. For completeness we present a proof below.

Lemma 3.6. *Let $d_1, d_2, \ldots, d_n$ be n real values, and let δ_i be i.i.d exponential random variables with parameter β. For all $t \in [n]$ denote by $D^{(t)}$ the t-th smallest value in the multiset $\{d_i - \delta_i \mid i \in [n]\}$. (e.g., $D^{(1)}$ is the smallest such value). Then, for all $k \geq 1$,*

$$\Pr[D^{(k)} - D^{(1)} \leq d] \leq (1 - \exp(-d \cdot \beta))^{k-1}$$

The above holds even if we condition on the index set $I \subseteq [n]$ that defines the smallest k values of $\{d_i - \delta_i\}$ and index i_k that defines the k-th smallest value. I.e., $\{d_i - \delta_i \mid i \in I\} = \{D^{(j)} \mid j \in [k]\}$ and $d_{i_k} - \delta_{i_k} = D^{(k)}$.

Proof. For simplicity, suppose $I = [k]$ and $D^{(k)} = d_k - \delta_k$ (for $j \neq k$ we make no assumption regarding which $i \in I$ satisfies $D^{(j)} = d_i - \delta_i$). Consider some $i \in [k-1]$. By definition of $D^{(k)}$ we have $D^{(k)} \geq d_i - \delta_i$. Put otherwise, $\Pr[\delta_i \geq d_i - D^{(k)}] = 1$. By memorylessness of the exponential we thus have

$$\begin{aligned}\Pr[\delta_i \leq d + d_i - D^{(k)}] &= \Pr[\delta_i \leq d + d_i - D^{(k)} \mid \delta_i \geq d_i - D^{(k)}] \\ &\leq \Pr[\delta_i \leq d] \\ &= 1 - \exp(-d\beta)\end{aligned}$$

Where the inequality is strict only if $d_i - D^{(k)}$ is negative. Either way, we have $\Pr[\delta_i \leq d + d_i - D^{(k)}] \leq 1 - \exp(-d\beta)$. Now, by independence of the random variables δ_i we have

$$\begin{aligned}\Pr[D^{(k)} - D^{(1)} \leq d] &= \Pr[\bigwedge_{i=1}^{k-1} \delta_i \leq d + d_i - D^{(k)}] \\ &= \prod_{i=1}^{k-1} \Pr[\delta_i \leq d + d_i - D^{(k)}] \\ &\leq (1 - \exp(-d\beta))^{k-1}\end{aligned}$$

□

Lemma 3.6 together with Observation 3.3 implies many useful properties of algorithm PARTITION(β), given by the following corollaries. In the proofs of these corollaries the distances to some prescribed node plus $\frac{2\log n}{\beta}$ will play the roles of the d_i in Lemma 3.6's statement.

Corollary 3.7. *The probability of a fixed edge (u, v) being cut by* PARTITION(β) *is at most $O(\beta)$.*

Proof. For the edge (u, v) to be cut, u and v must belong to different clusters. This implies that the two smallest shifted and rounded distances from v are at most one apart. But by Lemma 3.6 and Observation 3.3 this happens with probability at most $\Pr[D^{(2)} - D^{(1)} \leq 2] \leq 1 - \exp(-2\beta) \leq 2\beta$. □

The following useful property of PARTITION(β), proved to hold for the algorithm's sequential and parallel implementation in [14], follows from Lemma 3.6.

Corollary 3.8. *After running* PARTITION(β) *the probability of a fixed node u having nodes from t distinct clusters at distance d or less from u is at most $(1-\exp(-(2d+1)\cdot\beta))^{t-1}$.*

Proof. Let w be u's cluster center. Let v be some node at distance $d(u, v) \leq d$ from u, belonging to a different cluster whose cluster center is w'. Denote by $d_{-\delta}(v, w) \triangleq \frac{2\log n}{\beta} + d(v, w) - \lfloor \delta_w \rfloor$. Then $d_{-\delta}(v, w') \leq d_{-\delta}(v, w)$. Alternatingly applying triangle inequality and $d(u, v) \leq d$, we have

$$\begin{aligned} d_{-\delta}(u, w') &\leq d(u, v) + d_{-\delta}(v, w') \\ &\leq d + d_{-\delta}(v, w) \\ &\leq d + d(u, v) + d_{-\delta}(u, w) \\ &\leq 2d + d_{-\delta}(u, w) \end{aligned}$$

So, if u is at distance at most d from t different clusters, the t smallest values among $d_{-\delta}(u, w) = \frac{2\log n}{\beta} + d(u, w) - \lfloor \delta_w \rfloor$ differ by at most $2d$ from each other, so by Observation 3.3 the non-rounded shifted distances differ by at most $2d + 1$. Plugging these values into Lemma 3.6 yields the claimed bound. □

The following is a useful special case of the above corollary, given that we always run PARTITION(β) with $\beta = d^{-\Theta(1)}$.

Corollary 3.9. *For $\beta = d^{-\Theta(1)}$, with high probability, every node neighbors $O(\frac{\log n}{\log d})$ clusters.*

Lemma 3.10. *Let $d_1, d_2, \ldots, d_n$ be n real values, and let δ_i be i.i.d exponential random variables with parameter β. For all $t \in [n]$ denote by $D^{(t)}$ the t-th smallest value in the multiset $\{d_i - \delta_i \mid i \in [n]\}$. Furthermore, for any d, let A_d be the event that $D^{(1)} = d_i - \delta_i$ for some i with $d_i = d$. Then,*

$$\Pr[\left(D^{(2)} - D^{(1)} = O(1)\right) \wedge A_d] = O(\beta) \cdot \Pr[A_d]$$

Proof. Condition on the pair of indices $i_1, i_2 \in [n]$ such that $D^{(1)} = d_{i_1} - \delta_{i_1}$, $D^{(2)} = d_{i_2} - \delta_{i_2}$ and $d_{i_1} = d$. By Lemma 3.6, taking total expectation over all possible i_1 with $d_{i_1} = d$, we obtain $\Pr[D^{(2)} - D^{(1)} = O(1) \mid A_d] = O(\beta)$. □

The following lemma is key to our approach's effectiveness.

Lemma 3.11. *Let v be a node. For a run of* PARTITION(β) *with $\beta = (2\log n)^{-i}$, let $\mathbb{1}_v$ be an indicator random variable for the event that the lowest two values of $d(u, v) - \lfloor \delta_u \rfloor$ differ by some $O(1)$, and let $DCC(v)$ be the distance of v to its cluster center. Then, $\mathbb{E}[\mathbb{1}_v \cdot DCC(v)] = O(1 + \log k_i(v))$.*

Proof. For any integer d, let B_d be the event that v's distance to its cluster center is $DCC(v) = d$, and let E be the event that $\mathbb{1}_v = 1$. Then, by definition

$$\mathbb{E}[\mathbb{1}_v \cdot DCC(v)] = \sum_d d \cdot \Pr[E \wedge B_d]$$

For E to hold, the two smallest (non-rounded) shifted distances $d(u, v) - \delta_u$ must differ by $O(1)$, by Observation 3.3. On the other hand, for v's distance to cluster center to be d requires the smallest value $d(u, v) - \lfloor \delta_u \rfloor$ to be determined by a node u at distance $d(u, v) = d$. So, by Lemma 3.11 we have $\Pr[E \wedge B_d] = O(\beta) \cdot \Pr[B_d]$. Using this bound, we find

$$\begin{aligned} \mathbb{E}[\mathbb{1}_v \cdot DCC(v)] &= \sum_d d \cdot \Pr[E \wedge B_d] \\ &= \sum_d d \cdot O(\beta) \cdot \Pr[B_d] \\ &= O(\beta) \cdot \mathbb{E}[DCC(v)] \end{aligned}$$

which, by Corollary 3.5 is $O(\log k_i(v) + 1)$. □

In particular, by Lemma 3.2, we have the following.

Corollary 3.12. *Let $\mathbb{1}_v$ and $DCC(v)$ be as in Lemma 3.11. Then if $\beta = (2\log n)^{-i}$, with i chosen uniformly in $[s, t]$ with $t - s = \Theta(\log_{\log n} d)$, then $\mathbb{E}[\mathbb{1}_v \cdot DCC(v)] = O(\frac{\log n \cdot \log\log n}{\log d})$.*

As we transmit messages to and from the cluster center within clusters using Lemma 2.1's schedules and transmit across clusters using Decay in $O(\log^2 n)$ rounds (and spend at most $O(\log n)$ rounds until starting to use the cluster's schedule, by Lemma 2.1) the expected cost of informing a node at the end of a path p starting at an informed node is $\sum_{v \in p} \mathbb{E}[\mathbb{1}_v \cdot (DCC(v) + \log^2 n)]$, which together with Corollary 3.12 yields the following.

Lemma 3.13. *Let p be a path from an informed node to some node t. Assuming no collisions, t is informed after an expected $O(|p| \cdot \frac{\log n \cdot \log\log n}{\log d} + \log^{O(1)} n)$ rounds of step (6).*

The above approach as presented does not address the issue of potential collisions (indeed, Lemma 3.13 states as much explicitly) and therefore needs to be refined. In the next section we show how to obtain the same asymptotic behavior, while addressing potential collisions.

4. OVERCOMING COLLISIONS

In this section we show how to address potential collisions. The potential collisions can be divided into three kinds.

(1) Collisions during preprocessing – precomputing clusterings and schedules and transmitting I.

(2) Collisions when broadcasting using fine-grained clusters' schedules, due to other fine-grained clusters from different coarse clusters.

(3) Collisions when broadcasting using fine-grained clusters' schedules, due to other fine-grained clusters from the same coarse cluster.

In Sections 4.1, 4.2 and 4.3 we show how to deal with collisions of types 1, 2 and 3, respectively. For the first type of collisions we show that at a multiplicative polylogarithmic cost these collisions can be sidestepped. As the cost of the preprocessing steps will be $O(d/\log^{O(1)} n)$, this blowup will prove inconsequential. For the latter two kinds of collisions, this approach will prove too costly, as these collisions occur during the step whose running time dominates the algorithm's running time. Instead, we will consider a partition of every path p of length $|p| \in [d/2, d]$ from an informed node to an uninformed node t into disjoint subpaths of length $d^{0.1}$. By Lemma 3.13, the expected time to inform the last node of any such sub-path after the first node of this sub-path is informed (assuming no collisions) is $O(d^{0.1} \cdot \frac{\log n \log\log n}{\log n})$, so the expected time to inform the last node of p is $O(d \cdot \frac{\log n \log\log n}{\log n})$. In Sections 4.2 and 4.3 we show how to overcome collisions while guaranteeing the same expectation for the time to inform a node at the end of p.

An important tool we will rely on is correlated randomness within clusters. It may seem surprising that this could be achievable, but as we shall see, it is readily obtained by extending algorithm PARTITION(β).

Lemma 4.1. *For any b, at an $O(\frac{b}{\log n})$ multiplicative cost to PARTITION(β)'s running time, all nodes of each cluster can agree on b bits of randomness with high probability.*

Proof. The extra b bits can be transmitted by replacing every step of PARTITION(β) by $O(\frac{b}{\log n})$ steps, in each step broadcasting $\log n$ bits, originating at the cluster center. □

This implies Step (3) of our algorithm, in which we transmit $d^{0.3}$ values, blows up the coarse-grained clustering's running time by a factor of $O(d^{0.3})$.

4.1 Collisions During Precomputation

Lemma 2.1's and 2.2's respective algorithms' preprocessing take $O(D \cdot \log^{O(1)} n)$ rounds for a clustering of maximum diameter D. By our choices of β for the clusterings and Lemma 3.1, the coarse-grained clustering has maximum diameter $\sqrt{d} \log n$ and the $d^{0.3}$ fine-grained clusterings have maximum diameter $d^{0.01} \log n$. For the coarse-grained clusters, together with the blowup for step (3) mentioned above, this clustering's preprocessing takes $d^{0.8} \log n$ rounds. The preprocessing stages for the $d^{0.3}$ fine-grained clusterings take $O(d^{0.31} \log^{O(1)})$ rounds. Both bounds are $O(d/\log^{O(1)} n)$, so we can afford to blow up these algorithms' running time by a polylogarithmic factor in order to overcome potential collisions. As the next lemma asserts, this can be done.

Lemma 4.2. *Both the algorithms of Lemmas 2.1 and 2.2 can be implemented to succeed with high probability despite potential collisions, at a multiplicative cost of $\log^{O(1)} n$ to their preprocessing stages' running times.*

Proof. Collisions while running PARTITION(β) are addressed in the proof of Lemma 3.1. As for the Algorithm of Lemma 2.1, we replace every step of the algorithm of Lemma 2.1 by $O(\log^2 n)$-round meta-steps. In every constituent step of a meta-step, in any cluster C, with probability $\frac{1}{\log n}$, all nodes of the cluster C that broadcast in the original algorithm, do indeed broadcast. This is done by reusing $O(\log^2 n)$ random bits per cluster in round-robin order. (By Lemma 4.1, we may assume each cluster has $O(\log^2 n)$ bits corresponding to outcomes of such biased coin flips, by blowing up the running time of PARTITION(β) by a further $O(\log n)$ factor.) By Corollary 3.9, with high probability each node v neighbors at most $O(\frac{\log n}{\log d}) = O(\log n)$ different clusters. Consequently, the probability of a node v receiving a message it receives in the algorithm of Lemma 2.1 is $\Omega(1/\log n)$ and so with high probability this node will receive this message $\Omega(\log n)$ times, and in particular will receive it at least once, in the corresponding meta-step. Taking union bound over all nodes and steps of the algorithm, we find that with high probability this collision-overcoming strategy simulates the original algorithm despite potential collisions between clusters. □

4.2 Collisions Between Coarse Clusters

The following definition will prove constructive in addressing collisions of type 2.

Definition 4.1. *We say a node is* bad *if it has two different coarse-grained clusters within distance $d^{0.01} \cdot \log n$ of it. We say a path is* bad *if one of its nodes is bad.*

Consider a path p' of length $d^{0.1}$. By Corollary 3.8 and union bound, the probability of p' being bad is at most $\sum_{v \in p'} \Pr[v \text{ bad}] = O(d^{0.1} \cdot d^{0.01} \cdot \log n \cdot d^{-0.5}) = O(d^{-0.3})$. So, by linearity of expectation, the expected number of bad length-$d^{0.1}$ sub-paths of p in any partition of p into length-$d^{0.1}$ sub-paths is $O(\frac{d^{0.9}}{d^{0.3}}) = O(d^{0.6})$. Unfortunately, this expectation cannot be ascribed to the sum of independent random variables, so we cannot directly apply Chernoff bounds to obtain high concentration. Nonetheless, a more delicate analysis will yield the desired concentration, by writing the number of bad sub-paths as the sum of random variables which are themselves sums of independent random variables with high probability.

Lemma 4.3. *For any partition of a path p of total length $|p| \in [d/2, d]$ into length-$d^{0.1}$ sub-paths $p_1, p_2, \ldots, p_{d^{0.9}/|p|}$, the number of bad p_i is $O(d^{0.6})$ with high probability.*

Proof. By the above discussion $\Pr[p_i \text{ bad}] = O(d^{-0.3})$. Since all random shift values used to create the coarse-grained clustering by PARTITION(β) with $\beta = d^{-0.5}$ are at most $\frac{2 \log n}{\beta}$ with high probability, conditioning on $\max_u \delta_u \leq \frac{2 \log n}{\beta}$ does not change the probability space much; in particular, the probability of a sub-path p_i being bad remains $O(d^{-0.3})$. But, if $\max_u \delta_u \leq \frac{2 \log n}{\beta}$, then the events that any two sub-paths p_i, p_j of p at distance at least $\frac{5 \log n}{\beta} \geq \frac{4 \log n}{\beta} + 2d^{0.1}$ apart depend on a disjoint set of shift values. That is, the events that such distant sub-paths are bad are independent.

Denote by X the number of bad sub-paths in $p_1, \ldots, p_{d^{0.9}}$ and by X_i the bad sub-paths p_j indexed $j \equiv i \mod \frac{5 \log n}{\beta}$. By the above, if we condition on $\max_u \delta_u \leq \frac{2 \log n}{\beta}$, these X_i are sums of independent Bernoulli random variables with success probability $O(d^{-0.3})$, and are thus upper-bounded by binomials $Y_i \sim Bin(n', p')$, with parameters $n' = \frac{d^{0.9} \cdot \beta}{5 \log n}$ and $p' = \Theta(d^{-0.3})$. Plugging in $\beta = d^{-0.5}$, we find that $\mathbb{E}[Y_i] = n'p' = \Omega(d^{0.9} \cdot d^{-0.5}/\log n \cdot d^{-0.3}) = \Omega(\log n)$. By Chernoff bound each i satisfies $X_i \leq Y_i = O(\mathbb{E}[Y_i]) = O(n'/d^{0.3})$ with high probability. So, the number of bad sub-paths satisfies $X = O(d^{0.6})$ with high probability. □

The above lemma yields the following useful corollary.

Corollary 4.4. *On any path p of length $|p| \in [d/2, d]$ from an informed node to an uninformed node, the time spent by Divide and Chatter to transmit messages along bad sub-paths of p is $O(d)$ with high probability.*

Proof. By Lemma 4.3 p's bad sub-paths have overall length $O(d^{0.6} \cdot d^{0.1}) = O(\frac{d}{\log^2 n})$ with high probability. As our algorithm runs a step of Decay every two steps and Decay solves the 1-hop broadcast problem in $O(\log^2 n)$ rounds with high probability, transmitting along all bad sub-paths takes $O(d)$ rounds with high probability. □

4.3 Cutting out Collision-Prone Nodes

In this section we address collisions between fine-grained clusters within the same coarse-grained cluster when using their schedules; i.e., collisions of type 3.

The natural approach to overcome potential collisions between different fine-grained clusters in any coarse-grained cluster when running the schedules of Lemma 2.1 is simple: make nodes that border a cluster (other than their own) not participate in their clusters' fast schedule. That is, rather than taking entire clusters to be the induced subgraphs for which we run the schedules of Lemma 2.1, take the clusters (set)minus their nodes bordering other clusters, hoping that these new subgraphs have the same useful properties as the entire clusters. This approach, however, does not quite work, as these new subgraphs could have much higher diameter, and indeed need not even be connected. The following definition will prove useful in refining this approach.

Definition 4.2. *Consider a run of* PARTITION(β)*, and let* δ_v *be the exponential variables associated with each node. We say a node* v *is* risky *if the lowest two values in the (multi)set* $\{d(u,v) - \lfloor\delta_v\rfloor \mid u \in V\}$ *differ by at most one. Otherwise, we say the node* v *is* safe.

Recall that we condition on the (high probability) event that PARTITION(β) grows each cluster by one hop per epoch after the cluster's inception; that is, one hop every $O(\log^2 n)$ rounds, corresponding to one step of the sequential implementation. Given this conditioning, the set of safe nodes contains no nodes bordering other clusters, so running the fast schedules in their induced subgraphs avoids potential collisions between clusters. Crucially for our use, for any cluster $\mathcal{C}$, all safe nodes of $\mathcal{C}$ induce a connected component of diameter no greater than that of $\mathcal{C}$, as any safe node's path to its cluster center must be comprised solely of safe nodes. Therefore, the preprocessing stage of Lemma 2.1 can be run on subgraphs induced by the safe nodes in a cluster in the same time bounds as required to do the same for the entire cluster, namely $O(d)$ rounds. It remains to show how to notify risky nodes that they are risky without changing PARTITION(β)'s running time by too much.

Lemma 4.5. PARTITION(β) *can be run in* $O(\log^{O(1)} n/\beta)$ *rounds so that all risky nodes are informed that they are risky with high probability.*

Proof. We extend the radio network implementation discussed in Section 3.1. By Lemma 4.1 we may assume each cluster center sends some $O(\log^2 n)$ random bits to its cluster's nodes by blowing up the running time by $O(\log n)$.

Recall that each epoch of PARTITION(β) is implemented using $O(\log n)$ Decay phases in which clustered nodes inform their one-hop neighborhood of the fact. By a phase of Decay we mean broadcast with probability 2^{-i} for $i = 0, 1, 2, \ldots, \log_2 n - 1$. We modify the above in the following ways, using the random bits of each cluster in round-robin order: (1) during each Decay phase, for each cluster, all nodes of the cluster remain silent with probability $\frac{1}{2}$. (2) after each epoch, we run for a further $O(\log^2 n)$ phases of Decay during which for each cluster $\mathcal{C}$, with probability $\frac{1}{\log n}$, all risky nodes of $\mathcal{C}$ which have been notified of being risky broadcast one epoch after joining their cluster using a phase of Decay. As in our proof of Lemma 4.2, this guarantees that a node v neighboring such a risky node in its cluster will receive a message from one such neighbor with high probability within these $O(\log^2 n)$ Decay phases.

Consider a node v which borders a cluster other than its own, and is therefore risky. As each cluster is silent independently and with constant probability, the following hold with high probability: v receives $\Omega(\log n)$ message during any epoch neighbors of v may broadcast. Moreover, v receives a message from at least two distinct clusters either during the epoch in which v joins its cluster, or in the following epoch (depending on whether the two lowest values in $\{d(u,v) - \lfloor\delta_u\rfloor \mid u \in V\}$ differ by zero or one.) Either way, if v neighbors a cluster other than its own, v is notified that it is risky.

Now, consider a node w which does not border a cluster other than its own. Then, w is risky if and only if some node(s) v preceding w in a shortest path from w's cluster center u to w is (are) risky. As these risky nodes all have the same distance from the cluster center, they all broadcast at the end of the same epoch (the epoch following w's joining its cluster), and so w is notified of being risky one epoch after joining its cluster. Repeating the above, every risky node is notified of the fact by PARTITION(β)'s termination and no safe node is incorrectly notified of being risky. □

Lemma 4.6. *Let* p *be a path from an informed node to some node* t*. Then, if schedules are computed and run only for safe nodes of fine-grained clusters,* t *is informed after an expected* $O(|p| \cdot \frac{\log n \cdot \log\log n}{\log d})$ *rounds of step (6).*

Proof. Once a risky node is informed of the message the next node along p is informed in at most $O(\log^2 n)$ rounds, by virtue of the Decay steps. By Lemma 3.6 a node is risky with probability $O(\beta)$ and so the cost of informing risky nodes is $O(|p| \cdot \beta \cdot \log^2 n)$ rounds in expectation. For the largest possible β value we use in step (6), namely $\beta = O(1/d^{0.001})$, this is $O(|p|)$. We proceed to bound the cost incurred by safe nodes.

Consider some cluster of PARTITION(β). For a node v to be the first (resp., last) safe node along p in its cluster requires the next (resp., previous) node along p to be risky, hence the two lowest values of $\{d(u,v) - \lfloor\delta_v\rfloor \mid u \in V\}$ must differ by at most $O(1)$. By Lemma 3.11, if we denote by $\mathbb{1}_v$ an indicator for the event that v is a first or last safe node in its cluster along p, then for a fixed choice of i we have $\mathbb{E}[\mathbb{1}_v \cdot DCC(v)] = O(1 + \log k_i(v))$. As in our proof of Lemma 3.13, the time to transmit along p is commensurate to this expression, summed over all $v \in p$. By our bound on $\mathbb{E}_i[\log k_i(v)]$ of 3.2, the lemma follows. □

5. FINAL ANALYSIS

In this section we prove the main result of this paper. For succinctness, we say a path is *crossed* after r rounds if r rounds after the first node on this path is informed of a message, so is the last node. We will give a bound on the time to cross a path from an informed to an uniformed node.

Theorem 5.1. *The algorithm Divide and Chatter solves the* d*-hop broadcast problem in the radio network model in* $O(d \cdot \frac{\log n \log\log n}{\log d}) + \log^{O(1)} n$ *rounds with high probability.*

Proof. As discussed in Section 4, the preprocessing steps (1)-(5) all take $O(d)$ rounds despite potential collisions. It remains to prove $O(d \cdot \frac{\log n \log\log n}{\log d} + \log^{O(1)} n)$ rounds of step (6) suffice to solve the d-hop broadcast problem.

Consider a path p of length $|p| \in [d/2, d]$ from an informed node to an uninformed node, and let $p_1, p_2, \ldots, p_{|p|/d^{0.1}}$ be a partition of p into $\Theta(d^{0.9})$ sub-paths of length $d^{0.1}$. By Corollary 4.4, the time to cross all bad sub-paths is $O(d)$ with high probability. We proceed to bound the time spent on good sub-paths.

Now, consider X_j, the time to cross a good sub-path p_j. By Lemma 4.6, we know that $\mathbb{E}[X_j] = O(d^{0.1}\frac{\log n \log\log n}{\log d})$. We let the number of rounds spent using each random choice of $\beta = (2\log n)^{-i}$ in step (6) be twice this expectation. Therefore, by Markov's inequality the probability of crossing a sub-path within this many rounds is at least one half. As we ignore partial progress of the message along a sub-path when attempting to cross the same sub-path, these attempts are independent assuming independently-chosen i. Now, while the random choices of i are not strictly speaking independent, note that since we choose $d^{0.3}$ random i values and a sub-path of length $d^{0.1}$ is crossed with high probability within $O(\log n)$ attempts, the choices of i are independent w.h.p. for "close" sub-paths p_k, p_ℓ with $|k-\ell| \leq d^{0.2}/\log n$. Thus, by Chernoff bound, running step (6) for $2\mathbb{E}[X]$ rounds a total of $\Theta(d^{0.2}/\log n) = \Omega(\log n)$ times, we find that in any set of $d^{0.2}/\log n$ consecutive sub-paths of p we cross good sub-paths at least $d^{0.2}/\log n$ times with high probability; in particular, we cross *all* good sub-paths in this set. Summing over all such consecutive sets of sub-paths of p, we find that after $\Theta(d^{0.9})$ attempts to cross a path during $O(d^{0.1}\frac{\log n \log\log n}{\log d})$ rounds, we cross all good sub-paths of p. We conclude that for $d = \log^{\Omega(1)} n$, Divide and Chatter solves the d-hop broadcast problem in the radio network mode in $O(d\frac{\log n \log\log n}{\log d})$ rounds with high probability. □

6. ACKNOWLEDGMENTS

This research supported in part by NSF grant CCF-1527110 "Distributed Algorithms for Near Planar Networks" and NSF-BSF grant "Coding for Distributed Computing".

7. REFERENCES

[1] N. Alon, A. Bar-Noy, N. Linial, and D. Peleg, *A lower bound for radio broadcast*, Journal of Computer and System Sciences **43** (1991), no. 2, 290–298.

[2] R. Bar-Yehuda, O. Goldreich, and A. Itai, *On the time-complexity of broadcast in multi-hop radio networks: An exponential gap between determinism and randomization*, Journal of Computer and System Sciences **45** (1992), no. 1, 104–126.

[3] I. Chlamtac and S. Kutten., *On broadcasting in radio networks: Problem analysis and protocol design.*, IEEE Transactions on Communications **33** (1985), no. 12, 1240–1246.

[4] Ferdinando Cicalese, Fredrik Manne, and Qin Xin, *Faster centralized communication in radio networks*, Algorithms and Computation, Springer, 2006, pp. 339–348.

[5] A. Czumaj and W. Rytter, *Broadcasting algorithms in radio networks with unknown topology*, In Proc. IEEE Symp. on Foundations of Computer Science (2003), 492–501.

[6] Michael Elkin and Guy Kortsarz, *Improved schedule for radio broadcast*, Proceedings of the sixteenth annual ACM-SIAM symposium on Discrete algorithms, Society for Industrial and Applied Mathematics, 2005, pp. 222–231.

[7] Iris Gaber and Yishay Mansour, *Centralized broadcast in multihop radio networks*, Journal of Algorithms **46** (2003), no. 1, 1–20.

[8] Leszek Gasieniec, David Peleg, and Qin Xin, *Faster communication in known topology radio networks*, In Proc. ACM Symp. on Principles of Distributed Computing (2005), 129–137.

[9] M. Ghaffari and B. Haeupler, *Near-optimal leader election in multi-hop radio networks*, In Proc. ACM-SIAM Symp. on Discrete Algorithms (2013), 748–766.

[10] Mohsen Ghaffari, Bernhard Haeupler, and Majid Khabbazian, *Randomized broadcast in radio networks with collision detection*, Proceeding of the ACM SIGACT-SIGOPS Symposium on Principles of Distributed Computing (PODC) (2013), 325–334.

[11] D. Kowalski and A. Pelc, *Broadcasting in undirected ad hoc radio networks*, In Proc. ACM Symp. on Principles of Distributed Computing (2003), 73–82.

[12] Dariusz R Kowalski and Andrzej Pelc, *Optimal deterministic broadcasting in known topology radio networks*, Distributed Computing **19** (2007), no. 3, 185–195.

[13] E. Kushilevitz and Y. Mansour, *An $\Omega(d\log(n/d))$ lower bound for broadcast in radio networks*, SIAM Journal on Computing **27** (1998), no. 3, 702–712.

[14] Gary L Miller, Richard Peng, Adrian Vladu, and Shen Chen Xu, *Improved parallel algorithms for spanners and hopsets*, Proceedings of the 27th ACM on Symposium on Parallelism in Algorithms and Architectures, ACM, 2015, pp. 192–201.

[15] Gary L Miller, Richard Peng, and Shen Chen Xu, *Parallel graph decompositions using random shifts*, Proceedings of the twenty-fifth annual ACM symposium on Parallelism in algorithms and architectures, ACM, 2013, pp. 196–203.

[16] David Peleg, *Time-efficient broadcasting in radio networks: a review*, Distributed Computing and Internet Technology, Springer, 2007, pp. 1–18.

Broadcast Extensions with Optimal Communication and Round Complexity

Chaya Ganesh
Department of Computer Science
New York University
chaya.ganesh@gmail.com

Arpita Patra*
Department of Computer Science & Automation
Indian Institute of Science
arpita@csa.iisc.ernet.in

ABSTRACT

The problem of broadcast and Byzantine Agreement are of interest to both distributed computing and cryptography community. Often these primitives require prohibitive communication and round complexity. Broadcast extensions have been introduced to broadcast long messages at the cost of small number of broadcasts for bit. The latter are referred to as seed broadcasts.

In a setting with n parties and an adversary controlling at most t parties in Byzantine fashion such that $t < n$, we present a broadcast extension that is simultaneously optimal in terms of communication complexity and round complexity. Specifically, we achieve $\mathcal{O}(\ell n)$ bits of communication complexity for a message of length ℓ bits and $\mathcal{O}(n)$ round complexity. The known broadcast extension protocol in the same setting was only communication optimal.

A *concrete* broadcast extension protocol is obtained when the seed broadcasts are instantiated with broadcast protocols for bit. Our optimal broadcast extension protocol in $t < n$ setting leads to concrete extension protocols that improve the round complexity of existing concrete extension protocols by a factor of $\Omega(n)$. We also improve the state-of-the-art round complexity of the communication optimal concrete broadcast extension protocol in $t < n/2$ setting. The result comes as a corollary of a new extension protocol that improves both the round complexity as well as the *seed round complexity* of the existing extension protocols for $t < n/2$. The seed round complexity is defined as the number of rounds in which a broadcast for bit is invoked.

Keywords: Broadcast, Byzantine Agreement, Round complexity, Communication complexity, Seed Round Complexity

1. INTRODUCTION

Broadcast and Byzantine agreement (BA) are important primitives used widely in Multi-party computation (MPC) and distributed computing protocols in order to reach agreement on some messages. Most often, these higher level protocols need agreement to be reached on longer messages rather than single bits, which can be prohibitively expensive in terms of communication and round complexity. In a setting with n parties and an adversary controlling at most t parties in Byzantine fashion such that $t < n$, the best round complexity and communication complexity that can be achieved by a broadcast protocol for bit is $\Omega(\frac{n}{n-t})$ [GKKO07] and $\Omega(n^2)$ [DS83] respectively. Broadcast and BA extensions[1] are introduced and studied out of the need for efficient broadcast and BA protocols for *long messages*. The extension protocols achieve agreement for long messages relying on point-to-point communications and a small number of oracle access to a broadcast for bit. This is conceptually similar to Oblivious Transfer (OT) extension [IKNP03] where a large number of OTs are obtained at the cost of a small number of *seed* OTs and cheap symmetric key operations. It is well known that OT is a fundamental building block of MPC. We recall that OT [EGL85] is a protocol between a sender and a receiver where the sender with two inputs (x_0, x_1) can transmit x_σ to the receiver without knowing σ, where σ is the choice bit of the receiver. Following the OT extension literature, we too denote the broadcasts for bit used in the broadcast and BA extension protocols as *seed* broadcasts.

Four important parameters of extension protocols are: (i) communication complexity, (ii) round complexity, (iii) seed round complexity and (iv) seed communication complexity. The communication complexity of a protocol [Yao79] is defined to be the number of bits sent/received by the *honest* parties during the protocol execution. Note that, only the bits that should be received according to the protocol specification is counted. In any broadcast extension protocol, since each honest party must learn the message, a correct protocol will incur a communication complexity of at least $O(\ell n)$ where ℓ is the message length. We are interested in extensions that achieve this optimal communication complexity. The round complexity refers to the number of rounds taken by the protocol to terminate. In [HR14], it is shown that any broadcast extension protocol in dishonest majority setting requires $\Omega(n)$ rounds. The latter two complexity measures refer to the number of rounds in which a seed broadcast for bit is invoked and to the number of bits sent via seed broadcasts for bit. In any extension protocol, the optimal seed round complexity is one.

*Work partially supported by INSPIRE Faculty Fellowhsip (DST/INSPIRE/04/2014/015727) from Department of Science & Technology, India.

PODC'16, July 25-28, 2016, Chicago, IL, USA
© 2016 ACM. ISBN 978-1-4503-3964-3/16/07...$15.00
DOI: http://dx.doi.org/10.1145/2933057.2933082

[1] In the literature, they are known as multi-valued protocols.

1.1 Broadcast and Byzantine Agreement

In the Broadcast problem, a designated party (called the sender) holds an input message m, and the goal is for all parties to learn m and agree on it. In the related BA (consensus) problem, every party P_i holds a message m_i, and the goal is for all parties to agree on a common message. BA and broadcast have been studied in two settings: with or without a trusted set-up assumption. In the model where no set-up is assumed, information-theoretically secure BA (as well as broadcast) is achievable if and only if the number of corrupt parties t is at most $t < n/3$ where n is the total number of parties [PSL80, CW92, BGP92]. In the model where there is a set-up among the parties, BA is achievable for $t < n/2$ and broadcast is achievable for $t < n$ both cryptographically [DS83] and information theoretically [PW96]. The popular set-up assumption is a public-key infrastructure (PKI) set-up among n parties. By a PKI set-up among n parties, we mean the following: All parties hold a set of n public keys for a signature scheme where the ith key corresponds to the ith party. Every honest party holds the honestly-generated secret key associated with its own public key. The corrupted parties may generate their keys arbitrarily. The PKI set-up has been considered in two variants- (i) information-theoretic: a PKI set-up for an information-theoretically secure pseudo-signature scheme [PW96] (ii) cryptographic or computational: a PKI set-up for a cryptographically-secure unforgeable digital signature scheme [DS83].

1.2 Extension Protocols

Extension protocols for broadcast and BA are constructions from broadcast (of bit) and point-to-point communications. Historically, gaining communication efficiency motivated the study of such protocols. The seminal result of [DR85] shows that any BA or broadcast protocol must communicate $\Omega(n^2)$ bits. Since the message must be at least single bit, the lower bound on the communication complexity for single bit is $\Omega(n^2)$ bits. However, communication complexity of $\mathcal{O}(\ell n)$ bits can be achieved for large enough value of ℓ (at least $\ell \geq n$ bits) as shown in [FH06, LV11, Pat11, HR14]. Requiring large value for ℓ is practically motivated in many distributed computing applications, like reaching agreement on a large file in fault-tolerant distributed storage system, distributed voting where ballots containing gigabytes of data is to be handled [CGS97], Multi-party Computation [GMW87] where many broadcasts and agreements are invoked which can be combined into fewer executions of extension protocols.

A reduction of broadcast extension to broadcast for bit was first given in [TC84]. We denote the communication complexity of the broadcast of an s-bit message by $\mathcal{B}(s)$ or alternatively by $s\mathcal{B}(1)$. The protocol of [TC84] gives perfect security for $t < n/3$ and achieves a communication complexity of $O(\ell n^2 + n\mathcal{B}(1))$ bits for ℓ-bit message. The protocol given in [Pat11] gives perfect security for $t < n/3$ and achieves communication complexity of $\mathcal{O}(\ell n + n^2\mathcal{B}(1))$. A broadcast extension with information-theoretic security for the honest majority case with optimal communication complexity was given in [FH06]. More recently, in [HR14], the authors give constructions for a broadcast extension which achieve optimal communication complexity of $\mathcal{O}(\ell n)$ bits for $t < n$.

While it is known how to achieve optimal communication complexity in all the settings, the round and the seed round optimality has not been explored. Indeed, in some scenarios the latency associated with the communication rounds can be a huge bottleneck. The communication optimal protocol of [HR14] for $t < n$ has a round complexity of $\mathcal{O}(n^2)$ while the proven lower bound is $\mathcal{O}(n)$.

The seed round complexity of extension protocols is another measure that directly impacts the overall round complexity of extension protocols when broadcasts for bit are replaced with the corresponding protocols. This is because the broadcast protocols for bit have large round complexity as stated next. Any deterministic broadcast and BA protocol necessarily requires $(t+1)$ rounds [LF82, DR85]. Using randomization, the bound can be made constant in the honest majority setting [FM97, KK06]. But the round complexity is obtained in expected terms and importantly the constants are rather high for many practical purposes [KK06]. Specifically, the expected round complexity of the broadcast protocol of [KK06] in the honest majority setting is 56. If there are multiple sequential calls to the broadcast protocol, then, except the first call which takes expected 56 rounds, each additional call will cost expected 89 rounds. The usage of randomization does not help much in the dishonest majority setting which is considered to be the most practical setting. The proven lower bound on the round complexity for a broadcast protocol for bit is $\Omega(\frac{n}{n-t})$ [GKKO07]. The best known upper bound presented in [GKKO07] achieves expected $\mathcal{O}(k^2)$ round complexity when $t \leq n/2 + k$. The existing extension protocols invoke a broadcast protocol for bit in more than one round. The protocol of [HR14] for $t < n$ has a seed round complexity of $\mathcal{O}(n^2)$. The protocol of [FH06] for the $t < n/2$ case has a seed round complexity of 3. Extension protocols with optimal seed round complexity of one are thus highly desirable. On one hand, they lead to round efficient protocols in practice and on the other, they save us from any sequential compositional issues that arise for the sequential calls to the bit broadcasts.

1.3 Our Results

We present a broadcast extension protocol that is optimal in terms of both communication and round complexity beating the extension protocol of [HR14] that is only communication optimal. Our protocol has a round complexity and a seed round complexity of $\mathcal{O}(n)$. This is an $\Omega(n)$ improvement over the same complexities of the extension protocol of [HR14]. Next, we bring down the seed round complexity of communication optimal extension protocol to just 1 in $t < n/2$ setting. The round complexity of our protocol is 5. In $t < n/2$ setting, the best known communication optimal extension protocol has a round complexity of 6 and a seed round complexity of 3 [FH06]. All our protocols are cryptographically secure assuming a collision resistant hash function.

Our contributions put in context of other results are summarized in Table 1. We denote the communication complexity of a short s-bit message broadcast with $\mathcal{B}(s)$. κ denotes the cryptographic (statistical) security parameter for the cryptographic (information theoretic) primitives. 'i.t' denotes information theoretic.

A trivial construction to broadcast a long message is to broadcast bit by bit using a bit broadcast protocol. In Table 2, we list the complexities of the bit broadcast protocols when used to broadcast a ℓ bit message in various settings.

Table 1: Broadcast and BA Extension Protocols.

Threshold	Security	Communication Complexity	Round Complexity	Seed Round Complexity	Reference
$t < n/2$	i.t	$\mathcal{O}\left(\ell n + n^3\kappa + (n^2 + n\kappa)\mathcal{B}(1)\right)$	6	3	[FH06]
	cryptographic	$\mathcal{O}\left(\ell n + n^3\kappa + n\kappa\mathcal{B}(1)\right)$	5	1	This paper
$t < n$	i.t	$\mathcal{O}\left(\ell n + (n^4 + n^3\kappa)\mathcal{B}(1)\right)$	$\mathcal{O}(n^3)$	$\mathcal{O}(n^3)$	[HR14]
	cryptographic	$\mathcal{O}\left(\ell n + (n^2 + n\kappa)\mathcal{B}(1)\right)$	$\mathcal{O}(n^2)$	$\mathcal{O}(n^2)$	[HR14]
	cryptographic	$\mathcal{O}\left(\ell n + (n\kappa + n^3 \log n)\mathcal{B}(1)\right)$	$\mathcal{O}(n)$	$\mathcal{O}(n)$	This paper

Table 2: Broadcast protocols for bit.

Threshold	Security	Communication Complexity	Round complexity	Reference
$t < n/2$ and $t < n$	i.t	$\Omega\left(\ell n^2 + n^6\kappa\right)$	$\mathcal{O}(n)$	[PW96]
	cryptographic	$\Omega\left(\ell n^2 + n^3\kappa\right)$	$\mathcal{O}(n)$	[DS83]
$t < n/2$	cryptographic/i.t	$\mathcal{O}\left(\ell n^3 + n^6(\kappa + \log n)\right)$	56 (expected) for one call, $56 + 89c$ (expected) for $1 + c$ calls	[KK06]
$t \leq n/2 + k$	cryptographic	$\mathcal{O}\left(\ell(n^2k^2 + n^3) + n^6(\kappa + \log n)\right)$	$\mathcal{O}(k^2)$(expected)	[GKKO07]

Table 3: Concrete Broadcast and BA Extension Protocols.

Threshold	Security	Communication Complexity	Round complexity	Instantiation
$t < n/2$	i.t	$\mathcal{O}\left(\ell n + n^7\kappa\right)$	$\mathcal{O}(n)$	[FH06] with [PW96]
	cryptographic	$\mathcal{O}\left(\ell n + n^4(n + \kappa)\right)$	$\mathcal{O}(n)$	[FH06] with [DS83]
	cryptographic/i.t	$\mathcal{O}\left(\ell n + n^7\kappa(\kappa + \log n)\right)$	237 (expected)	[FH06] with [KK06]
	cryptographic	$\mathcal{O}\left(\ell n + n^4\kappa\right)$	$\mathcal{O}(n)$	This paper with [DS83]
	cryptographic	$\mathcal{O}\left(\ell n + n^7\kappa(\kappa + \log n)\right)$	60 (expected)	This paper with [KK06]
$t < n$	i.t	$\mathcal{O}\left(\ell n + n^{10}\kappa\right)$	$\mathcal{O}(n^4)$	[HR14] with [PW96]
	cryptographic	$\mathcal{O}\left(\ell n + n^5\kappa\right)$	$\mathcal{O}(n^3)$	[HR14] with [DS83]
	cryptographic	$\mathcal{O}\left(\ell n + n^6\kappa \log n\right)$	$\mathcal{O}(n^2)$	This paper with [DS83]
$t \leq n/2 + k$	cryptographic	$\mathcal{O}\left(\ell n + n^7\kappa(\kappa + \log n)\right)$	$\mathcal{O}(n^2k^2)$(expected)	[HR14] with [GKKO07]
	cryptographic	$\mathcal{O}\left(\ell n + (n^3k^2\kappa + n^9 \log n)(\kappa + \log n)\right)$	$\mathcal{O}(nk^2)$(expected)	This paper with [GKKO07]

A *concrete* broadcast extension protocol is obtained when the seed broadcasts are instantiated with broadcast protocols for bit. When our extension protocol is instantiated with an implementation of the bit broadcast oracle, the protocol also inherits assumptions from the implementation, for example, a PKI when instantiated with [DS83]. The complexity costs of possible instantiations after composing the bit broadcast protocols are summarized and compared with other protocols in Table 3. The security of the composed protocol is the 'minimal' security provided by the bit broadcast protocol and the extension protocol. Namely, the composed protocol will be information theoretically secure if and only if both the bit broadcast and the extension protocol are information theoretic. Otherwise, the composed protocol will be cryptographically secure. As seen from Table 3, our protocol that is simultaneously communication and round optimal leads to the *first* instantiation in dishonest majority setting with optimal $\mathcal{O}(\ell n)$ communication complexity and *overall* round complexity of $\mathcal{O}(n)$ after replacing the bit broadcasts with the protocol of [GKKO07] for some values of k. (For example, when $t \leq n/2 + k$ and k is a constant).

We leave as open questions, designing protocols for $t < n$ both in the information-theoretic and computational setting that are optimal in terms of all three major complexity measures: communication, round and seed round complexity.

2. MODELS AND DEFINITIONS

We work in the standard point-to-point network where the set of parties $\mathcal{P} = \{P_1, \cdots, P_n\}$ are connected by pairwise authenticated channels and communicate in synchronous rounds. The faultiness of the parties is modeled in terms of a monolithic adversary A corrupting t out of the n parties. A can make the corrupted parties deviate from the protocol in any desired manner. The parties who are not under the control of A are referred as *honest.* We now recall some definitions.

DEFINITION 1 (BROADCAST). *A protocol for a set of parties $\mathcal{P} = \{P_1, \cdots, P_n\}$, where a distinguished party called the sender, $P_s \in \mathcal{P}$ holds an initial input m is a broadcast protocol tolerating A, if the following properties are satisfied:*
- *Agreement. All the honest parties output the same value.*
- *Validity. If the sender is honest, all honest parties output the value m.*

DEFINITION 2 (BYZANTINE AGREEMENT). *A protocol for a set of parties $\mathcal{P} = \{P_1, \cdots, P_n\}$, where each party $P_i \in \mathcal{P}$ holds an initial input m_i is a Byzantine Agreement protocol tolerating A, if the following properties are satisfied:*
- *Agreement. All the honest parties output the same value.*
- *Validity. If every honest party P_i hold the same message $m_i = m$, then all honest parties output the value m.*

We consider two settings in this paper: (i) Dishonest majority: $n \geq t+1$ and (ii) Honest majority: $n \geq 2t+1$. In the former setting, only broadcast is possible and so we design a broadcast extension protocol with various optimal complexity measures. In the latter setting, a broadcast protocol can be obtained by making one call to a BA protocol plus $\mathcal{O}(\ell n)$ bits of communication over point-to-point channels. So we design a BA extension protocol with various optimal complexity measures. This implies a broadcast protocol with the optimal complexities in the latter setting.

Our protocols are cryptographically secure tolerating any polynomially bounded adversary A. Cryptographic or computational security guarantees that the protocol is secure based on some computational assumptions. Our protocols rely on a cryptographic collision-resistant hash function Hash. Collision resistance property guarantees that it is hard for a polynomially bounded adversary to come up with two preimages of Hash that hash to the same value.

A set-up assumption is needed in the setting $n \leq 3t$ for the bit broadcast oracle. Hence, our concrete protocols (after instantiation of the oracle) are secure assuming PKI and a collision-resistant hash function. The security analysis of our protocol is for a *static* adversary that corrupts parties at the beginning of the protocol.

3. BROADCAST EXTENSION IN DISHONEST MAJORITY SETTING

We present a broadcast extension protocol for ℓ bit message in the dishonest majority setting with two optimal measures: (i) communication complexity: $\mathcal{O}(\ell n)$ bits, (ii) round complexity: $\mathcal{O}(n)$. The protocol has a seed round complexity of $\mathcal{O}(n)$. In the same settings, the only known communication optimal broadcast extension protocol was given by [HR14] (will be referred as HR protocol henceforth). Both the round complexity and seed round complexity of the HR protocol are $\mathcal{O}(n^2)$. Our protocol is the first protocol that optimizes two significant parameters of a broadcast extension protocol simultaneously.

Like the HR protocol, our construction broadcasts the long message block by block sequentially using dispute control framework [BH06]. While overall communication complexity is guaranteed to be optimal, broadcasting each block may not be done with optimal communication complexity. Our dispute control framework ensures that a corrupted party gets a single chance to misbehave with an honest party. Once it is detected for wrong behaviour by an honest party in some execution of block broadcast, the corrupted party will be ignored by the honest party for the rest of the protocol. By maintaining a history of misbehaviours across block broadcasts, the dispute control framework help save expensive block communications between parties in dispute. At the heart of dispute control framework lies the art of maintaining history and using it carefully. Such a paradigm calls for sequential execution, and hence, often, the framework trades round complexity for communication complexity. When both the round and the communication overheads are of concern, the framework may not seem to be a wise choice. However, we hit the optimal communication and round complexity at the same time by implementing dispute control framework with overlapped sequential execution. At this point, we note a clear difference between our construction and HR construction. While the HR block broadcasts run sequentially without any overlap, our construction intertwines the block broadcasts cleverly, yet maintaining the optimal communication complexity. The result is our construction runs just for $\mathcal{O}(n)$ rounds beating the non-optimal $\mathcal{O}(n^2)$ round complexity of HR protocol.

Specifically, we divide the input message into n blocks. A broadcast round is then used to broadcast the hash values of the n blocks. The usage of broadcast ensures all the *honest* parties hold the same copies for the hash values. In an honest block broadcast protocol where everyone behaves honestly, it just requires $n-1$ point-to-point communication of the block in order to propagate it from the sender to the rest of the parties given that the hash value of the message block is already agreed upon and the underlying hash function is collision resistant. But the corrupted parties may behave arbitrarily. Although it may result in requiring more than $n-1$ point-to-point block communications, the honest parties will identify the corrupted parties who misbehaved and will ignore them for the rest of the protocol. Our protocol dmBC ('dm' stands for dishonest majority) is given below in Figure 1 which constitutes of two phases: (i) Hash Agreement Phase: It consists of just one round where P_s broadcasts the hashes $h^{(1)}, \ldots, h^{(n)}$ of the n message blocks using oracle access to broadcast bits so that the parties agree on the hash values of the blocks.; (ii) Block Agreement Phase: In this phase, the parties try to obtain the blocks from parties who already received it using *only* point-to-point communication such that the blocks verify against the agreed hash values.

We now concentrate on the block agreement phase where the agreement of blocks are done sequentially yet in an overlapped fashion. Specifically, a party P_i starts requesting for kth message block only when it has received the $(k-1)$th one. This reflects the sequential nature. The overlapping comes from the fact that the kth block agreement for P_i may run in parallel with the $(k-1)$th block agreement for P_j. This stems from the fact that a party P_i proceeds to kth block agreement once it receives the $(k-1)$th block and without waiting for others to receive the same. The protocol runs for $t+n$ rounds, where the earliest round to start asking for kth message block and the latest round to reach agreement on kth block are set to k and $t+k$ respectively. If no block matching the kth hash is received by the end of round $(t+k)$ round, then an honest party exits the while loop and outputs $\perp$. Our protocol guarantees that either all or none of the honest parties will get the message.

Every party maintains three kinds of sets. A local corrupt set $\mathcal{C}_i$ is used by party P_i to log the corrupted parties discovered across the blocks. For the kth block, every party P_i locally maintains a set of happy parties $\mathcal{H}_i^{(k)}$ and a set of unhappy parties $\overline{\mathcal{H}}_i^{(k)}$. From P_i's point of view, a party is happy if it declares to hold/receive a message block matching with the hash value $h^{(k)}$ and it broadcasts certain 'proof' along with the declaration. A party P_i promotes P_j to its happy set only when 'the proof verifies correctly'. Only P_s is considered to be happy initially for all the blocks.

Now let us understand how a particular block agreement is done. Consider the kth block. A party P_i who has received $(k-1)$th block and is still unhappy for the kth block checks if there is a party in its kth happy set $\mathcal{H}_i^{(k)}$ who it can ask for the kth message block. An unhappy (and *honest*) party P_i never requests a party for the message block more than once. Similarly, a happy (and *honest*) P_j does not entertain anyone more than once. To prevent the corrupted parties from making block request from multiple honest parties in a round, every party is made to broadcast the identity of its chosen party. A happy (and *honest*) P_j sends its message block to P_i over the point-to-point channel if and only if it receives a request from P_i via broadcast for the first time for a block. A matrix $\mathbf{T}^{(k)}$ is maintained by each party to dmBC

- **Input of P_s:** An ℓ bit message m.
- **Oracle:** Broadcast oracle for bits.
- **Cryptographic Assumption:** A collision resistant hash function Hash.

1. **Hash Agreement Phase:** The sender P_s does the following:
   1. Break the message m into n pieces by padding the end of the message if necessary so that all pieces are of the same length. Denote the n messages by $m^{(1)}, \cdots, m^{(n)}$.
   2. For $k = 1, \ldots, n$, compute $h^{(k)} = \mathsf{Hash}(m^{(k)})$ and broadcast $h^{(k)}$ to all parties.
2. **Block Agreement Phase:** Each party P_i does the following:
   1. Initialize
      - $\mathcal{C}_i$ to $\emptyset$, c_i to 1 and r to 1.
      - $\mathbf{T}_i^{(k)}[j,l] = 1$ for $j, l, k \in \{1, \ldots, n\}$
      - $\mathcal{H}_i^{(k)}, \overline{\mathcal{H}}_i^{(k)}$ to P_s and $\mathcal{P} \setminus P_s$ respectively for $k \in \{1, \ldots, n\}$
      - $o_i^{(k)}$ to $\perp$ if $P_i \neq P_s$, $o_i^{(k)} = m_i^{(k)}$ otherwise for $k \in \{1, \ldots, n\}$
   2. While $r \leq (n+t)$
      (a) If $P_i \in \overline{\mathcal{H}}_i^{(\mathsf{c}_i)}$, $\exists\, P_j \in \mathcal{H}_i^{(\mathsf{c}_i)} \setminus \mathcal{C}_i$ and $|\mathcal{H}_i^{(\mathsf{c}_i)} \cup \mathcal{C}_i| \geq r - \mathsf{c}_i + 1$, then broadcast $(\mathtt{send}, j, \mathsf{c}_i)$.
      (b) Let $(\mathtt{send}, x, y)$ be the output of the broadcast initiated by $P_j \notin \mathcal{C}_i$.
         i. if $\mathbf{T}_i^{(y)}[x,j] = 1$ and there is only one broadcast initiated by P_j, then set $\mathbf{T}_i^{(y)}[x,j] = 0$. If $x = i$ and $P_i \in \mathcal{H}_i^{(\mathsf{c}_i)}$, then send $o_i^{(\mathsf{c}_i)}$ to P_j over point-to-point channel.
         ii. else add P_j to $\mathcal{C}_i$.
      (c) If P_i broadcasted $(\mathtt{send}, j, \mathsf{c}_i)$ in step 2a: let $\overline{o_j^{(\mathsf{c}_i)}}$ denote the message block received from P_j over point-to-point channel.
         i. if $h^{(\mathsf{c}_i)} = \mathsf{Hash}(\overline{o_j^{(\mathsf{c}_i)}})$, then increment c_i by one, set $o_i^{(\mathsf{c}_i)} = \overline{o_j^{(\mathsf{c}_i)}}$ and finally broadcast $(\mathtt{happy}, \mathcal{H}_i^{(\mathsf{c}_i)}, \mathcal{C}_i, \mathsf{c}_i)$.
         ii. otherwise broadcast $(\mathtt{unhappy}, \mathsf{c}_i)$, add P_j to $\mathcal{C}_i$.
      (d) Let v be the output of the broadcast done by $P_j \notin \mathcal{C}_i$ in step 2c who broadcasted $(\mathtt{send}, *, *)$ in step 2a earlier this round:
         i. if $v = (\mathtt{happy}, \mathcal{H}_j^{x}, \mathcal{C}_j, x)$, $\mathcal{H}_j^{(x)} \cup \mathcal{C}_j \subseteq \mathcal{H}_i^{(x)} \cup \mathcal{C}_i$ and $|\mathcal{H}_j^{(x)} \cup \mathcal{C}_j| \geq r - x + 1$, then move P_j from $\overline{\mathcal{H}}_i^{(x)}$ to $\mathcal{H}_i^{(x)}$ and set $\mathcal{H}_i^{(x)} = \mathcal{H}_i^{(x)} \cup \mathcal{H}_j^{(x)}$.
         ii. if $v = (\mathtt{unhappy}, x)$, then do nothing.
         iii. else add P_j to $\mathcal{C}_i$.
      (e) If $r = \mathsf{c}_i + t$ and $P_i \in \overline{\mathcal{H}}_i^{(\mathsf{c}_i)}$, then exit *while* loop.
   3. If $o_i^{(k)} \neq \perp$ for all $1 \leq k \leq n$, then output $o_i^{(1)}|\cdots|o_i^{(n)}$. Else, output $\perp$.

Figure 1: Broadcast Protocol in Dishonest Majority Setting

detect repeated message send requests. A party who asks for the message block more than once from the same party is identified as corrupted. Next P_i, on receiving a message block from P_j can check if it matches with $h^{(k)}$. As $h^{(k)}$ is generated from a collision-resistant hash function, a corrupted P_j cannot trick an honest P_i by sending a wrong message block and yet pass the consistency check with $h^{(k)}$. Once P_i is happy, it prepares its proof and broadcasts the same. Intuitively, when P_s is corrupted, the proof enables to reach agreement on a block within the round limit fixed for the block. Namely, for the kth round, it is $k+t$. It ensures that the more the adversary delays the receipt of the block by the honest parties, the more it needs to expose the identities of the corrupted parties. We show that an honest party that moves to the kth happy set in round r will know at least $r-k$ corrupted parties. The proof further ensures that the delay cannot be beyond a limit. For the kth block, the first honest party must be allowed to be happy before round $k+t$. Otherwise all the honest parties will remain unhappy and would output a $\perp$ at the end of round $k+t$. More details follow.

Specifically, the proof of P_i for kth block in rth round is a happy set and corrupt set such that $|\mathcal{H}_i^{(k)} \cup \mathcal{C}_i| \geq r-k+1$ (excluding itself). If P_s is honest, then every honest party will get promoted to the kth happy sets of all the honest parties in the kth round itself as each one them can prepare a proof where the happy sets consists of P_s. For a corrupted P_s, the proof ensures that the first entry of an honest party in the kth happy sets of the honest parties *cannot* be in $(k+t)$th round. It must be in one of the previous rounds, because the proof in $(k+t)$th round requires $t+1$ distinct parties in the union of happy set and the corrupt set. Since an honest party will not belong to the corrupt set of another honest party, apart from self, the first honest entrant must include another honest party in its kth happy set. Therefore, there must be some other honest party who has become happy before $(k+t)$th round. We then show that if an honest party becomes happy in round r for the kth block such that $k \leq r < k+t$, then all the honest parties will be happy after running round $(k+t)$.

Lastly, to ensure that a corrupted party does not fake its proof by including parties that are not happy or corrupt, the proof is verified by checking if it is a subset of the union of the happy set and corrupt set of the verifier. An honest party's proof will always get verified by another honest party. We show that there is a one-to-one correspondence between the sets $\mathcal{H}_i^{(k)} \cup \mathcal{C}_i$ and $\mathcal{H}_j^{(k)} \cup \mathcal{C}_j$ of two honest parties P_i and P_j.

We now proceed to the proofs.

LEMMA 1 (COMPLEXITY). *Protocol* dmBC *has:*
(i) *a round complexity of* $\mathcal{O}(n)$,
(ii) *a seed round complexity of* $\mathcal{O}(n)$,
(iii) *a communication complexity of* $\mathcal{O}\big(\ell n+(n\kappa+n^3\log n)\mathcal{B}(1)\big)$ *bits and*
(iv) *a seed communication complexity of* $\mathcal{O}(n\kappa + n^3 \log n)$ *bits.*
for a message of ℓ*-bit length.*

PROOF. It is easy to verify the round complexity and the seed round complexity of the protocol.

We now compute the communication complexity by considering the communication received by each party. First, let us consider the communication received by an honest party. For every block of message, if an honest party eventually moves to the happy set, then it receives $\frac{\ell}{n}$ bits of message in order to move from the unhappy set to happy set. Across all the message blocks, it may in addition receive $\frac{\ell}{n}$ bits of wrong message block from each of the t corrupted parties. However, each such receipt will reveal the identity of one corrupted party. Thus, in total, the amount of communication received by an honest party in the protocol is $\mathcal{O}(\ell)$ bits. Now consider the communication received by a corrupted party. We need to focus on the communication made by the honest parties since a corrupted party can communicate as many bits as it wants to another corrupted party. A corrupted party cannot make an honest party to communicate any message block twice. Every honest party P_i keeps track of the list of parties it sends a message block to in the array $\mathbf{T}$. Once it sends the kth message block to P_x, it sets $\mathbf{T}^{(k)}[i,x]$ to 0. Thus, a corrupted party either moves to the happy set or creates a conflict with the honest party P_i. Irrespective of the case, the honest party P_i will not communicate the same message block to the same corrupted party for the second time. Thus, across all message blocks, a corrupted party can receive $\frac{\ell}{n}$ bits of message from each honest party to create conflicts with them. To move from unhappy set to happy set for each message block, it may receive $\frac{\ell}{n}$ bits of message from some honest party. Overall it counts to receipt of $\mathcal{O}(\ell)$ bits. Now counting over all parties, we get that the overall received message complexity is $\mathcal{O}(\ell n)$ bits. Since the communication complexity is same as the received bit complexity, we conclude that the communication complexity is $\mathcal{O}(\ell n)$ bits.

We now count the part of the communication complexity that is independent of ℓ and is broadcasted. In the Hash Agreement phase, P_s broadcasts n hash values corresponding to n message blocks. This requires a communication of $\mathcal{B}(n|h|)$ bits. Next, we consider the communication involved in the Block Agreement phase. For kth block, every party P_i will broadcast $(\texttt{happy}, \mathcal{H}_i^{(k)}, \mathcal{C}_i, k)$ only in the round when it moves from its unhappy set to happy set. In the worst case, it may broadcast $(\texttt{send}, j, \mathsf{c}_i)$ and $(\texttt{unhappy}, \mathsf{c}_i)$ in every round. We may assume the size of $\mathcal{H}_i^{(k)}$ and $\mathcal{C}_i$ to be $\mathcal{O}(t)$. This results in a communication of $\mathcal{B}(n \log n)$ bits per party per message block. Summing over all the blocks and all the parties, we get that a communication of $\mathcal{B}(n^3 \log n)$ bits is required. Assuming $|h^{(k)}| = \kappa$, the communication that is independent of ℓ turns out to be $\mathcal{B}(n\kappa + n^3 \log n)$ bits. Thus the ℓ independent communication complexity is $\mathcal{O}((n\kappa + n^3 \log n)\mathcal{B}(1))$ bits.

The communication complexity of protocol dmBC is, thus, $\mathcal{O}\big(\ell n+(n\kappa+n^3\log n)\mathcal{B}(1)\big)$ bits and the seed communication complexity is $\mathcal{O}(n\kappa + n^3 \log n)$ bits. □

LEMMA 2 (VALIDITY). *Assume that* Hash *is a collision-resistant hash function. In protocol* dmBC, *if* P_s *is honest then every honest party will output sender's message.*

PROOF. The validity follows from the fact that all the honest parties ask for and receive the kth message block from P_s in the kth round of the *while* loop and move to the kth happy set $\mathcal{H}^{(k)}$ of all the honest parties. Formally, the proof goes as follows. Before the start of the *while* loop, $\mathcal{H}_i^{(k)}$ is set to P_s for all $k \in \{1, \ldots, n\}$. Consider the kth message block. In the kth round of the *while* loop, the condition $|\mathcal{H}_i^{(k)}| \geq r - k + 1$ will hold for any honest party P_i, since both $|\mathcal{H}_i^{(k)}|$ and $r - k + 1$ are equal to 1. The latter is true because we are considering the kth round and hence $r = k$. Every honest party P_i does the following in the given order (i) It asks for the kth message block from P_s and will receive the same; (ii) It broadcasts $(\texttt{happy}, \mathcal{H}_i^{(k)}, \mathcal{C}_i, k)$ where, $\mathcal{H}_i^{(k)} = \{P_s\}$, sets $o_i^{(k)}$ to $m^{(k)}$ and increments block count c_i by one; (iii) At the end of kth round, it outputs $o_i^{(k)}$ which is the same as $m^{(k)}$, since P_s is honest. At the end of protocol dmBC, every honest P_i will output $m^{(1)}|\ldots|m^{(n)}$ which is same as the sender's message m. □

We now prove the agreement property via a sequence of lemmas on the dmBC protocol.

LEMMA 3. *In the start of any round* r *for* $1 \leq r \leq n+t$, *the condition* $\mathcal{H}_i^{(k)} \cup \mathcal{C}_i \subseteq \mathcal{H}_j^{(k)} \cup \mathcal{C}_j$ *is true for any two honest parties* P_i *and* P_j *for any* $k \in \{1, \ldots, n\}$.

PROOF. Consider any party P_α that enters $\mathcal{H}_i^{(k)}$ in round r for $1 \leq r \leq n+t$. We show that P_α will belong to $\mathcal{H}_j \cup \mathcal{C}_j$ in the same round r. Since P_α enters $\mathcal{H}_i$ in round r, the following must be true: (i) P_i has received P_α's broadcast $(\texttt{send}, x, y)$ such that $\mathbf{T}_i^{(y)}[x,\alpha] = 1$ and there is only one broadcast initiated by P_α in this round; and (ii) P_i has received P_α's broadcast $(\texttt{happy}, \mathcal{H}_\alpha^{(k)}, \mathcal{C}_\alpha, k)$ such that the conditions $\mathcal{H}_\alpha^{(k)} \cup \mathcal{C}_\alpha \subseteq \mathcal{H}_i^{(k)} \cup \mathcal{C}_i$ and $|\mathcal{H}_\alpha^{(k)} \cup \mathcal{C}_\alpha| \geq r - k + 1$ hold. P_j will also receive P_α's broadcast $(\texttt{send}, x, y)$ such that $\mathbf{T}_i^{(y)}[x,\alpha] = 1$ and this will be the only broadcast initiated by P_α in this round. Furthermore, P_j also receives P_α's broadcast $(\texttt{happy}, \mathcal{H}_\alpha^{(k)}, \mathcal{C}_\alpha, k)$. Now, if $\mathcal{H}_\alpha^{(k)} \cup \mathcal{C}_\alpha \subseteq \mathcal{H}_j^{(k)} \cup \mathcal{C}_j$, then P_j will move P_α to its happy set. Otherwise, P_j will add P_α to $\mathcal{C}_i$. It can never happen that P_α is moved to $\mathcal{H}_i^{(k)}$ by P_i, but P_j has neither moved it to $\mathcal{H}_j^{(k)}$ nor added to $\mathcal{C}_j$.

Consider any party P_α that enters $\mathcal{C}_i$ in round r for $1 \leq r \leq n+t$. We show that P_α belongs to $\mathcal{H}_j \cup \mathcal{C}_j$ in the same round r. P_α may enter $\mathcal{C}_i$ for an honest P_i because of one of the following reasons:

(i) P_i has received P_α's broadcast $(\texttt{send}, x, y)$ such that one of the following is true. Either $\mathbf{T}_i^{(y)}[x, \alpha]$ is already set to 0 (i.e. P_α has asked for the kth message block from P_x earlier) or there is more than one broadcast initiated by P_α in this round. In either case P_j will also add P_α to its corrupt set $\mathcal{C}_j$.

(ii) P_i has received P_α's broadcast $(\texttt{happy}, \mathcal{H}_\alpha^{(k)}, \mathcal{C}_\alpha, k)$ such that either of the conditions $\mathcal{H}_\alpha^{(k)} \cup \mathcal{C}_\alpha \subseteq \mathcal{H}_i^{(k)} \cup \mathcal{C}_i$ and $|\mathcal{H}_\alpha^{(k)} \cup \mathcal{C}_\alpha| \geq r-k+1$ are not true. P_j will also receive the same broadcast. Based on whether the conditions are true for P_j or not, P_j will either add P_α to $\mathcal{C}_j$ or move it to $\mathcal{H}_j^{(k)}$. But it cannot happen that P_j has not added P_α to either of the two sets.

(iii) P_i had requested P_α for the kth message block but has not received one matching with $h^{(k)}$. Then it must be the case that P_α belongs to the set $\mathcal{H}_i^{(k)}$ of P_i in the end of $(r-1)$th round itself. By the first part of our proof, P_j contains P_α in $\mathcal{H}_j \cup \mathcal{C}_j$ by the end of round $(r-1)$ too.

Together, we can conclude that every P_α belonging to $\mathcal{H}_i^{(k)} \cup \mathcal{C}_i$ belongs to $\mathcal{H}_j^{(k)} \cup \mathcal{C}_j$ for honest parties P_i and P_j at the start of any given round. Thus, the condition $\mathcal{H}_i^{(k)} \cup \mathcal{C}_i \subseteq \mathcal{H}_j^{(k)} \cup \mathcal{C}_j$ is true for any two honest parties P_i and P_j for any $k \in \{1, \ldots, n\}$. □

DEFINITION 3 (VALIDITY OF $\mathcal{C}_i$). *We say that a set $\mathcal{C}_i$ is valid if for honest P_i, and for all honest parties P_j $P_j \notin \mathcal{C}_i$.*

Below we prove that protocol dmBC ensures $\mathcal{C}_i$ remains valid throughout for an honest P_i.

LEMMA 4. *The set $\mathcal{C}_i$ is valid for an honest party P_i.*

PROOF. We note that an honest party adds a party P_j in corrupt set $\mathcal{C}_i$ when either of the following are true: (i) it receives multiple broadcasts from P_j of the form $(\texttt{send}, x, y)$ in different rounds or in the same round or (ii) it receives multiple broadcasts from P_j of the form $(\texttt{send}, x, y)$ and $(\texttt{send}, x', y')$ in the same round where $x \neq x'$ or (iii) it did not receive a message block from P_j upon request that matches with the corresponding hash value or (iv) it receives $(\texttt{happy}, \mathcal{H}_j^{(k)}, \mathcal{C}_j, k)$ for some k from P_j in round r such that either $|\mathcal{H}_j^{(k)} \cup \mathcal{C}_j| < r-k+1$ or $\mathcal{H}_j^{(k)} \cup \mathcal{C}_j \not\subseteq \mathcal{H}_i^{(k)} \cup \mathcal{C}_i$. P_j is clearly corrupted when any of the conditions stated in (i)-(iii) hold. Now, for the conditions in (iv), if P_j was honest it would not broadcast $(\texttt{happy}, \mathcal{H}_j^{(k)}, \mathcal{C}_j, k)$ such that $|\mathcal{H}_j^{(k)} \cup \mathcal{C}_j| < r-k+1$. By Lemma 3, for any two honest parties P_i and P_j, $\mathcal{H}_j^{(k)} \cup \mathcal{C}_j \subseteq \mathcal{H}_i^{(k)} \cup \mathcal{C}_i$ is true at the beginning of the round when $(\texttt{happy}, \mathcal{H}_j^{(k)}, \mathcal{C}_j, k)$ is broadcasted. If it is not true, then P_j is corrupted. □

The next lemma makes the following statements equivalent: For any k, in the kth block broadcast (i) an honest party moves from its kth unhappy set to kth happy set in round r (ii) an honest party moves from the kth unhappy set to the kth happy set of *every* honest party in round r.

LEMMA 5. *For any k, if an honest party P_i moves from $\overline{\mathcal{H}}_\alpha^{(k)}$ to $\mathcal{H}_\alpha^{(k)}$ for an honest party P_α in rth round, then it moves from $\overline{\mathcal{H}}_\beta^{(k)}$ to $\mathcal{H}_\beta^{(k)}$ for every other honest party P_β in the same round.*

PROOF. We note that the test done by P_α and P_β for promoting P_i to their happy sets are identical: P_α checks $\mathcal{H}_i^{(k)} \cup \mathcal{C}_i \subseteq \mathcal{H}_\alpha \cup \mathcal{C}_\alpha$ while P_β checks $\mathcal{H}_i^{(k)} \cup \mathcal{C}_i \subseteq \mathcal{H}_\beta^{(k)} \cup \mathcal{C}_\beta$. It follows from Lemma 3 that both will hold. □

We now prove the following lemma: For any k, if an honest and unhappy party moves a party to its kth happy set in rth round, then it will know at least $r-k+1$ corrupted parties by the end of rth round where $k \leq r \leq k+t$.

LEMMA 6. *For any k, if an honest party P_i is in $\mathcal{H}_i^{(k-1)}$ before rth round but in $\overline{\mathcal{H}}_i^{(k)}$ till the end of rth round and moved a party from $\overline{\mathcal{H}}_i^{(k)}$ to $\mathcal{H}_i^{(k)}$ in the rth round where $k \leq r \leq k+t$, then $|\mathcal{C}_i| \geq r-k+1$.*

PROOF. We prove the lemma using strong induction on r. We start with the following observation. Let P_j be the party that moved from $\overline{\mathcal{H}}_i$ to $\mathcal{H}_i$ in the rth round. This implies that the conditions $\mathcal{H}_j^{(k)} \cup \mathcal{C}_j \subseteq \mathcal{H}_i^{(k)} \cup \mathcal{C}_i$ and $|\mathcal{H}_j^{(k)} \cup \mathcal{C}_j| \geq r-k+1$ are true. From these two conditions, we can conclude that $|\mathcal{H}_i^{(k)} \cup \mathcal{C}_i| \geq r-k+1$ in the beginning of rth round itself (excluding P_j).

Base Case. Assume r to be the first round when P_i moved at least one party from $\overline{\mathcal{H}}_i^{(k)}$ to $\mathcal{H}_i^{(k)}$ and P_i is in $\overline{\mathcal{H}}_i$ till the end of rth round. We have $k \leq r \leq k+t$. Since before rth round no party has moved to $\mathcal{H}_i^{(k)}$, $\mathcal{H}_i^{(k)}$ consists of only P_s. Furthermore, P_s must be corrupted as P_i is still unhappy. Therefore, all the parties in $\mathcal{H}_i^{(k)}$ are corrupted. Since we have $|\mathcal{H}_i^{(k)} \cup \mathcal{C}_i| \geq r-k+1$ in the beginning of rth round, we can conclude that $|\mathcal{C}_i| \geq r-k+1$ in round r.

Induction Step. Assume the lemma statement is true for all the rounds starting from k to $r-1$. We will prove the statement for round r.

Now, assume that r' is the last round before r when P_i moved at least one party from $\overline{\mathcal{H}}_i^{(k)}$ to $\mathcal{H}_i^{(k)}$. We have $r' < r$. Since P_i must have been unhappy in round r' too, we have $|\mathcal{C}_i| \geq r'-k+1$ by the end of round r' via induction hypothesis. According to the protocol, the following condition will be satisfied for P_i in the end of round r': $|\mathcal{H}_i^{(k)} \cup \mathcal{C}_i| \geq r'-k+2$ after moving P_j to the happy set. Now we have two cases to consider.

(i) First, if P_i asks for the kth message block from some party in its happy set $\mathcal{H}_i^{(k)}$ in every round starting from round r' until round r, then P_i discovers $r-(r'-1)+1 = r-r'$ additional corrupt parties since it remains unhappy in the end of rth round. We therefore conclude that $|\mathcal{C}_i| \geq (r'-k+1)+(r-r') = r-k+1$ in this case.

(ii) The other possibility is that P_i asks for the kth message block for some rounds starting from round $r'+1$ but stops asking before round r. By assumption, the happy set $\mathcal{H}_i^{(k)}$ of P_i did not grow between r'th and rth round. In this case, we can conclude that all the parties that belong to $\mathcal{H}_i^{(k)}$ until the beginning of round r

are corrupted since none of them delivered P_i a message block that is consistent with $h^{(k)}$. Since we have $|\mathcal{H}_i^{(k)} \cup \mathcal{C}_i| \geq r - k + 1$ in the beginning of rth round and all the parties in $\mathcal{H}_i^{(k)}$ until the beginning of round r are corrupted, we have $|\mathcal{C}_i| \geq r - k + 1$.

□

We now prove a lemma that captures the fact that, the more an honest party is delayed in receiving a message block, the more the number of corrupted parties it discovers.

LEMMA 7. *For any k, if an honest party P_i moves to $\mathcal{H}_i^{(k)}$ in rth round where $k \leq r \leq k + t$, then $|\mathcal{C}_i| \geq r - k$.*

PROOF. We first prove the lemma assuming that P_i has not moved any party to $\mathcal{H}_i^{(k)}$ before round r. This means $\mathcal{H}_i^{(k)}$ contains P_s alone and P_i must have become happy on receiving the kth message block from P_s. This implies two things: first, it must have received all the previous message blocks from P_s too; second, r must be k. In this case, P_i knows zero corrupted parties. Since $r = k$, we have $|\mathcal{C}_i| \geq r - k$ at the end of round r. We now prove the lemma for the case when P_i does not receive the message blocks from P_s and has moved some party to $\mathcal{H}_i^{(k)}$ before rth round. We prove the lemma using induction on k.

Base Case. Assume $k = 1$. That is, we are considering the first message block. P_i has moved some party to $\mathcal{H}_i^{(k)}$ before rth round. Let r' be the last round when P_i does so. We have $1 \leq r' < r$. By Lemma 6, P_i knows at least $r' - k + 1 = r'$ corrupted parties by the end of r'th round. According to the protocol, by the end of round r', $|\mathcal{H}_i^{(1)} \cup \mathcal{C}_i| \geq r' - k + 2 = r' + 1$. Therefore, P_i will have parties in $\mathcal{H}_i^{(1)}$ that are not in $\mathcal{C}_i$ to ask for the message block. Since P_i has become happy in rth round, it must have been asking distinct parties for the message block, starting from round $(r' + 1)$ and upto round r. None of the parties that it asked for the message until round $r - 1$ delivered it a message block matching $h^{(1)}$. This implies it discovers $(r-1)-(r'+1)+1 = (r-r'-1)$ corrupted parties starting from round $(r'+1)$ and until round $(r-1)$. These identities are distinct from the r' parties it knew by the end of round r'. In total, P_i knows at least $r' + (r - r' - 1) = r - 1$ corrupted parties by the end of round r. Since $k = 1$, we have $|\mathcal{C}_i| \geq r - 1 = r - k$ at the end of round r.

Induction Step. Assume the lemma is true for all the message blocks upto $k - 1$. We now prove the lemma for the kth message block. Say, P_i moves to $\mathcal{H}_i^{(k-1)}$ in r_{k-1}th round where $(k - 1) \leq r \leq (k - 1 + t)$. By induction hypothesis, $|\mathcal{C}_i| \geq r_{k-1} - (k - 1)$ by the end of r_{k-1}th round. Now we consider two cases based on when P_i moves some party to $\mathcal{H}_i^{(k)}$ before round r.

(i) The last time P_i moves some party to its happy set $\mathcal{H}_i^{(k)}$ is in or before r_{k-1}th round. P_i had been asking for kth message block starting from round $(r_{k-1} + 1)$ to rth round. It has become happy only in round r. Until round $(r - 1)$, it discovers $(r - 1) - (r_{k-1} + 1) + 1 = r - r_{k-1} - 1$ corrupted parties which are different from $r_{k-1} - k + 1$ corrupted parties it knew by the end of round r_{k-1}. In total P_i now knows $(r - r_{k-1} - 1) + (r_{k-1} - k + 1) = r - k$ corrupted parties at the end of rth round.

(ii) The last time P_i moves some party to its happy set $\mathcal{H}_i^{(k)}$ is after r_{k-1}th round, say, in round r' such that $r_{k-1} < r' < r$. By Lemma 6, P_i knows at least $r' - k + 1$ corrupted parties by the end of r'th round. According to the protocol, by the end of round r', $|\mathcal{H}_i^{(k)} \cup \mathcal{C}_i| \geq r' - k + 2$. Hence, P_i will have parties in $\mathcal{H}_i^{(k)}$ that are not in $\mathcal{C}_i$ to ask for the message block starting from round $(r' + 1)$. Now, since P_i became happy in rth round, it must have been asking distinct parties for the message block starting from round $(r' + 1)$ and upto round r. None of the parties that it asked for the message until round $r - 1$ delivered it a message block matching with $h^{(k)}$. This implies it discovers $(r - 1) - (r' + 1) + 1 = (r - r' - 1)$ corrupted parties starting from round $(r' + 1)$ and until round $(r - 1)$. These identities are distinct from the r' parties it knew by the end of round r'. In total, P_i knows at least $(r' - k + 1) + (r - r' - 1) = r - k$ corrupted parties by the end of round r. We have $|\mathcal{C}_i| \geq r - k$ at the end of round r.

□

The following lemma states that for any k, if one honest party moves to the kth happy sets of the honest parties in rth round where $k \leq r < k + t$, then every honest party will move to the kth happy sets of the honest parties before round $(k+t)$. This lemma will let us prove that either all or none of the honest parties will be happy for the kth message block which in turn will lead us to the proof of the agreement property of our protocol dmBC.

LEMMA 8. *For any k, if some honest party P_i moves from $\overline{\mathcal{H}}_j^{(k)}$ to $\mathcal{H}_j^{(k)}$ for every honest party P_j in round r such that $k \leq r < k + t$, then every honest party will move from $\overline{\mathcal{H}}_j^{(k)}$ to $\mathcal{H}_j^{(k)}$ before $(k + t)$th round.*

PROOF. Let P_i be the first honest party that moves to the kth happy set $\mathcal{H}_j^{(k)}$ of honest P_j. Also let P_i moves to the happy set $\mathcal{H}_j^{(k)}$ of P_j in round r such that $k \leq r < k + t$. We now show that P_j will move to the kth happy sets of all the parties in or before $(k + t)$th round. Let r_{k-1} be the round number when P_j has moved to $\mathcal{H}_j^{(k-1)}$ where $(k - 1) \leq r_{k-1} \leq (k - 1) + t$. Now we complete our proof by considering the following two possible cases:

(i) $r_{k-1} < r$: By Lemma 6, P_j knows at least $r - k + 1$ corrupted parties by the end of rth round. At the end of rth round, honest P_j will have $|\mathcal{H}_j^{(k)} \cup \mathcal{C}_i| \geq r - k + 2$ after including P_i. Therefore, P_j will have at least one party to ask for the message block in $(r + 1)$th round. Now, if P_j talks to P_i in some round in or before $(k + t)$th round, then it moves to its happy set $\mathcal{H}_j^{(k)}$ after receiving the message block. So let us assume that P_j does not ask for the kth message block from P_i. This implies that P_j was requesting for the message block from parties other than P_i in each of the rounds starting from the $(r + 1)$th round. It is not possible that P_j has not asked for the block from anyone in some round after the rth round. This is because P_i will be in its happy set post rth round and by Lemma 4, P_i will not be in $\mathcal{C}_j$ as both P_i and P_j are honest. We therefore conclude that P_j talks to some party in its kth happy set in each of the rounds starting from the $(r+1)$th round and until $(k+t)$th round. Now P_j talks to $(k+t)-(r+1)+1 = k+t-r$ parties in its happy set starting from $(k+x)$th round to $(k+t)$th round. These $k+t-r$ parties are different from the $r-k+1$ corrupted parties P_j had in its corrupt list $\mathcal{C}_j$ at the end of rth round. If all the $k+t-r$ parties are corrupted, then total number of corrupted parties will be $x+t-x+1 = t+1$. This is a contradiction. One out of the $k+t-r$ parties must, therefore, be honest and belong to P_j's happy set $\mathcal{H}_j^{(k)}$. After getting the message block from the honest party in its happy set $\mathcal{H}_j^{(k)}$, P_j will move to its happy set too.

(ii) $r_{k-1} \geq r$: By Lemma 7, P_j will know at least $r_{k-1}-(k-1)$ corrupt parties by the end of round r_{k-1}. At the start of round $(r_{k-1}+1)$, P_i has $|\mathcal{C}_j| \geq r_{k-1}-(k-1)$ and its happy set $\mathcal{H}_j^{(k)}$ contains honest P_i that cannot belong to $\mathcal{C}_j$ by Lemma 4. So clearly $|\mathcal{H}_j^{(k)} \cup \mathcal{C}_j| \geq r_{k-1}-(k-1)+1 = (r_{k-1}+1)-k+1$ holds good in the beginning of round $(r_{k-1}+1)$. This implies P_j will ask for kth message block starting from round $(r_{k-1}+1)$. Now if it asks for the kth message block from P_i in some round before $k+t$, then it gets promoted to $\mathcal{H}_j^{(k)}$. If it does not ask P_i, then it must be asking other parties in its kth happy set in every round starting from round $(r_{k-1}+1)$ and until round $(k+t)$. By the end of $k+t$ rounds, if it has not got promoted to the kth happy set, then it discovers $(k+t)-(r_{k-1}+1)+1 = k+t-r_{k-1}$ corrupted parties. These are different from $r_{k-1}-(k-1)$ corrupt parties P_j knew by the end of round r_{k-1}. Therefore, the total corrupted parties will have to be $k+t-r_{k-1}+r_{k-1}-(k-1) = t+1$. This is a contradiction. Hence, we conclude P_j will talk to some honest party and get promoted to $\mathcal{H}_j^{(k)}$ by the end of round $(k+t)$.

Recall that by Lemma 5, an honest party will be promoted to the kth happy set respectively by all honest parties in the same round. P_j, will therefore, be promoted to the kth happy sets of all the honest parties. Now *every* honest P_j will move to the kth happy sets of all the parties since honest P_i will move to the kth happy set of every honest P_j in the same round (again due to Lemma 5). □

LEMMA 9. *For any k, either all or none of the honest parties will be in the kth happy sets of the honest parties.*

PROOF. By Lemma 8, if one honest party moves to the kth happy sets of the honest parties in rth round where $k \leq r < k+t$, then every honest party will move to the kth happy sets of the honest parties on or before $(k+t)$th round of the *while* loop. We now show that if at all an honest party moves to the kth happy set of the honest parties, the first such move happens in round r where $k \leq r < k+t$. Assume that P_i is the first honest party to enter to the kth happy sets of the honest parties. Also assume that P_i is moved to the kth happy sets in the $(k+t)$th round. Then P_i must have at least $(k+t)-k+1 = t+1$ parties in $\mathcal{H}_i^{(k)} \cup \mathcal{C}_i$ excluding itself during the broadcast of $(\texttt{happy}, \mathcal{H}_i^{(k)}, \mathcal{C}_i, k)$. Since there are at most t corrupted parties, there is already one honest party included in $\mathcal{H}_i^{(k)}\mathcal{C}_i$. By Lemma 4, the honest party cannot belong to $\mathcal{C}_i$. So it must be in $\mathcal{H}_i^{(k)}$. This contradicts our assumption that P_i is the first honest party to move to the kth happy set of every honest party.

We conclude that if one honest party moves to the kth happy set of the honest parties before $(k+t)$th round, then all the honest parties move to the kth happy sets by the end of $(k+t)$th round. Otherwise, none of the honest parties enter in the kth happy sets of the honest parties. □

LEMMA 10. *Assume that* Hash *is a collision-resistant hash function. For any k, all the honest parties in $\mathcal{H}_i^{(k)}$ for an honest P_i hold the same value.*

PROOF. This follows from the fact that Hash is a collision-resistant hash function and every honest party has an identical copy of $h^{(k)}$ (since it is broadcasted). Even a corrupted party cannot find a different image of $h^{(k)}$. Therefore, even if an honest party receives the kth message block from a corrupted party, the message block must be the same as the kth message block possessed by the honest parties in the happy set of an honest party (with very high probability). □

We are now ready to prove the agreement property of dmBC protocol.

LEMMA 11 (AGREEMENT). *In protocol* dmBC, *every honest party will output the same message.*

PROOF. By Lemma 9, either all or none of the honest parties are present in the kth happy sets of all the honest parties for any k. If all of them are present, then by Lemma 10 they will hold the same block. If none of them are present, then they will hold $\perp$. Agreement, therefore, holds for every block of message. Agreement over the entire message follows easily. □

THEOREM 4. *Assume that* Hash *is a collision-resistant hash function. The protocol* dmBC *satisfies:*

Agreement: Every honest party will output the same message.

Validity: If the sender is honest, all honest parties output the sender's message m.

Complexity: A round complexity and seed round complexity of $\mathcal{O}(n)$. A communication complexity and a seed communication complexity of $\mathcal{O}(\ell n + (n\kappa + n^3 \log n)\mathcal{B}(1))$ and $\mathcal{O}(n\kappa + n^3 \log n)$ bits respectively.

PROOF. The agreement, validity and complexity follows from Lemma 11, Lemma 2 and Lemma 1 respectively. □

4. BYZANTINE AGREEMENT EXTENSION IN HONEST MAJORITY SETTING

We present a Byzantine agreement (BA) extension protocol with $O(\ell n)$ communication complexity and one round of seed broadcast. Given a protocol for BA, a broadcast protocol can be constructed using the folklore transformation: The sender sends the message m to every party. The parties then run the BA protocol to achieve agreement among themselves. We point out that the broadcast protocol also has optimal communication complexity and requires one round of broadcast. The first round will take $O(\ell n)$, and the BA protocol will take $O(\ell n)$ making a broadcast protocol with overall $O(\ell n)$ communication complexity.

At a high level, our BA extension protocol closely follows the protocol of [FH06] (will be referred as FH protocol from now onwards) with the main difference in the seed round complexity. While [FH06] requires three seed rounds, our protocol requires just one seed round. A closer look will reveal that it is non-trivial to reduce the number of seed rounds in [FH06]. The FH protocol proceeds in three phases, where each phase brings the parties "closer" to agreement. The protocol may be aborted in the first two phases when some inconsistency is detected. In that case, the parties will output $\perp$. However, if the parties reach the third phase, agreement will be reached without any abort. In each of the first two phases, the parties must agree on whether to abort or to continue to the next phase. Otherwise the BA protocol will have no agreement property. This calls for at least two rounds of broadcast (one in each of the first two phases). FH protocol requires three seed rounds, one in the first phase and the other two in the second phase. Thus far, there is no known information-theoretic BA extension protocol with optimal communication complexity and one seed round in the honest majority setting. We propose a cryptographically secure protocol satisfying the above properties. Our protocol that appears in the full version of the paper improves both the round as well as the seed round complexity of FH protocol. We leave open the design of an information-theoretic protocol matching the complexities of our cryptographic protocol.

5. REFERENCES

[BGP92] Piotr Berman, Juan A Garay, and Kenneth J Perry. Bit optimal distributed consensus. In *Computer science*, pages 313–321. Springer, 1992.

[BH06] Zuzana Beerliová-Trubíniová and Martin Hirt. Efficient multi-party computation with dispute control. In *Theory of Cryptography*, pages 305–328. Springer, 2006.

[CGS97] Ronald Cramer, Rosario Gennaro, and Berry Schoenmakers. A secure and optimally efficient multi-authority election scheme. In *Advances in Cryptology - EUROCRYPT 1997*, pages 103–118. Springer, 1997.

[CW92] Brian A Coan and Jennifer L Welch. Modular construction of a byzantine agreement protocol with optimal message bit complexity. *Information and Computation*, 97(1):61–85, 1992.

[DR85] Danny Dolev and Rüdiger Reischuk. Bounds on information exchange for byzantine agreement. *J. ACM*, 32(1):191–204, 1985.

[DS83] Danny Dolev and H. Raymond Strong. Authenticated algorithms for byzantine agreement. *SIAM Journal on Computing*, 12(4):656–666, 1983.

[EGL85] Shimon Even, Oded Goldreich, and Abraham Lempel. A randomized protocol for signing contracts. *Communications of the ACM*, 28(6):637–647, 1985.

[FH06] Matthias Fitzi and Martin Hirt. Optimally efficient multi-valued byzantine agreement. In *Proceedings of the twenty-fifth annual ACM symposium on Principles of distributed computing*, pages 163–168. ACM, 2006.

[FM97] Pesech Feldman and Silvio Micali. An optimal probabilistic protocol for synchronous byzantine agreement. *SIAM Journal on Computing*, 26(4):873–933, 1997.

[GKKO07] Juan Garay, Jonathan Katz, Chiu-Yuen Koo, and Rafail Ostrovsky. Round complexity of authenticated broadcast with a dishonest majority. In *Foundations of Computer Science, 2007. FOCS'07*, pages 658–668. IEEE, 2007.

[GMW87] Oded Goldreich, Silvio Micali, and Avi Wigderson. How to play any mental game. In *Proceedings of the nineteenth annual ACM symposium on Theory of computing*, pages 218–229. ACM, 1987.

[HR14] Martin Hirt and Pavel Raykov. Multi-valued byzantine broadcast: The $t < n$ case. In *Advances in Cryptology–ASIACRYPT 2014*, pages 448–465. Springer, 2014.

[IKNP03] Yuval Ishai, Joe Kilian, Kobbi Nissim, and Erez Petrank. Extending oblivious transfers efficiently. In *Advances in Cryptology-CRYPTO 2003*, pages 145–161. Springer, 2003.

[KK06] Jonathan Katz and Chiu-Yuen Koo. On expected constant-round protocols for byzantine agreement. In *Advances in Cryptology - CRYPTO 2006*, pages 445–462, 2006.

[LF82] Leslie Lamport and Michael Fischer. Byzantine generals and transaction commit protocols. Technical report, Technical Report 62, SRI International, 1982.

[LV11] Guanfeng Liang and Nitin Vaidya. Error-free multi-valued consensus with byzantine failures. In *Proceedings of the 30th annual ACM SIGACT-SIGOPS symposium on Principles of distributed computing*, pages 11–20. ACM, 2011.

[Pat11] Arpita Patra. Error-free multi-valued broadcast and byzantine agreement with optimal communication complexity. In *Proceedings of Principles of Distributed Systems - 15th International Conference, OPODIS 2011*, pages 34–49, 2011.

[PSL80] Marshall Pease, Robert Shostak, and Leslie Lamport. Reaching agreement in the presence of faults. *Journal of the ACM (JACM)*, 27(2):228–234, 1980.

[PW96] Birgit Pfitzmann and Michael Waidner. *Information-theoretic pseudosignatures and byzantine agreement for $t \geq n/3$*. Technical Report RZ 2882, IBM Research, 1996.

[TC84] R. Turpin and B. A. Coan. Extending binary Byzantine Agreement to multivalued Byzantine Agreement. *Information Processing Letters*, 18(2):73–76, 1984.

[Yao79] Andrew Chi-Chih Yao. Some complexity questions related to distributive computing(preliminary report). In *Proceedings of the Eleventh Annual ACM Symposium on Theory of Computing*, STOC '79, pages 209–213. ACM, 1979.

Two-Bit Messages are Sufficient to Implement Atomic Read/Write Registers in Crash-prone Systems

Achour Mostéfaoui
LINA, Université de Nantes
44322 Nantes, France
Mostefaoui@univ-nantes.fr

Michel Raynal
Institut Universitaire de France
& IRISA, Université de Rennes
raynal@irisa.fr

ABSTRACT

Atomic registers are certainly the most basic objects of computing science. Their implementation on top of an n-process asynchronous message-passing system has received a lot of attention. It has been shown that $t < n/2$ (where t is the maximal number of processes that may crash) is a necessary and sufficient requirement to build an atomic register on top of a crash-prone asynchronous message-passing system. Considering such a context, this paper presents an algorithm which implements a single-writer multi-reader atomic register with four message types only, and where no message needs to carry control information in addition to its type. Hence, two bits are sufficient to capture all the control information carried by all the implementation messages. Moreover, the messages of two types need to carry a data value while the messages of the two other types carry no value at all. As far as we know, this algorithm is the first with such a sufficiency property on the size of control information carried by messages. It is also particularly efficient from a time complexity point of view.

General Terms:

Algorithms, Reliability, Theory

Keywords:

Asynchronous message-passing system, Atomic read-write register, Message type, Process crash failure, Sequence number, Upper bound.

PODC'16, July 25–28, 2016, Chicago, IL, USA.

© 2016 ACM. ISBN 978-1-4503-3964-3/16/07...$15.00

DOI: http://dx.doi.org/10.1145/2933057.2933095

1. INTRODUCTION

Since Sumer time [9], and –very much later– Turing's machine tape [20], read/write objects are certainly the most basic communication objects. Such an object, usually called a *register*, provides its users (processes) with a write operation which defines the new value of the register, and a read operation which returns the value of the register. When considering sequential computing, registers are universal in the sense they allow to solve any problem that can be solved [20].

Register in message-passing systems.

In a message-passing system, the computing entities communicate only by sending and receiving messages transmitted through a communication network. Hence, in such a system, a register is not a communication object given for free, but constitutes a communication abstraction which must be built with the help of the underlying communication network and the local memories of the processes.

Several types of registers can be defined according to which processes are allowed to read or write the register, and the quality (semantics) of the value returned by each read operation. We consider here registers which are single-writer multi-reader (SWMR), and atomic. Atomicity means that (a) each read or write operation appears as if it had been executed instantaneously at a single point of the time line, between its start event and its end event, (b) no two operations appear at the same point of the time line, and (c) a read returns the value written by the closest preceding write operation (or the initial value of the register if there is no preceding write) [10]. Algorithms building multi-writer multi-reader (MWMR) atomic registers from single-writer single-reader (SWSR) registers with a weaker semantics (safe or regular registers) have been introduced by L. Lamport in [10, 11] (such algorithms are described in several papers and textbooks, e.g., [4, 12, 18, 21]).

Many distributed algorithms have been proposed, which build a register on top of a message-passing system, be it failure-free or failure-prone. In the failure-prone case, the addressed failure models are the process crash failure model, or the Byzantine process failure model (see, the textbooks [4, 12, 16, 17]). The most famous of these algorithms was proposed by H. Attiya, A. Bar-Noy, and D. Dolev in [3]. This algorithm, which is usually called ABD according to the names of its authors, considers an n-process asynchronous system in which up to $t < n/2$ processes may crash (it is also shown in [3] that $t < n/2$ is an upper bound of the number of process crashes which can be tolerated). This simple and elegant algorithm, relies on (a) quorums [22], and (b) a simple broadcast/reply communication pattern. ABD uses this pattern once in a write operation, and twice in a read operation implementing an

SWMR register (informal presentations of ABD can be found in [2, 19]).

Content of the paper.

ABD and its successors (e.g., [1, 15, 22]) associate an increasing sequence number with each value that is written. This allows to easily identify each written value. Combined with the use of majority quorums, this value identification allows each read invocation to return a value that satisfies the atomicity property (intuitively, a read always returns the "last" written value).

Hence, from a communication point of view, in addition to the number of messages needed to implement a read or a write operation, important issues are the number of different message types, and the size of the control information that each of them has to carry. As sequence numbers increase according to the number of write invocations, this number is not bounded, and the size of a message that carries a sequence number can become arbitrarily large.

A way to overcome this drawback consists in finding a modulo-based implementation of sequence numbers [8], which can be used to implement read/write registers. Considering this approach, one of the algorithms presented in [3] uses messages that carry control information whose size is upper bounded by $O(n^5)$ bits (where n is the total number of processes). The algorithm presented in [1] reduced this size to $O(n^3)$ bits. Hence the natural question: "*How many bits of control information, a message has to carry, when one wants to implement an atomic read/write register?*".

This is the question that gave rise to this paper, which shows that it is possible to implement an SWMR atomic register with four types of message carrying no control information in addition to their type. Hence, the result: *messages carrying only two bits of control information are sufficient to implement an* SWMR *atomic register in the presence of asynchrony and up to $t < n/2$ unexpected process crashes.* Another important property of the proposed algorithm lies in its time complexity, namely, in a failure-free context and assuming a bound Δ on message transfer delays, a write operation requires at most 2Δ time units, and a read operation requires at most 4Δ time units.

Roadmap.

The paper is made up of 5 sections. The computing model and the notion of an atomic register are presented in Section 2. The algorithm building an SWMR atomic register, where messages carry only two bits of control information (their type), in an asynchronous message-passing system prone to any minority of process crashes is presented in Section 3. Its proof appears in Section 4. Finally, Section 5 concludes the paper, and we conjecture that two bits of control information are also necessary to solve the problem.

2. COMPUTATION MODEL AND ATOMIC READ/WRITE REGISTER

2.1 Computation model

Processes.

The computing model is composed of a set of n sequential processes denoted p_1, ..., p_n. Each process is asynchronous which means

that it proceeds at its own speed, which can be arbitrary and remains always unknown to the other processes.

A process may halt prematurely (crash failure), but executes correctly its local algorithm until it possibly crashes. The model parameter t denotes the maximal number of processes that may crash in a run. A process that crashes in a run is said to be *faulty*. Otherwise, it is *correct* or *non-faulty*. Given a run, $\mathcal{C}$ denotes the set of correct processes.

Communication.

Each pair of processes communicate by sending and receiving messages through two uni-directional channels, one in each direction. Hence, the communication network is a complete network: any process p_i can directly send a message to any process p_j.A process p_i invokes the operation "send TYPE(m) to p_j" to send to p_j the message m, whose type is TYPE. The operation "receive TYPE() from p_j" allows p_i to receive from p_j a message whose type is TYPE.

Each channel is reliable (no loss, corruption, nor creation of messages), not necessarily first-in/first-out, and asynchronous (while the transit time of each message is finite, there is no upper bound on message transit times).

Let us notice that, due to process and message asynchrony, no process can know if an other process crashed or is only very slow.

Notation.

The previous computation model is denoted $\mathcal{CAMP}_{n,t}[\emptyset]$ (unconstrained $\mathcal{C}$rash $\mathcal{A}$synchronous $\mathcal{M}$essage-$\mathcal{P}$assing).

2.2 Atomic read/write register

Definition.

A *concurrent object* is an object that can be accessed by several processes (possibly simultaneously). An SWMR *atomic* register (say REG) is a concurrent object which provides exactly one process (called the writer) with an operation denoted REG.write(), and all processes with an operation denoted REG.read(). When the writer invokes REG.write(v) it defines v as being the new value of REG. An SWMR atomic register is defined by the following set of properties [10].

- Liveness. An invocation of an operation by a correct process terminates.
- Consistency (safety). All the operations invoked by the processes, except possibly –for each faulty process– the last operation it invoked, appear as if they have been executed sequentially and this sequence of operations is such that:
  - each read returns the value written by the closest write that precedes it (or the initial value of REG if there is no preceding write),
  - if an operation $op1$ terminates before an operation $op2$ starts, then $op1$ appears before $op2$ in the sequence.

This set of properties states that, from an external observer point of view, the read/write register appears as if it is accessed sequentially by the processes, and this sequence (a) respects the real time access order, and (ii) belongs to the sequential specification of a register. More formal definitions can be found in [10, 14]. (When considering any object defined by a sequential specification, atomicity is also called linearizability [7], and it is then said that the object is *linearizable*.)

Necessary and sufficient condition.

The constraint ($t < n/2$) is a necessary and sufficient condition to implement an atomic read/write register in $\mathcal{CAMP}_{n,t}[\emptyset]$ [3]. Hence, the model $\mathcal{CAMP}_{n,t}[\emptyset]$ whose runs are constrained by $t < n/2$ is denoted $\mathcal{CAMP}_{n,t}[t < n/2]$.

3. AN ALGORITHM WITH TWO-BIT MESSAGES

A distributed algorithm implementing an SWMR atomic register in $\mathcal{CAMP}_{n,t}[t < n/2]$ is described in Figure 1. As already indicated, this algorithm uses only four types of messages, denoted WRITE0(), WRITE1(), READ(), and PROCEED(). The messages WRITE0() and WRITE1() carry a data value, while the messages READ() and PROCEED() carry only their type.

3.1 Notation and underlying principles

Notation.

p_w denotes the writer process, v_x denotes the xth value written by p_w, and v_0 is the initial value of the register REG that is built.

Underlying principles.

The principle that underlies the algorithm is the following. First, each process (a) manages a local copy of the sequential history made up of the values written by the writer, and (b) forwards, once to each process, each new value it learns. Then, so that all processes obtain the same sequential history, and be able to read up to date values, each process p_i follows rules to forward a value to another process p_j, and manages accordingly appropriate local variables, which store sequence numbers.

- Rule R1. When, while it knows the first $(x-1)$ written values, and only these values, p_i receives the xth written value, it forwards it to all the processes that, from its point of view, know the first $(x-1)$ written values and no more. In this way, these processes will learn the xth written value (if not yet done when they receive the corresponding message forwarded by p_i).
- Rule R2. The second forwarding rule is when p_i receives the xth written value from a process p_j, while it knows the first y written values, where $y > x$. In this case, p_i sends the $(x+1)^{th}$ written value to p_j, and only this value, in order p_j increases its local sequential history with its next value (if not yet done when it receives the message from p_i).
- Rule R3. To ensure a correct management of the local histories, and allow a process to help other processes in the construction of their local histories (Rules R1 and R2), each process manages a sequence number-based local view of the progress of each other process (as far as the construction of their local history is concerned).

As we are about to see, translating these rules into an algorithm, provides us with a distributed algorithm where, while each process locally manages sequence numbers, the only control information carried by each message is its type, the number of different message types being very small (namely 4, as already indicated)[1].

[1]Such a constant number of message types is not possible from a "modulo $f(n)$" implementation of sequence numbers carried by messages. This is because, from a control information point of view, each of the values in $\{0, 1, \ldots, f(n)-1\}$ defines a distinct message type. Let u insist on the fact that the problem we are interested in is not related to the size of counters (e.g., counters whose size is 4 bits, 32 bits, or more). The problem is to obtain message tags whose size is constant, and not a function of n.

3.2 Local data structures

Each process p_i manages the following local data structures.

- $history_i$: prefix sequence of the values already written, as known by p_i; $history_i$ is accessed with an array like-notation, and we have $history_i[0] = v_0$. As there is a single writer p_w, $history_w$ represents the history of the values written so far.
- $w\_sync_i[1..n]$: array of sequence numbers; $w\_sync_i[j] = \alpha$ means that, to p_i's knowledge, p_j knows the prefix of $history_w$ until $history_w[\alpha]$. Hence, $w\_sync_i[i]$ is the sequence number of the most recent value known by p_i, and $w\_sync_w[w]$ is the sequence number of the last value written.
- $r\_sync_i[1..n]$: array of sequence numbers; $r\_sync_i[j] = \alpha$ means that, to p_i's knowledge, p_j answered α of its read requests.
- wsn, rsn and sn: auxiliary local variables, the scope of each being restricted to the algorithm implementing an operation, or the processing of a message, in which it occurs.

3.3 Channel behavior with respect to the message types WRITE0() and WRITE1()

As far as the messages WRITE0() and WRITE1() are concerned, the notation WRITE$(0, v)$ is used for WRITE0(v), and similarly, WRITE$(1, v)$ is used for WRITE1(v).

When considering the two uni-directional channels connecting p_i and p_j, the algorithm, as we will see, requires (a) p_i to send to p_j the following sequence of messages WRITE$(1, v_1)$, WRITE0$(0, v_2)$, WRITE$(1, v_3)$, ..., WRITE$(x \bmod 2, v_x)$, etc., and (b) p_j to send to p_i the very same sequence of messages, namely WRITE$(1, v_1)$, WRITE0$(0, v_2)$, WRITE$(1, v_3)$, ..., WRITE$(x \bmod 2, v_x)$, etc.

Moreover, the algorithm forces process p_i to send to p_j the message WRITE$(x \bmod 2, v_x)$, only when it has received from p_j the message WRITE$((x-1) \bmod 2, v_{x-1})$. From the point of view of the write messages, these communication rules actually implement the *alternating bit* protocol [6, 13], which ensures the following properties:

- Property P1: each of the two uni-directional channels connecting p_i and p_j allows at most one message WRITE$(-,-)$ to bypass another message WRITE$(-,-)$, which, thanks to the single control bit carried by these messages allows the destination process (e.g., p_i) to process the messages WRITE() it receives from (e.g., p_j) in their sending order.
- Property P2: p_i and p_j are synchronized in such a way that $0 \leq |w\_sync_i[j] - w\_sync_j[i]| \leq 1$. This is the translation of Property P1 in terms of the pair of local synchronization-related variables $\langle w\_sync_i[j], w\_sync_j[i] \rangle$.

Let us insist on the fact that this "alternating bit" message exchange pattern is only on the write messages. It imposes no constraint on the messages of the types READ() and PROCEED() exchanged between p_i and p_j, which can come in between, at any place in the sequence of the write messages sent by a process p_i to a process p_j.

3.4 The algorithm implementing the write() operation

This algorithm is described at lines 1-4, executed by the writer p_w, and line 11-18, executed by any process.

local variables initialization:
$history_i[0] \leftarrow v_0$; $w\_sync_i[1..n] \leftarrow [0,\ldots,0]$; $r\_sync_i[1..n] \leftarrow [0,\ldots,0]$.

operation write(v) **is** % invoked by $p_i = p_w$ (the writer) %
(1) $wsn \leftarrow w\_sync_w[w]+1$; $w\_sync_w[w] \leftarrow wsn$; $history_w[wsn] \leftarrow v$; $b \leftarrow wsn \bmod 2$;
(2) **for each** j such that $w\_sync_w[j] = wsn-1$ **do** send WRITE(b,v) to p_j **end for**;
(3) wait $\big(z \geq (n-t)$ where z is the number of processes p_j such that $w\_sync_w[j] = wsn\big)$;
(4) return()
end operation.

operation read() **is** % the writer can directly returns $history_i[w\_synch_i[i]]$ %
(5) $rsn \leftarrow r\_sync_i[i]+1$; $r\_sync_i[i] \leftarrow rsn$;
(6) **for each** $j \in \{1,\ldots n\} \setminus \{i\}$ **do** send READ() to p_j **end for**;
(7) wait $\big(z \geq (n-t)$ where z is the number of processes p_j such that $r\_sync_i[j] = rsn\big)$;
(8) $sn \leftarrow w\_sync_i[i]$;
(9) wait $\big(z \geq (n-t)$ where z is the number of processes p_j such that $w\_sync_i[j] \geq sn\big)$;
(10) return($history_i[sn]$)
end operation.
%--

when WRITE(b,v) **is received from** p_j **do**
(11) wait $\big(b = (w\_sync_i[j]+1) \bmod 2\big)$;
(12) $wsn \leftarrow w\_sync_i[j]+1$;
(13) **if** $(wsn = w\_sync_i[i]+1)$
(14) **then** $w\_sync_i[i] \leftarrow wsn$; $history_i[wsn] \leftarrow v$; $b \leftarrow wsn \bmod 2$;
(15) **for each** ℓ such that $w\_sync_i[\ell] = wsn-1$ **do** send WRITE(b,v) to p_ℓ **end for**
(16) **else if** $(wsn < w\_sync_i[i])$ **then** $b \leftarrow (wsn+1) \bmod 2$; send WRITE$(b, history_i[wsn+1])$ to p_j **end if**
(17) **end if**;
(18) $w\_sync_i[j] \leftarrow wsn$.

when READ() **is received from** p_j **do**
(19) $sn \leftarrow w\_sync_i[i]$;
(20) wait $(w\_sync_i[j] \geq sn)$;
(21) send PROCEED() to p_j.

when PROCEED() **is received from** p_j **do**
(22) $r\_sync_i[j] \leftarrow r\_sync_i[j]+1$.

Figure 1: Single-writer multi-reader atomic register in $\mathcal{CAMP}_{n,t}[t < n/2]$ with counter-free messages

Invocation of the operation write().

When p_w invokes write(v_x) (we have then $w\_sync_w[w] = x-1$), it increases $w\_sync_w[w]$ and writes v_x at the tail of its local history variable (line 1). This value is locally identified by its sequence number $x = wsn$.

Then p_w sends WRITE(b, v_x), where $b = (wsn \bmod 2)$, to each process p_j that (from its point of view) knows all the previous write invocations, and only to these processes. According to the definition of $w\_sync_w[1..n]$, those are the processes p_j such that $w\_sync_w[j] = wsn-1 = w\_sync_w[w]-1$ (line 2). Let us notice that this ensures the requirement p_i needs to satisfy when it sends a message in order to benefit from the properties provided by the alternating bit communication pattern.

Finally, p_w waits until it knows that a quorum of at least $(n-t)$ processes knows the value v_x is it writing. The fact that a process p_j knows this x^{th} value is captured by the predicate $w\_sync_w[j] = wsn (= x)$ (line 3).

Reception of a message WRITE(b,v) *from a process* p_j.

When p_i receives a message WRITE(b,v) from a process p_j, it first waits until the waiting predicate of line 11 is satisfied. This waiting statement is nothing else than the the reception part of the alternating bit algorithm, which guarantees that the messages WRITE() from p_j are processed in their sending order. When this predicate is satisfied, all messages sent by p_j before WRITE(b,v) have been received and processed by p_i, and consequently the message WRITE(b,v) is the swn^{th} message sent by p_j (FIFO order), where $wsn = w\_sync_i[j]+1$, which means that $history_j[wsn] = v$ (line 12).

When this occurs, p_i learns that v is the next value to be added to its local history if additionally we have $w\_sync_i[i] = wsn-1$. In this case (predicate of line 13), p_i (a) adds v at the tail of its history (line 14), and (b) forwards the message WRITE(b,v) to the processes that, from its local point of view, know the first $(wsn-1)$ written values and no more (line 15, forwarding Rule R1).

If $wsn < w\_sync_i[i]$, from p_i's local point of view, the history known by p_j is a strict prefix of its own history. Consequently, p_i sends to p_j the message WRITE(b', v'), where $b' = ((wsn+1) \bmod 2)$ and $v' = history_i[wsn+1]$ (line 16 applies the forwarding Rule R2 in order to allow p_j to catch up its lag, if not yet done when it will receive the message WRITE(b',v') sent by p_i). Finally, as p_j sends to p_i a single message per write operation, whatever the value of wsn, p_i updates $w\_sync_i[j]$ (line 18).

Remark.

As far as the written values are concerned, the algorithm implementing the operation write() can be seen as a fault-tolerant "synchronizer" (in the spirit of [5]), which ensures the mutual consistency of the local histories between any two neighbors with the help of an alternating bit algorithm executed by each pair of neighbors [6, 13].

3.5 The algorithm implementing the read() operation

This algorithm is described at lines 5-10 executed by a reader p_i, and lines 19-22 executed by any process.

Invocation of the operation read().

The invoking process p_i first increments its local read request sequence number $r\_sync_i[i]$ and broadcasts its read request in a message READ(), which carries neither additional control information, nor a data value (lines 5-6). If p_i crashes during this broadcast, the message READ() is received by an arbitrary subset of processes (possibly empty). Otherwise, p_i waits until it knows that at least $(n-t)$ processes received its current request (line 7).

When this occurs, p_i considers the sequence number of the last value in its history, namely $sn = w\_sync_i[i]$ (line 8). This is the value it will return, namely $history_i[sn]$ (line 10). But in order to ensure atomicity, before returning $history_i[sn]$, p_i waits until at least $(n-t)$ processes know this value (and may be more). From p_i's point of view, the corresponding waiting predicate translates in "at least $(n-t)$ processes p_j are such that $w\_sync_i[j] \geq sn$".

Reception of a message READ() *sent by a process* p_j.

When a process p_i receives a message READ() from a process p_j (hence, p_j issued a read operation), it considers the most recent written value it knows (the sequence number of this value is $sn = w\_sync_i[i]$, line 19), and waits until it knows that p_j knows this value, which is locally captured by the sequence number-based predicate $w\_sync_i[j] \geq sn$ (line 20). When this occurs, p_i sends the message PROCEED() to p_j which is allowed to progress as far as p_i is concerned.

The control messages READ() and PROCEED() (whose sending is controlled by a predicate) implement a synchronization which – as far as p_i is concerned– forces the reader process p_j to wait until it knows a "fresh" enough value, where "freshness" is locally defined by p_i as the last value it was knowing when it received the message READ() from p_j (predicate of line 20).

Reception of a message PROCEED() *sent by a process* p_j.

When p_i receives a message PROCEED() from a process p_j, it learns that its local history is as fresh as p_j's history when p_j received its message READ(). Locally, this is captured by the incrementation of $r\_sync_i[j]$, namely p_j answered all the read requests of p_i until the $(r\_sync_i[j])^{th}$ one.

4. PROOF OF THE ALGORITHM

Let us remind that $\mathcal{C}$ is the set of correct processes, p_w the writer, and v_x the xth value written by p_w. Due to page limitation, the missing proofs are given in an Appendix.

LEMMA 1. $\forall i, j$: *$w\_sync_i[j]$ increases by steps equal to* 1.

As this lemma is used in all other lemmas, it will not be explicitly referenced.

Proof Let us first observe that, due to the sending predicates of line 2 (for the writer), and lines 15 and 16 for any process p_i, no process sends a message WRITE$(-,-)$ to itself.

As far as $w\_sync_i[i]$ is concerned, and according to the previous observation,we have the following. The writer increases the sequence number $w\_sync_w[w]$ only at line 1. Any reader process p_i increases $w\_sync_i[i]$ at line 14, and due to line 12 and the predicate of line 13, the increment is 1. Let us now consider the case of $w\_sync_i[j]$ when $i \neq j$. An incrementation of such a local variable occurs only at line 18, where (due to line 12) we have $wsn = w\_sync_i[j] + 1$, and the lemma follows. $\Box_{Lemma\ 1}$

LEMMA 2. $\forall i, j: w\_sync_i[i] \geq w\_sync_j[i]$.

Proof Let us first observe, that the predicate is initially true. Then, a local variable $w\_sync_j[i]$ is increased by 1, when p_j receives a message WRITE$(-,-)$ from p_i (lines 12 and 18). Process p_i sent this message at line 2 or 16 if $i = w$, and at lines 15 or 16 for any $i \neq w$. If the sending of the message WRITE$(b,-)$ by p_i occurs at line 2 or 15, p_i increased $w\_sync_i[i]$ at the previous line. If the sending occurs at line 16, $w\_sync_i[i]$ was increased during a previous message reception. $\Box_{Lemma\ 2}$

LEMMA 3. $\forall i$: $w\_sync_i[i] = \max\{w\_sync_i[j]\}_{1 \leq j \leq n}$.

Proof The lemma is trivially true for the writer process p_w. Let us consider any other process p_i, different from p_w. The proof is by induction on the number of messages WRITE$(-,-)$ received by p_i. Let

$$P(i,m) \stackrel{def}{=} w\_sync_i[i] = \max\{w\_sync_i[j]\}_{1 \leq j \leq n},$$

where m is the number of messages WRITE$(-,-)$ processed by p_i. The predicate $P(i,0)$ is true. Let us assume $P(i,m')$ is true for any m' such that $0 \leq m' \leq m$. Let p_j be the process that sends to p_i the $(m+1)^{th}$ message WRITE$(b,-)$, and let $w\_sync_i[i] = x$ when p_i starts processing this message. There are four cases to consider.

- Case 1. When the message WRITE$(-,-)$ from p_j is processed by p_i, we have $w\_sync_i[i] + 1 = w\_sync_i[j] + 1$. As the predicate of line 13 is satisfied when this message is processed, p_i updates $w\_sync_i[i]$ to the value $(x+1)$ at line 14. Moreover, it also updates $w\_sync_i[j]$ to the same value $(x+1)$ at line 18. As $P(i,m)$ is true, it follows that $P(i,m+1)$ is true after p_i processed the message.
- Case 2. When the message WRITE$(-,-)$ from p_j is processed by p_i, we have $w\_sync_i[j] + 1 < w\_sync_i[i] = x$. In this case, p_i does not modify $w\_sync_i[i]$. It only updates $w\_sync_i[j]$ to its next value (line 18), which is smaller than x. As $P(i,m)$ is true, it follows that $P(i,m+1)$ is true after p_i processed the message.
- Case 3. When the message WRITE$(-,-)$ from p_j is processed by p_i, we have $w\_sync_i[j] + 1 = w\_sync_i[i] = x$. In this case, both the predicates of lines 13 and 16 are false. It follows that p_i executes only the update of line 18, and we have then $w\_sync_i[j] = w\_sync_i[i] = x$. As $P(i,m)$ is true, $P(i,m+1)$ is true after p_i processed the message.
- Case 4. When the message WRITE$(-,-)$ from p_j is processed by p_i, we have $w\_sync_i[j]+1 > w\_sync_i[i]+1 = x+1$. In this case, due to (a) $w\_sync_i[j] \leq w\_sync_i[i]$ (induction assumption satisfied when the message WRITE$(-,-)$ arrives at p_i from p_j), and (b) the fact that $w\_sync_i[j]$ increases by 1 (Lemma 1), we necessarily have $w\_sync_i[i] + 1 \geq w\_sync_i[j] + 1$, when the message is received. Hence, we obtain $w\_sync_i[j]+1 > w\_sync_i[i]+1 \geq w\_sync_i[j]+1$, a contradiction. It follows that this case cannot occur.

$\Box_{Lemma\ 3}$

LEMMA 4. *$\forall i$: $history[0..w\_sync_i[i]]$ is a prefix of $history[0..w\_sync_w[w]]$.*

Proof The proof of this lemma rests on the properties P1 and P2 provided by the underlying "alternating bit" communication pattern imposed on the messages WRITE$(-,-)$ exchanged by any pair of processes p_i and p_j. If follows from these properties (obtained from the use of parity bits carried by every message WRITE$(-,-)$, and the associated wait statement of line 11) that, p_i sends to p_j the message WRITE$(-,v_x)$, only after it knows that p_j received WRITE$(-,v_{x-1})$. Moreover, it follows from the management of the local sequence numbers $w\_sync_i[1..n]$, that no process sends twice the same message WRITE$(-,v_x)$. Finally, due to the predicate of line 11, any two consecutive messages WRITE$(0,-)$ and WRITE$(1,-)$ sent by a process p_i to a process p_j are processed in their sending order.

The lemma then follows from these properties, and the fact that, when at lines 13-14 a process p_i assigns a value v to $history_i[x]$, this value was carried by x^{th} message WRITE$(-,v)$ sent by some process p_j, and is the value of $history_j[x]$. It follows that no two processes have different histories, from which we conclude that $history_i[x] = history_w[x]$. $\Box_{Lemma\ 4}$

LEMMA 5. *$\forall i \in \mathcal{C}, \forall j$: we have:*
R1: $(w\_sync_i[i] = w\_sync_i[j] = x) \Rightarrow p_i$ sent x messages WRITE$(-,-)$ to p_j,
R2: $(w\_sync_i[i] > w\_sync_i[j] = x) \Rightarrow p_i$ sent $x+1$ messages WRITE$(-,-)$ to p_j.

Proof Both predicates R1 and R2 are initially true ($w\_sync_i[i] = w\_sync_i[j] = 0$ and no message was previously sent by p_i to p_j). The variables involved in the premises of the predicates R1 and R2 can be modified in the execution of a write operation (if p_i is the writer), or when a message WRITE$(-,-)$ arrives at process p_i from process p_j. Let us suppose that R1 and R2 are true until the value x, and let us show that they remain true for the value $(x+1)$.

During the execution of a write operation, if $w\_sync_w[w] = w\_sync_w[j] = x$, the local variable $w\_sync_w[w]$ is incremented to $(x+1)$, and the $(x+1)^{th}$ message WRITE$(-,-)$ is sent by p_w to p_j (lines 1-2). R1 and R2 remain true. If $w\_sync_w[w] > w\_sync_w[j] = x$, the local variable $w\_sync_w[w]$ is incremented at line 1, but no message is sent to p_j at line 2, which falsifies neither R1 nor R2.

When a process p_i receives a message WRITE$(-,-)$ from a process p_j, there are also two cases, according to the values of $w\_sync_i[i]$ and $w\_sync_i[j]$ when p_i starts processing the message at line 12.

- Case 1. $w\_sync_i[i] = w\_sync_i[j] = x$. In this case, the predicate of line 13 is satisfied. It follows that both the counters $w\_sync_i[i]$ and $w\_sync_i[j]$ are incremented to $(x+1)$ (at line 14 for $w\_sync_i[i]$ and line 18 for $w\_sync_i[j]$). Moreover, when p_i executes line 15 we have $w\_sync_i[i] = w\_sync_i[j] - 1$, and consequently process p_i sends a message WRITE$(-,-)$ to p_j (the fact this message is the $(x+1)^{th}$ follows from the induction assumption). Hence, R1 and R2 are true when p_i terminates the processing of the message WRITE$(-,-)$ received from p_j.
- Case $w\_sync_i[i] > w\_sync_i[j] = x$. In this case, the counter $w\_sync_i[j]$ is incremented to $x+1$ at line 18, while the counter $w\_sync_i[i]$ is not (because the predicate of line 13 is false). Two sub-cases are considered according to the values of $w\_sync_i[i]$ and $w\_sync_i[j]$.
  - If $w\_sync_i[i] = x+1$ (this is the value $w\_sync_i[j]$ will obtain at line 18), the predicate of line 16 is false, and no message is sent to p_j. R1 and R2 remains true, as, by the induction assumption, p_i already sent $(x+1)$ messages WRITE$(-,-)$.
  - If $w\_sync_i[i] > x+1$, the predicate of line 16 is satisfied, and the $(x+2)^{th}$ message WRITE$(-,-)$ is sent to p_j at this line, maintaining satisfied the predicates R1 and R2.

$\Box_{Lemma\ 5}$

LEMMA 6. *No correct process blocks forever at line* 11.

Proof The fact that the waiting predicate of line 11 is eventually satisfied follows from the following observations.

- As the network is reliable, all the messages that are sent are received. Due to lines 2 and 15-16, this means that, for any x, if WRITE$(-,v_x)$ is received while m = WRITE$(-,v_{x-1})$ has not, then m will be eventually received.
- The message exchange pattern involving any two messages WRITE$(0,-)$ and WRITE$(1,-)$ sent consecutively and exchanged between each pair of processes is the "alternating bit pattern", from which it follows that no two messages WRITE$(b,-)$ (with the same b) can be received consecutively.
- It follows that the predicate of line 11 is a simple re-ordering predicate for any pair of messages such that WRITE$(-,v_x)$ was received before WRITE$(-,v_{x-1})$. When this predicate is not satisfied for a message m = WRITE$(b,-)$, this is because a message m' = WRITE$(1-b,-)$, will necessarily arrive and be processed before m. After that, the predicate of line 11 becomes true for m.

$\Box_{Lemma\ 6}$

LEMMA 7. *$\forall i,j \in \mathcal{C}$, if $w\_sync_i[i] = x$, there is a finite time after which $w\_sync_i[j] \geq x$.*

Proof Let us first notice that, due to Lemma 6, all WRITE$(-,-)$ messages received by correct processes will eventually satisfy the predicate line 11 and will be processed.

The proof is by contradiction. Let us assume that there exists some correct process p_j such that $w\_sync_i[j]$ stops increasing forever at some value $y < x$. Let us first notice that there is no message WRITE$(-,-)$ in transit from p_j to p_i otherwise its reception by p_i will entail the incrementation of $w\_sync_i[j]$ from y to $y+1$, contradicting the assumption. So, let us consider the last message WRITE$(-,-)$ sent by p_j to p_i and processed by p_i. There are three cases to consider when this message is received by p_i at line 11. (Let us remind that, due to to Lemma 3, $w\_sync_i[i] \geq w\_sync_i[j]$.)

- Case 1. $w\_sync_i[i] = w\_sync_i[j] = y - 1 < x - 1$. The variables $w\_sync_i[i]$ and $w\_sync_i[j]$ are both incremented at lines 14 and 18 respectively to the value $y < x$. As by assumption, $w\_sync_i[i]$ will attain the value x, it will be necessarily incremented in the future to reach x. The next time $w\_sync_i[i]$ is incremented, a message WRITE$(-,-)$ is sent by p_i to p_j (at line 15). Due to Lemma 5, p_i sent $y+1$ messages WRITE$(-,-)$ to p_j and eventually $w\_sync_j[i]$ will be equal to $y+1$. When the last of these messages arrives and is processed by p_j, there are two cases.

– Case $w\_sync_j[j] = y$ (as p_i sent $y+1$ messages WRITE$(-,-)$ to p_j, $w\_sync_j[j]$ cannot be smaller than y).
  In this case, $w\_sync_j[j] = y$ is increased, and a message WRITE$(-,-)$ is then sent by p_j to p_i (line 15). This contradicts the assumption that the message we considered was the last message sent by p_j to p_i.

– Case $w\_sync_j[j] \geq y+1$.
  In this case, as p_i sent previously y messages to p_j, we necessarily have $w\_sync_j[i] = y$. In this case, the predicate of line 13 is false, while the one of line 16 is satisfied. Hence, p_j sends a message WRITE$(-,-)$ to p_i. A contradiction.

- Case 2. $w\_sync_i[i] = w\_sync_i[j] + 1 = y < x$. In this case, when p_i receives the last message WRITE$(-,-)$ from p_j, the variable $w\_sync_i[j]$ is incremented at line 18 to the value $y < x$. Moreover, by the contradiction assumption, no more message WRITE$(-,-)$ is sent by p_j to p_i.

  Hence, we have now $w\_sync_i[i] = w\_sync_i[j] = y < x$, and the variable $w\_sync_i[i]$ will be incremented in the future to reach x. A reasoning similar to the previous one shows that p_j will send a message WRITE$(-,-)$ to p_i in the future, which contradicts the initial assumption.

- Case 3. $w\_sync_i[i] > w\_sync_i[j] + 1$. The reception by p_i of the last message WRITE$(-,-)$ from p_j entails the increase of $w\_sync_i[j]$ to its next value. However as the predicate $w\_sync_i[i] > w\_sync_i[j]$ remains true, a message WRITE$(-,-)$ is sent by p_i to p_j at line 16. Similarly to the previous cases, the reception of this message by p_j will direct it to send another message WRITE$(-,-)$ to p_i, contradicting the initial assumption.

Hence, $w\_sync_i[j]$ cannot stop increasing before reaching x, which proves the lemma. $\Box_{Lemma\ 7}$

LEMMA 8. *A writer that does not crash always terminates.*

Proof Let us first notice that, due to Lemma 6, the writer cannot block forever at line 11.

When it invokes a new write operation, the writer p_w first increases the write sequence number $w\_sync_w[w]$ to its next value wsn (line 1). If p_w does not crash, it follows from Lemma 7 that we eventually have $w\_sync_i[i] \geq w\_sync_w[i] = wsn$ at each correct process p_i. Consequently, the writer cannot block forever at line 3 and the lemma follows. $\Box_{Lemma\ 8}$

LEMMA 9. *A reader that does not crash always terminates.*

Proof Let us first notice that, due to Lemma 6, the reader cannot block forever at line 11.

Each time a process p_i executes a read operation it broadcasts a message READ() to all the other processes (line 6). Let us remind that its local variable $r\_sync_i[i]$ counts the number of messages READ() it has broadcast, while $r\_sync_i[j]$ counts the number of messages PROCEED() it has received from p_j (line 22) in response to its READ messages READ().

When the predicate of line 7 becomes true at the reader p_i, there are at least $(n-t)$ processes that answered the $r\_sync_i[i]$ messages READ() it sent (note that $r\_sync_i[i]$ is incremented line 5 and p_i does not send messages READ() to itself). We claim that each message READ() sent by p_i to a correct process p_j is eventually acknowledged by a a message PROCEED() send by p_j to p_i. It follows from this claim and line 22 executed by p_i when it receives a message PROCEED(), that the predicate of line 7 is eventually satisfied, and consequently, p_i cannot block forever at line 7.

Proof of the claim. Let us consider a correct process p_j when it receives a message READ() from p_i. It saves $w\_sync_i[i]$ in sn and waits until $w\_sync_j[i] \geq sn$ (lines 19-20). Due to Lemma 7, the predicate $w\_sync_j[i] \geq sn$ eventually becomes true at p_j. When this occurs, p_j sends the message PROCEED() to p_i (line 21), which proves the claim.

Let us now consider the wait statement at line 9, where sn is the value of $w\_sync_i[i]$ when the wait statement of line 7 terminates. Let p_j be a correct process. Due to Lemma 7 the predicate $w\_sync_i[j] \geq sn$ eventually holds. As this is true for any correct process p_j, p_i eventually exits the wait statement, which concludes the proof of the lemma. $\Box_{Lemma\ 9}$

LEMMA 10. *The implemented register is atomic.*

Proof Let $read[i,x]$ be a read operation issued by a process p_i which returns the value with sequence number x (i.e., $history_i[x]$), and $write[y]$ be the write operation which writes the value with sequence number y (i.e., $history_w[y]$). The proof of the lemma is the consequence of the three following claims.

- Claim 1. If $read[i,x]$ terminates before $write[y]$ starts, then $x < y$.
- Claim 2. If $write[x]$ terminates before $read[i,y]$ starts, then $x \leq y$.
- Claim 3. If $read[i,x]$ terminates before $read[j,y]$ starts, then $x \leq y$.

Claim 1 states that no process can read from the future. Claim 2 states that no process can read overwritten values. Claim 3 states that there is no new/old read inversion [4, 18].

Proof of Claim 1.
Due to Lemma 4, the value returned by $read[i,x]$ is $history_i[x] = history_w[x] = v_x$. As each write generate a greater sequence number, and p_w has not yet invoked write(v_y), we necessarily have $y > x$.

Proof of Claim 2.
It follows from lines 1-3 that when $write[x]$ terminates, there is a quorum Q_w of at least $(n-t)$ processes p_i such that $w\_sync_w[j] = x$. On another side, $read[i,y]$ obtains messages PROCEED() from a quorum Q_r at least $(n-t)$ processes (lines 22 and 7). As $|Q_w| \geq n-t$, $|Q_r| \geq n-t$, and $n-t > n/2$, we have $Q_w \cap Q_r \neq \emptyset$. Let p_k be a process of $Q_w \cap Q_r$. As $w\_sync_w[k] = x$, and $w\_sync_k[k] \geq w\_sync_w[k]$ (Lemma 2), and $write[x]$ is the last write before $read[i,y]$, we have $w\_sync_k[k] = x$ when $read[i,y]$ starts.

When p_k received the message READ() from p_i, $w\_sync_k[k]$ was equal to x, and p_k waited until $w\_sync_k[i] \geq x$ (line 20) before sending the message PROCEED() that allowed p_i to progress in its waiting at line 7. As $w\_sync_i[i] \geq w\_sync_k[i]$ (Lemma 2), it follows that we have $w\_sync_i[i] \geq x$, when p_i computes at line 8 the sequence number sn of the value it will return at line 10). Hence, the index $y = sn$ computed by p_i at line 8 is such that $y = sn = w\_sync_i[i] \geq x$.

line number	What is measured	ABD95 [3] unbounded seq. nb	ABD95 [3] bounded seq. nb	H. Attiya's algorithm [1]	Proposed algorithm
1	#msgs: write	$O(n)$	$O(n^2)$	$O(n)$	$O(n^2)$
2	#msgs: read	$O(n)$	$O(n^2)$	$O(n)$	$O(n)$
3	msg size (bits)	unbounded	$O(n^5)$	$O(n^3)$	2
4	local memory	unbounded	$O(n^6)$	$O(n^5)$	unbounded
5	Time: write	2Δ	12Δ	14Δ	2Δ
6	Time: read	4Δ	12Δ	18Δ	4Δ

Table 1: A few algorithms implementing an SWMR atomic register in $\mathcal{CAMP}_{n,t}[t < n/2]$

Proof of Claim 3.
On one side, when $read[i, x]$ stops waiting at line 9, there is a quorum Q_{ri} of at least $(n - t)$ processes p_k such that $w\_sync_i[k] \geq x$ (predicate of line 9 at p_i). Due to Lemma 2, we have then $w\_sync_k[k] \geq x$ for any process p_k of Q_{ri}, when $read[i, x]$ terminates.

On the other side, when $read[j, y]$ stops waiting at line 7 (which defines the value it returns, namely, $history_j[y]$), there is a quorum Q_{rj} of at least $(n - t)$ processes p_ℓ such that (due to the waiting predicate of line 20) $w\_sync_\ell[j] \geq sn(\ell)$, where $sn(\ell)$ is the value of $w\_sync_\ell[\ell]$ when p_ℓ receives the message READ() from p_j.

As each of Q_{ri} and Q_{rj} contains at least $(n - t)$ processes, and there is a majority of correct processes, there is at least one correct process in their intersection, say p_m. It follows that we have $w\_sync_m[m] \geq x$ when $read[i, x]$ terminates, and $w\_sync_m[j] \geq sn(m)$, where $sn(m)$ is the value of $w\_sync_m[m]$, when p_m received the message READ() from p_j. As $w\_sync_m[m]$ never decreases, and p_m receives READ() from p_j after $read[i, x]$ terminated, we necessarily have $sn(m) \geq x$. Hence, $w\_sync_m[j] \geq x$, when p_m sends PROCEED() to p_j. As (Lemma 2) $w\_sync_j[j] \geq w\_sync_m[j]$, it follows that the index sn computed by p_i at line 8 is such that $sn = y \geq x$. $\Box_{Lemma\ 10}$

THEOREM 1. *The algorithm described in Figure 1 implements an SWMR atomic register in the system model $\mathcal{CAMP}_{n,t}[t < n/2]$.*

Proof The theorem follows from Lemmas 8 and 9 (Termination properties), and Lemma 10 (Atomicity property). $\Box_{Theorem\ 1}$

THEOREM 2. *The algorithm described in Figure 1 uses only four types of messages, and those carry no additional control information. Moreover, a read operation requires $O(n)$ messages, and a write operation requires $O(n^2)$ messages.*

Proof The message content part of the theorem is trivial. A read generates n messages READ(), and each of them generates a message PROCEED(). A write operation generates $(n - 1)$ messages WRITE$(b, -)$ from the writer to the other processes, and then each process forward once this message to each process. $\Box_{Theorem\ 2}$

5. CONCLUDING REMARKS

The aim and the paper.

As indicated in the introduction, our aim was to investigate the following question: *"How many bits of control information messages have to carry to implement an atomic register in $\mathcal{CAMP}_{n,t}[t < n/2]$?"*.

As far as we know, all the previous works addressing this issue have reduced the size of control information with the use of a "modulo n" implementation technique. Table 1 presents three algorithms plus ours. These three algorithms are the unbounded version of the ABD algorithm [3], its bounded version, and the bounded algorithm due to H. Attiya [1]. They all associate a sequence number with each written value, but differently from ours, the last two require each message to carry a "modulo representative" of a sequence number.

For each algorithm, the table considers the number of messages it uses to implement the write operation (line 1), the read operation (line 2), the number of control bits carried by messages (line 3), the size of local memory used by each process (line 4), the time complexity of the write operation (line 5), and the time complexity of the read operation (line 6), both in a failure-free context. For time complexity it is assumed that message transfer delays are bounded by Δ, and local computations are instantaneous. The values appearing in the table for the bounded version of ABD and Attiya's algorithm are from [1, 19]. The reader can see that the proposed algorithm is particularly efficient from a time complexity point of view, namely, it is as good as the unbounded version of ABD.

The result presented in the paper.

As we have seen, our algorithm also uses sequence numbers, but those remain local. Only four types of messages are used, which means that each implementation message carries only two bits of control information. Moreover, only two message types carry a data value, the other two carry no data at all. Hence, this paper answers a long lasting question [19]: *"is it possible to implement an atomic register, despite asynchrony and crashes of a minority of processes, with messages whose control part is constant?"*.

The unbounded feature of the proposed algorithm (when looking at the local memory size) is due to the fact that the algorithm introduces a fault-tolerant version of a "synchronizer"[2] suited to the implementation of an atomic register, which disseminates new values, each traveling between each pair of processes in both directions, in such a way that a strong synchronization is ensured between any pair of processes, independently from the other processes, (namely, $\forall i, j : 0 \leq |w\_sync_i[j] - w\_sync_j[i]| \leq 1$). This fault-tolerant synchronization is strong enough to allow sequence numbers to be eliminated from messages. Unfortunately, it does not seem appropriate to allow a local modulo-based representation of sequence numbers at each process.

In addition to its theoretical interest, and thanks to its time complexity, the proposed algorithm is also interesting from a practical point of view. Due to the $O(n)$ message cost of its read operation, it can benefit to read-dominated applications and, more generally, to any setting where the communication cost (time and message size) is the critical parameter[3].

[2]As introduced in [5], and presented in textbooks such as [4, 12, 17].

[3]In addition to the way they use sequence numbers, an interesting design difference between our algorithm and ABD-like algorithms

A problem that remains open.

According to the previous discussion, a problem that still remains open is the following. Is it possible to design an implementation where (a) a constant number of bits is sufficient to encode the control information carried by messages, and (b) the sequence numbers have a local modulo-based implementation? We are inclined to think that this is not possible.

Acknowledgments

This work has been partially supported by the French ANR project DISPLEXITY, which is devoted to computability and complexity in distributed computing, and the Franco-German ANR project DISCMAT devoted to connections between mathematics and distributed computing.

6. REFERENCES

[1] Attiya H., Efficient and robust sharing of memory in message-passing systems. *Journal of Algorithms*, 34:109-127 (2000)

[2] Attiya H., Robust simulation of shared memory: 20 years after. *Bulletin of the EATCS*, 100:99-113 (2010)

[3] Attiya H., Bar-Noy A. and Dolev D., Sharing memory robustly in message passing systems. *Journal of the ACM*, 42(1):121-132 (1995)

[4] Attiya H. and Welch J., *Distributed computing: fundamentals, simulations and advanced topics*, (2d Edition), Wiley-Interscience, 414 pages (2004)

[5] Awerbuch B., Complexity of network synchronization. *Journal of the ACM*, 4:804-823 (1985)

[6] Bartlett K. A., Scantlebury S. A., and Wilkinson P. T., A note on reliable full-duplex transmission over half-duplex links. *Communications of the ACM*, 12(5):260-261 (1969)

[7] Herlihy M. P. and Wing J. M., Linearizability: a correctness condition for concurrent objects. *ACM Transactions on Programming Languages and Systems*, 12(3):463-492 (1990)

[8] Israeli A. and Li M., Bounded time-stamps, *Distributed Computing*, 6(4):205-209 (1993)

[9] Kramer S. N., *History Begins at Sumer: Thirty-Nine Firsts in Man's Recorded History*. University of Pennsylvania Press, 416 pages, ISBN 978-0-8122-1276-1 (1956)

[10] Lamport L., On interprocess communication, Part I: basic formalism. *Distributed Computing*, 1(2):77-85 (1986)

[11] Lamport L., On interprocess communication, Part II: Algorithms. *Distributed Computing*, 1(2):86-101 (1986)

[12] Lynch N. A., *Distributed algorithms*. Morgan Kaufmann Pub., San Francisco (CA), 872 pages, ISBN 1-55860-384-4 (1996)

[13] Lynch W. C., Reliable full-duplex file transmission over half-duplex telephone lines. *Communications of the ACM*, 11(6):407-410 (1968)

[14] Misra J., Axioms for memory access in asynchronous hardware systems. *ACM Transactions on Programming Languages and Systems*, 8(1):142-153 (1986)

[15] Mostéfaoui A. and Raynal M., Time-efficient read/write register in crash-prone asynchronous message-passing systems. *Proc. 4th Int'l Confernece on Networked Systems (NETYS'16)*, Springer LNCS, to appear (2016), https://hal.inria.fr/hal-01256067

[16] Raynal M., *Communication and agreement abstractions for fault-tolerant asynchronous distributed systems*. Morgan & Claypool Publishers, 251 pages, ISBN 978-1-60845-293-4 (2010)

[17] Raynal M., *Distributed algorithms for message-passing systems*. Springer, 510 pages, ISBN 978-3-642-38122-5 (2013)

[18] Raynal M., *Concurrent programming: algorithms, principles and foundations*. Springer, 515 pages, ISBN 978-3-642-32026-2 (2013)

[19] Ruppert E., Implementing shared registers in asynchronous message-passing systems. *Springer Encyclopedia of Algorithms*, pp. 400-403 (2008)

[20] Turing A. M., On computable numbers with an application to the Entscheidungsproblem. *Proc. of the London Mathematical Society*, 42:230-265, 1936.

[21] Vitányi P. M. B. and Awerbuch B., Atomic shared register access by asynchronous hardware (Detailed abstract). *Proc. 27th Annual Symposium on Foundations of Computer Science (FOCS'86)*, IEEE Press, pp. 233-243 (1986)

[22] Vukolic M., *Quorum systems, with applications to storage and consensus*. Morgan & Claypool Publishers, 132 pages, ISBN 978-1-60845-683-3 (2012)

is the following. When a process receives a message READ(), it has two possibilities. Either send by return the last written value it knows, as done in ABD-like algorithms. Or wait until it knows that the sender has a value as up to date as it own value, and only then send it a signal, as done in our algorithm with the message PROCEED().

How Proofs are Prepared at Camelot*

[Extended Abstract]†

Andreas Björklund
Department of Computer Science
Lund University
Lund, Sweden
andreas.bjorklund@yahoo.se

Petteri Kaski
Helsinki Institute for Information Technology HIIT
Department of Computer Science
Aalto University
Helsinki, Finland
petteri.kaski@aalto.fi

ABSTRACT

We study a design framework for robust, independently verifiable, and workload-balanced distributed algorithms working on a common input. The framework builds on recent noninteractive *Merlin–Arthur* proofs of batch evaluation of Williams [31st IEEE Colloquium on Computational Complexity (CCC'16, May 29–June 1, 2016, Tokyo), to appear] with the basic observation that Merlin's magic is not needed for batch evaluation: mere Knights can prepare the independently verifiable proof, in parallel, and with intrinsic error-correction.

As our main technical result, we show that the k-cliques in an n-vertex graph can be counted *and* verified in per-node $O(n^{(\omega+\epsilon)k/6})$ time and space on $O(n^{(\omega+\epsilon)k/6})$ compute nodes, for any constant $\epsilon > 0$ and positive integer k divisible by 6, where $2 \leq \omega < 2.3728639$ is the exponent of square matrix multiplication over the integers. This matches in total running time the best known sequential algorithm, due to Nešetřil and Poljak [*Comment. Math. Univ. Carolin.* 26 (1985) 415–419], and considerably improves its space usage and parallelizability. Further results (only partly presented in this extended abstract) include novel algorithms for counting triangles in sparse graphs, computing the chromatic polynomial of a graph, and computing the Tutte polynomial of a graph.

*The research leading to these results has received funding from the Swedish Research Council grant VR 2012-4730 "Exact Exponential-Time Algorithms" (A.B.) and the European Research Council under the European Union's Seventh Framework Programme (FP/2007-2013) / ERC Grant Agreement 338077 "Theory and Practice of Advanced Search and Enumeration" (P.K.). Work done in part while the authors were visiting the Simons Institute for the Theory of Computing.

†A full version of this paper is available at http://arxiv.org/abs/1602.01295

PODC'16, July 25–28, 2016, Chicago, IL, USA

ISBN 978-1-4503-3964-3/16/07...$15.00

DOI: http://dx.doi.org/10.1145/2933057.2933101

Keywords

batch evaluation; noninteractive proof; parameterized clique; Reed–Solomon; vector parallel; verification

1. INTRODUCTION

1.1 A scene of distress and relief at Camelot

Picture K Knights seated around the Round Table, distressed. At the center of the table stands the Input. The Knights have been tasked to prepare a Proof about the virtues of the input, and to make extreme haste: a proof must be prepared in time T/K, where T is the fastest time known in all of Britannia for any single soul to reveal such subtle virtues, let alone give uncontestable *proof* thereof.

Nigh impossible is the task in fact, for the Lady Morgana has enchanted many a poor Knight with her cunning dark magic, yet virtues must be revealed and proof thereof prepared. And not just any proof, but one that any lone soul can check, in time T/K and with a few tosses of a fair coin, and next to never be convinced if foul virtues it claims.

However, not all is lost, for the Knights recall the teachings of the wizard Merlin[1] and his powerful proofs that King Arthur so treasures. So the Knights agree to together evaluate in batch, and to individually decode-and-check for signs of the darkest of magic...

1.2 A template for community computation over common input

Building on Merlin–Arthur proofs [2] of *batch evaluation* of Williams [25], this paper documents a "Camelot template" for verifiable distributed computation that is robust against adversarial byzantine failures at the nodes and produces a static, independently verifiable proof that the computation succeeded. In essence, we observe that the act of *preparing* a proof in the Williams framework is magicless and robust against errors. Our contribution is in particular to show that for a number of problems such robust and correctness-proof-producing algorithms essentially match in total resource consumption the best known sequential algorithm for *solving* the problem.

We assume the following model for K distributed compute nodes with unique node identifiers. Each compute node has access to its own source of randomness that is independent

[1]Alas, the good wizard is taking a vacation, hence the distress at Camelot.

of the other nodes. The nodes are joined by a network that supports broadcast operations that take place (a) initially to all the nodes simultaneously, and, (b) after each node has finished computing, one short broadcast from the node to all the nodes. Here (a) is to broadcast the complete input (the problem instance) to the nodes, and (b) is to broadcast the encoded proof fragment that a node has computed to the other nodes. We assume sufficient synchronization exists in the network to coordinate the broadcasts so that each node knows when phases (a) and (b) are complete. Apart from this end-of-phase synchronization, broadcast operations may fail arbitrarily. For example, a broadcast may fail so that nodes may receive different and/or corrupt fragments in (b), or in (a) a node may receive an incorrect input that looks like a correct input. Furthermore, the nodes do not seek consensus. That is, at the end of phase (b), each node executes its own, individual check on the data it received and decides (probabilistically, using the random source at the node) whether to accept or reject the proof produced by the nodes.

Our subsequent algorithms guarantee that any entity (a compute node or an outside party) that has the correct input and a sufficient fraction of correctly encoded proof fragments will decode the correct proof and accept it. Furthermore, any entity that has the correct input will reject any incorrect proof presented to it (in encoded or decoded form) with high probability that can be controlled *after* the proof is presented for verification. In particular, any node with a correct proof can convince other nodes that it has a correct proof, but such subsequent consensus-seeking within the community after the algorithm has been executed is not within scope of the present paper.

1.3 How Camelot prepares, corrects, and checks a proof

We now review the Williams framework [25] and interpret it as a template for distributed computing in the assumed model with K computes nodes. The key idea is to task the K nodes to make *evaluations* of a univariate polynomial

$$P(x) = p_0 + p_1x + p_2x^2 + \ldots + p_dx^d \pmod{q},$$

where q is a prime that we assume each node can easily compute by looking at the input that it has received from the network. We also assume that each node can easily compute an upper bound for d from the input.

The polynomial $P(x)$ has been carefully constructed so that (a) it reveals[2] the desired properties of the input, and (b) the $d+1$ coefficients $p_0, p_1, \ldots, p_d \in \mathbb{Z}_q$ constitute a probabilistically verifiable *proof* that these properties have been correctly computed. In fact, the latter property is intrinsic to the template.

1. Proof preparation, in distributed encoded form. For a prime q and an integer e with $d+1 \le e \le q$, we task the K nodes to compute the sequence of e evaluations

$$P(0), P(1), \ldots, P(e-1) \pmod{q} \tag{1}$$

so that each node is responsible for about e/K evaluations, and broadcasts its evaluations to the other nodes once they are ready. This sequence of evaluations is, by definition, an encoding of the proof in the classical nonsystematic Reed–Solomon code [23] (see §2). From the perspective of community computation, this is a serendipitous property:

2. Error-correcting and decoding the proof. Since the nodes are tasked to produce entries in a Reed–Solomon codeword, each node can, *on its own*, run a fast Reed–Solomon decoder [15] (see §2) on the entries it has received from the network to recover both the actual proof $p_0, p_1, \ldots, p_d \in \mathbb{Z}_q$ and the evaluations $P(0), P(1), \ldots, P(e-1) \in \mathbb{Z}_q$ that failed, that is, the error locations identified by the decoder. In precise terms, to recover the correct proof using, e.g., the Gao [15] decoder, a node needs at least $(e+d+1)/2$ correct evaluations among the e evaluations for decoding to succeed at a node (see §2.2).

3. Checking a putative proof for correctness. Each node (or any other entity) that has available the correct input and a sequence $\tilde{p}_0, \tilde{p}_1, \ldots, \tilde{p}_d \in \mathbb{Z}_q$ can, probabilistically, check whether the sequence is in fact the correct proof $p_0, p_1, \ldots, p_d \in \mathbb{Z}_q$. This check is executed locally without any interaction with the network. All a node has to do is to select a uniform random integer $x_0 \in \mathbb{Z}_q$ and accept the proof if and only if

$$P(x_0) = \sum_{j=0}^{d} \tilde{p}_j x_0^j \pmod{q} \tag{2}$$

holds, at the cost of one evaluation of $P(x)$. (That is, the verifier executes the same algorithm that the nodes use for preparing the proof to obtain the left-hand side of (2); the right-hand side can be computed from $\tilde{p}_0, \tilde{p}_1, \ldots, \tilde{p}_d \in \mathbb{Z}_q$ using Horner's rule.) If the sequence $\tilde{p}_0, \tilde{p}_1, \ldots, \tilde{p}_d$ is the correct proof, the verifier always accepts. If the sequence is incorrect, it follows immediately from the fundamental theorem of algebra that $P(x_0) \neq \sum_{j=0}^{d} \tilde{p}_j x_0^j \pmod{q}$ holds with probability at least $1 - d/q$. Furthermore, since the verifier knows q and an upper bound for d, the verifier can control the probability of accepting an incorrect proof by independent repetitions of the test.

We stress that a node will, with high probability, not accept an incorrect proof even if arbitrary failures occur in the network and at the other nodes. Furthermore, assuming the failures are not extensive (remain below the decoding threshold) a correct proof will be decoded and accepted at each correctly functioning node that has the correct input. We refer to e.g. Tiwari *et al.* [24] for recent empirical data why robustness and proofs-of-correctness are increasingly desirable goals in algorithm design.

1.4 Optimality relative to best known sequential algorithms

Ideally, a Camelot algorithm should match in total running time the worst-case running time of the best known *sequential* algorithm for solving the problem. By design, such a Camelot algorithm not only solves the problem, but does so in *parallel*, *robustly*, and gives *an independently verifiable proof* that it succeeded. What is more, the parallel part of the computation (1) consists of evaluating the same polynomial P at distinct points, making the parallel computations intrinsically workload-balanced and ideal for vector-parallelization (single-instruction multiple-data (SIMD) parallelization) since each evaluation follows the same instruction stream.

[2]Possibly requiring iteration and postprocessing, e.g., the use of multiple distinct primes q and the Chinese Remainder Theorem to reconstruct large integers.

In essence, we seek the following optimal speedup tradeoff for a Camelot design. Assume that the best known sequential algorithm solves the problem essentially in time T. Then, an optimal Camelot design for K nodes should run in $E = T/K$ proof construction time and space for each node, and hence E evaluation (proof verification) time for a proof of size K, for any $K \leq T^{1/2}$. Here the upper bound $T^{1/2}$ is intrinsic to the framework since each node receives the whole proof for individual decoding and hence $E \geq K$. (This of course does not rule out variants where a single node does not work with the entire proof.)

In practice, our subsequent algorithm designs will not attain the optimal tradeoff for all problems considered. *However, for a number of canonical problems we are able to attain the optimal tradeoff.*

1.5 Our results—two highlights

This conference abstract highlights two examples of problems where we are able to attain the optimal tradeoff; the full version of this paper gives further highlights and an inventory of earlier algorithm designs that can be put into the Camelot framework.

For ease of exposition, we present our results as non-tradeoff versions with the maximum value of K (and hence the fastest wall-clock runtime E to prepare and check the proof) that we can attain, with the understanding that a smooth tradeoff up to the maximum K is possible and can be read off the proofs of our results.

When stating our results, we refer to K as the *proof size* and E as the *(running) time* of a Camelot algorithm. Put otherwise, the time E of a Camelot algorithm is the *wall-clock* time to prepare and verify the proof using K compute nodes working in parallel on the common input. The *total time* (sum of running times of all the nodes) is EK. The underlying precise degree d of the proof polynomial $P(x)$ is, up to factors suppressed by asymptotic notation, identically bounded as the stated proof size.[3] The stated proof size also bounds the amount of data the nodes in total broadcast across the network during proof preparation. With asymptotic notation we follow the convention that $\tilde{O}(\cdot)$ suppresses a factor polylogarithmic in the input size and $O^*(\cdot)$ suppresses a factor polynomial in the input size.

Each Camelot algorithm defines, as is, a *Merlin–Arthur* protocol [2], where Merlin's proof has the stated size, and Arthur's verification time is the stated time for the Camelot algorithm.

First highlight: counting small cliques. Our main result is that the problem of counting all the k-cliques in a graph admits a Camelot algorithm *that attains the optimal tradeoff relative to the best known sequential algorithm.* Let us write $2 \leq \omega < 2.3728639$ for the exponent of square matrix multiplication over the integers [20].

THEOREM 1. *For any constant $\epsilon > 0$ and any positive integer k divisible by 6, the number of k-cliques in an n-vertex graph can be computed with a Camelot algorithm that constructs a proof of size $O(n^{(\omega+\epsilon)k/6})$ in time $O(n^{(\omega+\epsilon)k/6})$.*

The best known sequential algorithm, due to Nešetřil and Poljak [22] (see also Eisenbrand and Grandoni [10]), runs in time $O(n^{(\omega+\epsilon)k/3})$. The algorithm in Theorem 1 is based on a novel, more space-efficient family of arithmetic circuits for evaluating a particular $\binom{6}{2}$-linear form that enables a very space-efficient design for counting 6-cliques in a graph.

Second highlight: graph coloring. As our second highlight result, we show that the problem of computing the chromatic polynomial of a given graph admits an optimal Camelot algorithm. Here the best known sequential algorithm runs in $O^*(2^n)$ time and $O^*(1.292^n)$ space [3, 4].

THEOREM 2. *The chromatic polynomial of an n-vertex graph can be computed with a Camelot algorithm that constructs a proof of size $O^*(2^{n/2})$ in time $O^*(2^{n/2})$.*

In particular, Theorem 2 gives an optimal tradeoff. The algorithm in Theorem 2 is a Kronecker-substitution-based polynomial lifting of the parallel partitioning sum-product algorithm of Björklund *et al.* [4].

Further Camelot designs. Many Camelot algorithms beyond the two highlight designs presented here are possible. We refer to the full version of this conference abstract for a detailed and more gradual exposition.

1.6 Overview of techniques and earlier work

The present Camelot framework can be seen as a continuation of two recent works aimed at understanding the fine-grained[4] complexity of computational problems and proof systems, initiated in a nondeterministic setting with a deterministic proof verifier by Carmosino *et al.* [7] and with the subsequent breakthrough by Williams [25] establishing non-trivial quantitative bounds for a *randomized verifier.* From this perspective, the Camelot framework pursues an even more fine-grained goal by focusing also on the effort of the *prover*, with the objective of relating the *total effort to prepare the proof* to the best known sequential algorithms for *solving* the problem at hand.

We recall the technical preliminaries underlying the framework in §2. To design an algorithm in the Camelot framework, all it takes is to come up with the proof polynomial P and a fast evaluation algorithm for P. To provide an accessible exposition towards our highlight results, we find it convenient to start (in §3) with an easier Camelot design and present the Merlin–Arthur protocol of Williams [25] for counting k-cliques in an n-vertex graph. Viewed as a Camelot algorithm, Williams's design runs in per-node time $\tilde{O}(n^{k/2+1})$ with a proof size of $\tilde{O}(n^{k/2})$, implying a total time that essentially meets the trivial sequential time $O(n^k)$. In particular, Williams's design admits a clean algebrization as the task of verifying a generalized matrix product (cf. Kruskal [18]) using a univariate polynomial extension of Freivalds's classical fingerprinting algorithm for verifying matrix products [13].

[3]The parameters e and q can be chosen with similar asymptotic bounds as d. We choose to omit the details of these parameters to keep the statement of our results concise, please consult the proofs for precise bounds on d to enable fine-tuning of selection of $d + 1 \leq e \leq q$ as appropriate for desired error-tolerance (during proof preparation) and soundness guarantee (for proof verification).

[4]*Fine-grained* in the sense that the objective is to obtain more precise *quantitative* bounds on resource usage compared with the more traditional coarse-grained and qualitative division between, e.g., polynomial time and exponential time in the context of classical Merlin–Arthur proofs [2].

Our design for Theorem 1 will also rely on a polynomial extension of an algebrization of the task of clique counting. Here the $\binom{6}{2}$-linear algebrization is essentially due to Nešetřil and Poljak [22], but we require a substantially different algebraic circuit design to evaluate the $\binom{6}{2}$-linear form. In §4 and §5 we present a new design that nests *four* levels of fast matrix multiplication so that the products at the top-level multiplication can (a) be evaluated in parallel and (b) extended to a proof polynomial P by careful use of Yates's algorithm [26] and fast matrix multiplication to enable efficient evaluation. The top-level multiplications rely on a trilinear representation of the matrix multiplication tensor $\langle n,n,n\rangle$ to assemble the monomials of a $\binom{6}{2}$-linear form out of a 3-linear base and three 4-linear parts, whose consistency is obtained via the trilinear representation. In essence, we show that 6-cliques can be counted with an arithmetic circuit of essentially the same size but with considerably more independence and depth than the Nešetřil–Poljak [22] design, which then enables the polynomial extension to a Camelot algorithm that attains the optimal speedup tradeoff relative to the Nešetřil–Poljak running time.

Our design for Theorem 2 is guided by the parallel algorithm of Björklund *et al.* [4] for computing the chromatic polynomial. In particular we rely on stardard inclusion–exclusion arguments [3] over tuples of independent sets, and split the domain (the vertex set) into two parts, using the ideas in [4] to sieve independent sets based on their intersections with the two parts. The key novelty in our present design is to lift the two-part approach into a univariate proof polynomial by means of Kronecker substitution, with two nested applications of Yates's algorithm to enable fast evaluation and an optimal Camelot design.

1.7 Related work

A Camelot algorithm seeks to *simultaneously* obtain essentially perfect parallelization on up to $K \le T^{1/2}$ parallel nodes, a noninteractive proof of correctness (probabilistically verifiable in no more time than each parallel node individually invests into the computation), robustness against errors, and to essentially match in total running time the best known sequential algorithm for solving the problem. To our knowledge, algorithm designs simultaneously meeting these goals have not been presented earlier. However, a large body of related work exists if one relaxes one or more of the goals; the following brief overview is not exhaustive.

McConnell, Mehlhorn, Näher, and Schweitzer [21] survey *certifiable algorithms* that produce, together with the output, an easy-to-verify correctness proof for the output. Many works study algorithms that are resilient to errors but do not in general produce a correctness proof. For example, Caminiti, Finocchi, Fusco, and Silvetri [6] study resilient dynamic programming, Chen, Grigorescy, and de Wolf [8] study error-correcting data structures for membership queries and polynomial evaluation, Cicalese [9] studies fault-tolerant search algorithms, and Finocchi, Grandoni, and Italiano [11] present resilient sorting and searching algorithms under memory faults.

Our focus on a magicless (honest) prover is not new. Goldwasser, Kalai, and Rothblum [17] study interactive proofs with a near-linear-time verifier in the input size and with a polynomial-time prover, however without a fine-grained running time goal and without a goal for parallelizability of proof preparation.

Fraigniaud, Korman, and Peleg [12] and Göös and Suomela [16] study proofs that can be verified locally at the nodes of a network of distributed processors but without detailed consideration of the complexity to prepare such a proof.

2. PRELIMINARIES

This section recalls the fast arithmetic primitives underlying the Camelot framework and our highlight results.

2.1 Fast polynomial arithmetic

Let us recall the fast arithmetic toolbox (see von zur Gathen and Gerhard [14]) for polynomials with coefficients in a finite field $\mathbb{F}_q$. Computational complexity is measured in the number of arithmetic operations in $\mathbb{F}_q$. Multiplication and division of two polynomials of degree at most d can be computed in $O(d \log d \log\log d)$ operations. The greatest common divisor of two polynomials of degree at most d can be computed in $O(d \log^2 d \log\log d)$ operations. Given a polynomial $P(x) = p_0 + p_1x + p_2x^2 \ldots + p_dx^d \in \mathbb{F}_q[x]$ and points $x_0, x_1, \ldots, x_d \in \mathbb{F}_q$ as input, the *evaluation map* $(P(x_0), P(x_1), \ldots, P(x_d)) \in \mathbb{F}_q^{d+1}$ can be computed in $O(d \log^2 d \log\log d)$ operations. Dually, given distinct points $x_0, x_1, \ldots, x_d \in \mathbb{F}_q$ and values $y_0, y_1, \ldots, y_d \in \mathbb{F}_q$ as input, the *interpolation map* computes the coefficients $(p_0, p_1, \ldots, p_d) \in \mathbb{F}_q^{d+1}$ of a polynomial $P(x)$ with $P(x_i) = y_i$ for all $i = 0, 1, \ldots, d$ in $O(d \log^2 d \log\log d)$ operations.

2.2 Reed–Solomon codes

We work with univariate polynomial codes in nonsystematic form as originally discovered by Reed and Solomon [23] to allow for fast decoding based on polynomial arithmetic (cf. Gao [15]).

Fix a finite field $\mathbb{F}_q$ and any $1 \le e \le q$ distinct elements $x_1, x_2, \ldots, x_e \in \mathbb{F}_q$. The parameter e is the *length* of the code. To *encode* a *message* $(p_0, p_1, \ldots, p_d) \in \mathbb{F}_q^{d+1}$ consisting of $d+1$ *symbols*, $1 \le d+1 \le e$, form the message polynomial $P(x) = p_0 + p_1x + p_2x^2 + \ldots + p_dx^d$ and the *codeword* $(P(x_1), P(x_2), \ldots, P(x_e)) \in \mathbb{F}_q^e$. The codeword can be computed from the message in $O(e \log^2 e \log\log e)$ operations using fast interpolation (see §2.1).

Since a nonzero polynomial of degree d has at most d roots, any two codewords either agree in at most d symbols or are identical. Thus, we can uniquely *decode* the message from any *received* word $(r_1, r_2, \ldots, r_e) \in \mathbb{F}_q^n$ that differs from the codeword in at most $(e-d-1)/2$ symbols.

To decode the received word (or assert decoding failure), we use the following algorithm of Gao [15]. As a precomputation step, compute the polynomial $G_0(x) = \prod_{i=1}^{e}(x - x_i) \in \mathbb{F}_q[x]$. (When $e = q$, we have $G_0(x) = x^q - x$ which suffices for our applications in this paper.) To decode $(r_1, r_2, \ldots, r_e) \in \mathbb{F}_q^e$, first interpolate the unique polynomial $G_1(x) \in \mathbb{F}_q[x]$ of degree at most $e-1$ with $G_1(x_i) = r_i$ for all $i = 1, 2, \ldots, e$. Second, apply the extended Euclidean algorithm to the polynomials $G_0(x)$ and $G_1(x)$, but stop as soon as the remainder $G(x)$ has degree less than $(e+d+1)/2$. At this point suppose that $U(x)G_0(x) + V(x)G_1(x) = G(x)$. Finally, divide $G(x)$ by $V(x)$ to obtain $G(x) = P(x)V(x) + R(x)$, where the degree of $R(x)$ is less than the degree of $V(x)$. If $R(x) = 0$ and $P(x)$ has degree at most d, output $P(x)$ as the result of decoding; otherwise assert decoding failure. We observe that decoding runs in $O(e \log^2 e \log\log e)$ operations using fast polynomial arithmetic.

2.3 Yates's algorithm

The following algorithm will be used as a subroutine of our fast evaluation algorithms in §5.3 and §7.1. For positive integers s, t, k, Yates's algorithm [26] multiplies a given $s^k \times 1$ vector x with a structured $t^k \times s^k$ matrix M to produce as output a $t^k \times 1$ vector $y = Mx$. The structural assumption about the matrix M is that it is a Kronecker power $M = A^{\otimes k}$ of a small $t \times s$ matrix A with entries α_{ij} for $i = 0, 1, \ldots, t-1$ and $j = 0, 1, \ldots, s-1$. All arithmetic takes place in a field $\mathbb{F}$. For a positive integer d, let us write $[d] = \{0, 1, \ldots, d-1\}$.

For positive integers d, k we shall tacitly identify each $j \in [d^k]$ with $(j_1, j_2, \ldots, j_k) \in [d]^k$. Indeed, we can view j as a k-digit integer in base d, where $j_1, j_2, \ldots, j_k$ are the k digits.

Given x and A as input, Yates's algorithm computes, for all $i \in [t^k]$, the value

$$y_i = \sum_{j \in [s^k]} \alpha_{i_1 j_1} \alpha_{i_2 j_2} \cdots \alpha_{i_k j_k} x_j \,. \tag{3}$$

Yates's algorithm employs dynamic programming to compute the k nested sums implicit in (3) one at a time. We refer to the full version of this conference abstract for a detailed exposition and extensions of Yates's algorithm. The classical version of the algorithm runs in $O((s^{k+1} + t^{k+1})k)$ operations, using working space for $O(s^k + t^k)$ field elements.

3. WILLIAMS'S MERLIN–ARTHUR PROTOCOL FOR COUNTING K-CLIQUES

This section interprets Williams's [25] Merlin–Arthur protocol for counting k-cliques as a Camelot algorithm. We stress that this section is for expositionary purposes only, in particular to demonstrate the Camelot framework with an easier design before proceeding to our highlight result.

3.1 A protocol for verifying (generalized) matrix products

Let us present a proof-polynomial version of Freivalds's classical protocol [13] to verify a matrix product and generalize it to m-linear products of $m > 2$ matrices; such generalized matrix products have been studied e.g. by Kruskal [18].

Suppose we have m integer matrices, $A^{(1)}, A^{(2)}, \ldots, A^{(m)}$, each of shape $s \times t$. We are to compute the

$$\underbrace{s \times s \times \cdots \times s}_{m}$$

array B, defined for all $i \in [s]^m$ by

$$b_i = \sum_{j=0}^{t-1} a^{(1)}_{i_1 j} a^{(2)}_{i_2 j} \cdots a^{(m)}_{i_m j} \,. \tag{4}$$

Observe that we can take $m = 2$ to recover the classical matrix product $B = A^{(1)}\big(A^{(2)}\big)^T$ It is immediate that we can compute B from the given input in $O(s^m tm)$ operations.

Now let us assume the role of Arthur. Suppose Merlin has computed $\tilde{B}$ (which Merlin claims to be B) and we are to check Merlin's work. Define the proof polynomial $P(x)$ as follows (5), and observe an equivalent definition (6):

$$\begin{aligned} P(x) &= \sum_{i \in [s]^m} b_i x^{s^{m-1} i_m + s^{m-2} i_{m-1} + \ldots + i_1} \qquad (5) \\ &= \sum_{i \in [s]^m} \sum_{j=0}^{t-1} a^{(1)}_{i_1 j} a^{(2)}_{i_2 j} \cdots a^{(m)}_{i_m j} x^{s^{m-1} i_m + s^{m-2} i_{m-1} + \ldots + i_1} \\ &= \sum_{j=0}^{t-1} \Bigg(\sum_{i_1=0}^{s-1} a^{(1)}_{i_1 j} x^{i_1} \Bigg) \cdots \Bigg(\sum_{i_m=0}^{s-1} a^{(m)}_{i_m j} x^{s^{m-1} i_m} \Bigg) . \qquad (6) \end{aligned}$$

It is immediate that $P(x)$ has degree at most $d \le s^m - 1$ and that the coefficients of $P(x)$ are precisely the entries of the array B. Thus, in essence, by handing us (what he claims to be) B, Merlin has handed us the polynomial $P(x)$ in coefficient form. Using (6), *without relying on Merlin's advice*, we can evaluate $P(x_0) \pmod q$ at any given $x_0 \in \mathbb{Z}_q$ in $O(tms)$ operations modulo q. Similarly, *but now relying on Merlin's advice*, using (5) and Horner's rule, we can evaluate $P(x_0) \pmod q$ in $O(s^m)$ operations. If Merlin has handed to us an incorrect B, we catch him with probability at least $1 - d/q$ by detecting that the two evaluations disagree; recall §1.3.

3.2 Williams's protocol for counting k-cliques

Let G be a graph with vertex set $[n]$ and let us assume that k is an even constant. Williams's protocol counts the cliques of size k in G via the observation that the complete graph K_k decomposes into two vertex-disjoint complete graphs $K_{k/2}$ and a complete bipartite graph $K_{k/2,k/2}$ joining the two. The key idea is to have Merlin assist to join the two halves in all possible ways via the protocol in §3.1. Let us assume the role of Arthur and proceed as follows. Construct a matrix A of shape $n \times n^{k/2}$ defined for all $i, j_1, j_2, \ldots, j_{k/2} \in [n]$ by $a_{i, j_1 j_2 \cdots j_{k/2}} = 1$ if both (a) $j_1, j_2, \ldots, j_{k/2}$ are distinct and form a $k/2$-clique in G and (b) i is distinct from and adjacent to each of $j_1, j_2, \ldots, j_{k/2}$ in G; otherwise $a_{i, j_1 j_2 \cdots j_{k/2}} = 0$. Have Merlin compute and send to us the

$$\underbrace{n \times n \times \cdots \times n}_{k/2}$$

array B defined by (4) for $s = n$, $t = n^{k/2}$, $m = k/2$, and $A^{(1)} = A^{(2)} = \ldots = A^{(m)} = A$. For a prime $q \ge n^{k/2} + 1$, use the protocol in §3.1 to check Merlin's work. (If the check fails, assert failure.) Take the sum of the values b_i for all distinct $i_1, i_2, \ldots, i_{k/2} \in \{0, 1, \ldots, n-1\}$ such that $i_1, i_2, \ldots, i_{k/2}$ form a $k/2$-clique in G. This sum is $k!$ times the number of k-cliques in G. The protocol runs in $\tilde{O}(n^{k/2+1})$ time.

4. FAST AND SPACE-EFFICIENT EVALUATION OF A MULTILINEAR FORM

We now proceed with the details of our highlight result, which is based on the study of a multilinear form that integrates over a function with only pairwise interactions between variables by decomposing the interactions into $\binom{6}{2} = 15$ parts. The advantage of such a decomposition is that one can use fast matrix multiplication to arrive at a nontrivial arithmetic circuit for fast integration. An example application is counting small subgraphs of a graph, which we will illustrate in more detail in the next section.

4.1 The form and the Nešetřil–Poljak formula

Let χ be an[5] $N \times N$ matrix over a commutative ring $\mathscr{R}$. We seek to compute the $\binom{6}{2}$-linear form

$$X_{\binom{6}{2}} = \sum_{\substack{a,b,c\\d,e,f}} \chi_{ab}\chi_{ac}\chi_{ad}\chi_{ae}\chi_{af}\chi_{bc}\chi_{bd}\chi_{be}\chi_{bf}\chi_{cd}\chi_{ce}\chi_{cf}\chi_{de}\chi_{df}\chi_{ef}\,. \quad (7)$$

A direct evaluation of (7) takes $O(N^6)$ operations. Nešetřil and Poljak [22] observe that we can precompute the three $N^2 \times N^2$ matrices

$$\begin{aligned} U_{ab,cd} &= \chi_{ab}\chi_{ac}\chi_{ad}\chi_{bc}\chi_{bd}\,, \\ S_{ab,ef} &= \chi_{ae}\chi_{af}\chi_{be}\chi_{bf}\chi_{ef}\,, \\ T_{cd,ef} &= \chi_{cd}\chi_{ce}\chi_{cf}\chi_{de}\chi_{df}\,, \end{aligned}$$

and then use fast matrix multiplication to compute

$$\begin{aligned} V_{ab,cd} &= \sum_{e,f} S_{ab,ef}T_{cd,ef}\,, \\ X_{\binom{6}{2}} &= \sum_{a,b,c,d} U_{ab,cd}V_{ab,cd}\,. \end{aligned}$$

This takes $O(N^{2\omega+\epsilon})$ arithmetic operations, using space for $O(N^4)$ scalars for any constant $\epsilon > 0$.

4.2 A new summation formula

Our main contribution in this section is a new circuit design that matches the Nešetřil–Poljak design in the asymptotic number of arithmetic operations but reduces the space complexity from $O(N^4)$ to $O(N^2)$ scalars. In particular, the space complexity is linear in the input size. Furthermore, the new design is easily parallelizable and extendable to a proof polynomial, as we will witness in the next section.

The new design works with the following decomposition of the matrix multiplication tensor. For $r = 1, 2, \ldots, R$, let $\alpha_{de}(r), \beta_{ef}(r), \gamma_{df}(r)$ be ring elements that satisfy the multivariate polynomial identity

$$\sum_{d,e,f} u_{de}v_{ef}w_{df} = \sum_{r=1}^{R}\Big(\sum_{d,e'}\alpha_{de'}(r)u_{de'}\Big)\Big(\sum_{e,f'}\beta_{ef'}(r)v_{ef'}\Big)\Big(\sum_{d',f}\gamma_{d'f}(r)w_{d'f}\Big)\,. \quad (8)$$

We can assume that $R = O(N^{\omega+\epsilon/2})$ for an arbitrary constant $\epsilon > 0$, where ω is the limiting exponent for the tensor rank of the matrix multiplication tensor $\langle n, n, n\rangle$ in $\mathscr{R}$ [5, 19].

The new design is as follows. For each $r = 1, 2, \ldots, R$, compute, using fast matrix multiplication,

$$\begin{aligned} H_{ad}(r) &= \sum_{e'} \alpha_{de'}(r)\chi_{ae'}\chi_{de'}\,, \\ K_{be}(r) &= \sum_{f'} \beta_{ef'}(r)\chi_{bf'}\chi_{ef'}\,, \\ L_{cf}(r) &= \sum_{d'} \gamma_{d'f}(r)\chi_{cd'}\chi_{d'f}\,, \\ A_{ab}(r) &= \sum_{d} \chi_{ad}\chi_{bd}H_{ad}(r)\,, \\ B_{bc}(r) &= \sum_{e} \chi_{be}\chi_{ce}K_{be}(r)\,, \\ C_{ac}(r) &= \sum_{f} \chi_{af}\chi_{cf}L_{cf}(r)\,. \end{aligned} \quad (9)$$

Finally, compute, again using fast matrix multiplication,

$$\begin{aligned} Q_{ab}(r) &= \sum_{c} \chi_{ac}\chi_{bc}B_{bc}(r)C_{ac}(r)\,, \\ P(r) &= \sum_{a,b} \chi_{ab}A_{ab}(r)Q_{ab}(r)\,. \end{aligned} \quad (10)$$

Each term $P(r)$ takes $O(N^{\omega+\epsilon/2})$ operations and space for $O(N^2)$ scalars to compute.

THEOREM 3. $X_{\binom{6}{2}} = \sum_{r=1}^{R} P(r)$.

PROOF. Expanding and applying (8) for each a, b, c in turn, we have

$$\begin{aligned} \sum_{r=1}^{R} P(r) &= \sum_{r=1}^{R}\sum_{a,b,c} \chi_{ab}\chi_{ac}\chi_{bc}A_{ab}(r)B_{bc}(r)C_{ac}(r) \\ &= \sum_{r=1}^{R}\sum_{a,b,c} \chi_{ab}\chi_{ac}\chi_{bc}\sum_{d,e'}\alpha_{de'}(r)\chi_{ad}\chi_{ae'}\chi_{bd}\chi_{de'} \\ &\qquad \sum_{e,f'}\beta_{ef'}(r)\chi_{be}\chi_{bf'}\chi_{ce}\chi_{ef'} \\ &\qquad \sum_{d',f,}\gamma_{d'f}(r)\chi_{af}\chi_{cd'}\chi_{cf}\chi_{d'f} \\ &= \sum_{a,b,c}\chi_{ab}\chi_{ac}\chi_{bc}\sum_{r=1}^{R}\Big(\sum_{d,e'}\alpha_{de'}(r)\chi_{ad}\chi_{ae'}\chi_{bd}\chi_{de'}\Big) \\ &\qquad \Big(\sum_{e,f'}\beta_{ef'}(r)\chi_{be}\chi_{bf'}\chi_{ce}\chi_{ef'}\Big) \\ &\qquad \Big(\sum_{d',f}\gamma_{d'f}(r)\chi_{af}\chi_{cd'}\chi_{cf}\chi_{d'f}\Big) \\ &= \sum_{a,b,c}\chi_{ab}\chi_{ac}\chi_{bc} \\ &\qquad \sum_{d,e,f}\chi_{ad}\chi_{ae}\chi_{af}\chi_{bd}\chi_{be}\chi_{bf}\chi_{cd}\chi_{ce}\chi_{cf}\chi_{de}\chi_{df}\chi_{ef}\,. \end{aligned}$$

□

Thus, we can compute (7) from χ in $O(N^{2\omega+\epsilon})$ operations and space for $O(N^2)$ scalars. Furthermore, easy parallelization using up to $O(N^{\omega+\epsilon/2})$ compute nodes is now possible since the values $P(r)$ can be computed independently of each other.

[5]The present formulation admits an immediate generalization to $\binom{6}{2}$ distinct $N \times N$ matrices, but to keep the notation concise, we work with a single matrix χ.

5. A CAMELOT ALGORITHM FOR COUNTING SMALL CLIQUES

This section proves Theorem 1. In particular, we demonstrate how to reduce counting k-cliques into an evaluation of the $\binom{6}{2}$-linear form, and then develop a proof polynomial $P(x)$ for the $\binom{6}{2}$-linear form, together with a fast evaluation algorithm that computes $P(x_0) \pmod{q}$ for given $x_0 \in \mathbb{Z}_q$.

5.1 Reduction to the multilinear form

Suppose that 6 divides k. We start with a routine reduction from counting k-cliques in a given n-vertex graph G to the task of evaluating the $\binom{6}{2}$-linear form for a particular matrix χ derived from G. (That is, G is the common input, from which each node individually derives χ.)

Let χ be an $N \times N$ matrix with $N = \binom{n}{k/6} \leq n^{k/6}$ and entries defined for all $A, B \in \binom{V(G)}{k/6}$ by

$$\chi_{AB} = \begin{cases} 1 & A \cup B \text{ is a clique in } G \text{ and } A \cap B = \emptyset; \\ 0 & \text{otherwise.} \end{cases}$$

That is, the entries of χ indicate all pairs of $k/6$-cliques in G that together form a $k/3$-clique.

The $\binom{6}{2}$-linear form $X_{\binom{6}{2}}$ with input χ now counts each k-clique in G exactly $\binom{k}{k/6,\, k/6,\, k/6,\, k/6,\, k/6,\, k/6}$ times.

5.2 A proof polynomial for the multilinear form

We now turn the counting algorithm in the previous section into a Camelot algorithm. First, we present a proof polynomial $P(x)$ in the Camelot framework that enables us to compute and verify the value $X_{\binom{6}{2}}$ from the input.

We define a univariate polynomial $P(x)$ so that we can recover $X_{\binom{6}{2}}$ via Theorem 3 using evaluations of $P(x)$ at integer points $x = 1, 2, \ldots, R$. We extend the coefficients $\alpha_{de}(r), \beta_{ef}(r), \gamma_{df}(r)$ into interpolation polynomials and then extend (9) and (10) into polynomials. Towards this end, for $r = 1, 2, \ldots, R$, let us write

$$\Lambda_r(x) = \prod_{\substack{j=1 \\ j \neq r}}^{R} \frac{x-j}{r-j} \tag{11}$$

for the Lagrange interpolation polynomials of degree at most R for the points $1, 2, \ldots, R$. The three univariate polynomials

$$\begin{aligned} \alpha_{de}(x) &= \sum_{r=1}^{R} \alpha_{de}(r)\Lambda_r(x)\,, \\ \beta_{ef}(x) &= \sum_{r=1}^{R} \beta_{ef}(r)\Lambda_r(x)\,, \\ \gamma_{df}(x) &= \sum_{r=1}^{R} \gamma_{df}(r)\Lambda_r(x) \end{aligned} \tag{12}$$

interpolate over the coefficients $\alpha_{de}(r), \beta_{ef}(r), \gamma_{df}(r)$ when $x = 1, 2, \ldots, R$. From (12), (9), and (10) it is immediate that the univariate polynomials

$$\begin{aligned} H_{ad}(x) &= \sum_{e'} \alpha_{de'}(x)\chi_{ae'}\chi_{de'}\,, \\ K_{be}(x) &= \sum_{f'} \beta_{ef'}(x)\chi_{bf'}\chi_{ef'}\,, \\ L_{cf}(x) &= \sum_{d'} \gamma_{d'f}(x)\chi_{cd'}\chi_{d'f}\,, \\ A_{ab}(x) &= \sum_{d} \chi_{ad}\chi_{bd}H_{ad}(x)\,, \\ B_{bc}(x) &= \sum_{e} \chi_{be}\chi_{ce}K_{be}(x)\,, \\ C_{ac}(x) &= \sum_{f} \chi_{af}\chi_{cf}L_{cf}(x)\,, \end{aligned} \tag{13}$$

and

$$\begin{aligned} Q_{ab}(x) &= \sum_{c} \chi_{ac}\chi_{bc}B_{bc}(x)C_{ac}(x)\,, \\ P(x) &= \sum_{a,b} \chi_{ab}A_{ab}(x)Q_{ab}(x)\,. \end{aligned} \tag{14}$$

have degree at most $3R$ and the evaluations of $P(x)$ at $x = 1, 2, \ldots, R$ satisfy Theorem 3. Thus, $P(x)$ is a proof polynomial that we can employ in the Camelot framework. For the modulus q we can select one or more primes $q \geq 3R + 1$ to enable interpolation and reconstruction of $X_{\binom{6}{2}}$ over the integers. In particular we can assume $q = O(R)$. Indeed, since $q \geq N^2$ and χ has entries in $\{0, 1\}$, we can recover the integer $0 \leq X_{\binom{6}{2}} = \sum_{r=1}^{R} P(r) \leq N^6$ from evaluations $\sum_{r=1}^{R} P(r) \pmod{q}$ for at most $O(1)$ distinct primes $q \geq 3R + 1$ using the Chinese Remainder Theorem. This gives proof size $\tilde{O}(R)$.

5.3 The evaluation algorithm

To complete the Camelot algorithm it remains to describe how each node evaluates, modulo q, the proof polynomial $P(x)$ at a given point. Let $x_0 \in \mathbb{Z}_q$ be given. We seek to compute $P(x_0) \pmod{q}$ in time $O(N^{\omega+\epsilon})$.

Let us assume that we have available the values $\alpha_{de}(x_0)$, $\beta_{ef}(x_0)$, $\gamma_{df}(x_0)$ for all d, e, f. (This is a nontrivial assumption that we will justify in what follows.) Then, using fast matrix multiplication to evaluate (13) and (14) at $x = x_0$, we obtain $P(x_0)$ in $O(N^{\omega+\epsilon/2})$ operations and $O(N^2)$ space.

Arithmetic operations on scalars modulo $q = O(R)$ can be implemented in $\tilde{O}(1)$ time and space, which is subsumed by the bound $O(N^{\omega+\epsilon})$. Thus, we are done assuming we can justify our earlier assumption.

To compute the values $\alpha_{de}(x_0)$, $\beta_{ef}(x_0)$, $\gamma_{df}(x_0)$ for all d, e, f, we proceed to take a look at the detailed structure of the coefficients $\alpha_{de}(r), \beta_{ef}(r), \gamma_{df}(r)$. We will focus on the coefficients $\alpha_{de}(r)$, the cases for $\beta_{ef}(r)$ and $\gamma_{df}(r)$ are symmetric.

By the properties of tensor rank and the fact that matrix multiplication tensors are closed under taking of Kronecker products, we can assume without loss of generality that $R = O(N^{\omega+\epsilon/2})$ and that there exist positive integer constants R_0, N_0 and a positive integer t such that $N = N_0^t$ and $R = R_0^t$. In particular, we may identify the indices d, e and the index r with t-digit integers in base N_0 and R_0, respectively, so that if we write d_j, e_j and r_j for the jth digit of d, e

and r, respectively, the coefficient $\alpha_{de}(r)$ has the Kronecker product form

$$\alpha_{de}(r) = \prod_{j=1}^{t} \alpha^{(0)}_{d_j e_j}(r_j)\,, \qquad (15)$$

where $\alpha^{(0)}$ is a matrix of size $N_0^2 \times R_0$ with integer entries. Thus, we may view (15) as an integer matrix of size $N^2 \times R$ which has been obtained as the t-fold Kronecker power of the constant-sized-and-entried matrix $\alpha^{(0)}$.

Let us now describe how to compute the N^2 coefficients $\alpha_{de}(x_0) \pmod q$ for all d, e. Let us recall from (12) that $\alpha_{de}(x)$ is an interpolating polynomial for the values (15). That is, we have, for all d, e,

$$\alpha_{de}(x_0) = \sum_{r=1}^{R} \alpha_{de}(r)\Lambda_r(x_0) \pmod q\,. \qquad (16)$$

We observe that (16) in fact describes a matrix-vector multiplication: we multiply the $N^2 \times R$ matrix with entries $\alpha_{de}(r)$ with the $R \times 1$ vector with entries $\Lambda_r(x_0)$. Because of the Kronecker structure (15), this matrix-vector product can be computed in $O(Rt)$ operations using Yates's algorithm (§2.3).

To initialize Yates's algorithm, we require the $R\times 1$ vector, so let us start by computing the values $\Lambda_r(x_0) \pmod q$ for $r = 1, 2, \ldots, R$. If $x_0 \in \{1, 2, \ldots, R\}$ the computation is immediate (insert a 1 to position x_0 and fill the rest of the vector with 0s), so let us assume that $x_0 \notin \{1, 2, \ldots, R\}$. First, precompute the values $F_0, F_1, \ldots, F_{R-1}$ with the recurrence $F_0 = 1$, $F_j = j \cdot F_{j-1} \pmod q$. Second, precompute the product $\Gamma(x_0) = \prod_{j=1}^{R}(x_0 - j) \pmod q$. Finally, observe from (11) that we can compute, for each $r = 1, 2, \ldots, R$,

$$\Lambda_r(x_0) = \frac{1}{(-1)^{R-r}F_{r-1}F_{R-r}} \cdot \frac{\Gamma(x_0)}{(x_0 - r)} \pmod q\,.$$

This initialization takes in total $O(R)$ operations and space modulo q.

Since $t = O(\log N)$ and $R = O(N^{\omega+\epsilon/2})$, the entire evaluation algorithm runs in $O(N^{\omega+\epsilon})$ time and space. This completes the Camelot framework for computing and verifying $X_{\binom{6}{2}}$ and thus proves Theorem 1.

6. A PROOF TEMPLATE FOR PARTITIONING SUM-PRODUCTS

This section supplies a template for proof polynomials that underlies our highlight result for the chromatic polynomial. We rely on Kronecker substitution to enable succinct univariate encoding of the partitioning property.

6.1 The problem

Let $U = \{1, 2, \ldots, n\}$ be an n-element ground set (or *universe*), and let us write 2^U for the set of all subsets of U. Let us call a function $f : 2^U \to \mathbb{Z}$ a *set function.*

Suppose the common input consists of at least n bits, known to all the nodes. Suppose the input defines a set function f such that for any given $X \subseteq U$ any node can compute the value $f(X)$ in time $O^*(1)$. *Furthermore, we assume that based on the input each node can in $O^*(1)$ time compute an upper bound ϕ such that $|f(X)| \leq \phi$ for all $X \subseteq U$.*

For a positive integer t with $t = O^*(1)$, the nodes would like to compute the value of the *t-part partitioning sum product*

$$\sum_{(X_1, X_2, \ldots, X_t)} f(X_1)f(X_2)\cdots f(X_t)\,, \qquad (17)$$

where the sum is over all t-tuples $(X_1, X_2, \ldots, X_t) \in 2^U \times 2^U \times \cdots \times 2^U$ such that

$$\begin{aligned} X_1 \cup X_2 \cup \cdots \cup X_t = U \\ \text{and } X_i \cap X_j = \emptyset \text{ holds for all } 1 \leq i < j \leq t. \end{aligned} \qquad (18)$$

That is, the t-tuple $(X_1, X_2, \ldots, X_t)$ partitions the universe U into t pairwise disjoint *parts* $X_1, X_2, \ldots, X_t$ so that the ordering of the parts is relevant and zero or more empty parts are permitted. On its own, a node can compute (17) in time $O^*(2^n)$ [3].

6.2 The proof polynomial

This section defines the proof polynomial $P(x)$ for partitioning sum-products. We start by partitioning the universe U into two disjoint parts, $U = E \cup B$, where E is the *explicit* set (whose subsets each node will track explicitly) and B is, by slight abuse of terminology, a set of *bits* (where the node will rely on advice from the other nodes).

Let us assume that the set B of bits is $\{0, 1, \ldots, 2^{|B|-1}\}$. With this assumption, select exactly $|B|$ bits, possibly with repetition. Observe that if your bits sum to $2^{|B|} - 1$, then you have selected each bit exactly once (without repetition).

Let us also recall that there are exactly $\binom{m+k-1}{k-1}$ ways to place m identical balls into k distinct bins. Put otherwise, we can form exactly $\binom{m+k-1}{k-1}$ distinct multisets of size m over a ground set of k elements. Let us write $\left(\!\binom{B}{k}\!\right)$ for the set of multisets of size k over B. In particular, $|\left(\!\binom{B}{|B|}\!\right)| = \binom{2|B|-1}{|B|-1}$ is precisely the number of ways we can select $|B|$ bits out of B, possibly with repetition. Let us write $\sum M$ for the sum of elements in $M \in \left(\!\binom{B}{|B|}\!\right)$. With this notation, our previous observation is equivalent the statement that for all $M \in \left(\!\binom{B}{|B|}\!\right)$ we have $\sum M = 2^{|B|} - 1$ if and only if $M = B$.

It will be convenient to present the proof polynomial first over the integers, and only then choose appropriate primes q. The proof polynomial is

$$P(x) = p_0 + p_1 x + p_2 x^2 + \ldots + p_d x^d \qquad (19)$$

whose coefficients are defined for all $s = 0, 1, \ldots, d$ with $d = 2^{|B|-1}|B|$ by

$$p_s = \sum_{(X_1, X_2, \ldots, X_t)} f(X_1)f(X_2)\cdots f(X_t)\,, \qquad (20)$$

where the sum is over all t-tuples $(X_1, X_2, \ldots, X_t) \in 2^U \times 2^U \times \cdots \times 2^U$ that satisfy the multiset equality

$$X_1 + X_2 + \ldots + X_t = E + M \qquad (21)$$

for a multiset $M \in \left(\!\binom{B}{|B|}\!\right)$ with $\sum M = s$. (We use additive notation for multisets to stress that the element multiplicities must agree for each element in the ground set U.)

We observe that $p_{2^{|B|-1}}$ agrees with (17). Indeed, (18) holds if and only if (21) holds with $B = M$. Furthermore, $B = M$ if and only if $\sum M = 2^{|B|-1}$. Thus, each node needs to get confidence that the coefficients $p_0, p_1, \ldots, p_d$ have been correctly computed, *over the integers.*

Since $P(x)$ has degree at most $2^{|B|-1}|B|$, it suffices to use primes q with $q = O^*(2^{|B|})$ to enable evaluation and reconstruction of the proof modulo q. Such primes can be found in time $O^*(1)$ [1].

Each node can use the upper bound ϕ on the absolute values of f to compute in time $O^*(1)$ the upper bound $2^{nt+1}\phi^t$ for the absolute values in (20). Assuming that $\log q = \Omega(n)$ and $\log q = \Omega(\phi)$, which will be the case in our instantiations of the template, it suffices to work with $O^*(1)$ distinct primes q to reconstruct the *integer* coefficients $p_0, p_1, \ldots, p_d$. Indeed, we have $t = O^*(1)$ and $\log \phi = O^*(1)$ since ϕ is computable from the common input in time $O^*(1)$.

6.3 A template for the evaluation algorithm

Let $x_0 \in \{0, 1, \ldots, q-1\}$ be given. We now describe how a node computes $P(x_0) \pmod q$, but will leave one implementation detail unspecified, namely how the function g is computed within the desired computational budget, with the understanding that such algorithms will be provided in subsequent sections when the template is instantiated. By "computing a function" we mean computing a table that contains the value of the function for every possible input to the function.

Let w_E, w_B be formal indeterminates. That is, each node will be computing with polynomials in w_E, w_B with integer coefficients normalized to $\{0, 1, \ldots, q-1\}$ modulo q. Each node computes the function $g : 2^E \to \mathbb{Z}_q[w_E, w_B]$ defined for all $Y \subseteq E$ by

$$g(Y) = \sum_{\substack{X \subseteq U \\ X \cap E \subseteq Y}} f(X) w_E^{|X \cap E|} w_B^{|X \cap B|} \prod_{b \in X \cap B} x_0^b \pmod q\,. \quad (22)$$

(Recall that $B = \{0, 1, \ldots, 2^{|B|-1}\}$ so the expression x_0^b is well-defined.) The time budget for computing the function g is $O^*(2^{|E|})$.

Assuming the node has computed g, it next computes the polynomial

$$\begin{aligned} a(w_E, w_B) &= \sum_{j_E, j_B} a_{j_E, j_B} w_E^{j_E} w_B^{j_B} \\ &= \sum_{Y \subseteq E} (-1)^{|E \setminus Y|} g(Y)^t \pmod q\,. \end{aligned} \quad (23)$$

The node is interested on $a_{|E|,|B|}$, the integer coefficient of the monomial $w_E^{|E|} w_B^{|B|}$ in $a(w)$. Using (23) and the computed g, the node can compute $a_{|E|,|B|}$ in time $O^*(2^{|E|})$.

From (22), (23), and standard inclusion–exclusion arguments [3] it follows that, modulo q,

$$a_{|E|,|B|} = \sum_{(X_1, X_2, \ldots, X_t)} f(X_1) f(X_2) \cdots f(X_t) \prod_{j=1}^{t} \prod_{b \in X_j \cap B} x_0^b\,, \quad (24)$$

where the sum is over all t-tuples $(X_1, X_2, \ldots, X_t) \in 2^U \times 2^U \times \cdots \times 2^U$ for which there exists a multiset $M \in \left(\!\binom{B}{|B|}\!\right)$ with

$$X_1 + X_2 + \ldots + X_t = E + M\,. \quad (25)$$

Furthermore, every multiset $M \in \left(\!\binom{B}{|B|}\!\right)$ satisfies $\sum M \in \{0, 1, \ldots, 2^{|B|-1}|B|\}$.

Comparing (20) and (21) with (24) and (25), we have

$$P(x_0) = a_{|E|,|B|} \pmod q\,.$$

That is, we have evaluated the polynomial $P(x)$ at the chosen point x_0 modulo q.

6.4 Running time for evaluation

Assuming the node keeps to its budget for computing the function g, we observe that $P(x_0) \pmod q$ for a given $x_0 \in \{0, 1, \ldots, q-1\}$ can be computed in time $O^*(2^{|B|} + 2^{|E|})$. This is minimized when $|B| = |E|$. Since $n = |U| = |E| + |B|$, we have $|E| = |B| = n/2$.

7. THE CHROMATIC POLYNOMIAL

We instantiate the template in §6 for the chromatic polynomial. Let G be an undirected graph with n vertices. The chromatic polynomial $\chi_G(t)$ is a polynomial in t of degree at most n. Thus the values of $\chi_G(t)$ at any $n+1$ points suffice to reconstruct G by interpolation.

The value $\chi_G(t)$ for a positive integer $t = 1, 2, \ldots, n+1$ counts the number of mappings $c : V(G) \to \{1, 2, \ldots, t\}$ such that $c(u) \neq c(v)$ holds for all edges $\{u, v\} \in E(G)$. Such mappings are in a bijective correspondence with the t-tuples $(X_1, X_2, \ldots, X_t)$ that partition $U = V(G)$ into t pairwise disjoint parts $X_1, X_2, \ldots, X_t$ such that each $X_i \subseteq U$ is an independent set of G.

Thus, $\chi_G(t)$ equals the partitioning sum-product (17) if we choose the set function $f : 2^U \to \mathbb{Z}$ to be the indicator function for independent sets in G. That is, for all $X \subseteq U$ we define

$$f(X) = \begin{cases} 1 & \text{if } X \text{ is independent in } G; \\ 0 & \text{otherwise.} \end{cases} \quad (26)$$

In particular, we can take $\phi = 1$ and use the template for $t = 1, 2, \ldots, n+1$ to interpolate the polynomial $\chi_G(t)$ from $\chi_G(1), \chi_G(2), \ldots, \chi_G(n+1)$.

7.1 Computing the node function

Suppose that $t = 1, 2, \ldots, n+1$ is fixed. It remains to complete the template for evaluating the function (22) with f defined by (26) in time $O^*(2^{n/2})$. In particular, we instantiate the template with $|E| = |B| = n/2$.

Computing (22) within the time budget requires a dedicated algorithm since G may have up to 2^n independent sets, and hence the sum (22) may have up to 2^n terms (for $Y = E$), which is well above our time budget.

The intuition that we pursue in what follows is that an arbitrary independent set $I \subseteq E \cup B$ in G remains independent in G when restricted to the induced subgraphs $G[E]$ and $G[B]$. Furthermore, $I \cap B$ is disjoint from the neighborhood of $I \cap E$ in B *but otherwise has no interactions with* $I \cap E$. These observations enable us to compute (22) in parts across the cut (E, B) with the help of Yates's algorithm (§2.3).

The node proceeds as follows. Let q and x_0 be as in the template. First, the node computes the function $\hat{f}_B : 2^B \to \mathbb{Z}_q[w_E, w_B]$ defined, modulo q, for all $X \subseteq B$ by

$$\hat{f}_B(X) = \begin{cases} \prod_{b \in X} w_B x_0^b & \text{if } X \text{ is independent in } G; \\ 0 & \text{otherwise.} \end{cases} \quad (27)$$

This takes time $O^*(2^{|B|})$. Next, using Yates's algorithm, the node computes in time $O^*(2^{|B|})$ the function $g_B : 2^B \to \mathbb{Z}_q[w_E, w_B]$ defined for all $Y \subseteq B$ by

$$g_B(Y) = \sum_{X \subseteq Y} \hat{f}_B(X) \pmod q\,. \quad (28)$$

For a subset $X \subseteq E$, let us write $\Gamma_{G,B}(X)$ for the set of all vertices $v \in B$ that have at least one neighbor in the set X in G. Next, using the function g_B that the node has computed, it computes the function $\hat{f}_E : 2^E \to \mathbb{Z}_q[w_E, w_B]$ defined, modulo q, for all $X \subseteq E$ by

$$\hat{f}_E(X) = \begin{cases} w_E^{|X|} g_B(B \setminus \Gamma_{G,B}(X)) & \text{if } X \text{ is ind. in } G; \\ 0 & \text{otherwise.} \end{cases} \tag{29}$$

Remark. The term $g_B(B \setminus \Gamma_{G,B}(X))$ in (29) extends an independent set $X \subseteq E$ with contributions from independent sets in B in all possible ways that are compatible with X. This aggregation of contributions across the cut (E, B) is the key to staying within the time budget $O^*(2^{n/2})$.

Finally, the node computes the function g in time $O^*(2^{|E|})$ using the function $\hat{f}_E$ and Yates's algorithm. Indeed, comparing (22) and (26) with (27), (28), and (29), we observe that

$$g(Y) = \sum_{X \subseteq Y} \hat{f}_E(X) \pmod{q}.$$

Acknowledgments

We thank Ryan Williams for useful discussions and giving us early access to his manuscript describing his batch evaluation framework [25] of which the present "Camelot" framework forms a special case. We also thank Stefan Schneider and Russell Impagliazzo for an inspiring exposition of the nondeterministic exponential time hypothesis and the Carmosino *et al.* [7] results at the Simons Institute in fall 2015. Finally, we thank Jukka Suomela and the anonymous referees for useful comments.

8. REFERENCES

[1] M. Agrawal, N. Kayal, N. Saxena, PRIMES is in P, *Ann. of Math. (2)* 160 (2004) 781–793.

[2] L. Babai, S. Moran, Arthur-Merlin games: a randomized proof system, and a hierarchy of complexity classes, *J. Comput. System Sci.* 36 (1988) 254–276.

[3] A. Björklund, T. Husfeldt, M. Koivisto, Set partitioning via inclusion-exclusion, *SIAM J. Comput.* 39 (2009) 546–563.

[4] A. Björklund, T. Husfeldt, P. Kaski, M. Koivisto, Covering and packing in linear space, *Inform. Process. Lett.* 111 (2011) 1033–1036.

[5] P. Bürgisser, M. Clausen, M. A. Shokrollahi, *Algebraic Complexity Theory*, Springer, 1997.

[6] S. Caminiti, I. Finocchi, E. G. Fusco, F. Silvestri, Resilient dynamic programming, *Algorithmica*, to appear.

[7] M. L. Carmosino, J. Gao, R. Impagliazzo, I. Mihajlin, R. Paturi, S. Schneider, Nondeterministic extensions of the strong exponential time hypothesis and consequences for non-reducibility, Proc. 2016 ACM Conference on Innovations in Theoretical Computer Science (ITCS'16, Cambridge, MA, January 14–16, 2016), ACM, 2016, pp. 261–270.

[8] V. Chen, E. Grigorescu, R. de Wolf, Error-correcting data structures, *SIAM J. Comput.* 42 (2013) 84–111.

[9] F. Cicalese, *Fault-Tolerant Search Algorithms*, Springer, Heidelberg, 2013.

[10] F. Eisenbrand, F. Grandoni, On the complexity of fixed parameter clique and dominating set, *Theoret. Comput. Sci.* 326 (2004) 57–67.

[11] I. Finocchi, F. Grandoni, G. F. Italiano, Optimal resilient sorting and searching in the presence of memory faults, *Theoret. Comput. Sci.* 410 (2009) 4457–4470.

[12] P. Fraigniaud, A. Korman, D. Peleg, Towards a complexity theory for local distributed computing, *J. ACM* 60 (2013), no. 5, Art. 35.

[13] R. Freivalds, Probabilistic machines can use less running time, *IFIP Congress* (1977) 839–842.

[14] J. von zur Gathen, J. Gerhard, *Modern Computer Algebra*, 3rd ed., Cambridge University Press, 2013.

[15] S. Gao, A new algorithm for decoding Reed–Solomon codes, in: V. K. Bhargava, H. V. Poor, V. Tarokh, S. Yoon, eds., *Communications, Information, and Network Security*, Springer, 2003, pp. 55–68.

[16] M. Göös, J. Suomela, Locally checkable proofs, Proc. 30th Annual ACM Symposium on Principles of Distributed Computing (PODC'11, San Jose, CA, June 6–8, 2011), ACM, 2011, pp. 159–168.

[17] S. Goldwasser, Y. T. Kalai, G. N. Rothblum, Delegating computation: Interactive proofs for muggles, *J. ACM* 62 (2015) Art. 27.

[18] J. B. Kruskal, Three-way arrays: rank and uniqueness of trilinear decompositions, with application to arithmetic complexity and statistics, *Linear Algebra and Appl.* 18 (1977) 95–138.

[19] J. M. Landsberg, *Tensors: Geometry and Applications*, American Mathematical Society, 2012.

[20] F. Le Gall, Powers of tensors and fast matrix multiplication, Proc. International Symposium on Symbolic and Algebraic Computation (ISSAC'14, Kobe, July 23–25, 2014), ACM, 2014, pp. 296–303.

[21] R. M. McConnell, K. Mehlhorn, S. Näher, P. Schweitzer, Survey: Certifying algorithms, *Computer Science Review* 5 (2011) 119–161.

[22] J. Nešetřil, S. Poljak, On the complexity of the subgraph problem, *Comment. Math. Univ. Carolin.* 26 (1985) 415–419.

[23] I. S. Reed, G. Solomon, Polynomial codes over certain finite fields, *J. Soc. Indust. Appl. Math.* 8 (1960) 300–304.

[24] D. Tiwari, S. Gupta, G. Gallarno, J. Rogers, D. Maxwell, Reliability lessons learned from GPU experience with the Titan supercomputer at Oak Ridge leadership computing facility, Proc. International Conference for High Performance Computing, Networking, Storage and Analysis (SC'15, Austin, TX, November 15–20, 2015), Art. 38.

[25] R. Williams, Strong ETH breaks with Merlin and Arthur: Short non-interactive proofs of batch evaluation, Proc. 31st IEEE Colloquium on Computational Complexity (CCC'16, Tokyo, May 29–June 1, 2016), to appear.

[26] F. Yates, *The Design and Analysis of Factorial Experiments*, Imperial Bureau of Soil Science, Harpenden, 1937.

Brief Announcement: Proactive Secret Sharing with a Dishonest Majority

Shlomi Dolev
Ben-Gurion University
Beer-Sheva, Israel
dolev@cs.bgu.ac.il

Karim ElDefrawy
HRL Laboratories
Malibu, California, USA
kmeldefrawy@hrl.com

Joshua Lampkins
HRL Laboratories
Malibu, California, USA
jdlampkins@hrl.com

Rafail Ostrovsky
University of California Los Angeles
Los Angeles, California, USA
rafail@cs.ucla.edu

Moti Yung
Snapchat & Columbia University
New York, New York, USA
moti@cs.columbia.edu

ABSTRACT

In a secret sharing scheme a dealer shares a secret s among n parties such that an adversary corrupting up to t parties does not learn s, while any $t+1$ parties can efficiently recover s. Over a long period of time all parties may be corrupted thus violating the threshold, which is accounted for in *Proactive Secret Sharing (PSS)*. PSS schemes periodically rerandomize (refresh) the shares of the secret and invalidate old ones. PSS retains confidentiality even when *all parties* are corrupted over the lifetime of the secret, but no more than t during a certain window of time, called the refresh period. Existing PSS schemes only guarantee secrecy in the presence of an honest majority with less than $n/2$ total corruptions during a refresh period; an adversary corrupting a single additional party, even if only passively, obtains the secret. This work is *the first feasibility result demonstrating PSS tolerating a dishonest majority*, it introduces the first PSS scheme secure against $t < n$ passive adversaries without recovery of lost shares, it can also recover from honest faulty parties losing their shares, and when tolerating e faults the scheme tolerates $t < n-e$ passive corruptions. A non-robust version of the scheme can tolerate $t < n/2 - e$ active adversaries, and mixed adversaries that control a combination of passively and actively corrupted parties that are a majority, but where less than $n/2 - e$ of such corruptions are active. We achieve these high thresholds with $O(n^4)$ communication when sharing a single secret, and $O(n^3)$ communication when sharing multiple secrets in batches.

Keywords

secret sharing, dishonest majority, proactive security, proactive secret sharing, non-robust secret sharing

PODC'16 July 25-28, 2016, Chicago, IL, USA

ACM ISBN 978-1-4503-3964-3/16/07.
DOI: http://dx.doi.org/10.1145/2933057.2933059

1. BACKGROUND AND RELATED WORK

Over a long period of time all parties in a secret sharing scheme [9, 3] may be compromised and the threshold may be temporarily violated. The *proactive security model* [7] deals with an adversary's ability to eventually compromise all the parties, it protects against a *mobile adversary* capable of corrupting all parties in a distributed system or protocol during the execution but with the following limitations: (1) only a constant fraction of parties can be corrupted during any round of the protocol; (2) parties are periodically rebooted (or reset) to a predictable and pristine initial state, guaranteeing a small fraction of corrupted parties, assuming that the corruption rate is not more than the reboot rate.

Existing Proactive Secret Sharing (PSS) schemes, e.g., [7, 5, 8, 1, 2], are insecure when a majority of the parties are compromised, even if the compromise is only passive. Such schemes typically store the secret as the free term in a polynomial of degree $t < n/2$, thus once an adversary compromises $t+1$ parties (even if only passively), it can reconstruct the polynomial and recover the secret. New and different techniques other than the above are required to construct PSS secure against dishonest majorities. Developing such techniques and the first PSS scheme secure against dishonest majorities is the main contribution of our work. Our PSS scheme provides security against $t < n$ passive adversaries without recovery of lost shares, it can also recover from honest faulty parties losing their shares, and when tolerating e faults it is secure against $t < n - e$ passive corruptions. A non-robust version of the scheme can tolerate $t < n/2 - e$ active adversaries, and mixed adversaries that control a combination of passively and actively corrupted parties that are a majority, but where less than $n/2 - e$ of such corruptions are active. Existing PSS schemes *cannot handle* such high combined corruption thresholds.

2. PRELIMINARIES

Below are preliminaries for the rest of the paper.

2.1 System and Network Model

We consider a set of n parties $\mathcal{P} = \{P_i\}_{i=1}^{n}$ connected via a synchronous network, and an authenticated broadcast channel. Each pair of parties also establish private secure authenticated communication channels which can be instantiated via appropriate encryption and digital signature schemes.

Time Periods and Refresh Phases: We assume that all parties are synchronized via a global clock. Time is divided into *time periods or epochs*; at the beginning of each period all parties engage in an interactive refresh protocol (also called refresh phase). At the end of the refresh phase all parties hold new shares for the same secret, and delete their old shares. We note that honest parties *must* delete their old shares so that if they get compromised in future periods, the adversary *cannot* recover their shares from old periods.

2.2 Variations of Secret Sharing

A Secret Sharing (SS) scheme consists of two protocols, `Share` and `Reconstruct`. `Share` allows a dealer to share a secret, s, among n parties such that it remains secure against an adversary that controls up to t parties, while allowing any group of $t+1$ or more uncorrupted parties to reconstruct the secrets via `Reconstruct`. A problem with standard secret sharing, e.g., Shamir's scheme [9], is that a dishonest dealer may deal inconsistent shares from which $t+1$ or more parties may not be able to reconstruct the secret. This malicious behavior can be prevented by augmenting the secret sharing scheme with homomorphic commitments; this is essentially what a Verifiable Secret Sharing (VSS) scheme achieves. A VSS scheme allows parties to verify that a dealer has correctly shared a secret. We utilize the VSS scheme of Feldman [4], where security is based on the hardness of computing discrete logarithms over $\mathbb{Z}_p$ for a large prime p. The definition of a Proactive Secret Sharing (PSS) scheme is similar to that of a standard SS scheme, with the addition of two new protocols to perform `Refresh` and `Recovery` for securing the secrets against a mobile adversary that can corrupt all n parties over a long period of time. The `Refresh` protocol refreshes data to prevent a mobile adversary from collecting (over a long period) a large number of shares that could exceed the reconstruction threshold and thus reveal the secret. The `Recovery` protocol allows rebooted parties, or faulty honest ones, to recover their shares and thus prevents the adversary from destroying the shared secret(s).

3. PROACTIVE SECRET SHARING SECURE AGAINST A DISHONEST MAJORITY

This section first overviews our PSS scheme and the intuition behind it, it then focuses on the two new protocols for refreshing and recovering shares; protocols for sharing and reconstructing a secret in our PSS scheme are similar to [6] and are briefly described due to space constraints. All protocols are secure against a dishonest majority.

3.1 Intuition and Overview of Operation

Field operations occur over a finite field $\mathbb{Z}_p$ for some prime p. Let α be a generator of $\mathbb{Z}_p^*$ and let $\beta = \alpha^{-1}$. In the case of multiple secrets, secrets will be stored at locations that are multiples of β, i.e., if $f(x)$ is a sharing polynomials then $f(\beta^1)$ and $f(\beta^2)$ will evaluate to secret 1 and secret 2 respectively, while shares will be computed as the evaluation of $f(x)$ at different values of α, i.e., $f(\alpha^1)$ and $f(\alpha^2)$ are the shares of party 1 and 2 respectively. We note that in the case of sharing a single secret, only one β is needed, and in that case it will not be the inverse of α, traditionally it has been the case that for single secrets $\beta = 0$, thus the secret s is stored at the free term of the sharing polynomial, i.e., $f(0) = s$. The shares for a single secret can be evaluations of $f(x)$ at indices of the parties, i.e. $f(1)$, $f(2)$ ... $f(n)$, or at pre-agreed upon points corresponding to each party such as $f(\alpha^1)$, $f(\alpha^2)$, ..., $f(\alpha^i)$.

To simplify the illustration we assume here and in description of our share, reconstruct and refresh protocols (`DM-Share`, `DM-Reconstruct`, and `DM-Refresh`), that the adversary only compromises nodes temporarily, so only refreshing of shares is needed. If parallel share recovery (`DM-Recover`) for rebooted nodes is required, the tolerated threshold is decreased by the maximum number of nodes to be rebooted in parallel or that can loose their shares (this can also be due to non-malicious faults). If nodes are serially rebooted such that only a single share is to be recovered at any instant, then the tolerated thresholds are decreased by 1.

Per the discussion in Section 1, to tolerate a dishonest majority it is not enough to store secrets in the free term, or as other points on a polynomial. What is needed is to encode secrets in a form resistant to a dishonest majority of up to $n-1$ parties. This can be achieved by first additively sharing the secret into n random summands (this provides security against $t < n$ passive adversaries), then those random additive summands may be shared and proactively refreshed using methods that can tolerate $t < n/2$ active adversaries with aborts, i.e., if less than $n/2$ of the parties are actively corrupted their misbehavior will be detected and flagged by the rest of the honest parties (constituting a majority) while ensuring confidentiality of the shared secret, even if up to $n/2$ passively corrupted parties exist among the remaining parties. This is the blueprint that we follow. Specifically, we start from the gradual secret sharing schemes from [6], develop two new protocols to verifiably generate random refreshing polynomials with the required properties, i.e., they have a random free term that encodes random additive shares that add up to zero. To recover shares with the above security guarantees, we observe that it is enough that the recovery protocol ensures security against $t < n/2$ ($t < n/2 - e$ with e faults) active adversaries, as passive adversaries only generate random polynomials and send them to the recovering party, i.e., if they respect the polynomial generation process, and as long as one party generates a random polynomial, the rest of the $n-1$ potentially passively corrupted parties will only see new random polynomials with the appropriate degrees.

3.2 Sharing and Reconstructing Secrets

`DM-Share`: to share a secret s the first step is to split it into n random summands, $s = rs_1 + rs_2 + \cdots + rs_n$. These n random summands are then each verifiably shared using a verifiable linear secret sharing scheme, e.g., using a verifiable version of Shamir's scheme (that relies on homomorphic commitments such as Feldman's scheme [4]) where each random summand rs_i is stored in the free term of a random polynomial of a specific degree. These n random sharing polynomials are of increasing degrees, where the degree of polynomial p_i is i where $i \in \{0, 1, 2, \ldots, n-2, n-2\}$; note that the first one is a constant and that two of the polynomials have degree $n-2$ if recovery of shares of one rebooted or faulty node is required. If only refreshing is required then degrees of the polynomials go up to $n-1$ instead.

`DM-Reconstruct`: to reconstruct a secret, each party broadcasts its shares, and each party then interpolates the n random sharing polynomials $p_i(x)$ and recovers the n random summands from the free terms, i.e., $rs_i = p_i(0)$. The secret is reconstructed as the summation of all the recovered free terms, $s = \sum_{i=0}^{n-1} rs_i = \sum_{i=0}^{n-1} p_i(0)$ when degrees are from 0 to $n-1$.

3.3 Refreshing Shares for Dishonest Majority

DM-Refresh: In our refresh protocol, each party generates n random refreshing polynomials with the appropriate degrees (i.e., from a single constant term, corresponding to degree 0, to degree $n-1$); each party then verifiably shares these refreshing polynomials with the other parties by committing to their coefficients and distributing shares of these polynomials as their evaluation at the indices of the parties similar to Feldman's VSS [4]. These refreshing polynomials should satisfy the following condition: they have random constant coefficients that add up to 0 (to match the case when a single secret is shared in the free term). This can be ensured by homomorphically checking that the polynomials shared by each party have this property. This condition ensures that the shared secret remains unchanged. Once each party receives all the shares generated by other parties, they add them to their local shares and delete the shares that resulted from the previous execution of the refresh protocol.

3.4 Recovering Shares for Dishonest Majority

DM-Recover: To be able to recover shares of a single party, then instead of initially sharing the n additive summands with polynomials of degrees $n-1$ to 0 (i.e., a single constant), the degrees will be $n-2$ to 0, with two of the summands shared with two different polynomials of degree $n-2$. This allows $n-1$ parties to recover shares of a single party that is rebooted. (For e parallel recoveries polynomial degrees will be $n-e-1$ to 0.) In each refresh period there are n current sharing polynomials with degrees ranging from $n-2$ to 0, and each party has a share for each of these polynomials. When a single party P_{rc} is rebooted and needs to recover its shares, i.e., the evaluation of each of the current sharing polynomials at P_{rc}'s evaluation point α^{rc}, the other parties need to generate and verifiably share n random polynomials that evaluate to the same values as the current sharing polynomials at α^{rc}. To achieve this, parties generate and verifiably share n random recovery polynomials that evaluate to 0 at α^{rc}. All parties add their local shares of the current sharing polynomials to the shares of these random recovery polynomials; this results in n shared random recovery polynomials that have only the point at α^{rc} in common with the current sharing polynomials. All parties then send their shares of these n shared random recovery polynomials to P_{rc}, and P_{rc} can then interpolate these polynomials without learning anything about the secret or the actual sharing polynomials of the current period. We note that passively corrupted parties in the recovery will execute the protocol correctly, and actively corrupted parties are limited to $t < n/2-e$ with e faults; we only need a recovery protocol secure against active adversaries because only the recovering party receives information. Every other party generates random data and shares it with the rest of the parties, so there is no information related to the secret that is revealed to any party. As long as there is a single honest party, the random recovery polynomials that party generates ensures randomness of the overall recovery polynomials; this ensures that the only information P_{rc} learns are its n shares at α^{rc}.

4. CONCLUSION AND OPEN QUESTIONS

We present the *first feasibility result for Proactive Secret Sharing (PSS) for a dishonest majority and the first such PSS scheme.* Our main PSS scheme is secure against $t < n$ passive adversaries without recovery of lost shares, and when tolerating e faults that result in lost shares the scheme resists $t < n-e$ passive corruptions. A non-robust version of the scheme can tolerate $t < n/2-e$ active adversaries, and mixed adversaries that control a combination of passively and actively corrupted parties that are a majority, but where less than $n/2-e$ of such corruptions are active. The following issues remain open: (i) It is unclear what is the lowest possible communication required for a PSS scheme secure against a dishonest majority. We achieve $O(n^3)$ for batches of secrets, it remains open if this can be reduced to $O(n)$ or $O(1)$. We conjecture that $O(n)$ is the lower bound for our PSS blueprint which first shares the secret via an additive sharing scheme. Such an additive scheme does not seem to be amenable to batching in a straightforward manner; it is currently not obvious to us how to batch it without destroying the secret. (ii) There are currently no PSS schemes secure against dishonest majorities of up to $n-1$ and that operate over asynchronous networks.

5. REFERENCES

[1] J. Baron, K. ElDefrawy, J. Lampkins, and R. Ostrovsky. How to withstand mobile virus attacks, revisited. In *Proceedings of the 2014 ACM Symposium on Principles of Distributed Computing*, PODC '14, pages 293–302, New York, NY, USA, 2014. ACM.

[2] J. Baron, K. ElDefrawy, J. Lampkins, and R. Ostrovsky. Communication-optimal proactive secret sharing for dynamic groups. In *Proceedings of the 2015 International Conference on Applied Cryptography and Network Security*, ACNS '15, 2015.

[3] G. R. Blakley. Safeguarding cryptographic keys. *Proc. of AFIPS National Computer Conference*, 48:313–317, 1979.

[4] P. Feldman. A practical scheme for non-interactive verifiable secret sharing. In *Proceedings of the 28th Annual Symposium on Foundations of Computer Science*, SFCS '87, pages 427–438, Washington, DC, USA, 1987. IEEE Computer Society.

[5] A. Herzberg, S. Jarecki, H. Krawczyk, and M. Yung. Proactive secret sharing or: How to cope with perpetual leakage. In *CRYPTO*, pages 339–352, 1995.

[6] M. Hirt, U. Maurer, and C. Lucas. A Dynamic Tradeoff between Active and Passive Corruptions in Secure Multi-Party Computation. In R. Canetti and J. A. Garay, editors, *Advances in cryptology - CRYPTO 2013 : 33rd Annual International Cryptology Conference, Santa Barbara, CA, USA, August 18-22, 2013 : proceedings*, volume 8043 of *Lecture notes in computer science*, pages 203–219, Heidelberg, 2013. Springer.

[7] R. Ostrovsky and M. Yung. How to withstand mobile virus attacks (extended abstract). In *PODC*, pages 51–59, 1991.

[8] D. Schultz. *Mobile Proactive Secret Sharing*. PhD thesis, Massachusetts Institute of Technology, 2007.

[9] A. Shamir. How to share a secret. *Commun. ACM*, 22(11):612–613, 1979.

Search on a Line with Faulty Robots

Jurek Czyzowicz[*]
Dept. d'informatique
Universite d'Outaouais
Gatineau, Canada
Jurek.Czyzowicz@uqo.ca

Evangelos Kranakis[†]
School of Computer Science
Carleton University, Ottawa
Ottawa, Canada
kranakis@scs.carleton.ca

Danny Krizanc
Dept. Math. and Comp. Sci.
Wesleyan University
Middletown CT, USA
dkrizanc@wesleyan.edu

Lata Narayanan[‡]
Dept. Comp. Sc. and
Software Eng.
Concordia University
Montreal, Canada
lata@cs.concordia.ca

Jaroslav Opatrny
Dept. Comp. Sc. and
Software Eng.
Concordia University
Montreal, Canada
opatrny@cs.concordia.ca

ABSTRACT

We consider the problem of searching on a line using n mobile robots, of which at most f are faulty, and the remaining are reliable. The robots start at the same location and move in parallel along the line with the same speed. There is a *target* placed on the line at a location unknown to the robots. Reliable robots can find the target when they reach its location, but faulty robots cannot detect the target. Our goal is to design a parallel algorithm minimizing the competitive ratio, represented by the worst case ratio between the time of arrival of the first reliable robot at the target, and the distance from the source to the target.

If $n \geq 2f+2$, there is a simple algorithm with competitive ratio 1. For $f < n < 2f+2$ we develop a new class of algorithms, called *proportional schedule algorithms*. For any given (n, f), we give a proportional schedule algorithm $A(n, f)$, whose competitive ratio is

$$\left(\frac{4f+4}{n}\right)^{\frac{2f+2}{n}} \left(\frac{4f+4}{n} - 2\right)^{1-\frac{2f+2}{n}} + 1.$$

Setting $a = n/f$ as a constant, the asymptotic competitive ratio is $(4/a)^{2/a}(4/a-2)^{1-2/a} + 1$.

Our search algorithm is easily seen to be optimal for the case $n = f+1$. We also show that as n tends to ∞ the competitive ratio of our algorithm for the case $n = 2f+1$ approaches 3 and this is optimal. More precisely, we show that asymptotically, the competitive ratio of our proportional schedule algorithm $A(2f+1, f)$ is at most $3 + \frac{4\ln n}{n}$, while any search algorithm has a lower bound $3 + \frac{2\ln n}{n}$ on its competitive ratio.

CCS Concepts

•**Computer systems organization** → **Embedded systems;** *Redundancy;* Robotics; •**Networks** → Network reliability;

Keywords

Search on a line; Faulty robots; Cow-path problem; Competitive ratio.

1. INTRODUCTION

Exploring an environment to find a target placed at an unknown location is a well studied problem in computer science, robotics, operations research, and mathematics. Starting with the work of Bellman [9] and Beck [7], many researchers have studied the optimal trajectory to be followed by a single robot searching for a target placed at an unknown location on a line. The goal of the robot is to minimize the competitive ratio, that is, the supremum, over all possible target locations, of the ratio between the distance travelled by the robot until it finds the target, and the distance of the target from the robot's starting position. It is well-known that, for the case of a single robot on a line, the optimal trajectory uses a doubling strategy: roughly, the robot travels some distance x to the left, then turns around and moves $2x$ to the right, and so on, until it finds the target. This trajectory has a competitive ratio of 9 (e.g. see Baeza-Yates et al. [6]).

In this paper, we study the problem of *parallel search* on a line, by n robots, of which some robots are *faulty*, and the remaining robots are *reliable*. All robots are assumed to start at a shared initial location, and to move at maximum speed 1 along the line. A robot can change the direction of its movement at some points defined by its algorithm. An algorithm for parallel search specifies a trajectory, e.g. the turning points, for each robot; the identities of robots are different, and they may have different trajectories. We assume that at most f of the robots are faulty. A faulty

[*]Supported in part by NSERC of Canada.
[†]Supported in part by NSERC of Canada.
[‡]Supported in part by NSERC of Canada.

PODC'16, July 25–28, 2016, Chicago, IL, USA.
© 2016 ACM. ISBN 978-1-4503-3964-3/16/07...$15.00
DOI: http://dx.doi.org/10.1145/2933057.2933102

robot follows its assigned trajectory and is indistinguishable from a reliable robot, except that *a faulty robot does not detect the target while visiting its location.* Thus, the target is detected only when its location is visited by a reliable robot. Therefore, an algorithm for a parallel search with f faulty robots must make sure that any point on the line can be visited by at least $f+1$ robots. Accordingly, we define the search time of a parallel search algorithm with faulty robots to be the time when the first reliable robot reaches the target, which could be, in the worst case, the visit of the $f+1$st robot. The competitive ratio of a search algorithm is defined to be the worst case ratio between the search time to the distance of the target from the starting position.

Since a faulty robot behaves the same as a reliable robot except that it does not detect the target, it follows that a robot can be deduced to be faulty only when the target is found by a reliable robot at a position previously visited by the faulty robot. It is therefore irrelevant if the robots were faulty at the beginning or later during the search. We note that the assumption of f faulty robots also models the situation when the target is hard to detect, and therefore we require visits by $f+1$ robots to the location of the target in order to assure the detection of the target. In our algorithms, we do not assume any communication among robots, but our lower bounds apply even in the presence of communication between the robots.

Observe that if $n \geq 2f+2$, we can simply partition the robots into two groups of $f+1$ robots each, and send the two groups in opposite directions from the starting position. Since each group has at least one reliable robot, a reliable robot is sure to discover the target in time d where d is the distance of the target from the starting position of the robots. This algorithm has competitive ratio one and is clearly optimal.

Thus, in the sequel we study the case when $f < n < 2f+2$. The trajectory of each robot can be defined by a possibly infinite sequence $x_0, x_1, x_2, \ldots$ of reals, called *turning points*, which are the points where the trajectory changes direction. Starting at the origin s the robot travels in one direction to reach x_0. At x_0 it turns around until x_1, where the direction is changed again, etc. In the sequel, a trajectory with an infinite number of turning points will be called a *zig-zag* strategy. It is natural to consider zig-zag strategies in which $x_{i+1} = \kappa x_i$ for every $i \geq c$ for some constant c; we call κ the *expansion factor* of the strategy. Indeed, the optimal doubling strategy for a single robot given in [7, 9] has expansion factor 2. In the context of parallel search, all robots could have different expansion factors, or have the same expansion factor, but start at different times or move at different speeds.

1.1 Our results

As mentioned earlier, when $n \geq 2f+2$, there is a trivial optimal solution. For $f < n < 2f+2$, we develop *proportional schedule algorithms*, a new class of algorithms for parallel search on a line with faulty robots. In Section 3, we prove the existence of this class of algorithms and show that for each pair (n, f), there exists a proportional schedule algorithm $A(n, f)$ with competitive ratio at most

$$\left(\frac{4f+4}{n}\right)^{\frac{2f+2}{n}} \left(\frac{4f+4}{n}-2\right)^{1-\frac{2f+2}{n}} + 1.$$

Setting $a = n/f$ as constant (i.e. when a fixed proportion of robots may be faulty), this gives us the asymptotic expression

$$(4/a)^{2/a} (4/a-2)^{1-2/a} + 1$$

for the competitive ratio.

When $n = f+1$, the proportional schedule algorithm $A(f+1, f)$ has a competitive ratio of 9. It is easy to see that this is optimal: if there is an algorithm $\mathcal{A}$ with a competitive ratio better than 9, then following the trajectory of the first robot in $\mathcal{A}$ would give a better competitive ratio than 9 for the case of a single robot, since it could be that in the execution of $\mathcal{A}$, the first robot is the only reliable robot. We remark that a competitive ratio of 9 is also achieved by all robots starting at the same time, and moving together while following a doubling strategy.

Finally, for $n = 2f+1$, the proportional schedule algorithm $A(2f+1, f)$ has competitive ratio at most $3 + \frac{4 \ln n}{n}$ (after excluding low order terms). In terms of lower bounds, in Section 4, we prove that any parallel search algorithm with $n < 2f+2$ robots has competitive ratio at least α where $\alpha > 3$ and satisfies $(\alpha-1)^n(\alpha-3) = 2^{n+1}$. Asymptotically, this yields a lower bound of $3 + \frac{2 \ln n}{n}$ (after excluding low order terms) on the competitive ratio. Thus, our proportional schedule algorithm $A(2f+1, f)$ is asymptotically optimal.

Table 1 gives our results for some specific values of n and f. Observe that the expansion factor for $A(n, f)$ changes when changing values of n or f. For $n = 2f+1$, it turns out that the expansion factor for $A(2f+1, f)$ is always $n+1$, and for $n = f+1$ the expansion factor is 2.

n	f	comp. ratio of $A(n,f)$	lower bound on comp. ratio	expansion factor of $A(n,f)$
2	1	9	9	2
3	1	5.24	3.76	4
3	2	9	9	2
4	1	1	1	
4	2	6.2	3.649	3
4	3	9	9	2
5	1	1	1	
5	2	4.43	3.57	6
5	3	6.76	3.57	2.67
5	4	9	9	2
11	5	3.73	3.345	12
41	20	3.24	3.12	42

Table 1: Upper and lower bounds for specific values of n and f

1.2 Related work

In general, search is concerned with minimizing the time to find a hidden target under various conditions on the environment and capabilities of the searcher(s). When the mobile robots do not know the environment in advance then search involves exploring [2, 3, 20, 25], and usually exploration is combined with mapping of the environment and positioning of the robots within it [29, 34]. Coordinating exploration by a team of robots is one of the core research themes in robotics [12, 23, 37, 38] and distributed computing [22]. Related search questions include the lost at sea problem [24, 27], the cow-path problem [7, 9], and the plane searching problem [6], to name a few.

The study of search on an infinite line, sometimes called

linear search, started with the independent works of Bellman [9] and Beck [7]. It consists of finding a motionless target on an infinite line in the smallest possible worst-case time expressed as a function of the distance of the target to the starting position. The competitive ratio of 9 was first shown to be optimal in [8] and numerous variations of this question have been studied. For example, when an upper bound on the distance to the target is known in advance, slightly better bounds were shown [10], while [19] studied the question when a cost is charged for changing the search direction. Recently, [14] showed that having many searchers, communicating upon meeting, does not improve the competitive ratio, when the search time is determined by the time of arrival of the last searcher at the target. Several papers considered the problem of searching in the two-dimensional plane by one or more searchers [5, 6]. The book [4] reviews most search games studied earlier.

Fault tolerance in distributed computing problems has been extensively studied in the past (see, e.g., [26, 31, 32]). Failures were most often related to static elements of the environment (network nodes and links) rather than mobile components. However such malfunctions are sometimes modelled by dynamic alteration of the network [13, 30]. The problems of having some faulty mobile robots were investigated in the context of the problems of gathering [1, 18, 21, 36], convergence [11, 15], flocking [39], and patrolling [17]. Some papers investigated the case of unreliable or inaccurate robot sensing devices, e.g., [16, 28, 36]. Perhaps the most related to our study is [17], where a collection of robots, some of which are unreliable, perform efficient patrolling of a fence.

2. PRELIMINARIES AND NOTATION

We assume that the n robots are named $a_0, a_1, \ldots a_{n-1}$. We first define a space/time 2D-representation of the movement of a robot on the line that will prove useful in arguing about the performance of the search algorithms proposed in this paper.

Consider the movement of a robot on an infinite line L. The trajectory of such a robot can be represented in the half-plane by a curve consisting of points (x, t) where x is the position of the robot on L at time t. As robots always use maximal available (unit) speed, each trajectory is composed of segments using slopes -1 and 1, see Figure 1.

Moreover, in our algorithms, we will require that the turning points of all the zig-zag strategies, are located on two lines forming a cone, as in Figure 2. This implies that all robots have the same expansion factor, though they may have different turning points.

For a fixed real number $\beta > 1$ we denote by C_β the cone delimited by a pair of lines $t = x\beta$ for $x \geq 0$, and $t = -x\beta$ for $x \leq 0$.

Definition 1. *Consider a point $(x_0, |x_0\beta|)$ on the boundary of the cone C_β, By a* zig-zag *movement of a robot defined by cone C_β and point $(x_0, |x_0\beta|)$ we mean the motion of the robot with unit speed inside the cone C_β that starts at $(x_0, |x_0\beta|)$ and that reverses its direction whenever it arrives at the boundary of C_β.*

The movement of a robot defined by a cone and a point on it boundary is depicted in Figure 2. Notice that this gives rise to a sequence $x_0, x_1, x_2, \ldots$ of *turning points* on the line at which the robot changes the direction of its movement.

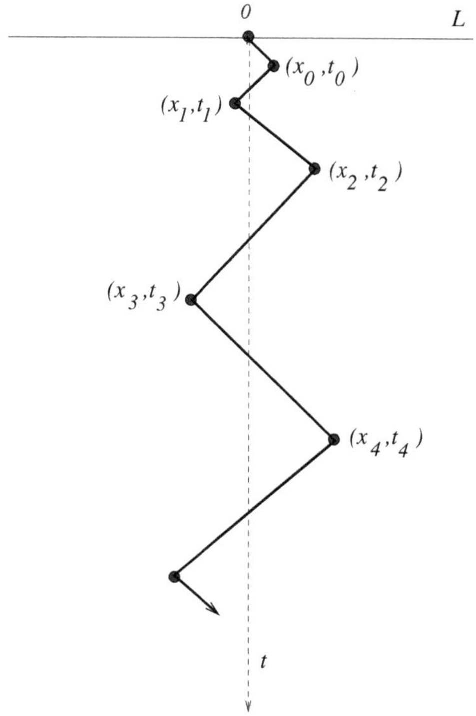

Figure 1: A general zig-zag strategy with turning points (x_i, t_i), $1 \leq i \leq 4$.

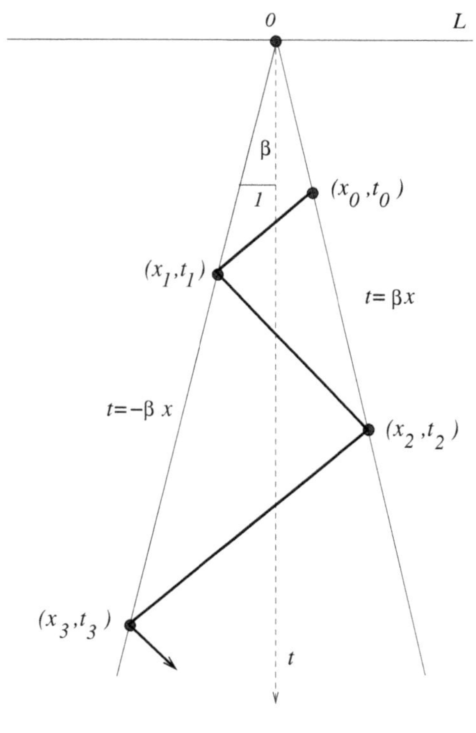

Figure 2: A zig-zag strategy defined by cone C_β, $\beta > 1$ (delimited by lines $t = \beta x$ for $x \geq 0$ and $t = -\beta x$ for $x \leq 0$) and point (x_0, t_0) on the cone.

Using the basic properties of triangles, it is easy to verify the following lemma which gives the expansion factor determined by C_β.

LEMMA 1. *Let x_0 be the initial position of a robot on the line at time t_0 which corresponds to point (x_0, t_0) on the boundary of the cone C_β, where $\beta > 1$. Then the turning points of the robot are given by the formula*

$$x_i = x_0 \left(\frac{\beta+1}{\beta-1} \right)^i (-1)^i \tag{1}$$

with corresponding expansion factor $(\beta+1)/(\beta-1)$.

3. UPPER BOUND

In this section we give a set of ziz-zag movements for a collection of n robots searching the line. We define set movements for all robots according to the same cone C_β. We also assume that two different robots will never share the same turning point. The collections of zigzag movements that we define for a set of robots will have a specific regularity that we define below. We call such collections of movements *proportional schedules.* The sets of turning points (taken by all robots) of proportional schedules will have the property that the distances between two consecutive turning points (corresponding to different robots) will behave according to some geometric sequence.

Let C_β be a cone for some fixed value of $\beta > 1$. Consider two robots a_0, a_1 and their zig-zag movements defined by C_β. Let $0 < \tau' < \tau"$ be two consecutive turning points of a_0 on the same side of the cone (by assumption above neither of them is a turning point of a_1). It is easy to see that there is exactly one point τ_1, which is a turning point of a_1 such that $\tau' < \tau_1 < \tau"$. By a similar argument, this is true for any pair of robots, hence, without loss of generality we can number the collection of n robots in such a way that for a sequence of turning points $0 < \tau_0 = \tau' < \tau_1 < \cdots < \tau_{n-1} < \tau_n = \tau''$, such that τ' and $\tau"$ are two consecutive turning points of a_0, we have that τ_i is a turning point of robot a_i for $i = 1, \ldots, n-1$. Observe that choosing a sequence of turning points $\tau_0, \tau_1, \cdots, \tau_n$, according to the condition above, entirely defines the schedule of complete ziz-zag movements of all robots. We call the schedule *proportional* if the ratio of consecutive differences of turning points on the same side of the cone remains the same. More precisely, we give the following definition.

DEFINITION 2. *Suppose that $0 < \tau_0 < \tau_1 < \cdots$ is the infinite sequence of positive turning points of all the robots in their respective zig-zag movements. We say that the schedule is* proportional *if for some real value r, the ratio $\frac{\tau_{i+1}-\tau_i}{\tau_i-\tau_{i-1}} = r$, for $i = 1, 2, \ldots$. We call r the proportionality ratio of the schedule.*

We denote by $S_\beta(n)$ the proportional schedule using n robots zig-zagging within the cone C_β. Given n and a value of $\beta > 1$, a turning point of one of the robots completely defines the proportional schedule $S_\beta(n)$. In the following technical lemma we determine the ratio of the proportional schedule $S_\beta(n)$ and establish some of its properties.

LEMMA 2. *Consider any $\beta > 1$ and n robots moving on the line according to the proportional schedule $S_\beta(n)$. The proportionality ratio of schedule $S_\beta(n)$ equals*

$$r = \left(\frac{\beta+1}{\beta-1} \right)^{2/n}. \tag{2}$$

Moreover, if $\tau_i > 0$ is a turning point of some robot at time t_i and $\tau_{i+1} > \tau_i$ is the next larger turning point by any robot visited at time t_{i+1} then we have $t_{i+1} = t_i + \tau_i \beta(r-1)$ and $\tau_{i+1} = r\tau_i$. [1]

PROOF. Let $A_i = (\tau_i, t_i)$, for $i = 0, 1, \ldots n-1$, be such that $\tau_0, \tau_1, \ldots, \tau_{n-1}$ be the consecutive turning points of robots $a_0, a_1, \ldots, a_{n-1}$ resulting from a proportional schedule, and $t_0, t_1, \ldots, t_{n-1}$ be the times of their respective visits. Let $d = |A_0 A_1|$ denote the length of the segment $A_0 A_1$ (see Figure 3). By the proportionality condition $\frac{\tau_2-\tau_1}{\tau_1-\tau_0} = r$

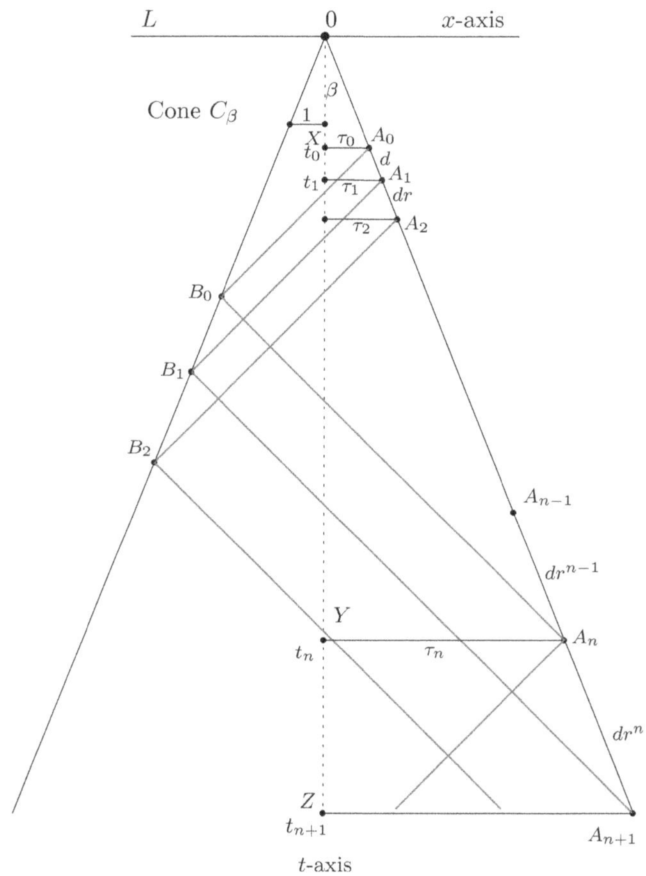

Figure 3: Proportional schedule for n robots $a_0, a_1, \ldots, a_{n-1}$, in the cone C_β .

and using similar triangles we conclude that $|A_1 A_2| = dr$, and consequently by induction $|A_i A_{i+1}| = dr^i$, for $i = 0, 1, \ldots, n-1$. Moreover, $|A_{n-1} A_n| = dr^{n-1}$ and $|A_n A_{n+1}| = dr^n$, where $A_n := (\tau_n, t_n)$, $A_{n+1} := (\tau_{n+1}, t_{n+1})$, and τ_n, τ_{n+1} are the next positive turning points after A_0, A_1 of robots a_0, a_1, respectively.

Consequently, the length of segment $A_0 A_n$ is given by the formula

[1]By symmetry the same result applies for negative turning points.

$$|A_0A_n| = d + dr + \cdots + dr^{n-1} = d\frac{r^n - 1}{r - 1}. \quad (3)$$

Denote by $B_0 = (\tau', t')$ the point on the cone C_β corresponding to the negative turning point τ' of robot a_0 at time t' such that $t_0 < t' < t_n$ (see Figure 3). By Lemma 1,

$$\begin{aligned} t_n - t_0 &= (t_n - t') + (t' - t_0) \\ &= \left(\tau_0 + \tau_0\frac{\beta+1}{\beta-1}\right) + \left(\tau_0\frac{\beta+1}{\beta-1} + \tau_0\left(\frac{\beta+1}{\beta-1}\right)^2\right) \\ &= \tau_0\left(1 + \frac{\beta+1}{\beta-1}\right)^2 = \tau_0\frac{4\beta^2}{(\beta-1)^2}. \end{aligned}$$

Consider points $X := (0, t_0), Y := (0, t_n)$. By similarity of triangles we have

$$\frac{|A_nA_0|}{|XY|} = \frac{|A_0O|}{|XO|}. \quad (4)$$

and since $|XO| = \tau_0\beta$ and $|A_0O| = \tau_0\sqrt{1+\beta^2}$ we get

$$|A_nA_0| = \frac{\tau_0\frac{4\beta^2}{(\beta-1)^2}\tau_0\sqrt{1+\beta^2}}{\tau_0\beta} = \frac{4\tau_0\beta\sqrt{\beta^2+1}}{(\beta-1)^2}. \quad (5)$$

Therefore

$$d\frac{r^n-1}{r-1} = \frac{4\tau_0\beta\sqrt{\beta^2+1}}{(\beta-1)^2}. \quad (6)$$

Robot a_1 visited its turning point τ_1 at time t_1 (depicted by point A_1 in Figure 3). Let t_{n+1} be its next turning point τ_{n+1} visited at t_{n+1} and let $A_{n+1} = (\tau_{n+1}, t_{n+1})$ and $Z = (0, t_{n+1})$. Note that

$$\begin{aligned} \frac{|OA_{n+1}|}{|OA_n|} &= \frac{\tau_0\sqrt{\beta^2+1} + d + dr + \cdots + dr^n}{\tau_0\sqrt{\beta^2+1} + d + dr + \cdots + dr^{n-1}} \quad (7) \\ &= 1 + \frac{dr^n}{\tau_0\sqrt{\beta^2+1} + d\frac{r^n-1}{r-1}} \end{aligned}$$

On the other hand we have

$$\begin{aligned} \frac{|OA_{n+1}|}{|OA_n|} &= \frac{|A_{n+1}B_1|}{|A_nB_0|} \\ &\quad \text{(by similarity of } \triangle OB_1A_{n+1} \text{ and } \triangle OB_0A_n\text{)}, \\ &= \frac{|A_{n+1}A_1|}{|A_nA_0|} \\ &\quad \text{(by similarity of } \triangle A_1B_1A_{n+1} \text{ and } \triangle A_0B_0A_n\text{)}, \\ &= \frac{\sum_{i=1}^{n} dr^i}{\sum_{i=0}^{n-1} dr^i} = r \quad (8) \end{aligned}$$

Combining Equations (7) and (8) we conclude that

$$r - 1 = \frac{dr^n}{\tau_0\sqrt{\beta^2+1} + d\frac{r^n-1}{r-1}} \quad (9)$$

To solve the system of Equations (6) and (9) for the unknowns r and d, we argue as follows. Substituting d from Equation (6) into Equation (9) we get

$$r - 1 = \frac{\frac{4\tau_0\beta\sqrt{\beta^2+1}}{(\beta-1)^2}\frac{r-1}{r^n-1}r^n}{\tau_0\sqrt{\beta^2+1} + \frac{4\tau_0\beta\sqrt{\beta^2+1}}{(\beta-1)^2}} \quad (10)$$

Simplifying Equation (10) we derive

$$1 = \frac{\frac{4\beta}{(\beta-1)^2}\frac{r^n}{r^n-1}}{1 + \frac{4\beta}{\beta^2-1}} \quad (11)$$

Multiplying out terms in Equation (11) and simplifying the expression we derive Equation (2). This proves the first part of Lemma 2.

We now prove the second part of Lemma 2. From Equation (6) we have

$$d = \frac{4\tau_0\beta\sqrt{\beta^2+1}}{(\beta-1)^2}\frac{r-1}{r^n-1} = \tau_0\sqrt{\beta^2+1}(r-1). \quad (12)$$

By similarity of triangles, observe that

$$\frac{t_1 - t_0}{d} = \frac{\beta}{\sqrt{\beta^2+1}}.$$

Hence, $t_1 = t_0 + \tau_0\beta(r-1)$. By similarity of triangles (see Figure 3) we have

$$\frac{\tau_1}{\tau_0} = \frac{|A_1O|}{|A_0O|} = \frac{d + \tau_0\sqrt{\beta^2+1}}{\tau_0\sqrt{\beta^2+1}}$$

After substituting in the last Equation the value of d as obtained from Equation (12) we get $\tau_1 = r\tau_0$. This concludes the proof of Lemma 2. □

Consider the proportional schedule for 3 robots when one of them may be faulty. The target is known to be found if at least two robots visited its position. Note the "tower-like" shape represented with bold lines on Figure 4. For any point (x, t) inside this shape we have that at time t point x was seen by at least two robots. Also if point (x, t) is outside this shape it means that at time t point x was seen by one robot or none. A similar tower-like shape may be constructed for a collection of n robots with up to f faulty robots for any n, f such that $f < n < 2f + 2$.

Definition 3. *Denote by $T_{f+1}(x)$ the time of the visit of point x by the $(f+1)$-st robot according to the schedule $S_\beta(n)$. Define the function*

$$K_\beta^{n,f}(x) := \frac{T_{f+1}(x)}{|x|},$$

and let

$$CR_\beta^{n,f} = \sup_{x \in \mathcal{R}} K_\beta^{n,f}(x)$$

denote the competitive ratio of the proportional schedule $S_\beta(n)$ when there are f faulty robots.

In the next two lemmas we establish properties of $K_\beta^{n,f}(x)$ and $T_{f+1}(x)$ needed to derive the competitive ratio of our algorithms.

Lemma 3. *The function $K_\beta^{n,f}(x)$ has discontinuities at turning points and it is continuous and decreasing in any interval not containing a turning point.*

Proof. Consider a vertical line, denoted by V, intersecting point x of the (infinite) line L. The line V intersects first the boundary of the cone C_β and subsequently the trajectories of the robots (see Figure 4.)

Clearly, the distance along line V from L to the intersection of the trajectory of the $(f+1)$st robot equals $T_{f+1}(x)$.

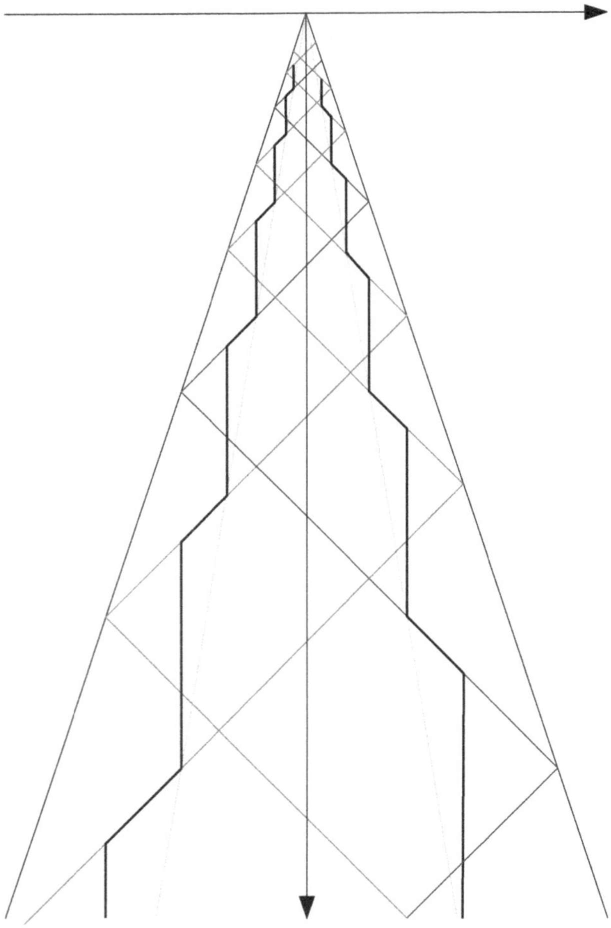

Figure 4: Searching by three robots one of which is faulty.

Observe that by moving line V continuously to the right, when it crosses a turning point of a robot, say a_0 without loss of generality, it ceases to intersect its trajectory. Consequently, the value of $T_{f+1}(x)$ increases by the vertical distance between the trajectories of the $(f+1)$st and $(f+2)$nd robots following a_0 at the moment of their visitation of point x, here denoted by a_f and a_{f+1}. This creates a discontinuity.

Consider now the values of $K_\beta^{n,f}(x)$ and $K_\beta^{n,f}(x+\epsilon)$ such that no turning point is in the interval $[x, x+\epsilon]$. As the $(f+1)$st robot at points x and $x+\epsilon$ remains the same (along V) we must have $T_{f+1}(x+\epsilon) = T_{f+1}(x)+\epsilon$. We claim that $K_\beta^{n,f}(x+\epsilon) < K_\beta^{n,f}(x)$. Indeed, observe that $x < T_{f+1}(x)$ since the point $(x, T_{f+1}(x))$ is inside the cone C_β. In turn this implies

$$\begin{aligned} K_\beta^{n,f}(x+\epsilon) &= \frac{T_{f+1}(x+\epsilon)}{x+\epsilon} = \frac{T_{f+1}(x)+\epsilon}{x+\epsilon} \\ &< \frac{T_{f+1}(x)}{x} = K_\beta^{n,f}(x), \end{aligned}$$

which proves the claim. □

LEMMA 4. *Suppose that robot a_0 visits its turning point τ_0 at time t_0. The time of the first visit of point τ_0 by robot a_{f+1} is*

$$T_{f+1} = \tau_0\left((\beta+1)^{\frac{2f+2}{n}}(\beta-1)^{1-\frac{2f+2}{n}}+1\right). \tag{13}$$

PROOF. Consider robot a_i arriving at time t_i at its first positive turning point τ_i for which $\tau_i > \tau_0$, $i = 1, 2, \ldots, f+1$. By Lemma 2 applied to robot a_i, we have that

$$\begin{aligned} t_i &= t_{i-1} + \tau_{i-1}\beta(r-1) \\ &= t_{i-2} + \tau_{i-2}\beta(r-1) + \tau_{i-1}\beta(r-1) \\ &\vdots \\ &= t_0 + (\tau_0 + \tau_1 + \cdots \tau_{i-1})\beta(r-1) \end{aligned}$$

By Lemma 2 (applied inductively) we have that $\tau_i = r^i\tau_0$ and

$$\begin{aligned} t_i &= t_0 + \tau_0(1 + r + \cdots + r^{i-1})\beta(r-1) \\ &= t_0 + \tau_0\beta(r^i - 1) \\ &= \tau_0\beta r^i \text{ (as } t_0 = \beta\tau_0) \end{aligned}$$

Note that before arriving at its turning point τ_{f+1} at time $t_{f+1} = \tau_0\beta r^{f+1}$, robot a_{f+1} visits point τ_0 at time $T_{f+1} = t_{f+1} - (\tau_{f+1} - \tau_0)$. Consequently, we have

$$T_{f+1} = \tau_0\beta r^{f+1} - \tau_0 r^{f+1} + \tau_0.$$

By Equation (2), we have that $r = \left(\frac{\beta+1}{\beta-1}\right)^{2/n}$. It follows that

$$\begin{aligned} T_{f+1} &= \tau_0\beta r^{f+1} - \tau_0 r^{f+1} + \tau_0 \\ &= \tau_0\left(r^{f+1}(\beta-1)+1\right) \\ &= \tau_0\left(\left(\frac{\beta+1}{\beta-1}\right)^{\frac{2f+2}{n}}(\beta-1)+1\right) \\ &= \tau_0\left((\beta+1)^{\frac{2f+2}{n}}(\beta-1)^{1-\frac{2f+2}{n}}+1\right). \end{aligned}$$

This proves Lemma 4. □

Using the two preceding lemmas we can derive the following upper bound on the competitive ratio of the proportional schedule $S_\beta(n)$.

LEMMA 5. *Consider n robots executing the proportional schedule $S_\beta(n)$. If up to f robots may be faulty where $f < n < 2f+2$ then*

$$CR_\beta^{n,f} = (\beta+1)^{\frac{2f+2}{n}}(\beta-1)^{1-\frac{2f+2}{n}}+1. \tag{14}$$

PROOF. By Lemma 3, we can subdivide line L into an infinite collection of intervals such that in each such interval the function $K_\beta^{n,f}(x)$ is continuous and decreasing and by Lemma 4, the suprema of the function $K_\beta^{n,f}(x)$ on these intervals are identical. Hence,

$$\begin{aligned} CR_\beta^{n,f} &= \sup_x K_\beta^{n,f}(x) \\ &= (\beta+1)^{\frac{2f+2}{n}}(\beta-1)^{1-\frac{2f+2}{n}}+1. \end{aligned}$$

This proves Lemma 5. □

We now choose the value of β as a function of f and n so as to minimize the function $F(\beta) := (\beta+1)^{\frac{2f+2}{n}}(\beta-1)^{1-\frac{2f+2}{n}}+1$, where $\beta > 1$. In turn, this can be optimized

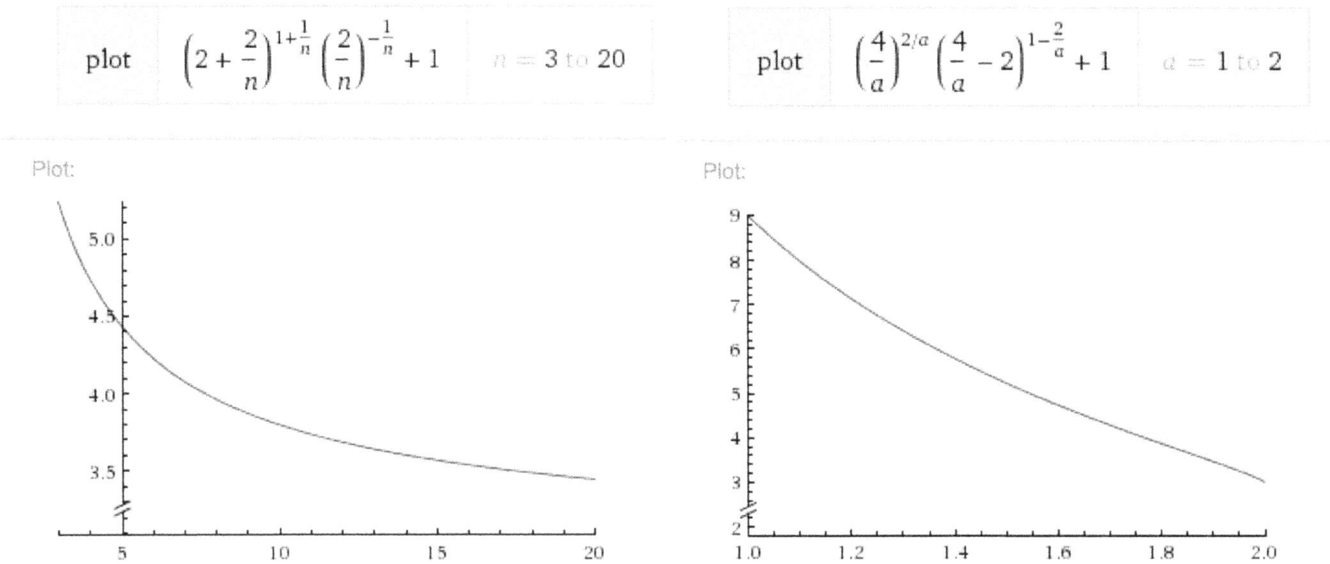

Figure 5: At left: plot of the competitive ratio $\left(2+\frac{2}{n}\right)^{1+\frac{1}{n}}\left(\frac{2}{n}\right)^{-\frac{1}{n}}+1$ of the proportional schedule algorithm for $n = 2f+1$ robots, f of which are faulty, At right: plot of $\left(\frac{4}{a}\right)^{\frac{2}{a}}\left(\frac{4}{a}-2\right)^{1-\frac{2}{a}}+1$, of the competitive ratio of our proportional schedule algorithm for $n = af$ robots f of which are faulty for $1 < a < 2$.

by taking the derivative of F with respect to β and setting it equal to 0. Indeed, we have that equation $F'(\beta) = 0$ is equivalent to the equation $0 = (\beta+1)^{\frac{2f+2}{n}-1}(\beta-1)^{-\frac{2f+2}{n}}\left(\frac{2f+2}{n}(\beta-1)+\left(1-\frac{2f+2}{n}\right)(\beta+1)\right)$. By solving this last equation for β we get the unique solution $\beta = \frac{4f+4}{n}-1$.

Next, we show how to convert a proportional schedule $S_\beta(n)$ into an algorithm for the above optimal value of β. Observe that the zig-zag movement of a robot having a turning point x_0 at time $t_0 > 0$ is infinite. It may also be extended backwards in the time interval $(0, t_0)$ by any number of steps. To make it into an algorithm, we need to determine the first part of the trajectory of each robot from the origin to the very first turning point on the cone C_β. The subsequent turning points are then fully determined by the cone. This requires the assumption that either an additive constant should be added to the competitive ratio, or that the minimal distance from the source to the target is known in advance (cf., [35][page 39]). We choose the second option and thus assume that the target is at distance at least one unit from the starting point 0.

Definition 4. *Fix $\beta = \frac{4f+4}{n}-1$. Set the turning point τ_0 of a_0 to 1, and let $\tau_1, \tau_2, \ldots, \tau_{n-1}$ be the turning points of $a_1, a_2, \ldots, a_{n-1}$ as determined by the proportional schedule $S_\beta(n)$. For any i, $1 \le i \le n-1$ let τ_i' be the first turning point of a_i less than 1 obtained by extending the trajectory of a_i backward inside the cone. Then in the* proportional schedule algorithm *$A(n, f)$, the trajectories of robots are defined as follows:*
Robot a_0 moves from 0 so that it reaches 1 at time β. Then it moves at speed 1 in the cone C_β. For $1 \le i \le n-1$, robot a_i moves from 0 so that it reaches τ_i' at time $\beta\tau_i'$. Then it moves at speed 1 in the cone C_β.

It is easy to observe that according to algorithm $A(n, f)$, at any time $t \ge \beta$, all robots are moving according to the proportional schedule $S_\beta(n)$ for the optimal value of β. We now give the main result of this section.

Theorem 1. *Consider a collection of n robots up to f of which are faulty. Then the competitive ratio of algorithm $A(n, f)$ is at most*

$$\left(\frac{4f+4}{n}\right)^{\frac{2f+2}{n}}\left(\frac{4f+4}{n}-2\right)^{1-\frac{2f+2}{n}}+1. \quad (15)$$

Proof. Our algorithm $A(n, f)$ is based on a proportional schedule $S_\beta(n)$ whose competitive ratio was shown to be at most

$$(\beta+1)^{\frac{2f+2}{n}}(\beta-1)^{1-\frac{2f+2}{n}}+1.$$

Substituting the value of $\beta = \frac{4f+4}{n}-1$ gives the result. □

In the sequel we compute some estimates of the resulting competitive ratio of our proportional schedule algorithms for various values of n and f, where $f < n < 2f+2$.

For $n = f+1$, the competitive ratio as given by Formula (15) is

$$\left(\frac{4f+4}{n}\right)^{\frac{2f+2}{n}}\left(\frac{4f+4}{n}-2\right)^{1-\frac{2f+2}{n}}+1 = 4^2(4-2)^{-1}+1$$
$$= 9,$$

i.e., the same as for $n = 1$ in [8] and as was observed earlier is optimal.

For $n = 3$ and $f = 1$ we have that $\beta = 8/3-1 = 5/3$ and the competitive ratio is $(\beta+1)^{1+\frac{1}{n}}(\beta-1)^{1-\frac{1}{n}}+1 = (8/3)4^{1/3} \sim 5.233$. More generally, for $n = 2f+1$, the resulting competitive ratio as given by Formula (15) is

$$\left(2+\frac{2}{n}\right)^{1+\frac{1}{n}}\left(\frac{2}{n}\right)^{-\frac{1}{n}}+1,$$

which tends to 3 as $n \to \infty$. The plot of this last function is depicted in Figure 5 (left). However, we can state and prove an even more precise upper bound as follows.

COROLLARY 1. *The optimal competitive ratio of a proportional schedule for $n = 2f + 1$ robots, exactly f of which are faulty, is at most $3 + \frac{4 \ln n}{n} + \frac{O(1)}{n}$.*

PROOF. Let $u_n = (n+1)^{1/n}$. Observe, that

$$u_n < \left(1 + \frac{\ln(n+1)}{n}\right)^2.$$

Indeed,

$$(u_n)^n = n + 1 = e^{\ln(n+1)} < \left(1 + \frac{\ln(n+1)}{n}\right)^{n+\ln(n+1)/2}.$$

The last inequality is based on $e^t < (1 + t/n)^{n+t/2}$ and can be found in [33][page 435]. Therefore,

$$u_n < \left(1 + \frac{\ln(n+1)}{n}\right)^{1+\ln(n+1)/2n} < \left(1 + \frac{\ln(n+1)}{n}\right)^2.$$

It follows that

$$\begin{aligned}
&\left(2 + \frac{2}{n}\right)^{1+\frac{1}{n}} (2/n)^{-1/n} + 1 \\
&= \left(2 + \frac{2}{n}\right) u_n + 1 \\
&< \left(2 + \frac{2}{n}\right)\left(1 + \frac{\ln(n+1)}{n}\right)^2 + 1 \\
&< \left(2 + \frac{2}{n}\right)\left(1 + 2\frac{\ln(n+1)}{n} + \text{low order terms}\right) + 1 \\
&< 3 + \frac{4 \ln n}{n} + \text{low order terms},
\end{aligned}$$

where the low order terms are in $O(1)/n$. This completes the proof of the corollary. □

Now assume that $1 < a := n/f < 2$. The resulting competitive ratio as given by Formula (15) is

$$\left(\frac{4}{a} + \frac{4}{n}\right)^{\frac{2}{a}+\frac{2}{n}} \left(\frac{4}{a} + \frac{4}{n} - 2\right)^{1-\frac{2}{a}-\frac{2}{n}} + 1,$$

which tends to $(4/a)^{2/a}(4/a - 2)^{1-2/a} + 1$ as $n \to \infty$. The plot of this last function is depicted in Figure 5 (right).

4. LOWER BOUND

In this section, we give a lower bound for the competitive ratio of any algorithm for search by $n < 2f + 2$ robots, of which f may be faulty. Let $x > 1$. We say that a robot has a *positive trajectory for x* if its *first* visits to the points in $\{-x, -1, 1, x\}$ are in the order $1, x, -1, -x$. Similarly, we say it has a *negative trajectory for x* if its first visits to the points in $\{-x, -1, 1, x\}$ are in the order $-1, -x, 1, x$. See Figure 6 for an illustration of positive and negative trajectories.

We start with a couple of simple observations about positive and negative trajectories, which we will use repeatedly in the proof of our lower bound.

LEMMA 6. *Let $x > 1$ and suppose a single robot visits both points $x, -x$ strictly before time $3x + 2$. Then it has to follow either a positive or a negative trajectory for x.*

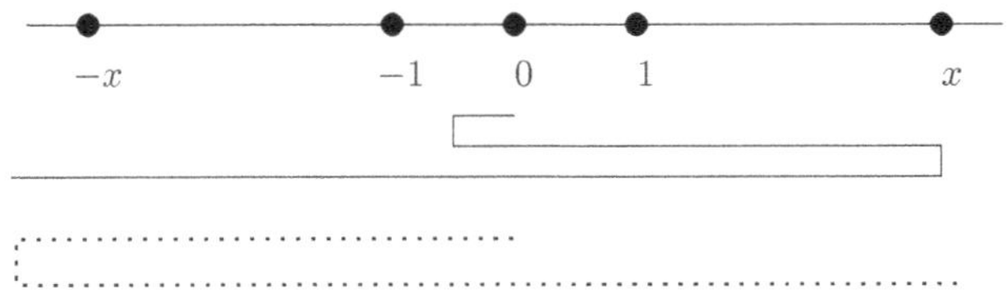

Figure 6: A positive trajectory for x is shown with a solid line: Robot visits $1, x, -1, -x$ in that order. A negative trajectory for x is shown with a dotted line: Robot visits $-1, -x, 1, x$ in that order.

PROOF. The robot has to visit either 1 or -1 first. Suppose it visits 1 before -1. If it visits $-x$ before x, then it takes time at least $3x + 2$ to reach x. Therefore it must first visit x (having visited 1 on the way), then -1 then $-x$, that is, it follows a positive trajectory for x. Similarly, if it visits -1 before 1, it must follow a negative trajectory for $-x$. □

LEMMA 7. *Let $x, y \geq 1$. If a robot follows a positive or negative trajectory for x, then it cannot reach both y and $-y$ before time $2x + y$.*

PROOF. If the robot follows a positive trajectory for x, it must visit x before it visits -1, and therefore needs time at least $2x + y$ to reach $-y$. Similarly if it follows a negative trajectory for x, it needs at least $2x + y$ time to reach y. □

We now present our main result. The key idea is as follows. First, we choose an $x > 1$ such that a single robot is forced to visit both $\pm x$ before a certain time in order for the algorithm to be competitive. Then we use Lemma 6 to show that the robot is forced to take a positive or negative trajectory for $\pm x$. Next we use Lemma 7 to show that the robot cannot possibly visit both $\pm y$ for some $y < x$. We repeat this argument for the other robots to derive a contradiction that the algorithm has the claimed competitive ratio.

THEOREM 2. *The competitive ratio of any algorithm for search by $n < 2f + 2$ robots, of which f are faulty, is at least α for any $\alpha > 3$ satisfying*

$$(\alpha - 1)^n (\alpha - 3) \leq 2^{n+1}$$

PROOF. Fix an α satisfying the conditions of the lemma. Assume the robots start at location 0. Depending on the movement of the robots, the adversary will place the target at one of the points $\pm 1, \pm x_{n-1}, \pm x_{n-2}, \ldots, \pm x_0$, where $x_i = \frac{2^{i+1}}{(\alpha-1)^i(\alpha-3)}$ for every i with $0 \leq i \leq n-1$, Observe that for all i such that $0 \leq i \leq n-2$,

$$x_i = \frac{\alpha - 1}{2} x_{i+1} \tag{16}$$

Furthermore,

$$\begin{aligned}
x_{n-1} &= \frac{2^n}{(\alpha-1)^{n-1}(\alpha-3)} &(17)\\
&= \frac{\alpha-1}{2} \frac{2^{n+1}}{(\alpha-1)^n(\alpha-3)} &(18)\\
&> \frac{\alpha-1}{2} &(19)
\end{aligned}$$

where the last inequality follows from the assumption on α.

Since $\alpha > 3$, it follows from Eqns 16 and 19 that:

$$x_0 > x_1 > \ldots x_{n-2} > x_{n-1} > 1 \tag{20}$$

See Figure 7 for an illustration. Suppose now, for the pur-

Figure 7: The adversary places the target at a location in $\{\pm 1, \pm x_{n-1}, \ldots, \pm x_0\}$, $x_0 > x_1 > x_2 \cdots > x_{n-1} > 1$.

pose of contradiction, that there is an algorithm $\mathcal{A}$ that has a competitive ratio $\rho < \alpha$.

First, we claim that for every i such that $0 \le i \le n-1$, at least $f+1$ of the robots must visit both $\pm x_i$ strictly before time αx_i. Suppose instead that at most f robots visit one of these points, say x_i, before time αx_i. The adversary makes them all faulty, and places the target at x_i. Therefore the earliest time a non-faulty robot visits x_i is at least αx_i, which implies that $\rho \ge \alpha$, a contradiction.

Furthermore, since there are at most $2f+1$ robots in all, by the pigeonhole principle, we conclude that there must be a robot that visits *both* $\pm x_i$ before time αx_i. Next we give a proof by induction that for every i with $0 \le i \le n-1$, it must be a *unique* robot that visits both $\pm x_i$ before time αx_i, and furthermore, it must use either a positive or a negative trajectory for x_i.

Inductively, we assume that for some i with $0 \le i < n-1$, and for each j such that $0 \le j \le i$, there is a unique robot a_j that visits both $\pm x_j$ before time αx_j, following either a positive or a negative trajectory for x_j. Now consider the points $\pm x_{i+1}$. By Lemma 7, such a robot a_j cannot visit both $\pm x_{i+1}$ before time $2x_j + x_{i+1}$. However, for all $1 \le j \le i$, since $x_j \ge x_i$, we have

$$\begin{aligned} 2x_j + x_{i+1} &\ge 2x_i + x_{i+1} \\ &= 2\frac{(\alpha-1)x_{i+1}}{2} + x_{i+1} \\ &= \alpha x_{i+1} \end{aligned}$$

where the first equality follows from (16). Therefore, none of the previous robots can visit both $\pm x_{i+1}$ before time αx_{i+1} and it must be a new robot, say a_{i+1}, that visits both $\pm x_{i+1}$ before time αx_{i+1}. Furthermore, since $x_{i+1} < x_0 = 2/(\alpha - 3)$, we conclude that $\alpha x_{i+1} < 3x_{i+1} + 2$, and so by Lemma 6, a_{i+1} must use a positive or a negative trajectory for x_{i+1}. This completes the proof by induction that there must be a unique robot visiting the points $\pm x_i$ for $0 \le i \le n-1$ before time αx_i, using either a positive or a negative trajectory for x_i.

Finally, consider the points ± 1. Following the same logic as for the points $\pm x_i$, there must be a single robot that visits both ± 1 before time α, otherwise $\rho \ge \alpha$. However, since for each j such that $0 \le j \le n-1$, the robot a_j follows either a positive or a negative trajectory for x_j, it cannot visit both ± 1 before time $2x_j + 1$. Since $x_j \ge x_{n-1}$, we have

$$\begin{aligned} 2x_j + 1 \ge 2x_{n-1} + 1 &= \frac{2^{n+1}}{(\alpha-1)^{n-1}(\alpha-3)} + 1 \\ &= (\alpha-1)\frac{2^{n+1}}{(\alpha-1)^n(\alpha-3)} + 1 \\ &\ge \alpha \end{aligned}$$

since $\frac{2^{n+1}}{(\alpha-1)^n(\alpha-3)} \ge 1$ by assumption. Thus, none of the n robots can visit ± 1 before time α, contradicting the assumption that the competitive ratio of $\mathcal{A}$ is less than α. □

Theorem 2 gives a lower bound of ≈ 3.76 on the competitive ratio of any algorithm for search by 3 robots, of which one may be faulty.

COROLLARY 2. *As n approaches ∞, the competitive ratio of an algorithm for search by $n < 2f+2$ robots, of which f may be faulty, is bounded from below by*

$$3 + \frac{2\ln n}{n} - \frac{2\ln\ln n}{n}.$$

PROOF. Take $\alpha = 3 + 2\frac{\ln n - \ln\ln n}{n}$ and observe that the following inequality holds $\frac{(\alpha-1)^n(\alpha-3)}{2^{n+1}} < 1$. □

5. CONCLUSION

Search on a line has been a source of numerous beautiful problems in robotics and our setting is no exception. In this paper, we analyzed the problem of search on a line by n robots. The novelty of our model is in that it allows $f < n$ robots to be faulty. We presented a new class of parallel search algorithms, called proportional schedule algorithms, and analyzed their competitive ratio. For every (n, f), we give a proportional schedule algorithm $A(n, f)$ whose expansion factor depends on the ratio n/f. For $n = f+1$ our algorithm is optimal. Finally, we showed a lower bound on the competitive ratio of any parallel search algorithm which shows our proportional schedule algorithm is asymptotically optimal when $n = 2f+1$.

6. REFERENCES

[1] N. Agmon and D. Peleg. Fault-tolerant gathering algorithms for autonomous mobile robots. *SIAM Journal on Computing*, 36(1):56–82, 2006.

[2] S. Albers and M. R. Henzinger. Exploring unknown environments. *SIAM Journal on Computing*, 29(4):1164–1188, 2000.

[3] S. Albers, K. Kursawe, and S. Schuierer. Exploring unknown environments with obstacles. *Algorithmica*, 32(1):123–143, 2002.

[4] S. Alpern and S. Gal. *The theory of search games and rendezvous*, volume 55. Kluwer Academic Publishers, 2002.

[5] R. Baeza Yates, J. Culberson, and G. Rawlins. Searching in the plane. *Information and Computation*, 106(2):234–252, 1993.

[6] R. Baeza-Yates and R. Schott. Parallel searching in the plane. *Computational Geometry*, 5(3):143–154, 1995.

[7] A. Beck. On the linear search problem. *Israel Journal of Mathematics*, 2(4):221–228, 1964.

[8] A. Beck and D. Newman. Yet more on the linear search problem. *Israel Journal of Mathematics*, 8(4):419–429, 1970.

[9] R. Bellman. An optimal search. *SIAM Review*, 5(3):274–274, 1963.

[10] P. Bose, J.-L. De Carufel, and S. Durocher. Revisiting the problem of searching on a line. In *Algorithms–ESA 2013, LNCS*, volume 8125, pages 205–216. Springer, 2013.

[11] Z. Bouzid, M.G. Potop-Butucaru, and S. Tixeuil. Optimal byzantine-resilient convergence in uni-dimensional robot network. *Theoretical Computer Science*, 411(34-36):3154–3168, 2010.

[12] W. Burgard, M. Moors, C. Stachniss, and F. E. Schneider. Coordinated multi-robot exploration. *IEEE Transactions on Robotics*, 21(3):376–386, 2005.

[13] A. Casteigts, P. Flocchini, W. Quattrociocchi, and N. Santoro. Time-varying graphs and dynamic networks. In *Ad-hoc, mobile, and wireless networks, LNCS*, volume 6811, pages 346–359. Springer, 2011.

[14] M. Chrobak, L. Gasieniec, Gorry T., and R. Martin. Group search on the line. In *Proceedings of SOFSEM 2015, LNCS 8939*, pages 164–176. Springer, 2015.

[15] R. Cohen and D. Peleg. Convergence properties of the gravitational algorithm in asynchronous robot systems. *SIAM Journal of Computing*, 41(1):1516–1528, 2005.

[16] R. Cohen and D. Peleg. Convergence of autonomous mobile robots with inaccurate sensors and movements. *SIAM Journal on Computing*, 38(1):276–302, 2008.

[17] J. Czyzowicz, L. Gasieniec, A. Kosowski, E. Kranakis, D. Krizanc, and N. Taleb. When patrolmen become corrupted: Monitoring a graph using faulty mobile robots. In *Algorithms and Computation - Proceedings of 26th International Symposium, ISAAC 2015*, pages 343–354, 2015.

[18] X. Défago, M. Gradinariu, S. Messika, and P.R. Parvédy. Fault-tolerant and self-stabilizing mobile robots gathering. In *Proceedings of DISC 2006*, pages 46–60, 2006.

[19] E. D. Demaine, S. P. Fekete, and S. Gal. Online searching with turn cost. *Theoretical Computer Science*, 361(2):342–355, 2006.

[20] X. Deng, T. Kameda, and C. Papadimitriou. How to learn an unknown environment. In *Proceedings of FOCS*, pages 298–303. IEEE, 1991.

[21] Y. Dieudonné, A. Pelc, and D. Peleg. Gathering despite mischief. *ACM Transactions on Algorithms (TALG)*, 11(1):1, 2014.

[22] O. Feinerman, A. Korman, Z. Lotker, and J. S. Sereni. Collaborative search on the plane without communication. In *Proceedings of the 2012 ACM symposium on Principles of distributed computing*, pages 77–86. ACM, 2012.

[23] P. Flocchini, D. Ilcinkas, A. Pelc, and N. Santoro. How many oblivious robots can explore a line. *Information processing letters*, 111:1027–1031, 2011.

[24] B. Gluss. An alternative solution to the lost at sea problem. *Naval Research Logistics Quarterly*, 8(1):117–122, 1961.

[25] F. Hoffmann, C. Icking, R. Klein, and K. Kriegel. The polygon exploration problem. *SIAM Journal on Computing*, 31(2):577–600, 2001.

[26] J. Hromkovič, R. Klasing, B. Monien, and R. Peine. Dissemination of information in interconnection networks (broadcasting & gossiping). In *Combinatorial network theory*, pages 125–212. Springer, 1996.

[27] J. R. Isbell. Pursuit around a hole. *Naval Research Logistics Quarterly*, 14(4):569–571, 1967.

[28] T. Izumi, S. Souissi, Y. Katayama, N. Inuzuka, X. Défago, K. Wada, and M. Yamashita. The gathering problem for two oblivious robots with unreliable compasses. *SIAM Journal on Computing*, 41(1):26–46, 2012.

[29] J. Kleinberg. On-line search in a simple polygon. In *Proceedings of SODA*, pages 8–15. SIAM, 1994.

[30] F. Kuhn, N. Lynch, and R. Oshman. Distributed computation in dynamic networks. In *Proceedings of the forty-second ACM symposium on Theory of computing*, pages 513–522. ACM, 2010.

[31] L. Lamport, R. Shostak, and M. Pease. The byzantine generals problem. *ACM Transactions on Programming Languages and Systems (TOPLAS)*, 4(3):382–401, 1982.

[32] N. A. Lynch. *Distributed algorithms*. Morgan Kaufmann, 1996.

[33] R. Motwani and P. Raghavan. *Randomized Algorithms*. Cambridge University Press, 1995.

[34] C. H Papadimitriou and M. Yannakakis. Shortest paths without a map. In *Proceedings of ICALP, LNCS*, volume 372, pages 610–620. Springer, 1989.

[35] S. Schuierer. Lower bounds in on-line geometric searching. *Computational Geometry*, 18(1):37–53, 2001.

[36] S. Souissi, X. Défago, and M. Yamashita. Gathering asynchronous mobile robots with inaccurate compasses. *Principles of Distributed Systems*, pages 333–349, 2006.

[37] S. Thrun. A probabilistic on-line mapping algorithm for teams of mobile robots. *The International Journal of Robotics Research*, 20(5):335–363, 2001.

[38] B. Yamauchi. Frontier-based exploration using multiple robots. In *Proceedings of 2nd international conference on Autonomous agents*, pages 47–53. ACM, 1998.

[39] Y. Yang, S. Souissi, X. Défago, and M. Takizawa. Fault-tolerant flocking for a group of autonomous mobile robots. *Journal of Systems and Software*, 84(1):29–36, 2011.

Uniform Deployment of Mobile Agents in Asynchronous Rings

Masahiro Shibata
Osaka University, Japan
m-sibata@ist.osaka-u.ac.jp

Toshiya Mega
Osaka University, Japan
t-mega@ist.osaka-u.ac.jp

Fukuhito Ooshita
NAIST, Japan
f-oosita@is.naist.jp

Hirotsugu Kakugawa
Osaka University, Japan
kakugawa@ist.osaka-u.ac.jp

Toshimitsu Masuzawa
Osaka University, Japan
masuzawa@ist.osaka-u.ac.jp

ABSTRACT

In this paper, we consider the uniform deployment problem of mobile agents in asynchronous unidirectional rings, which requires the agents to uniformly spread in the ring. The uniform deployment problem is striking contrast to the rendezvous problem which requires the agents to meet at the same node. While the rendezvous aims to break the symmetry, the uniform deployment aims to attain the symmetry. Hence, we are interested in clarifying how easily the uniform deployment problem can be solved compared to the rendezvous problem. We consider two problem settings. First, we consider agents with knowledge of k, where k is the number of agents. In this case, our proposed algorithm solves the uniform deployment problem with termination detection. This algorithm requires $O(\log n)$ memory per agent, $O(n \log k)$ time, and $O(kn)$ total moves, where n is the number of nodes. Next, we consider agents with no knowledge of k or n. In this case, we show that, when termination detection is required, there exists no algorithm to solve the uniform deployment problem. For this reason, we consider the relaxed uniform deployment problem that does not require termination detection, and we propose an algorithm to solve the relaxed uniform deployment problem. This algorithm requires $O(k/l \log(n/l))$ memory per agent, $O(n/l)$ time, and $O(kn/l)$ total moves, where l is the symmetry degree of the initial configuration ($l \geq 1$). Note that both the algorithms achieve the uniform deployment from any initial configuration, which is a striking difference from the rendezvous problem because the rendezvous problem is not solvable from some initial configurations.

Keywords

mobile agent, uniform deployment, ring networks, token, symmetry degree

PODC'16, July 25-28, 2016, Chicago, IL, USA

DOI: http://dx.doi.org/10.1145/2933057.2933093

1. INTRODUCTION

A *distributed system* is a system that consists of a set of computers (*nodes*) and communication links. As a way to design distributed systems, (mobile) agents have attracted a lot of attention [1]. Agents can traverse the system and process tasks on each node, and hence they can simplify design of distributed systems [2]. The *rendezvous problem* is a fundamental problem for cooperation of mobile agents. This problem requires all agents to meet at a single node. The rendezvous problem is considered in rings [3, 4], torus [5], trees [6], and arbitrary networks [7]. Some works assume that agents can use whiteboard on each node, and others assume that agents can use only tokens, which are markers that agents can release on nodes. As another fundamental problem, Flocchini et al. [8] and Elor et al. [9] considered the *uniform deployment* (or *uniform scattering*), which requires all agents to spread uniformly in the ring network, while Barriere et al. [10] considered it in the grid network. All of them propose uniform deployment algorithms under the assumption that agents are oblivious (or memoryless) but can observe multiple nodes within its visibility range. This assumption is often called a *Look-Compute-Move* model.

In this paper, we focus on the uniform deployment on asynchronous unidirectional rings. Different from [8, 9, 10], we consider agents that have memory but cannot observe nodes except for the currently located node. To our best knowledge, this is the first research considering the uniform deployment for such agents. From a practical point of view, the uniform deployment is useful for the network management. For instance, if agents can repair faulty nodes and are deployed uniformly, such agents can quickly reach and repair faulty nodes after the faults are detected. If agents with database replicas are deployed uniformly, each node can quickly access the database. Hence, we can regard the uniform deployment problem as a kind of the resource allocation problem. The uniform deployment is interesting to investigate also from a theoretical point of view. The problem exhibits a striking contrast to the rendezvous: the uniform deployment aims to attain the symmetry of agent locations while the rendezvous aims to break the symmetry. It is well known that the symmetry breaking is difficult (and sometimes impossible) in distributed systems. Hence, it is interesting to clarify how easily the uniform deployment can be achieved compared to the rendezvous.

Contributions of this paper are summarized in Table 1. We assume that each agent initially has a token and can release it on a node that it visits. After a token is released at some node, agents cannot remove the token. In addition, we assume that agents can

Table 1: Results in each model

	Trivial Algorithm (Appendix A)	Result 1 (Section 3)	Result 2 (Section 4.1)	Result 3 (Section 4.2)
Knowledge of k	Available	Available	Not Available	Not Available
Termination detection	Required	Required	Required	Not Required
Solvable / Unsolvable	Solvable	Solvable	Not Solvable	Solvable
Agent memory	$O(k \log n)$	$O(\log n)$	-	$O(k/l \log(n/l))$
Time complexity	$O(n)$	$O(n \log k)$	-	$O(n/l)$
Total agent moves	$O(kn)$	$O(kn)$	-	$O(kn/l)$

n: the number of nodes, k: the number of agents, l: the symmetry degree of the initial configuration

send a message to agents at the same node. We consider two problem settings. First, we consider agents with knowledge of k, where k is the number of agents. In this case, we propose two algorithms. The first algorithm is a trivial one and solves the uniform deployment with termination detection which requires $O(k \log n)$ memory per agent, $O(n)$ time, and $O(kn)$ total moves, where n is the number of nodes. The idea of this algorithm is as follows: 1) Each agent travels once around the ring and gets information about the initial locations of all the agents (i.e., distance sequence), and 2) each agent decides its target node (the node to stay at for the uniform deployment) from information and moves there. We explain the detail of this algorithm in Appendix A. The second algorithm solves the uniform deployment problem with termination detection. This algorithm reduces the memory per agent to $O(\log n)$, but allows $O(n \log k)$ time, and $O(kn)$ total moves. Next, we consider agents with no knowledge of k or n. In this case, we show that, when termination detection is required, there exists no algorithm to solve the uniform deployment problem. Intuitively, it is due to impossibility of finding k or n when some part of the initial configuration has symmetry: when an agent misestimates these at smaller numbers than actual ones, it prematurely terminates and the uniform deployment cannot be achieved. For this reason, we consider the relaxed uniform deployment problem that does not require termination detection, and we propose an algorithm to solve the relaxed uniform deployment problem. In this algorithm, each agent estimates k and n (possibly at smaller values than actual ones) and behaves based on the estimation. Thus, the efficiency of the algorithm depends on the estimation. To evaluate the efficiency, we introduce the following parameter l to denote the symmetry degree of an initial configuration: we say that an initial configuration has symmetry degree l when its distance sequence can be represented as l-times repetition of some aperiodic sequence. For example, an asymmetric initial configuration has symmetry degree 1, and the symmetry degree becomes larger for a higher symmetric initial configuration. Note that agents cannot know l but the efficiency depends on it. Using the symmetry degree parameter l, the efficiency of the algorithm is denoted as follows: this algorithm requires $O(k/l \log(n/l))$ memory per agent, $O(n/l)$ time, and $O(kn/l)$ total moves. This result shows a natural but interesting property: the algorithm achieves the uniform deployment more efficiently when the initial configuration has higher symmetry degree. For an asymmetric initial configuration, this algorithm requires $O(k \log n)$ memory per agent, $O(n)$ time, and $O(kn)$ total moves. However, when l is $\omega(1)$, this algorithm requires $o(k \log n)$ memory per agent, $o(n)$ time, and $o(kn)$ total moves. When l is $\Omega(n)$, this algorithm requires $O(1)$ memory per agent, $O(1)$ time, and $O(k)$ total moves.

Note that, for any initial configuration such that all agents are in the initial states and placed at the distinct nodes respectively, all proposed algorithms achieve the uniform deployment, which is a striking difference from the rendezvous problem because the rendezvous problem is not solvable from some initial configurations. Due to limitation of space, we omit several proofs of lemmas and theorems.

2. PRELIMINARIES

2.1 System model

A *unidirectional ring network* R is defined as 2-tuple $R = (V, E)$, where V is a set of anonymous nodes and E is a set of unidirectional links. We denote by $n\ (= |V|)$ the number of nodes. Then, we define $V = \{v_0, v_1, \ldots, v_{n-1}\}$ and $E = \{e_0, e_1, \ldots, e_{n-1}\}$ ($e_i = (v_i, v_{(i+1) \bmod n})$). For simplicity, operations to an index of a node assume calculation under modulo n, that is, $v_{(i+1) \bmod n}$ is simply represented by v_{i+1}. We define the direction from v_i to v_{i+1} as the *forward* direction. In addition, the *distance* from v_i to v_j ($0 \leq i, j \leq n-1$) is defined to be $(j - i) \bmod n$.

An agent is a state machine having an *initial state*. Let $A = \{a_0, a_1, \ldots, a_{k-1}\}$ be a set of $k\ (\leq n)$ anonymous agents. For simplicity, operations to an index of an agent assume calculation under modulo k. Since the ring is unidirectional, agents staying at v_i can move only to v_{i+1}. We consider two problem settings: agents with knowledge of k and agents with no knowledge of k or n. We assume that each agent initially has a 1-bit memory called a *token* and can release it on a node that it visits. Note that if agents are not allowed to have tokens, they cannot mark nodes in any way and this means that the uniform deployment problem cannot be solved. This is because if all agents move in a synchronous manner, they cannot get any information of other agents. After a token is released at some node, agents cannot remove the token. Note that since agents are anonymous, they cannot recognize the owner of each token. In addition, we assume that agents can send a message of any size to agents at the same node. We assume that agents move through a link in a FIFO manner, that is, when agent a_p leaves v_i after agent a_q leaves v_i, a_p reaches v_{i+1} after a_q reaches v_{i+1}. Note that such FIFO assumptions are natural because agents are implemented as messages in practice and FIFO assumptions of messages are natural and can be easily realized in distributed systems.

Each agent a_i executes the following five operations in an atomic action: 1) The agent reaches a node v (when a_i is in transit toward v), or it starts operations at v (when a_i is at v), 2) the agent receives all the messages (if any), 3) the agent executes local computation, 4) the agent broadcasts a message to all the agents staying at the same node v (if any) if it decides to send a message, and 5) the agent leaves v if it decides to move. After taking an atomic action, a_i has no message. Note that these assumptions of atomic actions are also natural because they can be implemented locally if each node has a

Table 2: Meaning of each element in configuration $C = \{S, T, M, P, Q\}$

Element	Meaning and example
$S = (s_0, s_1, \ldots, s_{k-1})$	Set of agent states (s_i is the state of agent a_i)
$T = (t_0, t_1, \ldots, t_{n-1})$	Set of node states (t_i is the state of node t_i)
$M = (m_0, m_1, \ldots, m_{k-1})$	Set of message sequences (m_i is a sequence of massages sent to a_i and not received by a_i)
$P = (p_0, p_1, \ldots, p_{n-1})$	Set of agents staying at nodes (p_i is a set of agents staying at node v_i)
$Q = (q_0, q_1, \ldots, q_{n-1})$	Set of agents residing on links (q_i is a set of agents in transit from v_{i-1} to v_i)

buffer that stores agents visiting the node and makes them execute processes in a FIFO order. We consider an *asynchronous* system, that is, the time for each agent to perform an operation is finite but unbounded.

A (global) *configuration* C is defined as a 5-tuple $C = (S, T, M, P, Q)$, and the correspondence table is in Table 2. The first element S is a k-tuple $S = (s_0, s_1, \ldots, s_{k-1})$, where s_i is the state (including the state of holding a token or not) of agent a_i $(0 \le i \le k-1)$. The second element T is an n-tuple $T = (t_0, t_1, \ldots, t_{n-1})$, where t_i is the state (i.e., the number of tokens) of node v_i $(0 \le i \le n-1)$. The third element M is a k-tuple $M = (m_0, m_1, \ldots m_{k-1})$, where m_i is a sequence of messages reached a_i but not consumed yet by a_i. The remaining elements P and Q represent the positions of agents. The element P is an n-tuple $P = (p_0, p_1, \ldots, p_{n-1})$, where p_i is a set of agents staying at node v_i $(0 \le i \le n-1)$. The element Q is an n-tuple $Q = (q_0, q_1, \ldots, q_{n-1})$, where q_i is a sequence of agents residing in the FIFO queue corresponding to link (v_{i-1}, v_i) $(0 \le i \le n-1)$. Hence, agents in q_i are those in transit from v_{i-1} to v_i.

We denote by $\mathcal{C}$ the set of all the possible configurations. In *initial configuration* $C_0 \in \mathcal{C}$, all agents are in the initial states and placed at distinct nodes respectively, and no node has any token. In addition, in C_0 the node where agent a stays is called the *home node* of a and denoted by $v_{HOME}(a)$. We assume that in C_0 agent a is stored at a buffer of its home node $v_{HOME}(a)$. This assures that agent a starts the algorithm at $v_{HOME}(a)$ before any other agent visits $v_{HOME}(a)$, that is, a is the first agent that takes an action at $v_{HOME}(a)$.

In addition, we define *periodic rings*. For initial configuration C_0, we assume that agents $a_0, a_1, \ldots, a_{k-1}$ exist in this order and we define the j-th $(j \ne 0)$ forward agent a' of agent a as the agent that exists in the a's forward direction and there are $j-1$ agents between a and a'. Then in C_0, we define the *distance sequence* of agent a_i as $D_i(C_0) = (d_0^i(C_0), \ldots, d_{k-1}^i(C_0))$, where $d_j^i(C_0)$ is the distance from the j-th forward agent of a_i to the $(j+1)$-th forward agent of a_i in C_0. In addition, we define the distance sequence of configuration C_0 as the lexicographically minimum sequence among $\{D_i(C_0) | a_i \in A\}$, and we denote it by $D(C_0)$. Moreover, let $shift(D, x) = (d_x, d_{x+1}, \ldots, d_{k-1}, d_0, d_1, \ldots, d_{x-1})$ for sequence $D = (d_0, d_1, \ldots, d_{k-1})$. Then, when $D(C_0) = shift(D(C_0), x)$ holds for some x such that $0 < x < k$ holds, we say the ring is *periodic*. Otherwise, we say the ring is *aperiodic*.

A *schedule* is an infinite sequence of agents. A schedule $X = \rho_1, \rho_2, \ldots$ is fair if every agent appears in X infinitely often. An infinite sequence of configurations $E = C_0, C_1, \ldots$ is called an *execution* from C_0 if there exists a fair schedule $X = \rho_1, \rho_2, \ldots$ that satisfies the following conditions for each h $(h > 0)$:

- If $\rho_h \in p_i$ holds for some i in a configuration C_h, the states of ρ_h and v_i in C_{h-1} are changed to those in C_h by a local computation of ρ_h. Let $a_j = \rho_h$. If $m_j \ne \emptyset$, all messages in m_j are delivered to a_j and consumed, that is, m_j becomes $\emptyset$. In addition, if ρ_h sends a message, the message is appended to each tail of m_l such that agent a_l is at v_i. Moreover, if ρ_h releases its token at v_i, The value of t_i increases by one. After this if ρ_h decides to move to v_{i+1}, ρ_h is removed from p_i and is appended to the tail of sequence q_{i+1}. If ρ_h decides to stay, ρ_h is still in p_i. The other elements in C_{h-1} are the same as those in C_h.
- If ρ_h is at the head of q_i for some i in a configuration C_h, ρ_h moves to v_i, that is, ρ_h is removed from q_i. Then, the states of ρ_h and v_i in C_{h-1} are changed to those in C_h by a local computation of ρ_h. If ρ_h sends a message, the message is appended to each tail of m_l such that agent a_l is at v_i. In addition, if ρ_h releases its token at v_i, the value of t_i increases by one. After this if ρ_h decides to move to v_{i+1}, ρ_h is appended to the tail of sequence q_{i+1}. If ρ_h decides to stay, ρ_h is inserted in p_i. The other elements in C_{h-1} are the same as those in C_h.
- Otherwise, C_{h-1} is the same as C_h.

2.2 The uniform deployment problem

The uniform deployment problem requires k (≥ 2) agents to spread uniformly in the ring, that is, the distance between any two *adjacent agents* should become identical. Here, we say two agents are adjacent when there exists no agent between them. However, we should consider the case that n is not a multiple of k. In this case, we aim to distribute the agents so that the distance d of any two adjacent agents should be $\lfloor n/k \rfloor$ or $\lceil n/k \rceil$.

We consider *the uniform deployment problem with termination detection* and *the uniform deployment problem without termination detection*. At first, we define the uniform deployment problem with termination detection. In this case, *a halt state* is defined as follows: when agent a_i enters a halt state, it terminates the algorithm, that is, a_i neither changes its state nor leaves the current node even if another agent sends a message to a_i. Hence if an agent enters a halt state, it can detect its termination. Now, we define the uniform deployment problem with termination detection as follows.

Definition 2.1 *An algorithm solves the uniform deployment problem* with *termination detection if any execution satisfies the following conditions.*

- *All agents change their states to the halt states in finite time.*
- *When all agents are in the halt states, $q_i = \emptyset$ holds for any $q_i \in Q$ and each distance d of two adjacent agents is $\lfloor n/k \rfloor$ or $\lceil n/k \rceil$.*

Next, we define the uniform deployment problem without termination detection. In this case, *a suspended state* is defined as follows: when agent a_i enters a suspended state, it neither changes its state nor leaves the current node unless another agent sends a message to a_i. If a_i receives a message, it can resume its behavior and leave the current node. The uniform deployment problem

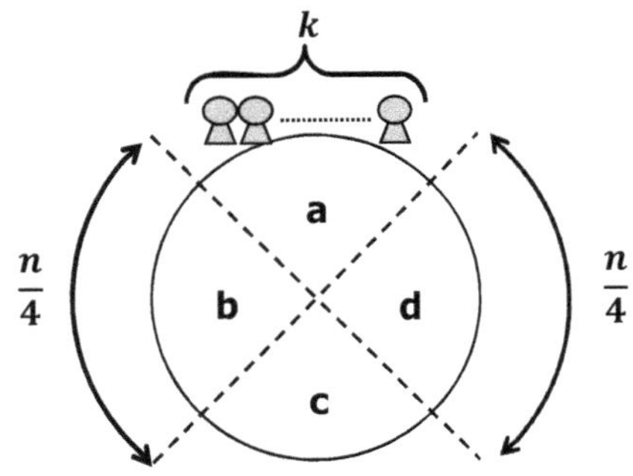

Figure 1: The initial configuration to derive a lower bound $\Omega(kn)$ of the total moves

without termination detection allows all agents to stop in suspended states, which is also known as communication deadlock.

Definition 2.2 *An algorithm solves the uniform deployment problem* without *termination detection if any execution satisfies the following conditions.*

- *All agents change their states to the suspended states in finite time.*
- *When all agents are in the suspended states, $q_i = \emptyset$ holds for any $q_i \in Q$ and each distance d of two adjacent agents satisfies $\lfloor n/k \rfloor$ or $\lceil n/k \rceil$.*

For the uniform deployment problem, the following theorem can be easily derived by considering the case that home nodes (or initial locations) of all k agents are continuous.

Theorem 2.1 *When $k \leq pn$ holds for some constant $p\,(p < 1)$, a lower bound of the total moves to solve the uniform deployment problem (with or without termination detection) is $\Omega(kn)$ even if agents have knowledge of k.*

PROOF. We assume $k \leq n/4$ holds and consider the initial configuration such that all agents stay in a quarter part of the ring like Fig. 1. In this case, the ring is divided into four quarter parts, and in the initial configuration, all agents are in the part a. To achieve the uniform deployment, $k/4$ agents need to move to the part c, the opposite part of a, and each of them must move at least $n/4$ times. Thus the total number of moves is at least $(k/4) \times (n/4) = kn/16$. □

Next, we evaluate the *time complexity* as the time required to achieve the uniform deployment. Since there is no assumption about the period of each action of agents in asynchronous systems, it is impossible to measure the exact time. Instead we consider the *ideal time complexity*, which is defined as the execution time under the following assumptions: 1) The time required for an agent to move from a node to its neighboring node is at most one, and 2) the time required for local computation is ignored (i.e., zero)[1]. In the following, we simply use terms "time complexity" and "time" instead of "ideal time complexity". Then, we can show the following theorem similarly to Theorem 2.1.

[1]This definition is based on the ideal time complexity for asynchronous message-passing systems [11].

Theorem 2.2 *A lower bound of the time complexity to solve the uniform deployment problem (with or without termination detection) is $\Omega(n)$.*

3. AGENTS WITH KNOWLEDGE OF K

In this section, we consider the uniform deployment problem for agents with knowledge of k.[2] We propose an algorithm to solve the uniform deployment problem with termination detection which requires $O(\log n)$ memory per agent, $O(n \log k)$ time, and $O(kn)$ total moves. The algorithm consists of two phases: selection phase and deployment phase. In the selection phase, multiple *base nodes* are selected as reference nodes for the uniform deployment. In the deployment phase, based on base nodes, each agent determines a *target node* where it should stay and moves there. For simplicity we assume $n = ck$ for some positive integer c in the following description, and this restriction is removed in Appendix B.

3.1 Selection phase

In this phase, some of home nodes are selected as the base nodes, and they are used as reference nodes for the uniform deployment. The selected base nodes should satisfy the following condition called the *base node condition*: 1) There exists at least one base node, 2) the distance between every pair of adjacent base nodes is identical, and 3) the number of the home nodes between every pair of adjacent base nodes is identical. The last condition is introduced to guarantee that the number of the selected base nodes is a divisor of k. When the selection phase is completed, each agent stays at its home node and knows whether its home node is selected as a base node or not. We call an agent a *leader* (but probably not unique) when its home node is selected as a base node, and call it a *follower* otherwise.

Now, we explain the way to select the base nodes satisfying the base node condition. The state of an agent is *active*, *leader* or *follower*. Active agents are candidates for leaders, and initially all agents are active. Once an agent becomes a follower or a leader, it never changes its state. In the following, we say that a node v is active (resp., a follower) when v is the home node of an active (resp., a follower) agent. At the beginning of the algorithm, each agent a_i releases its token at its home node $v_{HOME}(a_i)$. The selection phase consists of at most $\lceil \log k \rceil$ *sub-phases*. At the beginning of each sub-phase, each agent stays at its own home node. During the sub-phase, if the agent is a follower, it stays at its home node. If the agent is active, it travels once around the ring and decides whether it remains active or not in the next sub-phase using *IDs*.[3] Concretely, the ID (not necessarily unique) of an active agent a_i is given as $(d_i, fNum_i)$, where d_i is the distance from its home node $v_{HOME}(a_i)$ to the next active node in the sub-phase, say v_{next}, and $fNum_i$ is the number of follower nodes between $v_{HOME}(a_i)$ and v_{next}. For example in Fig. 2, when agent a_i moves from its home node v_j to the next active node v'_j, it visits five nodes and observes two follower nodes. Hence, a_i gets its own ID $ID_i = (5, 2)$. We compare two IDs by the lexicographical order: for $ID_1 = (d_1, fNum_1)$ and $ID_2 = (d_2, fNum_2)$, $ID_1 < ID_2$ if $(d_1 < d_2) \vee ((d_1 = d_2) \wedge (fNum_1 < fNum_2))$ holds. Each active agent decides whether it remains active or not using such IDs. Notice that in different sub-phases, the IDs of the same agent are different since the number of active agents is reduced in every sub-phase.

[2]We assume agents with knowledge of k, but agents with knowledge of n can similarly solve the problem.

[3]Active agents can detect they traveled once around the ring or not since they have knowledge of k.

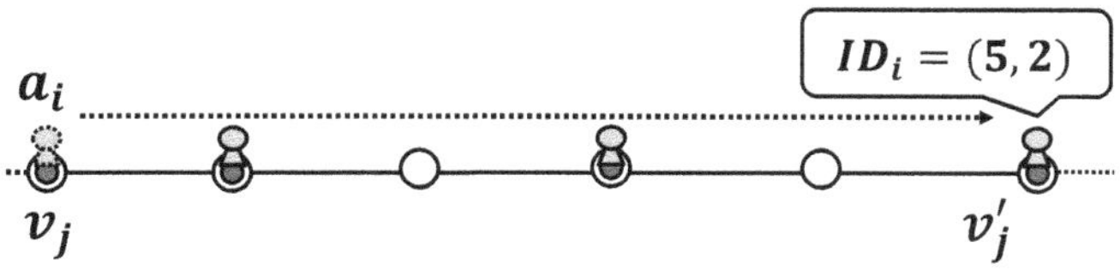

Figure 2: An ID of an active agent a_i

In the following, we explain the implementation of the sub-phase. In the sub-phase, each active agent a_i travels once around the ring. While travelling, a_i executes the followings:

1. Get its own ID $ID_i = (d_i, fNum_i)$: Agent a_i gets its own ID ID_i by moving from its home node $v_{HOME}(a_i)$ to the next active node v_{next} with counting the numbers of nodes and follower nodes (Fig. 2). Since all active agents are traversing the ring and all follower agents are staying at their home nodes, a_i can detect its arrival at the next active node when it visits a node with a token but with no agent. Note that this statement holds even in asynchronous systems because active agents do not pass other active agents from the FIFO property of links and the atomicity of the execution.

2. Get the ID $ID_{next} = (d_{next}, fNum_{next})$ of its next active agent: Similarly, with counting the numbers of nodes and follower nodes, a_i moves from v_{next} to the next active node (i.e., the node with a token but with no agent). Then, a_i gets the ID of $a_i's$ next active agent and stores it to ID_{next}.

3. Compare ID_i with those of all active agents: During the traversal of the ring, a_i compares ID_i with IDs of all active agents one by one, and checks 1) whether ID_i is the minimum and 2) whether the IDs of all active agents are identical. To check these, agent a_i keeps boolean variables *min* (*min* $=$ *true* means ID_i is the minimum among ever-found IDs) and *identical* (*identical* $=$ *true* means that ever-found IDs are identical), and it updates the variables (if necessary) every time it finds an ID of another active agent.

When a_i completes the traversal, it determines its state for the next sub-phase. If *identical* = *true* holds, this means that all active agents have the same IDs. In this case, a_i (and the other active agents) becomes a leader and completes the selection phase. If *identical* = *false* holds, a_i remains active if *min* = *true* and $ID_i < ID_{next}$ hold. The second condition means that, when active agents with the minimum ID appear consecutively, only one of them (or the last agent in the consecutive agents) remains active. This guarantees that the number of active agents is at least halved in each sub-phase. If a_i does not satisfy any of the above conditions, it becomes a follower. By repeating such sub-phase at most $\lceil \log k \rceil$ times, all the remaining active agents have the same IDs in some phase and they are selected as leaders so that their home nodes (or the base nodes) should satisfy the base node condition.

The pseudocode is described in Algorithm 1. Note that in the first sub-phase, each agent can get the number n of nodes when it finishes travelling once around the ring, but we omit the description.

3.2 Deployment phase

In this phase, each agent determines its target node and moves there. From the base node conditions, the base nodes are first selected as the target nodes. Hence, letting b be the number of the base nodes, other $k - b$ target nodes are selected so that the distance between two adjacent target nodes should be n/k.

While the leaders know the completion of the selection phase, followers do not know the fact. Hence, at the beginning of the deployment phase, each leader notifies followers that the selection phase is completed. To do this, each leader moves to the next base node. During the movement, if there exists an agent, the leader informs the agent of the distance *disBase* from the current node to the next base node. If the leader arrives at the next base node, it terminates the algorithm there since the current base node is its target node.

When each follower receives the value of *disBase*, it knows the completion of the selection phase. Then, it starts the deployment phase. Each follower moves *disBase* times and reaches the nearest base node. After this, the agent traverses the ring until it finds a vacant target node: every time the agent moves n/k times, it reaches a target node and stays there if the node is vacant (i.e., no agent is staying), otherwise (i.e., when the target node is already occupied by another agent) it keeps moving to the next target node. Note that from the FIFO property of links and the atomicity of the execution, it does not happen that two follower agents arrive at the same target node at the same time, that is, exactly one follower stays at each target node.

The pseudocode is described in Algorithm 2. We have the following theorem in Section 3.

Theorem 3.1 *For agents with knowledge of k, the proposed algorithm solves the uniform deployment problem with termination detection. This algorithm requires $O(\log n)$ memory per agent, $O(n \log k)$ time, and $O(kn)$ total moves.*

Algorithm 1 The behavior of active agent a_i

Behavior of Agent a_i

/*selection phase*/
phase = 1, *identical* = *true*, *min* = *true*
release a token at its home node $v_{HOME}(a_i)$
while *phase* $\neq \lceil \log k \rceil$ **do**
  move to the next active node and get its own ID $ID_i = (d_i, fNum_i)$
  if a_i is at $v_{HOME}(a_i)$ **then** change its state to a leader state // only a_i is active
  move to the next active node and get ID $ID_{next} = (d_{next}, fNum_{next})$ of the next active agent
  if $ID_i \neq ID_{next}$ **then** *identical* = *false*
  if $ID_i > ID_{next}$ **then** *min* = *false* // there exists an agent with smaller ID
  while a_i is not at $v_{HOME}(a_i)$ **do**
    move to the next active node and get ID $ID_{other} = (d_{other}, fNum_{other})$ of the next active agent
    if $ID_i \neq ID_{other}$ **then** *identical* =*false*
    if $ID_i > ID_{other}$ **then** *min* = *false* // there exists an agent with smaller ID
  end while
  if *identical* = *true* **then** change its state to a leader state // all active agents have the same IDs
  if (*min* = *false*) $\vee$ ($ID_i = ID_{next}$) **then** change its state to a follower state
  phase = *phase* + 1, *identical* = *true*, *min* = *true*
end while

Algorithm 2 The behavior of leader or follower agent a_i

```
Behavior of Agent a_i
/*deployment phase*/
// the behavior of leader agents
if a_i is in the leader state then
    t = 0
    while t ≠ fNum_i do
        move to the next node where a token exists // look for a follower agent
        send disBase to the agent at the current node
        t = t + 1
    end while
    move to the next node where a token exists // move to the next base node
    terminate the algorithm
end if

// the behavior of follower agents
if a_i is in the follower state then
    wait at the current node until a_i receives the value of disBase
    move disBase times // a_i reaches the nearest base node
    while true do
        move n/k times // move to the next target node
        if there exists no agent at the current node then terminate the algorithm
    end while
end if
```

4. AGENTS WITH NO KNOWLEDGE OF K OR N

In this section, we consider the uniform deployment problem for agents with no knowledge of k or n. We consider cases with termination detection and without termination detection in this order.

4.1 Uniform deployment problem with termination detection

When termination detection is required, we have the following theorem. Intuitively, it is due to impossibility of finding correct k or n when some part of the initial configuration has symmetry: when an agent misestimates these at smaller numbers than actual ones, it prematurely terminates and the uniform deployment cannot be achieved.

Theorem 4.1 *There exists no algorithm to solve the uniform deployment problem with termination detection even if agents can communicate with another agent at the same node.*

4.2 Uniform deployment problem without termination detection

In this section, we propose an algorithm to solve the uniform deployment problem without termination detection which requires $O(k/l\log(n/l))$ memory per agent, $O(n/l)$ time, and $O(kn/l)$ total moves, where l is the symmetry degree of the initial configuration. At first, we consider the case for aperiodic rings. After this, we show that our proposed algorithm achieves the uniform deployment also in periodic rings.

4.2.1 *Case for aperiodic rings*

In Section 3, since agents have knowledge of k, they can detect whether they traveled once around the ring or not. However in this section, agents cannot do this since they have no knowledge

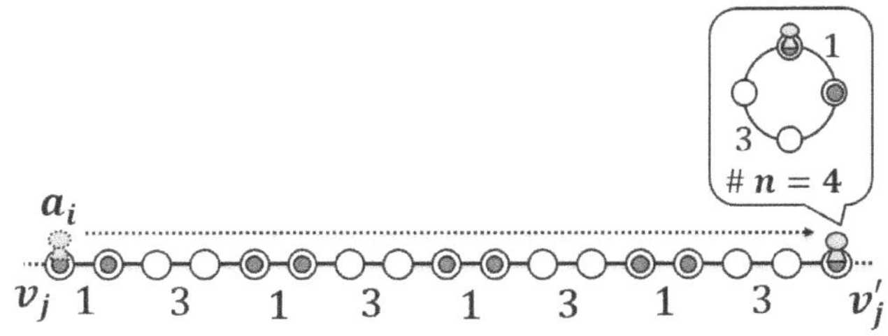

Figure 3: An example that an agent estimates the number of nodes

of k or n. Hence, at first agents estimate the number of nodes in the ring, and after this they move to their target nodes based on the estimations. Concretely, the algorithm consists of three phases: estimating phase, patrolling phase, and deployment phase. In the estimating phase, each agent a_i moves in the ring and estimates the number of nodes. At the end of this phase, we can show that at least one agent estimates the correct number n of nodes. In the patrolling phase, a_i moves in the ring several times depending on its estimated number of nodes. During the movement, if a_i visits the node where another agent exists, this agent may misestimate the number of nodes and prematurely stop at an incorrect target node. Hence, a_i sends its estimated number of nodes (with some information) to the agent. By this behavior, we can show that every agent eventually gets the correct number n of nodes and the location of its correct target node. In the deployment phase, a_i moves to its target node and enters a suspended state. After this, if a_i receives a message and recognizes that it misestimates the number of nodes, a_i decides its new target node from the message and moves there. For simplicity we assume $n = ck$ for some positive integer c in the following description, and this restriction can be removed similarly as in Section 3. In addition, for sequence Y, we define $Y^1 = Y$ and $Y^{l+1} = Y^l \cdot Y$ (or concatenation of $(l+1)$ Ys).

Estimating phase. In this phase, each agent a_i firstly releases its token at its home node $v_{HOME}(a_i)$. After this, a_i moves in the ring, memorizes the distance *dis* between two adjacent token nodes, and stores *dis* to an array D for memorizing the distance sequence. Agent a_i continues such a behavior until it completes estimating the number of nodes. Concretely, a_i continues to move until it observes the same distance sequence four times consecutively. Let $4n'$ be the number of nodes that a_i ever visited by the time. Then, a_i considers it travelled four times around the ring and estimates n' at the number of nodes in the ring. For example, let us consider Fig. 3. Each number in the figure represents the distance between two adjacent token nodes. Agent a_i moves from node v_j to v'_j and gets the distance sequence $D = (1,3,1,3,1,3,1,3) = (1,3)^4$. Then, a_i estimates 4 at the number of nodes. By this behavior, we can show that 1) at least one agent estimates the correct number n of nodes (in the aperiodic ring), and 2) if the estimated number n' is not correct, $n' \leq n/2$ holds. The pseudocode is given as Algorithm 3. During the estimating phase, a_i uses a variable k' for storing the estimated number of agents (tokens) and a variable *nodes* for storing the number of nodes that a_i has ever visited. These variables (including n' and D) are also used in the patrolling phase and the deployment phase.

The pseudocode is described in Algorithm 3. Variable k' represents the estimated number of agents (tokens) in the ring, and variable *nodes* represents the number of nodes a_i has ever visited.

Patrolling phase. In this phase, a_i moves $8n'$ times. Then, a_i considers it traveled twelve times around the ring from the begin-

Algorithm 3 The behavior of agent a_i in the estimating phase

Behavior of Agent a_i

/* estimating phase */
$n' = 0, k' = 0, \mathit{nodes} = 0, i = 0$
release a token at its home node $v_{HOME}(a_i)$
while $n' = 0$ **do**
  move to the next token node and get the distance *dis* between two token nodes
  $D[i] = \mathit{dis}, i = i + 1$
  if $(i \bmod 4 = 0) \wedge (\forall x\ (0 \le x \le i/4 - 1)\ D[x] = D[x + i/4] = D[x + 2 \times i/4] = D[x + 3 \times i/4])$ **then**
    // completing the estimation of the numbers of nodes and tokens
    $k' = i/4$
    $n' = D[0] + D[1] + \cdots + D[k' - 1]$
    $\mathit{nodes} = 4n'$
  end if
end while
change to the patrolling phase

Algorithm 4 The behavior of agent a_i in the patrolling phase

Behavior of Agent a_i

/* patrolling phase */
while $\mathit{nodes} \neq 12n'$ **do**
  move to the forward node
  $\mathit{nodes} = \mathit{nodes} + 1$
  if there exists another agent a_h **then** send $(n', k', \mathit{nodes}, D[\,])$ to a_h
end while
change to the deployment phase

ning with respect to its estimated number of nodes n'. During the movement, a_i may observe some agent a_h staying at some node. In this case, a_h may misestimate the number of nodes and prematurely stop at an incorrect target node. Hence if a_i observes such an agent, a_i sends n', k', nodes, and D to a_h. By this behavior, we can show that every agent eventually gets the correct number n of nodes and the location of its correct target node. The pseudocode is described in Algorithm 4.

Deployment phase. In this phase, a_i selects its target node and moves there as follows. Let $D = (d_0, d_1, \ldots, d_{k'-1})^4$ be the distance sequence that a_i obtained in the estimating phase, where d_j is the distance from the j-th token node it found to the $(j+1)$-st token node. Note that a_i's home node $v_{HOME}(a_i)$ is considered as the 0-th token node. In addition, let x be the minimum number such that $\mathit{shift}(D, x) = D_{min}$ holds, where D_{min} is the lexicographically minimum distance sequence among $\{\mathit{shift}(D, x) | 0 \le x \le k' - 1\}$. Then, a_i selects base node v_{base} where the agent whose distance sequence is D_{min} initially stays. In addition, a_i considers that it is *rank*-th agent $(0 \le \mathit{rank} \le k' - 1)$ from v_{base} (the agent staying at v_{base} is considered as the 0-th agent). Let *disBase* be the distance from the current node to v_{base} (if a_i already stays at v_{base}, we assume that $\mathit{disBase} = n'$). At first, a_i moves *disBase* times and reaches v_{base}. After this, a_i moves to its target node by moving $\mathit{rank} \times n'/k'$ times and enters a suspended state. When all agents enter suspended states, agents solve the uniform deployment problem.

However, a_i may stay at an incorrect target node when it misestimates the number of nodes. In this case, a_i eventually receives a message from another agent a_ℓ. Let n'_ℓ, k'_ℓ, nodes_ℓ, and D_ℓ be

Algorithm 5 The behavior of agent a_i in the deployment phase

Behavior of Agent a_i

/* deployment phase */
let D_{min} be the lexicographically minimum sequence among $\{\mathit{shift}(D, x) | 0 \le x \le k' - 1\}$
$\mathit{rank} = \min\{x \ge 0 | \mathit{shift}(D, x) = D_{min}\}$
$\mathit{disBase} = D[0] + D[1] + \cdots + D[k - 1 - \mathit{rank}]$
move *disBase* times
$\mathit{nodes} = \mathit{nodes} + \mathit{disBase}$
move $\mathit{rank} \times n'/k'$ times
$\mathit{nodes} = \mathit{nodes} + \mathit{rank} \times n'/k'$
change its state to a suspended state

/* behavior in the suspended state */
wait at the current node until a_i receives $(n'_\ell, k'_\ell, \mathit{nodes}_\ell, D_\ell[\,])$ from some agent a_ℓ
if $(n' \le n'_\ell/2) \wedge$ (there exists t such that $(\forall i\ (0 \le i \le 4k' - 1)\ D[i] = D_\ell[i + t]) \wedge (D_\ell[0] + \cdots D_\ell[t - 1] = \mathit{nodes}_\ell - \mathit{nodes})$ hold) **then**
  // a_i recognizes that it misunderstands the number of nodes
  $n' = n'_\ell, k' = k'_\ell, D[\,] = \mathit{shift}(D_\ell[\,], t)$
  move $12n' - \mathit{nodes}$ times
  $\mathit{nodes} = 12n'$
  go to line 2
end if

the estimated number of nodes, the estimated number of agents, the number of nodes ever visited, and the distance sequence included in a message from a_ℓ respectively. If $n' \le n'_\ell/2$ holds and there exists t such that $(\forall i\ (0 \le i \le 4k' - 1)\ D[i] = D_\ell[i + t]) \wedge (D_\ell[0] + \cdots D_\ell[t - 1] = \mathit{nodes}_\ell - \mathit{nodes})$ hold, it means that a_ℓ estimates at least twice number of nodes than a_i and memorizes a_i's whole distance sequence D as a part of D_ℓ. Then, a_i recognizes that it misestimates the number of nodes and resumes its behavior. Concretely, a_i firstly moves $12n'_\ell - \mathit{nodes}$ times We show later that $12n'_\ell - \mathit{nodes}$ is always positive. Then, a_i considers it traveled twelve times around the ring from the beginning with respect to the new estimated number of nodes n'_ℓ. This guarantees that agents can achieve the uniform deployment even in periodic rings, and we explain this later. After this, it decides the new base node and its new target node from n'_ℓ, k'_ℓ, nodes_ℓ and D_ℓ, moves to its new target node as mentioned before, and enters a suspended state again. When all agents enter suspended states, agents solve the uniform deployment problem. The pseudocode is described in Algorithm 5.

An example As an example, let us consider the ring in Fig. 4. This ring is aperiodic but has some *periodic subsequence*, that is, some agent observes a 4-times repeated subsequence before it travels once around the ring. In such a ring, some agent misestimates the number of nodes and enters a suspended state at an incorrect target node. However in this case, we can show that at least one agent a_i estimates the correct number n of nodes and informs prematurely suspending agents of n during the patrolling phase. Let us consider the behavior of agents a_1 and a_2. For simplicity, we assume that they behave in a synchronous manner. In the estimating phase, agent a_2 gets the distance sequence $D = (1, 3, 1, 3, 1, 3, 1, 3) = (1, 3)^4$ and estimates 4 at the number of nodes, which is incorrect (Fig. 4 (a) to Fig. 4 (b)). After this a_2 executes the patrolling and deployment phases, and enters a suspended state at incorrect target node v'_j (Fig. 4 (b) to Fig. 4 (c)). On the other hand, agent a_1 is still in the estimating phase. When a_1 observes $D = (11, 1, 3, 1, 3, 1, 3, 1, 3)^4$, it completes the estimating phase

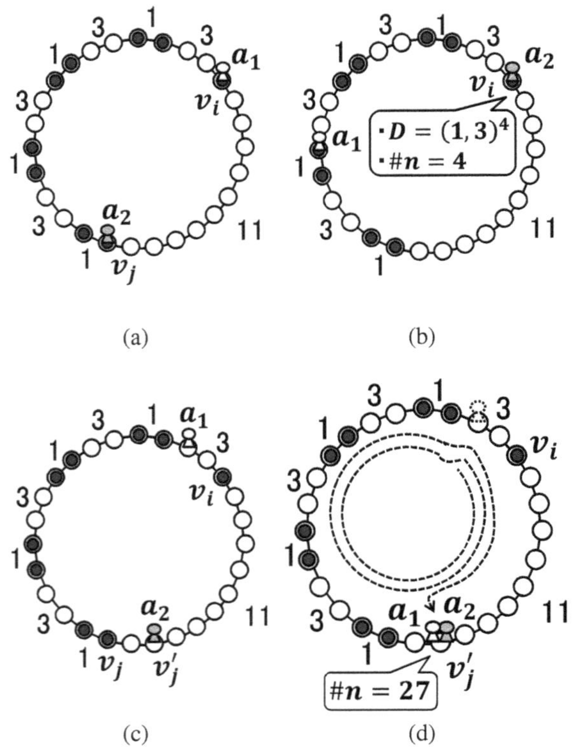

Figure 4: An example in the ring having some periodic subsequence ($n = 27, k = 9, d = 3$)

and estimates the correct number of nodes 27. After this in the patrolling phase, a_1 observes a_2 at v'_j, sends its estimated number of nodes with other information to a_2 (Fig. 4 (c) to Fig. 4 (d)), and moves to its target node. When a_2 receives the message from a_1, it recognizes that it misestimates the number of nodes and resumes its behavior.

We have the following lemmas for aperiodic rings.

Lemma 4.1 *If agent a_ℓ estimates the incorrect number of nodes n_ℓ (i.e., $n_\ell \neq n$ holds), $n_\ell \leq n/2$ holds.*

Lemma 4.2 *If ring R is aperiodic, at least one agent estimates the correct number n of nodes and gets distance sequence D of the initial configuration in R.*

Lemma 4.3 *If ring R is aperiodic, every agent eventually gets the correct number n of nodes and distance sequence D of the initial configuration in R.*

PROOF. We show that all agents eventually get the correct number n of nodes. Then from Algorithms 3 to 5, all agents can clearly get distance sequence D of the initial configuration in R. We prove the lemma by contradiction, that is, we assume that when all agents are in the suspended states, there exists at least one agent a_h whose estimated number of nodes n' is less than n. Then from Lemma 4.1, $n' \leq n/2$ holds. On the other hand from Lemma 4.2, at least one agent a_c estimates the correct number n of nodes. In the following we show that a_c observes a_h during the patrolling phase and sends its estimated number of nodes n to a_h, which contradicts the assumption of $n' < n$.

At first, let us consider the number of nodes a_h visits. Let n_1 be the number of nodes a_h estimates in the estimating phase. From Algorithms 3 to 5, a_h moves at most $14n_1$ times by the time a_h enters a suspended state for the first time. After this, we assume that a_h receives messages and updates its estimated number of nodes to $n_2, n_3, \ldots, n_l = n'$ in this order. When a_h updates it estimated number of node to n_2, a_h's total moves at that point (i.e, *nodes*) is at most $7n_2$ since $n_1 \leq n_2/2$ holds. Hence, $12n_2 -$ *nodes* is clearly positive. Then, a_h firstly moves in the ring until its total moves becomes $12n_2$ by moving $12n_2 -$ *nodes* times. After this, a_h moves to a new target node and enters a suspended state again. This requires at most $14n_2$ total moves. Then since $n_3 \leq n_2/2$ holds from Algorithm 5, *nodes* is at most $7n_3$ and $12n_3 -$ *nodes* is clearly positive. Thus recursively, we can show that $12n_i -$ *nodes* is always positive ($2 \leq i \leq l$) and a_h's total moves unless it does not get the correct number n of nodes is at most $14n' \leq 7n$. On the other hand, agent a_c moves $8n$ times in the patrolling phase. Thus, a_c clearly observes a_h during the patrolling phase and sends its estimated number n of nodes to a_h, which is a contradiction.

Therefore, we have the lemma. □

Lemma 4.4 *When ring R is aperiodic, agents solve the uniform deployment problem without termination detection.*

4.2.2 Case for periodic rings

Next, we consider the case for periodic rings. Let R' be a periodic ring and D' be the distance sequence of the initial configuration in R'. We say R' is a (N, l)-node ring if there exists an aperiodic distance sequence D such that $D' = D^l$ holds and the total sum of elements of D is N. Then, $n = Nl$ holds and l is equivalent to the symmetry degree of the initial configuration in R'. We call the ring R with the distance sequence D the *fundamental ring of* R' (e.g., Fig. 5). Note that an aperiodic ring can be denoted by a $(n, 1)$-node ring. In addition, for each agent a_i in R, there exist l agents in R' such that the distance sequence of each agent is l-times repetition of the distance sequence of a_i. We say such agents in R' are *corresponding agents* of agent a_i in R and denote by a_i^j ($0 \leq j \leq l-1$). We assume that agents $a_i^0, a_i^1, \ldots, a_i^{l-1}$ are deployed in this order and operations to an above index of a_i^j assume calculation under modulo l. Then, the distance from a_i^j to a_i^{j+1} is N. In this case, all agents eventually estimate the incorrect number $N = n/l$ of nodes, but we can show that agents can achieve the uniform deployment similarly to in R. Concretely from algorithms in Section 4.2.1, each agent moves to its target node after considering, based on the estimated number N of nodes, it traveled twelve times around the ring. This means that each agent stays at its target node during its twelfth or thirteenth circulations in the ring with respect to the estimated size N, which guarantees that when all agents are in the suspended states, no agents stay at the same node and they can achieve the uniform deployment. For example, let us consider rings in Fig. 5. Ring R' is the (6,2)-node periodic ring and R is the fundamental ring of R'. In R, each agent estimates the correct number 6 of nodes in the estimating phase and moves to its correct target node (Fig. 5 (a)). On the other hand in R', each agent also estimates the number 6 of nodes, which is incorrect (Fig. 5 (b)). By algorithms in Section 4.2.1, each agent moves to its target node after considering, based on the estimated size 6, it travelled twelve times around the ring, that is, after each agent moves 72 times (actually, each agent travelled six times around ring R'). This guarantees that when all agents are in the suspended states, no agents stay at the same node and they can achieve the uniform deployment (Fig. 5 (c)).

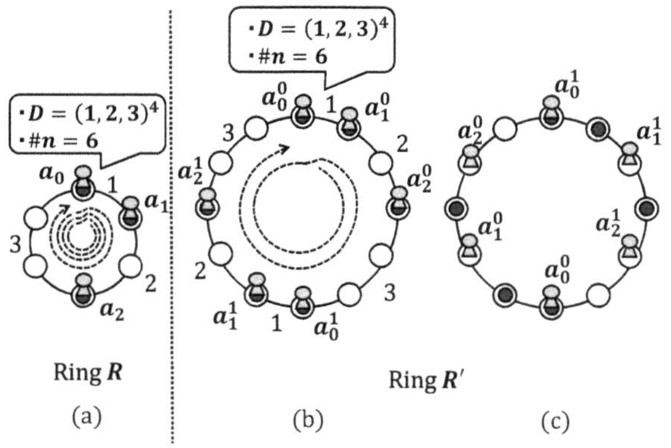

Figure 5: An example for the periodic ring

Now, we have the following lemmas, which can be proved similarly to the case of aperiodic rings.

Lemma 4.5 *Let R' be a (N, l)-node periodic ring and R be the fundamental ring of R'. Let a_i in R be the agent estimating the number N of nodes in the estimating phase. Then in R', agent a_i^j $(0 \le j \le l-1)$ corresponding to a_i also estimates the number N of nodes.*

Lemma 4.6 *Let R' be a (N, l)-node periodic ring and R be the fundamental ring of R'. Then in R', every agent eventually gets the number N of nodes and distance sequence D of the initial configuration in R.*

PROOF. We show that all agents eventually get the number N of nodes. Then from Algorithms 3 to 5, all agents can clearly get distance sequence D of the initial configuration in R. We prove the lemma by contradiction, that is, we assume that when all agents are in the suspended states, there exists at least one agent a_h whose estimated number of nodes n' is less than N. On the other hand from Lemma 4.5, there exists agent a_c^j $(0 \le j \le l-1)$ estimating the number N of nodes in the estimating phase. Let $A_c = \{a_c^0, a_c^1 \ldots, a_c^{l-1}\}$. In the following, we show that some agent in A_c observes a_h during the patrolling phase and sends its estimated number N of nodes to a_h, which contradicts the assumption of $n' < N$.

At first, let us consider the number of nodes a_h visits. Similarly to the case for aperiodic rings, when a_h updates its estimated number of nodes from n'' to n', it firstly moves in the ring until its total moves becomes $12n'$ by moving $12n' - nodes$ times. After this, a_h moves to a new target node and enters a suspended state again. This requires at most $14n'$ total moves. Hence unless a_h does not get the number N of nodes, its total moves is at most $14n' \le 7N$.

On the other hand from Lemma 4.5, there exists agent a_c^j in A_c such that it estimates N at the number of nodes and the distance from $v_{HOME}(a_c^j)$ to $v_{HOME}(a_h)$ is less than N. Recall that, $v_{HOME}(a)$ is the home node of agent a. Then, let us consider the behavior of agent a_c^{j-4}. Agent a_c^{j-4} firstly moves $4N$ times and finishes the estimating phase at node $v_{HOME}(a_c^j)$. After this, a_c^{j-4} moves $8N$ times from $v_{HOME}(a_c^j)$ in the patrolling phase. On the other hand, a_h moves at most $7N$ times from $v_{HOME}(a_h)$. Since the distance from $v_{HOME}(a_c^j)$ to $v_{HOME}(a_h)$ is less than N, a_c^{j-4} observes a_h during the patrolling phase and sends the number N of nodes to a_h, which is a contradiction.

Therefore, we have the lemma. □

Lemma 4.7 *Even when ring R' is periodic, agents solve the uniform deployment problem without termination detection.*

Finally, we have the following theorem for (N, l)-node rings.

Theorem 4.2 *For agents with no knowledge of k or n, the proposed algorithm solves the uniform deployment problem without termination detection. This algorithm requires $O(k/l \log(n/l))$ memory per agent, $O(n/l)$ time, and $O(kn/l)$ total moves.*

5. CONCLUSION

In this paper, we considered the uniform deployment problem of mobile agents in asynchronous unidirectional ring networks. The uniform deployment problem, which is a striking contrast to the rendezvous problem, is interesting to investigate. We proposed two algorithms to solve the uniform deployment problem in any initial configuration such that all agents are in the initial states and placed at the distinct nodes respectively. These algorithms utilize the essential characteristic of the uniform deployment problem: the problem aims to attain the symmetry, and these algorithms solve the problem without breaking symmetry that the initial agent locations have. Such an approach in designing mobile agent algorithms seems to be applicable to other problems that aim to attain the symmetry. As a future work, we want to consider the lower bound of memory requirement per agent. We conjecture that it is $\Omega(\log n)$, and if the conjecture is correct, we can show that the first algorithm is asymptotically optimal in terms of memory requirement.

6. ACKNOWLEDGMENTS

This work was supported by JSPS KAKENHI Grant Numbers 24500039, 26280022, 26330084, 15H00816, and 16K00018.

7. REFERENCES

[1] D. Kotz S. R. Gray, G. Cybenko, A.R. Peterson, and D. Rus. D'agents: Applications and performance of a mobile-agent system, Software: Practice and Experience. 32(6):543–573, 2002.

[2] D.B. Lange and M. Oshima. Seven good reasons for mobile agents, Communications of the ACM. 42(3):88–89, 1999.

[3] E. Kranakis, D. Krozanc, and E. Markou. The mobile agent rendezvous problem in the ring, Synthesis Lectures on Distributed Computing Theory, Vol. 1. pages 1–122, 2010.

[4] S. Kawai, F. Ooshita, H. Kakugawa, and T. Masuzawa. Randomized rendezvous of mobile agents in anonymous unidirectional ring networks, Proc. of the 19th International Colloquium on Structural Information and Communication Complexity, LNCS, Vol. 7355. pages 303–314, 2012.

[5] E. Kranakis, D. Krizanc, and E. Markou. Mobile agent rendezvous in a synchronous torus, Proc. of the 8th Latin American Theoretical Informatics, LNCS, Vol. 3887. pages 653–664, 2006.

[6] P. Fraigniaud and A. Pelc. Deterministic rendezvous in trees with little memory. Proc. of the 22nd International Symposium on Distributed Computing, LNCS, Vol. 6950. pages 242–256, 2008.

[7] A.Kosowski J. Czyzowicz and A. Pelc. How to meet when you forget: Log-space rendezvous in arbitrary graphs, Distributed Computing. 25(2):165–178, 2012.

[8] P. Flocchini, G. Prencipe, and N. Santoro. Self-deployment of mobile sensors on a ring, Theoretical Computer Science. 402(1):67–80, 2008.

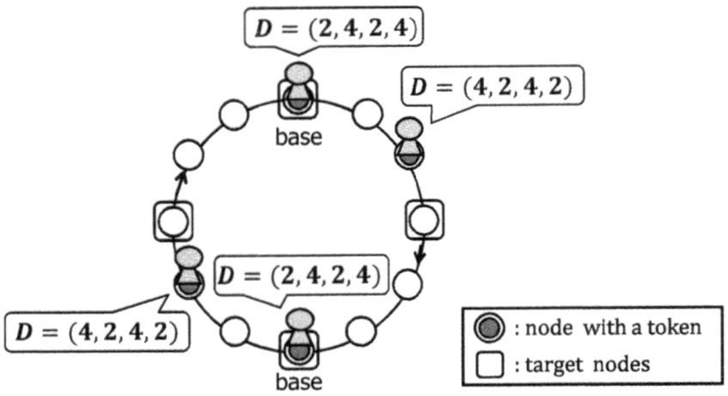

Figure 6: The base nodes and the target nodes

[9] Y. Elor and A.M. Bruckstein. Uniform multi-agent deployment on a ring, Theoretical Computer Science. 412(8):783–795, 2011.

[10] L. Barriere, P. Flocchini, E. Mesa-Barrameda, and N. Santoro. Uniform scattering of autonomous mobile robots in a grid, International Journal of Foundations of Computer Science. 22(03):679–697, 2011.

[11] G. Tel. Introduction to distributed algorithms. Cambridge university press, 2000.

APPENDIX

A. A TRIVIAL ALGORITHM FOR AGENTS WITH KNOWLEDGE OF K

In this section, we consider the uniform deployment problem for agents with knowledge of k, and propose a trivial algorithm to solve the uniform deployment problem with termination detection. This algorithm requires $O(k \log n)$ memory per agent, $O(n)$ time, $O(kn)$ total moves. For simplicity, we assume $n = ck$ for some positive integer c, and we can remove this assumption in Appendix B. The algorithm consists of the following two phases: the selection phase and the deployment phase. In the selection phase, each agent travels once around the ring and selects a base node. In the deployment phase, each agent moves to its target node based on the base node.

In the selection phase, each agent a_i releases its token at its home node $v_{HOME}(a_i)$, and after this travels once around the ring. Note that since agents have knowledge of k, they can detect they travelled once around the ring or not, and they can get the value of n when they finish travelling the ring. Then, a_i gets the distance sequence $D = \{d_0, d_1, \dots, d_{k-1}\}$ and selects the base node similarly to Section 4.2.1. That is, letting D_{min} be the lexicographically minimum distance sequence among $\{shift(D, x) | 0 \leq x \leq k-1\}$, a_i selects a base node v_{base} where the agent whose distance sequence is D_{min} initially exists. If D is aperiodic, all the agents select the same node as a base node. If D is periodic, multiple nodes are selected as base nodes (Fig. 6). However in this case, each agent can determine its base node and target node uniquely as explained later.

In the deployment phase, each agent a_i determines its target node and moves there similarly to Section 4.2.1. Let *disBase* be the distance from its home node $v_{HOME}(a_i)$ to v_{base}, and a_i can find from D that it is the *rank*-th agent ($0 \leq rank \leq k-1$) from v_{base} (the agent staying at v_{base} is considered as the 0-th agent). Then, agents firstly moves *disBase* times and reaches v_{base}. After this, a_i moves its target node by moving $rank \times n/k$ times and terminates

Algorithm 6 A trivial algorithm for agents with knowledge of k

Main behavior of Agent a_i

/* selection phase */
$i = 0$
release a token at its home node $v_{HOME}(a_i)$
while $i \neq k$ **do**
  move to the nearest token node and get the distance *dis* between two token nodes
  $D[i] = dis$
  $i = i + 1$
end while
// a_i completes travelling once around the ring and gets the number of node
$n = D[0] + D[1] + \cdots + D[k-1]$

/* deployment phase */
let D_{min} be the lexicographically minimum sequence among $\{shift(D, x) | 0 \leq x \leq k-1\}$
$rank = \min\{x \geq 0 | shift(D, x) = D_{min}\}$
$disBase = D[0] + D[1] + \cdots + D[k-1-rank]$
move $disBase + rank \times n/k$ times
terminate the algorithm

the algorithm. Note that if multiple base nodes are selected like Fig. 6, the following properties are satisfied: 1) The distance between every pair of two adjacent base nodes is identical, and 2) the number of agents and their locations between every pair of adjacent base nodes are also identical. Thus the base nodes can be reference nodes of the uniform deployment, and each agent can determine its base node and target node uniquely.

The pseudocode is described in Algorithm 6. We have the following theorem.

Theorem A.1 *For agents with knowledge of k, Algorithm 6 solves the uniform deployment problem with termination detection. This algorithm requires $O(k \log n)$ memory per agent, $O(n)$ time, and $O(kn)$ total moves.*

B. THE UNIFORM DEPLOYMENT FOR THE CASE OF $N \neq CK$

To remove the restriction of $n = ck$ imposed in Section 3, only the parts for determining the target nodes and for moving to a target node should be modified. In the case that n is not a multiple of k, the distance between some adjacent target nodes should be $\lceil n/k \rceil$ or $\lfloor n/k \rfloor$.

The target nodes should be determined by each agent so that the decisions of different agents should be identical. Since all the agents recognize the same nodes as the base nodes, the common target nodes can be determined using the base node as a reference node: Let b be the number of the base nodes, and $r = n \bmod k$. The distance of every pair of adjacent base nodes is identical even in the case of $n \neq ck$, and is $n/b = (\lfloor n/k \rfloor \times k + r)/b = \lfloor n/k \rfloor \times k/b + r/b$ (notice that k/b and r/b are integers). This implies that we should select $k/b - 1$ target nodes between two adjacent base nodes so that the first r/b intervals between adjacent target nodes should be $\lceil n/k \rceil$ and others should be $\lfloor n/k \rfloor$. With considering the above, each agent can determine its own target node by local computation so that all the agents can spread over the ring to achieve the uniform deployment.

Fault-Tolerant Multi-Agent Optimization: Optimal Iterative Distributed Algorithms *

Lili Su
Electrical and Computer Engineering
Coordinated Science Laboratory
University of Illinois at Urbana-Champaign
lilisu3@illinois.edu

Nitin H. Vaidya
Electrical and Computer Engineering
Coordinated Science Laboratory
University of Illinois at Urbana-Champaign
nhv@illinois.edu

ABSTRACT

This paper addresses the problem of distributed multi-agent optimization in which each agent i has a local cost function $h_i(x)$, and the goal is to optimize a global cost function consisting of an average of the local cost functions. Such optimization problems are of interest in many contexts, including distributed machine learning and distributed robotics.

We consider the distributed optimization problem in the presence of faulty agents. We focus primarily on Byzantine failures, but also briefly discuss some results for crash failures. For the Byzantine fault-tolerant optimization problem, the ideal goal is to optimize the average of local cost functions of the non-faulty agents. However, this goal also cannot be achieved. Therefore, we consider a relaxed version of the fault-tolerant optimization problem.

The goal for the relaxed problem is to generate an output that is an optimum of a global cost function formed as a *convex combination* of local cost functions of the non-faulty agents. More precisely, if $\mathcal{N}$ denotes the set of non-faulty agents in a given execution, then there must exist weights α_i for $i \in \mathcal{N}$ such that $\alpha_i \geq 0$ and $\sum_{i\in\mathcal{N}} \alpha_i = 1$, such that the output is an optimum of the cost function $\sum_{i\in\mathcal{N}} \alpha_i h_i(x)$. Ideally, we would like $\alpha_i = \frac{1}{|\mathcal{N}|}$ for all $i \in \mathcal{N}$, however, the maximum number of nonzero weights (α_i's) that can be guaranteed is $|\mathcal{N}| - f$, where f is the maximum number of Byzantine faulty agents.

The contribution of this paper is to present an *iterative* distributed optimization algorithm that achieves optimal fault-tolerance. Specifically, it ensures that at least $|\mathcal{N}| - f$ agents have weights that are bounded away from 0 (in particular, lower bounded by $\frac{1}{2(|\mathcal{N}|-f)}$). The proposed distributed algorithm has a simple iterative structure, with each agent maintaining only a small amount of local state. We show that the iterative algorithm ensures two properties as time goes to ∞: consensus (i.e., output of non-faulty agents becomes identical in the time limit), and optimality (in the sense that the output is the optimum of a suitably defined global cost function). After a finite number of iterations, the algorithm satisfies these properties approximately.

*This research is supported in part by National Science Foundation awards NSF 1329681 and 1421918. Any opinions, findings, and conclusions or recommendations expressed here are those of the authors and do not necessarily reflect the views of the funding agencies or the U.S. government.

PODC'16, July 25–28, 2016, Chicago, IL, USA.

DOI: http://dx.doi.org/10.1145/2933057.2933105

Keywords

Distributed optimization; Byzantine faults; complete networks; fault-tolerant computing

1. INTRODUCTION

Distributed optimization over multi-agent networks has received significant attention in recent years [9, 19, 31, 6, 13, 15]. Multi-agent optimization problems are of interest in many contexts, including distributed machine learning and distributed robotics. Most of the prior work in this area assumes that agents are cooperative (in the sense that agents try to follow the pre-specified rules or protocols). In contrast, in this work, we focus on the scenario when some agents may fail.

In the multi-agent optimization problem [9, 19], each agent has a *local* cost function, and when every agent is free from failures, the goal is to design algorithms that allow all the agents collectively minimize the average of the local cost functions. Specifically, let $h_i(x)$ be the local cost function of agent i, with x being the argument, for $i = 1, \cdots, n$. Under some regularity assumptions on the local functions, all the agents cooperatively identify an output x_o such that

$$\text{output } x_o \in \underset{x}{\text{argmin}} \ \frac{1}{n}\sum_{i=1}^{n} h_i(x). \qquad (1)$$

This paper explores the problem of distributed optimization in the presence of Byzantine faulty agents. In Section 7, we will also briefly discuss the case when the agents may crash. Byzantine faulty agents can behave arbitrarily. Unless fault-tolerance mechanisms are incorporated, the output of an optimization algorithm can be significantly affected by the faulty agents. In particular, a faulty agent may potentially send incorrect and incosistent messages to the non-faulty agents in order to bias the outcome. When agents may suffer Byzantine faults, instead of optimizing the global cost function defined above, ideally, the agents should attempt optimize the average of the local cost functions of just the non-faulty agents. It should be easy to see that, since the identity of the faulty agents is not known the non-faulty agents, it is not possible to optimize such a global cost function [22, 26]. Therefore, the goal must be relaxed when agents suffer Byzantine failures.

Several ways may be envisioned for relaxing the objective of fault-tolerant optimization. For instance, one way to relax the goal is to allow the output to deviate from the output of the ideal goal above, but to try to minimize the extent of this deviation in the worst-case. In general, we may formulate the relaxed optimization problem to allow a suitably chosen unique output from among the union of the set of optima of the local cost functions of all non-faulty agents. In our work, we are exploring the following relaxation of the fault-tolerant optimization problem [22, 23, 24, 25, 26]. Let $\mathcal{N}$ denote the set of non-faulty agents in a given execution. Let $\boldsymbol{\alpha}$ denote a vector with its i-th element being α_i. We only consider $\boldsymbol{\alpha}$ in which, for $i \notin \mathcal{N}$, $\alpha_i = 0$.

$$\text{output } x_o \text{ such that} \tag{2}$$
$$\text{there } \textbf{exists} \text{ weight vector } \boldsymbol{\alpha} \text{ for which}$$
$$x_o \in \underset{x}{\text{argmin}} \sum_{i \in \mathcal{N}} \alpha_i h_i(x),$$
$$\sum_{i \in \mathcal{N}} \alpha_i = 1, \quad \text{and} \quad \forall i, \ \alpha_i \geq 0$$

That is, the output of all the agents must be equal, and must equal an optimum of a weighted average of the local cost functions. Problem (2) does not require the non-faulty agents to learn the actual weights (α_i's) corresponding to the global cost function that was optimized. Observe that the above relaxation allows the output to be any value from a set of values, where each value potentially corresponds to a different choice of $\boldsymbol{\alpha}$.

To approximate the ideal goal of optimizing the average of local cost functions of just the non-faulty agents (in $\mathcal{N}$), it is desired that the weights (α_i's) above be non-zero for the largest possible number of non-faulty agents, and, preferably, these non-zero weights be as close to $\frac{1}{|\mathcal{N}|}$ as possible. This would ensure that the global cost function that is optimized has approximately equal representation for each agent's cost function. In particular, we define parameters β, γ to characterize the "goodness" of a weight vector $\boldsymbol{\alpha}$ [22, 26].

DEFINITION 1. (β,γ)**–admissibility:** *For $\beta > 0$ and $\gamma \geq 1$, vector $\boldsymbol{\alpha}$ is (β,γ)-admissible if:*
(1) $\sum_{i\in\mathcal{N}} \alpha_i = 1$, $\alpha_i \geq 0$, for each $i \in \mathcal{N}$;
(2) $\alpha_j = 0$ for each $j \notin \mathcal{N}$; and
(3) at least γ elements of $\boldsymbol{\alpha}$ are lower bounded by β.

The following impossibility result is easy to prove [22].

THEOREM 1. *[22] In a synchronous system, when up to f agents may be Byzantine faulty, for problem (2), for any $\beta > 0$, it is impossible to guarantee that $\boldsymbol{\alpha}$ is (β,γ)-admissible with $\gamma > |\mathcal{N}| - f$.*

Intuitively, the above theorem says that a convex combination of local objectives may not be admissible when the number of non-zero weights of the convex combination exceeds the threshold $|\mathcal{N}| - f$. This paper presents an iterative distributed algorithm that achieves the *optimal* number of non-zero weights. As discussed in Section 3, we have also designed a more complex algorithm that simulates a centralized solution to the fault-tolerant optimization problem [22, 26].

In its general form, in (2) above, the argument x of the cost function $h_i(x)$ is a k-dimensional vector of reals (i.e., $x \in \mathbb{R}^k$), where $k \geq 1$. In this paper, as a first step towards solving the fault-tolerant multi-agent optimization problem, we consider the special case when $k = 1$, i.e., x is a scalar. Problem (2) remains open for vector arguments with $k \geq 2$. Later in the paper, we discuss the technical difficulty in solving the problem with vector inputs.

The main contribution of this paper is as follows:

- For cost functions with real-valued (scalar) arguments, in a synchronous environment consisting of a completely connected network of $n > 3f$ agents, among which up to f agents may be Byzantine faulty, we present an *iterative distributed* algorithm that is optimal in the sense that it matches the bound in the impossibility result of Theorem 1. In particular, the proposed algorithm achieves $\boldsymbol{\alpha}$ that is $(\frac{1}{2(|\mathcal{N}|-f)}, |\mathcal{N}|-f)$-admissible. The iterative algorithm has a very simple structure, and requires each agent to maintain only a small amount of state. In particular, the algorithm allows a Byzantine faulty agent to send inconsistent messages to different agents.
- The above algorithm can also be extended to a *constrained* version of the optimization problem, to the crash failure model, and to asynchronous environments. While much of the paper addresses Byzantine faults in a synchronous completely connected network, Section 6 and Section 7 summarize the above extensions, as well as a few open problems.

Organization:.

The rest of this paper is organized as follows. Section 2 presents our system model, and assumptions regarding the cost functions. Related work is discussed in Section 3. Section 4 demonstrates a distributed gradient-based algorithm, named SBG, whose performance is analyzed in Section 5. Section 6 and Section 7 summarize extensions and discusse the open problems.

2. SYSTEM MODEL, ASSUMPTIONS AND NOTATIONS

The system under consideration is synchronous, and consists of $n > 3f$ agents, where f is the maximum number of agents that may be Byzantine faulty. The communication network is completely connected (i.e., each agent has a communication channel to each of the agents). We discuss some extensions of our results (e.g., for the crash failure model) in Sections 6 and 7. The set of n agents is denoted $\mathcal{V} = \{1, \cdots, n\}$. In a given execution, let $\mathcal{F}$ denote the set of Byzantine faulty agents, and let $\mathcal{N} = \mathcal{V} - \mathcal{F}$ denote the set of non-faulty agents. The set $\mathcal{F}$ of faulty agents may be chosen by an adversary arbitrarily, and may be different across executions.

We say that a function $h(\cdot) : \mathbb{R} \to \mathbb{R}$ is *admissible* if (i) $h(\cdot)$ is convex, and continuously differentiable, (ii) the set $\arg\min_{x\in\mathbb{R}} h(x)$ containing the optima of $h(\cdot)$ is non-empty and compact (i.e., bounded and closed), (iii) the magnitude of the gradients are bounded by L, i.e., $|h'(x)| \leq L$, and the derivatives $h'(\cdot)$ are L–Lipschitz continuous. Each agent $i \in \mathcal{V}$ is initially provided with an *admissible* local cost function $h_i(\cdot) : \mathbb{R} \to \mathbb{R}$. Similar assumptions on the local functions are standard in past literature on failure-free distributed optimization [9, 19, 31, 6, 13, 15].

3. RELATED WORK

The distributed optimization problem is related to Byzantine fault-tolerant consensus. In particular, the non-faulty agents are all required to produce (approximately) equal output, thus, consensus is part of the requirements satisfied by any solution for our problem. There is a significant body of work on fault-tolerant consensus, including our own prior work [7, 5, 18, 10, 14, 36, 11, 34, 30, 29, 12]. While much of the past work on Byzantine consensus has considered scalar inputs, there is recent work that addresses Byzantine consensus with vector (or multidimensional) inputs [17, 35].

Although convex optimization, including distributed optimization, also has a long history, we believe our work is the first to explore the problem of designing Byzantine fault-tolerant algorithms that achieve optimality in the sense defined earlier. Primal and dual decomposition methods that lend themselves naturally to a distributed paradigm have been known for at least fifty years, and their behavior is well understood [3]. The seminal work of Tsitsiklis and colleagues [33, 32] analyze algorithms for minimization of a smooth function $h(x)$ by distributing the processing of the components vector $x \in \mathbb{R}^n$ among n agents assuming $h(x)$ is separable. As noted earlier, there has been significant research on problem (1). The need for robustness for distributed optimization problems has received some attentions recently [9, 15, 28, 22]. Duchi et al. [9] and Lobel and Ozdaglar [15] study the impact of random communication link failures on the convergence of distributed variant of dual averaging algorithm and sub-gradient method, respectively. In particular, both [9] and [15] assume that each realizable link failure pattern admits a doubly-stochastic matrix which governs local estimates evolution dynamics.

Byzantine agents are first considered in the context of optimization in our series of four technical reports [22, 23, 24, 25]. In particular, in [26, 22], we explore an algorithm that requires all agents to perform *reliable broadcast* of all messages, essentially preventing the faulty agents from sending inconsistent messages to non-faulty agents. This approach effectively reduces the distributed optimization problem to a centralized problem, and allows a different class of solutions, with somewhat different properties, and requiring other proof techniques. In [23], we explore the special case when the optimum sets of the local cost functions of the non-faulty agents have a non-empty intersection. This property provides a form of redundnacy, which is exploited to solve the fault-tolerant optimization problem. In contrast, the algorithm presented in this paper is fully distributed, with a simple iterative structure (not requiring *reliable broadcast* and not making any assumptions about the intersection of the optimum sets).

Subsequent to our work, a somewhat weaker fault model (called *malicious* faults) was considered in [28] – they also obtain weaker guarantees on the behavior of their algorithm compared to those obtained in our work (including this paper).

4. BYZANTINE GRADIENT METHOD

A large number of *failure-free* optimization algorithms used in practice are *iterative* in nature, due to the practical benefits of implementing such algorithms [4, 2]. In an iterative algorithm, each agent maintains an estimate of the optimum, and the estimate converges to a true optimum in the limit as the number of iterations $\to \infty$. In this section, we present an iterative algorithm for problem (2). The algorithm satisfies the requirement in (2) in the limit as the number of iterations $\to \infty$. In practice, since the algorithm is terminated after a finite number of iterations, the algorithm will satisfy the requirements *approximately*. In particular, our algorithm will ensure that, after a sufficiently large number of iterations, the estimates maintained by the non-faulty agents become approximately equal (i.e., within some desired $\epsilon_1 > 0$), and the estimate of each agent is also approximately equal to (i.e., within some desired $\epsilon_2 > 0$) the optimum of a suitable weighted cost function (i.e., argmin in (2)). For brevity, our presentation below focusses on the limiting behavior as time $\to \infty$, although our algorithm does provably exhibit the desired behavior as above (i.e., approximate equality) after adequately large finite number of iterations.

The proposed iterative algorithm, *synchronous Byzantine gradient* method (SBG), is presented below. The pseudo-code describes the steps that should be performed by each agent $j \in \mathcal{V}$. A Byzantine faulty agent may deviate from the specification arbitrarily. Algorithm SBG combines features of iterative Byzantine consensus algorithms [16, 36] with elements of gradient-based optimization [4, 20]. We will show that the SBG algorithm solves (2) with $\left(\frac{1}{2(|\mathcal{N}|-f)}, |\mathcal{N}| - f\right)$–admissible weight vector $\boldsymbol{\alpha}$.

Algorithm SBG uses a trimming function (defined below) analogous to that used in previous Byzantine consensus algorithms.

Trim ($\mathcal{D}$)

Input: Multi-set $\mathcal{D}$ of real-valued scalars, with $|\mathcal{D}| \geq 2f+1$.

Output: Sort the elements in $\mathcal{D}$ in a non-decreasing order (breaking ties arbitrarily), and remove the smallest f values and the largest f values. Denote the minimum and the maximum of the remaining $|\mathcal{D}| - 2f$ values as y_s and y_l, respectively. Return the value below:

$$\frac{1}{2}(y_s + y_l)$$

Each agent j maintains a state variable x_j. We denote the value of x_j at the end of t iterations of SBG as $x_j[t]$, with the initial value being $x_j[0]$. The initial value may be chosen by each agent arbitrarily. Let $h'_j(x_j[t-1])$ denote the gradient of agent j's local cost function $h_j(\cdot)$ at $x_j[t-1]$.

$\lambda[t-1]$ used in Step 3 of the algorithm below is called the *step size*, which depends on the iteration index. The step sizes are known to all agents as a priori, and satisfy the following constraints: $\lambda[t-1] \geq \lambda[t]$ for $t \geq 1$, $\sum_{t=1}^{\infty} \lambda[t-1] = \infty$ and $\sum_{t=1}^{\infty} \lambda^2[t-1] < \infty$.

Algorithm **SBG** for agent j in iteration $t \geq 1$:

Step 1: Send the 2-tuple $(x_j[t-1], h'_j(x_j[t-1]))$ to all the other agents.

Step 2: Receive 2-tuples from all the other agents, with the first element of each tuple being a *state variable*, and the second element being a *gradient*. If such a tuple is not received from some agent, assume a default value for the tuple. Define:

$\mathcal{D}_j^x[t-1] \triangleq$ multi-set containing $x_j[t-1]$ and state variables received from other agents;

$\mathcal{D}_j^g[t-1] \triangleq$ multi-set containing $h_j'(x_j[t-1])$ and gradients received from other agents.

Step 3: Define $\widetilde{x}_j[t-1] \triangleq \mathsf{Trim}(\mathcal{D}_j^x[t-1])$, and $\widetilde{g}_j[t-1] \triangleq \mathsf{Trim}(\mathcal{D}_j^g[t-1])$. Update state as follows.

$$x_j[t] = \widetilde{x}_j[t-1] - \lambda[t-1]\widetilde{g}_j[t-1]. \quad (3)$$

In Algorithm SBG, in each iteration, an agent exchange both local estimate and local gradient with other agents. Although the information of gradient is contained in the local estimate, by exchanging gradients directly, a desired structural property of the update can be guaranteed. As seen above, each agent j maintains minimal state (namely, x_j) across iterations. Since the Trim function is applied to the state variables and gradients separately, it is possible that the values received from different sets of agents are removed in each of those trimming operations. The key difficulty in proving the desired (β, γ)-admissibility result arises due to the possibility that the Byzantine agents send different (erroneous) gradients to different non-faulty agents. Unlike the failure-free version of distributed optimization, the Byzantine faulty agents can effectively tamper with the global cost function being optimized. Thus, proving the lower bounds on β and γ requires us to show that the impact of the faulty behavior can be bounded. To delineate the impact of the faulty behavior, we now define a family $\mathcal{C}$ of "valid" global cost functions.

$$\mathcal{C} \triangleq \left\{ p(x) : p(x) = \sum_{i \in \mathcal{N}} \alpha_i h_i(x), \text{ where } \boldsymbol{\alpha} \text{ is } \left(\tfrac{1}{2(|\mathcal{N}|-f)}, |\mathcal{N}| - f\right)\text{-admissible} \right\} \quad (4)$$

Each $p(x) \in \mathcal{C}$ is said to be a *valid* function (a valid global objective). Note that each $p(x) \in \mathcal{C}$ is a convex combination of local cost functions of the non-faulty agents in $\mathcal{N}$ with $(\frac{1}{2(|\mathcal{N}|-f)}, |\mathcal{N}| - f)$-admissible weight vector $\boldsymbol{\alpha}$.

Time-varying step sizes, as in Step 3 above, are also used in previous algorithms for distributed optimization [9, 19, 31]. The key difference from the prior distributed optimization algorithms is in the use of the trimming function in Step 3 above. As seen later in Lemma 2, despite the adversarial behavior of the faulty agents, it is guaranteed that the *effective gradient* $\widetilde{g}_j[t-1]$ obtained in Step 3 has an important correspondence to a *time-dependent* (i.e., varying with iteration index t) *valid* cost function in $\mathcal{C}$.

Now let us define set Y to be the union of optimal solutions for all the valid functions in $\mathcal{C}$, i.e.,

$$Y \triangleq \bigcup_{p(\cdot) \in \mathcal{C}} \operatorname*{argmin}_{x \in \mathbb{R}} p(x). \quad (5)$$

Lemma 1 identifies an important property of set Y that is crucial in our convergence analysis. We will show that, as $t \to \infty$, for each agent j, its state variable $x_j[t]$ becomes trapped in set Y.

LEMMA 1. *Set Y is convex and closed.*

Lemma 1 is proved in Appendix A. As stated in Section 2, the argument x of the cost functions $h_j(x)$ is assumed to be a scalar in $\mathbb{R}$. In general, we would like to allow a vector argument for the cost functions (i.e., $x \in \mathbb{R}^k$, $k \geq 2$). However, set Y analogously defined for the case of vector arguments is *not necessarily convex*, making it difficult to extend our proof technique to vector arguments. In fact, the case of vector arguments remains an open problem presently.

The following distance metric will help state the main claim of this paper.

DEFINITION 2. *For any $x \in \mathbb{R}$, the distance between x and set Y is defined as follows*

$$Dist\,(x, Y) \triangleq \inf_{y \in Y} |x - y|.$$

Since Y is convex (Lemma 1), the function $Dist\,(\cdot, Y)$ is also convex. Theorem 2 states our main result, which summarizes the convergence behavior of algorithm SBG.

THEOREM 2. *Algorithm SBG achieves*

- *Consensus:* $\lim_{t \to \infty} (x_i[t] - x_j[t]) = 0$ *for all $i, j \in \mathcal{N}$, and*
- *Optimality:* $\lim_{t \to \infty} Dist\,(x_i[t], Y) = 0$ *for each $i \in \mathcal{N}$.*

Interpretation of Theorem 2.

Consensus: Property (i) in the above theorem implies consensus, since the state variables of all non-faulty agents become identical in the limit. However, property (i) does not imply that $x_j[t]$ for each $j \in \mathcal{N}$ itself has a limit. In fact, the value of the state variable $x_j[t]$ may change with t indefinitely. However, as property (i) states, in the limiting behavior, the state variables of all the non-faulty agents change in unison, maintaining consensus. This lack of a limit for each individual $x_j[t]$ is a direct result of the simple structure of algorithm SBG, which allows a faulty agent to send different gradients to different agents. If we were to require a *Byzantine broadcast* of $(x_j[t-1], h_j'(x_j[t-1]))$ in Step 1 of algorithm SBG at each agent j, then such duplicitous behavior by faulty agents can be precluded, as we have shown elsewhere [26]. With a higher cost (due to use of Byzantine broadcast), the modified algorithm can ensure that $x_j[t]$, $j \in \mathcal{N}$ has a limit as $t \to \infty$. However, the use of Byzantine broadcast essentially reduces the distributed optimization problem to the problem of centralized fault-tolerant optimization [26].

Despite the fact that the limit of $x_j[t]$ may not exist, the property (i) is useful in practice – if we were to terminate the algorithm after a sufficiently large number of iterations, then property (i) guarantees that the state of all non-faulty agents will be close to each other, thus achieving approximate consensus.

Optimality: Property (ii) in the above theorem makes guarantees about the "goodness" of the state of non-faulty agents as $t \to \infty$. In particular, observe that $Dist\,(x, Y) = 0$ if and only if $x \in Y$. Thus, property (ii) guarantees that, for sufficiently large t, state $x_j[t]$ for any non-faulty agent j approximately equals an optimum of a *valid* function in $\mathcal{C}$. That is, $x_j[t]$ approximately equals a solution of problem (2) with a $\left(\frac{1}{2(|\mathcal{N}|-f)}, |\mathcal{N}|-f\right)$-admissible weight vector $\boldsymbol{\alpha}$. Thus, Theorems 1 and 2 together imply that algorithm SBG achieves *optimal fault-tolerance* in the sense that an optimal number (i.e., $|\mathcal{N}|-f$) of local cost functions of non-faulty agents are guaranteed to be represented in the global cost function that is optimized. However, as the discussion of property (i) would suggest, this global cost function is time-varying. Secondly, when $|\mathcal{N}|-f$ weights are non-zero, if the weight distribution were to be uniform, then each weight would be $\frac{1}{|\mathcal{N}|-f}$. The fact that the $\boldsymbol{\alpha}$ vector achieved by algorithm SBG is $\left(\frac{1}{2(|\mathcal{N}|-f)}, |\mathcal{N}|-f\right)$-admissible implies that at least $|\mathcal{N}|-f$ weights are $\geq \frac{1}{2(|\mathcal{N}|-f)}$, which is within a factor of 2 of the uniform weight $\frac{1}{|\mathcal{N}|-f}$.

5. CORRECTNESS OF THEOREM 2

In this section, we present some key results that are useful in proving Theorem 2.

Recall that in Step 3 of algorithm SBG, each agent j applies the trimming function to compute the *effective gradient* $\widetilde{g}_j[t-1]$. Lemma 2 establishes a correspondence between this effective gradient and a valid function in $\mathcal{C}$.

LEMMA 2. *For each non-faulty agent $j \in \mathcal{N}$ and each iteration $t \geq 1$, there exists a valid function*

$$p_t^j(x) = \sum_{i \in \mathcal{N}} b_{ji}[t]\, h_i(x) \in \mathcal{C}$$

such that the effective gradient $\widetilde{g}_j[t-1]$ computed in Step 3 of algorithm SBG can be expressed as

$$\widetilde{g}_j[t-1] = \sum_{i \in \mathcal{N}} b_{ji}[t]\, h_i'(x_i[t-1]). \tag{6}$$

The proof of Lemma 2 can be found in [27, 24].

For agent $j \in \mathcal{N}$, the *weights* ($b_{ji}[t]$'s) in the interpolation on the right side of (6) correspond to the weights used to obtain a valid global cost function $p_t^j(x) \in \mathcal{C}$. Note that the vector formed by weights $b_{ji}[t]$ is $\left(\frac{1}{2(|\mathcal{N}|-f)}, |\mathcal{N}|-f\right)$-admissible. It is also important to note that, $h_i'(x_i[t-1])$ for each $i \in \mathcal{N}$ used in (6) is the gradient of agent i's local cost function $h_i(\cdot)$ computed at agent i's *own* state variable $x_i[t-1]$. Thus, the effective gradient $\widetilde{g}_j[t-1]$ is a linear interpolation of gradients of local cost functions at potentially *different* argument values. Despite this apparent discrepancy, algorithm SBG approximates the behavior of a gradient-based distributed optimization algorithm. Intuitively, the reason for this behavior is that the agents are guaranteed to eventually arrive at a consensus – thus, eventually, the gradients at different non-faulty agents are computed at approximately equal arguments. However, the weights $b_{ji}[t]$ in Lemma 2 are time-dependent, due to the potentially incorrect behavior by faulty agents (i.e., the weights correspond to potentially different functions in $\mathcal{C}$ in different iterations). More importantly, at different agents in $\mathcal{N}$, the weights corresponding to the effective gradients in a given iteration t can be different (i.e., for two different agents $k, j \in \mathcal{N}$, $p_t^k(x)$ and $p_t^j(x)$ may be different). Despite this difference, consensus is achieved due to the fact that set Y is convex (Lemma 1) and decreasing step sizes $\lambda[t-1]$ are used in algorithm SBG.

By a similar argument as in proving Lemma 2, we can obtain the result below for $\widetilde{x}_j[t-1]$ computed in Step 3 of algorithm SBG.

COROLLARY 1. *For each non-faulty agent $j \in \mathcal{N}$ and $t \geq 1$, there exists a $\left(\frac{1}{2(|\mathcal{N}|-f)}, |\mathcal{N}|-f\right)$-admissible weight vector $\mathbf{a}_j[t]$ (whose i-th element is $a_{ji}[t]$) such that $\widetilde{x}_j[t-1]$ computed in Step 3 of algorithm SBG can be expressed as*

$$\widetilde{x}_j[t-1] = \sum_{i \in \mathcal{N}} a_{ji}[t]\, x_i[t-1]. \tag{7}$$

Note that weights $b_{ji}[t]$ and $a_{ji}[t]$ in (6) and (7), respectively, are not necessarily identical, because the state variables and gradients are trimmed independently in Step 3 of algorithm SBG.

In Sections 5.1 and 5.2, we sketch the proofs of properties (i) and (ii) stated in Theorem 2. For complete proofs, please see [27, 24].

5.1 Asymptotic Consensus

We now sketch the proof that asymptotic consensus among the non-faulty agents is achieved under algorithm SBG. A complete proof can be found in the full version. Recall that $\lambda[t] \leq \lambda[t-1]$ and $\lim_{t\to\infty} \lambda[t] = 0$. The following proposition is used in proving consensus.

PROPOSITION 1. *Let $0 \leq b < 1$, and $\ell(t) = \sum_{r=0}^{t-1} \lambda[r] b^{t-r}$. Then $\lim_{t\to\infty} \ell(t) = 0$. Additionally, if $\lambda[t] = \frac{1}{t}$ for $t \geq 1$ and $\lambda[0] = 1$* [1], *then $\ell(t) = O(\frac{1}{t})$.*

Denote $M(t) = \max_{i \in \mathcal{N}} x_i[t]$ and $m(t) = \min_{i \in \mathcal{N}} x_i[t]$.

LEMMA 3. *Under algorithm SBG, $\lim_{t\to\infty}(M[t] - m[t]) = 0$. Additionally, if $\lambda[t] = \frac{1}{t}$ for $t \geq 1$ and $\lambda[0] = 1$, then $(M[t] - m[t]) = O(\frac{1}{t})$.*

From Corollary 1, we know that $\mathbf{a}_j$ is $\left(\frac{1}{2(|\mathcal{N}|-f)}, |\mathcal{N}|-f\right)$-admissible. Since $(|\mathcal{N}|-f) + (|\mathcal{N}|-f) - |\mathcal{N}| \geq 1$, for any $j, k \in \mathcal{N}$, there exists $i^* \in \mathcal{N}$ such that both $a_{ji^*}[t]$ and $a_{ki^*}[t]$ are lower bounded by $\frac{1}{2(|\mathcal{N}|-f)}$. Then the following holds.

$$\begin{aligned} &|\widetilde{x}_j[t-1] - \widetilde{x}_i[t-1]| \\ &\leq \left(1 - \frac{1}{2(|\mathcal{N}|-f)}\right)(M[t-1] - m[t-1]). \end{aligned} \tag{8}$$

Similarly, we have

$$|\widetilde{g}_j[t-1] - \widetilde{g}_k[t-1]| \leq \left(1 - \frac{1}{2(|\mathcal{N}|-f)}\right) 2L, \tag{9}$$

recalling that $|h_k'(x)| \leq L$ for any $k \in \mathcal{N}$ and any $x \in \mathbb{R}$.

From (3), (8) and (9), the disagreement $(M[t] - m[t])$ can

[1] As it can be seen from the proof of Proposition 1, $\lambda[0]$ can be chosen to be any positive constant.

be bounded as follows.

$$\begin{aligned}M[t]-m[t] &\le \left(1-\frac{1}{2(|\mathcal{N}|-f)}\right)(M[t-1]-m[t-1])\\ &\quad + 2L\lambda[t-1]\left(1-\frac{1}{2(|\mathcal{N}|-f)}\right)\\ &\le \left(1-\frac{1}{2(|\mathcal{N}|-f)}\right)^{t}(M[0]-m[0])\\ &\quad + 2L\sum_{r=0}^{t-1}\lambda[r]\left(1-\frac{1}{2(|\mathcal{N}|-f)}\right)^{t-r}. \quad (10)\end{aligned}$$

The first term in the right hand side of (10) diminishes exponentially fast, and by Proposition 1, the second term also goes to 0. Our next lemma (Lemma 4) says that the cumulative disagreement between two non-faulty agents is finite.

LEMMA 4. *Under algorithm SBG, it holds that*

$$\sum_{t=0}^{\infty}\lambda[t]\,(M[t]-m[t])<\infty.$$

The above results establish asymptotic consensus behavior of SBG.

5.2 Convergence Analysis

In this section, we sketch the proof that $x_j[t]$, where $j \in \mathcal{N}$, is trapped in Y asymptotically.

Lemma 3 shows that $\lim_{t\to\infty}(x_j[t]-x_i[t]) = 0$ for any $j, i \in \mathcal{N}$ – asymptotic consensus among the non-faulty agents is achieved. Thus, for sufficiently large t, (3) approximately equals

$$x_j[t] \;\approx\; x_j[t-1]-\lambda[t-1]p_t^j\,(x_j[t-1]),\forall j\in\mathcal{N}, \quad (11)$$

where $p_t^j(\cdot)$ is the valid function identified in Lemma 2. For a non-faulty agent j, one typical trajectory of x_j is as follows: (1) x_j first approaches set Y (defined in (5)), and (2) then bounces back and forth around set Y before completely being trapped in Y. The existence of disagreement in finite time (discussed above) complicates the convergence analysis significantly. To show the optimality of x_j for $j \in \mathcal{N}$, we use the auxiliary sequence $\{z[t]\}_{t=0}^{\infty}$ defined as follows.

DEFINITION 3. *Let $\{z[t]\}_{t=0}^{\infty}$ be a sequence of estimates such that*

$$z[t]=x_{j_t}[t], \quad \textit{where } j_t\in \operatorname{argmax}_{j\in\mathcal{N}} Dist\,(x_j[t],Y). \quad (12)$$

To show $\lim_{t\to\infty} Dist\,(x_j[t],Y)=0\,\forall j\in\mathcal{N}$, it is enough to show $\lim_{t\to\infty} Dist\,(z[t],Y)=0$, observing that $Dist\,(x_j[t],Y)\le Dist\,(z[t],Y)$ for each $j\in\mathcal{N}$ (formally proved in the full version). Moreover, a simple iteration relation can be obtained for $\{Dist\,(z[t],Y)\}_{t=0}^{\infty}$. Specifically,

$$\begin{aligned}Dist\,(z[t+1],Y) &\le \max\{\lambda[t]L,\ Dist\,(z[t],Y)\}\\ &\quad + L\lambda[t]\,(M[t]-m[t]), \quad \forall t\ge 0. \quad (13)\end{aligned}$$

The convexity of Y is crucial in establishing (13). Up to the disagreement adjustment term (i.e., $L\lambda[t]\,(M[t]-m[t])$ in (13)), the above iterative relation (13) is analogous to the basic evolution in the standard centralized gradient-based method [4]. Although the basic evolution relation has been obtained for failure-free distributed algorithms [9, 19, 31, 15], since our effective objective function is time-dependent ($p_t^j(\cdot)$ in (11)), their analysis does not apply directly to our problem.

It follows from Lemma 4 that

$$\lim_{t\to\infty} L\lambda[t]\,(M[t]-m[t])=0.$$

Thus, for sufficiently large t, (13) *roughly* equals

$$Dist\,(z[t+1],Y)\le\ \max\{\lambda[t]L,\ Dist\,(z[t],Y)\}.$$

Using the fact that $\lim_{t\to\infty}\lambda[t]=0$, and the "almost supermartingale" convergence theorem [21], Lemma 5 below can be proved.

LEMMA 5. *The sequence $\{Dist\,(z[t],Y)\}_{t=0}^{\infty}$ converges.*

Furthermore, we can show that the distance becomes 0 asymptotically, as stated in Lemma 6.

LEMMA 6. *The sequence $\{Dist\,(z[t],Y)\}_{t=0}^{\infty}$ converges to 0, i.e., $\lim_{t\to\infty} Dist\,(z[t],Y)=0$.*

Proof sketch for Lemma 6: Suppose $\lim_{t\to\infty} Dist\,(z[t],Y)=c$ with $c>0$. Then the sequence $\{z[t]\}_{t=0}^{\infty}$ will either accumulate to $(\max Y)+c$ or $(\min Y)-c$. *Roughly* speaking, there exists t_0, and $\rho>0$ such that

$$\begin{aligned}Dist\,(z[t+1],Y) &\le\ Dist\,(z[t],Y)-\lambda[t]\rho\\ &\le\ Dist\,(z[t_0],Y)-\rho\sum_{\tau=t_0}^{t}\lambda[\tau]. \quad (14)\end{aligned}$$

Since $\sum_{t=1}^{\infty}\lambda[t]=\infty$, taking limit on both sides of (14), we get $c\le-\infty$, proving a contradiction.

Lemma 6 is then used to establish that distance of $x_j[t]$ from Y converges to 0 as well.

6. CONSTRAINED OPTIMIZATION

We so far focussed on the *unconstrained* version of the optimization problem in (2). However, we can also generalize our results to the *constrained* version of problem (2) [25]. In particular, let $\mathcal{X}\subseteq\mathbb{R}$ such that $\mathcal{X}\neq$, and $\mathcal{X}$ is convex and closed. Then constrained version of (2) is stated below in (15). Observe that the output is now constrained to be in set $\mathcal{X}$.

$$\begin{aligned}&\text{output } x_o \text{ such that} \quad (15)\\ &\quad \text{there } \textbf{exists} \text{ weight vector } \boldsymbol{\alpha} \text{ for which}\\ &\quad x_o\ \in\ \operatorname*{argmin}_{x\in\mathcal{X}}\ \frac{1}{|\mathcal{N}|}\sum_{i\in\mathcal{N}}\alpha_i h_i(x),\\ &\quad \sum_{i\in\mathcal{N}}\alpha_i=1, \quad \text{and} \quad \forall i,\ \alpha_i\ge 0.\end{aligned}$$

The algorithm SBG can be adapted to solve (15) with a simple modification of the state update in (3), by projecting $\widetilde{x}_j[t-1]-\lambda[t-1]\widetilde{g}_j[t-1]$ on to set $\mathcal{X}$. This projection guarantees that $x_j[t]$ is within the constraint set $\mathcal{X}$. However, compared to the original algorithm, such a projection introduces a *projection error* at each iteration. Specifically, the update of x_j can be written as follows, where $e_i[t-1]$ denotes the projection error, and $Projection_{\mathcal{X}}$ denotes projection on to $\mathcal{X}$.

$$\begin{aligned}x_j[t] &= Projection_{\mathcal{X}}\,(\widetilde{x}_j[t-1]-\lambda[t-1]\widetilde{g}_j[t-1])\\ &= \widetilde{x}_j[t-1]-\lambda[t-1]\widetilde{g}_j[t-1]+e_i[t-1]. \quad (16)\end{aligned}$$

The projection error $e_i[t]$ can be shown to approach 0 as $t \to \infty$, and Theorem 2 holds true for the modified algorithm as well [25]. A complete algorithm description and analysis is presented in [25].

7. DISCUSSION AND FUTURE WORK

Compared with Byzantine failures, under the crash fault model, we can improve on the $\left(\frac{1}{2(|\mathcal{N}|-f|)}, |\mathcal{N}| - f\right)$- admissibility achieved in case of Byzantine faults. The algorithm SBG is modified in this case to perform *no trimming* at all, since the agents do not tamper with messages. For the modified algorithm, we have shown [24] that all the non-faulty agents (agents in $\mathcal{N}$) produce an output that equals an optimum of a global cost function of the form below.

$$c\left(\sum_{i\in\mathcal{N}} h_i(x) + \sum_{i\in\mathcal{F}} \alpha_i h_i(x)\right), \qquad (17)$$

where $\mathcal{F}$ is the set of faulty agents (that crash at some point during the execution), $0 \le \alpha_i \le 1$ for each $i \in \mathcal{F}$ and c is a normalization constant such that $c\left(|\mathcal{N}| + \sum_{i\in\mathcal{F}} \alpha_i\right) = 1$. Note that in (17), all the local functions associated with non-faulty agents have equal weights. A finite-time interpretation of the above results is also of practical interest.

We have only considered synchronous systems so far. In an asynchronous system as well, when there are up to f Byzantine faults, algorithm SBG can be modified to achieve fault-tolerant optimization. For instance, algorithm SBG may be combined with the reliable broadcast algorithm in [1]. Alternatively, we can require $n > 5f$, and combine SBG with the simpler asynchronous iterative Byzantine consensus algorithm in [8]. The two approaches will achieve a trade-off between communication cost and optimization performance.

Open Problems

Incomplete networks.

In this paper, we assumed that the underlying communication network is a completely connected. We have also explored SBG-like algorithms [25] for incomplete networks. However, our present approach is not believed to be optimal in general in incomplete network topologies. In particular, as seen previously, algorithm SBG achieves optimal fault tolerance, while also ensuring weights (α_i's) are bounded below by an adequately large constant (particularly, $\frac{1}{2(|\mathcal{N}|-f)}$). Obtaining equally strong results for incomplete networks remains an open problem.

Vector arguments.

Algorithm SBG assumes that the domain for the argument of the cost functions is $\mathbb{R}$ (or, in case of *constrained* optimization in (15) with $\mathcal{X} = \mathbb{R}$). In general, we would like to solve problem (2) for vector (i.e., multidimensional) arguments in $\mathbb{R}^k$ for $k \ge 2$ as well. In recent work, the problem of Byzantine *vector* consensus has been solved [17, 35]. However, a solution for Byzantine vector consensus by itself is *not* adequate to be able to solve the optimization problem of interest here. The difficulty lies in the geometry of the set of optima, when the argument is a higher dimensional vector. In particular, unlike the one-dimensional case where set Y defined in (5) is convex, it is not necessarily convex when the argument is higher dimensional.

Non-smooth cost functions.

In our work, we assumed continuously differentiable cost functions. In general, the cost functions may be non-smooth, and the optimization algorithm would need to use *subgradients* instead of *gradients*. For the *failure-free* case, distributed subgradient optimization algorithms indeed exist [9, 19], however, design and analysis of fault-tolerant optimization algorithms for non-smooth cost functions remain open.

8. ACKNOWLEDGMENTS

The authors would like to thank the reviewers for insightful comments and suggestions.

9. REFERENCES

[1] I. Abraham, Y. Amit, and D. Dolev. Optimal resilience asynchronous approximate agreement. In *Principles of Distributed Systems*, pages 229–239. Springer, 2005.

[2] D. P. Bertsekas. *Convex Optimization Algorithms.* Athena Scientific, 2015.

[3] S. Boyd, N. Parikh, E. Chu, B. Peleato, and J. Eckstein. Distributed optimization and statistical learning via the alternating direction method of multipliers. *Found. Trends Mach. Learn.*, 3(1):1–122, Jan. 2011.

[4] S. Boyd and L. Vandenberghe. *Convex optimization.* Cambridge university press, 2004.

[5] S. Chaudhuri. More choices allow more faults: Set consensus problems in totally asynchronous systems. *Information and Computation*, 105:132–158, 1992.

[6] J. Chen and A. Sayed. Diffusion adaptation strategies for distributed optimization and learning over networks. *Signal Processing, IEEE Transactions on*, 60(8):4289–4305, August 2012.

[7] D. Dolev, N. A. Lynch, S. S. Pinter, E. W. Stark, and W. E. Weihl. Reaching approximate agreement in the presence of faults. *J. ACM*, 33(3):499–516, May 1986.

[8] D. Dolev, N. A. Lynch, S. S. Pinter, E. W. Stark, and W. E. Weihl. Reaching approximate agreement in the presence of faults. *Journal of the ACM (JACM)*, 33(3):499–516, 1986.

[9] J. Duchi, A. Agarwal, and M. Wainwright. Dual averaging for distributed optimization: Convergence analysis and network scaling. *Automatic Control, IEEE Transactions on*, 57(3):592–606, March 2012.

[10] A. D. Fekete. Asymptotically optimal algorithms for approximate agreement. *Distributed Computing*, 4(1):9–29, 1990.

[11] R. Friedman, A. Mostefaoui, S. Rajsbaum, and M. Raynal. Asynchronous agreement and its relation with error-correcting codes. *Computers, IEEE Transactions on*, 56(7):865–875, 2007.

[12] M. Herlihy, S. Rajsbaum, M. Raynal, and J. Stainer. Computing in the presence of concurrent solo executions. In *LATIN 2014: Theoretical Informatics*, pages 214–225. Springer Berlin Heidelberg, 2014.

[13] B. Johansson. On distributed optimization in networked systems. 2008.

[14] H. J. LeBlanc, H. Zhang, S. Sundaram, and X. Koutsoukos. Consensus of multi-agent networks in the presence of adversaries using only local

information. In *Proceedings of the 1st International Conference on High Confidence Networked Systems*, HiCoNS '12, pages 1–10, New York, NY, USA, 2012. ACM.
[15] I. Lobel and A. Ozdaglar. Distributed subgradient methods for convex optimization over random networks. *Automatic Control, IEEE Transactions on*, 56(6):1291–1306, June 2011.
[16] N. A. Lynch. *Distributed Algorithms*. Morgan Kaufmann, 1996.
[17] H. Mendes and M. Herlihy. Multidimensional approximate agreement in byzantine asynchronous systems. In *Proceedings of the Forty-fifth Annual ACM Symposium on Theory of Computing*, STOC '13, pages 391–400, New York, NY, USA, 2013. ACM.
[18] A. Mostefaoui, S. Rajsbaum, and M. Raynal. Conditions on input vectors for consensus solvability in asynchronous distributed systems. *Journal of the ACM (JACM)*, 50(6):922–954, 2003.
[19] A. Nedic and A. Ozdaglar. Distributed subgradient methods for multi-agent optimization. *Automatic Control, IEEE Transactions on*, 54(1):48–61, Jan 2009.
[20] Y. Nesterov. *Introductory lectures on convex optimization*, volume 87. Springer Science & Business Media, 2004.
[21] H. Robbins and D. Siegmund. A convergence theorem for non negative almost supermartingales and some applications. In T. Lai and D. Siegmund, editors, *Herbert Robbins Selected Papers*, pages 111–135. Springer New York, 1985.
[22] L. Su and N. H. Vaidya. Byzantine multi-agent optimization: Part I. *arXiv preprint arXiv:1506.04681*, 2015.
[23] L. Su and N. H. Vaidya. Byzantine multi-agent optimization: Part II. *CoRR*, abs/1507.01845, 2015.
[24] L. Su and N. H. Vaidya. Byzantine multi-agent optimization: Part III. *Technical Report*, 2015.
[25] L. Su and N. H. Vaidya. Fault-tolerant distributed optimization (Part IV): Constrained optimization with arbitrary directed networks. *arXiv preprint arXiv:1511.01821*, 2015.
[26] L. Su and N. H. Vaidya. Multi-agent optimization in the presence of byzantine adversaries: Fundamental limits. In *Proceedings of IEEE American Control Conference (ACC)*, July, 2016.
[27] L. Su and N. H. Vaidya. Fault-tolerant multi-agent optimization: Optimal distributed algorithms (full version). In *Technical Report*, May, 2016.
[28] S. Sundaram and B. Gharesifard. Consensus-based distributed optimization with malicious nodes. In *Proceedings of the 53rd Annual Allerton Conference on Communication, Control and Computing*. IEEE, 2015.
[29] L. Tseng and N. H. Vaidya. Iterative approximate byzantine consensus under a generalized fault model. In *Distributed Computing and Networking*, pages 72–86. Springer, 2013.
[30] L. Tseng and N. H. Vaidya. Iterative approximate consensus in the presence of byzantine link failures. In *Networked Systems*, pages 84–98. Springer International Publishing, 2014.
[31] K. I. Tsianos, S. Lawlor, and M. G. Rabbat. Push-sum distributed dual averaging for convex optimization. In *Decision and Control (CDC), 2012 IEEE 51st Annual Conference on*, pages 5453–5458, Dec 2012.
[32] J. Tsitsiklis, D. Bertsekas, and M. Athans. Distributed asynchronous deterministic and stochastic gradient optimization algorithms. *Automatic Control, IEEE Transactions on*, 31(9):803–812, Sep 1986.
[33] J. N. Tsitsiklis. Problems in decentralized decision making and computation. Technical report, DTIC Document, 1984.
[34] N. H. Vaidya. Iterative byzantine vector consensus in incomplete graphs. In *Distributed Computing and Networking*, pages 14–28. Springer, 2014.
[35] N. H. Vaidya and V. K. Garg. Byzantine vector consensus in complete graphs. In *Proceedings of the 2013 ACM symposium on Principles of distributed computing*, pages 65–73. ACM, 2013.
[36] N. H. Vaidya, L. Tseng, and G. Liang. Iterative approximate byzantine consensus in arbitrary directed graphs. In *Proceedings of the 2012 ACM symposium on Principles of distributed computing*, pages 365–374. ACM, 2012.

APPENDIX

A. PROOF OF LEMMA 1

Proof that set Y is convex

We first prove that set Y is convex. Let $x_1, x_2 \in Y$ such that $x_1 \neq x_2$. By definition of Y, there exist valid functions $p_1(x) = \sum_{i \in \mathcal{N}} \alpha_i h_i(x) \in \mathcal{C}$ and $p_2(x) = \sum_{i \in \mathcal{N}} \beta_i h_i(x) \in \mathcal{C}$ such that $x_1 \in \text{argmin } p_1(x)$ and $x_2 \in \text{argmin } p_2(x)$, respectively. In addition, let $p(x) = \frac{1}{|\mathcal{N}|} \sum_{i \in \mathcal{N}} h_i(x)$. By definition of valid function in (4), it holds that $p(x) \in \mathcal{C}$. Note that it is possible that $p_1(\cdot) = p_2(\cdot)$, and that $p_i(\cdot) = p(\cdot)$ for $i = 1$ or $i = 2$.

Given $0 \leq \alpha \leq 1$, let $x_\alpha = \alpha x_1 + (1 - \alpha) x_2$. We consider two cases:

(i) $x_\alpha \in \text{argmin } p_1(x) \cup \text{argmin } p_2(x) \cup \text{argmin } p(x)$, and

(ii) $x_\alpha \notin \text{argmin } p_1(x) \cup \text{argmin } p_2(x) \cup \text{argmin } p(x)$.

Case (i): Suppose $x_\alpha \in \text{argmin } p_1(x) \cup \text{argmin } p_2(x) \cup \text{argmin } p(x)$.

When $x_\alpha \in \text{argmin } p_1(x) \cup \text{argmin } p_2(x) \cup \text{argmin } p(x)$, by definition of Y, we have

$$x_\alpha \in \text{argmin } p_1(x) \cup \text{argmin } p_2(x) \cup \text{argmin } p(x) \subseteq Y.$$

Thus, $x_\alpha \in Y$.

Case (ii): Suppose $x_\alpha \notin \text{argmin } p_1(x) \cup \text{argmin } p_2(x) \cup \text{argmin } p(x)$.

By symmetry, without loss of generality, assume that $x_1 < x_2$. By definition of x_α and the fact that $\text{argmin}_{x \in \mathbb{R}} p_1(x)$ is convex, it holds that $x_1 < x_\alpha < x_2$. By assumption of case (ii), it must be that $x_\alpha > \max(\text{argmin } p_1(x))$ and $x_\alpha < \min(\text{argmin } p_2(x))$, which imply that $p_1'(x_\alpha) > 0$ and $p_2'(x_\alpha) < 0$.

There are two possibilities for $p'(x_\alpha)$ (the gradient of $p(x_\alpha)$): $p'(x_\alpha) < 0$ or $p'(x_\alpha) > 0$. Note that $p'(x_\alpha) \neq 0$ because $x_\alpha \notin \text{argmin } p(x)$.

When $p'(x_\alpha) < 0$, there exists $0 \le \zeta \le 1$ such that

$$\zeta\ p_1'(x_\alpha) + (1-\zeta)\ p'(x_\alpha) = 0.$$

By definition of $p_1(x)$ and $p(x)$, we have

$$\begin{aligned} 0 &= \zeta\ p_1'(x_\alpha) + (1-\zeta)\ p'(x_\alpha) \\ &= \zeta \left(\sum_{i\in\mathcal{N}} \alpha_i h_i'(x_\alpha)\right) + (1-\zeta)\left(\frac{1}{|\mathcal{N}|}\sum_{i\in\mathcal{N}} h_i'(x_\alpha)\right) \\ &= \sum_{i\in\mathcal{N}} \left(\alpha_i\zeta + (1-\zeta)\frac{1}{|\mathcal{N}|}\right) h_i'(x_\alpha). \end{aligned}$$

Thus, x_α is an optimum of function

$$\sum_{i\in\mathcal{N}} \left(\alpha_i\zeta + (1-\zeta)\frac{1}{|\mathcal{N}|}\right) h_i(x). \tag{18}$$

Let $\mathcal{I}$ be the collection of indices defined by

$$\mathcal{I} \triangleq \{\ i:\ i\in\mathcal{N},\ \text{and}\ \alpha_i\zeta + (1-\zeta)\frac{1}{|\mathcal{N}|}\ \ge\ \frac{1}{2(|\mathcal{N}|-f)}\ \}.$$

Next we show that $|\mathcal{I}| \ge |\mathcal{N}| - f$. Let $\mathcal{I}_1$ be the collection of indices defined by

$$\mathcal{I}_1 \triangleq \{\ i:\ i\in\mathcal{N},\ \text{and}\ \alpha_i \ge \frac{1}{2(|\mathcal{N}|-f)}\ \}.$$

Since $p_1(x) \in \mathcal{C}$, then $|\mathcal{I}_1| \ge |\mathcal{N}| - f$. In addition, since $n > 3f$ and $|\mathcal{N}| = n - |\mathcal{F}| > 2f$, we have $|\mathcal{N}| < 2(|\mathcal{N}| - f)$. The following holds for each $j \in \mathcal{I}_1$.

$$\begin{aligned} \alpha_j\zeta + (1-\zeta)\frac{1}{|\mathcal{N}|} &\ge \zeta\frac{1}{2(|\mathcal{N}|-f)} + (1-\zeta)\frac{1}{|\mathcal{N}|} \\ &> \zeta\frac{1}{2(|\mathcal{N}|-f)} + (1-\zeta)\frac{1}{2(|\mathcal{N}|-f)} \\ &= \frac{1}{2(|\mathcal{N}|-f)}, \end{aligned}$$

i.e., $j \in \mathcal{I}$. Thus, $\mathcal{I}_1 \subseteq \mathcal{I}$.

Since $|\mathcal{I}_1| \ge |\mathcal{N}| - f$, we have $|\mathcal{I}| \ge |\mathcal{N}| - f$. So function (18) is a valid function in $\mathcal{C}$. Thus, $x_\alpha \in Y$.

Similarly, we can show that the above result holds when $p'(x_\alpha) > 0$.

Therefore, set Y is convex.

Proof that Y is closed

Auxiliary proposition

For each $x \in \mathbb{R}$, let $h'_{i_1(x)}(x), \cdots, h'_{i_{|\mathcal{N}|}(x)}(x)$ be a *non-increasing* order of $h_j'(x)$, for $j \in \mathcal{N}$, i.e.,

$$h'_{i_1(x)}(x) \ge \cdots \ge h'_{i_{|\mathcal{N}|}(x)}(x).$$

Note that associated with the gradient order, there is a corresponding list of non-faulty agents

$$\{i_1(x), i_2(x), \ldots, i_{|\mathcal{N}|}(x)\},$$

in which the relative ranks of non-faulty agents vary with x.

Define $r(x)$ as follows: For each $x \in \mathbb{R}$,

$$\begin{aligned} r(x) \triangleq &\left(1 - \frac{|\mathcal{N}|-f-1}{2(|\mathcal{N}|-f)}\right) h'_{i_1(x)}(x) \\ &+ \frac{1}{2(|\mathcal{N}|-f)} \sum_{j=2}^{|\mathcal{N}|-f} h'_{i_j(x)}(x). \end{aligned} \tag{19}$$

At each $x \in \mathbb{R}$, function $r(x)$ is the largest gradient value among all the valid functions in $\mathcal{C}$.

We now prove Proposition 2 that is useful in proving set Y is closed.

PROPOSITION 2. *$r(\cdot)$ is continuous and non-decreasing.*

PROOF. Recall that $\{i_1(x), i_2(x), \ldots, i_{|\mathcal{N}|}(x)\}$ is the list of non-faulty agents that corresponds to the non-increasing gradient order $h'_{i_1(x)}(x), \cdots, h'_{i_{|\mathcal{N}|}(x)}(x)$. By definition, function

$$\left(1 - \frac{|\mathcal{N}|-f-1}{2(|\mathcal{N}|-f)}\right) h_{i_1(x)}(\cdot) + \frac{1}{2(|\mathcal{N}|-f)} \sum_{j=2}^{|\mathcal{N}|-f} h_{i_j(x)}(\cdot)$$

is contained in $\mathcal{C}$. Since at each $x \in \mathbb{R}$, $r(x)$ is the largest gradient among gradients of all valid functions in $\mathcal{C}$, for any y (which may equal x) we have

$$\begin{aligned} r(y) \ge &\left(1 - \frac{|\mathcal{N}|-f-1}{2(|\mathcal{N}|-f)}\right) h'_{i_1(x)}(y) \\ &+ \frac{1}{2(|\mathcal{N}|-f)} \sum_{j=2}^{|\mathcal{N}|-f} h'_{i_j(x)}(y). \end{aligned} \tag{20}$$

Now, suppose $y \ge x \in \mathbb{R}$. Since $h_i'(\cdot)$ is non-decreasing, we have

$$\begin{aligned} r(y) &\ge \left(1 - \frac{|\mathcal{N}|-f-1}{2(|\mathcal{N}|-f)}\right) h'_{i_1(x)}(y) \\ &\quad + \frac{1}{2(|\mathcal{N}|-f)} \sum_{j=2}^{|\mathcal{N}|-f} h'_{i_j(x)}(y) \quad \text{by (20)} \\ &\ge \left(1 - \frac{|\mathcal{N}|-f-1}{2(|\mathcal{N}|-f)}\right) h'_{i_1(x)}(x) \\ &\quad + \frac{1}{2(|\mathcal{N}|-f)} \sum_{j=2}^{|\mathcal{N}|-f} h'_{i_j(x)}(x) \\ &= r(x) \quad \text{by (19)} \end{aligned}$$

Thus, function $r(\cdot)$ is non-decreasing.

Next we show that function $r(\cdot)$ is continuous.

For each $i \in \mathcal{V}$, since $h_i(\cdot)$ is continuously differentiable, it follows that $h_i'(\cdot)$ is continuous. That is, for each $i \in \mathcal{V}$ and $\forall\, \epsilon > 0$, $\exists\ \delta > 0$ such that

$$|x - c| < \delta \implies \left|h_i'(x) - h_i'(c)\right| \le \epsilon. \tag{21}$$

Assume $c \leq x < c + \delta$. Then

$$
\begin{aligned}
|r(x) - r(c)| &= r(x) - r(c) \quad \text{by monotonicity of } r(\cdot) \\
&\leq \left(1 - \frac{|\mathcal{N}| - f - 1}{2(|\mathcal{N}| - f)}\right) h'_{i_1(x)}(x) \\
&\quad + \frac{1}{2(|\mathcal{N}| - f)} \sum_{j=2}^{|\mathcal{N}|-f} h'_{i_j(x)}(x) \\
&\quad - \left(1 - \frac{|\mathcal{N}| - f - 1}{2(|\mathcal{N}| - f)}\right) h'_{i_1(x)}(c) \\
&\quad - \frac{1}{2(|\mathcal{N}| - f)} \sum_{j=2}^{|\mathcal{N}|-f} h'_{i_j(x)}(c) \quad \text{by (20)} \\
&\leq \left(1 - \frac{|\mathcal{N}| - f - 1}{2(|\mathcal{N}| - f)}\right) \left(h'_{i_1(x)}(x) - h'_{i_1(x)}(c)\right) \\
&\quad + \frac{1}{2(|\mathcal{N}| - f)} \sum_{j=2}^{|\mathcal{N}|-f} \left(h'_{i_j(x)}(x) - h'_{i_1(x)}(c)\right) \\
&\leq \left(1 - \frac{|\mathcal{N}| - f - 1}{2(|\mathcal{N}| - f)}\right) \epsilon + \frac{1}{2(|\mathcal{N}| - f)} \sum_{j=2}^{|\mathcal{N}|-f} \epsilon \quad \text{by (21)} \\
&= \left(\left(1 - \frac{|\mathcal{N}| - f - 1}{2(|\mathcal{N}| - f)}\right) + \frac{1}{2(|\mathcal{N}| - f)} \cdot (|\mathcal{N}| - f - 1)\right) \epsilon \\
&= \epsilon. \qquad (22)
\end{aligned}
$$

Similarly, we can show that when $c - \delta < x \leq c$, $|r(x) - r(c)| < \epsilon$.

Thus, function $r(\cdot)$ is continuous.

The proof of Proposition 2 is complete. □

Proof that Y is closed

With the auxiliary function $r(\cdot)$ at hand, we can show the closedness of set Y as follows.

Recall that Y is convex. To show Y is closed, it is enough to show that Y is bounded and both $\min Y$ and $\max Y$ exist.

It can be easily seen that $r(x)$ is negative for "sufficiently" small x, and positive for "sufficiently" large x. By Proposition 2, we know that function $r(x)$ is non-decreasing and continuous. Thus, there exists $x_0 \in \mathbb{R}$ such that

$$
\begin{aligned}
0 \; = \; r(x_0) &= \left(1 - \frac{|\mathcal{N}| - f - 1}{2(|\mathcal{N}| - f)}\right) h'_{i_1(x_0)}(x_0) \\
&\quad + \frac{1}{2(|\mathcal{N}| - f)} \sum_{j=2}^{|\mathcal{N}|-f} h'_{i_j(x_0)}(x_0).
\end{aligned}
$$

Let

$$
\begin{aligned}
q(x) &= \left(1 - \frac{|\mathcal{N}| - f - 1}{2(|\mathcal{N}| - f)}\right) h_{i_1(x_0)}(x) \\
&\quad + \frac{1}{2(|\mathcal{N}| - f)} \sum_{j=2}^{|\mathcal{N}|-f} h_{i_j(x_0)}(x). \qquad (23)
\end{aligned}
$$

Thus, $q'(x_0) = r(x_0) = 0$.

By construction, $q(x) \in \mathcal{C}$ is a valid function. Note that due to the possibility of existence of ties in top $|\mathcal{N}| - f$ rankings of the order $h'_{i_1(x)}(x), \cdots, h'_{i_{|\mathcal{N}|}(x)}(x)$, for a given x_0, there may be multiple orders over $h'_i(x_0), \forall i \in \mathcal{N}$ of the top $|\mathcal{N}| - f$ elements. Let $\mathcal{O}$ be the collection of all such orders. Note that there is an one-to-one correspondence of an order and a valid function defined in (23). Let

$$
a = \min_{o \in \mathcal{O}} \min \left(\operatorname{argmin} q_o(x)\right),
$$

which is well-defined since argmin $q_o(x)$ is compact, and $|\mathcal{O}|$ is finite.

By definition $a \in Y$. Next we show that $a = \min Y$.

Suppose, on the contrary that, there exists $\tilde{a} < a$ such that $\tilde{a} \in Y$. Since $\tilde{a} \in Y$, there exists $\tilde{q}(x) = \sum_{i \in \mathcal{N}} \alpha_i h_i(x) \in \mathcal{C}$ such that $\tilde{a} \in \operatorname{argmin} \tilde{q}(x)$. That is,

$$
\tilde{q}'(\tilde{a}) = 0. \qquad (24)
$$

We have

$$
\begin{aligned}
0 = q'(\tilde{a}) &= \sum_{i \in \mathcal{N}} \alpha_i h'_i(\tilde{a}) \\
&\leq \left(1 - \frac{|\mathcal{N}| - f - 1}{2(|\mathcal{N}| - f)}\right) h'_{i_1(\tilde{a})}(\tilde{a}) \\
&\quad + \frac{1}{2(|\mathcal{N}| - f)} \sum_{j=2}^{|\mathcal{N}|-f} h'_{i_j(\tilde{a})}(\tilde{a}) \\
&= r(\tilde{a}).
\end{aligned}
$$

From the definition of a and the assumption that $\tilde{a} < a$, we get $\tilde{a} < x_0$. Then, by monotonicity of $r(\cdot)$, we have

$$
r(\tilde{a}) \leq r(x_0).
$$

Thus, $r(\tilde{a}) = 0 = r(x_0)$. In addition, we have

$$
\begin{aligned}
0 = r(\tilde{a}) &= \left(1 - \frac{|\mathcal{N}| - f - 1}{2(|\mathcal{N}| - f)}\right) h'_{i_1(\tilde{a})}(\tilde{a}) \\
&\quad + \frac{1}{2(|\mathcal{N}| - f)} \sum_{j=2}^{|\mathcal{N}|-f} h'_{i_j(\tilde{a})}(\tilde{a}) \quad \text{by definition of } r(\tilde{a}) \\
&\leq \left(1 - \frac{|\mathcal{N}| - f - 1}{2(|\mathcal{N}| - f)}\right) h'_{i_1(\tilde{a})}(x_0) \\
&\quad + \frac{1}{2(|\mathcal{N}| - f)} \sum_{j=2}^{|\mathcal{N}|-f} h'_{i_j(\tilde{a})}(x_0) \quad \text{by monotonicity of } h'_i(\cdot) \\
&\leq \left(1 - \frac{|\mathcal{N}| - f - 1}{2(|\mathcal{N}| - f)}\right) h'_{i_1(x_0)}(x_0) \\
&\quad + \frac{1}{2(|\mathcal{N}| - f)} \sum_{j=2}^{|\mathcal{N}|-f} h'_{i_j(x_0)}(x_0), \quad \text{by (20)}
\end{aligned}
$$

which implies that $i_1(\tilde{a}), \cdots, i_{|\mathcal{N}|-f}(\tilde{a})$ is an order in $\mathcal{O}$. Thus, it can be seen that $\tilde{a} \geq a = \min_{o \in \mathcal{O}} \min \left(\operatorname{argmin} q_o(x)\right)$, contradicting the assumption that $\tilde{a} < a$.

Therefore, $a = \min Y$, i.e., $\min Y$ exists. Similarly, we can show that $\max Y$ also exists.

Therefore, set Y is closed.

Brief Announcement: Active Information Spread in Networks

Gennaro Cordasco
Department of Psicology,
Second Univ. of Naples, Italy
gennaro.cordasco@unina2.it

Luisa Gargano
Computer Science Dept.,
University of Salerno, Italy
lgargano@unisa.it

Adele A. Rescigno
Computer Science Dept.,
University of Salerno, Italy
arescigno@unisa.it

Ugo Vaccaro
Computer Science Dept.,
University of Salerno, Italy
uvaccaro@unisa.it

ABSTRACT

Identifying the most influential spreaders is an important issue for the study of the dynamics of information diffusion in complex networks. In this paper we analyze the following spreading model. Initially, a few nodes know a piece of information and are *active* spreaders of it. At subsequent rounds, spreaders communicate the information to their neighbors. Upon receiving the information, a node becomes *aware* of it but does not necessarily become a spreader; it starts spreading only if it gets the information from a sufficiently large number of its neighbors. We study the problem of choosing a small set of initial spreaders so as to maximize the final number of nodes that become aware of the information.

Keywords

Social Networks, Spread of Influence, Viral Marketing.

1. INTRODUCTION

Spreading processes in complex networks have recently gained a great deal of attention. There are many situations where members of a network may influence their neighbors' behavior and decisions, by swaying their opinions, by suggesting what products to buy, or simply by passing on a misinformation [1, 3, 10, 7]. A fundamental aspect to understand and control the spreading dynamics is the identification of influential spreaders that can diffuse information to a large portion of the network. This is the problem addressed in this paper. Our scenario posits a population consisting of n individuals that, with respect to the information, are subdivided into *ignorant, aware*, and *spreading.* Initially, all individuals are ignorant. Then an initial set of spreaders is selected. When a spreader informs an ignorant node v, the ignorant node v becomes aware; as soon as the individual v is informed by a number of spreaders greater than a threshold $t(v)$, it starts spreading the information itself. The motivations that lead us to consider this scenario come from experimental studies of how information spread in social networks [2].

We model the network as an undirected graph $G = (V, E)$, where V is the set of individuals and the set of edges E represents the relationships among members of the network, i.e., $(u, v) \in E$ if individuals u and v can directly communicate. We posit a threshold function $t : V \rightarrow \{0, 1, 2, \ldots\}$, and we denote by $N(v)$ the neighborhood of $v \in V$. An active diffusion process starting at $S \subseteq V$ is a sequence of node subsets: $\mathsf{Spreader}[S, \tau]$, $\tau = 0, 1, \ldots$, such that $\mathsf{Spreader}[S, 0] = S$ and

$$\mathsf{Spreader}[S,\tau] = \mathsf{Spreader}[S,\tau-1] \cup \Big\{u \,\Big|\, |N(u) \cap \mathsf{Spreader}[S,\tau-1]| \geq t(u)\Big\},$$

for $\tau \geq 1$. The process terminates when $\mathsf{Spreader}[S, \rho] = \mathsf{Spreader}[S, \rho-1]$ for some $\rho > 1$. We denote by $\mathsf{Spreader}[S] = \mathsf{Spreader}[S, \rho]$. Hence, when the process stops the set of aware nodes is

$$\mathsf{Aware}[S] = \mathsf{Spreader}[S] \cup \Big\{u \mid N(u) \cap \mathsf{Spreader}[S] \neq \emptyset\Big\}.$$

Given G, a threshold function $t(\cdot)$, and a budget β, we aim to identify a node set $S \subseteq V$, with $|S| \leq \beta$, such that the cardinality $|\mathsf{Aware}[S]|$ is *maximum.* We refer the problem as the AWARENESS MAXIMIZATION PROBLEM (AMP), and nodes in S are referred to as *seeds.* The related problem in which one asks for the smallest set S needed to achieve awareness of the whole network will be referred to as the PERFECT AWARENESS PROBLEM (PAP); analogously, S is referred as a perfect seed set.

1.1 Related Work

The above algorithmic problem has roots in the broad area of the *spread of influence* in Social Networks (see [5, 8] and references quoted therein). However, the papers appeared in the scientific literature considered the basic model in which *any* node, as soon as it is influenced by its neighbors, it also immediately starts spreading influence. The more refined model put forward in this paper, that differentiates among spreaders and plain aware (informed) nodes, appears to be new, to the best of our knowledge.

PODC'16 July 25-28, 2016, Chicago, IL, USA

ACM ISBN 978-1-4503-3964-3/16/07.
DOI: http://dx.doi.org/10.1145/2933057.2933069

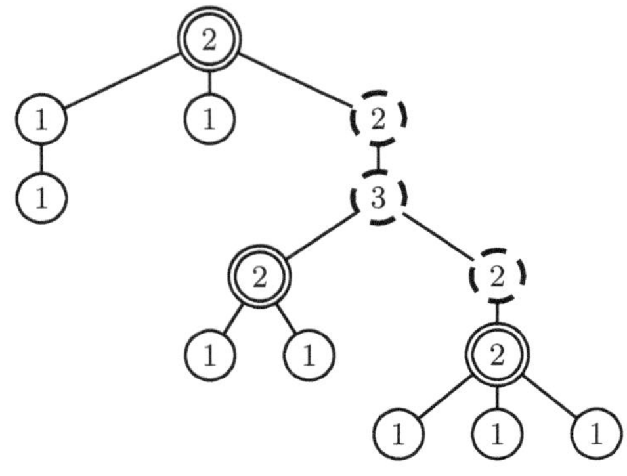

Figure 1. Numbers inside circles are the node thresholds, double–circled denote seeds, dashed–circled lines denote aware nodes, solid–circled nodes denote spreaders.

2. COMPLEXITY AND ALGORITHMS

We prove the hardness of AMP and PAP, by constructing gap-preserving reductions from the INFLUENCE MAXIMIZATION PROBLEM (i.e., given G, $t(\cdot)$, and β, identify set S, with $|S| \leq \beta$, such that $|\text{Spreader}[S]|$ is maximum) and the TARGET SET PROBLEM (given G and $t(\cdot)$, find a minimum size S s.t. $|\text{Spreader}[S]| = V$). Our Theorem 1 follows from the inapproximability results for the above problems given in [9] and [4].

THEOREM 1. *It is NP-Hard to approximate AMP within a ratio of* $n^{1-\epsilon}$, *for any fixed* $\epsilon > 0$.
PAP cannot be approximated within a ratio of $O(2^{log^{1-\epsilon} n})$, *for any* $\epsilon > 0$, *unless* $NP \subseteq DTIME(n^{polylog(n)})$.

Trees. On the positive side, we show that our problems becomes tractable if the graph is a tree. Let $T = (V, E)$ be a tree rooted at any node r, and let $T(v)$ the subtree rooted at v, for any $v \in V$. We have developed a dynamic programming algorithm for AMP. It makes a postorder traversal of the input tree T and for each node v, it solves all possible AMPs on $T(v)$, with bound $b \in \{0, \ldots, \beta\}$, and threshold for the root v in $\{t(v), t(v) - 1\}$, where $t(v) - 1$ corresponds to v made aware by its father in T.

While AMP can in general be used to solve PAP, simpler and much faster algorithms can be developed. An example of a perfect seed set is given in Figure 1. An optimal linear time algorithm which finds a perfect seed set of the input tree T can been devised. Algorithm 1 is a simplification of Algorithm 2 below, which can be shown optimal on trees.

THEOREM 2. *Given a tree with n nodes and maximum degree* Δ, AMP *with upper bound* β *can be solved in time* $O(n\beta^3 \min\{\Delta^2, n\})$; PAP *can be solved in linear time.*

Dense Graphs. We also study graphs characterized by large minimum degree. Real life social networks are characterized by the existence of highly connected communities and it was observed that in real networks, having high modularity [12], it is often difficult for information to flow from one community to another. This suggests that one should consider each (dense) community separately. We relate the graph minimum degree to the size of a perfect seed set. The idea is to show that, in any graph G with $t(v) \leq t$ for each node v, any independent set which is either maximal or has size $2t - 2$ is a perfect seed set for G. Establishing a significant lower bound on the size of the seed set has (so far) eluded our efforts. However, we noticed that deciding if there exists a perfect seed set of size less than t is a hard problem, indeed it admits a polynomial time reduction from the Set Cover problem.

Algorithm 1: TREE-PAP(T, t) $T = (V, E)$ is a tree

```
S = ∅;   A = ∅;   R = ∅;
// R is a set of required seeds, A is a set of aware nodes.
foreach v ∈ V in a BFS reverse order do
    if v ≠ r then
        if t(v) = 0 then
            t(f_v) = t(f_v) − 1;        // f_v denotes v's father
            A = A ∪ {f_v}
        else
            if v ∈ R AND t(v) ≥ 2 then
                S = S ∪ {v};
                t(f_v) = t(f_v) − 1;
                A = A ∪ {f_v}
            else
                if v ∉ A OR (v ∈ R AND t(v) = 1) then
                    R = R ∪ {f_v}        // f_v must spread
    if v = r AND t(v) > 0 AND v ∉ A − R then
        S = S ∪ {v}
return S
```

THEOREM 3. *Let* $G = (V, E)$ *be a graph with* $t(v) \leq t$ *and* $d(v) \geq \frac{|V|+t-3}{2}$, *for each* $v \in V$. *It is possible to efficiently find a perfect seed set for G of size at most* $2t - 2$.

2.1 A general graph algorithm for PAP.

For the Algorithm PAP(G, t) (see below) we can prove the following results.

THEOREM 4. *For any graph* $G = (V, E)$ *and threshold function* $t(\cdot)$, *the algorithm PAP(G,t) returns a perfect seed set for G in* $O(|E| \log |V|)$ *time.*

EXAMPLE 1. *Let G be a complete graph, the algorithm PAP(G,t) optimally returns a single seed: At the first iteration of the while loop, 3) applies and a node* v_1 *is selected; then a node* v_2 *is marked as required while all the others—being neighbors of* v_2*—are marked aware; during the successive iterations,* $|V| - t(v_2) - 1$ *nodes are removed from U; finally 2) holds for* v_2 *which is added to S and the algorithm returns* $S = \{v_2\}$.

If T is the tree in Figure 1 one can see that the algorithm PAP(T, t) returns a optimal seed set—consisting of the three double-circled nodes in the figure. Optimality holds for any tree.

THEOREM 5. *PAP(T,t) returns an* optimal *perfect seed set for any tree T and threshold function* $t(\cdot)$.

Due to Theorem 1, we cannot aim to any significant performance guaranteed on the seed set size for *general* graphs and threshold functions. Nonetheless, extensive experiments show that our algorithm performs very well on large real networks, both in terms of efficiency of the solution and of the running time. Experiments were performed on real networks, using the methodology employed in [6], with network

Algorithm 2: PAP(G, t) //$G = (V, E)$ is a graph with thresholds $t(v)$ for $v \in V$

```
S = ∅; // S is the seed set
R = ∅; // R a set of required seeds
A = ∅; // A is a set of aware nodes
Temp = ∅; // Temp is a temporary repository.
U = V;
foreach v ∈ V do k(v) = t(v); δ(v) = |N(v)|;
while A ≠ V OR R ≠ ∅ do
    if ∃v ∈ U s.t. k(v) ≤ 0 then            // 1): v is a spreader, thanks to its neighbors outside U
        foreach u ∈ N(v) ∩ U do
            k(u) = max(k(u) − 1, 0); A = A ∪ {u};
            if v ∉ Temp then δ(u) = δ(u) − 1;
        U = U − {v};   R = R − {v};   A = A ∪ {v};
    else
        if ∃v ∈ (U−Temp) ∩ R s.t. δ(v)<k(v) OR ∃v ∉ A s.t. δ(v) = 0 then      // 2): v must be in S
            foreach u ∈ N(v) ∩ U do k(u) = k(u) − 1; δ(u) = δ(u) − 1;  S = S ∪ {v};  U = U − {v};  R = R − {v};
            A = A ∪ {v};
        else
            if U − Temp − R ≠ ∅ then            // 3): v is moved in the temporary repository
                v = argmin_{w∈U−Temp−R} {δ(w)}
                if v ∉ A then
                    R = R ∪ {u} where u = argmax_{w∈N(v)∩(U−Temp)} {δ(w)}
                    foreach z ∈ N(u) ∩ U do A = A ∪ {z};
            else
                v = argmin_{w∈R} {δ(w)}; R = R − {v};
            foreach u ∈ N(v) ∩ U do δ(u) = δ(u) − 1; Temp = Temp ∪ {v};  A = A ∪ {v};
return S
```

sizes ranging from 4941 (Powergrid network [13]) to 154908 nodes (Douban network [14]). The experiments show that our algorithm strongly outperforms all previously known algorithms (that, however, aim to make each node a spreader). Just as an example, on the 5242 node ca-GrQc (General Relativity and Quantum Cosmology collaboration) network [11] with majority thresholds $t(v) = 0.5d(v)$, our PAP algorithm returns a seed set of 897 nodes, while the TSS algorithm of [6] gives a seed set 1023 of nodes. When all the thresholds $t(v)$ are equal to the node degrees $d(v)$, (and in such a case the PAP problem is equivalent to the well known DOMINATING SET problem) the results are of 1159 vs. 2785 nodes. The greedy algorithm for dominating set returns 1175 nodes.

3. REFERENCES

[1] S. Aral, D. Walker. Creating social contagion through viral product design: A randomized trial of peer influence in networks. *Management Science*, 57(9):1623–1639, 2011.

[2] E. Bakshy, I. Rosenn, C. Marlow, L. Adamic. The Role of Social Networks in Information Diffusion, *Proceedings of the 21st International Conference on World Wide Web*, 519–528, 2012.

[3] W. Chen, C. Castillo, L. Lakshmanan. *Information and Influence Propagation in Social Networks.* Morgan & Claypool, 2013.

[4] N. Chen. On the approximability of influence in social networks. *SIAM Journal on Discrete Mathematics*, 23(3):1400–1415, 2009.

[5] W. Chen, L, V.S. Lakshmanan, and C. Castillo. *Information and Influence Propagation in Social Networks.* Morgan & Claypool, (2013).

[6] G. Cordasco, L. Gargano, M. Mecchia, A. A. Rescigno, U. Vaccaro. A fast and effective heuristic for discovering small target sets in social networks. In *Proc. of COCOA 2015*, pages 193–208, 2015.

[7] M. Del Vicario, A. Bessi, F. Zollo, F. Petroni, A. Scala, G. Caldarelli, H. Stanley, W. Quattrociocchi. The spreading of misinformation onlines. *PNAS*, 113(3):554–559, 2016.

[8] D. Easley and J. Kleinberg. *Networks, Crowds, and Markets: Reasoning About a Highly Connected World.* Cambridge University Press, 2010.

[9] D. Kempe, J. Kleinberg, E. Tardos. Maximizing the spread of influence through a social network. *Theory of Computing*, 11(4):105–147, 2015.

[10] J. Leskovec, L. A. Adamic, B. A. Huberman. The dynamics of viral marketing. *ACM Trans. Web*, 1(1), 2007.

[11] J. Leskovec, A. Krevl. SNAP Datasets: Stanford large network dataset collection. http://snap.stanford.edu/data, 2015.

[12] M. E. J. Newman. Modularity and community structure in networks. *Proc. Natl. Acad. Sci. U.S.A.* 103 (23): 8577-8582, 2006.

[13] M. Newman. Network data, http://www-personal. umich.edu/ËIJmejn/netdata/, 2015.

[14] R. Zafarani, H. Liu. Social computing data repository at ASU, http://socialcomputing.asu.edu, 2009.

Brief Announcement: Certified Universal Gathering in $\mathbb{R}^2$ for Oblivious Mobile Robots

Pierre Courtieu
Cédric – CNAM
Paris, France
Pierre.Courtieu@cnam.fr

Lionel Rieg
Collège de France
Paris, France
Lionel.Rieg@college-de-france.fr

Sébastien Tixeuil
UPMC Sorbonne Universités,
LIP6-CNRS 7606,
Institut Universitaire de France
Paris, France
Sebastien.Tixeuil@lip6.fr

Xavier Urbain
ENSIIE,
LRI, CNRS UMR 8623,
Université Paris-Sud,
Université Paris-Saclay
Orsay, France
Xavier.Urbain@lri.fr

1. INTRODUCTION

Designing and proving mobile robot protocols is notoriously difficult. Since its initial presentation [13], this computing model has grown in popularity[1] and many refinements have been proposed (see [10] for a recent state of the art). The diversity of model variants makes it extremely onerous to check whether a particular property of a robot protocol holds in a particular setting. Even worse, checking whether a property that holds in a particular setting also holds in another setting that is not strictly contained in the first one often requires a completely new proof, even if the proof argument is very similar. The lack of proof reusability between model variants is a major problem for investigating the viability of new solutions or implementations of existing protocols (that are likely to execute in a more concrete execution model). Also, oblivious mobile robot protocols are mostly based on observing geometric constructions and deriving invariants from those observations. As the protocols are typically written in an informal high level language, assessing whether they conform to a particular model setting is particularly cumbersome, and may lead to hard to find mismatches. Hence, solely relying on handcrafted protocols, models and proofs is likely to introduce subtle errors that eventually lead to catastrophic failures when the system is actually deployed. Formal methods encompass a long-lasting path of research that is meant to overcome errors of human origin. Not surprisingly, this mechanised approach to protocol correctness was successively used in the context of mobile robots [5, 9, 2, 12, 7, 3, 4].

Model-checking proved useful to find bugs in existing literature [4] and assess formally published algorithms [9, 4], in a simpler setting where robots evolve in a *discrete space* where the number of possible positions is finite. Automatic program synthesis (for the problem of perpetual exclusive exploration in a ring-shaped discrete space) is due to Bonnet *et al.* [5], and can be used to obtain automatically algorithms that are "correct-by-design". The approach was refined by Millet *et al.* [12] for the problem of gathering in a discrete ring network. As all aforementioned approaches are designed for a discrete setting where both the number of positions and the number of robots are known, they cannot be used in the continuous space where robots positions take values in a set that is not enumerable, and they cannot permit to establish results that are valid for any number of robots.

Developed for the Coq proof assistant,[2] the Pactole framework enabled the use of higher-order logic to certify impossibility results [2] for the problem of convergence: for any positive ε, robots are required to reach locations that are at most ε apart. Another classical impossibility result that was certified using the Pactole framework is the impossibility of gathering starting from a bivalent configuration [7]. While the proof assistant approach seems a sensible path for establishing certified results for mobile robots that evolve in a continuous space, until this paper there exists no *positive* certified result in this context. Expressing mobile robot protocols in a formal framework that permits certification poses a double challenge: how to express the protocol (which can make use of complex geometric abstractions that must be properly defined within the framework), and how to write the proof?

Our contribution.

Our first contribution is a unified formal framework for expressing mobile robots models, protocols, and proofs. This framework is motivated by the fact that many of the observed errors in published papers come from a mismatch between

[1]The 2016 SIROCCO Prize for Innovation in Distributed Computing was awarded to Masafumi Yamashita for this line of work.

[2]http://coq.inria.fr

PODC'16, July 25–28, 2016, Chicago, IL, USA.

ACM ISBN 978-1-4503-3964-3/16/07.

DOI: http://dx.doi.org/2933057.2933070

the advertised model and the model that is actually used for writing the proofs. For example, some dining philosophers protocols were expressed and proved in a high-level atomicity model, but advertised as working in a lower-level atomicity model, revealed to be incorrect in the lower-level atomicity model (see the work of Adamek *et al.* [1] and references herein). Sometimes, the mismatch between the proof and the advertised model is more subtle: a perpetual exclusive exploration protocol the proof of which did not consider all possible behaviours in the advertised model ASYNC was used to exhibit a counter example in such a setting (See the work of Berard *et al.* [4] and references therein). A unified formalisation whose consistency can be mechanically assessed is a huge asset for designing correct solutions, whose correctness can be certified. As we used a subset of the same framework for certifying impossibility results [2, 7], consistency between negative and positive results is also guaranteed.

Our second contribution is a protocol design/proof methodology dedicated to mobile robots. We advocate the joint development of both the mobile robot protocol and its correctness proof, by taking advantage of the Coq proof assistant features. The proof assistant is typically able to check whether the proof of a particular theorem/lemma/corollary is valid. So replacing particular clauses of those theorems/lemmas/corollaries statements makes the proof assistant check whether the proof still is acceptable for the new statement. We used this feature to lift a preliminary version of this work (uni-dimensional setting [6]) to a Euclidean bi-dimensional space: the proof assistant checked which arguments were still valid in the new setting. This feature also proved useful when slightly changing parts of the algorithm: the impact of the changes on the proofs were immediate. Also, it becomes easy to remove or weaken hypotheses from the protocol, as the proof assistant makes it obvious if they are not used in the proof arguments. Finally, our methodology includes a formal way to guarantee whether the "global" view of the system (as seen from the protocol prover point of view) is effectively realisable given the hypotheses assumed in the model.

We instantiate our framework and methodology to actually design and prove correct a new protocol for the oblivious mobile robot universal gathering problem, that can be informally defined as follows: robots have to reach in a finite number of steps the same location, not known beforehand. In more details, *we present a new gathering algorithm* for robots operating in a continuous space that *(i)* can start from any configuration that is not bivalent (that is, the robots are not initially equally placed in exactly two locations, since gathering is impossible in this case), *(ii)* does not put restriction on the number of robots, *(iii)* does not assume that robots share a common chirality (no common notion of "left" and "right"). To our knowledge, this is the first certified positive (and constructive) result in the context of oblivious mobile robots.

2. OUR ALGORITHM

The protocol we propose uses multiplicity to build the set of towers of maximal height. If there is a unique tower of maximal height, i.e., a unique location of highest multiplicity, this location is the destination of each activated robot. Otherwise, the inhabited locations on the smallest enclosing circle (SEC) are taken into account to define a *target*.

The spectrum of a configuration is the multiset of all its robots' locations. It is *clean* if inhabited locations are either on the SEC or at target. When it is not clean (*dirty*), robots on SEC (or at target) stay where they are, the others move to the target, thus cleaning the spectrum. In a clean spectrum, any activated robot moves to the target. A configuration is said to be clean if and only if its spectrum is clean.

The important operation is thus to define a convenient target. Our target depends on how many inhabited locations are on the SEC. If there is only one, then the whole spectrum is reduced to a single location and all robots are gathered. When the number of towers on the SEC is not equal to 3, the target is the center of the SEC. Critical situations occur when towers on the SEC define a triangle. If this triangle is *equilateral*, the target is the center of the SEC (which is also the triangle's barycenter). If it is *isosceles* and not equilateral, the target is the vertex opposite to its base. Finally if the triangle is *scalene*, the target is the vertex opposite to its longest side.

A rephrase of that description in informal pseudo-code is presented as Figure 1. For a spectrum s, let $\text{support}(s)$ be the set of locations in s, let $\max(s)$ be the set of locations of maximal multiplicity in s, and let $\text{SEC}(s)$ be the smallest enclosing circle of s. Let *dest* be the destination to be computed. Remember that $(0, 0)$ is always the location of a robot in its own frame of reference.

Approach.

To certify results and to guarantee the soundness of theorems, we use Coq, a Curry-Howard-based interactive proof assistant enjoying a trustworthy kernel.

Developing a proof in a proof assistant may nonetheless be tedious, or require expertise from the user. To make this task easier, we are actively developing (under the name Pactole) a formal model, as well as lemmas and theorems, to specify and certify results about networks of autonomous mobile robots. It is designed to be robust and flexible enough to express most of the variety of assumptions in robots network, for example with reference to the considered space: discrete or continuous, bounded or unbounded... We want to stress that the framework eases the developer's task.

The Distributed Computing community is known to have fundamental algorithms tightly coupled with their proof of correctness. The mobile robot setting is no exception, as the minimal hypotheses a protocol must make to solve a given problem are extremely difficult to identify without actually writing the corresponding correctness proofs (that is, an intuitive approach is often detrimental to the correctness of the result to be established, as recent errors found in the literature proved [1]). In a formal proof approach to obtain mechanically certified protocols, our framework and methodology clearly contributes to two main phases in a verified development.

Firstly the *specification* phase, where all objects, definitions, algorithms, statements and expected properties are expressed without any ambiguity, in a higher order type theoretic functional environment. The lack of ambiguity is a key feature to enable the early detection of inconsistencies between the problem specification, the algorithmic proposal, and the execution model. We emphasise the fact that there is no need to be an expert with the Coq proof assistant to use our framework in this phase. Clear and unequivocal specifications are indeed a fundamental step towards correct algorithms.

```
if max(s) = ∅ then dest := (0,0)                                              (* absurd case *)
else  if max(s) = {p} then dest := p
else  begin                    (* first compute target then dest depending on cleanliness *)
      if support(s) ∩ SEC(s) = ∅ then dest := (0,0)                           (* absurd case *)
      else if  support(s) ∩ SEC(s) = {p} then target := p                (* already gathered *)
      else if  support(s) ∩ SEC(s) = {p1,p2,p3} then                        (* triangle cases *)
               if equilateral(p1,p2,p3) then target := barycenter(p1,p2,p3)
               else if isosceles(p1,p2,p3) then target := opposite of base(p1,p2,p3)
               else target := opposite of longest(p1,p2,p3)
      else target := center(SEC(s));
      if ∀p ∈ s, p ∈ SEC(s) or p = target  then dest := target      (* clean ⇒ go to target *)
      else if  (0,0) ∈ SEC(s) or (0,0) = target  then dest := (0,0) (* dirty ⇒ clean config *)
          else dest := target
      end
```

Figure 1: Our algorithm pseudocode

Secondly the *proof* phase, where properties are proved to hold for the relevant executions. This phase is of course more demanding on the expertise side, so our goal when constructing the framework was to provide useful libraries and proof techniques that can be reused in other contexts, enabling more automation to the protocol designer. Considering reusability, useful assets brought by the current work are the notions of gathering, SSYNC demons, etc., developments on geometry in $\mathbb{R}^2$ and smallest enclosing circles, as well as the proof that forbidden configurations can be reached from already forbidden configurations only [6]. Those will most likely prove useful in future developments. When developing the protocol for our case study, we decided to modify the protocol code several times, either to fix a newly discovered bug, or to ease the writeup of the proofs. This classical design stage was streamlined by the use of a formal language based on the Curry-Howard isomorphism [11] where both activities can be done in a uniform way. In such a setting, correcting the algorithm amounts to modifying the algorithm definition, and replaying the proofs certification process after adapting the proof scripts written previously. The mechanised verification of the proofs makes this process fast and trustworthy, compared to a purely handcrafted approach.

Resources.

A research report [8] describing our approach as well as the actual development and its `html` documentation are available from the project's webpage: http://pactole.lri.fr

3. REFERENCES

[1] J. Adamek, M. Nesterenko, and S. Tixeuil. Evaluating and optimizing stabilizing dining philosophers. In *11th European Dependable Computing Conference, EDCC 2015, Paris, France, September 7-11, 2015*, pages 233–244. IEEE, 2015.

[2] C. Auger, Z. Bouzid, P. Courtieu, S. Tixeuil, and X. Urbain. Certified Impossibility Results for Byzantine-Tolerant Mobile Robots. In T. Higashino, Y. Katayama, T. Masuzawa, M. Potop-Butucaru, and M. Yamashita, editors, *Stabilization, Safety, and Security of Distributed Systems - 15th International Symposium (SSS 2013)*, volume 8255 of *Lecture Notes in Computer Science*, pages 178–186, Osaka, Japan, Nov. 2013. Springer-Verlag.

[3] B. Bérard, P. Courtieu, L. Millet, M. Potop-Butucaru, L. Rieg, N. Sznajder, S. Tixeuil, and X. Urbain. Formal Methods for Mobile Robots: Current Results and Open Problems. *International Journal of Informatics Society*, 7(3):101–114, 2015. Invited Paper.

[4] B. Bérard, P. Lafourcade, L. Millet, M. Potop-Butucaru, Y. Thierry-Mieg, and S. Tixeuil. Formal verification of Mobile Robot Protocols. *Distributed Computing*, 2016.

[5] F. Bonnet, X. Défago, F. Petit, M. Potop-Butucaru, and S. Tixeuil. Discovering and assessing fine-grained metrics in robot networks protocols. In *33rd IEEE International Symposium on Reliable Distributed Systems Workshops, SRDS Workshops 2014, Nara, Japan, October 6-9, 2014*, pages 50–59. IEEE, 2014.

[6] P. Courtieu, L. Rieg, S. Tixeuil, and X. Urbain. A Certified Universal Gathering Algorithm for Oblivious Mobile Robots. *CoRR*, abs/1506.01603, 2015.

[7] P. Courtieu, L. Rieg, S. Tixeuil, and X. Urbain. Impossibility of Gathering, a Certification. *Information Processing Letters*, 115:447–452, 2015.

[8] P. Courtieu, L. Rieg, S. Tixeuil, and X. Urbain. Certified Universal Gathering Algorithm in $\mathbb{R}^2$ for Oblivious Mobile Robots. *CoRR*, abs/1602.08361, 2016.

[9] S. Devismes, A. Lamani, F. Petit, P. Raymond, and S. Tixeuil. Optimal Grid Exploration by Asynchronous Oblivious Robots. In A. W. Richa and C. Scheideler, editors, *Stabilization, Safety, and Security of Distributed Systems - 14th International Symposium (SSS 2012)*, volume 7596 of *Lecture Notes in Computer Science*, pages 64–76, Toronto, Canada, Oct. 2012. Springer-Verlag.

[10] P. Flocchini, G. Prencipe, and N. Santoro. *Distributed Computing by Oblivious Mobile Robots.* Synthesis Lectures on Distributed Computing Theory. Morgan & Claypool Publishers, 2012.

[11] W. A. Howard. The formulae-as-types notion of construction. In J. R. H. Jonathan P. Seldin, editor, *To H. B. Curry: Essays on Combinatory Logic, Lambda Calculus and Formalism*, pages 479–490. Academic Press, London, 1980.

[12] L. Millet, M. Potop-Butucaru, N. Sznajder, and S. Tixeuil. On the synthesis of mobile robots algorithms: The case of ring gathering. In P. Felber and V. K. Garg, editors, *Stabilization, Safety, and Security of Distributed Systems - 16th International Symposium, (SSS 2014)*, volume 8756 of *Lecture Notes in Computer Science*, pages 237–251, Paderborn, Germany, sep 2014. Springer-Verlag.

[13] I. Suzuki and M. Yamashita. Distributed Anonymous Mobile Robots: Formation of Geometric Patterns. *SIAM Journal of Computing*, 28(4):1347–1363, 1999.

Brief Announcement: Probabilistic Asynchronous Arbitrary Pattern Formation*

Quentin Bramas
Sorbonne Universités, UPMC Univ Paris 06, CNRS, LIP6 UMR 7606, 4 place Jussieu 75005 Paris
quentin.bramas@lip6.fr

Sébastien Tixeuil
Sorbonne Universités, UPMC Univ Paris 06, CNRS, LIP6 UMR 7606, 4 place Jussieu 75005 Paris
sebastien.tixeuil@lip6.fr

ABSTRACT

We propose a new probabilistic pattern formation algorithm for oblivious mobile robots that operates in the ASYNC model. Unlike previous work, our algorithm makes no assumptions about the local coordinate systems of robots (the robots do *not* share a common "North" nor a common "Right"), yet it preserves the ability from any initial configuration that contains at least 5 robots to form any general pattern (and not just patterns that satisfy symmetricity predicates). Our proposal also gets rid of the previous assumption (in the same model) that robots do not pause while moving (so, our robots really are fully asynchronous), and the amount of randomness is kept low – a single random bit per robot per Look-Compute-Move cycle is used. Our protocol consists in the combination of two phases, a probabilistic leader election phase, and a deterministic pattern formation one. As the deterministic phase does not use chirality, it may be of independent interest in the deterministic context. A noteworthy feature of our algorithm is the ability to form patterns with multiplicity points (except the gathering case due to impossibility results), a new feature in the context of pattern formation that we believe is an important asset of our approach.

1. INTRODUCTION

We consider a set of mobile robots that move freely in a continuous 2-dimensional Euclidian space. Each robot repeats asynchronously Look-Compute-Move (LCM) cycles [5]. First, it *Looks* at its surroundings to obtain a snapshot containing the locations of all robots as points in the plane, with respect to its ego-centered coordinate system. Based on this visual information, the robot *Computes* a destination and then *Moves* towards the destination. The robots are identical, anonymous and oblivious *i.e.*, the computed destination in each cycle depends only on the snapshot obtained in the current cycle (and not on the past history of execution). The snapshots obtained by the robots are not consistently oriented in any manner.

*This work was performed within the Labex SMART supported by French state funds managed by the ANR within the Investissements d'Avenir programme under reference ANR-11-IDEX-0004-02.

PODC'16 July 25-28, 2016, Chicago, IL, USA

ACM ISBN 978-1-4503-3964-3/16/07.
DOI: http://dx.doi.org/10.1145/2933057.2933074

In this particularly weak model it is interesting to characterize which additional assumptions are needed for the robots to cooperatively perform a given task. In this paper, we consider the pattern formation problem in the most general asynchronous (ASYNC) model. The robots start in an arbitrary initial configuration where no two robots occupy the same position, and are given the pattern to be formed as a set of coordinates in their own local coordinate system. An algorithm solves the pattern formation problem if within finite time the robots form the input pattern and remain stationary thereafter.

Related Work.

The pattern formation problem has been extensively studied in the deterministic setting [1, 6, 3, 5].

The best deterministic algorithm so far in the ASYNC model without a common coordinate system [6] proves the following: If ρ denotes the geometric symmetricity of a robot configuration (i.e., the maximum integer ρ such that the rotation by $2\pi/\rho$ is invariant for the configuration), and I and P denote the initial and target configurations, respectively, then P can be formed if and only if $\rho(I)$ divides $\rho(F)$.

To circumvent the impossibility to form any general pattern, the probabilistic path was taken by Yamauchi and Yamashita [7]. However, their approach makes use of three hypotheses that are not proved to be necessary: *(i)* all robots share a common chirality, *(ii)* a robot may not make an arbitrary long pause while moving (more precisely, it cannot be observed twice at the same position by the same robot in two different Look-Compute-Move cycles while it is moving), and *(iii)* infinitely many random bit are required (a robot requests a point chosen uniformly at random in a continuous segment) anytime access to a random source is performed. While the latter two are of more theoretical interest, the first one is intriguing, as a common chirality was also used extensively in the deterministic case.

Our Contribution.

In this paper, we propose a new probabilistic pattern formation algorithm for oblivious mobile robots that operate in the ASYNC model. Unlike previous work, our algorithm makes no assumptions about the local coordinate systems of robots (they do *not* share a common "North" nor a common "Right"), yet it preserves the ability from any initial configuration that contains at least 5 robots to form any general pattern (and not just patterns such that $\rho(I)$ divides $\rho(F)$). Besides relieving the chirality assumption, our proposal also gets rid of the previous assumption [7] that robots do not pause while moving (so, they really are fully asynchronous), and the amount of randomness is kept low – a single random bit per robot is used per use of the random source – (*vs.* infinitely many previously [7]). Our protocol consists in the combination of several phases, including a deterministic pattern formation one. As the deterministic phase does not use chirality, it may be of independent interest in the deterministic context.

A noteworthy property of our algorithm is that it permits to form patterns with multiplicity points (*without* assuming robots are endowed with multiplicity detection), a new feature in the context of pattern formation that we believe is an important asset of our approach. Of course, the case of gathering (a special pattern defined by a unique point of multiplicity n) remains impossible to solve in our settings [4].

2. MODEL

Robots operate in a 2-dimensional Euclidian space. Each robot has its own local coordinate system. For simplicity, we assume the existence (unknown from the robots) of a global coordinate system. Whenever it is clear from the context, we manipulate points in this global coordinate system, but each robot only sees the points in its local system. Two set of points A and B are *similar*, denoted $A \approx B$, if B can be obtained from A by translation, scaling, rotation, or symmetry. A *configuration* P is a set of positions of robots at a given time. Each robot that looks at this configuration may see different (but similar) set of points.

Each time a robot is activated it starts a Look/Compute/Move cycle. After the *look* phase, a robot obtains a configuration P representing the positions of the robots in its local coordinate system. After an arbitrary delay, the robot *computes* a path to a destination. Then, it *moves* toward the destination following the previously computed path. The duration of the move phase, and the delay between two phases, are chosen by an adversary and can be arbitrary long. The adversary decides when robots are activated assuming a *fair* scheduling *i.e.*, in any configuration, all robots are activated within finite time. The adversary also controls the robots movement along their target path and can stop a robot before reaching its destination, but not before traveling at least a distance $\delta > 0$ (δ being unknown to the robots).

An execution of an algorithm is an infinite sequence $P(0), P(1), \ldots$ of configurations. An algorithm ψ forms a pattern F if, for any execution $P(0), P(1), \ldots$, there exists a time t such that $P(t) \approx F$ and $P(t') = P(t)$ for all $t' \geq t$. In the sequel, the set of points F denotes the pattern to form. The coordinates of the points in F are given to the robots in an arbitrary coordinate system so that each robot may receive different, but equivalent, pattern F. If the pattern contains points of multiplicity, the robots receives a multiset, which is a set where each element is associated with its multiplicity. Even if the robots are not endowed with multiplicity detection, they know from the pattern what are the points of multiplicity to form. In particular, then can deduce from the pattern, the number n of robots, even if they do not see n robots.

3. ALGORITHM OVERVIEW

Our algorithm is divided into four phases. Since robots are oblivious and the scheduling is asynchronous, we cannot explicitly concatenate several phases to be executed in a specific order. However, one can simulate the effect of concatenation of two (or more) phases by inferring from the current configuration which phase to execute. Implementing this technique is feasible if phases are associated with disjoint sets of configurations where they are executed. Also, in order to simplify the proof of correctness, robots should not switch phases when placed in a configuration containing moving robots *i.e.*, a phase has to ensure that if the configuration resulting from a movement is associated with another phase, then all the robots are static (that is, none of them is moving). When this property holds, the first time a phase is executed, we can suppose that the configuration is static.

Our algorithm can form an arbitrary pattern. In particular, the pattern F can contain points of multiplicity. If this is the case, the robots create a new pattern $\tilde{F}$ from F where they remove the multiplicity, and add around each point p of multiplicity m, $m-1$ points really close to p, and located at the same distance to the center of the smallest circle enclosing F. The algorithm then proceed as usual with $\tilde{F}$ instead of F. The initial pattern F is formed by the termination phase, when $\tilde{F}$ is almost formed. So from now, we suppose that the pattern does not contains points of multiplicity.

In the following we define the phases of our algorithm and the set of associated configurations, starting from the more precise one (the phase we intuitively execute at the end to complete the pattern formation). Unless otherwise stated, the *center* of a configuration refers to the center of the smallest enclosing circle of this configuration.

Termination. The termination phase occurs when all robots, except the closest to the center, forms the target pattern (from which we remove one of the point closest to the center). The phase consists in moving the last robot towards its destination. While moving, the robot remains the closest to the center, so that the resulting configuration is associated to the same phase.

Almost Pattern Formation. Among the remaining configurations, we associate the guided ones to this phase. A configuration is *guided* when a unique robot is sufficiently close to the center and induces by its position a global sense of direction and orientation to every robot. In particular, when executing this phase, robots are totally ordered and have a unique destination assigned. The phase consists first in moving all the robots (except the one that is closest to the center), one by one, so that they are at the same distance to the center as their destination in the pattern. Secondly, the robots moves toward their destination, keeping their distance to the center and the ordering unchanged. The configuration has to remain guided until each robot, except the closest to the center, reaches its destination. A configuration obtained after executing this phase is either associated to the same phase, or to the termination phase.

Formation of a Guided Configuration 1 (FBC1). Among the remaining configurations, we associate the ones that contain a *centered equiangular or biangular* (CEB) set to this phase. A CEB-set is a subset of robots that exists when the configuration is symmetric or has a non-trivial symmetricity. Moreover it is constructed independently from the coordinate system (so it is unique when it exists), and is invariant when the robots in this set move toward (or away from) the center of the configuration. When the configuration contains a CEB-set, our algorithm consists in moving the robots in this set to obtain a guided configuration. The invariance property of the CEB-set is important to ensure that resulting configurations are still associated with this phase.

In more details, when this phase is executed, the robots in the CEB-set Q moves either toward or away from the center with probability $1/2$. We show that, with probability 1, a unique robot is elected after a finite number of activations. Then, the elected robot performs a special move to force the other robots in Q to terminate their movement. Once each robot is static, the elected robot moves toward the center to create a guided configuration. During the execution of this phase, it is possible that the configuration is associated with the termination phase. If this happens, our algorithm makes sure that all robots are static.

Formation of a Guided Configuration 2 (FBC2). We associate all remaining configurations to this phase. When executing this phase, the configuration does not have a CEB-set. This implies that

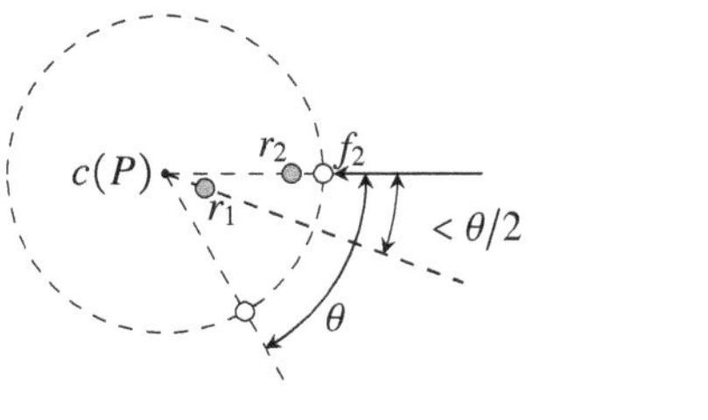

Figure 1: Positioning r_1 and r_2 to define a guided configuration.

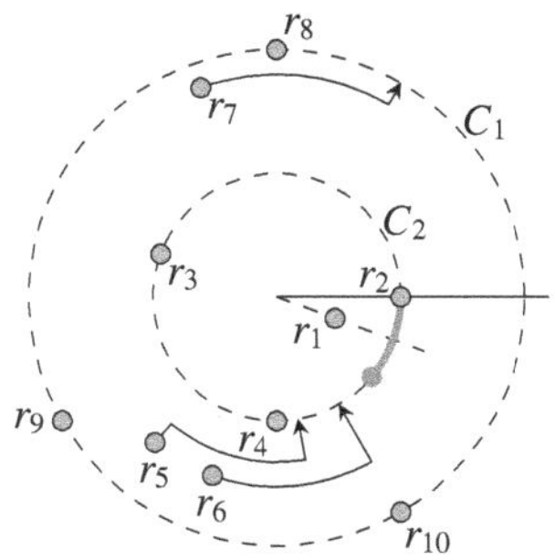

Figure 2: Moving robots to a correct distance from the center.

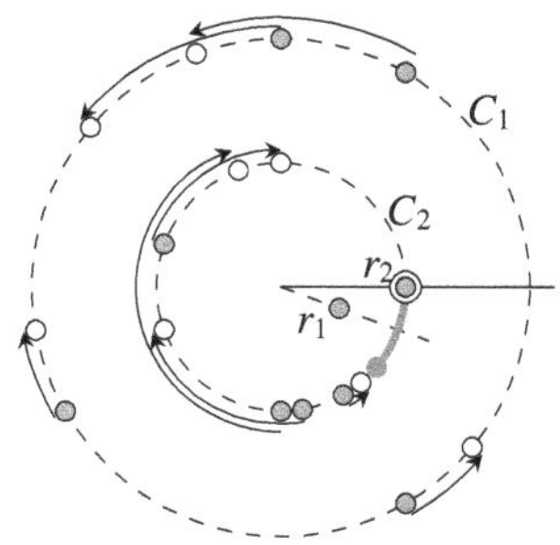

Figure 3: Robots move toward their final destination.

the configuration is not symmetric, so the robots are totally ordered. Therefore, the smallest robot moves toward the center to create a guided configuration (it remains the smallest robot while doing so). Before the movement, the robot checks if there exists a point in its path that creates a configuration containing a CEB-set. If it is the case, the robot chooses this point as its destination so that, when the configuration contains a CEB-set (and the robots switch to the FBC1 phase), all the robots are static.

4. ALGORITHM DETAILS

In this section we give some details about the main part of the deterministic pattern formation phase. Due to space constraints, the details of the other phases can be found in a technical report [2]. First we define some notations used in the remaining of the section.

For a set of positions P, $SEC(P)$ denotes its smallest enclosing circle. For a robot r, let $|r|$ be the distance between r and the center of the configuration (where the unit of distance is the radius of $SEC(P)$). Also, for a point $f \in F$, $|f|$ is the distance between f and the center of F. We denote by $ang(p_1, p_2, p_3)$ the angle formed by p_1, p_2 and p_3 (the orientation is chosen in order to minimize the angle).

We order the points in F, $f_1, \ldots, f_n$ such that $|f_1| \leq \ldots \leq |f_n|$, with $|f_i| = |f_{i+1}|$ implies $ang(f_i, c(F), f_n) \leq ang(f_{i+1}, c(P), f_n)$, and such that $ang(f_1, c(F), f_2)$ is minimal (where all angles have the same orientation). If several orders exist, we chose the one that minimize $ang(f_1, c(P), f_3)$. If again several orders exist we chose the have that minimize $ang(f_1, c(P), f_4)$ and so on. After that, if several orders minimize $ang(f_1, c(P), f_n)$, then the pattern is symmetric and the orders are equivalent. We order the robots $r_1, \ldots, r_n$ in the same way. However, when there are several equivalent orders for robots, it is not possible to match each robot with a destination in the pattern in an unambiguous way.

A configuration is *guided* if there is a unique ordering of robots (in the previously defined ordering), and we have: *(i)* $|r_1| \leq |r_2|/2$; *(ii)* $|r_2| \leq |f_2|$; *(iii)* $2ang(r_1, c(P), r_2) < \min_{f \in F, |f|=|f_2|} ang(f_2, c(F), f)$ (see Figure 1).

Almost Pattern Formation.

During this phase, it is important to keep the configuration guided. For that purpose, robots r_1 and r_2 must not move (r_2 can move radially so that $|r_2| = |f_2|$, but other robots cannot be closer than $|f_2|$). Also, no robot located at the same distance from the center than r_2 should form an angle smaller than $ang(f_1, c(P), f_2)$ (represented by a red arc in Figures 2 and 3). The phase starts by moving each robot r_i, $i \in [2..n]$ to the circle of radius $|f_i|$. For this, the greatest robot (in the ordering) that is strictly inside its circle moves toward its circle, while the ordering of robots remains unchanged (*cf.* the movement of robot r_7 in Figure 2). Then, the smallest robot that is outside its circle moves toward its circle while ensuring the ordering of robots remains unchanged (*cf.* the movement of robot r_5). Those actions are repeated until all robots reach their circles (*cf.* move of robot r_6).

Then each robot reaches its final destination, while staying on its circle (movement are performed along an arc) and while keeping the ordering of robots unchanged. In more details, when a robot r is activated and there is a robot r' on the path to its destination, r moves on its path toward r', but without reaching it. One can show that there cannot be a deadlock since there is no cycle in the waiting relation.

At the end of the phase, each robot (except r_1) is located on its destination. The termination phase consist in moving r_1 to its destination so that the configuration forms the pattern F.

5. REFERENCES

[1] Zohir Bouzid and Anissa Lamani. Robot networks with homonyms: The case of patterns formation. In Xavier Défago, Franck Petit, and Vincent Villain, editors, *Stabilization, Safety, and Security of Distributed Systems*, volume 6976 of *Lecture Notes in Computer Science*, pages 92–107. Springer Berlin Heidelberg, 2011.

[2] Quentin Bramas and Sébastien Tixeuil. Asynchronous pattern formation without chirality. *CoRR*, abs/1508.03714, 2015.

[3] Paola Flocchini, Giuseppe Prencipe, Nicola Santoro, and Peter Widmayer. Arbitrary pattern formation by asynchronous, anonymous, oblivious robots. *Theor. Comput. Sci.*, 407(1-3):412–447, 2008.

[4] Giuseppe Prencipe. Impossibility of gathering by a set of autonomous mobile robots. *Theoretical Computer Science*, 384(2):222–231, 2007.

[5] Ichiro Suzuki and Masafumi Yamashita. Distributed anonymous mobile robots: Formation of geometric patterns. *SIAM J. Comput.*, 28(4):1347–1363, 1999.

[6] Yukiko Yamauchi and Masafumi Yamashita. Pattern formation by mobile robots with limited visibility. In Thomas Moscibroda and Adele A. Rescigno, editors, *Structural Information and Communication Complexity - 20th International Colloquium, SIROCCO 2013, Ischia, Italy, July 1-3, 2013, Revised Selected Papers*, volume 8179 of *Lecture Notes in Computer Science*, pages 201–212. Springer, 2013.

[7] Yukiko Yamauchi and Masafumi Yamashita. Randomized pattern formation algorithm for asynchronous oblivious mobile robots. In Fabian Kuhn, editor, *Distributed Computing*, volume 8784 of *Lecture Notes in Computer Science*, pages 137–151. Springer Berlin Heidelberg, 2014.

Brief Announcement: Pattern Formation Problem for Synchronous Mobile Robots in the Three Dimensional Euclidean Space

Yukiko Yamauchi Taichi Uehara Masafumi Yamashita

Graduate School of Information Science and Electrical Engineering, Kyushu University, Japan

{yamauchi, taichi.uehara, mak}@inf.kyushu-u.ac.jp

ABSTRACT

We investigate the *pattern formation problem* that requires a swarm of autonomous mobile robots to form a given target pattern in the three-dimensional Euclidean space. We show a necessary and sufficient condition for synchronous robots to form a given target pattern from an initial configuration. We give a pattern formation algorithm for solvable instances that does not need any local memory at each robot.

Keywords

Mobile robots; pattern formation; rotation group; symmetry breaking

1. INTRODUCTION

Distributed coordination of autonomous mobile computing entities, called robots, agents, or sensor nodes, in the three dimensional Euclidean space (3D-space), is one of the most challenging problems in distributed computing theory and robotics since real robots move in 3D-space. This paper considers the *pattern formation problem* that requires a swarm of robots to form a given 3D target pattern. A robot is an anonymous point in 3D-space that autonomously moves according to a common algorithm. We consider the *fully-synchronous (FSYNC)* model where the robots synchronously repeat a Look-Compute-Move cycle. Each robot has neither any access to the global x-y-z coordinate system nor any explicit communication medium.

The pattern formation problem was first introduced by Suzuki and Yamashita for robots in the two-dimensional Euclidean space (2D-space) [2, 3]. Let P be an initial configuration (i.e., the positions) of the robots without any multiplicity. We consider the decomposition of P into regular m-gons centered at the center $c(P)$ of the smallest enclosing circle of P. The symmetricity $\rho(P)$ of P is the maximum value of such m with an exception that when a single point of P is at $c(P)$, $\rho(P) = 1$. This exception is derived from an easy symmetry breaking algorithm; the robot on the center leaves its current position. Then they showed that FSYNC robots can form a target pattern F from an initial configuration P if and only if $\rho(P)$ divides $\rho(F)$. The impossibility result implies these symmetric $\rho(P)$ robots cannot break their rotational symmetry. Fujinaga et al. showed that asynchrony among the robots does not interfere their formation ability [1].

Yamauchi et al. considered a kind of formation problem in 3D-space, called the *plane formation problem*, and measured the rotational symmetry of the robots in 3D-space by using the *rotation groups* each of which is defined by a set of rotation axes and their arrangement [4]. However the symmetricity in 3D-space has not been discussed.

The contribution of this paper is twofold. First, we define the symmetricity in 3D-space. Then we give a necessary and sufficient condition for the FSYNC robots to accomplish the pattern formation problem in 3D-space. For the solvable instances, we present a pattern formation algorithm that requires no local memory at each robot. We finally note that our results are generalization of existing results in 2D-space [2, 3] to 3D-space.

2. PRELIMINARY

Let R be a set of $n \geq 3$ robots each of which is represented by a point in 3D-space. By Z_0 we denote the global x-y-z coordinate system. A *configuration* $P(t)$ of R at time t is a multiset of positions of these n points observed in Z_0. We assume that the robots initially occupy distinct positions. The robots have no access to Z_0. Instead, each robot $r_i \in R$ observes the positions of other robots in its local x-y-z coordinate system Z_i, where the origin is always its current position, while the direction of each axis and the magnitude of the unit distance are arbitrary but never change. We assume that Z_0 and all Z_i are right-handed. Thus Z_i is either a uniform scaling, transformation, rotation, or their combination of Z_0.

We consider discrete time $0, 1, 2, \cdots$ and at each time step the robots execute a Look-Compute-Move cycle with each of the Look, Compute, and Move phases completely synchronized, i.e., we consider the *fully-synchronous (FSYNC)* model. At time t, each $r_i \in R$ obtains a multiset $Z_i(P(t))$ in the Look phase. Then r_i computes its next position by using an algorithm ψ, which is common to all robots. If ψ uses only $Z_i(P(t))$, we say that r_i is *oblivious*, and *non-oblivious* otherwise. Finally, r_i moves to $\psi(Z_i(P(t)))$ in Z_i before time $t + 1$. An infinite sequence of configurations $\mathcal{E} : P(0), P(1), \ldots$ is called an *execution* from an *initial configuration* $P(0)$.

The *pattern formation problem* requires the robots to form

PODC'16 July 25-28, 2016, Chicago, IL, USA

ACM ISBN 978-1-4503-3964-3/16/07.

DOI: http://dx.doi.org/10.1145/2933057.2933063

a given target pattern F from a given initial configuration. The target pattern F is given to each robot as a set of coordinates of n points in Z_0. Because the robots do not know Z_0, we allow rotation, translation, uniform scaling, and their combination on F. We say that the robots form a target pattern F from an initial configuration P, if, regardless of the choice of local coordinate systems and local memory contents (if any) of robots in the initial configuration, any execution $P(0)(= P), P(1), \ldots$ reaches a configuration $P(t)$ that is similar to F in finite time.

For any (multi)set of points P, by $B(P)$ and $b(P)$, we denote the *smallest enclosing ball* of P and its center, respectively. We say that a set of points form a polyhedron when the points occupy the vertices of the polyhedron.

3. SYMMETRICITY IN 3D-SPACE

The rotation group $SO(3)$ has five kinds of subgroups of finite order; the cyclic group C_k ($k = 2, 3, \cdots$), the dihedral group D_ℓ ($\ell = 2, 3, \cdots$), the tetrahedral group T, the octahedral group O, and the icosahedral group I, which are identified by the group formed by rotations on a regular pyramid with a regular k-gon base, a regular prism with regular ℓ-gon bases, a regular tetrahedron, a regular octahedron, and a regular icosahedron, respectively. (See Figure 1.) More precisely, each rotation group is defined by a set of *rotation axes* and their arrangement. A rotation axis that admits rotations by $2i\pi/k$ for $i = 0, 1, \cdots, k-1$ is called a k-fold axis.

Let $\mathbb{S} = \{C_k, D_\ell, T, O, I \mid k = 1, 2, \ldots, and\, \ell = 2, 3, \ldots\}$ be the set of rotation groups, where C_1 consists of the identity element (i.e., 1-fold rotation). We denote the order of $G \in \mathbb{S}$ by $|G|$. For example, $|T| = 12$, $|O| = 24$, and $|I| = 60$. When G' is a subgroup of G, we denote it by $G' \preceq G$.

DEFINITION 1. *Let P be a set of n points. The rotation group $\gamma(P)$ of P is the rotation group in $\mathbb{S}$ that acts on P and none of its proper supergroup in $\mathbb{S}$ acts on P.*

We say a rotation axis of $\gamma(P)$ is *occupied* when it contains some point of P and *unoccupied* otherwise. For a point $p \in P$, let $Orb(p) = \{g * p \in P : g \in \gamma(P)\}$ be the orbit of the group action of $\gamma(P)$ through p. Then we let $\{P_1, P_2, \ldots, P_m\} = \{Orb(p) : p \in P\}$ be its orbit space. Because $\gamma(P)$ is unique, such partition is also unique and we call it the *$\gamma(P)$-decomposition* of P [4]. When $\gamma(P)$-decomposition of P consists of one element, we say P is *transitive* regarding $\gamma(P)$.

For two groups $G, H \in \mathbb{S}$, an *embedding* of G to H is an embedding of each rotation axis of G to one of the rotation axes of H so that any k-fold axis of G overlaps a k'-fold axis of H satisfying $k|k'$ with keeping the arrangement, where $a|b$ represents that a divides b. Observe that we can embed G to H if and only if $G \preceq H$. For a set of points P, an embedding of $G \preceq \gamma(P)$ ($G \in \mathbb{S}$) to $\gamma(P)$ determines a decomposition of P into disjoint subsets by its group action in the same way as the $\gamma(P)$-decomposition of P. We call such decomposition a *G-decomposition* of P.

DEFINITION 2. *Let P be a set of n points. The symmetricity $\varrho(P)$ of P is the set of rotation groups $G \in \mathbb{S}$ that acts on P (thus $G \preceq \gamma(P)$) and there exists an embedding of G to $\gamma(P)$ such that each element of the G-decomposition of P is a $|G|$-set.*

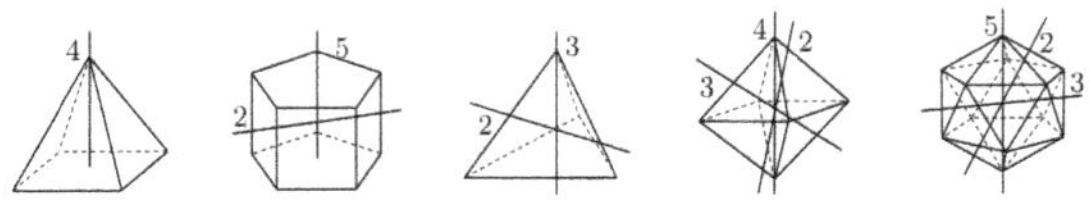

(a) C_4 (b) D_5 (c) T (d) O (e) I

Figure 1: Five kinds of rotation groups.

For each $G \in \varrho(P)$, there exists an arrangement of local coordinate systems of the robots on which G acts. Thus $\varrho(P)$ captures all rotation groups that the robots may forever keep. In other words, for each $G \in \varrho(P)$, $|G|$ robots may forever move symmetrically. From the definition, $\varrho(P)$ always contains C_1 and for any $G \in \varrho(P)$, $\varrho(P)$ contains every $G' \preceq G$ ($G' \in \mathbb{S}$). Because any initial configuration P is a set of n points, $\varrho(P)$ is the set of rotation groups $G \in \mathbb{S}$ that has an embedding to unoccupied rotation axes of $\gamma(P)$.

4. OUR RESULTS

In this section, we will show our main result that characterizes the pattern formation problem in 3D-space.

THEOREM 1. *Regardless of obliviousness, FSYNC robots can form a target pattern F from an initial configuration P if and only if $\varrho(P) \subseteq \varrho(F)$.*

We will show the necessity of Theorem 1 in Section 4.1 and the sufficiency in Section 4.2.

4.1 Necessity

LEMMA 1. *Regardless of obliviousness, FSYNC robots can form a target pattern F from an initial configuration P only if $\varrho(P) \subseteq \varrho(F)$.*

PROOF. (Sketch.) We first consider oblivious FSYNC robots. Assume that there exits a pattern formation algorithm ψ for an initial configuration P and a target pattern F such that $\varrho(P) \not\subseteq \varrho(F)$. There exists $G \in \varrho(P)$ such that $G \notin \varrho(F)$. There exists an arrangement of local coordinate systems of the robots such that G acts on P and the local coordinate systems of the robots. Let $P(0)(= P), P(1), \cdots$ be the execution starting from P with such local coordinate systems. For each element of the G-decomposition of P, these $|G|$ robots forever move symmetrically regarding G. Assume that the robots form F in $P(t^*)$. Thus $P(t^*)$ consists of $|H|$ symmetric points regarding any $H \in \varrho(F)$. However, we have $G \notin \varrho(F)$, a contradiction.

Even when the robots are equipped with memory, non-obliviousness does not help when the robots have common initial memory content. □

4.2 Sufficiency

We present a pattern formation algorithm ψ_{PF} that makes oblivious FSYNC robots form a target pattern F from an initial configuration P if P and F satisfy the condition of Theorem 1. Non-oblivious robots can also execute ψ_{PF} by ignoring local memory contents.

Algorithm ψ_{PF} consists of three phases: The first phase translates P into another configuration P' that satisfies $\gamma(P') \in \varrho(P)$. The second phase makes the robots agree on an embedding of F into P' so that the embedded target pattern $\widetilde{F}$ satisfies $b(\widetilde{F}) = b(P')$ and $B(\widetilde{F}) = B(P')$. Finally, the

Algorithm 4.1 `Go-to-center`(P) for robot $r_i \in R$

Notation

P: Configuration of the robots forming one of the seven polyhedra.

p_i: Current position of r_i.

ϵ: Arbitrarily small distance, e.g., $\ell/100$ where ℓ is the length of an edge of the polyhedron that P forms.

Algorithm

Switch (P) **do**

Case P forms a cuboctahedron:

Select an adjacent triangle face.

Destination d is the point ϵ before the center of the selected face on the line from p_i to the center.

Case P forms an icosidodecahedron:

Select an adjacent pentagon face.

Destination d is the point ϵ before the center of the selected face on the line from p_i to the center.

Default:

Select an adjacent face.

Destination d is the point ϵ before the center of the selected face on the line from p_i to the center.

Enddo

third phase gives each robot its final position by making the robots agree on a perfect matching between P' and $\widetilde{F}$, denoted by $M(P', \widetilde{F})$.

In [4], it has been shown that for a set of points P, there exists an ordering of the elements of the $\gamma(P)$-decomposition $\{P_1, P_2, \ldots, P_m\}$ of P so that P_1 is nearest to $b(P)$, P_m is on $B(P)$, and P_{i+1} is not in the interior of the ball centered at $b(P)$ and containing P_i on it. Additionally, the robots can agree on such ordering. This ordering allows ψ_{PF} to concentrate on each element of the $\gamma(P)$-decomposition of a current configuration P. In the following, we assume that $\{P_1, P_2, \ldots, P_m\}$ is ordered in this way.

4.2.1 First phase: Symmetry breaking

In the first phase, robots execute a symmetry breaking algorithm ψ_{SYM} that translates an initial configuration P into another configuration P' that satisfies $\gamma(P') \in \varrho(P)$. Hence we focus on the robots on the rotation axes of $\gamma(P)$.

We start with a symmetry breaking algorithm for transitive configurations regarding T, O, and I, i.e., when the robots form a regular tetrahedron, a regular octahedron, a cube, a cuboctahedron, a regular icosahedron, a regular dodecahedron, or an icosidodecahedron. Algorithm 4.1 shows the symmetry breaking algorithm for a configuration P forming one of these seven polyhedra, which is based on the "go-to-center" algorithm [4]. The resulting configuration P' satisfies $\gamma(P') \in \varrho(P)$. Intuitively, candidates of the next positions of the robots form a transitive set of points of size $|\gamma(P)|$. Thus, to keep $\gamma(P)$, there should be $|\gamma(P)|$ robots while the number of robots is less than $|\gamma(P)|$. By more careful argument, we can show the following lemma.

LEMMA 2. *Let P be an arbitrary initial configuration that forms one of the seven regular polyhedra. One step execution of Algorithm 4.1 translates P into another configuration P' that satisfies $\gamma(P') \in \varrho(P)$.*

Algorithm ψ_{SYM} determines the ordering among the occupied rotation axis of an initial configuration P and makes the robots on each type (i.e., fold) of the rotation axes leave them according to the order. Such robots form an element of the $\gamma(P)$-decomposition of P. If the robots are on the selected rotation axes form one of the above seven polyhedra, ψ_{SYM} makes them execute Algorithm 4.1. Otherwise the robots just leave the rotation axes. We can show that ψ_{SYM} gradually eliminates the occupied rotation axes of $\gamma(P)$ without adding any new rotation axis and translates P into another configuration P' that satisfies (i) $\gamma(P') \in \varrho(P)$ and (ii) all rotation axes of $\gamma(P')$ are unoccupied. Additionally, the robots can agree on the termination of ψ_{SYM}.

4.2.2 Second phase: Agreement of $\widetilde{F}$

Let P' be a terminal configuration of ψ_{SYM}. From the first property of the terminal configuration of ψ_{SYM}, we have $\gamma(P') \in \varrho(F)$. Thus there exists an embedding of $\gamma(P')$ to unoccupied rotation axes of $\gamma(F)$. Algorithm ψ_{PF} first embeds F into P' so that $\gamma(P')$ overlaps unoccupied rotation axes of $\gamma(F)$. We denote the embedded target pattern by $\widetilde{F}$. The size of $\widetilde{F}$ is determined so that $b(P') = b(\widetilde{F})$ and $B(P') = B(\widetilde{F})$ hold. Clearly, the robots can agree on $\widetilde{F}$.

4.2.3 Third phase: Matching $M(P', \widetilde{F})$

We consider the rotation group of $P' \cup \widetilde{F}$ that matches the points of P' to P' and those of $\widetilde{F}$ to $\widetilde{F}$. We have $\gamma(P' \cup \widetilde{F}) = \gamma(P')$. The group action of $\gamma(P')$ divides P' and $\widetilde{F}$ to disjoint subsets of size $|\gamma(P')|$ and the robots can agree on the ordering of these elements in the same way as [4]. Let $\{P'_1, P'_2, \ldots, P'_m\}$ and $\{\widetilde{F}_1, \widetilde{F}_2, \ldots, \widetilde{F}_m\}$ be the elements of P' and those of $\widetilde{F}$ that appear in the entire decomposition in this order. Then ψ_{PF} sends the robots forming P'_i to the positions of $\widetilde{F}_i$ for $1 \le i \le m$. In each element P'_i, each robot selects the nearest point in $\widetilde{F}_i$ as its destination. We denote the entire matching obtained with these rules by $M(P', \widetilde{F})$. Finally, the robots move to the corresponding positions in $M(P', \widetilde{F})$ to complete the pattern formation.

Acknowledgment

This work was supported by JSPS KAKENHI (No.15H00821 and No.15H02666) and Grant-in-Aid for Scientific Research on Innovative Areas " Molecular Robotics " (No.24104003) of MEXT, Japan.

5. REFERENCES

[1] N. Fujinaga, Y. Yamauchi, H. Ono, S. Kijima, and M. Yamashita, Pattern formation by oblivious asynchronous mobile robots, *SIAM J. Comput.*, 44, 3, pp.740–785, 2015.

[2] I. Suzuki and M. Yamashita, Distributed anonymous mobile robots: Formation of geometric patterns, *SIAM J. Comput.*, 28, 4, pp.1347–1363, 1999.

[3] M. Yamashita and I. Suzuki, Characterizing geometric patterns formable by oblivious anonymous mobile robots, *Theor. Comput. Sci.*, 411, pp.2433–2453, 2010.

[4] Y. Yamauchi, T. Uehara, S. Kijima, and M. Yamashita, Plane formation by synchronous mobile robots in the three dimensional Euclidean space, *In Proc. of DISC 2015*, pp.92-106, 2015.

Low-Congestion Shortcuts without Embedding*

Bernhard Haeupler
School of Computer Science
Carnegie Mellon University
Pittsburgh, PA 15213, USA
haeupler@cs.cmu.edu

Taisuke Izumi
Nagoya Institute of Technology
Nagoya, Aichi Prefecture
466-8555, Japan
t-izumi@nitech.ac.jp

Goran Zuzic
School of Computer Science
Carnegie Mellon University
Pittsburgh, PA 15213, USA
gzuzic@cs.cmu.edu

ABSTRACT

Distributed optimization algorithms are frequently faced with solving sub-problems on disjoint connected parts of a network. Unfortunately, the diameter of these parts can be significantly larger than the diameter of the underlying network, leading to slow running times. Recent work by [Ghaffari and Hauepler; SODA'16] showed that this phenomenon can be seen as the broad underlying reason for the pervasive $\Omega(\sqrt{n}+D)$ lower bounds that apply to most optimization problems in the CONGEST model. On the positive side, this work also introduced low-congestion shortcuts as an elegant solution to circumvent this problem in certain topologies of interest. Particularly, they showed that there exist good shortcuts for any planar network and more generally any bounded genus network. This directly leads to fast $O(D\log^{O(1)} n)$ distributed optimization algorithms on such topologies, e.g., for MST and Min-Cut approximation, given that one can efficiently construct these shortcuts in a distributed manner.

Unfortunately, the shortcut construction of [Ghaffari and Hauepler; SODA'16] relies heavily on having access to a bounded genus embedding of the network. Computing such an embedding distributedly, however, is a hard problem - even for planar networks. No distributed embedding algorithm for bounded genus graphs is in sight.

In this work, we side-step this problem by defining a slightly restricted and more structured form of shortcuts and giving a novel construction algorithm which efficiently finds a shortcut which is, up to a logarithmic factor, as good as the best shortcut that exists for a given network. This new construction algorithm directly leads to an $O(D\log^{O(1)} n)$-round algorithm for solving optimization problems like MST for any topology for which good restricted shortcuts exist - without the need to compute any embedding. This includes the first efficient algorithm for bounded genus graphs.

CCS Concepts

•**Mathematics of computing** → *Network optimization;*
•**Theory of computation** → *Distributed computing models; Graph algorithms analysis;*

Keywords

low-congestion shortcuts; planar graphs; bounded-genus graphs; MST; CONGEST model

1. INTRODUCTION

1.1 Background and Motivation

Consider the problem of finding the minimum spanning tree (MST) on a distributed network with n independent processing nodes. The network is abstracted as a graph $G=(V,E)$ with n nodes and diameter D. The nodes communicate by synchronously passing $O(\log n)$-bit messages to each of its direct neighbors. The goal is to design algorithms (protocols) that minimize the number of synchronous message passing rounds before the nodes collaboratively solve the optimization problem.

The message-passing setting we just described is a model called CONGEST [21]. The MST problem can be solved in such a setting using $O(\sqrt{n}\log^* n+D)$ rounds of communication [13]. Moreover, and perhaps more surprisingly, this bound was shown to be the best possible (up to polylogarithmic factors). Specifically, there are graphs in which one cannot do any better than $\tilde{\Omega}(\sqrt{n}+D)$ [1, 3, 22]. While clearly no algorithm can solve any global network optimization problem faster than $\Omega(D)$, the $\tilde{\Omega}(\sqrt{n})$ factor is harder to discern. To make matters worse, the $\tilde{\Omega}(\sqrt{n}+D)$ lower bound was shown to be far reaching. It applies to a multitude of important network optimization problems including MST, minimum-cut, weighted shortest-path, connectivity verification and so on [1]

While this bound precludes the existence of more efficient algorithms in the general case, it was not clear does it hold for special families of graphs. This question is especially important because any real-world application on huge networks should exploit the special structure that the network provides. The mere existence of "hard" networks for which one cannot design any fast algorithm might not be a limiting factor.

*This work was supported in part by KAKENHI No. 15H00852 and 16H02878 as well as NSF grants CCF-1527110 "Distributed Algorithms for Near Planar Networks" and NSF-BSF grant "Coding for Distributed Computing".

PODC'16, July 25 - 28, 2016, Chicago, IL, USA

ISBN 978-1-4503-3964-3/16/07...$15.00

DOI: http://dx.doi.org/10.1145/2933057.2933112

In the first result that utilizes network topology to circumvent the lower bound, Haeupler and Ghaffari designed an $O(D\log^{O(1)} n)$-round distributed MST algorithm for planar graphs [7]. Note that this algorithm offers a huge advantage over older results for planar graphs with small diameters.

They achieve this by introducing an elegant abstraction for designing distributed algorithms named **low-congestion shortcuts**. Their methods could in principle be used to achieve a similar result for genus-bounded graphs, but their presented algorithms have a major technical obstacle: they require a surface embedding of the planar/genus bounded graph to construct the low-congestion shortcuts. While computing a distributed embedding for planar graphs has a complex $O(D\log^{O(1)} n)$-round solution [6], this remains an open problem for genus-bounded graphs [7].

This paper side-steps the issue by vastly simplifying the construction of low-congestion shortcuts. We define a more structured version of low-congestion shortcuts called **tree-restricted shortcuts** and propose a simple and general distributed algorithm for finding them. The algorithm is completely oblivious to any intricacies of the underlying topology and finds universally near-optimal tree-restricted shortcuts. As a simple consequence of our construction technique we get a $O(gD\log^{O(1)} n)$-round algorithm for genus g graphs, which is a novel result. We believe that this simplicity makes the algorithm usable even in practice.

1.2 A Brief Overview of Low-Congestion Shortcuts

We now give a short introduction to the general low-congestion shortcuts as defined in [7]. Consider the following scenario, which is a recurring theme throughout distributed approaches for many network optimization problems:

> *A graph G is partitioned into a number of disjoint individually-connected* ***parts*** $P_1, P_2, ..., P_N$*, and we need to compute a (typically simple) function for each of the parts in isolation.*

A classical example for such a scenario is the 1926 algorithm of Boruvka [20] for computing Minimum Spanning Tree (MST): starting with a trivial partition of each node being its own part, in every iteration each part computes the minimum-weighted outgoing edge and merges with the part incident to this edge. After $O(\log n)$ iterations, we arrive at the MST, where n is the number of nodes in G.

A key concern in designing a distributed version of Boruvka's algorithm is finding good communication schemes that allow each part to collaborate with other nodes inside the same part and without interference from other parts. While a natural solution would be to allow communication only inside the same part, this could take a long time. The problem appears when the diameter of a part in isolation is much larger than the diameter D of the original graph G.

To overcome this issue, Ghaffari and Haeupler [7] introduced **low-congestion shortcuts**: each part P_i is given a subgraph of extra edges H_i that it can use to more efficiently communicate within itself. More precisely, each part P_i is associated with a **shortcut subgraph** H_i and is permitted to use $G[P_i] + H_i$ for communication.

To measure the quality of a shortcut, we characterize it with two quality parameters: **congestion** and **dilation**. A shortcut has congestion c and dilation d if *i)* the diameter of every subgraph $G[P_i] + H_i$ is at most d, and *ii)* every edge is assigned to at most c different subgraphs $G[P_i] + H_i$. Given a shortcut with congestion c and dilation d, we can solve problems such as MST and Min-Cut approximation in $O((c + d)\log^{O(1)} n)$ rounds [7]. Therefore, designing a distributed algorithm can be reduced to finding good-quality shortcuts.

While the pervasive $\Omega(\sqrt{n} + D)$ lower bound clearly implies we cannot find shortcuts with congestion + dilation = $O(D)$ on general graphs, this might not be the case on specific families of graphs. For example, planar graphs always offer $O(D\log^{O(1)} D)$ congestion and dilation shortcuts, thus bypassing the $\tilde{\Omega}(\sqrt{n} + D)$ lower bound[7].

1.3 Our Contribution

Roughly speaking, there are two challenges in the design of shortcut-based algorithms. Let $\mathcal{G}$ be the target class we want to design distributed algorithms. The first challenge is to identify the (small) values of c and d such that $\mathcal{G}$ has shortcuts with congestion c and dilation d. This is purely a graph-theoretic problem. The second challenge is to convert the existential result proved by the first challenge to the constructive result, i.e., we must design a distributed algorithm constructing efficient shortcuts for that class. This is a distinct problem of theoretical distributed computing.

A natural idea of lowering the barrier of the algorithm design is to invent a generic algorithm which finds a congestion c and dilation d shortcut for the best (or approximately best) c and d, which provides an automatic conversion of the existential result to the constructive one. Unfortunately, the known construction for planar graphs [7] is far from such a generality: as we already mentioned, It strongly depends on the distributed planar embedding algorithm [6], and thus not applicable to any other graph class. This is also a primary reason why the construction for planar graphs in [7] cannot be extended even for bounded genus graphs.

The primary contribution of this paper is to present a new generic algorithm for constructing shortcuts, which partially resolve the issue mentioned above. While our algorithm does not cover all existential results, it is applicable to an interesting and useful case – **tree-restricted shortcuts**, which is a class of shortcuts newly defined in this paper. The details of our contribution are summarized as follows:

- In Section 4 we introduce a new class of shortcuts, called tree-restricted shortcuts, which only use edges of some fixed spanning tree $T \subseteq G$. More precisely, $H_i \subseteq T$ for each part P_i. We introduce a new quality parameter called **block parameter**, which is defined as an upper bound on the number of connected components of H_i that intersect P_i (over all $i \in [N]$). Note that these components are subtrees of T. The block parameter can be seen as a stronger version of dilation and will often be used instead. In Section 4.3 we propose deterministic algorithms for broadcast, convergecast, and leader election (for all parts in parallel) utilizing tree-restricted shortcuts, which are, simpler and faster compared with the general-case randomized algorithms shown in [7].

- In Section 5 we present a generic algorithm for constructing tree-restricted shortcuts. Let T be a spanning tree of G with depth D and assume there exists a tree-restricted shortcut on $T \subseteq G$ with congestion c and block parameter b. We describe an algorithm that constructs a tree-restricted shortcut with congestion $O(c \log N)$ and block parameter $O(b)$ in $O(D \log n \log N + bD \log N + bc \log N)$ CONGEST rounds. It is also possible to run our algorithm in the environment where the system is not aware of the value of b and/or c with extra $\log(bc)$ factor, as described in Section 6.

- An important consequence of our algorithm is to provide the first distributed algorithm constructing a good shortcut for genus-g graphs. Fortunately, the known result for genus-g graphs exhibits the existence of tree-restricted shortcuts with congestion $O(gD \log D)$ and block parameter $O(\log D)$ for an arbitrary BFS tree T of depth D. Thus in Section 4.4 we can obtain a distributed algorithm constructing a tree-restricted shortcut with congestion $O(gD \log D \log N)$ and block $O(\log D)$ for graphs with genus at most g. For bounded genus graphs (i.e. $g = O(1)$), the algorithms based on our shortcut construction achieves the near-optimal time complexity (up to a polylogarithmic factor). According to the very recent unpublished result that is still in preparation, a similar result is obtained for graphs with bounded pathwidth and treewidth.

2. RELATED WORK

The complexity theoretic issues in the design of distributed graph algorithms for the CONGEST model have received much attention in the last decade, and got an extensive progress for many problems: Minimum-spanning tree [5, 12, 13, 22], Maximum flow [8], Minimum Cut [9, 19], Shortest paths and Diameter [4, 10, 11, 15, 16, 17, 18], and so on. Most of those problems have $\tilde{\Theta}(\sqrt{n} + D)$-round upper and lower bounds for some sort of approximation guarantee [1, 2, 9, 15, 22]. The guarantee of exact results sometimes yield a nearly liner-time bound [4]. Note that almost all lower bounds above holds for small diameter graphs. Thus, in any case, the general lower bound is more expensive than the universal lower bound of $\Omega(D)$ rounds.

On the positive side, distributed algorithms typically use a variety of ideas. In an effort to unify them in an elegant framework, Ghaffari and Haeupler introduced **low-congestion shortcuts** [7]. Specifically, their ideas can be turned into a very short and clean $O((D + \sqrt{n}) \log n)$ round MST algorithm for general graphs. Furthermore, low-congestion shortcuts can serve as a simple explanation of the pervasive $\tilde{\Omega}(D + \sqrt{n})$ lower bound. However, the main contribution of their techniques is a $\tilde{O}(D)$-round algorithm for planar graphs. To the best of our knowledge, it is the first attempt that considers a non-trivial popular graph class.

3. PRELIMINARIES

In this section, we formally define the CONGEST model and then recap the definitions of low-congestion shortcuts from [7].

3.1 CONGEST Model

We work in the classical CONGEST model [21]. In this setting, a network is given as a connected undirected graph $G = (V, E_G)$ with diameter D. Initially, nodes only know their immediate neighbors and they collaborate to compute some global function of the graph like the MST. Communication occurs in synchronous rounds; during a round, each node can send $O(\log n)$ bits to each of its neighbors (note that the nodes also know some polynomially tight bound on n, otherwise sending $O(\log n)$ bits does not make sense). The nodes always correctly follow the protocol and never fail. The goal is to design protocols that minimize the resource of time - the number of rounds before the nodes compute the solution.

We now precisely formalize the notion of solving a problem in this model, e.g. how is the input and output given. While the formalization is specifically given for the MST, any other problem is completely analogous. All nodes synchronously wake up in the first round and start executing some given protocol. Every node initially only knows its immediate neighbors and the weight of each of its incident edges. After a specific number of rounds, all nodes must simultaneously output *i)* the weight of the computed MST τ *ii)* for each edge e incident to it, a 0/1 bit indicating if $e \in \tau$.

3.2 Low-Congestion Shortcuts

Let G be a undirected graph along with a node partition $\mathcal{P} = (P_1, P_2, ..., P_N)$. **Low-congestion shortcuts** intuitively augment each part P_i with extra edges H_i that may be used to communicate within a part more efficiently. With a small abuse of notation, in the following we use the symbol H_i to indicate both the edge set and the subgraph induced by the set. As communication for part P_i occurs on $G[P_i] + H_i$, it is natural to try to minimize the diameters of those subgraphs. Hence we define **dilation** as an upper bound on the diameter of any shortcut subgraph $G[P_i] + H_i$. On the other hand, assigning an edge to almost every part will lead to over-congestion on that edge. Therefore, we define another quality measure of a shortcut, **congestion**, as an upper bound on the number of shortcut subgraphs $G[P_i] + H_i$ that contain any edge e.

Definition 1. Let $G = (V, E_G)$ be an undirected graph with vertices subdivided into **disjoint and connected** subsets $\mathcal{P} = (P_1, P_2, ..., P_N), P_i \subseteq V$. In other words, $G[P_i]$ is connected and $P_i \cap P_j = \emptyset$ for $i \neq j$. The subsets P_i are called **parts**. We define a **shortcut** $\mathcal{H}$ as a tuple of N **shortcut subgraphs** $(H_1, H_2, ..., H_N)$, $H_i \subseteq G$. A shortcut is characterized by the following parameters:

i) $\mathcal{H}$ has congestion c if each edge $e \in E_G$ is used in at most c different subgraphs $G[P_i] + H_i$, i.e. $\forall e \in E_T : |\{i : e \in H_i\}| \leq c$.

ii) $\mathcal{H}$ has dilation d if the diameter of any subgraph $G[P_i] + H_i$ is at most d.

The parameters determine the efficiency of communications facilitated by the shortcut. For example, Ghaffari and Haeupler show in [7] that one can solve the Minimum Spanning Tree and Min-Cut problems in $O((\text{congestion} + \text{dilation}) \log^{O(1)} n)$, given an efficient algorithm for finding shortcuts with parameters congestion and dilation. Note that congestion and dilation are traditional parameters that are extensively used in routing [7, 14].

4. TREE-RESTRICTED SHORTCUTS

In this section, we define tree-restricted shortcuts: a narrower notion of shortcuts which are *i)* simpler to work with,

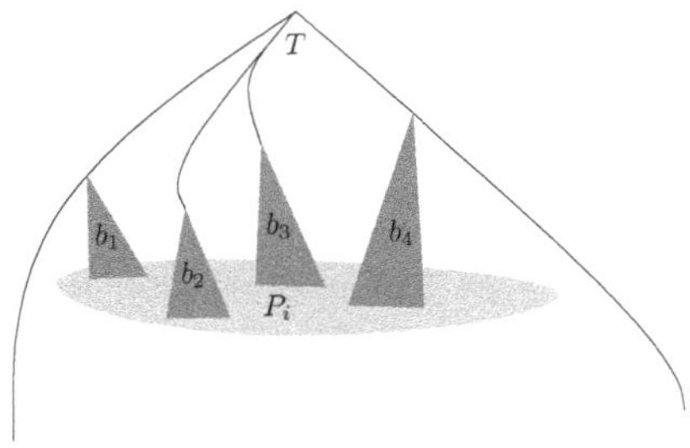

Figure 1: Illustration of a T-restricted shortcut subgraph with respect to the part P_i, composed of block components b_1, b_2, b_3 and b_4.

ii) often equally powerful as the general shortcuts, *iii)* offer deterministic routing schemes and, most importantly, *iv)* can be efficiently constructed on any graph that contains them. Following the definitions, we rephrase the results of [7] in our new terms, showcase an efficient deterministic routing scheme on them, and finally state our main result and show its applications.

4.1 Definition

Tree-restricted shortcuts are shortcuts with the additional property that any shortcut subgraph H_i is restricted to some spanning tree T. The user of the shortcut can typically fix any tree T, so a cogent choice would be the BFS tree because of its optimal depth.

Definition 2. Let $\mathcal{H} = (H_1, H_2, ..., H_N)$ be a T-restricted shortcut on the graph $G = (V, E_G)$ with respect to the parts $\mathcal{P} = (P_i)_{i=1}^N$. Given a rooted spanning tree $T = (V, E_T) \subseteq G$ we say that a shortcut $\mathcal{H}$ is **T-restricted** if for each $i \in [N], H_i \subseteq E_T$ i.e. every edge of H_i is a tree edge of T.

Congestion and dilation are still well-defined for tree-restricted shortcuts. However, it is more convenient to use an alternative **block parameter** in place of dilation. The block parameter upper-bounds the number of connected components of each H_i that intersects P_i. Note that, while $G[P_i]$ and therefore $G[P_i] + H$ are connected, H_i by itself might not be. The intersection property ensures that we do not count components that have no vertices in P_i.

Definition 3. Let $\mathcal{H} = (H_1, H_2, ..., H_N)$ be a T-restricted shortcut on the graph $G = (V, E_G)$ with respect to the parts $\mathcal{P} = (P_i)_{i=1}^N$. Fix a part P_i and consider the connected components of the spanning subgraph (V, H_i). If such a connected component intersects P_i we call it a **block component**. Furthermore, we define the **block parameter** b of $\mathcal{H}$ to be any upper bound to the number of block components for all parts.

A block parameter implies a bound on dilation, hence the block parameter can be seen as a stronger measure of quality. Lemma 1 argues that a block parameter of b implies the dilation of $b(2 \cdot \text{depth}(T) + 1)$. The Lemma also suggests that it is often beneficial to fix T to a BFS tree of G, thereby having asymptotically minimal depth. In that case, the depth of T is at most the diameter of the original graph, namely D. For this reason throughout this paper we denote the diameter of G and the depth of T by the same symbol D.

LEMMA 1. *Let T be a spanning tree with depth D and let $\mathcal{H} = (H_i : i \in [N])$ be a T-restricted shortcut with congestion c and block parameter b with respect to parts $\mathcal{P} = (P_i : i \in [N])$. Then the dilation of $\mathcal{H}$ is at most $b(2D + 1)$.*

PROOF. Fix $i \in [N]$. If we contract every block component of H_i into a supernode and remove all other nodes, supergraph will contain $b' \leq b$ supernodes and will be connected (because $G[P_i]$ is connected). Hence its diameter is $b' - 1 \leq b - 1$. Every supernode consists of a block component of diameter $2D$, so the diameter of H_i is at most $2bD + b - 1 < b(2D + 1)$. □

Distributed representation of a tree-restricted shortcut: Before we proceed to describe algorithms for shortcut routing and construction, we quickly specify here more precisely how a shortcut is represented distributively, i.e., what information regarding the shortcut any node is supposed to know in order to make the various routing algorithms on top of a shortcut efficient.

Formally, we say that a T-restricted shortcut $\mathcal{H}$ is computed when each node v knows *i)* T-depth each of its neighbors and itself *ii)* subset of incident edges that are tree edges of T *iii)* all the part IDs that can use v's parent edge as well as the depth of their respective block component root. For the sake of clarity, the described construction algorithms do not go into details about the computation of each of those properties. However, they can be easily augmented to compute them explicitly.

4.2 Shortcuts on Genus-Bounded and Planar Graphs

Tree-restricted shortcuts are particularly useful on genus-bounded (e.g. planar) graphs. In particular, we can reinterpret the low-congestion result of Haeupler and Ghaffari [7] using our notation.

THEOREM 1 (HAEUPLER AND GHAFFARI [7]). *Let G be a graph with genus g and diameter D, and let T be any tree with depth D (e.g. BFS tree). There exists a T-restricted shortcut with congestion $O(gD \log D)$ and block parameter $O(\log D)$.*

The paper originally also provided a $O(D \log D)$ upper bound on the dilation of the shortcut. However, this bound can be implicitly recovered from Lemma 1 and block parameter $O(\log D)$. Note that the Theorem proves only the existence of such shortcuts. While the original paper does describe an algorithm that can in principle be used to compute them, it requires an embedding of G on a surface of genus g. It is an open problem to compute such an embedding efficiently in the CONGEST model [7].

4.3 Routing on Tree-Restricted Shortcuts

In this section, we show how to use tree-restricted shortcuts to efficiently communicate within parts. The tree-restricted structure of the shortcut allows for simpler and more efficient routing methods than general shortcuts. The main reason for this is that distributed approaches for various network optimization problems often use broadcasting and convergecasting as primitives. However, such tasks can be efficiently and deterministically solved on subtrees, even when multiple (non-disjoint) subtrees have to execute the task in parallel. Lemma 2 formalizes this statement.

LEMMA 2 (ROUTING ON TREES). *Let T be a tree of depth D. Given a family of subtrees such that any edge of T is contained in at most c subtrees, there is a simple deterministic algorithm that can perform a convergecast/broadcast on all of the subtrees in $O(D+c)$ CONGEST rounds.*

Specifically, for convergecasts, if multiple messages are scheduled over the same edge, the algorithm forwards the packet with the smallest depth of the subtree root, breaking ties with the smallest ID of the subtree.

PROOF. The convergecast and broadcasts operations are symmetric, so we will only prove the Lemma for convergecasts.

Let v be a node of T. We will prove that no message gets transmitted along v's parent edge after $h_v + c$ rounds where h_v is the height of v (distance to the farthest leaf in its subtree). Note that any message that gets transmitted along v's parent edge must belong to a subtree that contains that edge. Let $\mathcal{S}_v = (s_1, s_2, ..., s_k)$ be the tuple of subtrees that contain v's parent edge, ordered by their priority (as described in the statement). In particular, we say that s_i has priority i in node v. The congestion condition stipulates that $k \leq c$.

We will prove by induction that for $i \in [k]$ the message associated with s_i will be transmitted no later than after $h_v + i$ rounds. The claim clearly holds for the leafs of T. Note that *i)* the relative priority-ordering between elements $\mathcal{S}_v$ is unchanged in any node of T *ii)* any subtree $s \notin \mathcal{S}_v$ that contains any child of v will have lower priority than any subtree in $\mathcal{S}_v$.

Fix s_i. By the time $h_v + i$, all of the messages corresponding to $\{s_1, ..., s_{i-1}\}$ will be sent by the induction hypothesis, so it is sufficient to argue that at time $h_v + i$, v has received messages corresponding to s_i from all of its children contained in s_i. But this is exactly the induction hypothesis as for any child w, its height $h_w \leq h_v - 1$ and the priority of s_i is at most i or $w \notin s_i$. Hence v will send the message corresponding to s_i in round h_v or before. □

Convergecasting/broadcasting on a tree is helpful in tree-restricted shortcut routing because we can intuitively envision each shortcut subgraph H_i as a family of subtrees (in our notation: block components). This communication within each block component will be the main building-block of primitives that operate on entire parts in parallel.

THEOREM 2 (ROUTING ON TREE-RESTRICTED SHORTCUTS). *On a T-restricted shortcut with congestion c and block parameter b there are deterministic distributed algorithms for:*

i) *Electing a leader for each of the parts in parallel.*

ii) *Convergecasting $O(\log n)$-bit messages to the leader of each part in parallel.*

iii) *Broadcasting a $O(\log n)$-bit message from the leader of each part in parallel.*

Each algorithm takes $O(b(D+c))$ CONGEST rounds.

PROOF. All of these algorithms have a common flavor: for each part we perceive its shortcut subgraph as a supergraph of at most b supernodes where each supernode is a block component. We proceed to describe each of the algorithms on the supergraph and implicitly assume that intra-block communication happens after each step of the algorithm.

Communication within block components can be done in parallel using Lemma 2: all the nodes of a block component convergecast the relevant information to the block-root and subsequently the block-root broadcasts the result back.

Electing a leader for each part is performed by electing a leader for each supernode (block component) and broadcasting the leader to all neighborhood supernodes for b steps. Every supernode keeps the smallest leader ID ever seen as its current leader. After b rounds all the supernodes have the same leader. The algorithm requires $O(b(D+c))$ rounds as each of the b broadcasting steps is followed by an $O(D+c)$ intra-block communication step.

Broadcasting/convergecasting from/to the leader can be done by building a BFS tree from the leader-supernode. We can utilize the standard distributed BFS algorithm on the supergraph requiring $O(b)$ steps. The algorithm similarly requires $O(b(D+c))$ rounds as each of the $O(b)$ BFS steps is followed by an $O(D+c)$ intra-block communication step. □

We also state a simple technical lemma that will be needed for the tree-restricted shortcut construction.

LEMMA 3. *Given a T-restricted shortcut with congestion c, a deterministic distributed algorithm can find all parts whose designated shortcut subgraph has at most b' block components. The algorithm executes in $O(b'(D+c))$ rounds.*

PROOF. Similarly to the proof of Theorem 2, we consider the supergraph of each shortcut subgraph for each part. We need to find all parts whose supergraphs have at most b' supernodes.

Each supernode broadcasts its leader for exactly b' rounds and every supernode keeps the minimum ID as their current leader. Subsequently, each leader r (there may be multiple ones as we have not bounded the block parameter) tries to build a BFS tree comprised of all the nodes that believe r is the leader. We can detect the existence of multiple leaders as in that case each BFS tree will contain two neighboring supernodes in different BFS trees and report failure. If this is not the case (all the supernodes of a part belong to the same BFS tree), we can convergecast the number of supernodes back to the root and subsequently broadcasts their count back. □

Comparison with routing on general shortcuts: Ghaffari and Haeupler [7] give a method for routing on general shortcuts in $O(\text{dilation} \cdot \log n + \text{congestion})$ rounds that is *i)* randomized and *ii)* assumes a leader is already elected for each part. They describe a process of leader election via a complicated randomized bootstrapping process that takes $O(\text{dilation} \cdot \log^2 n + \text{congestion} \cdot \log n)$ rounds. We contrast those results with our current tree-restricted shortcut routing where leader election is essentially no more difficult than broadcast/convergecasting and the routing is simpler and deterministic. The downside is that non-tree-restricted shortcuts sometimes offer better quality guarantees and therefore better performance.

4.4 Main Result and Applications

The main contribution of the paper is to introduce a general framework for finding good-quality shortcuts in graphs where the only assurance is that they exist. In other words, no topology assumption is assumed.

THEOREM 3. *Let G be a graph with a spanning tree $T \subseteq G$ such that there exists a T-restricted shortcut with congestion c and block parameter b. There exists a distributed algorithm that finds a T-restricted shortcut with congestion $O(c \log N)$ and block parameter $3b$ with high probability. The shortcut can be found in $O(D \log n \log N + bD \log N + bc \log N)$ rounds.*

We note that the Theorems 1 and 3 immediately give a novel result: an algorithm for constructing shortcuts on bounded genus graphs.

COROLLARY 1. *Given a genus-g graph with diameter D and N parts there is a distributed algorithm that computes a tree-restricted shortcut with congestion $O(gD \log D \log N)$ and block parameter $O(\log D)$ in $O(gD \log^2 D \log N)$ rounds.*

Next, we explain how to use tree-restricted shortcuts to distributively compute the Minimum Spanning Tree (MST) on genus-g graphs. Similarly to [7], we incorporate the shortcuts into the classic 1926 algorithm of Boruvka [20].

LEMMA 4. *Given a genus-g graph with n nodes and diameter D, there is a distributed algorithm that computes the Minimum Spanning Tree in $O(gD \log^2 D \log^2 n)$ rounds.*

For completeness we give a brief proof outline:

PROOF. Boruvka's algorithm runs in $O(\log n)$ phases. Each phase starts with a partition of the graph into connected parts and a computed MST for each part. Initially, the algorithm starts with the trivial partition in which each node is in its own part. At each phase, each part P_i suggests a merge along the minimum-weighted edge going out of P_i. It is well-known that all such edges belong to some MST. By computing a tree-restricted shortcut for each part in $O(gD \log^2 D \log n)$ rounds and using our convergecast algorithm on it in $O(gD \log^2 D)$ rounds we can compute the min-weight outgoing edges from each part. The only slight technical difficulty that remains is to assign IDs to parts which have merged. While we can communicate efficiently within each part, using the previously computed shortcuts, many parts could chain together to form a new part. This can be avoided by restricting the merge shapes to be star graphs: each part can become a **head** or **tail** with probability $\frac{1}{2}$ and we are only allowed to merge tails to heads. The number of phases remains $O(\log n)$ as every minimum-weighted outgoing edge will be used for merging with probability at least $\frac{1}{4}$, thus reducing the expected number of parts by a constant. □

5. CONSTRUCTING TREE-RESTRICTED SHORTCUTS

In this section, describe an algorithmic framework that solves the problem of finding near-optimal tree-restricted shortcuts.

5.1 Overview over the Algorithmic Framework

Our algorithm **FindShortcut** uses two separate subroutines:

- **Core:** This subroutine finds a good-quality shortcut with respect to at least a constant fraction of the parts. As a prerequisite, we must compute and fix a tree T with depth D such there exists a T-restricted shortcut with congestion c and block parameter b. Note that we only assume its existence.

LEMMA 5. *Let T be a spanning tree with depth D and assume there exists a T-restricted shortcut with congestion c and block parameter b. The subroutine* `CoreFast` *finds a T-restricted shortcut $\mathcal{H}' = (H'_i)_{i=1}^N$ with the following properties:*

i) *The congestion of $\mathcal{H}'$ is at most $8c$ with high probability.*

ii) *There exists a subset of parts $\mathcal{P}' \subseteq \mathcal{P}$ with size at least $|\mathcal{P}'| \geq \frac{N}{2}$ such that the shortcut subgraphs corresponding to parts in $\mathcal{P}'$ have block parameter $3b$.*

The subroutine takes $O(D \log n + c)$ CONGEST rounds to execute. Upon completion, each node knows for each of its incident edges which parts are they assigned to in $\mathcal{H}'$.

We divide out the exposition of the core subroutine in two versions: a deterministic and simper `CoreSlow` requiring $O(D \cdot c)$ rounds; and a randomized `CoreFast` requiring $O(D \log n + c)$ rounds. We note that the `CoreFast` subroutine is the only randomized building block of our framework. Therefore we can replace it with a deterministic (albeit slower) version at a cost of an addition $\frac{c}{\log n}$ factor.

- **Verification:** This subroutine is used to check which of the T-restricted shortcut subgraphs found by the core subroutine have sufficiently small block parameter (in particular, at most $3b$).

LEMMA 6. *Given a tree T with depth D and a tentative T-restricted shortcut $\mathcal{H}'$ with congestion c, the deterministic subroutine* `Verification` *finds all parts $\mathcal{P}' \subseteq \mathcal{P}$ whose designated shortcuts have at most b block components. The subroutine takes $O(b(D + c))$ CONGEST rounds to execute. Upon completion, each node knows whether its part is in the set $\mathcal{P}'$ or not.*

We call the parts whose designated shortcut subgraphs have this property as **good** and the rest as **bad**. **FindShortcut** runs the core subroutine followed by a verification step after which parts that have been marked as good are removed. This is repeated until no more bad parts remain.

5.2 FindShortcut Algorithm

Before we dive into the `FindShortcut` subroutine we must fix a spanning tree T. As the depth of T determines the efficiency of our framework, we can choose T to be a BFS tree rooted at any node of the graph G. This choice ensures that the depth of T is *i)* asymptotically optimal and *ii)* bounded by the diameter of G. For this reason throughout this paper we denote the diameter of G and the depth of T by the same symbol D.

Computing a BFS tree T in our distributed CONGEST model is a standard subroutine and can be computed in $O(D)$ rounds. Henceforth we assume that a tree T with depth D is computed.

`FindShortcut` subroutine: We run the `CoreFast` subroutine that computes a shortcut $\mathcal{H}'$ with congestion $8c$, but possibly an unacceptably large block parameter. The next step is to run the `Verification` subroutine that finds all parts whose computed shortcut subgraphs have at most $3b$ block components. We call those parts **good** and fix their computed shortcut subgraphs. The subroutine is iteratively repeated until all the parts have been marked as good. The check can be executed via a $O(D)$ convergecast on the entire tree T.

We next prove Theorem 3 properties of **FindShortcut** using Lemma 5 and Lemma 6.

THEOREM 4 (RESTATED THEOREM 3). *Let G be a graph with a spanning tree $T \subseteq G$ such that there exists a T-restricted shortcut with congestion c and block parameter b. There exists a distributed algorithm that finds a T-restricted shortcut with congestion $O(c \log N)$ and block parameter $3b$ with high probability.*
The shortcut can be found in $O(D \log n \log N + bD \log N + bc \log N)$ rounds.

PROOF. Let $\mathcal{H}'$ be the set of all shortcut subgraphs that have been marked as good through the lifetime of the entire subroutine. As any shortcut subgraph in $\mathcal{H}'$ has block parameter $3b$ and congestion $8c$ w.h.p. , it only remains to show that the algorithm terminates.

By Lemma 5 in each iteration we find a shortcut with congestion $8c$ and block parameter $3b$ for at least a half of the parts that have not been marked as good, w.h.p. This implies that after $O(\log N)$ iterations all the parts are marked as good. This further implies that the congestion of $\mathcal{H}'$ is $O(c \log N)$ as the congestion of the union of partial shortcuts is at most the sum of congestion of individual partial shortcuts.

Finally, the number of rounds is at most $O(\log N)$ times the combined number of rounds of the **CoreFast** and **Verification** subroutines, namely $O(\log N \cdot (D \log n + c + bD + bc)) = O(D \log N \log n + bD \log N + bc \log N)$. □

5.3 Warm-up: An $O(D \cdot c)$ Version of the Core Subroutine

In this section, we explain a simpler and deterministic, but slower version of the core subroutine named `CoreSlow` that takes $O(D \cdot c)$ rounds. This is improved in the next section where we present a $O(D \log n + c)$-round version of the same subroutine.

On a high level, the subroutine takes each part P_i and tries to assign all the T-ancestors of nodes in P_i to its shortcut subgraph. This may, however, lead to large congestions on some edges. We mitigate that issue by declaring an edge **unusable** if more than $2c$ parts try to use it. This ensures the congestion is $2c$. The process provably leads to a constant fraction parts having both small congestion and small block parameter.

Preliminaries: As standard, assume we fixed a spanning tree T of depth D such that G has a T-restricted shortcut with congestion c and block parameter b. During the execution of the algorithm some of the edges will be marked as **unusable**. Furthermore, we say that an tree edge $e \in E_T$ **can see** a node $v \in V$ if v is in the subtree of e and no edge on the unique simple path between the lower endpoint of e and v is unusable. Analogously, an edge can see a part ID i if it can see any node in P_i.

Outline of the `CoreSlow` subroutine: Initially, no edge is unusable. Process the (tree) edges of T in order of decreasing depth (bottom to top). An edge e is assigned to all the parts P_i such that e can see some node $v \in P_i$, but only if it would be assigned to at most $2c$ such parts. If this is not the case (more than $2c$ shortcut subgraphs would contain e), we mark this edge e as **unusable** and proceed without assigning any part to it.

Detailed description of the `CoreSlow` subroutine: Each node v maintains a list L_v of part IDs that its T-parent edge can see. All the L_v's are initially empty. The subroutine runs in depth(T) phases where in the kth phase all the nodes at depth depth(T) $- k$ update L_v in parallel and send L_v to its T-parent. The update for a node v works by first receiving $L_{v'}$ for all its T-children v'. We assign the union of all received lists and the singleton part ID of v (if any) to L_v. If $|L_v| \leq 2c$, we assign the parent edge of v to all the parts in L_v and transmit L_v to its parent (potentially requiring $2c$ rounds). Otherwise, if $|L_v| > 2c$, we declare the parent edge as unusable.

A direct implementation of this would lead to a subroutine that takes $O(D \cdot c)$ rounds in the CONGEST model. Each of the D levels must propagate at most $2c$ part IDs to their parent nodes. However, this bottleneck can be improved by random sampling, as we show in the next section with the subroutine `CoreFast`. A high-level pseudocode is given in Algorithm 1.

Algorithm 1 `CoreSlow`

1. At time k each node v at depth $depth(T) - k$ does the following in parallel:
   (a) if v is an element of P_i, set $L_v \leftarrow \{i\}$, otherwise $L_v \leftarrow \emptyset$
   (b) receive all the part IDs from v's children and assign their union to L'
   (c) $L_v \leftarrow L_v \cup L'$
   (d) if $|L_v| > 2c$, mark v's parent edge as unusable
   (e) otherwise (serially) send all the part IDs of L_v up to v's parent node
2. For each node v:
   (a) if the parent edge e of v is marked as unusable, e will not be assigned to any shortcut subgraphs
   (b) otherwise e will be assigned to all $H_i, \forall i \in L_v$

LEMMA 7. *Let T be a spanning tree with depth D and assume there exists a T-restricted shortcut with congestion c and block parameter b. The subroutine `CoreSlow` finds a T-restricted shortcut $\mathcal{H}' = (H'_1, H'_2, ..., H'_N)$ with the following properties:*

i) The congestion of $\mathcal{H}'$ is at most $2c$.

ii) There exists a subset of parts $\mathcal{P}' \subseteq \mathcal{P}$ with size at least $|\mathcal{P}'| \geq \frac{N}{2}$ such that the shortcut subgraphs corresponding to parts in $\mathcal{P}'$ have block parameter $3b$.

The subroutine takes $O(D \cdot c)$ CONGEST rounds to execute. Upon completion, each node knows for each of its incident edges which parts are they assigned to in $\mathcal{H}'$.

PROOF. Let $\mathcal{H} = (H_i)$ be any T-restricted shortcut with congestion c and block parameter b and let $\mathcal{H}' = (H'_i)$ be the shortcut computed by `CoreSlow`. We call $\mathcal{H}$ the **canonical** shortcut and $\mathcal{H}'$ the **computed** shortcut.

By construction, the congestion of $\mathcal{H}'$ is $2c$ as any edge that would be assigned to more than $2c$ shortcut subgraphs is marked as unusable. Hence we proved property *i)*.

Let $U \subseteq E_T$ be the set of unusable edges marked by the subroutine. In this paragraph we find an upper bound for $|U|$. Consider **blaming** a part P_i for congesting an unusable edge $e \in U$ when $e \notin G[P_i] + H_i$ and e can see P_i, i.e. edge e was not in the canonical shortcut subgraph H_i, but e was congested by part P_i (and ultimately declared unusable). Each part can be blamed at most b times because each block component can only be blamed for the first unusable edge in his T-tree path towards the T-root. Furthermore, if e is unusable, it takes at least $2c - c$ different block components (from different parts) to be blamed for congesting e. Therefore $|U| \le N\frac{b}{c}$.

We say that a part P_i **missed** an edge e when $e \in G[P_i] + H_i$ and $e \in U$ (consequently $e \notin H_i'$). Furthermore, call a part **bad** if it missed at least $2b$ edges and **good** otherwise. Note that if a part P_i is good, the block parameter of H_i' is at most $2b + \text{blockParameter}(\mathcal{H}) = 3b$. This is because each missed edge induces a new block component in $\mathcal{H}'$ (more precisely, we can identify each block component of $\mathcal{H}'$ by either an unique block component of $\mathcal{H}$ or an unique missed edge $e \in U$). Consequently, it is sufficient to prove that the subroutine finds at least $\frac{1}{2}N$ good parts.

As any unusable edge is contained in at most c canonical shortcut subgraphs and for a part to be bad we need at least $2b$ edges to be missed, we have that the number of bad parts is at most $|U|\frac{c}{2b} \le \frac{1}{2}N$. Hence, the subroutine finds at least $\frac{1}{2}N$ good shortcuts.

The number of rounds the subroutine takes is $O(D \cdot c)$: on each of the D depths of the tree T all the nodes in parallel must send the part IDs trying to use its parent edge up the tree. A node can send up to $2c$ IDs, each requiring a round for its transmission. □

5.4 A Faster $O(D \log n + c)$ Version of the Core Subroutine

In this section, we describe a faster version of the core subroutine named `CoreFast`. On a high level, we lower the running time of `CoreSlow` by estimating the number of parts trying to use an edge by random sampling. In particular, each part becomes **active** with probability p and we declare an edge unusable when $\Omega(c \cdot p)$ active parts try to use that edge.

Preliminaries: In addition to the preliminaries of `CoreSlow` we need shared randomness between all the nodes within a part. In other words, all the nodes of the same part must have access to the same seeds for a pseudorandom generator. This can be done by sharing $O(\log^2 n)$ random bits among all the nodes of G in $O(D + \log n)$ rounds, as described in [7].

Outline of the `CoreFast` subroutine: Each part becomes **active** with probability $p = \frac{\gamma \log n}{2c}$ where $\gamma > 0$ is sufficiently large constant. We basically do the same `CoreSlow` subroutine, but instead of propagating all part IDs of L_v, we propagate only the active ones and declare an edge **unusable** if at least $4c \cdot p = \Omega(\log n)$ (active) part IDs want to use it. Hence by a standard Chernoff bound argument we can claim with high probability that *i)* we never propagate more than $O(\log n)$ part IDs through an edge *ii)* each unusable edge has at least $2c$ part IDs trying to use that edge and *iii)* each usable (non-congested) edge has at most $8c$ part IDs. After determining which edges are unusable in $O(D \log n)$, `CoreFast` must nevertheless find the complete set of part IDs that can use each edge. This is a tree routing problem where each message (part ID) has to be routed up the tree T until the first unusable edge. No message needs to travel more than D edges and no edge needs to transmit more than $8c$ different part IDs w.h.p. Hence this routing can be done in $O(D + c)$ using Lemma 2.

Detailed description of the `CoreSlow` subroutine: Due to shared randomness, each part independently becomes **active** with probability $p = \frac{\gamma \log n}{2c}$ (all the nodes within the part agree on this label). Similarly as in `CoreSlow`, each node v maintains a list $\tilde{L}_v$ of active part IDs that its (T) parent edge can see. All the lists $\tilde{L}_v$ are initially empty. The subroutine runs in depth(T) phases where in the kth phase all the nodes at depth depth$(T) - k$ try to update $\tilde{L}_v$ in parallel and send $\tilde{L}_v$ to its T-parent. The update for a node v works by first receiving $\tilde{L}_{v'}$ for all its T-children v'. We assign the union of all received lists and the singleton part ID of v (if any) to $\tilde{L}_v$. If $|\tilde{L}_v| \le 4c \cdot p$, we assign the parent edge of v to all the parts in $\tilde{L}_v$ and transmit $\tilde{L}_v$ to its parent (requiring $O(\log n)$ rounds). This finalizes the first part of the subroutine where we determine all unusable edges. It remains to forward the complete set of part IDs (and not just the sampled ones) that can use some edge e to the endpoints of e. This is a classic tree routing problem where no route has its length larger than D and no edge intersects more than $8c$ paths w.h.p. Lemma 2 provides a method to route all part IDs in at most $O(D + c)$ rounds. Note that any two part IDs whose routes share an edge have the same endpoint (lowest unusable ancestor edge), so any routing priority between the messages gives the aforementioned $O(D + c)$ bound w.h.p. A high-level pseudocode is given in Algorithm 2

LEMMA 8 (RESTATED LEMMA 5). *Let T be a spanning tree with depth D and assume there exists a T-restricted shortcut with congestion c and block parameter b. The subroutine **CoreFast** finds a T-restricted shortcut $\mathcal{H}' = (H_i')_{i=1}^N$ with the following properties:*

i) *The congestion of $\mathcal{H}'$ is at most $8c$ with high probability.*

ii) *There exists a subset of parts $\mathcal{P}' \subseteq \mathcal{P}$ with size at least $|\mathcal{P}'| \ge \frac{N}{2}$ such that the shortcut subgraphs corresponding to parts in $\mathcal{P}'$ have block parameter $3b$.*

The subroutine takes $O(D \log n + c)$ CONGEST rounds to execute. Upon completion, each node knows for each of its incident edges which parts are they assigned to in $\mathcal{H}'$.

PROOF. This proof extensively utilizes methods used in the proof of Lemma 7. For completeness, we redefine all of the used terminologies and reprove all of the intermediate results.

Let $\mathcal{H} = (H_i)$ be any T-restricted shortcut with congestion c and block parameter b and let $\mathcal{H}' = (H_i')$ be the shortcut computed by `CoreFast`. We call $\mathcal{H}$ the **canonical** shortcut and $\mathcal{H}'$ the **computed** shortcut.

As $4c \cdot p = \Omega(\log n)$, a standard Chernoff bound argument demonstrates that any edge that is not marked as unusable can see at most $8c$ different part IDs w.h.p. Hence, the congestion of $\mathcal{H}'$ is $8c$ w.h.p.

Algorithm 2 `CoreFast`

1. Each part becomes active with probability $p = \frac{\gamma \log n}{2c}$
2. At time k each node v at depth $depth(T) - k$ does the following in parallel:
   (a) if v is an element of P_i and P_i is active, set $\tilde{L}_v \leftarrow \{i\}$, otherwise $\tilde{L}_v \leftarrow \emptyset$
   (b) receive all the active part IDs from v's children and assign their union to L'
   (c) $\tilde{L}_v \leftarrow \tilde{L}_v \cup L'$
   (d) if $|\tilde{L}_v| \geq 4c \cdot p$, mark v's parent edge as unusable
   (e) otherwise send all the part IDs $\tilde{L}_v$ up to v's parent node
3. Each node v initializes Q_v with its part ID (or $\emptyset$ if not in any part)
4. Each node v does the following in parallel:
   (a) add all received IDs to the Q_v
   (b) if parent edge of v is not unusable and $\exists i \in Q_v$ that was never forwarded
      i. forward minimum such i along the parent edge
5. Each part ID in Q_v can use the parent edge of v, unless it is unusable

Let $U \subseteq E_T$ be the set of unusable edges marked by the subroutine. In this paragraph we find an upper bound for $|U|$. Consider **blaming** a part P_i for congesting an unusable edge $e \in U$ when $e \notin G[P_i] + H_i$ and e can see P_i, i.e. edge e was not in the canonical shortcut subgraph $G[P_i] + H_i$, but e was congested by part P_i (and ultimately declared unusable). We can similarly argue via a Chernoff bound that each unusable edge $e \in U$ can see at least $2c$ parts, hence we blame at least $2c - \text{congestion}(\mathcal{H}) = c$ parts for congesting e. Each part can be blamed at most b times because each block component can only be blamed for the first unusable edge in his T-tree path towards the T-root. Furthermore, if e is unusable, it takes at least $2c-c$ different block components (from different parts) to be blamed for congesting e. Therefore $|U| \leq N\frac{b}{c}$.

We say that a part P_i **missed** an edge e when $e \in G[P_i] + H_i$ and $e \in U$ (consequently $e \notin H_i'$). Furthermore, call a part **bad** if it missed at least $2b$ edges and **good** otherwise. Note that if a part P_i is good, the block parameter of H_i' is at most $2b + \text{blockParameter}(\mathcal{H}) = 3b$. This is because each missed edge induces a new block component in $\mathcal{H}'$ (more precisely, we can identify each block component of $\mathcal{H}'$ by either an unique block component of $\mathcal{H}$ or an unique missed edge $e \in U$). Consequently, it is sufficient to prove that the subroutine finds at least $\frac{1}{2}N$ good parts.

As any unusable edge is contained in at most c canonical shortcut subgraphs and for a part to be bad we need at least $2b$ edges to be missed, we have that the number of bad parts is at most $|U|\frac{c}{2b} \leq \frac{1}{2}N$. Hence, the subroutine finds at least $\frac{1}{2}N$ good shortcuts.

The number of rounds the subroutine takes is $O(D \log n + c)$: on each of the D depths of the tree T all the nodes in parallel must send the active part IDs that its parent edge can see. If an edge e is not unusable, a Chernoff bound proves that at most $O(c \cdot p) = O(\log n)$ active part IDs can be seen from e, hence the number of rounds for determining unusable edges is $O(D \log n)$ w.h.p.

Propagating the part IDs upwards along T described in Lemma 2 takes $O(D + c)$ rounds, bringing the total number of rounds to $O(D \log n + c)$. □

5.5 Verification Subroutine

In this section, we describe the `Verification` subroutine. Given a tree-restricted shortcut with congestion c and possibly unbounded block parameter, it inspects each of the shortcut subgraphs in parallel and marks the ones that have at most b block components.

The subroutine runs precisely the algorithm described in Lemma 3 which we restate here.

LEMMA 9 (RESTATED LEMMA 3). *Given a T-restricted shortcut with congestion c, a deterministic distributed algorithm can find all parts whose designated shortcut subgraph has at most b' block components. The algorithm executes in $O(b'(D + c))$ rounds.*

The Lemma provides a direct method to implement the formal requirements of the `Verification` subroutine which we restate here for clarity.

LEMMA 10 (RESTATED LEMMA 6). *Given a tree T with depth D and a tentative T-restricted shortcut $\mathcal{H}'$ with congestion c, the deterministic subroutine `Verification` finds all parts $\mathcal{P}' \subseteq \mathcal{P}$ whose designated shortcuts have at most b block components. The subroutine takes $O(b(D + c))$ CONGEST rounds to execute. Upon completion, each node knows whether its part is in the set $\mathcal{P}'$ or not.*

6. SHORTCUT CONSTRUCTION IN THE CASE OF UNKNOWN PARAMETERS

The algorithm presented in Section 5 assume that upper-bound values on b and c are available. That is, each node must know those values before starting the algorithm. Fortunately, in our algorithm, the lack of that knowledge is not a problem. A key property of our construction algorithm is that it inherently includes termination detection, which allows us to use a simple doubling mechanism: We first start the first trial with a small estimated value of parameters, and if we fail the construction, the next trial is executed after doubling the values of parameters. This mechanism removes the requirement of the knowledge on b and/or c with a potential extra log-factor of the running time. It should be noted that utilizing this mechanism can yield much better shortcuts than the theoretical bound. For example, even for graphs with large genus g, the algorithm can find a good (i.e. $o(gD \log D \log N)$-congestion) shortcut if it luckily exists.

References

[1] A. Das Sarma, S. Holzer, L. Kor, A. Korman, D. Nanongkai, G. Pandurangan, D. Peleg, and R. Wattenhofer. Distributed verification and hardness of distributed approximation. In *Proc. of the Symp. on Theory of Comp. (STOC)*, pages 363–372, 2011.

[2] M. Elkin. Unconditional lower bounds on the time-approximation tradeoffs for the distributed minimum spanning tree problem. In *Proc. of the Symp. on Theory of Comp. (STOC)*, pages 331–340, 2004.

[3] M. Elkin. An unconditional lower bound on the time-approximation trade-off for the distributed minimum spanning tree problem. *SIAM Journal on Computing*, 36(2):433–456, 2006.

[4] S. Frischknecht, S. Holzer, and R. Wattenhofer. Networks cannot compute their diameter in sublinear time. In *Proc. of ACM-SIAM Symp. on Disc. Alg. (SODA)*, pages 1150–1162, 2012.

[5] J. Garay, S. Kutten, and D. Peleg. A sub-linear time distributed algorithm for minimum-weight spanning trees. In *Proc. of the Symp. on Found. of Comp. Sci. (FOCS)*, 1993.

[6] M. Ghaffari and B. Haeupler. Distributed algorithms for planar networks I: Planar embedding. Manuscript, 2015.

[7] M. Ghaffari and B. Haeupler. Distributed algorithms for planar networks II: Low-congestion shortcuts, mst, and min-cut. In *Proc. of ACM-SIAM Symp. on Disc. Alg. (SODA)*, pages 202–219. SIAM, 2016.

[8] M. Ghaffari, A. Karrenbauer, F. Kuhn, C. Lenzen, and B. Patt-Shamir. Near-optimal distributed maximum flow: Extended abstract. In *the Proc. of the Int'l Symp. on Princ. of Dist. Comp. (PODC)*, pages 81–90, 2015.

[9] M. Ghaffari and F. Kuhn. Distributed minimum cut approximation. In *Proc. of the Int'l Symp. on Dist. Comp. (DISC)*, pages 1–15, 2013.

[10] S. Holzer and R. Wattenhofer. Optimal distributed all pairs shortest paths and applications. In *the Proc. of the Int'l Symp. on Princ. of Dist. Comp. (PODC)*, pages 355–364, 2012.

[11] T. Izumi and R. Wattenhofer. Time lower bounds for distributed distance oracles. In *Proc. of the International Conference on Principles of Distributed Systems*, pages 60–75, 2014.

[12] M. Khan and G. Pandurangan. A fast distributed approximation algorithm for minimum spanning trees. *Distributed Computing*, 20(6):391–402, 2008.

[13] S. Kutten and D. Peleg. Fast distributed construction of k-dominating sets and applications. In *the Proc. of the Int'l Symp. on Princ. of Dist. Comp. (PODC)*, pages 238–251, 1995.

[14] F. T. Leighton, B. M. Maggs, and S. B. Rao. Packet routing and job-shop scheduling in O(congestion+ dilation) steps. *Combinatorica*, 14(2):167–186, 1994.

[15] C. Lenzen and B. Patt-Shamir. Fast routing table construction using small messages: Extended abstract. In *Proc. of the Symp. on Theory of Comp. (STOC)*, pages 381–390, 2013.

[16] C. Lenzen and B. Patt-Shamir. Fast partial distance estimation and applications. In *the Proc. of the Int'l Symp. on Princ. of Dist. Comp. (PODC)*, pages 153–162, 2015.

[17] C. Lenzen and D. Peleg. Efficient distributed source detection with limited bandwidth. In *the Proc. of the Int'l Symp. on Princ. of Dist. Comp. (PODC)*, pages 375–382, 2013.

[18] D. Nanongkai. Distributed approximation algorithms for weighted shortest paths. In *Proc. of the Symp. on Theory of Comp. (STOC)*, pages 565–573, 2014.

[19] D. Nanongkai and H.-H. Su. Almost-tight distributed minimum cut algorithms. In *Proc. of the Int'l Symp. on Dist. Comp. (DISC)*, pages 439–453, 2014.

[20] J. Nešetřil, E. Milková, and H. Nešetřilová. Otakar boruvka on minimum spanning tree problem translation of both the 1926 papers, comments, history. *Discrete Math.*, 233(1):3–36, 2001.

[21] D. Peleg. *Distributed Computing: A Locality-sensitive Approach.* Society for Industrial and Applied Mathematics, Philadelphia, PA, USA, 2000.

[22] D. Peleg and V. Rubinovich. A near-tight lower bound on the time complexity of distributed MST construction. In *Proc. of the Symp. on Found. of Comp. Sci. (FOCS)*, pages 253–, 1999.

The Coalescing-Branching Random Walk on Expanders and the Dual Epidemic Process

Colin Cooper
Department of Informatics
King's College London
London, WC2R 2LS, UK
colin.cooper@kcl.ac.uk

Tomasz Radzik
Department of Informatics
King's College London
London, WC2R 2LS, UK
tomasz.radzik@kcl.ac.uk

Nicolás Rivera
Department of Informatics
King's College London
London, WC2R 2LS, UK
nicolas.rivera@kcl.ac.uk

ABSTRACT

Information propagation on graphs is a fundamental topic in distributed computing. One of the simplest models of information propagation is the push protocol in which at each round each agent independently pushes the current knowledge to a random neighbour. In this paper we study the so-called coalescing-branching random walk (COBRA), in which each vertex pushes the information to k randomly selected neighbours and then stops passing information until it receives the information again. The aim of COBRA is to propagate information fast but with a limited number of transmissions per vertex per step. In this paper we study the cover time of the COBRA process defined as the minimum time until each vertex has received the information at least once. Our main result says that if G is an n-vertex r-regular graph whose transition matrix has second eigenvalue λ, then the COBRA cover time of G is $\mathcal{O}(\log n)$, if $1-\lambda$ is greater than a positive constant, and $\mathcal{O}((\log n)/(1-\lambda)^3))$, if $1-\lambda \gg \sqrt{\log(n)/n}$. These bounds are independent of r and hold for $3 \le r \le n-1$. They improve the previous bound of $O(\log^2 n)$ for expander graphs [Dutta et al., SPAA 2013].

Our main tool in analysing the COBRA process is a novel duality relation between this process and a discrete epidemic process, which we call a biased infection with persistent source (BIPS). A fixed vertex v is the source of an infection and remains permanently infected. At each step each vertex u other than v selects k neighbours, independently and uniformly, and u is infected in this step if and only if at least one of the selected neighbours has been infected in the previous step. We show the duality between COBRA and BIPS which says that the time to infect the whole graph in the BIPS process is of the same order as the cover time of the COBRA process.

PODC'16, July 25-28, 2016, Chicago, IL, USA

DOI: http://dx.doi.org/10.1145/2933057.2933119

CCS Concepts

•**Mathematics of computing → Probabilistic algorithms;** *Markov processes;* •**Theory of computation → Distributed algorithms; Random walks and Markov chains;**

Keywords

Random processes on graphs; epidemic processes; cover time

1. INTRODUCTION

Dutta et al. [5, 6] studied the following *coalescing-branching* random walk process for propagating information through a connected n-vertex graph. At the start of a round each vertex containing information "pushes" this information to k randomly selected neighbours, then it stops passing the information until it receives the information again. At the end of a round if a vertex receives information from two or more vertices, then the information coalesces into one. Thus it does not help if a vertex receives the same information from more than one neighbour. The continuous act of coalescing and branching gives the name COBRA to this process.

The aim of the COBRA process is to rapidly propagate information to all vertices but to limit the number of transmissions per vertex per step and without requiring that vertices store information for longer than one round. In the special case that $k = 1$, the COBRA process is a simple random walk, which achieves a low transmission rate but does not satisfy the fast propagation condition.

The main quantity of interest in information propagation processes is the time taken to inform (or visit) all vertices. By analogy with a random walk, this is referred to as the *cover time*. The w.h.p.[1] cover time results for the COBRA process obtained in [5, 6] for the case $k = 2$ include the following. (i) For the complete graph K_n all vertices are visited in $\mathcal{O}(\log n)$ rounds. (ii) For regular constant degree expanders, the cover time is $\mathcal{O}(\log^2 n)$. (iii) For the d-dimensional grid, the cover time is $\tilde{O}(n^{1/d})$. By comparison with the complete graph, it might seem that the cover time of any r-regular expander by the COBRA process (with $k = 2$) should be $\mathcal{O}(\log n)$ for any degree r between 3 and $n-1$. The proof of this is the main content of this paper (see Theorem 1 below). This is the best possible asymptotic bound since the number of visited vertices at most doubles in each round.

[1] "With high probability," which means in this paper probability at most n^{-c}, for some positive constant c.

The COBRA process imitates a type of epidemic process but with an upper bound k on the number of contacts. Indeed, the COBRA process turns out to be a discrete version of the *contact process*, which is a continuous model with exponential waiting times, in which (typically) a particle at vertex v infects each neighbour with rate μ, and becomes extinct with rate 1. One difference between the processes is that a contact process can die out, whereas the COBRA one does not. The contact process was introduced by Harris in 1974 [8], and has been extensively studied on infinite lattices and trees. A major topic of study is, given the initial spread of infection, to determine the values of μ for which the process is transient, recurrent, and stationary. See for example, Madras and Schinazi [12] for a concise summary, and also Liggett [10]; Pemantle [13] gives a more detailed analysis on trees, Liggett for finite trees [11]. The work of Bezuidenhout and Grimmett [2] was a breakthrough paper for lattices.

We proceed with the formal definition of the COBRA process and the statement of our main results.

Coalescing Branching Random Walk (COBRA): Consider a graph $G = (V, E)$ and an integer $k \geq 1$. Let $C \subseteq V$ and consider the set process $(C_t)_{t\geq 0}$ with $C_0 = C$ and C_{t+1} is defined as follows. Let C_t be the vertices chosen at round t (not necessarily for the first time). Each vertex $v \in C_t$ independently chooses k neighbours uniformly at random with replacement and all the chosen vertices belong to C_{t+1}.

For $C_0 = \{u\}$, let $\mathbf{cov}(u) = \min\{T : \bigcup_{t=1}^{T} C_t = V\}$ be the number of steps needed for the COBRA process to visit all vertices of the graph G starting from vertex u; and let $\mathrm{COV}(u) = \mathbf{E}(\mathbf{cov}(u))$. By analogy with the cover time of a random walk, which measures the worst case starting vertex, we let $\mathrm{COV}(G) = \max_{u\in V} \mathrm{COV}(u)$ be the cover time of the COBRA process.

Let G be a connected n-vertex r-regular graph with adjacency matrix $A(G)$ and random-walk transition matrix $P = A(G)/r$. Let $\lambda_1, \lambda_2, ..., \lambda_n$ be the eigenvalues of the transition matrix ordered in a non-increasing sequence. Thus $\lambda_1 = 1$, $\lambda_n \geq -1$. Let $\lambda = \lambda_{\max} = \max_{i=2,...,n} |\lambda_i|$ be the second largest eigenvalue (in absolute value). If the graph G is not bipartite, then $\lambda < 1$. In which case we have the following theorem.

THEOREM 1. *Let G be a connected regular n-vertex graph with $1 - \lambda \gg \sqrt{(\log n)/n}$.* [2] *Let*

$$T = \frac{\log(n)}{(1-\lambda)^3}.$$

Let $COV(G) = \max_{u\in V} COV(u)$ be the cover time of G by a COBRA process with branching factor $k = 2$. Then $COV(G) = \mathcal{O}(T)$ and for all $u \in V$, w.h.p. $\mathbf{cov}(u) = \mathcal{O}(T)$.

The COBRA process is a type of a multiple random walk processes, so it is tempting to try to analyse COBRA using techniques developed for such processes. Previous work on multiple random walks includes [1, 3, 4, 7], where cover times were analysed for various classes of graphs. The analysis of the COBRA process given in Dutta et al. [5, 6] uses a number of tools from multiple random walks, but applicability of those tools turns out to be limited because the random walks in COBRA are highly dependent. In order to prove Theorem 1, we introduce a related epidemic process BIPS, which is a dual of COBRA under time reversal, and work on this new process instead of the original one. The formal duality between BIPS and COBRA used in the proof of Theorem 1 is established in Theorem 4.

Biased Infection with Persistent Source (BIPS): Consider a graph $G = (V, E)$ and an integer $k \geq 1$. Consider a vertex v which is the source of an infection. We consider the process A_t defined by $A_0 = \{v\}$. Given A_t each vertex $u \in V$, other than v, independently and uniformly with replacement selects k neighbours and becomes a member of A_{t+1} if and only if at least one of the selected neighbours is in A_t. Additionally, $v \in A_t$ for all $t \geq 0$. We call A_t the infected set at time t. Observe the source v is always infected. Finally, if $A_0 = \{v\}$ then it is clear that v is the source of the infection process.

The BIPS process is a discrete epidemic process of the SIS (Susceptible-Infected-Susceptible) type, in which vertices (other than the source v) refresh their infected state at each step by contacting k randomly chosen neighbours. The presence of a persistent (or corrupted) source means that w.h.p. all vertices of the underlying graph eventually become infected. The BIPS process is of independent interest since in the context of epidemics, certain viruses exhibit the property that a particular host can become persistently infected. For example, in animals the BVDV (Bovine viral diarrhea virus) is of this type and a model that mimics the spread of BVDV was described in [9]. The model is able to simulate the spread of infection when a persistently infected animal is introduced into an infection-free herd.

If we define $\mathbf{infec}(v)$ as the first time when all vertices are infected when the source is v, $\mathrm{Infec}(v) = \mathbf{E}(\mathbf{infec}(v))$, and $\mathrm{Infec}(G) = \max_{u\in V} \mathrm{Infec}(v)$, then we have the analogue theorem of Theorem 1.

THEOREM 2. *Let G be a connected n-vertex r-regular graph with $1 - \lambda \gg \sqrt{(\log n)/n}$. Then for every $v \in V$, the infection time, $\mathbf{infec}(v)$, by a BIPS process with $k = 2$ satisfies $\mathbf{infec}(v) = \mathcal{O}(\log(n)/(1-\lambda)^3)$ in expectation and with probability at least $1 - \mathcal{O}(1/n^3)$. Moreover $Infec(G) = \mathcal{O}(\log(n)/(1-\lambda)^3)$.*

Although Theorem 1 is proved for a COBRA process with branching factor $k = 2$, it seems natural to ask if, for expanders, a cover time of $\mathcal{O}(\log n)$ can be obtained with less branching. Clearly $k = 1$ is not enough; the cover time of any n vertex graph by a random walk is $\Omega(n \log n)$. Suppose that at the start of each step, each particle divides in two with probability ρ. This gives an expected branching factor of $1+\rho$. The following result shows that any constant $\rho > 0$ will do. The proof of Theorem 3 follows from the proof of Theorem 1, by using Corollary 1 of Lemma 1 in Section 3.

THEOREM 3. *Let G be a connected n-vertex r-regular graph with $\lambda < 1$ constant and let $v \in V(G)$. Provided $\rho > 0$ constant, for all $v \in V$, the cover time of G by the COBRA process with branching factor $1 + \rho$ and $C_0 = \{v\}$ is $\mathbf{cov}(v) = \mathcal{O}(\log(n))$ rounds in expectation and with high probability.*

Overview of the proof of Theorem 1

For a connected graph $G = (V, E)$, denote $\mathrm{Hit}_C(v) = \min\{t : v \in C_t, C_0 = C\}$ the hitting time of vertex v for a COBRA process starting from C. In particular, $\mathrm{Hit}_u(v)$ is the hitting

[2] $(1-\lambda) \geq C\sqrt{(\log n)/n}$ for some suitably large constant C.

time of v starting from u. Suppose there exists $T > 0$ such that for any fixed pair (u, v) it holds that $\text{Hit}_u(v) > T$ with probability at most $\mathcal{O}(1/n^2)$. By the union bound we get $\mathbf{cov}(u) = \max_{v\in V} \text{Hit}_u(v) > T$ with probability at most $\mathcal{O}(1/n)$. Thus $\mathbf{cov}(u) < T$ with high probability. This results also holds in expectation. To see this, observe that by restarting the process after T steps with any of the existing particles, we have that

$$\begin{aligned}\text{COV}(u) \quad &\leq \quad T + \mathcal{O}(1/n)2T + \cdots \\ &\quad + \mathcal{O}(1/n^j)(j+1)T + \cdots \;=\; \mathcal{O}(T). \quad (1)\end{aligned}$$

Thus obtaining that $\text{COV}(u) = \mathcal{O}(T)$. In our case $T = \mathcal{O}(\log(n)/(1-\lambda)^3)$.

We give an overview of the Proof of Theorem 1.

1. In Section 2 we prove Theorem 4 which relates hitting times in the COBRA process to the membership of elements of the infected set at a given step of the BIPS process as follows

$$\mathbf{P}(\text{Hit}_u(v) > t) = \mathbf{P}(u \notin A_t | A_0 = \{v\}). \qquad (2)$$

   The probability on the left hand side is for COBRA process staring from u, and on the right hand side for a BIPS process with persistent source v, and where A_t the infected set at step t.

2. From Theorem 2 we obtain that for T as above, $\mathbf{P}(u \notin A_T | A_0 = v) \leq \mathbf{P}(A_T \neq V | A_0 = v) = \mathcal{O}(1/n^3)$. This together with the above duality implies Theorem 1. Sections 3–5 are devoted to the proof of Theorem 2.

3. In Section 3 we prove a lower bound on $\mathbf{E}(|A_{t+1}| \mid |A_t|)$, the expected size of the infected set at round $t+1$ of a BIPS process given the size at step t.

4. The proof of Theorem 2 is split into two parts. In Section 4 we show that in $\mathcal{O}(T)$ rounds the infected set A_t increases its size from 1 to $\Omega(T)$ (we refer here only to the case when $1-\lambda$ is constant). In Section 5 we prove that in $\mathcal{O}(T)$ extra rounds the whole graph is infected. Both parts of the proof of Theorem 2 use the bound on $\mathbf{E}(|A_{t+1}| \mid |A_t|)$.

Notation. For a vertex $x \in V$, $N(x)$ denotes the set of neighbours of x and $d(x) = |N(x)|$. More generally, for $A \subseteq V$, $d_A(x) = |N(x) \cap A|$. We also define $d(A) = \sum_{x\in A} d(x)$. If there is no ambiguity, we write A in place of $|A|$. Let $\Gamma(A) = \{x \in V : \exists u \in A, \{x, u\} \in E(G)\}$ be the inclusive neighbourhood of A. By replacing each undirected edge $\{x, u\}$ with directed edges (x, u) and (u, x) and counting the edges with the second vertex in A, it follows that $\sum_{u\in\Gamma(A)} d_A(u) = r|A|$.

2. DUALITY BETWEEN COBRA AND BIPS PROCESSES

The intuition for the next theorem can be seen as follows. Replace each edge in the graph by a pair of directed edges. Let v be a distinguished vertex. Delete all out edges of v and replace them with a loop. Let $k = 1$. Any random walk which arrives at v at or before step t remains at v. A walk W starting at u which arrives at v at step $s < t$ corresponds to a BIPS process which remains at v for $t-s$ steps and then follows the edges of W back to u in s steps. This correspondence generalizes to the COBRA and BIPS processes with the parameter $k \geq 2$.

Recall that $(C_t)_{t\geq 0}$ and $(A_t)_{t\geq 0}$ denote the COBRA and BIPS processes, respectively. To avoid confusion, we use the notation $\mathbf{P}(\cdot)$ for probabilities in the BIPS process, and $\widehat{\mathbf{P}}(\cdot)$ in the COBRA process. Our main Theorem 1 follows from the duality between these two processes expressed in (2). To prove (2), we generalize this relation in the following theorem to a form which is convenient for an inductive proof. To simplify notation, we will write "$A_0 = v$" for the frequently appearing condition "$A_0 = \{v\}$."

THEOREM 4. *Let G be a connected regular graph and consider the COBRA and BIPS processes on G with parameter $k \geq 1$. For each $v \in V$, $C \subseteq V$ and $t \geq 0$ we have*

$$\widehat{\mathbf{P}}(Hit_C(v) > t | C_0 = C) \;=\; \mathbf{P}(C \cap A_t = \emptyset | A_0 = v).$$

PROOF. Observe that the claim is trivial if $v \in C$, since both probabilities are 0. We assume that $v \notin C$ and proceed by induction on t. For $t = 0$ the claim is true because both probabilities are 1. Assume the claim is true for a fixed $t \geq 0$, we will prove it for $t+1$.

Consider the BIPS process at step $t+1$. Denote by B_x the random k-set of neighbours chosen by vertex x. Note that $B_v = \{v\}$ always. Define $X(C) = \bigcup_{x\in C} B_x$. It is an assumption of the model that, at step $t+1$, for any fixed set B, the event $X(C) = B$ is independent of A_t and thus of the event $B \cap A_t = \emptyset$. Thus,

$$\begin{aligned}&\mathbf{P}(B \cap A_t = \emptyset \text{ and } X(C) = B | A_0 = v) \\ &\quad = \mathbf{P}(B \cap A_t = \emptyset | A_0 = v)\mathbf{P}(X(C) = B | A_0 = v).\end{aligned}$$

Let $N^X(C)$ be the set of possible $B = X(C)$ generated by C in one step: $N^X(C) = \{B \subseteq V : \mathbf{P}(X(C) = B) > 0\}$. The events $X(C) = B$ are mutually exclusive and exhaustive, so

$$\begin{aligned}&\mathbf{P}(C \cap A_{t+1} = \emptyset | A_0 = v) \\ &= \sum_{B\in N^X(C)} \mathbf{P}(B \cap A_t = \emptyset | A_0 = v)\mathbf{P}(X(C) = B | A_0 = v).\end{aligned}$$

For any set B, the induction hypothesis gives

$$\mathbf{P}(B \cap A_t = \emptyset | A_0 = v) \;=\; \widehat{\mathbf{P}}(\text{Hit}(v) > t | C_0 = B).$$

Let $B = Y(C)$ be the random set chosen (to push to) by C in the COBRA process, and let $N^Y(C)$ be the set of possible B resulting from this. If $v \notin C$, then for any $u \in C$

$$\mathbf{P}(X(u) = B_u) = \widehat{\mathbf{P}}(Y(u) = B_u).$$

The events $B_u, u \in C$ are independent, so

$$\mathbf{P}(X(C) = B | A_0 = v) = \widehat{\mathbf{P}}(Y(C) = B).$$

Moreover $N^X(C) = N^Y(C)$. Thus for $v \notin C$,

$$\begin{aligned}&\mathbf{P}(C \cap A_{t+1} = \emptyset | A_0 = v) \\ &= \sum_{B\in N^X(C)} \mathbf{P}(B \cap A_t = \emptyset | A_0 = v)\mathbf{P}(X(C) = B | A_0 = v) \\ &= \sum_{B\in N^Y(C)} \widehat{\mathbf{P}}(\text{Hit}(v) > t | C_0 = B)\widehat{\mathbf{P}}(Y(C) = B) \\ &= \widehat{\mathbf{P}}(\text{Hit}(v) > t+1 | C_0 = C).\end{aligned}$$

□

PROOF OF THEOREM 1. From Theorem 4 for $C = \{u\}$ and the union bound we get that for any two vertices $u, v \in V$, and any $T \geq 0$,

$$\begin{aligned} \widehat{\mathbf{P}}(\text{Hit}_u(v) > T) &= \mathbf{P}(u \notin A_T | A_0 = v) \\ &\leq \mathbf{P}(A_T \neq V | A_0 = v) \\ &= \mathbf{P}(\mathbf{infec}(v) > T). \end{aligned}$$

For $T = \mathcal{O}((\log n)/(1-\lambda)^3)$, Theorem 2 tells us that $\mathbf{P}(\mathbf{infec}(u) > T) = \mathcal{O}(1/n^3)$, so $\widehat{\mathbf{P}}(\text{Hit}_u(v) > T) = \mathcal{O}(1/n^3)$. Therefore

$$\mathbf{P}(\mathbf{cov}(u) > T) \leq \sum_{v \in V} \mathbf{P}(\text{Hit}_u(v) > T) = \mathcal{O}\left(\frac{1}{n^2}\right).$$

Concluding that $\mathbf{cov}(u) \leq T$ with probability at least $1 - O(1/n^2)$. From Equation (1) we get the result in expectation. □

3. EXPECTED GROWTH OF THE BIPS PROCESS

The following lemma, which gives a lower bound on the expected increase of infection in one step of the BIPS process, is the basis for our analysis of this process.

LEMMA 1. *Let G be a connected r-regular graph on n vertices, with $\lambda < 1$ where λ is the absolute second eigenvalue of the random-walk transition matrix. Let A_t be the size of the infected set after step t of the BIPS process with $k = 2$, then*

$$\mathbf{E}(|A_{t+1}| \mid A_t = A) \geq |A|(1 + (1-\lambda^2)(1 - |A|/n)). \quad (3)$$

PROOF. Note that $\sum_{u \in \Gamma(A)} d_A(u) = r|A|$. Thus

$$\begin{aligned} &\mathbf{E}(|A_{t+1}| \mid A_t = A) && (4)\\ &= 1 + \sum_{u \in \Gamma(A) \setminus \{v\}} (1 - (1 - d_A(u)/r)^2) && (5)\\ &\geq \sum_{u \in \Gamma(A)} \left(\frac{2}{r} d_A(u) - \frac{1}{r^2} d_A^2(u)\right) && (6)\\ &= 2|A| - \frac{1}{r^2} \sum_{u \in \Gamma(A)} d_A^2(u). && (7) \end{aligned}$$

For the inequality in (3) we argue as follows. Let $P = P(G)$ be the transition matrix of a simple random walk on G. Let $P(x, A) = \sum_{y \in A} P(x, y) = d_A(x)/r$. From (4)-(7) we have

$$\mathbf{E}(|A_{t+1}| \,|A_t = A) \geq 2A - \sum_{x \in V} P(x, A)^2. \quad (8)$$

Observe that $\sum_{x \in V} P(x, A)^2 = \langle P1_A, P1_A \rangle = \|P1_A\|^2$, where $1_A = (1_{\{x \in A\}} : x \in V)$ and $P1_A = (P(x, A) : x \in V)$. As P is symmetric, it has an orthonormal basis of right eigenvectors $f_1, ..., f_n$, i.e. $\|f_i\| = 1$, $\langle f_i, f_j \rangle = 0$ for $i \neq j$. For any vector g, $g = \sum_{i=1}^n \langle f, f_i \rangle f_i$ and $\|g\|^2 = \sum_{i=1}^n \langle g, f_i \rangle^2$. Here $f_1 = (1/\sqrt{n})$ is the unique eigenvector with eigenvalue 1, and $\langle 1_A, f_1 \rangle = A/\sqrt{n}$. Thus

$$\begin{aligned} \|P1_A\|^2 &= \|P \sum_{i=1}^n \langle 1_A, f_i \rangle f_i\|^2 = \|\sum_{i=1}^n \langle 1_A, f_i \rangle P f_i\|^2 \\ &= \|\sum_{i=1}^n \langle 1_A, f_i \rangle \lambda_i f_i\|^2 = \sum_{i=1}^n \langle 1_A, f_i \rangle^2 \lambda_i^2 \|f_i\|^2 \\ &\leq (1-\lambda^2)\langle 1_A, f_1 \rangle^2 + \lambda^2 \sum_{i=1}^n \langle 1_A, f_i \rangle^2 \\ &= (1-\lambda^2)\frac{|A|^2}{n} + \lambda^2 \|1_A\|^2 \\ &= (1-\lambda^2)\frac{|A|^2}{n} + \lambda^2 |A|. \end{aligned} \quad (9)$$

Thus (8) and (9) imply

$$\mathbf{E}(|A_{t+1}| \,|A_t = A) \geq 2|A| - \lambda^2|A| - (1-\lambda^2)\frac{|A|^2}{n},$$

which is equivalent to (3). □

The following corollary is easily obtained from the proof of Lemma 1. In a BIPS process with $k = 1 + \rho$, each vertex contacts one randomly chosen neighbour, and with probability $\rho > 0$ randomly chooses a second neighbour, with replacement.

COROLLARY 1. *Let A_t be the size of the infected set after step t of the BIPS process with expected branching factor $k = 1 + \rho$, then*

$$\mathbf{E}(|A_{t+1}| \mid |A_t = A) \geq |A|(1 + \rho(1-\lambda^2)(1 - |A|/n)).$$

PROOF. The probability that x chooses at least one vertex in the infected set A, is

$$\begin{aligned} 1 - (1 - P(x, A))(1 - \rho P(x, A)) \\ = (1+\rho)P(x, A) - \rho P(x, A)^2. \end{aligned}$$

The rest of the proof is the same. □

4. BIPS PROCESS FOR SMALL SETS

Consider a BIPS process A_t with source v on a graph G. Thus at $t = 0$, $A_0 = \{v\}$.

LEMMA 2. *Let G be a connected r-regular graph on n vertices, with $\lambda = \lambda(n) < 1$, and let $m \leq n/2$. Then with probability at least $1 - \mathcal{O}(1/n^C)$, we have that $A_t > m$ for some $t \leq T$, where $T = 13m/(1-\lambda) + 24C\log(n)/(1-\lambda)^2$.*

PROOF. Let A_0 be the initial infected set and A_t be the infected set at the end of round t. For convenience we denote by A_t the size of the set A_t, instead of $|A_t|$.

Denote the event $E_t = \{A_0 < m+1, \ldots, A_t < m+1\}$. We need to find an upper bound for $\mathbf{P}(E_t)$ for any t. Observe $\mathbf{P}(E_0) = 1$, so we concentrate on $t \geq 1$. Let $\phi > 0$ (to be chosen later), then

$$\begin{aligned} \mathbf{P}(E_t) &= \mathbf{P}(E_{t-1}, A_t < m+1) \\ &= \mathbf{P}(E_{t-1}, A_t - A_0 < m) \\ &= \mathbf{P}(E_{t-1}, e^{-\phi(A_t - A_0)} > e^{-\phi m}) \\ &= \mathbf{P}(e^{-\phi(A_t - A_0)} 1_{\{E_{t-1}\}} > e^{-\phi m}) \\ &\leq e^{\phi m}\, \mathbf{E}(e^{-\phi(A_t - A_0)} 1_{\{E_{t-1}\}}). \end{aligned} \quad (10)$$

Because $1_{\{E_{t-1}\}} = 1_{\{E_{t-2}\}} 1_{\{A_{t-1}<m+1\}}$, and assuming $1_{\{E_{-1}\}} \equiv 1$, we can write

$$G_t(\phi) \equiv \mathbf{E}(e^{-\phi(A_t - A_0)} 1_{\{E_{t-1}\}})$$
$$= \mathbf{E}(e^{-\phi(A_t - A_{t-1})} e^{-\phi(A_{t-1}-A_0)} 1_{\{E_{t-2}\}} 1_{\{A_{t-1}<m+1\}}) \quad (11)$$

Observe that $G_0(\phi) \equiv 1$. Denote the sigma algebra $\mathcal{F}_t = \sigma(A_0, \ldots, A_t)$. By taking expectation conditional on $\mathcal{F}_{t-1}$ we rewrite (11) as

$$\begin{aligned} G_t(\phi) &= \mathbf{E}\,(\,\mathbf{E}\,(\,e^{-\phi(A_{t-1}-A_0)} 1_{\{E_{t-2}\}} 1_{\{A_{t-1}<m+1\}} \\ &\qquad \times e^{-\phi(A_t - A_{t-1})} | \mathcal{F}_{t-1}\,)\,) \\ &= \mathbf{E}\,(\,e^{-\phi(A_{t-1}-A_0)} 1_{\{E_{t-2}\}} 1_{\{A_{t-1}<m+1\}} \\ &\qquad \times \mathbf{E}(e^{-\phi(A_t - A_{t-1})} | \mathcal{F}_{t-1}\,)\,). \qquad (12) \end{aligned}$$

We derive an upper bound on $\mathbf{E}(e^{-\phi(A_t - A_{t-1})} | \mathcal{F}_{t-1})$. Observe that

$$E(e^{-\phi(A_t - A_{t-1})} | \mathcal{F}_{t-1}) = e^{\phi A_{t-1}}\, \mathbf{E}(e^{-\phi A_t} | \mathcal{F}_{t-1}). \quad (13)$$

For $x \in V$ the events $\{x \in A_t | \mathcal{F}_{t-1}\}$ are independent, and since A_t is a Markov chain, they depend only on A_{t-1}. Thus

$$\begin{aligned} &\mathbf{E}(e^{-\phi A_t} | \mathcal{F}_{t-1}) \\ &= \prod_{x \in V} \mathbf{E}(e^{-\phi 1_{\{x \in A_t\}}} | \mathcal{F}_{t-1}) \\ &= \prod_{x \in V} \left(e^{-\phi} \mathbf{P}(x \in A_t | A_{t-1}) + 1 - \mathbf{P}(x \in A_t | A_{t-1})\right) \\ &= \prod_{x \in V} \left(1 - (1 - e^{-\phi}) \mathbf{P}(x \in A_t | A_{t-1})\right) \\ &\leq \prod_{x \in V} \exp\{-(1 - e^{-\phi}) \mathbf{P}(x \in A_t | A_{t-1})\} \\ &= \exp\{-(1 - e^{-\phi}) \sum_{x \in V} \mathbf{P}(x \in A_t | A_{t-1})\} \\ &= \exp\{-(1 - e^{-\phi}) \mathbf{E}(A_t | A_{t-1})\}. \qquad (14) \end{aligned}$$

Substitute (14) into (13) and (12) to get

$$\begin{aligned} &G_t(\phi) \\ &\leq \mathbf{E}\left[\, e^{-\phi(A_{t-1}-A_0)} 1_{\{E_{t-2}\}} \right. \\ &\qquad \left. \times 1_{\{A_{t-1}<m+1\}} e^{\phi A_{t-1}} \exp\{-(1 - e^{-\phi}) \mathbf{E}(A_t | A_{t-1})\}\right]. \end{aligned} \quad (15)$$

Define

$$\Psi(A) = 1_{\{A<m+1\}} e^{\phi A} \exp\{-(1 - e^{-\phi}) \mathbf{E}(A_t | A_{t-1} = A)\}.$$

Remember that, due to the source, we have $A_t > 0$ for all $t \geq 0$, thus we consider A with size at least 1 in $\Psi(A)$. Denote by $\delta = \delta(A) = (\mathbf{E}(A_t | A_{t-1} = A))/A$. Then

$$\Psi(A) = 1_{\{1 \leq A \leq m\}} \exp\left(-A((1 - e^{-\phi})\delta - \phi)\right). \quad (16)$$

Our next step is to find an upper bound of $\Psi(A)$ independent of A. For $k \in \{1, \ldots, n\}$ define $\delta_\lambda(k) = 1 + (1 - \lambda^2)(1 - k/n)$. We now choose $\phi = \log(1 + x)$ where $x = \frac{1-\lambda}{2}$. Since $|A| \leq n/2$ from (3) of Lemma 1 we get

$$\begin{aligned} \delta(A) &\geq \delta_\lambda(|A|) = 1 + (1 - \lambda^2)(1 - |A|/n) \\ &\geq 1 + (1 - \lambda)(1 + \lambda)/2 \\ &\geq 1 + \frac{1 - \lambda}{2} = e^\phi. \end{aligned}$$

Using this with (16), we get that

$$\begin{aligned} \Psi(A) &= 1_{\{1 \leq A \leq m\}} \exp\left(-A((1 - e^{-\phi})\delta - \phi)\right) \\ &\leq 1_{\{1 \leq A \leq m\}} \exp\left(-A(e^\phi - 1 - \phi)\right). \qquad (17) \end{aligned}$$

Observe that $f(y) = e^y - 1 - y > 0$, thus we take $A = 1$ in the above quantity to get

$$\Psi(A) \leq e^{1 + \phi - e^\phi} = e^{\log(1+x) - x}. \quad (18)$$

From Inequality (15) and the fact that $\Psi(A) \leq e^{\log(1+x)-x}$, we get

$$\begin{aligned} &G_t(\phi) \\ &\leq \mathbf{E}\left[e^{-\phi(A_{t-1}-A_0)} 1_{\{E_{t-2}\}} \right. \\ &\qquad \left. \times 1_{\{A_{t-1}<m+1\}} e^{\phi A_{t-1}} \exp\{-(1 - e^{-\phi}) \mathbf{E}(A_t | A_{t-1})\}\right] \\ &= \mathbf{E}(e^{-\phi(A_{t-1}-A_0)} 1_{\{E_{t-2}\}} \Psi(A_{t-1})) \\ &\leq \mathbf{E}(e^{-\phi(A_{t-1}-A_0)} 1_{\{E_{t-2}\}}) \exp(\log(1 + x) - x) \\ &= G_{t-1}(\phi) \exp(\log(1 + x) - x). \end{aligned}$$

Using $G_0(\phi) \equiv 1$ and induction we get

$$G_t(\phi) \leq e^{t(\log(1+x)-x)}.$$

Putting $G_t(\phi)$ into Inequality (10), we obtain

$$\mathbf{P}(E_t) \leq G_t(\phi) e^{\phi m} \leq e^{m\phi + t(\log(1+x)-x)}. \quad (19)$$

We need to estimate the exponent. Recall that $\phi = (1 + x)$ with $x = \frac{1-\lambda}{2} \leq 1/2$. For $x < 1$ the terms of $\log(1 + x)$ are monotone decreasing in absolute value, so that $\log(1 + x) \leq x - x^2/2 + x^3/3$. From this, and $x \leq 1/2$, the exponent can be bounded as follows,

$$\begin{aligned} &(t + m)\log(1 + x) - tx \\ &\leq -tx + (t + m)\left(x - \frac{x^2}{2} + \frac{x^3}{3}\right) \\ &= x\left(m\left(1 - \frac{x}{2} + \frac{x^2}{3}\right) - \frac{tx}{2}\left(1 - \frac{2x}{3}\right)\right) \\ &\leq x\left(\frac{13m}{12} - \frac{tx}{6}\right). \end{aligned}$$

Put $x = (1 - \lambda)/2$ and choose

$$t = 13m/(1 - \lambda) + (24C\log(n))/(1 - \lambda)^2$$

to obtain the result. □

5. BIPS PROCESS FOR LARGE SETS

In this section we analyze the growth of A_t in the BIPS process from $A_{t'} = \Theta(\log n/(1 - \lambda)^2)$ up to $A_{t''} = n$. We start by applying Lemma 2 with $m = K\log(n)/(1 - \lambda)^2$, for some (large) constant K, to have w.h.p. $A_t \geq K\log n/(1 - \lambda)^2$ for some $t = \mathcal{O}(\log n/(1 - \lambda)^3)$. Lemma 3 shows that from this point additional $\mathcal{O}(\log(n)/(1 - \lambda))$ rounds bring the infection size A_t up to at least $(9/10)n$ w.h.p. Lemma 4 shows that when A_t becomes $\geq (9/10)n$, then w.h.p. the whole graph becomes infected at some point within the subsequent $\mathcal{O}(\log(n)/(1 - \lambda))$ rounds.

LEMMA 3. *Let G be a connected n-vertex r-regular graph with $\lambda < 1$. Suppose that $|A_t| \geq K\log(n)/(1 - \lambda)^2$, with*

$K = 4000$. *Then the BIPS process infects at least* $9/10$ *of the whole graph in* $\mathcal{O}(\log(n)/(1-\lambda))$ *extra rounds with probability at least* $1-\mathcal{O}(1/n^3)$.

PROOF. Assume A_t has size less or equal than $9n/10$ but greater than $K\log(n)/(1-\lambda)^2$, then from Lemma 1

$$\begin{aligned}\mathbf{E}(A_{t+1}|A_t) &\geq A_t(1+(1-\lambda^2)(1-9/10)) \\ &\geq A_t\left(1+\frac{1-\lambda}{10}\right).\end{aligned}$$

Let $\varepsilon = \sqrt{10\log(n)/A_t}$. Observe that, given A_t, the size of A_{t+1} is the sum of independent Bernoulli random variables. Using Chernoff bound for the lower tail of the sum of Bernoulli random variables, we get

$$\begin{aligned}&\mathbf{P}(A_{t+1} < (1-\varepsilon)\mathbf{E}(A_{t+1}|A_t)|A_t) \\ &\leq e^{-\varepsilon^2\mathbf{E}(A_{t+1}|A_t)/2} = e^{-5\log(n)} = \frac{1}{n^5}. \qquad (20)\end{aligned}$$

By hypothesis $A_t \geq 4000\log n/(1-\lambda)^2$, so $\varepsilon \leq (1-\lambda)/20$. Therefore, with probability at least $1-n^{-5}$ we have

$$\begin{aligned}A_{t+1} &\geq (1-\varepsilon)\mathbf{E}(A_{t+1}|A_t) \\ &\geq A_t\left(1+\frac{1-\lambda}{10}\right)\left(1-\frac{1-\lambda}{20}\right) \\ &\geq A_t\left(1+\frac{1-\lambda}{23}\right).\end{aligned}$$

Finally, we have that after $23/(1-\lambda)$ rounds, the size of infection has at least doubled. Hence, with probability at least $1-23\log(n)n^{-5}/(1-\lambda) \geq 1-n^{-4}$, after $23\log(n)/(1-\lambda)$ rounds, the infection covers at least $9n/10$ vertices. □

LEMMA 4. *Let* G *be a connected* n*-vertex* r*-regular graph with* $1-\lambda \gg \sqrt{\log(n)/n}$. *With probability at least* $1-n^{-5}$, *after* $T \leq 8\log(n)/(1-\lambda)$ *rounds the BIPS process infects the whole graph.*

PROOF. For convenience, let A_0 and B_0 be the size of the infected and non-infected sets at the beginning of this phase and denote $q = 9/10$. Clearly $A_0 \geq qn$. Let A_t and B_t be their respective sizes after t rounds. From (3) we get

$$\mathbf{E}(A_{t+1}|A_t = A) \geq A + (n-A)(1-\lambda^2)A/n. \quad (21)$$

The corresponding inequality for B_{t+1} is

$$\begin{aligned}\mathbf{E}(B_{t+1}|B_t) &\leq B_t - B_t(1-\lambda^2)A_t/n \\ &= B_t(1-(1-\lambda^2)A_t/n). \qquad (22)\end{aligned}$$

Let $|A_t| = k$. By applying the law of total probability and equation (22), we get

$$\begin{aligned}\mathbf{E}(B_{t+1}) &= \sum_{k=qn}^{n}\mathbf{E}(B_{t+1}|B_t = n-k)\mathbf{P}(B_t = n-k) \\ &\quad + \mathbf{E}(B_{t+1}|A_t < qn)\mathbf{P}(A_t < qn) \\ &\leq \sum_{k=qn}^{n}(n-k)(1-(1-\lambda^2)k/n)\mathbf{P}(B_t = n-k) \\ &\quad + n\mathbf{P}(A_t < qn) \\ &\leq \sum_{k=qn}^{n}(n-k)(1-(1-\lambda^2)q)\mathbf{P}(B_t = n-k) \\ &\quad + n\mathbf{P}(A_t < qn) \\ &\leq (1-(1-\lambda^2)q)\mathbf{E}(B_t) + n\mathbf{P}(A_t < qn). \qquad (23)\end{aligned}$$

We next prove that

$$\mathbf{P}(A_t < qn) \leq tn^{-8}. \qquad (24)$$

To check the last inequality consider the event $E_t = \{A_t \geq qn, i = 0,\ldots,t\}$. We are going to prove that E_t has high probability. Indeed

$$\begin{aligned}\mathbf{P}(E_t) &= \mathbf{P}(E_t|E_{t-1})\mathbf{P}(E_{t-1}) + \mathbf{P}(E_t|E_{t-1}^c)\mathbf{P}(E_{t-1}^c) \\ &\geq \mathbf{P}(E_t|E_{t-1})\mathbf{P}(E_{t-1}).\end{aligned}$$

Observe that A_t depends only on A_{t-1} since it is a Markov chain, then

$$\mathbf{P}(E_t|E_{t-1}) = \mathbf{P}(A_t \geq qn|A_{t-1} \geq qn),$$

and by a standard coupling argument

$$\mathbf{P}(A_t \geq qn|A_{t-1} \geq qn) \geq \mathbf{P}(A_t \geq qn|A_{t-1} = qn).$$

Choose $\varepsilon = \sqrt{16\log(n)/qn}$, then, by Chernoff bound

$$\begin{aligned}&\mathbf{P}(A_{t+1} < (1-\varepsilon)\mathbf{E}(A_{t+1}|A_t = qn)|A_t = qn) \\ &\leq e^{-\varepsilon^2\mathbf{E}(A_{t+1}|A_t = qn)/2} = e^{-8\log(n)} = \frac{1}{n^8}.\end{aligned}$$

Since we assume that $1-\lambda \gg \sqrt{\log(n)/n}$, we have $A_t = qn \geq 4000\log(n)/(1-\lambda)^2$, so $\varepsilon \leq (1-\lambda)/15$. Thus with probability at least $1-n^{-8}$ we have

$$\begin{aligned}A_{t+1} &\geq (1-\varepsilon)\mathbf{E}(A_{t+1}|A_t = qn) \\ &\geq qn\left(1+\frac{1-\lambda}{10}\right)\left(1-\frac{1-\lambda}{15}\right) \geq qn.\end{aligned}$$

Therefore $\mathbf{P}(A_t \geq qn|A_{t-1} = qn) \geq 1-n^{-8}$. We conclude that

$$\mathbf{P}(E_t) \geq (1-n^{-8})^t \geq 1-tn^{-8}.$$

Observe that $\mathbf{P}(A_t \geq qn) \geq \mathbf{P}(E_t) \geq 1-tn^{-8}$, so (24) holds.

Returning to our analysis, from Inequalities (23) and (24) we have

$$\mathbf{E}(B_{t+1}) \leq (1-(1-\lambda^2)q)\mathbf{E}(B_t) + tn^{-7}. \qquad (25)$$

Denote $\theta = (1-(1-\lambda^2)q)$, then by iterating (25) and using $B_0 = (1-q)n$, we get

$$\mathbf{E}(B_t) \leq \theta^t(1-q)n + \mathcal{O}(t^2n^{-7}) \leq n\theta^t + \mathcal{O}(t^2n^{-7}).$$

Choosing $T = 5\log(n)/\log(1/\theta)$ and applying Markov's inequality give

$$\begin{aligned}\mathbf{P}(B_T \geq 1) &\leq \mathbf{E}(B_T) \leq \theta^T + \mathcal{O}(T^2n^{-7}) \\ &= n^{-5} + \mathcal{O}(T^2n^{-7}). \qquad (26)\end{aligned}$$

Finally, observe that for $0 < \theta < 1$ we have $(1-\theta) \leq \log(1/\theta)$ and thus

$$\begin{aligned}T &= 6\log(n)/(\log(1/\theta)) \leq 6\log(n)/(1-\theta) \\ &\leq 6\log(n)/(q(1-\lambda^2)) \leq 6\log(n)/(q(1-\lambda)) \\ &\leq 8\log(n)/(1-\lambda) = \mathcal{O}(n), \qquad (27)\end{aligned}$$

where the last bound follows from the assumption $1-\lambda \gg \sqrt{(\log n)/n}$. We obtain $\mathbf{P}(B_T \geq 1) = \mathcal{O}(n^{-5})$ from (26) and (27). □

PROOF OF THEOREM 2. Apply Lemma 2 with $m = 4000(\log n)/(1-\lambda^2)$. Observe that since we assume $1-\lambda \gg \sqrt{(\log n)/n}$, there is no problem with the restriction $m \leq n/2$ in this lemma. After that a straightforward application of Lemmas 3 and 4 gives us the result. □

6. ACKNOWLEDGMENTS

The research presented in this paper has been supported by EPSRC grant EP/M005038/1, "Randomized algorithms for computer networks". Nicolás Rivera was supported by funding from Becas CHILE.

7. REFERENCES

[1] N. Alon, C. Avin, M. Koucký, G. Kozma, Z. Lotker, and M. R. Tuttle. Many random walks are faster than one. *Combinatorics, Probability & Computing*, 20(4):481–502, 2011.

[2] C. Bezuidenhout and G. Grimmett. The critical contact process dies out. *The Annals of Probability*, pages 1462–1482, 1990.

[3] A. Z. Broder, A. R. Karlin, P. Raghavan, and E. Upfal. Trading space for time in undirected s-t connectivity. In *STOC*, pages 543–549. ACM, 1989.

[4] C. Cooper, A. M. Frieze, and T. Radzik. Multiple random walks in random regular graphs. *SIAM J. Discrete Math.*, 23(4):1738–1761, 2009.

[5] C. Dutta, G. Pandurangan, R. Rajaraman, and S. Roche. Coalescing-branching random walks on graphs. In *Proceedings of the Twenty-fifth Annual ACM Symposium on Parallelism in Algorithms and Architectures*, SPAA '13, pages 176–185, New York, NY, USA, 2013. ACM.

[6] C. Dutta, G. Pandurangan, R. Rajaraman, and S. Roche. Coalescing-branching random walks on graphs. *ACM Trans. Parallel Comput.*, 2(3):20:1–20:29, Nov. 2015.

[7] R. Elsässer and T. Sauerwald. Tight bounds for the cover time of multiple random walks. In S. Albers, A. Marchetti-Spaccamela, Y. Matias, S. E. Nikoletseas, and W. Thomas, editors, *Automata, Languages and Programming, 36th International Colloquium, ICALP 2009, Rhodes, Greece, July 5-12, 2009, Proceedings, Part I*, volume 5555 of *Lecture Notes in Computer Science*, pages 415–426. Springer, 2009.

[8] T. E. Harris. Contact interactions on a lattice. *Ann. Probab.*, 2(6):969–988, 12 1974.

[9] G. Innocent, I. Morrison, J. Brownlie, and G. Gettinby. A computer simulation of the transmission dynamics and the effects of duration of immunity and survival of persistently infected animals on the spread of bovine viral diarrhoea virus in dairy cattle. *Epidemiology and Infection*, 119:91–100, 8 1997.

[10] T. Liggett. *Stochastic Interacting Systems: Contact, Voter and Exclusion Processes*. Die Grundlehren der mathematischen Wissenschaften in Einzeldarstellungen. Springer, 1999.

[11] T. M. Liggett. *Perplexing Problems in Probability: Festschrift in Honor of Harry Kesten*, chapter Branching Random Walks on Finite Trees, pages 315–330. Birkhäuser Boston, Boston, MA, 1999.

[12] N. Madras and R. Schinazi. Branching random walks on trees. *Stochastic Processes and their Applications*, 42(2):255 – 267, 1992.

[13] R. Pemantle. The contact process on trees. *Ann. Probab.*, 20(4):2089–2116, 10 1992.

Ant-Inspired Density Estimation via Random Walks

[Extended Abstract]*

Cameron Musco
Massachusetts Institute of Technology
32 Vassar Street
Cambridge, MA
cnmusco@mit.edu

Hsin-Hao Su
Massachusetts Institute of Technology
32 Vassar Street
Cambridge, MA
hsinhao@mit.edu

Nancy Lynch
Massachusetts Institute of Technology
32 Vassar Street
Cambridge, MA
lynch@csail.mit.edu

ABSTRACT

Many ant species employ distributed population density estimation in applications ranging from quorum sensing [21], to task allocation [9], to appraisal of enemy colony strength [1]. It has been shown that ants estimate density by tracking encounter rates – the higher the population density, the more often the ants bump into each other [21, 10].

We study distributed density estimation from a theoretical perspective. We show that a group of anonymous agents randomly walking on a grid are able to estimate their density d to within a multiplicative factor $1 \pm \epsilon$ with probability $1-\delta$ in just $\tilde{O}\left(\frac{\log(1/\delta)\log(1/d\epsilon)}{d\epsilon^2}\right)$ steps by measuring their encounter rates with other agents. Despite dependencies inherent in the fact that nearby agents may collide repeatedly (and, worse, cannot recognize when this happens), this bound nearly matches what is required to estimate d by independently sampling grid locations.

From a biological perspective, our work helps shed light on how ants and other social insects can obtain relatively accurate density estimates via encounter rates. From a technical perspective, our analysis provides new tools for understanding complex dependencies in the collision probabilities of multiple random walks. We bound the strength of these dependencies using *local mixing properties* of the underlying graph. Our results extend beyond the grid to more general graphs and we discuss applications to social network size estimation, density estimation by robot swarms, and random walked-based sampling of sensor networks.

1. INTRODUCTION

The ability to sense local population density is an important tool used by many ant species. When a colony must relocate to a new nest, scouts search for potential nest sites, assess their quality, and recruit other scouts to high quality locations. A high enough density of scouts at a potential new nest (a *quorum threshold*) triggers those ants to decide on the site and transport the rest of the colony there [21]. When neighboring colonies compete for territory, a high relative density of a colony's ants in a contested area will cause those ants to attack enemies in the area, while a low relative density will cause the colony to retreat [1]. Varying densities of ants performing certain tasks such as foraging or brood care can trigger other ants to switch tasks, maintaining proper worker allocation within in the colony [9, 22].

It has been shown that ants estimate density in a distributed manner, via encounter rates [21, 10]. As ants randomly walk around an area, if they bump into a larger number of other ants, this indicates a higher population density. By tracking encounters with specific types of ants, e.g. successful foragers or enemies, ants can estimate more specific densities. This strategy allows each ant to obtain an accurate density estimate and requires very little communication – ants must simply detect when they collide and do not perform any higher level data aggregation.

1.1 Density Estimation on the Grid

We study distributed density estimation from a theoretical perspective. We model a colony of ants as a set of anonymous agents randomly distributed on a two-dimensional grid. Computation proceeds in rounds, with each agent stepping in a random direction in each round. A *collision* occurs when two agents reach the same position in the same round and encounter rate is measured as the number of collisions an agent is involved in during a sequence of rounds divided by the number of rounds. Aside from collision detection, the agents have no other means of communication.

The intuition that encounter rate tracks density is clear. It is easy to show that the *expected* encounter rate measured by each agent is exactly the density d – the number of agents divided by the grid size (see Lemma 2). However, it is unclear if encounter rate actually gives a good density estimate – i.e., if it concentrates around its expectation.

Consider agents positioned not on the grid, but on a complete graph. In each round, each agent steps to a uniformly random position and in expectation, the number of other agents they collide with in this step is d. Since each agent chooses its new location uniformly at random in each step, collisions are essentially *independent* between rounds. The agents are effectively taking independent Bernoulli samples with success probability d, and by a standard Chernoff bound, within $O\left(\frac{\log(1/\delta)}{d\epsilon^2}\right)$ rounds obtain a $(1 \pm \epsilon)$ multiplicative approximation to d with probability $1-\delta$.

*Full version available at http://arxiv.org/abs/1603.02981

PODC'16, July 25 - 28, 2016, Chicago, IL, USA

ISBN 978-1-4503-3964-3/16/07...$15.00

DOI: http://dx.doi.org/10.1145/2933057.2933106

On the grid graph, the picture is significantly more complex. If two agents are initially located near each other, they are more likely to collide via random walking. After a first collision, due to their proximity, they are likely to collide repeatedly in future rounds. The agents cannot recognize repeat collisions since they are anonymous and even if they could, it is unclear that it would help. On average, compared to the complete graph, agents collide with fewer individuals and collide multiple times with those individuals that they do encounter, causing an increase in encounter rate variance and making density estimation more difficult.

Mathematically speaking, on a graphs with *fast mixing times* [14], like the complete graph, each agent's location is weakly correlated with its previous locations. This ensures that collisions are also weakly correlated between rounds and encounter rate serves as a very accurate estimate of density. The grid graph on the other hand is *slow mixing* – agents' positions and hence collisions are highly correlated between rounds. This correlation increases encounter rate variance.

1.2 Our Contributions

Surprisingly, despite this increased variance, encounter rate-based density estimation on the grid is nearly as accurate as on the complete graph. $O\left(\frac{\log(1/\delta)\log\log(1/\delta)\log(1/d\epsilon)}{d\epsilon^2}\right)$ rounds suffices for each agent's encounter rate to be a $(1\pm\epsilon)$ approximation to d with probability $1-\delta$ (see Theorem 1).

Technically, to bound accuracy on the grid, we obtain moment bounds on the number of times that two randomly walking agents repeatedly collide over a set of rounds. These bounds also apply to the number of equalizations (returns to starting location) of a single walk. While *expected* random walk hitting times, return times, and collision rates are well understood [14, 5], higher moment bounds and high probability results are much less common. We hope our bounds are of general use in the theoretical study of random walks and random-walk based algorithms.

Our moment bounds show that, while the grid graph is slow mixing, it has sufficiently strong *local mixing* to make random walk-based density estimation accurate. Random walks tend to spread quickly over a local area and not repeatedly cover the same nodes. Significant work has focused on showing that random walk sampling is nearly as good as independent sampling for fast mixing expander graphs [7, 4]. We are the first to extend this type of analysis to slowly mixing graphs, showing that strong local mixing is sufficient in many applications.

Beyond the grid, we show how to generate moment bounds from a bound on the probability that two random walks re-collide (analogously, that a single random walk equalizes) after a certain number of steps, and apply this technique to d-dimensional grids, regular expanders, and hypercubes. We discuss applications of our results to social network size estimation via random walk [11], obtaining significant improvements over known work for networks with slow global mixing time, but strong local mixing. We also discuss connections to robot swarm density estimation by robot swarms and random walk-based sensor network sampling [3, 13].

2. THEORETICAL MODEL

We consider a two-dimensional torus with A nodes (dimensions $\sqrt{A}\times\sqrt{A}$) populated with identical anonymous agents. We assume that A is large – larger than the area agents traverse over the runtimes of our algorithms. We feel that this torus model successfully captures the dynamics of density estimation on a surface, while avoiding complicating factors of boundary behavior.

Initially each agent is placed independently at a uniform random node in the torus. This placement is important for our bounds – otherwise adversarial positioning could force the agents to walk for the mixing time of the grid $O(A\log A)$ before obtaining good density estimates. We believe the assumption is a reasonable model for the positioning of a colony of active agents looking to perform density estimation, however weakening it would be interesting.

Computation proceeds in discrete, synchronous rounds. Each agent has an ordered pair *position* which it updates in each round with a step chosen uniformly at random from $\{(0,1),(0,-1),(1,0),(-1,0)\}$. Of course, in reality ants do not move via pure random walk – observed encounter rates seem to actually be lower than predicted by a pure random walk model [10, 20]. However, we feel that our model sufficiently captures the highly random movement of ants while remaining tractable to analysis and applicable to ant-inspired random walk-based algorithms (Section 5).

Aside from the ability to move in each round, agents can sense the number of agents other than themselves at their position at the *end of each round*, formally through calling *count(position)*. We say that two agents *collide in round* r if they have the same position at the end of the round. Outside of collision counting, agents have no means of communication. They are anonymous (cannot uniquely identify each other) and all execute identical density estimation routines.

Density Estimation Problem.

Let $(n+1)$ be the number of agents and define population density as $d \stackrel{\text{def}}{=} n/A$. Each agent's goal is to estimate d to $(1\pm\epsilon)$ accuracy with probability $1-\delta$ for $\epsilon,\delta\in(0,1)$ – i.e., to return an estimate $\tilde{d}$ with $\mathbb{P}\left[\tilde{d}\in[(1-\epsilon)d,(1+\epsilon)d]\right]\geq 1-\delta$. As a technicality, with $n+1$ agents we define $d=n/A$ instead of $d=(n+1)/A$ for convenience of calculation. In the natural case, when n is large, the distinction is minor.

3. DENSITY ESTIMATION VIA RANDOM WALK COLLISION RATES

As discussed, the challenge in analyzing random walk-based density estimation arises from increased variance due to repeated collisions of nearby agents. In our full paper [19], we show that, if not restricted to random walking, agents can avoid collision correlations by splitting into 'stationary' and 'mobile' groups and only counting collisions between members of different groups. This allows them to essentially simulate independent sampling of grid locations to estimate density. This method is extremely simple to analyze, however is not 'natural' in a biological sense or useful in the applications of Section 5. Further, independent sampling is unnecessary! Algorithm 1 describes a simple random walk-based approach that gives a nearly matching bound.

3.1 Random Walk Algorithm Analysis

Our main result follows; its proof appears at the end of Section 3 after some preliminary lemmas.

Algorithm 1 Encounter Rate-Based Density Estimation

```
input: runtime t
  c := 0
  for r = 1, ..., t do
    position := position + rand{(0,1), (0,−1), (1,0), (−1,0)}
    c := c + count(position)          ▷ Update collision count.
  end for
  return d̃ = c/t
```

THEOREM 1 (DENSITY ESTIMATION ACCURACY). *After running for t rounds, for $t \leq A$, Algorithm 1 returns $\tilde{d}$ such that, for any $\delta > 0$, with probability $\geq 1-\delta$, $\tilde{d} \in [(1-\epsilon)d, (1+\epsilon)d]$ for $\epsilon = \sqrt{\frac{\log(1/\delta)\log(t)}{td}}$. In other words, for any $\epsilon,\delta \in (0,1)$ if $t = \Theta\left(\frac{\log(1/\delta)\log\log(1/\delta)\log(1/d\epsilon)}{d\epsilon^2}\right)$, $\tilde{d}$ is a $(1 \pm \epsilon)$ multiplicative estimate of d with probability $\geq 1-\delta$.*

Throughout our analysis, we take the viewpoint of a single agent executing Algorithm 1, referred to as 'agent a'. To start, we show that the encounter rate $\tilde{d}$ is an unbiased estimator of d:

LEMMA 2 (UNBIASED ESTIMATOR). *$\mathbb{E}\,\tilde{d} = d$.*

PROOF. We can decompose c as the sum of collisions with different agents over different rounds. Specifically, give the n other agents arbitrary ids $1, 2, ..., n$ and let $c_j(r)$ equal 1 if agent a collides with agent j in round r, and 0 otherwise. By linearity of expectation: $\mathbb{E}\,c = \sum_{j=1}^{n}\sum_{r=1}^{t}\mathbb{E}\,c_j(r)$.

Since each agent is initially at a uniform random location and after any number of steps, is still at uniform random location, for all j, r, $\mathbb{E}\,c_j(r) = 1/A$. Thus, $\mathbb{E}\,c = nt/A = dt$ and $\mathbb{E}\,\tilde{d} = \mathbb{E}\,c/t = d$. □

With Lemma 2 in place, we now must show that the encounter rate is close to its expectation with high probability and hence provides a good estimate of density.

3.2 Bounding Effects of Repeat Collisions

Let $c_j = \sum_{r=1}^{t} c_j(r)$ be the total number of collisions with agent j. Due to the initial uniform distribution of the agents, the c_j's are all independent and identically distributed.

Each c_j is the sum of highly correlated random variables – due to the slow mixing of the grid, if two agents collide at round r, they are much more likely to collide in successive rounds. However, by bounding the strength of this correlation, we are able to give strong bounds on the moments of the distribution of each c_j, showing that it is sub-exponential. It follows that $\tilde{d} = \frac{1}{t}\sum_{j=1}^{n} c_j$, is also sub-exponential and hence concentrates strongly around its expectation, the true density d.

We first bound the probability of a re-collision in round $r+m$, assuming a collision in round r.

LEMMA 3 (RE-COLLISION PROBABILITY BOUND). *Consider two agents a_1 and a_2 randomly walking on a two-dimensional torus of dimensions $\sqrt{A} \times \sqrt{A}$. If a_1 and a_2 collide again in round r, for any $m \geq 0$, the probability that a_1 and a_2 collide in round $r+m$ is $\Theta\left(\frac{1}{m+1}\right) + O\left(\frac{1}{A}\right)$.*

PROOF. From round r to round $r+m$, a_1 and a_2 take $2m$ random steps in total. Let M_x be the total number of steps they take in the x direction and M_y be the total number in the y direction. $M_x + M_y = 2m$.

We start by computing the probability that the agents collide in round $r+m$ conditioned on the values of M_x and M_y. All steps are chosen independently, so we can consider movement in the x and y directions separately. Specifically, let $\mathcal{C}$ be the event that the a_1 and a_2 collide in round $r+m$, $\mathcal{C}_x$ be the event that they have the same x position, and $\mathcal{C}_y$ be the event that they have the same y position. We have:

$$\mathbb{P}[\mathcal{C}|M_x = m_x, M_y = m_y] = \mathbb{P}[\mathcal{C}_x|M_x = m_x] \cdot \mathbb{P}[\mathcal{C}_y|M_y = m_y]. \tag{1}$$

We first consider $\mathbb{P}[\mathcal{C}_x|M_x = m_x]$. All bounds will hold symmetrically for the y dimension. We split our analysis into two cases. Let $\mathcal{C}_x^1$ be the event that the two agents have the same x position after round $r+m$ and have identical displacements from their starting locations. Let $\mathcal{C}_x^2$ be the event that the two agents have the same x position after round $r+m$ but *do not* have identical displacements. This requires that the agents 'wrap' around the torus, ending at the same position despite moving different amounts in the x direction. We have $\mathbb{P}[\mathcal{C}_x|M_x = m_x] = \mathbb{P}[\mathcal{C}_x^1|M_x = m_x] + \mathbb{P}[\mathcal{C}_x^2|M_x = m_x]$.

$\mathbb{P}[\mathcal{C}_x^1|M_x = m_x]$ is identical to the probability that a single random walk takes m_x steps and has 0 overall displacement – i.e. takes an equal number of clockwise and counterclockwise steps. This is well known [6] and given by:

$$\mathbb{P}[\mathcal{C}_x^1|M_x = m_x] = \binom{m_x}{m_x/2}\left(\frac{1}{2}\right)^{m_x} = \frac{m_x!}{(\frac{m_x}{2}!)^2}\left(\frac{1}{2}\right)^{m_x}. \tag{2}$$

Above we assume m_x is even – otherwise $\mathcal{C}_x^1$ cannot occur. By Stirling's approximation for any $n > 0$, $n! = \sqrt{2\pi n}\left(\frac{n}{e}\right)^n\left(1 + O\left(\frac{1}{n}\right)\right)$. Plugging this into 2:

$$\begin{aligned}\mathbb{P}[\mathcal{C}_x^1|M_x = m_x] &= \frac{m_x!}{(\frac{m_x}{2}!)^2}\left(\frac{1}{2}\right)^{m_x}\\ &= \frac{\sqrt{2\pi m_x}\left(\frac{m_x}{e}\right)^{m_x}\left(1+O\left(\frac{1}{m_x}\right)\right)}{\pi m_x\left(\frac{m_x/2}{e}\right)^{m_x}\left(1+O\left(\frac{1}{m_x/2}\right)\right)^2}\cdot\left(\frac{1}{2}\right)^{m_x}\\ &= \Theta\left(\frac{1}{\sqrt{m_x+1}}\right).\end{aligned}$$

(We use $m_x + 1$ instead of m_x in the denominator so that the bound holds in the case when $m_x = 0$.)

$\mathbb{P}[\mathcal{C}_x^2|M_x = m_x]$ is the probability that two agents have the same x position after round $r+m$ but have different total displacements. It is identical to the probability that a single m_x step random walk has overall displacement $\pm c\sqrt{A}$ for some integer $c \geq 1$ (and so 'wraps around' the torus, ending at its starting location). Roughly, we bound the probability of this event by the probability that the random walk ends at *any* other location on the torus. There are $\sqrt{A}$ such locations, so the probability is bounded by $O\left(\frac{1}{\sqrt{A}}\right)$.

$$\mathbb{P}[\mathcal{C}_x^2|M_x = m_x] = 2\cdot\left(\frac{1}{2}\right)^{m_x}\cdot\sum_{c=1}^{\lfloor\frac{m_x}{\sqrt{A}}\rfloor}\binom{m_x}{\frac{m_x - c\sqrt{A}}{2}} \tag{3}$$

where the extra factor of 2 comes from the fact that the displacement may be either clockwise or counterclockwise. (Note that if $\frac{m_x - c\sqrt{A}}{2}$ is not an integer we just define the binomial coefficient to equal 0.)

For $i \in [1, ..., \sqrt{A}-1]$, let $\mathcal{D}_x^i$ be the event that a single random walk is i steps clockwise from its starting location after taking M_x steps. We have:

$$\begin{aligned}
&\mathbb{P}[\mathcal{D}_x^i | M_x = m_x] \\
&= \left(\frac{1}{2}\right)^{m_x} \cdot \sum_{c=-\left\lfloor \frac{m_x+i}{\sqrt{A}} \right\rfloor}^{\left\lfloor \frac{m_x-i}{\sqrt{A}} \right\rfloor} \binom{m_x}{\frac{m_x+i+c\sqrt{A}}{2}} \\
&\geq \left(\frac{1}{2}\right)^{m_x} \cdot \sum_{c=-\left\lfloor \frac{m_x+i}{\sqrt{A}} \right\rfloor}^{-1} \binom{m_x}{\frac{m_x+i+c\sqrt{A}}{2}} \\
&\geq \left(\frac{1}{2}\right)^{m_x} \cdot \sum_{c=1}^{\left\lfloor \frac{m_x}{\sqrt{A}} \right\rfloor} \binom{m_x}{\frac{m_x+i-c\sqrt{A}}{2}}. \qquad (4)
\end{aligned}$$

For any $i \in [1, ..., \sqrt{A}-1]$, and any $c \geq 1$, $\frac{m_x+i-c\sqrt{A}}{2}$ is closer to $\frac{m_x}{2}$ than $\frac{m_x-c\sqrt{A}}{2}$ is, so

$$\binom{m_x}{\frac{m_x+i-c\sqrt{A}}{2}} > \binom{m_x}{\frac{m_x-c\sqrt{A}}{2}} \qquad (5)$$

as long as $\frac{m_x+i-c\sqrt{A}}{2}$ is an integer. This allows us to lower bound $\mathbb{P}[\mathcal{D}_x^i | M_x = m_x]$ using $\mathbb{P}\left[\mathcal{C}_x^2 | M_x = m_x\right]$. Let $\mathcal{E}_{i,c}$ equal 1 if $\frac{m_x+i-c\sqrt{A}}{2}$ is an integer and 0 otherwise. Since $\mathcal{C}_x^2$ and each $\mathcal{D}_x^i$ are disjoint events:

$$\mathbb{P}\left[\mathcal{C}_x^2 | M_x = m_x\right] + \sum_{i=1}^{\sqrt{A}-1} \mathbb{P}\left[\mathcal{D}_x^i | M_x = m_x\right] \leq 1$$

$$\mathbb{P}\left[\mathcal{C}_x^2 | M_x = m_x\right] + \left(\frac{1}{2}\right)^{m_x} \sum_{i=1}^{\sqrt{A}-1} \sum_{c=1}^{\left\lfloor \frac{m_x}{\sqrt{A}} \right\rfloor} \binom{m_x}{\frac{m_x+i-c\sqrt{A}}{2}} \leq 1$$

(applying (4))

$$\mathbb{P}\left[\mathcal{C}_x^2 | M_x = m_x\right] + \left(\frac{1}{2}\right)^{m_x} \sum_{c=1}^{\left\lfloor \frac{m_x}{\sqrt{A}} \right\rfloor} \left(\binom{m_x}{\frac{m_x-c\sqrt{A}}{2}} \sum_{i=1}^{\sqrt{A}-1} \mathcal{E}_{i,c} \right) \leq 1$$

(by (5) and switching summations)

$$\mathbb{P}\left[\mathcal{C}_x^2 | M_x = m_x\right] \cdot \Theta(\sqrt{A}) \leq 1.$$

The last step follows from combining (3) with the fact that $\sum_{i=1}^{\sqrt{A}-1} \mathcal{E}_{i,c} = \Theta\left(\sqrt{A}\right)$ for all c since $\frac{m_x+i-c\sqrt{A}}{2}$ is integral for half the possible $i \in [1, ..., \sqrt{A}-1]$. Rearranging, we have $\mathbb{P}\left[\mathcal{C}_x^2 | M_x = m_x\right] = O\left(\frac{1}{\sqrt{A}}\right)$.

Combining our bounds for $\mathcal{C}_x^1$ and $\mathcal{C}_x^2$, $\mathbb{P}\left[\mathcal{C}_x | M_x = m_x\right] = \Theta\left(\frac{1}{\sqrt{m_x+1}}\right) + O\left(\frac{1}{\sqrt{A}}\right)$. Identical bounds hold for the y direction and by (1) we have:

$$\begin{aligned}
\mathbb{P}\left[\mathcal{C} | M_x = m_x, M_y = m_y\right] &= \Theta\left(\frac{1}{\sqrt{(m_x+1)(m_y+1)}}\right) \\
+ O\left(\frac{1}{\sqrt{A(m_x+1)}} + \frac{1}{\sqrt{A(m_y+1)}}\right) &+ O\left(\frac{1}{A}\right). \qquad (6)
\end{aligned}$$

Finally, we remove the conditioning on M_x and M_y. Since direction is chosen independently and uniformly at random for each step, $\mathbb{E}\, M_x = \mathbb{E}\, M_y = m$. By a Chernoff bound:

$$\mathbb{P}[M_x \leq m/2] \leq 2e^{-(1/2)^2 \cdot m/2} = O\left(\frac{1}{m+1}\right).$$

(Again using $m+1$ instead of m to cover the $m=0$ case). An identical bound holds for M_y, and so, except with probability $O\left(\frac{1}{m+1}\right)$ both are $\geq m/2$. Plugging into (6) gives:

$$\begin{aligned}
\mathbb{P}\left[\mathcal{C}\right] &= \Theta\left(\frac{1}{m+1}\right) + O\left(\frac{1}{\sqrt{A(m+1)}}\right) + O\left(\frac{1}{A}\right) \\
&= \Theta\left(\frac{1}{m+1}\right) + O\left(\frac{1}{A}\right).
\end{aligned}$$

□

We note that the techniques of Lemma 3 also apply to bounding the probability that a single random walk returns to its origin (equalizes) after m steps (proof in full paper).

COROLLARY 4 (EQUALIZATION PROBABILITY BOUND). *Consider agent a_1 randomly walking on a two-dimensional torus of dimensions $\sqrt{A} \times \sqrt{A}$. If a_1 is located at position p after round r, for any even $m \geq 0$, the probability that a_1 is again at position p after round $r+m$ is $\Theta\left(\frac{1}{m+1}\right) + O\left(\frac{1}{A}\right)$.*

Roughly, assuming as in Theorem 1 that $t \leq A$, by Lemma 3, in t rounds, a expects to re-collide with any agent it encounters $\sum_{m=0}^{t-1} \Theta\left(\frac{1}{m+1}\right) = \Theta(\log t)$ times. By Lemma 2, a expects to be involved in $dt = nt/A$ total collisions. So accounting for re-collisions, it expects to collide with $\Theta\left(\frac{nt}{A \log t}\right)$ unique individuals. This is formalized in Lemma 5 (proof in full paper).

LEMMA 5 (FIRST COLLISION PROBABILITY). *Assuming $t \leq A$, for all $j \in [1, ..., n]$, $\mathbb{P}\left[c_j \geq 1\right] = \Theta\left(\frac{t}{A \log t}\right)$.*

We now give our main technical lemma – a strong moment bound on the distribution of c_j. Intuitively, not only does an agent *expect* to collide at most $O(\log t)$ times with any other agent it encounters, but this bound extends to the higher moments of the collision distribution, and so holds with high probability. In this sense, the grid has strong *local mixing* – random walks spread quickly over a local area and do not cover the same nodes too many times.

LEMMA 6. *(Collision Moment Bound) For $j \in [1, ..., n]$, let $\bar{c}_j \overset{\text{def}}{=} c_j - \mathbb{E}\, c_j$. For all $k \geq 2$, assuming $t \leq A$, $\mathbb{E}\left[\bar{c}_j^k\right] = O\left(\frac{t}{A} \cdot k! \log^{k-1} t\right)$.*

PROOF. We expand $\mathbb{E}[\bar{c}_j^k] = \mathbb{P}[c_j \geq 1] \cdot \mathbb{E}[\bar{c}_j^k | c_j \geq 1] + \mathbb{P}[c_j = 0] \cdot \mathbb{E}[\bar{c}_j^k | c_j = 0]$, and so by Lemma 5:

$$\mathbb{E}\left[\bar{c}_j^k\right] = O\left(\frac{t}{A \log t} \cdot \mathbb{E}\left[\bar{c}_j^k | c_j \geq 1\right] + \mathbb{E}\left[\bar{c}_j^k | c_j = 0\right]\right).$$

$\mathbb{E}\left[\bar{c}_j^k | c_j = 0\right] = (\mathbb{E}\, c_j)^k = (t/A)^k \leq \frac{t}{A} k! \log^{k-1} t$ for all $k \geq 2$. Further, $\mathbb{E}\left[\bar{c}_j^k | c_j \geq 1\right] \leq \mathbb{E}\left[c_j^k | c_j \geq 1\right]$, since $\mathbb{E}\, c_j = \frac{t}{A} \leq 1$. So to prove the lemma, it just remains to show that $\mathbb{E}\left[c_j^k | c_j \geq 1\right] = O\left(k! \log^k t\right)$.

Conditioning on $c_j \geq 1$, we know the agents have an initial collision in some round $t' \leq t$. We split c_j over rounds: $c_j = \sum_{r=t'}^{t} c_j(r) \leq \sum_{r=t'}^{t'+t-1} c_j(r)$. To simplify notation we relabel round t' round 1 and so round $t'+t-1$ becomes round t. Expanding c_j^k out fully using the summation:

$$\mathbb{E}\left[c_j^k\right] = \mathbb{E}\left[\sum_{r_1=1}^{t}\sum_{r_2=1}^{t}...\sum_{r_k=1}^{t} c_j(r_1)c_j(r_2)...c_j(r_k)\right]$$
$$= \sum_{r_1=1}^{t}\sum_{r_2=1}^{t}...\sum_{r_k=1}^{t}\mathbb{E}\left[c_j(r_1)c_j(r_2)...c_j(r_k)\right].$$

$\mathbb{E}\left[c_j(r_1)c_j(r_2)...c_j(r_k)\right]$ is just the probability that the two agents collide in each of rounds $r_1, r_2, ...r_k$. Assume w.l.o.g. that $r_1 \leq r_2 \leq ... \leq r_k$. By Lemma 3 this is:

$$O\left(\frac{1}{r_1(r_2-r_1+1)(r_3-r_2+1)...(r_k-r_{k-1}+1)}\right).$$

So we can rewrite, by linearity of expectation:

$$\mathbb{E}\left[c_j^k\right] = k!\sum_{r_1=1}^{t}...\sum_{r_k=r_{k-1}}^{t} O\left(\frac{1}{r_1...(r_k-r_{k-1}+1)}\right).$$

We multiply by $k!$ since in this sum we only have *ordered* k-tuples, whereas the original sum is over *unordered* k-tuples. We can bound:

$$\sum_{r_k=r_{k-1}}^{t}\frac{1}{r_k-r_{k-1}+1} = 1+\frac{1}{2}+...+\frac{1}{t} = O(\log t)$$

so rearranging the sum and simplifying gives:

$$\mathbb{E}\left[c_j^k\right] = k!\sum_{r_1=1}^{t}\frac{1}{r_1}...\sum_{r_k=r_{k-1}}^{t}\frac{1}{r_k-r_{k-1}+1}$$
$$= k!\sum_{r_1=1}^{t}\frac{1}{r_1}...\sum_{r_{k-1}=r_{k-2}}^{t}\frac{1}{r_{k-2}-r_{k-1}+1}\cdot O(\log t).$$

We repeat this simplification for each level of summation replacing $\sum_{r_i=r_{i-1}}^{t}\frac{1}{r_i-r_{i-1}+1}$ with $O(\log t)$. Iterating through the k levels gives $\mathbb{E}\left[c_j^k\right] = O(k!\log^k t)$ giving the lemma. □

As with Lemma 3, the techniques used in Lemmas 5 and 6 can be applied to a single walk. We give two bounds that may be of independent interest (proofs in full paper)

COROLLARY 7 (RE-VISIT MOMENT BOUND). *Consider an agent a_1 randomly walking on a two-dimensional $\sqrt{A}\times\sqrt{A}$ torus that is initially located at a uniformly random location and takes $t \leq A$ steps. Let c_j be the number of times a_1 visits node j. For $j \in [1,...A]$ and all $k \geq 2$,*

$$\mathbb{E}\left[\bar{c}_j^k\right] = O\left(\frac{t}{A}\cdot k!\log^{k-1} t\right).$$

COROLLARY 8 (EQUALIZATION MOMENT BOUND). *Consider an agent a_1 randomly walking on a two-dimensional $\sqrt{A}\times\sqrt{A}$ torus. If a_1 takes $t \leq A$ steps and c is the number of times it returns to its starting position (the number of equalizations), for all $k \geq 2$, $\mathbb{E}\left[\bar{c}^k\right] = O\left(k!\log^k t\right)$.*

3.3 Concentration of Density Estimate

Armed with the moment bound of Lemma 6 we can finally show that $\sum_{j=1}^{n}\bar{c}_j$ concentrates strongly about its expectation. Since $\sum_{j=1}^{n}\bar{c}_j$ is just a mean-centered and scaled version of $\tilde{d} = \frac{1}{t}\sum_{j=1}^{n}c_j$, this is enough to prove the accuracy of encounter rate-based density estimation. We start by showing that $\sum_{j=1}^{n}\bar{c}_j$ is a sub-exponential random variable.

COROLLARY 9 ($\sum_{j=1}^{n}\bar{c}_j$ IS SUB-EXPONENTIAL). *Assuming $t \leq A$, $\sum_{j=1}^{n}\bar{c}_j$ is sub-exponential with parameters $b = \Theta(\log t)$ and $\sigma^2 = \Theta\,(td\log t)$. Specifically, for any λ with $|\lambda| < \frac{1}{b}$ $\mathbb{E}\left[e^{\lambda\sum_{j=1}^{n}\bar{c}_j}\right] \leq e^{\frac{\sigma^2\lambda^2}{2}}$.*

PROOF. By Lemma 6, for $\sigma^2 = \Theta\left(\frac{t\log t}{A}\right)$ and $b = \Theta(\log t)$, $\bar{c}_j$ satisfies the Bernstein condition: $\mathbb{E}\left[\bar{c}_j^k\right] \leq \frac{1}{2}k!\sigma^2 b^{k-2}$. This implies that $\bar{c}_j$ is sub-exponential with parameters $\sigma^2 = \Theta(\frac{t\log t}{A})$ and $b = \Theta(\log t)$ (see [23], Chapter 2). Since each $\bar{c}_j$ is independent, this gives us, for all λ with $|\lambda| \leq \frac{1}{b}$:

$$\mathbb{E}\left[e^{\lambda\sum_{j=1}^{n}\bar{c}_j}\right] = \prod_{j=1}^{n}\mathbb{E}\,e^{\lambda\bar{c}_j} \leq e^{n\cdot\frac{\lambda^2}{2}\cdot\Theta\left(\frac{t\log t}{A}\right)} = e^{\Theta(\lambda^2 td\log t)}.$$

This completes the proof by the definition of a sub-exponential random variable. □

We finally apply a standard sub-exponential tail bound [23] to prove our main result.

LEMMA 10 (SUB-EXPONENTIAL TAIL). *Suppose that X is sub-exponential with parameters (σ^2, b). Then, for any $\Delta \leq \frac{\sigma^2}{b}$, $\mathbb{P}[|X-\mathbb{E}\,X| \geq \Delta] \leq 2e^{-\frac{\Delta^2}{2\sigma^2}}$.*

PROOF OF THEOREM 1. Since $\bar{c}_j$ is just a mean-centered version of c_j, $\sum_{j=1}^{n}\bar{c}_j$ deviates from its mean exactly the same amount as $\sum_{j=1}^{n}c_j$. Further, $\tilde{d} = \frac{1}{t}\sum_{j=1}^{n}c_j$, so the probability that it falls within an ϵ multiplicative factor of its mean is the same as the probability that $\sum_{j=1}^{n}c_j$ falls within an ϵ multiplicative factor of its mean. By Corollary 9 and Lemma 10:

$$\delta = \mathbb{P}\left[\left|\sum_{j=1}^{n}c_j - \mathbb{E}\left[\sum_{j=1}^{n}c_j\right]\right| \geq \epsilon\,\mathbb{E}\left[\sum_{j=1}^{n}c_j\right]\right]$$
$$= \mathbb{P}\left[\left|\sum_{j=1}^{n}c_j - td\right| \geq \epsilon td\right] \leq 2e^{\Theta\left(-\frac{\epsilon^2 td}{\log t}\right)}.$$

$\frac{\epsilon^2 td}{\log t} = \Theta\left(\log(1/\delta)\right)$ and so $\epsilon = \Theta\left(\sqrt{\frac{\log(1/\delta)\log t}{td}}\right)$. □

4. MORE GENERAL TOPOLOGIES

We now extend our results to a broader set of graph topologies, demonstrating the generality of the local mixing analysis discussed above. We illustrate divergence between local and global mixing properties, which can have significant effects on random walk-based algorithms.

4.1 From Repeat Collision Bounds to Estimation Accuracy

Our proofs are largely independent of graph structure, using just a re-collision probability bound (Lemma 3) and the regularity (uniform node degrees) of the grid, so agents remain uniformly distributed in each round. Hence, extending our results to other regular graphs primarily involves obtaining re-collision probability bounds for these graphs.

We consider agents on A node graphs that execute analogously to Algorithm 1, stepping to a random neighbor in each round. Again, we focus on the multi-agent case but similar bounds (resembling Corollaries 7, 8) hold for single walks. We start with a general lemma, giving density estimation accuracy in terms of re-collision probability. The proof (see full paper) closely follows our grid analysis.

LEMMA 11 (GENERAL ACCURACY BOUND). *Consider a regular graph with A nodes such that, if two randomly walking agents a_1 and a_2 collide in round r, for any $0 \leq m \leq t$, the probability that they collide again in round $r+m$ is $\Theta(\beta(m))$ for some non-increasing function $\beta(m)$. Let $B(t) \stackrel{\text{def}}{=} \sum_{m=0}^{t} \beta(m)$. After running for $t \leq A$ steps, Algorithm 1 returns $\tilde{d}$ such that, for any $\delta > 0$, with probability $\geq 1-\delta$, $\tilde{d} \in [(1-\epsilon)d, (1+\epsilon)d]$ for $\epsilon = O\left(\sqrt{\frac{\log(1/\delta)B(t)}{td}}\right)$.*

Note that in the special case of the grid, by Lemma 3, we can set $\beta(m) = 1/(m+1)$ and hence $B(t) = \Theta(\log t)$, yielding Theorem 1.

Applying the above bound requires a constant factor approximation to the re-collision probability – the probability is$\Theta(\beta(m))$. Sometimes however, it is much easier to give just an upper bound – so the probability is $O(\beta(m))$. In this case a slightly weaker bound holds:

LEMMA 12 (GENERAL ACCURACY BOUND 2). *Consider a regular graph with A nodes such that, if two randomly walking agents a_1 and a_2 collide in round r, for any $0 \leq m \leq t$, the probability that they collide again in round $r+m$ is $O(\beta(m))$ for some non-increasing function $\beta(m)$. Let $B(t) \stackrel{\text{def}}{=} \sum_{m=0}^{t} \beta(m)$. After running for $t \leq A$ steps, Algorithm 1 returns $\tilde{d}$ such that, for any $\delta > 0$, with probability $\geq 1-\delta$ $\tilde{d} \in [(1-\epsilon)d, (1+\epsilon)d]$ for $\epsilon = O\left(\sqrt{\frac{\log(1/\delta)\cdot B(t)^2}{td}}\right)$.*

4.2 k-Dimensional Tori

We consider general k-dimensional tori. As k increases, local mixing becomes stronger, fewer re-collisions occur, and density estimation becomes easier. For $k \geq 3$, although the torus still mixes slowly, density estimation is as accurate as on the complete graph! We first study the ring:

LEMMA 13 (RE-COLLISION BOUND – RING). *If two randomly walking agents a_1 and a_2 are located on a 1-dimensional torus (a ring) with A nodes, and collide in round r, for any $m \geq 0$, the probability that a_1 and a_2 collide again in round $r+m$ for $k \geq 1$ is $\Theta\left(\frac{1}{\sqrt{m+1}}\right) + O\left(\frac{1}{A}\right)$.*

PROOF. We have already shown this re-collision bound in the proof of Lemma 3. It is identical to $\mathbb{P}[\mathcal{C}_x|M_x = m]$ on an $A \times A$ grid, which is bounded by$\Theta\left(\frac{1}{\sqrt{m+1}}\right) + O\left(\frac{1}{A}\right)$. □

For $m \leq A$, the $O\left(\frac{1}{A}\right)$ is absorbed into the$\Theta\left(\frac{1}{\sqrt{m+1}}\right)$ term. We estimate the sum of repeat collision probabilities using $\frac{1}{\sqrt{x}} \leq 2(\sqrt{x} - \sqrt{x-1})$ (derivation in full paper). So:

$$\sum_{m=0}^{t} \frac{1}{\sqrt{m+1}} \leq 1 + 2\left(\sqrt{2} - \sqrt{1}) + ... + (\sqrt{t+1} - \sqrt{t}\right)$$
$$= 2\sqrt{t+1} - 1.$$

Similarly, $\frac{1}{\sqrt{x-1}} \geq 2(\sqrt{x} - \sqrt{x-1})$ and so:

$$\sum_{m=0}^{t} \frac{1}{\sqrt{m+1}} \geq 2\left(\sqrt{2} - \sqrt{1}) + ... + (\sqrt{t+2} - \sqrt{t+1}\right)$$
$$= 2\sqrt{t+2} - 2.$$

So, overall $\sum_{m=0}^{t} \frac{1}{\sqrt{m+1}} = \Theta(\sqrt{t})$. Plugging into Lemma 11, on a ring, random walk-based density estimation gives: $\epsilon = O\left(\sqrt{\frac{\log(1/\delta)\sqrt{t}}{td}}\right) = O\left(\sqrt{\frac{\log(1/\delta)}{\sqrt{t}d}}\right)$. Rearranging, $t = \Theta\left(\left(\frac{\log(1/\delta)}{\epsilon^2 d}\right)^2\right)$ rounds are necessary to obtain a $1 \pm \epsilon$ approximation with probability $\geq 1-\delta$. Local mixing on the ring is much worse than on the torus– we expect to see $\Theta(\sqrt{t})$ rather than $\Theta(\log t)$ repeat collisions with every agent interacted with. Hence, density estimation is much more difficult, requiring t to be quadratic rather than linear in $1/d$.

4.2.1 Higher Dimensional Tori

We now cover $k \geq 3$. While global mixing time is on the order of $A^{2/k}$ [2] and so is slow if $k << A$, local mixing is so strong that our accuracy bounds actually match those of independent sampling! Throughout this section, we assume that k is a small constant and hide it in asymptotic notation.

LEMMA 14 (RE-COLLISION BOUND – TORUS). *If two randomly walking agents a_1 and a_2 are located on a k-dimensional torus with A nodes, and collide in round r, for any constant $k \geq 3$, $m \geq 0$, the probability that a_1 and a_2 collide in round $r+m$ is $\Theta\left(\frac{1}{(m+1)^{k/2}}\right) + O\left(\frac{1}{A}\right)$.*

PROOF. We closely follow the proof of Lemma 3. a_1 and a_2 take $2m$ total steps: M_i in each dimension for $i \in [1, ..., k]$. Let $\mathcal{C}_i$ be the event that the agents have the same position in the ith dimension in round $r+m$. Following Lemma 3,

$$\mathbb{P}[\mathcal{C}_i|M_i = m_i] = \Theta\left(\frac{1}{\sqrt{m_i+1}}\right) + O\left(\frac{1}{A^{1/k}}\right).$$

So,

$$\mathbb{P}[\mathcal{C}|M_1 = m_1, ..., M_k = m_k]$$
$$= \left[\Theta\left(\frac{1}{\sqrt{m_1+1}}\right) + O\left(\frac{1}{A^{1/k}}\right)\right] \cdot$$
$$.... \cdot \left[\Theta\left(\frac{1}{\sqrt{m_k+1}}\right) + O\left(\frac{1}{A^{1/k}}\right)\right]. \tag{7}$$

In expectation, $M_i = 2m/k$. So by a Chernoff bound,

$$\mathbb{P}[M_i \leq m/k] \leq 2e^{-(1/2)^2 \cdot 2m/3k} = O\left(\frac{1}{(m+1)^{k/2}}\right)$$

again assuming k is a small constant. Union bounding over all k dimensions, we have $M_i \geq m/k$ for all i except with probability $O\left(\frac{1}{(m+1)^{k/2}}\right)$ and hence by (7):

$$\mathbb{P}[\mathcal{C}] = O\left(\frac{1}{(m+1)^{k/2}}\right) + \left[\Theta\left(\frac{1}{\sqrt{\frac{m}{k}+1}}\right) + O\left(\frac{1}{A^{\frac{1}{k}}}\right)\right]^k$$
$$= \Theta\left(\frac{1}{(m+1)^{k/2}}\right) + O\left(\frac{1}{A}\right)$$

giving the lemma (again, asymptotic notation hides multiplicative factors in k since it is constant). □

We can plug the above bound into Lemma 12. For $t \leq A$ and $k \geq 3$, $\sum_{m=0}^{t}\left(\frac{1}{(m+1)^{k/2}} + \frac{1}{A}\right) < 1 + \sum_{m=0}^{\infty} \frac{1}{(m+1)^{k/2}} = O(1)$. So we can set $B(t) = 1$ and have $\epsilon = O\left(\frac{\sqrt{\log(1/\delta)}}{td}\right)$. Rearranging, we require $t = \Theta\left(\frac{\log(1/\delta)}{\epsilon^2 d}\right)$. This matches the performance of independent sampling up to constants.

4.3 Regular Expanders

When a graph *does* mix well globally, it also mixes well locally. The number of repeat collisions is low and accurate density estimation is possible. The most obvious example is the complete graph, on which random-walk based density estimation is equivalent to density estimation via independent sampling. We generalize to any regular expander.

LEMMA 15 (RE-COLLISION BOUND – EXPANDER). *Let G be a k-regular expander with A nodes and adjacency matrix $\mathbf{M}$. Let $\mathbf{W} = \frac{1}{k} \cdot \mathbf{M}$ be its random walk matrix, with eigenvalues $\lambda_1 \geq \lambda_2 \geq \ldots \geq \lambda_A$. Let $\lambda = \max\{|\lambda_2|, |\lambda_A|\}$. If two randomly walking agents a_1 and a_2 collide in round r, for any $m \geq 0$, the probability that they collide again in round $r+m$ is at most $\lambda^m + 2/A$.*

PROOF. Suppose that a_1 and a_2 collide at node i in round r. The probability they re-collide at round $r+m$ is $||\mathbf{W}^m \mathbf{e}_i||_2^2$, since for each j, $\mathbf{W}_{i,j}^m = (\mathbf{W}^m \mathbf{e}_i)_j$ is the probability an agent is at node j after round $r+m$ given that it is at node i after round r. We bound this norm using the following lemma on how rapidly an expander random walk converges to its stable distribution:

LEMMA 16 ([14]). *Let G be a k-regular expander with A nodes, adjacency matrix $\mathbf{M}$, and random walk matrix $\mathbf{W} = \frac{1}{k} \cdot \mathbf{M}$. Let $\lambda_1 \geq \lambda_2 \geq \ldots \geq \lambda_A$ be the eigenvalues of $\mathbf{W}$ and $\lambda = \max\{|\lambda_2|, |\lambda_A|\}$. For each $1 \leq j \leq n$,*

$$\left|(\mathbf{W}^m \cdot e_i)_j - \frac{1}{A}\right| \leq \lambda^m.$$

Now we can bound $||\mathbf{W}^m \mathbf{e}_i||_2^2$ by:

$$||\mathbf{W}^m \mathbf{e}_i||_2^2 = \sum_{j=1}^{A} (\mathbf{W}^m \mathbf{e}_i)_j^2 = \sum_{j=1}^{A} \left(\frac{1}{A} + \chi_j\right)^2$$

where $\chi_j \stackrel{\text{def}}{=} (\mathbf{W}^m \cdot \mathbf{e}_i)_j - \frac{1}{A}$ so that $\chi_j \in [-1/A, \lambda^m]$ by Lemma 16. Thus $\sum_j \chi_j = \sum_j (\mathbf{W}^m \mathbf{e}_i)_j - A \cdot (1/A) = 0$ and

$$\begin{aligned} ||\mathbf{W}^m \mathbf{e}_i||_2^2 &= \sum_{j=1}^{A} \left(\frac{1}{A} + \chi_j\right)^2 \\ &\leq \sum_{j=1}^{A} \left(\left(\frac{1}{A}\right)^2 + \frac{2\chi_j}{A} + \chi_j^2\right) = \frac{1}{A} + \sum_{j=1}^{A} \chi_j^2. \end{aligned}$$

$\sum_j \chi_j^2$ is maximized when the number of possible j with $\chi_j = \lambda^m$ is maximized. Let $S \subset [1, A]$ be the indices j with $\chi_j = \lambda^m$. Since $\sum_j \chi_j = 0$, we have $\sum_{j \in S} \lambda^m + \sum_{j \notin S} \chi_j = 0$. Therefore, $|S| \cdot \lambda^m \leq -\sum_{j \notin A} \chi_j \leq 1 - |S|/A$ and so $|S| \leq \frac{1}{\lambda^m + 1/A}$. Therefore,

$$\begin{aligned} \sum_{j=1}^{A} \chi_j^2 &\leq \sum_{j \in S} \lambda^{2m} + \sum_{j \notin S} \chi_j^2 \\ &\leq \frac{\lambda^{2m}}{\lambda^m + 1/A} + \frac{A - |S|}{A^2} \leq \lambda^m + 1/A. \end{aligned}$$

Thus, $||\mathbf{W}^m \mathbf{e}_i||_2^2 \leq \lambda^m + 2/A$, giving the lemma. □

We now apply Lemma 12, with $B(t) = \sum_{m=0}^{t} \beta(m) \leq \frac{1}{1-\lambda} + 2t/A$. Assuming $t = O(A)$,

$$\begin{aligned} \epsilon &= O\left(\sqrt{\frac{\log(1/\delta)(1/(1-\lambda) + 2t/A)^2}{td}}\right) \\ &= O\left(\sqrt{\frac{\log(1/\delta)}{td(1-\lambda)^2}}\right). \end{aligned}$$

Rearranging, $t = \Theta\left(\frac{\log(1/\delta)}{\epsilon^2 d(1-\lambda)^2}\right)$, matching independent sampling up to a factor of $O(1/(1-\lambda)^2)$.

4.4 k-Dimensional Hypercube

Finally, we give bounds for a k-dimensional hypercube. Such a graph has $A = 2^k$ vertices mapped to the elements of $\{\pm 1\}^k$, with an edge between any two vertices that differ by hamming distance 1. The hypercube is relatively fast mixing. Its adjacency matrix eigenvalues are $[-k, -k+2, -k+4, \ldots, k-4, k-2, k]$. Since it is bipartite, we can effectively ignore the negative eigenvalues and apply Lemma 15 with $\lambda = \Theta(1 - 2/k) = \Theta(1 - 1/\log A)$. This yields $t = \Theta\left(\frac{\log(1/\delta)\log^2(A)}{\epsilon^2 d}\right)$. However, it is possible to remove the dependence on A via a more refined analysis – while the global mixing time of the graph increases as A grows, local mixing becomes stronger!

LEMMA 17 (RE-COLLISION BOUND – HYPERCUBE). *If two randomly walking agents a_1 and a_2 are located on a k-dimensional hypercube with $A = 2^k$ vertices and collide in round r, for any $m \geq 0$, the probability that a_1 and a_2 collide in round $r+m$ is at most $(7/10)^m + O\left(\frac{1}{\sqrt{A}}\right)$.*

PROOF. A node of the hypercube can be represented as a k-bit string and each random walk step seen as choosing one of the bits uniformly at random and flipping it. If a_1 and a_2 collide, for each of the bit, the total number of times a_1 and a_2 chose that bit must be even. The total number of possible ways for re-collision to occur at round $r+m$ is exactly the number of ways $2m$ flips can be placed into k buckets, where each bucket has even number of elements:

$$\sum_{\substack{a_1 + \ldots + a_k = 2m \\ (a_i \mod 2) \equiv 0}} \frac{(2m)!}{a_1! \cdot \ldots \cdot a_k!}.$$

This value is equal to the coefficient of x^{2m} in the exponential generating function

$$\begin{aligned} &(2m)!\left(1 + \frac{x^2}{2!} + \frac{x^4}{4!} + \ldots\right)^k \\ &= (2m)!\left(\frac{e^x + e^{-x}}{2}\right)^k = \frac{(2m)!}{2^k} \sum_{i=0}^{k} \binom{k}{i} e^{x(2i-k)}. \end{aligned}$$

Differentiating $2m$ times, we see the coefficient of x^{2m} is:

$$\frac{1}{2^k} \sum_{i=0}^{k} \binom{k}{i} (2i-k)^{2m} = \sum_{i=0}^{k} \left(\binom{k}{i} / 2^k\right) \cdot (2i-k)^{2m}.$$

This summation is exactly $\mathbb{E}[X^{2m}]$, where X is a sum of k i.i.d. random variables each equal to 1 with probability 1/2 and -1 otherwise. For any $c \in (0,1]$, we can write:

$$\begin{aligned}\mathbb{E}[X^{2m}] &= \mathbb{E}[X^{2m}||X| \geq ck] \cdot \mathbb{P}[|X| \geq ck] \\ &\quad + \mathbb{E}[X^{2m}||X| \leq ck] \cdot \mathbb{P}[|X| \leq ck] \\ &\leq k^{2m}\,\mathbb{P}[|X| \geq ck] + (ck)^{2m}.\end{aligned}$$

To bound the return probability bound, we this count by the the total number of possible paths taken by a_1 and a_2 in m steps, k^{2m}, giving an upper bound of:

$$\mathbb{P}[|X| \geq ck] + c^{2m}.$$

By a Hoeffding bound, $\mathbb{P}[|X| \geq ck] \leq 2e^{-c^2 k/2}$. If we set $c = \sqrt{\ln A/k} = \sqrt{\ln 2}$ then $\mathbb{P}[|X| \geq ck] \leq 1/\sqrt{A}$. So our final probability bound is:

$$\mathbb{P}[|X| \geq ck] + c^{2m} \leq \frac{1}{\sqrt{A}} + (\sqrt{\ln 2})^{2m} < \frac{1}{\sqrt{A}} + (7/10)^m.$$

Note that, by adjusting c, it is possible trade off the terms in the above bound, giving stronger inverse dependence on A at the expense of slower exponential decay in m. □

Using Lemma 12, we have $B(t) = \sum_{m=0}^{t} \beta(m) \leq \frac{10}{3} + \frac{t}{\sqrt{A}}$. Assuming $t = O(\sqrt{A})$, this gives $\epsilon = O\left(\sqrt{\frac{\log(1/\delta)}{td}}\right)$ and so $t = \Theta\left(\frac{\log(1/\delta)}{\epsilon^2 d}\right)$, matching independent sampling.

5. APPLICATIONS

We conclude by discussing algorithmic applications of our ant-inspired density estimation algorithm (Algorithm 1), variations on this algorithm, and our analysis techniques.

5.1 Social Network Size Estimation

Random walk-based density estimation is closely related to work on estimating the size of social networks and other massive graphs using random walks [11, 12, 15, 16]. In these applications, one does not have access to the full graph (so cannot exactly count the nodes), but can simulate random walks by following links between nodes [17, 8]. One approach is to run a single random walk and count repeat node visits [15, 12]. Alternatively, [11] proposes running multiple random walks and counting their collisions. This can be significantly more efficient since the dominant cost is typically in link queries to the network. With multiple random walks, this cost can be trivially distributed to multiple servers.

Walks are first run for a 'burn-in' period so their locations are distributed approximately by the stable distribution of the network. The walks are then halted, and the number of collisions in this final round are counted. The collision count gives an estimate of the walks' density and since the number of walks is known, an estimate for network size.

We show that ant-inspired algorithms can give runtime improvements over this method. After burn-in, instead of halting the walks, we run them for *multiple rounds*, recording encounter rates as in Algorithm 1. This allows the use of fewer random walks, decreasing total burn-in cost, and leading to faster runtimes when mixing time is relatively slow, as is common in social network graphs [18].

5.1.1 Random Walk-Based Network Size Estimation

Consider an undirected, connected, non-bipartite graph $G = (V, E)$. Let S be the set of vertices of G that are 'known'. Initially, $S = \{v\}$ where v is a seed vertex. We can access G by looking up the neighborhood $\Gamma(v_i)$ of any vertex $v_i \in S$ and adding $\Gamma(v_i)$ to S.

To compute the number of nodes $|V|$ in the network, we could scan S, looking up the neighbors of each vertex and adding them to the set. After querying all nodes in S we will have $S = V$ and will know the network size. However, the number of queries required equals $|V|$. The goal is to estimate network size using a significantly more efficient random-walk based approach.

A number of challenges are introduced by this application. While we can simulate many random walks on G, we can no longer assume these random walks start at randomly chosen nodes, as we do not have the ability to uniformly sample nodes from the network. Instead, we must allow the random walks to run for a burn-in phase of length proportional to the mixing time of G. After this phase, the walks are distributed approximately according to the stable distribution of G.

In general, G is not regular. In the stable distribution, a random walk is located at a vertex with probability proportional to its degree. Hence, collisions tend to occur more at higher degree vertices. To correct for this bias, we count a collision at vertex v_i with weight $1/\deg(v_i)$. As we will see, with this modification, we must adjust our final estimate by the average degree of the graph, which we must estimate.

We use a natural generalization of re-collision probability. For any $i, j \in |V|$, let $p(v_i, v_j, m)$ be the probability of an m step random walk starting at v_i ending at v_j. Define:

$$\beta(m) \stackrel{\text{def}}{=} \frac{\max_{i,j} p(v_i, v_j, m)}{\deg(v_j)}$$

Intuitively, this is the maximum m step collision probability, weighted by degree since higher degree vertices are more likely to be visited in the stable distribution. Let $B(t) = \sum_{m=1}^{t} \beta(m)$. Note that this weighted $B(t)$ is upper bounded by the unweighted $B(t)$ used in Lemmas 11 and 12.

For simplicity, we ignore burn-in and assume that our walks start distributed exactly by the stable distribution of G. A walk starts at vertex v_i with probability $p_i \stackrel{\text{def}}{=} \frac{\deg(v_i)}{\sum_i \deg(v_i)} = \frac{\deg(v_i)}{2|E|}$ and initial locations are independent. We also assume knowledge of the average degree $\overline{\deg} = 2|E|/|V|$. In our full paper we rigorously analyze burn-in and show to estimate $\overline{\deg}$, completing our analysis.

Algorithm 2 Random Walk Network Size Estimation

input: step count t, average degree $\overline{\deg}$, n random starting locations $[w_1, ..., w_n]$ distributed according to the network's stable distribution

$[c_1, ..., c_n] := [0, 0, ..., 0]$
for $r = 1, ..., t$ **do**
  $\forall j$, set $w_j := randomElement(\Gamma(w_j))$
    ▷ $\Gamma(w_j)$ denotes the neighborhood of w_j.
  $\forall j$, set $c_j := c_j + \frac{count(w_j)}{\deg(w_j)}$
    ▷ $count(w_j)$ returns # other walkers at w_j.
end for
$C := \frac{\overline{\deg} \sum c_j}{\cdot n(n-1)t}$
return $\tilde{A} = 1/C$

THEOREM 18. *If* $n^2 t = \Theta\left(\frac{B(t)\overline{\deg}}{\epsilon^2 \delta}|V|\right)$, *with probability* $1-\delta$, *Algorithm 2 returns* $\tilde{A} \in [(1-\epsilon)|V|, (1+\epsilon)|V|]$.

Throughout this section, we work directly with the weighted total collision count C, showing that it is close to its expectation with high probability and hence giving the accuracy bound for $\tilde{A}$. As in the density estimation case, we start by showing that C is correct in expectation.

LEMMA 19. $\mathbb{E}\, C = 1/|V|$.

PROOF. Let $c_j(r)$ be the number of collisions, weighted by inverse vertex degree, walk j expects to be involved in at round r. In each round all walks are at vertex v_i with probability $p_i = \frac{\deg(v_i)}{2|E|}$, so:

$$\mathbb{E}\, c_j(r) = \sum_{i=1}^{|V|} \left[\frac{\deg(v_i)}{2|E|} \cdot \frac{(n-1)\deg(v_i)}{2|E|} \cdot \frac{1}{\deg(v_i)}\right]$$
$$= \frac{n-1}{4|E|^2} \sum_{i=1}^{|V|} \deg(v_i) = \frac{n-1}{2|E|}.$$

By linearity of expectation: $\mathbb{E}\, c_j = \frac{t(n-1)}{2|E|}$, $\mathbb{E} \sum c_j = \frac{tn(n-1)}{2|E|}$ and hence, $\mathbb{E}\, C = \frac{\overline{\deg}}{2|E|} = 1/|V|$. □

We now need to show concentration of C about its expectation. Let $c_{i,j}$ be the weighted collision count between walks w_i and w_j where $i \neq j$. It is possible to closely follow the moment bound proof of Lemma 6 and show that $c_{i,j}$ is sub-exponential. However, unlike in the case of regular graphs, we will not be able to claim that the different $c_{i,j}$'s are independent. Hence, we will not be able to use the same sub-exponential tail bounds employed in Section 3.3.

Instead, we bound the second moment (the variance) of each $c_{i,j}$ and show concentration via Chebyshev's inequality. This leads to a linear rather than logarithmic dependence on the failure probability $1/\delta$. However, note that we can simply perform $\log(1/\delta)$ estimates each with failure probability 1/3 and return the median, which will be correct with probability $1-\delta$. Variance proofs are deferred to our full paper, with the upshot being:

LEMMA 20 (TOTAL COLLISION VARIANCE BOUND). *Let* $\bar{C} = \frac{\overline{\deg} \sum_j \bar{c}_j}{n(n-1)t}$. $\mathbb{E}\left[\bar{C}^2\right] = O\left(\frac{1}{n^2 t} \cdot \frac{B(t)|E|}{|V|^2}\right)$.

With this variance bound, we can prove Theorem 18.

PROOF OF THEOREM 18. Note that $\bar{C} = C - \mathbb{E}\, C$. By Chebyshev's inequality Lemma 20 gives:

$$\mathbb{P}\left[|C - \mathbb{E}\, C| \geq \epsilon \mathbb{E}\, C\right] \leq \frac{1}{\epsilon^2 n^2 t} \cdot B(t)|E|.$$

Rearranging gives that, in order to have $\bar{C} \in \left[\frac{(1-\epsilon)}{|V|}, \frac{1+\epsilon}{|V|}\right]$ with probability δ, we must have:

$$n^2 t = \Theta\left(\frac{1}{\epsilon^2 \delta} B(t)|E|\right).$$

Assuming $\epsilon < 1/4$ this gives $\tilde{A} \in [(1-2\epsilon)|V|, (1+2\epsilon)|V|]$, giving the lemma after adjusting constants on ϵ. □

5.1.2 *Runtime and Comparision to Previous Work*

Let $M = O\left(\frac{\log(|E|/\delta)}{1-\lambda}\right)$ denote the burn-in time required before running Algorithm 2 (see full paper for derivation). Ignoring average degree estimation, which is typically of lower order (see full paper), to obtain a $(1 \pm \epsilon)$ estimate of network size with probability $1-\delta$ we must run n random walks for $M+t$ steps, making $n(M+t)$ link queries, where by Theorem 18, $n = \Theta\left(\sqrt{\frac{|V| \cdot B(t)\overline{\deg}}{t \cdot \epsilon^2 \delta}}\right)$. In the special case with $t=1$ we obtain a somewhat simpler bound (proof in full paper), requiring $n = \Theta\left(\sqrt{\frac{|V| \cdot \overline{\deg}}{\epsilon^2 \delta}}\right)$.

[11] also uses $t=1$, but uses a different estimator tracking degrees, inverse degrees, and collisions. Roughly, they require: $n = \Theta\left(\max\left\{\sqrt{\frac{1}{\epsilon^2 \delta \sum p_i^2}}, \frac{\sum p_i^3}{\epsilon^2 \delta (\sum p_i^2)^2}\right\}\right)$ where $p_i = \frac{\deg(v_i)}{2|E|}$. Their first term can be rewritten as

$$\sqrt{\frac{2|E|}{\sum_{i=1}^{|V|} \deg(v_i)^2}} \cdot \sqrt{\frac{|V| \cdot \overline{\deg}}{\epsilon^2 \delta}}.$$

This will always be somewhat smaller than our bound term as $2|E| \leq \sum_{i=1}^{|V|} \deg(v_i)^2$. Their second term is harder to compare but is upper bounded by:

$$\frac{\sum p_i^3}{\epsilon^2 \delta \left(\sum p_i^2\right)^2} \leq \frac{\deg_{\max}^3}{\overline{\deg}^4 |V|^2} \cdot \frac{2|E|}{\epsilon^2 \delta} = \frac{\deg_{\max}^3}{\overline{\deg}^3} \cdot \frac{1}{\epsilon^2 \delta |V|}.$$

Assuming $\deg_{\max} / \overline{\deg}$ is not too large, this term will be small. However, a few very high degree nodes in an otherwise sparse graph can make it very large.

In sum, not directly comparable to [11], in the $t=1$ case, assuming reasonable node degrees, our bounds are of the same order of magnitude. Further, the bound of Theorem 18 gives an important tradeoff for graphs with slow mixing time – we can increase the number of steps in our random walks, decreasing the total number of walks.

In our full paper we demonstrate that on a torus with ≥ 3 dimensions, our bounds give a polynomial speed up over [11]. We leave it as an open question to compare our bounds with those of [11] on more natural classes of graphs, and to determine either experimentally or theoretically, typical values of $B(t)$ on these graphs.

5.2 Robot Swarm Density Estimation

Algorithm 1 can be directly applied for simple and robust density estimation in robot swarms. Additionally, the algorithm can be used to estimate the frequency of certain properties within the swarm. Let d be the overall population density and d_P be the density of agents with some property P. Let $f_P = d_P/d$ be the relative frequency of P.

Assuming that agents with property P are distributed uniformly in population and that agents can detect this property (through direct communication or some other signal), then they can separately track encounters with these agents. They can compute an estimate $\tilde{d}$ of d and $\tilde{d}_P$ of d_P. By Theorem 1, after running for $t = \Theta\left(\frac{\log(1/\delta)\log\log(1/\delta)\log(1/d\epsilon)}{d_P \epsilon^2}\right)$ steps, with prob $1-2\delta$, $\tilde{d}_P/\tilde{d} \in \left[\left(\frac{1-\epsilon}{1+\epsilon}\right) f_P, \left(\frac{1+\epsilon}{1-\epsilon}\right) f_P\right] = [(1-O(\epsilon))f_P, (1+O(\epsilon))f_P]$ for small ϵ.

In a biological setting, properties may include if an ant has recently completed a food foraging trip [9], or if an ant is a nestmate or enemy [1]. In a robotics setting, properties may include whether a robot is part of a certain task group, whether a robot has completed a task, or whether a robot has detected a certain event or environmental property.

5.3 Random Walk Sensor Network Sampling

Finally, we believe our moment bounds for a single random walk (Corollaries 7 and 8) can be applied to random walk-based distributed algorithms for sensor network sampling. We leave obtaining rigorous bounds to future work.

Random walk-based sensor network sampling [13, 3] is a technique in which a query message (a 'token') is initially sent by a base station to a sensor. The token is relayed randomly between sensors, which are connected via a grid network, and its value is updated appropriately at each step to give an answer to the query. This scheme is robust and efficient - it adapts to node failures and does not require setting up or storing spanning tree communication structures.

However, if attempting to estimate some quantity, such as the percentage of sensors that have recorded a specific condition, as in density estimation, unless an effort is made to record which sensors have been previously visited, additional variance is added due to repeat sensor visits. Recording previous visits introduces computational burden – either the token message size must increase or nodes themselves must remember which tokens they have seen. We are hopeful that our moment bounds can be used to show that this is unnecessary – due to strong local mixing, the number of repeat sensor visits will be low, and increased variance due to random walking will be limited.

6. ACKNOWLEDGEMENTS

We thank Amartya Shankha Biswas, Christopher Musco, and Mira Radeva for helpful discussions. This work was partially supported by NSF Grants BIO-1455983 and CCF-1461559, the NSF Center for Science of Information grant CCF-0939370, and AFOSR grant FA9550-13-1-0042.

7. REFERENCES

[1] E. S. Adams. Boundary disputes in the territorial ant *Azteca trigona*: effects of asymmetries in colony size. *Animal Behaviour*, 39(2):321–328, 1990.

[2] D. Aldous and J. Fill. Reversible Markov chains and random walks on graphs, 2002.

[3] C. Avin and C. Brito. Efficient and robust query processing in dynamic environments using random walk techniques. In *Proceedings of the 3rd International Symposium on Information Processing in Sensor Networks*, pages 277–286. ACM, 2004.

[4] K.-M. Chung, H. Lam, Z. Liu, and M. Mitzenmacher. Chernoff-Hoeffding bounds for Markov chains: Generalized and simplified. *arXiv:1201.0559*, 2012.

[5] R. Elsässer and T. Sauerwald. Tight bounds for the cover time of multiple random walks. In *Automata, Languages and Programming*, pages 415–426. Springer, 2009.

[6] W. Feller. An introduction to probability theory and its applications. vol. i. 1950.

[7] D. Gillman. A Chernoff bound for random walks on expander graphs. *SIAM Journal on Computing*, 27(4):1203–1220, 1998.

[8] M. Gjoka, M. Kurant, C. T. Butts, and A. Markopoulou. A walk in Facebook: Uniform sampling of users in online social networks. *arXiv:0906.0060*, 2009.

[9] D. M. Gordon. Interaction patterns and task allocation in ant colonies. In *Information Processing in Social Insects*, pages 51–67. Springer, 1999.

[10] D. M. Gordon, R. E. Paul, and K. Thorpe. What is the function of encounter patterns in ant colonies? *Animal Behaviour*, 45(6):1083–1100, 1993.

[11] L. Katzir, E. Liberty, and O. Somekh. Estimating sizes of social networks via biased sampling. In *Proceedings of the 20th International Conference on World Wide Web*, pages 597–606. ACM, 2011.

[12] M. Kurant, C. T. Butts, and A. Markopoulou. Graph size estimation. *arXiv:1210.0460*, 2012.

[13] L. Lima and J. Barros. Random walks on sensor networks. In *5th International Symposium on Modeling and Optimization in Mobile, Ad Hoc and Wireless Networks and Workshops, 2007*, pages 1–5. IEEE, 2007.

[14] L. Lovász. Random walks on graphs: A survey. *Combinatorics, Paul Erdos is Eighty*, 2(1):1–46, 1993.

[15] J. Lu and D. Li. Sampling online social networks by random walk. In *Proceedings of the First ACM International Workshop on Hot Topics on Interdisciplinary Social Networks Research*, pages 33–40. ACM, 2012.

[16] J. Lu and H. Wang. Variance reduction in large graph sampling. *Information Processing & Management*, 50(3):476–491, 2014.

[17] A. Mislove, M. Marcon, K. P. Gummadi, P. Druschel, and B. Bhattacharjee. Measurement and analysis of online social networks. In *Proceedings of the 7th ACM SIGCOMM Conference on Internet Measurement*, pages 29–42. ACM, 2007.

[18] A. Mohaisen, A. Yun, and Y. Kim. Measuring the mixing time of social graphs. In *Proceedings of the 10th ACM SIGCOMM Conference on Internet Measurement*, pages 383–389. ACM, 2010.

[19] C. Musco, H.-H. Su, and N. Lynch. Ant-inspired density estimation via random walks. *arXiv:1603.02981*, 2016.

[20] S. C. Nicolis, G. Theraulaz, and J.-L. Deneubourg. The effect of aggregates on interaction rate in ant colonies. *Animal Behaviour*, 69(3):535–540, 2005.

[21] S. Pratt. Quorum sensing by encounter rates in the ant *Temnothorax albipennis*. *Behavioral Ecology*, 16(2):488–496, 2005.

[22] R. J. Schafer, S. Holmes, and D. M. Gordon. Forager activation and food availability in harvester ants. *Animal Behaviour*, 71(4):815–822, 2006.

[23] M. J. Wainwright. High-dimensional statistics: A non-asymptotic viewpoint, draft. http://www.stat.berkeley.edu/~mjwain/stat210b/Chap2_TailBounds_Jan22_2015.pdf, 2015.

Brief Announcement: Multi-Broadcasting under the SINR Model *

Sai Praneeth Reddy
Department of Computer Science
Indian Institute of Technology Delhi
New Delhi, India
saipraneet@gmail.com

Shailesh Vaya
Xerox Research Center India
Prestige Tech Park, Marathalli
Bangalore, India
shailesh.vaya@xerox.com

ABSTRACT

We study the multi-broadcast problem in multi-hop ad-hoc wireless networks, under the SINR model, deployed in the 2D Euclidean plane. In multi-broadcast, there are k initial messages, potentially belonging to different nodes, that must be forwarded to all n nodes of the network. We present deterministic algorithms for multi-broadcast for the different settings reflecting the different types of knowledge, about the topology of the network, available to the nodes: (i) the whole network topology (ii) their own coordinates and coordinates of their neighbors (iii) only their own physical coordinates (iv) only their own ids and the ids of their neighbors, but not actual physical co-ordinates. The last result is specially interesting, as it is the first deterministic protocol, for the SINR model, that does not require nodes to know their coordinates in the plane (a very specialized type of knowledge), but intricately exploits the fact that they lie on a two dimensional plane.

Keywords

Multi-broadcasting; SINR Model; Distributed Algorithms

1. INTRODUCTION

We consider a wireless network on a 2D plane with the *Euclidean metric* [1], which consists of n *stations* which are referred to as *nodes*. Each node is assigned a label in the range $\{1, \ldots, N\}$. The *transmission power* of station v is noted by P_v and is a positive real number. The communication graph of the network is a graph defined on the nodes; an edge (u, w) exists in communication graph if node w can successfully receive the message transmitted by u when no other node is simultaneously transmitting. The diameter of the communication graph is referred to by D and the maximum degree by Δ. The Signal-To-Noise-Interference-Ratio Model, aka SINR model, is characterized by three parameters: path loss $\alpha > 2$, ambient noise $\mathcal{N} > 0$, and threshold $\beta \geq 1$. For simplicity, we assume that $\beta = 1$ from now on. For a set of stations, transmitting in the same round $\mathcal{T}$, the success of transmission from a transmitting node v to a receiving node u depends on the signal strength to noise ratio or $SINR(v, u, \mathcal{T})$, defined as:

$$SINR(v, u, \mathcal{T}) = \frac{P_v \text{dist}(v, u)^{-\alpha}}{\mathcal{N} + \sum_{w \in \mathcal{T} \setminus \{v\}} P_w \text{dist}(w, u)^{-\alpha}} \quad (1)$$

A station u successfully receives a message from a station v in a round if it is true that $v \in \mathcal{T}$, $u \notin \mathcal{T}$ and the following conditions hold true

a) $P_v \text{dist}^{-\alpha}(v, u) \geq (1 + \varepsilon)\beta\mathcal{N}$ b) $SINR(v, u, \mathcal{T}) \geq \beta$

where $\mathcal{T}$ denotes the set of stations which are transmitting concurrently and $\varepsilon > 0$ is a fixed *signal sensitivity parameter* of the model. The weak devices model (as opposed to the strong devices model, where only condition (a) is sufficient) is well motivated [6] with a rich body of literature on it. Let r be the radius within which the transmission of a node succeeds, assuming that no other node is transmitting. Two nodes of the underlying communication graph $G(V, E)$ are connected if they lie within a distance of r from each other. In the *multi-broadcast* problem, there is a set of *source nodes* K that are active at the start of the protocol, each of them with a message. The goal is to deliver all messages stored with source nodes to all nodes in the network. In this work, we study the multi-broadcast problem in SINR model with unit-size restriction on message size i.e. it contains at most one original message, with at most $O(\log n)$ additional control bits. Furthermore, we assume the *non-spontaneous* setting, in which all nodes except the nodes in set K are asleep in the beginning. The asleep nodes cannot transmit a message till they receive a message from some neighboring node. We consider *round complexity* as the sole metric for measuring the efficiency of the distributed protocols developed in this work.

Related works.

Several algorithms were developed for deterministic *single* broadcast in [6] - an $O(n \log n)$ algorithm with knowledge of only own coordinates and $O(D \log^2 n)$ if nodes know also coordinates of their neighbors, amongst others. Our study goes even further in two aspects: first, we study more general problem of multi-broadcasting, and second, we analyze the impact of knowledge of coordinates on algorithm's

*Full version of the paper is available at arxiv[7]

[1]All results state here can be generalized to more general metric spaces such as those with bounded growth.

PODC'16 July 25-28, 2016, Chicago, IL, USA

ACM ISBN 978-1-4503-3964-3/16/07.

DOI: http://dx.doi.org/10.1145/2933057.2933064

performance, which brings a new perspective of wireless devices not equipped with GPS (in some settings like network of wireless devices etc., GPS gives approximate knowledge of coordinates which is not sufficient). In a recent work, [2] study broadcasting and building of the backbone in the same model as ours, but with even lesser knowledge, though present randomized algorithms. They show slightly slower broadcasting protocols when the nodes do not even the labels of their own neighbors or any of the graph parameters, as assumed here.

2. OUR RESULTS

The general structure of our algorithms is as follows - initially all the nodes containing rumors are active, and then leader(s are elected from amongst them. Then, a tree structure, which is both well spread out and well connected to the entire network, is constructed in a distributed manner. This tree acts as a back-bone and can be utilized to collect and disseminate information. The speed with which we can construct the tree and elect the leader depends on the amount of (initial) *knowledge* each node has, giving us different algorithms for each setting:

Knowledge only of neighbor's labels.

This is our most interesting and technically sophisticated result. It is for the setting when nodes have no knowledge of their physical location and know only their own labels and the labels of their neighbors, besides the standard knowledge of parameters n, N, k, D, Δ. It seems somewhat hard to fathom that one could develop a fast algorithm for this setting considering that nothing is known about the underlying geometric positions of the node. No deterministic results have been known for this setting in the literature.

The high-level idea of the protocol consists of two subprotocols: BTD_Traversals and BTD_MB. In BTD_Traversals, each of the nodes with messages with them issue a token. Whenever a node receives multiple tokens, they compete with each other and only one of them remains. This token is then passed on. The game ends when there is a single token left, thus electing a *leader*. The leader then starts a distributed traversal of the entire graph using a DFS approach (called a BTD-traversal in literature). This is conducted again using tokens where each node possessing tokens passes on its tokens to all of its hitherto unvisited children (in a DFS manner). This traversal creates a tree.

The internal nodes of the resultant tree can be shown to be both well connected to the entire network, as well as well spread out, enabling us to utilize it as a backbone structure. For an intuition about why the resulting tree is well spread out, suppose that some node of the tree (say w) has more than 6 children who are internal nodes. This means that at some round of the token passing, there were 7 nodes, all within a distance of $2r$ of each other. Because the nodes are within a 2D plane, there exist 2 nodes (say $v1$ and $v2$) within a distance of r of each other, i.e. they are neighbors of each other. W.l.o.g. assume that $v1$ received the token before $v2$. Then, because we follow a DFS approach, $v1$ upon receiving its token would have passed on its token to all its unvisited neighbors before w's next transmission occurs. Thus, $v2$ would have become the child of $v1$ and not w, giving us a contradiction.

In the second protocol BTD_MB, the leaves of the tree transmit their messages to the internal nodes by initiating an Eulerian walk. Since the tree is well spread out, we can efficiently propagate these messages across the network. Using a suitable *strongly-selective family*, transmissions succeed as long as they are well spread out (refer Lemma 1 in [7] for a formal statement). The final result is captured by the following theorem:

Theorem 1. *Execution of the deterministic protocol BTD_Traversals, followed by BTD_MB accomplishes multi-broadcast task for k messages in $O((n+k)\log n)$ rounds in a network of size n on a 2D plane, where each node only contains information about the list of its neighbors and graph parameters, and no knowledge of coordinates.*

For the next three settings, we leverage two theorems (Corollary 1 and 2) from [6]. The first states we can *always* ensure that at least one transmission succeeds, and the second that if the nodes which are transmitting in any round are sufficiently *spread-out* across the 2D plane, then all the transmissions succeed (refer Appendix **??** for more details).

Knowledge of only one's own coordinates and label.

We run two threads in *parallel*, operating in alternative rounds to prevent interference. Initially, only the set of k nodes with rumors are *active*. The first thread conducts leader election by using selective families as in the Corollary 1 previously mentioned. In each round, when two *active* nodes communicate with each other, the one with the larger label drops out. Since we are guaranteed that two closest neighbors successfully communicate in $O(\log n)$ rounds, repeating this Δ times ensures election of one leader for each neighborhood. In the second thread, the trees implicitly formed in thread 1 (the node which drops out of the election is the child of the other node) are used by the respective roots (leaders) to coordinate transmissions of all the coordinates and labels of the children nodes. These transmissions succeed by Corollary 2 because only one node per tree transmits at any point in time, ensuring that the transmissions are well spread out. Thus, in this way each root learns the co-ordinates and labels of all of its neighbors, transforming this setting into the next.

Theorem 2. *Protocol* General-Multicast *accomplishes deterministic multi-Broadcast in the non-spontaneous wake-up setting in $O((n+k)\log N)$ rounds, given that each node is aware of its label and coordinates.*

Knowledge of co-ordinates and labels of only neighbors.

Given an initial set of k active nodes with rumors, we need to first wake up all the nodes, and construct a backbone structure. The Gen-Inter-Box-Broadcast protocol from [6] gives us a method to ensure that all the neighbors of an active node are activated and received its message in $O(\log^2 n)$ rounds. Thus, repeating this procedure D times ensures that all the nodes of the network become active. Then, each set of neighbors can run a leader election algorithm to elect a leader from amongst themselves. These leaders are stitched together to form a backbone structure which are used to disseminate messages, giving us the following result:

Theorem 3. *Protocol* Local-Multicast *accomplishes multi-Broadcast in the non-spontaneous wake-up setting in $O(D\log^2 n$*

$k \log \Delta$) *rounds, given that each node is only aware of its neighbors.*

Knowledge of co-ordinates and labels of entire network.

In this setting, the main difficulty is that the set of nodes which are initially awake, i.e. the nodes with the messages is initially unknown. It is possible that most of these active nodes are very close to each other so that their transmissions interfere with each other. To overcome this, a protocol for leader election can be conducted using selector families in time $O(k \log \Delta)$ or in $O(\log g)$, where g is the *granularity* of the network i.e. the ratio between r and the smallest distance between two neighbors. The backbone structure can then be easily computed by each node and all the messages disseminated in time D. This gives us the following result:

Theorem 4. *There exists a protocol that accomplishes deterministic multi-Broadcast in* $O(D + k \log \Delta)$ *rounds or in* $O(D + k + \log g)$ *rounds when the granularity* g *is known when every node is aware of all the labels and coordinates of the entire network.*

3. REFERENCES

[1] B. S. Chlebus, D. R. Kowalski, A. Pelc, and M. A. Rokicki. Efficient distributed communication in ad-hoc radio networks. In *ICALP*, pages 613–624, 2011.

[2] B. S. Chlebus, D. R. Kowalski, and S. Vaya. Distributed communication in bare-bones wireless networks. *arXiv preprint arXiv:1510.07357*, 2015.

[3] A. E. F. Clementi, A. Monti, and R. Silvestri. Selective families, superimposed codes, and broadcasting on unknown radio networks. In S. R. Kosaraju, editor, *SODA*, pages 709–718. ACM/SIAM, 2001.

[4] A. Dessmark and A. Pelc. Broadcasting in geometric radio networks. *J. Discrete Algorithms*, 5(1):187–201, 2007.

[5] Y. Emek, L. Gasieniec, E. Kantor, A. Pelc, D. Peleg, and C. Su. Broadcasting in udg radio networks with unknown topology. *Distributed Computing*, 21(5):331–351, 2009.

[6] T. Jurdzinski, D. R. Kowalski, and G. Stachowiak. Distributed deterministic broadcasting in wireless networks of weak devices. In *ICALP*, 2013. Full version available at: CoRR, abs/1210.1804.

[7] S. P. Reddy, D. R. Kowalski, and S. Vaya. Multi-broadcasting under the SINR model. *CoRR*, abs/1504.01352, 2015.

Brief Announcement: Using Read-k Inequalities to Analyze a Distributed MIS Algorithm *

Sriram V. Pemmaraju
Department of Computer Science
The University of Iowa
Iowa City, IA 52242-1419, USA
sriram-pemmaraju@uiowa.edu

Talal Riaz
Department of Computer Science
The University of Iowa
Iowa City, IA 52242-1419, USA
talal-riaz@uiowa.edu

ABSTRACT

Until recently, the fastest distributed MIS algorithm, even for simple graphs, e.g., unoriented trees, has been the simple randomized algorithm discovered in the 80s. This algorithm (commonly called *Luby's algorithm*) computes an MIS in $O(\log n)$ rounds (with high probability). This situation changed when Lenzen and Wattenhofer (PODC 2011) presented a randomized $O(\sqrt{\log n} \cdot \log\log n)$-round MIS algorithm for unoriented trees. This algorithm was improved by Barenboim et al. (FOCS 2012), resulting in an MIS algorithm running in $O(\sqrt{\log n \cdot \log\log n})$ rounds.

The analyses of these tree MIS algorithms depends on "near independence" of probabilistic events, a feature of the tree structure of the network. In their paper, Lenzen and Wattenhofer hope that their algorithm and analysis could be extended to graphs with bounded arboricity. We show how to do this in this note. By using a new tail inequality for *read-k families* of random variables due to Gavinsky et al. (*Random Struct Algorithms*, 2015), we show how to deal with dependencies induced by the recent tree MIS algorithms when they are executed on bounded arboricity graphs. Specifically, we analyze a version of the tree MIS algorithm of Barenboim et al. and show that it runs in $O(\text{poly}(\alpha) \cdot \sqrt{\log n \cdot \log\log n})$ rounds in the $\mathcal{CONGEST}$ model for arboricity-α graphs.

Keywords

Bounded Arboricity Graphs, CONGEST model, Luby's Algorithm, Maximal Independent Set, Read-k Inequality

1. INTRODUCTION

Computing a *maximal independent set* (MIS) is a fundamental problem in distributed computing because it nicely captures the essential challenge of distributed symmetry breaking. The fastest algorithm for MIS, commonly called *Luby's algorithm* [1, 7, 5], is randomized and it computes an MIS of an n-node graph in $O(\log n)$ rounds, with high probability (whp), i.e., with probability at least $1 - 1/n$. In PODC 2011, Lenzen and Wattenhofer [6] showed that an MIS in an n-node *unoriented* tree can be computed in $O(\sqrt{\log n} \cdot \log\log n)$ rounds whp. More recently in FOCS 2012, Barenboim et al. [2, 3] presented a slightly faster tree MIS algorithm (similar to the Lenzen-Wattenhofer algorithm) that runs in $O(\sqrt{\log n \cdot \log\log n})$ rounds whp.

A natural question that arises (and asked by Lenzen and Wattenhofer [6]) is whether these tree MIS algorithms and analyses can be extended to *bounded arboricity graphs*. A graph G is said to have *arboricity* α if α is the minimum number of forests that the edges of G can be partitioned into. From this it follows that the edges of an arboricity-α graph can be oriented in such a manner that each node has at most α outgoing edges. Clearly, forests have arboricity 1, and the family of graphs with constant arboricity includes planar graphs, graphs with constant treewidth, graphs with constant genus, family of graphs that exclude a fixed minor, etc. Unfortunately, the Lenzen-Wattenhofer analysis and the Barenboim et al. analysis runs into trouble for graphs with even *constant arboricity* because of the nature of dependencies between probabilistic events in the algorithm.

The source of the difficulty can be explained as follows. Even though these algorithms [6, 2, 3] run on unoriented trees, *for the purposes of analysis* it can be assumed that the input tree is rooted at an arbitrary node. Because the graph is a tree, probabilistic events at children of a node v are essentially independent, the only slight dependency being caused by the interaction via their parent, namely v. For graphs with arboricity greater than 1 the dependency structure among the probabilistic events can be much more complicated. Suppose (for the purposes of the analysis) that we orient the edges of an arboricity-α graph such that each node has at most α out-neighbors. Let us call the out-neighbors of a node v its *parents* (denoted $\texttt{Parent}(v)$) and the in-neighbors, its *children* (denoted $\texttt{Child}(v)$). For a node v, consider the set $\texttt{Child}(v)$ and the dependencies among probabilistic events at nodes in $\texttt{Child}(v)$. The events we are referring to are of the type "w joins the MIS" or "a neighbor of w joins the MIS" for $w \in \texttt{Child}(v)$. Even though each node has at most α parents, a node $w \in \texttt{Child}(v)$ may share children with every other node in $\texttt{Child}(v)$ and as a result there could be dependencies between events at w and events at any of the other nodes in $\texttt{Child}(v)$. Thus it is not clear how to take advantage of the structure of bounded arboricity graphs in order to mimic the analysis in [6, 2, 3].

The main purpose of this note is to show that recent

*This work is supported in part by National Science Foundation grant CCF-1318166.

PODC'16 July 25-28, 2016, Chicago, IL, USA

ACM ISBN 978-1-4503-3964-3/16/07.
DOI: http://dx.doi.org/10.1145/2933057.2933062

results on *read-k families of random variables* deal with roughly this type of dependency structure and therefore provide a new approach to analyzing randomized distributed algorithms with more complicated dependency structure. Using analysis based on *read-k inequalities*, we show that the tree MIS algorithms of Lenzen and Wattenhofer [6] and Barenboim et al. [3, 2] work for bounded arboricity graphs as well.

1.1 Read-k Inequalities

Let $\{Y_j \mid 1 \leq j \leq n\}$ be a set of random variables such that each random variable Y_j is a function of some subset of the set of independent random variables $\{X_i \mid 1 \leq i \leq m\}$. For each $1 \leq j \leq n$, let $P_j \subseteq \{1, 2, \ldots, m\}$, let f_j be a boolean function of $\{X_i \mid i \in P_j\}$, and define $Y_j := f_j((X_i)_{i \in P_j})$. The collection of random variables Y_j is called a *read-k family* if every $1 \leq i \leq m$ appears in at most k of the P_j's. In other words, each X_i is allowed to influence at most k of the Y_j's. Note that the Y_j's can have a complicated dependency structure amongst themselves – it is their dependency on the X_i's that is bounded. For example, the dependency graph of the Y_j's can even be a clique! The first of the two inequalities from Gavinsky et al. [4] is the following.

THEOREM 1.1 (THEOREM 1.2, [4]). *Let $Y_1, Y_2, \cdots, Y_n$ be a family of read-k indicator variables with $\Pr[Y_i = 1] = p$. Then, $\Pr[Y_1 = Y_2 = \cdots = Y_n = 1] \leq p^{n/k}$.*

If the Y_j's were independent, then the probability that $Y_1 = Y_2 = \cdots = Y_n = 1$ would simply be p^n. Thus Theorem 1.1 is essentially saying that the read-k family structure of the dependencies among the Y_j's allows us to obtain an upper bound on the probability that is an exponential factor $1/k$ worse than what is possible had the Y_j's been independent.

Gavinsky et al. [4] use Theorem 1.1 and information-theoretic arguments to derive the following tail inequality on the sum of indicator random variables that form a read-k family.

THEOREM 1.2 (THEOREM 1.1, [4]). *Let $Y_1, \cdots, Y_n$ be a family of read-k indicator variables with $\Pr[Y_i = 1] = p_i$. Define $p := \frac{1}{n}\sum_{i=1}^{n} p_i$ and $Y := \sum_{i=1}^{n} Y_i$. Then for any $\epsilon, \delta > 0$,*

$$\Pr(Y \leq (p - \epsilon)n) \leq \exp\left(-2\epsilon^2 \frac{n}{k}\right).$$

As in Theorem 1.1, these tail inequalities are also an exponential $1/k$ factor worse than corresponding Chernoff bounds that we might have used, had the Y_j's been independent.

To see that the above tools are well-suited for analyzing tree MIS algorithms [6, 3, 2] consider a graph G with arboricity α, fix a node v in G, and consider the set $\texttt{Child}(v)$. For a node $w \in \texttt{Child}(v)$, let Y_w be an indicator variable for a probabilistic event at node w. Now suppose that Y_w depends on independent random choices made by w and its children. The structure of an arboricity-α graph and the associated edge-orientation ensures that each node has at most α parents and therefore the random choice at each node can influence at most α of the Y_w's. Thus the set $\{Y_w \mid w \in \texttt{Child}(v)\}$ forms a read-α family and we can apply Theorems 1.1 and 1.2 to bound $Pr(\cap_w Y_w = 1)$ and to show that $\sum_w Y_w$ is concentrated about its expectation.

The above example illustrates the simplest application of read-k inequalities in our analysis. We use read-k inequalities to evaluate probabilistic interactions between a node and its parents also. This may seem difficult to do given that a parent can have arbitrarily many children and thus a random choice at a parent can influence events at arbitrarily many children. However, in our algorithm nodes with extremely high degree opt out of the competition (temporarily) and this turns out to be sufficient for the use of read-k inequalities, with appropriate k, to analyze the interaction between nodes and their parents. Finally, our analysis also relies on interactions between a node and its grandchildren, leading to our use of read-$\Theta(\alpha^2)$ families as well.

1.2 Our Result

We apply read-k-inequality-based analysis to the execution of the tree MIS algorithm of Barenboim et al. [3, 2] on bounded arboricity graphs and obtain the following result.

THEOREM 1.3. *The tree MIS algorithm of Barenboim et al. [3, 2] (with appropriate parameter values) can be used to compute an MIS in the $\mathcal{CONGEST}$ model on the family of graphs with arboricity α in $O(poly(\alpha) \cdot \sqrt{\log n \cdot \log\log n})$ rounds, whp.*

This result can also be seen as an improvement over the MIS result on bounded arboricity graphs due to Barenboim et el. [3, 2]. In their paper, Barenboim et al. have a separate algorithm (distinct from their tree MIS) algorithm that computes an MIS on graphs with arboricity α in $O(\log^2 \alpha + \log^{2/3} n)$ rounds. The dependency on n of the running time of our algorithm is asymptotically better, implying that for small α (i.e., $\alpha = O(\log^c n)$ for a small enough constant c) our algorithm is asymptotically faster. In this context, it should be noted that recently (in SODA 2016) Gaffari presented a novel distributed MIS algorithm for general graphs that runs in $O(\log \Delta) + 2^{O(\sqrt{\log\log n})}$ rounds and a corollary of this algorithm is an $O(\log \alpha + \sqrt{\log n})$-round MIS algorithm on graphs with arboricity α.

2. MIS ON BOUNDED ARBORICITY GRAPHS

We present an algorithm that we call BOUNDEDARBINDEPENDENTSET, which is essentially identical to the TREEINDEPENDENTSET algorithm of Barenboim et al. (Section 8, [3]), except for parameter values (Θ, Λ, ρ_k) which now depend on α as well.

I denotes the set of nodes which have joined the MIS and B stores a set of so-called "bad" nodes. As nodes join I, they and their neighbors become *inactive*; additionally, nodes in B also become inactive. We use V_{IB} to denote the set of nodes which are currently active, $\Gamma_{IB}(u)$ to denote the neighborhood of node u, restricted to nodes in V_{IB}, and $deg_{IB}(u) := |\Gamma_{IB}(u)|$. The algorithm proceeds in $\Theta := \lfloor \log\left(\frac{\Delta}{1176 \cdot 16\alpha^{10} \ln^2 \Delta}\right) \rfloor$ *scales*. For any scale k, $1 \leq k \leq \Theta$, a node in V_{IB} that has degree more than $\Delta/2^k + \alpha$ is called a *high degree* node for that scale. In each scale, we start by performing $O(\alpha^8(\log \alpha + \log\log \Delta))$ *iterations* of Luby's algorithm [7]. The exact number of iterations (denoted by Λ) is $\lceil p \cdot 8\alpha^2(32\alpha^6 + 1) \cdot \ln(260\alpha^4 \ln^2 \Delta) \rceil$. Here p is a large enough constant.

In a single iteration, every node $v \in V_{IB}$ chooses a real number $r(v) \in [0, 1)$ called a *priority*. If v has more than $\rho_k := 8 \ln \Delta \cdot \Delta/2^{k+1}$ neighbors in any iteration, its priority is (deterministically) set to 0, otherwise, it chooses a priority uniformly at random in $(0, 1)$ (denote $UAR(0, 1)$ in the pseudocode). After each iteration, nodes in I and neighbors of these nodes (i.e., $\Gamma_{IB}(I)$) are removed from V_{IB}. If, after

Algorithm 1: BOUNDEDARBINDEPENDENTSET(G):

1: Initialize sets $I, B \subseteq V(G)$: $I \leftarrow \phi$; $B \leftarrow \phi$

2: **for** *each scale* $k \leftarrow 1$ *to* $\Theta := \left\lfloor \log\left(\frac{\Delta}{1176 \cdot 16\alpha^{10} \ln^2 \Delta}\right) \right\rfloor$ **do**

$\rho_k \leftarrow 8 \ln \Delta \cdot \Delta / 2^{k+1}$

$\Lambda \leftarrow \lceil p \cdot 8\alpha^2(32\alpha^6 + 1) \cdot \ln(260\alpha^4 \ln^2 \Delta) \rceil$

2(a) Repeat Λ times

- Each node $v \in V_{IB}$ chooses a priority $r(v)$:

$$r(v) \leftarrow \begin{cases} 0, & \text{if } \deg_{IB}(v) > \rho_k \\ UAR(0,1) & \text{otherwise} \end{cases}$$

- Mark v if $r(v) > max\{r(w) | w \in \Gamma_{IB}(v)\}$
- $I \leftarrow I \cup \{v \in V_{IB} | v \text{ is marked }\}$
- $V_{IB} \leftarrow V_{IB} \setminus (I \cup \Gamma_{IB}(I))$

2(b) Each node v is labeled "bad" if $|\{w \in \Gamma_{IB}(v) | deg_{IB}(w) > \Delta/2^k + \alpha\}| > \Delta/2^{k+2}$

$B \leftarrow B \cup \{v \in V_{IB} \mid v \text{ is labeled "bad"}\}$

$V_{IB} \leftarrow V_{IB} \setminus B$

end

3: **return** (I, B, V_{IB})

all Λ iterations in the current scale, a node $v \in V_{IB}$ has more than $\Delta/2^{k+2}$ high-degree neighbors then it is designated a "bad" node and added to the set B. It is worth emphasizing that this algorithm has no access to an edge-orientation or a forest-decomposition of the given α-arboricity graph.

THEOREM 2.1. *Using* BOUNDEDARBINDEPENDENTSET *in* $O\left(\alpha^8(\log\alpha + \log\log\Delta) \cdot \log\Delta + \log\log n \log\alpha\right)$ *rounds whp we can compute an MIS on a graph with arboricity* α. *This leads to an algorithm that computes an MIS on a graph with arboricity* α *in* $O(\alpha^9 \sqrt{\log n} \cdot \log\log n)$ *rounds whp.*

2.1 Finishing Up

Algorithm BOUNDEDARBINDEPENDENTSET returns an independent set I (which need not be maximal), a set B of "bad" nodes, and a set V_{IB}, that need not be empty. So after the algorithm has completed, we still need to process the sets B and V_{IB}. The "finishing up" algorithm is aided by two results shown by our analysis: (i) the subgraph induced by B has small connected components and (ii) the graph induced by V_{IB} has the property that no node has too many high degree neighbors (otherwise, they would have been placed in B). For details of the "finishing up" see the full paper [8].

3. OVERVIEW OF ANALYSIS

The heart of the analysis shows that the following invariant is maintained (at the end of each scale) at every active node, with sufficiently high probability.

INVARIANT: At the end of scale k, for all $v \in V_{IB}$,

$$\left|\{w \in \Gamma_{IB}(v) | \deg_{IB}(w) > \Delta/2^k + \alpha\}\right| \leq \Delta/2^{k+2}$$

The INVARIANT bounds the number of high degree neighbors a node has after k scales of the algorithm. Let N denote the set on the left-hand side of the INVARIANT above. The goal is to show that, with probability at least $1 - 1/\Delta^{2p}$, in Scale k, (i) either v becomes inactive in Step 2(a) because it or its neighbor joins the MIS or (ii) $|N|$ falls to $\Delta/2^{k+2}$ or below by the end of Scale k. Showing this leads to the result that after Scale k, each active node satisfies the invariant with probability at least $1 - 1/\Delta^{2p}$ and is therefore placed in B with probability at most $1/\Delta^{2p}$. Using the proof in Barenboim et al. [2, 3], we conclude from this result that all connected components in the graph induced by B are small.

We partition the analysis needed to show (i) and (ii) above into the analysis of three key probabilistic events. The first event concerns the interaction between nodes and their children and the second concerns the interaction between nodes and their parents. The third event is more complicated and it concerns the interaction between nodes and their children, their grandchildren and their children's other parents. Let us fix a Scale k and an iteration within that scale. Let $M \subseteq V_{IB}$ be an active subset of nodes just before the start of this iteration. The three probabilistic events we analyze can be informally described as follows. For Events (1) and (2), we assume that all nodes in M have degree at most ρ_k and are therefore competitive. The analysis of these three events makes critical use of read-k inequalities, for different values of k and leads to the claimed result. See [8] for details.

Event (1) Among the set of nodes M, there exists a node whose priority is larger than the priority of all its children.
Event (2) Suppose that M is sufficiently large. Then a large fraction of the nodes in M have priority greater than priorities of all their parents.
Event (3) Suppose that every node in M has sufficiently high degree. Then a large fraction of the nodes in M become inactive due to their children joining the MIS.

4. REFERENCES

[1] N. Alon, L. Babai, and A. Itai. A fast and simple randomized parallel algorithm for the maximal independent set problem. *J. Algorithms*, 7(4):567–583, 1986.

[2] L. Barenboim, M. Elkin, S. Pettie, and J. Schneider. The locality of distributed symmetry breaking. In *53rd Annual IEEE Symposium on Foundations of Computer Science, FOCS 2012, New Brunswick, NJ, USA, October 20-23, 2012*, pages 321–330, 2012.

[3] L. Barenboim, M. Elkin, S. Pettie, and J. Schneider. The locality of distributed symmetry breaking. *CoRR*, abs/1202.1983, 2015.

[4] D. Gavinsky, S. Lovett, M. Saks, and S. Srinivasan. A tail bound for read-k families of functions. *Random Structures & Algorithms*, 47:99–108, 2015.

[5] A. Israeli and A. Itai. A fast and simple randomized parallel algorithm for maximal matching. *Inf. Process. Lett.*, 22(2):77–80, 1986.

[6] C. Lenzen and R. Wattenhofer. MIS on trees. In *Proceedings of the 30th annual ACM SIGACT-SIGOPS symposium on Principles of distributed computing*, PODC '11, pages 41–48, New York, NY, USA, 2011. ACM.

[7] M. Luby. A simple parallel algorithm for the maximal independent set. *SIAM Journal on Computing*, 15:1036–1053, 1986.

[8] S. V. Pemmaraju and T. Riaz. Using Read-k Inequalities to Analyze a Distributed MIS Algorithm. *ArXiv e-prints*, May 2016.

Brief Announcement: A Key-Value Map for Massive Real-Time Analytics

Dmitry Basin
Yahoo Research
Haifa, Israel
dbasin@yahoo-inc.com

Edward Bortnikov
Yahoo Research
Haifa, Israel
ebortnik@yahoo-inc.com

Anastasia Braginsky
Yahoo Research
Haifa, Israel
anastas@yahoo-inc.com

Guy Golan Gueta
Yahoo Research
Haifa, Israel
ggolan@yahoo-inc.com

Eshcar Hillel
Yahoo Research
Haifa, Israel
eshcar@yahoo-inc.com

Idit Keidar
Technion and Yahoo Research
Haifa, Israel
idish@ee.technion.ac.il

Moshe Sulamy*
Tel-Aviv University
Tel-Aviv, Israel
msulamy@gmail.com

ABSTRACT

Modern big data processing platforms employ huge in-memory key-value (KV-) maps. Their applications simultaneously drive high-rate data ingestion *and* large-scale analytics. These two scenarios expect KV-map implementations that scale well with both real-time updates and massive atomic scans triggered by range queries. However, today's state-of-the art concurrent KV-maps fall short of satisfying these requirements – they either provide only limited or non-atomic scans, or severely hamper updates when scans are ongoing.

We present KiWi, the first atomic KV-map to efficiently support simultaneous massive data retrieval and real-time access. The key to achieving this is treating scans as first class citizens, whereas most existing concurrent KV-maps do not provide atomic scans, and some others add them to existing maps without rethinking the design anew.

1. INTRODUCTION

The ordered *key-value* (KV) map abstraction has been recognized as a popular programming interface since the dawn of computer science, and remains an essential component of virtually any computing system today. It is not surprising, therefore, that with the advent of multi-core computing, many scalable concurrent implementations have emerged, e.g., [2, 3, 4, 9, 10, 12].

Today, KV-maps have become centerpiece to web-scale data processing systems, e.g., Google's F1 [15], which powers its AdWords[1] business, and Yahoo's Flurry[2], the technology behind its Mobile Developer Analytics business. These applications raise novel use cases and push scalability requirements to new levels. Namely, they require real-time performance for both (1) ingestion of the incoming data streams, and (2) analytics of the resulting dataset. For example, as of early 2016, the Flurry platform systematically collected data of 830,000 mobile apps[3] running on 1.6 billion user devices[4]. Flurry streams this data into a massive index, and provides application developers with tools that produce a wealth of reports over the collected data.

Analytics platforms exploit KV-stores like Google's Bigtable [7] and Apache HBase [1]. These technologies combine on-disk indices for persistence with an in-memory KV-map for real-time data acquisition [7]. The latter's scalability has a major impact on overall system performance, (as shown in [8]). The stream scenario requires the KV-map to support fast *put* operations, whereas the analytics aspect relies on (typically large) scans (i.e., range queries). The consistency (atomicity) of scans is essential for correct analytics. The new challenge that arises in this environment is allowing consistent scans to be obtained *while the data is being updated in real-time.*

In this brief announcement we present KiWi, the first KV map to efficiently support large atomic scans as required for data analytics, alongside real-time updates. Most existing concurrent KV-maps do not support atomic scans at all [2, 11, 3, 4, 9, 12, 10]. Others support a single scan at a time [13], do not ensure progress for scans [5, 14, 6, 11], or severely hamper updates when scans are ongoing [5, 14]. Table 1 summarizes the properties of state-of-the-art concurrent data structures that support scans, and compares them to KiWi.

*This work was done in part while interning with Yahoo Research, Haifa.

PODC'16, July 25-28, 2016, Chicago, IL, USA
ACM 978-1-4503-3964-3/16/07.
http://dx.doi.org/10.1145/2933057.2933061

[1] https://www.google.com/adwords/
[2] https://developer.yahoo.com/flurry/docs/analytics/
[3] http://flurrymobile.tumblr.com/post/144245637325/appmatrix
[4] http://flurrymobile.tumblr.com/post/117769261810/the-phablet-revolution

	atomic scans	balanced	multi-scan	wait-free scans	fast puts
snapshot iterator [13]	✓	✓	✗	✓	✓
SnapTree [5]	✓	✓	✓	✗	✗
Ctrie [14]	✓	✓	✓	✗	✗
k-ary tree [6]	✓	✗	✓	✗	✓
BW-Tree [11]	✗	✓	✓	✗	✓
Java-Skiplist [2]	✗	✓	✓	✓	✓
KiWi	**✔**	**✔**	**✔**	**✔**	**✔**

Table 1: Comparison of concurrent data structures that support scans. Fast puts means not hampering updates (e.g., by cloning nodes) when scans are ongoing.

An important emphasis in KiWi's design is on facilitating synchronization between scans and updates. Since scans are typically long, our solution avoids livelock and wasted work by always allowing them to complete (without ever needing to restart). On the other hand, updates are short (since only single-key puts are supported), therefore restarting them in cases of conflicts is practically "good enough" – restarts are rare and when they do occur, little work is wasted. Formally, KiWi opts to provide *wait-free* scans and *lock-free* put operations.

2. DESIGN PRINCIPLES

To support atomic wait-free scans, KiWi employs multi-versioning. But in contrast to the standard approach where each put creates a new version for the updated key, KiWi only keeps old versions that are needed for ongoing scans, and otherwise over-writes the existing version. Moreover, version numbers are managed by scans rather than updates, and thus put operations may over-write data without changing its version number. This unorthodox approach offers significant performance gains given that scans typically retrieve large amounts of data and hence take much longer than updates. It also necessitates a fresh approach to synchronizing updates an scans, which is a staple of KiWi's design.

A second important feature of KiWi's design is its efficient memory management. Data in KiWi is organized as a collection of *chunks*, which are large blocks of contiguous key ranges. Such data layout is cache-friendly and suitable for non-uniform memory architectures (NUMA), as it allows long scans to proceed with few fetches of new data to cache or local memory. Chunks regularly undergo maintenance to improve their space utilization (via *compaction*) and internal organization, as well as the distribution of key ranges into chunks (via splits and merges). All these issues are handled by KiWi's *rebalance* abstraction, which performs batch processing of multiple maintenance operations that are vital for the data structure's health. The synchronization of rebalance operations with ongoing puts and scans is subtle, and much of the KiWi algorithm is dedicated to handling possible races in this context.

KiWi is a balanced data structure, providing logarithmic access latency in the absence of contention. This is achieved via a combination of (1) indexing chunks for fast lookup and (2) partially sorting keys in each chunk to allow for fast in-chunk binary search. To facilitate concurrency control, we separate chunk management from indexing: KiWi employs a *search index* separately from the (chunk-based) data storage layer. The index is updated lazily after rebalancing of the data storage layer completes.

3. RESULTS

KiWi is a practical algorithm, with multiple optimizations implemented on top of the theoretical underpinnings. We benchmark its Java implementation extensively under multiple representative workloads. In the vast majority of experiments, KiWi significantly surpasses the best-in-class concurrent algorithms. KiWi's advantages are particularly pronounced in our target scenario with long scans in the presence of concurrent puts, where KiWi's atomic scans are twice as fast as the non-atomic scans offered by the Java Skiplist [2], and compared to existing atomic solutions [6, 5], KiWi not only performs all operations faster, but actually executes either updates or scans an order of magnitude faster than every other solution.

Figure 1 presents evaluation results for a *mixed* workload – half the threads perform scans, whereas the second half perform puts. Each scan picks the range's lower bound uniformly at random, and iterates through S keys for a parameter S. We compare KiWi with other state-of-the art KV-maps supporting scans.. Figure 1(a) shows the throughput scalability with scan size, with maximal parallelism (32 threads). KiWi dominates universally except for very short scans, for which k-ary tree [6] is 10% faster. For long scans, the latter deteriorates fast (Figure 1 (b)). This happens because k-ary tree restarts iterating every time a put falls within the scanned range – i.e., puts make progress but scans get starved. For large values of S, SnapTree [5] is the second-fastest because it shared-locks the scanned ranges in advance and scans unobstructed. From the puts perspective (Figure 1 (c)-(d)), KiWi is the fastest again, whereas SnapTree is the slowest since its locking starves concurrent updates. In contrast to its competitors, KiWi serves both scans and puts well.

Finally, KiWi implements a balanced data structure, which allows operations to run orders of magnitude faster than unbalanced ones in case insertion order is not random. For example, if we build the map from an ordered stream of keys, KiWi's throughput is close to that obtained in experiments with a random insertion order. In contrast, implementations that do not address balancing directly fail to provide adequate performance – e.g., k-ary tree's get/put throughput is 700 times slower than KiWi's in this scenario.

4. REFERENCES

[1] Apache HBase – a Distributed Hadoop Database. https://hbase.apache.org/.

[2] Java Concurrent Skip List. https://docs.oracle.com/javase/7/docs/api/java/util/concurrent/ConcurrentSkipListMap.html.

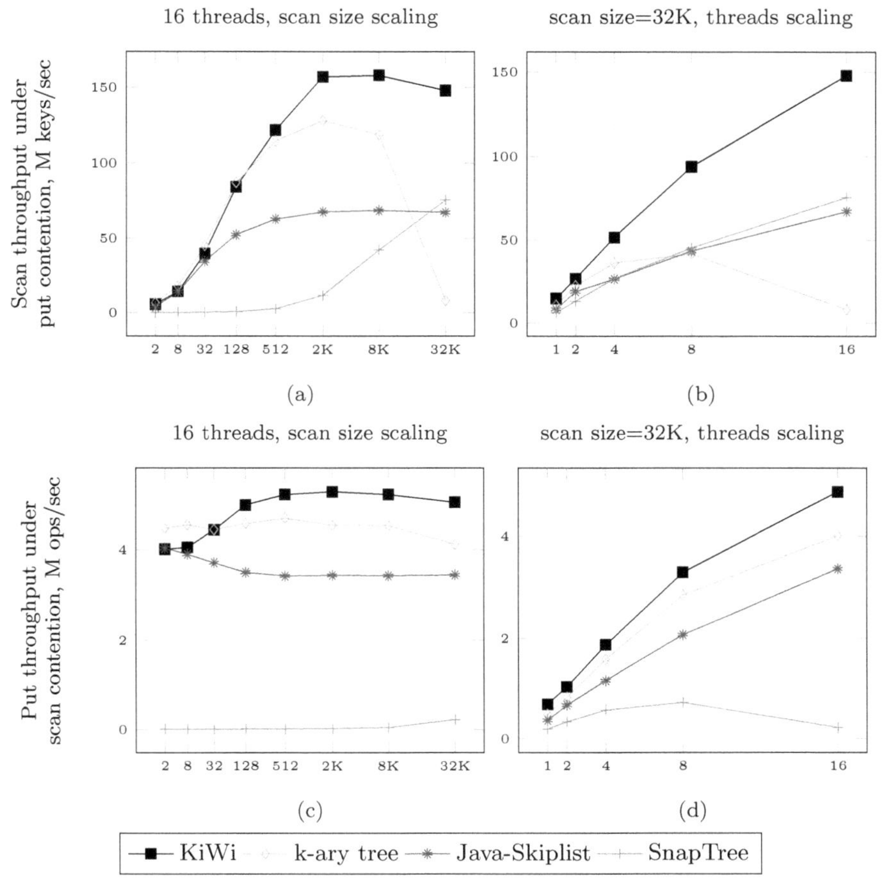

Figure 1: KiWi's throughput: (a-b) Scans with background put contention, (c-d) Puts with background scan contention.

[3] A. Braginsky and E. Petrank. Locality-conscious lock-free linked lists. In *ICDCN*, pages 107–118, 2011.

[4] A. Braginsky and E. Petrank. A lock-free B+tree. In *SPAA*, pages 58–67, 2012.

[5] N. G. Bronson, J. Casper, H. Chafi, and K. Olukotun. A practical concurrent binary search tree. In *PPOPP*, pages 257–268, 2010.

[6] T. Brown and H. Avni. Range queries in non-blocking k-ary search trees. In *OPODIS*, pages 31–45, 2012.

[7] F. Chang, J. Dean, S. Ghemawat, W. C. Hsieh, D. A. Wallach, M. Burrows, T. Chandra, A. Fikes, and R. E. Gruber. Bigtable: A distributed storage system for structured data. *ACM Trans. Comput. Syst.*, 26(2):4:1–4:26, June 2008.

[8] G. Golan-Gueta, E. Bortnikov, E. Hillel, and I. Keidar. Scaling concurrent log-structured data stores. In *EuroSys*, pages 32:1–32:14, 2015.

[9] D. Hendler, N. Shavit, and L. Yerushalmi. A scalable lock-free stack algorithm. In *SPAA*, pages 206–215, 2004.

[10] A. Kogan and E. Petrank. A methodology for creating fast wait-free data structures. In *PPoPP*, pages 141–150, 2012.

[11] D. B. Lomet, S. Sengupta, and J. J. Levandoski. The bw-tree: A b-tree for new hardware platforms. In *ICDE*, pages 302–313, 2013.

[12] A. Natarajan and N. Mittal. Fast concurrent lock-free binary search trees. In *PPoPP*, pages 317–328, 2014.

[13] E. Petrank and S. Timnat. Lock-free data-structure iterators. In *DISC*, pages 224–238, 2013.

[14] A. Prokopec, N. G. Bronson, P. Bagwell, and M. Odersky. Concurrent tries with efficient non-blocking snapshots. In *PPoPP*, pages 151–160, 2012.

[15] J. Shute, R. Vingralek, B. Samwel, B. Handy, C. Whipkey, E. Rollins, M. Oancea, K. Littlefield, D. Menestrina, S. Ellner, J. Cieslewicz, I. Rae, T. Stancescu, and H. Apte. F1: A distributed sql database that scales. In *VLDB*, 2013.

Author Index

www.ingramcontent.com/pod-product-compliance
Ingram Content Group UK Ltd.
Pitfield, Milton Keynes, MK11 3LW, UK
UKHW051414290926
15471UKWH00009B/1604